UNLOCKING THE
OLD
TESTAMENT

UNLOCKING THE
OLD TESTAMENT

A SIDE-BY-SIDE COMMENTARY

ED J. PINEGAR · RICHARD J. ALLEN

Covenant Communications, Inc.

Cover image: *The Prophet Isaiah Foretells of Christ's Birth* by Harry Anderson © Intellectual Reserve, Inc. Courtesy of the Church History Museum.
Cover and book design © 2009 by Covenant Communications, Inc.

Published by Covenant Communications, Inc.
American Fork, Utah

Copyright © 2009 by Ed J. Pinegar and Richard J. Allen

Printed in U.S.A.
Second Printing: September 2013

15 14 13   10 9 8 7 6 5 4 3

ISBN-13 978-1-59811-851-3
ISBN-10 1-59811-851-X

Introduction

⚜

THE OLD TESTAMENT

For many, the journey of life is an aimless quest on the seas of doubt. But for others, upheld by the gospel of light and secured by the compass of faith, there is joy in the passing of time toward a sure and certain goal—return to the glorious presence of the Father and the Son. If we belong to the latter group, then our ship is the word of God, our sails are moved by His Spirit, and our travel companions consist of the loved ones dear to our heart.

On this journey of life, we prepare ourselves in the harbor of hope and the cove of the covenant. We venture out on the surging waves of adversity and challenge, energized by the vision of better things to come. The eternal plan of happiness is not a fuzzy and abstract Utopian dream dancing in our fantasy beyond the distant horizon; instead, it is a clear and concise plan of power and action for today—this very hour and all the hours to come until we reach our destination. The voice of the Lord, conveyed through the words of His chosen prophets, calls to us through the pages of holy writ—the panoramic record of the Old and New Testaments, the fulness of the gospel preserved in the Book of Mormon, and the fundamentals of exaltation unfolded through the Doctrine and Covenants and the Pearl of Great Price in our own dispensation. These comprise the essence of truth concerning the bread of life and the living waters of the Atonement of Jesus Christ.

For some, the Old Testament represents a vast ocean of complexity that is obscured by the shadows of antiquity, masked by the unfamiliar patterns of distant cultures, and diluted by the claims of unsympathetic interpreters who say it represents only legend and myth. But viewed through the lens of gospel truth and illuminated by the light of continuing revelation, the Old Testament emerges for what it truly is—the wellspring document of God's design for bringing to pass the immortality and eternal life of His faithful children through priesthood blessings of redeeming truth, saving ordinances, and the power to endure to the end. The Old Testament is the opening chapter of God's book of life—the overture of ever-unfolding evidence of His love, compassion, and mercy bestowed upon all who receive it with thanksgiving and courage as we travel through mortality, moving ever closer to our heavenly home.

Magnificent in scope and detail, inspiring in thematic content, and riveting in its anecdotal abundance, the Old Testament is the foundational scripture of the divine canon. Above all else in terms of mission and purpose, the Old Testament—augmented by the books of Moses and Abraham from the Pearl of Great Price—constitutes a grand and glorious exposition of the character, qualities, and mission of Jesus Christ. The thoughtful and prayerful reader cannot ponder the ancient passages of scripture about the Savior without being touched spiritually with the profound significance of His love, the mercy of His longsuffering, and the majesty of His divine intercession on behalf of mankind.

Considered separately, one at a time, any one of the prophets of the Old Testament—whether Adam, Enoch, Noah, Melchizedek, Abraham, Jacob, Moses, Isaiah, Jeremiah, or any of the rest—presents a vivid memorial, inspiring and unforgettable, of the truths of the gospel of Jesus Christ. But considered together—their testimonies blended as one as if in a constellation of heavenly lights configured around the central glory of the Father and the Son—the prophets offer an eternal array of witnesses to the truth of God's saving principles and ordinances. It is in the blending of their testimonies—just as Nephi stood forth to offer his testimony, intermingled with that of his brother Jacob and the prophet Isaiah, all three having seen the Lord in person (see 2 Ne. 2:1–4)—that we have irrefutable evidence of the truth of the plan of happiness as confirmed by multiple witnesses and the whisperings of the Spirit. In our world of confusing and conflicting byways, we can thank our Heavenly Father and His Only Begotten Son for prophets to open up the pathway of truth before us. The witness of those prophets is preserved as an endowment of truth in the canon of scripture, starting with the Old Testament and continuing with the word of God poured out once again in our own day of Restoration.

Across the vast landscape of the Old Testament we see a panoramic view of mixed scenes, encompassing alternately both a wasteland patchwork of wilderness as well as fertile pastures of splendor. At times we see the wasteland of man's prideful intemperance and sin. At other times we see the pastures of penitence, humility, and covenant devotion. Both are present, intermingled in the experiences of the human condition.

As travelers across this terrain, we labor in grief and sorrow (as did Enoch in Moses 7:20–40) over the accounts of Israel's travail under the burdens of wickedness. But we also rejoice from time to time through scenes of grandeur and triumph as the Lord's prophets and disciples, leaders and Saints, men and women both, rise on eagle's wings to the potential of their God-given destiny. Such are the spiritual oases that beckon the anxious traveler seeking the fountains of living water to quench their thirst for truth, truth that is embedded in the sacred chronicles of the Lord's dealings with His children.

Jeremiah discerned the need for, and explained the satisfaction of, attaining the thirst-quenching power of such spiritual oases in these words:

Thus saith the LORD; Cursed be the man that trusteth in man, and maketh flesh his arm, and whose heart departeth from the LORD.

For he shall be like the heath in the desert, and shall not see when good cometh; but shall inhabit the parched places in the wilderness, in a salt land and not inhabited.

Blessed is the man that trusteth in the LORD, and whose hope the LORD is.

For he shall be as a tree planted by the waters, and that spreadeth out her roots by the river, and shall not see when heat cometh, but her leaf shall be green; and shall not be careful in the year of drought, neither shall cease from yielding fruit. (Jer. 17:5–8)

Truly there is much to be learned from the experience and testimony of the prophets whose words are found in the Old Testament. What edifying insights and truths we can bring into our lives from a careful review of the lives and witness of such men of strength and valor! In addition, there are women whose lives and character reflect transcendent qualities of nobility and valor of the type reflected in President Joseph F. Smith's state- ment about those he saw in his vision of the spirit world, in- cluding "our glorious Mother Eve, with many of her faithful daughters who had lived through the ages and worshiped the true and living God" (D&C 138:39). We learn much from studying the lives of such noble women and taking to heart their example of righteousness and devotion!

In the Old Testament, themes and doctrines are illustrated or expounded in the character, associations, and/or circum- stances of people whose stories are told. Throughout its pages are found life-changing lessons on faith, repentance, baptism, and the Holy Ghost—plus courage, covenants, deliverance, de- votion, fasting, forgiveness, gratitude, humility, joy, leadership, love, mercy, obedience, peace, prayer, restoration, strength of the Lord, and many others. Relationships of all kinds are found throughout the Old Testament—brotherly, sisterly, parental, spousal, and many variations. Examples of teaching and family instruction abound. Stories of the victory of good over evil are well represented. Principles of leadership (of lack thereof) are illustrated in the accounts of kings both righteous and wicked —including those who shifted dominantly from righteous to wicked. In all, the scope of the Old Testament provides a cur- riculum of breathtaking power for those interested in spiritual development and eternal growth in all its dimensions.

From the divine dawning of the Creation, to the glories of Sinai, to the pervasive flame of prophecy illuminating the mis- sion of the coming Redeemer—the Old Testament is a book of light, even the light of the word of God and the light of His eternal plan of salvation. "It is written, Man shall not live by bread alone, but by every word that proceedeth out of the mouth of God" (Matt. 4:4). Thus responded the mortal Mes- siah, quoting from Deuteronomy 8:4, to the temptations of Satan, over whom He had already prevailed in the premortal councils of heaven (see Abr. 3:27–28). And so it is.

The banquet of endowed truth is incomplete without the spiritual nourishment provided by the Old Testament, the foun- dational library of the holy canon. This priceless scripture is an essential part of the word of God. Through the power and light of the Old Testament, we gain precious and enduring benefits: a deeper understanding of the origins and nature of God's de- sign for the immortality and eternal life of man, life-sustaining insights into the covenant process of sanctification and purifi- cation, a treasured witness of the truth of Christ's calling and Atonement, and a greater abundance of strength and courage to "seek the face of the Lord always," as we are reminded in the Doctrine and Covenants, "that in patience ye may possess your souls, and ye shall have eternal life" (D&C 101:38).

But the radiance of the Old Testament does not flow to us without our devoted effort and humble dependence on the inpsiration of the Holy Ghost. By study and faith, we can drink from the refreshing well of truth that awaits us from this source. By prayer and pondering we can avail ourselves of the message of the Old Testament, which John A. Widt- soe summarized eloquently as follows:

What is the message of the Old Testament? From the first to the last, in the Pentateuch, in the histori- cal books, in the poetical books, and in the prophets, it teaches the existence of a personal God, the Maker of the heavens and the earth, the Father of the human race. It teaches that the earth and all things upon it are provided for man's benefit but that man must obey law, divine law, to secure the blessings he desires. It teaches that obedience to the moral law, given by God for human conduct, involving faith in God, not to be compared with man-made, ethical, selfish codes of ac- tion, is the most important concern of man. It is the message of messages for humankind. (*Evidences and Reconciliations* [Salt Lake City: Improvement Era], 135)

The Old Testament's "message of messages" is centered in the atoning mission of Jesus Christ as our Redeemer and Savior. That is the primary purpose of the Old Testament: to provide a divine witness of the Son of God, the great Je- hovah, and show us how we can move forward to be more like Him through covenant fidelity and obedience. Indeed, our view of the Savior in His sacred role as Jehovah, Mes- siah, Christ, Creator, Emmanuel, Jesus, and King provides a lens for us to perceive more fully the mother lode of di- vine truth that is presented to us in the Old Testament record.

Our objective in providing this commentary has cen- tered chiefly on the hope that this material may be helpful to those who want to strengthen their testimonies of the truthfulness of the gospel of Jesus Christ and magnify the desire to honor covenant obligations with faith and valor. We are grateful to Covenant Communications for their service in bringing this work into circulation. We are espe- cially grateful to our wives, Patricia Pinegar and Carol Lynn Allen, for their encouragement and support during the process of research and writing.

—Ed J. Pinegar and Richard J. Allen

THE PEARL OF GREAT PRICE

As students of the scriptural abundance of the Pearl of Great Price, we are permitted to go with Abraham into the circle of the Lord, where resplendent truth is unfolded to our senses. With Moses we walk to the Mount to learn firsthand the saving principles of the gospel as taught by the Master Himself. What a singular blessing that the Lord has seen fit to preserve the record of these priceless teaching moments and allow us to participate in the visions of grandeur that confirm in such a vivid and compelling way the purposes of life and the mission of the Savior. Our experience is a vicarious involvement in the reality of what Abraham and Moses experienced in person—but through the Spirit, our conviction of the verity of these events and our confirmation of the truth of these principles can be real and enduring.

By studying these scriptures faithfully and prayerfully, we can rekindle in our memories the comforting assurance that we too were once in the halls of glory with our Father in Heaven and His Son, where the "first lessons in the world of spirits" (D&C 138:56) were taught us in preparation for our sojourn on earth. It was there that we first learned how to see with godly vision, how to magnify our divinely endowed intelligence, how to prepare for future mortal tasks assigned us there, how to honor and cherish the earth that had been prepared specifically as our temporal (and eventually spiritual) home, how to strengthen ourselves in anticipation of our probationary earth life, how to follow the will of the Father and the Son in all respects and at all times, and how to cultivate humility and meekness as an antidote to pride.

The memory of our early lessons in the premortal existence has been graciously masked, so that we can learn line upon line, precept upon precept how to be faithful agents unto ourselves in making the correct choices in life. Through the promptings of the Spirit, we can look forward to the blessings that follow the covenant promises, and see with our inner eye the time where we can return once again to the presence of the Maker from whom all blessings flow.

—Ed J. Pinegar and Richard J. Allen

CITATIONS USED IN THIS BOOK

AGQ—Joseph Fielding Smith, *Answers to Gospel Questions,* 5 volumes, Joseph Fielding Smith, Jr., comp. and ed. (Salt Lake City: Deseret Book Co., 1980)

CR—*Conference Report*

FAR—Kent P. Jackson, *From Apostasy to Restoration* (Salt Lake City, Deseret Book Co., 1996)

HC—*History of the Church,* 7 volumes

JD—*Journal of Discourses,* 26 volumes

TPJS—Joseph Fielding Smith, comp., *Teachings of the Prophet Joseph Smith* (Salt Lake City: Deseret Book Co., 1938)

HOW TO USE THIS BOOK

The left column on each page contains the actual text of the Pearl of Great Price or the Old Testament without chapter headings or footnotes. The scriptural text in this book contains only those scriptures that are included in the Gospel Doctrine class reading assignments, so the full text of the Old Testament is not included here.

The right column on each page contains commentary that corresponds to the scriptural text to its left.

In some places, the abundance of rich information on people of the Old Testament was too long to fit in the right column adjacent to the scriptural text. In these cases, information on such people—primarily the prophets of the Old Testament—is contained in appendices at the back of the book; references to these appendices are found in the text where appropriate. As you have the time and interest, you can consult these appendices for more information about the people described in the Old Testament.

Throughout the book, *Points of Interest* are indicated by an open-book icon. These include charts, illustrations, photographs, and text that might enrich your study of the Pearl of Great Price and the Old Testament.

Finally, space has been provided in various places throughout the book so you can take notes or write your impressions as you study the Pearl of Great Price and the Old Testament.

Abbreviations Used in This Book

The Books of the Old Testament	Abbreviation
Genesis	Gen.
Exodus	Ex.
Leviticus	Lev.
Numbers	Num.
Deuteronomy	Deut.
Joshua	Josh.
Judges	Judg.
Ruth	
1 Samuel	1 Sam.
2 Samuel	2 Sam.
1 Kings	1 Kgs.
2 Kings	2 Kgs.
1 Chronicles	1 Chron.
2 Chronicles	2 Chron.
Ezra	
Nehemiah	Neh.
Esther	Esth.
Job	
Psalms	Ps.
Proverbs	Prov.
Ecclesiastes	Eccl.
The Song of Solomon	Song.
Isaiah	Isa.
Jeremiah	Jer.
Lamentations	Lam.
Ezekiel	Ezek.
Daniel	Dan.
Hosea	
Joel	
Amos	
Obadiah	Obad.
Jonah	
Micah	
Nahum	
Habakkuk	Hab.
Zephaniah	Zeph.
Haggai	Hag.
Zechariah	Zech.
Malachi	Mal.
Moses	
Abraham	Abr.

Pronunciation Guide

For proper names that may be difficult to pronounce, a general guide, using everyday English vowel applications, is provided. Note that the use of the letter "y" in these applications always implies a long "i" (as in the vowel sound in words like try, high, eye, or sky). An example is the pronunciation of the name Adonijah as ad'-uh-ny̆'-juh.

An accented syllable is marked with an apostrophe (') following the syllable.

The pronunciations suggested in this volume are not intended to be definitive but to serve only as a general aid based on recommendations adapted from a variety of general sources.

THE
PEARL OF GREAT PRICE

SELECTIONS FROM THE BOOK OF MOSES

CHAPTER 1
(June 1830)

1 THE words of God, which he spake unto Moses at a time when Moses was caught up into an exceedingly high mountain,

2 And he saw God face to face, and he talked with him, and the glory of God was upon Moses; therefore Moses could endure his presence.

3 And God spake unto Moses, saying: Behold, I am the Lord God Almighty, and Endless is my name; for I am without beginning of days or end of years; and is not this endless?

4 And, behold, thou art my son; wherefore look, and I will show thee the workmanship of mine hands; but not all, for my works are without end, and also my words, for they never cease.

5 Wherefore, no man can behold all my works, except he behold all my glory; and no man can behold all my glory, and afterwards remain in the flesh on the earth.

6 And I have a work for thee, Moses, my son; and thou art in the similitude of mine Only Begotten; and mine Only Begotten is and shall be the Savior, for he is full of grace and truth; but there is no God beside me, and all things are present with me, for I know them all.

7 And now, behold, this one thing I show unto thee, Moses, my son, for thou art in the world, and now I show it unto thee.

8 And it came to pass that Moses looked, and beheld the world upon which he was created; and Moses beheld the world and the ends thereof, and all the children of men which are, and which were created; of the same he greatly marveled and wondered.

9 And the presence of God withdrew from Moses, that his glory was not upon Moses; and Moses was left unto himself. And as he was left unto himself, he fell unto the earth.

10 And it came to pass that it was for the space of many hours before Moses did again receive his natural strength like unto man; and he said unto himself: Now, for this cause I know that man is nothing, which thing I never had supposed.

11 But now mine own eyes have beheld God; but not my natural, but my spiritual eyes, for my natural eyes could not have beheld; for I should have withered and died in his presence; but his glory was upon me; and I beheld his face, for I was transfigured before him.

12 And it came to pass that when Moses had said these words, behold, Satan came tempting him, saying: Moses, son of man, worship me.

13 And it came to pass that Moses looked upon Satan and said: Who art thou? For behold, I am a son of God, in the similitude of his Only Begotten; and where is thy glory, that I should worship thee?

THE
PEARL OF GREAT PRICE

CHAPTER 1

Moses 1:1–4—The Nature of God and Our Divine Parentage

God is endless and infinite in His wisdom and His works. He is our Father in Heaven, and like Moses, we are the literal children of our Heavenly Father, who knows us personally. Each of us is a divine being having a mortal experience to prove ourselves worthy of returning to our Heavenly Father's presence (see Abr. 3:25). We have the potential to become perfect like our Heavenly Father and our Savior Jesus Christ and receive of Their fulness (see 3 Ne. 12:48; D&C 84:38).

As God spoke with Moses face to face, Moses came to understand the character and the attributes of God. We can also come to know these truths through study, prayer, and by the witness of the Holy Ghost. This knowledge of His goodness and power is necessary for us to act with faith, to show love, and to be obedient. Understanding the nature of God will help us come to know Him.

In verse 6 we are told, "… there is no God beside me" (Moses 1:6). In Moses' day idolatry was rampant, with many gods of all descriptions. The Lord wanted to be sure that Moses knew that there was ONE GOD to worship, a concept that was reiterated in the Ten Commandments.

Moses 1:10—Humility, the Heavenly Virtue

We are dependent on the Lord for strength. Without God, we are nothing. With God, we have the promise of unending blessings.

Moses came to realize the greatness of God after having this magnificent spiritual experience on the mount. His strength was gone. It took hours before he could return to his "strength like unto man" (Moses 1:10).

Moses had been a prince in Egypt—brought up in the courts of Pharaoh surrounded by worldly splendor and power. Now, under the tutelage of the Creator, he learns the truth about mankind—that enduring strength comes only through God, and that man is totally dependent on divine power for his vitality and his very being.

This knowledge gave Moses an understanding of the virtue of humility. Humility is the beginning virtue of exaltation (see Matt. 23:12). Humility is the quality that brings into our hearts a love of our fellow men and a feeling of connectedness to all mankind. Humility causes us to relate to God in prayerful gratitude and love because we realize that we are His children and acknowledge our dependence on Him. Moses learned on the mount—as we must learn—that we need an enduring attitude of humility if we are to succeed in helping to build the Kingdom of God (D&C 12:8).

14 For behold, I could not look upon God, except his glory should come upon me, and I were transfigured before him. But I can look upon thee in the natural man. Is it not so, surely?

15 Blessed be the name of my God, for his Spirit hath not altogether withdrawn from me, or else where is thy glory, for it is darkness unto me? And I can judge between thee and God; for God said unto me: Worship God, for him only shalt thou serve.

16 Get thee hence, Satan; deceive me not; for God said unto me: Thou art after the similitude of mine Only Begotten.

17 And he also gave me commandments when he called unto me out of the burning bush, saying: Call upon God in the name of mine Only Begotten, and worship me.

18 And again Moses said: I will not cease to call upon God, I have other things to inquire of him: for his glory has been upon me, wherefore I can judge between him and thee. Depart hence, Satan.

19 And now, when Moses had said these words, Satan cried with a loud voice, and ranted upon the earth, and commanded, saying: I am the Only Begotten, worship me.

20 And it came to pass that Moses began to fear exceedingly; and as he began to fear, he saw the bitterness of hell. Nevertheless, calling upon God, he received strength, and he commanded, saying: Depart from me, Satan, for this one God only will I worship, which is the God of glory.

21 And now Satan began to tremble, and the earth shook; and Moses received strength, and called upon God, saying: In the name of the Only Begotten, depart hence, Satan.

22 And it came to pass that Satan cried with a loud voice, with weeping, and wailing, and gnashing of teeth; and he departed hence, even from the presence of Moses, that he beheld him not.

23 And now of this thing Moses bore record; but because of wickedness it is not had among the children of men.

24 And it came to pass that when Satan had departed from the presence of Moses, that Moses lifted up his eyes unto heaven, being filled with the Holy Ghost, which beareth record of the Father and the Son;

25 And calling upon the name of God, he beheld his glory again, for it was upon him; and he heard a voice, saying: Blessed art thou, Moses, for I, the Almighty, have chosen thee, and thou shalt be made stronger than many waters; for they shall obey thy command as if thou wert God.

26 And lo, I am with thee, even unto the end of thy days; for thou shalt deliver my people from bondage, even Israel my chosen.

27 And it came to pass, as the voice was still speaking, Moses cast his eyes and beheld the earth, yea, even all of it; and there was not a particle of it which he did not behold, discerning it by the spirit of God.

28 And he beheld also the inhabitants thereof, and there was not a soul which he beheld not; and he discerned them by the Spirit of God; and their numbers were great, even numberless as the sand upon the sea shore.

29 And he beheld many lands; and each land was called earth, and there were inhabitants on the face thereof.

30 And it came to pass that Moses called upon God, saying: Tell me, I pray thee, why these things are so, and by what thou madest them?

31 And behold, the glory of the Lord was upon Moses, so that Moses stood in the presence of God, and talked with him face to face. And the Lord God said unto Moses: For mine own purpose

Moses 1:15—Spiritual Strength in the Face of Opposition

Our moral agency makes us free to choose between good and evil. Moses, like all mankind (even Christ), had to be tempted. There is opposition in all things; it is a test of life and it is part of the Plan of Happiness. Without it there could be no happiness (see 2 Ne. 2:11).

What is the level of our spiritual vitality in the face of temptation and opposition? Moses was able to overcome the temptation because he knew the glory of God, and so can we. He had a portion of the Spirit, which enabled him to judge righteously (see D&C 11:12), and the Spirit could show him all things to do (2 Ne. 32:5). We, too, can enjoy spiritual guidance. Moses was righteous, and righteousness binds Satan; we, too, can choose righteousness (see 1 Ne. 22:15, 26).

Temptation is a part of opposition in all things. The gift of God called *agency* gives us the power to choose, and there will be blessings or consequence according to our choices. For the gift of agency to work, there must be (1) eternal laws, (2) knowledge of good and evil, (3) opposition in all things, (4) power to choose, and (5) consequences to our choices here and in the hereafter. Recognizing these elements of agency gives us perspective to choose righteousness, for it magnifies our spiritual strength in the face of opposition and it leads to happiness and eternal life.

As we study these scriptural passages, we see that there is the promise of great joy in *choosing the right* and potentially great sorrow in *not choosing the right*.

Moses 1:20—Courage through Prayer and Priesthood Power

When we pray for the Spirit of the Lord to be with us, we shall not fear. In this world, with all its iniquity, we are continually being bombarded by the adversary and the hosts of Heaven who were cast down to the earth. Fear is so destructive if we do not confront it with positive action. We must have *faith in God* (see Matt. 8:26), *perfect love* (see 1 John 4:18), *preparation* (see D&C 38:30), *knowledge* (see Prov. 24:5), *experience* to build confidence, and, above all, we must *pray to God always* (see Moses 1:20). We see the pattern for overcoming fear in our lives: the prayer of faith and the power of God unite to dispel fear and replace it with confidence, hope, and a feeling of strength and courage.

Moses 1:31—Purpose of the Lord in Creating the Earth

"The Lord never created this world at random. He has never done any of His work at random. The earth was created for certain purposes; and one of these was its final redemption and the establishment of His government and kingdom upon it in the latter days, to prepare it for the reign of the Lord Jesus Christ." —Wilford Woodruff (JD 15:8)

The creation is perfect; the plan behind it is perfect; the majestic ebb and flow of life attest to the perfection of the Maker. In this chapter we identify six interdependent, indispensable aspects of the creative signature: the Savior's

have I made these things. Here is wisdom and it remaineth in me.

32 And by the word of my power, have I created them, which is mine Only Begotten Son, who is full of grace and truth.

33 And worlds without number have I created; and I also created them for mine own purpose; and by the Son I created them, which is mine Only Begotten.

34 And the first man of all men have I called Adam, which is many.

35 But only an account of this earth, and the inhabitants thereof, give I unto you. For behold, there are many worlds that have passed away by the word of my power. And there are many that now stand, and innumerable are they unto man; but all things are numbered unto me, for they are mine and I know them.

36 And it came to pass that Moses spake unto the Lord, saying: Be merciful unto thy servant, O God, and tell me concerning this earth, and the inhabitants thereof, and also the heavens, and then thy servant will be content.

37 And the Lord God spake unto Moses, saying: The heavens, they are many, and they cannot be numbered unto man; but they are numbered unto me, for they are mine.

38 And as one earth shall pass away, and the heavens thereof even so shall another come, and there is no end to my works, neither to my words.

39 For behold, this is my work and my glory—to bring to pass the immortality and eternal life of man.

40 And now, Moses, my son, I will speak unto thee concerning this earth upon which thou standest; and thou shalt write the things which I shall speak.

41 And in a day when the children of men shall esteem my words as naught and take many of them from the book which thou shalt write, behold, I will raise up another like unto thee; and they shall be had again among the children of men—among as many as shall believe.

42 (These words were spoken unto Moses in the mount, the name of which shall not be known among the children of men. And now they are spoken unto you. Show them not unto any except them that believe. Even so. Amen.)

MOSES CHAPTER 2
(June–October 1830)

1 AND it came to pass that the Lord spake unto Moses, saying: Behold, I reveal unto you concerning this heaven, and this earth; write the words which I speak. I am the Beginning and the End, the Almighty God; by mine Only Begotten I created these things; yea, in the beginning I created the heaven, and the earth upon which thou standest.

2 And the earth was without form, and void; and I caused darkness to come up upon the face of the deep; and my Spirit moved upon the face of the water; for I am God.

3 And I, God, said: Let there be light; and there was light.

4 And I, God, saw the light; and that light was good. And I, God, divided the light from the darkness.

5 And I, God, called the light Day; and the darkness, I called Night; and this I did by the word of my power, and it was done as I spake; and the evening and the morning were the first day.

central role in all of it, the goodness and glory of the plan of creation, man being created in the image of God, the harmony and unity of man and woman in the grand scheme of life, the principle of free agency, and the everlasting covenant pattern of Sabbath rest as the crowning seal upon the creative act.

Moses 1:33—The Savior as Creator

The Savior is the steward of all life, under the Father, being both Creator and Redeemer, the beginning and the end. Moses was taught that Jesus Christ is the Only Begotten Son of God the Father, also known as Jehovah, God of the Old Testament, Creator and Redeemer of the world. He did everything the Father asked Him to do. God the Eternal Father, by the Word of His power, even by His Only Begotten Son, created the earth (Moses 1:32). Heavenly Father delegated this part of the Plan of Happiness to His Only Begotten Son and other noble spirits. This doctrine of stewardship is vital for the growth and development of the children of God. Heavenly Father loves us so much that He allows us to act for Him in His great work.

Moses 1:39—Divine Mission

Moses was taught that the purpose of our Heavenly Father and our Savior is to bring about the immortality and eternal life of man. This is the work and glory of God — the happiness of His children. He loves us. He wants us to return home to His presence to live forever. We, like Moses, have a work to do. We are disciples of Jesus Christ. We stand as witnesses. We are here to build up the Kingdom of God. Our work then is our Heavenly Father's work: the immortality and eternal life of our brothers and sisters.

MOSES CHAPTER 2
(June–October 1830)

Moses 2:1—Father In Heaven

Our Father in Heaven—as presented in holy writ and confirmed to the devout and faithful through the Holy Ghost—is the Supreme Lord and God of all Creation, the Eternal Source of light and truth, the benevolent and everloving Father of our spirits (see Hebrews 12:9; 1 John 4:7-8), the Author of the glorious gospel plan of happiness (see Abraham 3:23, 27), the Exemplar of the pattern for all holiness and perfection, the merciful Grantor of agency unto His children, and the Benefactor of all mankind through the gift of His Only Begotten Son, whose atoning sacrifice empowers the process for achieving immortality and exaltation. *(For more inights on Father in Heaven and the Holy Ghost, see Appendix A.)*

6 And again, I, God, said: Let there be a firmament in the midst of the water, and it was so, even as I spake; and I said: Let it divide the waters from the waters; and it was done;

7 And I, God, made the firmament and divided the waters, yea, the great waters under the firmament from the waters which were above the firmament, and it was so even as I spake.

8 And I, God, called the firmament Heaven; and the evening and the morning were the second day.

9 And I, God, said: Let the waters under the heaven be gathered together unto one place, and it was so; and I, God, said: Let there be dry land; and it was so.

10 And I, God, called the dry land Earth; and the gathering together of the waters, called I the Sea; and I, God, saw that all things which I had made were good.

11 And I, God, said: Let the earth bring forth grass, the herb yielding seed, the fruit tree yielding fruit, after his kind, and the tree yielding fruit, whose seed should be in itself upon the earth, and it was so even as I spake.

12 And the earth brought forth grass, every herb yielding seed after his kind, and the tree yielding fruit, whose seed should be in itself, after his kind; and I, God, saw that all things which I had made were good;

13 And the evening and the morning were the third day.

14 And I, God, said: Let there be lights in the firmament of the heaven, to divide the day from the night, and let them be for signs, and for seasons, and for days, and for years;

15 And let them be for lights in the firmament of the heaven to give light upon the earth; and it was so.

16 And I, God, made two great lights; the greater light to rule the day, and the lesser light to rule the night, and the greater light was the sun, and the lesser light was the moon; and the stars also were made even according to my word.

17 And I, God, set them in the firmament of the heaven to give light upon the earth,

18 And the sun to rule over the day, and the moon to rule over the night, and to divide the light from the darkness; and I, God, saw that all things which I had made were good;

19 And the evening and the morning were the fourth day.

20 And I, God, said: Let the waters bring forth abundantly the moving creature that hath life, and fowl which may fly above the earth in the open firmament of heaven.

21 And I, God, created great whales, and every living creature that moveth, which the waters brought forth abundantly, after their kind, and every winged fowl after his kind; and I, God, saw that all things which I had created were good.

22 And I, God, blessed them, saying: Be fruitful, and multiply, and fill the waters in the sea; and let fowl multiply in the earth;

23 And the evening and the morning were the fifth day.

24 And I, God, said: Let the earth bring forth the living creature after his kind, cattle, and creeping things, and beasts of the earth after their kind, and it was so;

25 And I, God, made the beasts of the earth after their kind, and cattle after their kind, and everything which creepeth upon the earth after his kind; and I, God, saw that all these things were good.

26 And I, God, said unto mine Only Begotten, which was with me from the beginning: Let us make man in our image, after our likeness; and it was so. And I, God, said: Let them have dominion over the fishes of the sea, and over the fowl of the air, and over the cattle,

Moses 2:26—In the Image of God

We are literally the spiritual children of God, the Eternal Father, Elohim. Our first parents in mortality were Adam and Eve. They were created in the image and likeness of our Heavenly Father and our Savior Jesus Christ. This knowledge brings to us the vision that each of us as a divine child of God has the potential for limitless growth, the capacity to be even as our Heavenly Parents. This understanding changes not only our perspective on life but also our thought process. It brings us the knowledge of where we came from, why we are here, and where we are going. As mortals our image and likeness are a close counterpart, a personification or embodiment, and literally a representation of God.

This divine parentage becomes a power in our lives. We were born with self-esteem, self-respect, and self-worth because of our innate makeup. We do not require external or worldly victories to maintain a sense of value or a belief in self.

Moses 2:27—Adam

From holy writ we know that Adam (meaning: man or many) was the first man. Abraham referred to Adam as the "first father" (Abraham 1:3; compare D&C 107:40-53), meaning the head of the descending lineage of priesthood authority in the succession of dispensations upon the earth. Modern revelation speaks of "Michael, or Adam, the father of all, the prince of all, the ancient of days" (D&C 27:11).

In latter-day revelation, Adam is also identified with the title *archangel* (see D&C 107:54). The name Michael in Hebrew has the meaning "one who is like God." Thus "Michael, mine archangel" (D&C 29:26) will have the assignment to accomplish the final defeat of Satan and his hosts at the end of the millennial period (see D&C 88:112–115)—just as he defeated Lucifer (Satan) and his followers in the premortal realm (see Rev. 12:7–8). Adam is a figure of supernal importance in the work and glory of God, beginning in the premortal realm, continuing throughout mortality, and extending into the eternities.

For more information on Adam, see Appendix B.

Eve

Eve (meaning: the mother of all living), the first woman of humankind and divine "help meet" given unto Adam, is mentioned by name 16 times in the scriptures. From the latter-day vision of President Joseph F. Smith concerning the work of salvation in the spirit world, we have the most satisfying one-word attribute used to summarize the character and person of Eve: "glorious" (see D&C 138:39).

For more information on Eve, see Appendix B.

and over all the earth, and over every creeping thing that creepeth upon the earth.

27 And I, God, created man in mine own image, in the image of mine Only Begotten created I him; male and female created I them.

28 And I, God, blessed them, and said unto them: Be fruitful, and multiply, and replenish the earth, and subdue it, and have dominion over the fish of the sea, and over the fowl of the air, and over every living thing that moveth upon the earth.

29 And I, God, said unto man: Behold, I have given you every herb bearing seed, which is upon the face of all the earth, and every tree in the which shall be the fruit of a tree yielding seed; to you it shall be for meat.

30 And to every beast of the earth, and to every fowl of the air, and to everything that creepeth upon the earth, wherein I grant life, there shall be given every clean herb for meat; and it was so, even as I spake.

31 And I, God, saw everything that I had made, and, behold, all things which I had made were very good; and the evening and the morning were the sixth day.

MOSES CHAPTER 3
(June–October 1830)

1 THUS the heaven and the earth were finished, and all the host of them.

2 And on the seventh day I, God, ended my work, and all things which I had made; and I rested on the seventh day from all my work, and all things which I had made were finished, and I, God, saw that they were good;

3 And I, God, blessed the seventh day, and sanctified it; because that in it I had rested from all my work which I, God, had created and made.

4 And now, behold, I say unto you, that these are the generations of the heaven and of the earth, when they were created, in the day that I, the Lord God, made the heaven and the earth,

5 And every plant of the field before it was in the earth, and every herb of the field before it grew. For I, the Lord God, created all things, of which I have spoken, spiritually, before they were naturally upon the face of the earth. For I, the Lord God, had not caused it to rain upon the face of the earth. And I, the Lord God, had created all the children of men; and not yet a man to till the ground; for in heaven created I them; and there was not yet flesh upon the earth, neither in the water, neither in the air;

6 But I, the Lord God, spake, and there went up a mist from the earth, and watered the whole face of the ground.

7 And I, the Lord God, formed man from the dust of the ground, and breathed into his nostrils the breath of life; and man became a living soul, the first flesh upon the earth, the first man also; nevertheless, all things were before created; but spiritually were they created and made according to my word.

8 And I, the Lord God, planted a garden eastward in Eden, and there I put the man whom I had formed.

9 And out of the ground made I, the Lord God, to grow every tree, naturally, that is pleasant to the sight of man; and man could behold it. And it became also a living soul. For it was spiritual in the day

Moses 2:30—The Majesty of the Creation and the Plan of Life

Looking at the Creation from the Lord's perspective, we can see the grand scope and the divine goodness of the plan of life, and can appreciate our world as a manifestation of the power and glory of God at work.

We learn from the Hebrew that the word *create* refers to "organize." Matter has always existed. The earth and firmament were organized in six periods of time. The creation was concluded in the crowning moment where Adam and Eve were placed here upon the earth.

While Moses and Abraham were granted divine vision of the creation, the knowledge and methodology for creating the earth have not yet been made known to mankind. We are finite mortals and in this state it would be impossible to comprehend such truth (see Isa. 55: 8–9). The time will come, if we are true and faithful, when all things will be made known to those who honor the oath and covenant of the priesthood.

The earth has a singular purpose—to be a place for Heavenly Father's children to live, be tested, and prepared to reside in the celestial kingdom if found worthy. And thus we see that gratitude for the earth comes as we understand and appreciate its glory and the purpose for which it was created.

MOSES CHAPTER 3
(June–October 1830)

Moses 3:2—The Beauties of Nature

The gratitude we feel when immersed in the glories of nature gives peace to the soul and rest to the mind. With thanks we view the grandeur of the Creation and we partake of God's spirit of satisfaction upon completion of His creative work. We humbly recognize the wondrous truth that all these good things were made "for the benefit and the use of man, both to please the eye and to gladden the heart" (D&C 59:18) and that "it pleaseth God that he hath given all these things unto man; for unto this end were they made to be used, with judgment" (D&C 59:20). With the spirit of thanksgiving and joy we "confess…his hand in all things" (D&C 59:21) and commit ourselves more fully to honor the Creation and the divine purpose for which it was instituted.

This magnificent Creation—with its endless manifestations of fertility and fruitfulness—is evidence supreme of the dynamic operation of the creative life-sustaining light of Christ, which not only informs the sun, the moon, the stars, and the earth, but also serves to enlighten our minds and quicken our understandings as it fills the immensity of space (see D&C 88:7–12). It is this surpassing light that sustains the flame of gratitude burning in our hearts.

that I created it; for it remaineth in the sphere in which I, God, created it, yea, even all things which I prepared for the use of man; and man saw that it was good for food. And I, the Lord God, planted the tree of life also in the midst of the garden, and also the tree of knowledge of good and evil.

10 And I, the Lord God, caused a river to go out of Eden to water the garden; and from thence it was parted, and became into four heads.

11 And I, the Lord God, called the name of the first Pison, and it compasseth the whole land of Havilah, where I, the Lord God, created much gold;

12 And the gold of that land was good, and there was bdellium and the onyx stone.

13 And the name of the second river was called Gihon; the same that compasseth the whole land of Ethiopia.

14 And the name of the third river was Hiddekel; that which goeth toward the east of Assyria. And the fourth river was the Euphrates.

15 And I, the Lord God, took the man, and put him into the Garden of Eden, to dress it, and to keep it.

16 And I, the Lord God, commanded the man, saying: Of every tree of the garden thou mayest freely eat,

17 But of the tree of the knowledge of good and evil, thou shalt not eat of it, nevertheless, thou mayest choose for thyself, for it is given unto thee; but, remember that I forbid it, for in the day thou eatest thereof thou shalt surely die.

18 And I, the Lord God, said unto mine Only Begotten, that it was not good that the man should be alone; wherefore, I will make an help meet for him.

19 And out of the ground I, the Lord God, formed every beast of the field, and every fowl of the air; and commanded that they should come unto Adam, to see what he would call them; and they were also living souls; for I, God, breathed into them the breath of life, and commanded that whatsoever Adam called every living creature, that should be the name thereof.

20 And Adam gave names to all cattle, and to the fowl of the air, and to every beast of the field; but as for Adam, there was not found an help meet for him.

21 And I, the Lord God, caused a deep sleep to fall upon Adam; and he slept, and I took one of his ribs and closed up the flesh in the stead thereof;

22 And the rib which I, the Lord God, had taken from man, made I a woman, and brought her unto the man.

23 And Adam said: This I know now is bone of my bones, and flesh of my flesh; she shall be called Woman, because she was taken out of man.

24 Therefore shall a man leave his father and his mother, and shall cleave unto his wife; and they shall be one flesh.

25 And they were both naked, the man and his wife, and were not ashamed.

Moses 3:24—Marriage

The ordained unity of man and woman in the divine plan was confirmed again by the Savior during His earthly ministry:

> But from the beginning of the creation God made them male and female.
>
> For this cause shall a man leave his father and mother, and cleave to his wife;
>
> And they twain shall be one flesh: so then they are no more twain, but one flesh.
>
> What therefore God hath joined together, let not man put asunder. (Mark 10:6–9.)

Paul spoke of this doctrine as follows: "Nevertheless neither is the man without the woman, neither the woman without the man, in the Lord (1 Cor. 11:11).

POINT OF INTEREST

This fresco from Vittskövle Church in Sweden depicts God creating the animals. "Adam was the first *flesh on the earth and the* first *man also (see Moses 3:7). By flesh is meant mortality. . . . Adam was placed on the earth* after *all other creatures were here. He came when the earth was prepared for him. . . . The Lord speaks of his becoming the* first *'flesh,' or mortal, because of his fall. He was, of course, the first man on the earth, contrary to the teachings of our evolutionists. His name means 'many,' in reference to the greatness of his posterity as the human father of mankind"* (Joseph Fielding Smith, *Doctrines of Salvation* 1:92; emphasis in original).

MOSES CHAPTER 4
(June–October 1830)

1 AND I, the Lord God, spake unto Moses, saying: That Satan, whom thou hast commanded in the name of mine Only Begotten, is the same which was from the beginning, and he came before me, saying—Behold, here am I, send me, I will be thy son, and I will redeem all mankind, that one soul shall not be lost, and surely I will do it; wherefore give me thine honor.

2 But, behold, my Beloved Son, which was my Beloved and Chosen from the beginning, said unto me—Father, thy will be done, and the glory be thine forever.

3 Wherefore, because that Satan rebelled against me, and sought to destroy the agency of man, which I, the Lord God, had given him, and also, that I should give unto him mine own power; by the power of mine Only Begotten, I caused that he should be cast down;

4 And he became Satan, yea, even the devil, the father of all lies, to deceive and to blind men, and to lead them captive at his will, even as many as would not hearken unto my voice.

5 And now the serpent was more subtle than any beast of the field which I, the Lord God, had made.

6 And Satan put it into the heart of the serpent, (for he had drawn away many after him,) and he sought also to beguile Eve, for he knew not the mind of God, wherefore he sought to destroy the world.

7 And he said unto the woman: Yea, hath God said—Ye shall not eat of every tree of the garden? (And he spake by the mouth of the serpent.)

8 And the woman said unto the serpent: We may eat of the fruit of the trees of the garden;

9 But of the fruit of the tree which thou beholdest in the midst of the garden, God hath said—Ye shall not eat of it, neither shall ye touch it, lest ye die.

10 And the serpent said unto the woman: Ye shall not surely die;

11 For God doth know that in the day ye eat thereof, then your eyes shall be opened, and ye shall be as gods, knowing good and evil.

12 And when the woman saw that the tree was good for food, and that it became pleasant to the eyes, and a tree to be desired to make her wise, she took of the fruit thereof, and did eat, and also gave unto her husband with her, and he did eat.

13 And the eyes of them both were opened, and they knew that they had been naked. And they sewed fig-leaves together and made themselves aprons.

14 And they heard the voice of the Lord God, as they were walking in the garden, in the cool of the day; and Adam and his wife went to hide themselves from the presence of the Lord God amongst the trees of the garden.

15 And I, the Lord God, called unto Adam, and said unto him: Where goest thou?

16 And he said: I heard thy voice in the garden, and I was afraid, because I beheld that I was naked, and I hid myself.

17 And I, the Lord God, said unto Adam: Who told thee thou wast naked? Hast thou eaten of the tree whereof I commanded thee that thou shouldst not eat, if so thou shouldst surely die?

18 And the man said: The woman thou gavest me, and commandest that she should remain with me, she gave me of the fruit of the tree and I did eat.

MOSES CHAPTER 4
(June–October 1830)

Moses 4:1—Avoiding Pride
The primordial example of prideful rebellion is Lucifer, who shows all discerning onlookers the pattern of behavior that inexorably leads to a fall from the grace of God.

Moses sees that Satan wanted to be sent as the Son of God, that he professed that he would redeem all mankind, and that he wanted the glory. First, he was not chosen. Second, he sought to take away our agency. Third, he wanted to usurp the glory of the Father. Satan was full of pride. Satan rebelled against three eternal verities: (1) Heavenly Father chooses His servants. They must be called of God. (2) Agency is eternal—and Satan sought to destroy it. (3) Avoiding pride is essential to salvation. Pride is the universal sin. It is the primary motivation or attribute of those who are carnal, sensual, and devilish. Only in putting the enemy of pride under our feet can we hope to become like the Savior and rise to the hope of eternal life.

Moses 4:2—Doing the Father's Will
The supernal prototype of godly obedience is the Savior, who, in perfect and humble submission to the will of the Father, offered Himself as Redeemer.

Moses was taught that our beloved brother Jesus Christ was chosen from the beginning to be the Savior of the world. The Savior showed forth two magnificent attributes: obedience ("Thy will be done") and humility ("the glory be thine for ever"). All good comes from God and the Holy Spirit, who lead us to do good and inspire all the good we do. We show our love by doing the will of our Father . . . even as the Lord Jesus Christ.

Moses 4:3—Agency is God-given
In His omniscience and infinite wisdom, the Lord saw from the beginning the pathway that man would have to follow in order to fulfill his potential as the bearer of the image of God. A central part of the mortal experience is the opportunity to exercise freedom of choice—to choose to love God and obey His will, or to love Satan and follow the byways of worldly enticements and sin. This ability to choose was God-given. It was a key part of the plan. All mortals are under strict command to teach their children the gospel plan, including the principles and ordinances of saving power. Those who choose the correct pathway, raising their families in light and truth, will move upward toward a state where the Atonement will be operative in their lives and ultimately lead to deliverance from spiritual death.

19 And I, the Lord God, said unto the woman: What is this thing which thou hast done? And the woman said: The serpent beguiled me, and I did eat.

20 And I, the Lord God, said unto the serpent: Because thou hast done this thou shalt be cursed above all cattle, and above every beast of the field; upon thy belly shalt thou go, and dust shalt thou eat all the days of thy life;

21 And I will put enmity between thee and the woman, between thy seed and her seed; and he shall bruise thy head, and thou shalt bruise his heel.

22 Unto the woman, I, the Lord God, said: I will greatly multiply thy sorrow and thy conception. In sorrow thou shalt bring forth children, and thy desire shall be to thy husband, and he shall rule over thee.

23 And unto Adam, I, the Lord God, said: Because thou hast hearkened unto the voice of thy wife, and hast eaten of the fruit of the tree of which I commanded thee, saying—Thou shalt not eat of it, cursed shall be the ground for thy sake; in sorrow shalt thou eat of it all the days of thy life.

24 Thorns also, and thistles shall it bring forth to thee, and thou shalt eat the herb of the field.

25 By the sweat of thy face shalt thou eat bread, until thou shalt return unto the ground—for thou shalt surely die—for out of it wast thou taken: for dust thou wast, and unto dust shalt thou return.

26 And Adam called his wife's name Eve, because she was the mother of all living; for thus have I, the Lord God, called the first of all women, which are many.

27 Unto Adam, and also unto his wife, did I, the Lord God, make coats of skins, and clothed them.

28 And I, the Lord God, said unto mine Only Begotten: Behold, the man is become as one of us to know good and evil; and now lest he put forth his hand and partake also of the tree of life, and eat and live forever,

29 Therefore I, the Lord God, will send him forth from the Garden of Eden, to till the ground from whence he was taken;

30 For as I, the Lord God, liveth, even so my words cannot return void, for as they go forth out of my mouth they must be fulfilled.

31 So I drove out the man, and I placed at the east of the Garden of Eden, cherubim and a flaming sword, which turned every way to keep the way of the tree of life.

32 (And these are the words which I spake unto my servant Moses, and they are true even as I will; and I have spoken them unto you. See thou show them unto no man, until I command you, except to them that believe. Amen.)

MOSES CHAPTER 5
(June–October 1830)

1 AND it came to pass that after I, the Lord God, had driven them out, that Adam began to till the earth, and to have dominion over all the beasts of the field, and to eat his bread by the sweat of his brow, as I the Lord had commanded him. And Eve, also, his wife, did labor with him.

2 And Adam knew his wife, and she bare unto him sons and daughters, and they began to multiply and to replenish the earth.

Moses 4:31—The Fall

The Lord anticipated the fall of mankind as a necessary part of man's journey toward immortality and eternal life. Prior to the fall, Adam and Eve were in a state of innocence. They were in the presence of God, did not know good from evil, were unable to have children, and were not subject to death. They were commanded to multiply and replenish the earth; they were also commanded not to partake of the forbidden fruit. They had the power to choose. In this state of innocence, they did not realize that they couldn't have children.

Eve was beguiled by Satan and partook of the forbidden fruit. Knowing consequently good from evil, she realized that she would be cast out from the Garden of Eden and that, no longer being with Adam, they would not be able to have children (see Moses 5:11). Adam, now aware of his fate, made the choice and knowingly partook of the fruit that man may be (see 2 Ne. 2:25).

The results of the fall, with the following outcomes, proved to be a blessing for all mankind:

• Spirit children of God the Father are provided mortal tabernacles (see Moses 5:11).

• All mankind experience physical and spiritual death (see 2 Ne. 9:6).

• We experience opposition, which is necessary for our growth (see 2 Ne. 2:11).

• We have the capacity to choose good or evil and receive the blessings or consequences (see 2 Ne. 2:27).

• The Plan of Redemption brings joy and eternal life if we follow it and obey (see Moses 5:10–11).

For insights into cherubim, which were placed to guard the Garden of Eden, see Appendix C.

MOSES CHAPTER 5
(June–October 1830)

Introduction: "If thou doest well . . ."

A motto for this chapter might well be, "If thou doest well, thou shalt be accepted" (Moses 5:23). This motto encompasses three main dimensions: (1) Bringing before the Lord an acceptable offering—when we follow the Lord's counsel, we are favored of Him; but He is displeased with those who reject his counsel; (2) Understanding the difference between the bondage of darkness and the freedom of light—the gospel of light and love is sent to dispel the darkness of hate and the secret combinations of death; and (3) Aligning ourselves with Zion, a righteous people—to be of one heart and one mind with one another and with the Lord is to be a Zion people.

Moses 5:1—Mortality

Adam and Eve were cast out of the garden and began their life as mortals. They were given the right to choose good or evil and began to provide for themselves. They started their family and kept the commandment of multiplying and replenishing the earth. They called upon God in prayer, and the Lord gave them commandments to worship God and offer sacrifice. Adam did not understand why he

3 And from that time forth, the sons and daughters of Adam began to divide two and two in the land, and to till the land, and to tend flocks, and they also begat sons and daughters.

4 And Adam and Eve, his wife, called upon the name of the Lord, and they heard the voice of the Lord from the way toward the Garden of Eden, speaking unto them, and they saw him not; for they were shut out from his presence.

5 And he gave unto them commandments, that they should worship the Lord their God, and should offer the firstlings of their flocks, for an offering unto the Lord. And Adam was obedient unto the commandments of the Lord.

6 And after many days an angel of the Lord appeared unto Adam, saying: Why dost thou offer sacrifices unto the Lord? And Adam said unto him: I know not, save the Lord commanded me.

7 And then the angel spake, saying: This thing is a similitude of the sacrifice of the Only Begotten of the Father, which is full of grace and truth.

8 Wherefore, thou shalt do all that thou doest in the name of the Son, and thou shalt repent and call upon God in the name of the Son forevermore.

9 And in that day the Holy Ghost fell upon Adam, which beareth record of the Father and the Son, saying: I am the Only Begotten of the Father from the beginning, henceforth and forever, that as thou hast fallen thou mayest be redeemed, and all mankind, even as many as will.

10 And in that day Adam blessed God and was filled, and began to prophesy concerning all the families of the earth, saying: Blessed be the name of God, for because of my transgression my eyes are opened, and in this life I shall have joy, and again in the flesh I shall see God.

11 And Eve, his wife, heard all these things and was glad, saying: Were it not for our transgression we never should have had seed, and never should have known good and evil, and the joy of our redemption, and the eternal life which God giveth unto all the obedient.

12 And Adam and Eve blessed the name of God, and they made all things known unto their sons and their daughters.

13 And Satan came among them, saying: I am also a son of God; and he commanded them, saying: Believe it not; and they believed it not, and they loved Satan more than God. And men began from that time forth to be carnal, sensual, and devilish.

14 And the Lord God called upon men by the Holy Ghost everywhere and commanded them that they should repent;

15 And as many as believed in the Son, and repented of their sins, should be saved; and as many as believed not and repented not, should be damned; and the words went forth out of the mouth of God in a firm decree; wherefore they must be fulfilled.

16 And Adam and Eve, his wife, ceased not to call upon God. And Adam knew Eve his wife, and she conceived and bare Cain, and said: I have gotten a man from the Lord; wherefore he may not reject his words. But behold, Cain hearkened not, saying: Who is the Lord that I should know him?

17 And she again conceived and bare his brother Abel. And Abel hearkened unto the voice of the Lord. And Abel was a keeper of sheep, but Cain was a tiller of the ground.

18 And Cain loved Satan more than God. And Satan commanded him, saying: Make an offering unto the Lord.

19 And in process of time it came to pass that Cain brought of the fruit of the ground an offering unto the Lord.

offered the firstlings of the flock, but he obeyed. (That is a lesson within itself: obey and then seek understanding—not the other way around.)

Thus we see that mortality is the time for us to prepare to meet God. Mortality should not be the time for amassing the wealth of the world or for acquiring fame and fortune, position or status, or the honors of men. We learn from Moses 5 the simple truth about mortality: As a family we are to work, have children, call upon God, keep His commandments, remember the Savior's Atoning sacrifice, apply the Atonement to our lives, and teach these things to our children. These are simple truths with everlasting blessings.

Moses 5:11—The Joy Of Life

Adam and Eve truly had the vision of life. They saw the joy that mortals can have because of the goodness of God, the Plan of Redemption, and the promised blessings through obedience. Truly this moment of truth in their lives must also be part of our lives. Adam fell that we might have joy (see 2 Ne. 2:25)—joy now and eternal joy in the life to come in the presence of our Heavenly Father.

Life is exactly what we make of it. We can find joy in the Lord and the Plan of Happiness. If we lose sight of the joys of life we can become filled with discouragement rather than hope, fear and doubt rather than faith, sorrow and guilt beyond repair rather than repentance through the Lord Jesus Christ.

Moses 5:11—Family

The family is a safe haven, a place of strength, a retreat from the turmoil of the world, a fortress of God where Zion's kin—mothers and fathers, sons and daughters—can grow and abound in the spirit of love and truth. We stand all amazed to know, first of all, that we were created in the image of God, and then, even more, to realize that our family was created in the sacred image of *His* family—preserved through bonds of everlasting love and priesthood power.

Moses 5:11—Children

We look into the eyes of a child and we are grateful. To us this experience is a miraculous unfolding of our inner vision, the wondrous magnifying of our hope. Of all the tasks on earth, nothing is so challenging yet rewarding as raising a child. Surely our joy lies in our posterity. The trials seem almost overwhelming at times. But in the eyes of a child we see clearly the heavenly vision of how to proceed. And we know that in the strength of the Lord we can do all things. With John the Beloved we will yet say, gratefully, "I have no greater joy than to hear that my children walk in truth" (3 John 1:4).

Moses 5:13—Love of God, or Love of Satan and the World

We can choose whom and how much we love and receive the blessings or consequences of our actions.

20 And Abel he also brought of the firstlings of his flock, and of the fat thereof. And the Lord had respect unto Abel, and to his offering;

21 But unto Cain, and to his offering, he had not respect. Now Satan knew this, and it pleased him. And Cain was very wroth, and his countenance fell.

22 And the Lord said unto Cain: Why art thou wroth? Why is thy countenance fallen?

23 If thou doest well, thou shalt be accepted. And if thou doest not well, sin lieth at the door, and Satan desireth to have thee; and except thou shalt hearken unto my commandments, I will deliver thee up, and it shall be unto thee according to his desire. And thou shalt rule over him;

24 For from this time forth thou shalt be the father of his lies; thou shalt be called Perdition; for thou wast also before the world.

25 And it shall be said in time to come—That these abominations were had from Cain; for he rejected the greater counsel which was had from God; and this is a cursing which I will put upon thee, except thou repent.

26 And Cain was wroth, and listened not any more to the voice of the Lord, neither to Abel, his brother, who walked in holiness before the Lord.

27 And Adam and his wife mourned before the Lord, because of Cain and his brethren.

28 And it came to pass that Cain took one of his brothers' daughters to wife, and they loved Satan more than God.

29 And Satan said unto Cain: Swear unto me by thy throat, and if thou tell it thou shalt die; and swear thy brethren by their heads, and by the living God, that they tell it not; for if they tell it, they shall surely die; and this that thy father may not know it; and this day I will deliver thy brother Abel into thine hands.

30 And Satan sware unto Cain that he would do according to his commands. And all these things were done in secret.

31 And Cain said: Truly I am Mahan, the master of this great secret, that I may murder and get gain. Wherefore Cain was called Master Mahan, and he gloried in his wickedness.

32 And Cain went into the field, and Cain talked with Abel, his brother. And it came to pass that while they were in the field, Cain rose up against Abel, his brother, and slew him.

33 And Cain gloried in that which he had done, saying: I am free; surely the flocks of my brother falleth into my hands.

34 And the Lord said unto Cain: Where is Abel, thy brother? And he said: I know not. Am I my brother's keeper?

35 And the Lord said: What hast thou done? The voice of thy brother's blood cries unto me from the ground.

36 And now thou shalt be cursed from the earth which hath opened her mouth to receive thy brother's blood from thy hand.

37 When thou tillest the ground it shall not henceforth yield unto thee her strength. A fugitive and a vagabond shalt thou be in the earth.

38 And Cain said unto the Lord: Satan tempted me because of my brother's flocks. And I was wroth also; for his offering thou didst accept and not mine; my punishment is greater than I can bear.

39 Behold thou hast driven me out this day from the face of the Lord, and from thy face shall I be hid; and I shall be a fugitive and a vagabond in the earth; and it shall come to pass, that he that findeth me will slay me, because of mine iniquities, for these things are not hid from the Lord.

When Satan tempted the children of Adam and Eve, some of them chose to believe Satan instead of their parents concerning the plan of redemption. They loved Satan more than God. The results were devastating. They became carnal, sensual, and devilish. Cain and his wife were some of those who loved Satan more than God (see Moses 5:28). When one is carnal, sensual, and devilish one is subject to the lusts and passions of the flesh. Such become worldly. The world and the things of the world become their god. They are in a state of enmity with God (see Rom. 8:7).

The moment one chooses the world — thus choosing Satan — over God, he separates himself from God. We can choose the world or Satan over God…things, positions, titles, stations, possessions, honors of men, fame, money and fortunes, and even our occupation, hobbies, TV, and our daily work.

Moses 5:25—Rejecting the Lord's Counsel

The manner and type of proper sacrifice had been taught Adam and his children. Cain loved Satan more than God, and Satan commanded Cain to make an offering unto the Lord. Cain, choosing to follow the counsel of Satan, offered the fruit of the field, which was not in similitude of the atoning sacrifice. Despite warnings (see Moses 5:23), Cain persisted in following Satan, and his choices showed that he loved Satan more than God.

Cain has provided us an example so dramatic we cannot miss the results of failing to follow the counsel of the Lord. The Lord is boud when we do what He asks. His blessings are ours as we choose to follow Him and make an appropriate offering in righteousness—with our heart, with our mind, or in good works.

Moses 5:32—Cain and Abel
For insights about Cain and Abel, see Appendix D.

The Death of Abel by Gustave Doré

40 And I the Lord said unto him: Whosoever slayeth thee, vengeance shall be taken on him sevenfold. And I the Lord set a mark upon Cain, lest any finding him should kill him.

41 And Cain was shut out from the presence of the Lord, and with his wife and many of his brethren dwelt in the land of Nod, on the east of Eden.

42 And Cain knew his wife, and she conceived and bare Enoch, and he also begat many sons and daughters. And he builded a city, and he called the name of the city after the name of his son, Enoch.

43 And unto Enoch was born Irad, and other sons and daughters. And Irad begat Mahujael, and other sons and daughters. And Mahujael begat Methusael, and other sons and daughters. And Methusael begat Lamech.

44 And Lamech took unto himself two wives; the name of one being Adah, and the name of the other, Zillah.

45 And Adah bare Jabal; he was the father of such as dwell in tents, and they were keepers of cattle; and his brother's name was Jubal, who was the father of all such as handle the harp and organ.

46 And Zillah, she also bare Tubal Cain, an instructor of every artificer in brass and iron. And the sister of Tubal Cain was called Naamah.

47 And Lamech said unto his wives, Adah and Zillah: Hear my voice, ye wives of Lamech, hearken unto my speech; for I have slain a man to my wounding, and a young man to my hurt.

48 If Cain shall be avenged sevenfold, truly Lamech shall be seventy and seven fold;

49 For Lamech having entered into a covenant with Satan, after the manner of Cain, wherein he became Master Mahan, master of that great secret which was administered unto Cain by Satan; and Irad, the son of Enoch, having known their secret, began to reveal it unto the sons of Adam;

50 Wherefore Lamech, being angry, slew him, not like unto Cain, his brother Abel, for the sake of getting gain, but he slew him for the oath's sake.

51 For, from the days of Cain, there was a secret combination, and their works were in the dark, and they knew every man his brother.

52 Wherefore the Lord cursed Lamech, and his house, and all them that had covenanted with Satan; for they kept not the commandments of God, and it displeased God, and he ministered not unto them, and their works were abominations, and began to spread among all the sons of men. And it was among the sons of men.

53 And among the daughters of men these things were not spoken, because that Lamech had spoken the secret unto his wives, and they rebelled against him, and declared these things abroad, and had not compassion;

54 Wherefore Lamech was despised, and cast out, and came not among the sons of men, lest he should die.

55 And thus the works of darkness began to prevail among all the sons of men.

56 And God cursed the earth with a sore curse, and was angry with the wicked, with all the sons of men whom he had made;

57 For they would not hearken unto his voice, nor believe on his Only Begotten Son, even him whom he declared should come in the meridian of time, who was prepared from before the foundation of the world.

58 And thus the Gospel began to be preached, from the beginning, being declared by holy angels sent forth from the presence of God, and by his own voice, and by the gift of the Holy Ghost.

Moses 5:43—Lamech

Lamech is the fifth in descent from Cain, son of Adam. The account in the Pearl of Great Price extends our knowledge about Lamech, he being a principal facilitator of Satanic secret combinations in the early history of mankind (see Moses 5:49–55).

Moses 5:58—The Gospel of Love

The gospel of light and love is sent to dispel the darkness of hate and the secret combinations of death.

The pattern for revelation has always been the same from the beginning of time. God, angels, or living prophets, seers, and revelators moved upon by the power of the Holy Ghost have brought us the word of God—even the gospel of Jesus Christ. Within the gospel are the principles and ordinances of salvation. Adam preached repentance to his sons as the voice of God came unto him (see Moses 6:1). Enoch, likewise, preached repentance, having been commanded by a voice from heaven (see Moses 6:27).

Of all the gospel themes, faith unto repentance has been preached the most. It follows that man, being in a fallen state, needs to change. He needs to become a Saint through the atonement of Christ (see Mos. 3:19). This happens as we yield to the enticings of the Holy Spirit (see D&C 50:17–22) and accept Christ and partake of baptism and the gift of the Holy Ghost. The purpose of revelation is to reveal the will of God to mankind, thus helping them return to His presence.

Thus we see that the light of the Lord is the key to receiving knowledge from the Lord. The knowledge of God is the knowledge that saves. We cannot live without it. We would be left to ourselves. "Where there is no vision, the people perish" (Prov. 29:18). Where there is no light, there is darkness; if that is the case, we cannot see and we cannot comprehend all things (see D&C 88:67). The goodness of God is continually before us as we receive direction for our lives. Our challenge is: do we follow the Spirit, the living prophets, angels, and the voice of the Lord? When we do, we will be free, for we will live by the light of the Lord.

 POINT OF INTEREST

Hebrew scholar Robert Alter says of the meaning of the original "mark upon Cain"—in Gen. 4:15 and Moses 5:40—that "it is of course a mark of protection, not a stigma as the English idiom 'mark of Cain' suggests." This is further reinforced by the Lord's statement in the same verses "lest any finding him should kill him" (The Five Books of Moses [New York: W. W. Norton & Company, 2004]).

59 And thus all things were confirmed unto Adam, by an holy ordinance, and the Gospel preached, and a decree sent forth, that it should be in the world, until the end thereof; and thus it was. Amen.

MOSES CHAPTER 6
(November–December 1830)

1 AND Adam hearkened unto the voice of God, and called upon his sons to repent.

2 And Adam knew his wife again, and she bare a son, and he called his name Seth. And Adam glorified the name of God; for he said: God hath appointed me another seed, instead of Abel, whom Cain slew.

3 And God revealed himself unto Seth, and he rebelled not, but offered an acceptable sacrifice, like unto his brother Abel. And to him also was born a son, and he called his name Enos.

4 And then began these men to call upon the name of the Lord, and the Lord blessed them;

5 And a book of remembrance was kept, in the which was recorded, in the language of Adam, for it was given unto as many as called upon God to write by the spirit of inspiration;

6 And by them their children were taught to read and write, having a language which was pure and undefiled.

7 Now this same Priesthood, which was in the beginning, shall be in the end of the world also.

8 Now this prophecy Adam spake, as he was moved upon by the Holy Ghost, and a genealogy was kept of the children of God. And this was the book of the generations of Adam, saying: In the day that God created man, in the likeness of God made he him;

9 In the image of his own body, male and female, created he them, and blessed them, and called their name Adam, in the day when they were created and became living souls in the land upon the footstool of God.

10 And Adam lived one hundred and thirty years, and begat a son in his own likeness, after his own image, and called his name Seth.

11 And the days of Adam, after he had begotten Seth, were eight hundred years, and he begat many sons and daughters;

12 And all the days that Adam lived were nine hundred and thirty years, and he died.

13 Seth lived one hundred and five years, and begat Enos, and prophesied in all his days, and taught his son Enos in the ways of God; wherefore Enos prophesied also.

14 And Seth lived, after he begat Enos, eight hundred and seven years, and begat many sons and daughters.

15 And the children of men were numerous upon all the face of the land. And in those days Satan had great dominion among men, and raged in their hearts; and from thenceforth came wars and bloodshed; and a man's hand was against his own brother, in administering death, because of secret works, seeking for power.

16 All the days of Seth were nine hundred and twelve years, and he died.

17 And Enos lived ninety years, and begat Cainan. And Enos and the residue of the people of God came out from the land, which was called Shulon, and dwelt in a land of promise, which he called after his own son, whom he had named Cainan.

MOSES CHAPTER 6
(November–December 1830)

Moses 6:2—Seth
Seth was a son of Adam and Eve. According to the biblical account, his mother "called his name Seth: For God, *said she*, hath appointed me another seed instead of Abel, whom Cain slew" (Gen. 4:25). Seth, who lived 912 years, was the father of Enos as well as other sons and daughters. Latter-day scripture gives a fuller understanding of the character and importance of Seth:

> . . . [Seth] received the promise of God by his father, that his posterity should be the chosen of the Lord, and that they should be preserved unto the end of the earth;
>
> Because he (Seth) was a perfect man, and his likeness was the express likeness of his father, insomuch that he seemed to be like unto his father in all things, and could be distinguished from him only by his age. (D&C 107:42–43; see also D&C 107:51)

Additionally, Seth is mentioned as a participant in the august assembly of elect individuals gathered together by Adam to receive his benedictory blessing at Adam-ondi-Ahman (see D&C 107:53). Seth is also mentioned as one of the noble personages viewed by President Joseph F. Smith in his vision of the spirit realm (see D&C 138:40). Moreover, the Pearl of Great Price confirms that God revealed himself unto Seth (see Moses 6:3).

Moses 6:5—Book of Remembrance
From the beginning, the preservation of family history has been a pattern set by the prophets of the Lord. The sons and daughters of God are precious, and each is of divine importance. Our commission is to keep a record of our own family experiences—even a "book of remembrance" that contributes to the archive of progress in the Kingdom of God.

Moses 6:17–19—Enos, Cainan, and Mahalaleel
Enos (meaning: mortal man) was the son of Seth and grandson of Adam and Eve; the Old Testament gives scant information about the life of Enos beyond the fact that he had sons and daughters (including Cainan) and lived 905 years (see Genesis 5:6–11). The account in Genesis indicates that after the birth of Enos "began men to call upon the name of the LORD" (Genesis 4:26).

In comparison with the brief account in Genesis, the Pearl of Great Price broadens our understanding of the ministry and valor of Enos as a prophet (see Moses 6:13–18.)

The Doctrine and Covenants sheds additional light on the life of Enos, Cainan, and Mahalaleel (pronounced "muh-hay'-luh-lee'-uhl"). All three are mentioned twice in that work: once in connection with the descent of the priesthood lineage (see D&C 107:44–46) and again as participants in the assembly of elect individuals gathered together by Adam

18 And Enos lived, after he begat Cainan, eight hundred and fifteen years, and begat many sons and daughters. And all the days of Enos were nine hundred and five years, and he died.

19 And Cainan lived seventy years, and begat Mahalaleel; and Cainan lived after he begat Mahalaleel eight hundred and forty years, and begat sons and daughters. And all the days of Cainan were nine hundred and ten years, and he died.

20 And Mahalaleel lived sixty-five years, and begat Jared; and Mahalaleel lived, after he begat Jared, eight hundred and thirty years, and begat sons and daughters. And all the days of Mahalaleel were eight hundred and ninety-five years, and he died.

21 And Jared lived one hundred and sixty-two years, and begat Enoch; and Jared lived, after he begat Enoch, eight hundred years, and begat sons and daughters. And Jared taught Enoch in all the ways of God.

22 And this is the genealogy of the sons of Adam, who was the son of God, with whom God, himself, conversed.

23 And they were preachers of righteousness, and spake and prophesied, and called upon all men, everywhere, to repent; and faith was taught unto the children of men.

24 And it came to pass that all the days of Jared were nine hundred and sixty-two years, and he died.

25 And Enoch lived sixty-five years, and begat Methuselah.

26 And it came to pass that Enoch journeyed in the land, among the people; and as he journeyed, the Spirit of God descended out of heaven, and abode upon him.

27 And he heard a voice from heaven, saying: Enoch, my son, prophesy unto this people, and say unto them—Repent, for thus saith the Lord: I am angry with this people, and my fierce anger is kindled against them; for their hearts have waxed hard, and their ears are dull of hearing, and their eyes cannot see afar off;

28 And for these many generations, ever since the day that I created them, have they gone astray, and have denied me, and have sought their own counsels in the dark; and in their own abominations have they devised murder, and have not kept the commandments, which I gave unto their father, Adam.

29 Wherefore, they have foresworn themselves, and, by their oaths, they have brought upon themselves death; and a hell I have prepared for them, if they repent not;

30 And this is a decree, which I have sent forth in the beginning of the world, from my own mouth, from the foundation thereof, and by the mouths of my servants, thy fathers, have I decreed it, even as it shall be sent forth in the world, unto the ends thereof.

31 And when Enoch had heard these words, he bowed himself to the earth, before the Lord, and spake before the Lord, saying: Why is it that I have found favor in thy sight, and am but a lad, and all the people hate me; for I am slow of speech; wherefore am I thy servant?

32 And the Lord said unto Enoch: Go forth and do as I have commanded thee, and no man shall pierce thee. Open thy mouth, and it shall be filled, and I will give thee utterance, for all flesh is in my hands, and I will do as seemeth me good.

33 Say unto this people: Choose ye this day, to serve the Lord God who made you.

34 Behold my Spirit is upon you, wherefore all thy words will I justify; and the mountains shall flee before you, and the rivers shall turn from their course; and thou shalt abide in me, and I in you; therefore walk with me.

to receive his benedictory blessing (see D&C 107:53). The name Mahalaleel is rendered *Maleleel* in Luke 3:37.

Moses 6:21—Enoch

The record of the life of Enoch, seventh from Adam is fairly sparse as presented in the Old Testament (see Gen. 5:18–24). The apostle Paul gives additional insight when he explained that Enoch "pleased God" and was translated (see Heb. 11:5). Beyond that, however, we have few salient details of his character from these references.

However, from the light shed on Enoch in the Pearl of Great Price we begin to grasp the extraordinary dignity and importance of this prophet.

For more insights into the life of Enoch, see Appendix E.

Moses 6:22–36—The Calling of a Prophet

The humility of Enoch in connection with his calling as a prophet of God is a quality that emerged in a similar way when others were called to this same office. Moses, who was "very meek, above all the men which *were* upon the face of the earth" (Num. 12:3), needed the reassurance of the Almighty when he was called to liberate the Israelites (see Ex. 3:11–12). Isaiah was burdened with feelings of incapacity and lowliness when he was called (see Isa. 6:5–7), but immediately experienced a confirmation that his instrumentality would, through the blessing of the Lord, be equal to the daunting task. Jeremiah was overcome with feelings of inadequacy when called as a prophet:

> Then said I, Ah, Lord GOD! behold, I cannot speak: for I am a child.
>
> But the LORD said unto me, Say not, I am a child: for thou shalt go to all that I shall send thee, and whatsoever I command thee thou shalt speak.
>
> Be not afraid of their faces: for I am with thee to deliver thee, saith the LORD.
>
> Then the LORD put forth his hand, and touched my mouth. And the LORD said unto me, Behold, I have put my words in thy mouth.
>
> See, I have this day set thee over the nations and over the kingdoms, to root out, and to pull down, and to destroy, and to throw down, to build, and to plant. (Jer. 1:6–10)

Similarly, anyone called to a position in the kingdom of God—and all have a role to play—will feel touched by a sense of needing to rise to a higher level of performance and worthiness. Through the blessings of the Spirit, eyes can be opened to a vision of fulfillment and hearts can be strengthened in the measure needed to "go and do the things which the Lord hath commanded" (1 Ne. 3:7).

35 And the Lord spake unto Enoch, and said unto him: Anoint thine eyes with clay, and wash them, and thou shalt see. And he did so.

36 And he beheld the spirits that God had created; and he beheld also things which were not visible to the natural eye; and from thenceforth came the saying abroad in the land: A seer hath the Lord raised up unto his people.

37 And it came to pass that Enoch went forth in the land, among the people, standing upon the hills and the high places, and cried with a loud voice, testifying against their works; and all men were offended because of him.

38 And they came forth to hear him, upon the high places, saying unto the tent-keepers: Tarry ye here and keep the tents, while we go yonder to behold the seer, for he prophesieth, and there is a strange thing in the land; a wild man hath come among us.

39 And it came to pass when they heard him, no man laid hands on him; for fear came on all them that heard him; for he walked with God.

40 And there came a man unto him, whose name was Mahijah, and said unto him: Tell us plainly who thou art, and from whence thou comest?

41 And he said unto them: I came out from the land of Cainan, the land of my fathers, a land of righteousness unto this day. And my father taught me in all the ways of God.

42 And it came to pass, as I journeyed from the land of Cainan, by the sea east, I beheld a vision; and lo, the heavens I saw, and the Lord spake with me, and gave me commandment; wherefore, for this cause, to keep the commandment, I speak forth these words.

43 And Enoch continued his speech, saying: The Lord which spake with me, the same is the God of heaven, and he is my God, and your God, and ye are my brethren, and why counsel ye yourselves, and deny the God of heaven?

44 The heavens he made; the earth is his footstool; and the foundation thereof is his. Behold, he laid it, an host of men hath he brought in upon the face thereof.

45 And death hath come upon our fathers; nevertheless we know them, and cannot deny, and even the first of all we know, even Adam.

46 For a book of remembrance we have written among us, according to the pattern given by the finger of God; and it is given in our own language.

47 And as Enoch spake forth the words of God, the people trembled, and could not stand in his presence.

48 And he said unto them: Because that Adam fell, we are; and by his fall came death; and we are made partakers of misery and woe.

49 Behold Satan hath come among the children of men, and tempteth them to worship him; and men have become carnal, sensual, and devilish, and are shut out from the presence of God.

50 But God hath made known unto our fathers that all men must repent.

51 And he called upon our father Adam by his own voice, saying: I am God; I made the world, and men before they were in the flesh.

52 And he also said unto him: If thou wilt turn unto me, and hearken unto my voice, and believe, and repent of all thy transgressions, and be baptized, even in water, in the name of mine Only Begotten Son, who is full of grace and truth, which is Jesus Christ, the only name which shall be given under heaven, whereby salvation shall come unto the children of men, ye shall receive the gift

Moses 6:46—Book of Remembrance

Scriptures are the journals of God's prophets regarding their dealings with God and man. The lesson applies to all of us, for we should keep a journal and write our personal history.

Adam and all his seed kept a record—a book of remembrance that contained words written under the spirit of inspiration in the language of Adam (see Moses 6:5). Abraham also recorded his history back to the beginning of the creation. Abraham had in his possession the record, and as he wrote, his purpose was clear. It was "for the benefit of my posterity that shall come after me" (Abr. 1:31).

The Lord has commanded his servants since the beginning of time to record the dealings of God with man. Christ, when visiting the American continent, reminded the people to record the words of Samuel the Lamanite, for they were so precious concerning the prophecies of our Savior. Under commandment of God the Father, the Savior also gave the Nephites the words of Malachi concerning Elijah and the work of family history and genealogy—for the Nephites had left Jerusalem prior to the ministry of the Prophet Malachi (approximately 430 BC). It is imperative to leave the word of God with the children of God so they will have direction in their lives. Without it they fall away (see Mosiah 1:3–7).

Moses 6:52—Salvation through the Lord

Through the Prophet Joseph Smith we have preserved for our day the words of Moses—who was recording in turn the words of Enoch, reporting on what the Lord had said to Adam concerning the plan of salvation brought about through the Atonement of Jesus Christ. What is remarkable about this verse, so pure and plain in its essence, is that it confirms many of the fundamental truths of the gospel of Jesus Christ that have been lost from the Old Testament canon—those "plain and precious things" restored by the Lord in the latter days through the Book of Mormon, the Pearl of Great Price, and the Doctrine and Covenants.

It is instructive that our present Old Testament (King James version) does not contain the words "baptism," "Holy Ghost," "Only Begotten," or "Only Begotten Son." Nowhere in the Old Testament does the name *Jesus Christ* appear. Yet all of these principles, truths, and identities were at work in Old Testament dispensations as evidenced repeatedly in the Pearl of Great Price and the Book of Mormon, the prophets of old bearing continual witness of the divine mission of the Son of God, even Jesus Christ.

The coming together of precious precepts and principles of truth in the latter days through the design of the Almighty proves "that the holy scriptures are true, and that God does inspire men and call them to his holy work in this age and generation, as well as in generations of old; Thereby showing that he is the same God yesterday, today, and forever" (D&C 20:11–12).

of the Holy Ghost, asking all things in his name, and whatsoever ye shall ask, it shall be given you.

53 And our father Adam spake unto the Lord, and said: Why is it that men must repent and be baptized in water? And the Lord said unto Adam: Behold I have forgiven thee thy transgression in the Garden of Eden.

54 Hence came the saying abroad among the people, that the Son of God hath atoned for original guilt, wherein the sins of the parents cannot be answered upon the heads of the children, for they are whole from the foundation of the world.

55 And the Lord spake unto Adam, saying: Inasmuch as thy children are conceived in sin, even so when they begin to grow up, sin conceiveth in their hearts, and they taste the bitter, that they may know to prize the good.

56 And it is given unto them to know good from evil; wherefore they are agents unto themselves, and I have given unto you another law and commandment.

57 Wherefore teach it unto your children, that all men, everywhere, must repent, or they can in nowise inherit the kingdom of God, for no unclean thing can dwell there, or dwell in his presence; for, in the language of Adam, Man of Holiness is his name, and the name of his Only Begotten is the Son of Man, even Jesus Christ, a righteous Judge, who shall come in the meridian of time.

58 Therefore I give unto you a commandment, to teach these things freely unto your children, saying:

59 That by reason of transgression cometh the fall, which fall bringeth death, and inasmuch as ye were born into the world by water, and blood, and the spirit, which I have made, and so became of dust a living soul, even so ye must be born again into the kingdom of heaven, of water, and of the Spirit, and be cleansed by blood, even the blood of mine Only Begotten; that ye might be sanctified from all sin, and enjoy the words of eternal life in this world, and eternal life in the world to come, even immortal glory;

60 For by the water ye keep the commandment; by the Spirit ye are justified, and by the blood ye are sanctified;

61 Therefore it is given to abide in you; the record of heaven; the Comforter; the peaceable things of immortal glory; the truth of all things; that which quickeneth all things, which maketh alive all things; that which knoweth all things, and hath all power according to wisdom, mercy, truth, justice, and judgment.

62 And now, behold, I say unto you: This is the plan of salvation unto all men, through the blood of mine Only Begotten, who shall come in the meridian of time.

63 And behold, all things have their likeness, and all things are created and made to bear record of me, both things which are temporal, and things which are spiritual; things which are in the heavens above, and things which are on the earth, and things which are in the earth, and things which are under the earth, both above and beneath: all things bear record of me.

64 And it came to pass, when the Lord had spoken with Adam, our father, that Adam cried unto the Lord, and he was caught away by the Spirit of the Lord, and was carried down into the water, and was laid under the water, and was brought forth out of the water.

65 And thus he was baptized, and the Spirit of God descended upon him, and thus he was born of the Spirit, and became quickened in the inner man.

66 And he heard a voice out of heaven, saying: Thou art baptized with fire, and with the Holy Ghost. This is the record of the Father,

Moses 6:58—Teach Your Children

"Teach your children" has been the clarion call to parents since the beginning of time. Here, Adam and Eve were commanded to teach the gospel of Jesus Christ and the Plan of Salvation "freely" to their children. As we note in the dictionary of Noah Webster in 1828—the edition in circulation during the time the Prophet Joseph Smith was translating the Book of Mormon and working on the Pearl of Great Price—the word "freely" connotes the following:

- Voluntary, yet under a moral agent accountable, he must act freely.
- Plentifully in abundance—always.
- Without scruple or reserve—with no doubt or hesitation.
- Without impediment or hindrance—with no obstruction or things of life getting in one's way.
- Spontaneously—anytime there is a teaching moment.
- Liberally and generously—truth of all things always.
- Gratuitously—free with no claim of merit or compensation.

We realize that the word the Prophet choose to use to explain the responsibility of teaching truly magnifies the greatest role of parents—to love and teach their children.

Moses 6:59—The Atonement

The mission of the Savior assures the resurrection for all and opens the way for the obedient and faithful to return to God's presence.

As a result of the Fall man became mortal. In this fallen state it was necessary to provide a way for us to return to the presence of our Heavenly Father. Jesus Christ became our Savior; it was through His blood that we were provided with the way back—if we would follow Christ. This is the way and the truth—the *ultimate moment of truth* in our life. This is the truth upon which Eternal life is founded.

The Atonement not only brings forgiveness to those who repent, but it also makes possible immortality and eternal life through the resurrection. The power of the Atonement illuminates every aspect of our lives as Christ nourishes us and comforts us. He takes upon Himself our pains, afflictions, infirmities, and sickness, and in reality succors us in all things (see Alma 7:11–12). It is the Atonement that binds us to Christ through gratitude and the covenants of His doctrine.

The doctrine of Christ includes the first four principles and ordinance of the gospel, which apply the Atonement to our lives. The gospel is, in fact, simply this: "I came into the world to do the will of my Father . . . that I might be lifted up upon the cross, that I might draw all men unto me" (3 Ne. 27:13–14). Yes, the Atonement draws us to Christ in every way that we might come back to the presence of our Heavenly Father.

and the Son, from henceforth and forever;

67 And thou art after the order of him who was without beginning of days or end of years, from all eternity to all eternity.

68 Behold, thou art one in me, a son of God; and thus may all become my sons. Amen.

MOSES CHAPTER 7
(December 1830)

1 AND it came to pass that Enoch continued his speech, saying: Behold, our father Adam taught these things, and many have believed and become the sons of God, and many have believed not, and have perished in their sins, and are looking forth with fear, in torment, for the fiery indignation of the wrath of God to be poured out upon them.

2 And from that time forth Enoch began to prophesy, saying unto the people, that: As I was journeying, and stood upon the place Mahujah, and cried unto the Lord, there came a voice out of heaven, saying—Turn ye, and get ye upon the mount Simeon.

3 And it came to pass that I turned and went up on the mount; and as I stood upon the mount, I beheld the heavens open, and I was clothed upon with glory;

4 And I saw the Lord; and he stood before my face, and he talked with me, even as a man talketh one with another, face to face; and he said unto me: Look, and I will show unto thee the world for the space of many generations.

5 And it came to pass that I beheld in the valley of Shum, and lo, a great people which dwelt in tents, which were the people of Shum.

6 And again the Lord said unto me: Look; and I looked towards the north, and I beheld the people of Canaan, which dwelt in tents.

7 And the Lord said unto me: Prophesy; and I prophesied, saying: Behold the people of Canaan, which are numerous, shall go forth in battle array against the people of Shum, and shall slay them that they shall utterly be destroyed; and the people of Canaan shall divide themselves in the land, and the land shall be barren and unfruitful, and none other people shall dwell there but the people of Canaan;

8 For behold, the Lord shall curse the land with much heat, and the barrenness thereof shall go forth forever; and there was a blackness came upon all the children of Canaan, that they were despised among all people.

9 And it came to pass that the Lord said unto me: Look; and I looked, and I beheld the land of Sharon, and the land of Enoch, and the land of Omner, and the land of Heni, and the land of Shem, and the land of Haner, and the land of Hanannihah, and all the inhabitants thereof;

10 And the Lord said unto me: Go to this people, and say unto them—Repent, lest I come out and smite them with a curse, and they die.

11 And he gave unto me a commandment that I should baptize in the name of the Father, and of the Son, which is full of grace and truth, and of the Holy Ghost, which beareth record of the Father and the Son.

12 And it came to pass that Enoch continued to call upon all the people, save it were the people of Canaan, to repent;

13 And so great was the faith of Enoch that he led the people of

Summary of Precepts and Principles

By studying the scriptures, especially the Pearl of Great Price and the words of the Old Testament prophets such as Moses and Enoch, we gain insight into the matchless gifts of love granted us by our Father in Heaven and His Son Jesus Christ. For these gifts we are asked only to bring a broken heart and a contrite spirit (see 2 Ne. 2:7). This offering can take a variety of forms in our daily lives. We are promised immortality and eternal life if we will but bring an acceptable offering of obedience before the Lord. We are promised the light of the gospel if we will but follow the prophets and the Holy Spirit. We are promised that we can be a Zion society if we will only be unified and pure in heart. We are promised the compassion of the Atonement if we will show our gratitude and thanksgiving through righteousness. We are given the holy scriptures as our guide and asked only to follow them and to keep and share our own book of remembrance with our families and friends. By honoring and obeying the commandments of our Father in Heaven, we can have joy and peace in this life and eternal life in the world to come through the "merits, and mercy, and grace of the Holy Messiah" (2 Ne. 2:8).

MOSES CHAPTER 7
(December 1830)

Moses 7:18—Becoming a Zion People

To be of one heart and one mind with one another and with the Lord is to be a Zion people. The word *heart* in Hebrew is "leb" or "lebab." It refers to the inner man—his character, the whole man, the governing center of all his actions, the seat of his will, his emotions, his attention and reflection and understanding, his purpose and his desires.

Enoch's people literally gave their heart to the Lord—and in so doing, gave themselves and their will to Him. This should be what we strive for: to become pure in heart as a person, a family, a ward, a stake, and a church. It all begins with the individual. Some things we can do to become pure in heart and a Zion people are:

- Feast upon the word of God—search the scriptures.
- Know His will and do His will (see 2 Ne. 32:3).
- Fast and pray to receive direction and strength and to avoid and overcome temptation (see 3 Ne. 18:15,18).
- Become as Christ (see 3 Ne. 27:27) and give Christ-like service (see D&C 103:9–10).
- Keep ourselves unspotted from the world (see D&C 59:9).
- Build up the kingdom of God (see D&C 81:5; 25:6; 18:10).

The blessings are great: "And blessed [how happy] are all the pure in heart, for they shall see God" (3 Ne. 12:8).

Though the heavens wept over the pervasive wickedness among mankind, yet there was unfolded the vision of joy through the mission of the Savior.

Enoch rejoiced as he saw the day of the coming of our Savior Jesus Christ. Why was his soul rejoicing so? Enoch

God, and their enemies came to battle against them; and he spake the word of the Lord, and the earth trembled, and the mountains fled, even according to his command; and the rivers of water were turned out of their course; and the roar of the lions was heard out of the wilderness; and all nations feared greatly, so powerful was the word of Enoch, and so great was the power of the language which God had given him.

14 There also came up a land out of the depth of the sea, and so great was the fear of the enemies of the people of God, that they fled and stood afar off and went upon the land which came up out of the depth of the sea.

15 And the giants of the land, also, stood afar off; and there went forth a curse upon all people that fought against God;

16 And from that time forth there were wars and bloodshed among them; but the Lord came and dwelt with his people, and they dwelt in righteousness.

17 The fear of the Lord was upon all nations, so great was the glory of the Lord, which was upon his people. And the Lord blessed the land, and they were blessed upon the mountains, and upon the high places, and did flourish.

18 And the Lord called his people ZION, because they were of one heart and one mind, and dwelt in righteousness; and there was no poor among them.

19 And Enoch continued his preaching in righteousness unto the people of God. And it came to pass in his days, that he built a city that was called the City of Holiness, even ZION.

20 And it came to pass that Enoch talked with the Lord; and he said unto the Lord: Surely Zion shall dwell in safety forever. But the Lord said unto Enoch: Zion have I blessed, but the residue of the people have I cursed.

21 And it came to pass that the Lord showed unto Enoch all the inhabitants of the earth; and he beheld, and lo, Zion, in process of time, was taken up into heaven. And the Lord said unto Enoch: Behold mine abode forever.

22 And Enoch also beheld the residue of the people which were the sons of Adam; and they were a mixture of all the seed of Adam save it was the seed of Cain, for the seed of Cain were black, and had not place among them.

23 And after that Zion was taken up into heaven, Enoch beheld, and lo, all the nations of the earth were before him;

24 And there came generation upon generation; and Enoch was high and lifted up, even in the bosom of the Father, and of the Son of Man; and behold, the power of Satan was upon all the face of the earth.

25 And he saw angels descending out of heaven; and he heard a loud voice saying: Wo, wo be unto the inhabitants of the earth.

26 And he beheld Satan; and he had a great chain in his hand, and it veiled the whole face of the earth with darkness; and he looked up and laughed, and his angels rejoiced.

27 And Enoch beheld angels descending out of heaven, bearing testimony of the Father and Son; and the Holy Ghost fell on many, and they were caught up by the powers of heaven into Zion.

28 And it came to pass that the God of heaven looked upon the residue of the people, and he wept; and Enoch bore record of it, saying: How is it that the heavens weep, and shed forth their tears as the rain upon the mountains?

29 And Enoch said unto the Lord: How is it that thou canst weep, seeing thou art holy, and from all eternity to all eternity?

knew the condition of man. He comprehended the Fall, the Atonement, and the plight of man, should there be no atonement (see 2 Ne. 9). Because Enoch understood and appreciated the Savior's infinite atonement and His power of resurrection, he was filled with gratitude. This gratitude caused his attitude to be one of rejoicing, and his life reflected Christ in all he did through his behavior. The joy in one's life comes from an appreciation for the goodness of God and His love for us expressed in the giving of His Only Begotten Son. When we, like Enoch, act with faith, we can return to the presence of our Heavenly Father.

POINT OF INTEREST

"And the giants of the land . . ." (Moses 7:15; see also Gen. 6:4) Gen. 6:4 calls these giants Nephilim. *Some interpreters translate this as "fallen ones," implying a divine connection. Enoch himself "spoke of them as a depraved lot who sought to murder him. . . . The Nephilim were described as giants—how big we do not know. Were they like Goliath? In any case, the giants who lived in Enoch's day were a depraved lot who sought to murder him. But part divine and part human they were not, for neither God, angels, nor 'the sons of the gods' consorted with earthly women as implied"* (Mark E. Petersen, *Noah and the Flood* [Salt Lake City, UT: Deseret Book, 1982]).

Did giants really exist? A decayed human skeleton claimed by eyewitnesses to measure around 10 feet 9 inches tall was discovered in November 1856 in West Virginia. Another measuring 12 feet tall was unearthed in California in 1833. A farmer in Louisiana dug up a 9-foot 11-inch skeleton in 1928, and in 1931 a boy burying his dog found a 10-foot 2-inch skeleton, also in Louisiana.

30 And were it possible that man could number the particles of the earth, yea, millions of earths like this, it would not be a beginning to the number of thy creations; and thy curtains are stretched out still; and yet thou art there, and thy bosom is there; and also thou art just; thou art merciful and kind forever;

31 And thou hast taken Zion to thine own bosom, from all thy creations, from all eternity to all eternity; and naught but peace, justice, and truth is the habitation of thy throne; and mercy shall go before thy face and have no end; how is it thou canst weep?

32 The Lord said unto Enoch: Behold these thy brethren; they are the workmanship of mine own hands, and I gave unto them their knowledge, in the day I created them; and in the Garden of Eden, gave I unto man his agency;

33 And unto thy brethren have I said, and also given commandment, that they should love one another, and that they should choose me, their Father; but behold, they are without affection, and they hate their own blood;

34 And the fire of mine indignation is kindled against them; and in my hot displeasure will I send in the floods upon them, for my fierce anger is kindled against them.

35 Behold, I am God; Man of Holiness is my name; Man of Counsel is my name; and Endless and Eternal is my name, also.

36 Wherefore, I can stretch forth mine hands and hold all the creations which I have made; and mine eye can pierce them also, and among all the workmanship of mine hands there has not been so great wickedness as among thy brethren.

37 But behold, their sins shall be upon the heads of their fathers; Satan shall be their father, and misery shall be their doom; and the whole heavens shall weep over them, even all the workmanship of mine hands; wherefore should not the heavens weep, seeing these shall suffer?

38 But behold, these which thine eyes are upon shall perish in the floods; and behold, I will shut them up; a prison have I prepared for them.

39 And That which I have chosen hath pled before my face. Wherefore, he suffereth for their sins; inasmuch as they will repent in the day that my Chosen shall return unto me, and until that day they shall be in torment;

40 Wherefore, for this shall the heavens weep, yea, and all the workmanship of mine hands.

41 And it came to pass that the Lord spake unto Enoch, and told Enoch all the doings of the children of men; wherefore Enoch knew, and looked upon their wickedness, and their misery, and wept and stretched forth his arms, and his heart swelled wide as eternity; and his bowels yearned; and all eternity shook.

42 And Enoch also saw Noah, and his family; that the posterity of all the sons of Noah should be saved with a temporal salvation;

43 Wherefore Enoch saw that Noah built an ark; and that the Lord smiled upon it, and held it in his own hand; but upon the residue of the wicked the floods came and swallowed them up.

44 And as Enoch saw this, he had bitterness of soul, and wept over his brethren, and said unto the heavens: I will refuse to be comforted; but the Lord said unto Enoch: Lift up your heart, and be glad; and look.

45 And it came to pass that Enoch looked; and from Noah, he beheld all the families of the earth; and he cried unto the Lord, saying: When shall the day of the Lord come? When shall the blood of the Righteous be shed, that all they that mourn may be sanctified and have eternal life?

Moses 7:32–35—Dialogue Between Enoch and the Lord

The dialogue between the Enoch and the Lord is a supreme example of the personal relationship between the Creator and His children. Though the Lord is God, yet He designs to have a one-on-one communion with His sons and daughters. That is the purpose of mortality—to prepare the way for this eternal communion and everlasting presence in the realms of glory with Father and Son. The Prophet Joseph Smith declared: "And seek the face of the Lord always, that in patience ye may possess your souls, and ye shall have eternal life" (D&C 101:38).

46 And the Lord said: It shall be in the meridian of time, in the days of wickedness and vengeance.

47 And behold, Enoch saw the day of the coming of the Son of Man, even in the flesh; and his soul rejoiced, saying: The Righteous is lifted up, and the Lamb is slain from the foundation of the world; and through faith I am in the bosom of the Father, and behold, Zion is with me.

48 And it came to pass that Enoch looked upon the earth; and he heard a voice from the bowels thereof, saying: Wo, wo is me, the mother of men; I am pained, I am weary, because of the wickedness of my children. When shall I rest, and be cleansed from the filthiness which is gone forth out of me? When will my Creator sanctify me, that I may rest, and righteousness for a season abide upon my face?

49 And when Enoch heard the earth mourn, he wept, and cried unto the Lord, saying: O Lord, wilt thou not have compassion upon the earth? Wilt thou not bless the children of Noah?

50 And it came to pass that Enoch continued his cry unto the Lord, saying: I ask thee, O Lord, in the name of thine Only Begotten, even Jesus Christ, that thou wilt have mercy upon Noah and his seed, that the earth might never more be covered by the floods.

51 And the Lord could not withhold; and he covenanted with Enoch, and sware unto him with an oath, that he would stay the floods; that he would call upon the children of Noah;

52 And he sent forth an unalterable decree, that a remnant of his seed should always be found among all nations, while the earth should stand;

53 And the Lord said: Blessed is he through whose seed Messiah shall come; for he saith—I am Messiah, the King of Zion, the Rock of Heaven, which is broad as eternity; whoso cometh in at the gate and climbeth up by me shall never fall; wherefore, blessed are they of whom I have spoken, for they shall come forth with songs of everlasting joy.

54 And it came to pass that Enoch cried unto the Lord, saying: When the Son of Man cometh in the flesh, shall the earth rest? I pray thee, show me these things.

55 And the Lord said unto Enoch: Look, and he looked and beheld the Son of Man lifted up on the cross, after the manner of men;

56 And he heard a loud voice; and the heavens were veiled; and all the creations of God mourned; and the earth groaned; and the rocks were rent; and the saints arose, and were crowned at the right hand of the Son of Man, with crowns of glory;

57 And as many of the spirits as were in prison came forth, and stood on the right hand of God; and the remainder were reserved in chains of darkness until the judgment of the great day.

58 And again Enoch wept and cried unto the Lord, saying: When shall the earth rest?

59 And Enoch beheld the Son of Man ascend up unto the Father; and he called unto the Lord, saying: Wilt thou not come again upon the earth? Forasmuch as thou art God, and I know thee, and thou hast sworn unto me, and commanded me that I should ask in the name of thine Only Begotten; thou hast made me, and given unto me a right to thy throne, and not of myself, but through thine own grace; wherefore, I ask thee if thou wilt not come again on the earth.

60 And the Lord said unto Enoch: As I live, even so will I come in the last days, in the days of wickedness and vengeance, to fulfil the oath which I have made unto you concerning the children of Noah;

Moses 7:47—Jesus Christ, Jehovah of the Old Testament

In the meridian of time, the Son of God walked among a people who were looking for the Messiah—but they failed to recognize Him. His presence and influence had been confirmed from the foundations of the earth. His glory and counsel had been resounding through all the generations of time, unfolding with power in the records of the Old Testament. But the people were blind to His coming and His mission. Enoch saw in vision with utter plainness the condescension of the Son of God coming forth to bring about His atoning sacrifice. It was Jesus Christ whom he saw. Modern Christendom has lost touch with the verity that Jesus Christ was the Jehovah of the Old Testament. It is Jesus Christ who is "a stone, a tried stone, a precious corner *stone*, a sure foundation" (Isa. 28:16)—even the cornerstone of salvation and exaltation.

POINT OF INTEREST

Biblical Longevity

Name	Age
Methuselah	*969*
Jared	*962*
Noah	*950*
Adam	*930*
Seth	*912*
Enos	*905*
Mahalalel	*895*
Lamech	*777*
Shem	*600*
Enoch	*365*
Peleg	*239*
Job	*210?*
Isaac	*180*
Abraham	*175*
Nahor	*148*
Jacob	*147*
Esau	*147?*
Ishmael	*137*
Levi	*137*
Laban	*130+*
Deborah	*130+*
Sarah	*127*
Miriam	*125+*
Aaron	*123*
Rebecca	*120+*
Moses	*120*
Joseph	*110*
Joshua	*110*

61 And the day shall come that the earth shall rest, but before that day the heavens shall be darkened, and a veil of darkness shall cover the earth; and the heavens shall shake, and also the earth; and great tribulations shall be among the children of men, but my people will I preserve;

62 And righteousness will I send down out of heaven; and truth will I send forth out of the earth, to bear testimony of mine Only Begotten; his resurrection from the dead; yea, and also the resurrection of all men; and righteousness and truth will I cause to sweep the earth as with a flood, to gather out mine elect from the four quarters of the earth, unto a place which I shall prepare, an Holy City, that my people may gird up their loins, and be looking forth for the time of my coming; for there shall be my tabernacle, and it shall be called Zion, a New Jerusalem.

63 And the Lord said unto Enoch: Then shalt thou and all thy city meet them there, and we will receive them into our bosom, and they shall see us; and we will fall upon their necks, and they shall fall upon our necks, and we will kiss each other;

64 And there shall be mine abode, and it shall be Zion, which shall come forth out of all the creations which I have made; and for the space of a thousand years the earth shall rest.

65 And it came to pass that Enoch saw the day of the coming of the Son of Man, in the last days, to dwell on the earth in righteousness for the space of a thousand years;

66 But before that day he saw great tribulations among the wicked; and he also saw the sea, that it was troubled, and men's hearts failing them, looking forth with fear for the judgments of the Almighty God, which should come upon the wicked.

67 And the Lord showed Enoch all things, even unto the end of the world; and he saw the day of the righteous, the hour of their redemption, and received a fulness of joy;

68 And all the days of Zion, in the days of Enoch, were three hundred and sixty-five years.

69 And Enoch and all his people walked with God, and he dwelt in the midst of Zion; and it came to pass that Zion was not, for God received it up into his own bosom; and from thence went forth the saying, ZION IS FLED.

MOSES CHAPTER 8
(February 1831)

1 And all the days of Enoch were four hundred and thirty years.

2 And it came to pass that Methuselah, the son of Enoch, was not taken, that the covenants of the Lord might be fulfilled, which he made to Enoch; for he truly covenanted with Enoch that Noah should be of the fruit of his loins.

3 And it came to pass that Methuselah prophesied that from his loins should spring all the kingdoms of the earth (through Noah), and he took glory unto himself.

4 And there came forth a great famine into the land, and the Lord cursed the earth with a sore curse, and many of the inhabitants thereof died.

5 And it came to pass that Methuselah lived one hundred and eighty-seven years, and begat Lamech;

6 And Methuselah lived, after he begat Lamech, seven hundred and eighty-two years, and begat sons and daughters;

Moses 7:67—Office of the Prophet

The profound magnitude of the office of the prophet—being blessed to see "all things"—is the key to counsel and guidance for the people of the Lord. To live in an age when there is a prophet of the Lord on the earth to convey the wisdom of the Almighty as a pattern and example for conducting one's life is a blessing of inestimable worth. In our day, this pattern was confirmed and exemplified by the Prophet Joseph Smith, who guided the Restoration of the Church according to the Lord's way of leading: teaching correct principles, following the Holy Spirit, acting in love, and serving with devotion. The kingdom of God will unfold and prosper with inexorable power, leading up to the time of the Second Coming, when the Zion of Enoch's day—the Zion that was fled—will return and meet up with the Saints of the Lord who have prepared themselves for that grand reunion foretold by all the Lord's prophets who have been blessed to see "all things" from the beginning to the end of time—and beyond.

MOSES CHAPTER 8
(February 1831)

Moses 8:1–5—Methuselah, Lamech, and Noah

Methuselah (meaning: man of the javelin, or dart), son of Enoch, was the longest surviving of the ancient patriarchs (see Gen. 5:21–27; 1 Chron. 1:3; and Luke 3:37—where the name is rendered *Mathusala*).

Lamech was the seventh in descent from Seth, son of Adam, as follows: Seth, Enos, Cainan, Mahalaleel, Jared, Enoch, Methuselah, Lamech (see Gen. 5:6–25). Lamech was the father of Noah (see Gen. 5:25–31; 1 Chron. 1:3; compare Luke 3:36; Moses 8:5–11).

Noah (meaning: rest), son of Lamech, was a leading patriarch of the Old Testament.

From latter-day scripture, we learn that Noah, when ten years old, was ordained to the priesthood by Methuselah (see D&C 107:52). From that moment on he honored his priesthood calling with valor. Everyone is familiar with the story of Noah and the ark. But there is more there than meets the eye. The story is an intimate and revealing source of knowledge about the nature of spirituality and obedience to the covenants—precisely the kinds of qualities that are required for each of us to preserve life for ourselves and our families from day to day.

For more insights on Methuselah, Lamech, and Noah, see Appendix F.

7 And all the days of Methuselah were nine hundred and sixty-nine years, and he died.

8 And Lamech lived one hundred and eighty-two years, and begat a son,

9 And he called his name Noah, saying: This son shall comfort us concerning our work and toil of our hands, because of the ground which the Lord hath cursed.

10 And Lamech lived, after he begat Noah, five hundred and ninety-five years, and begat sons and daughters;

11 And all the days of Lamech were seven hundred and seventy-seven years, and he died.

12 And Noah was four hundred and fifty years old, and begat Japheth; and forty-two years afterward he begat Shem of her who was the mother of Japheth, and when he was five hundred years old he begat Ham.

13 And Noah and his sons hearkened unto the Lord, and gave heed, and they were called the sons of God.

14 And when these men began to multiply on the face of the earth, and daughters were born unto them, the sons of men saw that those daughters were fair, and they took them wives, even as they chose.

15 And the Lord said unto Noah: The daughters of thy sons have sold themselves; for behold mine anger is kindled against the sons of men, for they will not hearken to my voice.

16 And it came to pass that Noah prophesied, and taught the things of God, even as it was in the beginning.

17 And the Lord said unto Noah: My Spirit shall not always strive with man, for he shall know that all flesh shall die; yet his days shall be an hundred and twenty years; and if men do not repent, I will send in the floods upon them.

18 And in those days there were giants on the earth, and they sought Noah to take away his life; but the Lord was with Noah, and the power of the Lord was upon him.

19 And the Lord ordained Noah after his own order, and commanded him that he should go forth and declare his Gospel unto the children of men, even as it was given unto Enoch.

20 And it came to pass that Noah called upon the children of men that they should repent; but they hearkened not unto his words;

21 And also, after that they had heard him, they came up before him, saying: Behold, we are the sons of God; have we not taken unto ourselves the daughters of men? And are we not eating and drinking, and marrying and giving in marriage? And our wives bear unto us children, and the same are mighty men, which are like unto men of old, men of great renown. And they hearkened not unto the words of Noah.

22 And God saw that the wickedness of men had become great in the earth; and every man was lifted up in the imagination of the thoughts of his heart, being only evil continually.

23 And it came to pass that Noah continued his preaching unto the people, saying: Hearken, and give heed unto my words;

24 Believe and repent of your sins and be baptized in the name of Jesus Christ, the Son of God, even as our fathers, and ye shall receive the Holy Ghost, that ye may have all things made manifest; and if ye do not this, the floods will come in upon you; nevertheless they hearkened not.

25 And it repented Noah, and his heart was pained that the Lord had made man on the earth, and it grieved him at the heart.

26 And the Lord said: I will destroy man whom I have created, from the face of the earth, both man and beast, and the creeping things,

Moses 8:13–19

Noah, like all the Lord's chosen prophets, was a just and righteous man. Knowing of the calamity that rampant wickedness was bringing upon His wayward children, the Lord gave them a chance to repent by sending His prophet Noah to speak plainly words of repentance. According to divine instruction, Noah prepared an ark of safety for his family. The Lord established with him and his family a covenant whereby they might enjoy the spiritual safety of the gospel and the priesthood of God. The ark is thus a symbol of refuge through the covenant. The vain ambition of the post-diluvian population gathering at Babel and wanting to make "a name" for themselves caused the Lord to intervene to thwart their conspiracy of pride by scattering them abroad. Noah and his family, plus the Jaredites, were preserved and guided by the Lord.

Moses 8:20–24—The warning voice of prophecy

As has been the case with all of God's chosen prophets, those in the early dispensations called the people to repentance. In the time of Noah, wickedness had become epidemic. The people had become nefarious even in the thoughts of their hearts (see Gen. 6:5). Noah's time preceded the destruction of other nations for gross wickedness—the Jaredites and the Nephites. In this state the people did not yield to the warnings of Noah. Surely their "hearts were past feeling" (1 Ne. 17:45). The whole earth had ripened in iniquity. This time the Lord warned through Noah that the people must repent, or "I will destroy all flesh from off the earth" (Moses 8:30).

As was the case with Noah, the words of the Lord's prophets will always be fulfilled. Nothing is more sure than the word of God—whether delivered by God himself, His Son Jesus Christ, angels of God, or by the gift and power of the Holy Ghost through His servants (see D&C 1:38). Recognizing this, it is imperative that we listen to the voice of warning. The consequences are great for not listening to the Savior's words or those of His servants: "And wo be unto him that will not hearken unto the words of Jesus, and also to them whom he hath chosen and sent among them; for whoso receiveth not the words of Jesus and the words of those whom he hath sent receiveth not him; and therefore he will not receive them at the last day; And it would be better for them if they had not been born. For do ye suppose that ye can get rid of the justice of an offended God, who hath been trampled under feet of men, that thereby salvation might come?" (3 Ne. 28:34–35).

and the fowls of the air; for it repenteth Noah that I have created them, and that I have made them; and he hath called upon me; for they have sought his life.

27 And thus Noah found grace in the eyes of the Lord; for Noah was a just man, and perfect in his generation; and he walked with God, as did also his three sons, Shem, Ham, and Japheth.

28 The earth was corrupt before God, and it was filled with violence.

29 And God looked upon the earth, and, behold, it was corrupt, for all flesh had corrupted its way upon the earth.

30 And God said unto Noah: The end of all flesh is come before me, for the earth is filled with violence, and behold I will destroy all flesh from off the earth.

THE
BOOK OF ABRAHAM

TRANSLATED FROM THE PAPYRUS, BY JOSEPH SMITH

ABRAHAM CHAPTER 1

1 IN the land of the Chaldeans, at the residence of my fathers, I, Abraham, saw that it was needful for me to obtain another place of residence;

2 And, finding there was greater happiness and peace and rest for me, I sought for the blessings of the fathers, and the right whereunto I should be ordained to administer the same; having been myself a follower of righteousness, desiring also to be one who possessed great knowledge, and to be a greater follower of righteousness, and to possess a greater knowledge, and to be a father of many nations, a prince of peace, and desiring to receive instructions, and to keep the commandments of God, I became a rightful heir, a High Priest, holding the right belonging to the fathers.

3 It was conferred upon me from the fathers; it came down from the fathers, from the beginning of time, yea, even from the beginning, or before the foundation of the earth, down to the present time, even the right of the firstborn, or the first man, who is Adam, or first father, through the fathers unto me.

4 I sought for mine appointment unto the Priesthood according to the appointment of God unto the fathers concerning the seed.

5 My fathers having turned from their righteousness, and from the holy commandments which the Lord their God had given unto them, unto the worshiping of the gods of the heathen, utterly refused to hearken to my voice;

6 For their hearts were set to do evil, and were wholly turned to the god of Elkenah, and the god of Libnah, and the god of Mahmackrah, and the god of Korash, and the god of Pharaoh, king of Egypt;

Moses 8:25–27—The Lord's Dealings with His Children

We see In Moses 8 that the Lord calls and empowers just and holy men like Noah to serve as His prophetic emissaries on earth. He then commands these servants to raise the voice of warning and preach repentance to the world. He causes that places of refuge and resort are established to afford safety and security to His obedient Saints. From time to time, we see that He also scatters and re-gathers the people for their own protection or to diffuse prideful intent and bring about needful correction.

The prophets can be an example for us. We, like them, can achieve the attributes and qualities as described in Moses 8:27. Remember that the Lord assists us in being able to "become" as He is.

THE
BOOK OF ABRAHAM

Overview

There are a number of important themes in the life of Abraham to help us conduct our lives in accordance with divine principles, including the following:

(1) Mortality gives indispensable experience that make us better able to fulfill the Lord's errand.

(2) All things are possible with God: The Lord will fulfill all of His promises to His children—despite every challenge or obstacle.

(3) The Lord requires the heart and a willing mind: Abraham was commanded to offer up the thing most dear to his heart—his own son.

(4) The Lord will provide the means whereby we can obey: Abraham demonstrated complete devotion and obedience, and the Lord, in His mercy and goodness, provided the ram for the sacrifice.

For more insights on Abraham, see Appendix G.

ABRAHAM CHAPTER 1

Abraham 1:1–2—High Priest

The office of high priest in the Melchizedek priesthood has been a cardinal position in the governance of the kingdom of God from the beginning. The ancient patriarchs, beginning with Adam, were high priests: "Three years previous to the death of Adam, he called Seth, Enos, Cainan, Mahalaleel, Jared, Enoch, and Methuselah, who were all high priests, with the residue of his posterity who were righteous, into the valley of Adam-ondi-Ahman, and there bestowed upon them his last blessing" (D&C 107:54). Abraham was also a high priest.

When the preparatory priesthood (Aaronic or Levitical) was instituted during the post-Sinai days of Moses, the presiding officer was designated as a high priest. Aaron was the first such officer to bear that title in the Aaronic priesthood.

7 Therefore they turned their hearts to the sacrifice of the heathen in offering up their children unto these dumb idols, and hearkened not unto my voice, but endeavored to take away my life by the hand of the priest of Elkenah. The priest of Elkenah was also the priest of Pharaoh.

8 Now, at this time it was the custom of the priest of Pharaoh, the king of Egypt, to offer up upon the altar which was built in the land of Chaldea, for the offering unto these strange gods, men, women, and children.

9 And it came to pass that the priest made an offering unto the god of Pharaoh, and also unto the god of Shagreel, even after the manner of the Egyptians. Now the god of Shagreel was the sun.

10 Even the thank-offering of a child did the priest of Pharaoh offer upon the altar which stood by the hill called Potiphar's Hill, at the head of the plain of Olishem.

11 Now, this priest had offered upon this altar three virgins at one time, who were the daughters of Onitah, one of the royal descent directly from the loins of Ham. These virgins were offered up because of their virtue; they would not bow down to worship gods of wood or of stone, therefore they were killed upon this altar, and it was done after the manner of the Egyptians.

12 And it came to pass that the priests laid violence upon me, that they might slay me also, as they did those virgins upon this altar; and that you may have a knowledge of this altar, I will refer you to the representation at the commencement of this record.

13 It was made after the form of a bedstead, such as was had among the Chaldeans, and it stood before the gods of Elkenah, Libnah, Mahmackrah, Korash, and also a god like unto that of Pharaoh, king of Egypt.

14 That you may have an understanding of these gods, I have given you the fashion of them in the figures at the beginning, which manner of figures is called by the Chaldeans Rahleenos, which signifies hieroglyphics.

15 And as they lifted up their hands upon me, that they might offer me up and take away my life, behold, I lifted up my voice unto the Lord my God, and the Lord hearkened and heard, and he filled me with the vision of the Almighty, and the angel of his presence stood by me, and immediately unloosed my bands;

16 And his voice was unto me: Abraham, Abraham, behold, my name is Jehovah, and I have heard thee, and have come down to deliver thee, and to take thee away from thy father's house, and from all thy kinsfolk, into a strange land which thou knowest not of;

17 And this because they have turned their hearts away from me, to worship the god of Elkenah, and the god of Libnah, and the god of Mahmackrah, and the god of Korash, and the god of Pharaoh, king of Egypt; therefore I have come down to visit them, and to destroy him who hath lifted up his hand against thee, Abraham, my son, to take away thy life.

18 Behold, I will lead thee by my hand, and I will take thee, to put upon thee my name, even the Priesthood of thy father, and my power shall be over thee.

19 As it was with Noah so shall it be with thee; but through thy ministry my name shall be known in the earth forever, for I am thy God.

20 Behold, Potiphar's Hill was in the land of Ur, of Chaldea. And the Lord broke down the altar of Elkenah, and of the gods of the land, and utterly destroyed them, and smote the priest that he died; and there was great mourning in Chaldea, and also in the court of Pharaoh; which Pharaoh signifies king by royal blood.

Later, Hilkiah, Eliashib, Joshua (during the days of Darius), and others were called high priests (see 2 Kings 22:8; Neh. 3:1; Haggai 1:1).

During the days of Abraham, Melchizedek was a great high priest of such valor and honor that his name was appropriated in the designation for the high priesthood (see D&C 107:1-4).

Abraham 1:3–15—All These Things Shall Give Thee Experience

Abraham survived a youth fraught with abuse and danger. Similarly, the challenges and adversities of life give us training and experience in those qualities of faith, persistence, resilience, and problem-solving that make us better able to carry on the Lord's errand.

Abraham had within his heart the vision of future service through the priesthood of God; however, his circumstances stood at odds with his hope and yearning to be a valiant servant. Abuse, evil, ignorance, cruelty, superstition, false gods—all of these conspired to thwart his mission. Thus, he had to depend on faith and on the Lord for his own safety and deliverance. His experiences were to prepare him for future challenges and tests that established him as the father of many nations and the great patriarch of coming generations. Just like Joseph Smith in our day (see D&C 122:7–9), Abraham had to tread the path of sacrifice that the Savior so willingly trod in bringing about the Atonement.

Thus we see that dealing with adversity is truly the test of life. Our Savior endured all, submitting to the Father's will. The Prophet Joseph, in this dispensation, endured all things, and then martyrdom at age thirty-eight. Now each of us in our own way will be tried and tested by adversity and opposition in all things. We too must endure—not just endure, but endure to the end and endure well.

 POINT OF INTEREST

This is the reconstructed facade of the Ziggurat of Ur, the original structure being visible from the top. "The Babylonian city of Ur was home to Abraham's family before they began their journey to the Promised Land. Excavations of the site (at Tel el-Muqayyar in modern-day southern Iraq) in the early 20th century revealed many examples of beautiful craftsmanship, including gold weapons and figurines from the royal tombs (c. 2500 BCE). A large number of inscribed tablets have provided valuable information about the history of the city" (John Bowker, *The Complete Bible Handbook* [New York: DK Publishing, 1998]).

21 Now this king of Egypt was a descendant from the loins of Ham, and was a partaker of the blood of the Canaanites by birth.

22 From this descent sprang all the Egyptians, and thus the blood of the Canaanites was preserved in the land.

23 The land of Egypt being first discovered by a woman, who was the daughter of Ham, and the daughter of Egyptus, which in the Chaldean signifies Egypt, which signifies that which is forbidden;

24 When this woman discovered the land it was under water, who afterward settled her sons in it; and thus, from Ham, sprang that race which preserved the curse in the land.

25 Now the first government of Egypt was established by Pharaoh, the eldest son of Egyptus, the daughter of Ham, and it was after the manner of the government of Ham, which was patriarchal.

26 Pharaoh, being a righteous man, established his kingdom and judged his people wisely and justly all his days, seeking earnestly to imitate that order established by the fathers in the first generations, in the days of the first patriarchal reign, even in the reign of Adam, and also of Noah, his father, who blessed him with the blessings of the earth, and with the blessings of wisdom, but cursed him as pertaining to the Priesthood.

27 Now, Pharaoh being of that lineage by which he could not have the right of Priesthood, notwithstanding the Pharaohs would fain claim it from Noah, through Ham, therefore my father was led away by their idolatry;

28 But I shall endeavor, hereafter, to delineate the chronology running back from myself to the beginning of the creation, for the records have come into my hands, which I hold unto this present time.

29 Now, after the priest of Elkenah was smitten that he died, there came a fulfilment of those things which were said unto me concerning the land of Chaldea, that there should be a famine in the land.

30 Accordingly a famine prevailed throughout all the land of Chaldea, and my father was sorely tormented because of the famine, and he repented of the evil which he had determined against me, to take away my life.

31 But the records of the fathers, even the patriarchs, concerning the right of Priesthood, the Lord my God preserved in mine own hands; therefore a knowledge of the beginning of the creation, and also of the planets, and of the stars, as they were made known unto the fathers, have I kept even unto this day, and I shall endeavor to write some of these things upon this record, for the benefit of my posterity that shall come after me.

ABRAHAM CHAPTER 2

1 NOW the Lord God caused the famine to wax sore in the land of Ur, insomuch that Haran, my brother, died; but Terah, my father, yet lived in the land of Ur, of the Chaldees.

2 And it came to pass that I, Abraham, took Sarai to wife, and Nahor, my brother, took Milcah to wife, who was the daughter of Haran.

3 Now the Lord had said unto me: Abraham, get thee out of thy country, and from thy kindred, and from thy father's house, unto a land that I will show thee.

Abraham 1:23—Egyptus/Daughter of Egyptus

A woman is identified in the Book of Abraham as "the daughter of Ham, and the daughter of Egyptus, which in the Chaldean signifies Egypt, which signifies that which is forbidden" (Abr. 1:23). According to the record, this woman (also named Egyptus) discovered the land of Egypt and, as specified in verse 25, was the mother of the first Pharaoh.

Abraham 1:31—Patriarch/Patriarchs

The word *patriarch* is not used in the King James version of the Old Testament; however, in reference to Old Testament figures, it is used twice in the New Testament: "the patriarch David" (Acts 2:12) and "the patriarch Abraham" (Heb. 7:4). The word *patriarchs* (plural) is likewise not used in the Old Testament, but occurs twice in the New Testament in Stephen's recounting of the history of Israel— ". . . and Jacob *begat* the twelve patriarchs. And the patriarchs, moved with envy, sold Joseph into Egypt: but God was with him, . . ." (Acts 7:8–9)—and once in the Pearl of Great Price in the statement by Abraham found in verse 31.

Patriarch is an ordained office in the Melchizedek priesthood: "The order of this priesthood was confirmed to be handed down from father to son, and rightly belongs to the literal descendants of the chosen seed, to whom the promises were made. This order was instituted in the days of Adam, and came down by lineage. . . . " (D&C 107:49–41).

As confirmed in the Bible Dictionary: "The fathers from Adam to Jacob were all patriarchs of this kind. The word as used in the Bible seems to denote also a title of honor to early leaders of the Israelites. . . . The word is of Greek derivation and means father-ruler; the Hebrew word it translates is simply *father*."

The word *patriarchal* is used three times in holy writ: twice in the Book of Abraham concerning a pattern for government (as in the "patriarchal reign" of Adam, Noah, Ham, and by appropriation Pharaoh—see Abr. 1:25, 26) and once in the Doctrine and Covenants concerning "the keys of the patriarchal blessings" (D&C 124:92).

ABRAHAM CHAPTER 2

"If there is anything calculated to interest the mind of the Saints, to awaken in them the finest sensibilities, and arouse them to enterprise and exertion, surely it is the great and precious promises made by our heavenly Father to the children of Abraham." — Joseph Smith, HC 4:128.

For insights on the Abrahamic Covenant, see Appendix H.

4 Therefore I left the land of Ur, of the Chaldees, to go into the land of Canaan; and I took Lot, my brother's son, and his wife, and Sarai my wife; and also my father followed after me, unto the land which we denominated Haran.

5 And the famine abated; and my father tarried in Haran and dwelt there, as there were many flocks in Haran; and my father turned again unto his idolatry, therefore he continued in Haran.

6 But I, Abraham, and Lot, my brother's son, prayed unto the Lord, and the Lord appeared unto me, and said unto me: Arise, and take Lot with thee; for I have purposed to take thee away out of Haran, and to make of thee a minister to bear my name in a strange land which I will give unto thy seed after thee for an everlasting possession, when they hearken to my voice.

7 For I am the Lord thy God; I dwell in heaven; the earth is my footstool; I stretch my hand over the sea, and it obeys my voice; I cause the wind and the fire to be my chariot; I say to the mountains—Depart hence—and behold, they are taken away by a whirlwind, in an instant, suddenly.

8 My name is Jehovah, and I know the end from the beginning; therefore my hand shall be over thee.

9 And I will make of thee a great nation, and I will bless thee above measure, and make thy name great among all nations, and thou shalt be a blessing unto thy seed after thee, that in their hands they shall bear this ministry and Priesthood unto all nations;

10 And I will bless them through thy name; for as many as receive this Gospel shall be called after thy name, and shall be accounted thy seed, and shall rise up and bless thee, as their father;

11 And I will bless them that bless thee, and curse them that curse thee; and in thee (that is, in thy Priesthood) and in thy seed (that is, thy Priesthood), for I give unto thee a promise that this right shall continue in thee, and in thy seed after thee (that is to say, the literal seed, or the seed of the body) shall all the families of the earth be blessed, even with the blessings of the Gospel, which are the blessings of salvation, even of life eternal.

ABRAHAM CHAPTER 3

1 AND I, Abraham, had the Urim and Thummim, which the Lord my God had given unto me, in Ur of the Chaldees;

2 And I saw the stars, that they were very great, and that one of them was nearest unto the throne of God; and there were many great ones which were near unto it;

3 And the Lord said unto me: These are the governing ones; and the name of the great one is Kolob, because it is near unto me, for I am the Lord thy God: I have set this one to govern all those which belong to the same order as that upon which thou standest.

4 And the Lord said unto me, by the Urim and Thummim, that Kolob was after the manner of the Lord, according to its times and seasons in the revolutions thereof; that one revolution was a day unto the Lord, after his manner of reckoning, it being one thousand years according to the time appointed unto that whereon thou standest. This is the reckoning of the Lord's time, according to the reckoning of Kolob.

5 And the Lord said unto me: The planet which is the lesser light, lesser than that which is to rule the day, even the night, is above or greater than that upon which thou standest in point of reckoning,

ABRAHAM CHAPTER 3

Abraham 3:1–4—Our Time on Earth

If a day to the Lord is equivalent to one thousand years in the time reckoning of man, then how long is the life of an average person from the perspective of the Lord? If we assume that the average person lives 75 years, then in the time reckoning of the Lord, the average person will live *one hour and 48 minutes*. Can we be obedient and faithful to our Father in Heaven for one hour and 48 minutes? The challenge is to make the best use of our time during our short mortal probation on earth, as in the following set of guidelines:

Build on a spiritual foundation by seeing things in the eternal context (see Moses 1:39; Alma 12:24; 34:33; D&C 72:4), establishing worthy priorities (see Matt. 6:33; 8:21–22; 18:9; 46:12), making a master plan for spiritual action (see Moses 3:5; Abr. 3:17), and cultivating contingencies to overcome challenges and roadblocks (see 1 Ne. 9:5–6; compare D&C 10:39–41; D&C 42:10).

Prepare wisely and thoroughly by putting your life in order (see D&C 89:21; 93:28; D&C 121:45–46), organizing your approach (see D&C 38:30; 88:119; 109:8; 132:8), delegating wisely (see Ex. 18:23; D&C 1:38; 46:11–12; Moro. 10, Eph. 4), and using the best helps and tools available (see 1 Ne. 16:10–16; Alma 37:7–8; D&C 130:8, 11).

Act with prudence and courage by using spiritual power (see 2 Ne. 32:3, 5; Moro. 10:4–5; D&C 58:27–28), being positive and patient (see 2 Ne. 28:30; Isa. 28:10, 13; D&C 6:36; 64:33–34), seeking quality solutions (see Matt. 7:24–27; Moro. 10:32), and defeating procrastination (see John 13:17; Mosiah 4:10; Alma 34:31–32).

Achieve optimum leverage of your time by using time layering—the ability to accomplish multiple goals at the same time—as did the Savior (see John 4:13–14; Luke 24:17, 32; see also Mosiah 2:17; Alma 19:6; 34:27; D&C 100:8), using the correct pace (see Mosiah 4:27; Alma 26:12; D&C 60:13; 136:35); using time patterning (doing things during those times when we are most effective and efficient—see D&C 88:124; 3 Ne. 18:18; D&C 20:77, 79), and using time relativity to our advantage with patience and discernment (understanding that time passes at different "rates" for different people—see Gen. 29:20; D&C 38:2; 54:10; 88:41; 121:41).

for it moveth in order more slow; this is in order because it standeth above the earth upon which thou standest, therefore the reckoning of its time is not so many as to its number of days, and of months, and of years.

6 And the Lord said unto me: Now, Abraham, these two facts exist, behold thine eyes see it; it is given unto thee to know the times of reckoning, and the set time, yea, the set time of the earth upon which thou standest, and the set time of the greater light which is set to rule the day, and the set time of the lesser light which is set to rule the night.

7 Now the set time of the lesser light is a longer time as to its reckoning than the reckoning of the time of the earth upon which thou standest.

8 And where these two facts exist, there shall be another fact above them, that is, there shall be another planet whose reckoning of time shall be longer still;

9 And thus there shall be the reckoning of the time of one planet above another, until thou come nigh unto Kolob, which Kolob is after the reckoning of the Lord's time; which Kolob is set nigh unto the throne of God, to govern all those planets which belong to the same order as that upon which thou standest.

10 And it is given unto thee to know the set time of all the stars that are set to give light, until thou come near unto the throne of God.

11 Thus I, Abraham, talked with the Lord, face to face, as one man talketh with another; and he told me of the works which his hands had made;

12 And he said unto me: My son, my son (and his hand was stretched out), behold I will show you all these. And he put his hand upon mine eyes, and I saw those things which his hands had made, which were many; and they multiplied before mine eyes, and I could not see the end thereof.

13 And he said unto me: This is Shinehah, which is the sun. And he said unto me: Kokob, which is star. And he said unto me: Olea, which is the moon. And he said unto me: Kokaubeam, which signifies stars, or all the great lights, which were in the firmament of heaven.

14 And it was in the night time when the Lord spake these words unto me: I will multiply thee, and thy seed after thee, like unto these; and if thou canst count the number of sands, so shall be the number of thy seeds.

15 And the Lord said unto me: Abraham, I show these things unto thee before ye go into Egypt, that ye may declare all these words.

16 If two things exist, and there be one above the other, there shall be greater things above them; therefore Kolob is the greatest of all the Kokaubeam that thou hast seen, because it is nearest unto me.

17 Now, if there be two things, one above the other, and the moon be above the earth, then it may be that a planet or a star may exist above it; and there is nothing that the Lord thy God shall take in his heart to do but what he will do it.

18 Howbeit that he made the greater star; as, also, if there be two spirits, and one shall be more intelligent than the other, yet these two spirits, notwithstanding one is more intelligent than the other, have no beginning; they existed before, they shall have no end, they shall exist after, for they are gnolaum, or eternal.

19 And the Lord said unto me: These two facts do exist, that there are two spirits, one being more intelligent than the other; there shall be another more intelligent than they; I am the Lord thy God, I am more intelligent than they all.

POINT OF INTEREST

"Abraham's story . . . mirrors the migration of the Aramaic nomads: In the second half of the second millennium B.C., Abraham led his tribe out of Mesopotamia at God's behest and into Palestine, where the settled despite the resistance of the previous inhabitants. In the traditional Islamic version, he led them to Mecca, where he constructed the Ka'aba and founded the pilgrimage tradition" (Visual History of the World [Washington D.C.: National Geographic Society, 2005]). *This image shows pilgrims at the Ka'aba in Mecca, considered "the most sacred site in the Islamic world, . . . the point toward which the Muslims pray five times a day. . . . The Ka'aba is located in the center of the Grand Mosque and is accessed through twenty-four gateways"* (Spencer J. Palmer and Roger R. Keller, Religions of the Word: A Latter-day Saint View [Provo, UT: Brigham Young University, 1990]).

Pilgrims at Mecca

20 The Lord thy God sent his angel to deliver thee from the hands of the priest of Elkenah.

21 I dwell in the midst of them all; I now, therefore, have come down unto thee to declare unto thee the works which my hands have made, wherein my wisdom excelleth them all, for I rule in the heavens above, and in the earth beneath, in all wisdom and prudence, over all the intelligences thine eyes have seen from the beginning; I came down in the beginning in the midst of all the intelligences thou hast seen.

22 Now the Lord had shown unto me, Abraham, the intelligences that were organized before the world was; and among all these there were many of the noble and great ones;

23 And God saw these souls that they were good, and he stood in the midst of them, and he said: These I will make my rulers; for he stood among those that were spirits, and he saw that they were good; and he said unto me: Abraham, thou art one of them; thou wast chosen before thou wast born.

24 And there stood one among them that was like unto God, and he said unto those who were with him: We will go down, for there is space there, and we will take of these materials, and we will make an earth whereon these may dwell;

25 And we will prove them herewith, to see if they will do all things whatsoever the Lord their God shall command them;

26 And they who keep their first estate shall be added upon; and they who keep not their first estate shall not have glory in the same kingdom with those who keep their first estate; and they who keep their second estate shall have glory added upon their heads for ever and ever.

27 And the Lord said: Whom shall I send? And one answered like unto the Son of Man: Here am I, send me. And another answered and said: Here am I, send me. And the Lord said: I will send the first.

28 And the second was angry, and kept not his first estate; and, at that day, many followed after him.

THE
FIRST BOOK OF MOSES CALLED GENESIS

CHAPTER 6

1 AND it came to pass, when men began to multiply on the face of the earth, and daughters were born unto them,

2 That the sons of God saw the daughters of men that they were fair; and they took them wives of all which they chose.

3 And the LORD said, My spirit shall not always strive with man, for that he also is flesh: yet his days shall be an hundred and twenty years.

4 There were giants in the earth in those days; and also after that, when the sons of God came in unto the daughters of men, and they bare children to them, the same became mighty men which were of old, men of renown.

Abraham 3:17—Godly Vision

Abraham was given many visions from the Lord that enlightened his mind and soul. He could see clearly things as they were and would be. He had a vision of life and the work of the Lord. We need a clear vision too. We must have a vision of who we are and what we can do. We can do all things in the strength of the Lord. We can do all things that are expedient if we exercise faith. We can be instruments in the hand of the Lord. We can do whatsoever the Lord commands, for He will prepare a way for us. We can see and envision the work and glory of God—and our role is to help bring this about.

Abraham 3:19—Intelligence

Intelligence is an eternal attribute of God and His spirit children; it is light and truth, which are also attributes of God. They are through and in all things created by the Lord. This light enlightens all things. Christ is the light, the way, the truth, and the life of the world. When our eye is single to the glory of God we will be filled with this light and we will comprehend all things (D&C 88:67).

The intelligence we acquire here on earth will rise with us in the resurrection and will be to our advantage in the hereafter (see D&C 130:18–19). As children of God we are to be seekers of light and truth; if we do not seek these things we will not be able to comprehend all things; we will not keep the commandments, and will thus be unable to receive more light and truth. This is the time to prepare to meet God.

Abraham 3:23—Foreordination

In the premortal realm, God chose many noble leaders to guide His work on the earth. Each of us was chosen to fulfill an important calling of service and love.

Abraham was one of the noble and great premortal spirits and was called to lead a dispensation of time. What did Abraham and others do premortally to be foreordained? They were called and prepared from the foundation of the world on account of their exceeding faith and good works; they chose good and exercised exceedingly great faith (see Alma 13:3). Everything is predicated on obedience. Blessings and opportunities come to those who choose to follow the Lord.

We were prepared during the premortal phase of our existence for our mortal experience today, as we learn from latter-day revelation (see D&C 138:56). Our life does not unfold in a vacuum, with no anchor and no connection to higher purpose, but rather in the divine context of a divine plan laid down before the foundations of the world, a plan in which we participated with the full awareness of our role in coming to earth to experience mortality, assist in building up the Kingdom of God, and set the stage, with our loved ones, for a return to our Father in Heaven. By the principle of foreordination we obtained the promise for glorious opportunities and blessings in mortality and beyond, predicated upon our valiant devotion to the cause of helping the Lord in bringing to pass the immortality and eternal life of man.

5 ¶ And GOD saw that the wickedness of man was great in the earth, and that every imagination of the thoughts of his heart was only evil continually.

6 And it repented the LORD that he had made man on the earth, and it grieved him at his heart.

7 And the LORD said, I will destroy man whom I have created from the face of the earth; both man, and beast, and the creeping thing, and the fowls of the air; for it repenteth me that I have made them.

8 But Noah found grace in the eyes of the LORD.

9 ¶ These are the generations of Noah: Noah was a just man and perfect in his generations, and Noah walked with God.

10 And Noah begat three sons, Shem, Ham, and Japheth.

11 The earth also was corrupt before God, and the earth was filled with violence.

12 And God looked upon the earth, and, behold, it was corrupt; for all flesh had corrupted his way upon the earth.

13 And God said unto Noah, The end of all flesh is come before me; for the earth is filled with violence through them; and, behold, I will destroy them with the earth.

14 ¶ Make thee an ark of gopher wood; rooms shalt thou make in the ark, and shalt pitch it within and without with pitch.

15 And this is the fashion which thou shalt make it of: The length of the ark shall be three hundred cubits, the breadth of it fifty cubits, and the height of it thirty cubits.

16 A window shalt thou make to the ark, and in a cubit shalt thou finish it above; and the door of the ark shalt thou set in the side thereof; with lower, second, and third stories shalt thou make it.

17 And, behold, I, even I, do bring a flood of waters upon the earth, to destroy all flesh, wherein is the breath of life, from under heaven; and every thing that is in the earth shall die.

18 But with thee will I establish my covenant; and thou shalt come into the ark, thou, and thy sons, and thy wife, and thy sons' wives with thee.

19 And of every living thing of all flesh, two of every sort shalt thou bring into the ark, to keep them alive with thee; they shall be male and female.

20 Of fowls after their kind, and of cattle after their kind, of every creeping thing of the earth after his kind, two of every sort shall come unto thee, to keep them alive.

21 And take thou unto thee of all food that is eaten, and thou shalt gather it to thee; and it shall be for food for thee, and for them.

22 Thus did Noah; according to all that God commanded him, so did he.

Noah's Ark by Matthaeus Merian (the Elder)

GENESIS CHAPTER 6

Genesis 6:10—Ham

Ham (meaning: hot) was a son of Noah. After the flood, the families of Noah came forth from the ark. Tragically, Ham and his progeny were cursed for indiscrete and offensive behavior (see Gen. 9:18-22).

The offspring of Ham are listed as follows: "And the sons of Ham; Cush, and Mizraim, and Phut, and Canaan" (Gen. 10:6; see also 1 Chron. 1:8). The geographical destinations of these peoples are given in the Bible Dictionary, p. 698: "Cush = the dark-skinned race of eastern Africa and southern Arabia; Mizraim = Egyptians; Phut = Libyans; Canaan = inhabitants of Palestine before arrival of the Semitic races."

Modern scripture discloses that Ham's wife and daughter were both named Egyptus and that some of Ham's descendants settled in Egypt (see Abr. 1:21–27): "When this woman [Egyptus, daughter of Egyptus] discovered the land [Egypt] it was under water, who afterward settled her sons in it; and thus, from Ham, sprang that race which preserved the curse in the land" (Abr. 1:24).

Genesis 6:18—The Ark: A Symbol of Refuge Through the Covenant

According to divine instruction, Noah prepared an ark of safety for his family. The Lord established with him and his family a covenant whereby they might enjoy the spiritual safety of the Gospel and the Priesthood of God.

The Joseph Smith translation makes clear the covenant the Lord established with Noah's great-grandfather, Enoch, "… that of thy posterity shall come all nations …." (JST Gen. 8:23). Noah and his sons and their wives were saved from the flood.

Covenants with the Lord truly save people, a truth that is symbolized in the ark—a refuge from the flood. The ark was a refuge for Noah; so likewise for us our refuge is a "gathering place"—the Kingdom of God . . . a promised land . . . a Zion . . . a New Jerusalem.

The covenants of the Lord are always kept by the Lord. It is up to us to be faithful, thus receiving the blessings of the covenants. The greatest example is the blessing of the marriage covenant. When this covenant is kept faithfully, the sealing power is made evident by bonding families together for time and all eternity; and then the blessings of eternal increase will unfold forever (see D&C 131).

POINT OF INTEREST

Tevah or Teba, the word translated as "ark" is rare in the Bible, the only other reference being to the reed boat in which the infant Moses was abandoned in Exodus 2:3.

CHAPTER 7

1 AND the LORD said unto Noah, Come thou and all thy house into the ark; for thee have I seen righteous before me in this generation.

2 Of every clean beast thou shalt take to thee by sevens, the male and his female: and of beasts that are not clean by two, the male and his female.

3 Of fowls also of the air by sevens, the male and the female; to keep seed alive upon the face of all the earth.

4 For yet seven days, and I will cause it to rain upon the earth forty days and forty nights; and every living substance that I have made will I destroy from off the face of the earth.

5 And Noah did according unto all that the LORD commanded him.

6 And Noah was six hundred years old when the flood of waters was upon the earth.

7 ¶ And Noah went in, and his sons, and his wife, and his sons' wives with him, into the ark, because of the waters of the flood.

8 Of clean beasts, and of beasts that are not clean, and of fowls, and of every thing that creepeth upon the earth,

9 There went in two and two unto Noah into the ark, the male and the female, as God had commanded Noah.

10 And it came to pass after seven days, that the waters of the flood were upon the earth.

11 ¶ In the six hundredth year of Noah's life, in the second month, the seventeenth day of the month, the same day were all the fountains of the great deep broken up, and the windows of heaven were opened.

12 And the rain was upon the earth forty days and forty nights.

13 In the selfsame day entered Noah, and Shem, and Ham, and Japheth, the sons of Noah, and Noah's wife, and the three wives of his sons with them, into the ark;

14 They, and every beast after his kind, and all the cattle after their kind, and every creeping thing that creepeth upon the earth after his kind, and every fowl after his kind, every bird of every sort.

15 And they went in unto Noah into the ark, two and two of all flesh, wherein is the breath of life.

16 And they that went in, went in male and female of all flesh, as God had commanded him: and the LORD shut him in.

17 And the flood was forty days upon the earth; and the waters increased, and bare up the ark, and it was lift up above the earth.

18 And the waters prevailed, and were increased greatly upon the earth; and the ark went upon the face of the waters.

19 And the waters prevailed exceedingly upon the earth; and all the high hills, that were under the whole heaven, were covered.

20 Fifteen cubits upward did the waters prevail; and the mountains were covered.

21 And all flesh died that moved upon the earth, both of fowl, and of cattle, and of beast, and of every creeping thing that creepeth upon the earth, and every man:

22 All in whose nostrils was the breath of life, of all that was in the dry land, died.

23 And every living substance was destroyed which was upon the face of the ground, both man, and cattle, and the creeping things, and the fowl of the heaven; and they were destroyed from the earth: and Noah only remained alive, and they that were with him in the ark.

GENESIS CHAPTER 7

Genesis 7:5—Obedience

What more sterling epithet than this could be found to summarize the life of one of God's chosen servants? If we aspire to an elect ultimate judgment about our pattern of life in this mortal sphere, then let it be the quest to earn the worthy reputation that we faithfully "did according unto all that the LORD commanded."

Genesis 7:6–24—A Worldwide Flood

The sanitizing flooding of the earth at the time of Noah was not a localized phenomenon, but worldwide in scope, as Moroni confirmed in his statement about the mission of the prophet Ether on the American continent: "For behold, they rejected all the words of Ether; for he truly told them of all things, from the beginning of man; and that after the waters had receded from off the face of this land [America] it became a choice land above all other lands, a chosen land of the Lord; wherefore the Lord would have that all men should serve him who dwell upon the face thereof" (Ether 13:1).

 POINT OF INTEREST

According to Babylonian scholar H. W. F. Saggs, "It is beyond doubt . . . that certain of the stories in Genesis have some relationship to Babylonian or Sumerian myths. The Flood story has a very close relationship, with so many details in common, such as the sending out of birds from the Ark, that there can be no doubt that the accounts of the Flood in Genesis and in the 'Gilgamesh Epic' have ultimately a common source" (The Babylonians [London: Folio Society, 2007]). Biblical scholar John Bowker describes the Mesopotamian story: "The . . . Epic of Gilgamesh discovered in 1878 written on clay tablets [a detail of the cuneiform flood tablet is shown above] in the library of Ashurbanipal at Nineveh . . . concerns a hero called Utnapishtim, who . . . is the parallel figure to Noah, and like him is saved from the coming deluge with his wife, family, and selected animals in an ark, while the rest of humankind is destroyed. The similarities in the circumstantial details of the stories are striking and open up the possibility of dependence of some kind. The ark is constructed in a similar way, the birds sent out from the ark are the same, and the ark lands on a high mountain. Equally striking, however, are the theological differences: the gods of the Epic of Gilgamesh squabble and fight; they decide to destroy humans because of the noise they are making" (The Complete Bible Handbook [New York: DK Publishing, 1998]).

24 And the waters prevailed upon the earth an hundred and fifty days.

CHAPTER 8

The flood ceases—Noah sends forth a dove, which returns with an olive leaf—He releases all living things from the ark—He offers sacrifices—Seedtime and harvest and seasons assured.

1 AND God remembered Noah, and every living thing, and all the cattle that was with him in the ark: and God made a wind to pass over the earth, and the waters asswaged;

2 The fountains also of the deep and the windows of heaven were stopped, and the rain from heaven was restrained;

3 And the waters returned from off the earth continually: and after the end of the hundred and fifty days the waters were abated.

4 And the ark rested in the seventh month, on the seventeenth day of the month, upon the mountains of Ararat.

5 And the waters decreased continually until the tenth month: in the tenth month, on the first day of the month, were the tops of the mountains seen.

6 ¶ And it came to pass at the end of forty days, that Noah opened the window of the ark which he had made:

7 And he sent forth a raven, which went forth to and fro, until the waters were dried up from off the earth.

8 Also he sent forth a dove from him, to see if the waters were abated from off the face of the ground;

9 But the dove found no rest for the sole of her foot, and she returned unto him into the ark, for the waters were on the face of the whole earth: then he put forth his hand, and took her, and pulled her in unto him into the ark.

10 And he stayed yet other seven days; and again he sent forth the dove out of the ark;

11 And the dove came in to him in the evening; and, lo, in her mouth was an olive leaf pluckt off: so Noah knew that the waters were abated from off the earth.

12 And he stayed yet other seven days; and sent forth the dove; which returned not again unto him any more.

13 ¶ And it came to pass in the six hundredth and first year, in the first month, the first day of the month, the waters were dried up from off the earth: and Noah removed the covering of the ark, and looked, and, behold, the face of the ground was dry.

14 And in the second month, on the seven and twentieth day of the month, was the earth dried.

15 ¶ And God spake unto Noah, saying,

16 Go forth of the ark, thou, and thy wife, and thy sons, and thy sons' wives with thee.

17 Bring forth with thee every living thing that is with thee, of all flesh, both of fowl, and of cattle, and of every creeping thing that creepeth upon the earth; that they may breed abundantly in the earth, and be fruitful, and multiply upon the earth.

18 And Noah went forth, and his sons, and his wife, and his sons' wives with him:

19 Every beast, every creeping thing, and every fowl, and whatsoever creepeth upon the earth, after their kinds, went forth out of the ark.

20 ¶ And Noah builded an altar unto the LORD; and took of every

GENESIS CHAPTER 8

Genesis 8:20–22—Joseph Smith Perspective

The Joseph Smith translation of the verses in Genesis 8 provides a change in perspective, showing that it was Noah perceiving the aroma of the burnt offering and bringing supplication before the Lord to guard against any future flood:

> And Noah builded an altar unto the Lord, and took of every clean beast, and of every clean fowl, and offered burnt offerings on the altar; and gave thanks unto the Lord, and rejoiced in his heart.
>
> And the Lord spake unto Noah, and he blessed him. And Noah smelled a sweet savor, and he said in his heart;
>
> I will call on the name of the Lord, that he will not again curse the ground any more for man's sake, for the imagination of man's heart is evil from his youth; and he will not again smite any more every thing living, as he hath done, while the earth remaineth;
>
> And, that seed-time and harvest, and cold and heat, and summer and winter, and day and night, may not cease with man. (JST Gen. 9:4–6)

In fact, it was the design of the Lord that the cleansing flood at the time of Noah was to be a unique and one-time event (see Gen. 9:11–17; Isa. 54:9; 3 Ne. 22:9). The earth had been, in effect, baptized with water in anticipation of the future transformation when it would be baptized with fire to receive its paradisiacal stature of eternal glory:

> The earth, the Lord says, abides its creation; it has been baptized with water, and will, in the future, be baptized with fire and the Holy Ghost, to be prepared to go back into the celestial presence of God, with all things that dwell upon it which have, like the earth, abided the law of their creation. (Brigham Young, *Discourses of Brigham Young* [Salt Lake City: Deseret Book Company, 1971], 393)

Noah at an Altar with Sacrifice, chromolithograph

clean beast, and of every clean fowl, and offered burnt offerings on the altar.

21 And the LORD smelled a sweet savour; and the LORD said in his heart, I will not again curse the ground any more for man's sake; for the imagination of man's heart is evil from his youth; neither will I again smite any more every thing living, as I have done.

22 While the earth remaineth, seedtime and harvest, and cold and heat, and summer and winter, and day and night shall not cease.

CHAPTER 9

1 AND God blessed Noah and his sons, and said unto them, Be fruitful, and multiply, and replenish the earth.

2 And the fear of you and the dread of you shall be upon every beast of the earth, and upon every fowl of the air, upon all that moveth upon the earth, and upon all the fishes of the sea; into your hand are they delivered.

3 Every moving thing that liveth shall be meat for you; even as the green herb have I given you all things.

4 But flesh with the life thereof, which is the blood thereof, shall ye not eat.

5 And surely your blood of your lives will I require; at the hand of every beast will I require it, and at the hand of man; at the hand of every man's brother will I require the life of man.

6 Whoso sheddeth man's blood, by man shall his blood be shed: for in the image of God made he man.

7 And you, be ye fruitful, and multiply; bring forth abundantly in the earth, and multiply therein.

8 ¶ And God spake unto Noah, and to his sons with him, saying,

9 And I, behold, I establish my covenant with you, and with your seed after you;

10 And with every living creature that is with you, of the fowl, of the cattle, and of every beast of the earth with you; from all that go out of the ark, to every beast of the earth.

11 And I will establish my covenant with you; neither shall all flesh be cut off any more by the waters of a flood; neither shall there any more be a flood to destroy the earth.

12 And God said, This is the token of the covenant which I make between me and you and every living creature that is with you, for perpetual generations:

13 I do set my bow in the cloud, and it shall be for a token of a covenant between me and the earth.

14 And it shall come to pass, when I bring a cloud over the earth, that the bow shall be seen in the cloud:

15 And I will remember my covenant, which is between me and you and every living creature of all flesh; and the waters shall no more become a flood to destroy all flesh.

16 And the bow shall be in the cloud; and I will look upon it, that I may remember the everlasting covenant between God and every living creature of all flesh that is upon the earth.

17 And God said unto Noah, This is the token of the covenant, which I have established between me and all flesh that is upon the earth.

GENESIS CHAPTER 9

Genesis 9:1–17—The Rainbow

Note the Joseph Smith Translation of the passages concerning the rainbow. The text is augmented to include more specific references to the fulfillment of the everlasting covenant of old in the last days when the city of Enoch Zion) will return and "the general assembly of the church of the firstborn" (JST Gen. 9:23) will assume control of the earth. During these final events, it is of interest that the faithful will look *upward* and Zion will look *downward* amidst an all-encompassing state of gladness and joy (see JST Gen. 9:18–25).

And God made a covenant with Noah, and said, This shall be the token of the covenant I make between me and you, and for every living creature with you, and for perpetual generations;

I will set my bow in the cloud; and it shall be for a token of a covenant between me and the earth.

And it shall come to pass, when I bring a cloud over the earth, that the bow shall be seen in the cloud; and I will remember my covenant, which I have made between me and you, for every living creature of all flesh. And the waters shall no more become a flood to destroy all flesh.

And the bow shall be in the cloud; and I will look upon it, that I may remember the everlasting covenant, which I made unto thy father Enoch; that, when men should keep all my commandments, Zion should again come on the earth, the city of Enoch which I have caught up unto myself.

And this is mine everlasting covenant, that when thy posterity shall embrace the truth, and look upward, then shall Zion look downward, and all the heavens shall shake with gladness, and the earth shall tremble with joy;

And the general assembly of the church of the firstborn shall come down out of heaven, and possess the earth, and shall have place until the end come. And this is mine everlasting covenant, which I made with thy father Enoch.

And the bow shall be in the cloud, and I will establish my covenant unto thee, which I have made between me and thee, for every living creature of all flesh that shall be upon the earth.

And God said unto Noah, This is the token of the covenant which I have established between me and thee; for all flesh shall be upon the earth. (JST Genesis 9:18–25)

18 ¶ And the sons of Noah, that went forth of the ark, were Shem, and Ham, and Japheth: and Ham is the father of Canaan.

19 These are the three sons of Noah: and of them was the whole earth overspread.

20 And Noah began to be an husbandman, and he planted a vineyard:

21 And he drank of the wine, and was drunken; and he was uncovered within his tent.

22 And Ham, the father of Canaan, saw the nakedness of his father, and told his two brethren without.

23 And Shem and Japheth took a garment, and laid it upon both their shoulders, and went backward, and covered the nakedness of their father; and their faces were backward, and they saw not their father's nakedness.

24 And Noah awoke from his wine, and knew what his younger son had done unto him.

25 And he said, Cursed be Canaan; a servant of servants shall he be unto his brethren.

26 And he said, Blessed be the LORD God of Shem; and Canaan shall be his servant.

27 God shall enlarge Japheth, and he shall dwell in the tents of Shem; and Canaan shall be his servant.

28 ¶ And Noah lived after the flood three hundred and fifty years.

29 And all the days of Noah were nine hundred and fifty years: and he died.

CHAPTER 11

1 AND the whole earth was of one language, and of one speech.

2 And it came to pass, as they journeyed from the east, that they found a plain in the land of Shinar; and they dwelt there.

3 And they said one to another, Go to, let us make brick, and burn them throughly. And they had brick for stone, and slime had they for morter.

4 And they said, Go to, let us build us a city and a tower, whose top may reach unto heaven; and let us make us a name, lest we be scattered abroad upon the face of the whole earth.

5 And the LORD came down to see the city and the tower, which the children of men builded.

6 And the LORD said, Behold, the people is one, and they have all one language; and this they begin to do: and now nothing will be restrained from them, which they have imagined to do.

7 Go to, let us go down, and there confound their language, that they may not understand one another's speech.

8 So the LORD scattered them abroad from thence upon the face of all the earth: and they left off to build the city.

9 Therefore is the name of it called Babel; because the LORD did there confound the language of all the earth: and from thence did the LORD scatter them abroad upon the face of all the earth.

Genesis 9:18–27—Japheth

Japheth (pronounced "jay'-feth" or "jay'-futh") was the oldest son of Noah. On one occasion Noah was sedated under the influence of wine when Ham came upon him in his nakedness and then informed his brothers, Shem and Japheth. These two discretely covered their father without viewing him. Noah later pronounced a curse on Ham for his indiscretion and blessed the other two sons. The descendents of Japheth settled in a region extending from the eastern Mediterranean coasts to the Black Sea and the Caspian Sea. The sons of Japheth included "Gomer, and Magog, and Madai, and Javan, and Tubal, and Meshech, and Tiras" (1 Chron. 1:5).

Genesis 9:28–29—Elias

How does Noah relate to Elias? The name Elias does not occur in the Old Testament (King James Version). However, Elias is the Greek form of the name of the Old Testament prophet Elijah as it is rendered in the New Testament (see for example Matt. 17:1–4, Luke 4:25–26, and James 5:17). From modern scripture we learn that Elias is both an individual prophet as well as a title. Elias the individual appeared to Joseph Smith and Oliver Cowdery in the Kirtland Temple on April 3, 1836, "and committed the dispensation of the gospel of Abraham, saying that in us and our seed all generations after us should be blessed" (D&C 110:12). President Joseph Fielding Smith taught that in this extraordinary appearance, Elias was Noah, also known as the Angel Gabriel (see AGQ 3:339-341).

The title Elias implies a forerunner, such as John the Baptist—who, in the authority of the Aaronic Priesthood, prepared the way in "the spirit of Elias" (D&C 27:7) for the Savior in the meridian of time. Elias, as a title, also can refer to all the heavenly messengers who came to restore keys and authorities in the dispensation of the fulness of times leading up to the Second Coming.

The title Elias can also refer to the Savior Jesus Christ, as John the Baptist confirmed: "He it is of whom I bear record. He is that prophet, even Elias, who, coming after me, is preferred before me, whose shoe's latchet I am not worthy to unloose, or whose place I am not able to fill; for he shall baptize, not only with water, but with fire, and with the Holy Ghost" (JST John 1:28).

GENESIS CHAPTER 11

Genesis 11:1–9—The Scattering

The vain ambition of the post-diluvian population gathering at Babel caused the Lord to thwart their conspiracy of pride by scattering them abroad. Noah and his family, and eventually the Jaredites, were preserved and guided by the Lord.

The word *babel* has a Hebrew root meaning "to confuse or mix." When man takes upon himself the way back to God, and through pride wants to establish a name for himself, God will usually, and most generally, cause the people to be humbled.

CHAPTER 12

1 NOW the LORD had said unto Abram, Get thee out of thy country, and from thy kindred, and from thy father's house, unto a land that I will shew thee:

2 And I will make of thee a great nation, and I will bless thee, and make thy name great; and thou shalt be a blessing:

3 And I will bless them that bless thee, and curse him that curseth thee: and in thee shall all families of the earth be blessed.

4 So Abram departed, as the LORD had spoken unto him; and Lot went with him: and Abram was seventy and five years old when he departed out of Haran.

5 And Abram took Sarai his wife, and Lot his brother's son, and all their substance that they had gathered, and the souls that they had gotten in Haran; and they went forth to go into the land of Canaan; and into the land of Canaan they came.

6 ¶ And Abram passed through the land unto the place of Sichem, unto the plain of Moreh. And the Canaanite was then in the land.

7 And the LORD appeared unto Abram, and said, Unto thy seed will I give this land: and there builded he an altar unto the LORD, who appeared unto him.

8 And he removed from thence unto a mountain on the east of Beth-el, and pitched his tent, having Beth-el on the west, and Hai on the east: and there he builded an altar unto the LORD, and called upon the name of the LORD.

CHAPTER 13

1 AND Abram went up out of Egypt, he, and his wife, and all that he had, and Lot with him, into the south.

2 And Abram was very rich in cattle, in silver, and in gold.

3 And he went on his journeys from the south even to Beth-el, unto the place where his tent had been at the beginning, between Beth-el and Hai;

4 Unto the place of the altar, which he had made there at the first: and there Abram called on the name of the LORD.

The Lord has a divine strategy for preserving the temporal and spiritual well-being of His children, while allowing them to exercise their innate and God-given free agency. That strategy is built around the "word" — both the word of truth through angels and prophets, as well as the Word Himself, who is the Only Begotten. The message of the gospel of redemption is promulgated through just and holy men like Noah and his prophetic colleagues throughout all the dispensations of time. The central core of the message is repentance based on faith, covenanted through baptism, confirmed through the gift of the Holy Ghost, and proven by a willingness to endure to the end. Places of refuge are established, symbolized perfectly by the ark of old times. These places of resort may be lands of promise ordained to receive the faithful, or they may be stakes of Zion to which the faithful can flee for counsel and protection, or temples where saving ordinances are provided. When the covenant Saints obey and follow the will of the Lord, wherever it might take them, they are blessed with safety and His protecting hand.

GENESIS CHAPTER 12

Genesis 12:1–3—A Covenant Of Righteousness

The Lord establishes with Abraham and his posterity a covenant of righteousness, with an eternal promise of grand earthly and heavenly blessings based on obedience and service.

For additional insights on the Abrahamic Covenant, see Appendix H.

GENESIS CHAPTER 13

From the story of Abraham we glean mighty themes and principles to guide our lives. First, there is the portrait of Abraham as the paragon of righteousness, his noble life serving as the worthy exemplum for all who honor and embrace the covenant program of the Lord. Second, we see in Melchizedek, the "King of Salem," a further exemplary prophetic leader whose faith and sterling character were so perfect that the higher priesthood is named in his honor. Third, we remember from the fate of Sodom and Gomorrah the warning to avoid the allure of worldliness: we are to exercise extreme caution, while living in the world, not to partake of worldly practices. We see that the Lord will guide His saints away from the destructive forces of evil.

Genesis 13:12–13—Avoiding Worldliness

We are to exercise extreme caution, while living in the world, not to partake of worldly practices. Let us be cautious not to overlook the subtle inference of Lot pitching his tent toward Sodom. Sodom was a city of sin. We should abhor sin, and stay away and avoid the road to sin. Having pitched his tent toward Sodom, it wasn't long before Lot lived in Sodom (see Gen. 14:12). As is often the case when people ripen in iniquity, the result was war and bloodshed; caught up, Lot lost it all. Abraham came to his

5 ¶ And Lot also, which went with Abram, had flocks, and herds, and tents.

6 And the land was not able to bear them, that they might dwell together: for their substance was great, so that they could not dwell together.

7 And there was a strife between the herdmen of Abram's cattle and the herdmen of Lot's cattle: and the Canaanite and the Perizzite dwelled then in the land.

8 And Abram said unto Lot, Let there be no strife, I pray thee, between me and thee, and between my herdmen and thy herdmen; for we be brethren.

9 Is not the whole land before thee? separate thyself, I pray thee, from me: if thou wilt take the left hand, then I will go to the right; or if thou depart to the right hand, then I will go to the left.

10 And Lot lifted up his eyes, and beheld all the plain of Jordan, that it was well watered every where, before the LORD destroyed Sodom and Gomorrah, even as the garden of the LORD, like the land of Egypt, as thou comest unto Zoar.

11 Then Lot chose him all the plain of Jordan; and Lot journeyed east: and they separated themselves the one from the other.

12 Abram dwelled in the land of Canaan, and Lot dwelled in the cities of the plain, and pitched his tent toward Sodom.

13 But the men of Sodom were wicked and sinners before the LORD exceedingly.

14 ¶ And the LORD said unto Abram, after that Lot was separated from him, Lift up now thine eyes, and look from the place where thou art northward, and southward, and eastward, and westward:

15 For all the land which thou seest, to thee will I give it, and to thy seed for ever.

16 And I will make thy seed as the dust of the earth: so that if a man can number the dust of the earth, then shall thy seed also be numbered.

17 Arise, walk through the land in the length of it and in the breadth of it; for I will give it unto thee.

18 Then Abram removed his tent, and came and dwelt in the plain of Mamre, which is in Hebron, and built there an altar unto the LORD.

CHAPTER 14

1 AND it came to pass in the days of Amraphel king of Shinar, Arioch king of Ellasar, Chedorlaomer king of Elam, and Tidal king of nations;

2 That these made war with Bera king of Sodom, and with Birsha king of Gomorrah, Shinab king of Admah, and Shemeber king of Zeboiim, and the king of Bela, which is Zoar.

3 All these were joined together in the vale of Siddim, which is the salt sea.

4 Twelve years they served Chedorlaomer, and in the thirteenth year they rebelled.

5 And in the fourteenth year came Chedorlaomer, and the kings that were with him, and smote the Rephaims in Ashteroth Karnaim, and the Zuzims in Ham, and the Emims in Shaveh Kiriathaim,

6 And the Horites in their mount Seir, unto El-paran, which is by the wilderness.

rescue and saved Lot as well as his family, friends, and goods. We *must not* be of the world, for Satan desires to sift us as wheat. Never assume you have the power to resist *all* temptation. You must stay on the straight and narrow, for broad is the way that leads to destruction (see Matt. 7:14). One little degree can change the course of a mighty ship over its course in a few days; so likewise can our lives be ruined with just a simple turn toward the world and Satan.

Lot (meaning: a covering), son of Haran and nephew of Abraham, joined with the family entourage leaving Ur of the Chaldees for their journey to the land of Canaan. The estates of Abraham and Lot were so abundant that the two family groups had to be separated to find terrain of sufficient size for both. When Abraham granted Lot a choice of where he would reside, Lot favored the verdant plains, and pitched his tent toward Sodom. That location exposed Lot to the battle that rocked the area in due time.

Lot and his family dwelt by choice in a wicked city. Thus messengers were sent to warn Lot to remove his family from the midst of evil, lest they should be present when the impending destruction from heaven should take place (see Gen. 19). When Lot seemed to resist, the messengers took forceful action (see Gen. 19:16). The escape was just in time.

We can look back on the experience of Lot and remember to avoid following his example when he "pitched *his* tent toward Sodom" (Gen. 13:12). We are counseled well to focus our view on eternal things rather than on the enticements of the world. We can also remember to avoid the experience of Lot's wife when she disobeyed the counsel of the messengers of God by looking back. At the same time, we can garner from the story of Lot the mercy and compassion of the Lord in taking steps to save Lot and his family from the fiery destruction of Sodom and Gomorrah.

GENESIS CHAPTER 14

Genesis 14:1—Chedorlaomer

Chedorlaomer (pronounced "ked-or-lay-o'-mer" or "ked-or-lay'-omer") was a king of Elam in the time of Abraham. Elam was an ancient country lying in the southwest region of what is today Iran. In league with three princes of Babylon, Chedorlaomer defeated the kings of Sodom, Gomorrah, and several other cities in that area of the land; in the battle, the victors took all the goods of Sodom and Gomorrah and several prisoners, including Lot. Learning of this abduction, Abraham went out with 318 of his own men, routed the forces of Chedorlaomer, and regained all the goods, as well as the prisoners (see Gen. 14:16).

Genesis 14:2–5—Rephaim/Rephaims

The Rephaim (pronounced "ref'-ay-im"; meaning: giants) were a pre-Israelite people who were especially large of stature. At the time of Abraham, Chedorlaomer defeated this tribe and several others. According to the covenant promises given by the Lord to Abraham and his seed, the Rephaim and other indigenous peoples were to be supplanted or subjected by the Israelites (see Gen. 15:18–21).

7 And they returned, and came to En-mishpat, which is Kadesh, and smote all the country of the Amalekites, and also the Amorites, that dwelt in Hazezon-tamar.

8 And there went out the king of Sodom, and the king of Gomorrah, and the king of Admah, and the king of Zeboiim, and the king of Bela (the same is Zoar;) and they joined battle with them in the vale of Siddim;

9 With Chedorlaomer the king of Elam, and with Tidal king of nations, and Amraphel king of Shinar, and Arioch king of Ellasar; four kings with five.

10 And the vale of Siddim was full of slimepits; and the kings of Sodom and Gomorrah fled, and fell there; and they that remained fled to the mountain.

11 And they took all the goods of Sodom and Gomorrah, and all their victuals, and went their way.

12 And they took Lot, Abram's brother's son, who dwelt in Sodom, and his goods, and departed.

13 ¶ And there came one that had escaped, and told Abram the Hebrew; for he dwelt in the plain of Mamre the Amorite, brother of Eshcol, and brother of Aner: and these were confederate with Abram.

14 And when Abram heard that his brother was taken captive, he armed his trained servants, born in his own house, three hundred and eighteen, and pursued them unto Dan.

15 And he divided himself against them, he and his servants, by night, and smote them, and pursued them unto Hobah, which is on the left hand of Damascus.

16 And he brought back all the goods, and also brought again his brother Lot, and his goods, and the women also, and the people.

17 ¶ And the king of Sodom went out to meet him after his return from the slaughter of Chedorlaomer, and of the kings that were with him, at the valley of Shaveh, which is the king's dale.

18 And Melchizedek king of Salem brought forth bread and wine: and he was the priest of the most high God.

19 And he blessed him, and said, Blessed be Abram of the most high God, possessor of heaven and earth:

20 And blessed be the most high God, which hath delivered thine enemies into thy hand. And he gave him tithes of all.

21 And the king of Sodom said unto Abram, Give me the persons, and take the goods to thyself.

22 And Abram said to the king of Sodom, I have lift up mine hand unto the LORD, the most high God, the possessor of heaven and earth,

23 That I will not take from a thread even to a shoelatchet, and that I will not take any thing that is thine, lest thou shouldest say, I have made Abram rich:

24 Save only that which the young men have eaten, and the portion of the men which went with me, Aner, Eshcol, and Mamre; let them take their portion.

CHAPTER 15

1. After these things the word of the LORD came unto Abram in a vision, saying, Fear not, Abram: I *am* thy shield, *and* thy exceeding great reward.

2. And Abram said, LORD GOD, what wilt thou give me, seeing I go childless, and the steward of my house *is* this Eliezer of Damascus?

Genesis 14:6–11—Amalekites

The Amalekites (pronounced "uh-mal'-uh-kites") were an ancient Arab tribe that existed at the time of Abraham and continued on to the time of Moses and beyond. The Amalekites were constantly at war with the Hebrews in connection with the Exodus and the return to the Holy Land. The power of the Amalekites was eventually broken by Saul and David (see 1 Sam. 15; 27:8; 2 Sam. 8:12). The Simeonites later eradicated the last vestige of the Amalekites (see 1 Chron. 4:43). The Amalekites do not derive their name from Amalek, grandson of Esau, who lived much later.

Genesis 14:13—Hebrews

Abraham was identified as a Hebrew, as was Joseph in Egypt and all of the Israelites during their sojourn in that country. The derivation of the word *Hebrew* may relate to the word *eber* ("to cross," as go to the other side of a river)—implying that Abraham and his seed were those who had come from the other side of the river (Euphrates). Alternately, the word Hebrew may derive from the name Eber (or Heber), one of the ancestors of Abraham (see Gen. 10:21–25). In general, the word Hebrews has come to refer to the whole House of Israel, including the Jews in modern times.

Genesis 14:13—Mamre

Mamre (pronounced "mam'-ree") was an Amorite ally of Abraham in Canaan. He was among the 318 men Abraham used to route the forces of Chedorlaomer. The name Mamre was also used to signify the place where Abraham settled when he first came to Canaan and separated his estate from that of Lot (see Gen. 13:18). It was there that Abraham acquired property for a burial place for his family and where many notable ones were buried, including Sarah, Abraham, Isaac, Rebekah, Leah, and Jacob (see Gen. 23:19; 25:9; 49:30–31; 50:13).

Genesis 14:18—Melchizedek

The "King of Salem" is an exemplary prophetic leader whose faith and nobility of character were so perfect that the higher priesthood is named in his honor.

For more insights on Melchizedek, see Appendix I.

Genesis 14:18— "The most high God"

El Elyon is the Hebrew expression for Deity rendered in the passage where it occurs for the first time in the Old Testament: "And Melchizedek king of Salem brought forth bread and wine: and he *was* the priest of the most high God" (Gen. 14:18). The expression "the most high God" occurs rather frequently thereafter in the Old Testament, New Testament, Book of Mormon, and Doctrine and Covenants; see, for example, "Wherefore, go forth, crying with a loud voice, saying: The kingdom of heaven is at hand; crying: Hosanna! blessed be the name of the Most High God" (D&C 39:19).

3. And Abram said, Behold, to me thou hast given no seed: and, lo, one born in my house is mine heir.

4. And, behold, the word of the LORD came unto him, saying, This shall not be thine heir; but he that shall come forth out of thine own bowels shall be thine heir.

5. And he brought him forth abroad, and said, Look now toward heaven, and tell the stars, if thou be able to number them: and he said unto him, So shall thy seed be.

6. And he believed in the LORD; and he counted it to him for righteousness.

7. And he said unto him, I am the LORD that brought thee out of Ur of the Chaldees, to give thee this land to inherit it.

8. And he said, LORD GOD, whereby shall I know that I shall inherit it?

9. And he said unto him, Take me an heifer of three years old, and a she goat of three years old, and a ram of three years old, and a turtledove, and a young pigeon.

10. And he took unto him all these, and divided them in the midst, and laid each piece one against another: but the birds divided he not.

11. And when the fowls came down upon the carcases, Abram drove them away.

12. And when the sun was going down, a deep sleep fell upon Abram; and, lo, an horror of great darkness fell upon him.

13. And he said unto Abram, Know of a surety that thy seed shall be a stranger in a land that is not theirs, and shall serve them; and they shall afflict them four hundred years;

14. And also that nation, whom they shall serve, will I judge: and afterward shall they come out with great substance.

15. And thou shalt go to thy fathers in peace; thou shalt be buried in a good old age.

16. But in the fourth generation they shall come hither again: for the iniquity of the Amorites is not yet full.

17. And it came to pass, that, when the sun went down, and it was dark, behold a smoking furnace, and a burning lamp that passed between those pieces.

18. In the same day the LORD made a covenant with Abram, saying, Unto thy seed have I given this land, from the river of Egypt unto the great river, the river Euphrates:

19. The Kenites, and the Kenizzites, and the Kadmonites,

20. And the Hittites, and the Perizzites, and the Rephaims,

21. And the Amorites, and the Canaanites, and the Girgashites, and the Jebusites.

POINT OF INTEREST

Arabs are descendants of Abraham through Hagar's son Ishmael. While not all Arabs are Muslims, those who are perform the traditional hajj, *which includes* sa'ye, *a ritual walk commemorating Hagar's search for water as she wandered in the desert with her son, Ishmael. It is carried out by walking rapidly back and forth seven times between two low hills called Al-Marwah and Al-Safa while praising Allah.*

GENESIS CHAPTER 15

Genesis 15:2—Eliezer

Eliezer (pronounced el-ih-ee'-zer"; meaning: God is help) is the man whom Abram (later named Abraham) identified as steward of his house—apparently the same steward who later acted as emissary in the quest to obtain a wife for Isaac (see Gen. 24). This devoted man in the circle of Abraham was commissioned to go to the city of Nahor in the region of Padan-aram in Mesopotamia where Abraham's kin were located. According to the familiar story, it was Rebekah who came forth and offered water to the weary traveler and received of him gifts from the estate of Abram. When the servant presented the invitation for Rebekah to journey to the abode of Abraham and Isaac, her answer was in the affirmative (see Gen. 24:58–61).

The servant of Abraham was thus able to complete his commission with honor and success, and Isaac received a wife in fulfillment of the promise of the Abrahamic covenant. Rebekah subsequently gave birth to Esau and Jacob (see Gen. 25:24–26).

The Expulsion of Ishmael and His Mother by Gustave Doré

CHAPTER 16

4 ¶ And he went in unto Hagar, and she conceived: and when she saw that she had conceived, her mistress was despised in her eyes.

5 And Sarai said unto Abram, My wrong be upon thee: I have given my maid into thy bosom; and when she saw that she had conceived, I was despised in her eyes: the LORD judge between me and thee.

6 But Abram said unto Sarai, Behold, thy maid is in thy hand; do to her as it pleaseth thee. And when Sarai dealt hardly with her, she fled from her face.

7 ¶ And the angel of the LORD found her by a fountain of water in the wilderness, by the fountain in the way to Shur.

8 And he said, Hagar, Sarai's maid, whence camest thou? and whither wilt thou go? And she said, I flee from the face of my mistress Sarai.

9 And the angel of the LORD said unto her, Return to thy mistress, and submit thyself under her hands.

10 And the angel of the LORD said unto her, I will multiply thy seed exceedingly, that it shall not be numbered for multitude.

11 And the angel of the LORD said unto her, Behold, thou art with child, and shalt bear a son, and shalt call his name Ishmael; because the LORD hath heard thy affliction.

12 And he will be a wild man; his hand will be against every man, and every man's hand against him; and he shall dwell in the presence of all his brethren.

13 And she called the name of the LORD that spake unto her, Thou God seest me: for she said, Have I also here looked after him that seeth me?

14 Wherefore the well was called Beer-lahai-roi; behold, it is between Kadesh and Bered.

15 ¶ And Hagar bare Abram a son: and Abram called his son's name, which Hagar bare, Ishmael.

16 And Abram was fourscore and six years old, when Hagar bare Ishmael to Abram.

CHAPTER 17

1 AND when Abram was ninety years old and nine, the LORD appeared to Abram, and said unto him, I am the Almighty God; walk before me, and be thou perfect.

2 And I will make my covenant between me and thee, and will multiply thee exceedingly.

3 And Abram fell on his face: and God talked with him, saying,

4 As for me, behold, my covenant is with thee, and thou shalt be a father of many nations.

5 Neither shall thy name any more be called Abram, but thy name shall be Abraham; for a father of many nations have I made thee.

6 And I will make thee exceeding fruitful, and I will make nations of thee, and kings shall come out of thee.

7 And I will establish my covenant between me and thee and thy seed after thee in their generations for an everlasting covenant, to be a God unto thee, and to thy seed after thee.

8 And I will give unto thee, and to thy seed after thee, the land wherein thou art a stranger, all the land of Canaan, for an everlasting possession; and I will be their God.

9 ¶ And God said unto Abraham, Thou shalt keep my covenant therefore, thou, and thy seed after thee in their generations.

GENESIS CHAPTER 16

Genesis 16:1—Hagar

Hagar (meaning: flight) was an Egyptian handmaiden to Sarah and was also later the mother of Abraham's son Ishmael (see Gen. 16:1–16; 21:9–21; 25:12; Gal. 4:24). Hagar is also mentioned three times in the Doctrine and Covenants, each time in connection with the principle of plural marriage (see D&C 132:34, 65).

GENESIS CHAPTER 17

Genesis 17:1–4—All Things Are Possible with God

The Lord will fulfill all of His promises to His children—despite every challenge or obstacle.

The Lord had promised Abraham that he would multiply and be the father of many nations (see Gen. 17:1–4). The Lord, through holy men, reminded Abraham and his wife that Sarah would bear a son (see Gen. 18:10). And the Lord said, "Is any thing too hard for the Lord? At the time appointed I will return unto thee, according to the time of life, and Sarah shall have a son." Sarah bore a son, and Abraham named him Isaac (see Gen. 21:2–3). We can observe the hand of the Lord in all things—from the creation, to the Atonement, to the nurturing and blessing of His children in all things, to the resurrection and eternal life for His obedient children. Yes, the Lord can do all things . . . and we can do all things He requests of us in His strength (see Alma 26:11–12), with faith (see Moroni 7:33), and He will prepare a way for us to accomplish His commandments (see 1 Ne. 3:7).

Genesis 17:5–8—Promised Land

The Abrahamic covenant embraces the divine promise to grant to the faithful special gathering places of refuge upon the earth, as well as an ultimate home among the mansions of the Father on high.

From time to time, the Lord sets apart certain lands and locations as ordained gathering places for His covenant people; in the Middle East it was the Holy Land; in the Book of Mormon context, it was the Americas; in the latter days, it is the stakes of Zion, and eventually the New Jerusalem. All of this mortal geography is but a type and symbol for the eternal abode of the righteous in the eventual heavenly courts of the Father and Son.

Thus we see that the promises of God are always honored. The only question for us is this: will we keep the covenants? All promised blessings are predicated upon obedience to the law upon which the blessing rests (see D&C 130:19–21). The Abrahamic Covenant with all of its promised blessings awaits the faithful.

10 This is my covenant, which ye shall keep, between me and you and thy seed after thee; Every man child among you shall be circumcised.

11 And ye shall circumcise the flesh of your foreskin; and it shall be a token of the covenant betwixt me and you.

12 And he that is eight days old shall be circumcised among you, every man child in your generations, he that is born in the house, or bought with money of any stranger, which is not of thy seed.

13 He that is born in thy house, and he that is bought with thy money, must needs be circumcised: and my covenant shall be in your flesh for an everlasting covenant.

14 And the uncircumcised man child whose flesh of his foreskin is not circumcised, that soul shall be cut off from his people; he hath broken my covenant.

15 ¶ And God said unto Abraham, As for Sarai thy wife, thou shalt not call her name Sarai, but Sarah shall her name be.

16 And I will bless her, and give thee a son also of her: yea, I will bless her, and she shall be a mother of nations; kings of people shall be of her.

17 Then Abraham fell upon his face, and laughed, and said in his heart, Shall a child be born unto him that is an hundred years old? and shall Sarah, that is ninety years old, bear?

18 And Abraham said unto God, O that Ishmael might live before thee!

19 And God said, Sarah thy wife shall bear thee a son indeed; and thou shalt call his name Isaac: and I will establish my covenant with him for an everlasting covenant, and with his seed after him.

20 And as for Ishmael, I have heard thee: Behold, I have blessed him, and will make him fruitful, and will multiply him exceedingly; twelve princes shall he beget, and I will make him a great nation.

21 But my covenant will I establish with Isaac, which Sarah shall bear unto thee at this set time in the next year.

22 And he left off talking with him, and God went up from Abraham.

23 ¶ And Abraham took Ishmael his son, and all that were born in his house, and all that were bought with his money, every male among the men of Abraham's house; and circumcised the flesh of their foreskin in the selfsame day, as God had said unto him.

24 And Abraham was ninety years old and nine, when he was circumcised in the flesh of his foreskin.

25 And Ishmael his son was thirteen years old, when he was circumcised in the flesh of his foreskin.

26 In the selfsame day was Abraham circumcised, and Ishmael his son.

27 And all the men of his house, born in the house, and bought with money of the stranger, were circumcised with him.

CHAPTER 18

1 AND the LORD appeared unto him in the plains of Mamre: and he sat in the tent door in the heat of the day;

2 And he lift up his eyes and looked, and, lo, three men stood by him: and when he saw them, he ran to meet them from the tent door, and bowed himself toward the ground,

3 And said, My Lord, if now I have found favour in thy sight, pass not away, I pray thee, from thy servant:

Abraham and the Three Angels by Gustave Doré

GENESIS CHAPTER 18

Genesis 18:1–14—The Omnipotent Almighty

The question "Is any thing too hard for the Lord" resounds down through the ages as a reminder of the omnipotence of the Almighty. Though our mortal eyes too often fail to penetrate the veil of incredulity deployed by our own self-doubt, the eye of the Lord sees all and the word of the Lord confirms to our understanding that His plans will move forward inexorably. Consider the expression of faith declared by the prophet Jeremiah: "Ah Lord GOD! behold, thou hast made the heaven and the earth by thy great power and stretched out arm, *and* there is nothing too hard for thee" (Jer. 32:17); the well-known statement by King Lamoni: "I know, in the strength of the Lord thou canst do all things" (Alma 20:4); and the assurance given by the Savior Himself concerning the power of salvation: "With men *it is* impossible, but not with God: for with God all things are possible" (Mark 10:27).

4 Let a little water, I pray you, be fetched, and wash your feet, and rest yourselves under the tree:

5 And I will fetch a morsel of bread, and comfort ye your hearts; after that ye shall pass on: for therefore are ye come to your servant. And they said, So do, as thou hast said.

6 And Abraham hastened into the tent unto Sarah, and said, Make ready quickly three measures of fine meal, knead it, and make cakes upon the hearth.

7 And Abraham ran unto the herd, and fetcht a calf tender and good, and gave it unto a young man; and he hasted to dress it.

8 And he took butter, and milk, and the calf which he had dressed, and set it before them; and he stood by them under the tree, and they did eat.

9 ¶ And they said unto him, Where is Sarah thy wife? And he said, Behold, in the tent.

10 And he said, I will certainly return unto thee according to the time of life; and, lo, Sarah thy wife shall have a son. And Sarah heard it in the tent door, which was behind him.

11 Now Abraham and Sarah were old and well stricken in age; and it ceased to be with Sarah after the manner of women.

12 Therefore Sarah laughed within herself, saying, After I am waxed old shall I have pleasure, my lord being old also?

13 And the LORD said unto Abraham, Wherefore did Sarah laugh, saying, Shall I of a surety bear a child, which am old?

14 Is any thing too hard for the LORD? At the time appointed I will return unto thee, according to the time of life, and Sarah shall have a son.

15 Then Sarah denied, saying, I laughed not; for she was afraid. And he said, Nay; but thou didst laugh.

16 ¶ And the men rose up from thence, and looked toward Sodom: and Abraham went with them to bring them on the way.

17 And the LORD said, Shall I hide from Abraham that thing which I do;

18 Seeing that Abraham shall surely become a great and mighty nation, and all the nations of the earth shall be blessed in him?

19 For I know him, that he will command his children and his household after him, and they shall keep the way of the LORD, to do justice and judgment; that the LORD may bring upon Abraham that which he hath spoken of him.

20 And the LORD said, Because the cry of Sodom and Gomorrah is great, and because their sin is very grievous;

21 I will go down now, and see whether they have done altogether according to the cry of it, which is come unto me; and if not, I will know.

22 And the men turned their faces from thence, and went toward Sodom: but Abraham stood yet before the LORD.

23 ¶ And Abraham drew near, and said, Wilt thou also destroy the righteous with the wicked?

24 Peradventure there be fifty righteous within the city: wilt thou also destroy and not spare the place for the fifty righteous that are therein?

25 That be far from thee to do after this manner, to slay the righteous with the wicked: and that the righteous should be as the wicked, that be far from thee: Shall not the Judge of all the earth do right?

26 And the LORD said, If I find in Sodom fifty righteous within the city, then I will spare all the place for their sakes.

Genesis 18:16–19—Abraham: A Portrait of Righteousness

The righteous life of the patriarch and prophet Abraham serves as a worthy exemplum for all who honor and embrace the covenant program of the Lord.

Abraham sought after a happier and more peaceful place to live, since the land of the Chaldeans was fraught with wickedness and idolatry. He wanted the blessings of the fathers. He was a follower of righteousness. He had a desire to gain great knowledge and receive direction from the Lord and keep the commandments.

We later learn from the Lord that Abraham was a righteous father and leader, for he would teach his family and his household in the ways of the Lord. He would teach them the justice and judgment of the Lord. They would learn that the Lord is full of mercy and justice; thus if they followed in the ways of the Lord they would be blessed. Conversely, if they chose evil, the judgment of God was the result.

Abraham's classic demonstration of "peacemaking" is an example to us all. The herdsmen of Lot and Abraham had a concern — they had strife one with another over the land. Abraham, full of wisdom and charity, suggested that there be peace. Since there was adequate land available, he suggested, "if thou wilt take the left hand, then I will go to the right; of if thou depart to the right hand, then I will go to the left" (Gen. 13:9). He was basically saying that it didn't matter to him, but let there be peace—"for we be brethren" (Gen. 13:8). Lot chose the plain of Jordan and Abraham then took Canaan. This is where the real win-win principle began. If it is good for you, then it is good for me (see Gen. 13:6–12).

Abraham, like all the righteous, paid his tithes and offerings to the high priest, Melchizedek (see Gen. 14:20). He would not even partake of the spoils of war from the King of Sodom (see Gen. 14:23). Abraham's heart was pure; therefore, he was a just man, and his behavior was merely a reflection of his inner self. Because he was pure, he was righteous in his behavior.

Through him, we see that examples of righteousness bless all who know or who partake of the righteousness. Every good deed lasts forever, and righteous examples can teach a thousand lessons. Thus, the words of our Savior echo in our soul: "And know ye that ye shall be judges of this people, according to the judgment which I shall give unto you, which shall be just. Therefore, what manner of men ought ye to be? Verily I say unto you, even as I am" (3 Ne. 27:27).

27 And Abraham answered and said, Behold now, I have taken upon me to speak unto the Lord, which am but dust and ashes:

28 Peradventure there shall lack five of the fifty righteous: wilt thou destroy all the city for lack of five? And he said, If I find there forty and five, I will not destroy it.

29 And he spake unto him yet again, and said, Peradventure there shall be forty found there. And he said, I will not do it for forty's sake.

30 And he said unto him, Oh let not the Lord be angry, and I will speak: Peradventure there shall thirty be found there. And he said, I will not do it, if I find thirty there.

31 And he said, Behold now, I have taken upon me to speak unto the Lord: Peradventure there shall be twenty found there. And he said, I will not destroy it for twenty's sake.

32 And he said, Oh let not the Lord be angry, and I will speak yet but this once: Peradventure ten shall be found there. And he said, I will not destroy it for ten's sake.

33 And the LORD went his way, as soon as he had left communing with Abraham: and Abraham returned unto his place.

CHAPTER 19

1 AND there came two angels to Sodom at even; and Lot sat in the gate of Sodom: and Lot seeing them rose up to meet them; and he bowed himself with his face toward the ground;

2 And he said, Behold now, my lords, turn in, I pray you, into your servant's house, and tarry all night, and wash your feet, and ye shall rise up early, and go on your ways. And they said, Nay; but we will abide in the street all night.

3 And he pressed upon them greatly; and they turned in unto him, and entered into his house; and he made them a feast, and did bake unleavened bread, and they did eat.

4 ¶ But before they lay down, the men of the city, even the men of Sodom, compassed the house round, both old and young, all the people from every quarter:

5 And they called unto Lot, and said unto him, Where are the men which came in to thee this night? bring them out unto us, that we may know them.

6 And Lot went out at the door unto them, and shut the door after him,

7 And said, I pray you, brethren, do not so wickedly.

8 Behold now, I have two daughters which have not known man; let me, I pray you, bring them out unto you, and do ye to them as is good in your eyes: only unto these men do nothing; for therefore came they under the shadow of my roof.

9 And they said, Stand back. And they said again, This one fellow came in to sojourn, and he will needs be a judge: now will we deal worse with thee, than with them. And they pressed sore upon the man, even Lot, and came near to break the door.

10 But the men put forth their hand, and pulled Lot into the house to them, and shut to the door.

11 And they smote the men that were at the door of the house with blindness, both small and great: so that they wearied themselves to find the door.

12 ¶ And the men said unto Lot, Hast thou here any besides? son in law, and thy sons, and thy daughters, and whatsoever thou hast in the city, bring them out of this place:

GENESIS CHAPTER 19

Genesis 19:17—Sodom and Gomorrah: Portrait of Wickedness

In this verse, we see that the Lord will guide His saints away from the destructive forces of evil.

Abraham bargained with the Lord to spare Sodom and Gomorrah if there was an element of righteousness remaining within the depraved walls of these archetypal cities of evil. Lot chose to be in proximity with worldliness and its beauty, and seemed reluctant at first to leave. The angels of the Lord retrieved the only righteous souls and then destroyed the wicked. We need to heed the warnings of the prophets to flee Babylon and not look back as did Lot's wife (see Gen. 19:26), whose commitment to righteousness was apparently imperfect.

Wickedness has a price. When a person or group becomes so wicked that their iniquity is virtually full, the Lord does not allow them to live upon the earth unless they repent. There are dramatic cases where the Lord has destroyed the wicked, such as during the time of Noah, toward the end of the Jaredite period, the final chapter of the Nephite chronicle, and at other isolated times and places (such as Sodom and Gomorrah). On an individual basis, when people do not repent, they become "chained" to the devil (see Alma 12:9–11).

Interesting Note: Did Lot really offer up his own daughters to distract the depraved citizens of Sodom (see Gen. 19:8)? Just the opposite was the case. The Joseph Smith Translation makes clear that Lot made an impassioned attempt to *protect* his daughters from the mob (see JST Gen. 19:9–15).

Genesis 19:26—Pillar of Salt

What is meant when it says that Lot's wife "became a pillar of salt" (Gen. 19:26)? Elder Bruce R. McConkie gave insight when he wrote, "Luke 17:32: 'Look not back to Sodom and the wealth and luxury you are leaving. Stay not in the burning house, in the hope of salvaging your treasures, lest the flame destroy you; but flee, flee to the mountains.' Luke 17:33: 'Seek temporal things and lose eternal life; sacrifice the things of this life and gain eternal life'" (Bruce R. McConkie, *Doctrinal New Testament Commentary* [Salt Lake City: Bookcraft, 1965], 1:645).

It seems clear that Lot's wife turning back was a symbol of her lack of faith and devotion to the Lord . . . hence she returned to that type of life and perished. And thus we see that wickedness never was righteousness or happiness, and it only leads to destruction. There is no reward for sin—only sorrow and misery.

Genesis 19:37–38—Moab/Moabites

Moab was the son of Lot by his oldest daughter, conceived by an incestuous union unbeknownst to the sedated and sleeping Lot. Out of this happening arose the cultures of the Moabites and Ammonites, peoples who constantly warred with the Israelites.

13 For we will destroy this place, because the cry of them is waxen great before the face of the LORD; and the LORD hath sent us to destroy it.

14 And Lot went out, and spake unto his sons in law, which married his daughters, and said, Up, get you out of this place; for the LORD will destroy this city. But he seemed as one that mocked unto his sons in law.

15 ¶ And when the morning arose, then the angels hastened Lot, saying, Arise, take thy wife, and thy two daughters, which are here; lest thou be consumed in the iniquity of the city.

16 And while he lingered, the men laid hold upon his hand, and upon the hand of his wife, and upon the hand of his two daughters; the LORD being merciful unto him: and they brought him forth, and set him without the city.

17 ¶ And it came to pass, when they had brought them forth abroad, that he said, Escape for thy life; look not behind thee, neither stay thou in all the plain; escape to the mountain, lest thou be consumed.

18 And Lot said unto them, Oh, not so, my Lord:

19 Behold now, thy servant hath found grace in thy sight, and thou hast magnified thy mercy, which thou hast shewed unto me in saving my life; and I cannot escape to the mountain, lest some evil take me, and I die:

20 Behold now, this city is near to flee unto, and it is a little one: Oh, let me escape thither, (is it not a little one?) and my soul shall live.

21 And he said unto him, See, I have accepted thee concerning this thing also, that I will not overthrow this city, for the which thou hast spoken.

22 Haste thee, escape thither; for I cannot do any thing till thou be come thither. Therefore the name of the city was called Zoar.

23 ¶ The sun was risen upon the earth when Lot entered into Zoar.

24 Then the LORD rained upon Sodom and upon Gomorrah brimstone and fire from the LORD out of heaven;

25 And he overthrew those cities, and all the plain, and all the inhabitants of the cities, and that which grew upon the ground.

26 ¶ But his wife looked back from behind him, and she became a pillar of salt.

27 ¶ And Abraham gat up early in the morning to the place where he stood before the LORD:

28 And he looked toward Sodom and Gomorrah, and toward all the land of the plain, and beheld, and, lo, the smoke of the country went up as the smoke of a furnace.

29 ¶ And it came to pass, when God destroyed the cities of the plain, that God remembered Abraham, and sent Lot out of the midst of the overthrow, when he overthrew the cities in the which Lot dwelt.

30 ¶ And Lot went up out of Zoar, and dwelt in the mountain, and his two daughters with him; for he feared to dwell in Zoar: and he dwelt in a cave, he and his two daughters.

31 And the firstborn said unto the younger, Our father is old, and there is not a man in the earth to come in unto us after the manner of all the earth:

32 Come, let us make our father drink wine, and we will lie with him, that we may preserve seed of our father.

33 And they made their father drink wine that night: and the firstborn went in, and lay with her father; and he perceived not when she lay down, nor when she arose.

The most-often cited episode concerning conflict with the Moabites is the campaign of Barak, king of the Moabites, to bring down a curse upon the Israelites. When the hosts of Israel were encamped on the plains of Moab, east of the Jordan River near Jericho, Balak took action to retain the services of Balaam—who apparently had the reputation of divine influence—for the purpose of cursing Israel (see Num. 22:6). Israel was perceived as a distinct threat to the Moabites and their confederate associates, the Midianites. Balaam agreed to approach the Lord on their behalf. But the message was not to their liking, for the Lord adjured Balaam: "Thou shalt not go with them; thou shalt not curse the people: for they *are* blessed" (Num. 22:12). Still, Balak insisted, so Balaam supplicated the Lord again and received permission to go, provided he would do according to the Lord's command. Balaam went, though "God's anger was kindled because he went" (Num. 22:22). It was then that the famous event took place manifesting that Balaam's means of transportation (his donkey) had more spiritual discernment than Balaam himself. Seeing the angel of the Lord blocking the way, the donkey repeatedly held back (see Num. 22:27–35). Thereafter, Balak enjoined Balaam three times to view the hosts of Israel and perform the cursing that he had paid for. But each time the answer came back that Israel was to be blessed by the Lord, rather than cursed (see Num. 23:19–24; 24:4–9, 17–19).

Balak and Balaam went their separate ways. But the Israelites had intimate contact with the Moabites and began to assimilate their pagan practices and immoral ways. Thus the Lord commanded Moses to strike out against the indigenous peoples and eliminate the evil influence of the Moabites and Midianites (see Num. 31:8; also Josh. 24:9–10; Neh. 13:2; Micah 6:5; 2 Pet. 2:15; Jude 1:11; Rev. 2:14).

On other occasions the Moabites continued their succession of confrontations with the Israelites:

The Moabites were sent by the Lord as a scourge against the wayward Israelites, who, having repented, were then delivered by the Benjamite Ehud (see Judges 3:12–30).

During the days of David, the Moabites were subjugated as a tributary people (see 2 Sam. 8:2; 1 Chron. 18:2).

Jehoram of Israel and Jehoshaphat of Judah achieved a decisive victory over the rebelling Moabites (see 2 Kings 3:6–27).

Jehoshaphat importuned the Lord for help in overcoming the attacking confederation of Ammonites and Moabites (see 2 Chron. 20:1–25).

The Moabites played a supporting role (along with the Ammonites) in the process of the Babylonian defeat of the Jewish people under Nebuchadnezzar (see 2 Kings 24:1–2).

Eventually, the Moabites and Ammonites came under the yoke of Assyria and Chaldea according to the judgments of the Lord (see Zeph. 2:8–11; compare Amos 1; 2 Kings 24:2;

34 And it came to pass on the morrow, that the firstborn said unto the younger, Behold, I lay yesternight with my father: let us make him drink wine this night also; and go thou in, and lie with him, that we may preserve seed of our father.

35 And they made their father drink wine that night also: and the younger arose, and lay with him; and he perceived not when she lay down, nor when she arose.

36 Thus were both the daughters of Lot with child by their father.

37 And the firstborn bare a son, and called his name Moab: the same is the father of the Moabites unto this day.

38 And the younger, she also bare a son, and called his name Benammi: the same is the father of the children of Ammon unto this day.

CHAPTER 21

1 AND the LORD visited Sarah as he had said, and the LORD did unto Sarah as he had spoken.

2 For Sarah conceived, and bare Abraham a son in his old age, at the set time of which God had spoken to him.

3 And Abraham called the name of his son that was born unto him, whom Sarah bare to him, Isaac.

4 And Abraham circumcised his son Isaac being eight days old, as God had commanded him.

5 And Abraham was an hundred years old, when his son Isaac was born unto him.

6 ¶ And Sarah said, God hath made me to laugh, so that all that hear will laugh with me.

7 And she said, Who would have said unto Abraham, that Sarah should have given children suck? for I have born him a son in his old age.

8 And the child grew, and was weaned: and Abraham made a great feast the same day that Isaac was weaned.

9 ¶ And Sarah saw the son of Hagar the Egyptian, which she had born unto Abraham, mocking.

10 Wherefore she said unto Abraham, Cast out this bondwoman and her son: for the son of this bondwoman shall not be heir with my son, even with Isaac.

11 And the thing was very grievous in Abraham's sight because of his son.

12 ¶ And God said unto Abraham, Let it not be grievous in thy sight because of the lad, and because of thy bondwoman; in all that Sarah hath said unto thee, hearken unto her voice; for in Isaac shall thy seed be called.

13 And also of the son of the bondwoman will I make a nation, because he is thy seed.

14 And Abraham rose up early in the morning, and took bread, and a bottle of water, and gave it unto Hagar, putting it on her shoulder, and the child, and sent her away: and she departed, and wandered in the wilderness of Beer-sheba.

15 And the water was spent in the bottle, and she cast the child under one of the shrubs.

16 And she went, and sat her down over against him a good way off, as it were a bowshot: for she said, Let me not see the death of the child. And she sat over against him, and lift up her voice, and wept.

Ezek. 25). In cultures such as that of the Moabites we have a defining emblem of practices and patterns of life that are antithetical to the covenant principles of the Lord's kingdom. In the conflict of opposites we can gain greater understanding of what is required for eternal blessings.

GENESIS CHAPTER 21

Genesis 21:1–13—Ishmael

Ishmael was the oldest son of Abram (soon thereafter called Abraham), being born of Hagar, the Egyptian handmade of Sarai (soon thereafter Sarah) (see Gen. 16; 17:15–26; compare 1 Chron. 1:28–31). On the weaning of Isaac, a separation occurred in the household of Abraham:

> And Sarah saw the son of Hagar the Egyptian, which she had born unto Abraham, mocking.
>
> Wherefore she said unto Abraham, Cast out this bondwoman and her son: for the son of this bondwoman shall not be heir with my son, even with Isaac.
>
> And the thing was very grievous in Abraham's sight because of his son.
>
> And God said unto Abraham, Let it not be grievous in thy sight because of the lad, and because of thy bondwoman; in all that Sarah hath said unto thee, hearken unto her voice; for in Isaac shall thy seed be called.
>
> And also of the son of the bondwoman will I make a nation, because he is thy seed. (Gen. 21:9–13)

Abraham dispatched Hagar and Ishmael into the wilderness with bread and water. When the provisions were spent, Hagar mourned helplessly, fearing that the child would perish. When God heard the cry of the boy, He sent an angel to comfort the mother (see Gen. 21:18–21.)

Later, upon the passing of Abraham, Isaac and Ishmael came together again to bury their father (see Gen. 25:9). Ishmael passed away at age 137 (see Gen. 25:17–18). His descendants seem to have become a wandering people who related to, and intermingled with, the nations of Canaan. Joseph was sold by his brethren into the hands of "Ishmeelites" who took him to Egypt (see Gen. 37:25–28; 39:1). Paul refers to the situation with Isaac and Ishmael with these words: "But he who was of the bondwoman was born after the flesh; but he of the freewoman was by promise" (Gal. 4:21; see also Gal. 4:22–31).

Genesis 21:14–20—Blessings of the Lord

This event illustrates the all-encompassing design of the Lord to bless His children—even those not of the declared primary lineage. He had a plan for Ishmael, and blessings were in store to be poured out upon the descendants of this Abrahamic stock in rich measure. The Lord opened the eyes of Hagar, that she found life-sustaining water for her child. In a similar way, the vision of parents of faith can be opened so that they perceive the blessings of living water provided by the gospel of Jesus Christ for their sons and daughters. All children can be blessed with the

17 And God heard the voice of the lad; and the angel of God called to Hagar out of heaven, and said unto her, What aileth thee, Hagar? fear not; for God hath heard the voice of the lad where he is.

18 Arise, lift up the lad, and hold him in thine hand; for I will make him a great nation.

19 And God opened her eyes, and she saw a well of water; and she went, and filled the bottle with water, and gave the lad drink.

20 And God was with the lad; and he grew, and dwelt in the wilderness, and became an archer.

21 And he dwelt in the wilderness of Paran: and his mother took him a wife out of the land of Egypt.

22 ¶ And it came to pass at that time, that Abimelech and Phichol the chief captain of his host spake unto Abraham, saying, God is with thee in all that thou doest:

23 Now therefore swear unto me here by God that thou wilt not deal falsely with me, nor with my son, nor with my son's son: but according to the kindness that I have done unto thee, thou shalt do unto me, and to the land wherein thou hast sojourned.

24 And Abraham said, I will swear.

25 And Abraham reproved Abimelech because of a well of water, which Abimelech's servants had violently taken away.

26 And Abimelech said, I wot not who hath done this thing: neither didst thou tell me, neither yet heard I of it, but to day.

27 And Abraham took sheep and oxen, and gave them unto Abimelech; and both of them made a covenant.

28 And Abraham set seven ewe lambs of the flock by themselves.

29 And Abimelech said unto Abraham, What mean these seven ewe lambs which thou hast set by themselves?

30 And he said, For these seven ewe lambs shalt thou take of my hand, that they may be a witness unto me, that I have digged this well.

31 Wherefore he called that place Beer-sheba; because there they sware both of them.

32 Thus they made a covenant at Beer-sheba: then Abimelech rose up, and Phichol the chief captain of his host, and they returned into the land of the Philistines.

33 ¶ And Abraham planted a grove in Beer-sheba, and called there on the name of the LORD, the everlasting God.

34 And Abraham sojourned in the Philistines' land many days.

CHAPTER 22

1 AND it came to pass after these things, that God did tempt Abraham, and said unto him, Abraham: and he said, Behold, here I am.

2 And he said, Take now thy son, thine only son Isaac, whom thou lovest, and get thee into the land of Moriah; and offer him there for a burnt offering upon one of the mountains which I will tell thee of.

3 ¶ And Abraham rose up early in the morning, and saddled his ass, and took two of his young men with him, and Isaac his son, and clave the wood for the burnt offering, and rose up, and went unto the place of which God had told him.

4 Then on the third day Abraham lifted up his eyes, and saw the place afar off.

5 And Abraham said unto his young men, Abide ye here with the ass; and I and the lad will go yonder and worship, and come again to you.

vitality of eternal life, no matter what their station in mortality might be. All are beloved of the Father and Son. All can have the abundance of immortality and exaltation through obedience to the gospel plan of happiness. All Saints of every provenance and culture can participate in the glory and joy of the Abrahamic covenant by admission to the fold of Christ through faith, repentance, baptism, and the gift of the Holy Ghost, together with all the higher ordinances of the priesthood.

Genesis 21:34—Philistines

The Philistines (pronounced "fih'-luh-steens" or "fih-lis'-teens") were an ancient tribe, or group of tribes, that contended from time to time with the Israelites, particularly during the time of King Saul and, to a declining degree, King David. They are first mentioned in the Old Testament in connection with Abraham, who made a covenant of peace with Abimelech, king of the Philistines in Gerar, a region located in the Western Negev not far from Gaza to the northwest and Beersheba to the southeast (see Gen. 21:32–34).

It was rarely such an amicable spirit that characterized the relationship between the Philistines and the people of the Lord. The intense and lethal conflict between the Philistines and Samson is well known (see Judges 14–16). David encountered and defeated the Philistine giant Goliath (see 1 Sam. 17:49–51). It was later in battle against the Philistines that Saul and his three sons (Jonathan, Abinadab, and Malchi-shua) were slain (see 1 Sam. 31). Upon his being anointed king of Israel, David subjected the Philistines to a definitive defeat (see 2 Sam. 5). Under Hezekiah, king of Judah, the Philistines were again brought under subjection (see 2 Kings 18:8), though their animosity against the Israelites continued to fester without cease (see Ezek. 25:15–17).

Originally, the Philistines resided in "Caphtor" (Amos 9:7), thought to be the island of Crete or perhaps part of the Egyptian delta. Eventually they established a powerful confederacy of five key cities (Ashdod, Gaza, Askelon, Gath, and Ekron) in the territory between Judea and Egypt (see 1 Sam. 6:17). The name "Palestine," a word designating the Holy Land itself, derives from the name of the Philistines—an ironic reminder that the Philistine phenomenon is an enduring emblem of the opposition perpetually encountered by the Kingdom of God in its forward advance toward the time when it will fill the entire world (see Dan. 2:35; D&C 65:2).

The Philistines are mentioned three times in the Book of Mormon, in each case as part of Nephi's inclusion of the writings of Isaiah: 2 Ne. 12:6 (compare Isa. 2:6); 2 Ne. 19:12 (compare Isa. 9:12); and 2 Ne. 21:14 (compare Isa. 11:14).

6 And Abraham took the wood of the burnt offering, and laid it upon Isaac his son; and he took the fire in his hand, and a knife; and they went both of them together.

7 And Isaac spake unto Abraham his father, and said, My father: and he said, Here am I, my son. And he said, Behold the fire and the wood: but where is the lamb for a burnt offering?

8 And Abraham said, My son, God will provide himself a lamb for a burnt offering: so they went both of them together.

9 And they came to the place which God had told him of; and Abraham built an altar there, and laid the wood in order, and bound Isaac his son, and laid him on the altar upon the wood.

10 And Abraham stretched forth his hand, and took the knife to slay his son.

11 And the angel of the LORD called unto him out of heaven, and said, Abraham, Abraham: and he said, Here am I.

12 And he said, Lay not thine hand upon the lad, neither do thou any thing unto him: for now I know that thou fearest God, seeing thou hast not withheld thy son, thine only son from me.

13 And Abraham lifted up his eyes, and looked, and behold behind him a ram caught in a thicket by his horns: and Abraham went and took the ram, and offered him up for a burnt offering in the stead of his son.

14 And Abraham called the name of that place Jehovah-jireh: as it is said to this day, In the mount of the LORD it shall be seen.

15 ¶ And the angel of the LORD called unto Abraham out of heaven the second time,

16 And said, By myself have I sworn, saith the LORD, for because thou hast done this thing, and hast not withheld thy son, thine only son:

17 That in blessing I will bless thee, and in multiplying I will multiply thy seed as the stars of the heaven, and as the sand which is upon the sea shore; and thy seed shall possess the gate of his enemies;

18 And in thy seed shall all the nations of the earth be blessed; because thou hast obeyed my voice.

19 So Abraham returned unto his young men, and they rose up and went together to Beer-sheba; and Abraham dwelt at Beer-sheba.

20 ¶ And it came to pass after these things, that it was told Abraham, saying, Behold, Milcah, she hath also born children unto thy brother Nahor;

21 Huz his firstborn, and Buz his brother, and Kemuel the father of Aram,

22 And Chesed, and Hazo, and Pildash, and Jidlaph, and Bethuel.

23 And Bethuel begat Rebekah: these eight Milcah did bear to Nahor, Abraham's brother.

24 And his concubine, whose name was Reumah, she bare also Tebah, and Gaham, and Thahash, and Maachah.

GENESIS CHAPTER 22

Genesis 22:1–2—The Lord Requires the Heart and a Willing Mind

Abraham was commanded to offer up the thing most dear to his heart—his own son. Only through a commitment to sacrifice all that we have, if required to do so, can we manifest to the Lord that our love for Him and His divine cause is perfect.

God did tempt (prove) Abraham by commanding him to sacrifice his only son. Abraham took Isaac and two other young men on the journey to Moriah, where he was to offer Isaac as a burnt offering, even a sacrifice to the Lord. On the third day Abraham and Isaac went to worship. Isaac carried the wood as they journeyed. Isaac asked about the sacrifice, and Abraham replied, ". . . my son, God will provide himself a lamb for a burn offering . . ." (Gen. 22:8). Abraham bound Isaac and laid him on the altar preparing for the ultimate sacrifice. As he took the knife, an angel of the Lord forbade him and said, ". . . for now I know that thou fearest [i.e., showest reverence to] God, seeing thou hast not withheld thy son . . ." (Gen. 22:12). A ram was provided for the burnt offering. The Lord then promised Abraham, ". . . in thy seed shall all the nations of the earth be blessed . . ." (Gen. 22:18).

Thus we see that during our life here on earth we must offer all. In our day, the Lord requires a broken heart and a contrite spirit. He requires our will, and that is what we can give the giver of all—then the Lord can make of us all that we were intended to be, exalted sons and daughters of God the Father, Elohim.

For more insights on Isaac, see Appendix J.

Genesis 22:3–12—The Lord Will Provide the Means Whereby We Can Obey

Abraham demonstrated complete devotion and obedience, and the Lord, in His mercy and goodness, provided the ram for the sacrifice. Thus it is for all the Lord's faithful children.

The test was in Abraham's willingness and then, as usual, the Lord provided a way—even prepared the way for the sacrifice to be completed. The Lord truly does provide the means to do all things he commands us. We simply must act with love and faith and do as He has commanded. He strengthens us to do all things (see Alma 26:11–12). He gives us weaknesses so that we will be humbled, thus turning to Him for strength (see Ether 12:27). He gives us His word, which gives direction (see 2 Ne. 32:3; Alma 37:37–47). He blesses us with the Holy Ghost, which shows us all things to do (see 2 Ne. 32:5). Yes, the Lord is there with all things to bless our lives—the Plan of Happiness, the gospel, the priesthood, and the temple. He is our strength, He is our all, He goes before our face, He is on the right and on the left, His Spirit is in our heart, and His angels round about to bear us up.

CHAPTER 24

1 AND Abraham was old, and well stricken in age: and the LORD had blessed Abraham in all things.
2 And Abraham said unto his eldest servant of his house, that ruled over all that he had, Put, I pray thee, thy hand under my thigh:
3 And I will make thee swear by the LORD, the God of heaven, and the God of the earth, that thou shalt not take a wife unto my son of the daughters of the Canaanites, among whom I dwell:
4 But thou shalt go unto my country, and to my kindred, and take a wife unto my son Isaac.
5 And the servant said unto him, Peradventure the woman will not be willing to follow me unto this land: must I needs bring thy son again unto the land from whence thou camest?
6 And Abraham said unto him, Beware thou that thou bring not my son thither again.
7 ¶ The LORD God of heaven, which took me from my father's house, and from the land of my kindred, and which spake unto me, and that sware unto me, saying, Unto thy seed will I give this land; he shall send his angel before thee, and thou shalt take a wife unto my son from thence.
8 And if the woman will not be willing to follow thee, then thou shalt be clear from this my oath: only bring not my son thither again.
9 And the servant put his hand under the thigh of Abraham his master, and sware to him concerning that matter.
10 ¶ And the servant took ten camels of the camels of his master, and departed; for all the goods of his master were in his hand: and he arose, and went to Mesopotamia, unto the city of Nahor.
11 And he made his camels to kneel down without the city by a well of water at the time of the evening, even the time that women go out to draw water.
12 And he said, O LORD God of my master Abraham, I pray thee, send me good speed this day, and shew kindness unto my master Abraham.
13 Behold, I stand here by the well of water; and the daughters of the men of the city come out to draw water:
14 And let it come to pass, that the damsel to whom I shall say, Let down thy pitcher, I pray thee, that I may drink; and she shall say, Drink, and I will give thy camels drink also: let the same be she that thou hast appointed for thy servant Isaac; and thereby shall I know that thou hast shewed kindness unto my master.
15 ¶ And it came to pass, before he had done speaking, that, behold, Rebekah came out, who was born to Bethuel, son of Milcah, the wife of Nahor, Abraham's brother, with her pitcher upon her shoulder.

GENESIS CHAPTER 24

Overview
"It (celestial marriage) is one of the greatest blessings that ever was conferred upon the human family. It is an eternal law which has always existed in other worlds as well as in this world." — John Taylor, *JD* 24:229

In all dispensations of time from Adam on, eternal marriage has been the gateway to the highest covenant blessings of the Lord. Thus Abraham and his patriarchal successors, as well as all of God's chosen prophets, have taught the preeminence of celestial marriage and the wisdom of choosing mates who are worthy of this blessing. The portrait given in the scriptures of the loyalty and leadership of Abraham's chief steward is a remarkable illustration of faith, righteousness, obedience, and valor in the quest to honor righteous principles of covenant marriage. His successful mission to obtain a wife for Isaac assured the continuity of the covenant lineage.

Genesis 24:1–4—Marriage in the Covenant
Abraham and his patriarchal successors, as well as all of God's chosen prophets, have taught the preeminence of celestial marriage and the wisdom of choosing mates who are worthy of this blessing.

Abraham labored diligently to prepare the way for his son Isaac to marry in the covenant. Isaac and Rebekah were saddened when Esau married out of the covenant (see Gen. 26:34–35), and took great pains to see that Jacob followed the ordained pathway of the Abrahamic Covenant in marriage (see Gen. 28:1–5). A divinely-ordained partnership of man and wife participating in the Lord's mission to bring to pass "the immortality and eternal life of man" (Moses 1:39), marriage in the covenant (temple marriage) is essential as the foundation for the bringing about and continuation of "eternal lives" (see D&C 132:24). Great care must be given in the selection of a mate.

All men and women who have chosen Christ and chosen to enter into or accept the covenant of everlasting marriage can enjoy the blessings of exaltation. Marriage in any other way can result in failure to receive all the blessings of the Abrahamic covenant.

Genesis 24:15—Rebekah
Rebekah (meaning: that which binds or secures) was the wife of Isaac, the son of Abraham. The story of how Abraham arranged for his servant to seek a wife for Isaac within the extended family circle is a familiar and uplifting account of courtship and marriage (see Gen. 24).
For more insights on Rebekah, see Appendix K.

16 And the damsel was very fair to look upon, a virgin, neither had any man known her: and she went down to the well, and filled her pitcher, and came up.

17 And the servant ran to meet her, and said, Let me, I pray thee, drink a little water of thy pitcher.

18 And she said, Drink, my lord: and she hasted, and let down her pitcher upon her hand, and gave him drink.

19 And when she had done giving him drink, she said, I will draw water for thy camels also, until they have done drinking.

20 And she hasted, and emptied her pitcher into the trough, and ran again unto the well to draw water, and drew for all his camels.

21 And the man wondering at her held his peace, to wit whether the LORD had made his journey prosperous or not.

22 And it came to pass, as the camels had done drinking, that the man took a golden earring of half a shekel weight, and two bracelets for her hands of ten shekels weight of gold;

23 And said, Whose daughter art thou? tell me, I pray thee: is there room in thy father's house for us to lodge in?

24 And she said unto him, I am the daughter of Bethuel the son of Milcah, which she bare unto Nahor.

25 She said moreover unto him, We have both straw and provender enough, and room to lodge in.

26 And the man bowed down his head, and worshipped the LORD.

27 And he said, Blessed be the LORD God of my master Abraham, who hath not left destitute my master of his mercy and his truth: I being in the way, the LORD led me to the house of my master's brethren.

28 And the damsel ran, and told them of her mother's house these things.

29 ¶ And Rebekah had a brother, and his name was Laban: and Laban ran out unto the man, unto the well.

30 And it came to pass, when he saw the earring and bracelets upon his sister's hands, and when he heard the words of Rebekah his sister, saying, Thus spake the man unto me; that he came unto the man; and, behold, he stood by the camels at the well.

31 And he said, Come in, thou blessed of the LORD; wherefore standest thou without? for I have prepared the house, and room for the camels.

32 ¶ And the man came into the house: and he ungirded his camels, and gave straw and provender for the camels, and water to wash his feet, and the men's feet that were with him.

33 And there was set meat before him to eat: but he said, I will not eat, until I have told mine errand. And he said, Speak on.

34 And he said, I am Abraham's servant.

35 And the LORD hath blessed my master greatly; and he is become great: and he hath given him flocks, and herds, and silver, and gold, and menservants, and maidservants, and camels, and asses.

36 And Sarah my master's wife bare a son to my master when she was old: and unto him hath he given all that he hath.

37 And my master made me swear, saying, Thou shalt not take a wife to my son of the daughters of the Canaanites, in whose land I dwell:

38 But thou shalt go unto my father's house, and to my kindred, and take a wife unto my son.

39 And I said unto my master, Peradventure the woman will not follow me.

40 And he said unto me, The LORD, before whom I walk, will send his angel with thee, and prosper thy way; and thou shalt take a wife for my son of my kindred, and of my father's house:

Genesis 24:16–27—Portrait of Loyal Stewardship

The loyalty and leadership of Abraham's chief steward is a remarkable illustration of faith, righteousness, obedience, and valor. His successful mission to obtain a wife for Isaac assured the continuity of the covenant lineage.

Marriage customs and practices in Old Testament times differed from our current patterns. A young man's parents generally chose his wife and arranged for the marriage, which was the case with Abraham. He, being old, sent his eldest servant on the errand to secure for Isaac a wife from among their kindred, thus making it possible to marry in the covenant. Abraham assured his servant that the Lord would send angels before him in order that he night take a wife for his son. The servant made an oath with Abraham to do as he requested, and he ended up obtaining Rebekah as a wife for Isaac.

The account of how Abraham's chief steward obtained the hand of Rebekah for his master's son is remarkably complete. He demonstrated all the qualities of stewardship that a servant of the Lord in our day would do well to emulate: allegiance, resourcefulness, prayerfulness, faith, thoroughness, strict obedience to commandments, thoughtfulness, gratitude, unwavering devotion to the cause, and wisdom. This attitude and devotion is the example for all those who have stewardships—and this includes all of us, especially parents who are guiding their children to marry in the temple and honor their birthright.

Eliezer and Rebekah by Gustave Doré

41 Then shalt thou be clear from this my oath, when thou comest to my kindred; and if they give not thee one, thou shalt be clear from my oath.

42 And I came this day unto the well, and said, O LORD God of my master Abraham, if now thou do prosper my way which I go:

43 Behold, I stand by the well of water; and it shall come to pass, that when the virgin cometh forth to draw water, and I say to her, Give me, I pray thee, a little water of thy pitcher to drink;

44 And she say to me, Both drink thou, and I will also draw for thy camels: let the same be the woman whom the LORD hath appointed out for my master's son.

45 And before I had done speaking in mine heart, behold, Rebekah came forth with her pitcher on her shoulder; and she went down unto the well, and drew water: and I said unto her, Let me drink, I pray thee.

46 And she made haste, and let down her pitcher from her shoulder, and said, Drink, and I will give thy camels drink also: so I drank, and she made the camels drink also.

47 And I asked her, and said, Whose daughter art thou? And she said, The daughter of Bethuel, Nahor's son, whom Milcah bare unto him: and I put the earring upon her face, and the bracelets upon her hands.

48 And I bowed down my head, and worshipped the LORD, and blessed the LORD God of my master Abraham, which had led me in the right way to take my master's brother's daughter unto his son.

49 And now if ye will deal kindly and truly with my master, tell me: and if not, tell me; that I may turn to the right hand, or to the left.

50 Then Laban and Bethuel answered and said, The thing proceedeth from the LORD: we cannot speak unto thee bad or good.

51 Behold, Rebekah is before thee, take her, and go, and let her be thy master's son's wife, as the LORD hath spoken.

52 And it came to pass, that, when Abraham's servant heard their words, he worshipped the LORD, bowing himself to the earth.

53 And the servant brought forth jewels of silver, and jewels of gold, and raiment, and gave them to Rebekah: he gave also to her brother and to her mother precious things.

54 And they did eat and drink, he and the men that were with him, and tarried all night; and they rose up in the morning, and he said, Send me away unto my master.

55 And her brother and her mother said, Let the damsel abide with us a few days, at the least ten; after that she shall go.

56 And he said unto them, Hinder me not, seeing the LORD hath prospered my way; send me away that I may go to my master.

57 And they said, We will call the damsel, and enquire at her mouth.

58 And they called Rebekah, and said unto her, Wilt thou go with this man? And she said, I will go.

59 And they sent away Rebekah their sister, and her nurse, and Abraham's servant, and his men.

60 And they blessed Rebekah, and said unto her, Thou art our sister, be thou the mother of thousands of millions, and let thy seed possess the gate of those which hate them.

61 ¶ And Rebekah arose, and her damsels, and they rode upon the camels, and followed the man: and the servant took Rebekah, and went his way.

Genesis 24:50—Laban

Laban (meaning: white) was the son of Bethuel, who in turn was the youngest son of Nahor, brother of Abraham (see Gen. 22:22–23). When the servant of Abraham came to Haran in search of a wife for Isaac, he was led to Rebekah by inspiration. Therefore, Bethuel and Laban (Rebekah's brother) concluded: "The thing proceedeth from the LORD: we cannot speak unto thee bad or good. Behold, Rebekah *is* before thee, take *her,* and go, and let her be thy master's son's wife, as the LORD hath spoken" (Gen. 24:50–51). Years later, Isaac sent his son Jacob to Laban, Rebekah's brother, to seek a wife (see Gen. 28:1–5). Jacob was well received:

And it came to pass, when Laban heard the tidings of Jacob his sister's son, that he ran to meet him, and embraced him, and kissed him, and brought him to his house. And he told Laban all these things.

And Laban said to him, Surely thou *art* my bone and my flesh. And he abode with him the space of a month.

And Laban said unto Jacob, Because thou *art* my brother, shouldest thou therefore serve me for nought? tell me, what *shall* thy wages *be?*

And Laban had two daughters: the name of the elder *was* Leah, and the name of the younger *was* Rachel.

Leah *was* tender eyed; but Rachel *was* beautiful and well favoured.

And Jacob loved Rachel; and said, I will serve thee seven years for Rachel thy younger daughter.

And Laban said, *It is* better that I give her to thee, than that I should give her to another man: abide with me.

And Jacob served seven years for Rachel; and they seemed unto him *but* a few days, for the love he had to her. (Gen. 29:13–20)

On the day of the wedding, Laban unilaterally adjusted the terms of the marriage agreement by sending the veiled Leah that evening to be Jacob's wife, her true identity being something that Jacob did not discover until the following morning: "And it came to pass, that in the morning, behold, it *was* Leah: and he said to Laban, What *is* this thou hast done unto me? did not I serve with thee for Rachel? wherefore then hast thou beguiled me? And Laban said, It must not be so done in our country, to give the younger before the firstborn" (Gen. 29:25–26). Jacob then agreed to serve Laban yet another seven years and was soon thereafter favored with the girl of his choice, having now two wives for his labors. In all Jacob served Laban for a total of twenty years before returning to Canaan (see Gen. 31:38, 41). The two had their points of difference over the years but separated with a covenant of friendship (see Gen. 31:43–55).

62 And Isaac came from the way of the well Lahai-roi; for he dwelt in the south country.

63 And Isaac went out to meditate in the field at the eventide: and he lifted up his eyes, and saw, and, behold, the camels were coming.

64 And Rebekah lifted up her eyes, and when she saw Isaac, she lighted off the camel.

65 For she had said unto the servant, What man is this that walketh in the field to meet us? And the servant had said, It is my master: therefore she took a vail, and covered herself.

66 And the servant told Isaac all things that he had done.

67 And Isaac brought her into his mother Sarah's tent, and took Rebekah, and she became his wife; and he loved her: and Isaac was comforted after his mother's death.

CHAPTER 25

1 THEN again Abraham took a wife, and her name was Keturah.

2 And she bare him Zimran, and Jokshan, and Medan, and Midian, and Ishbak, and Shuah.

3 And Jokshan begat Sheba, and Dedan. And the sons of Dedan were Asshurim, and Letushim, and Leummim.

4 And the sons of Midian; Ephah, and Epher, and Hanoch, and Abida, and Eldaah. All these were the children of Keturah.

5 ¶ And Abraham gave all that he had unto Isaac.

6 But unto the sons of the concubines, which Abraham had, Abraham gave gifts, and sent them away from Isaac his son, while he yet lived, eastward, unto the east country.

7 And these are the days of the years of Abraham's life which he lived, an hundred threescore and fifteen years.

8 Then Abraham gave up the ghost, and died in a good old age, an old man, and full of years; and was gathered to his people.

9 And his sons Isaac and Ishmael buried him in the cave of Machpelah, in the field of Ephron the son of Zohar the Hittite, which is before Mamre;

10 The field which Abraham purchased of the sons of Heth: there was Abraham buried, and Sarah his wife.

11 ¶ And it came to pass after the death of Abraham, that God blessed his son Isaac; and Isaac dwelt by the well Lahai-roi.

12 ¶ Now these are the generations of Ishmael, Abraham's son, whom Hagar the Egyptian, Sarah's handmaid, bare unto Abraham:

13 And these are the names of the sons of Ishmael, by their names, according to their generations: the firstborn of Ishmael, Nebajoth; and Kedar, and Adbeel, and Mibsam,

14 And Mishma, and Dumah, and Massa,

15 Hadar, and Tema, Jetur, Naphish, and Kedemah:

16 These are the sons of Ishmael, and these are their names, by their towns, and by their castles; twelve princes according to their nations.

17 And these are the years of the life of Ishmael, an hundred and thirty and seven years: and he gave up the ghost and died; and was gathered unto his people.

18 And they dwelt from Havilah unto Shur, that is before Egypt, as thou goest toward Assyria: and he died in the presence of all his brethren.

GENESIS CHAPTER 25

Genesis 25:1—Keturah

Keturah (pronounced "kih-too'-ruh" or "kih'-tyoor-uh"; meaning: incense) was a wife of Abraham, who remarried following the passing of Sarah. The posterity of Abraham and Keturah included various tribes, among them the Midianites (after their son Midian—see Gen. 25:4; 1 Chron. 1:33).

Genesis 25:22–23—Personal Revelation

We are not left on our own in this mortal realm of shadows and tribulation. The Lord has prepared a way to guide the prayerful at decisive moments—especially faithful and dedicated parents—through the blessings of His Holy Spirit.

Revelation is given to all mankind. There is a requirement, and Rebekah fulfilled that requirement—she asked. The Lord revealed to her concerning Jacob and Esau. So likewise has the Lord revealed truth to all His children since time began. There is a pattern for revelation. We must ask with a sincere heart, with faith, having done our part according to our role and stewardship. One does not receive revelation for others outside one's stewardship. And thus we see that revelation is the "rock" upon which we build a sure foundation on the Lord Jesus Christ. This is how Peter knew that Jesus was the Christ (see Matt. 16:17–18). This is how we know that Jesus is the Christ, the Book of Mormon is true, Joseph Smith was the Prophet of the restoration, and this is the true Church led by a living prophet today. Without revelation we would lose not only the knowledge of God, but also the direction for our lives today. We cannot live and gain eternal life without revelation as a Church and as individuals.

Genesis 25:24–34—Esau

Esau (meaning: hairy) was the older of two twin sons born to Isaac and Rebekah. The story of how Esau sold his birthright to Jacob for "pottage" (see Gen. 25:29–34) has become famous.

Contrary to the wishes of his parents, Esau married non-Israelite women (see Gen. 26:34–35). Later, when Isaac was old and frail, he desired to pronounce a blessing upon the head of his firstborn, Esau. But Rebekah counseled Jacob to manage the circumstances in such a way that he, rather than Esau, received the primary blessing, much to Esau's dismay (see Gen. 27:38–44).

Unlike his brother, Jacob was obedient in seeking a wife from among his Israelite kin, according to the covenant blessing given to him by his father Isaac (see Gen. 28:3–5).

Eventually Esau and Jacob became reconciled (see Gen. 33). Their ancestors constituted two rival nations, the Israelites and the Edomites (from "edom," meaning red).

There is honor and glory in being true to the birthright and calling as servants of the Lord, commissioned to be exemplars of obedience and righteousness in carrying the

19 ¶ And these are the generations of Isaac, Abraham's son: Abraham begat Isaac:

20 And Isaac was forty years old when he took Rebekah to wife, the daughter of Bethuel the Syrian of Padan-aram, the sister to Laban the Syrian.

21 And Isaac intreated the LORD for his wife, because she was barren: and the LORD was intreated of him, and Rebekah his wife conceived.

22 And the children struggled together within her; and she said, If it be so, why am I thus? And she went to enquire of the LORD.

23 And the LORD said unto her, Two nations are in thy womb, and two manner of people shall be separated from thy bowels; and the one people shall be stronger than the other people; and the elder shall serve the younger.

24 ¶ And when her days to be delivered were fulfilled, behold, there were twins in her womb.

25 And the first came out red, all over like an hairy garment; and they called his name Esau.

26 And after that came his brother out, and his hand took hold on Esau's heel; and his name was called Jacob: and Isaac was threescore years old when she bare them.

27 And the boys grew: and Esau was a cunning hunter, a man of the field; and Jacob was a plain man, dwelling in tents.

28 And Isaac loved Esau, because he did eat of his venison: but Rebekah loved Jacob.

29 ¶ And Jacob sod pottage: and Esau came from the field, and he was faint:

30 And Esau said to Jacob, Feed me, I pray thee, with that same red pottage; for I am faint: therefore was his name called Edom.

31 And Jacob said, Sell me this day thy birthright.

32 And Esau said, Behold, I am at the point to die: and what profit shall this birthright do to me?

33 And Jacob said, Swear to me this day; and he sware unto him: and he sold his birthright unto Jacob.

34 Then Jacob gave Esau bread and pottage of lentiles; and he did eat and drink, and rose up, and went his way: thus Esau despised his birthright.

CHAPTER 26

1 AND there was a famine in the land, beside the first famine that was in the days of Abraham. And Isaac went unto Abimelech king of the Philistines unto Gerar.

2 And the LORD appeared unto him, and said, Go not down into Egypt; dwell in the land which I shall tell thee of:

3 Sojourn in this land, and I will be with thee, and will bless thee; for unto thee, and unto thy seed, I will give all these countries, and I will perform the oath which I sware unto Abraham thy father;

4 And I will make thy seed to multiply as the stars of heaven, and will give unto thy seed all these countries; and in thy seed shall all the nations of the earth be blessed;

5 Because that Abraham obeyed my voice, and kept my charge, my commandments, my statutes, and my laws.

6 ¶ And Isaac dwelt in Gerar:

7 And the men of the place asked him of his wife; and he said, She is my sister: for he feared to say, She is my wife; lest, said he, the

gospel to the world. Esau had confused priorities and valued his temporal comforts above his spiritual birthright. Thus the Lord saw to it that the birthright blessings fell to Jacob, the younger son. We must have the faith and the humility to follow the Lord's counsel by seeking first His kingdom, and then He will bless us and multiply our gifts in righteousness and justice. As we honor our heritage by honoring our God, we can receive all the blessings of God—a simple truth with profound results when understood, appreciated, and applied to life.

GENESIS CHAPTER 26

Genesis 26:1–5—Blessings of the Covenant
In these significant verses, the Lord extends the promises and blessings of the Abrahamic covenant to Isaac, the birthright son of the patriarch Abraham. Through Isaac, the blessings of an abundant noble lineage would be preserved, including promises of a chosen homeland and commissions of carrying the gospel and priesthood blessings to the world. The Abrahamic covenant would have a dual essence:

Blessings in this mortal realm—a promised land of refuge and safety; a fruitful lineage comprising many nations; the gospel plan of salvation and the blessings of the Holy Spirit, with access to priesthood keys and ordinances; and the divine mission of blessing all the earth, that the faithful might endure to the end

Blessings in the world to come—a heavenly home with "all that my father hath" (D&C 84:38); eternal increase through eternal marriage; immortality and eternal life; and the divine destiny of perfection and godhood

Genesis 26:6–8—Abimelech
Abimelech was king of Gerar during the days of Isaac, son of Abraham. This Abimelech might be the same as the one who interacted earlier with Abraham (see Gen. 20), or might perhaps be that person's son (see Gen. 26).

Following the death of Sarah and Abraham, Isaac was instructed of the Lord to go for relief and blessing to Gerar during a sore famine in the land (see Gen. 26:1–5). Just as Abraham had done earlier concerning Sarah, Isaac represented to the people of the land that Rebekah was his sister. When Abimelech observed from his window that "Isaac *was* sporting with Rebekah" (Gen. 26:8), he realized the true state of affairs and reproachfully asked Isaac why he had acted with deception. Isaac declared: "Because I said, Lest I die for her" (Gen. 26:9). Abimelech was appeased and commanded his people to leave Rebekah alone.

Isaac was permitted to remain in the land—until his growing prosperity began to awaken a sense of envy in his landsmen, the Philistines. Abimelech then ordered him to leave, but came to visit him later at Beersheba, where they entered into a covenant of peace much like the one established with Abraham years earlier (see Gen. 26:26–33).

men of the place should kill me for Rebekah; because she was fair to look upon.

8 And it came to pass, when he had been there a long time, that Abimelech king of the Philistines looked out at a window, and saw, and, behold, Isaac was sporting with Rebekah his wife.

9 And Abimelech called Isaac, and said, Behold, of a surety she is thy wife: and how saidst thou, She is my sister? And Isaac said unto him, Because I said, Lest I die for her.

10 And Abimelech said, What is this thou hast done unto us? one of the people might lightly have lien with thy wife, and thou shouldest have brought guiltiness upon us.

11 And Abimelech charged all his people, saying, He that toucheth this man or his wife shall surely be put to death.

12 Then Isaac sowed in that land, and received in the same year an hundredfold: and the LORD blessed him.

13 And the man waxed great, and went forward, and grew until he became very great:

14 For he had possession of flocks, and possession of herds, and great store of servants: and the Philistines envied him.

15 For all the wells which his father's servants had digged in the days of Abraham his father, the Philistines had stopped them, and filled them with earth.

16 And Abimelech said unto Isaac, Go from us; for thou art much mightier than we.

17 ¶ And Isaac departed thence, and pitched his tent in the valley of Gerar, and dwelt there.

18 And Isaac digged again the wells of water, which they had digged in the days of Abraham his father; for the Philistines had stopped them after the death of Abraham: and he called their names after the names by which his father had called them.

19 And Isaac's servants digged in the valley, and found there a well of springing water.

20 And the herdmen of Gerar did strive with Isaac's herdmen, saying, The water is ours: and he called the name of the well Esek; because they strove with him.

21 And they digged another well, and strove for that also: and he called the name of it Sitnah.

22 And he removed from thence, and digged another well; and for that they strove not: and he called the name of it Rehoboth; and he said, For now the LORD hath made room for us, and we shall be fruitful in the land.

23 And he went up from thence to Beer-sheba.

24 And the LORD appeared unto him the same night, and said, I am the God of Abraham thy father: fear not, for I am with thee, and will bless thee, and multiply thy seed for my servant Abraham's sake.

25 And he builded an altar there, and called upon the name of the LORD, and pitched his tent there: and there Isaac's servants digged a well.

26 ¶ Then Abimelech went to him from Gerar, and Ahuzzath one of his friends, and Phichol the chief captain of his army.

27 And Isaac said unto them, Wherefore come ye to me, seeing ye hate me, and have sent me away from you?

28 And they said, We saw certainly that the LORD was with thee: and we said, Let there be now an oath betwixt us, even betwixt us and thee, and let us make a covenant with thee;

29 That thou wilt do us no hurt, as we have not touched thee, and as we have done unto thee nothing but good, and have sent thee away in peace: thou art now the blessed of the LORD.

Tomb of Abraham

POINT OF INTEREST

Abraham purchased the cave of Machpelah (Abraham's tomb in its current form is above) from Ephron the Hittite. The presence of Hittites in Palestine, however, is the subject of much debate. Hittite scholar O. R. Gurney says: "Whereas the Hittites appear in the Old Testament as a Palestinian tribe, increasing knowledge of the history of the ancient people of Hatti has led us even further from Palestine. . . . Although Hittite armies reached Damascus, they never entered Palestine itself. . . . The presence of Hittites in Palestine before the Israelite conquest thus presents a curious problem. So far from explaining it, all our accumulated knowledge of the people of Hatti has only made it more perplexing. The stories of Abraham's purchase of the cave of Machpelah (Genesis 23) and of Esau's Hittite wives (Genesis 26:34; 36:1–3) have, it is true, been ascribed by critics to the post-exilic 'Priestly' writer, and are therefore not of much value as historical evidence; nor are the various lists of Canaanite tribes thought to be very much earlier in their date of composition. But the important passage, Numbers 13:29, cannot be explained away. Here it is stated quite definitely that the Hittites occupied the hill-country, with Amorites in the coastal plain and the Jordan valley, and Amalekites in the south. . . . Since the location of the Hittites agrees with the story about the purchase of the cave of Machpelah near Hebron from a Hittite, we may assume that the latter is based on an early source" (The Hittites [London: Folio Society, 2007]).

30 And he made them a feast, and they did eat and drink.

31 And they rose up betimes in the morning, and sware one to another: and Isaac sent them away, and they departed from him in peace.

32 And it came to pass the same day, that Isaac's servants came, and told him concerning the well which they had digged, and said unto him, We have found water.

33 And he called it Shebah: therefore the name of the city is Beersheba unto this day.

34 ¶ And Esau was forty years old when he took to wife Judith the daughter of Beeri the Hittite, and Bashemath the daughter of Elon the Hittite:

35 Which were a grief of mind unto Isaac and to Rebekah.

CHAPTER 27

1 AND it came to pass, that when Isaac was old, and his eyes were dim, so that he could not see, he called Esau his eldest son, and said unto him, My son: and he said unto him, Behold, here am I.

2 And he said, Behold now, I am old, I know not the day of my death:

3 Now therefore take, I pray thee, thy weapons, thy quiver and thy bow, and go out to the field, and take me some venison;

4 And make me savoury meat, such as I love, and bring it to me, that I may eat; that my soul may bless thee before I die.

5 And Rebekah heard when Isaac spake to Esau his son. And Esau went to the field to hunt for venison, and to bring it.

6 ¶ And Rebekah spake unto Jacob her son, saying, Behold, I heard thy father speak unto Esau thy brother, saying,

7 Bring me venison, and make me savoury meat, that I may eat, and bless thee before the LORD before my death.

8 Now therefore, my son, obey my voice according to that which I command thee.

9 Go now to the flock, and fetch me from thence two good kids of the goats; and I will make them savoury meat for thy father, such as he loveth:

10 And thou shalt bring it to thy father, that he may eat, and that he may bless thee before his death.

11 And Jacob said to Rebekah his mother, Behold, Esau my brother is a hairy man, and I am a smooth man:

12 My father peradventure will feel me, and I shall seem to him as a deceiver; and I shall bring a curse upon me, and not a blessing.

13 And his mother said unto him, Upon me be thy curse, my son: only obey my voice, and go fetch me them.

14 And he went, and fetched, and brought them to his mother: and his mother made savoury meat, such as his father loved.

GENESIS CHAPTER 27

Genesis 27:1–8—The Will of the Lord

Rebekah had not forgotten the promptings of the Lord concerning her two sons: "And the LORD said unto her, Two nations are in thy womb, and two manner of people shall be separated from thy bowels; and the one people shall be stronger than the other people; and the elder shall serve the younger" (Gen. 25:23). Esau, though having the right of primogeniture as the older son, had not demonstrated unfailing commitment to the cause of the Lord's design for humankind, but had sold his birthright for naught. The Lord knew of his weakness—as did his mother. Hence her strategy to ensure that the commission of the Abrahamic covenant would devolve upon her more faithful son Jacob. Such was the design of the Almighty. Rebekah was not acting out of cunning or deception, but in accommodation with the will of the Lord.

Clearly evident in the actions of Rebekah was the commitment to serve in the role as protector over her son—not only in regard to physical security, but also spiritual security. With an indomitable maternal desire, she yearned for Jacob to have the blessings of a marriage with a woman brought up in an environment where the highest spiritual standards were observed and honored. As such, Rebekah is the exemplum of motherly care and nurture.

POINT OF INTEREST

This relief from the side gallery at Yazilikaya, Turkey, depicts twelve Hittite gods from the underworld in procession.

15 And Rebekah took goodly raiment of her eldest son Esau, which were with her in the house, and put them upon Jacob her younger son:

16 And she put the skins of the kids of the goats upon his hands, and upon the smooth of his neck:

17 And she gave the savoury meat and the bread, which she had prepared, into the hand of her son Jacob.

18 ¶ And he came unto his father, and said, My father: and he said, Here am I; who art thou, my son?

19 And Jacob said unto his father, I am Esau thy firstborn; I have done according as thou badest me: arise, I pray thee, sit and eat of my venison, that thy soul may bless me.

20 And Isaac said unto his son, How is it that thou hast found it so quickly, my son? And he said, Because the LORD thy God brought it to me.

21 And Isaac said unto Jacob, Come near, I pray thee, that I may feel thee, my son, whether thou be my very son Esau or not.

22 And Jacob went near unto Isaac his father; and he felt him, and said, The voice is Jacob's voice, but the hands are the hands of Esau.

23 And he discerned him not, because his hands were hairy, as his brother Esau's hands: so he blessed him.

24 And he said, Art thou my very son Esau? And he said, I am.

25 And he said, Bring it near to me, and I will eat of my son's venison, that my soul may bless thee. And he brought it near to him, and he did eat: and he brought him wine, and he drank.

26 And his father Isaac said unto him, Come near now, and kiss me, my son.

27 And he came near, and kissed him: and he smelled the smell of his raiment, and blessed him, and said, See, the smell of my son is as the smell of a field which the LORD hath blessed:

28 Therefore God give thee of the dew of heaven, and the fatness of the earth, and plenty of corn and wine:

29 Let people serve thee, and nations bow down to thee: be lord over thy brethren, and let thy mother's sons bow down to thee: cursed be every one that curseth thee, and blessed be he that blesseth thee.

30 ¶ And it came to pass, as soon as Isaac had made an end of blessing Jacob, and Jacob was yet scarce gone out from the presence of Isaac his father, that Esau his brother came in from his hunting.

31 And he also had made savoury meat, and brought it unto his father, and said unto his father, Let my father arise, and eat of his son's venison, that thy soul may bless me.

32 And Isaac his father said unto him, Who art thou? And he said, I am thy son, thy firstborn Esau.

33 And Isaac trembled very exceedingly, and said, Who? where is he that hath taken venison, and brought it me, and I have eaten of all before thou camest, and have blessed him? yea, and he shall be blessed.

34 And when Esau heard the words of his father, he cried with a great and exceeding bitter cry, and said unto his father, Bless me, even me also, O my father.

35 And he said, Thy brother came with subtilty, and hath taken away thy blessing.

36 And he said, Is not he rightly named Jacob? for he hath supplanted me these two times: he took away my birthright; and, behold, now he hath taken away my blessing. And he said, Hast thou not reserved a blessing for me?

37 And Isaac answered and said unto Esau, Behold, I have made

NOTES:

him thy lord, and all his brethren have I given to him for servants; and with corn and wine have I sustained him: and what shall I do now unto thee, my son?

38 And Esau said unto his father, Hast thou but one blessing, my father? bless me, even me also, O my father. And Esau lifted up his voice, and wept.

39 And Isaac his father answered and said unto him, Behold, thy dwelling shall be the fatness of the earth, and of the dew of heaven from above;

40 And by thy sword shalt thou live, and shalt serve thy brother; and it shall come to pass when thou shalt have the dominion, that thou shalt break his yoke from off thy neck.

41 ¶ And Esau hated Jacob because of the blessing wherewith his father blessed him: and Esau said in his heart, The days of mourning for my father are at hand; then will I slay my brother Jacob.

42 And these words of Esau her elder son were told to Rebekah: and she sent and called Jacob her younger son, and said unto him, Behold, thy brother Esau, as touching thee, doth comfort himself, purposing to kill thee.

43 Now therefore, my son, obey my voice; and arise, flee thou to Laban my brother to Haran;

44 And tarry with him a few days, until thy brother's fury turn away;

45 Until thy brother's anger turn away from thee, and he forget that which thou hast done to him: then I will send, and fetch thee from thence: why should I be deprived also of you both in one day?

46 And Rebekah said to Isaac, I am weary of my life because of the daughters of Heth: if Jacob take a wife of the daughters of Heth, such as these which are of the daughters of the land, what good shall my life do me?

CHAPTER 28

1 AND Isaac called Jacob, and blessed him, and charged him, and said unto him, Thou shalt not take a wife of the daughters of Canaan.

2 Arise, go to Padan-aram, to the house of Bethuel thy mother's father; and take thee a wife from thence of the daughters of Laban thy mother's brother.

3 And God Almighty bless thee, and make thee fruitful, and multiply thee, that thou mayest be a multitude of people;

4 And give thee the blessing of Abraham, to thee, and to thy seed with thee; that thou mayest inherit the land wherein thou art a stranger, which God gave unto Abraham.

5 And Isaac sent away Jacob: and he went to Padan-aram unto Laban, son of Bethuel the Syrian, the brother of Rebekah, Jacob's and Esau's mother.

6 ¶ When Esau saw that Isaac had blessed Jacob, and sent him away to Padan-aram, to take him a wife from thence; and that as he blessed him he gave him a charge, saying, Thou shalt not take a wife of the daughters of Canaan;

GENESIS CHAPTER 28

Genesis 28:1–15—Abrahamic Covenant

In these verses we see that the promises and blessings of the Abrahamic covenant (see Gen. 17:1–8; Abr. 2:8–11) are extended to Jacob, just as they were extended to his father Isaac (see Gen. 26:1–5). Thus Jacob was to have the blessings of an abundant noble lineage, including promises of a chosen homeland and commissions of carrying the gospel and priesthood blessings to the world (see also Gen. 35:9–13; 48:3–4).

For more insight on the Abrahamic covenant, see Appendix H.

Isaac Blessing Jacob by Gustave Doré

7 And that Jacob obeyed his father and his mother, and was gone to Padan-aram;

8 And Esau seeing that the daughters of Canaan pleased not Isaac his father;

9 Then went Esau unto Ishmael, and took unto the wives which he had Mahalath the daughter of Ishmael Abraham's son, the sister of Nebajoth, to be his wife.

10 ¶ And Jacob went out from Beer-sheba, and went toward Haran.

11 And he lighted upon a certain place, and tarried there all night, because the sun was set; and he took of the stones of that place, and put them for his pillows, and lay down in that place to sleep.

12 And he dreamed, and behold a ladder set up on the earth, and the top of it reached to heaven: and behold the angels of God ascending and descending on it.

13 And, behold, the LORD stood above it, and said, I am the LORD God of Abraham thy father, and the God of Isaac: the land whereon thou liest, to thee will I give it, and to thy seed;

14 And thy seed shall be as the dust of the earth, and thou shalt spread abroad to the west, and to the east, and to the north, and to the south: and in thee and in thy seed shall all the families of the earth be blessed.

15 And, behold, I am with thee, and will keep thee in all places whither thou goest, and will bring thee again into this land; for I will not leave thee, until I have done that which I have spoken to thee of.

16 ¶ And Jacob awaked out of his sleep, and he said, Surely the LORD is in this place; and I knew it not.

17 And he was afraid, and said, How dreadful is this place! this is none other but the house of God, and this is the gate of heaven.

18 And Jacob rose up early in the morning, and took the stone that he had put for his pillows, and set it up for a pillar, and poured oil upon the top of it.

19 And he called the name of that place Beth-el: but the name of that city was called Luz at the first.

20 And Jacob vowed a vow, saying, If God will be with me, and will keep me in this way that I go, and will give me bread to eat, and raiment to put on,

21 So that I come again to my father's house in peace; then shall the LORD be my God:

22 And this stone, which I have set for a pillar, shall be God's house: and of all that thou shalt give me I will surely give the tenth unto thee.

CHAPTER 29

1 Then Jacob went on his journey, and came into the land of the people of the east.

2 And he looked, and behold a well in the field, and, lo, there *were* three flocks of sheep lying by it; for out of that well they watered the flocks: and a great stone *was* upon the well's mouth.

3 And thither were all the flocks gathered: and they rolled the stone from the well's mouth, and watered the sheep, and put the stone again upon the well's mouth in his place.

4 And Jacob said unto them, My brethren, whence *be* ye? And they said, Of Haran *are* we.

5 And he said unto them, Know ye Laban the son of Nahor? And they said, We know *him*.

6 And he said unto them, *Is* he well? And they said, *He is* well: and, behold, Rachel his daughter cometh with the sheep.

GENESIS CHAPTER 29

Genesis 29:1–9—Rachel

Rachel (meaning: ewe) was the younger of the two daughters of Laban, son of Bethuel, the latter being the youngest son of Nahor, brother of Abraham (see Gen. 22:22–23). When Isaac sent his son Jacob to Laban (who was the brother of Rebekah, Isaac's wife), Jacob was well received. The story of his encounter with Rachel is among the most memorable courtship chronicles in the Old Testament.

Though he had promised the hand of Rachel to Jacob in exchange for seven years of service, Laban conceived of a plan to ensure that the marriage of his oldest daughter, Leah, came first. After Jacob had served his seven years for the hand of Rachel, Laban adjusted the unfolding of events on the marriage day by sending the veiled Leah that evening to be Jacob's wife. The next morning the truth was discovered by Jacob. Jacob, having agreed to serve Laban yet another seven years, was soon thereafter favored with the bride of his choice—Rachel.

Leah bore Jacob six sons: Reuben, Simeon, Levi, Judah (see Gen. 29:32–35), and later Issachar and Zebulun (see Gen. 30:17–20). Leah also bore a daughter by the name of Dinah (see Gen. 30:21). All of these children having been born before Rachel was able to conceive, Rachel gave unto Jacob her maid Bilhah, who bore two sons, Dan and Naphtali (see Gen. 30:1–8). Thereafter, Rachel was also blessed to have children.

Both Rachel and Leah accompanied Jacob back to Canaan (see Gen. 31:17–18). After Jacob's wondrous encounter with God at Beth-el, where he was renamed Israel and heard the divine promise confirming the Abrahamic covenant upon him and his seed (see Gen. 35:1–20), he again became a father through Rachel—but not without tragic suffering, when Rachel died in childbirth (see Gen. 35:16–20).

The spirit of Rachel and Leah was invoked by the compatriots of Boaz when he married Ruth and ensured that the lineage of Israel would be carried on down to the time of the Savior.

The hope that Jeremiah unfolds for his listeners in reference to Rachel is none other than the Restoration of the gospel of Jesus Christ in the latter days:

> Behold, the days come, saith the LORD, that I will make a new covenant with the house of Israel, and with the house of Judah:
>
> Not according to the covenant that I made with their fathers in the day *that* I took them by the hand to bring them out of the land of Egypt; which my covenant they brake, although I was an husband unto them, saith the LORD:
>
> But this *shall be* the covenant that I will make with the house of Israel; After those days, saith the LORD, I will put my law in their inward parts, and write it in their hearts; and will be their God, and they shall be my people.

7 And he said, Lo, *it is* yet high day, neither *is it* time that the cattle should be gathered together: water ye the sheep, and go *and* feed *them*.

8 And they said, We cannot, until all the flocks be gathered together, and *till* they roll the stone from the well's mouth; then we water the sheep.

9 ¶ And while he yet spake with them, Rachel came with her father's sheep: for she kept them.

10 And it came to pass, when Jacob saw Rachel the daughter of Laban his mother's brother, and the sheep of Laban his mother's brother, that Jacob went near, and rolled the stone from the well's mouth, and watered the flock of Laban his mother's brother.

11 And Jacob kissed Rachel, and lifted up his voice, and wept.

12 And Jacob told Rachel that he *was* her father's brother, and that he *was* Rebekah's son: and she ran and told her father.

13 And it came to pass, when Laban heard the tidings of Jacob his sister's son, that he ran to meet him, and embraced him, and kissed him, and brought him to his house. And he told Laban all these things.

14 And Laban said to him, Surely thou *art* my bone and my flesh. And he abode with him the space of a month.

15 ¶ And Laban said unto Jacob, Because thou *art* my brother, shouldest thou therefore serve me for nought? tell me, what *shall* thy wages *be?*

16 And Laban had two daughters: the name of the elder *was* Leah, and the name of the younger *was* Rachel.

17 Leah *was* tender eyed; but Rachel *was* beautiful and well favoured.

18 And Jacob loved Rachel; and said, I will serve thee seven years for Rachel thy younger daughter.

19 And Laban said, *It is* better that I give her to thee, than that I should give her to another man: abide with me.

20 And Jacob served seven years for Rachel; and they seemed unto him *but* a few days, for the love he had to her.

21 ¶ And Jacob said unto Laban, Give *me* my wife, for my days are fulfilled, that I may go in unto her.

22 And Laban gathered together all the men of the place, and made a feast.

23 And it came to pass in the evening, that he took Leah his daughter, and brought her to him; and he went in unto her.

24 And Laban gave unto his daughter Leah Zilpah his maid *for* an handmaid.

25 And it came to pass, that in the morning, behold, it *was* Leah: and he said to Laban, What *is* this thou hast done unto me? did not I serve with thee for Rachel? wherefore then hast thou beguiled me?

26 And Laban said, It must not be so done in our country, to give the younger before the firstborn.

27 Fulfil her week, and we will give thee this also for the service which thou shalt serve with me yet seven other years.

28 And Jacob did so, and fulfilled her week: and he gave him Rachel his daughter to wife also.

29 And Laban gave to Rachel his daughter Bilhah his handmaid to be her maid.

30 And he went in also unto Rachel, and he loved also Rachel more than Leah, and served with him yet seven other years.

31 ¶ And when the LORD saw that Leah *was* hated, he opened her womb: but Rachel *was* barren.

32 And Leah conceived, and bare a son, and she called his name Reuben: for she said, Surely the LORD hath looked upon my affliction; now therefore my husband will love me.

And they shall teach no more every man his neighbour, and every man his brother, saying, Know the LORD: for they shall all know me, from the least of them unto the greatest of them, saith the LORD: for I will forgive their iniquity, and I will remember their sin no more. (Jer. 31:31–34)

It was especially through Joseph, son of Rachel and Jacob, that the power and blessings of the Abrahamic covenant would be made available to all quarters of the earth in the latter days.

Genesis 29:29—Bilhah

Bilhah (meaning: bashful, wavering) was a maidservant of Laban whom he gave to his daughter Rachel when she became Jacob's wife (see Gen. 29:29; 46:25). When Rachel was at first not able to bear children, she gave Bilhah unto Jacob to wife (see Gen. 30:1–5). Bilhah bore two sons, Dan and Naphtali. Later, Jacob's son Reuben by Leah was immoral with Bilhah (see Gen. 35:22) and thus condemned of his father (see Gen. 49:4), even to the loss of his birthright as the firstborn son. Reuben's birthright was given to the sons of Joseph—Ephraim and Manasseh (see 1 Chron. 5:1).

Genesis 29:30–32—Reuben

Reuben (meaning: behold a son) was Jacob's firstborn son. Reuben's life was marked by compass points of conflicting character: the nobility of primogeniture (being the firstborn son and heir to the primary blessings of the lineage) versus the degradation of his immoral act with Bilhah, his father's concubine, that cost him his birthright; his vile conspiracy with his brethren to do away with their brother Joseph versus his decision to intercede and abandon Joseph in a pit with the intention of retrieving him later and returning him to Jacob; his pattern of impulsiveness (as with Bilhah) versus his sense of principle in protectively guaranteeing the life of Benjamin should Jacob permit this youngest son to return with the brothers to the court of Joseph.

When Jacob and his family moved to Egypt, Reuben had a total of four sons (see Gen. 46:9). Reuben having been displaced out of his birthright position, Jacob transferred that blessing to Joseph (see 1 Chron. 5:1–2) and accepted Joseph's two sons, Ephraim and Manasseh, as participants in the right of inheritance (see Gen. 48:5). The tribe of Reuben inherited a fertile area east of the Jordan River (see Num. 32).

Genesis 29:33–34—Levi

Levi (meaning: joined or adhered to) was the third son of Jacob by Leah (see Gen. 29:34; 35:23). The motivation for giving his that name (see v. 34) related to Leah's self-consciousness about Jacob's favoring her sister, Rachel, though she (Rachel) had not been able to bear children. Later in their careers, Levi and Simeon were responsible for the callous campaign of vengeance against the Hivite community when Shechem, the son of Hamor the Hivite,

33. And she conceived again, and bare a son; and said, Because the LORD hath heard that I *was* hated, he hath therefore given me this *son* also: and she called his name Simeon.

34. And she conceived again, and bare a son; and said, Now this time will my husband be joined unto me, because I have born him three sons: therefore was his name called Levi.

35. And she conceived again, and bare a son: and she said, Now will I praise the LORD: therefore she called his name Judah; and left bearing.

CHAPTER 34

1 AND Dinah the daughter of Leah, which she bare unto Jacob, went out to see the daughters of the land.

2 And when Shechem the son of Hamor the Hivite, prince of the country, saw her, he took her, and lay with her, and defiled her.

3 And his soul clave unto Dinah the daughter of Jacob, and he loved the damsel, and spake kindly unto the damsel.

4 And Shechem spake unto his father Hamor, saying, Get me this damsel to wife.

5 And Jacob heard that he had defiled Dinah his daughter: now his sons were with his cattle in the field: and Jacob held his peace until they were come.

6 ¶ And Hamor the father of Shechem went out unto Jacob to commune with him.

7 And the sons of Jacob came out of the field when they heard it: and the men were grieved, and they were very wroth, because he had wrought folly in Israel in lying with Jacob's daughter; which thing ought not to be done.

8 And Hamor communed with them, saying, The soul of my son Shechem longeth for your daughter: I pray you give her him to wife.

9 And make ye marriages with us, and give your daughters unto us, and take our daughters unto you.

10 And ye shall dwell with us: and the land shall be before you; dwell and trade ye therein, and get you possessions therein.

11 And Shechem said unto her father and unto her brethren, Let me find grace in your eyes, and what ye shall say unto me I will give.

12 Ask me never so much dowry and gift, and I will give according as ye shall say unto me: but give me the damsel to wife.

13 And the sons of Jacob answered Shechem and Hamor his father deceitfully, and said, because he had defiled Dinah their sister:

14 And they said unto them, We cannot do this thing, to give our sister to one that is uncircumcised; for that were a reproach unto us:

15 But in this will we consent unto you: If ye will be as we be, that every male of you be circumcised;

16 Then will we give our daughters unto you, and we will take your daughters to us, and we will dwell with you, and we will become one people.

17 But if ye will not hearken unto us, to be circumcised; then will we take our daughter, and we will be gone.

18 And their words pleased Hamor, and Shechem Hamor's son.

fell in love with Dinah (Levi's sister) and defiled her. Executing the ultimate response to this misdeed, Simeon and Levi fell upon the Hivite community, killed all of the males, "and took Dinah out of Shechem's house, and went out" (Gen. 34:26). They then despoiled the city and took all the survivors captive. When Jacob learned of their actions, he was greatly distressed and gathered his people together and moved away to Bethel at the command of God (see Gen. 34:30; 35:1–5).

The blessing pronounced by Moses on the tribe of Levi (of which he and Aaron were members) included the promise of priestly assignments (see Deut. 33:10–11). These words reflect the perpetual assignment given to the sons of Levi to provide service in support of the work of the priesthood on behalf of the House of Israel under the direction of Aaron and his sons (see Num. 3, 4, 8).

Genesis 29:35—Judah

Judah (meaning: praise), fourth son of Jacob and Leah, was a principal figure in the perpetuity of the Abrahamic lineage as it extended down to Jesus Christ. Judah was the one who stepped forward among the sons of Jacob to advance an alternative to slaying their brother Joseph (see Gen. 37:26–27). It was Judah who assumed the role of protector and guarantor of Benjamin when Jacob was persuaded to allow his youngest son to return to the Egyptian court where Joseph was in charge (see Gen. 43:8). When Joseph received the birthright by virtue of the moral laxity of Reuben, Judah nevertheless maintained a vital role (see 1 Chron. 5:2).

From the word of the Lord to Joseph of Egypt included in the Book of Mormon we find confirmed the fact that the legacy of Judah is to serve as the wellspring of the Bible, just as the legacy of Joseph is contained in the Book of Mormon (see 2 Ne. 3:12–13.)

GENESIS CHAPTER 34

Genesis 34:1–26—Dinah

Dinah (meaning: judged and vindicated) was the daughter of Jacob and Leah. Shechem, the son of Hamor the Hivite, fell in love with Dinah and defiled her. Angered over this act, the sons of Jacob deceitfully pretended to accept the peace overtures of Hamor by requiring the males of the Hivites to be circumcised in exchange for the hand of Dinah and assurance of cooperation and intermarriage with the Israelites. When Hamor and Shechem and their circle had agreed to the arrangement and carried out the requirement, two of the sons of Jacob, Simeon and Levi, fell upon the Hivite community, killed all of the males, "and took Dinah out of Shechem's house, and went out" (Gen. 34:26). They then despoiled the city and took all the survivors captive.

When Jacob learned what had happened, he was greatly distressed: "And Jacob said to Simeon and Levi, Ye have troubled me to make me to stink among the inhabitants of the land, among the Canaanites and the Perizzites: and I *being* few in number, they shall gather themselves together against me, and slay me; and I shall be destroyed, I

19 And the young man deferred not to do the thing, because he had delight in Jacob's daughter: and he was more honourable than all the house of his father.

20 ¶ And Hamor and Shechem his son came unto the gate of their city, and communed with the men of their city, saying,

21 These men are peaceable with us; therefore let them dwell in the land, and trade therein; for the land, behold, it is large enough for them; let us take their daughters to us for wives, and let us give them our daughters.

22 Only herein will the men consent unto us for to dwell with us, to be one people, if every male among us be circumcised, as they are circumcised.

23 Shall not their cattle and their substance and every beast of theirs be ours? only let us consent unto them, and they will dwell with us.

24 And unto Hamor and unto Shechem his son hearkened all that went out of the gate of his city; and every male was circumcised, all that went out of the gate of his city.

25 ¶ And it came to pass on the third day, when they were sore, that two of the sons of Jacob, Simeon and Levi, Dinah's brethren, took each man his sword, and came upon the city boldly, and slew all the males.

26 And they slew Hamor and Shechem his son with the edge of the sword, and took Dinah out of Shechem's house, and went out.

27 The sons of Jacob came upon the slain, and spoiled the city, because they had defiled their sister.

28 They took their sheep, and their oxen, and their asses, and that which was in the city, and that which was in the field,

29 And all their wealth, and all their little ones, and their wives took they captive, and spoiled even all that was in the house.

30 And Jacob said to Simeon and Levi, Ye have troubled me to make me to stink among the inhabitants of the land, among the Canaanites and the Perizzites: and I being few in number, they shall gather themselves together against me, and slay me; and I shall be destroyed, I and my house.

31 And they said, Should he deal with our sister as with an harlot?

CHAPTER 37

1 AND Jacob dwelt in the land wherein his father was a stranger, in the land of Canaan.

2 These are the generations of Jacob. Joseph, being seventeen years old, was feeding the flock with his brethren; and the lad was with the sons of Bilhah, and with the sons of Zilpah, his father's wives: and Joseph brought unto his father their evil report.

3 Now Israel loved Joseph more than all his children, because he was the son of his old age: and he made him a coat of many colours.

4 And when his brethren saw that their father loved him more than all his brethren, they hated him, and could not speak peaceably unto him.

5 ¶ And Joseph dreamed a dream, and he told it his brethren: and they hated him yet the more.

6 And he said unto them, Hear, I pray you, this dream which I have dreamed:

and my house" (Gen. 34:30). He then gathered his people together and moved away to Bethel at the command of God (see Gen. 35:1–5). Dinah later journeyed to Egypt with Jacob's family circle (see Gen. 46:8, 15).

Genesis 34:25—Simeon

Simeon (meaning: that hears) was the second son of Jacob by his wife Leah. When Simeon and Levi inflicted drastic retribution upon the Shechemites for the mistreatment of Dinah, daughter of Jacob and Leah (see Gen. 30:21), Jacob was greatly distressed and feared the destruction of his own family as a result (see Gen. 34:30). He then gathered his people together and moved away to Bethel at the command of God (see Gen. 35:1–5).

Simeon also figures into the dramatic encounter between Joseph of Egypt and his brothers, by whom he had been sold into slavery and who now came appealing for provisions during the famine in Canaan. Simeon was retained by Joseph (who was still not recognized by his brothers) as hostage collateral to guarantee the delivery of Benjamin, being eventually released when reconciliation and forgiveness came about (see Gen. 42:24, 36; 43:23).

GENESIS CHAPTER 37

Genesis 37—Overview

The story of Joseph and his brothers provides a memorable contrast between two opposing patterns of life. In the brothers, for the most part, we perceive evidence that envy, jealousy, and greed exact dire penalties. When Joseph's brethren conspire to destroy the lad, they provide a bleak memorial to the consequences of sibling rivalry and wickedness. Preserved in the scriptural account are candid portraits of the moral lassitude and debauchery of several of Jacob's sons. The painful consequences of their misdeeds serve as valuable lessons about the importance of following the commandments of God. By contrast, Joseph's example of moral uprightness in Egypt is among the most celebrated instances of strength of character in all of holy writ.

In the contrast between the character of Joseph and the character of his brothers, we see played out in the starkest terms the preeminence of integrity over envy, honesty over jealousy, and (in the case of some of the brothers) virtue over moral laxity. Joseph built his life upon a foundation of enduring principles and a commitment to follow the guidance of the Spirit. As such, his moral courage and leadership reflect the kind of strength, discipline, and stability that a great leader must always have.

Genesis 37:1–8—Joseph

The jealousy and disdain of the older brothers of Joseph is similar to that harbored by Laman and Lemuel against Nephi in the Book of Mormon. Such reactions are typical of those who encounter the workings of the Spirit in others and, out of hardness of heart, fail to discern the light of higher truth granted by the Lord to those with the eye of faith.

For more insight on Joseph, see Appendix L.

7 For, behold, we were binding sheaves in the field, and, lo, my sheaf arose, and also stood upright; and, behold, your sheaves stood round about, and made obeisance to my sheaf.

8 And his brethren said to him, Shalt thou indeed reign over us? or shalt thou indeed have dominion over us? And they hated him yet the more for his dreams, and for his words.

9 ¶ And he dreamed yet another dream, and told it his brethren, and said, Behold, I have dreamed a dream more; and, behold, the sun and the moon and the eleven stars made obeisance to me.

10 And he told it to his father, and to his brethren: and his father rebuked him, and said unto him, What is this dream that thou hast dreamed? Shall I and thy mother and thy brethren indeed come to bow down ourselves to thee to the earth?

11 And his brethren envied him; but his father observed the saying.

12 ¶ And his brethren went to feed their father's flock in Shechem.

13 And Israel said unto Joseph, Do not thy brethren feed the flock in Shechem? come, and I will send thee unto them. And he said to him, Here am I.

14 And he said to him, Go, I pray thee, see whether it be well with thy brethren, and well with the flocks; and bring me word again. So he sent him out of the vale of Hebron, and he came to Shechem.

15 ¶ And a certain man found him, and, behold, he was wandering in the field: and the man asked him, saying, What seekest thou?

16 And he said, I seek my brethren: tell me, I pray thee, where they feed their flocks.

17 And the man said, They are departed hence; for I heard them say, Let us go to Dothan. And Joseph went after his brethren, and found them in Dothan.

18 And when they saw him afar off, even before he came near unto them, they conspired against him to slay him.

19 And they said one to another, Behold, this dreamer cometh.

20 Come now therefore, and let us slay him, and cast him into some pit, and we will say, Some evil beast hath devoured him: and we shall see what will become of his dreams.

21 And Reuben heard it, and he delivered him out of their hands; and said, Let us not kill him.

22 And Reuben said unto them, Shed no blood, but cast him into this pit that is in the wilderness, and lay no hand upon him; that he might rid him out of their hands, to deliver him to his father again.

23 ¶ And it came to pass, when Joseph was come unto his brethren, that they stript Joseph out of his coat, his coat of many colours that was on him;

24 And they took him, and cast him into a pit: and the pit was empty, there was no water in it.

25 And they sat down to eat bread: and they lifted up their eyes and looked, and, behold, a company of Ishmeelites came from Gilead with their camels bearing spicery and balm and myrrh, going to carry it down to Egypt.

26 And Judah said unto his brethren, What profit is it if we slay our brother, and conceal his blood?

27 Come, and let us sell him to the Ishmeelites, and let not our hand be upon him; for he is our brother and our flesh. And his brethren were content.

28 Then there passed by Midianites merchantmen; and they drew and lifted up Joseph out of the pit, and sold Joseph to the Ishmeelites for twenty pieces of silver: and they brought Joseph into Egypt.

Genesis 37:9–28—Midianites

The Midianites were a dominant nomadic people associated with the lineage of Midian (son of Abraham and Keturah) living principally in the northern region of the Arabian Peninsula and emerging from time to time in the chronicles of Israelite history. Joseph was sold to a caravan of Midianites by his jealous brethren (see Gen. 37:28), this caravan group subsequently selling him into Egyptian hands (see Gen. 37:36).

When Moses fled from Egypt he lived among the Midianites and married Zipporah, daughter of Reuel (or Jethro), the prince of Midian (see Ex. 2:11–21; 3:1; 4:19). Following the Exodus (see Ex. 18:1), the Midianites provided guidance to Moses and the Israelites during their wanderings in the wilderness, acting in their behalf "instead of eyes" (Num. 10:31). The history of the relationship between the Israelites and the Midianites from that time forward was marked from time to time by milestones of severe conflict.

Divine injunction brought about the elimination of the kings of Midian—plus Balaam—and all their cities (see Num. 31:1–2). Later, having recovered their stature, the Midianites subjected the people of Israel to dominance for seven years (see Judges 6:1–6)—until Gideon, the warrior-judge, was commissioned of the Lord to defeat the enemy forces in a decisive battle (see Judges 6–8). This victory over the Midianites is celebrated in later scriptural references as an exemplum of the supremacy of divine justice over worldly forces (see Psalms 83:9; Isa. 9:4; 10:26).

Genesis 37:29–32—The Wages of Envy

Envy, jealousy, and greed exact dire penalties. When Joseph's brethren conspire to destroy him, they provide a bleak memorial to the consequences of sibling rivalry and wickedness.

Joseph, being favored of Jacob "because he was the son of his old age" (Gen. 37:3), became a target of malice on the part of his older brothers. Joseph was not reluctant to share his dreams, which indicated his future leadership, something that contributed to his brothers' feelings of jealousy and their selling him into slavery.

The story of Joseph shows the results of jealousy, envy, greed, and hatred, yet shows the power of God in all things. Through it we see the results of envy, jealousy, and greed can be devastating and can result in acts of violence and hatred. The Lord teaches us that where jealousy is we cannot see God (see D&C 67:10).

Genesis 37:36—Potiphar

Potiphar (pronounced "pot'-uh-fahr" or "pot'-uh-fuhr"; meaning: he whom Ra [the sun-god] gave), mentioned only twice in the Old Testament, was captain of the bodyguard of the Pharaoh and benefactor of Joseph when he was sold into slavery.

When Potiphar's licentious wife sought to entice Joseph, he fled in keeping with his righteous character, causing her to accuse him falsely before her husband (see Gen. 39:7–19). As a result, Joseph was imprisoned. Thus

29 ¶ And Reuben returned unto the pit; and, behold, Joseph was not in the pit; and he rent his clothes.

30 And he returned unto his brethren, and said, The child is not; and I, whither shall I go?

31 And they took Joseph's coat, and killed a kid of the goats, and dipped the coat in the blood;

32 And they sent the coat of many colours, and they brought it to their father; and said, This have we found: know now whether it be thy son's coat or no.

33 And he knew it, and said, It is my son's coat; an evil beast hath devoured him; Joseph is without doubt rent in pieces.

34 And Jacob rent his clothes, and put sackcloth upon his loins, and mourned for his son many days.

35 And all his sons and all his daughters rose up to comfort him; but he refused to be comforted; and he said, For I will go down into the grave unto my son mourning. Thus his father wept for him.

36 And the Midianites sold him into Egypt unto Potiphar, an officer of Pharaoh's, and captain of the guard.

CHAPTER 38

1 AND it came to pass at that time, that Judah went down from his brethren, and turned in to a certain Adullamite, whose name was Hirah.

2 And Judah saw there a daughter of a certain Canaanite, whose name was Shuah; and he took her, and went in unto her.

3 And she conceived, and bare a son; and he called his name Er.

4 And she conceived again, and bare a son; and she called his name Onan.

5 And she yet again conceived, and bare a son; and called his name Shelah: and he was at Chezib, when she bare him.

6 And Judah took a wife for Er his firstborn, whose name was Tamar.

7 And Er, Judah's firstborn, was wicked in the sight of the LORD; and the LORD slew him.

8 And Judah said unto Onan, Go in unto thy brother's wife, and marry her, and raise up seed to thy brother.

9 And Onan knew that the seed should not be his; and it came to pass, when he went in unto his brother's wife, that he spilled it on the ground, lest that he should give seed to his brother.

10 And the thing which he did displeased the LORD: wherefore he slew him also.

11 Then said Judah to Tamar his daughter in law, Remain a widow at thy father's house, till Shelah my son be grown: for he said, Lest peradventure he die also, as his brethren did. And Tamar went and dwelt in her father's house.

12 ¶ And in process of time the daughter of Shuah Judah's wife died; and Judah was comforted, and went up unto his sheepshearers to Timnath, he and his friend Hirah the Adullamite.

13 And it was told Tamar, saying, Behold thy father in law goeth up to Timnath to shear his sheep.

14 And she put her widow's garments off from her, and covered her with a vail, and wrapped herself, and sat in an open place, which is by the way to Timnath; for she saw that Shelah was grown, and she was not given unto him to wife.

was laid the foundation for Joseph's rise in the eyes of Pharaoh and his eventual attainment of the position of leadership that enabled him to save his family from the effects of the regional famine.

GENESIS CHAPTER 38

Genesis 38:1–26—Portraits of Moral Weakness

Preserved in the scriptures are candid accounts of the moral lassitude and debauchery of several of Jacob's sons or associates. The painful consequences of their misdeeds serve as valuable lessons about the importance of following the commandments of God.

When Jacob's daughter, Dinah, is defiled by Shechem, a Hivite prince, Jacob arranges to redress the situation by bringing all the Hivites under certain provisions of the covenant; however, Simeon and Levi destroy the offenders and their community, thus laying the groundwork for lasting enmity in the land. Furthermore, Reuben and Judah commit serious moral sins that cast shadows over the landscape of this unfolding record of the work of the Lord. In the case of Reuben, he loses his birthright as the oldest son to Joseph (see 1 Chron. 5:1–2).

The lesson overshadowing these chronicles of moral turpitude is the fact that the Lord's purposes are not defeated, for Joseph's sons inherit the birthright and thus his lineage carries on the leadership role under the Abrahamic Covenant. Similarly, the Savior is to come from the preserved lineage of Judah as the light and life of the world. No matter what some of the Lord's children do in defiance of His laws, the Lord is still in charge of the process whereby the Plan of Salvation can unfold to its ultimate destiny.

Thus we see that the problems of society are exacerbated by the lack of purity in individual lives. Some people choose immorality as a way of life, ignoring the truth that their individual desires are reflected in the moral fiber of society. Let us therefore make a commitment to a moral and pure pattern of living.

 POINT OF INTEREST

A kid from the flock. "Though this is plausible enough payment coming from a prosperous pastoralist in a barter culture, it also picks up the motif of the slaughtered kid whose blood was used by Judah and his brothers to deceive Jacob (as Jacob before them used a kid to deceive his father). This connection was aptly perceived a millennium and a half ago in the Midrash Bereishit Rabba. The other material element in the brothers' deception of their father was a garment; Tamar uses a garment—the whore's dress and veil—to deceive her father-in-law" (Robert Alter, *The Five Books of Moses* [New York: W. W. Norton & Company, 2004]).

15 When Judah saw her, he thought her to be an harlot; because she had covered her face.

16 And he turned unto her by the way, and said, Go to, I pray thee, let me come in unto thee; (for he knew not that she was his daughter in law.) And she said, What wilt thou give me, that thou mayest come in unto me?

17 And he said, I will send thee a kid from the flock. And she said, Wilt thou give me a pledge, till thou send it?

18 And he said, What pledge shall I give thee? And she said, Thy signet, and thy bracelets, and thy staff that is in thine hand. And he gave it her, and came in unto her, and she conceived by him.

19 And she arose, and went away, and laid by her vail from her, and put on the garments of her widowhood.

20 And Judah sent the kid by the hand of his friend the Adullamite, to receive his pledge from the woman's hand: but he found her not.

21 Then he asked the men of that place, saying, Where is the harlot, that was openly by the way side? And they said, There was no harlot in this place.

22 And he returned to Judah, and said, I cannot find her; and also the men of the place said, that there was no harlot in this place.

23 And Judah said, Let her take it to her, lest we be shamed: behold, I sent this kid, and thou hast not found her.

24 ¶ And it came to pass about three months after, that it was told Judah, saying, Tamar thy daughter in law hath played the harlot; and also, behold, she is with child by whoredom. And Judah said, Bring her forth, and let her be burnt.

25 When she was brought forth, she sent to her father in law, saying, By the man, whose these are, am I with child: and she said, Discern, I pray thee, whose are these, the signet, and bracelets, and staff.

26 And Judah acknowledged them, and said, She hath been more righteous than I; because that I gave her not to Shelah my son. And he knew her again no more.

27 ¶ And it came to pass in the time of her travail, that, behold, twins were in her womb.

28 And it came to pass, when she travailed, that the one put out his hand: and the midwife took and bound upon his hand a scarlet thread, saying, This came out first.

29 And it came to pass, as he drew back his hand, that, behold, his brother came out: and she said, How hast thou broken forth? this breach be upon thee: therefore his name was called Pharez.

30 And afterward came out his brother, that had the scarlet thread upon his hand: and his name was called Zarah.

CHAPTER 39

1 AND Joseph was brought down to Egypt; and Potiphar, an officer of Pharaoh, captain of the guard, an Egyptian, bought him of the hands of the Ishmeelites, which had brought him down thither.

2 And the LORD was with Joseph, and he was a prosperous man; and he was in the house of his master the Egyptian.

3 And his master saw that the LORD was with him, and that the LORD made all that he did to prosper in his hand.

4 And Joseph found grace in his sight, and he served him: and he made him overseer over his house, and all that he had he put into his hand.

GENESIS CHAPTER 39

Genesis 39:1–12—Honesty

Honesty has luster. It rings true. It has the touch of majesty. It is the essence of our citizenship in the kingdom of God, for it confirms our obedience to the covenants made with our Father in Heaven and defines our promise to endure to the end. When we are honest with God, we are on the pathway to exaltation and eternal life. When we are honest with our families and friends, we earn their esteem and trust. When we are honest with ourselves, we have peace and joy. Thank heaven for the ageless pattern of Jesus Christ, our Master and Lord, whose infinite grace and matchless honesty made Him the light and the life of the world and the Savior for all mankind.

Verily Christ is the paragon, now and forever, of all that is honest. He has given us His word as a sacred gift from God—holy and profound—bringing us joy as we use it to bless and sanctify others. Honesty abounds in using the word with valor and truth. Of all the creatures under heaven's crown, man alone has been endowed with the power of speech, after the manner of the Creator. Our charge is to use our word with honesty, for our word is our bond.

Honesty comes in many hues: integrity and trust, nobility and valor, honor and reliability. Predictably, the honest soul is upright, fair, sincere, truthful, virtuous, chaste, authentic, genuine, and faithfully obedient. Obedience is, indeed, the signal key of honest lives. Adam was honest in sacrificing unto God, without knowing why, until an angel taught him that it was done as "a similitude of the sacrifice of the Only Begotten of the Father, which is full of grace and truth" (Moses 5:7). Noah was honest when he obeyed the Lord in making the ark to save a righteous remnant of humankind. Joseph of Egypt was honest in rejecting the enticements of Potiphar's wife and honoring his covenant vows of virtue and obedience. Moses, Isaiah, and Jeremiah were likewise honest when they humbly expressed inadequacy for their prophetic callings—but allowed the Lord to make of them worthy servants for saving souls. Lehi was honest in proclaiming repentance to his prideful landsmen, then leading his family to safety abroad in the Promised Land. The people of Ammon were honest when they refused to break their solemn oath to remain forever at peace; their noble sons, warriors of Helaman, were honest in obeying the counsel of their mothers to exercise faith—and thus uphold the liberty of their people. Abinadi was honest when he refused to recall his warning words and thus gave his life as a witness for truth. Joseph Smith was honest in refusing to recant his testimony of the First Vision and then going forward undaunted, in faith, to fulfill his role as the prophet of God in bringing to pass the restoration of truth in the latter days. The pioneers were honest and bold in their willingness to "gather together, and stand in holy places" (D&C 101:22). And so it goes.

Honesty is the expression of one's true character. Honesty is the core of integrity. Honesty binds and preserves relationships. Honesty exalts communication and edifies

5 And it came to pass from the time that he had made him overseer in his house, and over all that he had, that the LORD blessed the Egyptian's house for Joseph's sake; and the blessing of the LORD was upon all that he had in the house, and in the field.

6 And he left all that he had in Joseph's hand; and he knew not ought he had, save the bread which he did eat. And Joseph was a goodly person, and well favoured.

7 ¶ And it came to pass after these things, that his master's wife cast her eyes upon Joseph; and she said, Lie with me.

8 But he refused, and said unto his master's wife, Behold, my master wotteth not what is with me in the house, and he hath committed all that he hath to my hand;

9 There is none greater in this house than I; neither hath he kept back any thing from me but thee, because thou art his wife: how then can I do this great wickedness, and sin against God?

10 And it came to pass, as she spake to Joseph day by day, that he hearkened not unto her, to lie by her, or to be with her.

11 And it came to pass about this time, that Joseph went into the house to do his business; and there was none of the men of the house there within.

12 And she caught him by his garment, saying, Lie with me: and he left his garment in her hand, and fled, and got him out.

13 And it came to pass, when she saw that he had left his garment in her hand, and was fled forth,

14 That she called unto the men of her house, and spake unto them, saying, See, he hath brought in an Hebrew unto us to mock us; he came in unto me to lie with me, and I cried with a loud voice:

15 And it came to pass, when he heard that I lifted up my voice and cried, that he left his garment with me, and fled, and got him out.

16 And she laid up his garment by her, until his lord came home.

17 And she spake unto him according to these words, saying, The Hebrew servant, which thou hast brought unto us, came in unto me to mock me:

18 And it came to pass, as I lifted up my voice and cried, that he left his garment with me, and fled out.

19 And it came to pass, when his master heard the words of his wife, which she spake unto him, saying, After this manner did thy servant to me; that his wrath was kindled.

20 And Joseph's master took him, and put him into the prison, a place where the king's prisoners were bound: and he was there in the prison.

21 ¶ But the LORD was with Joseph, and shewed him mercy, and gave him favour in the sight of the keeper of the prison.

22 And the keeper of the prison committed to Joseph's hand all the prisoners that were in the prison; and whatsoever they did there, he was the doer of it.

23 The keeper of the prison looked not to any thing that was under his hand; because the LORD was with Joseph, and that which he did, the LORD made it to prosper.

promises. Honesty is a governing principle—because it generates lasting trust and enduring loyalty.

We can be grateful for the eternal foundation of transcendent honesty upon which to build our future lives. We can be grateful for the fruits of honesty: peace, freedom, self-respect, and the favor of God. Honesty is an enduring, perennial source of vitality; dishonesty is like a weed—it grows up quickly but is soon scorched in the sun of disclosure and blown away in the winds of discontent. We can be grateful that honesty is taught in the home by gentle persuasion, by kindness, and love—for honesty is the quintessence of charity and the enlivening spirit of the Golden Rule. Let us draw a line in the sand. Let us stand up for the principle of honesty in all our undertakings. Honesty is at the heart of our covenant with God. Honesty is the best policy—the *only* policy. It is our quest in all things. It leads to a life that is sweet and full of joy.

Genesis 39:23—Portrait of Leadership and Virtue

Joseph's example of moral uprightness in Egypt is among the most celebrated instances of strength of character in all of Holy Writ.

Joseph's flight at the adulterous overtures of Potiphar's wife stands in stark contrast with the moral weakness of some of his brothers. The story of his strength of character is a beacon of light that still shines today in our world of moral relativity characterized by the loss of the anchor of enduring principles. Moreover, Joseph's resiliency, positive leadership, and creative problem-solving cause him to be elevated in stature and office in his Egyptian setting, thus laying the groundwork for his future role of preserver of his heritage under the Abrahamic Covenant.

Through his example, we see that one of the best ways to keep from sinning is to avoid the situation or the road that leads to sin. Joseph ran from sin; so should we.

POINT OF INTEREST

"The term 'Pharaoh' . . . has come to us from our Bible: the stories of Joseph and of Moses use it as a general term for the reigning Egyptian monarch; the second book of Kings describes a ruler of Dynasty XXI as 'Pharaoh Neko', adding the personal name as was sometimes done in the native literature from Dynasty XXII onwards. . . . The Egyptian original Per-'o . . . meant simply 'great house' and was one of the many ways of referring to the royal palace. Then, in the reign of Tuthmosis III, the term began to be used for the king himself. . . . Hence the word 'Pharaoh' passed into the Hebrew scriptures, and out of these into our own vocabulary" (Alan Gardiner, *The Egyptians* [London: Folio Society, 2007]).

CHAPTER 40

Joseph interprets the dreams of Pharaoh's chief butler and chief baker— The butler fails to tell Pharaoh of Joseph.

1 AND it came to pass after these things, that the butler of the king of Egypt and his baker had offended their lord the king of Egypt.

2 And Pharaoh was wroth against two of his officers, against the chief of the butlers, and against the chief of the bakers.

3 And he put them in ward in the house of the captain of the guard, into the prison, the place where Joseph was bound.

4 And the captain of the guard charged Joseph with them, and he served them: and they continued a season in ward.

5 ¶ And they dreamed a dream both of them, each man his dream in one night, each man according to the interpretation of his dream, the butler and the baker of the king of Egypt, which were bound in the prison.

6 And Joseph came in unto them in the morning, and looked upon them, and, behold, they were sad.

7 And he asked Pharaoh's officers that were with him in the ward of his lord's house, saying, Wherefore look ye so sadly to day?

8 And they said unto him, We have dreamed a dream, and there is no interpreter of it. And Joseph said unto them, Do not interpretations belong to God? tell me them, I pray you.

9 And the chief butler told his dream to Joseph, and said to him, In my dream, behold, a vine was before me;

10 And in the vine were three branches: and it was as though it budded, and her blossoms shot forth; and the clusters thereof brought forth ripe grapes:

11 And Pharaoh's cup was in my hand: and I took the grapes, and pressed them into Pharaoh's cup, and I gave the cup into Pharaoh's hand.

12 And Joseph said unto him, This is the interpretation of it: The three branches are three days:

13 Yet within three days shall Pharaoh lift up thine head, and restore thee unto thy place: and thou shalt deliver Pharaoh's cup into his hand, after the former manner when thou wast his butler.

14 But think on me when it shall be well with thee, and shew kindness, I pray thee, unto me, and make mention of me unto Pharaoh, and bring me out of this house:

15 For indeed I was stolen away out of the land of the Hebrews: and here also have I done nothing that they should put me into the dungeon.

16 When the chief baker saw that the interpretation was good, he said unto Joseph, I also was in my dream, and, behold, I had three white baskets on my head:

17 And in the uppermost basket there was of all manner of bakemeats for Pharaoh; and the birds did eat them out of the basket upon my head.

18 And Joseph answered and said, This is the interpretation thereof: The three baskets are three days:

19 Yet within three days shall Pharaoh lift up thy head from off thee, and shall hang thee on a tree; and the birds shall eat thy flesh from off thee.

20 ¶ And it came to pass the third day, which was Pharaoh's birthday, that he made a feast unto all his servants: and he lifted up the head of the chief butler and of the chief baker among his servants.

21 And he restored the chief butler unto his butlership again; and he gave the cup into Pharaoh's hand:

GENESIS CHAPTER 40

Genesis 40—Overview

The fruitful and noble life partakes of the gifts of God. Joseph was richly blessed with gifts of leadership and the ability to discern the patterns of divine intervention in human affairs. He used his gifts for the glory of God and the preservation of his people.

The fruitful and noble life also reflects the light of redeeming love. Joseph is the unsurpassed paragon of brotherly kindness and love of parents in holy writ. Can one find, outside the example of the Savior, a greater demonstration of genuine love for one's family members, and compassionate concern for their welfare, than in the life of Joseph?

The fruitful and noble life also provides evidence of the hand of God at work in this mortal realm. Joseph's vision of the heavenly workings in the affairs of mankind allows him to overlook the petty intrigues of his brethren, though they conspired to exile him in a strange land. Though he started out as a prisoner in Egypt, he was never confined to a negative world of grudge-bearing, recriminations, and blame. Instead, Joseph had the miraculous power to see the good in all that transpired, and to become a partner with God in bringing about divine purposes.

 POINT OF INTEREST

"The name Djoser is first recorded on an . . . ivory plaque where it appears as the king's nebty-*name, but definite proof of the identity of Netjrikhe with the Djoser of the hieroglyphs and the Tosorthros of Manetho is found no earlier than in a long rock inscription of Ptolemaic date on the island of Sehêl in the First Cataract. This inscription relates that King Netjrikhe Djoser [above], being in deep sorrow because of a seven-year famine that had afflicted the land, sought counsel from the wise Imhotep"* (Alan Gardiner, *The Egyptians* [London: Folio Society, 2007]). *Is Djoser the Pharaoh of Joseph's time? Did Imhotep alter the records to take the credit for preserving Egypt? With the Egyptian penchant for changing historical records it's possible. It's just as likely that Joseph helped another Pharaoh through a different famine.*

22 But he hanged the chief baker: as Joseph had interpreted to them.

23 Yet did not the chief butler remember Joseph, but forgat him.

CHAPTER 41

1 AND it came to pass at the end of two full years, that Pharaoh dreamed: and, behold, he stood by the river.

2 And, behold, there came up out of the river seven well favoured kine and fatfleshed; and they fed in a meadow.

3 And, behold, seven other kine came up after them out of the river, ill favoured and leanfleshed; and stood by the other kine upon the brink of the river.

4 And the ill favoured and leanfleshed kine did eat up the seven well favoured and fat kine. So Pharaoh awoke.

5 And he slept and dreamed the second time: and, behold, seven ears of corn came up upon one stalk, rank and good.

6 And, behold, seven thin ears and blasted with the east wind sprung up after them.

7 And the seven thin ears devoured the seven rank and full ears. And Pharaoh awoke, and, behold, it was a dream.

8 And it came to pass in the morning that his spirit was troubled; and he sent and called for all the magicians of Egypt, and all the wise men thereof: and Pharaoh told them his dream; but there was none that could interpret them unto Pharaoh.

9 ¶ Then spake the chief butler unto Pharaoh, saying, I do remember my faults this day:

10 Pharaoh was wroth with his servants, and put me in ward in the captain of the guard's house, both me and the chief baker:

11 And we dreamed a dream in one night, I and he; we dreamed each man according to the interpretation of his dream.

12 And there was there with us a young man, an Hebrew, servant to the captain of the guard; and we told him, and he interpreted to us our dreams; to each man according to his dream he did interpret.

13 And it came to pass, as he interpreted to us, so it was; me he restored unto mine office, and him he hanged.

14 ¶ Then Pharaoh sent and called Joseph, and they brought him hastily out of the dungeon: and he shaved himself, and changed his raiment, and came in unto Pharaoh.

15 And Pharaoh said unto Joseph, I have dreamed a dream, and there is none that can interpret it: and I have heard say of thee, that thou canst understand a dream to interpret it.

16 And Joseph answered Pharaoh, saying, It is not in me: God shall give Pharaoh an answer of peace.

17 And Pharaoh said unto Joseph, In my dream, behold, I stood upon the bank of the river:

18 And, behold, there came up out of the river seven kine, fatfleshed and well favoured; and they fed in a meadow:

19 And, behold, seven other kine came up after them, poor and very ill favoured and leanfleshed, such as I never saw in all the land of Egypt for badness:

20 And the lean and the ill favoured kine did eat up the first seven fat kine:

21 And when they had eaten them up, it could not be known that they had eaten them; but they were still ill favoured, as at the beginning. So I awoke.

GENESIS CHAPTER 41

Genesis 41:1–38—An Eye Single to the Glory of God

Joseph is a prime example of one with *an eye single to the glory of God*. This precise phrase is used several times in the scriptures. For example, the prophet Mormon, referring to the record of Joseph, of which he was a chief compiler and curator, declares: "For none can have power to bring it to light save it be given him of God; for God wills that it shall be done with an eye single to his glory, or the welfare of the ancient and long dispersed covenant people of the Lord" (Morm. 8:15).

Similarly, the phrase is used in the Doctrine and Covenants in regard to the qualifications of those who embark in the service of the Lord: "And faith, hope, charity and love, with an eye single to the glory of God, qualify him for the work" (D&C 4:5). In addition, it is used to describe the relationship that a covenant people should cultivate among one another: "Every man seeking the interest of his neighbor, and doing all things with an eye single to the glory of God" (D&C 82:19). Moreover, it is also used to characterize the person who is filled with light, which light "comprehendeth all things" (D&C 88:67).

What does one see when one has an eye single to the glory of God, as did he? One discerns, first of all, how to deploy the spiritual gifts that God has imparted for the blessing of the Saints; next, one discerns continually the daily opportunities to exercise forgiving love of the kind shown by the Redeemer; third, one discerns with the spiritual eye the hand of God outstretched over the affairs of men, leading and guiding His people in the unfolding of the Plan of Salvation.

Genesis 41:28, 38—The Gifts of God

Joseph was richly blessed with gifts of leadership and the ability to discern the patterns of divine intervention in human affairs. He used his gifts for the glory of God and the preservation of his people.

All leaders must be visionary. From his youth Joseph had the ability to interpret spiritual phenomena, such as inspired dreams. He combined this gift with an uncanny understanding of how to rise in favor with those over him, whether it was the warden of the prison or the Pharaoh of the land. Moreover, he had an unerring sense of confidence in devising and carrying out practical solutions to challenging problems, such as the coming famine in the land. As a leader among men—politically as well as spiritually—Joseph showed a better way, one that gave glory and honor to God and followed the principles of harmony, love, forgiveness, productivity, and the Redeemer's touch.

Following Joseph's interpretation of Pharaoh's dream, the Pharaoh praised Joseph as one with the Spirit of God—intimating that no one was as wise as Joseph. Pharaoh gave unto Joseph the power to rule the people of Egypt. Joseph's interpretation was fulfilled—after seven years of plenty, the seven years of famine began.

22 And I saw in my dream, and, behold, seven ears came up in one stalk, full and good:

23 And, behold, seven ears, withered, thin, and blasted with the east wind, sprung up after them:

24 And the thin ears devoured the seven good ears: and I told this unto the magicians; but there was none that could declare it to me.

25 ¶ And Joseph said unto Pharaoh, The dream of Pharaoh is one: God hath shewed Pharaoh what he is about to do.

26 The seven good kine are seven years; and the seven good ears are seven years: the dream is one.

27 And the seven thin and ill favoured kine that came up after them are seven years; and the seven empty ears blasted with the east wind shall be seven years of famine.

28 This is the thing which I have spoken unto Pharaoh: What God is about to do he sheweth unto Pharaoh.

29 Behold, there come seven years of great plenty throughout all the land of Egypt:

30 And there shall arise after them seven years of famine; and all the plenty shall be forgotten in the land of Egypt; and the famine shall consume the land;

31 And the plenty shall not be known in the land by reason of that famine following; for it shall be very grievous.

32 And for that the dream was doubled unto Pharaoh twice; it is because the thing is established by God, and God will shortly bring it to pass.

33 Now therefore let Pharaoh look out a man discreet and wise, and set him over the land of Egypt.

34 Let Pharaoh do this, and let him appoint officers over the land, and take up the fifth part of the land of Egypt in the seven plenteous years.

35 And let them gather all the food of those good years that come, and lay up corn under the hand of Pharaoh, and let them keep food in the cities.

36 And that food shall be for store to the land against the seven years of famine, which shall be in the land of Egypt; that the land perish not through the famine.

37 ¶ And the thing was good in the eyes of Pharaoh, and in the eyes of all his servants.

38 And Pharaoh said unto his servants, Can we find such a one as this is, a man in whom the Spirit of God is?

39 And Pharaoh said unto Joseph, Forasmuch as God hath shewed thee all this, there is none so discreet and wise as thou art:

40 Thou shalt be over my house, and according unto thy word shall all my people be ruled: only in the throne will I be greater than thou.

41 And Pharaoh said unto Joseph, See, I have set thee over all the land of Egypt.

42 And Pharaoh took off his ring from his hand, and put it upon Joseph's hand, and arrayed him in vestures of fine linen, and put a gold chain about his neck;

43 And he made him to ride in the second chariot which he had; and they cried before him, Bow the knee: and he made him ruler over all the land of Egypt.

44 And Pharaoh said unto Joseph, I am Pharaoh, and without thee shall no man lift up his hand or foot in all the land of Egypt.

45 And Pharaoh called Joseph's name Zaphnath-paaneah; and he gave him to wife Asenath the daughter of Potipherah priest of On. And Joseph went out over all the land of Egypt.

Heavenly Father's hand is in all things to bring about His eternal purpose—the Plan of happiness. All of Joseph's work was designed to bless the House of Israel.

Genesis 41:45—Asenath

Asenath (pronounced "as'-un-nath"; meaning: gift of the sun-god) was the wife of Joseph. Only three references are given in the scriptures concerning this important woman (see Gen. 41:45; 41:50; 46:20).

Genesis 41:45—Zaphnath-Paaneah

Zaphnath-paaneah was a name give to Joseph by the Pharaoh. While the meaning of the name is uncertain, it surely implies something of dignity and honor.

Genesis 41:51–52—Ephraim

Ephraim (meaning: fruitful) was the younger of the two sons born to Joseph and Asenath. When the aged Israel (Jacob) was about to give a blessing to Joseph's sons, he placed his hands in such a way as to favor Ephraim (see Gen. 48:17–20.)

Since Joseph received the birthright ahead of Reuben, because of the latter's transgression, Ephraim was given the birthright in Israel (see 1 Chron. 5:1–2). In terms of an inheritance in the Promised Land, Joseph received two portions, one for each of his two sons (the tribe of Levi, as ministering servants, received support but no territorial land grant). The inheritance of Manasseh and Ephraim consisted of prime and fertile regions of the Promised Land (see Josh. 16–17).

The tribe of Ephraim had a colorful history marked at times by an envious nature concerning the other tribes. Isaiah prophesied of a time when such feelings would be supplanted by the harmony of a new era of gospel illumination (see Isa. 11:13).

To Ephraim is given the primary responsibility for conveying the truths of the gospel of Jesus Christ to all the world under provisions of the Abrahamic covenant. In this context, latter-day scripture sheds further light on the position of Ephraim in the designs of the Almighty (see especially D&C 64:33–36).

Ephraim is also mentioned in connection with the "rod" that should come forth "out of the stem of Jesse" (see Isa. 11:1, D&C 113:4). The term "rod" very likely refers to the Prophet Joseph Smith. Ephraim is also mentioned three times in connection with the return of the ten tribes and the glorious blessings to be poured out upon Israel at that time—and especially upon Ephraim, who holds the birthright and serves in a leadership capacity to further the cause of the Abrahamic covenant in bringing the message of the restored gospel of Jesus Christ to the world in the latter days (see D&C 133:30–34).

Genesis 41:51–52—Manasseh

Manasseh (pronounced "muh-na'-suh" or "muh-nas'uh"; meaning: forgetting) was the firstborn son of Joseph of Egypt. In his ailing years, Jacob (Israel) was visited by Joseph, with these two sons, who received blessings from the patriarch. The scene is touching and poignant:

46 ¶ And Joseph was thirty years old when he stood before Pharaoh king of Egypt. And Joseph went out from the presence of Pharaoh, and went throughout all the land of Egypt.

47 And in the seven plenteous years the earth brought forth by handfuls.

48 And he gathered up all the food of the seven years, which were in the land of Egypt, and laid up the food in the cities: the food of the field, which was round about every city, laid he up in the same.

49 And Joseph gathered corn as the sand of the sea, very much, until he left numbering; for it was without number.

50 And unto Joseph were born two sons before the years of famine came, which Asenath the daughter of Potipherah priest of On bare unto him.

51 And Joseph called the name of the firstborn Manasseh: For God, said he, hath made me forget all my toil, and all my father's house.

52 And the name of the second called he Ephraim: For God hath caused me to be fruitful in the land of my affliction.

53 ¶ And the seven years of plenteousness, that was in the land of Egypt, were ended.

54 And the seven years of dearth began to come, according as Joseph had said: and the dearth was in all lands; but in all the land of Egypt there was bread.

55 And when all the land of Egypt was famished, the people cried to Pharaoh for bread: and Pharaoh said unto all the Egyptians, Go unto Joseph; what he saith to you, do.

56 And the famine was over all the face of the earth: And Joseph opened all the storehouses, and sold unto the Egyptians; and the famine waxed sore in the land of Egypt.

57 And all countries came into Egypt to Joseph for to buy corn; because that the famine was so sore in all lands.

CHAPTER 42

1 NOW when Jacob saw that there was corn in Egypt, Jacob said unto his sons, Why do ye look one upon another?

2 And he said, Behold, I have heard that there is corn in Egypt: get you down thither, and buy for us from thence; that we may live, and not die.

3 ¶ And Joseph's ten brethren went down to buy corn in Egypt.

4 But Benjamin, Joseph's brother, Jacob sent not with his brethren; for he said, Lest peradventure mischief befall him.

5 And the sons of Israel came to buy corn among those that came: for the famine was in the land of Canaan.

6 And Joseph was the governor over the land, and he it was that sold to all the people of the land: and Joseph's brethren came, and bowed down themselves before him with their faces to the earth.

7 And Joseph saw his brethren, and he knew them, but made himself strange unto them, and spake roughly unto them; and he said unto them, Whence come ye? And they said, From the land of Canaan to buy food.

And he blessed Joseph, and said, God, before whom my fathers Abraham and Isaac did walk, the God which fed me all my life long unto this day.

The Angel which redeemed me from all evil, bless the lads; and let my name be named on them, and the name of my fathers Abraham and Isaac; and let them grow into a multitude in the midst of the earth.

And when Joseph saw that his father laid his right hand upon the head of Ephraim, it displeased him: and he held up his father's hand, to remove it from Ephraim's head unto Manasseh's head.

And Joseph said unto his father, Not so, my father: for this *is* the firstborn; put thy right hand upon his head.

And his father refused, and said, I know *it,* my son, I know *it:* he also shall become a people, and he also shall be great: but truly his younger brother shall be greater than he, and his seed shall become a multitude of nations.

And he blessed them that day, saying, In thee shall Israel bless, saying, God make thee as Ephraim and as Manasseh: and he set Ephraim before Manasseh. (Gen. 48:15–20)

Thus Ephraim, the younger son, was placed in the primary position regarding the blessing of his posterity. Concerning their inheritance in the Promised Land, Joshua provided an expanded view (see Josh. 17:17–18). Gideon, the warrior/judge, was of the tribe of Manasseh (see Judges 6:15).

In a statement by Amulek, missionary companion to Alma, we learn from the Book of Mormon that Lehi was a descendant of Joseph, through the latter's son, Manasseh (see Alma 10:3). Manasseh is also mentioned, along with Ephraim, in one other passage from the Book of Mormon where Nephi is quoting Isaiah (see 2 Ne. 19:2).

GENESIS CHAPTER 42

Genesis 42:1–24—Motives Guided by Mission

Why was Joseph weeping? Because his fundamental constitution was one of love. He perceived from a high perspective the workings of his brethren—their weakness and yet their promise as sons of Israel, their shortcomings and yet their feelings of remorse and penitence for their vile actions. Joseph knew that his mission was one of both forgiveness and sustenance, forbearance and redemption. He had the power within his grasp and soon would deliver his family from the chains of starvation and collapse.

Joseph loved his brethren. Just as the Savior (who, like the heavens, wept over the sufferings of mankind—see Moses 7:37), Joseph wept over his family. But inherent in his tears—as in the tears of the Redeemer—was the joy he discerned in his vision of the coming succor and recovery of the beloved members of his family.

8 And Joseph knew his brethren, but they knew not him.

9 And Joseph remembered the dreams which he dreamed of them, and said unto them, Ye are spies; to see the nakedness of the land ye are come.

10 And they said unto him, Nay, my lord, but to buy food are thy servants come.

11 We are all one man's sons; we are true men, thy servants are no spies.

12 And he said unto them, Nay, but to see the nakedness of the land ye are come.

13 And they said, Thy servants are twelve brethren, the sons of one man in the land of Canaan; and, behold, the youngest is this day with our father, and one is not.

14 And Joseph said unto them, That is it that I spake unto you, saying, Ye are spies:

15 Hereby ye shall be proved: By the life of Pharaoh ye shall not go forth hence, except your youngest brother come hither.

16 Send one of you, and let him fetch your brother, and ye shall be kept in prison, that your words may be proved, whether there be any truth in you: or else by the life of Pharaoh surely ye are spies.

17 And he put them all together into ward three days.

18 And Joseph said unto them the third day, This do, and live; for I fear God:

19 If ye be true men, let one of your brethren be bound in the house of your prison: go ye, carry corn for the famine of your houses:

20 But bring your youngest brother unto me; so shall your words be verified, and ye shall not die. And they did so.

21 ¶ And they said one to another, We are verily guilty concerning our brother, in that we saw the anguish of his soul, when he besought us, and we would not hear; therefore is this distress come upon us.

22 And Reuben answered them, saying, Spake I not unto you, saying, Do not sin against the child; and ye would not hear? therefore, behold, also his blood is required.

23 And they knew not that Joseph understood them; for he spake unto them by an interpreter.

24 And he turned himself about from them, and wept; and returned to them again, and communed with them, and took from them Simeon, and bound him before their eyes.

25 ¶ Then Joseph commanded to fill their sacks with corn, and to restore every man's money into his sack, and to give them provision for the way: and thus did he unto them.

26 And they laded their asses with the corn, and departed thence.

27 And as one of them opened his sack to give his ass provender in the inn, he espied his money; for, behold, it was in his sack's mouth.

28 And he said unto his brethren, My money is restored; and, lo, it is even in my sack: and their heart failed them, and they were afraid, saying one to another, What is this that God hath done unto us?

29 ¶ And they came unto Jacob their father unto the land of Canaan, and told him all that befell unto them; saying,

30 The man, who is the lord of the land, spake roughly to us, and took us for spies of the country.

31 And we said unto him, We are true men; we are no spies:

32 We be twelve brethren, sons of our father; one is not, and the youngest is this day with our father in the land of Canaan.

33 And the man, the lord of the country, said unto us, Hereby shall I know that ye are true men; leave one of your brethren here with me, and take food for the famine of your households, and be gone:

 POINT OF INTEREST

Thoth (above) is the Egyptian god of letters, science, and astronomy, and is considered the scribe of the gods. He was inserted in many tales as the wise counsel and persuader, and his association with learning, and measurement, led him to be connected with Seshat, the earlier deification of wisdom, who was said to be his daughter, or variably his wife. Thoth is credited by the ancient Egyptians as the inventor of writing, and is also considered to have been the scribe of the underworld. For this reason Thoth was universally worshiped by ancient Egyptian scribes.

34 And bring your youngest brother unto me: then shall I know that ye are no spies, but that ye are true men: so will I deliver you your brother, and ye shall traffick in the land.

35 ¶ And it came to pass as they emptied their sacks, that, behold, every man's bundle of money was in his sack: and when both they and their father saw the bundles of money, they were afraid.

36 And Jacob their father said unto them, Me have ye bereaved of my children: Joseph is not, and Simeon is not, and ye will take Benjamin away: all these things are against me.

37 And Reuben spake unto his father, saying, Slay my two sons, if I bring him not to thee: deliver him into my hand, and I will bring him to thee again.

38 And he said, My son shall not go down with you; for his brother is dead, and he is left alone: if mischief befall him by the way in the which ye go, then shall ye bring down my gray hairs with sorrow to the grave.

CHAPTER 43

1 AND the famine was sore in the land.

2 And it came to pass, when they had eaten up the corn which they had brought out of Egypt, their father said unto them, Go again, buy us a little food.

3 And Judah spake unto him, saying, The man did solemnly protest unto us, saying, Ye shall not see my face, except your brother be with you.

4 If thou wilt send our brother with us, we will go down and buy thee food:

5 But if thou wilt not send him, we will not go down: for the man said unto us, Ye shall not see my face, except your brother be with you.

6 And Israel said, Wherefore dealt ye so ill with me, as to tell the man whether ye had yet a brother?

7 And they said, The man asked us straitly of our state, and of our kindred, saying, Is your father yet alive? have ye another brother? and we told him according to the tenor of these words: could we certainly know that he would say, Bring your brother down?

8 And Judah said unto Israel his father, Send the lad with me, and we will arise and go; that we may live, and not die, both we, and thou, and also our little ones.

9 I will be surety for him; of my hand shalt thou require him: if I bring him not unto thee, and set him before thee, then let me bear the blame for ever:

10 For except we had lingered, surely now we had returned this second time.

11 And their father Israel said unto them, If it must be so now, do this; take of the best fruits of the land in your vessels, and carry down the man a present, a little balm, and a little honey, spices, and myrrh, nuts, and almonds:

12 And take double money in your hand; and the money that was brought again in the mouth of your sacks, carry it again in your hand; peradventure it was an oversight:

13 Take also your brother, and arise, go again unto the man:

14 And God Almighty give you mercy before the man, that he may send away your other brother, and Benjamin. If I be bereaved of my children, I am bereaved.

GENESIS CHAPTER 43

Genesis 43:1–30—Benjamin

Benjamin (meaning: son of my right hand), son of Jacob and Rachel (as was Joseph), was born during a time of travel between Bethel and Bethlehem. His mother died in childbirth while giving birth to him (see Gen. 35:18). Later, when a serious famine came over the land and Jacob sent his ten sons to Egypt to obtain grain, Benjamin was too young to travel. The story of the sons' encounters with the governor of Egypt—their brother in disguise—is one of the most magnificent and dramatic scenes in the Old Testament (see Gen. 42–45).

Still unrecognized, Joseph retained Simeon as surety and sent the rest home with supplies, having given them the order to return with their youngest brother, Benjamin. Jacob was reluctant to allow Benjamin to go (see Gen. 42:36). But Jacob finally relented, and his eleven sons were again granted an audience before Joseph of Egypt (see Gen. 43:27–31).

After the banquet, Joseph sent his brothers forth laden with supplies, but concealed their payments (as before) in their sacks and his silver cup in the sack of Benjamin. Upon an investigation, the cup was retrieved and the brothers were accused of treachery. Benjamin was to be retained. Judah beseeched Joseph to accept him (Judah) in the place of Benjamin (see Gen. 44:31). In compassion Joseph suspended the charade and revealed his true identity, counseling his shocked brethren to have peace (see Gen. 45:5–7). Joseph then received Benjamin in love:

Jacob's final blessing upon the head of Benjamin included the following words: "Benjamin shall ravin *as a* wolf: in the morning he shall devour the prey, and at night he shall divide the spoil" (Gen. 49:27). Benjamin and his posterity were indeed aggressive in standing against the enemies of Israel and developed a reputation as skillful archers and slingers (see 1 Chron. 8:40; 12:2).

Moses bestowed the following blessing upon the tribe of Benjamin: "The beloved of the LORD shall dwell in safety by him; *and the LORD* shall cover him all the day long, and he shall dwell between his shoulders" (Deut. 33:12).

Following their return from Babylonian captivity, the tribes of Benjamin and Judah comprised the main body of the Jewish nation (see Ezra 1:5; 10:9). The most famous of the Benjamites down through the generations were king Saul (see 1 Sam. 9:1) and the Apostle Paul (see Rom. 11:1).

15 ¶ And the men took that present, and they took double money in their hand, and Benjamin; and rose up, and went down to Egypt, and stood before Joseph.

16 And when Joseph saw Benjamin with them, he said to the ruler of his house, Bring these men home, and slay, and make ready; for these men shall dine with me at noon.

17 And the man did as Joseph bade; and the man brought the men into Joseph's house.

18 And the men were afraid, because they were brought into Joseph's house; and they said, Because of the money that was returned in our sacks at the first time are we brought in; that he may seek occasion against us, and fall upon us, and take us for bondmen, and our asses.

19 And they came near to the steward of Joseph's house, and they communed with him at the door of the house,

20 And said, O sir, we came indeed down at the first time to buy food:

21 And it came to pass, when we came to the inn, that we opened our sacks, and, behold, every man's money was in the mouth of his sack, our money in full weight: and we have brought it again in our hand.

22 And other money have we brought down in our hands to buy food: we cannot tell who put our money in our sacks.

23 And he said, Peace be to you, fear not: your God, and the God of your father, hath given you treasure in your sacks: I had your money. And he brought Simeon out unto them.

24 And the man brought the men into Joseph's house, and gave them water, and they washed their feet; and he gave their asses provender.

25 And they made ready the present against Joseph came at noon: for they heard that they should eat bread there.

26 ¶ And when Joseph came home, they brought him the present which was in their hand into the house, and bowed themselves to him to the earth.

27 And he asked them of their welfare, and said, Is your father well, the old man of whom ye spake? Is he yet alive?

28 And they answered, Thy servant our father is in good health, he is yet alive. And they bowed down their heads, and made obeisance.

29 And he lifted up his eyes, and saw his brother Benjamin, his mother's son, and said, Is this your younger brother, of whom ye spake unto me? And he said, God be gracious unto thee, my son.

30 And Joseph made haste; for his bowels did yearn upon his brother: and he sought where to weep; and he entered into his chamber, and wept there.

31 And he washed his face, and went out, and refrained himself, and said, Set on bread.

32 And they set on for him by himself, and for them by themselves, and for the Egyptians, which did eat with him, by themselves: because the Egyptians might not eat bread with the Hebrews; for that is an abomination unto the Egyptians.

33 And they sat before him, the firstborn according to his birthright, and the youngest according to his youth: and the men marvelled one at another.

34 And he took and sent messes unto them from before him: but Benjamin's mess was five times so much as any of theirs. And they drank, and were merry with him.

NOTES:

CHAPTER 44

1 AND he commanded the steward of his house, saying, Fill the men's sacks with food, as much as they can carry, and put every man's money in his sack's mouth.

2 And put my cup, the silver cup, in the sack's mouth of the youngest, and his corn money. And he did according to the word that Joseph had spoken.

3 As soon as the morning was light, the men were sent away, they and their asses.

4 And when they were gone out of the city, and not yet far off, Joseph said unto his steward, Up, follow after the men; and when thou dost overtake them, say unto them, Wherefore have ye rewarded evil for good?

5 Is not this it in which my lord drinketh, and whereby indeed he divineth? ye have done evil in so doing.

6 ¶ And he overtook them, and he spake unto them these same words.

7 And they said unto him, Wherefore saith my lord these words? God forbid that thy servants should do according to this thing:

8 Behold, the money, which we found in our sacks' mouths, we brought again unto thee out of the land of Canaan: how then should we steal out of thy lord's house silver or gold?

9 With whomsoever of thy servants it be found, both let him die, and we also will be my lord's bondmen.

10 And he said, Now also let it be according unto your words: he with whom it is found shall be my servant; and ye shall be blameless.

11 Then they speedily took down every man his sack to the ground, and opened every man his sack.

12 And he searched, and began at the eldest, and left at the youngest: and the cup was found in Benjamin's sack.

13 Then they rent their clothes, and laded every man his ass, and returned to the city.

14 ¶ And Judah and his brethren came to Joseph's house; for he was yet there: and they fell before him on the ground.

15 And Joseph said unto them, What deed is this that ye have done? wot ye not that such a man as I can certainly divine?

16 And Judah said, What shall we say unto my lord? what shall we speak? or how shall we clear ourselves? God hath found out the iniquity of thy servants: behold, we are my lord's servants, both we, and he also with whom the cup is found.

17 And he said, God forbid that I should do so: but the man in whose hand the cup is found, he shall be my servant; and as for you, get you up in peace unto your father.

18 ¶ Then Judah came near unto him, and said, Oh my lord, let thy servant, I pray thee, speak a word in my lord's ears, and let not thine anger burn against thy servant: for thou art even as Pharaoh.

19 My lord asked his servants, saying, Have ye a father, or a brother?

20 And we said unto my lord, We have a father, an old man, and a child of his old age, a little one; and his brother is dead, and he alone is left of his mother, and his father loveth him.

21 And thou saidst unto thy servants, Bring him down unto me, that I may set mine eyes upon him.

22 And we said unto my lord, The lad cannot leave his father: for if he should leave his father, his father would die.

GENESIS CHAPTER 44

Genesis 44—Love of Family

In the dynamic vortex of forces displayed in this story shines forth the glow of love and concern of an aged father for his sons. Jacob, convinced that his beloved Joseph had been torn to pieces in the desert, would now sink into the shadows of death should he learn that Benjamin, too, was lost from his grasp forever. Thus Judah stands forth to plead before the governor of Egypt that he be allowed to offer himself as a bondsman and servant in the place of the youngest brother—all to protect the well-being of the father. This would prove too much for Joseph to bear. The charade—instigated as a teaching process—would have to be suspended. The truth would have to emerge to bless the lives of the senior brothers—weighed down under the burden of remorse and self-incrimination—with new-found hope and joy.

Joseph Makes Himself Known to His Brethren by Gustave Doré

23 And thou saidst unto thy servants, Except your youngest brother come down with you, ye shall see my face no more.

24 And it came to pass when we came up unto thy servant my father, we told him the words of my lord.

25 And our father said, Go again, and buy us a little food.

26 And we said, We cannot go down: if our youngest brother be with us, then will we go down: for we may not see the man's face, except our youngest brother be with us.

27 And thy servant my father said unto us, Ye know that my wife bare me two sons:

28 And the one went out from me, and I said, Surely he is torn in pieces; and I saw him not since:

29 And if ye take this also from me, and mischief befall him, ye shall bring down my gray hairs with sorrow to the grave.

30 Now therefore when I come to thy servant my father, and the lad be not with us; seeing that his life is bound up in the lad's life;

31 It shall come to pass, when he seeth that the lad is not with us, that he will die: and thy servants shall bring down the gray hairs of thy servant our father with sorrow to the grave.

32 For thy servant became surety for the lad unto my father, saying, If I bring him not unto thee, then I shall bear the blame to my father for ever.

33 Now therefore, I pray thee, let thy servant abide instead of the lad a bondman to my lord; and let the lad go up with his brethren.

34 For how shall I go up to my father, and the lad be not with me? lest peradventure I see the evil that shall come on my father.

CHAPTER 45

1 THEN Joseph could not refrain himself before all them that stood by him; and he cried, Cause every man to go out from me. And there stood no man with him, while Joseph made himself known unto his brethren.

2 And he wept aloud: and the Egyptians and the house of Pharaoh heard.

3 And Joseph said unto his brethren, I am Joseph; doth my father yet live? And his brethren could not answer him; for they were troubled at his presence.

4 And Joseph said unto his brethren, Come near to me, I pray you. And they came near. And he said, I am Joseph your brother, whom ye sold into Egypt.

5 Now therefore be not grieved, nor angry with yourselves, that ye sold me hither: for God did send me before you to preserve life.

6 For these two years hath the famine been in the land: and yet there are five years, in the which there shall neither be earing nor harvest.

7 And God sent me before you to preserve you a posterity in the earth, and to save your lives by a great deliverance.

8 So now it was not you that sent me hither, but God: and he hath made me a father to Pharaoh, and lord of all his house, and a ruler throughout all the land of Egypt.

9 Haste ye, and go up to my father, and say unto him, Thus saith thy son Joseph, God hath made me lord of all Egypt: come down unto me, tarry not:

10 And thou shalt dwell in the land of Goshen, and thou shalt be near unto me, thou, and thy children, and thy children's children, and thy flocks, and thy herds, and all that thou hast:

GENESIS CHAPTER 45

Genesis 45:1–5—Forgiveness

The forgiving spirit of Joseph is manifested with remarkable clarity, he being a shadow and type of the Redeemer Himself—sent from God to preserve the life of all of God's children. Like Joseph, any individual touched by a redeeming spirit can never restrain the exercise of forgiveness.

Genesis 45:6–7—The Hand of God

Joseph's vision of the heavenly workings in the affairs of mankind allow him to overlook the petty intrigues of his brethren, though they conspired to exile him in a strange land. Though he started out as a prisoner in Egypt, he was never confined to a negative world of grudge-bearing, recriminations, and blame. Instead, Joseph had the miraculous power to see the good in all that transpired, and to become a partner with God in bringing about divine purposes.

Joseph sees clearly the hand of God in all that transpires. He is at once the nourisher, the forgiver, the guide, the mentor, the man of grace, the uniter, the family man. In Joseph we see a prototype of the Savior Himself, who provides the bread of life at times of spiritual famine, the water of life at times of spiritual thirst. Joseph is the purveyor of peace, the harbinger of spiritual harmony. He is the theme of life, the essence of restored vitality. Like the Savior, he is easy to love and easy to follow. Jacob, now Israel, said it best: "It is enough, Joseph my son is yet alive; I will go and see him before I die" (Gen. 45:28).

To act with an eye single to the glory of God, as did Joseph, means we must humbly seek after the best gifts and invest them in the service of our fellow beings; we must learn to kindle the Redeemer's love in our daily lives; we must look for and discern the hand of God at work in our lives and give Him heartfelt thanks for the marvelous work and a wonder that the gospel of Jesus Christ brings within the reach of every penitent and faithful Saint. When we begin to do this, we begin to catch the vision of the scope of God's covenant plan.

Genesis 45:8–15—Redeeming Love

Joseph is the unsurpassed paragon of brotherly kindness and love of parents in all of holy writ. Can one find, outside the example of the Savior, a greater demonstration of genuine love for one's family members, and compassionate concern for their welfare, than in the life of Joseph?

The dramatic account of the interaction between Joseph and his brothers, who come seeking food to preserve their families' lives, never loses its capacity to rivet the reader and generate unforgettable images of greatness of character. Joseph's leadership and integrity, his forgiving nature and genuine love combine to make the reader want to be better, want to improve, want to emulate such a Christlike example. We have on the one hand the deep and profound yearning of the father Israel who waits anxiously in his homeland to know of the safety and preservation of all his

11 And there will I nourish thee; for yet there are five years of famine; lest thou, and thy household, and all that thou hast, come to poverty.

12 And, behold, your eyes see, and the eyes of my brother Benjamin, that it is my mouth that speaketh unto you.

13 And ye shall tell my father of all my glory in Egypt, and of all that ye have seen: and ye shall haste and bring down my father hither.

14 And he fell upon his brother Benjamin's neck, and wept; and Benjamin wept upon his neck.

15 Moreover he kissed all his brethren, and wept upon them: and after that his brethren talked with him.

16 ¶ And the fame thereof was heard in Pharaoh's house, saying, Joseph's brethren are come: and it pleased Pharaoh well, and his servants.

17 And Pharaoh said unto Joseph, Say unto thy brethren, This do ye; lade your beasts, and go, get you unto the land of Canaan;

18 And take your father and your households, and come unto me: and I will give you the good of the land of Egypt, and ye shall eat the fat of the land.

19 Now thou art commanded, this do ye; take you wagons out of the land of Egypt for your little ones, and for your wives, and bring your father, and come.

20 Also regard not your stuff; for the good of all the land of Egypt is yours.

21 And the children of Israel did so: and Joseph gave them wagons, according to the commandment of Pharaoh, and gave them provision for the way.

22 To all of them he gave each man changes of raiment; but to Benjamin he gave three hundred pieces of silver, and five changes of raiment.

23 And to his father he sent after this manner; ten asses laden with the good things of Egypt, and ten she asses laden with corn and bread and meat for his father by the way.

24 So he sent his brethren away, and they departed: and he said unto them, See that ye fall not out by the way.

25 ¶ And they went up out of Egypt, and came into the land of Canaan unto Jacob their father,

26 And told him, saying, Joseph is yet alive, and he is governor over all the land of Egypt. And Jacob's heart fainted, for he believed them not.

27 And they told him all the words of Joseph, which he had said unto them: and when he saw the wagons which Joseph had sent to carry him, the spirit of Jacob their father revived:

28 And Israel said, It is enough; Joseph my son is yet alive: I will go and see him before I die.

sons—even those whose youthful indiscretions caused him untold grief. On the other hand we have the outbound love of Joseph for his father and brethren. The two forces of love arch toward each other in this account, and provide the cupola of grandeur in which this divine family story plays itself out. And thus we see that the great commandment of love can truly fulfill all the law and the prophets (see Matt. 22:36–40). It is the essence of our life, for when one has charity he or she will truly act like Christ.

Genesis 45:8–15—Forgiveness

We are grateful indeed when others cross our mortal path who are willing to share our burdens in life. We are thankful when friends lift away the heaviness of the journey, for burdens there are not a few. That is why the people of the Lord, as part of Zion's covenant bond, "are willing to bear one another's burdens" (Mosiah 18:8). Of all such burdens, there is none in life to exceed the weight of our own sense of imperfection. When pride or sin or anguish over personal faults settles upon our shoulders and presses downward upon our heart, that is indeed a great weight. If others are forgiving and supportive in our quest to unfold our spiritual wings of penitence, heaven-bound, then we thank them from the depths of our being.

Some will lift and some encourage, but there is only one with the power to free us from the persistent ponderousness of sin. Said the Lord: "Come unto me, all ye that labour and are heavy laden, and I will give you rest. Take my yoke upon you, and learn of me; for I am meek and lowly in heart: and ye shall find rest unto your souls. For my yoke is easy, and my burden is light" (Matt. 11:28–30).

Our desire is to have the buoyancy of hope through Jesus Christ "rest in [our] minds forever" (Moro. 9:25). That is the easy yoke. That is the light burden. To be forgiven, and to be forgiving, brings peace, unity, enduring happiness, and the promise of eternal life.

Genesis 45:16–28—He Lives!

What greater joy could a parent have than to learn that a child, long believed dead, yet lives? In even greater measure, how supreme is the joy of any parent to learn that a child who has strayed from the strait and narrow pathway has come back into the fold once again. Said John, "I have no greater joy than to hear that my children walk in truth" (3 John 1:4).

THE
SECOND BOOK OF MOSES CALLED EXODUS

CHAPTER 1

1 NOW these are the names of the children of Israel, which came into Egypt; every man and his household came with Jacob.

2 Reuben, Simeon, Levi, and Judah,

3 Issachar, Zebulun, and Benjamin,

4 Dan, and Naphtali, Gad, and Asher.

5 And all the souls that came out of the loins of Jacob were seventy souls: for Joseph was in Egypt already.

6 And Joseph died, and all his brethren, and all that generation.

7 ¶ And the children of Israel were fruitful, and increased abundantly, and multiplied, and waxed exceeding mighty; and the land was filled with them.

8 Now there arose up a new king over Egypt, which knew not Joseph.

9 And he said unto his people, Behold, the people of the children of Israel are more and mightier than we:

10 Come on, let us deal wisely with them; lest they multiply, and it come to pass, that, when there falleth out any war, they join also unto our enemies, and fight against us, and so get them up out of the land.

11 Therefore they did set over them taskmasters to afflict them with their burdens. And they built for Pharaoh treasure cities, Pithom and Raamses.

12 But the more they afflicted them, the more they multiplied and grew. And they were grieved because of the children of Israel.

13 And the Egyptians made the children of Israel to serve with rigour:

14 And they made their lives bitter with hard bondage, in morter, and in brick, and in all manner of service in the field: all their service, wherein they made them serve, was with rigour.

15 ¶ And the king of Egypt spake to the Hebrew midwives, of which the name of the one was Shiphrah, and the name of the other Puah:

16 And he said, When ye do the office of a midwife to the Hebrew women, and see them upon the stools; if it be a son, then ye shall kill him: but if it be a daughter, then she shall live.

17 But the midwives feared God, and did not as the king of Egypt commanded them, but saved the men children alive.

18 And the king of Egypt called for the midwives, and said unto them, Why have ye done this thing, and have saved the men children alive?

19 And the midwives said unto Pharaoh, Because the Hebrew women are not as the Egyptian women; for they are lively, and are delivered ere the midwives come in unto them.

20 Therefore God dealt well with the midwives: and the people multiplied, and waxed very mighty.

21 And it came to pass, because the midwives feared God, that he made them houses.

EXODUS CHAPTER 1

Exodus—Overview

The story of the Exodus is a story of deliverance through the power of God. The liberation of Israel from Egyptian bondage is parallel to our own deliverance from the consequences of sin through the process of faith, repentance, baptism, and the gift of the Holy Ghost—the atoning principles and ordinances established for our blessing through the redemption of the Savior. Spiritual liberation involves a number of aspects, five of which are featured in this chapter: (1) the prayer of faith; (2) the calling of prophets to declare the will of the Lord—just as we, too, receive callings in the Church as a blessing for ourselves and others; (3) bringing about the effects of the Atonement through our obedience; (4) remembering our covenants in ways the Lord has prescribed (in particular the sacrament); and (5) receiving constant nourishment and guidance through the Holy Spirit.

Just as the Lord heard the cries of ancient Israel suffering from their bondage, He will also listen to our sincere prayers for strength and guidance to overcome the challenges of mortality and to lead our families to spiritual well-being. He will call us into service. When the Lord extends a calling, He supplies the power and guidance to carry it out.

Just as the Lord liberated the captive Israelites from Egyptian bondage, He has also put in place the saving truths, ordinances, and powers to bless our lives with redeeming grace through the Atonement of Jesus Christ. Just as the Lord remembered His covenant promises to Abraham, Isaac, and Jacob by delivering Israel, so can we show through our daily obedience that we remember His goodness and honor His commandments. The Lord provided means to guide the Israelites in their journey out of Egypt. Similarly, He provides for us the light of the gospel and the voice of prophecy so that we might find our way safely back into His presence.

POINT OF INTEREST

"In Egypt, during the period of the New Kingdom (1550–1200 B.C.), it was not unusual for foreign boys, many of whom were the sons of Egypt's vassals in Palestine, to be brought up at the court of Pharaoh together with the royal children. Moses itself is a common Egyptian name. The Egyptian word ms, meaning 'to be born,' is usually associated with the name of a god (e.g. Rameses means 'son of Ra' and Thutmosis means 'son of Thoth'). . . . Scholars generally believe that the Biblical description of the living and working conditions of the Israelites best fits the reign of Pharaoh Rameses II (1290–1224 B.C.). Egyptian sources are of no help with regard to the events of the Exodus narrative" (Bruce Metzer, David Goldstein, and John Ferguson, *Great Events of Bible Times* [New York: Fall River Press, 2009]).

22 And Pharaoh charged all his people, saying, Every son that is born ye shall cast into the river, and every daughter ye shall save alive.

CHAPTER 2

1 AND there went a man of the house of Levi, and took to wife a daughter of Levi.

2 And the woman conceived, and bare a son: and when she saw him that he was a goodly child, she hid him three months.

3 And when she could not longer hide him, she took for him an ark of bulrushes, and daubed it with slime and with pitch, and put the child therein; and she laid it in the flags by the river's brink.

4 And his sister stood afar off, to wit what would be done to him.

5 ¶ And the daughter of Pharaoh came down to wash herself at the river; and her maidens walked along by the river's side; and when she saw the ark among the flags, she sent her maid to fetch it.

6 And when she had opened it, she saw the child: and, behold, the babe wept. And she had compassion on him, and said, This is one of the Hebrews' children.

7 Then said his sister to Pharaoh's daughter, Shall I go and call to thee a nurse of the Hebrew women, that she may nurse the child for thee?

8 And Pharaoh's daughter said to her, Go. And the maid went and called the child's mother.

9 And Pharaoh's daughter said unto her, Take this child away, and nurse it for me, and I will give thee thy wages. And the woman took the child, and nursed it.

10 And the child grew, and she brought him unto Pharaoh's daughter, and he became her son. And she called his name Moses: and she said, Because I drew him out of the water.

15 Now when Pharaoh heard this thing, he sought to slay Moses. But Moses fled from the face of Pharaoh, and dwelt in the land of Midian: and he sat down by a well.

16 Now the priest of Midian had seven daughters: and they came and drew water, and filled the troughs to water their father's flock.

17 And the shepherds came and drove them away: but Moses stood up and helped them, and watered their flock.

18 And when they came to Reuel their father, he said, How is it that ye are come so soon to day?

19 And they said, An Egyptian delivered us out of the hand of the shepherds, and also drew water enough for us, and watered the flock.

20 And he said unto his daughters, And where is he? why is it that ye have left the man? call him, that he may eat bread.

21 And Moses was content to dwell with the man: and he gave Moses Zipporah his daughter.

25 And God looked upon the children of Israel, and God had respect unto them.

EXODUS CHAPTER 2

For insights about Moses, see Appendix M; for insights about Jethro, see Appendix N.

Exodus 2:1–3—Jochebed

Jochebed (pronounced "jock'-uh-bed") was the wife of Amram and the mother of Moses. It was Jochebed who hid the infant Moses in the bulrushes when Pharaoh ordered the execution of all the male children born to the Israelites (see Ex. 2:1–3). When Pharaoh's daughter rescued the son of Jochebed and arranged for her to nurse the child, history was in the making.

Exodus 2:4–10—Daughter of Pharaoh

The daughter of Pharaoh was the one who discovered the babe Moses hidden in an ark of bulrushes on the bank of the river and had compassion on him. We know little more about this daughter of the Pharaoh, except that she performed a supremely important task of preserving the life of Moses, thus enabling him to rise to the station of liberator of his people and prophet of the Lord.

Exodus 2:16—Zipporah

Zipporah (pronounced "zih-pohr'-uh") was the wife of Moses and the daughter of Jethro (or Reuel), priest of Midian (see Ex. 2:21; 4:20, 25; 18:2). She was the mother of the two sons of Moses, Gershom and Eliezer. Of her life we know very little, except that she intervened when the Lord was angry with Moses for failing to circumcise his son as commanded. As the Lord was about to fall upon Moses, Zipporah accomplished the circumcision herself and Moses was spared, humbly repenting before the Lord (see Ex. 4:24–26; see also JST Ex. 4:24–27, in the Appendix of the Church's edition of the Bible).

EXODUS CHAPTER 3

Exodus 3—God Hears Our Prayers

Just as the Lord heard the cries of ancient Israel suffering from their bondage, He will also listen to our sincere prayers for strength and guidance to overcome the challenges of mortality and lead our families to spiritual well-being.

After the death of Joseph and the Pharaoh, the Israelites began to suffer under successor regimes. Their burdens became heavy, their oppression painful. They cried to the Lord for relief, and He heard their prayers and intervened to bring a new situation into their lives and redress the wrongs that had befallen them.

In this, as in many other situations, we see the power of prayer in all things. As just a few examples, prayer helps us:

Receive the blessing of the Holy Ghost (see 3 Ne. 19:9; D&C 19:38; D&C 42:14)

Avoid and overcome temptation (see 3 Ne. 18:15–18; D&C 31:12)

Receive strength (see Moses 1:20)

CHAPTER 3

1 NOW Moses kept the flock of Jethro his father in law, the priest of Midian: and he led the flock to the backside of the desert, and came to the mountain of God, even to Horeb.

2 And the angel of the LORD appeared unto him in a flame of fire out of the midst of a bush: and he looked, and, behold, the bush burned with fire, and the bush was not consumed.

3 And Moses said, I will now turn aside, and see this great sight, why the bush is not burnt.

4 And when the LORD saw that he turned aside to see, God called unto him out of the midst of the bush, and said, Moses, Moses. And he said, Here am I.

5 And he said, Draw not nigh hither: put off thy shoes from off thy feet, for the place whereon thou standest is holy ground.

6 Moreover he said, I am the God of thy father, the God of Abraham, the God of Isaac, and the God of Jacob. And Moses hid his face; for he was afraid to look upon God.

7 ¶ And the LORD said, I have surely seen the affliction of my people which are in Egypt, and have heard their cry by reason of their taskmasters; for I know their sorrows;

8 And I am come down to deliver them out of the hand of the Egyptians, and to bring them up out of that land unto a good land and a large, unto a land flowing with milk and honey; unto the place of the Canaanites, and the Hittites, and the Amorites, and the Perizzites, and the Hivites, and the Jebusites.

9 Now therefore, behold, the cry of the children of Israel is come unto me: and I have also seen the oppression wherewith the Egyptians oppress them.

10 Come now therefore, and I will send thee unto Pharaoh, that thou mayest bring forth my people the children of Israel out of Egypt.

11 ¶ And Moses said unto God, Who am I, that I should go unto Pharaoh, and that I should bring forth the children of Israel out of Egypt?

12 And he said, Certainly I will be with thee; and this shall be a token unto thee, that I have sent thee: When thou hast brought forth the people out of Egypt, ye shall serve God upon this mountain.

13 And Moses said unto God, Behold, when I come unto the children of Israel, and shall say unto them, The God of your fathers hath sent me unto you; and they shall say to me, What is his name? what shall I say unto them?

14 And God said unto Moses, I AM THAT I AM: and he said, Thus shalt thou say unto the children of Israel, I AM hath sent me unto you.

15 And God said moreover unto Moses, Thus shalt thou say unto the children of Israel, The LORD God of your fathers, the God of Abraham, the God of Isaac, and the God of Jacob, hath sent me unto you: this is my name for ever, and this is my memorial unto all generations.

16 Go, and gather the elders of Israel together, and say unto them, The LORD God of your fathers, the God of Abraham, of Isaac, and of Jacob, appeared unto me, saying, I have surely visited you, and seen that which is done to you in Egypt:

17 And I have said, I will bring you up out of the affliction of Egypt unto the land of the Canaanites, and the Hittites, and the Amorites,

Petition the Lord for others (see Matt. 5:44; Mosiah 27:14)

Receive forgiveness (see Enos 1:4-6; JS–H 1:29)

Gain faith and humility (see Hel. 3:35)

Express gratitude (see Dan. 6:10)

Receive knowledge and understanding (see James 1:5–6)

Receive charity (see Moro. 7:48)

Exodus 3:11–12—Divine Calling/Divine Power

When the Lord extends a calling, He supplies the power and guidance to carry it out. When God called Moses to liberate His people, Moses was at first reluctant to accept, feeling inadequate to influence worldly powers and events to bring about the divine purposes. But God made clear that He was all-powerful—I AM is His name—and that when I AM sends you, you go with inexorable power to perform the commissioned deeds.

The Lord is Jehovah. The Lord is able to soften hearts and cause that the enemies should feel favor toward His people. He is also able to intervene with awesome force, if necessary, to open the way for His will to be carried out. We need have no fear of answering a calling from the Lord, for He will fight our battles for us and provide means for us to carry out the assignments. And thus we see that it is essential in acting with faith and hope to have the perception of the strength of the Lord in our lives. For in all reality, He *is* our strength. Whether it is on a daily matter of life itself or as we "cry unto the Lord" for our special needs, He is there and He will help. As we seek to do His will, He will strengthen us in all things.

For more insights about the Savior Jesus Christ from the perspective of the Old Testament, see Appendix O.

Moses before Pharaoh by Haydar Hatemi

and the Perizzites, and the Hivites, and the Jebusites, unto a land flowing with milk and honey.

18 And they shall hearken to thy voice: and thou shalt come, thou and the elders of Israel, unto the king of Egypt, and ye shall say unto him, The LORD God of the Hebrews hath met with us: and now let us go, we beseech thee, three days' journey into the wilderness, that we may sacrifice to the LORD our God.

19 ¶ And I am sure that the king of Egypt will not let you go, no, not by a mighty hand.

20 And I will stretch out my hand, and smite Egypt with all my wonders which I will do in the midst thereof: and after that he will let you go.

21 And I will give this people favour in the sight of the Egyptians: and it shall come to pass, that, when ye go, ye shall not go empty:

22 But every woman shall borrow of her neighbour, and of her that sojourneth in her house, jewels of silver, and jewels of gold, and raiment: and ye shall put them upon your sons, and upon your daughters; and ye shall spoil the Egyptians.

CHAPTER 5

1 AND afterward Moses and Aaron went in, and told Pharaoh, Thus saith the LORD God of Israel, Let my people go, that they may hold a feast unto me in the wilderness.

2 And Pharaoh said, Who is the LORD, that I should obey his voice to let Israel go? I know not the LORD, neither will I let Israel go.

3 And they said, The God of the Hebrews hath met with us: let us go, we pray thee, three days' journey into the desert, and sacrifice unto the LORD our God; lest he fall upon us with pestilence, or with the sword.

4 And the king of Egypt said unto them, Wherefore do ye, Moses and Aaron, let the people from their works? get you unto your burdens.

5 And Pharaoh said, Behold, the people of the land now are many, and ye make them rest from their burdens.

6 And Pharaoh commanded the same day the taskmasters of the people, and their officers, saying,

7 Ye shall no more give the people straw to make brick, as heretofore: let them go and gather straw for themselves.

8 And the tale of the bricks, which they did make heretofore, ye shall lay upon them; ye shall not diminish ought thereof: for they be idle; therefore they cry, saying, Let us go and sacrifice to our God.

9 Let there more work be laid upon the men, that they may labour therein; and let them not regard vain words.

10 ¶ And the taskmasters of the people went out, and their officers, and they spake to the people, saying, Thus saith Pharaoh, I will not give you straw.

11 Go ye, get you straw where ye can find it: yet not ought of your work shall be diminished.

12 So the people were scattered abroad throughout all the land of Egypt to gather stubble instead of straw.

13 And the taskmasters hasted them, saying, Fulfil your works, your daily tasks, as when there was straw.

EXODUS CHAPTER 5

Exodus 5—Freedom and the Atonement

Just as the Lord liberated the captive Israelites from Egyptian bondage, He has also put in place the saving truths, ordinances, and powers to bless our lives with redeeming grace through the Atonement of Jesus Christ.

The historical Israelite exodus and deliverance is a pattern for the journey of liberation that each of us must complete as we accomplish the exodus from the bondage of sin and worldly entanglements toward a state of spiritual freedom. The journey toward the Promised Land is symbolic of our passage toward Zion, where we can raise our families in truth and light, and taste the joys of the gospel through obedience and righteousness. Just as the Lord liberated Israel through the shedding of the blood of the first-born of the Egyptians, so He liberated us through the shedding of blood of His Only Begotten, that we might not perish, but have everlasting life. The consequences of sin pass over us through the process of faith, repentance, baptism and the blessings of the gift of the Holy Ghost.

Exodus 5—Coming to an Understanding and Appreciation of the Atonement

The Passover was in all things intended to symbolize and embody the future sacrifice of our Lord and Savior Jesus Christ (see 2 Ne. 11:4) The children of Israel were in slavery. Egypt held them in bondage. So likewise we are in slavery and bondage to Satan because of sin. When the final plague was instituted during the Passover, the first-born sons of Pharaoh and the Egyptians were taken and Israel was granted its freedom. We, likewise, are made free by the atoning blood of the Lord Jesus Christ.

Our very eternal life is totally dependent on the Atonement of the Lord Jesus Christ. Our freedom from sin, our sanctification and justification, are bought through the Lord's infinite and eternal and vicarious sacrifice. Until one comes to a knowledge of the doctrine of the Atonement, one cannot understand and appreciate the Savior and His sacrifice (see 2 Ne. 9; D&C 19:25–19; Alma 34).

Exodus 5—Freedom

Freedom is a seed within, placed there by a just and loving Father, Creator of us all, to bring about the immortality and eternal life of His children. Freedom is a sprouting gift of agency to choose the way of light and life according to the gospel plan enabled by the Holy One of Israel: Messiah, Lord, and King. Freedom is the rising stem of our unfolding childlike faith, nourished by the sacred word of truth, quickened by the rays of warming sunshine from above, and anchored in the soils of time endowed by earthly fathers—through their courage, toil, and vision—with the rights of liberating choice. Freedom is the tree of Zion's growth, the reaching out of branches, limbs, and leaves in keeping with the plan of God to multiply upon the earth the families of the Saints, the "children of the prophets, ... the children of the covenant" (3 Ne. 20:25, 26). Freedom is the fruit of everlasting life, the gathered

14 And the officers of the children of Israel, which Pharaoh's taskmasters had set over them, were beaten, and demanded, Wherefore have ye not fulfilled your task in making brick both yesterday and to day, as heretofore?

15 ¶ Then the officers of the children of Israel came and cried unto Pharaoh, saying, Wherefore dealest thou thus with thy servants?

16 There is no straw given unto thy servants, and they say to us, Make brick: and, behold, thy servants are beaten; but the fault is in thine own people.

17 But he said, Ye are idle, ye are idle: therefore ye say, Let us go and do sacrifice to the LORD.

18 Go therefore now, and work; for there shall no straw be given you, yet shall ye deliver the tale of bricks.

19 And the officers of the children of Israel did see that they were in evil case, after it was said, Ye shall not minish ought from your bricks of your daily task.

20 ¶ And they met Moses and Aaron, who stood in the way, as they came forth from Pharaoh:

21 And they said unto them, The LORD look upon you, and judge; because ye have made our savour to be abhorred in the eyes of Pharaoh, and in the eyes of his servants, to put a sword in their hand to slay us.

22 And Moses returned unto the LORD, and said, Lord, wherefore hast thou so evil entreated this people? why is it that thou hast sent me?

23 For since I came to Pharaoh to speak in thy name, he hath done evil to this people; neither hast thou delivered thy people at all.

CHAPTER 6

1 THEN the LORD said unto Moses, Now shalt thou see what I will do to Pharaoh: for with a strong hand shall he let them go, and with a strong hand shall he drive them out of his land.

2 And God spake unto Moses, and said unto him, I am the LORD:

3 And I appeared unto Abraham, unto Isaac, and unto Jacob, by the name of God Almighty, but by my name JEHOVAH was I not known to them.

4 And I have also established my covenant with them, to give them the land of Canaan, the land of their pilgrimage, wherein they were strangers.

5 And I have also heard the groaning of the children of Israel, whom the Egyptians keep in bondage; and I have remembered my covenant.

6 Wherefore say unto the children of Israel, I am the LORD, and I will bring you out from under the burdens of the Egyptians, and I will rid you out of their bondage, and I will redeem you with a stretched out arm, and with great judgments:

7 And I will take you to me for a people, and I will be to you a God: and ye shall know that I am the LORD your God, which bringeth you out from under the burdens of the Egyptians.

8 And I will bring you in unto the land, concerning the which I did swear to give it to Abraham, to Isaac, and to Jacob; and I will give it you for an heritage: I am the LORD.

9 ¶ And Moses spake so unto the children of Israel: but they hearkened not unto Moses for anguish of spirit, and for cruel bondage.

10 And the LORD spake unto Moses, saying,

yield from choices wise and true, empowered by the atoning Exemplar of the way of life for all who follow in His paths: "But behold, they are in the hands of the Lord of the harvest, and they are his; and he will raise them up at the last day" (Alma 26:7).

Freedom is the fiber of our very being, the joy of our existence, the purpose of our life. The principles of heaven do not confine, but rather make us free. The plan of God is not to force us home again—"that one soul shall not be lost" (Moses 4:1)—but rather to impart to all the gift of independent choice to come unto the Lord, "and none of them is lost," said Christ (John 17:12), save only those who choose the ultimate decline, "Having denied the Holy Spirit after having received it, and having denied the Only Begotten Son of the Father" (D&C 76:35). Freedom would have us rise, not fall; blossom, not fade; learn the wisdom of self-determination, not the anguish of internment through pride and sin.

The light of freedom opens our eyes; the sounds of freedom echo in our minds; the savor of freedom fills our yearning for lasting joy; the touch of freedom guides our relationships with family, friends, and neighbors; the hope of eternal freedom in the mansions of the Lord lifts us above the trials of life with resilience and courage. "I, the Lord God, make you free, therefore ye are free indeed" (D&C 98:8). For this sacred gift of freedom we are grateful and pledge to Him our time and talents, our love and devotion, our honor and faith, that it might become "a tree springing up unto everlasting life" (Alma 32:41).

EXODUS CHAPTER 6

Exodus 6:2–3—Jehovah

Jehovah is a principal name for Jesus Christ, generally rendered in small caps as "LORD" or "GOD" in the King James Version of the Bible. The sublime and eternal implication of the name was expressed to Moses by the Lord Himself: "And Moses said unto God, Behold, *when* I come unto the children of Israel, and shall say unto them, The God of your fathers hath sent me unto you; and they shall say to me, What *is* his name? what shall I say unto them? And God said unto Moses, I AM THAT I AM: and he said, Thus shalt thou say unto the children of Israel, I AM hath sent me unto you" (Ex. 3:14). The name *Jehovah* is used only four times in the KJV of the Old Testament (see Ex. 6:2–3; Ps. 83:18; Isa. 12:2; 26:4).

In addition, the Old Testament mentions the place name "Jehovah-jireh" (Gen. 22:14), so named by Abraham to memorialize the spot where he was about to sacrifice his son Isaac when the Lord intervened to provide a ram. *Jehovah-jireh* means "the Lord will see or provide."

The name *Jehovah* appears six times in the Doctrine and Covenants (see D&C 109:34, 42, 56, 68; 110:3; 128:9), twice in the Pearl of Great Price where the Lord is instructing Abraham (see Abr. 1:16; 2:8), and twice in the Book of Mormon (see 2 Ne. 22:2 and Moro. 10:34).

11 Go in, speak unto Pharaoh king of Egypt, that he let the children of Israel go out of his land.

12 And Moses spake before the LORD, saying, Behold, the children of Israel have not hearkened unto me; how then shall Pharaoh hear me, who am of uncircumcised lips?

13 And the LORD spake unto Moses and unto Aaron, and gave them a charge unto the children of Israel, and unto Pharaoh king of Egypt, to bring the children of Israel out of the land of Egypt.

14 ¶ These be the heads of their fathers' houses: The sons of Reuben the firstborn of Israel; Hanoch, and Pallu, Hezron, and Carmi: these be the families of Reuben.

15 And the sons of Simeon; Jemuel, and Jamin, and Ohad, and Jachin, and Zohar, and Shaul the son of a Canaanitish woman: these are the families of Simeon.

16 ¶ And these are the names of the sons of Levi according to their generations; Gershon, and Kohath, and Merari: and the years of the life of Levi were an hundred thirty and seven years.

17 The sons of Gershon; Libni, and Shimi, according to their families.

18 And the sons of Kohath; Amram, and Izhar, and Hebron, and Uzziel: and the years of the life of Kohath were an hundred thirty and three years.

19 And the sons of Merari; Mahali and Mushi: these are the families of Levi according to their generations.

20 And Amram took him Jochebed his father's sister to wife; and she bare him Aaron and Moses: and the years of the life of Amram were an hundred and thirty and seven years.

21 ¶ And the sons of Izhar; Korah, and Nepheg, and Zichri.

22 And the sons of Uzziel; Mishael, and Elzaphan, and Zithri.

23 And Aaron took him Elisheba, daughter of Amminadab, sister of Naashon, to wife; and she bare him Nadab, and Abihu, Eleazar, and Ithamar.

24 And the sons of Korah; Assir, and Elkanah, and Abiasaph: these are the families of the Korhites.

25 And Eleazar Aaron's son took him one of the daughters of Putiel to wife; and she bare him Phinehas: these are the heads of the fathers of the Levites according to their families.

26 These are that Aaron and Moses, to whom the LORD said, Bring out the children of Israel from the land of Egypt according to their armies.

27 These are they which spake to Pharaoh king of Egypt, to bring out the children of Israel from Egypt: these are that Moses and Aaron.

28 ¶ And it came to pass on the day when the LORD spake unto Moses in the land of Egypt,

29 That the LORD spake unto Moses, saying, I am the LORD: speak thou unto Pharaoh king of Egypt all that I say unto thee.

30 And Moses said before the LORD, Behold, I am of uncircumcised lips, and how shall Pharaoh hearken unto me?

Exodus 6:8—Promise of the Lord

The Israelites were being sorely tried and tested as they approached the hour of deliverance. Would they have the faith and confidence in the Lord and His servants? The promise of that moment was: You shall *know* that I am the Lord. They would have a witness of His power that would extend thereafter through their generations forever, and they would have an inheritance of their own where their children could grow up under the aegis of spiritual liberation. How could He accomplish this miracle? Because He is the Lord.

Exodus 6:18—Kohath

Kohath (meaning: assembly) was the second of the three sons of Levi, son of Jacob (see Gen. 46:11). Kohath had four sons, the first of whom was Amram (see Ex. 6:18). Amram, who married his father's sister Jochebed, was the father of Moses and Aaron (see Ex. 6:20). The Kohathite line of Levitical priests performed important duties associated with the Tabernacle (see Num. 3:27, 30; 4:18, 34, 37; 10:21; 1 Chron. 15:5) and received a number of cities in the Promised Land (see 1 Chron. 6:61, 70).

Moses and Aaron before Pharaoh by Gustave Doré

CHAPTER 11

1 AND the LORD said unto Moses, Yet will I bring one plague more upon Pharaoh, and upon Egypt; afterwards he will let you go hence: when he shall let you go, he shall surely thrust you out hence altogether.

2 Speak now in the ears of the people, and let every man borrow of his neighbour, and every woman of her neighbour, jewels of silver, and jewels of gold.

3 And the LORD gave the people favour in the sight of the Egyptians. Moreover the man Moses was very great in the land of Egypt, in the sight of Pharaoh's servants, and in the sight of the people.

4 And Moses said, Thus saith the LORD, About midnight will I go out into the midst of Egypt:

5 And all the firstborn in the land of Egypt shall die, from the firstborn of Pharaoh that sitteth upon his throne, even unto the firstborn of the maidservant that is behind the mill; and all the firstborn of beasts.

6 And there shall be a great cry throughout all the land of Egypt, such as there was none like it, nor shall be like it any more.

7 But against any of the children of Israel shall not a dog move his tongue, against man or beast: that ye may know how that the LORD doth put a difference between the Egyptians and Israel.

8 And all these thy servants shall come down unto me, and bow down themselves unto me, saying, Get thee out, and all the people that follow thee: and after that I will go out. And he went out from Pharaoh in a great anger.

9 And the LORD said unto Moses, Pharaoh shall not hearken unto you; that my wonders may be multiplied in the land of Egypt.

10 And Moses and Aaron did all these wonders before Pharaoh: and the LORD hardened Pharaoh's heart, so that he would not let the children of Israel go out of his land.

CHAPTER 12

1 AND the LORD spake unto Moses and Aaron in the land of Egypt, saying,

2 This month shall be unto you the beginning of months: it shall be the first month of the year to you.

3 ¶ Speak ye unto all the congregation of Israel, saying, In the tenth day of this month they shall take to them every man a lamb, according to the house of their fathers, a lamb for an house:

4 And if the household be too little for the lamb, let him and his neighbour next unto his house take it according to the number of the souls; every man according to his eating shall make your count for the lamb.

5 Your lamb shall be without blemish, a male of the first year: ye shall take it out from the sheep, or from the goats:

6 And ye shall keep it up until the fourteenth day of the same month: and the whole assembly of the congregation of Israel shall kill it in the evening.

7 And they shall take of the blood, and strike it on the two side posts and on the upper door post of the houses, wherein they shall eat it.

EXODUS CHAPTER 11

Exodus 11:3—A Great Man in the Land of Egypt

This verse is a reminder of the great stature of Moses in the land of Egypt. Additionally, his position in the history of post-exodus Israel is of undisputed importance (see Deut. 4:10). Nephi would use the example of Moses to inspire his hesitating brothers: "Therefore let us go up; let us be strong like unto Moses; for he truly spake unto the waters of the Red Sea and they divided hither and thither, and our fathers came through, out of captivity, on dry ground, and the armies of Pharaoh did follow and were drowned in the waters of the Red Sea" (1 Ne. 4:2). When Joseph of Egypt prophesied of a seer in the latter days who would do a great work (referring to Joseph Smith), he said: "And he shall be great like unto Moses, whom I have said I would raise up unto you, to deliver my people, O house of Israel" (2 Ne. 3:9). In our day, the president of the Church is compared to Moses: "And again, the duty of the President of the office of the High Priesthood is to preside over the whole church, and to be like unto Moses—" (D&C 107:91).

EXODUS CHAPTER 12

Exodus 12:1–14—Passover

The feast of the Passover was established in commemoration of the "passing over" of the angels of destruction, sent to perform the ultimate judgment on the Egyptian leadership for refusing to liberate the Israelite nation. The preservation of the Israelites through the sacramental disposition of a lamb without blemish in each household, and the marking of the side posts and door posts with the sacrificial blood, was a type and a shadow of the ultimate sacrifice of the Son of God—Himself perfect and without blemish, the Lamb of God, whose blood was shed, according to the will of the Father, to bring about the Atonement and redemption of mankind. It was during the week of the Passover that Christ, during His earthly ministry, established the ordinance of the sacrament, supplanting the age-old practice of sacrificing the Paschal lamb, before going forth to give His life as Redeemer.

Exodus 12:19—Stranger

The term *stranger* occurs 121 times in the Old Testament (plus 65 times in the plural form), usually in relation to a person or persons of Israelite extraction coming into non-Israelite environments (such as Abraham in Canaan or the Israelites in Egypt)—or the opposite: those of non-Israelite extraction living among the Israelites. In the latter case there were protocols in the law concerning how to integrate such people in authorized and accommodating ways. The following sentence covers the spirit of the matter: "Love ye therefore the stranger: for ye were strangers in the land of Egypt" (Deut. 10:19). A famous use of the word *stranger* in the New Testament is this passage from the Savior: "For I was an hungred, and ye gave me meat: I was thirsty, and ye gave me drink: I was a stranger, and ye took me in" (Matt. 25:35).

8 And they shall eat the flesh in that night, roast with fire, and unleavened bread; and with bitter herbs they shall eat it.

9 Eat not of it raw, nor sodden at all with water, but roast with fire; his head with his legs, and with the purtenance thereof.

10 And ye shall let nothing of it remain until the morning; and that which remaineth of it until the morning ye shall burn with fire.

11 ¶ And thus shall ye eat it; with your loins girded, your shoes on your feet, and your staff in your hand; and ye shall eat it in haste: it is the LORD's passover.

12 For I will pass through the land of Egypt this night, and will smite all the firstborn in the land of Egypt, both man and beast; and against all the gods of Egypt I will execute judgment: I am the LORD.

13 And the blood shall be to you for a token upon the houses where ye are: and when I see the blood, I will pass over you, and the plague shall not be upon you to destroy you, when I smite the land of Egypt.

14 And this day shall be unto you for a memorial; and ye shall keep it a feast to the LORD throughout your generations; ye shall keep it a feast by an ordinance for ever.

15 Seven days shall ye eat unleavened bread; even the first day ye shall put away leaven out of your houses: for whosoever eateth leavened bread from the first day until the seventh day, that soul shall be cut off from Israel.

16 And in the first day there shall be an holy convocation, and in the seventh day there shall be an holy convocation to you; no manner of work shall be done in them, save that which every man must eat, that only may be done of you.

17 And ye shall observe the feast of unleavened bread; for in this selfsame day have I brought your armies out of the land of Egypt: therefore shall ye observe this day in your generations by an ordinance for ever.

18 ¶ In the first month, on the fourteenth day of the month at even, ye shall eat unleavened bread, until the one and twentieth day of the month at even.

19 Seven days shall there be no leaven found in your houses: for whosoever eateth that which is leavened, even that soul shall be cut off from the congregation of Israel, whether he be a stranger, or born in the land.

20 Ye shall eat nothing leavened; in all your habitations shall ye eat unleavened bread.

21 ¶ Then Moses called for all the elders of Israel, and said unto them, Draw out and take you a lamb according to your families, and kill the passover.

22 And ye shall take a bunch of hyssop, and dip it in the blood that is in the bason, and strike the lintel and the two side posts with the blood that is in the bason; and none of you shall go out at the door of his house until the morning.

23 For the LORD will pass through to smite the Egyptians; and when he seeth the blood upon the lintel, and on the two side posts, the LORD will pass over the door, and will not suffer the destroyer to come in unto your houses to smite you.

24 And ye shall observe this thing for an ordinance to thee and to thy sons for ever.

25 And it shall come to pass, when ye be come to the land which the LORD will give you, according as he hath promised, that ye shall keep this service.

26 And it shall come to pass, when your children shall say unto you, What mean ye by this service?

Exodus 12:20—Leaven

What was the significance of avoiding leavened bread during the Passover? It might have had a connection with the Lord's injunction to be prepared to act without delay, for the Israelites were to eat "in haste" (Ex. 12:7), remaining ever ready for action associated with the promised liberation. Leaven added to bread would, as a fermenting process, cause the dough to rise and expand—but that would take time, and time was of the essence in that critical era when speed was required. The principle worked on the opposing side as well, for the Egyptians, observing in horror that all their firstborn were destroyed, directed that Moses should remove the Israelite "in haste" (Ex. 12:33).

Another symbolic aspect related to leaven might have been its association with corruption (fermentation in the literal sense, moral degradation in the spiritual sense). Down through the ages, the Israelites were indeed enjoined to avoid all corrupting influences—and the annual Passover practice would remind them of that counsel. During His earthly ministry, the Savior warned His disciples: "Take heed and beware of the leaven of the Pharisees and of the Sadducees" (Matt. 16:6), meaning the toxic influence their misguided philosophies could have on the people (see also Mark 8:15). Paul also applied this same simile: "Know ye not that a little leaven leaveneth the whole lump? Purge out therefore the old leaven, that ye may be a new lump, as ye are unleavened. For even Christ our passover is sacrificed for us: Therefore let us keep the feast, not with old leaven, neither with the leaven of malice and wickedness; but with the unleavened *bread* of sincerity and truth" (1 Cor. 5:6–8).

At the same time, leaven was used in a positive sense, as in the Savior's short parable: "The kingdom of heaven is like unto leaven, which a woman took, and hid in three measures of meal, till the whole was leavened" (Matt. 13:33). The positive influence of gospel light and truth would become pervasively nurturing in facilitating the growth of the kingdom of Heaven. Why "three" measures of meal? The Prophet Joseph Smith provided this explanation in a letter to the elders of the Church published in September of 1835: "It may be understood that the Church of the Latter-day Saints has taken its rise from a little leaven that was put into three witnesses. Behold, how much this is like the parable! It is fast leavening the lump, and will soon leaven the whole" (*HC* 2:270).

On a later occasion, December 20, 1842, the Prophet was asked about the meaning of the same parable from Matthew 13. Invoking once again the principle of "three," he replied that "it alluded expressly to the last days, when there should be but little faith on the earth, and it should leaven the whole world; also there shall be safety in Zion and Jerusalem, and in the remnants whom the Lord our God shall call. The three measures refer directly to the Priesthood, truth springing up on a fixed principle, to the three in the Grand Presidency, confining the oracles to a certain head on the principle of three" (*HC* 5:207).

27 That ye shall say, It is the sacrifice of the LORD's passover, who passed over the houses of the children of Israel in Egypt, when he smote the Egyptians, and delivered our houses. And the people bowed the head and worshipped.

28 And the children of Israel went away, and did as the LORD had commanded Moses and Aaron, so did they.

29 ¶ And it came to pass, that at midnight the LORD smote all the firstborn in the land of Egypt, from the firstborn of Pharaoh that sat on his throne unto the firstborn of the captive that was in the dungeon; and all the firstborn of cattle.

30 And Pharaoh rose up in the night, he, and all his servants, and all the Egyptians; and there was a great cry in Egypt; for there was not a house where there was not one dead.

31 ¶ And he called for Moses and Aaron by night, and said, Rise up, and get you forth from among my people, both ye and the children of Israel; and go, serve the LORD, as ye have said.

32 Also take your flocks and your herds, as ye have said, and be gone; and bless me also.

33 And the Egyptians were urgent upon the people, that they might send them out of the land in haste; for they said, We be all dead men.

34 And the people took their dough before it was leavened, their kneadingtroughs being bound up in their clothes upon their shoulders.

35 And the children of Israel did according to the word of Moses; and they borrowed of the Egyptians jewels of silver, and jewels of gold, and raiment:

36 And the LORD gave the people favour in the sight of the Egyptians, so that they lent unto them such things as they required. And they spoiled the Egyptians.

37 ¶ And the children of Israel journeyed from Rameses to Succoth, about six hundred thousand on foot that were men, beside children.

38 And a mixed multitude went up also with them; and flocks, and herds, even very much cattle.

39 And they baked unleavened cakes of the dough which they brought forth out of Egypt, for it was not leavened; because they were thrust out of Egypt, and could not tarry, neither had they prepared for themselves any victual.

40 ¶ Now the sojourning of the children of Israel, who dwelt in Egypt, was four hundred and thirty years.

41 And it came to pass at the end of the four hundred and thirty years, even the selfsame day it came to pass, that all the hosts of the LORD went out from the land of Egypt.

42 It is a night to be much observed unto the LORD for bringing them out from the land of Egypt: this is that night of the LORD to be observed of all the children of Israel in their generations.

43 ¶ And the LORD said unto Moses and Aaron, This is the ordinance of the passover: There shall no stranger eat thereof:

44 But every man's servant that is bought for money, when thou hast circumcised him, then shall he eat thereof.

45 A foreigner and an hired servant shall not eat thereof.

46 In one house shall it be eaten; thou shalt not carry forth ought of the flesh abroad out of the house; neither shall ye break a bone thereof.

47 All the congregation of Israel shall keep it.

NOTES:

48 And when a stranger shall sojourn with thee, and will keep the passover to the LORD, let all his males be circumcised, and then let him come near and keep it; and he shall be as one that is born in the land: for no uncircumcised person shall eat thereof.

49 One law shall be to him that is homeborn, and unto the stranger that sojourneth among you.

50 Thus did all the children of Israel; as the LORD commanded Moses and Aaron, so did they.

51 And it came to pass the selfsame day, that the LORD did bring the children of Israel out of the land of Egypt by their armies.

CHAPTER 13

1 AND the LORD spake unto Moses, saying,

2 Sanctify unto me all the firstborn, whatsoever openeth the womb among the children of Israel, both of man and of beast: it is mine.

3 ¶ And Moses said unto the people, Remember this day, in which ye came out from Egypt, out of the house of bondage; for by strength of hand the LORD brought you out from this place: there shall no leavened bread be eaten.

4 This day came ye out in the month Abib.

5 ¶ And it shall be when the LORD shall bring thee into the land of the Canaanites, and the Hittites, and the Amorites, and the Hivites, and the Jebusites, which he sware unto thy fathers to give thee, a land flowing with milk and honey, that thou shalt keep this service in this month.

6 Seven days thou shalt eat unleavened bread, and in the seventh day shall be a feast to the LORD.

7 Unleavened bread shall be eaten seven days; and there shall no leavened bread be seen with thee, neither shall there be leaven seen with thee in all thy quarters.

8 ¶ And thou shalt shew thy son in that day, saying, This is done because of that which the LORD did unto me when I came forth out of Egypt.

9 And it shall be for a sign unto thee upon thine hand, and for a memorial between thine eyes, that the LORD's law may be in thy mouth: for with a strong hand hath the LORD brought thee out of Egypt.

10 Thou shalt therefore keep this ordinance in his season from year to year.

11 ¶ And it shall be when the LORD shall bring thee into the land of the Canaanites, as he sware unto thee and to thy fathers, and shall give it thee,

12 That thou shalt set apart unto the LORD all that openeth the matrix, and every firstling that cometh of a beast which thou hast; the males shall be the LORD's.

13 And every firstling of an ass thou shalt redeem with a lamb; and if thou wilt not redeem it, then thou shalt break his neck: and all the firstborn of man among thy children shalt thou redeem.

14 ¶ And it shall be when thy son asketh thee in time to come, saying, What is this? that thou shalt say unto him, By strength of hand the LORD brought us out from Egypt, from the house of bondage:

15 And it came to pass, when Pharaoh would hardly let us go, that the LORD slew all the firstborn in the land of Egypt, both the firstborn of man, and the firstborn of beast: therefore I sacrifice to the LORD all that openeth the matrix, being males; but all the firstborn of my children I redeem.

EXODUS CHAPTER 13

"If you want to know how to be saved, I can tell you: it is by keeping the commandments of God. No power on earth, no power beneath the earth, will ever prevent you or me or any Latter-day Saint from being saved, except ourselves." —Heber J. Grant, *Improvement Era* 48:123.

Exodus 13:1–3—Remember the Covenant

Just as the Lord remembered His covenant promises to Abraham, Isaac, and Jacob by delivering Israel, so must we show through our daily obedience that we remember His goodness and honor His commandments.

The Lord remembered Israel. He kept His covenant promises. To help the Israelites remember His miraculous intervention on their behalf, He instituted the Passover, with detailed rules and observances that reminded the people of His blessings to them and pointed to the atoning sacrifice of the Son. Following the infinite sacrifice of the Savior, the sacrament was instituted as a lasting memorial to His atoning redemption and as a means for us to remember our covenant promises and renew our commitment to obey the Lord's commandments.

The Lord will always remember us (see Isa. 49:15–16; 3 Nephi 10:6; D&C 10:65). The question is, will we always remember Him? This is part of the test. The Lord has provided the temple covenants, the garment, and the sacrament as regular covenant-making reminders. Yet in all of our lives there are things to see and feel that should cause us to remember. Everything connotes there is a God. Therefore, every day should be a reminder of the goodness of God in our lives.

Exodus 13:4–22—Guiding Light of the Gospel

The Lord provided means to guide the Israelites in their journey out of Egypt. Similarly, He provides for us the light of the gospel and the voice of prophecy so that we might find our way safely back into His presence.

The Lord supplied miraculous means for marking the path of liberation and showing the Israelites the way to safety. No less miraculous are His blessings to us today that lead us from one milestone to the next in our journey for spiritual liberation. We have the scriptures, including the Book of Mormon; we have the voice of living prophets to shed light on our condition and provide saving truths; we have the priesthood to provide authorized ordinances of salvation; we have the sealing ordinances of the temple; we have the Holy Spirit to illuminate our souls. Our blessings are overwhelming. Who are the pillars of light in the family? They are the parents of Zion who raise their children in light and truth and remind them always of the goodness of God in the past, the covenants of the present, and the hope of the future through the atonement of Jesus Christ.

The Lord has never left us alone, but has been constant in providing us direction through His light, His word (the gospel of Jesus Christ), and the Holy Spirit. On a personal basis, our Savior has been more explicit: "And whoso

16 And it shall be for a token upon thine hand, and for frontlets between thine eyes: for by strength of hand the LORD brought us forth out of Egypt.

17 ¶ And it came to pass, when Pharaoh had let the people go, that God led them not through the way of the land of the Philistines, although that was near; for God said, Lest peradventure the people repent when they see war, and they return to Egypt:

18 But God led the people about, through the way of the wilderness of the Red sea: and the children of Israel went up harnessed out of the land of Egypt.

19 And Moses took the bones of Joseph with him: for he had straitly sworn the children of Israel, saying, God will surely visit you; and ye shall carry up my bones away hence with you.

20 ¶ And they took their journey from Succoth, and encamped in Etham, in the edge of the wilderness.

21 And the LORD went before them by day in a pillar of a cloud, to lead them the way; and by night in a pillar of fire, to give them light; to go by day and night:

22 He took not away the pillar of the cloud by day, nor the pillar of fire by night, from before the people.

CHAPTER 14

1 AND the LORD spake unto Moses, saying,

2 Speak unto the children of Israel, that they turn and encamp before Pi-hahiroth, between Migdol and the sea, over against Baal-zephon: before it shall ye encamp by the sea.

3 For Pharaoh will say of the children of Israel, They are entangled in the land, the wilderness hath shut them in.

4 And I will harden Pharaoh's heart, that he shall follow after them; and I will be honoured upon Pharaoh, and upon all his host; that the Egyptians may know that I am the LORD. And they did so.

5 ¶ And it was told the king of Egypt that the people fled: and the heart of Pharaoh and of his servants was turned against the people, and they said, Why have we done this, that we have let Israel go from serving us?

6 And he made ready his chariot, and took his people with him:

7 And he took six hundred chosen chariots, and all the chariots of Egypt, and captains over every one of them.

8 And the LORD hardened the heart of Pharaoh king of Egypt, and he pursued after the children of Israel: and the children of Israel went out with an high hand.

9 But the Egyptians pursued after them, all the horses and chariots of Pharaoh, and his horsemen, and his army, and overtook them encamping by the sea, beside Pi-hahiroth, before Baal-zephon.

10 ¶ And when Pharaoh drew nigh, the children of Israel lifted up their eyes, and, behold, the Egyptians marched after them; and they were sore afraid: and the children of Israel cried out unto the LORD.

11 And they said unto Moses, Because there were no graves in Egypt, hast thou taken us away to die in the wilderness? wherefore hast thou dealt thus with us, to carry us forth out of Egypt?

12 Is not this the word that we did tell thee in Egypt, saying, Let us alone, that we may serve the Egyptians? For it had been better for us to serve the Egyptians, than that we should die in the wilderness.

13 ¶ And Moses said unto the people, Fear ye not, stand still, and see the salvation of the LORD, which he will shew to you to day: for the Egyptians whom ye have seen to day, ye shall see them again no more for ever.

receiveth you, there I will be also, for I will go before your face. I will be on your right hand and on your left, and my Spirit shall be in your hearts, and mine angels round about you, to bear you up" (D&C 84:88). He not only goes before us, He pays for our sins, nurtures us, and comforts us in all things (see Alma 7:11–12). If we but look, we can see His light. He is the life and light of the world (see D&C 6:21; 10:71). And when we have our eyes single to the glory of our Father, our whole bodies will be filled with light, and we will be able to comprehend all things (see D&C 88:67).

Exodus 13—Summary of Precepts and Principles

From the scriptural account of the Exodus we renew our acquaintance with the miraculous way the Lord delivered Israel from bondage through the leadership of a great prophet. In no less miraculous a way, we can be delivered from the bondage of carnality and sin through the Redemption of Jesus Christ. The process of deliverance is simple and straightforward. Our Heavenly Father hears our sincere prayers of faith and declares His will through the scriptures and the word of living prophets. Through obedience to the principles of the gospel, and through the saving ordinances administered by authorized priesthood leaders, we are blessed with the effects of the atonement of the Savior in our lives. Partaking of the sacrament allows us to renew our covenants and our commitment to obedience so that the Holy Ghost can always be with us as we humbly take upon ourselves the name of Jesus Christ and attempt to emulate His example. Such are the steps of spiritual liberation in our daily lives.

The Egyptians Urge Moses to Depart by Gustave Doré

14 The LORD shall fight for you, and ye shall hold your peace.

15 ¶ And the LORD said unto Moses, Wherefore criest thou unto me? speak unto the children of Israel, that they go forward:

16 But lift thou up thy rod, and stretch out thine hand over the sea, and divide it: and the children of Israel shall go on dry ground through the midst of the sea.

17 And I, behold, I will harden the hearts of the Egyptians, and they shall follow them: and I will get me honour upon Pharaoh, and upon all his host, upon his chariots, and upon his horsemen.

18 And the Egyptians shall know that I am the LORD, when I have gotten me honour upon Pharaoh, upon his chariots, and upon his horsemen.

19 ¶ And the angel of God, which went before the camp of Israel, removed and went behind them; and the pillar of the cloud went from before their face, and stood behind them:

20 And it came between the camp of the Egyptians and the camp of Israel; and it was a cloud and darkness to them, but it gave light by night to these: so that the one came not near the other all the night.

21 And Moses stretched out his hand over the sea; and the LORD caused the sea to go back by a strong east wind all that night, and made the sea dry land, and the waters were divided.

22 And the children of Israel went into the midst of the sea upon the dry ground: and the waters were a wall unto them on their right hand, and on their left.

23 ¶ And the Egyptians pursued, and went in after them to the midst of the sea, even all Pharaoh's horses, his chariots, and his horsemen.

24 And it came to pass, that in the morning watch the LORD looked unto the host of the Egyptians through the pillar of fire and of the cloud, and troubled the host of the Egyptians,

25 And took off their chariot wheels, that they drave them heavily: so that the Egyptians said, Let us flee from the face of Israel; for the LORD fighteth for them against the Egyptians.

26 ¶ And the LORD said unto Moses, Stretch out thine hand over the sea, that the waters may come again upon the Egyptians, upon their chariots, and upon their horsemen.

27 And Moses stretched forth his hand over the sea, and the sea returned to his strength when the morning appeared; and the Egyptians fled against it; and the LORD overthrew the Egyptians in the midst of the sea.

28 And the waters returned, and covered the chariots, and the horsemen, and all the host of Pharaoh that came into the sea after them; there remained not so much as one of them.

29 But the children of Israel walked upon dry land in the midst of the sea; and the waters were a wall unto them on their right hand, and on their left.

30 Thus the LORD saved Israel that day out of the hand of the Egyptians; and Israel saw the Egyptians dead upon the sea shore.

31 And Israel saw that great work which the LORD did upon the Egyptians: and the people feared the LORD, and believed the LORD, and his servant Moses.

EXODUS CHAPTER 14

Exodus 14:13–14—Salvation of the Lord

The supreme victory of the divine cause on that unforgettable day would resonate and echo down through the generations of time. The words "salvation of the Lord" (see also 2 Chron. 20:17; Lam. 3:26; 1 Ne. 19:17; Mosiah 15:28; 16:1; 17:15) and "salvation of God" (see also Ps. 50:23; Luke 3:6; Acts 28:28; 3 Ne. 16:20; D&C 123:17) would become an emblematic maxim for engendering hope and courage in the lives of God's children ever after.

An episode from the history of Zion's Camp provides a modern illustration of the promise that the "Lord shall fight for you, and ye shall hold your peace" (Ex. 14:14). Under certain conditions God commands His people to defend themselves, while at other times He declares that He will fight their battles for them. On Thursday, June 19, 1834, Zion's Camp was protected by divine authority in the form of a severe thunderstorm at Fishing River in Clay County, Missouri. A mob of nearly 400 men who had vowed "to kill Joe Smith and his army" (*HC* 2:104) were converging upon the Saints' location. Five scouts from the mob visited the camp, threatening that the Mormons would "see hell before morning" (*HC* 2:103). Some of the brethren desired to load their weapons and fight, but Joseph Smith told them, "Stand still, and see the salvation of God" (*Church History in the Fulness of Times*, rev. ed. [Salt Lake City: Corporation of the President of The Church of Jesus Christ of Latter-day Saints, 1993], 148; cf. Ex. 14:13).

Wilford Woodruff recorded what appeared in the previously clear skies moments after the scouts' departure: "A small cloud like a black spot appeared in the north west, and it began to unroll itself like a scroll, and in a few minutes the whole heavens were covered with a pall as black as ink" (*HC* 2:104). The ensuing storm, of unprecedented violence, entirely frustrated the schemes of the scattering mob. Joseph declared, "God is in this storm." The surviving mobocrats decided that "when Jehovah fights they would rather be absent."

Exodus 14:31—Miracles

One can only imagine the effect this awe-inspiring miracle had on the hearts and minds of the observing Israelites. It is little wonder, under the circumstances, that the "people feared the LORD and believed the LORD, and his servant Moses." The challenge for us today is to fear the Lord, believe the Lord, and follow the prophets of today—all on the basis of our own internal miracle of the might change and the whisperings of the Holy Ghost.

CHAPTER 15

1 THEN sang Moses and the children of Israel this song unto the LORD, and spake, saying, I will sing unto the LORD, for he hath triumphed gloriously: the horse and his rider hath he thrown into the sea.

2 The LORD is my strength and song, and he is become my salvation: he is my God, and I will prepare him an habitation; my father's God, and I will exalt him.

3 The LORD is a man of war: the LORD is his name.

4 Pharaoh's chariots and his host hath he cast into the sea: his chosen captains also are drowned in the Red sea.

5 The depths have covered them: they sank into the bottom as a stone.

6 Thy right hand, O LORD, is become glorious in power: thy right hand, O LORD, hath dashed in pieces the enemy.

7 And in the greatness of thine excellency thou hast overthrown them that rose up against thee: thou sentest forth thy wrath, which consumed them as stubble.

8 And with the blast of thy nostrils the waters were gathered together, the floods stood upright as an heap, and the depths were congealed in the heart of the sea.

9 The enemy said, I will pursue, I will overtake, I will divide the spoil; my lust shall be satisfied upon them; I will draw my sword, my hand shall destroy them.

10 Thou didst blow with thy wind, the sea covered them: they sank as lead in the mighty waters.

11 Who is like unto thee, O LORD, among the gods? who is like thee, glorious in holiness, fearful in praises, doing wonders?

12 Thou stretchedst out thy right hand, the earth swallowed them.

13 Thou in thy mercy hast led forth the people which thou hast redeemed: thou hast guided them in thy strength unto thy holy habitation.

14 The people shall hear, and be afraid: sorrow shall take hold on the inhabitants of Palestina.

15 Then the dukes of Edom shall be amazed; the mighty men of Moab, trembling shall take hold upon them; all the inhabitants of Canaan shall melt away.

16 Fear and dread shall fall upon them; by the greatness of thine arm they shall be as still as a stone; till thy people pass over, O LORD, till the people pass over, which thou hast purchased.

17 Thou shalt bring them in, and plant them in the mountain of thine inheritance, in the place, O LORD, which thou hast made for thee to dwell in, in the Sanctuary, O Lord, which thy hands have established.

18 The LORD shall reign for ever and ever.

19 For the horse of Pharaoh went in with his chariots and with his horsemen into the sea, and the LORD brought again the waters of the sea upon them; but the children of Israel went on dry land in the midst of the sea.

20 ¶ And Miriam the prophetess, the sister of Aaron, took a timbrel in her hand; and all the women went out after her with timbrels and with dances.

21 And Miriam answered them, Sing ye to the LORD, for he hath triumphed gloriously; the horse and his rider hath he thrown into the sea.

EXODUS CHAPTER 15

Exodus 15—Perspective on Exodus

The successful exodus of Israel was marked with a universal celebration of praise and thanksgiving. Our relationship with our Heavenly Father and His Son is incomplete without our constant expression of gratitude and thanksgiving for blessings received. Our relationship with our Heavenly Father and His Son is incomplete without our constant expression of gratitude and thanksgiving for blessings received.

Through His prophets, such as Moses, the Lord provides universal laws to govern all human behavior. The giving of these laws is a gift designed to bring peace, harmony, well-being, and rich spiritual blessings into the lives of God's children. The Lord commands Israel to seek Him and His presence, to be His peculiar covenant people (His "own"), and to be holy in their walk of life. To abdicate this divine directive is to provoke the Lord and relinquish promised blessings. The Lord imparts to us truth and blessings according to our willingness and capacity to receive, adding grace for grace, line upon line—"as the dews from heaven" (D&C 121:45).

The experiences of the liberated Israelites in the wilderness, following their Exodus from Egypt at the hand of God, provide valuable lessons for us today. In many respects, Israel was like a tender growth being transplanted to a new environment, or like seeds being placed into a strange new growth terrain. Perhaps we can liken this circumstance to a garden, and ask what essential conditions of growth to look for. Perhaps we can discern the following six aspects of spiritual horticulture: (1) The freedom to grow is similar to the deliverance of Israel from foreign bondage, an event evoking the most heartfelt feelings of gratitude and praise. (2) The essential nutrients relate to the continual flow of divine nurture in our lives. (3) The caretakers of the garden are the prophets and stewards called to prepare the way and build up the Kingdom of God. (4) The principles of vitality sustaining all natural growth are like the commandments of the Lord, which sustain our spiritual development and well-being. (5) The sunshine on which all life depends has its symbolic counterpart in the radiant image of God and His glorious presence — just as we are commanded to "seek the face of the Lord always" (D&C 101:38). (6) The indispensable moisture for the growing plants is similar to the doctrines of the Priesthood, which distil upon our souls "as the dews from heaven" (D&C 121:45).

Exodus 15:20–21—Miriam

Miriam, daughter of Amram and his wife Jochebed, was the sister of Moses and Aaron. It was Miriam who, observing the daughter of Pharaoh as she discovered her younger brother hidden in the bulrushes, arranged for "a nurse of the Hebrew women" (her own mother, Jochebed) to come into service to care for Moses (Ex. 1:7). It was later Miriam who raised an anthem of praise to the Lord following the deliverance of Israel through the Red Sea.

22 So Moses brought Israel from the Red sea, and they went out into the wilderness of Shur; and they went three days in the wilderness, and found no water.

23 ¶ And when they came to Marah, they could not drink of the waters of Marah, for they were bitter: therefore the name of it was called Marah.

24 And the people murmured against Moses, saying, What shall we drink?

25 And he cried unto the LORD; and the LORD shewed him a tree, which when he had cast into the waters, the waters were made sweet: there he made for them a statute and an ordinance, and there he proved them,

26 And said, If thou wilt diligently hearken to the voice of the LORD thy God, and wilt do that which is right in his sight, and wilt give ear to his commandments, and keep all his statutes, I will put none of these diseases upon thee, which I have brought upon the Egyptians: for I am the LORD that healeth thee.

27 ¶ And they came to Elim, where were twelve wells of water, and threescore and ten palm trees: and they encamped there by the waters.

CHAPTER 16

1 AND they took their journey from Elim, and all the congregation of the children of Israel came unto the wilderness of Sin, which is between Elim and Sinai, on the fifteenth day of the second month after their departing out of the land of Egypt.

2 And the whole congregation of the children of Israel murmured against Moses and Aaron in the wilderness:

3 And the children of Israel said unto them, Would to God we had died by the hand of the LORD in the land of Egypt, when we sat by the flesh pots, and when we did eat bread to the full; for ye have brought us forth into this wilderness, to kill this whole assembly with hunger.

4 ¶ Then said the LORD unto Moses, Behold, I will rain bread from heaven for you; and the people shall go out and gather a certain rate every day, that I may prove them, whether they will walk in my law, or no.

5 And it shall come to pass, that on the sixth day they shall prepare that which they bring in; and it shall be twice as much as they gather daily.

6 And Moses and Aaron said unto all the children of Israel, At even, then ye shall know that the LORD hath brought you out from the land of Egypt:

7 And in the morning, then ye shall see the glory of the LORD; for that he heareth your murmurings against the LORD: and what are we, that ye murmur against us?

8 And Moses said, This shall be, when the LORD shall give you in the evening flesh to eat, and in the morning bread to the full; for that the LORD heareth your murmurings which ye murmur against him: and what are we? your murmurings are not against us, but against the LORD.

9 ¶ And Moses spake unto Aaron, Say unto all the congregation of the children of Israel, Come near before the LORD: for he hath heard your murmurings.

On one occasion during the wandering in the wilderness, Miriam and Aaron murmured against Moses for having taken to wife an Ethiopian woman (see Num. 12:2). As a result, the Lord confirmed to them both the preeminence of Moses the prophet. For her lapse, Miriam was rendered leprous, causing the anguished Aaron to appeal to Moses to intercede with the Lord on her behalf—which he did, resulting in her return after seven days of recovery (see Num. 12:10–16). Miriam passed away at Kadesh and was buried there (see Num. 20:1).

Though her life was marked by an occasion of murmuring, Miriam nevertheless remained stalwart and noble in the history of the covenant people—and thus remembered of the Lord as one who was sent before the people along with her brothers.

EXODUS CHAPTER 16

"Here, then, is eternal life—to know the only wise and true God; and you have got to learn how to be gods yourselves, and to be kings and priests to God, the same as all gods have done before you, namely, by going from one small degree to another, and from a small capacity to a great one; from grace to grace, from exaltation to exaltation. . . ." —Joseph Smith, King Follett Discourse, *HC* 6:306.

Exodus 16:1–15—Divine Nurture

The Lord heard the murmuring of the Israelites wandering in the wilderness and provided water, quail, and manna for their nourishment. As long as they abided by His statutes and directives and followed the counsel of His prophet, they were sustained in well-being on their journey toward the Promised Land.

Moses turned to the Lord with each challenge he faced. With a tree He made the waters of Marah sweet. When they needed bread, the Lord told Moses He would "rain" bread from the sky and prove the people if they would be obedient. In the evening, the Lord gave them flesh—quail was provided. Surely these temporal nourishments provided a daily reminder of not only the goodness of God, but also our total dependence upon Him, which normally would keep us in a state of humility.

Just as the Lord provided nourishment for the Israelites in the wilderness, He provides spiritual manna for all the faithful who hunger and thirst after righteousness. Through the nurturing of our Lord and Savior and our Heavenly Father can we be sustained in this life. For They truly do nurture and sustain us in all things—whether of the earth, for it is Theirs, for our temporal needs, or by the goodness of God through His Word, our Savior, or the Holy Spirit. We are nurtured now and forever because of our God —even our very eternal Father in Heaven who begat us as spirit sons and daughters. He is the supreme nurturer in all things.

10 And it came to pass, as Aaron spake unto the whole congregation of the children of Israel, that they looked toward the wilderness, and, behold, the glory of the LORD appeared in the cloud.

11 ¶ And the LORD spake unto Moses, saying,

12 I have heard the murmurings of the children of Israel: speak unto them, saying, At even ye shall eat flesh, and in the morning ye shall be filled with bread; and ye shall know that I am the LORD your God.

13 And it came to pass, that at even the quails came up, and covered the camp: and in the morning the dew lay round about the host.

14 And when the dew that lay was gone up, behold, upon the face of the wilderness there lay a small round thing, as small as the hoar frost on the ground.

15 And when the children of Israel saw it, they said one to another, It is manna: for they wist not what it was. And Moses said unto them, This is the bread which the LORD hath given you to eat.

16 ¶ This is the thing which the LORD hath commanded, Gather of it every man according to his eating, an omer for every man, according to the number of your persons; take ye every man for them which are in his tents.

17 And the children of Israel did so, and gathered, some more, some less.

18 And when they did mete it with an omer, he that gathered much had nothing over, and he that gathered little had no lack; they gathered every man according to his eating.

19 And Moses said, Let no man leave of it till the morning.

20 Notwithstanding they hearkened not unto Moses; but some of them left of it until the morning, and it bred worms, and stank: and Moses was wroth with them.

21 And they gathered it every morning, every man according to his eating: and when the sun waxed hot, it melted.

22 ¶ And it came to pass, that on the sixth day they gathered twice as much bread, two omers for one man: and all the rulers of the congregation came and told Moses.

23 And he said unto them, This is that which the LORD hath said, To morrow is the rest of the holy sabbath unto the LORD: bake that which ye will bake to day, and seethe that ye will seethe; and that which remaineth over lay up for you to be kept until the morning.

24 And they laid it up till the morning, as Moses bade: and it did not stink, neither was there any worm therein.

25 And Moses said, Eat that to day; for to day is a sabbath unto the LORD: to day ye shall not find it in the field.

26 Six days ye shall gather it; but on the seventh day, which is the sabbath, in it there shall be none.

27 ¶ And it came to pass, that there went out some of the people on the seventh day for to gather, and they found none.

28 And the LORD said unto Moses, How long refuse ye to keep my commandments and my laws?

29 See, for that the LORD hath given you the sabbath, therefore he giveth you on the sixth day the bread of two days; abide ye every man in his place, let no man go out of his place on the seventh day.

30 So the people rested on the seventh day.

31 And the house of Israel called the name thereof Manna: and it was like coriander seed, white; and the taste of it was like wafers made with honey.

32 ¶ And Moses said, This is the thing which the LORD commandeth, Fill an omer of it to be kept for your generations; that they

NOTES:

may see the bread wherewith I have fed you in the wilderness, when I brought you forth from the land of Egypt.

33 And Moses said unto Aaron, Take a pot, and put an omer full of manna therein, and lay it up before the LORD, to be kept for your generations.

34 As the LORD commanded Moses, so Aaron laid it up before the Testimony, to be kept.

35 And the children of Israel did eat manna forty years, until they came to a land inhabited; they did eat manna, until they came unto the borders of the land of Canaan.

36 Now an omer is the tenth part of an ephah.

CHAPTER 17

1 AND all the congregation of the children of Israel journeyed from the wilderness of Sin, after their journeys, according to the commandment of the LORD, and pitched in Rephidim: and there was no water for the people to drink.

2 Wherefore the people did chide with Moses, and said, Give us water that we may drink. And Moses said unto them, Why chide ye with me? wherefore do ye tempt the LORD?

3 And the people thirsted there for water; and the people murmured against Moses, and said, Wherefore is this that thou hast brought us up out of Egypt, to kill us and our children and our cattle with thirst?

4 And Moses cried unto the LORD, saying, What shall I do unto this people? they be almost ready to stone me.

5 And the LORD said unto Moses, Go on before the people, and take with thee of the elders of Israel; and thy rod, wherewith thou smotest the river, take in thine hand, and go.

6 Behold, I will stand before thee there upon the rock in Horeb; and thou shalt smite the rock, and there shall come water out of it, that the people may drink. And Moses did so in the sight of the elders of Israel.

7 And he called the name of the place Massah, and Meribah, because of the chiding of the children of Israel, and because they tempted the LORD, saying, Is the LORD among us, or not?

8 ¶ Then came Amalek, and fought with Israel in Rephidim.

9 And Moses said unto Joshua, Choose us out men, and go out, fight with Amalek: to morrow I will stand on the top of the hill with the rod of God in mine hand.

10 So Joshua did as Moses had said to him, and fought with Amalek: and Moses, Aaron, and Hur went up to the top of the hill.

11 And it came to pass, when Moses held up his hand, that Israel prevailed: and when he let down his hand, Amalek prevailed.

EXODUS CHAPTER 17

Exodus 17:10–13—Hur

Hur was a leading official in Israel who assisted Aaron in supporting the hands of Moses on a hill during the battle in which Joshua prevailed against the Amalekites. Hur also assisted Aaron in overseeing the people while Moses was on Mount Sinai (see Ex. 24:14).

Aaron's service with Hur in holding up the hands of Moses during the battle with Amalek is a memorable exercise in supporting God's leaders: "But Moses' hands *were* heavy; and they took a stone, and put *it* under him, and he sat thereon; and Aaron and Hur stayed up his hands, the one on the one side, and the other on the other side; and his hands were steady until the going down of the sun. And Joshua discomfited Amalek and his people with the edge of the sword" (Ex. 17:12–13)

Victory O Lord! by John Everett Millais

12 But Moses' hands were heavy; and they took a stone, and put it under him, and he sat thereon; and Aaron and Hur stayed up his hands, the one on the one side, and the other on the other side; and his hands were steady until the going down of the sun.

13 And Joshua discomfited Amalek and his people with the edge of the sword.

14 And the LORD said unto Moses, Write this for a memorial in a book, and rehearse it in the ears of Joshua: for I will utterly put out the remembrance of Amalek from under heaven.

15 And Moses built an altar, and called the name of it Jehovah-nissi:

16 For he said, Because the LORD hath sworn that the LORD will have war with Amalek from generation to generation.

CHAPTER 18

1 WHEN Jethro, the priest of Midian, Moses' father in law, heard of all that God had done for Moses, and for Israel his people, and that the LORD had brought Israel out of Egypt;

2 Then Jethro, Moses' father in law, took Zipporah, Moses' wife, after he had sent her back,

3 And her two sons; of which the name of the one was Gershom; for he said, I have been an alien in a strange land:

4 And the name of the other was Eliezer; for the God of my father, said he, was mine help, and delivered me from the sword of Pharaoh:

5 And Jethro, Moses' father in law, came with his sons and his wife unto Moses into the wilderness, where he encamped at the mount of God:

6 And he said unto Moses, I thy father in law Jethro am come unto thee, and thy wife, and her two sons with her.

7 ¶ And Moses went out to meet his father in law, and did obeisance, and kissed him; and they asked each other of their welfare; and they came into the tent.

8 And Moses told his father in law all that the LORD had done unto Pharaoh and to the Egyptians for Israel's sake, and all the travail that had come upon them by the way, and how the LORD delivered them.

9 And Jethro rejoiced for all the goodness which the LORD had done to Israel, whom he had delivered out of the hand of the Egyptians.

10 And Jethro said, Blessed be the LORD, who hath delivered you out of the hand of the Egyptians, and out of the hand of Pharaoh, who hath delivered the people from under the hand of the Egyptians.

11 Now I know that the LORD is greater than all gods: for in the thing wherein they dealt proudly he was above them.

12 And Jethro, Moses' father in law, took a burnt offering and sacrifices for God: and Aaron came, and all the elders of Israel, to eat bread with Moses' father in law before God.

13 ¶ And it came to pass on the morrow, that Moses sat to judge the people: and the people stood by Moses from the morning unto the evening.

EXODUS CHAPTER 18

Exodus 18:19, 21—Stewardship and Accountability

The kingdom of God is a kingdom of order, organized according to a structure of participatory teamwork and delegation, with a prophet at the head to carry out the will of the Lord.

In the battle against the offender, Amalek, the Israelites under Joshua prevailed as long as Moses' hands were outstretched on top of the hill, supported on either side by Aaron and Hur (see Ex. 17:9–13). Thus we see the importance of noble "counselors" in the grand program of God's kingdom. Similarly, Moses is able to sustain the awesome burden of presiding over so vast a people as the Israelites only because his father-in-law, Jethro, wisely teaches him the art and practice of careful delegation and prioritizing of the work (see Ex. 18:17–26).

Delegating a responsibility or stewardship always requires an accounting. The doctrine of moral agency requires blessings and/or consequences for our actions. This is an accounting or a judgment as the case may be. The beautiful part that we must all understand is that people grow with responsibilities and stewardships. This is what helps us become better instruments in the hands of the Lord as well as becoming more like our Savior Jesus Christ. As leaders we must always remember delegation always requires a follow-up and accounting of one's duty.

POINT OF INTEREST

Every great matter (Ex. 18:22). *"Matter' is the polyvalent Hebrew* davar, *which means 'word,' 'thing,' 'matter,' 'affair,' 'mission,' and more. . . .* Davar *in the singular occurs exactly ten times in this episode and . . . it might be a kind of coded prelude to the immediately following episode of the Ten Commandments, which in the Hebrew are called the Ten Words"* (Robert Alter, *The Five Books of Moses* [New York: W. W. Norton & Company, 2004]).

14 And when Moses' father in law saw all that he did to the people, he said, What is this thing that thou doest to the people? why sittest thou thyself alone, and all the people stand by thee from morning unto even?

15 And Moses said unto his father in law, Because the people come unto me to enquire of God:

16 When they have a matter, they come unto me; and I judge between one and another, and I do make them know the statutes of God, and his laws.

17 And Moses' father in law said unto him, The thing that thou doest is not good.

18 Thou wilt surely wear away, both thou, and this people that is with thee: for this thing is too heavy for thee; thou art not able to perform it thyself alone.

19 Hearken now unto my voice, I will give thee counsel, and God shall be with thee: Be thou for the people to God-ward, that thou mayest bring the causes unto God:

20 And thou shalt teach them ordinances and laws, and shalt shew them the way wherein they must walk, and the work that they must do.

21 Moreover thou shalt provide out of all the people able men, such as fear God, men of truth, hating covetousness; and place such over them, to be rulers of thousands, and rulers of hundreds, rulers of fifties, and rulers of tens:

22 And let them judge the people at all seasons: and it shall be, that every great matter they shall bring unto thee, but every small matter they shall judge: so shall it be easier for thyself, and they shall bear the burden with thee.

23 If thou shalt do this thing, and God command thee so, then thou shalt be able to endure, and all this people shall also go to their place in peace.

24 So Moses hearkened to the voice of his father in law, and did all that he had said.

25 And Moses chose able men out of all Israel, and made them heads over the people, rulers of thousands, rulers of hundreds, rulers of fifties, and rulers of tens.

26 And they judged the people at all seasons: the hard causes they brought unto Moses, but every small matter they judged themselves.

27 ¶ And Moses let his father in law depart; and he went his way into his own land.

CHAPTER 19

1 IN the third month, when the children of Israel were gone forth out of the land of Egypt, the same day came they into the wilderness of Sinai.

2 For they were departed from Rephidim, and were come to the desert of Sinai, and had pitched in the wilderness; and there Israel camped before the mount.

3 And Moses went up unto God, and the LORD called unto him out of the mountain, saying, Thus shalt thou say to the house of Jacob, and tell the children of Israel;

4 Ye have seen what I did unto the Egyptians, and how I bare you on eagles' wings, and brought you unto myself.

5 Now therefore, if ye will obey my voice indeed, and keep my covenant, then ye shall be a peculiar treasure unto me above all people: for all the earth is mine:

EXODUS CHAPTER 19

Exodus 19:1–5—The Commandments of God

Through His prophet, Moses, the Lord provides universal laws to govern all human behavior. The giving of these laws is a gift designed to bring peace, harmony, well-being, and rich spiritual blessings into the lives of God's children.

The Lord established his covenant with Israel. The Ten Commandments were given. These commandments are repeated in the Book of Mormon (see Mosiah 12:33–36; 13:12–24), the Doctrine and Covenants (see D&C 42:18–27; 59:5–16), and the New Testament (see Matt. 5:17–37). These commandments deal with relationships of eternal significance—God, family, and fellow man. It is fitting that the Gospel of John records, "And this is life eternal, that they might know thee the only true God, and Jesus Christ, whom thou hast sent" (John 17:3). We are taught that eternal life is establishing a relationship with our Heavenly Father and our Savior.

The basic unit of the Church is the family. The Proclamation on the Family makes clear the role of family here and in the hereafter. The sealing ordinance makes clear the priority that marriage and family play in our eternal lives (see D&C 131, 132). The way we treat our fellowmen is truly a demonstration of our feelings for the Lord Jesus Christ (see Matt. 25:40). The moment of truth in regard to the ten commandments is one eternal verity—we should love God and our fellowmen because it does fulfill all the law and the prophets (see Matt. 22:36–40).

The commandments of God are clear. We have them before us. There is no excuse. "I didn't know" or "I didn't understand" will not suffice at judgment day. The blessings of obedience are clear as well—life eternal in the presence of our Heavenly Father. Eternal increase and the blessings of Abraham are our reward.

6 And ye shall be unto me a kingdom of priests, and an holy nation. These are the words which thou shalt speak unto the children of Israel.

7 ¶ And Moses came and called for the elders of the people, and laid before their faces all these words which the LORD commanded him.

8 And all the people answered together, and said, All that the LORD hath spoken we will do. And Moses returned the words of the people unto the LORD.

9 And the LORD said unto Moses, Lo, I come unto thee in a thick cloud, that the people may hear when I speak with thee, and believe thee for ever. And Moses told the words of the people unto the LORD.

10 ¶ And the LORD said unto Moses, Go unto the people, and sanctify them to day and to morrow, and let them wash their clothes,

11 And be ready against the third day: for the third day the LORD will come down in the sight of all the people upon mount Sinai.

12 And thou shalt set bounds unto the people round about, saying, Take heed to yourselves, that ye go not up into the mount, or touch the border of it: whosoever toucheth the mount shall be surely put to death:

13 There shall not an hand touch it, but he shall surely be stoned, or shot through; whether it be beast or man, it shall not live: when the trumpet soundeth long, they shall come up to the mount.

14 ¶ And Moses went down from the mount unto the people, and sanctified the people; and they washed their clothes.

15 And he said unto the people, Be ready against the third day: come not at your wives.

16 ¶ And it came to pass on the third day in the morning, that there were thunders and lightnings, and a thick cloud upon the mount, and the voice of the trumpet exceeding loud; so that all the people that was in the camp trembled.

17 And Moses brought forth the people out of the camp to meet with God; and they stood at the nether part of the mount.

18 And mount Sinai was altogether on a smoke, because the LORD descended upon it in fire: and the smoke thereof ascended as the smoke of a furnace, and the whole mount quaked greatly.

19 And when the voice of the trumpet sounded long, and waxed louder and louder, Moses spake, and God answered him by a voice.

20 And the LORD came down upon mount Sinai, on the top of the mount: and the LORD called Moses up to the top of the mount; and Moses went up.

21 And the LORD said unto Moses, Go down, charge the people, lest they break through unto the LORD to gaze, and many of them perish.

22 And let the priests also, which come near to the LORD, sanctify themselves, lest the LORD break forth upon them.

23 And Moses said unto the LORD, The people cannot come up to mount Sinai: for thou chargedst us, saying, Set bounds about the mount, and sanctify it.

24 And the LORD said unto him, Away, get thee down, and thou shalt come up, thou, and Aaron with thee: but let not the priests and the people break through to come up unto the LORD, lest he break forth upon them.

25 So Moses went down unto the people, and spake unto them.

Moses with the Tablets by Rembrandt van Rijn

CHAPTER 20

1 AND God spake all these words, saying,

2 I am the LORD thy God, which have brought thee out of the land of Egypt, out of the house of bondage.

3 Thou shalt have no other gods before me.

4 Thou shalt not make unto thee any graven image, or any likeness of any thing that is in heaven above, or that is in the earth beneath, or that is in the water under the earth:

5 Thou shalt not bow down thyself to them, nor serve them: for I the LORD thy God am a jealous God, visiting the iniquity of the fathers upon the children unto the third and fourth generation of them that hate me;

6 And shewing mercy unto thousands of them that love me, and keep my commandments.

7 Thou shalt not take the name of the LORD thy God in vain; for the LORD will not hold him guiltless that taketh his name in vain.

8 Remember the sabbath day, to keep it holy.

9 Six days shalt thou labour, and do all thy work:

10 But the seventh day is the sabbath of the LORD thy God: in it thou shalt not do any work, thou, nor thy son, nor thy daughter, thy manservant, nor thy maidservant, nor thy cattle, nor thy stranger that is within thy gates:

11 For in six days the LORD made heaven and earth, the sea, and all that in them is, and rested the seventh day: wherefore the LORD blessed the sabbath day, and hallowed it.

12 ¶ Honour thy father and thy mother: that thy days may be long upon the land which the LORD thy God giveth thee.

13 Thou shalt not kill.

14 Thou shalt not commit adultery.

15 Thou shalt not steal.

16 Thou shalt not bear false witness against thy neighbour.

17 Thou shalt not covet thy neighbour's house, thou shalt not covet thy neighbour's wife, nor his manservant, nor his maidservant, nor his ox, nor his ass, nor any thing that is thy

18 ¶ And all the people saw the thunderings, and the lightnings, and the noise of the trumpet, and the mountain smoking: and when the people saw it, they removed, and stood afar off.

19 And they said unto Moses, Speak thou with us, and we will hear: but let not God speak with us, lest we die.

20 And Moses said unto the people, Fear not: for God is come to prove you, and that his fear may be before your faces, that ye sin not.

21 And the people stood afar off, and Moses drew near unto the thick darkness where God was.

22 ¶ And the LORD said unto Moses, Thus thou shalt say unto the children of Israel, Ye have seen that I have talked with you from heaven.

23 Ye shall not make with me gods of silver, neither shall ye make unto you gods of gold.

24 ¶ An altar of earth thou shalt make unto me, and shalt sacrifice thereon thy burnt offerings, and thy peace offerings, thy sheep, and thine oxen: in all places where I record my name I will come unto thee, and I will bless thee.

25 And if thou wilt make me an altar of stone, thou shalt not build it of hewn stone: for if thou lift up thy tool upon it, thou hast polluted it.

EXODUS CHAPTER 20

Exodus 20:4–5—Idols

Idols were representations of personalities or aspects of nature that became the objects of worship among the heathen nations (and at times among the wayward Israelites)—as contrasted with the worship of the true God.

The Lord warned against mingling receptively with idol worshippers and called for the overthrow of such regimes (see for example Ex. 34:10–17; Deut. 7; 12:29–32; 20:10–18; 1 Sam. 15:23). Though the names *Baal* and *Molech* and *Elkenah* are no longer in vogue, the same sinister evil associated with idol worship is still rampant in today's world. Idolatry thrives in the contours of obsession with lucre, addiction to power as an end in itself, and commitment to immoral carnality in endless forms. The Savior taught: "No man can serve two masters: for either he will hate the one, and love the other; or else he will hold to the one, and despise the other. Ye cannot serve God and mammon" (Matt. 6:24). "Thou shalt have no other gods before me" is still the operant commandment of a jealous God—but one who nevertheless receives the penitent and devout with mercy and ever-loving kindness.

Exodus 20:6–17—The Ten Commandments Today

1. *Thou shalt have no other Gods before me* (Ex. 20:3).

God is first and foremost, and His purpose is His family's happiness. Therefore, in putting Heavenly Father first we build up the Kingdom of God first—hence, we bless our brothers and sisters.

2. *Thou shalt not make unto thee any graven image* (Ex. 20:4–6).

Idolatry has been a problem with mankind since the beginning of time. You cannot place any other god, thing, material possession, position, station, fame, fortune, vocation, hobby, or cause before God.

3. *Thou shalt not take the name of the Lord thy God in vain* (Ex. 20:7).

Reverence for God is demonstrated by not profaning the name of God, swearing, or by making oaths in the name of God in light-minded manners. Our behavior can demonstrate our feelings in regard to our oaths and covenants with our Savior and Heavenly Father whereby we could take His name in vain by not honoring our covenants.

4. *Remember the Sabbath day to keep it holy* (Ex. 20:8–11).

The Sabbath day is to rest from your temporal affairs, symbolize your covenant with God, allow the Lord to sanctify you on His day, renew your covenants, and prepare and renew yourself for the coming week.

5. *Honor thy father and thy mother* (Ex. 20:12).

This is demonstrated by a reverential attitude toward your parents, by obedience in righteousness, and by bringing joy and honor to their name.

6. *Thou shalt not kill* (Ex. 20:13).

The wanton act of destroying the life of a child of God is wrong. We each have the right to protect our homes, our

26 Neither shalt thou go up by steps unto mine altar, that thy nakedness be not discovered thereon.

CHAPTER 32

1 AND when the people saw that Moses delayed to come down out of the mount, the people gathered themselves together unto Aaron, and said unto him, Up, make us gods, which shall go before us; for as for this Moses, the man that brought us up out of the land of Egypt, we wot not what is become of him.

2 And Aaron said unto them, Break off the golden earrings, which are in the ears of your wives, of your sons, and of your daughters, and bring them unto me.

3 And all the people brake off the golden earrings which were in their ears, and brought them unto Aaron.

4 And he received them at their hand, and fashioned it with a graving tool, after he had made it a molten calf: and they said, These be thy gods, O Israel, which brought thee up out of the land of Egypt.

5 And when Aaron saw it, he built an altar before it; and Aaron made proclamation, and said, To morrow is a feast to the LORD.

6 And they rose up early on the morrow, and offered burnt offerings, and brought peace offerings; and the people sat down to eat and to drink, and rose up to play.

7 ¶ And the LORD said unto Moses, Go, get thee down; for thy people, which thou broughtest out of the land of Egypt, have corrupted themselves:

8 They have turned aside quickly out of the way which I commanded them: they have made them a molten calf, and have worshipped it, and have sacrificed thereunto, and said, These be thy gods, O Israel, which have brought thee up out of the land of Egypt.

9 And the LORD said unto Moses, I have seen this people, and, behold, it is a stiffnecked people:

10 Now therefore let me alone, that my wrath may wax hot against them, and that I may consume them: and I will make of thee a great nation.

11 And Moses besought the LORD his God, and said, LORD, why doth thy wrath wax hot against thy people, which thou hast brought forth out of the land of Egypt with great power, and with a mighty hand?

12 Wherefore should the Egyptians speak, and say, For mischief did he bring them out, to slay them in the mountains, and to consume them from the face of the earth? Turn from thy fierce wrath, and repent of this evil against thy people.

13 Remember Abraham, Isaac, and Israel, thy servants, to whom thou swarest by thine own self, and saidst unto them, I will multiply your seed as the stars of heaven, and all this land that I have spoken of will I give unto your seed, and they shall inherit it for ever.

14 And the LORD repented of the evil which he thought to do unto his people.

15 ¶ And Moses turned, and went down from the mount, and the two tables of the testimony were in his hand: the tables were written on both their sides; on the one side and on the other were they written.

16 And the tables were the work of God, and the writing was the writing of God, graven upon the tables.

religion, and our families. The death of an individual is not necessarily wrong (as in defensive response), but rather the reason for the death as the result of another's actions is the factor in determining whether it is a sin.

7. *Thou shalt not commit adultery* (Ex. 20:14).

This is crystal clear. The real problem is staying off the road toward adultery and fornication. This requires staying on the straight and narrow path with absolutely NO flirtatious behavior.

8. *Thou shalt not steal* (Ex. 20:15).

This applies to all acts of integrity and honesty. One cannot claim another's possessions, ideas, or what is due another in any form.

9. *Thou shalt not bear false witness* (Ex. 20:16).

One cannot in any form pass any information as if it were true to another that would harm or hurt another. Lies, gossip, rumor, and so-called truth must be stopped with you. A good test—Is it kind? Is it true? And is it necessary?

10. *Thou shalt not covet* (Ex. 20:17).

When one becomes covetous it can be the beginning of so many sins. The Ten Commandments, as well as all the commandments of God, are interrelated and interwoven to such an extent that in breaking one causes us to break another or leads to another sin. Such is covetousness.

Exodus 20:20—Seek the Face of the Lord Always

The Lord commands Israel to seek Him and His presence, to be His peculiar covenant people (i.e., His 'own'), and to be holy in their walk of life. The test of life (the proving of ourselves worthy) is ongoing and difficult. Surely that is why Nephi as he was closing 2 Nephi said these immortal words, "Wherefore, ye must press forward with a steadfastness in Christ, having a perfect brightness of hope, and a love of God and of all men. Wherefore, if ye shall press forward, feasting upon the word of Christ, and endure to the end, behold, thus saith the Father: Ye shall have eternal life. And now, behold, my beloved brethren, this is the way: and there is none other way nor name given under heaven whereby man can be saved in the kingdom of God. And now, behold, this is the doctrine of Christ, and the only and true doctrine of the Father, and of the Son, and of the Holy Ghost, which is one God, without end. Amen" (2 Ne. 31:20–21).

EXODUS CHAPTER 32

Exodus 32:12—JST

The Joseph Smith Translation renders this verse as follows: "Wherefore should the Egyptians speak, and say, For mischief did he bring them out, to slay them in the mountains, and to consume them from the face of the earth? Turn from thy fierce wrath. Thy people will repent of this evil; therefore come thou not out against them" (JST Ex. 32:12).

Exodus 32:12–13—Moses as Advocate

The wrath of the Lord was kindled when He beheld that the people had arranged for the creation of a golden calf to worship while the prophet was away in the mount.

17 And when Joshua heard the noise of the people as they shouted, he said unto Moses, There is a noise of war in the camp.

18 And he said, It is not the voice of them that shout for mastery, neither is it the voice of them that cry for being overcome: but the noise of them that sing do I hear.

19 ¶ And it came to pass, as soon as he came nigh unto the camp, that he saw the calf, and the dancing: and Moses' anger waxed hot, and he cast the tables out of his hands, and brake them beneath the mount.

20 And he took the calf which they had made, and burnt it in the fire, and ground it to powder, and strawed it upon the water, and made the children of Israel drink of it.

21 And Moses said unto Aaron, What did this people unto thee, that thou hast brought so great a sin upon them?

22 And Aaron said, Let not the anger of my lord wax hot: thou knowest the people, that they are set on mischief.

23 For they said unto me, Make us gods, which shall go before us: for as for this Moses, the man that brought us up out of the land of Egypt, we wot not what is become of him.

24 And I said unto them, Whosoever hath any gold, let them break it off. So they gave it me: then I cast it into the fire, and there came out this calf.

25 ¶ And when Moses saw that the people were naked; (for Aaron had made them naked unto their shame among their enemies:)

26 Then Moses stood in the gate of the camp, and said, Who is on the LORD's side? let him come unto me. And all the sons of Levi gathered themselves together unto him.

27 And he said unto them, Thus saith the LORD God of Israel, Put every man his sword by his side, and go in and out from gate to gate throughout the camp, and slay every man his brother, and every man his companion, and every man his neighbour.

28 And the children of Levi did according to the word of Moses: and there fell of the people that day about three thousand men.

29 For Moses had said, Consecrate yourselves to day to the LORD, even every man upon his son, and upon his brother; that he may bestow upon you a blessing this day.

30 ¶ And it came to pass on the morrow, that Moses said unto the people, Ye have sinned a great sin: and now I will go up unto the LORD; peradventure I shall make an atonement for your sin.

31 And Moses returned unto the LORD, and said, Oh, this people have sinned a great sin, and have made them gods of gold.

32 Yet now, if thou wilt forgive their sin—; and if not, blot me, I pray thee, out of thy book which thou hast written.

33 And the LORD said unto Moses, Whosoever hath sinned against me, him will I blot out of my book.

34 Therefore now go, lead the people unto the place of which I have spoken unto thee: behold, mine Angel shall go before thee: nevertheless in the day when I visit I will visit their sin upon them.

35 And the LORD plagued the people, because they made the calf, which Aaron made.

But Moses, in the role of advocate, quickly puts forth a valid reason for having the Lord refrain from destroying the people: the Egyptians would render a judgment of "mischief" against the Lord for having delivered the people from Egypt only to destroy them. Moses then invokes the spirit of the Abraham covenant, which provided for the unfolding of a mighty nation from the patriarchal lineage. The Lord responds with a specifically covenant position: If the people repent, they shall not be destroyed.

Exodus 32:14—JST
The Joseph Smith Translation renders this verse as follows: "And the Lord said unto Moses, If they will repent of the evil which they have done, I will spare them, and turn away my fierce wrath; but, behold, thou shalt execute judgment upon all that will not repent of this evil this day. Therefore, see thou do this thing that I have commanded thee, or I will execute all that which I had thought to do unto my people" (JST Ex. 32:14).

Exodus 32:15–35—Aaron
Aaron's life was marked at times by the spirit of penitence and remorse. During the time Moses spent upon the holy mount receiving the tablets of the covenant, Aaron yielded to the enticings of the people in their desire for idols by preparing for them a golden calf, which the people welcomed with the words, "These be thy gods, O Israel, which brought thee up out of the land of Egypt" (Ex. 32:4). When Moses returned and chastised his brother, Aaron supplicated: "Let not the anger of my lord wax hot: thou knowest the people, that they are set on mischief" (Ex. 32:22). It took then the atoning intervention of Moses before the Lord to settle the matter, but not before the erring Israelites were severely punished (see Ex. 32:33–35; Deut. 9:20–26; compare the words of Stephen in Acts 7:37–42).

Apis the Bull of Memphis

CHAPTER 33

1 AND the LORD said unto Moses, Depart, and go up hence, thou and the people which thou hast brought up out of the land of Egypt, unto the land which I sware unto Abraham, to Isaac, and to Jacob, saying, Unto thy seed will I give it:

2 And I will send an angel before thee; and I will drive out the Canaanite, the Amorite, and the Hittite, and the Perizzite, the Hivite, and the Jebusite:

3 Unto a land flowing with milk and honey: for I will not go up in the midst of thee; for thou art a stiffnecked people: lest I consume thee in the way.

4 ¶ And when the people heard these evil tidings, they mourned: and no man did put on him his ornaments.

5 For the LORD had said unto Moses, Say unto the children of Israel, Ye are a stiffnecked people: I will come up into the midst of thee in a moment, and consume thee: therefore now put off thy ornaments from thee, that I may know what to do unto thee.

6 And the children of Israel stripped themselves of their ornaments by the mount Horeb.

7 And Moses took the tabernacle, and pitched it without the camp, afar off from the camp, and called it the Tabernacle of the congregation. And it came to pass, that every one which sought the LORD went out unto the tabernacle of the congregation, which was without the camp.

8 And it came to pass, when Moses went out unto the tabernacle, that all the people rose up, and stood every man at his tent door, and looked after Moses, until he was gone into the tabernacle.

9 And it came to pass, as Moses entered into the tabernacle, the cloudy pillar descended, and stood at the door of the tabernacle, and the Lord talked with Moses.

10 And all the people saw the cloudy pillar stand at the tabernacle door: and all the people rose up and worshipped, every man in his tent door.

11 And the LORD spake unto Moses face to face, as a man speaketh unto his friend. And he turned again into the camp: but his servant Joshua, the son of Nun, a young man, departed not out of the tabernacle.

12 ¶ And Moses said unto the LORD, See, thou sayest unto me, Bring up this people: and thou hast not let me know whom thou wilt send with me. Yet thou hast said, I know thee by name, and thou hast also found grace in my sight.

13 Now therefore, I pray thee, if I have found grace in thy sight, shew me now thy way, that I may know thee, that I may find grace in thy sight: and consider that this nation is thy people.

14 And he said, My presence shall go with thee, and I will give thee rest.

15 And he said unto him, If thy presence go not with me, carry us not up hence.

16 For wherein shall it be known here that I and thy people have found grace in thy sight? is it not in that thou goest with us? so shall we be separated, I and thy people, from all the people that are upon the face of the earth.

17 And the LORD said unto Moses, I will do this thing also that thou hast spoken: for thou hast found grace in my sight, and I know thee by name.

18 And he said, I beseech thee, shew me thy glory.

EXODUS CHAPTER 33

Exodus 33:1–14—The Lesser Order

The Lord imparts to us truth and blessings according to our willingness and capacity to receive, adding grace for grace, line upon line.

The Israelites were unwilling to abide by the higher order (Melchizedek) and thus were given a lesser order of outward commandments, principles, and covenants called the "Law of Moses." This was to be their schoolmaster until such time as their hearts and minds were prepared to receive more light and truth. They were content to let Moses be their intermediary with the Lord, and noted with trepidation that Moses' face shone with glory after he spoke with the Lord.

We are given blessings according to our obedience. And likewise, blessings are withheld because of our disobedience (see D&C 82:10; 130:19–21). King Benjamin made it clear when he said, "And moreover I would desire that ye should consider on the blessed and happy state of those that keep the commandments of God. For behold, they are blessed in all things, both temporal and spiritual; and if they hold out faithful to the end they are received into heaven, that thereby they may dwell with God in a state of never-ending happiness. O remember, remember that these things are true; for the Lord God hath spoken it" (Mosiah 2:41).

19 And he said, I will make all my goodness pass before thee, and I will proclaim the name of the LORD before thee; and will be gracious to whom I will be gracious, and will shew mercy on whom I will shew mercy.

20 And he said, Thou canst not see my face: for there shall no man see me, and live.

21 And the LORD said, Behold, there is a place by me, and thou shalt stand upon a rock:

22 And it shall come to pass, while my glory passeth by, that I will put thee in a clift of the rock, and will cover thee with my hand while I pass by:

23 And I will take away mine hand, and thou shalt see my back parts: but my face shall not be seen.

CHAPTER 34

1 AND the LORD said unto Moses, Hew thee two tables of stone like unto the first: and I will write upon these tables the words that were in the first tables, which thou brakest.

2 And be ready in the morning, and come up in the morning unto mount Sinai, and present thyself there to me in the top of the mount.

3 And no man shall come up with thee, neither let any man be seen throughout all the mount; neither let the flocks nor herds feed before that mount.

4 ¶ And he hewed two tables of stone like unto the first; and Moses rose up early in the morning, and went up unto mount Sinai, as the LORD had commanded him, and took in his hand the two tables of stone.

5 And the LORD descended in the cloud, and stood with him there, and proclaimed the name of the LORD.

6 And the LORD passed by before him, and proclaimed, The LORD, The LORD God, merciful and gracious, longsuffering, and abundant in goodness and truth,

7 Keeping mercy for thousands, forgiving iniquity and transgression and sin, and that will by no means clear the guilty; visiting the iniquity of the fathers upon the children, and upon the children's children, unto the third and to the fourth generation.

8 And Moses made haste, and bowed his head toward the earth, and worshipped.

9 And he said, If now I have found grace in thy sight, O Lord, let my Lord, I pray thee, go among us; for it is a stiffnecked people; and pardon our iniquity and our sin, and take us for thine inheritance.

10 ¶ And he said, Behold, I make a covenant: before all thy people I will do marvels, such as have not been done in all the earth, nor in any nation: and all the people among which thou art shall see the work of the LORD: for it is a terrible thing that I will do with thee.

EXODUS CHAPTER 34

Exodus 34:1–2—JST

The Joseph Smith translation of the Bible provides an expanded rendition of the opening verses of Exodus 34, as follows:

And the Lord said unto Moses, Hew thee two other tables of stone, like unto the first, and I will write upon them also, the words of the law, according as they were written at the first on the tables which thou brakest; but it shall not be according to the first, for I will take away the priesthood out of their midst; therefore my holy order, and the ordinances thereof, shall not go before them; for my presence shall not go up in their midst, lest I destroy them.

But I will give unto them the law as at the first, but it shall be after the law of a carnal commandment; for I have sworn in my wrath, that they shall not enter into my presence, into my rest, in the days of their pilgrimage. Therefore do as I have commanded thee, and be ready in the morning, and come up in the morning unto mount Sinai, and present thyself there to me, in the top of the mount. (JST Ex. 34:1–2)

Moses Breaking the Tables of the Law by Gustave Doré

11 Observe thou that which I command thee this day: behold, I drive out before thee the Amorite, and the Canaanite, and the Hittite, and the Perizzite, and the Hivite, and the Jebusite.

12 Take heed to thyself, lest thou make a covenant with the inhabitants of the land whither thou goest, lest it be for a snare in the midst of thee:

13 But ye shall destroy their altars, break their images, and cut down their groves:

14 For thou shalt worship no other god: for the LORD, whose name is Jealous, is a jealous God:

15 Lest thou make a covenant with the inhabitants of the land, and they go a whoring after their gods, and do sacrifice unto their gods, and one call thee, and thou eat of his sacrifice;

16 And thou take of their daughters unto thy sons, and their daughters go a whoring after their gods, and make thy sons go a whoring after their gods.

17 Thou shalt make thee no molten gods.

18 ¶ The feast of unleavened bread shalt thou keep. Seven days thou shalt eat unleavened bread, as I commanded thee, in the time of the month Abib: for in the month Abib thou camest out from Egypt.

19 All that openeth the matrix is mine; and every firstling among thy cattle, whether ox or sheep, that is male.

20 But the firstling of an ass thou shalt redeem with a lamb: and if thou redeem him not, then shalt thou break his neck. All the firstborn of thy sons thou shalt redeem. And none shall appear before me empty.

21 ¶ Six days thou shalt work, but on the seventh day thou shalt rest: in earing time and in harvest thou shalt rest.

22 ¶ And thou shalt observe the feast of weeks, of the firstfruits of wheat harvest, and the feast of ingathering at the year's end.

23 ¶ Thrice in the year shall all your men children appear before the Lord GOD, the God of Israel.

24 For I will cast out the nations before thee, and enlarge thy borders: neither shall any man desire thy land, when thou shalt go up to appear before the LORD thy God thrice in the year.

25 Thou shalt not offer the blood of my sacrifice with leaven; neither shall the sacrifice of the feast of the passover be left unto the morning.

26 The first of the firstfruits of thy land thou shalt bring unto the house of the LORD thy God. Thou shalt not seethe a kid in his mother's milk.

27 And the LORD said unto Moses, Write thou these words: for after the tenor of these words I have made a covenant with thee and with Israel.

28 And he was there with the LORD forty days and forty nights; he did neither eat bread, nor drink water. And he wrote upon the tables the words of the covenant, the ten commandments.

29 ¶ And it came to pass, when Moses came down from mount Sinai with the two tables of testimony in Moses' hand, when he came down from the mount, that Moses wist not that the skin of his face shone while he talked with him.

30 And when Aaron and all the children of Israel saw Moses, behold, the skin of his face shone; and they were afraid to come nigh him.

31 And Moses called unto them; and Aaron and all the rulers of the congregation returned unto him: and Moses talked with them.

 POINT OF INTEREST

Commandment	Then	Now
1. No other gods.	Ex. 34:10–14 Deut. 5:6–7	D&C 76:1–4
2. Not make graven image.	Ex. 34:17 Deut. 4:15–19	D&C 1:15–16
3. Not take the name of the Lord in vain.	Lev. 19:12 Deut. 5:11	D&C 63:61–62
4. Keep the Sabbath holy.	Ex. 31:12–17 Deut. 5:12–15	D&C 59:9–13
5. Honor father and mother.	Ex. 21:15, 17 Deut. 21:18–21	D&C 27:9
6. Not kill.	Ex. 21:12–14 Deut. 5:17	D&C 42:18–19, 79
7. Not commit adultery.	Ex. 22:16–17 Deut. 5:18	D&C 42:22–26, 74–81
8. Not steal.	Lev. 19:13 Deut. 5:19	D&C 42:20, 84–85
9. Not bear false witness.	Ps. 101:7 Deut. 5:20	D&C 42:21, 27, 86
10. Not covet.	Prov. 28:16 Deut. 5:21–22	D&C 19:25–26

32 And afterward all the children of Israel came nigh: and he gave them in commandment all that the LORD had spoken with him in mount Sinai.

33 And till Moses had done speaking with them, he put a vail on his face.

34 But when Moses went in before the LORD to speak with him, he took the vail off, until he came out. And he came out, and spake unto the children of Israel that which he was commanded.

35 And the children of Israel saw the face of Moses, that the skin of Moses' face shone: and Moses put the vail upon his face again, until he went in to speak with him.

THE
FOURTH BOOK OF MOSES CALLED NUMBERS

CHAPTER 11

1 AND when the people complained, it displeased the LORD: and the LORD heard it; and his anger was kindled; and the fire of the LORD burnt among them, and consumed them that were in the uttermost parts of the camp.

2 And the people cried unto Moses; and when Moses prayed unto the LORD, the fire was quenched.

3 And he called the name of the place Taberah: because the fire of the LORD burnt among them.

4 ¶ And the mixt multitude that was among them fell a lusting: and the children of Israel also wept again, and said, Who shall give us flesh to eat?

5 We remember the fish, which we did eat in Egypt freely; the cucumbers, and the melons, and the leeks, and the onions, and the garlick:

6 But now our soul is dried away: there is nothing at all, beside this manna, before our eyes.

7 And the manna was as coriander seed, and the colour thereof as the colour of bdellium.

8 And the people went about, and gathered it, and ground it in mills, or beat it in a mortar, and baked it in pans, and made cakes of it: and the taste of it was as the taste of fresh oil.

9 And when the dew fell upon the camp in the night, the manna fell upon it.

Exodus 34:35—Illumination of Moses

The being of Moses was illuminated with the glory of the Lord, causing his face to radiate light. From the account of Moses on the mount (Pearl of Great Price) we learn more about this process of transfiguration:

And the presence of God withdrew from Moses, that his glory was not upon Moses; and Moses was left unto himself. And as he was left unto himself, he fell unto the earth.

And it came to pass that it was for the space of many hours before Moses did again receive his natural strength like unto man; and he said unto himself: Now, for this cause I know that man is nothing, which thing I never had supposed.

But now mine own eyes have beheld God; but not my natural, but my spiritual eyes, for my natural eyes could not have beheld; for I should have withered and died in his presence; but his glory was upon me; and I beheld his face, for I was transfigured before him. (Moses 1:911)

NUMBERS CHAPTER 11

"Remember all thy church, O Lord, with all their families. . . . That thy church may come forth out of the wilderness of darkness, and shine forth fair as the moon, clear as the sun, and terrible as an army with banners."
—Joseph Smith, Dedication of the Kirtland Temple, D&C 109:72

Numbers 11—Overview of Precepts and Principles

The kingdom of God is an effective matrix of organized leadership with the prophet at the head and many inspired workers to move the work forward. The priesthood of God operates on principles of humility and meekness. Pride and arrogance have no place in spiritual leadership. The Lord's choicest blessings are reserved for the faithful. Murmuring and fear are not qualities of the righteous. By keeping our vision focused on the Savior and His gospel, we will have the sure guidance needed to complete our mortal journey successfully.

When the Israelite nation was liberated from Egyptian bondage, it must have presented an ominous and impressive spectacle as it moved across the wilderness and toward the Promised Land. The ancient image of the army of God has been used in modern times as a reminder of the strength and forward thrust of God's purposes in establishing His kingdom in the latter-days (see D&C 10:31).

The idea of Israel's banners is also well established in the scriptures. Isaiah exclaims: "Lift ye up a banner upon the high mountain, exalt the voice unto them, shake the hand, that they may go into the gates of the nobles" (Isa. 13:2). General Moroni lifted up the banner (title) of liberty (see Alma 46:12–13, 36). Moses lifted up the brass image of a fiery serpent to remind the Israelites to think of the Savior and be saved (see Num. 21:9). We might also

10 ¶ Then Moses heard the people weep throughout their families, every man in the door of his tent: and the anger of the LORD was kindled greatly; Moses also was displeased.

11 And Moses said unto the LORD, Wherefore hast thou afflicted thy servant? and wherefore have I not found favour in thy sight, that thou layest the burden of all this people upon me?

12 Have I conceived all this people? have I begotten them, that thou shouldest say unto me, Carry them in thy bosom, as a nursing father beareth the sucking child, unto the land which thou swarest unto their fathers?

13 Whence should I have flesh to give unto all this people? for they weep unto me, saying, Give us flesh, that we may eat.

14 I am not able to bear all this people alone, because it is too heavy for me.

15 And if thou deal thus with me, kill me, I pray thee, out of hand, if I have found favour in thy sight; and let me not see my wretchedness.

16 ¶ And the LORD said unto Moses, Gather unto me seventy men of the elders of Israel, whom thou knowest to be the elders of the people, and officers over them; and bring them unto the tabernacle of the congregation, that they may stand there with thee.

17 And I will come down and talk with thee there: and I will take of the spirit which is upon thee, and will put it upon them; and they shall bear the burden of the people with thee, that thou bear it not thyself alone.

18 And say thou unto the people, Sanctify yourselves against to morrow, and ye shall eat flesh: for ye have wept in the ears of the LORD, saying, Who shall give us flesh to eat? for it was well with us in Egypt: therefore the LORD will give you flesh, and ye shall eat.

19 Ye shall not eat one day, nor two days, nor five days, neither ten days, nor twenty days;

20 But even a whole month, until it come out at your nostrils, and it be loathsome unto you: because that ye have despised the LORD which is among you, and have wept before him, saying, Why came we forth out of Egypt?

21 And Moses said, The people, among whom I am, are six hundred thousand footmen; and thou hast said, I will give them flesh, that they may eat a whole month.

22 Shall the flocks and the herds be slain for them, to suffice them? or shall all the fish of the sea be gathered together for them, to suffice them?

23 And the LORD said unto Moses, Is the LORD's hand waxed short? thou shalt see now whether my word shall come to pass unto thee or not.

24 ¶ And Moses went out, and told the people the words of the LORD, and gathered the seventy men of the elders of the people, and set them round about the tabernacle.

25 And the LORD came down in a cloud, and spake unto him, and took of the spirit that was upon him, and gave it unto the seventy elders: and it came to pass, that, when the spirit rested upon them, they prophesied, and did not cease.

26 But there remained two of the men in the camp, the name of the one was Eldad, and the name of the other Medad: and the spirit rested upon them; and they were of them that were written, but went not out unto the tabernacle: and they prophesied in the camp.

27 And there ran a young man, and told Moses, and said, Eldad and Medad do prophesy in the camp.

suppose that the liberated Israel had flags and banners hoisted during its march. If so, what those banners may have depicted is unknown; however, if we allow our imagination some license, we could suppose that such banners would represent some of the principles that should govern the movement of the army of God—such as (1) *teamwork* (everyone bearing a fair part of the load), (2) *loyalty* (rather than pridefully finding fault with the leaders or usurping their power), (3) *faith* (rather than murmuring and complaining), and (4) *vision* (keeping our eyes focused on the Savior, as on the brazen serpent that Moses lifted up on the pole).

Numbers 11:24–29—Shared Leadership: Many Hands to Bear the Load

The Kingdom of God is an effective matrix of organized leadership with the prophet at the head and many inspired workers to move the work forward.

Moses was weighed down with the responsibilities of leading the increasingly resistant and murmuring Israel. The Lord provided seventy elders to lighten his load. Joshua appealed to Moses to restrain two of the elders who were prophesying in the camp, but Moses saw it quite differently—he wished that all the Lord's people would be moved by the spirit of prophesy, for that is the way the Lord would have it.

Spiritual teamwork is a hallmark of a Zion society. If we choose to work alone we suffer lack of support, burn-out, and inability to complete the task. But together we gain added insight and wisdom, strength of numbers, comradery of fellowship in a common cause, enthusiasm from others, and the list goes on. Reflect on how Heavenly Father deals with mankind, and you can see the principle at work. If we are obedient we will become part of the "eternal team" to assist others to gain immortality and eternal life. Let us remember that all are entitled to revelation within their own role and stewardship.

Numbers 11:26–29—Eldad and Medad

Eldad (meaning: whom God has loved) and Medad (meaning: love) were two of the seventy elders called to give assistance to Moses during the sojourn in the wilderness (see Num. 11:25–26.)

It was reported to Moses by a young man that these two were prophesying, even though they failed to go to the tabernacle as appointed. When Joshua asked Moses to forbid them from prophesying, he responded with a statement that has since become a celebrated dictum: "And Moses said unto him, Enviest thou for my sake? would God that all the LORD's people were prophets, *and* that the LORD would put his spirit upon them! And Moses gat him into the camp, he and the elders of Israel" (Num. 11:29–30).

For more insight into Joshua, see Appendix P.

28 And Joshua the son of Nun, the servant of Moses, one of his young men, answered and said, My lord Moses, forbid them.

29 And Moses said unto him, Enviest thou for my sake? would God that all the LORD's people were prophets, and that the LORD would put his spirit upon them!

30 And Moses gat him into the camp, he and the elders of Israel.

31 ¶ And there went forth a wind from the LORD, and brought quails from the sea, and let them fall by the camp, as it were a day's journey on this side, and as it were a day's journey on the other side, round about the camp, and as it were two cubits high upon the face of the earth.

32 And the people stood up all that day, and all that night, and all the next day, and they gathered the quails: he that gathered least gathered ten homers: and they spread them all abroad for themselves round about the camp.

33 And while the flesh was yet between their teeth, ere it was chewed, the wrath of the LORD was kindled against the people, and the LORD smote the people with a very great plague.

34 And he called the name of that place Kibroth-hattaavah: because there they buried the people that lusted.

35 And the people journeyed from Kibroth-hattaavah unto Hazeroth; and abode at Hazeroth.

CHAPTER 12

1 AND Miriam and Aaron spake against Moses because of the Ethiopian woman whom he had married: for he had married an Ethiopian woman.

2 And they said, Hath the LORD indeed spoken only by Moses? hath he not spoken also by us? And the LORD heard it.

3 (Now the man Moses was very meek, above all the men which were upon the face of the earth.)

4 And the LORD spake suddenly unto Moses, and unto Aaron, and unto Miriam, Come out ye three unto the tabernacle of the congregation. And they three came out.

5 And the LORD came down in the pillar of the cloud, and stood in the door of the tabernacle, and called Aaron and Miriam: and they both came forth.

6 And he said, Hear now my words: If there be a prophet among you, I the LORD will make myself known unto him in a vision, and will speak unto him in a dream.

7 My servant Moses is not so, who is faithful in all mine house.

8 With him will I speak mouth to mouth, even apparently, and not in dark speeches; and the similitude of the LORD shall he behold: wherefore then were ye not afraid to speak against my servant Moses?

9 And the anger of the LORD was kindled against them; and he departed.

10 And the cloud departed from off the tabernacle; and, behold, Miriam became leprous, white as snow: and Aaron looked upon Miriam, and, behold, she was leprous.

11 And Aaron said unto Moses, Alas, my lord, I beseech thee, lay not the sin upon us, wherein we have done foolishly, and wherein we have sinned.

NUMBERS CHAPTER 12

Numbers 12:3—Humility Versus Taking Authority unto Ourselves

Miriam and Aaron complained against Moses and arrogated to themselves equal prophetic gifts. They were rebuked by the Lord, and Miriam was exiled for a week with leprosy. The Lord upheld his servant Moses as the chosen prophet and extolled his greatness as one who could speak face-to-face with the Lord. In our day, we must avoid finding fault with the Lord's anointed and instead sustain and uphold our ordained leaders with faith and humility.

The priesthood of God operates on principles of humility and meekness. Pride and arrogance have no place in spiritual leadership. Within the kingdom we truly must be careful, for we separate ourselves from our God when we separate ourselves from our prophets and leaders. Pride and self-sufficiency must be overcome with humility and becoming easily entreated so as to be willing to follow the brethren.

The house of humility is the grand venue for the outpouring of God's choicest blessings. To receive the gospel in humble meekness, and come unto Christ, is to make of our house a fortress built upon a rock—the solid foundation of eternal truth. We can think of the walls of the house of humility as holy emblems of four magnificent gifts: *divine guidance, revelation, grace,* and *strength.* When we are humble, the Lord will guide us and reveal to us His will in loving response to our earnest supplication.

From the windows of a humble house we are blessed with a glorious view of our possibilities as sons and daughters of God. As worthy tenants in the house of humility, we sacrifice "a broken heart and a contrite spirit" (3 Ne. 9:20), leading in turn to a "mighty change" (Mosiah 5:2) in our hearts through the atoning grace of Christ the Lord. As a result, we "always abound in good works" (Alma 7:24) and our inner vision is wondrously opened: "And we, ourselves, also, through the infinite goodness of God, and the manifestations of his Spirit, have great views of that which is to come; and were it expedient, we could prophesy of all things" (Mosiah 5:3).

Numbers 12:6–8—Moses' Prophetic Calling

Both Aaron and his sister Miriam had reprimanded Moses for taking an Ethiopian woman to wife. For this insubordination, the Lord called them to task by confirming the divine prophetic calling of Moses. In the remarkable words of theses verses, the Lord confirmed the authority and supreme commission of Moses, who did not learn the word of God just through visions and dreams, but in personal communion with the Almighty. Aaron turned away humbly from his offence and appealed for the healing of Miriam, who had been struck with leprosy. Through the intercession of Moses, the infraction was settled and Miriam was cured after a seven-day separation from the camp (see Num. 12:9–16).

12 Let her not be as one dead, of whom the flesh is half consumed when he cometh out of his mother's womb.

13 And Moses cried unto the LORD, saying, Heal her now, O God, I beseech thee.

14 ¶ And the LORD said unto Moses, If her father had but spit in her face, should she not be ashamed seven days? let her be shut out from the camp seven days, and after that let her be received in again.

15 And Miriam was shut out from the camp seven days: and the people journeyed not till Miriam was brought in again.

16 And afterward the people removed from Hazeroth, and pitched in the wilderness of Paran.

CHAPTER 13

1 AND the LORD spake unto Moses, saying,

2 Send thou men, that they may search the land of Canaan, which I give unto the children of Israel: of every tribe of their fathers shall ye send a man, every one a ruler among them.

3 And Moses by the commandment of the LORD sent them from the wilderness of Paran: all those men were heads of the children of Israel.

4 And these were their names: of the tribe of Reuben, Shammua the son of Zaccur.

5 Of the tribe of Simeon, Shaphat the son of Hori.

6 Of the tribe of Judah, Caleb the son of Jephunneh.

7 Of the tribe of Issachar, Igal the son of Joseph.

8 Of the tribe of Ephraim, Oshea the son of Nun.

9 Of the tribe of Benjamin, Palti the son of Raphu.

10 Of the tribe of Zebulun, Gaddiel the son of Sodi.

11 Of the tribe of Joseph, namely, of the tribe of Manasseh, Gaddi the son of Susi.

12 Of the tribe of Dan, Ammiel the son of Gemalli.

13 Of the tribe of Asher, Sethur the son of Michael.

14 Of the tribe of Naphtali, Nahbi the son of Vophsi.

15 Of the tribe of Gad, Geuel the son of Machi.

16 These are the names of the men which Moses sent to spy out the land. And Moses called Oshea the son of Nun Jehoshua.

17 ¶ And Moses sent them to spy out the land of Canaan, and said unto them, Get you up this way southward, and go up into the mountain:

18 And see the land, what it is; and the people that dwelleth therein, whether they be strong or weak, few or many;

19 And what the land is that they dwell in, whether it be good or bad; and what cities they be that they dwell in, whether in tents, or in strong holds;

20 And what the land is, whether it be fat or lean, whether there be wood therein, or not. And be ye of good courage, and bring of the fruit of the land. Now the time was the time of the firstripe grapes.

21 ¶ So they went up, and searched the land from the wilderness of Zin unto Rehob, as men come to Hamath.

22 And they ascended by the south, and came unto Hebron; where Ahiman, Sheshai, and Talmai, the children of Anak, were. (Now Hebron was built seven years before Zoan in Egypt.)

23 And they came unto the brook of Eshcol, and cut down from thence a branch with one cluster of grapes, and they bare it between two upon a staff; and they brought of the pomegranates, and of the figs.

NUMBERS CHAPTER 13

Numbers 13:30—Caleb

Caleb was one of the twelve princes, or heads of the tribes of Israel, whom Moses sent, by command of the Lord, to spy out the land of Canaan. Despite the fear of the people, Caleb wanted to go at once (see Num. 13:30). His companions resisted, saying: "We be not able to go up against the people; for they *are* stronger than we" (Num. 13:31). Thus all Israel shrank in fear and lamented the situation facing them in Canaan—even wanting at that moment to return to Egypt.

The anger of the Lord was kindled against the Israelites for their murmuring and lack of faith in His power. It took the earnest supplication of Moses to dissuade the Lord from sending destruction upon the people in that very hour. Though the murmurers were pardoned, those twenty years of age and older were disenfranchised as to their right to enter the Promised Land at the conclusion of the sojourn in the wilderness (see Num. 14:29). Those of faith and courage would, however, enter therein (see Num. 14:24, 30). As to the other scouts who returned a report of fear to the people: they perished according to the judgment of God:

Caleb of the tribe of Judah received an inheritance in the Promised Land and, as man of 85 years, left his testimony as a legacy of faith and courage (see Josh. 14:6–14; see also Josh. 15:13–18, 42–49; 21:12; Num. 34:19; Judges 1:12–15, 20; 1 Chron. 4:15; 6:56.)

24 The place was called the brook Eshcol, because of the cluster of grapes which the children of Israel cut down from thence.

25 And they returned from searching of the land after forty days.

26 ¶ And they went and came to Moses, and to Aaron, and to all the congregation of the children of Israel, unto the wilderness of Paran, to Kadesh; and brought back word unto them, and unto all the congregation, and shewed them the fruit of the land.

27 And they told him, and said, We came unto the land whither thou sentest us, and surely it floweth with milk and honey; and this is the fruit of it.

28 Nevertheless the people be strong that dwell in the land, and the cities are walled, and very great: and moreover we saw the children of Anak there.

29 The Amalekites dwell in the land of the south: and the Hittites, and the Jebusites, and the Amorites, dwell in the mountains: and the Canaanites dwell by the sea, and by the coast of Jordan.

30 And Caleb stilled the people before Moses, and said, Let us go up at once, and possess it; for we are well able to overcome it.

31 But the men that went up with him said, We be not able to go up against the people; for they are stronger than we.

32 And they brought up an evil report of the land which they had searched unto the children of Israel, saying, The land, through which we have gone to search it, is a land that eateth up the inhabitants thereof; and all the people that we saw in it are men of a great stature.

33 And there we saw the giants, the sons of Anak, which come of the giants: and we were in our own sight as grasshoppers, and so we were in their sight.

CHAPTER 14

1 AND all the congregation lifted up their voice, and cried; and the people wept that night.

2 And all the children of Israel murmured against Moses and against Aaron: and the whole congregation said unto them, Would God that we had died in the land of Egypt! or would God we had died in this wilderness!

3 And wherefore hath the LORD brought us unto this land, to fall by the sword, that our wives and our children should be a prey? were it not better for us to return into Egypt?

4 And they said one to another, Let us make a captain, and let us return into Egypt.

5 Then Moses and Aaron fell on their faces before all the assembly of the congregation of the children of Israel.

6 ¶ And Joshua the son of Nun, and Caleb the son of Jephunneh, which were of them that searched the land, rent their clothes:

POINT OF INTEREST

Each of the Twelve Tribes is described allegorically in Gen. 49, and symbols for the tribes have been derived from these descriptions, as well as from other biblical passages. The emblems are arranged in a number of different ways, depending on your source. These are clockwise, according to a bar mitzvah medal.

1) *Simeon is a tower. "And the tribes of Israel were gathered together" (Deut. 33:5).*

2) *Levi is the ephod or breastplate of the high priest. "They shall teach Jacob thy judgments, and Israel thy law" (Deut. 33:10).*

3) *"Judah is a lion's whelp" (Gen. 49:9).*

4) *Zebulun is a ship. "Zebulun shall dwell at the haven of the sea; and he shall be for an haven of ships" (Gen. 49:13).*

5) *"Issachar is a strong ass couching down between two burdens" (Gen. 49:14).*

6) *Dan is the scales of justice. "Dan shall judge his people" (Gen. 49:16).*

7) *Gad is a tent. "He shall overcome at the last" (Gen. 49:19).*

8) *"Naftali is a hind [deer] let loose" (Gen. 49:21).*

9) *Benjamin is a wolf. "In the morning he shall devour the prey" (Gen. 49:27).*

10) *Asher is an olive tree. "Out of Asher his bread shall be fat" (Gen. 49:20).*

11) *Joseph is a sheaf of wheat. "Blessed of the Lord be his land" (Deut. 49:13).*

12) *Reuben is the sun. "Thou art . . . the excellency of dignity, and the excellency of power" (Gen. 49:3).*

7 And they spake unto all the company of the children of Israel, saying, The land, which we passed through to search it, is an exceeding good land.

8 If the LORD delight in us, then he will bring us into this land, and give it us; a land which floweth with milk and honey.

9 Only rebel not ye against the LORD, neither fear ye the people of the land; for they are bread for us: their defence is departed from them, and the LORD is with us: fear them not.

10 But all the congregation bade stone them with stones. And the glory of the LORD appeared in the tabernacle of the congregation before all the children of Israel.

11 ¶ And the LORD said unto Moses, How long will this people provoke me? and how long will it be ere they believe me, for all the signs which I have shewed among them?

12 I will smite them with the pestilence, and disinherit them, and will make of thee a greater nation and mightier than they.

13 ¶ And Moses said unto the LORD, Then the Egyptians shall hear it, (for thou broughtest up this people in thy might from among them;)

14 And they will tell it to the inhabitants of this land: for they have heard that thou LORD art among this people, that thou LORD art seen face to face, and that thy cloud standeth over them, and that thou goest before them, by day time in a pillar of a cloud, and in a pillar of fire by night.

15 ¶ Now if thou shalt kill all this people as one man, then the nations which have heard the fame of thee will speak, saying,

16 Because the LORD was not able to bring this people into the land which he sware unto them, therefore he hath slain them in the wilderness.

17 And now, I beseech thee, let the power of my LORD be great, according as thou hast spoken, saying,

18 The LORD is longsuffering, and of great mercy, forgiving iniquity and transgression, and by no means clearing the guilty, visiting the iniquity of the fathers upon the children unto the third and fourth generation.

19 Pardon, I beseech thee, the iniquity of this people according unto the greatness of thy mercy, and as thou hast forgiven this people, from Egypt even until now.

20 And the LORD said, I have pardoned according to thy word:

21 But as truly as I live, all the earth shall be filled with the glory of the LORD.

22 Because all those men which have seen my glory, and my miracles, which I did in Egypt and in the wilderness, and have tempted me now these ten times, and have not hearkened to my voice;

23 Surely they shall not see the land which I sware unto their fathers, neither shall any of them that provoked me see it:

24 But my servant Caleb, because he had another spirit with him, and hath followed me fully, him will I bring into the land whereinto he went; and his seed shall possess it.

25 (Now the Amalekites and the Canaanites dwelt in the valley.) To morrow turn you, and get you into the wilderness by the way of the Red sea.

26 ¶ And the LORD spake unto Moses and unto Aaron, saying,

27 How long shall I bear with this evil congregation, which murmur against me? I have heard the murmurings of the children of Israel, which they murmur against me.

28 Say unto them, As truly as I live, saith the LORD, as ye have spoken in mine ears, so will I do to you:

NUMBERS CHAPTER 14

Numbers 14:9—Faith Does Not Murmur

The Lord's choicest blessings are reserved for the faithful. Murmuring and fear are not qualities of the righteous.

The children of Israel displayed a chronic tendency to murmur, find fault, focus on memories of the abundance of their former Egyptian life, and complain against Moses and the Lord. In his wrath, the Lord plagued them a surfeit of meat so that they can be consumed in their greed. When their twelve captains were sent to spy out the Promised Land, ten of them succumbed to fear in the face of the enemy and brought back news of hopelessness. Only Joshua and Caleb had the faith to see Israel victorious with the help of the Lord.

The Lord swore that the murmuring people would not enter the Promised Land. When we exercise our **faith** we will overcome doubt and fear. When we **love** our Heavenly Father we will recognize our strength through Him and the power to do all things (see 1 John 4:18). As we **prepare** we will not fear (see D&C 38:30). **Knowledge** of the Plan of Happiness fills us with hope to carry us through those difficult times. **Experience** builds within us the confidence of our abilities to do all things that the Lord would have us do.

29 Your carcases shall fall in this wilderness; and all that were numbered of you, according to your whole number, from twenty years old and upward, which have murmured against me,

30 Doubtless ye shall not come into the land, concerning which I sware to make you dwell therein, save Caleb the son of Jephunneh, and Joshua the son of Nun.

31 But your little ones, which ye said should be a prey, them will I bring in, and they shall know the land which ye have despised.

32 But as for you, your carcases, they shall fall in this wilderness.

33 And your children shall wander in the wilderness forty years, and bear your whoredoms, until your carcases be wasted in the wilderness.

34 After the number of the days in which ye searched the land, even forty days, each day for a year, shall ye bear your iniquities, even forty years, and ye shall know my breach of promise.

35 I the LORD have said, I will surely do it unto all this evil congregation, that are gathered together against me: in this wilderness they shall be consumed, and there they shall die.

36 And the men, which Moses sent to search the land, who returned, and made all the congregation to murmur against him, by bringing up a slander upon the land,

37 Even those men that did bring up the evil report upon the land, died by the plague before the LORD.

38 But Joshua the son of Nun, and Caleb the son of Jephunneh, which were of the men that went to search the land, lived still.

39 And Moses told these sayings unto all the children of Israel: and the people mourned greatly.

40 ¶ And they rose up early in the morning, and gat them up into the top of the mountain, saying, Lo, we be here, and will go up unto the place which the LORD hath promised: for we have sinned.

41 And Moses said, Wherefore now do ye transgress the commandment of the LORD? but it shall not prosper.

42 Go not up, for the LORD is not among you; that ye be not smitten before your enemies.

43 For the Amalekites and the Canaanites are there before you, and ye shall fall by the sword: because ye are turned away from the LORD, therefore the LORD will not be with you.

44 But they presumed to go up unto the hill top: nevertheless the ark of the covenant of the LORD, and Moses, departed not out of the camp.

45 Then the Amalekites came down, and the Canaanites which dwelt in that hill, and smote them, and discomfited them, even unto Hormah.

Return of the Spies from the Land of Promise by Gustave Doré

POINT OF INTEREST

Just a few months after the people of Israel had left Egypt and had been given the law, they were told that it was time for them to take possession of the promised land. Following that commandment from the Lord, a group was sent to Canaan to determine conditions there. They returned, reporting that the land was rich and fertile—and as an indication of exactly how fertile it was, they carried back a cluster of grapes as evidence of the verdant produce that grew there (see Num. 13:23). Despite their glowing report, all but Joshua and Caleb felt that there was no possibility the current inhabitants could be driven out. When Joshua and Caleb argued differently, the people wanted to have them stoned (see Num. 14:10). At that point, feeling the great anger of the Lord, Moses pleaded in prayer for mercy on behalf of the people (see Num. 14:13–14). As a result, the Israelites were not destroyed—but neither were they able to enter and possess the promised land at that time. Instead, they had to wander in the wilderness of Sinai for the next thirty-eight years. All of those over the age of twenty who dismissed the possibility that the Lord could have helped them gain possession of the promised land—which, of course, did not include Joshua and Caleb—died while they wandered in the wilderness.

CHAPTER 21

1 AND when king Arad the Canaanite, which dwelt in the south, heard tell that Israel came by the way of the spies; then he fought against Israel, and took some of them prisoners.

2 And Israel vowed a vow unto the LORD, and said, If thou wilt indeed deliver this people into my hand, then I will utterly destroy their cities.

3 And the LORD hearkened to the voice of Israel, and delivered up the Canaanites; and they utterly destroyed them and their cities: and he called the name of the place Hormah.

4 ¶ And they journeyed from mount Hor by the way of the Red sea, to compass the land of Edom: and the soul of the people was much discouraged because of the way.

5 And the people spake against God, and against Moses, Wherefore have ye brought us up out of Egypt to die in the wilderness? for there is no bread, neither is there any water; and our soul loatheth this light bread.

6 And the LORD sent fiery serpents among the people, and they bit the people; and much people of Israel died.

7 ¶ Therefore the people came to Moses, and said, We have sinned, for we have spoken against the LORD, and against thee; pray unto the LORD, that he take away the serpents from us. And Moses prayed for the people.

8 And the LORD said unto Moses, Make thee a fiery serpent, and set it upon a pole: and it shall come to pass, that every one that is bitten, when he looketh upon it, shall live.

9 And Moses made a serpent of brass, and put it upon a pole, and it came to pass, that if a serpent had bitten any man, when he beheld the serpent of brass, he lived.

10 ¶ And the children of Israel set forward, and pitched in Oboth.

11 And they journeyed from Oboth, and pitched at Ije-abarim, in the wilderness which is before Moab, toward the sunrising.

12 ¶ From thence they removed, and pitched in the valley of Zared.

13 From thence they removed, and pitched on the other side of Arnon, which is in the wilderness that cometh out of the coasts of the Amorites: for Arnon is the border of Moab, between Moab and the Amorites.

14 Wherefore it is said in the book of the wars of the LORD, What he did in the Red sea, and in the brooks of Arnon,

15 And at the stream of the brooks that goeth down to the dwelling of Ar, and lieth upon the border of Moab.

16 And from thence they went to Beer: that is the well whereof the LORD spake unto Moses, Gather the people together, and I will give them water.

17 ¶ Then Israel sang this song, Spring up, O well; sing ye unto it:

18 The princes digged the well, the nobles of the people digged it, by the direction of the lawgiver, with their staves. And from the wilderness they went to Mattanah:

19 And from Mattanah to Nahaliel: and from Nahaliel to Bamoth:

20 And from Bamoth in the valley, that is in the country of Moab, to the top of Pisgah, which looketh toward Jeshimon.

21 ¶ And Israel sent messengers unto Sihon king of the Amorites, saying,

22 Let me pass through thy land: we will not turn into the fields, or into the vineyards; we will not drink of the waters of the well: but we will go along by the king's high way, until we be past thy borders.

NUMBERS CHAPTER 21

Numbers 21:9—Look to Christ and Live

The Lord responded to the faithless murmuring of the Israelites by sending fiery serpents to humble them. He commanded Moses to set up a token of safety in the form of a brass serpent—signifying the Redeemer—so that all who would focus their eyes on this sign would live. The symbolism, which has endured over the millennia, is a powerful reminder that we must take upon ourselves the name of Christ and live by all the principles and ordinances of the gospel if we are to have the hope of salvation.

The only name under heaven whereby man can be saved is Jesus Christ. We live by His gospel, His priesthood, and His Church and kingdom. We take upon us His name and make life-saving covenants always to remember Him and keep His commandments. Then, in His Holy House, the Temple of our Lord, we make sacred covenants, which will bless us for time and all eternity. This is life eternal to know God and Jesus Christ whom he has sent (see John 17:3). Yes, we must look to Christ and God our Father and then we can live now and forever in righteousness. By keeping our vision focused on the Savior and His gospel, we will have the sure guidance needed to complete our mortal journey successfully.

Numbers 21:33–35—Og

Og (pronounced "ahg" or "ohg"; meaning: giant, or long-necked) was king of Bashan—"the land of giants" (Deut. 3:13)—at the time Moses and the Israelites were advancing into Canaanite territory. After the defeat of the Amorites, Moses and his army were assaulted by Og and his forces, who were of a race of large-statured people.

The territories of the Amorites and Og were given by Moses to the tribes of Gad and Reuben and half the tribe of Manasseh (see Num. 32:33–34; Deut. 3:12–13; Josh. 13:12; 30–31; Neh. 9:22), with Manasseh receiving, in general, the territory that had been possessed by Og.

Og was iconic in his size: "For only Og king of Bashan remained of the remnant of giants; behold, his bedstead [or possibly sarcophagus] *was* a bedstead of iron; *is* it not in Rabbath of the children of Ammon? nine cubits *was* the length thereof [over 13 feet], and four cubits the breadth of it [nearly six feet], after the cubit of a man" (Deut. 3:11). Despite his imposing stature, Og and his giant warriors were readily removed by the Israelite forces and became for generations a symbol of the inexorable advance of the kingdom of the Lord (see Ps. 135:10–12; compare Ps. 136:18–21).

Numbers 21:34—Sihon

Sihon was king of the Amorites. When he refused to allow the Israelites to pass through his land and instead rose up in battle against them, Moses and his armies defeated them decisively and possessed their territory (see Num. 21:21–35). This triumph over the enemy became an ensign of God's power of deliverance for generations (see Deut. 1:4; 2:26–32; 3:2, 6; 29:7; 31:4; Josh. 2:10; 9:10; 12:2, 5; 13:10, 21, 27; Judges 11:19–21; 1 Kings 4:19; Neh. 9:22; Ps. 135:11; 136:19; Jer. 48:45).

23 And Sihon would not suffer Israel to pass through his border: but Sihon gathered all his people together, and went out against Israel into the wilderness: and he came to Jahaz, and fought against Israel.

24 And Israel smote him with the edge of the sword, and possessed his land from Arnon unto Jabbok, even unto the children of Ammon: for the border of the children of Ammon was strong.

25 And Israel took all these cities: and Israel dwelt in all the cities of the Amorites, in Heshbon, and in all the villages thereof.

26 For Heshbon was the city of Sihon the king of the Amorites, who had fought against the former king of Moab, and taken all his land out of his hand, even unto Arnon.

27 Wherefore they that speak in proverbs say, Come into Heshbon, let the city of Sihon be built and prepared:

28 For there is a fire gone out of Heshbon, a flame from the city of Sihon: it hath consumed Ar of Moab, and the lords of the high places of Arnon.

29 Woe to thee, Moab! thou art undone, O people of Chemosh: he hath given his sons that escaped, and his daughters, into captivity unto Sihon king of the Amorites.

30 We have shot at them; Heshbon is perished even unto Dibon, and we have laid them waste even unto Nophah, which reacheth unto Medeba.

31 ¶ Thus Israel dwelt in the land of the Amorites.

32 And Moses sent to spy out Jaazer, and they took the villages thereof, and drove out the Amorites that were there.

33 ¶ And they turned and went up by the way of Bashan: and Og the king of Bashan went out against them, he, and all his people, to the battle at Edrei.

34 And the LORD said unto Moses, Fear him not: for I have delivered him into thy hand, and all his people, and his land; and thou shalt do to him as thou didst unto Sihon king of the Amorites, which dwelt at Heshbon.

35 So they smote him, and his sons, and all his people, until there was none left him alive: and they possessed his land.

CHAPTER 22

Balak offers money and cattle and great honors to Balaam to curse Israel—The Lord forbids Balaam so to do—An angel opposes Balaam on the way.

1 AND the children of Israel set forward, and pitched in the plains of Moab on this side Jordan by Jericho.

2 ¶ And Balak the son of Zippor saw all that Israel had done to the Amorites.

3 And Moab was sore afraid of the people, because they were many: and Moab was distressed because of the children of Israel.

4 And Moab said unto the elders of Midian, Now shall this company lick up all that are round about us, as the ox licketh up the grass of the field. And Balak the son of Zippor was king of the Moabites at that time.

5 He sent messengers therefore unto Balaam the son of Beor to Pethor, which is by the river of the land of the children of his people, to call him, saying, Behold, there is a people come out from Egypt: behold, they cover the face of the earth, and they abide over against me:

NUMBERS CHAPTER 22

The Story of Balaam

Great blessings flow when we aspire to the honor and glory of God, rather than to the honor and pride of the world. The purposes of God cannot be thwarted or altered by the hand of man. Our mission is to align ourselves with full devotion to the will of God and do all in our power to carry it out faithfully.

From the sad commentary about Balaam, the fallen prophet, we learn valuable lessons about motivation—both the kind that leads to destruction as well as the kind that will lead to great spiritual blessings. People who are spiritually motivated aspire to the honor of God and seek to do the will of God. They know that spiritual wealth is infinitely more glorious than the ephemeral accumulations of worldly goods and titles. They fear God in that they respect His justice; they love God in that they keep His commandments and strive to emulate His Son in all things. The honor of God, the will of God, and the justice of God are the interacting themes of the story of Balaam.

Numbers 22:5–41—Balaam

Balaam was a prophet who lived in Pethor, a city by the Euphrates (see Deut. 23:4; Num. 22:5). When the hosts of Israel were encamped on the plains of Moab, east of the Jordan River near Jericho, the king of the Moabites, Balak, took action to hire Balaam—who apparently had the reputation of divine influence—for the purpose of cursing Israel. Israel was perceived as a distinct threat to the Moabites and their confederate associates, the Midianites. Balak said therefore to Balaam: "Come now therefore, I pray thee, curse me this people; for they *are* too mighty for me: peradventure I shall prevail, *that* we may smite them, and *that* I may drive them out of the land: for I wot that he whom thou blessest *is* blessed, and he whom thou cursest is cursed" (Num. 22:6). Because Balak's delegation came "with the rewards of divination in their hand" (Num. 22:7), Balaam agreed to approach the Lord on their behalf. But the message was not to their liking, for the Lord adjured Balaam: "Thou shalt not go with them; thou shalt not curse the people: for they *are* blessed" (Num. 22:12). Still, Balak insisted, so Balaam supplicated the Lord again and received permission to go, provided he would do according to the Lord's command. So Balaam went, though "God's anger was kindled because he went" (Num. 22:22).

It was then that the famous event took place manifesting that Balaam's means of transportation (his donkey) had more spiritual discernment than Balaam himself (see Num. 22:27–35.)

Thereafter, Balak enjoined Balaam three times to view the hosts of Israel and perform the cursing that he had paid for. But each time the answer came back in almost rhapsodic affirmation that Israel was to be blessed by the Lord, rather than cursed (see Num. 23:19–24; 24:4–9.)

6 Come now therefore, I pray thee, curse me this people; for they are too mighty for me: peradventure I shall prevail, that we may smite them, and that I may drive them out of the land: for I wot that he whom thou blessest is blessed, and he whom thou cursest is cursed.

7 And the elders of Moab and the elders of Midian departed with the rewards of divination in their hand; and they came unto Balaam, and spake unto him the words of Balak.

8 And he said unto them, Lodge here this night, and I will bring you word again, as the LORD shall speak unto me: and the princes of Moab abode with Balaam.

9 And God came unto Balaam, and said, What men are these with thee?

10 And Balaam said unto God, Balak the son of Zippor, king of Moab, hath sent unto me, saying,

11 Behold, there is a people come out of Egypt, which covereth the face of the earth: come now, curse me them; peradventure I shall be able to overcome them, and drive them out.

12 And God said unto Balaam, Thou shalt not go with them; thou shalt not curse the people: for they are blessed.

13 And Balaam rose up in the morning, and said unto the princes of Balak, Get you into your land: for the LORD refuseth to give me leave to go with you.

14 And the princes of Moab rose up, and they went unto Balak, and said, Balaam refuseth to come with us.

15 ¶ And Balak sent yet again princes, more, and more honourable than they.

16 And they came to Balaam, and said to him, Thus saith Balak the son of Zippor, Let nothing, I pray thee, hinder thee from coming unto me:

17 For I will promote thee unto very great honour, and I will do whatsoever thou sayest unto me: come therefore, I pray thee, curse me this people.

18 And Balaam answered and said unto the servants of Balak, If Balak would give me his house full of silver and gold, I cannot go beyond the word of the LORD my God, to do less or more.

19 Now therefore, I pray you, tarry ye also here this night, that I may know what the LORD will say unto me more.

20 And God came unto Balaam at night, and said unto him, If the men come to call thee, rise up, and go with them; but yet the word which I shall say unto thee, that shalt thou do.

21 And Balaam rose up in the morning, and saddled his ass, and went with the princes of Moab.

22 ¶ And God's anger was kindled because he went: and the angel of the LORD stood in the way for an adversary against him. Now he was riding upon his ass, and his two servants were with him.

23 And the ass saw the angel of the LORD standing in the way, and his sword drawn in his hand: and the ass turned aside out of the way, and went into the field: and Balaam smote the ass, to turn her into the way.

24 But the angel of the LORD stood in a path of the vineyards, a wall being on this side, and a wall on that side.

25 And when the ass saw the angel of the LORD, she thrust herself unto the wall, and crushed Balaam's foot against the wall: and he smote her again.

26 And the angel of the LORD went further, and stood in a narrow place, where was no way to turn either to the right hand or to the left.

The last straw for Balak was this ultimate prophecy from Balaam:

> . . . there shall come a Star out of Jacob, and a Sceptre shall rise out of Israel, and shall smite the corners of Moab, and destroy all the children of Sheth.
>
> And Edom shall be a possession, Seir also shall be a possession for his enemies; and Israel shall do valiantly.
>
> Out of Jacob shall come he that shall have dominion, and shall destroy him that remaineth of the city.
>
> Out of Jacob shall come he [i.e., the Messiah] that shall have dominion, and shall destroy him that remaineth of the city." (Num. 24:17–19)

Thereafter Balak and Balaam went their separate ways. But the Israelites had intimate contact with the Moabites and began to assimilate their pagan practices and immoral ways. Thus the Lord commanded Moses to strike out against the indigenous peoples and eliminate the evil influence of the Moabites and Midianites. The result was decisive: "And they slew the kings of Midian, beside the rest of them that were slain; *namely*, Evi, and Rekem, and Zur, and Hur, and Reba, five kings of Midian: Balaam also the son of Beor they slew with the sword" (Num. 31:8). Joshua later summarized the moral of the story, speaking in the words of the Lord: "Then Balak the son of Zippor, king of Moab, arose and warred against Israel, and sent and called Balaam the son of Beor to curse you: But I would not hearken unto Balaam; therefore he blessed you still: so I delivered you out of his hand" (Josh. 24:9–10).

Balaam is an exemplar of one with a grand potential but a lowly agenda. The Lord did not reach out to him as His mouthpiece, but graciously listened and responded when supplicated. The word of the Lord through Balaam served the divine interests of preparing the way for the people of Israel.

The Lord blesses His chosen people as they act in righteousness; those who act in His name in honor are enabled to proclaim the blessings of the covenant and uphold the divine purposes of heaven. Those who associate too closely with groups and individuals of an idolatrous cast, as did Balaam, will suffer the same fate as their masters.

Numbers 22:32—The Honor of God

Balaam was outwardly committed to uphold the honor of God, but in his heart he heeded the beckoning enticements of worldly wealth and prestige. Thus his vision was impaired as he set out on his journey, and he could not at first see the angel of the Lord standing to prevent his own self-destruction. To allow the entanglements of pride and vain ambition to take root in our hearts will obscure our view of heavenly objectives so apparent to the pure and faithful.

We cannot fool God, for He knows our hearts. We will not only be judged by our outward expressions of service, but even more so by the desires of our heart (see Alma 41:3–7). Surely this is why the Brethren speak so much

27 And when the ass saw the angel of the LORD, she fell down under Balaam: and Balaam's anger was kindled, and he smote the ass with a staff.

28 And the LORD opened the mouth of the ass, and she said unto Balaam, What have I done unto thee, that thou hast smitten me these three times?

29 And Balaam said unto the ass, Because thou hast mocked me: I would there were a sword in mine hand, for now would I kill thee.

30 And the ass said unto Balaam, Am not I thine ass, upon which thou hast ridden ever since I was thine unto this day? was I ever wont to do so unto thee? And he said, Nay.

31 Then the LORD opened the eyes of Balaam, and he saw the angel of the LORD standing in the way, and his sword drawn in his hand: and he bowed down his head, and fell flat on his face.

32 And the angel of the LORD said unto him, Wherefore hast thou smitten thine ass these three times? behold, I went out to withstand thee, because thy way is perverse before me:

33 And the ass saw me, and turned from me these three times: unless she had turned from me, surely now also I had slain thee, and saved her alive.

34 And Balaam said unto the angel of the LORD, I have sinned; for I knew not that thou stoodest in the way against me: now therefore, if it displease thee, I will get me back again.

35 And the angel of the LORD said unto Balaam, Go with the men: but only the word that I shall speak unto thee, that thou shalt speak. So Balaam went with the princes of Balak.

36 ¶ And when Balak heard that Balaam was come, he went out to meet him unto a city of Moab, which is in the border of Arnon, which is in the utmost coast.

37 And Balak said unto Balaam, Did I not earnestly send unto thee to call thee? wherefore camest thou not unto me? am I not able indeed to promote thee to honour?

38 And Balaam said unto Balak, Lo, I am come unto thee: have I now any power at all to say any thing? the word that God putteth in my mouth, that shall I speak.

39 And Balaam went with Balak, and they came unto Kirjath-huzoth.

40 And Balak offered oxen and sheep, and sent to Balaam, and to the princes that were with him.

41 And it came to pass on the morrow, that Balak took Balaam, and brought him up into the high places of Baal, that thence he might see the utmost part of the people.

CHAPTER 23

1 AND Balaam said unto Balak, Build me here seven altars, and prepare me here seven oxen and seven rams.

2 And Balak did as Balaam had spoken; and Balak and Balaam offered on every altar a bullock and a ram.

3 And Balaam said unto Balak, Stand by thy burnt offering, and I will go: peradventure the LORD will come to meet me: and whatsoever he sheweth me I will tell thee. And he went to an high place.

4 And God met Balaam: and he said unto him, I have prepared seven altars, and I have offered upon every altar a bullock and a ram.

5 And the LORD put a word in Balaam's mouth, and said, Return unto Balak, and thus thou shalt speak.

about "becoming" pure in heart, making our thoughts more pure, and preventing us from taking in or harboring evil thoughts of any nature. Surely Alma was right when he asked the question, "Have ye experienced this mighty change in your hearts?" (Alma 5:14). Without a pure heart we will eventually succumb to unrighteous thoughts and deeds.

Great blessings flow when we aspire to the honor and glory of God, rather than to the honor and pride of the world.

NUMBERS CHAPTER 23

Numbers 23:7—Syrians

The Syrians were a people of Semitic origin (see Gen. 10:22; 22:21) living in the ancient realm of Syria, north and northeast of Palestine, originally called "Aram," meaning highlands—hence the term *Aramaeans* is a general equivalent to the term Syrians. Aramaic became the language of diplomatic communication in the days of Hezekiah and gradually became the language of daily life among the Jewish people, thus the native language spoken by Jesus. The Syrians (or Aramaeans) were generally rivals of Israel.

Damascus was one of the chief cities of the Syrians. It was destroyed by the Assyrians (see 2 Kings 16:7–9). Syria later regained its prominence with Antioch as its capital. During the time of Jesus Syria was a Roman province.

6 And he returned unto him, and, lo, he stood by his burnt sacrifice, he, and all the princes of Moab.

7 And he took up his parable, and said, Balak the king of Moab hath brought me from Aram, out of the mountains of the east, saying, Come, curse me Jacob, and come, defy Israel.

8 How shall I curse, whom God hath not cursed? or how shall I defy, whom the LORD hath not defied?

9 For from the top of the rocks I see him, and from the hills I behold him: lo, the people shall dwell alone, and shall not be reckoned among the nations.

10 Who can count the dust of Jacob, and the number of the fourth part of Israel? Let me die the death of the righteous, and let my last end be like his!

11 And Balak said unto Balaam, What hast thou done unto me? I took thee to curse mine enemies, and, behold, thou hast blessed them altogether.

12 And he answered and said, Must I not take heed to speak that which the LORD hath put in my mouth?

13 And Balak said unto him, Come, I pray thee, with me unto another place, from whence thou mayest see them: thou shalt see but the utmost part of them, and shalt not see them all: and curse me them from thence.

14 ¶ And he brought him into the field of Zophim, to the top of Pisgah, and built seven altars, and offered a bullock and a ram on every altar.

15 And he said unto Balak, Stand here by thy burnt offering, while I meet the LORD yonder.

16 And the LORD met Balaam, and put a word in his mouth, and said, Go again unto Balak, and say thus.

17 And when he came to him, behold, he stood by his burnt offering, and the princes of Moab with him. And Balak said unto him, What hath the LORD spoken?

18 And he took up his parable, and said, Rise up, Balak, and hear; hearken unto me, thou son of Zippor:

19 God is not a man, that he should lie; neither the son of man, that he should repent: hath he said, and shall he not do it? or hath he spoken, and shall he not make it good?

20 Behold, I have received commandment to bless: and he hath blessed; and I cannot reverse it.

21 He hath not beheld iniquity in Jacob, neither hath he seen perverseness in Israel: the LORD his God is with him, and the shout of a king is among them.

22 God brought them out of Egypt; he hath as it were the strength of an unicorn.

23 Surely there is no enchantment against Jacob, neither is there any divination against Israel: according to this time it shall be said of Jacob and of Israel, What hath God wrought!

24 Behold, the people shall rise up as a great lion, and lift up himself as a young lion: he shall not lie down until he eat of the prey, and drink the blood of the slain.

25 ¶ And Balak said unto Balaam, Neither curse them at all, nor bless them at all.

26 But Balaam answered and said unto Balak, Told not I thee, saying, All that the LORD speaketh, that I must do?

27 ¶ And Balak said unto Balaam, Come, I pray thee, I will bring thee unto another place; peradventure it will please God that thou mayest curse me them from thence.

Balaam and His Ass by Rembrandt van Rijn

POINT OF INTEREST

"This is the only talking animal . . . in the entire Bible. . . . But the talking ass is perfectly in accord with the theological assumptions of the story: if God absolutely controls blessings and curses and vision, He can do the same for speech. . . . The wonderful absurdity of [Balaam's] response to [his mount's question 'What have I done unto thee?'] is that Balaam doesn't miss a beat. Confronted with the articulated speech of his ass's eminently justified complaint, he answers irascibly as though he were thoroughly accustomed to conducting debates with his beast. . . . Even as he harangues his ass, Balaam remains perfectly blind to something the ass had no difficulty seeing all along: he wishes he had a sword at the very moment the Lord's messenger stands in front of him wielding an unsheathed sword" (Robert Alter, *The Five Books of Moses* [New York: W. W. Norton & Company, 2004]).

28 And Balak brought Balaam unto the top of Peor, that looketh toward Jeshimon.

29 And Balaam said unto Balak, Build me here seven altars, and prepare me here seven bullocks and seven rams.

30 And Balak did as Balaam had said, and offered a bullock and a ram on every altar.

CHAPTER 24

1 AND when Balaam saw that it pleased the LORD to bless Israel, he went not, as at other times, to seek for enchantments, but he set his face toward the wilderness.

2 And Balaam lifted up his eyes, and he saw Israel abiding in his tents according to their tribes; and the spirit of God came upon him.

3 And he took up his parable, and said, Balaam the son of Beor hath said, and the man whose eyes are open hath said:

4 He hath said, which heard the words of God, which saw the vision of the Almighty, falling into a trance, but having his eyes open:

5 How goodly are thy tents, O Jacob, and thy tabernacles, O Israel!

6 As the valleys are they spread forth, as gardens by the river's side, as the trees of lign aloes which the LORD hath planted, and as cedar trees beside the waters.

7 He shall pour the water out of his buckets, and his seed shall be in many waters, and his king shall be higher than Agag, and his kingdom shall be exalted.

8 God brought him forth out of Egypt; he hath as it were the strength of an unicorn: he shall eat up the nations his enemies, and shall break their bones, and pierce them through with his arrows.

9 He couched, he lay down as a lion, and as a great lion: who shall stir him up? Blessed is he that blesseth thee, and cursed is he that curseth thee.

10 ¶ And Balak's anger was kindled against Balaam, and he smote his hands together: and Balak said unto Balaam, I called thee to curse mine enemies, and, behold, thou hast altogether blessed them these three times.

11 Therefore now flee thou to thy place: I thought to promote thee unto great honour; but, lo, the LORD hath kept thee back from honour.

12 And Balaam said unto Balak, Spake I not also to thy messengers which thou sentest unto me, saying,

13 If Balak would give me his house full of silver and gold, I cannot go beyond the commandment of the LORD, to do either good or bad of mine own mind; but what the LORD saith, that will I speak?

14 And now, behold, I go unto my people: come therefore, and I will advertise thee what this people shall do to thy people in the latter days.

15 ¶ And he took up his parable, and said, Balaam the son of Beor hath said, and the man whose eyes are open hath said:

16 He hath said, which heard the words of God, and knew the knowledge of the most High, which saw the vision of the Almighty, falling into a trance, but having his eyes open:

17 I shall see him, but not now: I shall behold him, but not nigh: there shall come a Star out of Jacob, and a Sceptre shall rise out of Israel, and shall smite the corners of Moab, and destroy all the children of Sheth.

NUMBERS CHAPTER 24

Numbers 24:19—The Will of God

Balaam, enticed by promises of worldly rewards, succumbed three times to the entreaties of Balak to seek from the Lord a cursing of Israel. Was Balaam expecting the Lord to alter His decreed purposes? Was he somehow expecting the Lord to let him "have his cake and eat it too"— as if divine approval could ever flow out of imperfect devotion? It was not to be. He had no recourse but to declare the word of the Lord as it was given.

As demonstated here, the will of God will always eventually come to pass. The only true gift one can give to Him is our "own will." That's why we offer a broken heart and contrite spirit (see 3 Ne. 9:20). That's why we submit to all things (see Mosiah 3:19). That's why we pray for His will to be done and not our own (see Mark 14:36). Remember that we cannot fool God, for He knows the intent of our heart.

The purposes of God cannot be thwarted or altered by the hand of man. Our mission is to align ourselves with full devotion to the will of God and do all in our power to carry it out faithfully.

18 And Edom shall be a possession, Seir also shall be a possession for his enemies; and Israel shall do valiantly.

19 Out of Jacob shall come he that shall have dominion, and shall destroy him that remaineth of the city.

20 ¶ And when he looked on Amalek, he took up his parable, and said, Amalek was the first of the nations; but his latter end shall be that he perish for ever.

21 And he looked on the Kenites, and took up his parable, and said, Strong is thy dwellingplace, and thou puttest thy nest in a rock.

22 Nevertheless the Kenite shall be wasted, until Asshur shall carry thee away captive.

23 And he took up his parable, and said, Alas, who shall live when God doeth this!

24 And ships shall come from the coast of Chittim, and shall afflict Asshur, and shall afflict Eber, and he also shall perish for ever.

25 And Balaam rose up, and went and returned to his place: and Balak also went his way.

CHAPTER 31

1 AND the LORD spake unto Moses, saying,

2 Avenge the children of Israel of the Midianites: afterward shalt thou be gathered unto thy people.

3 And Moses spake unto the people, saying, Arm some of yourselves unto the war, and let them go against the Midianites, and avenge the LORD of Midian.

4 Of every tribe a thousand, throughout all the tribes of Israel, shall ye send to the war.

5 So there were delivered out of the thousands of Israel, a thousand of every tribe, twelve thousand armed for war.

6 And Moses sent them to the war, a thousand of every tribe, them and Phinehas the son of Eleazar the priest, to the war, with the holy instruments, and the trumpets to blow in his hand.

7 And they warred against the Midianites, as the LORD commanded Moses; and they slew all the males.

8 And they slew the kings of Midian, beside the rest of them that were slain; namely, Evi, and Rekem, and Zur, and Hur, and Reba, five kings of Midian: Balaam also the son of Beor they slew with the sword.

9 And the children of Israel took all the women of Midian captives, and their little ones, and took the spoil of all their cattle, and all their flocks, and all their goods.

10 And they burnt all their cities wherein they dwelt, and all their goodly castles, with fire.

11 And they took all the spoil, and all the prey, both of men and of beasts.

12 And they brought the captives, and the prey, and the spoil, unto Moses, and Eleazar the priest, and unto the congregation of the children of Israel, unto the camp at the plains of Moab, which are by Jordan near Jericho.

13 ¶ And Moses, and Eleazar the priest, and all the princes of the congregation, went forth to meet them without the camp.

14 And Moses was wroth with the officers of the host, with the captains over thousands, and captains over hundreds, which came from the battle.

15 And Moses said unto them, Have ye saved all the women alive?

NUMBERS CHAPTER 31

"Each and every intelligent being will be judged according to the deeds done in the body, according to his works, faith, desires, and honesty or dishonesty before God; every trait of his character will receive its just merit or demerit, and he will be judged according to the law of heaven." —Brigham Young, JD 8:154.

Numbers 31:1–2—The Justice of God

There is always a consequence for action. Good follows good, and evil follows evil. The justice of God is inexorable.

The inhabitants of the Promised Land, ripened in iniquity, were to be removed by the Israelites. Balaam, evidently behind a campaign to cause the Israelites to compromise their covenant promises, was destroyed along with the Midianites. His example of infamy lives on as the prototype of the prophetic figure who was "called" of God for a great work, but not "chosen," because of his lack of pure devotion and his inability to turn away from the temptations of worldly honor and glory. By heeding the warning footprints he left in the sands of time, we can go a different way and cultivate an obedient walk in life that will lead to harmony, peace, and spiritual acceptance of the Lord.

From his example we see that those who seek to destroy will themselves be destroyed. Consequences from the Lord are poured out upon the children of men for their disobedience, either on earth or in the hereafter. No one escapes the judgment of God. Every sin must be repented of in order for the atonement to make us free from sin. Balaam was killed as the Israelites destroyed the Midianites. Each of us must come to grips with our own hearts. Is our heart pure? Do we continually want the things of the world? Balaam was destroyed not only in physical death—he was destroyed by a wanton and greedy heart.

Numbers 31:3–8—Summary of Precepts and Principles Concerning Balaam

The best summary of the doctrine reflected in the life of Balaam is the statement made by the Savior: "But seek ye first the kingdom of God, and his righteousness and all these things shall be added unto you" (Matt. 6:33; 3 Ne. 13:33). Furthermore, in the words of Paul: "Be not deceived; God is not mocked: for whatsoever a man soweth, that shall he also reap" (Gal. 6:7). Balaam placed the honor of God in second place after worldly honors; he put his own desires and longings before the will of God, and therefore experienced the justice of God. It is the same for us all—for the eternal purposes of the Lord are inexorable: they will come about, with or without our participation. Far better for us to cultivate spiritual motivation and bring our will into harmony with the principles of righteousness and salvation.

16 Behold, these caused the children of Israel, through the counsel of Balaam, to commit trespass against the LORD in the matter of Peor, and there was a plague among the congregation of the LORD.

17 Now therefore kill every male among the little ones, and kill every woman that hath known man by lying with him.

18 But all the women children, that have not known a man by lying with him, keep alive for yourselves.

19 And do ye abide without the camp seven days: whosoever hath killed any person, and whosoever hath touched any slain, purify both yourselves and your captives on the third day, and on the seventh day.

20 And purify all your raiment, and all that is made of skins, and all work of goats' hair, and all things made of wood.

21 ¶ And Eleazar the priest said unto the men of war which went to the battle, This is the ordinance of the law which the LORD commanded Moses;

22 Only the gold, and the silver, the brass, the iron, the tin, and the lead,

23 Every thing that may abide the fire, ye shall make it go through the fire, and it shall be clean: nevertheless it shall be purified with the water of separation: and all that abideth not the fire ye shall make go through the water.

24 And ye shall wash your clothes on the seventh day, and ye shall be clean, and afterward ye shall come into the camp.

25 ¶ And the LORD spake unto Moses, saying,

26 Take the sum of the prey that was taken, both of man and of beast, thou, and Eleazar the priest, and the chief fathers of the congregation:

27 And divide the prey into two parts; between them that took the war upon them, who went out to battle, and between all the congregation:

28 And levy a tribute unto the LORD of the men of war which went out to battle: one soul of five hundred, both of the persons, and of the beeves, and of the asses, and of the sheep:

29 Take it of their half, and give it unto Eleazar the priest, for an heave offering of the LORD.

30 And of the children of Israel's half, thou shalt take one portion of fifty, of the persons, of the beeves, of the asses, and of the flocks, of all manner of beasts, and give them unto the Levites, which keep the charge of the tabernacle of the LORD.

31 And Moses and Eleazar the priest did as the LORD commanded Moses.

32 And the booty, being the rest of the prey which the men of war had caught, was six hundred thousand and seventy thousand and five thousand sheep,

33 And threescore and twelve thousand beeves,

34 And threescore and one thousand asses,

35 And thirty and two thousand persons in all, of women that had not known man by lying with him.

36 And the half, which was the portion of them that went out to war, was in number three hundred thousand and seven and thirty thousand and five hundred sheep:

37 And the LORD's tribute of the sheep was six hundred and threescore and fifteen.

38 And the beeves were thirty and six thousand; of which the LORD's tribute was threescore and twelve.

NOTES:

39 And the asses were thirty thousand and five hundred; of which the LORD's tribute was threescore and one.

40 And the persons were sixteen thousand; of which the LORD's tribute was thirty and two persons.

41 And Moses gave the tribute, which was the LORD's heave offering, unto Eleazar the priest, as the LORD commanded Moses.

42 And of the children of Israel's half, which Moses divided from the men that warred,

43 (Now the half that pertained unto the congregation was three hundred thousand and thirty thousand and seven thousand and five hundred sheep,

44 And thirty and six thousand beeves,

45 And thirty thousand asses and five hundred,

46 And sixteen thousand persons;)

47 Even of the children of Israel's half, Moses took one portion of fifty, both of man and of beast, and gave them unto the Levites, which kept the charge of the tabernacle of the LORD; as the LORD commanded Moses.

48 ¶ And the officers which were over thousands of the host, the captains of thousands, and captains of hundreds, came near unto Moses:

49 And they said unto Moses, Thy servants have taken the sum of the men of war which are under our charge, and there lacketh not one man of us.

50 We have therefore brought an oblation for the LORD, what every man hath gotten, of jewels of gold, chains, and bracelets, rings, earrings, and tablets, to make an atonement for our souls before the LORD.

51 And Moses and Eleazar the priest took the gold of them, even all wrought jewels.

52 And all the gold of the offering that they offered up to the LORD, of the captains of thousands, and of the captains of hundreds, was sixteen thousand seven hundred and fifty shekels.

53 (For the men of war had taken spoil, every man for himself.)

54 And Moses and Eleazar the priest took the gold of the captains of thousands and of hundreds, and brought it into the tabernacle of the congregation, for a memorial for the children of Israel before the LORD.

THE
FIFTH BOOK OF MOSES CALLED DEUTERONOMY

CHAPTER 6

1 NOW these are the commandments, the statutes, and the judgments, which the LORD your God commanded to teach you, that ye might do them in the land whither ye go to possess it:

2 That thou mightest fear the LORD thy God, to keep all his statutes and his commandments, which I command thee, thou, and thy son, and thy son's son, all the days of thy life; and that thy days may be prolonged.

DEUTERONOMY CHAPTER 6

"The building up of Zion is a cause that has interested the people of God in every age; it is a theme upon which prophets, priests and kings have dwelt with peculiar delight; they have looked forward with joyful anticipation to the day in which we live; and fired with heavenly and joyful anticipations they have sung and written and prophesied of this our day; but they died without the sight; we are the favored people that God has made choice of to bring about the Latter-day glory." —Joseph Smith, HC 4:609–610

Deuteronomy 6—Preview of Principles for Righteous Living

With salvation at stake, let us make every needful preparation in order to create a spiritual environment, cultivate a righteous walk, and assure that our hearts and minds are set upon the Lord and His goodness so that we keep His commandments. When we forget to recognize the hand of God in all things, and instead take credit for our own prosperity, then surely the days of our security are shortened, and destruction is at the door.

With so much baseness rampant in the world, it is imperative that we beware of negative influences and misguided peer pressures. It is imperative that we elevate our minds to God through edifying expressions of praise and celebration. Songs of glory, language of praise, poetry of honor, sayings of truth, artwork of beauty and dignity—all these are reminders of our divine heritage and our noble birthright.

Deuteronomy 6:5–7—Remember Your Covenants; Fear God and Keep His Commandments

Moses provided for Israel his final instructions, his last sermon. He memorialized the pattern of godly living that will edify and save Israel. Within Moses' address lies the counsel that each of us must take into our hearts: We must fear God in that we keep His commandments and honor the covenant promises. We must show our love for God through devotion and obedience. We must constantly remind ourselves to have an eye single to the glory of God. We must teach our children these things diligently.

It is interesting that all the prophets teach the same doctrine. They all speak for the same God. They teach of the goodness of God, our Savior Jesus Christ, life-saving doctrine, principles, commandments and covenants, and the importance of these truths being given to our families.

With salvation at stake, every needful preparation must be made to create a spiritual environment, cultivate a righteous walk, and assure that our hearts and minds are set upon the Lord and His goodness in order that we keep His commandments.

3 ¶ Hear therefore, O Israel, and observe to do it; that it may be well with thee, and that ye may increase mightily, as the LORD God of thy fathers hath promised thee, in the land that floweth with milk and honey.

4 Hear, O Israel: The LORD our God is one LORD:

5 And thou shalt love the LORD thy God with all thine heart, and with all thy soul, and with all thy might.

6 And these words, which I command thee this day, shall be in thine heart:

7 And thou shalt teach them diligently unto thy children, and shalt talk of them when thou sittest in thine house, and when thou walkest by the way, and when thou liest down, and when thou risest up.

8 And thou shalt bind them for a sign upon thine hand, and they shall be as frontlets between thine eyes.

9 And thou shalt write them upon the posts of thy house, and on thy gates.

10 And it shall be, when the LORD thy God shall have brought thee into the land which he sware unto thy fathers, to Abraham, to Isaac, and to Jacob, to give thee great and goodly cities, which thou buildedst not,

11 And houses full of all good things, which thou filledst not, and wells digged, which thou diggedst not, vineyards and olive trees, which thou plantedst not; when thou shalt have eaten and be full;

12 Then beware lest thou forget the LORD, which brought thee forth out of the land of Egypt, from the house of bondage.

13 Thou shalt fear the LORD thy God, and serve him, and shalt swear by his name.

14 Ye shall not go after other gods, of the gods of the people which are round about you;

15 (For the LORD thy God is a jealous God among you) lest the anger of the LORD thy God be kindled against thee, and destroy thee from off the face of the earth.

16 ¶ Ye shall not tempt the LORD your God, as ye tempted him in Massah.

17 Ye shall diligently keep the commandments of the LORD your God, and his testimonies, and his statutes, which he hath commanded thee.

18 And thou shalt do that which is right and good in the sight of the LORD: that it may be well with thee, and that thou mayest go in and possess the good land which the LORD sware unto thy fathers,

19 To cast out all thine enemies from before thee, as the LORD hath spoken.

20 And when thy son asketh thee in time to come, saying, What mean the testimonies, and the statutes, and the judgments, which the LORD our God hath commanded you?

21 Then thou shalt say unto thy son, We were Pharaoh's bondmen in Egypt; and the LORD brought us out of Egypt with a mighty hand:

22 And the LORD shewed signs and wonders, great and sore, upon Egypt, upon Pharaoh, and upon all his household, before our eyes:

23 And he brought us out from thence, that he might bring us in, to give us the land which he sware unto our fathers.

24 And the LORD commanded us to do all these statutes, to fear the LORD our God, for our good always, that he might preserve us alive, as it is at this day.

25 And it shall be our righteousness, if we observe to do all these commandments before the LORD our God, as he hath commanded us.

Deuteronomy 6:7–9—Frontlets: Instruments of Remembering

Parental instruction in gospel living is essential in the development and upbringing of children. Loving reminders and encouragement are indispensable. The "frontlets" (or phylacteries) used in earlier times were small strips of parchment upon which key scriptures were written. These memory strips were attached to small leather holders and worn around the arm or forehead as a demonstration of faithfulness. Somewhat in the same spirit, young people today wear their CTR rings to remind them to "choose the right."

The scriptures teach the principle of *remembering* again and again. The word *remember* in its various forms in used in more than 550 verses. Remembering is a dynamic spiritual process of bringing important spiritual truths to mind on a continual basis in order to cultivate "a godly walk and conversation" (D&C 20:69). To "remember" is to align oneself with the will of God in order to become, on a daily basis, more and more like Him. Thoughts lead to action; thus "remembering" in a faithful and obedient way leads to living in a faithful and obedient way. President Spencer W. Kimball stated, "When you look in the dictionary for the most important word, do you know what it is?…'Remember' is the word" ("Circles of Exaltation," Address to Religious Educators, BYU, 28 June 1968, 8).

 POINT OF INTEREST

Teffilin (phylacteries or frontlets) are a pair of black leather boxes containing scrolls of parchment inscribed with verses from the Bible. The hand-tefillin, or shel yad, is worn by Jews wrapped around the arm, hand and fingers, while the head-tefillin, or shel rosh, is placed above the forehead. They serve as reminders that God brought the children of Israel out of Egypt and serve several purposes in the fulfillment of scriptural commandments prescribing them to be worn by Jews.

CHAPTER 8

1 ALL the commandments which I command thee this day shall ye observe to do, that ye may live, and multiply, and go in and possess the land which the LORD sware unto your fathers.

2 And thou shalt remember all the way which the LORD thy God led thee these forty years in the wilderness, to humble thee, and to prove thee, to know what was in thine heart, whether thou wouldest keep his commandments, or no.

3 And he humbled thee, and suffered thee to hunger, and fed thee with manna, which thou knewest not, neither did thy fathers know; that he might make thee know that man doth not live by bread only, but by every word that proceedeth out of the mouth of the LORD doth man live.

4 Thy raiment waxed not old upon thee, neither did thy foot swell, these forty years.

5 Thou shalt also consider in thine heart, that, as a man chasteneth his son, so the LORD thy God chasteneth thee.

6 Therefore thou shalt keep the commandments of the LORD thy God, to walk in his ways, and to fear him.

7 For the LORD thy God bringeth thee into a good land, a land of brooks of water, of fountains and depths that spring out of valleys and hills;

8 A land of wheat, and barley, and vines, and fig trees, and pomegranates; a land of oil olive, and honey;

9 A land wherein thou shalt eat bread without scarceness, thou shalt not lack any thing in it; a land whose stones are iron, and out of whose hills thou mayest dig brass.

10 When thou hast eaten and art full, then thou shalt bless the LORD thy God for the good land which he hath given thee.

11 Beware that thou forget not the LORD thy God, in not keeping his commandments, and his judgments, and his statutes, which I command thee this day:

12 Lest when thou hast eaten and art full, and hast built goodly houses, and dwelt therein;

13 And when thy herds and thy flocks multiply, and thy silver and thy gold is multiplied, and all that thou hast is multiplied;

14 Then thine heart be lifted up, and thou forget the LORD thy God, which brought thee forth out of the land of Egypt, from the house of bondage;

15 Who led thee through that great and terrible wilderness, wherein were fiery serpents, and scorpions, and drought, where there was no water; who brought thee forth water out of the rock of flint;

16 Who fed thee in the wilderness with manna, which thy fathers knew not, that he might humble thee, and that he might prove thee, to do thee good at thy latter end;

17 And thou say in thine heart, My power and the might of mine hand hath gotten me this wealth.

18 But thou shalt remember the LORD thy God: for it is he that giveth thee power to get wealth, that he may establish his covenant which he sware unto thy fathers, as it is this day.

19 And it shall be, if thou do at all forget the LORD thy God, and walk after other gods, and serve them, and worship them, I testify against you this day that ye shall surely perish.

20 As the nations which the LORD destroyeth before your face, so shall ye perish; because ye would not be obedient unto the voice of the LORD your God.

DEUTERONOMY CHAPTER 8

Deuteronomy 8:11, 17—Avoid Pride and Self-Righteousness; Remember God

When we forget to recognize the hand of God in all things, and instead take credit for our own prosperity, then surely the days of our security are shortened, and destruction is at the door.

It is God's desire that we flourish spiritually and temporally. His covenant promises provide for an increase in our posterity, a gathering place for our security, and a bounteous outpouring of truth and enlightenment. But all is contingent on our obedience and faithfulness.

God will have a humble people. When pride enters into the picture, instability and disharmony are inevitable consequences (the curse that Moses refers to in Deut. 11:26–28). We must avoid pride and instead give honor and glory to God as the font of all our blessings. Thus, we assure our continued blessings in this life and eternal life in the world to come.

Through this example we see that forgetting God leads to sorrow and sin due to the unsteadiness of the hearts of men.

 POINT OF INTEREST

Class	Clean	Unclean
Mammals	Two qualifications: 1. Cloven hoofs 2. Chewing of the cud	Carnivores and those not meeting both "clean" qualifications
Birds	Those not specifically listed as forbidden	Birds of prey or scavengers
Reptiles	None	All
Water Animals	Two qualifications: 1. Fish 2. Scales	Those not meeting both "clean" qualifications
Insects	Those in the grasshopper family	All except grasshoppers

CHAPTER 11

1 THEREFORE thou shalt love the LORD thy God, and keep his charge, and his statutes, and his judgments, and his commandments, alway.

2 And know ye this day: for I speak not with your children which have not known, and which have not seen the chastisement of the LORD your God, his greatness, his mighty hand, and his stretched out arm,

3 And his miracles, and his acts, which he did in the midst of Egypt unto Pharaoh the king of Egypt, and unto all his land;

4 And what he did unto the army of Egypt, unto their horses, and to their chariots; how he made the water of the Red sea to overflow them as they pursued after you, and how the LORD hath destroyed them unto this day;

5 And what he did unto you in the wilderness, until ye came into this place;

6 And what he did unto Dathan and Abiram, the sons of Eliab, the son of Reuben: how the earth opened her mouth, and swallowed them up, and their households, and their tents, and all the substance that was in their possession, in the midst of all Israel:

7 But your eyes have seen all the great acts of the LORD which he did.

8 Therefore shall ye keep all the commandments which I command you this day, that ye may be strong, and go in and possess the land, whither ye go to possess it;

9 And that ye may prolong your days in the land, which the LORD sware unto your fathers to give unto them and to their seed, a land that floweth with milk and honey.

10 ¶ For the land, whither thou goest in to possess it, is not as the land of Egypt, from whence ye came out, where thou sowedst thy seed, and wateredst it with thy foot, as a garden of herbs:

11 But the land, whither ye go to possess it, is a land of hills and valleys, and drinketh water of the rain of heaven:

12 A land which the LORD thy God careth for: the eyes of the LORD thy God are always upon it, from the beginning of the year even unto the end of the year.

13 ¶ And it shall come to pass, if ye shall hearken diligently unto my commandments which I command you this day, to love the LORD your God, and to serve him with all your heart and with all your soul,

14 That I will give you the rain of your land in his due season, the first rain and the latter rain, that thou mayest gather in thy corn, and thy wine, and thine oil.

15 And I will send grass in thy fields for thy cattle, that thou mayest eat and be full.

16 Take heed to yourselves, that your heart be not deceived, and ye turn aside, and serve other gods, and worship them;

17 And then the LORD's wrath be kindled against you, and he shut up the heaven, that there be no rain, and that the land yield not her fruit; and lest ye perish quickly from off the good land which the LORD giveth you.

DEUTERONOMY CHAPTER 11

Deuteronomy 11—Agency and Consequences

There are consequences associated with the commandments of God: blessings through obedience and cursings through disobedience. One is free to use one's God-given agency, but not free to determine the consequences. The consequences flow according to divine decree.

As Lehi made clear to his sons: "Wherefore, men are free according to the flesh; and all things are given them which are expedient unto man. And they are free to choose liberty and eternal life, through the great Mediator of all men, or to choose captivity and death, according to the captivity and power of the devil; for he seeketh that all men might be miserable like unto himself" (2 Ne. 2:27).

Modern revelation confirms the same principle with plainness: "There is a law, irrevocably decreed in heaven before the foundations of this world, upon which all blessings are predicated—And when we obtain any blessing from God, it is by obedience to that law upon which it is predicated" (D&C 130:20–21).

Moses

POINT OF INTEREST

The Hebrew title of Deuteronomy is Debarim *from the first line, "These be the words* [debarim] *which Moses spake." "The book is presented as the last will and testament of Moses, addressing the people on the plains of Moab just before his death [translation]. . . . The book of Deuteronomy was perhaps first compiled at sanctuaries, such as Shechem and Shiloh in the north; after the fall of the Northern Kingdom in* 722 B.C.E., *it would have been taken down to Judah. . . . It is possible that all or part of Deuteronomy was the law book discovered during the restoration of the Temple during the reign of Josiah* (John Bowker, *The Complete Bible Handbook* [New York: DK Publishing, 2001]).

18 ¶ Therefore shall ye lay up these my words in your heart and in your soul, and bind them for a sign upon your hand, that they may be as frontlets between your eyes.

19 And ye shall teach them your children, speaking of them when thou sittest in thine house, and when thou walkest by the way, when thou liest down, and when thou risest up.

20 And thou shalt write them upon the door posts of thine house, and upon thy gates:

21 That your days may be multiplied, and the days of your children, in the land which the LORD sware unto your fathers to give them, as the days of heaven upon the earth.

22 ¶ For if ye shall diligently keep all these commandments which I command you, to do them, to love the LORD your God, to walk in all his ways, and to cleave unto him;

23 Then will the LORD drive out all these nations from before you, and ye shall possess greater nations and mightier than yourselves.

24 Every place whereon the soles of your feet shall tread shall be yours: from the wilderness and Lebanon, from the river, the river Euphrates, even unto the uttermost sea shall your coast be.

25 There shall no man be able to stand before you: for the LORD your God shall lay the fear of you and the dread of you upon all the land that ye shall tread upon, as he hath said unto you.

26 ¶ Behold, I set before you this day a blessing and a curse;

27 A blessing, if ye obey the commandments of the LORD your God, which I command you this day:

28 And a curse, if ye will not obey the commandments of the LORD your God, but turn aside out of the way which I command you this day, to go after other gods, which ye have not known.

29 And it shall come to pass, when the LORD thy God hath brought thee in unto the land whither thou goest to possess it, that thou shalt put the blessing upon mount Gerizim, and the curse upon mount Ebal.

30 Are they not on the other side Jordan, by the way where the sun goeth down, in the land of the Canaanites, which dwell in the champaign over against Gilgal, beside the plains of Moreh?

31 For ye shall pass over Jordan to go in to possess the land which the LORD your God giveth you, and ye shall possess it, and dwell therein.

32 And ye shall observe to do all the statutes and judgments which I set before you this day.

CHAPTER 32

1 GIVE ear, O ye heavens, and I will speak; and hear, O earth, the words of my mouth.

2 My doctrine shall drop as the rain, my speech shall distil as the dew, as the small rain upon the tender herb, and as the showers upon the grass:

3 Because I will publish the name of the LORD: ascribe ye greatness unto our God.

4 He is the Rock, his work is perfect: for all his ways are judgment: a God of truth and without iniquity, just and right is he.

DEUTERONOMY CHAPTER 32

Deuteronomy 32—Overview

The message of Moses' final exhortation to the people of Israel has keen relevance for us today. He enjoined the Saints of his day to cultivate and maintain a spiritual environment where they would remember to keep their covenant promises, avoid prideful self-righteousness, protect themselves and their families from polluting influences, and allow the gratitude of their minds and hearts to overflow in expressions of love and celebration for the goodness of God.

Deuteronomy 32:4—The "Rock"

The language given in verse four about the "Rock"—incorporating perfection, truth, and that which is just and right—is magnificent. The metaphor of the "Rock," as applied to the Son of God, is used often in the scriptures (see Deut. 32:15, 18, 30–31; 2 Sam. 22:2–3, 47; 23:3; Ps. 18:2, 32, 46; 28:1; 31:2–3; 42:9; 62:2, 6-7; 71:3; 78:35; 89:26; 92:15; 94:22; 95:1; 1 Cor. 10:4; 1 Ne. 13:36; 15:15; 2 Ne. 4:30, 35; 9:45; 28:28; Jacob 7:25; Hel. 5:12; 3 Ne. 11:39–40; 18:12–13; D&C 6:34; 10:69; 11:16, 24; 18:4–5, 17; 33:13; 50:44; Moses 7:53; Abr. 2:16). Some of the most striking and memorable passages are the following:

> And the Father and I are one. I am in the Father and the Father in me; and inasmuch as ye have received me, ye are in me and I in you. Wherefore, I am in your midst, and I am the good shepherd, and the stone of Israel. He that buildeth upon this rock shall never fall. (D&C 50:43–44; compare Matt. 7:24–27)

> And the Lord said: Blessed is he through whose seed Messiah shall come; for he saith—I am Messiah, the King of Zion, the Rock of Heaven, which is broad as eternity; whoso cometh in at the gate and climbeth up by me shall never fall; wherefore, blessed are they of whom I have spoken, for they shall come forth with songs of everlasting joy. (Moses 7:53)

Deuteronomy 32:5–14—Anthem of Praise

The magnificent sentiments of this portion of the anthem of praise constitute a poetic rendition of the Lord's declaration to Moses on the mount: "For behold, this is my work and my glory—to bring to pass the immortality and eternal life of man" (Moses 1:39). The Lord's portion—His "inheritance"—is His people. His mission is His people. He leads, delivers, protects, carries, nurtures. It is breathtaking to realize that what the Lord does is done for and on our behalf as His sons and daughters.

Deuteronomy 32:15–44—Celebrate God's Goodness

It is imperative that we elevate our minds to God through edifying expressions of praise and celebration. Songs of glory, language of praise, poetry of honor, sayings

5 They have corrupted themselves, their spot is not the spot of his children: they are a perverse and crooked generation.

6 Do ye thus requite the LORD, O foolish people and unwise? is not he thy father that hath bought thee? hath he not made thee, and established thee?

7 ¶ Remember the days of old, consider the years of many generations: ask thy father, and he will shew thee; thy elders, and they will tell thee.

8 When the most High divided to the nations their inheritance, when he separated the sons of Adam, he set the bounds of the people according to the number of the children of Israel.

9 For the LORD's portion is his people; Jacob is the lot of his inheritance.

10 He found him in a desert land, and in the waste howling wilderness; he led him about, he instructed him, he kept him as the apple of his eye.

11 As an eagle stirreth up her nest, fluttereth over her young, spreadeth abroad her wings, taketh them, beareth them on her wings:

12 So the LORD alone did lead him, and there was no strange god with him.

13 He made him ride on the high places of the earth, that he might eat the increase of the fields; and he made him to suck honey out of the rock, and oil out of the flinty rock;

14 Butter of kine, and milk of sheep, with fat of lambs, and rams of the breed of Bashan, and goats, with the fat of kidneys of wheat; and thou didst drink the pure blood of the grape.

15 ¶ But Jeshurun waxed fat, and kicked: thou art waxen fat, thou art grown thick, thou art covered with fatness; then he forsook God which made him, and lightly esteemed the Rock of his salvation.

16 They provoked him to jealousy with strange gods, with abominations provoked they him to anger.

17 They sacrificed unto devils, not to God; to gods whom they knew not, to new gods that came newly up, whom your fathers feared not.

18 Of the Rock that begat thee thou art unmindful, and hast forgotten God that formed thee.

19 And when the LORD saw it, he abhorred them, because of the provoking of his sons, and of his daughters.

20 And he said, I will hide my face from them, I will see what their end shall be: for they are a very froward generation, children in whom is no faith.

21 They have moved me to jealousy with that which is not God; they have provoked me to anger with their vanities: and I will move them to jealousy with those which are not a people; I will provoke them to anger with a foolish nation.

22 For a fire is kindled in mine anger, and shall burn unto the lowest hell, and shall consume the earth with her increase, and set on fire the foundations of the mountains.

23 I will heap mischiefs upon them; I will spend mine arrows upon them.

24 They shall be burnt with hunger, and devoured with burning heat, and with bitter destruction: I will also send the teeth of beasts upon them, with the poison of serpents of the dust.

25 The sword without, and terror within, shall destroy both the young man and the virgin, the suckling also with the man of gray hairs.

26 I said, I would scatter them into corners, I would make the remembrance of them to cease from among men:

of truth, artwork of beauty and dignity—all these are reminders of our divine heritage and our noble birthright.

Moses taught the people to cultivate the highest form of expression in remembering and celebrating God's goodness. He taught them songs of praise that kept the covenant ideas and commitment alive in their hearts. He taught them to think in terms of the "Rock of their salvation" (Jesus Christ) (see Deut. 32:15, 18, 30–31). He used words that edified and lifted. He rehearsed God's triumph in unforgettable terms: "He found them in a desert land, and in the waste howling wilderness; he led him about, he instructed him, he kept him as the apple of his eye. As an eagle stirreth up her nest, fluttereth over her young, spreadeth abroad her wings, taketh then, beareth them on her wings: So the Lord alone did lead him . . ." (Deut. 32:10–12). Moses also was explicit in his images of warning for Israel, that they might be stirred up to remembering the Lord their God.

When we are grateful and celebrate in every way possible the goodness of God, it perpetuates our desire to do good. When singing the hymns of Zion or the songs of praise to God we are filled with the Spirit, and the results are expressed so well in the Doctrine and Covenants: "And now, verily, verily, I say unto thee, put your trust in that Spirit which leadeth to do good – yea, to do justly, to walk humbly, to judge righteously; and this is my Spirit. Verily, Verily, I say unto you, I will impart unto you of my Spirit, which shall enlighten your mind, which shall fill your soul with joy . . ." (D&C 11:12–13).

Deuteronomy—Summary of Precepts and Principles

The greatest agency of change is the purifying, ennobling influence of the Holy Spirit of God in our lives. Therefore, our every thought and deed should be aligned with the aspiration of creating a positive spiritual environment in our homes and communities where the Spirit can touch our lives with truth and reinforce our fervent desire to go good.

Moses taught a comprehensive program of spiritual redemption centered on the coming Atonement of Jesus Christ. The program can be summarized in four steps: (1) honor the covenant through obedience to gospel principles, (2) avoid pride and destructive self-righteousness, (3) defend against unrighteous influences, and (4) cultivate a life of gratitude and thanksgiving as expressed through a spiritual walk and celebratory expressions of praise and glory unto God. We can learn much from the chronicles of God's dealings with his ancient covenant people. All of the principles taught by the prophets of God in those days are eternal in nature and central to the restored gospel in our times.

27 Were it not that I feared the wrath of the enemy, lest their adversaries should behave themselves strangely, and lest they should say, Our hand is high, and the LORD hath not done all this.

28 For they are a nation void of counsel, neither is there any understanding in them.

29 O that they were wise, that they understood this, that they would consider their latter end!

30 How should one chase a thousand, and two put ten thousand to flight, except their Rock had sold them, and the LORD had shut them up?

31 For their rock is not as our Rock, even our enemies themselves being judges.

32 For their vine is of the vine of Sodom, and of the fields of Gomorrah: their grapes are grapes of gall, their clusters are bitter:

33 Their wine is the poison of dragons, and the cruel venom of asps.

34 Is not this laid up in store with me, and sealed up among my treasures?

35 To me belongeth vengeance, and recompence; their foot shall slide in due time: for the day of their calamity is at hand, and the things that shall come upon them make haste.

36 For the LORD shall judge his people, and repent himself for his servants, when he seeth that their power is gone, and there is none shut up, or left.

37 And he shall say, Where are their gods, their rock in whom they trusted,

38 Which did eat the fat of their sacrifices, and drank the wine of their drink offerings? let them rise up and help you, and be your protection.

39 See now that I, even I, am he, and there is no god with me: I kill, and I make alive; I wound, and I heal: neither is there any that can deliver out of my hand.

40 For I lift up my hand to heaven, and say, I live for ever.

41 If I whet my glittering sword, and mine hand take hold on judgment; I will render vengeance to mine enemies, and will reward them that hate me.

42 I will make mine arrows drunk with blood, and my sword shall devour flesh; and that with the blood of the slain and of the captives, from the beginning of revenges upon the enemy.

43 Rejoice, O ye nations, with his people: for he will avenge the blood of his servants, and will render vengeance to his adversaries, and will be merciful unto his land, and to his people.

44 ¶ And Moses came and spake all the words of this song in the ears of the people, he, and Hoshea the son of Nun.

45 And Moses made an end of speaking all these words to all Israel:

46 And he said unto them, Set your hearts unto all the words which I testify among you this day, which ye shall command your children to observe to do, all the words of this law.

47 For it is not a vain thing for you; because it is your life: and through this thing ye shall prolong your days in the land, whither ye go over Jordan to possess it.

48 And the LORD spake unto Moses that selfsame day, saying,

49 Get thee up into this mountain Abarim, unto mount Nebo, which is in the land of Moab, that is over against Jericho; and behold the land of Canaan, which I give unto the children of Israel for a possession:

50 And die in the mount whither thou goest up, and be gathered unto thy people; as Aaron thy brother died in mount Hor, and was gathered unto his people:

POINT OF INTEREST

Give ear, O ye heavens. *"The high stylistic solemnity of the poem [in Deut. 32] is signaled by a formal beginning that calls attention to the poet's own act of uttering sublime speech. This convention constitutes an approximate analogy to the invocation of the muse and the proclamation of the subject of the poem at the beginning of the Homeric epics. The address here to heaven and earth as witnesses is replicated, as many commentators have noted, by the opening lines of Isaiah 1. The Song of Moses (traditionally referred to in Hebrew . . . as Shirat [the song of] Ha'azinu) is certainly older than the body of Deuteronomy, though how much older is a matter of scholarly debate. Many (though not all) of the grammatical and morphological features of the language as well as certain aspects of the syntax are archaic, and numerous formulaic word pairs in the parallel members of the lines are ones that also occur in the prebiblical poetry of Ugarit. On stylistic grounds, then, the poem—or at least much of it—could be as early as the period of the Judges, that is, the eleventh century B.C.E.* (Robert Alter, *The Five Books of Moses* [New York: W. W. Norton & Company, 2004]).

Rejoice, O ye nations. *"Though the formulation of the Hebrew is a little obscure, the sense seems to be something like 'Nations, congratulate God's people as He exacts vengeance from their enemies and restores them to their place in their land.' The [Dead Sea Scrolls], . . .approximately confirming the Septuagint, has a partly divergent reading: 'Gladden, O heavens, His people / and let all divine beings bow before him. // For His sons' blood He will avenge / and vengeance turn back on His foes. // And His enemies He will requite / and purge His people's soil.' There are grounds for thinking this reading might be more authentic than the Masoretic Text. The invocation of the heavens at the end of the poem would correspond neatly to the apostrophe to the heavens at the beginning, whereas turning to the nations at the end is a little odd. As in the probable substitution of 'sons of israel' for 'sundry gods' in verse 8, later editors for reasons of monotheistic rigor might have been impelled to delete the reference that follows to all divine beings (kol'elohim) bowing before the triumphant Lord"* (Robert Alter, *The Five Books of Moses* [New York: W. W. Norton & Company, 2004]).

51 Because ye trespassed against me among the children of Israel at the waters of Meribah-Kadesh, in the wilderness of Zin; because ye sanctified me not in the midst of the children of Israel.

52 Yet thou shalt see the land before thee; but thou shalt not go thither unto the land which I give the children of Israel.

THE
BOOK OF JOSHUA

CHAPTER 1

1 NOW after the death of Moses the servant of the LORD it came to pass, that the LORD spake unto Joshua the son of Nun, Moses' minister, saying,

2 Moses my servant is dead; now therefore arise, go over this Jordan, thou, and all this people, unto the land which I do give to them, even to the children of Israel.

3 Every place that the sole of your foot shall tread upon, that have I given unto you, as I said unto Moses.

4 From the wilderness and this Lebanon even unto the great river, the river Euphrates, all the land of the Hittites, and unto the great sea toward the going down of the sun, shall be your coast.

5 There shall not any man be able to stand before thee all the days of thy life: as I was with Moses, so I will be with thee: I will not fail thee, nor forsake thee.

6 Be strong and of a good courage: for unto this people shalt thou divide for an inheritance the land, which I sware unto their fathers to give them.

7 Only be thou strong and very courageous, that thou mayest observe to do according to all the law, which Moses my servant commanded thee: turn not from it to the right hand or to the left, that thou mayest prosper whithersoever thou goest.

8 This book of the law shall not depart out of thy mouth; but thou shalt meditate therein day and night, that thou mayest observe to do according to all that is written therein: for then thou shalt make thy way prosperous, and then thou shalt have good success.

9 Have not I commanded thee? Be strong and of a good courage; be not afraid, neither be thou dismayed: for the LORD thy God is with thee whithersoever thou goest.

10 ¶ Then Joshua commanded the officers of the people, saying,

11 Pass through the host, and command the people, saying, Prepare you victuals; for within three days ye shall pass over this Jordan, to go in to possess the land, which the LORD your God giveth you to possess it.

12 ¶ And to the Reubenites, and to the Gadites, and to half the tribe of Manasseh, spake Joshua, saying,

13 Remember the word which Moses the servant of the LORD commanded you, saying, The LORD your God hath given you rest, and hath given you this land.

14 Your wives, your little ones, and your cattle, shall remain in the land which Moses gave you on this side Jordan; but ye shall pass before your brethren armed, all the mighty men of valour, and help them;

JOSHUA CHAPTER 1

Joshua 1:1–9—Joshua's Commission

The commission of Joshua is inspiring in its promises and assurances. The Lord will be with him. The successor of Moses is to be strong and courageous, observing the law of the Lord with precision, thus prospering wherever he should go. He is to follow the word of the Lord, meditating on it day and night. He is not to fear, for the Lord will be with Him always.

Any calling in the Church and kingdom of God can appropriately incorporate such principles of courage, obedience, living by the word, and having continual faith in the support and blessing of the Lord.

The Angel Appearing to Joshua by Gustave Doré

15 Until the LORD have given your brethren rest, as he hath given you, and they also have possessed the land which the LORD your God giveth them: then ye shall return unto the land of your possession, and enjoy it, which Moses the LORD's servant gave you on this side Jordan toward the sunrising.

16 ¶ And they answered Joshua, saying, All that thou commandest us we will do, and whithersoever thou sendest us, we will go.

17 According as we hearkened unto Moses in all things, so will we hearken unto thee: only the LORD thy God be with thee, as he was with Moses.

18 Whosoever he be that doth rebel against thy commandment, and will not hearken unto thy words in all that thou commandest him, he shall be put to death: only be strong and of a good courage.

CHAPTER 2

1 AND Joshua the son of Nun sent out of Shittim two men to spy secretly, saying, Go view the land, even Jericho. And they went, and came into an harlot's house, named Rahab, and lodged there.

2 And it was told the king of Jericho, saying, Behold, there came men in hither to night of the children of Israel to search out the country.

3 And the king of Jericho sent unto Rahab, saying, Bring forth the men that are come to thee, which are entered into thine house: for they be come to search out all the country.

4 And the woman took the two men, and hid them, and said thus, There came men unto me, but I wist not whence they were:

5 And it came to pass about the time of shutting of the gate, when it was dark, that the men went out: whither the men went I wot not: pursue after them quickly; for ye shall overtake them.

6 But she had brought them up to the roof of the house, and hid them with the stalks of flax, which she had laid in order upon the roof.

7 And the men pursued after them the way to Jordan unto the fords: and as soon as they which pursued after them were gone out, they shut the gate.

8 ¶ And before they were laid down, she came up unto them upon the roof;

9 And she said unto the men, I know that the LORD hath given you the land, and that your terror is fallen upon us, and that all the inhabitants of the land faint because of you.

10 For we have heard how the LORD dried up the water of the Red sea for you, when ye came out of Egypt; and what ye did unto the two kings of the Amorites, that were on the other side Jordan, Sihon and Og, whom ye utterly destroyed.

JOSHUA CHAPTER 2

"Every man should be willing to be presided over; and he is not fit to preside over others until he can submit sufficiently to the presidency of his brethren." —Joseph F. Smith, *Improvement Era* 21:105

Joshua 2:1–3—Rahab

Rahab (pronounced "ray'-hab"; meaning: broad or large) was a woman in Jericho who sequestered the two spies sent by Joshua to survey the city in preparation for the Israelite advance into Canaan (see Josh. 2:1–3).

Courageously, Rahab, having concealed the men under stalks of flax on her roof, claimed that the fugitives had escaped in the night. Why would she have rescued the Israelite enemy spies in this fashion? According to her own witness to them, she and her household were persuaded that the Israelite cause was of divine making (see Josh. 2:9–11). She then requested of the men that they spare her family during the impending invasion, something they agree to do in exchange for her silence concerning their mission. To secure the members of her family gathered within the walls of her house, which was located on the wall of the city, she was to tie a scarlet thread in the window through which she bid the spies escape (see Josh. 2:12–22). In honor of this oath, her family was withdrawn to safety on the day that Jericho was destroyed by the armies of Joshua (see Josh. 6:17–25).

Paul later recounted this event in his lecture on the principle of faith: "By faith the walls of Jericho fell down, after they were compassed about seven days. By faith the harlot Rahab perished not with them that believed not, when she had received the spies with peace" (Heb. 11:30–31). In another passage, James uses the incident concerning Rahab's decisive initiative to illustrate the principle that "faith without works is dead" (James 2:26). In other passages of scripture, the word *Rahab* is used in a different sense—to identify, symbolically, a force of worldly pride, such as Egypt (see Ps. 87:4; 98:10; Isa. 51:9).

11 And as soon as we had heard these things, our hearts did melt, neither did there remain any more courage in any man, because of you: for the LORD your God, he is God in heaven above, and in earth beneath.

12 Now therefore, I pray you, swear unto me by the LORD, since I have shewed you kindness, that ye will also shew kindness unto my father's house, and give me a true token:

13 And that ye will save alive my father, and my mother, and my brethren, and my sisters, and all that they have, and deliver our lives from death.

14 And the men answered her, Our life for yours, if ye utter not this our business. And it shall be, when the LORD hath given us the land, that we will deal kindly and truly with thee.

15 Then she let them down by a cord through the window: for her house was upon the town wall, and she dwelt upon the wall.

16 And she said unto them, Get you to the mountain, lest the pursuers meet you; and hide yourselves there three days, until the pursuers be returned: and afterward may ye go your way.

17 And the men said unto her, We will be blameless of this thine oath which thou hast made us swear.

18 Behold, when we come into the land, thou shalt bind this line of scarlet thread in the window which thou didst let us down by: and thou shalt bring thy father, and thy mother, and thy brethren, and all thy father's household, home unto thee.

19 And it shall be, that whosoever shall go out of the doors of thy house into the street, his blood shall be upon his head, and we will be guiltless: and whosoever shall be with thee in the house, his blood shall be on our head, if any hand be upon him.

20 And if thou utter this our business, then we will be quit of thine oath which thou hast made us to swear.

21 And she said, According unto your words, so be it. And she sent them away, and they departed: and she bound the scarlet line in the window.

22 And they went, and came unto the mountain, and abode there three days, until the pursuers were returned: and the pursuers sought them throughout all the way, but found them not.

23 ¶ So the two men returned, and descended from the mountain, and passed over, and came to Joshua the son of Nun, and told him all things that befell them:

24 And they said unto Joshua, Truly the LORD hath delivered into our hands all the land; for even all the inhabitants of the country do faint because of us.

CHAPTER 3

1 AND Joshua rose early in the morning; and they removed from Shittim, and came to Jordan, he and all the children of Israel, and lodged there before they passed over.

2 And it came to pass after three days, that the officers went through the host;

3 And they commanded the people, saying, When ye see the ark of the covenant of the LORD your God, and the priests the Levites bearing it, then ye shall remove from your place, and go after it.

4 Yet there shall be a space between you and it, about two thousand cubits by measure: come not near unto it, that ye may know the way by which ye must go: for ye have not passed this way heretofore.

Joshua 2:12—Save Your Family by Sustaining Your Leaders

To follow the counsel of the prophet and protect and sustain the work of the kingdom is a spiritual insurance policy for your family.

Just as the woman Rahab protected Israel's emissaries at Jericho, and thus secured for all her kindred the protection of the Lord, even so can we mark out a line of defense for our families as we keep the commandments and live in the world but not of the world. Cultivating a character of obedience and faithfulness sets up a bulwark of fortifications for our children. We can say, with the Savior, "And for their sakes I sanctify myself, that they also might be sanctified through the truth" (John 17:19). We can teach our children the saving principles of righteousness and prepare them for the challenges of life. We can set up memorials like Joshua did to remind the Israelites of their miraculous passage over Jordan, or of the covenant of obedience that Israel made unto the Lord.

One of the first steps to apostasy is criticizing the Lord's anointed and failing to follow their counsel. When we openly criticize our leaders in front of our children, the sin becomes twice as devastating, for we sow the seeds of doubt in our children. They grow up to criticize, find fault, and complain about their leaders. Their sins come back to haunt them. Just the opposite can be true—when we praise, honor, follow, and sustain our leaders, our children will grow up to do likewise.

JOSHUA CHAPTER 3

Joshua 3:1–7—The Lord Will Magnify His Leaders

Each person in his or her own way plays a vital leadership role in the kingdom of God. The obedient and faithful are sustained by the Lord and magnified in the eyes of others—parents in their families, teachers in their classes, bishops in their wards, missionaries in the field, prophets in their callings—that all might be edified and prosper spiritually.

The Lord magnified Joshua in the eyes of the people by giving him the spirit of obedience, righteousness, and priesthood power. The waters of the Jordan were turned back in miraculous fashion to allow Israel to pass over into the Promised Land. In no less miraculous fashion, the Lord's leaders in the homes, wards, and stakes of Zion can open the passageways of spiritual opportunity so that individuals can cross the challenging frontiers of mortal experience into a state of higher perfectness according to the patterns of gospel living.

There are miracles happening around us every day in the transformations of souls brought about through humble obedience to the Lord's commandments. As leaders show humility and prayerfully seek the Spirit, the way will be opened for them, too, to fulfill their callings successfully and be accepted by those who depend on their example and courage.

5 And Joshua said unto the people, Sanctify yourselves: for to morrow the LORD will do wonders among you.

6 And Joshua spake unto the priests, saying, Take up the ark of the covenant, and pass over before the people. And they took up the ark of the covenant, and went before the people.

7 ¶ And the LORD said unto Joshua, This day will I begin to magnify thee in the sight of all Israel, that they may know that, as I was with Moses, so I will be with thee.

8 And thou shalt command the priests that bear the ark of the covenant, saying, When ye are come to the brink of the water of Jordan, ye shall stand still in Jordan.

9 ¶ And Joshua said unto the children of Israel, Come hither, and hear the words of the LORD your God.

10 And Joshua said, Hereby ye shall know that the living God is among you, and that he will without fail drive out from before you the Canaanites, and the Hittites, and the Hivites, and the Perizzites, and the Girgashites, and the Amorites, and the Jebusites.

11 Behold, the ark of the covenant of the LORD of all the earth passeth over before you into Jordan.

12 Now therefore take you twelve men out of the tribes of Israel, out of every tribe a man.

13 And it shall come to pass, as soon as the soles of the feet of the priests that bear the ark of the LORD, the Lord of all the earth, shall rest in the waters of Jordan, that the waters of Jordan shall be cut off from the waters that come down from above; and they shall stand upon an heap.

14 ¶ And it came to pass, when the people removed from their tents, to pass over Jordan, and the priests bearing the ark of the covenant before the people;

15 And as they that bare the ark were come unto Jordan, and the feet of the priests that bare the ark were dipped in the brim of the water, (for Jordan overfloweth all his banks all the time of harvest,)

16 That the waters which came down from above stood and rose up upon an heap very far from the city Adam, that is beside Zaretan: and those that came down toward the sea of the plain, even the salt sea, failed, and were cut off: and the people passed over right against Jericho.

17 And the priests that bare the ark of the covenant of the LORD stood firm on dry ground in the midst of Jordan, and all the Israelites passed over on dry ground, until all the people were passed clean over Jordan.

CHAPTER 4

1 AND it came to pass, when all the people were clean passed over Jordan, that the LORD spake unto Joshua, saying,

2 Take you twelve men out of the people, out of every tribe a man,

3 And command ye them, saying, Take you hence out of the midst of Jordan, out of the place where the priests' feet stood firm, twelve stones, and ye shall carry them over with you, and leave them in the lodging place, where ye shall lodge this night.

4 Then Joshua called the twelve men, whom he had prepared of the children of Israel, out of every tribe a man:

5 And Joshua said unto them, Pass over before the ark of the LORD your God into the midst of Jordan, and take ye up every man of you a stone upon his shoulder, according unto the number of the tribes of the children of Israel:

Joshua 3:13–17—Dry Bed of the River Jordan

This miracle, reminiscent of the passage of the Israelites through the parting Red Sea, marks the beginning of a new era in the national history of the chosen people of the Lord. It was the Lord who opened the passage to the Promised Land; it was the faithful remnants of the mighty hosts of Israel who crossed the threshhold and took the steps forward in fulfilment of the promises given to Moses.

Those steps were real, just as our daily steps along the strait and narrow are authentic transitional movements toward a homeland promised to all who honor their covenant obligations and look forward in faith to the time when they are welcomed home into the rest of the Lord, "which rest is the fulness of his glory" (D&C 84:24).

6 That this may be a sign among you, that when your children ask their fathers in time to come, saying, What mean ye by these stones?

7 Then ye shall answer them, That the waters of Jordan were cut off before the ark of the covenant of the LORD; when it passed over Jordan, the waters of Jordan were cut off: and these stones shall be for a memorial unto the children of Israel for ever.

8 And the children of Israel did so as Joshua commanded, and took up twelve stones out of the midst of Jordan, as the LORD spake unto Joshua, according to the number of the tribes of the children of Israel, and carried them over with them unto the place where they lodged, and laid them down there.

9 And Joshua set up twelve stones in the midst of Jordan, in the place where the feet of the priests which bare the ark of the covenant stood: and they are there unto this day.

10 ¶ For the priests which bare the ark stood in the midst of Jordan, until every thing was finished that the LORD commanded Joshua to speak unto the people, according to all that Moses commanded Joshua: and the people hasted and passed over.

11 And it came to pass, when all the people were clean passed over, that the ark of the LORD passed over, and the priests, in the presence of the people.

12 And the children of Reuben, and the children of Gad, and half the tribe of Manasseh, passed over armed before the children of Israel, as Moses spake unto them:

13 About forty thousand prepared for war passed over before the LORD unto battle, to the plains of Jericho.

14 ¶ On that day the LORD magnified Joshua in the sight of all Israel; and they feared him, as they feared Moses, all the days of his life.

15 And the LORD spake unto Joshua, saying,

16 Command the priests that bear the ark of the testimony, that they come up out of Jordan.

17 Joshua therefore commanded the priests, saying, Come ye up out of Jordan.

18 And it came to pass, when the priests that bare the ark of the covenant of the LORD were come up out of the midst of Jordan, and the soles of the priests' feet were lifted up unto the dry land, that the waters of Jordan returned unto their place, and flowed over all his banks, as they did before.

19 ¶ And the people came up out of Jordan on the tenth day of the first month, and encamped in Gilgal, in the east border of Jericho.

20 And those twelve stones, which they took out of Jordan, did Joshua pitch in Gilgal.

21 And he spake unto the children of Israel, saying, When your children shall ask their fathers in time to come, saying, What mean these stones?

22 Then ye shall let your children know, saying, Israel came over this Jordan on dry land.

23 For the LORD your God dried up the waters of Jordan from before you, until ye were passed over, as the LORD your God did to the Red sea, which he dried up from before us, until we were gone over:

24 That all the people of the earth might know the hand of the LORD, that it is mighty: that ye might fear the LORD your God for ever.

JOSHUA CHAPTER 4

Joshua 4:9—Twelve Stones

The memorial of twelve stones set up to commemorate the passage of the tribes of Israel through the Jordan is a reminder to families of today to find appropriate ways to mark the milestones of family progress: whether the memory devices are cherished objects, choice pictures, framed documents, family histories, plaques, or the like, is a matter of choice. What is central is the quest to recapture the essence of family joys in ways that stimulate good conversation and raise in the minds of young people thoughtful questions about the principles and values that contribute to spiritual strength and unity—particularly faith in and reverence for our Heavenly Father and His beloved Son.

Joshua and the Israeli People by Karolingischer Buchmaler

CHAPTER 5

1 AND it came to pass, when all the kings of the Amorites, which were on the side of Jordan westward, and all the kings of the Canaanites, which were by the sea, heard that the LORD had dried up the waters of Jordan from before the children of Israel, until we were passed over, that their heart melted, neither was there spirit in them any more, because of the children of Israel.

2 ¶ At that time the LORD said unto Joshua, Make thee sharp knives, and circumcise again the children of Israel the second time.

3 And Joshua made him sharp knives, and circumcised the children of Israel at the hill of the foreskins.

4 And this is the cause why Joshua did circumcise: All the people that came out of Egypt, that were males, even all the men of war, died in the wilderness by the way, after they came out of Egypt.

5 Now all the people that came out were circumcised: but all the people that were born in the wilderness by the way as they came forth out of Egypt, them they had not circumcised.

6 For the children of Israel walked forty years in the wilderness, till all the people that were men of war, which came out of Egypt, were consumed, because they obeyed not the voice of the LORD: unto whom the LORD sware that he would not shew them the land, which the LORD sware unto their fathers that he would give us, a land that floweth with milk and honey.

7 And their children, whom he raised up in their stead, them Joshua circumcised: for they were uncircumcised, because they had not circumcised them by the way.

8 And it came to pass, when they had done circumcising all the people, that they abode in their places in the camp, till they were whole.

9 And the LORD said unto Joshua, This day have I rolled away the reproach of Egypt from off you. Wherefore the name of the place is called Gilgal unto this day.

10 ¶ And the children of Israel encamped in Gilgal, and kept the passover on the fourteenth day of the month at even in the plains of Jericho.

11 And they did eat of the old corn of the land on the morrow after the passover, unleavened cakes, and parched corn in the selfsame day.

12 ¶ And the manna ceased on the morrow after they had eaten of the old corn of the land; neither had the children of Israel manna any more; but they did eat of the fruit of the land of Canaan that year.

13 ¶ And it came to pass, when Joshua was by Jericho, that he lifted up his eyes and looked, and, behold, there stood a man over against him with his sword drawn in his hand: and Joshua went unto him, and said unto him, Art thou for us, or for our adversaries?

14 And he said, Nay; but as captain of the host of the LORD am I now come. And Joshua fell on his face to the earth, and did worship, and said unto him, What saith my lord unto his servant?

15 And the captain of the LORD'S host said unto Joshua, Loose thy shoe from off thy foot; for the place whereon thou standest is holy. And Joshua did so.

JOSHUA CHAPTER 5

Joshua 5:14—The Lord Will Fight the Battles of the Faithful

When we put our shoulder to the wheel and join with the forces of righteousness, we will triumph, for the Lord will fight our battles and sustain our efforts.

The battle of Jericho is a lasting memorial to the guidance and protecting care of the Lord. As Israel did all that was asked by the Lord, she prospered and secured a place of refuge for her Saints. Even so today, as we follow the commandments and seek the face of the Lord always, we can have the hope of being led to places of refuge: sanctuaries of our own hearts when they are broken and humble, homes of sanctity and peace, stakes of Zion that afford strength in the face of the world's challenges and Temples of Holiness before the Lord.

Thus we see that one must do all that lies within one's power in order to please God and accomplish His will. "Therefore, dearly beloved brethren, let us cheerfully do all things that lie in our power; and then may we stand still, with the utmost assurance, to see the salvation of God, and for his arm to be revealed" (D&C 123:17). The arm of the Lord will always be extended in His way and in His time to help His children grow and become worthy of eternal life.

Joshua and the Fall of Jericho, chromolithograph

CHAPTER 6

1 NOW Jericho was straitly shut up because of the children of Israel: none went out, and none came in.

2 And the LORD said unto Joshua, See, I have given into thine hand Jericho, and the king thereof, and the mighty men of valour.

3 And ye shall compass the city, all ye men of war, and go round about the city once. Thus shalt thou do six days.

4 And seven priests shall bear before the ark seven trumpets of rams' horns: and the seventh day ye shall compass the city seven times, and the priests shall blow with the trumpets.

5 And it shall come to pass, that when they make a long blast with the ram's horn, and when ye hear the sound of the trumpet, all the people shall shout with a great shout; and the wall of the city shall fall down flat, and the people shall ascend up every man straight before him.

6 ¶ And Joshua the son of Nun called the priests, and said unto them, Take up the ark of the covenant, and let seven priests bear seven trumpets of rams' horns before the ark of the LORD.

7 And he said unto the people, Pass on, and compass the city, and let him that is armed pass on before the ark of the LORD.

8 ¶ And it came to pass, when Joshua had spoken unto the people, that the seven priests bearing the seven trumpets of rams' horns passed on before the LORD, and blew with the trumpets: and the ark of the covenant of the LORD followed them.

9 ¶ And the armed men went before the priests that blew with the trumpets, and the rereward came after the ark, the priests going on, and blowing with the trumpets.

10 And Joshua had commanded the people, saying, Ye shall not shout, nor make any noise with your voice, neither shall any word proceed out of your mouth, until the day I bid you shout; then shall ye shout.

11 So the ark of the LORD compassed the city, going about it once: and they came into the camp, and lodged in the camp.

12 ¶ And Joshua rose early in the morning, and the priests took up the ark of the LORD.

13 And seven priests bearing seven trumpets of rams' horns before the ark of the LORD went on continually, and blew with the trumpets: and the armed men went before them; but the rereward came after the ark of the LORD, the priests going on, and blowing with the trumpets.

14 And the second day they compassed the city once, and returned into the camp: so they did six days.

15 And it came to pass on the seventh day, that they rose early about the dawning of the day, and compassed the city after the same manner seven times: only on that day they compassed the city seven times.

16 And it came to pass at the seventh time, when the priests blew with the trumpets, Joshua said unto the people, Shout; for the LORD hath given you the city.

17 ¶ And the city shall be accursed, even it, and all that are therein, to the LORD: only Rahab the harlot shall live, she and all that are with her in the house, because she hid the messengers that we sent.

18 And ye, in any wise keep yourselves from the accursed thing, lest ye make yourselves accursed, when ye take of the accursed thing, and make the camp of Israel a curse, and trouble it.

JOSHUA CHAPTER 6

Joshua 6:1–20—Walls of Jericho

The walls of Jericho symbolically represent any daunting impediment we might encounter in our quest to rise to our potential when following the principles of the gospel. How do we surmount such obstacles? By heeding the whisperings of the Spirit and following the counsel of the Lord and His chosen prophets. Through faith, obedience, and wise action, we can overcome the barriers that attempt to divert us from the appointed path.

Jericho, Israel

POINT OF INTEREST

"Apart from its biblical importance, Jericho provides one of the first examples of a continuously inhabited site. Although there is evidence of earlier human remains, the first development was a Neolithic settlement from about 8000 B.C.E. of mud-brick houses, a stone-built surrounding wall, and, remarkably for this period, a large central tower. . . . From the third and fourth millennia B.C.E., the town was defended by mud walls; 17 different phases have been traced by archaeologists. Other inhabitants of the site include the Canaanites, who probably lived at Jericho from c. 1900 B.C.E." (John Bowker, *The Complete Bible Handbook* [New York: DK Publishing, 2001]).

19 But all the silver, and gold, and vessels of brass and iron, are consecrated unto the LORD: they shall come into the treasury of the LORD.

20 So the people shouted when the priests blew with the trumpets: and it came to pass, when the people heard the sound of the trumpet, and the people shouted with a great shout, that the wall fell down flat, so that the people went up into the city, every man straight before him, and they took the city.

21 And they utterly destroyed all that was in the city, both man and woman, young and old, and ox, and sheep, and ass, with the edge of the sword.

22 But Joshua had said unto the two men that had spied out the country, Go into the harlot's house, and bring out thence the woman, and all that she hath, as ye sware unto her.

23 And the young men that were spies went in, and brought out Rahab, and her father, and her mother, and her brethren, and all that she had; and they brought out all her kindred, and left them without the camp of Israel.

24 And they burnt the city with fire, and all that was therein: only the silver, and the gold, and the vessels of brass and of iron, they put into the treasury of the house of the LORD.

25 And Joshua saved Rahab the harlot alive, and her father's household, and all that she had; and she dwelleth in Israel even unto this day; because she hid the messengers, which Joshua sent to spy out Jericho.

26 ¶ And Joshua adjured them at that time, saying, Cursed be the man before the LORD, that riseth up and buildeth this city Jericho: he shall lay the foundation thereof in his firstborn, and in his youngest son shall he set up the gates of it.

27 So the LORD was with Joshua; and his fame was noised throughout all the country.

CHAPTER 23

1 AND it came to pass a long time after that the LORD had given rest unto Israel from all their enemies round about, that Joshua waxed old and stricken in age.

2 And Joshua called for all Israel, and for their elders, and for their heads, and for their judges, and for their officers, and said unto them, I am old and stricken in age:

3 And ye have seen all that the LORD your God hath done unto all these nations because of you; for the LORD your God is he that hath fought for you.

4 Behold, I have divided unto you by lot these nations that remain, to be an inheritance for your tribes, from Jordan, with all the nations that I have cut off, even unto the great sea westward.

5 And the LORD your God, he shall expel them from before you, and drive them from out of your sight; and ye shall possess their land, as the LORD your God hath promised unto you.

6 Be ye therefore very courageous to keep and to do all that is written in the book of the law of Moses, that ye turn not aside therefrom to the right hand or to the left;

7 That ye come not among these nations, these that remain among you; neither make mention of the name of their gods, nor cause to swear by them, neither serve them, nor bow yourselves unto them:

Joshua 6:21–25—Spiritual Deliverance

The preservation of Rahab and her family stands as a marker of the spirit of deliverance associated with those who, with courage and commitment, sustain and support the ongoing progress of the kingdom of God. The story of Rahab is also a reminder that the faithful daughters and sons of God, from whatever cultural or demographic background, are today, through obedience to the laws and commandments, welcomed into the covenant circle of those appointed to carry on the work of the Lord.

JOSHUA CHAPTER 23

Joshua 23:1–16—Testimony of Joshua

Joshua gives the people his benedictory counsel in the form of a firm testimony of the reality of God: "for the LORD your God is he that hath fought for you" (Josh. 23:3). He enjoins the people to keep the commandments with courage, to cleave unto the Lord rather than to the tribal gods of the local inhabitants, and to love the Lord with all their heart and soul. His prophetic counsel comes in the form of a promise and a warning: the good things that the Lord has done for them will surely continue, provided they honor their covenants; failure to do so will bring about their certain destruction in the land.

Precisely the same kind of counsel was given by the prophet Lehi to his children in his final blessing: "For the Lord God hath said that: Inasmuch as ye shall keep my commandments ye shall prosper in the land; and inasmuch as ye will not keep my commandments ye shall be cut off from my presence" (2 Ne. 4:4).

8 But cleave unto the LORD your God, as ye have done unto this day.

9 For the LORD hath driven out from before you great nations and strong: but as for you, no man hath been able to stand before you unto this day.

10 One man of you shall chase a thousand: for the LORD your God, he it is that fighteth for you, as he hath promised you.

11 Take good heed therefore unto yourselves, that ye love the LORD your God.

12 Else if ye do in any wise go back, and cleave unto the remnant of these nations, even these that remain among you, and shall make marriages with them, and go in unto them, and they to you:

13 Know for a certainty that the LORD your God will no more drive out any of these nations from before you; but they shall be snares and traps unto you, and scourges in your sides, and thorns in your eyes, until ye perish from off this good land which the LORD your God hath given you.

14 And, behold, this day I am going the way of all the earth: and ye know in all your hearts and in all your souls, that not one thing hath failed of all the good things which the LORD your God spake concerning you; all are come to pass unto you, and not one thing hath failed thereof.

15 Therefore it shall come to pass, that as all good things are come upon you, which the LORD your God promised you; so shall the LORD bring upon you all evil things, until he have destroyed you from off this good land which the LORD your God hath given you.

16 When ye have transgressed the covenant of the LORD your God, which he commanded you, and have gone and served other gods, and bowed yourselves to them; then shall the anger of the LORD be kindled against you, and ye shall perish quickly from off the good land which he hath given unto you.

CHAPTER 24

1 AND Joshua gathered all the tribes of Israel to Shechem, and called for the elders of Israel, and for their heads, and for their judges, and for their officers; and they presented themselves before God.

2 And Joshua said unto all the people, Thus saith the LORD God of Israel, Your fathers dwelt on the other side of the flood in old time, even Terah, the father of Abraham, and the father of Nachor: and they served other gods.

3 And I took your father Abraham from the other side of the flood, and led him throughout all the land of Canaan, and multiplied his seed, and gave him Isaac.

4 And I gave unto Isaac Jacob and Esau: and I gave unto Esau mount Seir, to possess it; but Jacob and his children went down into Egypt.

5 I sent Moses also and Aaron, and I plagued Egypt, according to that which I did among them: and afterward I brought you out.

6 And I brought your fathers out of Egypt: and ye came unto the sea; and the Egyptians pursued after your fathers with chariots and horsemen unto the Red sea.

NOTES:

_____

_____

_____

_____

_____

_____

_____

_____

_____

_____

_____

_____

JOSHUA CHAPTER 24

Joshua 24:15—Choose to Follow the Lord

There is a fundamental choice in life whether to pledge allegiance to the Lord and follow in His pathways, or to cater to the patterns and behaviors of worldliness. The way of holiness is the way of peace, harmony and salvation.

Joshua, in his final testimony and counsel, adjured the Israelites to follow the Lord, and charged them strictly to avoid the false gods of the indigenous peoples of Canaan. Israel then made a covenant to choose the Lord and remain on the pathway of righteousness. Joshua set up a memorial to the sacred event as a reminder to Israel to honor their pledge forever.

Through examples like this one, we see that our real purpose here upon the earth is to be like Joshua as he instructed the Israelites to choose the Lord's way. We are to serve God with all our heart, might, mind, and strength and to "cleave" unto the Lord in all things—and thus we shall enjoy eternal life.

7 And when they cried unto the LORD, he put darkness between you and the Egyptians, and brought the sea upon them, and covered them; and your eyes have seen what I have done in Egypt: and ye dwelt in the wilderness a long season.

8 And I brought you into the land of the Amorites, which dwelt on the other side Jordan; and they fought with you: and I gave them into your hand, that ye might possess their land; and I destroyed them from before you.

9 Then Balak the son of Zippor, king of Moab, arose and warred against Israel, and sent and called Balaam the son of Beor to curse you:

10 But I would not hearken unto Balaam; therefore he blessed you still: so I delivered you out of his hand.

11 And ye went over Jordan, and came unto Jericho: and the men of Jericho fought against you, the Amorites, and the Perizzites, and the Canaanites, and the Hittites, and the Girgashites, the Hivites, and the Jebusites; and I delivered them into your hand.

12 And I sent the hornet before you, which drave them out from before you, even the two kings of the Amorites; but not with thy sword, nor with thy bow.

13 And I have given you a land for which ye did not labour, and cities which ye built not, and ye dwell in them; of the vineyards and oliveyards which ye planted not do ye eat.

14 ¶ Now therefore fear the LORD, and serve him in sincerity and in truth: and put away the gods which your fathers served on the other side of the flood, and in Egypt; and serve ye the LORD.

15 And if it seem evil unto you to serve the LORD, choose you this day whom ye will serve; whether the gods which your fathers served that were on the other side of the flood, or the gods of the Amorites, in whose land ye dwell: but as for me and my house, we will serve the LORD.

16 And the people answered and said, God forbid that we should forsake the LORD, to serve other gods;

17 For the LORD our God, he it is that brought us up and our fathers out of the land of Egypt, from the house of bondage, and which did those great signs in our sight, and preserved us in all the way wherein we went, and among all the people through whom we passed:

18 And the LORD drave out from before us all the people, even the Amorites which dwelt in the land: therefore will we also serve the LORD; for he is our God.

19 And Joshua said unto the people, Ye cannot serve the LORD: for he is an holy God; he is a jealous God; he will not forgive your transgressions nor your sins.

20 If ye forsake the LORD, and serve strange gods, then he will turn and do you hurt, and consume you, after that he hath done you good.

21 And the people said unto Joshua, Nay; but we will serve the LORD.

22 And Joshua said unto the people, Ye are witnesses against yourselves that ye have chosen you the LORD, to serve him. And they said, We are witnesses.

23 Now therefore put away, said he, the strange gods which are among you, and incline your heart unto the LORD God of Israel.

24 And the people said unto Joshua, The LORD our God will we serve, and his voice will we obey.

25 So Joshua made a covenant with the people that day, and set them a statute and an ordinance in Shechem.

Joshua 24—Summary of Precepts and Principles

Joshua, as the successor to Moses, was a great prophet leader at a time when righteous leadership was especially needed among the Israelites. Like Joshua, we also have our Jerichos to conquer. We need to remember that God will sustain his leaders and magnify them to be the equal of any test. To save our families in light and truth, we must sustain our leadership in their efforts to fulfill the Lord's errand and thus open the way for the Lord to fight our battles on a daily basis. We must choose decisively to be on the Lord's side and emulate the Savior's mission: "And for their sakes I sanctify myself, that they also might be sanctified through the truth" (John 17:19). As we apply the Lord's leadership principles, He will bless and sanctify our hearts and minds through His Spirit so that we will not be afraid, but know that the Lord is with us.

Joshua 24—Agency

Agency is a marvelous gift from our Father in Heaven. We look upon our agency as a choice blessing from our Creator, and we are deeply grateful. Agency gives us the right to choose the way of happiness, rather than the way of misery (see 2 Ne. 2:27). We understand and know that our agency is necessary for our growth. True, it is a bit daunting at times to look at the many pathways stretching before us over the landscape of our lives. But the Lord has given us clear directions for finding the gospel pathway—and the right to choose. He warms our heart and enlightens our mind when we follow the straight and narrow pathway leading to eternal happiness. We find peace in making wise choices based on eternal principles.

Counseled Joshua: "Choose you this day whom ye will serve; . . . but as for me and my house, we will serve the LORD" (Josh. 24:15). Praise be to God that we have the power to make our own choices. We feel the light of Christ burning within us to guide our footsteps (see Moro. 7:15–17). We hear the whisperings of the Spirit when we seek answers to life's challenges (see 2 Ne. 32:5). We feel the comforting joy of doing what the Lord would have us do.

Agency is to our lives what the sun is to the world in which we live. Agency is the light of wisdom and the glow of our divine potential to become like Jesus Christ, our Redeemer. Of all of the blessings given to us by God, the freedom to choose is one of the most choice and ennobling. Being agents of the Lord, we are grateful. Being wise servants, we are filled with thanksgiving. Our willingness to learn and do as the Lord would have us do brings quiet confirmation to our souls that our freedom to choose comes to us because we are created in the very image of God.

26 ¶ And Joshua wrote these words in the book of the law of God, and took a great stone, and set it up there under an oak, that was by the sanctuary of the LORD.

27 And Joshua said unto all the people, Behold, this stone shall be a witness unto us; for it hath heard all the words of the LORD which he spake unto us: it shall be therefore a witness unto you, lest ye deny your God.

28 So Joshua let the people depart, every man unto his inheritance.

29 ¶ And it came to pass after these things, that Joshua the son of Nun, the servant of the LORD, died, being an hundred and ten years old.

30 And they buried him in the border of his inheritance in Timnath-serah, which is in mount Ephraim, on the north side of the hill of Gaash.

31 And Israel served the LORD all the days of Joshua, and all the days of the elders that overlived Joshua, and which had known all the works of the LORD, that he had done for Israel.

32 ¶ And the bones of Joseph, which the children of Israel brought up out of Egypt, buried they in Shechem, in a parcel of ground which Jacob bought of the sons of Hamor the father of Shechem for an hundred pieces of silver: and it became the inheritance of the children of Joseph.

33 And Eleazar the son of Aaron died; and they buried him in a hill that pertained to Phinehas his son, which was given him in mount Ephraim.

THE
BOOK OF JUDGES

CHAPTER 2

1 AND an angel of the LORD came up from Gilgal to Bochim, and said, I made you to go up out of Egypt, and have brought you unto the land which I sware unto your fathers; and I said, I will never break my covenant with you.

2 And ye shall make no league with the inhabitants of this land; ye shall throw down their altars: but ye have not obeyed my voice: why have ye done this?

3 Wherefore I also said, I will not drive them out from before you; but they shall be as thorns in your sides, and their gods shall be a snare unto you.

4 And it came to pass, when the angel of the LORD spake these words unto all the children of Israel, that the people lifted up their voice, and wept.

5 And they called the name of that place Bochim: and they sacrificed there unto the LORD.

6 ¶ And when Joshua had let the people go, the children of Israel went every man unto his inheritance to possess the land.

JUDGES CHAPTER 2

"We are here to cooperate with God in the salvation of the living, in the redemption of the dead, in the blessings of our ancestors, in the pouring out [of] blessings upon our children; we are here for the purpose of redeeming and generating the earth on which we live, and God has placed His authority and His counsels here upon the earth for that purpose, that men may learn to do the will of God on the earth as it is done in heaven. This is the object of our existence. —John Taylor, *JD* 21:94

Preview—Precepts and Principles in the Book of Judges

The Lord gives us our free agency, and allows us to be tested and tried through various influences—"thorns in your sides" (see Judges 2:3) when we become forgetful—as a means of proving our faithfulness. The Lord provides sources of light and leadership to keep us on the straight and narrow—prophets, angels, righteous civil leaders (judges), according to our circumstances, all to kindle and keep alive the fire of righteousness in our lives. To be worthy instruments in the hands of God, we are to honor our covenant promises and be true to the principles of righteousness. Once committed, Gideon was ever a faithful servant of God. As with Samson, those who deviate from the appointed pathway will fail to measure up to the potential inherent within them. Nevertheless, the Lord strives mightily with men and women, giving them every opportunity to overcome their weaknesses and bring about good results.

The 200-year period of the judges—between Joshua and Samuel—was a time of great turmoil in Israel. It was a period that reflected many variations of the cycles of obedience and falling away, faithfulness and forgetting the covenants, sin and recovery, weakness and valor. The diverse portraits of leadership emerging from this period are mixed: at times they give us encouragement and inspiration; at other times they sound the warning voice. The message is clear: when we remember the Lord and His commandments, then all will be well; when we venture into forbidden pathways, then we relinquish peace, harmony, and the favor of God.

The pathway of life takes us through the tests of time, where we have the opportunity to overcome challenges, learn from hardships, resist temptation, rise above oppression, measure up to trials, and transcend adversity. To guide us along the way, the Lord provides beacons of light in the form of angels, prophets, teachers, mentors, and leaders of all kinds (in this case judges). To exemplify courage and strength, He raises up individuals of uncommon stature, such as Deborah and Gideon—and, yes, the controversial Samson. All of this serves to bring about His divine mission of perfecting the Saints and preparing them for the completion of their journey, which is to end with salvation and immortality in His eternal rest.

7 And the people served the LORD all the days of Joshua, and all the days of the elders that outlived Joshua, who had seen all the great works of the LORD, that he did for Israel.

8 And Joshua the son of Nun, the servant of the LORD, died, being an hundred and ten years old.

9 And they buried him in the border of his inheritance in Timnath-heres, in the mount of Ephraim, on the north side of the hill Gaash.

10 And also all that generation were gathered unto their fathers: and there arose another generation after them, which knew not the LORD, nor yet the works which he had done for Israel.

11 ¶ And the children of Israel did evil in the sight of the LORD, and served Baalim:

12 And they forsook the LORD God of their fathers, which brought them out of the land of Egypt, and followed other gods, of the gods of the people that were round about them, and bowed themselves unto them, and provoked the LORD to anger.

13 And they forsook the LORD, and served Baal and Ashtaroth.

14 ¶ And the anger of the LORD was hot against Israel, and he delivered them into the hands of spoilers that spoiled them, and he sold them into the hands of their enemies round about, so that they could not any longer stand before their enemies.

15 Whithersoever they went out, the hand of the LORD was against them for evil, as the LORD had said, and as the LORD had sworn unto them: and they were greatly distressed.

16 ¶ Nevertheless the LORD raised up judges, which delivered them out of the hand of those that spoiled them.

17 And yet they would not hearken unto their judges, but they went a whoring after other gods, and bowed themselves unto them: they turned quickly out of the way which their fathers walked in, obeying the commandments of the LORD; but they did not so.

18 And when the LORD raised them up judges, then the LORD was with the judge, and delivered them out of the hand of their enemies all the days of the judge: for it repented the LORD because of their groanings by reason of them that oppressed them and vexed them.

19 And it came to pass, when the judge was dead, that they returned, and corrupted themselves more than their fathers, in following other gods to serve them, and to bow down unto them; they ceased not from their own doings, nor from their stubborn way.

20 ¶ And the anger of the LORD was hot against Israel; and he said, Because that this people hath transgressed my covenant which I commanded their fathers, and have not hearkened unto my voice;

21 I also will not henceforth drive out any from before them of the nations which Joshua left when he died:

22 That through them I may prove Israel, whether they will keep the way of the LORD to walk therein, as their fathers did keep it, or not.

23 Therefore the LORD left those nations, without driving them out hastily; neither delivered he them into the hand of Joshua.

Judges 2:11–12—Ashtaroth/Ashtoreth

Ashtaroth (pronounced "ash'-tuh-roth") is the plural form of the name Ashtoreth (pronounced "ash'-tuh-reth"), the principal female goddess of the Phoenicians. The principal male god was Baal (plural Baalim). During the days of Joshua, the Israelites served the Lord according to the covenant: "And the people served the LORD all the days of Joshua, and all the days of the elders that outlived Joshua, who had seen all the great works of the LORD, that he did for Israel" (Judges 2:7). But after the passing of Joshua, a sinister change gradually occurred as the people began to worship other gods (see Judges 2:11–12).

This idolatry continued from time to time as the Israelites struggled to find the pathway of righteousness (see Judges 10:6). The prophet Samuel persuaded the people to abandon such evil and return to the Lord (see 1 Sam. 7:3–4), but they all too soon forgot their promise (see 1 Sam. 12:10; 31:10). During the days of Solomon, the singular form *Ashtoreth* was commonly used (see 1 Kings 11:5, 33). Josiah the reformer destroyed the "high places" that Solomon had erected in honor of Ashtoreth (see 2 Kings 23:11).

Judges 2:22—The Tests of Time

The Lord gives us our free agency, and allows us to be tested and tried through various influences—"thorns in your sides" (see Judges 2:3) when we become forgetful—as a means of proving our faithfulness.

Just as the Lord allowed segments of Canaanite civilization to be preserved in proximity to Israel as a standing test of loyalty and fidelity, similarly He allows us to make our journey through the world's highways and byways in order that we might have the opportunity to choose the right according to His precepts and commandments, and remain free of worldly taint.

The lack of proper teaching, an unwillingness to accept good teaching, or choosing to do according to our own will always result in apostasy, whether the apostasy is individual or as a group. There is a responsibility to insure against it. It falls on everyone. We must be good teachers, teaching by the Spirit, and we must be easily entreated and receive the teachings by the spirit of truth—in which case it is of God and both teacher and learner are edified (see D&C 50:17–22).

CHAPTER 4

1 AND the children of Israel again did evil in the sight of the LORD, when Ehud was dead.

2 And the LORD sold them into the hand of Jabin king of Canaan, that reigned in Hazor; the captain of whose host was Sisera, which dwelt in Harosheth of the Gentiles.

3 And the children of Israel cried unto the LORD: for he had nine hundred chariots of iron; and twenty years he mightily oppressed the children of Israel.

4 ¶ And Deborah, a prophetess, the wife of Lapidoth, she judged Israel at that time.

5 And she dwelt under the palm tree of Deborah between Ramah and Beth-el in mount Ephraim: and the children of Israel came up to her for judgment.

6 And she sent and called Barak the son of Abinoam out of Kedesh-naphtali, and said unto him, Hath not the LORD God of Israel commanded, saying, Go and draw toward mount Tabor, and take with thee ten thousand men of the children of Naphtali and of the children of Zebulun?

7 And I will draw unto thee to the river Kishon Sisera, the captain of Jabin's army, with his chariots and his multitude; and I will deliver him into thine hand.

8 And Barak said unto her, If thou wilt go with me, then I will go: but if thou wilt not go with me, then I will not go.

9 And she said, I will surely go with thee: notwithstanding the journey that thou takest shall not be for thine honour; for the LORD shall sell Sisera into the hand of a woman. And Deborah arose, and went with Barak to Kedesh.

10 ¶ And Barak called Zebulun and Naphtali to Kedesh; and he went up with ten thousand men at his feet: and Deborah went up with him.

11 Now Heber the Kenite, which was of the children of Hobab the father in law of Moses, had severed himself from the Kenites, and pitched his tent unto the plain of Zaanaim, which is by Kedesh.

12 And they shewed Sisera that Barak the son of Abinoam was gone up to mount Tabor.

13 And Sisera gathered together all his chariots, even nine hundred chariots of iron, and all the people that were with him, from Harosheth of the Gentiles unto the river of Kishon.

14 And Deborah said unto Barak, Up; for this is the day in which the LORD hath delivered Sisera into thine hand: is not the LORD gone out before thee? So Barak went down from mount Tabor, and ten thousand men after him.

15 And the LORD discomfited Sisera, and all his chariots, and all his host, with the edge of the sword before Barak; so that Sisera lighted down off his chariot, and fled away on his feet.

16 But Barak pursued after the chariots, and after the host, unto Harosheth of the Gentiles: and all the host of Sisera fell upon the edge of the sword; and there was not a man left.

17 Howbeit Sisera fled away on his feet to the tent of Jael the wife of Heber the Kenite: for there was peace between Jabin the king of Hazor and the house of Heber the Kenite.

18 ¶ And Jael went out to meet Sisera, and said unto him, Turn in, my lord, turn in to me; fear not. And when he had turned in unto her into the tent, she covered him with a mantle.

JUDGES CHAPTER 4

Judges 4—Beacons of Light

During this period of time, the Lord raised up a sequence of wise leaders—judges—to maintain some sense of godly order among the tribes of Israel. He also sent angels and prophets from time to time to stir the Israelites up to a sense of their commitments and to remind them of the marvelous blessings that were part of their heritage. For the most part, the judges worked righteousness and brought about progress in the quality of life. Deborah stands out as an example—a beacon of light, friendship, and courage in a sometimes confusing and unstable historical terrain—and reflects the strength and power of divine leadership.

Having good friends and being a good friend is an important aspect of life. Our Savior made the relationship between friends based on love (see John 15:13–15). Our Savior loved us. He gave His life for us. He taught us, nurtured us, and is all things unto us. He is our friend. We likewise can be a friend to all, and by so doing are friends of Christ (see Matt. 25:40).

Judges 4:4–24—Deborah

Deborah (meaning: a bee) was a celebrated leader who served as judge over Israel and unified the people in strength to defeat their enemies (see Judges 4:4–5). She commissioned Barak, the son of Abinoam, to wage battle against the encroaching Canaanites under the command of Sisera. Barak agreed to gather the forces and attack, provided Deborah would consent to accompany him. That she did (see Judges 4:14). That day the Canaanites, with their much larger force, were annihilated, along with their king, whose name was Jabin (see Judges 4:23–24). Thereafter Deborah and Barak joined in singing a glorious anthem of praise to the Lord:

> *The inhabitants of* the villages ceased, they ceased in Israel, until that I Deborah arose, that I arose a mother in Israel. . . .
>
> *They that are delivered* from the noise of archers in the places of drawing water, there shall they rehearse the righteous acts of the LORD, *even* the righteous acts *toward the inhabitants* of his villages in Israel: then shall the people of the LORD go down to the gates.
>
> Awake, awake, Deborah: awake, awake, utter a song: arise, Barak, and lead thy captivity captive, thou son of Abinoam. (Judges 5:7, 11–12)

The essence of Deborah's service is summarized thus: "So let all thine enemies perish, O LORD: but *let* them that love him *be* as the sun when he goeth forth in his might. And the land had rest forty years" (Judges 5:31).

Judges 4:7—Sisera

Sisera (pronounced "sis'-uh-ruh") was the captain of the army of Jabin, king of Canaan, during the time of Deborah. After the Canaanites were annhilated, Sisera fled to

19 And he said unto her, Give me, I pray thee, a little water to drink; for I am thirsty. And she opened a bottle of milk, and gave him drink, and covered him.

20 Again he said unto her, Stand in the door of the tent, and it shall be, when any man doth come and enquire of thee, and say, Is there any man here? that thou shalt say, No.

21 Then Jael Heber's wife took a nail of the tent, and took an hammer in her hand, and went softly unto him, and smote the nail into his temples, and fastened it into the ground: for he was fast asleep and weary. So he died.

22 And, behold, as Barak pursued Sisera, Jael came out to meet him, and said unto him, Come, and I will shew thee the man whom thou seekest. And when he came into her tent, behold, Sisera lay dead, and the nail was in his temples.

23 So God subdued on that day Jabin the king of Canaan before the children of Israel.

24 And the hand of the children of Israel prospered, and prevailed against Jabin the king of Canaan, until they had destroyed Jabin king of Canaan.

CHAPTER 6

1 AND the children of Israel did evil in the sight of the LORD: and the LORD delivered them into the hand of Midian seven years.

2 And the hand of Midian prevailed against Israel: and because of the Midianites the children of Israel made them the dens which are in the mountains, and caves, and strong holds.

3 And so it was, when Israel had sown, that the Midianites came up, and the Amalekites, and the children of the east, even they came up against them;

4 And they encamped against them, and destroyed the increase of the earth, till thou come unto Gaza, and left no sustenance for Israel, neither sheep, nor ox, nor ass.

5 For they came up with their cattle and their tents, and they came as grasshoppers for multitude; for both they and their camels were without number: and they entered into the land to destroy it.

6 And Israel was greatly impoverished because of the Midianites; and the children of Israel cried unto the LORD.

7 ¶ And it came to pass, when the children of Israel cried unto the LORD because of the Midianites,

8 That the LORD sent a prophet unto the children of Israel, which said unto them, Thus saith the LORD God of Israel, I brought you up from Egypt, and brought you forth out of the house of bondage;

9 And I delivered you out of the hand of the Egyptians, and out of the hand of all that oppressed you, and drave them out from before you, and gave you their land;

10 And I said unto you, I am the LORD your God; fear not the gods of the Amorites, in whose land ye dwell: but ye have not obeyed my voice.

11 ¶ And there came an angel of the LORD, and sat under an oak which was in Ophrah, that pertained unto Joash the Abi-ezrite: and his son Gideon threshed wheat by the winepress, to hide it from the Midianites.

12 And the angel of the LORD appeared unto him, and said unto him, The LORD is with thee, thou mighty man of valour.

the house of Heber the Kenite (a supposed ally), whose wife Jael strategically extended hospitality to Sisera but then slew him as he was sleeping (see Judges 4:18–22). Thereafter Deborah and Barak joined in singing a glorious anthem of praise to the Lord in which the memory of Sisera is repeatedly invoked (see Judges 5:20, 26, 28, 30).

Judges 4:22–24—Jael

When the Israelites came against Jabin, king of the Canaanites, with his invading hosts under command of Sisera, the victory was with Deborah and her commander Barak (see Judges 4:14, 23–24). The fleeing Sisera took refuge in the tent of Jael (pronounced "jay'-uhl"; meaning: mountain goat), wife of Heber the Kenite (a tribe related to the Midianites and friendly toward the Israelites). In the guise of serving and hiding Sisera, Jael stealthily brought an end to his life (see Judges 4:22–24).

In their hymn of praise and celebration following the victory over the Canaanites, Deborah and Barak remembered the woman who silenced Sisera: "Blessed above women shall Jael the wife of Heber the Kenite be, blessed shall she be above women in the tent" (Judges 5:24).

JUDGES CHAPTER 6

Judges 6:11–14—Gideon

Gideon (meaning: warrior) was one of the leading figures represented in the Book of Judges covering the turbulent period of time commencing with the death of Joshua (around 1477 BC) and extending to the birth of Samuel (around 1125 BC). The judgeship of Gideon began around 1263 BC, when he was called to deliver Israel from bondage under the Midianites (see Judges 6:14). Gideon obeyed the command of the Lord to destroy the altar of Baal and the associated ceremonial grove (see Judges 6:28)—thus earning the alternative name *Jerubbaal* (meaning: he that striveth against Baal—see Judges 6:32; 7:1; 1 Sam. 12:11). He then prevailed over the forces of the Midianites by applying an abundance of strategic know-how to compensate for the smallness of his own army.

Though triumphant, Gideon refused the kingship: "And Gideon said unto them, I will not rule over you, neither shall my son rule over you: the LORD shall rule over you" (Judges 8:23). His son Abimelech was born around 1223 BC. As Judges 9 relates, when Abimelech aspired to and obtained the office of king, following the death of his father, he murdered his paternal brethren (numbering "threescore and ten"—Judges 9:5) to preserve his power and office (see Judges 9:53–56). Abimelech ruled with treachery and cunning, generating many enemies in the process. On one occasion, in bringing destruction to one of the towns in his realm, he was slain (see Judges 9:53–56; compare 2 Sam. 11:21). Gideon is remembered fondly as an exemplar of the victorious champion of right (see Isa. 9:4).

13 And Gideon said unto him, Oh my Lord, if the LORD be with us, why then is all this befallen us? and where be all his miracles which our fathers told us of, saying, Did not the LORD bring us up from Egypt? but now the LORD hath forsaken us, and delivered us into the hands of the Midianites.

14 And the LORD looked upon him, and said, Go in this thy might, and thou shalt save Israel from the hand of the Midianites: have not I sent thee?

15 And he said unto him, Oh my Lord, wherewith shall I save Israel? behold, my family is poor in Manasseh, and I am the least in my father's house.

16 And the LORD said unto him, Surely I will be with thee, and thou shalt smite the Midianites as one man.

17 And he said unto him, If now I have found grace in thy sight, then shew me a sign that thou talkest with me.

18 Depart not hence, I pray thee, until I come unto thee, and bring forth my present, and set it before thee. And he said, I will tarry until thou come again.

19 ¶ And Gideon went in, and made ready a kid, and unleavened cakes of an ephah of flour: the flesh he put in a basket, and he put the broth in a pot, and brought it out unto him under the oak, and presented it.

20 And the angel of God said unto him, Take the flesh and the unleavened cakes, and lay them upon this rock, and pour out the broth. And he did so.

21 ¶ Then the angel of the LORD put forth the end of the staff that was in his hand, and touched the flesh and the unleavened cakes; and there rose up fire out of the rock, and consumed the flesh and the unleavened cakes. Then the angel of the LORD departed out of his sight.

22 And when Gideon perceived that he was an angel of the LORD, Gideon said, Alas, O Lord GOD! for because I have seen an angel of the LORD face to face.

23 And the LORD said unto him, Peace be unto thee; fear not: thou shalt not die.

24 Then Gideon built an altar there unto the LORD, and called it Jehovah-shalom: unto this day it is yet in Ophrah of the Abi-ezrites.

25 ¶ And it came to pass the same night, that the LORD said unto him, Take thy father's young bullock, even the second bullock of seven years old, and throw down the altar of Baal that thy father hath, and cut down the grove that is by it:

26 And build an altar unto the LORD thy God upon the top of this rock, in the ordered place, and take the second bullock, and offer a burnt sacrifice with the wood of the grove which thou shalt cut down.

27 Then Gideon took ten men of his servants, and did as the LORD had said unto him: and so it was, because he feared his father's household, and the men of the city, that he could not do it by day, that he did it by night.

28 ¶ And when the men of the city arose early in the morning, behold, the altar of Baal was cast down, and the grove was cut down that was by it, and the second bullock was offered upon the altar that was built.

Deborah by Gustave Doré

 POINT OF INTEREST

"The Hebrew word that we translate as 'judge'—shophet—is a participle of the Hebrew verb shaphat. In the Hebrew Bible, shaphat is used to describe roles that include a giver of the law, a judge, or a governor. These people would be responsible for making decisions in controversial situations, executing judgment, discriminating, condemning, punishing, and vindicating. There are only two instances in the book of Judges where the word is used in its legal sense—first, when the Israelites come to Deborah 'for judgment' (4:5), and second, when Jephthah warns the king of the Ammonites to 'Let the Lord, who is judge, decide today for the Israelites or for the Ammonites' (11:27)." (John Bowker, *The Complete Bible Handbook* [New York: DK Publishing, 2001]).

29 And they said one to another, Who hath done this thing? And when they enquired and asked, they said, Gideon the son of Joash hath done this thing.

30 Then the men of the city said unto Joash, Bring out thy son, that he may die: because he hath cast down the altar of Baal, and because he hath cut down the grove that was by it.

31 And Joash said unto all that stood against him, Will ye plead for Baal? will ye save him? he that will plead for him, let him be put to death whilst it is yet morning: if he be a god, let him plead for himself, because one hath cast down his altar.

32 Therefore on that day he called him Jerubbaal, saying, Let Baal plead against him,

33 ¶ Then all the Midianites and the Amalekites and the children of the east were gathered together, and went over, and pitched in the valley of Jezreel.

34 But the Spirit of the LORD came upon Gideon, and he blew a trumpet; and Abi-ezer was gathered after him.

35 And he sent messengers throughout all Manasseh; who also was gathered after him: and he sent messengers unto Asher, and unto Zebulun, and unto Naphtali; and they came up to meet them.

36 ¶ And Gideon said unto God, If thou wilt save Israel by mine hand, as thou hast said,

37 Behold, I will put a fleece of wool in the floor; and if the dew be on the fleece only, and it be dry upon all the earth beside, then shall I know that thou wilt save Israel by mine hand, as thou hast said.

38 And it was so: for he rose up early on the morrow, and thrust the fleece together, and wringed the dew out of the fleece, a bowl full of water.

39 And Gideon said unto God, Let not thine anger be hot against me, and I will speak but this once: let me prove, I pray thee, but this once with the fleece; let it now be dry only upon the fleece, and upon all the ground let there be dew.

40 And God did so that night: for it was dry upon the fleece only, and there was dew on all the ground.

CHAPTER 7

1 THEN Jerubbaal, who is Gideon, and all the people that were with him, rose up early, and pitched beside the well of Harod: so that the host of the Midianites were on the north side of them, by the hill of Moreh, in the valley.

2 And the LORD said unto Gideon, The people that are with thee are too many for me to give the Midianites into their hands, lest Israel vaunt themselves against me, saying, Mine own hand hath saved me.

3 Now therefore go to, proclaim in the ears of the people, saying, Whosoever is fearful and afraid, let him return and depart early from mount Gilead. And there returned of the people twenty and two thousand; and there remained ten thousand.

4 And the LORD said unto Gideon, The people are yet too many; bring them down unto the water, and I will try them for thee there: and it shall be, that of whom I say unto thee, This shall go with thee, the same shall go with thee; and of whomsoever I say unto thee, This shall not go with thee, the same shall not go.

5 So he brought down the people unto the water: and the LORD said unto Gideon, Every one that lappeth of the water with his tongue, as a dog lappeth, him shalt thou set by himself; likewise every one that boweth down upon his knees to drink.

Judges 6:29—Joash (Jehoash)

Joash was the father of Gideon, the warrior/judge (see Judges 6:11). When during the nighttime Gideon destroyed the altar of Baal and grove (idol of nature worship) associated with it, the citizens demanded next morning to know the identity of the perpetrator. Learning that it was Gideon, they called for his execution. The answer of Joash is unforgettable:

> And Joash said unto all that stood against him, Will ye plead for Baal? will ye save him? he that will plead for him, let him be put to death whilst it is yet morning: if he be a god, let him plead for himself, because one hath cast down his altar.
>
> Therefore on that day he called him Jerubbaal, saying, Let Baal plead against him, because he hath thrown down his altar. (Judges 6:31–32)

Thereafter, with the dissenting population silenced, Gideon (now also called Jerubbaal) received a divine commission to deliver Israel—and he promptly defeated the Midianite enemies (see Judges 7–8). We can remember Joash as the father of principle who stood up for his son at a time of national crisis.

Judges 6:32—Jerubbaal

Jerubbaal (pronounced "jeh'-ruh-bay'-uhl"; meaning: he that contends with Baal) was the name that Gideon, the judge, received from his father Joash after Gideon had destroyed the altar of Baal according to a commandment from an angel of God (see Judges 6:32; 7:1; 9:1; 1 Sam. 12:11).

JUDGES CHAPTER 7

Judges 7—The Strength of the Lord

The army of Israel, no matter how small, is invincible when going forth in the strength of the Lord. With the Lord on our side, there is no enemy that can vanquish or prevail.

The story of Gideon and his three hundred stalwart men, armed with trumpets and pitchers and operating under guidance of the Almighty, is a memorable testimony to the fulfillment of the designs of the Lord on behalf of His people. Elisha, likewise, would in later times confirm the supremacy of the hosts of the Lord over any worldly foe. When the young servant observed with fear the power of the enemy forces arrayed, Elisha said: "Fear not: for they that be with us are more than they that be with them. And Elisha prayed, and said, LORD, I pray thee, open his eyes, that he may see. And the LORD opened the eyes of the young man; and he saw: and, behold, the mountain was full of horses and chariots of fire round about Elisha" (2 Kings 6:16–17). The Syrians were then defeated, just as the Midianites when confronting Gideon and the Lord's army.

The lesson is plain: In our challenges and tribulations, let us seek the Lord's guidance and pray for the vision to see the inevitable victory that blesses the lives of the faithful and valiant when they go forth "in the strength of the Lord" (Alma 20:4).

6 And the number of them that lapped, putting their hand to their mouth, were three hundred men: but all the rest of the people bowed down upon their knees to drink water.

7 And the LORD said unto Gideon, By the three hundred men that lapped will I save you, and deliver the Midianites into thine hand: and let all the other people go every man unto his place.

8 So the people took victuals in their hand, and their trumpets: and he sent all the rest of Israel every man unto his tent, and retained those three hundred men: and the host of Midian was beneath him in the valley.

9 ¶ And it came to pass the same night, that the LORD said unto him, Arise, get thee down unto the host; for I have delivered it into thine hand.

10 But if thou fear to go down, go thou with Phurah thy servant down to the host:

11 And thou shalt hear what they say; and afterward shall thine hands be strengthened to go down unto the host. Then went he down with Phurah his servant unto the outside of the armed men that were in the host.

12 And the Midianites and the Amalekites and all the children of the east lay along in the valley like grasshoppers for multitude; and their camels were without number, as the sand by the sea side for multitude.

13 And when Gideon was come, behold, there was a man that told a dream unto his fellow, and said, Behold, I dreamed a dream, and, lo, a cake of barley bread tumbled into the host of Midian, and came unto a tent, and smote it that it fell, and overturned it, that the tent lay along.

14 And his fellow answered and said, This is nothing else save the sword of Gideon the son of Joash, a man of Israel: for into his hand hath God delivered Midian, and all the host.

15 ¶ And it was so, when Gideon heard the telling of the dream, and the interpretation thereof, that he worshipped, and returned into the host of Israel, and said, Arise; for the LORD hath delivered into your hand the host of Midian.

16 And he divided the three hundred men into three companies, and he put a trumpet in every man's hand, with empty pitchers, and lamps within the pitchers.

17 And he said unto them, Look on me, and do likewise: and, behold, when I come to the outside of the camp, it shall be that, as I do, so shall ye do.

18 When I blow with a trumpet, I and all that are with me, then blow ye the trumpets also on every side of all the camp, and say, The sword of the LORD, and of Gideon.

19 ¶ So Gideon, and the hundred men that were with him, came unto the outside of the camp in the beginning of the middle watch; and they had but newly set the watch: and they blew the trumpets, and brake the pitchers that were in their hands.

20 And the three companies blew the trumpets, and brake the pitchers, and held the lamps in their left hands, and the trumpets in their right hands to blow withal: and they cried, The sword of the LORD, and of Gideon.

21 And they stood every man in his place round about the camp: and all the host ran, and cried, and fled.

22 And the three hundred blew the trumpets, and the LORD set every man's sword against his fellow, even throughout all the host: and the host fled to Beth-shittah in Zererath, and to the border of Abel-meholah, unto Tabbath.

NOTES:

23 And the men of Israel gathered themselves together out of Naphtali, and out of Asher, and out of all Manasseh, and pursued after the Midianites.

24 ¶ And Gideon sent messengers throughout all mount Ephraim, saying, Come down against the Midianites, and take before them the waters unto Beth-barah and Jordan. Then all the men of Ephraim gathered themselves together, and took the waters unto Beth-barah and Jordan.

25 And they took two princes of the Midianites, Oreb and Zeeb; and they slew Oreb upon the rock Oreb, and Zeeb they slew at the winepress of Zeeb, and pursued Midian, and brought the heads of Oreb and Zeeb to Gideon on the other side Jordan.

CHAPTER 13

1 AND the children of Israel did evil again in the sight of the LORD; and the LORD delivered them into the hand of the Philistines forty years.

2 ¶ And there was a certain man of Zorah, of the family of the Danites, whose name was Manoah; and his wife was barren, and bare not.

3 And the angel of the LORD appeared unto the woman, and said unto her, Behold now, thou art barren, and bearest not: but thou shalt conceive, and bear a son.

4 Now therefore beware, I pray thee, and drink not wine nor strong drink, and eat not any unclean thing:

5 For, lo, thou shalt conceive, and bear a son; and no razor shall come on his head: for the child shall be a Nazarite unto God from the womb: and he shall begin to deliver Israel out of the hand of the Philistines.

6 ¶ Then the woman came and told her husband, saying, A man of God came unto me, and his countenance was like the countenance of an angel of God, very terrible: but I asked him not whence he was, neither told he me his name:

7 But he said unto me, Behold, thou shalt conceive, and bear a son; and now drink no wine nor strong drink, neither eat any unclean thing: for the child shall be a Nazarite to God from the womb to the day of his death.

8 Then Manoah intreated the LORD, and said, O my Lord, let the man of God which thou didst send come again unto us, and teach us what we shall do unto the child that shall be born.

9 And God hearkened to the voice of Manoah; and the angel of God came again unto the woman as she sat in the field: but Manoah her husband was not with her.

10 And the woman made haste, and ran, and shewed her husband, and said unto him, Behold, the man hath appeared unto me, that came unto me the other day.

11 And Manoah arose, and went after his wife, and came to the man, and said unto him, Art thou the man that spakest unto the woman? And he said, I am.

12 And Manoah said, Now let thy words come to pass. How shall we order the child, and how shall we do unto him?

13 And the angel of the LORD said unto Manoah, Of all that I said unto the woman let her beware.

14 She may not eat of any thing that cometh of the vine, neither let her drink wine or strong drink, nor eat any unclean thing: all that I commanded her let her observe.

JUDGES CHAPTER 13

Judges 13:5—Nazarite

An individual under the vow of a Nazarite (meaning: one separated unto the Lord, a consecrated man) would abstain from strong drink, avoid cutting the hair of the head, and avoid any contact with dead people (see Num. 6). The Nazarite vow could be for life (as in the case of Samson—see Judges 13:5, 7; 16:17; or Samuel—see 1 Sam. 1:11) or for only a shorter, defined period of time (see Amos 2:11–12). Note also the reference to John the Baptist in the New Testament: "For he shall be great in the sight of the Lord, and shall drink neither wine nor strong drink; and he shall be filled with the Holy Ghost, even from his mother's womb" (Luke 1:15).

Judges 13:24—Samson

Samson (meaning: of the sun), famous for his astounding strength, was the twelfth in a sequence of judges serving in Israel (see Judges 13–16). At a time when the Israelites had been in bondage to the Philistines for four decades, an angel of the Lord came to the wife of Manoah, a member of the tribe of Dan, and pronounced a wondrous blessing upon her head (for she had been barren) that she would bear a son (see Judges 13:5, 24). Samson was that son.

The rise of Samson was marked by several notable milestones: his slaying of a lion with his bare hands during the time he was courting a Philistine woman (see Judges 14); his slaying of a thousand Philistines with the jawbone of an ass in connection with bitter disappointments concerning his marriage (see Judges 15); and his fatal interaction with Delilah, a woman from the valley of Sorek whom he loved (see Judges 16:4).

The Philistines bribed Delilah to discover the secret of Samson's astounding strength. Three times in sequence she induced him deceitfully to share the information with her—but each time it proved to be a fiction. She persisted, learning that his srength came from the fact that he had kept the vows of the Nazarites and had never cut his hair (see Judges 16:17.)

Then Delilah made her move by causing his hair to be shaved, leaving him enervated and powerless: "And he wist not that the LORD was departed from him" (Judges 16:20). The Philistines then put out Samson's eyes and imprisoned him at Gaza. Later—after Samson's hair had grown long once again (see Judges 16:22)—the Philistines assembled a vast throng of people to celebrate their victory and to make sport of Samson. It was then that he called one last time upon the Lord and pulled down the pillars of the house, destroying himself and all three thousand of the celebrants who were therein (see Judges 16:28–30).

Gideon and Samson—Instruments of God

To be worthy instruments in the hands of God, we are to honor our covenant promises and be true to the principles of righteousness. Once committed, Gideon was ever a faithful servant of God. As with Samson, those who deviate from the appointed pathway will fail to measure up to

15 ¶ And Manoah said unto the angel of the LORD, I pray thee, let us detain thee, until we shall have made ready a kid for thee.

16 And the angel of the LORD said unto Manoah, Though thou detain me, I will not eat of thy bread: and if thou wilt offer a burnt offering, thou must offer it unto the LORD. For Manoah knew not that he was an angel of the LORD.

17 And Manoah said unto the angel of the LORD, What is thy name, that when thy sayings come to pass we may do thee honour?

18 And the angel of the LORD said unto him, Why askest thou thus after my name, seeing it is secret?

19 So Manoah took a kid with a meat offering, and offered it upon a rock unto the LORD: and the angel did wondrously; and Manoah and his wife looked on.

20 For it came to pass, when the flame went up toward heaven from off the altar, that the angel of the LORD ascended in the flame of the altar. And Manoah and his wife looked on it, and fell on their faces to the ground.

21 But the angel of the LORD did no more appear to Manoah and to his wife. Then Manoah knew that he was an angel of the LORD.

22 And Manoah said unto his wife, We shall surely die, because we have seen God.

23 But his wife said unto him, If the LORD were pleased to kill us, he would not have received a burnt offering and a meat offering at our hands, neither would he have shewed us all these things, nor would as at this time have told us such things as these.

24 ¶ And the woman bare a son, and called his name Samson: and the child grew, and the LORD blessed him.

25 And the Spirit of the LORD began to move him at times in the camp of Dan between Zorah and Eshtaol.

CHAPTER 14

1 AND Samson went down to Timnath, and saw a woman in Timnath of the daughters of the Philistines.

2 And he came up, and told his father and his mother, and said, I have seen a woman in Timnath of the daughters of the Philistines: now therefore get her for me to wife.

3 Then his father and his mother said unto him, Is there never a woman among the daughters of thy brethren, or among all my people, that thou goest to take a wife of the uncircumcised Philistines? And Samson said unto his father, Get her for me; for she pleaseth me well.

4 But his father and his mother knew not that it was of the LORD, that he sought an occasion against the Philistines: for at that time the Philistines had dominion over Israel.

5 ¶ Then went Samson down, and his father and his mother, to Timnath, and came to the vineyards of Timnath: and, behold, a young lion roared against him.

6 And the Spirit of the LORD came mightily upon him, and he rent him as he would have rent a kid, and he had nothing in his hand: but he told not his father or his mother what he had done.

7 And he went down, and talked with the woman; and she pleased Samson well.

8 ¶ And after a time he returned to take her, and he turned aside to see the carcase of the lion: and, behold, there was a swarm of bees and honey in the carcase of the lion.

the potential inherent within them. Nevertheless, the Lord strives mightily with men and women, giving them every opportunity to overcome their weaknesses and bring about good results.

Gideon became an instrument in the hands of the Lord. The Lord used him and directed him to do things the Lord's way. When Gideon realized the Lord was not only with him but would insure the victory, he was full of faith . . . and his men shared that faith and also became instruments in the hand of the Lord.

Samson's parents were imbued with a desire to provide the best environment for his appointed development as a Nazarite, devoted to the cause of righteousness. Samson presents a mixed portrait of great promise and power as well as weakness and appetite. As long as the Spirit of the Lord was with him, he remained poised to be a productive instrument in the hands of God When he deviated from the course, then carnal desire, rancor, anger, and the spirit of vengeance were allowed to flourish and drive out spiritual motivation. We can learn great lessons from his example as we strive to cultivate harmony, balance, humility and spirituality as the predominant forces in our lives.

Judges 13—Summary of Precepts and Principles

To meet the tests of time and complete the journey of life with honor and allegiance to heavenly principles is to earn the crown of glory in the mansions of the Father. We can count our blessings when we discern the hand of the Lord in our everyday lives: the scriptures containing the fullness of the gospel, living prophets and other devoted teachers—the beacons of light and instruments of God who are placed along our pathway as guides and mentors—and above all, the inspiration of the Spirit. If we are faithful, the Lord's message to Gideon will be His message to us: "Surely I will be with thee" (Judges 6:16).

JUDGES CHAPTER 14

Judges 14—Striving of the Lord

The influence of the Spirit of the Lord in Samson's life from time to time—despite his disposition toward impulsiveness and untethered reaction—is an indication that the Lord was working with Samson to help shape his service on behalf of the Israelites.

As is always the case, the Lord gives ample leeway for the imperfect (a quality that applies to all) to rise to their potential and bring about good results. Samson, as it turns out, was less than perfect in honoring his Nazarite beginnings, and was to come to an ignominious end—but not before being instrumental in causing the power of God to prevail over the Philistine leaders and their minions (see Judges 16:28–30).

9 And he took thereof in his hands, and went on eating, and came to his father and mother, and he gave them, and they did eat: but he told not them that he had taken the honey out of the carcase of the lion.

10 ¶ So his father went down unto the woman: and Samson made there a feast; for so used the young men to do.

11 And it came to pass, when they saw him, that they brought thirty companions to be with him.

12 ¶ And Samson said unto them, I will now put forth a riddle unto you: if ye can certainly declare it me within the seven days of the feast, and find it out, then I will give you thirty sheets and thirty change of garments:

13 But if ye cannot declare it me, then shall ye give me thirty sheets and thirty change of garments. And they said unto him, Put forth thy riddle, that we may hear it.

14 And he said unto them, Out of the eater came forth meat, and out of the strong came forth sweetness. And they could not in three days expound the riddle.

15 And it came to pass on the seventh day, that they said unto Samson's wife, Entice thy husband, that he may declare unto us the riddle, lest we burn thee and thy father's house with fire: have ye called us to take that we have? is it not so?

16 And Samson's wife wept before him, and said, Thou dost but hate me, and lovest me not: thou hast put forth a riddle unto the children of my people, and hast not told it me. And he said unto her, Behold, I have not told it my father nor my mother, and shall I tell it thee?

17 And she wept before him the seven days, while their feast lasted: and it came to pass on the seventh day, that he told her, because she lay sore upon him: and she told the riddle to the children of her people.

18 And the men of the city said unto him on the seventh day before the sun went down, What is sweeter than honey? and what is stronger than a lion? And he said unto them, If ye had not plowed with my heifer, ye had not found out my riddle.

19 ¶ And the Spirit of the LORD came upon him, and he went down to Ashkelon, and slew thirty men of them, and took their spoil, and gave change of garments unto them which expounded the riddle. And his anger was kindled, and he went up to his father's house.

20 But Samson's wife was given to his companion, whom he had used as his friend.

Likeness of a lion carved on stone in India

 POINT OF INTEREST

The type of lion that Samson would have fought is now endangered, with only 359 reported at Gir National Forest in India. It is one of the three major big cats found in India, the others being the Bengal tiger and the Indian leopard. Asiatic lions once ranged from the Mediterranean to the northeastern parts of the Indian subcontinent, but excessive hunting, water pollution, and decline in natural prey reduced their habitat. Historically Asiatic lions were classified into three kinds—Bengal, Arabian and Persian lions. Asiatic lion are smaller and lighter than their African counterparts but are equally aggressive.

CHAPTER 15

1 BUT it came to pass within a while after, in the time of wheat harvest, that Samson visited his wife with a kid; and he said, I will go in to my wife into the chamber. But her father would not suffer him to go in.

2 And her father said, I verily thought that thou hadst utterly hated her; therefore I gave her to thy companion: is not her younger sister fairer than she? take her, I pray thee, instead of her.

3 ¶ And Samson said concerning them, Now shall I be more blameless than the Philistines, though I do them a displeasure.

4 And Samson went and caught three hundred foxes, and took firebrands, and turned tail to tail, and put a firebrand in the midst between two tails.

5 And when he had set the brands on fire, he let them go into the standing corn of the Philistines, and burnt up both the shocks, and also the standing corn, with the vineyards and olives.

6 ¶ Then the Philistines said, Who hath done this? And they answered, Samson, the son in law of the Timnite, because he had taken his wife, and given her to his companion. And the Philistines came up, and burnt her and her father with fire.

7 ¶ And Samson said unto them, Though ye have done this, yet will I be avenged of you, and after that I will cease.

8 And he smote them hip and thigh with a great slaughter: and he went down and dwelt in the top of the rock Etam.

9 ¶ Then the Philistines went up, and pitched in Judah, and spread themselves in Lehi.

10 And the men of Judah said, Why are ye come up against us? And they answered, To bind Samson are we come up, to do to him as he hath done to us.

11 Then three thousand men of Judah went to the top of the rock Etam, and said to Samson, Knowest thou not that the Philistines are rulers over us? what is this that thou hast done unto us? And he said unto them, As they did unto me, so have I done unto them.

12 And they said unto him, We are come down to bind thee, that we may deliver thee into the hand of the Philistines. And Samson said unto them, Swear unto me, that ye will not fall upon me yourselves.

13 And they spake unto him, saying, No; but we will bind thee fast, and deliver thee into their hand: but surely we will not kill thee. And they bound him with two new cords, and brought him up from the rock.

14 ¶ And when he came unto Lehi, the Philistines shouted against him: and the Spirit of the LORD came mightily upon him, and the cords that were upon his arms became as flax that was burnt with fire, and his bands loosed from off his hands.

15 And he found a new jawbone of an ass, and put forth his hand, and took it, and slew a thousand men therewith.

16 And Samson said, With the jawbone of an ass, heaps upon heaps, with the jaw of an ass have I slain a thousand men.

17 And it came to pass, when he had made an end of speaking, that he cast away the jawbone out of his hand, and called that place Ramath-lehi.

18 ¶ And he was sore athirst, and called on the LORD, and said, Thou hast given this great deliverance into the hand of thy servant: and now shall I die for thirst, and fall into the hand of the uncircumcised?

JUDGES CHAPTER 15

Judges 15—Samson

The Spirit of the Lord imparts strength without measure to overcome obstacles. Again, Samson, despite his tendency toward excess and bravado, is granted relief from his bonds and allowed to take action against those who would confine and oppress him.

Many episodes in the scriptures speak of bands being miraculously rendered powerless to hold back the servants of the Lord: Paul was released from his prison bands (see Acts 16:26); Nephi was freed of the tethers imposed by his murmuring brothers (see 1 Ne. 7:18; 18:15); and Alma and Amulek were liberated from confinement in prison (see Alma 14:28).

Symbolically, the scriptures speak of the effects of sin being as bands that confine and render immobile. Alma spoke of the liberation of his own father and his father's associates from such bands:

And now I ask of you on what conditions are they saved? Yea, what grounds had they to hope for salvation? What is the cause of their being loosed from the bands of death, yea, and also the chains of hell?

Behold, I can tell you—did not my father Alma believe in the words which were delivered by the mouth of Abinadi? And was he not a holy prophet? Did he not speak the words of God, and my father Alma believe them?

And according to his faith there was a mighty change wrought in his heart. Behold I say unto you that this is all true. (Alma 5:10–12)

Alma the younger himself had been delivered from such bands (see Mosiah 27:29). We can see from such experiences of deliverance, including that of Samson, that the Lord gives us all a chance, despite our imperfections, to be liberated from all oppressive circumstances according to our faith and devotion.

19 But God clave an hollow place that was in the jaw, and there came water thereout; and when he had drunk, his spirit came again, and he revived: wherefore he called the name thereof En-hakkore, which is in Lehi unto this day.

20 And he judged Israel in the days of the Philistines twenty years.

CHAPTER 16

1 THEN went Samson to Gaza, and saw there an harlot, and went in unto her.

2 And it was told the Gazites, saying, Samson is come hither. And they compassed him in, and laid wait for him all night in the gate of the city, and were quiet all the night, saying, In the morning, when it is day, we shall kill him.

3 And Samson lay till midnight, and arose at midnight, and took the doors of the gate of the city, and the two posts, and went away with them, bar and all, and put them upon his shoulders, and carried them up to the top of an hill that is before Hebron.

4 ¶ And it came to pass afterward, that he loved a woman in the valley of Sorek, whose name was Delilah.

5 And the lords of the Philistines came up unto her, and said unto her, Entice him, and see wherein his great strength lieth, and by what means we may prevail against him, that we may bind him to afflict him: and we will give thee every one of us eleven hundred pieces of silver.

6 ¶ And Delilah said to Samson, Tell me, I pray thee, wherein thy great strength lieth, and wherewith thou mightest be bound to afflict thee.

7 And Samson said unto her, If they bind me with seven green withs that were never dried, then shall I be weak, and be as another man.

8 Then the lords of the Philistines brought up to her seven green withs which had not been dried, and she bound him with them.

9 Now there were men lying in wait, abiding with her in the chamber. And she said unto him, The Philistines be upon thee, Samson. And he brake the withs, as a thread of tow is broken when it toucheth the fire. So his strength was not known.

10 And Delilah said unto Samson, Behold, thou hast mocked me, and told me lies: now tell me, I pray thee, wherewith thou mightest be bound.

11 And he said unto her, If they bind me fast with new ropes that never were occupied, then shall I be weak, and be as another man.

12 Delilah therefore took new ropes, and bound him therewith, and said unto him, The Philistines be upon thee, Samson. And there were liers in wait abiding in the chamber. And he brake them from off his arms like a thread.

13 And Delilah said unto Samson, Hitherto thou hast mocked me, and told me lies: tell me wherewith thou mightest be bound. And he said unto her, If thou weavest the seven locks of my head with the web.

14 And she fastened it with the pin, and said unto him, The Philistines be upon thee, Samson. And he awaked out of his sleep, and went away with the pin of the beam, and with the web.

15 ¶ And she said unto him, How canst thou say, I love thee, when thine heart is not with me? thou hast mocked me these three times, and hast not told me wherein thy great strength lieth.

JUDGES CHAPTER 16

Judges 16:4—Delilah

Delilah (meaning: weak, languishing) was a woman from the valley of Sorek whom Samson loved (see Judges 16:4). The Philistines bribed her to discover the secret of Samson's astounding strength. Acting on this conspiracy, she induced Samson three times in sequence to share the information with her—but each time it proved to be a fiction. She persisted, and finally learned that his strength was due to the keeping of his Nazarite vow, which resulted in his never cutting his hair (see Judges 16:17.)

Then Delilah made her move:

> And she made him sleep upon her knees; and she called for a man, and she caused him to shave off the seven locks of his head; and she began to afflict him, and his strength went from him.
>
> And she said, The Philistines *be* upon thee, Samson. And he awoke out of his sleep, and said, I will go out as at other times before, and shake myself. And he wist not that the LORD was departed from him. (Judges 16:19–20)

16 And it came to pass, when she pressed him daily with her words, and urged him, so that his soul was vexed unto death;

17 That he told her all his heart, and said unto her, There hath not come a razor upon mine head; for I have been a Nazarite unto God from my mother's womb: if I be shaven, then my strength will go from me, and I shall become weak, and be like any other man.

18 And when Delilah saw that he had told her all his heart, she sent and called for the lords of the Philistines, saying, Come up this once, for he hath shewed me all his heart. Then the lords of the Philistines came up unto her, and brought money in their hand.

19 And she made him sleep upon her knees; and she called for a man, and she caused him to shave off the seven locks of his head; and she began to afflict him, and his strength went from him.

20 And she said, The Philistines be upon thee, Samson. And he awoke out of his sleep, and said, I will go out as at other times before, and shake myself. And he wist not that the LORD was departed from him.

21 ¶ But the Philistines took him, and put out his eyes, and brought him down to Gaza, and bound him with fetters of brass; and he did grind in the prison house.

22 Howbeit the hair of his head began to grow again after he was shaven.

23 Then the lords of the Philistines gathered them together for to offer a great sacrifice unto Dagon their god, and to rejoice: for they said, Our god hath delivered Samson our enemy into our hand.

24 And when the people saw him, they praised their god: for they said, Our god hath delivered into our hands our enemy, and the destroyer of our country, which slew many of us.

25 And it came to pass, when their hearts were merry, that they said, Call for Samson, that he may make us sport. And they called for Samson out of the prison house; and he made them sport: and they set him between the pillars.

26 And Samson said unto the lad that held him by the hand, Suffer me that I may feel the pillars whereupon the house standeth, that I may lean upon them.

27 Now the house was full of men and women; and all the lords of the Philistines were there; and there were upon the roof about three thousand men and women, that beheld while Samson made sport.

28 And Samson called unto the LORD, and said, O Lord GOD, remember me, I pray thee, and strengthen me, I pray thee, only this once, O God, that I may be at once avenged of the Philistines for my two eyes.

29 And Samson took hold of the two middle pillars upon which the house stood, and on which it was borne up, of the one with his right hand, and of the other with his left.

30 And Samson said, Let me die with the Philistines. And he bowed himself with all his might; and the house fell upon the lords, and upon all the people that were therein. So the dead which he slew at his death were more than they which he slew in his life.

31 Then his brethren and all the house of his father came down, and took him, and brought him up, and buried him between Zorah and Eshtaol in the buryingplace of Manoah his father. And he judged Israel twenty years.

Death of Samson by Gustave Doré

THE
BOOK OF RUTH

CHAPTER 1

1 NOW it came to pass in the days when the judges ruled, that there was a famine in the land. And a certain man of Beth-lehem-judah went to sojourn in the country of Moab, he, and his wife, and his two sons.

2 And the name of the man was Elimelech, and the name of his wife Naomi, and the name of his two sons Mahlon and Chilion, Ephrathites of Beth-lehem-judah. And they

3 And Elimelech Naomi's husband died; and she was left, and her two sons.

4 And they took them wives of the women of Moab; the name of the one was Orpah, and the name of the other Ruth: and they dwelled there about ten years.

5 And Mahlon and Chilion died also both of them; and the woman was left of her two sons and her husband.

6 ¶ Then she arose with her daughters in law, that she might return from the country of Moab: for she had heard in the country of Moab how that the LORD had visited his people in giving them bread.

7 Wherefore she went forth out of the place where she was, and her two daughters in law with her; and they went on the way to return unto the land of Judah.

8 And Naomi said unto her two daughters in law, Go, return each to her mother's house: the LORD deal kindly with you, as ye have dealt with the dead, and with me.

9 The LORD grant you that ye may find rest, each of you in the house of her husband. Then she kissed them; and they lifted up their voice, and wept.

10 And they said unto her, Surely we will return with thee unto thy people.

11 And Naomi said, Turn again, my daughters: why will ye go with me? are there yet any more sons in my womb, that they may be your husbands?

12 Turn again, my daughters, go your way; for I am too old to have an husband. If I should say, I have hope, if I should have an husband also to night, and should also bear sons;

13 Would ye tarry for them till they were grown? would ye stay for them from having husbands? nay, my daughters; for it grieveth me much for your sakes that the hand of the LORD is gone out against me.

14 And they lifted up their voice, and wept again: and Orpah kissed her mother in law; but Ruth clave unto her.

15 And she said, Behold, thy sister in law is gone back unto her people, and unto her gods: return thou after thy sister in law.

16 And Ruth said, Intreat me not to leave thee, or to return from following after thee: for whither thou goest, I will go; and where thou lodgest, I will lodge: thy people shall be my people, and thy God my God:

17 Where thou diest, will I die, and there will I be buried: the LORD do so to me, and more also, if ought but death part thee and me.

RUTH CHAPTER 1

Ruth 1—Overview

For millennia, the story of Ruth's devotion to her mother-in-law, Naomi, has inspired those who value the jewel of loyal friendship as among the greatest of human character traits. The traits of kindness and love, so enduringly reflected in the story of the relationship of Boaz and Ruth, add a glow of the divine to our temporal lives of challenge and trial.

Life is full of adversity and trial, but we have within us the ability to respond with courage and hope, knowing that in time spring will follow winter, sunshine will follow rain, and the blessings of the Lord will prevail over the burdens of our worldly sojourn if we remember our covenants and live by faith.

From the beginning, God's chosen people were to be a royal lineage with a special divine mission of bringing the blessings of the gospel to all the world. Through the process of "adoption" (as in the case of Ruth), all peoples everywhere are welcome to become part of God's family by accepting and living the gospel principles.

The word of the Lord contained in Ruth is a handbook on the abundant life, as seen many centuries before the coming of Christ at the time of His mortal ministry. We see in these pages of scripture many of the building blocks of the abundant life, including the loyalty and devotion of Ruth, the kindness and love of Boaz, the effulgent joy that the hopeful Naomi experienced to see her emptied home filled again with loved ones, the tolerance and respect that the Israelites learned to cultivate for one of their Moabite adoptees.

For more insight into Ruth, see Appendix Q.

Ruth 1:1–2—Naomi

Naomi (pronounced "nay-oh'-mee" or "nah'-oh-mee"; meaning: pleasant) was the wife of Elimelech, the mother of two sons (Mahlon and Chilion), and the mother-in-law of Ruth. When this family moved from Bethlehem-Judah to Moab to seek relief during a severe famine, Elimelech of the house passed away, leaving his wife Naomi and her two sons to fare for themselves. The two sons each married a Moabite woman and then, tragically, also passed away.

When Naomi decided to return alone to Bethlehem, one of her two daughters-in-law, Ruth, widow of Mahlon, was desirous of remaining with her: "And Ruth said, Intreat me not to leave thee, *or* to return from following after thee: for whither thou goest, I will go; and where thou lodgest, I will lodge: thy people *shall be* my people, and thy God my God" (Ruth 1:16). Naomi gladly consented, and when they returned to Bethlehem, Ruth went forth to glean in the fields of their kinsman, Boaz.

Boaz admired Ruth for her noble character (see Ruth 2:11–12) and was generous and protective on her behalf (see Ruth 2:16), causing Naomi to catch the vision of their future union. As a near kinsman, Boaz did come forward to pursue the possibility of stepping into the role of benefactor and husband, which was the legal custom of the people

18 When she saw that she was stedfastly minded to go with her, then she left speaking unto her.

19 ¶ So they two went until they came to Beth-lehem. And it came to pass, when they were come to Beth-lehem, that all the city was moved about them, and they said, Is this Naomi?

20 And she said unto them, Call me not Naomi, call me Mara: for the Almighty hath dealt very bitterly with me.

21 I went out full, and the LORD hath brought me home again empty: why then call ye me Naomi, seeing the LORD hath testified against me, and the Almighty hath afflicted me?

22 So Naomi returned, and Ruth the Moabitess, her daughter in law, with her, which returned out of the country of Moab: and they came to Beth-lehem in the beginning of barley harvest.

CHAPTER 2

1 AND Naomi had a kinsman of her husband's, a mighty man of wealth, of the family of Elimelech; and his name was Boaz.

2 And Ruth the Moabitess said unto Naomi, Let me now go to the field, and glean ears of corn after him in whose sight I shall find grace. And she said unto her, Go, my daughter.

3 And she went, and came, and gleaned in the field after the reapers: and her hap was to light on a part of the field belonging unto Boaz, who was of the kindred of Elimelech.

4 ¶ And, behold, Boaz came from Beth-lehem, and said unto the reapers, The LORD be with you. And they answered him, The LORD bless thee.

5 Then said Boaz unto his servant that was set over the reapers, Whose damsel is this?

6 And the servant that was set over the reapers answered and said, It is the Moabitish damsel that came back with Naomi out of the country of Moab:

7 And she said, I pray you, let me glean and gather after the reapers among the sheaves: so she came, and hath continued even from the morning until now, that she tarried a little in the house.

8 Then said Boaz unto Ruth, Hearest thou not, my daughter? Go not to glean in another field, neither go from hence, but abide here fast by my maidens:

9 Let thine eyes be on the field that they do reap, and go thou after them: have I not charged the young men that they shall not touch thee? and when thou art athirst, go unto the vessels, and drink of that which the young men have drawn.

10 Then she fell on her face, and bowed herself to the ground, and said unto him, Why have I found grace in thine eyes, that thou shouldest take knowledge of me, seeing I am a stranger?

11 And Boaz answered and said unto her, It hath fully been shewed me, all that thou hast done unto thy mother in law since the death of thine husband: and how thou hast left thy father and thy mother, and the land of thy nativity, and art come unto a people which thou knewest not heretofore.

12 The LORD recompense thy work, and a full reward be given thee of the LORD God of Israel, under whose wings thou art come to trust.

13 Then she said, Let me find favour in thy sight, my lord; for that thou hast comforted me, and for that thou hast spoken friendly unto thine handmaid, though I be not like unto one of thine handmaidens.

(see Deut. 25:5–10). When the nearest male relative of Naomi's deceased husband declined the opportunity to redeem the family estate (see Ruth 4:6), Boaz, as the next in line, was legally able to take charge of the situation (see Ruth 4:9–10). Boaz and Ruth were married and soon favored with a son (see Ruth 4:17). Thus the marriage of Boaz and Ruth provided a direct linkage to the future descendant of David, Jesus Christ.

Ruth 1:13–16—Devotion and Loyalty: Hallmarks of True Friends

When Naomi's husband and her two sons passed away, she was left with her sorrow and the care of her two Moabite daughters-in-law. She wanted to send them back to their own cultural setting, but one of them, Ruth, decides out of friendship and loyalty to remain with her, expressing the now celebrated passage that begins, ". . . for whither thou goest, I will go . . ." (Ruth 1:16). In Ruth, Naomi found spiritual support and sustenance to help her over the years after her bereavement.

Thus we see the blessings that come from the deeds of a devoted and loyal friend. In our desire to be ". . . even as He is" (3 Ne. 27:27) it behooves us to become devoted and loyal to our God, our family, and our friends. Nothing is so reassuring as the devoted mate or the loyal and supportive family member. When this support is felt from others, you truly have power to go on in the face of sorrow, death and temptations of all kinds and depths.

RUTH CHAPTER 2

Ruth 2—The Universal Gospel

Ruth was of the Moabite lineage, one of the indigenous cultures remaining in the Holy Land after the return of Israel from Egypt. The original Moab was the son of Lot's oldest daughter (see Gen. 19:37), and thus the Moabites were akin to the Israelites, but represented a different way of life and religion. Ruth represented the local culture at its best, being a pure and virtuous individual with the highest aspirations and character, and she embraced wholeheartedly the Israelite way of life. She was welcomed into her new environment and became instrumental in continuing the promised lineage via David to the Savior himself. What a fitting unfolding of history that the Author of universal salvation should have come from a line that combined in Ruth and Boaz, the confluence of two cultures—one Israelite and the other non-Israelite, but both from the same Maker and Creator. It is a reminder that converts to the Church and kingdom of God are welcome from all kindreds, nations, tongues, and peoples—and that the fullness of joy here and in the hereafter is given to all that choose to come unto Christ.

Ruth 2:3—Boaz

Boaz (meaning: in him is might, or splendor) was a prosperous farmer in Bethlehem and a near-relative of the Elimelech family. When Naomie and Ruth returned to

14 And Boaz said unto her, At mealtime come thou hither, and eat of the bread, and dip thy morsel in the vinegar. And she sat beside the reapers: and he reached her parched corn, and she did eat, and was sufficed, and left.

15 And when she was risen up to glean, Boaz commanded his young men, saying, Let her glean even among the sheaves, and reproach her not:

16 And let fall also some of the handfuls of purpose for her, and leave them, that she may glean them, and rebuke her not.

17 So she gleaned in the field until even, and beat out that she had gleaned: and it was about an ephah of barley.

18 ¶ And she took it up, and went into the city: and her mother in law saw what she had gleaned: and she brought forth, and gave to her that she had reserved after she was sufficed.

19 And her mother in law said unto her, Where hast thou gleaned to day? and where wroughtest thou? blessed be he that did take knowledge of thee. And she shewed her mother in law with whom she had wrought, and said, The man's name with whom I wrought to day is Boaz.

20 And Naomi said unto her daughter in law, Blessed be he of the LORD, who hath not left off his kindness to the living and to the dead. And Naomi said unto her, The man is near of kin unto us, one of our next kinsmen.

21 And Ruth the Moabitess said, He said unto me also, Thou shalt keep fast by my young men, until they have ended all my harvest.

22 And Naomi said unto Ruth her daughter in law, It is good, my daughter, that thou go out with his maidens, that they meet thee not in any other field.

23 So she kept fast by the maidens of Boaz to glean unto the end of barley harvest and of wheat harvest; and dwelt with her mother in law.

CHAPTER 3

1 THEN Naomi her mother in law said unto her, My daughter, shall I not seek rest for thee, that it may be well with thee?

2 And now is not Boaz of our kindred, with whose maidens thou wast? Behold, he winnoweth barley to night in the threshingfloor.

3 Wash thyself therefore, and anoint thee, and put thy raiment upon thee, and get thee down to the floor: but make not thyself known unto the man, until he shall have done eating and drinking.

4 And it shall be, when he lieth down, that thou shalt mark the place where he shall lie, and thou shalt go in, and uncover his feet, and lay thee down; and he will tell thee what thou shalt do.

5 And she said unto her, All that thou sayest unto me I will do.

6 ¶ And she went down unto the floor, and did according to all that her mother in law bade her.

7 And when Boaz had eaten and drunk, and his heart was merry, he went to lie down at the end of the heap of corn: and she came softly, and uncovered his feet, and laid her down.

8 ¶ And it came to pass at midnight, that the man was afraid, and turned himself: and, behold, a woman lay at his feet.

9 And he said, Who art thou? And she answered, I am Ruth thine handmaid: spread therefore thy skirt over thine handmaid; for thou art a near kinsman.

Bethlehem, Ruth went forth to glean in the fields of their kinsman, Boaz. Boaz admired Ruth for her noble character:

> . . . It hath fully been shewed me, all that thou hast done unto thy mother in law since the death of thine husband: and *how* thou hast left thy father and thy mother, and the land of thy nativity, and art come unto a people which thou knewest not heretofore.
>
> The LORD recompense thy work, and a full reward be given thee of the LORD God of Israel, under whose wings thou art come to trust." (Ruth 2:11–12)

As a near kinsman, Boaz came forward to pursue the possibility of his stepping into the role of benefactor and husband according to the legal custom of the people; when Elimelech's nearest male relative of Elimelech declined the opportunity to redeem the family estate, Boaz and Ruth married.

Boaz and Ruth were soon favored with a son: "And the women her neighbours gave it a name, saying, There is a son born to Naomi; and they called his name Obed [one who serves]: he *is* the father of Jesse, the father of David" (Ruth 4:17). Thus the marriage of Boaz and Ruth provided a direct link to the future descendant of David, Jesus Christ. (Boaz is rendered *Booz* in the New Testament passage detailing this lineage—see Matt. 1:5; Boaz, for an unknown reason, was also the name of one of the two great pillars in the temple of Solomon, the other being Jachin—see 1 Kings 7:21; 2 Chron. 3:17.)

RUTH CHAPTER 3

Ruth 3:11—Kindness and Love

The traits of kindness and love, so enduringly reflected in the story of the relationship of Boaz and Ruth, add a glow of the divine to our temporal lives of challenge and trial.

As a gleaner, Ruth works tirelessly to provide food for herself and the widow Naomi. The landholder Boaz, a kinsman to Naomi's deceased husband, takes note of Ruth's love and industry and has compassion and admiration for her. He is as kind and loving a person as Ruth is, and through the advice of Naomi, Ruth is able to facilitate the developing relationship.

Boaz works through long-standing social customs to lay the foundation for a proper and community-sanctioned marriage with Ruth. It is one of the great happy-ending stories in all of literature. And thus we see the power of love and kindness demonstrated by Ruth.

Surely in our lives we can bless all we come in contact with by being more kind. It will defuse difficult moments. It can brighten another day. It can heal a troubled heart. Kindness is truly an expression of charity.

10 And he said, Blessed be thou of the LORD, my daughter: for thou hast shewed more kindness in the latter end than at the beginning, inasmuch as thou followedst not young men, whether poor or rich.

11 And now, my daughter, fear not; I will do to thee all that thou requirest: for all the city of my people doth know that thou art a virtuous woman.

12 And now it is true that I am thy near kinsman: howbeit there is a kinsman nearer than I.

13 Tarry this night, and it shall be in the morning, that if he will perform unto thee the part of a kinsman, well; let him do the kinsman's part: but if he will not do the part of a kinsman to thee, then will I do the part of a kinsman to thee, as the LORD liveth: lie down until the morning.

14 ¶ And she lay at his feet until the morning: and she rose up before one could know another. And he said, Let it not be known that a woman came into the floor.

15 Also he said, Bring the vail that thou hast upon thee, and hold it. And when she held it, he measured six measures of barley, and laid it on her: and she went into the city.

16 And when she came to her mother in law, she said, Who art thou, my daughter? And she told her all that the man had done to her.

17 And she said, These six measures of barley gave he me; for he said to me, Go not empty unto thy mother in law.

18 Then said she, Sit still, my daughter, until thou know how the matter will fall: for the man will not be in rest, until he have finished the thing this day.

CHAPTER 4

1 THEN went Boaz up to the gate, and sat him down there: and, behold, the kinsman of whom Boaz spake came by; unto whom he said, Ho, such a one! turn aside, sit down here. And he turned aside, and sat down.

2 And he took ten men of the elders of the city, and said, Sit ye down here. And they sat down.

3 And he said unto the kinsman, Naomi, that is come again out of the country of Moab, selleth a parcel of land, which was our brother Elimelech's:

4 And I thought to advertise thee, saying, Buy it before the inhabitants, and before the elders of my people. If thou wilt redeem it, redeem it: but if thou wilt not redeem it, then tell me, that I may know: for there is none to redeem it beside thee; and I am after thee. And he said, I will redeem it.

5 Then said Boaz, What day thou buyest the field of the hand of Naomi, thou must buy it also of Ruth the Moabitess, the wife of the dead, to raise up the name of the dead upon his inheritance.

6 ¶ And the kinsman said, I cannot redeem it for myself, lest I mar mine own inheritance: redeem thou my right to thyself; for I cannot redeem it.

7 Now this was the manner in former time in Israel concerning redeeming and concerning changing, for to confirm all things; a man plucked off his shoe, and gave it to his neighbour: and this was a testimony in Israel.

RUTH CHAPTER 4

Ruth 4:14–15—Joy After Sorrow

Life is full of adversity and trial, but we have within us the ability to respond with courage and hope, knowing that in time spring will follow winter, sunshine will follow rain, and the blessings of the Lord will prevail over the burdens of our worldly sojourn if we remember our covenants and live by faith.

Naomi lost her husband as well as both of her sons. She became the prototype for all widows everywhere, and suffered greatly because of her loss and her sorrow. Added to that was the burden of having to support herself and her daughter-in-law Ruth. But Ruth was the source of sunshine in her life, and eventually the marriage of Ruth and Boaz brought harmony and stability into their family circle where before there was only despair and longing.

In time, the sorrows in Naomi's life passed and things improved. Moreover, the fruit of the new marriage was a continuation of the covenant lineage, leading to David, and beyond, to Christ himself.

This story demonstrates the rich reality that following sorrow in death and the hardships that it entails, we must press forward. The Balm of Gilead will be brought to us through the goodness of the Lord. He is over all and in all and through all things. In our moment of despair if we but turn it over to the Lord, He will bless us, and our joy will be full.

8 Therefore the kinsman said unto Boaz, Buy it for thee. So he drew off his shoe.

9 ¶ And Boaz said unto the elders, and unto all the people, Ye are witnesses this day, that I have bought all that was Elimelech's, and all that was Chilion's and Mahlon's, of the hand of Naomi.

10 Moreover Ruth the Moabitess, the wife of Mahlon, have I purchased to be my wife, to raise up the name of the dead upon his inheritance, that the name of the dead be not cut off from among his brethren, and from the gate of his place: ye are witnesses this day.

11 And all the people that were in the gate, and the elders, said, We are witnesses. The LORD make the woman that is come into thine house like Rachel and like Leah, which two did build the house of Israel: and do thou worthily in Ephratah, and be famous in Bethlehem:

12 And let thy house be like the house of Pharez, whom Tamar bare unto Judah, of the seed which the LORD shall give thee of this young woman.

13 ¶ So Boaz took Ruth, and she was his wife: and when he went in unto her, the LORD gave her conception, and she bare a son.

14 And the women said unto Naomi, Blessed be the LORD, which hath not left thee this day without a kinsman, that his name may be famous in Israel.

15 And he shall be unto thee a restorer of thy life, and a nourisher of thine old age: for thy daughter in law, which loveth thee, which is better to thee than seven sons, hath born him.

16 And Naomi took the child, and laid it in her bosom, and became nurse unto it.

17 And the women her neighbours gave it a name, saying, There is a son born to Naomi; and they called his name Obed: he is the father of Jesse, the father of David.

18 ¶ Now these are the generations of Pharez: Pharez begat Hezron,

19 And Hezron begat Ram, and Ram begat Amminadab,

20 And Amminadab begat Nahshon, and Nahshon begat Salmon,

21 And Salmon begat Boaz, and Boaz begat Obed,

22 And Obed begat Jesse, and Jesse begat David.

Ruth and Boaz by Gustave Doré

THE
FIRST BOOK OF SAMUEL

OTHERWISE CALLED THE FIRST BOOK OF THE KINGS

CHAPTER 1

1 NOW there was a certain man of Ramathaim-zophim, of mount Ephraim, and his name was Elkanah, the son of Jeroham, the son of Elihu, the son of Tohu, the son of Zuph, an Ephrathite:

2 And he had two wives; the name of the one was Hannah, and the name of the other Peninnah: and Peninnah had children, but Hannah had no children.

3 And this man went up out of his city yearly to worship and to sacrifice unto the LORD of hosts in Shiloh. And the two sons of Eli, Hophni and Phinehas, the priests of the LORD, were there.

4 ¶ And when the time was that Elkanah offered, he gave to Peninnah his wife, and to all her sons and her daughters, portions:

5 But unto Hannah he gave a worthy portion; for he loved Hannah: but the LORD had shut up her womb.

6 And her adversary also provoked her sore, for to make her fret, because the LORD had shut up her womb.

7 And as he did so year by year, when she went up to the house of the LORD, so she provoked her; therefore she wept, and did not eat.

8 Then said Elkanah her husband to her, Hannah, why weepest thou? and why eatest thou not? and why is thy heart grieved? am not I better to thee than ten sons?

9 ¶ So Hannah rose up after they had eaten in Shiloh, and after they had drunk. Now Eli the priest sat upon a seat by a post of the temple of the LORD.

10 And she was in bitterness of soul, and prayed unto the LORD, and wept sore.

11 And she vowed a vow, and said, O LORD of hosts, if thou wilt indeed look on the affliction of thine handmaid, and remember me, and not forget thine handmaid, but wilt give unto thine handmaid a man child, then I will give him unto the LORD all the days of his life, and there shall no razor come upon his head.

12 And it came to pass, as she continued praying before the LORD, that Eli marked her mouth.

13 Now Hannah, she spake in her heart; only her lips moved, but her voice was not heard: therefore Eli thought she had been drunken.

14 And Eli said unto her, How long wilt thou be drunken? put away thy wine from thee.

15 And Hannah answered and said, No, my lord, I am a woman of a sorrowful spirit: I have drunk neither wine nor strong drink, but have poured out my soul before the LORD.

16 Count not thine handmaid for a daughter of Belial: for out of the abundance of my complaint and grief have I spoken hitherto.

17 Then Eli answered and said, Go in peace: and the God of Israel grant thee thy petition that thou hast asked of him.

1 SAMUEL CHAPTER 1

"… it is impossible to speak of the abundant life without speaking of life as a continuum. This life, this narrow sphere we call mortality, does not, within the short space of time we are allowed here, give to all of us perfect justice, perfect health, or perfect opportunities. Perfect justice, however, will come eventually through a divine plan, as will the perfection of all other conditions and blessings—to those who have lived to merit them." —Spencer W. Kimball, *Ensign*, July 1978

1 Samuel 1:1–2—Hannah

Hannah (pronounced "han'-uh"; meaning: grace) was the wife of Elkanah (pronounced "el-kay'-nuh" or "el'-kay-nuh"), a devout Ephraimite who lived in the central mountainous district of Israel (see 1 Sam. 1:1–3). Hannah mourned over her childless status and prayed one day, near the temple, for a special blessing (see 1 Sam. 1:11). When the priest Eli observed her struggles and came to understand her burden, he had compassion on her and promised her that God would grant her petition (see 1 Sam. 1:17). Indeed, the Lord did remember her with a blessing of fruitfulness when Samuel was born (see 1 Sam. 1:20). After Samuel was weaned, Hannah brought him to the house of the Lord and promised her child to the Lord (see 1 Sam. 1:26–28). Subsequently, Hannah uttered a glorious song of praise unto the Lord for His mercy unto her (see 1 Sam. 2:10—the first reference to the Messiah in the Old Testament).

Samuel grew in stature as he "ministered unto the Lord" (1 Sam. 2:18). His mother remembered him caringly and "made him a little coat, and brought *it* to him from year to year, when she came up with her husband to offer the yearly sacrifice" (1 Sam. 2:19). Just as Hannah clothed her son regularly in a coat of maternal protection, so the Lord clothed him in the fatherly mantle of prophetic authority. Soon Samuel took upon himself the stature of one of the Lord's greatest prophets. His life and ministry partook of the love and grace of his mother, one of the choicest of the righteous and valiant women celebrated in the scriptures. Hannah was also blessed thereafter with five more children, three sons and two daughters (see 1 Sam. 2:21).

1 Samuel 1:27–28—Child of the Temple

Everyone has deep-seated longings and desires to have a life of fulfillment and productivity. Like Hanna, who longed to be a mother, we can take our hopes and aspirations to the Lord, especially in the temples of God, and ask in faith and love that He might grant the righteous blessings of our heart—and He will hear.

Hannah's heartfelt desire was to become a mother. Her devotion and pleading before the Lord at His temple were heard, and the Lord's servant promised her that her prayers would be answered. When she conceived and bore Samuel, the coming prophet of the Lord, she was filled with joy and thanksgiving, pleased to dedicate her son to the service of

18 And she said, Let thine handmaid find grace in thy sight. So the woman went her way, and did eat, and her countenance was no more sad.

19 ¶ And they rose up in the morning early, and worshipped before the LORD, and returned, and came to their house to Ramah: and Elkanah knew Hannah his wife; and the LORD remembered her.

20 Wherefore it came to pass, when the time was come about after Hannah had conceived, that she bare a son, and called his name Samuel, saying, Because I have asked him of the LORD.

21 And the man Elkanah, and all his house, went up to offer unto the LORD the yearly sacrifice, and his vow.

22 But Hannah went not up; for she said unto her husband, I will not go up until the child be weaned, and then I will bring him, that he may appear before the LORD, and there abide for ever.

23 And Elkanah her husband said unto her, Do what seemeth thee good; tarry until thou have weaned him; only the LORD establish his word. So the woman abode, and gave her son suck until she weaned him.

24 ¶ And when she had weaned him, she took him up with her, with three bullocks, and one ephah of flour, and a bottle of wine, and brought him unto the house of the LORD in Shiloh: and the child was young.

25 And they slew a bullock, and brought the child to Eli.

26 And she said, O my lord, as thy soul liveth, my lord, I am the woman that stood by thee here, praying unto the LORD.

27 For this child I prayed; and the LORD hath given me my petition which I asked of him:

28 Therefore also I have lent him to the LORD; as long as he liveth he shall be lent to the LORD. And he worshipped the LORD there.

CHAPTER 2

1 AND Hannah prayed, and said, My heart rejoiceth in the LORD, mine horn is exalted in the LORD: my mouth is enlarged over mine enemies; because I rejoice in thy salvation.

2 There is none holy as the LORD: for there is none beside thee: neither is there any rock like our God.

3 Talk no more so exceeding proudly; let not arrogancy come out of your mouth: for the LORD is a God of knowledge, and by him actions are weighed.

4 The bows of the mighty men are broken, and they that stumbled are girded with strength.

5 They that were full have hired out themselves for bread; and they that were hungry ceased: so that the barren hath born seven; and she that hath many children is waxed feeble.

6 The LORD killeth, and maketh alive: he bringeth down to the grave, and bringeth up.

7 The LORD maketh poor, and maketh rich: he bringeth low, and lifteth up.

8 He raiseth up the poor out of the dust, and lifteth up the beggar from the dunghill, to set them among princes, and to make them inherit the throne of glory: for the pillars of the earth are the LORD's, and he hath set the world upon them.

9 He will keep the feet of his saints, and the wicked shall be silent in darkness; for by strength shall no man prevail.

10 The adversaries of the LORD shall be broken to pieces; out of heaven shall he thunder upon them: the LORD shall judge the ends

holiness. And thus we see that as we give ourselves to the Lord He will bless us in all things.

Remember that when our motives are pure and our purposes are in harmony with the Lord's, we can and will receive the blessings of the Lord. If we seek the will of God in all things and then ask with real intent and exercise faith, the blessings can be ours. The blessings of our God are waiting for the faithful.

1 Samuel 1—Summary of Precepts and Principles

The purpose of thegospel is to bring about the abundant life for God's children—even eternal life and exaltation. We learn line upon line, precept upon precept. We build the edifice of our evolving spiritual life one block at a time. We learn to be loyal, kind and loving, hopeful, tolerant, and full of faith, even as the Father and Son epitomize these same qualities to us on a divine scale. We discern in the preserved records of our forebears the spirit of these building blocks of spiritual abundance at work. Just as Ruth, Naomi, Boaz, and Hannah exemplified these qualities, we too, by the grace of God, can leave behind for our children and our children's children a legacy of obedience and honor. Let us open our hearts to receive the guidance of the Spirit in fulfilling such a calling: "For unto him that receiveth it shall be given more abundantly, even power" (D&C 71:6).

1 SAMUEL CHAPTER 2

"There is no substitute for the home. Its foundation is as ancient as the world, and its mission has been ordained of God from the earliest times. . . . The home then is more than a habitation, it is an institution which stands for stability and love in individuals as well as in nations. . . . A Latter-day Saint who has no ambition to establish a home and give it permanency has not a full conception of a sacred duty the gospel imposes upon him." —Joseph F. Smith, *Juvenile Instructor* 38:144.

1 Samuel 2—Overview of Precepts and Principles

Embedded in these priceless passages of scripture is a checklist of indispensable items for all parents and leaders in Zion to internalize and apply to the sacred commission of teaching children to understand in a timely and enduring way "the doctrine of repentance, faith in Christ the Son of the living God, and of baptism and the gift of the Holy Ghost by the laying on of the hands" (D&C 68:25). First of all, we find here persuasive evidence that the favor of God is drawn toward those who seek to follow His will in all diligence. Next, in the contrast between the faithful commitment of Samuel's parents and the unwise fatherly indulgence of Eli we perceive clearly the ordained pathway that parents are to follow in teaching their children the boundaries that heavenly law marks out as the frontiers of safety and wise behavior. Third, the remarkable calling of Samuel reinforces the doctrine that the Lord has a mission for each of us to perform—in most cases many missions. An

of the earth; and he shall give strength unto his king, and exalt the horn of his anointed.

11 And Elkanah went to Ramah to his house. And the child did minister unto the LORD before Eli the priest.

12 ¶ Now the sons of Eli were sons of Belial; they knew not the LORD.

13 And the priests' custom with the people was, that, when any man offered sacrifice, the priest's servant came, while the flesh was in seething, with a flesh-hook of three teeth in his hand;

14 And he struck it into the pan, or kettle, or caldron, or pot; all that the fleshhook brought up the priest took for himself. So they did in Shiloh unto all the Israelites that came thither.

15 Also before they burnt the fat, the priest's servant came, and said to the man that sacrificed, Give flesh to roast for the priest; for he will not have sodden flesh of thee, but raw.

16 And if any man said unto him, Let them not fail to burn the fat presently, and then take as much as thy soul desireth; then he would answer him, Nay; but thou shalt give it me now: and if not, I will take it by force.

17 Wherefore the sin of the young men was very great before the LORD: for men abhorred the offering of the LORD.

18 ¶ But Samuel ministered before the LORD, being a child, girded with a linen ephod.

19 Moreover his mother made him a little coat, and brought it to him from year to year, when she came up with her husband to offer the yearly sacrifice.

20 ¶ And Eli blessed Elkanah and his wife, and said, The LORD give thee seed of this woman for the loan which is lent to the LORD. And they went unto their own home.

21 And the LORD visited Hannah, so that she conceived, and bare three sons and two daughters. And the child Samuel grew before the LORD.

22 ¶ Now Eli was very old, and heard all that his sons did unto all Israel; and how they lay with the women that assembled at the door of the tabernacle of the congregation.

23 And he said unto them, Why do ye such things? for I hear of your evil dealings by all this people.

24 Nay, my sons; for it is no good report that I hear: ye make the LORD's people to transgress.

25 If one man sin against another, the judge shall judge him: but if a man sin against the LORD, who shall intreat for him? Notwithstanding they hearkened not unto the voice of their father, because the LORD would slay them.

26 And the child Samuel grew on, and was in favour both with the LORD, and also with men.

27 ¶ And there came a man of God unto Eli, and said unto him, Thus saith the LORD, Did I plainly appear unto the house of thy father, when they were in Egypt in Pharaoh's house?

28 And did I choose him out of all the tribes of Israel to be my priest, to offer upon mine altar, to burn incense, to wear an ephod before me? and did I give unto the house of thy father all the offerings made by fire of the children of Israel?

29 Wherefore kick ye at my sacrifice and at mine offering, which I have commanded in my habitation; and honourest thy sons above me, to make yourselves fat with the chiefest of all the offerings of Israel my people?

30 Wherefore the LORD God of Israel saith, I said indeed that thy house, and the house of thy father, should walk before me for ever:

important part of the parental commission is to teach children to prepare for and accept such callings with enthusiasm and thanksgiving. Finally, these passages reinforce the truth that the Lord is our King—and that any allegiance to worldly patterns of living rather than heavenly principles will lead away from the pathways of peace, harmony, and enduring joy that we all seek in life.

1 Samuel 2:12—Eli

Eli (meaning: ascending) was a high priest and judge in Israel during the days of Samuel the prophet. Eli was of the lineage of Ithamar, the youngest surviving son of Aaron. The priestly office remained with Eli's family and the lineage of Ithamar until Abiathar was removed from office by Solomon because of his conflicting loyalty to Solomon's brother, Adonijah, who aspired to the throne (see 1 Kings 1:7; 2:26–27). At that point in time, the office was conveyed by Solomon to Zadok of the family of Eleazar, oldest surviving son of Aaron (see 1 Kings 2:35).

Eli's history is recorded in 1 Samuel chapters 1–4. It was Eli who pronounced a blessing upon Hannah, wife of Elkanah, when she was grieving over her lack of a son (see 1 Sam. 2:20). It was not for his piety and compassion that Eli was to encounter the judgment of God, but rather for his indulgence and passivity concerning his sons, Hophni and Phinehas, both priests (see 1 Sam. 2:12). These two sons selfishly misused the offerings brought before the Lord by the people (see 1 Sam. 2:12–17) and were guilty of gross immorality with the women who came before the tabernacle (see 1 Sam. 2:22).

While Eli confronted his sons (see 1 Sam. 2:23–25), his words were not enough to induce Hophni and Phinehas to repent. Therefore, the Lord sent a man of God to Eli to speak in somewhat more unmistakable terms (see 1 Sam. 2:30–31, 34–35). Soon thereafter, the Lord confirmed His word by speaking to the young Samuel during the night in the household of Eli (see 1 Sam. 3:11–14). When Samuel got up the courage to share these truths with Eli the following morning, the aging priest responded in mildness: "It *is* the LORD: let him do what seemeth him good" (1 Sam. 3:18.)

In due time the Philistines fell upon Israel and exacted a great slaughter. The ark of the covenant, which had been taken from its resting place in Shiloh as a means to deter the enemy, was then stolen by the Philistines, and "the two sons of Eli, Hophni and Phinehas, were slain" (1 Sam. 4:11). When a messenger reported these calamities to the anxious Eli, waiting on the sidelines, "he fell from off the seat backward by the side of the gate, and his neck brake, and he died: for he was an old man, and heavy" (1 Sam. 4:18). Thus ended the forty-year tenure of Eli, who had attained the age of ninety-eight and departed without the glow of joy about him.

1 Samuel 2:24—Principles and Responsibilities of Parenthood

Parents are to illuminate the pathway of progress for their children, using the light of gospel truths. At the same

but now the LORD saith, Be it far from me; for them that honour me I will honour, and they that despise me shall be lightly esteemed.

31 Behold, the days come, that I will cut off thine arm, and the arm of thy father's house, that there shall not be an old man in thine house.

32 And thou shalt see an enemy in my habitation, in all the wealth which God shall give Israel: and there shall not be an old man in thine house for ever.

33 And the man of thine, whom I shall not cut off from mine altar, shall be to consume thine eyes, and to grieve thine heart: and all the increase of thine house shall die in the flower of their age.

34 And this shall be a sign unto thee, that shall come upon thy two sons, on Hophni and Phinehas; in one day they shall die both of them.

35 And I will raise me up a faithful priest, that shall do according to that which is in mine heart and in my mind: and I will build him a sure house; and he shall walk before mine anointed for ever.

36 And it shall come to pass, that every one that is left in thine house shall come and crouch to him for a piece of silver and a morsel of bread, and shall say, Put me, I pray thee, into one of the priests' offices, that I may eat a piece of bread.

CHAPTER 3

1 AND the child Samuel ministered unto the LORD before Eli. And the word of the LORD was precious in those days; there was no open vision.

2 And it came to pass at that time, when Eli was laid down in his place, and his eyes began to wax dim, that he could not see;

3 And ere the lamp of God went out in the temple of the LORD, where the ark of God was, and Samuel was laid down to sleep;

4 That the LORD called Samuel: and he answered, Here am I.

5 And he ran unto Eli, and said, Here am I; for thou calledst me. And he said, I called not; lie down again. And he went and lay down.

6 And the LORD called yet again, Samuel. And Samuel arose and went to Eli, and said, Here am I; for thou didst call me. And he answered, I called not, my son; lie down again.

7 Now Samuel did not yet know the LORD, neither was the word of the LORD yet revealed unto him.

8 And the LORD called Samuel again the third time. And he arose and went to Eli, and said, Here am I; for thou didst call me. And Eli perceived that the LORD had called the child.

9 Therefore Eli said unto Samuel, Go, lie down: and it shall be, if he call thee, that thou shalt say, Speak, LORD; for thy servant heareth. So Samuel went and lay down in his place.

10 And the LORD came, and stood, and called as at other times, Samuel, Samuel. Then Samuel answered, Speak; for thy servant heareth.

11 ¶ And the LORD said to Samuel, Behold, I will do a thing in Israel, at which both the ears of every one that heareth it shall tingle.

12 In that day I will perform against Eli all things which I have spoken concerning his house: when I begin, I will also make an end.

13 For I have told him that I will judge his house for ever for the iniquity which he knoweth; because his sons made themselves vile, and he restrained them not.

time, parents are to mark clearly the boundaries and limits for appropriate behavior, and restrain their children from crossing the mark.

Eli learned of his sons' wicked behavior and reproved them, but not with sufficient sharpness. The Lord sorely chastised Eli, condemned the family, and shortened its tenure.

1 Samuel 2:26—Favored of God: Goodness of Samuel and Wickedness of Eli's Sons

Those who seek after the principles of integrity, service, and holiness are favored of the Lord. He withdraws His hand of sustaining power from those who dishonor His word and His institutions. This is amply illustrated in the contrasting lives of the young Samuel and the sinful sons of Eli. *For more insight on Samuel, see Appendix R.*

Hannah gives praise to the Lord for His goodness as her son Samuel grows and prospers, ministering before the Lord and increasing in favor and righteousness. By way of contrast, Eli's two sons, Hophni and Phinehas, exercise unrighteous dominion as priests of God, being both greedy and immoral, thus bringing shame upon their family and calling forth the justice of God.

Oh, how careful we all need to be, for there are eyes watching and ears hearing at every moment. Each of us is an example to someone somewhere. We should seek to live a life beyond reproach—and we should seek to bless and help rather than condemn.

1 SAMUEL CHAPTER 3

1 Samuel 3:4—Honoring the Lord's Call

It is wisdom do to be prepared to receive the Lord's callings to consecrate our time, gifts, and resources for the building up of His kingdom.

The boy Samuel received a divine commission during the night and began his role as a prophet of God by conveying the Lord's sanction of Eli and his family for their unrighteousness. Through this example, we see that we have been and shall be called to many important assignments. One thing must be clear—it is not the title, position, or station that matters, but rather how well we serve in the callings we have been given. No position exalts—only righteousness.

14 And therefore I have sworn unto the house of Eli, that the iniquity of Eli's house shall not be purged with sacrifice nor offering for ever.

15 ¶ And Samuel lay until the morning, and opened the doors of the house of the LORD. And Samuel feared to shew Eli the vision.

16 Then Eli called Samuel, and said, Samuel, my son. And he answered, Here am I.

17 And he said, What is the thing that the LORD hath said unto thee? I pray thee hide it not from me: God do so to thee, and more also, if thou hide any thing from me of all the things that he said unto thee.

18 And Samuel told him every whit, and hid nothing from him. And he said, It is the LORD: let him do what seemeth him good.

19 ¶ And Samuel grew, and the LORD was with him, and did let none of his words fall to the ground.

20 And all Israel from Dan even to Beer-sheba knew that Samuel was established to be a prophet of the LORD.

21 And the LORD appeared again in Shiloh: for the LORD revealed himself to Samuel in Shiloh by the word of the LORD.

CHAPTER 8

1 AND it came to pass, when Samuel was old, that he made his sons judges over Israel.

2 Now the name of his firstborn was Joel; and the name of his second, Abiah: they were judges in Beer-sheba.

3 And his sons walked not in his ways, but turned aside after lucre, and took bribes, and perverted judgment.

4 Then all the elders of Israel gathered themselves together, and came to Samuel unto Ramah,

5 And said unto him, Behold, thou art old, and thy sons walk not in thy ways: now make us a king to judge us like all the nations.

6 ¶ But the thing displeased Samuel, when they said, Give us a king to judge us. And Samuel prayed unto the LORD.

7 And the LORD said unto Samuel, Hearken unto the voice of the people in all that they say unto thee: for they have not rejected thee, but they have rejected me, that I should not reign over them.

8 According to all the works which they have done since the day that I brought them up out of Egypt even unto this day, wherewith they have forsaken me, and served other gods, so do they also unto thee.

9 Now therefore hearken unto their voice: howbeit yet protest solemnly unto them, and shew them the manner of the king that shall reign over them.

10 ¶ And Samuel told all the words of the LORD unto the people that asked of him a king.

11 And he said, This will be the manner of the king that shall reign over you: He will take your sons, and appoint them for himself, for his chariots, and to be his horsemen; and some shall run before his chariots.

12 And he will appoint him captains over thousands, and captains over fifties; and will set them to ear his ground, and to reap his harvest, and to make his instruments of war, and instruments of his chariots.

1 SAMUEL CHAPTER 8

1 Samuel 8:18—Earthly King/Heavenly King

When a people supplant their Heavenly King with a preference for an earthly king, then adversity and oppression are at the door. We must seek the face of the Lord always, and honor Him as our King, Ruler and Redeemer.

Israel pleaded to have a king, like other nations—one who would fight their battles. Samuel (himself a father with rebellious sons) resisted, but the Lord told him to indulge the Israelites with their desire. Samuel declared what manner of royal oppression the Israelites had to look forward to if they honored earthly institutions, but they insisted. Thus Israel rejected the Lord as sovereign and sought earthly justice and power.

Through this example, we see that we as individuals and society must honor God in all things. The Book of Mormon has recorded these immortal words: " . . . Inasmuch as ye shall keep my commandments ye shall prosper in the land" (Jarom 1:9). These clarion words are repeated over and over in the Book of Mormon. We cannot have anything or anyone before us that would dictate our moral behavior or give us the codes to live by save it is our God.

1 Samuel 8—Summary of Precepts and Principles

Even though the Lord loves all of His children, His honor is reserved for those who honor Him, as the scriptures attest. We honor Him by keeping His commandments. We honor him by teaching our children to follow in His footsteps. As parents and leaders in Zion, we honor Him by infusing our lives with the light of the gospel. We consecrate our time, talents, and resources to the building up of His kingdom. We fulfill our missions with diligence and valor. We teach allegiance to the Heavenly King rather than to worldly practices based on temporal principles. All of this brings glory to our Heavenly Father and blessings of light and truth into our family circles. The families of Zion are the units of eternal increase in the Lord's plan, the places where holiness is learned and practiced, but it must be done in the Lord's way, and according to the principles of spiritual truth.

13 And he will take your daughters to be confectionaries, and to be cooks, and to be bakers.

14 And he will take your fields, and your vineyards, and your oliveyards, even the best of them, and give them to his servants.

15 And he will take the tenth of your seed, and of your vineyards, and give to his officers, and to his servants.

16 And he will take your menservants, and your maidservants, and your goodliest young men, and your asses, and put them to his work.

17 He will take the tenth of your sheep: and ye shall be his servants.

18 And ye shall cry out in that day because of your king which ye shall have chosen you; and the LORD will not hear you in that day.

19 ¶ Nevertheless the people refused to obey the voice of Samuel; and they said, Nay; but we will have a king over us;

20 That we also may be like all the nations; and that our king may judge us, and go out before us, and fight our battles.

21 And Samuel heard all the words of the people, and he rehearsed them in the ears of the LORD.

22 And the LORD said to Samuel, Hearken unto their voice, and make them a king. And Samuel said unto the men of Israel, Go ye every man unto his city.

CHAPTER 9

1 NOW there was a man of Benjamin, whose name was Kish, the son of Abiel, the son of Zeror, the son of Bechorath, the son of Aphiah, a Benjamite, a mighty man of power.

2 And he had a son, whose name was Saul, a choice young man, and a goodly: and there was not among the children of Israel a goodlier person than he: from his shoulders and upward he was higher than any of the people.

3 And the asses of Kish Saul's father were lost. And Kish said to Saul his son, Take now one of the servants with thee, and arise, go seek the asses.

4 And he passed through mount Ephraim, and passed through the land of Shalisha, but they found them not: then they passed through the land of Shalim, and there they were not: and he passed through the land of the Benjamites, but they found them not.

5 And when they were come to the land of Zuph, Saul said to his servant that was with him, Come, and let us return; lest my father leave caring for the asses, and take thought for us.

6 And he said unto him, Behold now, there is in this city a man of God, and he is an honourable man; all that he saith cometh surely to pass: now let us go thither; peradventure he can shew us our way that we should go.

7 Then said Saul to his servant, But, behold, if we go, what shall we bring the man? for the bread is spent in our vessels, and there is not a present to bring to the man of God: what have we?

8 And the servant answered Saul again, and said, Behold, I have here at hand the fourth part of a shekel of silver: that will I give to the man of God, to tell us our way.

1 SAMUEL CHAPTER 9

1 Samuel 9—Preview of the Story of Saul and David

The scriptural account of the early days of Saul and the calling of young David to become king of Israel is a study in aspects of the heart. We learn, as in the case of Saul in the beginning, that the Lord can work with willing and renewable hearts, hearts that are humble and receptive. At the same time, we learn that such hearts must continue in reverent sanctity and pure obedience lest the spirit of pride and arrogant self-containment supplant the commitment to do God's will. Saul is our witness of the danger of such a defection of heart, and the consequence of his self-justification is a sad commentary on what happens when we are no longer a person after the Lord's "own heart" (1 Sam. 13:14). At the same time, we learn from these scriptures that the Lord sees the heart, not the outward appearance, when He calls His servants on His errand, as in the case of the young David. We see, moreover, that the Lord gives courage to the faithful and the valiant. Such do not experience fear in the face of the Goliaths of the world, because they go in the power of God.

For more insight into the lives of David and Saul, see Appendix S and Appendix T.

1 Samuel 9:19—Seer

The designation *seer* is used in the Old Testament a number of times in reference to various individuals: Samuel (see 1 Sam. 9:19), Zadok (see 2 Sam. 15:27), Gad (see 2 Sam. 24:11), Heman (see 1 Chron. 25:5), Iddo (see 2 Chron. 9:29), Hanani (see 2 Chron. 16:7, 10), Asaph (see 2 Chron. 29:30), Jeduthun (see 2 Chron. 35:15), and Amos (see Amos 7:12). The first time the word *seer* is used in the Old Testament (KJV) it appears in a commentary statement (within parentheses) in the context of the emergence of Saul as the initial king of Israel during the days of Samuel (see 1 Sam. 9:9).

In the context of Ammon's discussion with King Limhi, the Book of Mormon provides more express information on the office of seer:

> Now Ammon said unto him: I can assuredly tell thee, O king, of a man that can translate the records; for he has wherewith that he can look, and translate all records that are of ancient date; and it is a gift from God. And the things are called interpreters, and no man can look in them except he be commanded, lest he should look for that he ought not and he should perish. And whosoever is commanded to look in them, the same is called seer.
>
> And behold, the king of the people who are in the land of Zarahemla is the man that is commanded to do these things, and who has this high gift from God.
>
> And the king said that a seer is greater than a prophet.

9 (Beforetime in Israel, when a man went to enquire of God, thus he spake, Come, and let us go to the seer: for he that is now called a Prophet was beforetime called a Seer.)

10 Then said Saul to his servant, Well said; come, let us go. So they went unto the city where the man of God was.

11 ¶ And as they went up the hill to the city, they found young maidens going out to draw water, and said unto them, Is the seer here?

12 And they answered them, and said, He is; behold, he is before you: make haste now, for he came to day to the city; for there is a sacrifice of the people to day in the high place:

13 As soon as ye be come into the city, ye shall straightway find him, before he go up to the high place to eat: for the people will not eat until he come, because he doth bless the sacrifice; and afterwards they eat that be bidden. Now therefore get you up; for about this time ye shall find him.

14 And they went up into the city: and when they were come into the city, behold, Samuel came out against them, for to go up to the high place.

15 ¶ Now the LORD had told Samuel in his ear a day before Saul came, saying,

16 To morrow about this time I will send thee a man out of the land of Benjamin, and thou shalt anoint him to be captain over my people Israel, that he may save my people out of the hand of the Philistines: for I have looked upon my people, because their cry is come unto me.

17 And when Samuel saw Saul, the LORD said unto him, Behold the man whom I spake to thee of! this same shall reign over my people.

18 Then Saul drew near to Samuel in the gate, and said, Tell me, I pray thee, where the seer's house is.

19 And Samuel answered Saul, and said, I am the seer: go up before me unto the high place; for ye shall eat with me to day, and to morrow I will let thee go, and will tell thee

20 And as for thine asses that were lost three days ago, set not thy mind on them; for they are found. And on whom is all the desire of Israel? Is it not on thee, and on all thy father's house?

21 And Saul answered and said, Am not I a Benjamite, of the smallest of the tribes of Israel? and my family the least of all the families of the tribe of Benjamin? wherefore then speakest thou so to me?

22 And Samuel took Saul and his servant, and brought them into the parlour, and made them sit in the chiefest place among them that were bidden, which were about thirty persons.

23 And Samuel said unto the cook, Bring the portion which I gave thee, of which I said unto thee, Set it by thee.

24 And the cook took up the shoulder, and that which was upon it, and set it before Saul. And Samuel said, Behold that which is left! set it before thee, and eat: for unto this time hath it been kept for thee since I said, I have invited the people. So Saul did eat with Samuel that day.

25 ¶ And when they were come down from the high place into the city, Samuel communed with Saul upon the top of the house.

26 And they arose early: and it came to pass about the spring of the day, that Samuel called Saul to the top of the house, saying, Up, that I may send thee away. And Saul arose, and they went out both of them, he and Samuel, abroad.

27 And as they were going down to the end of the city, Samuel said to Saul, Bid the servant pass on before us, (and he passed on,) but stand thou still a while, that I may shew thee the word of God.

And Ammon said that a seer is a revelator and a prophet also; and a gift which is greater can no man have, except he should possess the power of God, which no man can; yet a man may have great power given him from God.

But a seer can know of things which are past, and also of things which are to come, and by them shall all things be revealed, or, rather, shall secret things be made manifest, and hidden things shall come to light, and things which are not known shall be made known by them, and also things shall be made known by them which otherwise could not be known.

Thus God has provided a means that man, through faith, might work mighty miracles; therefore he becometh a great benefit to his fellow beings. (Mosiah 8:13–18)

Additionally, the role of seer in relationship to the Prophet Joseph Smith is referenced in Lehi's quotation of the prophetic words of Joseph of Egypt concerning a like-named seer of the latter days (see 2 Ne. 3:6–7, 11, 14; see also D&C 124:94 concerning Hyrum Smith as assistant president). In the Pearl of Great Price Enoch is identified as a seer (see Moses 6:36, 38). In the leadership of The Church of Jesus Christ of Latter-day Saints, the First Presidency and Council of the Twelve are sustained as prophets, seers, and revelators.

POINT OF INTEREST

The Bible Dictionary places the commencement of Saul's reign at 1095 B.C., but other sources have him crowned as late as 1020 B.C. "In Judah and Israel, as elsewhere in the ancient Near East, events were dated according the regnal years of the kings. . . . Since antiquity, scholars have tried to reconcile the various dating contradictions in the Books of Kings. There are a number of reasons for these discrepancies. During the exile in Babylon, extensive chronographic works were composed. The compiler of the Books of Kings, using these as well as other, older chronicles and lists of kings, would also from time to time have added his own calculations where there were gaps or confusions. . . . In establishing absolute dates, modern scholars use synchronisms from sources elsewhere, in general from Mesopotamia. . . . Chronologies for the first millennium B.C. . . . based on continuous lists of years down to the Hellenistic period . . . can be verified by astronomical reckoning. For example, from the evidence of the Bible and the Babylonian Chronicle it is possible to date Nebuchadnezzar's capture of Jerusalem to the eighth year of Nebuchadnezzar; that is 597 B.C. But many dates, like those of Saul's reign, are not known. Original oral methods of transmitting dates and other information adds further difficulty to reaching a reliable chronology" (Bruce Metzer, David Goldstein, and John Ferguson, *Great Events of Bible Times* [New York: Fall River Press, 1990]).

CHAPTER 10

1 THEN Samuel took a vial of oil, and poured it upon his head, and kissed him, and said, Is it not because the LORD hath anointed thee to be captain over his inheritance?

2 When thou art departed from me to day, then thou shalt find two men by Rachel's sepulchre in the border of Benjamin at Zelzah; and they will say unto thee, The asses which thou wentest to seek are found: and, lo, thy father hath left the care of the asses, and sorroweth for you, saying, What shall I do for my son?

3 Then shalt thou go on forward from thence, and thou shalt come to the plain of Tabor, and there shall meet thee three men going up to God to Beth-el, one carrying three kids, and another carrying three loaves of bread, and another carrying a bottle of wine:

4 And they will salute thee, and give thee two loaves of bread; which thou shalt receive of their hands.

5 After that thou shalt come to the hill of God, where is the garrison of the Philistines: and it shall come to pass, when thou art come thither to the city, that thou shalt meet a company of prophets coming down from the high place with a psaltery, and a tabret, and a pipe, and a harp, before them; and they shall prophesy:

6 And the Spirit of the LORD will come upon thee, and thou shalt prophesy with them, and shalt be turned into another man.

7 And let it be, when these signs are come unto thee, that thou do as occasion serve thee; for God is with thee.

8 And thou shalt go down before me to Gilgal; and, behold, I will come down unto thee, to offer burnt offerings, and to sacrifice sacrifices of peace offerings: seven days shalt thou tarry, till I come to thee, and shew thee what thou shalt do.

9 ¶ And it was so, that when he had turned his back to go from Samuel, God gave him another heart: and all those signs came to pass that day.

10 And when they came thither to the hill, behold, a company of prophets met him; and the Spirit of God came upon him, and he prophesied among them.

11 And it came to pass, when all that knew him beforetime saw that, behold, he prophesied among the prophets, then the people said one to another, What is this that is come unto the son of Kish? Is Saul also among the prophets?

12 And one of the same place answered and said, But who is their father? Therefore it became a proverb, Is Saul also among the prophets?

13 And when he had made an end of prophesying, he came to the high place.

14 ¶ And Saul's uncle said unto him and to his servant, Whither went ye? And he said, To seek the asses: and when we saw that they were no where, we came to Samuel.

15 And Saul's uncle said, Tell me, I pray thee, what Samuel said unto you.

16 And Saul said unto his uncle, He told us plainly that the asses were found. But of the matter of the kingdom, whereof Samuel spake, he told him not.

17 ¶ And Samuel called the people together unto the LORD to Mizpeh;

18 And said unto the children of Israel, Thus saith the LORD God of Israel, I brought up Israel out of Egypt, and delivered you out of

1 SAMUEL CHAPTER 10

"I heard the Prophet Joseph say, in speaking the Twelve on one occasion: 'You will have all kinds of trials to pass through. And it is quite as necessary for you to be tried as it was for Abraham and other men of God, and (said he) God will feel after you, and He will take hold of you and wrench your very heart strings, and if you cannot stand it you will not be fit for an inheritance in the celestial kingdom of God.'" —John Taylor, JD 24:197

1 Samuel 10:6—The Lord Can Work with Willing and Renewable Hearts

Just as in the case of the young Saul, the Lord favors the humble and spiritually malleable, and blesses them in their callings by giving them a transformed and rejuvenated heart.

When Israel rejected the Lord as their king and insisted on having a worldly king like the neighboring cultures, the Lord caused the prophet Samuel to anoint the young Saul to be king of Israel. Saul had many good qualities, including (at the beginning) a humble nature. The Lord gave him "another heart" (1 Sam. 10:9)—Saul was illuminated by divine purpose and became spiritually committed. The Spirit of the Lord came upon him and he then prophesied with power. Samuel adjured the Israelites and their new king to be obedient to the Lord's commandments lest He reject them.

From this example we learn that to assist the Lord one surely must be humble, full of charity, and willing to submit to the will of the Father: "And no one can assist in the work except he shall be humble and full of love, having faith, hope, and charity, being temperate in all things, whatsoever shall be entrusted to his care" (D&C 12:8). With these qualities the Lord can truly use us to bless His children.

1 Samuel 10:7–25—Secular versus Eternal

The Lord granted the people that which they demanded—a king. When people prefer a secular king over the Almighty King, He shows forth mercy sufficient to grant unto them their desire, knowing that justice will prevail in the event such a worldly king will lead them into the pathway of unrighteousness. When the people exclaimed "God save the king" in affirmation of the reign of the towering Saul, they could scarcely understand how appropriate their supplication would become—for Saul would sooner than later be rejected of the Lord for his disobedience and prideful arrogance.

the hand of the Egyptians, and out of the hand of all kingdoms, and of them that oppressed you:

19 And ye have this day rejected your God, who himself saved you out of all your adversities and your tribulations; and ye have said unto him, Nay, but set a king over us. Now therefore present yourselves before the LORD by your tribes, and by your thousands.

20 And when Samuel had caused all the tribes of Israel to come near, the tribe of Benjamin was taken.

21 When he had caused the tribe of Benjamin to come near by their families, the family of Matri was taken, and Saul the son of Kish was taken: and when they sought him, he could not be found.

22 Therefore they enquired of the LORD further, if the man should yet come thither. And the LORD answered, Behold, he hath hid himself among the stuff.

23 And they ran and fetched him thence: and when he stood among the people, he was higher than any of the people from his shoulders and upward.

24 And Samuel said to all the people, See ye him whom the LORD hath chosen, that there is none like him among all the people? And all the people shouted, and said, God save the king.

25 Then Samuel told the people the manner of the kingdom, and wrote it in a book, and laid it up before the LORD. And Samuel sent all the people away, every man to his house.

26 ¶ And Saul also went home to Gibeah; and there went with him a band of men, whose hearts God had touched.

27 But the children of Belial said, How shall this man save us? And they despised him, and brought him no presents. But he held his peace.

CHAPTER 11

1 THEN Nahash the Ammonite came up, and encamped against Jabesh-gilead: and all the men of Jabesh said unto Nahash, Make a covenant with us, and we will serve thee.

2 And Nahash the Ammonite answered them, On this condition will I make a covenant with you, that I may thrust out all your right eyes, and lay it for a reproach upon all Israel.

3 And the elders of Jabesh said unto him, Give us seven days' respite, that we may send messengers unto all the coasts of Israel: and then, if there be no man to save us, we will come out to thee.

4 ¶ Then came the messengers to Gibeah of Saul, and told the tidings in the ears of the people: and all the people lifted up their voices, and wept.

5 And, behold, Saul came after the herd out of the field; and Saul said, What aileth the people that they weep? And they told him the tidings of the men of Jabesh.

6 And the Spirit of God came upon Saul when he heard those tidings, and his anger was kindled greatly.

7 And he took a yoke of oxen, and hewed them in pieces, and sent them throughout all the coasts of Israel by the hands of messengers, saying, Whosoever cometh not forth after Saul and after Samuel, so shall it be done unto his oxen. And the fear of the LORD fell on the people, and they came out with one consent.

Samuel Blessing Saul by Gustave Doré

1 SAMUEL CHAPTER 11

1 Samuel 11:6–13—Saul's Strategy

When operating under the influence of the Spirit of the Lord, Saul was able to obtain a decisive victory over the Ammonite enemies of Israel. His striking iconic display of the remains of the slaughtered oxen—a persuasive warning against the effects of timidity and cowardice—was a powerful strategy for galvanizing unity and commitment among the people: "And the fear of the LORD fell on the people, and they came out with one consent" (1 Sam. 11:7).

Such direct engagement is characteristic of a bold and effective leader. Captain Moroni in the Book of Mormon used a powerful display of the Title of Liberty throughout the country to instill courage and commitment in the hearts of the people beset by the assault of enemy forces (see Alma 46:13, 36).

8 And when he numbered them in Bezek, the children of Israel were three hundred thousand, and the men of Judah thirty thousand.

9 And they said unto the messengers that came, Thus shall ye say unto the men of Jabesh-gilead, To morrow, by that time the sun be hot, ye shall have help. And the messengers came and shewed it to the men of Jabesh; and they were glad.

10 Therefore the men of Jabesh said, To morrow we will come out unto you, and ye shall do with us all that seemeth good unto you.

11 And it was so on the morrow, that Saul put the people in three companies; and they came into the midst of the host in the morning watch, and slew the Ammonites until the heat of the day: and it came to pass, that they which remained were scattered, so that two of them were not left together.

12 ¶ And the people said unto Samuel, Who is he that said, Shall Saul reign over us? bring the men, that we may put them to death.

13 And Saul said, There shall not a man be put to death this day: for to day the LORD hath wrought salvation in Israel.

14 Then said Samuel to the people, Come, and let us go to Gilgal, and renew the kingdom there.

15 And all the people went to Gilgal; and there they made Saul king before the LORD in Gilgal; and there they sacrificed sacrifices of peace offerings before the LORD; and there Saul and all the men of Israel rejoiced greatly.

1 Samuel 11:15—Saul Becomes King

Saul becomes king in Israel—the first of a long sequence of monarchs of various stripes, with wide-ranging levels of righteousness.

CHAPTER 13

1 SAUL reigned one year; and when he had reigned two years over Israel,

2 Saul chose him three thousand men of Israel; whereof two thousand were with Saul in Michmash and in mount Beth-el, and a thousand were with Jonathan in Gibeah of Benjamin: and the rest of the people he sent every man to his tent.

3 And Jonathan smote the garrison of the Philistines that was in Geba, and the Philistines heard of it. And Saul blew the trumpet throughout all the land, saying, Let the Hebrews hear.

4 And all Israel heard say that Saul had smitten a garrison of the Philistines, and that Israel also was had in abomination with the Philistines. And the people were called together after Saul to Gilgal.

5 ¶ And the Philistines gathered themselves together to fight with Israel, thirty thousand chariots, and six thousand horsemen, and people as the sand which is on the sea shore in multitude: and they came up, and pitched in Michmash, eastward from Beth-aven.

6 When the men of Israel saw that they were in a strait, (for the people were distressed,) then the people did hide themselves in caves, and in thickets, and in rocks, and in high places, and in pits.

7 And some of the Hebrews went over Jordan to the land of Gad and Gilead. As for Saul, he was yet in Gilgal, and all the people followed him trembling.

1 SAMUEL CHAPTER 13

1 Samuel 13:14—Saul's Decline

The insubordination of Saul in brashly taking upon himself the authority to perform a sacrificial offering unto the Lord brought about a precipitous decline in his stature and station before the Lord, and eventually, as a result of fuedture misjudgments, result in his being replaced by David.

8 ¶ And he tarried seven days, according to the set time that Samuel had appointed: but Samuel came not to Gilgal; and the people were scattered from him.

9 And Saul said, Bring hither a burnt offering to me, and peace offerings. And he offered the burnt offering.

10 And it came to pass, that as soon as he had made an end of offering the burnt offering, behold, Samuel came; and Saul went out to meet him, that he might salute him.

11 ¶ And Samuel said, What hast thou done? And Saul said, Because I saw that the people were scattered from me, and that thou camest not within the days appointed, and that the Philistines gathered themselves together at Michmash;

12 Therefore said I, The Philistines will come down now upon me to Gilgal, and I have not made supplication unto the LORD: I forced myself therefore, and offered a burnt offering.

13 And Samuel said to Saul, Thou hast done foolishly: thou hast not kept the commandment of the LORD thy God, which he commanded thee: for now would the LORD have established thy kingdom upon Israel for ever.

14 But now thy kingdom shall not continue: the LORD hath sought him a man after his own heart, and the LORD hath commanded him to be captain over his people, because thou hast not kept that which the LORD commanded thee.

15 And Samuel arose, and gat him up from Gilgal unto Gibeah of Benjamin. And Saul numbered the people that were present with him, about six hundred men.

16 And Saul, and Jonathan his son, and the people that were present with them, abode in Gibeah of Benjamin: but the Philistines encamped in Michmash.

17 ¶ And the spoilers came out of the camp of the Philistines in three companies: one company turned unto the way that leadeth to Ophrah, unto the land of Shual:

18 And another company turned the way to Beth-horon: and another company turned to the way of the border that looketh to the valley of Zeboim toward the wilderness.

19 ¶ Now there was no smith found throughout all the land of Israel: for the Philistines said, Lest the Hebrews make them swords or spears:

20 But all the Israelites went down to the Philistines, to sharpen every man his share, and his coulter, and his axe, and his mattock.

21 Yet they had a file for the mattocks, and for the coulters, and for the forks, and for the axes, and to sharpen the goads.

22 So it came to pass in the day of battle, that there was neither sword nor spear found in the hand of any of the people that were with Saul and Jonathan: but with Saul and with Jonathan his son was there found.

23 And the garrison of the Philistines went out to the passage of Michmash.

CHAPTER 15

1 SAMUEL also said unto Saul, The LORD sent me to anoint thee to be king over his people, over Israel: now therefore hearken thou unto the voice of the words of the LORD.

2 Thus saith the LORD of hosts, I remember that which Amalek did to Israel, how he laid wait for him in the way, when he came up from Egypt.

Death of Agag by Gustave Doré

3 Now go and smite Amalek, and utterly destroy all that they have, and spare them not; but slay both man and woman, infant and suckling, ox and sheep, camel and ass.

4 And Saul gathered the people together, and numbered them in Telaim, two hundred thousand footmen, and ten thousand men of Judah.

5 And Saul came to a city of Amalek, and laid wait in the valley.

6 ¶ And Saul said unto the Kenites, Go, depart, get you down from among the Amalekites, lest I destroy you with them: for ye shewed kindness to all the children of Israel, when they came up out of Egypt. So the Kenites departed from among the Amalekites.

7 And Saul smote the Amalekites from Havilah until thou comest to Shur, that is over against Egypt.

8 And he took Agag the king of the Amalekites alive, and utterly destroyed all the people with the edge of the sword.

9 But Saul and the people spared Agag, and the best of the sheep, and of the oxen, and of the fatlings, and the lambs, and all that was good, and would not utterly destroy them: but every thing that was vile and refuse, that they destroyed utterly.

10 ¶ Then came the word of the LORD unto Samuel, saying,

11 It repenteth me that I have set up Saul to be king: for he is turned back from following me, and hath not performed my commandments. And it grieved Samuel; and he cried unto the LORD all night.

12 And when Samuel rose early to meet Saul in the morning, it was told Samuel, saying, Saul came to Carmel, and, behold, he set him up a place, and is gone about, and passed on, and gone down to Gilgal.

13 And Samuel came to Saul: and Saul said unto him, Blessed be thou of the LORD: I have performed the commandment of the LORD.

14 And Samuel said, What meaneth then this bleating of the sheep in mine ears, and the lowing of the oxen which I hear?

15 And Saul said, They have brought them from the Amalekites: for the people spared the best of the sheep and of the oxen, to sacrifice unto the LORD thy God; and the rest we have utterly destroyed.

16 Then Samuel said unto Saul, Stay, and I will tell thee what the LORD hath said to me this night. And he said unto him, Say on.

17 And Samuel said, When thou wast little in thine own sight, wast thou not made the head of the tribes of Israel, and the LORD anointed thee king over Israel?

18 And the LORD sent thee on a journey, and said, Go and utterly destroy the sinners the Amalekites, and fight against them until they be consumed.

19 Wherefore then didst thou not obey the voice of the LORD, but didst fly upon the spoil, and didst evil in the sight of the LORD?

20 And Saul said unto Samuel, Yea, I have obeyed the voice of the LORD, and have gone the way which the LORD sent me, and have brought Agag the king of Amalek, and have utterly destroyed the Amalekites.

21 But the people took of the spoil, sheep and oxen, the chief of the things which should have been utterly destroyed, to sacrifice unto the LORD thy God in Gilgal.

22 And Samuel said, Hath the LORD as great delight in burnt offerings and sacrifices, as in obeying the voice of the LORD? Behold, to obey is better than sacrifice, and to hearken than the fat of rams.

1 SAMUEL CHAPTER 15

1 Samuel 15:9—Agag

Agag (possible meaning: flame; the name was probably a general designation for the Amalekite kings, similar to "Pharaoh" among the Egyptians) was king of the Amalekites when Saul was purging the country of the enemies of Israel (sometime after 1095 BC). At the time of Moses, the Amalekites under Amalek came against Israel. Israel responded in the strength of the Lord and won the battle, the arms of Moses being held aloft by Aaron and Hur (see Ex. 17:8–14). It was then that the Lord proclaimed He would work against the Amalekites during the coming generations (see Ex. 17:14–16). When Saul took up the ensign of Israel, Samuel reminded him of his commission (see 1 Sam. 15:1–3).

Saul and his armies went forward with great force: "And he took Agag the king of the Amalekites alive, and utterly destroyed all the people with the edge of the sword. But Saul and the people spared Agag, and the best of the sheep, and of the oxen, and of the fatlings, and the lambs, and all *that was* good, and would not utterly destroy them: but every thing *that was* vile and refuse, that they destroyed utterly" (1 Sam. 15:8–9).

Samuel then came forward and reported to Saul the displeasure of the Lord for Saul's disobedience to the commandment to destroy everything of the Amalekites, sparing nothing. When Saul defended himself for having saved the best of the spoil to sacrifice unto the Lord, Samuel declared the divine judgment upon the king:

> . . . Hath the LORD *as great* delight in burnt offerings and sacrifices, as in obeying the voice of the LORD? Behold, to obey *is* better than sacrifice, *and* to hearken than the fat of rams.
>
> For rebellion *is as* the sin of witchcraft, and stubbornness *is as* iniquity and idolatry. Because thou hast rejected the word of the LORD, he hath also rejected thee from *being* king. (1 Sam. 15:22–23)

From that moment on, Saul's tenure began its irreversible decline—and Samuel proceeded to slay Agag to fulfill the commandment of the Lord against the enemy of Israel (see 1 Sam. 15:33).

1 Samuel 15:22–23—The Nobility of Pure Obedience

When we begin to govern our lives according to our own desires and judgment rather than acting in the spirit of our commission as servants of God, then we begin to falter and lose favor with the Lord. Only by obedience to the commandments and will of God can we hope to have the blessings of heaven and prosper in our duties and service.

Soon after assuming the role of king in Israel, Saul began to forget the Lord and arrogate to himself the abilities of righteous judgment and priesthood authority. When Samuel delayed his arrival to offer sacrifice to the Lord, Saul took it upon himself to perform the priestly duties and

23 For rebellion is as the sin of witchcraft, and stubbornness is as iniquity and idolatry. Because thou hast rejected the word of the LORD, he hath also rejected thee from being king.

24 ¶ And Saul said unto Samuel, I have sinned: for I have transgressed the commandment of the LORD, and thy words: because I feared the people, and obeyed their voice.

25 Now therefore, I pray thee, pardon my sin, and turn again with me, that I may worship the LORD.

26 And Samuel said unto Saul, I will not return with thee: for thou hast rejected the word of the LORD, and the LORD hath rejected thee from being king over Israel.

27 And as Samuel turned about to go away, he laid hold upon the skirt of his mantle, and it rent.

28 And Samuel said unto him, The LORD hath rent the kingdom of Israel from thee this day, and hath given it to a neighbour of thine, that is better than thou.

29 And also the Strength of Israel will not lie nor repent: for he is not a man, that he should repent.

30 Then he said, I have sinned: yet honour me now, I pray thee, before the elders of my people, and before Israel, and turn again with me, that I may worship the LORD thy God.

31 So Samuel turned again after Saul; and Saul worshipped the LORD.

32 ¶ Then said Samuel, Bring ye hither to me Agag the king of the Amalekites. And Agag came unto him delicately. And Agag said, Surely the bitterness of death is past.

33 And Samuel said, As thy sword hath made women childless, so shall thy mother be childless among women. And Samuel hewed Agag in pieces before the LORD in Gilgal.

34 ¶ Then Samuel went to Ramah; and Saul went up to his house to Gibeah of Saul.

35 And Samuel came no more to see Saul until the day of his death: nevertheless Samuel mourned for Saul: and the LORD repented that he had made Saul king over Israel.

CHAPTER 16

1 AND the LORD said unto Samuel, How long wilt thou mourn for Saul, seeing I have rejected him from reigning over Israel? fill thine horn with oil, and go, I will send thee to Jesse the Bethlehemite: for I have provided me a king among his sons.

2 And Samuel said, How can I go? if Saul hear it, he will kill me. And the LORD said, Take an heifer with thee, and say, I am come to sacrifice to the LORD.

3 And call Jesse to the sacrifice, and I will shew thee what thou shalt do: and thou shalt anoint unto me him whom I name unto thee.

4 And Samuel did that which the LORD spake, and came to Bethlehem. And the elders of the town trembled at his coming, and said, Comest thou peaceably?

5 And he said, Peaceably: I am come to sacrifice unto the LORD: sanctify yourselves, and come with me to the sacrifice. And he sanctified Jesse and his sons, and called them to the sacrifice.

was rejected of the Lord as no longer "a man after his own heart" (1 Sam. 13:14).

Later Saul disobeyed the Lord by saving the spoils from the battle with the Amalekites, thus sealing his rejection by the Lord as king over Israel. Thereafter he was plagued with an evil spirit not of the Lord, and only the music of young David could give him relief. Obedience is not just the first law of heaven, but the governing principle of all blessings from God. It is obedience that brings righteousness, which qualifies us for eternal lives.

1 Samuel 15:23—The Consequences of Our Self-Justification

The Lord "requireth the heart and a willing mind" (D&C 64:34). When we rationalize our misbehavior and sins and justify our unrighteous behavior, the Lord is displeased and we relinquish great spiritual blessings. Willing obedience makes all rationalization unnecessary and brings greater harmony, peace, and confidence into our lives.

When Saul disobeyed the Lord by saving out the spoils of war after battle, Samuel called him to repentance. Disobedience is a terrible sin. But Saul went even further. He justified his behavior at first by laying the blame on his people, and then by claiming to want to use the spoils as a sacrifice to the Lord.

Saul's response in the face of the truth has become the enduring prototype of the self-justifying act, and stands as a memorial to the dire consequences of unrighteous rationalization. We must be careful lest we fall away. Remember: Saul's life was circumspect and righteous in the beginning. The problem came in time. Enduring to the end in steadfastness and continued righteousness was his problem—and ours, too, lest we forget. We must always look to the Lord and remember it is His strength and His will that will bless, help, and guide us back to His presence.

SAMUEL CHAPTER 16

1 Samuel 16:7—The Lord Looks Upon the Heart

While mankind tends to evaluate based on outward appearance and temporal standards, the Lord discerns one's potential for doing good and judges by the heart (the desire and capacity for righteous service).

When Samuel was sent to prepare the way for a new king in Israel, he went at first according to standard protocol by looking at the oldest of Jesse's eight sons. But the Lord guided him to discern the individual chosen for the throne—David, the youngest. Thus we learn how the Lord makes his selections—by looking at the heart and seeing with the inner eye of spiritual vision. Samuel, having been inspired to do so, anointed David king of Israel prior to the death of Saul.

David was called to play the harp for Saul that he might be relieved of the evil spirit. David found favor in the sight of Saul and became his armor-bearer. Through this we see that the Lord looks upon our hearts (the real us) to determine the character of our soul. We, as mortals, must never judge.

6 ¶ And it came to pass, when they were come, that he looked on Eliab, and said, Surely the LORD's anointed is before him.

7 But the LORD said unto Samuel, Look not on his countenance, or on the height of his stature; because I have refused him: for the LORD seeth not as man seeth; for man looketh on the outward appearance, but the LORD looketh on the heart.

8 Then Jesse called Abinadab, and made him pass before Samuel. And he said, Neither hath the LORD chosen this.

9 Then Jesse made Shammah to pass by. And he said, Neither hath the LORD chosen this.

10 Again, Jesse made seven of his sons to pass before Samuel. And Samuel said unto Jesse, The LORD hath not chosen these.

11 And Samuel said unto Jesse, Are here all thy children? And he said, There remaineth yet the youngest, and, behold, he keepeth the sheep. And Samuel said unto Jesse, Send and fetch him: for we will not sit down till he come hither.

12 And he sent, and brought him in. Now he was ruddy, and withal of a beautiful countenance, and goodly to look to. And the LORD said, Arise, anoint him: for this is he.

13 Then Samuel took the horn of oil, and anointed him in the midst of his brethren: and the Spirit of the LORD came upon David from that day forward. So Samuel rose up, and went to Ramah.

14 ¶ But the Spirit of the LORD departed from Saul, and an evil spirit from the LORD troubled him.

15 And Saul's servants said unto him, Behold now, an evil spirit from God troubleth thee.

16 Let our lord now command thy servants, which are before thee, to seek out a man, who is a cunning player on an harp: and it shall come to pass, when the evil spirit from God is upon thee, that he shall play with his hand, and thou shalt be well.

17 And Saul said unto his servants, Provide me now a man that can play well, and bring him to me.

18 Then answered one of the servants, and said, Behold, I have seen a son of Jesse the Beth-lehemite, that is cunning in playing, and a mighty valiant man, and a man of war, and prudent in matters, and a comely person, and the LORD is with him.

19 ¶ Wherefore Saul sent messengers unto Jesse, and said, Send me David thy son, which is with the sheep.

20 And Jesse took an ass laden with bread, and a bottle of wine, and a kid, and sent them by David his son unto Saul.

21 And David came to Saul, and stood before him: and he loved him greatly; and he became his armourbearer.

22 And Saul sent to Jesse, saying, Let David, I pray thee, stand before me; for he hath found favour in my sight.

23 And it came to pass, when the evil spirit from God was upon Saul, that David took an harp, and played with his hand: so Saul was refreshed, and was well, and the evil spirit departed from him.

1 Samuel 16:12—"This Is He"

"This is he." What more definitive commission could there be than the word of God declaring an individual to be the chosen one. We think of instances such as this to be transcendent and unique—but the expression "This is he" or "This is she" has relevance to every one of God's sons and daughters, for every one has unique responsibilities and commissions relating to the building up of the kingdom of God and its families, branches, and stakes. To realize that our individual assignments from the Lord render us chosen before Him is humbling and energizing at the same time.

1 Samuel 16:14—JST

The Joseph Smith Translation renders this verse: "But the Spirit of the Lord departed from Saul, and an evil spirit which was not of the Lord troubled him." The same correction applies to verses 15, 16, and 23.

David Slaying Goliath, chromolithograph

CHAPTER 17

1 NOW the Philistines gathered together their armies to battle, and were gathered together at Shochoh, which belongeth to Judah, and pitched between Shochoh and Azekah, in Ephes-dammim.

2 And Saul and the men of Israel were gathered together, and pitched by the valley of Elah, and set the battle in array against the Philistines.

3 And the Philistines stood on a mountain on the one side, and Israel stood on a mountain on the other side: and there was a valley between them.

4 ¶ And there went out a champion out of the camp of the Philistines, named Goliath, of Gath, whose height was six cubits and a span.

5 And he had an helmet of brass upon his head, and he was armed with a coat of mail; and the weight of the coat was five thousand shekels of brass.

6 And he had greaves of brass upon his legs, and a target of brass between his shoulders.

7 And the staff of his spear was like a weaver's beam; and his spear's head weighed six hundred shekels of iron: and one bearing a shield went before him.

8 And he stood and cried unto the armies of Israel, and said unto them, Why are ye come out to set your battle in array? am not I a Philistine, and ye servants to Saul? choose you a man for you, and let him come down to me.

9 If he be able to fight with me, and to kill me, then will we be your servants: but if I prevail against him, and kill him, then shall ye be our servants, and serve us.

10 And the Philistine said, I defy the armies of Israel this day; give me a man, that we may fight together.

11 When Saul and all Israel heard those words of the Philistine, they were dismayed, and greatly afraid.

12 ¶ Now David was the son of that Ephrathite of Beth-lehem-judah, whose name was Jesse; and he had eight sons: and the man went among men for an old man in the days of Saul.

13 And the three eldest sons of Jesse went and followed Saul to the battle: and the names of his three sons that went to the battle were Eliab the firstborn, and next unto him Abinadab, and the third Shammah.

14 And David was the youngest: and the three eldest followed Saul.

15 But David went and returned from Saul to feed his father's sheep at Beth-lehem.

16 And the Philistine drew near morning and evening, and presented himself forty days.

17 And Jesse said unto David his son, Take now for thy brethren an ephah of this parched corn, and these ten loaves, and run to the camp to thy brethren;

18 And carry these ten cheeses unto the captain of their thousand, and look how thy brethren fare, and take their pledge.

19 Now Saul, and they, and all the men of Israel, were in the valley of Elah, fighting with the Philistines.

20 ¶ And David rose up early in the morning, and left the sheep with a keeper, and took, and went, as Jesse had commanded him; and he came to the trench, as the host was going forth to the fight, and shouted for the battle.

21 For Israel and the Philistines had put the battle in array, army against army.

1 SAMUEL CHAPTER 17

1 Samuel 17:1–4—Goliath

Goliath of Gath was the notorious Philistine giant slain by the young David. Goliath's imposing stature (some ten feet tall) and confrontational tone had struck fear into the hearts of Saul's warriors (see 1 Sam. 17:8–10).

But young David had armor far beyond the efficacy of Goliath's lofty helmet, impenetrable coat of mail, and massive spear—for David was armed with the strength of the Lord. Said the young lad to the incredulous king Saul:

Thy servant slew both the lion and the bear: and this uncircumcised Philistine shall be as one of them, seeing he hath defied the armies of the living God.

David said moreover, The LORD that delivered me out of the paw of the lion, and out of the paw of the bear, he will deliver me out of the hand of this Philistine. (1 Sam. 17:36–37)

Given permission by Saul, David encountered Goliath in the valley while two armies watched with rapt attention from opposing mountain slopes. Said David to the disdainful giant man of war. David took his sling and sent a stone missile against Goliath with deadly accuracy. He then decapitated the giant with the latter's own sword (see 1 Sam. 17:49–51)—and became a legendary emblem of the victory of good over evil. The sword of Goliath was preserved as a religious trophy at the city of Nob, and David later retrieved it when, during his flight before the murderous Saul, he visited there with the priest Ahimelech to obtain nourishment (see 1 Sam. 21:6).

Goliath was also the possible name of another Philistine giant slain by Elhahan (like David, a Bethlehemite) as reported in 2 Sam. 21:19. This same giant is identified as "Lahmi the brother of Goliath" in 1 Chron. 20:5.

The term *giants* is used thirteen times in the Old Testament and twice in the Pearl of Great Price (Book of Moses). Additionally, the term *giant* (in the singular) is used eight times in the Old Testament. These references are to individuals of unusually large stature and strength. The most famous of the "giants" was Goliath.

22 And David left his carriage in the hand of the keeper of the carriage, and ran into the army, and came and saluted his brethren.

23 And as he talked with them, behold, there came up the champion, the Philistine of Gath, Goliath by name, out of the armies of the Philistines, and spake according to the same words: and David heard them.

24 And all the men of Israel, when they saw the man, fled from him, and were sore afraid.

25 And the men of Israel said, Have ye seen this man that is come up? surely to defy Israel is he come up: and it shall be, that the man who killeth him, the king will enrich him with great riches, and will give him his daughter, and make his father's house free in Israel.

26 And David spake to the men that stood by him, saying, What shall be done to the man that killeth this Philistine, and taketh away the reproach from Israel? for who is this uncircumcised Philistine, that he should defy the armies of the living God?

27 And the people answered him after this manner, saying, So shall it be done to the man that killeth him.

28 ¶ And Eliab his eldest brother heard when he spake unto the men; and Eliab's anger was kindled against David, and he said, Why camest thou down hither? and with whom hast thou left those few sheep in the wilderness? I know thy pride, and the naughtiness of thine heart; for thou art come down that thou mightest see the battle.

29 And David said, What have I now done? Is there not a cause?

30 And he turned from him toward another, and spake after the same manner: and the people answered him again after the former manner.

31 And when the words were heard which David spake, they rehearsed them before Saul: and he sent for him.

32 ¶ And David said to Saul, Let no man's heart fail because of him; thy servant will go and fight with this Philistine.

33 And Saul said to David, Thou art not able to go against this Philistine to fight with him: for thou art but a youth, and he a man of war from his youth.

34 And David said unto Saul, Thy servant kept his father's sheep, and there came a lion, and a bear, and took a lamb out of the flock:

35 And I went out after him, and smote him, and delivered it out of his mouth: and when he arose against me, I caught him by his beard, and smote him, and slew him.

36 Thy servant slew both the lion and the bear: and this uncircumcised Philistine shall be as one of them, seeing he hath defied the armies of the living God.

37 David said moreover, The LORD that delivered me out of the paw of the lion, and out of the paw of the bear, he will deliver me out of the hand of this Philistine. And Saul said unto David, Go, and the LORD be with thee.

38 ¶ And Saul armed David with his armour, and he put an helmet of brass upon his head; also he armed him with a coat of mail.

39 And David girded his sword upon his armour, and he assayed to go; for he had not proved it. And David said unto Saul, I cannot go with these; for I have not proved them. And David put them off him.

40 And he took his staff in his hand, and chose him five smooth stones out of the brook, and put them in a shepherd's bag which he had, even in a scrip; and his sling was in his hand: and he drew near to the Philistine.

1 Samuel 17:45–46—Victory in the Strength of the Lord

When we go about the Lord's errand by relying on His power and following His Spirit, we are assured of ultimate victory, for the purposes of the Lord cannot be thwarted or compromised.

All the mighty men of Israel quaked at the Philistine hordes and cowered at the defiant strength of the giant, Goliath. But the anointed youth, David, going in the strength of the Lord, used his inspired skill to thwart the arrogant enemy at his one place of weakness. The story of David and Goliath is perhaps the supreme emblem in all of world literature of how the weak things of the earth can vanquish the strong through the help of the Lord. No story has so inspired the hearts of people everywhere—especially young people—to take courage in carrying out their mortal assignments with hope and faith. The power of God is exercised through his servants as they act with faith and trust in the Lord. All of us can be strengthened beyond our own capabilities through the Lord. We must live worthy of this opportunity to be able to be of service to the Lord and our fellowmen.

1 Samuel 17:55—Abner

Abner (meaning: father of light) was the commander over the army of King Saul and cousin of the king (Saul's father Kish being a brother to Abner's father, Ner—see 1 Sam. 14:51). Abner was one of the many key figures who played a role in the epic drama of David's ascent to the throne of Israel. It was he who introduced David to Saul following the defeat of Goliath (see 1 Sam. 17:55–58.)

Saul's aggressive disposition toward David over the ensuing period of time forced the David to retreat into the wilderness for safety. By virtue of his office, Abner accompanied Saul in an attempt to remove David from the scene (see 1 Sam. 26:5). But David avoided bringing hurt to Saul, even when the opportunity presented itself during a nocturnal incursion into Saul's camp (see 1 Sam. 26:9–10). Later, David rebuked Abner for his failure to protect Saul on that occasion (see 1 Sam. 25:15–16).

After the death of Saul, David was anointed king over Judah at Hebron (see 2 Sam. 2:4), but Abner elevated Ish-bosheth, son of Saul, as king over Israel (see 2 Sam. 2:8–9) and thus cultivated a movement contrary to David's interests. When Ish-bosheth was defeated and perished in battle, Abner made gestures of support toward David (see 2 Sam. 3:12, 18), and David responded with courtesy and in the spirit of peace (see 2 Sam. 3:21). But a state of harmony was not to be, for Abner had earlier slain Asahel, the brother of Joab, David's army commander, and Joab then took action on his own to end the life of Abner (see 2 Sam. 3:27). David lamented the death of Abner and mourned before the people (see 2 Sam. 3:36–38).

David's interactions with Abner revealed much about David's character and honor. Soon after the death of Abner, David was anointed king over Israel (see 2 Sam. 5:3).

41 And the Philistine came on and drew near unto David; and the man that bare the shield went before him.

42 And when the Philistine looked about, and saw David, he disdained him: for he was but a youth, and ruddy, and of a fair countenance.

43 And the Philistine said unto David, Am I a dog, that thou comest to me with staves? And the Philistine cursed David by his gods.

44 And the Philistine said to David, Come to me, and I will give thy flesh unto the fowls of the air, and to the beasts of the field.

45 Then said David to the Philistine, Thou comest to me with a sword, and with a spear, and with a shield: but I come to thee in the name of the LORD of hosts, the God of the armies of Israel, whom thou hast defied.

46 This day will the LORD deliver thee into mine hand; and I will smite thee, and take thine head from thee; and I will give the carcases of the host of the Philistines this day unto the fowls of the air, and to the wild beasts of the earth; that all the earth may know that there is a God in Israel.

47 And all this assembly shall know that the LORD saveth not with sword and spear: for the battle is the LORD's, and he will give you into our hands.

48 And it came to pass, when the Philistine arose, and came and drew nigh to meet David, that David hasted, and ran toward the army to meet the Philistine.

49 And David put his hand in his bag, and took thence a stone, and slang it, and smote the Philistine in his forehead, that the stone sunk into his forehead; and he fell upon his face to the earth.

50 So David prevailed over the Philistine with a sling and with a stone, and smote the Philistine, and slew him; but there was no sword in the hand of David.

51 Therefore David ran, and stood upon the Philistine, and took his sword, and drew it out of the sheath thereof, and slew him, and cut off his head therewith. And when the Philistines saw their champion was dead, they fled.

52 And the men of Israel and of Judah arose, and shouted, and pursued the Philistines, until thou come to the valley, and to the gates of Ekron. And the wounded of the Philistines fell down by the way to Shaaraim, even unto Gath, and unto Ekron.

53 And the children of Israel returned from chasing after the Philistines, and they spoiled their tents.

54 And David took the head of the Philistine, and brought it to Jerusalem; but he put his armour in his tent.

55 ¶ And when Saul saw David go forth against the Philistine, he said unto Abner, the captain of the host, Abner, whose son is this youth? And Abner said, As thy soul liveth, O king, I cannot tell.

56 And the king said, Enquire thou whose son the stripling is.

57 And as David returned from the slaughter of the Philistine, Abner took him, and brought him before Saul with the head of the Philistine in his hand.

58 And Saul said to him, Whose son art thou, thou young man? And David answered, I am the son of thy servant Jesse the Bethlehemite.

1 Samuel 17:58—Jesse

Jesse was the father of David and therefore in the direct line of descent leading to Christ.

After Saul had witnessed the miraculous conquest over Goliath by the fearless young man with the sling, he said: "Whose son *art* thou, *thou* young man? And David answered, *I am* the son of thy servant Jesse the Bethlehemite" (1 Sam. 17:58). From that moment on, Jesse, as the father of David, was renowned throughout the land—just as his son was. Jesse is mentioned repeatedly in the scriptural accounts of the early history of David and also in the writings of Isaiah (see Isa. 11:1).

1 Samuel 17—Summary of Precepts and Principles

The classic story of David and Goliath teaches many truths. David showed humility, trust, faith, and dependence upon the strength in the Lord. By way of contrast, Goliath's boastful nature and trust in the arm of the flesh were evident.

The Lord will truly fight our battles and provide a way for us to accomplish His righteous purposes. Like David, we can protect ourselves with the armor of God. The story of David and Goliath is a classic tale of the encounter with opposition. There is opposition in all things (see 2 Ne. 2:11); there can be no growth and progression without it. Temptation is part of opposition, and without temptation we could not be agents unto ourselves (see D&C 29:39). Satan tempts us in a variety of ways: making us think that our decisions really don't matter, creating doubt and unbelief, enticing us with the lusts of the flesh (see James 1:12–15), and deploying many other devious and insidious tactics. He knows our weaknesses. When we love the world and its allurements more than God, we are more susceptible to temptation—we become carnal, sensual, and devilish (see Moses 5:13). To understand and recognize the winds of temptation and the storm clouds of evil enticements that surround us is to prepare ourselves for the battle to resist such destructive forces. In the strength of the Lord we can erect the defenses of covenant valor and activate the protecting influence of the Spirit of God.

The Lord can transform our weaknesses into strengths. By all appearances, David was no match for Goliath—but the young lad prevailed for the cause of Israel because he acted in the strength of the Lord. Once more the record gives evidence of the power of God to do all things—to deliver David (see 1 Sam. 17:37), to strengthen Paul (see 2 Cor. 12:9), to empower Ammon (see Alma 26:12), to guide the missionaries of today as we proclaim the gospel (see D&C 1:23)—and the list goes on, with many examples of the Lord strengthening His children. As to ourselves, we are nothing; but in the strength of the Lord we can do all things (see 1 Ne. 21:5; Alma 20:4; 26:12; Ether 12:27). The lesson of David is that we can overcome our vulnerabilities, follow the Spirit, cultivate humility, and act in faith—thus emerging victorious.

CHAPTER 18

1 AND it came to pass, when he had made an end of speaking unto Saul, that the soul of Jonathan was knit with the soul of David, and Jonathan loved him as his own soul.

2 And Saul took him that day, and would let him go no more home to his father's house.

3 Then Jonathan and David made a covenant, because he loved him as his own soul.

4 And Jonathan stripped himself of the robe that was upon him, and gave it to David, and his garments, even to his sword, and to his bow, and to his girdle.

5 ¶ And David went out whithersoever Saul sent him, and behaved himself wisely: and Saul set him over the men of war, and he was accepted in the sight of all the people, and also in the sight of Saul's servants.

6 And it came to pass as they came, when David was returned from the slaughter of the Philistine, that the women came out of all cities of Israel, singing and dancing, to meet king Saul, with tabrets, with joy, and with instruments of musick.

7 And the women answered one another as they played, and said, Saul hath slain his thousands, and David his ten thousands.

8 And Saul was very wroth, and the saying displeased him; and he said, They have ascribed unto David ten thousands, and to me they have ascribed but thousands: and what can he have more but the kingdom?

9 And Saul eyed David from that day and forward.

10 ¶ And it came to pass on the morrow, that the evil spirit from God came upon Saul, and he prophesied in the midst of the house: and David played with his hand, as at other times: and there was a javelin in Saul's hand.

11 And Saul cast the javelin; for he said, I will smite David even to the wall with it. And David avoided out of his presence twice.

12 ¶ And Saul was afraid of David, because the LORD was with him, and was departed from Saul.

13 Therefore Saul removed him from him, and made him his captain over a thousand; and he went out and came in before the people.

14 And David behaved himself wisely in all his ways; and the LORD was with him.

15 Wherefore when Saul saw that he behaved himself very wisely, he was afraid of him.

16 But all Israel and Judah loved David, because he went out and came in before them.

17 ¶ And Saul said to David, Behold my elder daughter Merab, her will I give thee to wife: only be thou valiant for me, and fight the LORD's battles. For Saul said, Let not mine hand be upon him, but let the hand of the Philistines be upon him.

18 And David said unto Saul, Who am I? and what is my life, or my father's family in Israel, that I should be son in law to the king?

19 But it came to pass at the time when Merab Saul's daughter should have been given to David, that she was given unto Adriel the Meholathite to wife.

20 And Michal Saul's daughter loved David: and they told Saul, and the thing pleased him.

21 And Saul said, I will give him her, that she may be a snare to him, and that the hand of the Philistines may be against him. Wherefore Saul said to David, Thou shalt this day be my son in law in the one of the twain.

1 SAMUEL CHAPTER 18

1 Samuel 18—The Story of David and Jonathan

The friendship of Jonathan and David is rightly celebrated as one of the most exemplary brotherly relationships recorded in the scriptures. Friendship between and among individuals united on the basis of the covenant always reflects faith and righteousness — faith that nothing can detract from, or interfere with, the loyalty and all-weather support of true friends; and righteousness in that genuine friendship is based on principles of truth and love.

In our dispensation of time the Lord established a greeting of friendship for use in the School of the Prophets: "Art thou a brother or brethren? I salute you in the name of the Lord Jesus Christ, in token or remembrance of the everlasting covenant, in which covenant I receive you to fellowship, in a determination that is fixed, immovable, and unchangeable, to be your friend and brother through the grace of God in the bonds of love, to walk in all the commandments of God blameless, in thanksgiving, forever and ever. Amen" (D&C 88:133). Friendship of this lustrous kind cannot be eclipsed by the envy, greed, or malice of others (such as that which King Saul harbored for the forgiving David).

1 Samuel 18:1—Jonathan

Jonathan loved David as much as Saul hated him. Time and again, Jonathan defended, protected, and rescued the son of Jesse from the king's assassination plots. Never for a moment stooping to jealousy or envy, Jonathan saw in David the future king of Israel (see 1 Sam. 23:17) and did all in his power to facilitate his preservation for that destined role. True friends are actively involved in strengthening and protecting their friend's life, that they might enjoy eternal life together.

For more insights on Jonathan, see Appendix U.

1 Samuel 18:20–21—Michal

Michal (pronounced like "Michael") was the younger of Saul's two daughters, the first-born being Merab (see 1 Sam. 14:9). Michal loved David and was given to him by the king to be his wife.

22 ¶ And Saul commanded his servants, saying, Commune with David secretly, and say, Behold, the king hath delight in thee, and all his servants love thee: now therefore be the king's son in law.

23 And Saul's servants spake those words in the ears of David. And David said, Seemeth it to you a light thing to be a king's son in law, seeing that I am a poor man, and lightly esteemed?

24 And the servants of Saul told him, saying, On this manner spake David.

25 And Saul said, Thus shall ye say to David, The king desireth not any dowry, but an hundred foreskins of the Philistines, to be avenged of the king's enemies. But Saul thought to make David fall by the hand of the Philistines.

26 And when his servants told David these words, it pleased David well to be the king's son in law: and the days were not expired.

27 Wherefore David arose and went, he and his men, and slew of the Philistines two hundred men; and David brought their foreskins, and they gave them in full tale to the king, that he might be the king's son in law. And Saul gave him Michal his daughter to wife.

28 ¶ And Saul saw and knew that the LORD was with David, and that Michal Saul's daughter loved him.

29 And Saul was yet the more afraid of David; and Saul became David's enemy continually.

30 Then the princes of the Philistines went forth: and it came to pass, after they went forth, that David behaved himself more wisely than all the servants of Saul; so that his name was much set by.

CHAPTER 19

1 AND Saul spake to Jonathan his son, and to all his servants, that they should kill David.

2 But Jonathan Saul's son delighted much in David: and Jonathan told David, saying, Saul my father seeketh to kill thee: now therefore, I pray thee, take heed to thyself until the morning, and abide in a secret place, and hide thyself:

3 And I will go out and stand beside my father in the field where thou art, and I will commune with my father of thee; and what I see, that I will tell thee.

4 ¶ And Jonathan spake good of David unto Saul his father, and said unto him, Let not the king sin against his servant, against David; because he hath not sinned against thee, and because his works have been to thee-ward very good:

5 For he did put his life in his hand, and slew the Philistine, and the LORD wrought a great salvation for all Israel: thou sawest it, and didst rejoice: wherefore then wilt thou sin against innocent blood, to slay David without a cause?

6 And Saul hearkened unto the voice of Jonathan: and Saul sware, As the LORD liveth, he shall not be slain.

7 And Jonathan called David, and Jonathan shewed him all those things. And Jonathan brought David to Saul, and he was in his presence, as in times past.

8 ¶ And there was war again: and David went out, and fought with the Philistines, and slew them with a great slaughter; and they fled from him.

9 And the evil spirit from the LORD was upon Saul, as he sat in his house with his javelin in his hand: and David played with his hand.

1 Samuel 18:28–29—The Treachery of a Jealous Mind

Saul was plagued by the spirit of jealousy and continually plotted for the death of David. But David deftly followed the course of safety opened up for him by the Lord and thus repeatedly escaped harm. Saul had been abandoned by the Lord, just as David had been taken into the Lord's favor—thus it was inevitable that David would ultimately ascend the throne of Israel.

Envy and jealousy are the ways of the devil. They are not innocuous in their effects on us. They lead to destruction. Once one learns to love others, to truly love them—the ultimate concern that brings about righteous service—one will overcome all envy and jealousy.

Pride and arrogance of the type that consumed King Saul are the fuels of lethal envy and jealousy. Only by cultivating a life of humility and penitence can we hope to avoid such an invidious state of pride and greed, and qualify for the spirit of harmony, peace, and joy in this life and eternal rest in the life to come.

1 SAMUEL CHAPTER 19

1 Samuel 19:9—JST

The Joseph Smith Translation renders this verse as follows: "And the evil spirit which was not of the Lord was upon Saul, as he sat in his house with his javelin in his hand; and David played with his hand" (JST 1 Sam. 19:9).

10 And Saul sought to smite David even to the wall with the javelin; but he slipped away out of Saul's presence, and he smote the javelin into the wall: and David fled, and escaped that night.

11 Saul also sent messengers unto David's house, to watch him, and to slay him in the morning: and Michal David's wife told him, saying, If thou save not thy life to night, to morrow thou shalt be slain.

12 ¶ So Michal let David down through a window: and he went, and fled, and escaped.

13 And Michal took an image, and laid it in the bed, and put a pillow of goats' hair for his bolster, and covered it with a cloth.

14 And when Saul sent messengers to take David, she said, He is sick.

15 And Saul sent the messengers again to see David, saying, Bring him up to me in the bed, that I may slay him.

16 And when the messengers were come in, behold, there was an image in the bed, with a pillow of goats' hair for his bolster.

17 And Saul said unto Michal, Why hast thou deceived me so, and sent away mine enemy, that he is escaped? And Michal answered Saul, He said unto me, Let me go; why should I kill thee?

18 ¶ So David fled, and escaped, and came to Samuel to Ramah, and told him all that Saul had done to him. And he and Samuel went and dwelt in Naioth.

19 And it was told Saul, saying, Behold, David is at Naioth in Ramah.

20 And Saul sent messengers to take David: and when they saw the company of the prophets prophesying, and Samuel standing as appointed over them, the Spirit of God was upon the messengers of Saul, and they also prophesied.

21 And when it was told Saul, he sent other messengers, and they prophesied likewise. And Saul sent messengers again the third time, and they prophesied also.

22 Then went he also to Ramah, and came to a great well that is in Sechu: and he asked and said, Where are Samuel and David? And one said, Behold, they be at Naioth in Ramah.

23 And he went thither to Naioth in Ramah: and the Spirit of God was upon him also, and he went on, and prophesied, until he came to Naioth in Ramah.

24 And he stripped off his clothes also, and prophesied before Samuel in like manner, and lay down naked all that day and all that night. Wherefore they say, Is Saul also among the prophets?

CHAPTER 20

1 AND David fled from Naioth in Ramah, and came and said before Jonathan, What have I done? what is mine iniquity? and what is my sin before thy father, that he seeketh my life?

2 And he said unto him, God forbid; thou shalt not die: behold, my father will do nothing either great or small, but that he will shew it me: and why should my father hide this thing from me? it is not so.

3 And David sware moreover, and said, Thy father certainly knoweth that I have found grace in thine eyes; and he saith, Let not Jonathan know this, lest he be grieved: but truly as the LORD liveth, and as thy soul liveth, there is but a step between me and death.

4 Then said Jonathan unto David, Whatsoever thy soul desireth, I will even do it for thee.

1 Samuel 19:10–14—Saul's Efforts to Eliminate David

Committed to the elimination of David, Saul took steps to fulfill his evil purpose, not understanding the intense loyalty of his daughter to her husband:

> Saul also sent messengers unto David's house, to watch him, and to slay him in the morning: and Michal David's wife told him, saying, If thou save not thy life to night, to morrow thou shalt be slain.
>
> So Michal let David down through a window: and he went, and fled, and escaped.
>
> And Michal took an image, and laid *it* in the bed, and put a pillow of goats' *hair* for his bolster, and covered *it* with a cloth.
>
> And when Saul sent messengers to take David, she said, He *is* sick. (1 Sam. 19:11–14)

When the messengers ultimately took possession of the bed-ridden "David," they learned that they had seized a mannequin, much to the disappointment of Saul (see 1 Sam. 19:15–17). Subsequently Saul gave Michal to another man (see 1 Sam. 25:44); however, David later reclaimed her from her second husband (see 2 Sam. 3:13–16).

Then, on the occasion of supreme joy for David—the return of the ark to Jerusalem—Michal was distressed, apparently offended by David's outspoken celebratory display (see 2 Sam. 6:15–16; see also 1 Chron. 15:29). Upon David's return, she reproached him with the words: "How glorious was the king of Israel to day, who uncovered himself to day in the eyes of the handmaids of his servants, as one of the vain fellows shamelessly uncovereth himself!" (2 Sam. 6:20). Thereafter Michal had no offspring (see 2 Sam. 6:23; compare 2 Sam. 21:8, where *Michal* should likely have been rendered *Merab*).

1 SAMUEL CHAPTER 20

1 Samuel 20—Covenant of Friendship

Few examples of friendship in holy writ resonate with greater fervor or authenticity than the covenant that Jonathan established with his friend, David.

What greater test is there for a proclaimed covenant of friendship than the specter of the countenance of death hovering over the stage of life during any given hour? The lives of both Jonathan and David were at stake, but they still honored their covenant of companionship and loyalty.

How strong today are the bands that join us in association with our own loved ones? When families are joined together through the blessings of temple covenants, then nothing should have the power to weaken the unity of love and loyalty that belongs to such a relationship—not even the threat of mortal danger. From Jonathan and David we can learn a lesson about invincible friendship and oneness.

5 And David said unto Jonathan, Behold, to morrow is the new moon, and I should not fail to sit with the king at meat: but let me go, that I may hide myself in the field unto the third day at even.

6 If thy father at all miss me, then say, David earnestly asked leave of me that he might run to Beth-lehem his city: for there is a yearly sacrifice there for all the family.

7 If he say thus, It is well; thy servant shall have peace: but if he be very wroth, then be sure that evil is determined by him.

8 Therefore thou shalt deal kindly with thy servant; for thou hast brought thy servant into a covenant of the LORD with thee: notwithstanding, if there be in me iniquity, slay me thyself; for why shouldest thou bring me to thy father?

9 And Jonathan said, Far be it from thee: for if I knew certainly that evil were determined by my father to come upon thee, then would not I tell it thee?

10 Then said David to Jonathan, Who shall tell me? or what if thy father answer thee roughly?

11 ¶ And Jonathan said unto David, Come, and let us go out into the field. And they went out both of them into the field.

12 And Jonathan said unto David, O LORD God of Israel, when I have sounded my father about to morrow any time, or the third day, and, behold, if there be good toward David, and I then send not unto thee, and shew it thee;

13 The LORD do so and much more to Jonathan: but if it please my father to do thee evil, then I will shew it thee, and send thee away, that thou mayest go in peace: and the LORD be with thee, as he hath been with my father.

14 And thou shalt not only while yet I live shew me the kindness of the LORD, that I die not:

15 But also thou shalt not cut off thy kindness from my house for ever: no, not when the LORD hath cut off the enemies of David every one from the face of the earth.

16 So Jonathan made a covenant with the house of David, saying, Let the LORD even require it at the hand of David's enemies.

17 And Jonathan caused David to swear again, because he loved him: for he loved him as he loved his own soul.

18 Then Jonathan said to David, To morrow is the new moon: and thou shalt be missed, because thy seat will be empty.

19 And when thou hast stayed three days, then thou shalt go down quickly, and come to the place where thou didst hide thyself when the business was in hand, and shalt remain by the stone Ezel.

20 And I will shoot three arrows on the side thereof, as though I shot at a mark.

21 And, behold, I will send a lad, saying, Go, find out the arrows. If I expressly say unto the lad, Behold, the arrows are on this side of thee, take them; then come thou: for there is peace to thee, and no hurt; as the LORD liveth.

22 But if I say thus unto the young man, Behold, the arrows are beyond thee; go thy way: for the LORD hath sent thee away.

23 And as touching the matter which thou and I have spoken of, behold, the LORD be between thee and me for ever.

24 ¶ So David hid himself in the field: and when the new moon was come, the king sat him down to eat meat.

25 And the king sat upon his seat, as at other times, even upon a seat by the wall: and Jonathan arose, and Abner sat by Saul's side, and David's place was empty.

26 Nevertheless Saul spake not any thing that day: for he thought, Something hath befallen him, he is not clean; surely he is not clean.

The Escape of David through a Window by Gustave Doré

27 And it came to pass on the morrow, which was the second day of the month, that David's place was empty: and Saul said unto Jonathan his son, Wherefore cometh not the son of Jesse to meat, neither yesterday, nor to day?

28 And Jonathan answered Saul, David earnestly asked leave of me to go to Beth-lehem:

29 And he said, Let me go, I pray thee; for our family hath a sacrifice in the city; and my brother, he hath commanded me to be there: and now, if I have found favour in thine eyes, let me get away, I pray thee, and see my brethren. Therefore he cometh not unto the king's table.

30 Then Saul's anger was kindled against Jonathan, and he said unto him, Thou son of the perverse rebellious woman, do not I know that thou hast chosen the son of Jesse to thine own confusion, and unto the confusion of thy mother's nakedness?

31 For as long as the son of Jesse liveth upon the ground, thou shalt not be established, nor thy kingdom. Wherefore now send and fetch him unto me, for he shall surely die.

32 And Jonathan answered Saul his father, and said unto him, Wherefore shall he be slain? what hath he done?

33 And Saul cast a javelin at him to smite him: whereby Jonathan knew that it was determined of his father to slay David.

34 So Jonathan arose from the table in fierce anger, and did eat no meat the second day of the month: for he was grieved for David, because his father had done him shame.

35 ¶ And it came to pass in the morning, that Jonathan went out into the field at the time appointed with David, and a little lad with him.

36 And he said unto his lad, Run, find out now the arrows which I shoot. And as the lad ran, he shot an arrow beyond him.

37 And when the lad was come to the place of the arrow which Jonathan had shot, Jonathan cried after the lad, and said, Is not the arrow beyond thee?

38 And Jonathan cried after the lad, Make speed, haste, stay not. And Jonathan's lad gathered up the arrows, and came to his master.

39 But the lad knew not any thing: only Jonathan and David knew the matter.

40 And Jonathan gave his artillery unto his lad, and said unto him, Go, carry them to the city.

41 ¶ And as soon as the lad was gone, David arose out of a place toward the south, and fell on his face to the ground, and bowed himself three times: and they kissed one another, and wept one with another, until David exceeded.

42 And Jonathan said to David, Go in peace, forasmuch as we have sworn both of us in the name of the LORD, saying, The LORD be between me and thee, and between my seed and thy seed for ever. And he arose and departed: and Jonathan went into the city.

CHAPTER 23

1 THEN they told David, saying, Behold, the Philistines fight against Keilah, and they rob the threshingfloors.

2 Therefore David enquired of the LORD, saying, Shall I go and smite these Philistines? And the LORD said unto David, Go, and smite the Philistines, and save Keilah.

3 And David's men said unto him, Behold, we be afraid here in Judah: how much more then if we come to Keilah against the armies of the Philistines?

1 SAMUEL CHAPTER 23

1 Samuel 23:1–4—War

When does a contingent of warriors wage war? When it is decreed by the Lord. Confronted by circumstances of lethal danger for his people, David inquired of the Lord and was given leave to take defensive action. When David's men demurred, he again inquired of the Lord and received assurances of victory—which then was achieved.

In modern revelation, the Lord counseled the Saints during the dislocations and turmoil of the early Restoration period as follows: "And again, this is the law that I gave unto mine ancients, that they should not go out unto battle against any nation, kindred, tongue, or people, save I, the Lord, commanded them" (D&C 98:33).

Amidst the persecutions and violence heaped upon the Saints in those years unfolds this dawning light of wisdom from the Lord in answer to the question: How should we protect our families when they are attacked? Central to the revealed response (see D&C 98:23–48) are three principles: (1) We are to do all we can to protect our families and secure their safety and well-being; (2) we are to infuse our strategies for response with genuine forgiveness and forbearance when the enemy repents and desists; and (3) we are to await the command of God when the hour for justified proactive retribution arrives.

Thus the Saints were told not to revile against their enemies, but to forgive them even after the second and third offences, warning them in the name of the Lord not to come against them again. Nevertheless, after this process, the enemies are given into the hands of the Saints, just as in ancient times, provided the Saints lift a standard of peace consistently and leave it to the Lord to justify a response. Should the enemies repent, they are to be forgiven without limit. Should they not repent a second and third time, they are still to be forgiven—until beyond the third time, when the testimonies against them shall be brought before the Lord and He will avenge the Saints— unless the enemies should then repent with all their heart, unto the third and fourth generations.

President Joseph Fielding Smith gave this helpful summary of the principles given in the revealed word of the Lord:

> The law of forgiveness and retribution depicted in the latter half of this revelation is most worthy of careful study. This law applies to individuals and to families, as well as to the Church at large. We are under commandment to forgive our enemies and suffer their abuse and smiting the first time and second time, also the third time. This is to be done in patience, and in humility and prayer, hoping that the enemy might repent. If the enemy come upon us for the fourth time we are justified in meting out retribution, but even then there is to come a reward if we patiently endure, and the Lord will reward us abundantly. For all these abuses we will be rewarded if we endure them in patience. Perchance the enemy may repent, and that we should

4 Then David enquired of the LORD yet again. And the LORD answered him and said, Arise, go down to Keilah; for I will deliver the Philistines into thine hand.

5 So David and his men went to Keilah, and fought with the Philistines, and brought away their cattle, and smote them with a great slaughter. So David saved the inhabitants of Keilah.

6 And it came to pass, when Abiathar the son of Ahimelech fled to David to Keilah, that he came down with an ephod in his hand.

7 ¶ And it was told Saul that David was come to Keilah. And Saul said, God hath delivered him into mine hand; for he is shut in, by entering into a town that hath gates and bars.

8 And Saul called all the people together to war, to go down to Keilah, to besiege David and his men.

9 ¶ And David knew that Saul secretly practised mischief against him; and he said to Abiathar the priest, Bring hither the ephod.

10 Then said David, O LORD God of Israel, thy servant hath certainly heard that Saul seeketh to come to Keilah, to destroy the city for my sake.

11 Will the men of Keilah deliver me up into his hand? will Saul come down, as thy servant hath heard? O LORD God of Israel, I beseech thee, tell thy servant. And the LORD said, He will come down.

12 Then said David, Will the men of Keilah deliver me and my men into the hand of Saul? And the LORD said, They will deliver thee up.

13 ¶ Then David and his men, which were about six hundred, arose and departed out of Keilah, and went whithersoever they could go. And it was told Saul that David was escaped from Keilah; and he forbare to go forth.

14 And David abode in the wilderness in strong holds, and remained in a mountain in the wilderness of Ziph. And Saul sought him every day, but God delivered him not into his hand.

15 And David saw that Saul was come out to seek his life: and David was in the wilderness of Ziph in a wood.

16 ¶ And Jonathan Saul's son arose, and went to David into the wood, and strengthened his hand in God.

17 And he said unto him, Fear not: for the hand of Saul my father shall not find thee; and thou shalt be king over Israel, and I shall be next unto thee; and that also Saul my father knoweth.

18 And they two made a covenant before the LORD: and David abode in the wood, and Jonathan went to his house.

19 ¶ Then came up the Ziphites to Saul to Gibeah, saying, Doth not David hide himself with us in strong holds in the wood, in the hill of Hachilah, which is on the south of Jeshimon?

20 Now therefore, O king, come down according to all the desire of thy soul to come down; and our part shall be to deliver him into the king's hand.

21 And Saul said, Blessed be ye of the LORD; for ye have compassion on me.

22 Go, I pray you, prepare yet, and know and see his place where his haunt is, and who hath seen him there: for it is told me that he dealeth very subtilly.

23 See therefore, and take knowledge of all the lurking places where he hideth himself, and come ye again to me with the certainty, and I will go with you: and it shall come to pass, if he be in the land, that I will search him out throughout all the thousands of Judah.

24 And they arose, and went to Ziph before Saul: but David and his men were in the wilderness of Maon, in the plain on the south of Jeshimon.

most sincerely desire. This may to the most ordinary human being be a hard law to follow; but nevertheless it is the word of the Lord. One of the best illustrations of this spirit of enduring wrong rather than retaliating is found in the story of the people of Ammon in the Book of Mormon. Because they refused to take up arms to defend themselves, but would rather lay down their lives than shed blood in their own defense, they brought many of their enemies to repentance and to the kingdom of God. [Alma 24:17-25; 27:3.] This is the doctrine of Jesus Christ as taught in his Sermon on the Mount. [Matt. 5:21-22, 43-44.] If all peoples would accept this doctrine there could be no war and all difficulties could be adjusted in righteousness. This doctrine was taught, so the Lord declared, to his people anciently. There are many things in the Old Testament in relation to the wars and battles of the Israelites in the meagre record which has come down to us, which are made to appear to us that these people were cruel and vengeful, but the Lord says they went out to battle when they were guided by prophets and the spirit of revelation when the Lord commanded them. (Joseph Fielding Smith, *Church History and Modern Revelation*, 4 vols. [Salt Lake City: Deseret Book, 1947–1950], 2:193)

25 Saul also and his men went to seek him. And they told David: wherefore he came down into a rock, and abode in the wilderness of Maon. And when Saul heard that, he pursued after David in the wilderness of Maon.

26 And Saul went on this side of the mountain, and David and his men on that side of the mountain: and David made haste to get away for fear of Saul; for Saul and his men compassed David and his men round about to take them.

27 ¶ But there came a messenger unto Saul, saying, Haste thee, and come; for the Philistines have invaded the land.

28 Wherefore Saul returned from pursuing after David, and went against the Philistines: therefore they called that place Selahammahlekoth.

29 ¶ And David went up from thence, and dwelt in strong holds at En-gedi.

CHAPTER 24

1 AND it came to pass, when Saul was returned from following the Philistines, that it was told him, saying, Behold, David is in the wilderness of En-gedi.

2 Then Saul took three thousand chosen men out of all Israel, and went to seek David and his men upon the rocks of the wild goats.

3 And he came to the sheepcotes by the way, where was a cave; and Saul went in to cover his feet: and David and his men remained in the sides of the cave.

4 And the men of David said unto him, Behold the day of which the LORD said unto thee, Behold, I will deliver thine enemy into thine hand, that thou mayest do to him as it shall seem good unto thee. Then David arose, and cut off the skirt of Saul's robe privily.

5 And it came to pass afterward, that David's heart smote him, because he had cut off Saul's skirt.

6 And he said unto his men, The LORD forbid that I should do this thing unto my master, the LORD's anointed, to stretch forth mine hand against him, seeing he is the anointed of the LORD.

7 So David stayed his servants with these words, and suffered them not to rise against Saul. But Saul rose up out of the cave, and went on his way.

8 David also arose afterward, and went out of the cave, and cried after Saul, saying, My lord the king. And when Saul looked behind him, David stooped with his face to the earth, and bowed himself.

9 ¶ And David said to Saul, Wherefore hearest thou men's words, saying, Behold, David seeketh thy hurt?

10 Behold, this day thine eyes have seen how that the LORD had delivered thee to day into mine hand in the cave: and some bade me kill thee: but mine eye spared thee; and I said, I will not put forth mine hand against my lord; for he is the LORD's anointed.

11 Moreover, my father, see, yea, see the skirt of thy robe in my hand: for in that I cut off the skirt of thy robe, and killed thee not, know thou and see that there is neither evil nor transgression in mine hand, and I have not sinned against thee; yet thou huntest my soul to take it.

12 The LORD judge between me and thee, and the LORD avenge me of thee: but mine hand shall not be upon thee.

13 As saith the proverb of the ancients, Wickedness proceedeth from the wicked: but mine hand shall not be upon thee.

1 SAMUEL CHAPTER 24

"Ever keep in exercise the principle of mercy and be ready to forgive our brother on the first intimations of repentance, and asking forgiveness; and should we even forgive our brother, or even our enemy, before he repent or ask forgiveness, our Heavenly Father would be equally as merciful unto us." —Joseph Smith, *DHC* 3:383

1 Samuel 24:10—The Forgiveness of a Magnanimous Heart

Though repeatedly the target of Saul's murderous intrigues, David displays the spirit of ultimate forgiveness and becomes, with Joseph of Egypt, the prototypical practitioner of mercy and clemency among the Lord's chosen.

David has every reason to loathe Saul, who seeks repeatedly to kill him out of jealousy and treachery. However, David avoided even the hint of vengeance and chose to spare Saul's life, even after the Lord delivered the king into his hands, saying that he will leave judgment in the hands of the Lord. So we see that to forgive is divine—the ultimate act of being Christlike. It truly is a reflection of our heart. Remember, it is given to us to forgive everyone.

1 Samuel 24—Summary of Precepts and Principles

David exemplified the epitome of a forgiving spirit. The Lord has told us in our day, "I, the Lord, will forgive whom I will forgive, but of you it is required to forgive all men" (D&C 63:10). David was able to forgive even the one who continually plotted to have his life taken away. Saul, on the other hand, exemplified the basest form of envy, greed, pride, and malice. We have in the contrast an enduring lesson in how to conduct our walk of life so as to find favor with God. Additionally, David and Jonathan display an admirable quality of friendship that was able to survive every conceivable deterrent and twist of circumstance. As such, their story is a lasting monument to friendship based on faith and righteousness.

At thirty years of age, David was anointed king over Israel; his reign lasted a total of forty years. Among other tribulations, David had to suffer the hatred and murderous attacks of Saul. David had every reason to loathe Saul, his deposed predecessor on the throne, for Saul sought repeatedly to kill him out of jealousy and treachery. However, David avoided even the hint of vengeance and chose to spare Saul's life again and again, even after the Lord had delivered the king into his hands. David's position was to leave judgment in the hands of the Lord. David displayed the spirit of ultimate forgiveness and became, along with Joseph of Egypt, the prototypical practitioner of mercy and clemency among the Lord's chosen: "I will not put forth my hand against my lord, for he is the Lord's anointed" (1 Sam. 24:10).

David was also compassionate and forgiving in the case of his rebellious son, Absalom. Absalom was guilty of fratricide in the case of Amnon (David's oldest son; see 2 Sam. 13:14) and rose up in insurrection to depose David for a time (see 2 Sam. 15:1–5; 15–17; 15:37; 19:10; compare Ps. 3). In a massive battle between the forces of David and the

14 After whom is the king of Israel come out? after whom dost thou pursue? after a dead dog, after a flea.

15 The LORD therefore be judge, and judge between me and thee, and see, and plead my cause, and deliver me out of thine hand.

16 ¶ And it came to pass, when David had made an end of speaking these words unto Saul, that Saul said, Is this thy voice, my son David? And Saul lifted up his voice, and wept.

17 And he said to David, Thou art more righteous than I: for thou hast rewarded me good, whereas I have rewarded thee evil.

18 And thou hast shewed this day how that thou hast dealt well with me: forasmuch as when the LORD had delivered me into thine hand, thou killedst me not.

19 For if a man find his enemy, will he let him go well away? wherefore the LORD reward thee good for that thou hast done unto me this day.

20 And now, behold, I know well that thou shalt surely be king, and that the kingdom of Israel shall be established in thine hand.

21 Swear now therefore unto me by the LORD, that thou wilt not cut off my seed after me, and that thou wilt not destroy my name out of my father's house.

22 And David sware unto Saul. And Saul went home; but David and his men gat them up unto the hold.

THE
SECOND BOOK OF SAMUEL

OTHERWISE CALLED
THE SECOND BOOK OF THE KINGS

CHAPTER 11

1 AND it came to pass, after the year was expired, at the time when kings go forth to battle, that David sent Joab, and his servants with him, and all Israel; and they destroyed the children of Ammon, and besieged Rabbah. But David tarried still at Jerusalem.

2 ¶ And it came to pass in an eveningtide, that David arose from off his bed, and walked upon the roof of the king's house: and from the roof he saw a woman washing herself; and the woman was very beautiful to look upon.

forces of Absalom at Gilead, in the forest of Ephraim, Absalom's forces were destroyed or routed, and Joab (contrary to David's instructions) slew Absalom, who has been caught in the branches of a tree while escaping on a mule (see 2 Sam. 18:9, 14–15). David was heartbroken upon hearing the news: "And the king was much moved, and went up to the chamber over the gate, and wept: and as he went, thus he said, O my son Absalom, my son, my son Absalom! would God I had died for thee, O Absalom, my son, my son!" (2 Sam. 18:33; compare 2 Sam. 19:1, 4). Subsequently, David returned to his throne in Jerusalem, still anguished over the loss of Absalom.

2 SAMUEL CHAPTER 11

2 Samuel 11—The David and Bathsheba Story
The account of David and his agonizing ordeal in confronting the effects of sin is a compelling argument on behalf of remembering the covenant and avoiding the pitfalls of ungodly behavior. The Lord has promised us that our confidence in His presence will wax strong if we will faithfully let virtue "garnish" our thoughts unceasingly (see D&C 121:45). Such was not the case with David. The process of his fall is abundantly clear: He failed to heed the warnings against temptation and found himself ensnared in not just one but a chain of misdeeds that compromised his very exaltation. Thus he experienced the intense suffering of one who has to contend with the ominous and harrowing reality of looking up from the deep pit of egregious moral transgression—"how sore you know not," said the Lord, speaking of this kind of ordeal, "how exquisite you know not, yea, how hard to bear you know not" (D&C 18:15). The agony of such suffering can only be matched in intensity by the joy of those who are able to avoid such missteps and remain valiant in the faith.

2 Samuel 11:2—Heed Early Warnings Against Temptation
When circumstances present the opportunity for sin, we must, like Joseph of Egypt—and unlike David—flee to higher moral ground. Character is first displayed in the choice between principle and fleeting pleasure.

David happened to observe Bathsheba at a distance one evening and was enticed. Rather than turning back and putting away bad thoughts, he yielded to the temptation. Though at the time triumphantly victorious on the field of battle against the enemies of Israel, he was tragically vanquished in the battle for his own soul—for he relinquished the power to heed the early warnings against sin.

Temptation is ever present, and we *must* take steps to avoid and overcome it. Anyone can be tempted. It behooves us to flee from temptation rather than see how much we can handle, for then it is often too late.

For additional insight on Bathsheba and her husband, Uriah, see Appendix V.

3 And David sent and enquired after the woman. And one said, Is not this Bath-sheba, the daughter of Eliam, the wife of Uriah the Hittite?

4 And David sent messengers, and took her; and she came in unto him, and he lay with her; for she was purified from her uncleanness: and she returned unto her house.

5 And the woman conceived, and sent and told David, and said, I am with child.

6 ¶ And David sent to Joab, saying, Send me Uriah the Hittite. And Joab sent Uriah to David.

7 And when Uriah was come unto him, David demanded of him how Joab did, and how the people did, and how the war prospered.

8 And David said to Uriah, Go down to thy house, and wash thy feet. And Uriah departed out of the king's house, and there followed him a mess of meat from the king.

9 But Uriah slept at the door of the king's house with all the servants of his lord, and went not down to his house.

10 And when they had told David, saying, Uriah went not down unto his house, David said unto Uriah, Camest thou not from thy journey? why then didst thou not go down unto thine house?

11 And Uriah said unto David, The ark, and Israel, and Judah, abide in tents; and my lord Joab, and the servants of my lord, are encamped in the open fields; shall I then go into mine house, to eat and to drink, and to lie with my wife? as thou livest, and as thy soul liveth, I will not do this thing.

12 And David said to Uriah, Tarry here to day also, and to morrow I will let thee depart. So Uriah abode in Jerusalem that day, and the morrow.

13 And when David had called him, he did eat and drink before him; and he made him drunk: and at even he went out to lie on his bed with the servants of his lord, but went not down to his house.

14 ¶ And it came to pass in the morning, that David wrote a letter to Joab, and sent it by the hand of Uriah.

15 And he wrote in the letter, saying, Set ye Uriah in the forefront of the hottest battle, and retire ye from him, that he may be smitten, and die.

16 And it came to pass, when Joab observed the city, that he assigned Uriah unto a place where he knew that valiant men were.

17 And the men of the city went out, and fought with Joab: and there fell some of the people of the servants of David; and Uriah the Hittite died also.

18 ¶ Then Joab sent and told David all the things concerning the war;

19 And charged the messenger, saying, When thou hast made an end of telling the matters of the war unto the king,

20 And if so be that the king's wrath arise, and he say unto thee, Wherefore approached ye so nigh unto the city when ye did fight? knew ye not that they would shoot from the wall?

21 Who smote Abimelech the son of Jerubbesheth? did not a woman cast a piece of a millstone upon him from the wall, that he died in Thebez? why went ye nigh the wall? then say thou, Thy servant Uriah the Hittite is dead also.

22 ¶ So the messenger went, and came and shewed David all that Joab had sent him for.

23 And the messenger said unto David, Surely the men prevailed against us, and came out unto us into the field, and we were upon them even unto the entering of the gate.

2 Samuel 11—David's Experience with Sorrow and Repentance

In the midst of his ascendancy as a righteous king, temptation stole into David's life. He did not, as Joseph of Egypt, flee to higher moral ground; in the case of David, a great man was brought down on the basis of a character flaw—a chink in the armor of self-discipline—and the consequences were immeasurably tragic.

David's temptation did not end with sexual sin, but extended to further evil machinations beyond his lasciviousness (see 2 Sam. 11:14–15). In the wake of his immorality, David committed a greater crime in arranging for the death of Bathsheba's husband, Uriah. David then married Bathsheba—but God knew his sin. Nathan, the prophet, came to David and said, "Wherefore hast thou despised the commandment of the LORD, to do evil in his sight? thou hast killed Uriah the Hittite with the sword, and hast taken his wife to be thy wife, and hast slain him with the sword of the children of Ammon" (2 Sam. 12:9).

This bleak and treacherous circumstance leads David to the devastating insight that he has committed sin of gross measure. Slowly but surely the seeds of repentance begin to sprout (see 2 Sam. 12:13), but the consequence of his action was unspeakably far-reaching (see D&C 132:39).

From David we learn a priceless lesson: In considering how to avoid sin we need to understand the principle of accountability. When we succumb to sin, we subject ourselves to the consequences of the sin according to the natural law that applies—we lose the Spirit (see Mosiah 2:36), and then we lose all the blessings associated with keeping the commandment. When we sin, we withdraw ourselves from the Spirit (see Mosiah 2:36) and become more easily influenced by the devil and his temptations (see D&C 29:40). All have sinned (see 1 John 1:8–10)—but we are free to choose righteousness rather than sin (see 2 Ne. 2:27). The test of life is to make good choices and to repent of our sins by exercising faith unto repentance (see Alma 34:15–17), and when we confess and forsake our sins, the Lord remembers them no more (see D&C 58:42–43). The Lord makes no allowance for sin, but is compassionate and merciful to the repentant sinner (see D&C 1:31–32)—for we cannot be saved in our sins (see Alma 11:37; Hel. 5:10).

The matter of repentance and overcoming sin is a daily exercise in the fundamentals of the gospel of Jesus Christ. The process is clear and unmistakable: faith, repentance, keeping the commitments made at baptism, and living worthy of the gift of the Holy Ghost by enduring to the end.

All are invited by the Lord to seek justification before God and sanctification through the Atonement and the blessing of the Holy Ghost, or else they cannot be empowered from on high to do all requisite things (see Moses 6:58–62). Surely repentance is the single greatest thing we can do in regard to our individual salvation; helping others repent becomes the greatest good we can do for our fellowmen (see D&C 15:6; 31:5; James 5:20).

Our salvation, exaltation, and eternal life depend on our overcoming and forsaking our sins. We are to repent—and we are clearly told that there is no other way back into

24 And the shooters shot from off the wall upon thy servants; and some of the king's servants be dead, and thy servant Uriah the Hittite is dead also.

25 Then David said unto the messenger, Thus shalt thou say unto Joab, Let not this thing displease thee, for the sword devoureth one as well as another: make thy battle more strong against the city, and overthrow it: and encourage thou him.

26 ¶ And when the wife of Uriah heard that Uriah her husband was dead, she mourned for her husband.

27 And when the mourning was past, David sent and fetched her to his house, and she became his wife, and bare him a son. But the thing that David had done displeased the LORD.

CHAPTER 12

1 AND the LORD sent Nathan unto David. And he came unto him, and said unto him, There were two men in one city; the one rich, and the other poor.

2 The rich man had exceeding many flocks and herds:

3 But the poor man had nothing, save one little ewe lamb, which he had bought and nourished up: and it grew up together with him, and with his children; it did eat of his own meat, and drank of his own cup, and lay in his bosom, and was unto him as a daughter.

4 And there came a traveller unto the rich man, and he spared to take of his own flock and of his own herd, to dress for the wayfaring man that was come unto him; but took the poor man's lamb, and dressed it for the man that was come to him.

5 And David's anger was greatly kindled against the man; and he said to Nathan, As the LORD liveth, the man that hath done this thing shall surely die:

6 And he shall restore the lamb fourfold, because he did this thing, and because he had no pity.

7 ¶ And Nathan said to David, Thou art the man. Thus saith the LORD God of Israel, I anointed thee king over Israel, and I delivered thee out of the hand of Saul;

8 And I gave thee thy master's house, and thy master's wives into thy bosom, and gave thee the house of Israel and of Judah; and if that had been too little, I would moreover have given unto thee such and such things.

9 Wherefore hast thou despised the commandment of the LORD, to do evil in his sight? thou hast killed Uriah the Hittite with the sword, and hast taken his wife to be thy wife, and hast slain him with the sword of the children of Ammon.

10 Now therefore the sword shall never depart from thine house; because thou hast despised me, and hast taken the wife of Uriah the Hittite to be thy wife.

11 Thus saith the LORD, Behold, I will raise up evil against thee out of thine own house, and I will take thy wives before thine eyes, and give them unto thy neighbour, and he shall lie with thy wives in the sight of this sun.

12 For thou didst it secretly: but I will do this thing before all Israel, and before the sun.

13 And David said unto Nathan, I have sinned against the LORD. And Nathan said unto David, The LORD also hath put away thy sin; thou shalt not die.

14 Howbeit, because by this deed thou hast given great occasion to the enemies of the LORD to blaspheme, the child also that is born unto thee shall surely die.

the presence of our Heavenly Father. The process of repentance through the Atonement of our Savior is a wonderful gift—yet how much less painful it is to make righteous choices and learn from the scriptures and our leaders than to learn everything on the earth by trial and error. Alma said it correctly when he said, " O, remember, my son, and learn wisdom in thy youth; yea, learn in thy youth to keep the commandments of God" (Alma 37:35). Jacob counseled us in regard to repentance and staying on the straight and narrow path, "O be wise; what can I say more?" (Jacob 6:12). In the case of Bathsheba and Uriah, David was not wise—but we can learn wisdom from his example by avoiding the pitfalls that caused him so much suffering.

2 SAMUEL CHAPTER 12

2 Samuel 12:9—The Ominous Consequences of Sin

Sin draws the participant ever deeper into the quicksands of its captivity: one thing leads to another until salvation itself is placed at risk. The story of David's pitiful fall reminds all who aspire to the honor of God that sin cannot be hidden or dismissed—for there is always a price to be paid, sometimes very dear.

After David yielded to temptation and crossed the threshold into the realm of immorality, he attempted to manipulate circumstances by bringing Uriah, Bathsheba's husband, back from battle and into his family circle again where he would appear to be the father of David's coming child. But Uriah's loyalty to his battle colleagues got in the way of David's strategy to hide his sin, thus David felt constrained to plot the murder of the husband. This horrible deed completed, David finds himself face to face with Nathan, prophet of the Lord, sent to convey the awful truth that spiritual death would surely follow, for the Lord knows all and cannot be mocked. Thus David forfeited his exaltation (see D&C 132:39).

For insights on Nathan, see Appendix W.

2 Samuel 12:9—Ammon/Ammonites

The name *Ammon* occurs no fewer than ninety-one times throughout the Old Testament, usually in the expression "children of Ammon," meaning the tribal people of that name who were descended from Lot, the nephew of Abraham (see Gen. 19:38; Deut. 2:19).

From the Ammonites we can surely learn a lesson of persistence and perseverance—for as enemies to Israel, for the most part, they endured multiple repulsions and defeats over centuries of time and still managed to emerge as a people of hard-core longevity. They were located beyond the Jordan, northeast of the Dead Sea, in an area eastward from the mountainous Gilead region and south of the Jabbok River. Their capital city was known as Rabbah ("chief city") or Rabbath-Ammon ("city of the Ammonites")—located on the site currently within the bounds of the modern city of Amman, Jordan.

Because they laid claim to the fertile Gilead area, they were usually at odds with the Israelites (see Judges 11). As

15 ¶ And Nathan departed unto his house. And the LORD struck the child that Uriah's wife bare unto David, and it was very sick.

16 David therefore besought God for the child; and David fasted, and went in, and lay all night upon the earth.

17 And the elders of his house arose, and went to him, to raise him up from the earth: but he would not, neither did he eat bread with them.

18 And it came to pass on the seventh day, that the child died. And the servants of David feared to tell him that the child was dead: for they said, Behold, while the child was yet alive, we spake unto him, and he would not hearken unto our voice: how will he then vex himself, if we tell him that the child is dead?

19 But when David saw that his servants whispered, David perceived that the child was dead: therefore David said unto his servants, Is the child dead? And they said, He is dead.

20 Then David arose from the earth, and washed, and anointed himself, and changed his apparel, and came into the house of the LORD, and worshipped: then he came to his own house; and when he required, they set bread before him, and he did eat.

21 Then said his servants unto him, What thing is this that thou hast done? thou didst fast and weep for the child, while it was alive; but when the child was dead, thou didst rise and eat bread.

22 And he said, While the child was yet alive, I fasted and wept: for I said, Who can tell whether GOD will be gracious to me, that the child may live?

23 But now he is dead, wherefore should I fast? can I bring him back again? I shall go to him, but he shall not return to me.

24 ¶ And David comforted Bath-sheba his wife, and went in unto her, and lay with her: and she bare a son, and he called his name Solomon: and the LORD loved him.

25 And he sent by the hand of Nathan the prophet; and he called his name Jedidiah, because of the LORD.

26 ¶ And Joab fought against Rabbah of the children of Ammon, and took the royal city.

27 And Joab sent messengers to David, and said, I have fought against Rabbah, and have taken the city of waters.

28 Now therefore gather the rest of the people together, and encamp against the city, and take it: lest I take the city, and it be called after my name.

29 And David gathered all the people together, and went to Rabbah, and fought against it, and took it.

30 And he took their king's crown from off his head, the weight whereof was a talent of gold with the precious stones: and it was set on David's head. And he brought forth the spoil of the city in great abundance.

31 And he brought forth the people that were therein, and put them under saws, and under harrows of iron, and under axes of iron, and made them pass through the brickkiln: and thus did he unto all the cities of the children of Ammon. So David and all the people returned unto Jerusalem.

such, they were repulsed by the tribal leader Jephthah and also by King Saul (see 1 Sam. 11). David was able to bring the Ammonites under his control (see 2 Sam. 11:1). It was during the time of the battle with the Ammonites that David became involved with Bathsheba and caused the death of her husband Uriah, an atrocity with dire consequences.

After the time of David, the Ammonites regained their independence. Among the wives of Solomon was Naamah, an Ammonitess, who was the mother of Rehoboam (see 1 Kings 14:31; 2 Chron. 12:13). Solomon offended the Lord by choosing to adopt the idolatrous practices of Ammonite worship:

> For Solomon went after Ashtoreth the goddess of the Zidonians, and after Milcom the abomination of the Ammonites.
>
> And Solomon did evil in the sight of the LORD, and went not fully after the LORD, as *did* David his father.
>
> Then did Solomon build an high place for Chemosh, the abomination of Moab, in the hill that *is* before Jerusalem, and for Molech, the abomination of the children of Ammon. (1 Kings 11:5–7)

Eventually, the Ammonites came under the yoke of Assyria and Chaldea according to the judgments of the Lord:

> I have heard the reproach of Moab, and the revilings of the children of Ammon, whereby they have reproached my people, and magnified *themselves* against their border.
>
> Therefore *as* I live, saith the LORD of hosts, the God of Israel, Surely Moab shall be as Sodom, and the children of Ammon as Gomorrah, *even* the breeding of nettles, and saltpits, and a perpetual desolation: the residue of my people shall spoil them, and the remnant of my people shall possess them.
>
> This shall they have for their pride, because they have reproached and magnified *themselves* against the people of the LORD of hosts.
>
> The LORD *will be* terrible unto them: for he will famish all the gods of the earth; and *men* shall worship him, every one from his place, *even* all the isles of the heathen. (Zeph. 2:8–11; compare Amos 1; 2 Kings 24:2; Ezek. 25)

Thus we can learn a second lesson from the Ammonites: in addition to their perseverance and endurance as a people, they embodied a culture of unrighteousness that brought down upon them the inexorable judgments of God, for they were eventually absorbed by the onward advancement of Arabs centuries after Christ's ministry in the Holy Land.

THE
FIRST BOOK OF THE KINGS

COMMONLY CALLED
THE THIRD BOOK OF THE KINGS

CHAPTER 3

1 AND Solomon made affinity with Pharaoh king of Egypt, and took Pharaoh's daughter, and brought her into the city of David, until he had made an end of building his own house, and the house of the LORD, and the wall of Jerusalem round about.

2 Only the people sacrificed in high places, because there was no house built unto the name of the LORD, until those days.

3 And Solomon loved the LORD, walking in the statutes of David his father: only he sacrificed and burnt incense in high places.

4 And the king went to Gibeon to sacrifice there; for that was the great high place: a thousand burnt offerings did Solomon offer upon that altar.

5 ¶ In Gibeon the LORD appeared to Solomon in a dream by night: and God said, Ask what I shall give thee.

6 And Solomon said, Thou hast shewed unto thy servant David my father great mercy, according as he walked before thee in truth, and in righteousness, and in uprightness of heart with thee; and thou hast kept for him this great kindness, that thou hast given him a son to sit on his throne, as it is this day.

7 And now, O LORD my God, thou hast made thy servant king instead of David my father: and I am but a little child: I know not how to go out or come in.

8 And thy servant is in the midst of thy people which thou hast chosen, a great people, that cannot be numbered nor counted for multitude.

9 Give therefore thy servant an understanding heart to judge thy people, that I may discern between good and bad: for who is able to judge this thy so great a people?

10 And the speech pleased the Lord, that Solomon had asked this thing.

11 And God said unto him, Because thou hast asked this thing, and hast not asked for thyself long life; neither hast asked riches for thyself, nor hast asked the life of thine enemies; but hast asked for thyself understanding to discern judgment;

12 Behold, I have done according to thy words: lo, I have given thee a wise and an understanding heart; so that there was none like thee before thee, neither after thee shall any arise like unto thee.

13 And I have also given thee that which thou hast not asked, both riches, and honour: so that there shall not be any among the kings like unto thee all thy days.

14 And if thou wilt walk in my ways, to keep my statutes and my commandments, as thy father David did walk, then I will lengthen thy days.

15 And Solomon awoke; and, behold, it was a dream. And he came to Jerusalem, and stood before the ark of the covenant of the LORD,

1 KINGS CHAPTER 3

1 Kings 3—Preview of the Life of Solomon

One of the greatest tests of character is how we use the talents, gifts, and means with which the Lord has blessed us. The better part of wisdom is to aspire to outcomes of service and honor that will merit the judgment cited by the Savior in His parable of the talents: "Well done, good and faithful servant; thou hast been faithful over a few things, I will make thee ruler over many things: enter into the joy of thy lord" (Matt. 25:21, 23). Few in the history of the world have been blessed with gifts and means to exceed those of Solomon, the son of David. As long as he used these resources to bless the lives of others and further God's purposes—rendering sound judgment among the people and erecting the Temple of the Lord—he prospered and enjoyed the blessings of heaven. When he lost balance in his life and elevated worldly goods and honors above the principles of heaven, he was supplanted.

1 Kings 3:12—Wisdom as a Gift of God

Just as Solomon sought for the best gifts to serve the people, we too should aspire for that which promotes the cause of salvation and brings blessings into the lives of our loved ones.

The Lord appeared to Solomon in a dream and offered to give him whatever he might desire. Rather than seeking after selfish gifts, Solomon asked for an understanding heart to judge the people effectively. The Lord was pleased and gave Solomon the gift of unsurpassed wisdom, which Solomon used to cultivate peace and prosperity in Israel. As long as Solomon remained wise in spiritual matters, he flourished in his leadership.

We must remember that the Lord stands ready to bless His children as we come to Him in meekness and humility desiring to serve and bless our fellowmen.

 POINT OF INTEREST

1 Kgs. 3:1 and 1 Kgs. 9: 16 refer to Solomon's relationship with Egypt. "All these statements read like authentic history, but no confirmation is obtainable from the Egyptian side, and chronological uncertainties, though confined within fairly narrow limits, are sufficient to render it doubtful which particular Pharaohs were in question; also Tahpenes is unidentifiable in the hieroglyphs" (Alan Gardiner, *The Egyptians* [London: Folio Society, 2007]).

and offered up burnt offerings, and offered peace offerings, and made a feast to all his servants.

16 ¶ Then came there two women, that were harlots, unto the king, and stood before him.

17 And the one woman said, O my lord, I and this woman dwell in one house; and I was delivered of a child with her in the house.

18 And it came to pass the third day after that I was delivered, that this woman was delivered also: and we were together; there was no stranger with us in the house, save we two in the house.

19 And this woman's child died in the night; because she overlaid it.

20 And she arose at midnight, and took my son from beside me, while thine handmaid slept, and laid it in her bosom, and laid her dead child in my bosom.

21 And when I rose in the morning to give my child suck, behold, it was dead: but when I had considered it in the morning, behold, it was not my son, which I did bear.

22 And the other woman said, Nay; but the living is my son, and the dead is thy son. And this said, No; but the dead is thy son, and the living is my son. Thus they spake before the king.

23 Then said the king, The one saith, This is my son that liveth, and thy son is the dead: and the other saith, Nay; but thy son is the dead, and my son is the living.

24 And the king said, Bring me a sword. And they brought a sword before the king.

25 And the king said, Divide the living child in two, and give half to the one, and half to the other.

26 Then spake the woman whose the living child was unto the king, for her bowels yearned upon her son, and she said, O my lord, give her the living child, and in no wise slay it. But the other said, Let it be neither mine nor thine, but divide it.

27 Then the king answered and said, Give her the living child, and in no wise slay it: she is the mother thereof.

28 And all Israel heard of the judgment which the king had judged; and they feared the king: for they saw that the wisdom of God was in him, to do judgment.

CHAPTER 5

1 AND Hiram king of Tyre sent his servants unto Solomon; for he had heard that they had anointed him king in the room of his father: for Hiram was ever a lover of David.

2 And Solomon sent to Hiram, saying,

3 Thou knowest how that David my father could not build an house unto the name of the LORD his God for the wars which were about him on every side, until the LORD put them under the soles of his feet.

4 But now the LORD my God hath given me rest on every side, so that there is neither adversary nor evil occurrent.

5 And, behold, I purpose to build an house unto the name of the LORD my God, as the LORD spake unto David my father, saying, Thy son, whom I will set upon thy throne in thy room, he shall build an house unto my name.

1 Kings 3:16–28—Solomon's Judgment

The celebrated judgment of Solomon concerning the authentic mother and the grieving woman with specious claims still resounds with resilience and power. The strategy involving the sword was designed to arouse and expose genuine maternal feelings—and once the true mother had supplicated the king to allow the child to be given away in order to preserve its life, he knew how to render a wise and prudent judgment.

The Savior said, "For where your treasure is, there will your heart be also" (Matt. 6:21). The mother's treasure was her child, and her heart was with the child—thus her willingness to give up her child in order to save its life. The other mother was understandably grieved over the loss of her own child, but her deed of deception revealed her blindness to the happiness of the genuine mother. Her attitude was chilling: "Let it be neither mine nor thine, but divide it" (verse 26). In other words: "If I cannot have the child, then neither can you." Thus Solomon could be confirmed in his decision to return the child to the true mother.

1 KINGS CHAPTER 5

1 Kings 5:1—Hiram

Hiram (or Huram) was the king of Tyre who had befriended David as the new king of Israel—"for Hiram was ever a lover of David" (1 Kings 5:1)—and assisted him in building his palace (see 2 Sam. 5:11; 1 Chron. 14:1). Hiram also assisted Solomon, David's successor, in the construction of the temple (see 1 Kings 5:2–12; 9:11) and in maritime commercial undertakings (see 1 Kings 10:11). The name *Hiram* was also rendered *Huram* (see 2 Chron. 2:5–12; 8:2, 18; 9:10–21).

6 Now therefore command thou that they hew me cedar trees out of Lebanon; and my servants shall be with thy servants: and unto thee will I give hire for thy servants according to all that thou shalt appoint: for thou knowest that there is not among us any that can skill to hew timber like unto the Sidonians.

7 ¶ And it came to pass, when Hiram heard the words of Solomon, that he rejoiced greatly, and said, Blessed be the LORD this day, which hath given unto David a wise son over this great people.

8 And Hiram sent to Solomon, saying, I have considered the things which thou sentest to me for: and I will do all thy desire concerning timber of cedar, and concerning timber of fir.

9 My servants shall bring them down from Lebanon unto the sea: and I will convey them by sea in floats unto the place that thou shalt appoint me, and will cause them to be discharged there, and thou shalt receive them: and thou shalt accomplish my desire, in giving food for my household.

10 So Hiram gave Solomon cedar trees and fir trees according to all his desire.

11 And Solomon gave Hiram twenty thousand measures of wheat for food to his household, and twenty measures of pure oil: thus gave Solomon to Hiram year by year.

12 And the LORD gave Solomon wisdom, as he promised him: and there was peace between Hiram and Solomon; and they two made a league together.

13 ¶ And king Solomon raised a levy out of all Israel; and the levy was thirty thousand men.

14 And he sent them to Lebanon, ten thousand a month by courses: a month they were in Lebanon, and two months at home: and Adoniram was over the levy.

15 And Solomon had threescore and ten thousand that bare burdens, and fourscore thousand hewers in the mountains;

16 Beside the chief of Solomon's officers which were over the work, three thousand and three hundred, which ruled over the people that wrought in the work.

17 And the king commanded, and they brought great stones, costly stones, and hewed stones, to lay the foundation of the house.

18 And Solomon's builders and Hiram's builders did hew them, and the stonesquarers: so they prepared timber and stones to build the house.

CHAPTER 6

1 AND it came to pass in the four hundred and eightieth year after the children of Israel were come out of the land of Egypt, in the fourth year of Solomon's reign over Israel, in the month Zif, which is the second month, that he began to build the house of the LORD.

2 And the house which king Solomon built for the LORD, the length thereof was threescore cubits, and the breadth thereof twenty cubits, and the height thereof thirty cubits.

3 And the porch before the temple of the house, twenty cubits was the length thereof, according to the breadth of the house; and ten cubits was the breadth thereof before the house.

4 And for the house he made windows of narrow lights.

5 ¶ And against the wall of the house he built chambers round about, against the walls of the house round about, both of the temple and of the oracle: and he made chambers round about:

POINT OF INTEREST

"The literature of the ancient Near East had a tradition of writings containing wise sayings and proverbs. These writings of the wisdom of the past, and the wisdom literature of Egypt and Mesopotamia in particular, provide many close cultural parallels with that of Israel. The tradition in these countries is older than the tradition in Israel, some of the Egyptian Instructions dating from the third millennium B.C.E. Such comparisons are often used to illuminate the possible context of Israelite wisdom. For example, on the basis of a close parallel with the Egyptian Instruction of Amenemope, a school textbook, it is argued that Proverbs 22:14–24:22 was probably used as a handbook for training administrators in a school context, paralleling the Egyptian one. Such a context may have been in 'wisdom school' at the court of King Solomon during a period of Solomonic Enlightenment, when a class of administrators may have needed to service a growing monarchic state" (John Bowker, *The Complete Bible Handbook* [New York: DK Publishing, 2001]).

1 KINGS CHAPTER 6

1 Kings 6:1—The Temple of Solomon

The erection of a temple, the House of the Lord, is a covenant undertaking of the most sacred kind. Obedience to the statutes and commandments of the Lord brings His presence among the faithful. The covenant foundation of the gospel of Jesus Christ is the means, through the Atonement, whereby the sons and daughters of God can have access to the presence of Father and Son in the eternities. The temple is the venue where sacred priesthood ordinances endow the faithful with the privilege of entering the pathway leading to an eternal homecoming. The temple of Solomon was a milestone in the unfolding saga of temple blessings flowing to the people of the Lord.

6 The nethermost chamber was five cubits broad, and the middle was six cubits broad, and the third was seven cubits broad: for without in the wall of the house he made narrowed rests round about, that the beams should not be fastened in the walls of the house.

7 And the house, when it was in building, was built of stone made ready before it was brought thither: so that there was neither hammer nor axe nor any tool of iron heard in the house, while it was in building.

8 The door for the middle chamber was in the right side of the house: and they went up with winding stairs into the middle chamber, and out of the middle into the third.

9 So he built the house, and finished it; and covered the house with beams and boards of cedar.

10 And then he built chambers against all the house, five cubits high: and they rested on the house with timber of cedar.

11 ¶ And the word of the LORD came to Solomon, saying,

12 Concerning this house which thou art in building, if thou wilt walk in my statutes, and execute my judgments, and keep all my commandments to walk in them; then will I perform my word with thee, which I spake unto David thy father:

13 And I will dwell among the children of Israel, and will not forsake my people Israel.

14 So Solomon built the house, and finished it.

15 And he built the walls of the house within with boards of cedar, both the floor of the house, and the walls of the cieling: and he covered them on the inside with wood, and covered the floor of the house with planks of fir.

16 And he built twenty cubits on the sides of the house, both the floor and the walls with boards of cedar: he even built them for it within, even for the oracle, even for the most holy place.

17 And the house, that is, the temple before it, was forty cubits long.

18 And the cedar of the house within was carved with knops and open flowers: all was cedar; there was no stone seen.

19 And the oracle he prepared in the house within, to set there the ark of the covenant of the LORD.

20 And the oracle in the forepart was twenty cubits in length, and twenty cubits in breadth, and twenty cubits in the height thereof: and he overlaid it with pure gold; and so covered the altar which was of cedar.

21 So Solomon overlaid the house within with pure gold: and he made a partition by the chains of gold before the oracle; and he overlaid it with gold.

22 And the whole house he overlaid with gold, until he had finished all the house: also the whole altar that was by the oracle he overlaid with gold.

23 ¶ And within the oracle he made two cherubims of olive tree, each ten cubits high.

24 And five cubits was the one wing of the cherub, and five cubits the other wing of the cherub: from the uttermost part of the one wing unto the uttermost part of the other were ten cubits.

25 And the other cherub was ten cubits: both the cherubims were of one measure and one size.

26 The height of the one cherub was ten cubits, and so was it of the other cherub.

27 And he set the cherubims within the inner house: and they stretched forth the wings of the cherubims, so that the wing of the one touched the one wall, and the wing of the other cherub touched

NOTES:

the other wall; and their wings touched one another in the midst of the house.

28 And he overlaid the cherubims with gold.

29 And he carved all the walls of the house round about with carved figures of cherubims and palm trees and open flowers, within and without.

30 And the floor of the house he overlaid with gold, within and without.

31 ¶ And for the entering of the oracle he made doors of olive tree: the lintel and side posts were a fifth part of the wall.

32 The two doors also were of olive tree; and he carved upon them carvings of cherubims and palm trees and open flowers, and overlaid them with gold, and spread gold upon the cherubims, and upon the palm trees.

33 So also made he for the door of the temple posts of olive tree, a fourth part of the wall.

34 And the two doors were of fir tree: the two leaves of the one door were folding, and the two leaves of the other door were folding.

35 And he carved thereon cherubims and palm trees and open flowers: and covered them with gold fitted upon the carved work.

36 ¶ And he built the inner court with three rows of hewed stone, and a row of cedar beams.

37 ¶ In the fourth year was the foundation of the house of the LORD laid, in the month Zif:

38 And in the eleventh year, in the month Bul, which is the eighth month, was the house finished throughout all the parts thereof, and according to all the fashion of it. So was he seven years in building it.

CHAPTER 7

1 BUT Solomon was building his own house thirteen years, and he finished all his house.

2 ¶ He built also the house of the forest of Lebanon; the length thereof was an hundred cubits, and the breadth thereof fifty cubits, and the height thereof thirty cubits, upon four rows of cedar pillars, with cedar beams upon the pillars.

3 And it was covered with cedar above upon the beams, that lay on forty five pillars, fifteen in a row.

4 And there were windows in three rows, and light was against light in three ranks.

5 And all the doors and posts were square, with the windows: and light was against light in three ranks.

6 ¶ And he made a porch of pillars; the length thereof was fifty cubits, and the breadth thereof thirty cubits: and the porch was before them: and the other pillars and the thick beam were before them.

7 ¶ Then he made a porch for the throne where he might judge, even the porch of judgment: and it was covered with cedar from one side of the floor to the other.

Cutting Down Cedars for the . . . Temple by Gustave Doré

8 ¶ And his house where he dwelt had another court within the porch, which was of the like work. Solomon made also an house for Pharaoh's daughter, whom he had taken to wife, like unto this porch.

9 All these were of costly stones, according to the measures of hewed stones, sawed with saws, within and without, even from the foundation unto the coping, and so on the outside toward the great court.

10 And the foundation was of costly stones, even great stones, stones of ten cubits, and stones of eight cubits.

11 And above were costly stones, after the measures of hewed stones, and cedars.

12 And the great court round about was with three rows of hewed stones, and a row of cedar beams, both for the inner court of the house of the LORD, and for the porch of the house.

13 ¶ And king Solomon sent and fetched Hiram out of Tyre.

14 He was a widow's son of the tribe of Naphtali, and his father was a man of Tyre, a worker in brass: and he was filled with wisdom, and understanding, and cunning to work all works in brass. And he came to king Solomon, and wrought all his work.

15 For he cast two pillars of brass, of eighteen cubits high apiece: and a line of twelve cubits did compass either of them about.

16 And he made two chapiters of molten brass, to set upon the tops of the pillars: the height of the one chapiter was five cubits, and the height of the other chapiter was five cubits:

17 And nets of checker work, and wreaths of chain work, for the chapiters which were upon the top of the pillars; seven for the one chapiter, and seven for the other chapiter.

18 And he made the pillars, and two rows round about upon the one network, to cover the chapiters that were upon the top, with pomegranates: and so did he for the other chapiter.

19 And the chapiters that were upon the top of the pillars were of lily work in the porch, four cubits.

20 And the chapiters upon the two pillars had pomegranates also above, over against the belly which was by the network: and the pomegranates were two hundred in rows round about upon the other chapiter.

21 And he set up the pillars in the porch of the temple: and he set up the right pillar, and called the name thereof Jachin: and he set up the left pillar, and called the name thereof Boaz.

22 And upon the top of the pillars was lily work: so was the work of the pillars finished.

23 ¶ And he made a molten sea, ten cubits from the one brim to the other: it was round all about, and his height was five cubits: and a line of thirty cubits did compass it round about.

24 And under the brim of it round about there were knops compassing it, ten in a cubit, compassing the sea round about: the knops were cast in two rows, when it was cast.

25 It stood upon twelve oxen, three looking toward the north, and three looking toward the west, and three looking toward the south, and three looking toward the east: and the sea was set above upon them, and all their hinder parts were inward.

26 And it was an hand breadth thick, and the brim thereof was wrought like the brim of a cup, with flowers of lilies: it contained two thousand baths.

27 ¶ And he made ten bases of brass; four cubits was the length of one base, and four cubits the breadth thereof, and three cubits the height of it.

1 KINGS CHAPTER 7

1 Kings 7:23—The "Molten Sea"

The ancient structure of the "molten sea" resting upon twelve outward-facing oxen is a primordial symbol that has endured until the present time. According to the passage in 2 Chron. 4:6, this "sea" was used "for the priests to wash in." The record does not indicate that it was used for baptismal purposes as the similar structures are used in the temples today.

The baptismal font of the Nauvoo Temple was dedicated by Brigham Young on Monday, November 8, 1841, with the Prophet Joseph Smith in attendance. The first baptism for the dead in this dispensation had been performed on August 15, 1840, in the Mississippi River, with others following over the next few weeks (see *Church History in the Fulness of Times*, 251). On January 19, 1841, the Lord commanded that a temple be built for this purpose: "For this ordinance belongeth to my house, and cannot be acceptable to me, only in the days of your poverty, wherein ye are not able to build a house unto me" (D&C 124:30).

On October 3, 1841, the Prophet announced that the Lord had commanded that no further baptisms for the dead be performed until they could be done in the temple (see HC 4:426). On November 8, 1841, the provisional baptismal font was finally ready for dedication.

The font was described in this way: "The font stands upon twelve oxen, four on each side, and two at each end, their heads, shoulders, and fore legs projecting out from under the font; they are carved out of pine plank, glued together, and copied after the most beautiful five-year-old steer that could be found in the country, and they are an excellent striking likeness of the original; the horns were formed after the most perfect horn that could be procured. The oxen and ornamental mouldings of the font were carved by Elder Elijah Fordham, from the city of New York, which occupied eight months of time. . . . The water was supplied from a well thirty feet deep in the east end of the basement" (HC 4:446). Thus the Saints were joyfully able to present themselves before the Lord in obedience to His commandment.

POINT OF INTEREST

Molten Sea *"The basin was cast by Hiram of Tyre who was responsible for all the bronze work in the temple. . . . The basin was over 14 feet in diameter, over 7 feet high, and over 43 feet in circumference. It was about 3 inches thick. The estimated weight is about 30 tons, and the estimated volume is about 12,000 gallons. . . . The oxen were later removed by Ahaz and replaced with a stone base"* (Illustrated Bible Dictionary [Nashville, Tenn.: Holman Bible Publishers, 2003]).

28 And the work of the bases was on this manner: they had borders, and the borders were between the ledges:

29 And on the borders that were between the ledges were lions, oxen, and cherubims: and upon the ledges there was a base above: and beneath the lions and oxen were certain additions made of thin work.

30 And every base had four brasen wheels, and plates of brass: and the four corners thereof had undersetters: under the laver were undersetters molten, at the side of every addition.

31 And the mouth of it within the chapiter and above was a cubit: but the mouth thereof was round after the work of the base, a cubit and an half: and also upon the mouth of it were gravings with their borders, foursquare, not round.

32 And under the borders were four wheels; and the axletrees of the wheels were joined to the base: and the height of a wheel was a cubit and half a cubit.

33 And the work of the wheels was like the work of a chariot wheel: their axletrees, and their naves, and their felloes, and their spokes, were all molten.

34 And there were four undersetters to the four corners of one base: and the undersetters were of the very base itself.

35 And in the top of the base was there a round compass of half a cubit high: and on the top of the base the ledges thereof and the borders thereof were of the same.

36 For on the plates of the ledges thereof, and on the borders thereof, he graved cherubims, lions, and palm trees, according to the proportion of every one, and additions round about.

37 After this manner he made the ten bases: all of them had one casting, one measure, and one size.

38 ¶ Then made he ten lavers of brass: one laver contained forty baths: and every laver was four cubits: and upon every one of the ten bases one laver.

39 And he put five bases on the right side of the house, and five on the left side of the house: and he set the sea on the right side of the house eastward over against the south.

40 ¶ And Hiram made the lavers, and the shovels, and the basons. So Hiram made an end of doing all the work that he made king Solomon for the house of the LORD:

41 The two pillars, and the two bowls of the chapiters that were on the top of the two pillars; and the two networks, to cover the two bowls of the chapiters which were upon the top of the pillars;

42 And four hundred pomegranates for the two networks, even two rows of pomegranates for one network, to cover the two bowls of the chapiters that were upon the pillars;

43 And the ten bases, and ten lavers on the bases;

44 And one sea, and twelve oxen under the sea;

45 And the pots, and the shovels, and the basons: and all these vessels, which Hiram made to king Solomon for the house of the LORD, were of bright brass.

46 In the plain of Jordan did the king cast them, in the clay ground between Succoth and Zarthan.

47 And Solomon left all the vessels unweighed, because they were exceeding many: neither was the weight of the brass found out.

48 And Solomon made all the vessels that pertained unto the house of the LORD: the altar of gold, and the table of gold, whereupon the shewbread was,

49 And the candlesticks of pure gold, five on the right side, and five on the left, before the oracle, with the flowers, and the lamps, and the tongs of gold,

POINT OF INTEREST

Below is a basic layout of Solomon's temple, based on historical documents, minus the molten sea and altar.

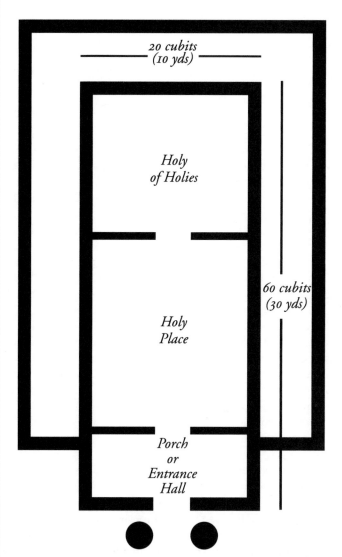

50 And the bowls, and the snuffers, and the basons, and the spoons, and the censers of pure gold; and the hinges of gold, both for the doors of the inner house, the most holy place, and for the doors of the house, to wit, of the temple.

51 So was ended all the work that king Solomon made for the house of the LORD. And Solomon brought in the things which David his father had dedicated; even the silver, and the gold, and the vessels, did he put among the treasures of the house of the LORD.

CHAPTER 8

1 THEN Solomon assembled the elders of Israel, and all the heads of the tribes, the chief of the fathers of the children of Israel, unto king Solomon in Jerusalem, that they might bring up the ark of the covenant of the LORD out of the city of David, which is Zion.

2 And all the men of Israel assembled themselves unto king Solomon at the feast in the month Ethanim, which is the seventh month.

3 And all the elders of Israel came, and the priests took up the ark.

4 And they brought up the ark of the LORD, and the tabernacle of the congregation, and all the holy vessels that were in the tabernacle, even those did the priests and the Levites bring up.

5 And king Solomon, and all the congregation of Israel, that were assembled unto him, were with him before the ark, sacrificing sheep and oxen, that could not be told nor numbered for multitude.

6 And the priests brought in the ark of the covenant of the LORD unto his place, into the oracle of the house, to the most holy place, even under the wings of the cherubims.

7 For the cherubims spread forth their two wings over the place of the ark, and the cherubims covered the ark and the staves thereof above.

8 And they drew out the staves, that the ends of the staves were seen out in the holy place before the oracle, and they were not seen without: and there they are unto this day.

9 There was nothing in the ark save the two tables of stone, which Moses put there at Horeb, when the LORD made a covenant with the children of Israel, when they came out of the land of Egypt.

10 And it came to pass, when the priests were come out of the holy place, that the cloud filled the house of the LORD,

11 So that the priests could not stand to minister because of the cloud: for the glory of the LORD had filled the house of the LORD.

12 ¶ Then spake Solomon, The LORD said that he would dwell in the thick darkness.

13 I have surely built thee an house to dwell in, a settled place for thee to abide in for ever.

14 And the king turned his face about, and blessed all the congregation of Israel: (and all the congregation of Israel stood;)

15 And he said, Blessed be the LORD God of Israel, which spake with his mouth unto David my father, and hath with his hand fulfilled it, saying,

16 Since the day that I brought forth my people Israel out of Egypt, I chose no city out of all the tribes of Israel to build an house, that my name might be therein; but I chose David to be over my people Israel.

NOTES:

17 And it was in the heart of David my father to build an house for the name of the LORD God of Israel.

18 And the LORD said unto David my father, Whereas it was in thine heart to build an house unto my name, thou didst well that it was in thine heart.

19 Nevertheless thou shalt not build the house; but thy son that shall come forth out of thy loins, he shall build the house unto my name.

20 And the LORD hath performed his word that he spake, and I am risen up in the room of David my father, and sit on the throne of Israel, as the LORD promised, and have built an house for the name of the LORD God of Israel.

21 And I have set there a place for the ark, wherein is the covenant of the LORD, which he made with our fathers, when he brought them out of the land of Egypt.

22 ¶ And Solomon stood before the altar of the LORD in the presence of all the congregation of Israel, and spread forth his hands toward heaven:

23 And he said, LORD God of Israel, there is no God like thee, in heaven above, or on earth beneath, who keepest covenant and mercy with thy servants that walk before thee with all their heart:

24 Who hast kept with thy servant David my father that thou promisedst him: thou spakest also with thy mouth, and hast fulfilled it with thine hand, as it is this day.

25 Therefore now, LORD God of Israel, keep with thy servant David my father that thou promisedst him, saying, There shall not fail thee a man in my sight to sit on the throne of Israel; so that thy children take heed to their way, that they walk before me as thou hast walked before me.

26 And now, O God of Israel, let thy word, I pray thee, be verified, which thou spakest unto thy servant David my father.

27 But will God indeed dwell on the earth? behold, the heaven and heaven of heavens cannot contain thee; how much less this house that I have builded?

28 Yet have thou respect unto the prayer of thy servant, and to his supplication, O LORD my God, to hearken unto the cry and to the prayer, which thy servant prayeth before thee to day:

29 That thine eyes may be open toward this house night and day, even toward the place of which thou hast said, My name shall be there: that thou mayest hearken unto the prayer which thy servant shall make toward this place.

30 And hearken thou to the supplication of thy servant, and of thy people Israel, when they shall pray toward this place: and hear thou in heaven thy dwelling place: and when thou hearest, forgive.

31 ¶ If any man trespass against his neighbour, and an oath be laid upon him to cause him to swear, and the oath come before thine altar in this house:

32 Then hear thou in heaven, and do, and judge thy servants, condemning the wicked, to bring his way upon his head; and justifying the righteous, to give him according to his righteousness.

33 ¶ When thy people Israel be smitten down before the enemy, because they have sinned against thee, and shall turn again to thee, and confess thy name, and pray, and make supplication unto thee in this house:

34 Then hear thou in heaven, and forgive the sin of thy people Israel, and bring them again unto the land which thou gavest unto their fathers.

1 KINGS CHAPTER 8

1 Kings 8:22–53—Dedication of the Temple

Solomon pronounced the prayer of dedication of the House of the Lord in these verses, supplicating the Lord for His blessings, guidance, and forgiveness. In our day, the inspired prayer of dedication of the Kirtland Temple delivered by Joseph Smith on March 27, 1836 (see D&C 109), is a reminder that the solemn procedure of offering temple structures to the Lord for His acceptance and blessing continues in the dispensation of the fulness of times.

Solomon's Prayer at the Consecration of the Temple

35 ¶ When heaven is shut up, and there is no rain, because they have sinned against thee; if they pray toward this place, and confess thy name, and turn from their sin, when thou afflictest them:

36 Then hear thou in heaven, and forgive the sin of thy servants, and of thy people Israel, that thou teach them the good way wherein they should walk, and give rain upon thy land, which thou hast given to thy people for an inheritance.

37 ¶ If there be in the land famine, if there be pestilence, blasting, mildew, locust, or if there be caterpiller; if their enemy besiege them in the land of their cities; whatsoever plague, whatsoever sickness there be;

38 What prayer and supplication soever be made by any man, or by all thy people Israel, which shall know every man the plague of his own heart, and spread forth his hands toward this house:

39 Then hear thou in heaven thy dwelling place, and forgive, and do, and give to every man according to his ways, whose heart thou knowest; (for thou, even thou only, knowest the hearts of all the children of men;)

40 That they may fear thee all the days that they live in the land which thou gavest unto our fathers.

41 Moreover concerning a stranger, that is not of thy people Israel, but cometh out of a far country for thy name's sake;

42 (For they shall hear of thy great name, and of thy strong hand, and of thy stretched out arm;) when he shall come and pray toward this house;

43 Hear thou in heaven thy dwelling place, and do according to all that the stranger calleth to thee for: that all people of the earth may know thy name, to fear thee, as do thy people Israel; and that they may know that this house, which I have builded, is called by thy name.

44 ¶ If thy people go out to battle against their enemy, whithersoever thou shalt send them, and shall pray unto the LORD toward the city which thou hast chosen, and toward the house that I have built for thy name:

45 Then hear thou in heaven their prayer and their supplication, and maintain their cause.

46 If they sin against thee, (for there is no man that sinneth not,) and thou be angry with them, and deliver them to the enemy, so that they carry them away captives unto the land of the enemy, far or near;

47 Yet if they shall bethink themselves in the land whither they were carried captives, and repent, and make supplication unto thee in the land of them that carried them captives, saying, We have sinned, and have done perversely, we have committed wickedness;

48 And so return unto thee with all their heart, and with all their soul, in the land of their enemies, which led them away captive, and pray unto thee toward their land, which thou gavest unto their fathers, the city which thou hast chosen, and the house which I have built for thy name:

49 Then hear thou their prayer and their supplication in heaven thy dwelling place, and maintain their cause,

50 And forgive thy people that have sinned against thee, and all their transgressions wherein they have transgressed against thee, and give them compassion before them who carried them captive, that they may have compassion on them:

51 For they be thy people, and thine inheritance, which thou broughtest forth out of Egypt, from the midst of the furnace of iron:

NOTES:

52 That thine eyes may be open unto the supplication of thy servant, and unto the supplication of thy people Israel, to hearken unto them in all that they call for unto thee.

53 For thou didst separate them from among all the people of the earth, to be thine inheritance, as thou spakest by the hand of Moses thy servant, when thou broughtest our fathers out of Egypt, O Lord GOD.

54 And it was so, that when Solomon had made an end of praying all this prayer and supplication unto the LORD, he arose from before the altar of the LORD, from kneeling on his knees with his hands spread up to heaven.

55 And he stood, and blessed all the congregation of Israel with a loud voice, saying,

56 Blessed be the LORD, that hath given rest unto his people Israel, according to all that he promised: there hath not failed one word of all his good promise, which he promised by the hand of Moses his servant.

57 The LORD our God be with us, as he was with our fathers: let him not leave us, nor forsake us:

58 That he may incline our hearts unto him, to walk in all his ways, and to keep his commandments, and his statutes, and his judgments, which he commanded our fathers.

59 And let these my words, wherewith I have made supplication before the LORD, be nigh unto the LORD our God day and night, that he maintain the cause of his servant, and the cause of his people Israel at all times, as the matter shall require:

60 That all the people of the earth may know that the LORD is God, and that there is none else.

61 Let your heart therefore be perfect with the LORD our God, to walk in his statutes, and to keep his commandments, as at this day.

62 ¶ And the king, and all Israel with him, offered sacrifice before the LORD.

63 And Solomon offered a sacrifice of peace offerings, which he offered unto the LORD, two and twenty thousand oxen, and an hundred and twenty thousand sheep. So the king and all the children of Israel dedicated the house of the LORD.

64 The same day did the king hallow the middle of the court that was before the house of the LORD: for there he offered burnt offerings, and meat offerings, and the fat of the peace offerings: because the brasen altar that was before the LORD was too little to receive the burnt offerings, and meat offerings, and the fat of the peace offerings.

65 And at that time Solomon held a feast, and all Israel with him, a great congregation, from the entering in of Hamath unto the river of Egypt, before the LORD our God, seven days and seven days, even fourteen days.

66 On the eighth day he sent the people away: and they blessed the king, and went unto their tents joyful and glad of heart for all the goodness that the LORD had done for David his servant, and for Israel his people.

1 Kings 8:54–62—The Royal Blessing

In beautiful and eloquent language Solomon pronounces a blessing upon his audience, enjoining them to walk in the ways of the Lord and obey His commandments. The people were to sustain the cause of the Lord as a testimony to the entire world that "the LORD is God, and that there is none else" (verse 60). The people were to let their hearts be "perfect with the Lord" (verse 61).

Similarly, we of today can engage with full devotion in the sacred work of the temples, not only for the blessing of our families, but also as a witness to the world that the Lord lives, and that His House is the precinct where sacred blessings are available to all who walk in His ways with hearts that are perfect in the Lord.

POINT OF INTEREST

Below is a model of the Second Temple by Michael Osnis.

CHAPTER 9

1 AND it came to pass, when Solomon had finished the building of the house of the LORD, and the king's house, and all Solomon's desire which he was pleased to do,

2 That the LORD appeared to Solomon the second time, as he had appeared unto him at Gibeon.

3 And the LORD said unto him, I have heard thy prayer and thy supplication, that thou hast made before me: I have hallowed this house, which thou hast built, to put my name there for ever; and mine eyes and mine heart shall be there perpetually.

4 And if thou wilt walk before me, as David thy father walked, in integrity of heart, and in uprightness, to do according to all that I have commanded thee, and wilt keep my statutes and my judgments:

5 Then I will establish the throne of thy kingdom upon Israel for ever, as I promised to

6 But if ye shall at all turn from following me, ye or your children, and will not keep my commandments and my statutes which I have set before you, but go and serve other gods, and worship them:

7 Then will I cut off Israel out of the land which I have given them; and this house, which I have hallowed for my name, will I cast out of my sight; and Israel shall be a proverb and a byword among all people:

8 And at this house, which is high, every one that passeth by it shall be astonished, and shall hiss; and they shall say, Why hath the LORD done thus unto this land, and to this house?

9 And they shall answer, Because they forsook the LORD their God, who brought forth their fathers out of the land of Egypt, and have taken hold upon other gods, and have worshipped them, and served them: therefore hath the LORD brought upon them all this evil.

10 ¶ And it came to pass at the end of twenty years, when Solomon had built the two houses, the house of the LORD, and the king's house,

11 (Now Hiram the king of Tyre had furnished Solomon with cedar trees and fir trees, and with gold, according to all his desire,) that then king Solomon gave Hiram twenty cities in the land of Galilee.

12 And Hiram came out from Tyre to see the cities which Solomon had given him; and they pleased him not.

13 And he said, What cities are these which thou hast given me, my brother? And he called them the land of Cabul unto this day.

14 And Hiram sent to the king sixscore talents of gold.

15 ¶ And this is the reason of the levy which king Solomon raised; for to build the house of the LORD, and his own house, and Millo, and the wall of Jerusalem, and Hazor, and Megiddo, and Gezer.

16 For Pharaoh king of Egypt had gone up, and taken Gezer, and burnt it with fire, and slain the Canaanites that dwelt in the city, and given it for a present unto his daughter, Solomon's wife.

17 And Solomon built Gezer, and Beth-horon the nether,

18 And Baalath, and Tadmor in the wilderness, in the land,

19 And all the cities of store that Solomon had, and cities for his chariots, and cities for his horsemen, and that which Solomon desired to build in Jerusalem, and in Lebanon, and in all the land of his dominion.

20 And all the people that were left of the Amorites, Hittites, Perizzites, Hivites, and Jebusites, which were not of the children of Israel,

1 KINGS CHAPTER 9

1 Kings 9:1–3—The House of the Lord: Eternal Symbol of Righteousness

We should look to the House of the Lord as the enduring icon of God's mission to bring about the immortality and eternal life of mankind. By keeping our eye on the temple and remembering our covenant promises, we prepare the way for great spiritual blessings in our lives.

The Lord had promised David that his son would build a house to the Lord. Solomon followed through with this destined project and erected a magnificent temple complex for sacred worship. The dedicatory program was replete with utterances importuning the Lord to accept His people as His own and prosper their way as long as they heeded His word and kept His commandments, looking toward the temple as a continual reminder of their covenant commitments. The temple edifice became renowned throughout the region, and rulers and potentates came from all around to admire it and bask in the opulence and wisdom of Solomon's court.

To this day, the temple is a place of worship, of making lifesaving covenants, of receiving blessings from God, of instruction, and of serving our fellowmen. We must live worthy of entering this sacred house. We must make plans to attend regularly, thus blessing others and ourselves.

1 Kings 9:4–5—David's Leadership in Establishing a Unified Kingdom Grounded in Righteous Principles

Despite his private transgression, David succeeded admirably as the one who elevated the nation of Israel in unity and grandeur during its golden age (see 1 Kings 11:38; compare 2 Chron. 7:17–20).

The governance of Israel under David became a type and symbol for the eventual reign of the Son of God, as Isaiah prophesied (see Isa. 16:5). Said Jeremiah:

> Behold, the days come, saith the LORD, that I will raise unto David a righteous Branch, and a King shall reign and prosper, and shall execute judgment and justice in the earth.
>
> In his days Judah shall be saved, and Israel shall dwell safely: and this is his name whereby he shall be called, THE LORD OUR RIGHTEOUSNESS. (Jer. 23:5–6)

1 Kings 9:26–28—Arabia/Arabians

Arabia, the vast territory to the east of the Holy Land—bounded by the Red Sea on the west, the Indian Ocean on the south, and the Persian Gulf and Euphrates River on the east—was occupied over generations by a variety of peoples. In the southern region of Arabia lived the Joktanites, a trading people who were descendants of Joktan, the son of Eber, who was a great-grandson of Shem (see Gen. 10:26–30). In the central region of Arabia were found the Ishmaelites, the supposed descendants of Abraham through Ishmael, son of Abraham and Hagar (see Gen. 21:14–21; 25:13–14). In the northern region of Arabia

21 Their children that were left after them in the land, whom the children of Israel also were not able utterly to destroy, upon those did Solomon levy a tribute of bondservice unto this day.

22 But of the children of Israel did Solomon make no bondmen: but they were men of war, and his servants, and his princes, and his captains, and rulers of his chariots, and his horsemen.

23 These were the chief of the officers that were over Solomon's work, five hundred and fifty, which bare rule over the people that wrought in the work.

24 ¶ But Pharaoh's daughter came up out of the city of David unto her house which Solomon had built for her: then did he build Millo.

25 ¶ And three times in a year did Solomon offer burnt offerings and peace offerings upon the altar which he built unto the LORD, and he burnt incense upon the altar that was before the LORD. So he finished the house.

26 ¶ And king Solomon made a navy of ships in Ezion-geber, which is beside Eloth, on the shore of the Red sea, in the land of Edom.

27 And Hiram sent in the navy his servants, shipmen that had knowledge of the sea, with the servants of Solomon.

28 And they came to Ophir, and fetched from thence gold, four hundred and twenty talents, and brought it to king Solomon.

CHAPTER 10

1 AND when the queen of Sheba heard of the fame of Solomon concerning the name of the LORD, she came to prove him with hard questions.

2 And she came to Jerusalem with a very great train, with camels that bare spices, and very much gold, and precious stones: and when she was come to Solomon, she communed with him of all that was in her heart.

3 And Solomon told her all her questions: there was not any thing hid from the king, which he told her not.

4 And when the queen of Sheba had seen all Solomon's wisdom, and the house that he had built,

5 And the meat of his table, and the sitting of his servants, and the attendance of his ministers, and their apparel, and his cupbearers, and his ascent by which he went up unto the house of the LORD; there was no more spirit in her.

6 And she said to the king, It was a true report that I heard in mine own land of thy acts and of thy wisdom.

7 Howbeit I believed not the words, until I came, and mine eyes had seen it: and, behold, the half was not told me: thy wisdom and prosperity exceedeth the fame which I heard.

8 Happy are thy men, happy are these thy servants, which stand continually before thee, and that hear thy wisdom.

9 Blessed be the LORD thy God, which delighted in thee, to set thee on the throne of Israel: because the LORD loved Israel for ever, therefore made he thee king, to do judgment and justice.

10 And she gave the king an hundred and twenty talents of gold, and of spices very great store, and precious stones: there came no more such abundance of spices as these which the queen of Sheba gave to king Solomon.

were various wandering tribes (including the Midianites) who traced their descent from Abraham and Keturah (see Gen. 25:1–4).

Contacts with the Arabian peoples were of a diverse nature throughout Israelite history. The Israelites wandered forty years in the deserts of Arabia before accessing the Promised Land. During the time of the judges, the Midianites of Arabia displayed aggression toward Israel, but Gideon was guided by the Lord to defeat them (see Judges 6–7). Solomon was visited by the queen of Sheba, who came to him from Arabia with gold, precious stones, and spices (see 1 Kings 10:1–14; 2 Chron. 9:1–14). Indeed, Arabia was the source of much gold for Solomon in his building projects (see 1 Kings 9:26–28; 2 Chron. 9:10). The Arabians brought tributes to Jehoshaphat, king of Judah (see 2 Chron. 17:10–12), but they desisted after his death and instead invaded Jerusalem and made off with the wealth and family of Jehoram, his son and successor (see 2 Chron. 21:16–17).

Isaiah prophesied of the Lord's judgments against some of the Arabian tribes (see Isa. 21:13–17), as did Jeremiah (see Jer. 25:23–27; 49:28–33). Nehemiah, while working to rebuild the walls of Jerusalem after the Babylonian conquest, faced opposition from the Arabian chief Geshem and his allies, but was able to overcome them and prevail (see Neh. 2:19; 4:7–13; 6). At Pentecost there were Arabians present in Jerusalem (see Acts 2:11), and Paul spent some time in Arabia following his conversion (see Gal. 1:17).

1 KINGS CHAPTER 10

1 Kings 10:1—The Queen of Sheba

The Queen of Sheba visited King Solomon at his court and acclaimed his renowned wisdom and justice:

> And she said to the king, It was a true report that I heard in mine own land of thy acts and of thy wisdom.
>
> Howbeit I believed not the words, until I came, and mine eyes had seen it: and, behold, the half was not told me: thy wisdom and prosperity exceedeth the fame which I heard.
>
> Happy are thy men, happy are these thy servants, which stand continually before thee, and that hear thy wisdom.
>
> Blessed be the LORD thy God, which delighted in thee, to set thee on the throne of Israel: because the LORD loved Israel for ever, therefore made he thee king, to do judgment and justice. (1 Kings 10:6–9; compare 2 Chron. 9:5–8)

The queen came from Sheba, a country in southern Arabia. The Savior referred to the queen of Sheba as the "queen of the south" who came to confirm and admire the wisdom of Solomon: ". . . and behold, a greater than Solomon is here" (Matt. 12:42).

11 And the navy also of Hiram, that brought gold from Ophir, brought in from Ophir great plenty of almug trees, and precious stones.

12 And the king made of the almug trees pillars for the house of the LORD, and for the king's house, harps also and psalteries for singers: there came no such almug trees, nor were seen unto this day.

13 And king Solomon gave unto the queen of Sheba all her desire, whatsoever she asked, beside that which Solomon gave her of his royal bounty. So she turned and went to her own country, she and her servants.

14 ¶ Now the weight of gold that came to Solomon in one year was six hundred threescore and six talents of gold,

15 Beside that he had of the merchantmen, and of the traffick of the spice merchants, and of all the kings of Arabia, and of the governors of the country.

16 ¶ And king Solomon made two hundred targets of beaten gold: six hundred shekels of gold went to one target.

17 And he made three hundred shields of beaten gold; three pound of gold went to one shield: and the king put them in the house of the forest of Lebanon.

18 ¶ Moreover the king made a great throne of ivory, and overlaid it with the best gold.

19 The throne had six steps, and the top of the throne was round behind: and there were stays on either side on the place of the seat, and two lions stood beside the stays.

20 And twelve lions stood there on the one side and on the other upon the six steps: there was not the like made in any kingdom.

21 ¶ And all king Solomon's drinking vessels were of gold, and all the vessels of the house of the forest of Lebanon were of pure gold; none were of silver: it was nothing accounted of in the days of Solomon.

22 For the king had at sea a navy of Tharshish with the navy of Hiram: once in three years came the navy of Tharshish, bringing gold, and silver, ivory, and apes, and peacocks.

23 So king Solomon exceeded all the kings of the earth for riches and for wisdom.

24 ¶ And all the earth sought to Solomon, to hear his wisdom, which God had put in his heart.

25 And they brought every man his present, vessels of silver, and vessels of gold, and garments, and armour, and spices, horses, and mules, a rate year by year.

26 ¶ And Solomon gathered together chariots and horsemen: and he had a thousand and four hundred chariots, and twelve thousand horsemen, whom he bestowed in the cities for chariots, and with the king at Jerusalem.

27 And the king made silver to be in Jerusalem as stones, and cedars made he to be as the sycomore trees that are in the vale, for abundance.

28 ¶ And Solomon had horses brought out of Egypt, and linen yarn: the king's merchants received the linen yarn at a price.

29 And a chariot came up and went out of Egypt for six hundred shekels of silver, and an horse for an hundred and fifty: and so for all the kings of the Hittites, and for the kings of Syria, did they bring them out by their means.

 POINT OF INTEREST

This Renaissance relif of Sheba's visit to Solomon is found on a Florence baptistry gate.

CHAPTER 11

1 BUT king Solomon loved many strange women, together with the daughter of Pharaoh, women of the Moabites, Ammonites, Edomites, Zidonians, and Hittites;

2 Of the nations concerning which the LORD said unto the children of Israel, Ye shall not go in to them, neither shall they come in unto you: for surely they will turn away your heart after their gods: Solomon clave unto these in love.

3 And he had seven hundred wives, princesses, and three hundred concubines: and his wives turned away his heart.

4 For it came to pass, when Solomon was old, that his wives turned away his heart after other gods: and his heart was not perfect with the LORD his God, as was the heart of David his father.

5 For Solomon went after Ashtoreth the goddess of the Zidonians, and after Milcom the abomination of the Ammonites.

6 And Solomon did evil in the sight of the LORD, and went not fully after the LORD, as did David his father.

7 Then did Solomon build an high place for Chemosh, the abomination of Moab, in the hill that is before Jerusalem, and for Molech, the abomination of the children of Ammon.

8 And likewise did he for all his strange wives, which burnt incense and sacrificed unto their gods.

9 ¶ And the LORD was angry with Solomon, because his heart was turned from the LORD God of Israel, which had appeared unto him twice,

10 And had commanded him concerning this thing, that he should not go after other gods: but he kept not that which the LORD commanded.

11 Wherefore the LORD said unto Solomon, Forasmuch as this is done of thee, and thou hast not kept my covenant and my statutes, which I have commanded thee, I will surely rend the kingdom from thee, and will give it to thy servant.

12 Notwithstanding in thy days I will not do it for David thy father's sake: but I will rend it out of the hand of thy son.

13 Howbeit I will not rend away all the kingdom; but will give one tribe to thy son for David my servant's sake, and for Jerusalem's sake which I have chosen.

14 ¶ And the LORD stirred up an adversary unto Solomon, Hadad the Edomite: he was of the king's seed in Edom.

15 For it came to pass, when David was in Edom, and Joab the captain of the host was gone up to bury the slain, after he had smitten every male in Edom;

16 (For six months did Joab remain there with all Israel, until he had cut off every male in Edom:)

17 That Hadad fled, he and certain Edomites of his father's servants with him, to go into Egypt; Hadad being yet a little child.

18 And they arose out of Midian, and came to Paran: and they took men with them out of Paran, and they came to Egypt, unto Pharaoh king of Egypt; which gave him an house, and appointed him victuals, and gave him land.

19 And Hadad found great favour in the sight of Pharaoh, so that he gave him to wife the sister of his own wife, the sister of Tahpenes the queen.

20 And the sister of Tahpenes bare him Genubath his son, whom Tahpenes weaned in Pharaoh's house: and Genubath was in Pharaoh's household among the sons of Pharaoh.

1 KINGS CHAPTER 11

"The worst fear that I have about [members of this Church] is that they will get rich in this country, forget God and his people, wax fat, and kick themselves out of the Church and go to hell. This people will stand mobbing, robbing, poverty, and all manner of persecution, and be true. But my greater fear for them is that they cannot stand wealth; and yet they have to be tried with riches, for they will become the richest people on this earth." —Brigham Young, in Preston Nibley, *Brigham Young: The Man and His Work* (1936), 128

1 Kings 11:4—Earthly Wealth in the Balance of Life: The Folly of Solomon's Descent

The consequence of allowing worldly influences to assume the upper hand in our lives is all too clear from the example of Solomon. When idolatry and moral decadence displace the statutes and ordinances of God, then man falls from God's favor and destruction lurks at the gate.

The Lord had given Solomon the blessing of riches and honor, even though he had not asked for these (see 1 Kings 3:13). Therein was a test for Solomon—a test that he was not able to pass, giving in as he did to the idolatry of his wives and an intemperate (unbalanced) affection for material things. For this reason, the Lord was not pleased with Solomon, and declared that a new situation would be introduced in Israel through the intervention of her enemies.

The prophet Ahijah informed Jeroboam that the kingdom would be rent in twain, and that he would become King of Israel, with the lesser part to remain with the lineage of David (see 1 Kings 11:36). Thus once again the forgetfulness of Israel would give occasion for much dislocation and trial in the future, just as our own slowness to heed the commandments of God can bring difficulties into our lives.

It is clear from this example that money and wealth and the use of it becomes a true test in life. All of us have increase. We have a duty to build up the kingdom of God. We all can do our part with our tithes and offerings, and should we be blessed with great surpluses, our test continues in regard to the use of our monies and whether we will use it to bless our fellowmen.

1 Kings 11:5—Milcom

Milcom (meaning: their king) was a heathen god whose worship Solomon facilitated among his people (see 1 Kings 11:5). Because of this wickedness, the Lord sent word through the prophet Ahijah that Jeroboam would displace Solomon and his followers (see 1 Kings 11:33).

In due time, Jeroboam did indeed become king over the northern kingdom (see 1 Kings 12:20), although he did not entirely cleanse the culture of idolatry, thus evoking the rebuke of the prophet Ahijah (see 1 Kings 14:6–16). Generations later, Josiah, the great reform king, eradicated the worship of false gods and destroyed their sanctuaries "which Solomon the king of Israel had builded

21 And when Hadad heard in Egypt that David slept with his fathers, and that Joab the captain of the host was dead, Hadad said to Pharaoh, Let me depart, that I may go to mine own country.

22 Then Pharaoh said unto him, But what hast thou lacked with me, that, behold, thou seekest to go to thine own country? And he answered, Nothing: howbeit let me go in any wise.

23 ¶ And God stirred him up another adversary, Rezon the son of Eliadah, which fled from his lord Hadadezer king of Zobah:

24 And he gathered men unto him, and became captain over a band, when David slew them of Zobah: and they went to Damascus, and dwelt therein, and reigned in Damascus.

25 And he was an adversary to Israel all the days of Solomon, beside the mischief that Hadad did: and he abhorred Israel, and reigned over Syria.

26 ¶ And Jeroboam the son of Nebat, an Ephrathite of Zereda, Solomon's servant, whose mother's name was Zeruah, a widow woman, even he lifted up his hand against the king.

27 And this was the cause that he lifted up his hand against the king: Solomon built Millo, and repaired the breaches of the city of David his father.

28 And the man Jeroboam was a mighty man of valour: and Solomon seeing the young man that he was industrious, he made him ruler over all the charge of the house of Joseph.

29 And it came to pass at that time when Jeroboam went out of Jerusalem, that the prophet Ahijah the Shilonite found him in the way; and he had clad himself with a new garment; and they two were alone in the field:

30 And Ahijah caught the new garment that was on him, and rent it in twelve pieces:

31 And he said to Jeroboam, Take thee ten pieces: for thus saith the LORD, the God of Israel, Behold, I will rend the kingdom out of the hand of Solomon, and will give ten tribes to thee:

32 (But he shall have one tribe for my servant David's sake, and for Jerusalem's sake, the city which I have chosen out of all the tribes of Israel:)

33 Because that they have forsaken me, and have worshipped Ashtoreth the goddess of the Zidonians, Chemosh the god of the Moabites, and Milcom the god of the children of Ammon, and have not walked in my ways, to do that which is right in mine eyes, and to keep my statutes and my judgments, as did David his father.

34 Howbeit I will not take the whole kingdom out of his hand: but I will make him prince all the days of his life for David my servant's sake, whom I chose, because he kept my commandments and my statutes:

35 But I will take the kingdom out of his son's hand, and will give it unto thee, even ten tribes.

36 And unto his son will I give one tribe, that David my servant may have a light alway before me in Jerusalem, the city which I have chosen me to put my name there.

37 And I will take thee, and thou shalt reign according to all that thy soul desireth, and shalt be king over Israel.

38 And it shall be, if thou wilt hearken unto all that I command thee, and wilt walk in my ways, and do that is right in my sight, to keep my statutes and my commandments, as David my servant did; that I will be with thee, and build thee a sure house, as I built for David, and will give Israel unto thee.

39 And I will for this afflict the seed of David, but not for ever.

for Ashtoreth the abomination of the Zidonians, and for Chemosh the abomination of the Moabites, and for Milcom the abomination of the children of Ammon" (2 Kings 23:13). The canon of scripture makes clear the dire consequences of advocating and embracing allegiance to any worldly deities such as Milcom—also identified with such terms as *Molech* (see Lev. 18:21; 20:2–5), *Moloch* (see Amos 5:26), and *Malcham* (see Zeph. 1:5).

1 Kings 11:26—Jeroboam

Jeroboam (pronounced "jer'-uh-boh'-uhm"; meaning: whose people are many) was the first in a long sequence of kings over the northern part of the house of Israel. Israel became divided into two parts around 975 BC, largely as a result of a revolt of the people against the heavy tax burden imposed by King Solomon. The northern part of the kingdom, headquartered at Shechem, comprised ten of the tribes, with Ephraim as the dominant group. The southern part of the kingdom, headquartered at Jerusalem, consisted chiefly of the tribes of Judah and Benjamin.

Jeroboam, son of Nebat, the Ephraimite, being "a mighty man of valour," began his career in the court of Solomon, who, "seeing the young man that he was industrious, he made him ruler over all the charge of the house of Joseph" (1 Kings 11:28).

For more insights on Jeroboam, see Appendix X.

1 Kings 11:29—Ahijah

Ahijah (pronounced "uh-hy'-juh"; meaning: brother or friend of Jehovah) was a prophet from the town of Shiloh (north of Jerusalem, in the land of Ephraim) who lived during the days of Jeroboam, the servant of Solomon who was to ascend the throne of Israel. Ahijah delivered to Jeroboam the extraordinary word of the Lord concerning the division of the tribes of Israel (see 1 Kings 11:29–38). In addition, Ahijah also prophesied of the judgments of God upon Jeroboam for his subsequent wickedness and idolatry. Jeroboam's son took ill, so he dispatched his wife in disguise to inquire of Ahijah about their boy's fate. When she arrived at Ahijah's home, he revealed to her the tragic news that her boy would die upon her return, and that the Lord would bring an end to the reign of Jeroboam in due time because of his evil ways (see 1 Kings 14:1–18; 15:29; 2 Chron. 9:29).

1 Kings 11:40—Shishak

Shishak (pronounced "shy'-shak") was the king of Egypt to whom Jeroboam fled to escape the sword of Solomon until the Solomon's death (see 1 Kings 11:40), after which Jeroboam was elevated to the throne of the northern kingdom of Israel (see 1 Kings 12:20). Subsequently, in the fifth year of the reign of Rehoboam, successor to Solomon, Shishak invaded the southern kingdom (see 2 Chron. 12:5–9; see also 1 Kings 14:25–28).

Shishak is therefore a memorable emblem of the hand of God—in both justice and mercy—shaping and guiding the affairs of the children of promise in their challenge to rise to their potential.

40 Solomon sought therefore to kill Jeroboam. And Jeroboam arose, and fled into Egypt, unto Shishak king of Egypt, and was in Egypt until the death of Solomon.

41 ¶ And the rest of the acts of Solomon, and all that he did, and his wisdom, are they not written in the book of the acts of Solomon?

42 And the time that Solomon reigned in Jerusalem over all Israel was forty years.

43 And Solomon slept with his fathers, and was buried in the city of David his father: and Rehoboam his son reigned in his stead.

CHAPTER 12

1 AND Rehoboam went to Shechem: for all Israel were come to Shechem to make him king.

2 And it came to pass, when Jeroboam the son of Nebat, who was yet in Egypt, heard of it, (for he was fled from the presence of king Solomon, and Jeroboam dwelt in Egypt;)

3 That they sent and called him. And Jeroboam and all the congregation of Israel came, and spake unto Rehoboam, saying,

4 Thy father made our yoke grievous: now therefore make thou the grievous service of thy father, and his heavy yoke which he put upon us, lighter, and we will serve thee.

5 And he said unto them, Depart yet for three days, then come again to me. And the people departed.

6 ¶ And king Rehoboam consulted with the old men, that stood before Solomon his father while he yet lived, and said, How do ye advise that I may answer this people?

7 And they spake unto him, saying, If thou wilt be a servant unto this people this day, and wilt serve them, and answer them, and speak good words to them, then they will be thy servants for ever.

8 But he forsook the counsel of the old men, which they had given him, and consulted with the young men that were grown up with him, and which stood before him:

9 And he said unto them, What counsel give ye that we may answer this people, who have spoken to me, saying, Make the yoke which thy father did put upon us lighter?

10 And the young men that were grown up with him spake unto him, saying, Thus shalt thou speak unto this people that spake unto thee, saying, Thy father made our yoke heavy, but make thou it lighter unto us; thus shalt thou say unto them, My little finger shall be thicker than my father's loins.

11 And now whereas my father did lade you with a heavy yoke, I will add to your yoke: my father hath chastised you with whips, but I will chastise you with scorpions.

12 ¶ So Jeroboam and all the people came to Rehoboam the third day, as the king had appointed, saying, Come to me again the third day.

13 And the king answered the people roughly, and forsook the old men's counsel that they gave him;

14 And spake to them after the counsel of the young men, saying, My father made your yoke heavy, and I will add to your yoke: my father also chastised you with whips, but I will chastise you with scorpions.

15 Wherefore the king hearkened not unto the people; for the cause was from the LORD, that he might perform his saying, which the LORD spake by Ahijah the Shilonite unto Jeroboam the son of Nebat.

1 KINGS CHAPTER 12

1 Kings 12—The Story of Rehoboam and Jeroboam

It is abundantly clear from the history being discussed in this chapter that iniquity in the seat of government could have no wholesome outcomes for Israel. When the kings (like Rehoboam or Jeroboam) followed a wicked agenda, the people suffered.

The same was true on the American continent during Book of Mormon times. Righteous General Moroni had to hoist the title of liberty to rally the people against the evil onslaughts of the cunning Amalickiah.

The message is lucid for our times: "Thus we see how quick the children of men do forget the Lord their God, yea, how quick to do iniquity, and to be led away by the evil one. Yea, and we also see the great wickedness one very wicked man can cause to take place among the children of men" (Alma 46:8–9). At the same time, it is apparent that an upright leader of influence like Moses, Joshua, or Jehoshaphat—one who is anchored in righteous principles—has rather awesome power to bring about good for many, many people, sometimes for generations. We can see in the portrait honoring General Moroni, for example, a summary statement about the enduring truth concerning spiritual leadership: "Yea, verily, verily I say unto you, if all men had been, and were, and ever would be, like unto Moroni, behold, the very powers of hell would have been shaken forever; yea, the devil would never have power over the hearts of the children of men" (Alma 48:17).

The contrasting consequences of covenant leadership (based on divine purpose and godly principles) versus non-covenant leadership (based on worldly pride and idolatry) are made abundantly clear in the scriptural account of the kings of Israel and Judah.

For more insights on Jeroboam, see Appendix X.
For more insights on Rehoboam, see Appendix Y.

16 ¶ So when all Israel saw that the king hearkened not unto them, the people answered the king, saying, What portion have we in David? neither have we inheritance in the son of Jesse: to your tents, O Israel: now see to thine own house, David. So Israel departed unto their tents.

17 But as for the children of Israel which dwelt in the cities of Judah, Rehoboam reigned over them.

18 Then king Rehoboam sent Adoram, who was over the tribute; and all Israel stoned him with stones, that he died. Therefore king Rehoboam made speed to get him up to his chariot, to flee to Jerusalem.

19 So Israel rebelled against the house of David unto this day.

20 And it came to pass, when all Israel heard that Jeroboam was come again, that they sent and called him unto the congregation, and made him king over all Israel: there was none that followed the house of David, but the tribe of Judah only.

21 ¶ And when Rehoboam was come to Jerusalem, he assembled all the house of Judah, with the tribe of Benjamin, an hundred and fourscore thousand chosen men, which were warriors, to fight against the house of Israel, to bring the kingdom again to Rehoboam the son of Solomon.

22 But the word of God came unto Shemaiah the man of God, saying,

23 Speak unto Rehoboam, the son of Solomon, king of Judah, and unto all the house of Judah and Benjamin, and to the remnant of the people, saying,

24 Thus saith the LORD, Ye shall not go up, nor fight against your brethren the children of Israel: return every man to his house; for this thing is from me. They hearkened therefore to the word of the LORD, and returned to depart, according to the word of the LORD.

25 ¶ Then Jeroboam built Shechem in mount Ephraim, and dwelt therein; and went out from thence, and built Penuel.

26 And Jeroboam said in his heart, Now shall the kingdom return to the house of David:

27 If this people go up to do sacrifice in the house of the LORD at Jerusalem, then shall the heart of this people turn again unto their lord, even unto Rehoboam king of Judah, and they shall kill me, and go again to Rehoboam king of Judah.

28 Whereupon the king took counsel, and made two calves of gold, and said unto them, It is too much for you to go up to Jerusalem: behold thy gods, O Israel, which brought thee up out of the land of Egypt.

29 And he set the one in Beth-el, and the other put he in Dan.

30 And this thing became a sin: for the people went to worship before the one, even unto Dan.

31 And he made an house of high places, and made priests of the lowest of the people, which were not of the sons of Levi.

32 And Jeroboam ordained a feast in the eighth month, on the fifteenth day of the month, like unto the feast that is in Judah, and he offered upon the altar. So did he in Beth-el, sacrificing unto the calves that he had made: and he placed in Beth-el the priests of the high places which he had made.

33 So he offered upon the altar which he had made in Beth-el the fifteenth day of the eighth month, even in the month which he had devised of his own heart; and ordained a feast unto the children of Israel: and he offered upon the altar, and burnt incense.

1 Kings 12:22—Shemaiah

Shemaiah (pronounced "shem-y'-uh"; meaning: the Lord heareth) was a prophet who admonished Rehoboam, king of Judah, not to rise up against the northern tribes, though they had defied the heavy tax burden imposed by the regime of Solomon and continued by Rehoboam (his son and successor):

> But the word of God came unto Shemaiah the man of God, saying,
>
> Speak unto Rehoboam, the son of Solomon, king of Judah, and unto all the house of Judah and Benjamin, and to the remnant of the people, saying,
>
> Thus saith the LORD, Ye shall not go up, nor fight against your brethren the children of Israel: return every man to his house; for this thing is from me. They hearkened therefore to the word of the LORD, and returned to depart, according to the word of the LORD. (1 Kings 12:22–24)

Rehoboam heeded the counsel, but his power was greatly weakened not long thereafter as a result of an invasion by the Egyptians under Shishak, king of Egypt—something Shemaiah had warned him about (see 2 Chron. 12:5–12). Shemaiah recorded the acts of Rehoboam in a book called "the book of Shemaiah" (2 Chron. 12:15).

1 Kings 12:31—Non-Covenant Leadership: The Consequences of Government Based on Worldly Pride and Idolatry

When Israel's kings ignored principles of righteousness, the nation became divided and the people were led into iniquity. We can learn valuable lessons in proper leadership by studying these accounts.

After the death of Solomon, his son Rehoboam came to power in Jerusalem. Jeroboam, one of the leaders in Solomon's court, became the king of the separated tribes of Israel (all except Judah and Benjamin). Jeroboam's ascendancy had been foretold by the prophet Ahijah, the Lord promising him a "sure house" (1 Kings 11:38) if he would heed the covenant promises and commandments. Regretfully, he led the people astray, as did Rehoboam, who ignored the advice of the older men and increased the oppression on the people. Both of these kings—one over Judah and one over Israel—failed to walk in footsteps of their righteous predecessors among the rulers of the covenant people, and thus the Lord withdrew his support.

Throughout the history of the world mankind has suffered from poor or heinous leadership. As individuals and groups we have an obligation and responsibility for the welfare of all mankind. We must take action. If no action is taken, apathy results in torpidity and lives suffer. The consequences are real for sins of omission.

CHAPTER 13

1 AND, behold, there came a man of God out of Judah by the word of the LORD unto Beth-el: and Jeroboam stood by the altar to burn incense.

2 And he cried against the altar in the word of the LORD, and said, O altar, altar, thus saith the LORD; Behold, a child shall be born unto the house of David, Josiah by name; and upon thee shall he offer the priests of the high places that burn incense upon thee, and men's bones shall be burnt upon thee.

3 And he gave a sign the same day, saying, This is the sign which the LORD hath spoken; Behold, the altar shall be rent, and the ashes that are upon it shall be poured out.

4 And it came to pass, when king Jeroboam heard the saying of the man of God, which had cried against the altar in Beth-el, that he put forth his hand from the altar, saying, Lay hold on him. And his hand, which he put forth against him, dried up, so that he could not pull it in again to him.

5 The altar also was rent, and the ashes poured out from the altar, according to the sign which the man of God had given by the word of the LORD.

6 And the king answered and said unto the man of God, Intreat now the face of the LORD thy God, and pray for me, that my hand may be restored me again. And the man of God besought the LORD, and the king's hand was restored him again, and became as it was before.

7 And the king said unto the man of God, Come home with me, and refresh thyself, and I will give thee a reward.

8 And the man of God said unto the king, If thou wilt give me half thine house, I will not go in with thee, neither will I eat bread nor drink water in this place:

9 For so was it charged me by the word of the LORD, saying, Eat no bread, nor drink water, nor turn again by the same way that thou camest.

10 So he went another way, and returned not by the way that he came to Beth-el.

11 ¶ Now there dwelt an old prophet in Beth-el; and his sons came and told him all the works that the man of God had done that day in Beth-el: the words which he had spoken unto the king, them they told also to their father.

12 And their father said unto them, What way went he? For his sons had seen what way the man of God went, which came from Judah.

13 And he said unto his sons, Saddle me the ass. So they saddled him the ass: and he rode thereon,

14 And went after the man of God, and found him sitting under an oak: and he said unto him, Art thou the man of God that camest from Judah? And he said, I am.

15 Then he said unto him, Come home with me, and eat bread.

16 And he said, I may not return with thee, nor go in with thee: neither will I eat bread nor drink water with thee in this place:

17 For it was said to me by the word of the LORD, Thou shalt eat no bread nor drink water there, nor turn again to go by the way that thou camest.

18 He said unto him, I am a prophet also as thou art; and an angel spake unto me by the word of the LORD, saying, Bring him back with thee into thine house, that he may eat bread and drink water. But he lied unto him.

 POINT OF INTEREST

This relief at Karnak in Egypt shows Shoshenq I ready to club a group of foreigners in the presence of Egypt's chief god, Amun. The row of cartouches surrounding him list captured towns in the Jezreel Valley and on the Via Maris trade route through Palestine, including Gibeon, Mahanaim, Israel's capital on the east side of the Jordan, Hapharaim, Rehab, Beth-Shean, Shunem, and Taanach. "Although Shoshenq I is usually thought to be the Biblical Shishak who attacked the southern kingdom of Judah, few Judaean towns are listed. Most of the places mentioned were within the northern kingdom of Israel, while Jerusalem, target of Shishak's campaign according to the Bible, is missing. Although the inscription is heavily damaged, it is certain that Jerusalem was not included because the list is arranged into geographical sequences which allow no space for the name Jerusalem" (Bruce Metzer, David Goldstein, John Ferguson, Great Events of Bible Times [New York: Fall River Press, 1990]).

19 So he went back with him, and did eat bread in his house, and drank water.

20 ¶ And it came to pass, as they sat at the table, that the word of the LORD came unto the prophet that brought him back:

21 And he cried unto the man of God that came from Judah, saying, Thus saith the LORD, Forasmuch as thou hast disobeyed the mouth of the LORD, and hast not kept the commandment which the LORD thy God commanded thee,

22 But camest back, and hast eaten bread and drunk water in the place, of the which the LORD did say to thee, Eat no bread, and drink no water; thy carcase shall not come unto the sepulchre of thy fathers.

23 ¶ And it came to pass, after he had eaten bread, and after he had drunk, that he saddled for him the ass, to wit, for the prophet whom he had brought back.

24 And when he was gone, a lion met him by the way, and slew him: and his carcase was cast in the way, and the ass stood by it, the lion also stood by the carcase.

25 And, behold, men passed by, and saw the carcase cast in the way, and the lion standing by the carcase: and they came and told it in the city where the old prophet dwelt.

26 And when the prophet that brought him back from the way heard thereof, he said, It is the man of God, who was disobedient unto the word of the LORD: therefore the LORD hath delivered him unto the lion, which hath torn him, and slain him, according to the word of the LORD, which he spake unto him.

27 And he spake to his sons, saying, Saddle me the ass. And they saddled him.

28 And he went and found his carcase cast in the way, and the ass and the lion standing by the carcase: the lion had not eaten the carcase, nor torn the ass.

29 And the prophet took up the carcase of the man of God, and laid it upon the ass, and brought it back: and the old prophet came to the city, to mourn and to bury him.

30 And he laid his carcase in his own grave; and they mourned over him, saying, Alas, my brother!

31 And it came to pass, after he had buried him, that he spake to his sons, saying, When I am dead, then bury me in the sepulchre wherein the man of God is buried; lay my bones beside his bones:

32 For the saying which he cried by the word of the LORD against the altar in Beth-el, and against all the houses of the high places which are in the cities of Samaria, shall surely come to pass.

33 ¶ After this thing Jeroboam returned not from his evil way, but made again of the lowest of the people priests of the high places: whosoever would, he consecrated him, and he became one of the priests of the high places.

34 And this thing became sin unto the house of Jeroboam, even to cut it off, and to destroy it from off the face of the earth.

The Disobedient Prophet Slain by a Lion by Gustave Doré

CHAPTER 14

1 AT that time Abijah the son of Jeroboam fell sick.

2 And Jeroboam said to his wife, Arise, I pray thee, and disguise thyself, that thou be not known to be the wife of Jeroboam; and get thee to Shiloh: behold, there is Ahijah the prophet, which told me that I should be king over this people.

3 And take with thee ten loaves, and cracknels, and a cruse of honey, and go to him: he shall tell thee what shall become of the child.

4 And Jeroboam's wife did so, and arose, and went to Shiloh, and came to the house of Ahijah. But Ahijah could not see; for his eyes were set by reason of his age.

5 ¶ And the LORD said unto Ahijah, Behold, the wife of Jeroboam cometh to ask a thing of thee for her son; for he is sick: thus and thus shalt thou say unto her: for it shall be, when she cometh in, that she shall feign herself to be another woman.

6 And it was so, when Ahijah heard the sound of her feet, as she came in at the door, that he said, Come in, thou wife of Jeroboam; why feignest thou thyself to be another? for I am sent to thee with heavy tidings.

7 Go, tell Jeroboam, Thus saith the LORD God of Israel, Forasmuch as I exalted thee from among the people, and made thee prince over my people Israel,

8 And rent the kingdom away from the house of David, and gave it thee: and yet thou hast not been as my servant David, who kept my commandments, and who followed me with all his heart, to do that only which was right in mine eyes;

9 But hast done evil above all that were before thee: for thou hast gone and made thee other gods, and molten images, to provoke me to anger, and hast cast me behind thy back:

10 Therefore, behold, I will bring evil upon the house of Jeroboam, and will cut off from Jeroboam him that pisseth against the wall, and him that is shut up and left in Israel, and will take away the remnant of the house of Jeroboam, as a man taketh away dung, till it be all gone.

11 Him that dieth of Jeroboam in the city shall the dogs eat; and him that dieth in the field shall the fowls of the air eat: for the LORD hath spoken it.

12 Arise thou therefore, get thee to thine own house: and when thy feet enter into the city, the child shall die.

13 And all Israel shall mourn for him, and bury him: for he only of Jeroboam shall come to the grave, because in him there is found some good thing toward the LORD God of Israel in the house of Jeroboam.

14 Moreover the LORD shall raise him up a king over Israel, who shall cut off the house of Jeroboam that day: but what? even now.

15 For the LORD shall smite Israel, as a reed is shaken in the water, and he shall root up Israel out of this good land, which he gave to their fathers, and shall scatter them beyond the river, because they have made their groves, provoking the LORD to anger.

16 And he shall give Israel up because of the sins of Jeroboam, who did sin, and who made Israel to sin.

17 ¶ And Jeroboam's wife arose, and departed, and came to Tirzah: and when she came to the threshold of the door, the child died;

18 And they buried him; and all Israel mourned for him, according to the word of the LORD, which he spake by the hand of his servant Ahijah the prophet.

 POINT OF INTEREST

The Bible's Pharaoh Shishak was likely Shoshenq I, also known as Shoshenk I, a Libyan mercenary who founded Egypt's 22nd dynasty. "After Solomon's death, Jeroboam, an upstart pretender to his throne, fled to Egypt under Shishak (1 Kings 11:40) only to return later as the king of the ten tribes, while Rehoboam, Solomon's son, had to content himself with kingship over Judah." A similar incident is recorded a half-century earlier when "Joab, in command of King David's forces, had devastated Edom and put its entire male population to the sword. Hadad, a child of the Edomite royal family, had escaped to Egypt and as he grew up found favour with the Pharaoh, who gave him to wife the sister of Tahpenes his queen. Later, Hadad returned to his own country against Pharaoh's will, and became a lifelong enemy of Solomon." As mentioned on page 193, "no mention of either Gezer or Jerusalem is made in the surviving names accompanying the great scene of the Bubastite portal [in Karnak]. These names are presented in the traditional fashion, . . . namely, attached to the busts of prisoners whom the gigantic figure of Pharaoh leads forward for presentation to his father Amen-Re'. The enumeration is disappointing; of the 150 and more places named only a few are well enough preserved to suggest definite routes and these skirt around the hill-country of Samaria without reaching the centre of the Israelite kingdom; nor is there any hint that they ever touched Judah at all. There are, however, some indications of a raid into Edomite territory. The long-accepted belief that a 'field of Abraham' was to be read in the list is now rejected. However, the discovery at Megiddo of a fragment mentioning Shoshenk leaves no doubt as to the reality of his campaign, though it remains wholly obscure whether it was an attempt to revive ancient glories, whether it was designed for support of Jeroboam, or whether it was a mere plundering raid. That both Shoshenk and his successor Osorkon I renewed the secular friendship of Egypt with the princes of Byblos is confirmed by the presence of statues of them there, probably gifts sent by those Pharaohs themselves" (Alan Gardiner, *The Egyptians* [London: Folio Society, 2007]).

19 And the rest of the acts of Jeroboam, how he warred, and how he reigned, behold, they are written in the book of the chronicles of the kings of Israel.

20 And the days which Jeroboam reigned were two and twenty years: and he slept with his fathers, and Nadab his son reigned in his stead.

21 ¶ And Rehoboam the son of Solomon reigned in Judah. Rehoboam was forty and one years old when he began to reign, and he reigned seventeen years in Jerusalem, the city which the LORD did choose out of all the tribes of Israel, to put his name there. And his mother's name was Naamah an Ammonitess.

22 And Judah did evil in the sight of the LORD, and they provoked him to jealousy with their sins which they had committed, above all that their fathers had done.

23 For they also built them high places, and images, and groves, on every high hill, and under every green tree.

24 And there were also sodomites in the land: and they did according to all the abominations of the nations which the LORD cast out before the children of Israel.

25 ¶ And it came to pass in the fifth year of king Rehoboam, that Shishak king of Egypt came up against Jerusalem:

26 And he took away the treasures of the house of the LORD, and the treasures of the king's house; he even took away all: and he took away all the shields of gold which Solomon had made.

27 And king Rehoboam made in their stead brasen shields, and committed them unto the hands of the chief of the guard, which kept the door of the king's house.

28 And it was so, when the king went into the house of the LORD, that the guard bare them, and brought them back into the guard chamber.

29 ¶ Now the rest of the acts of Rehoboam, and all that he did, are they not written in the book of the chronicles of the kings of Judah?

30 And there was war between Rehoboam and Jeroboam all their days.

31 And Rehoboam slept with his fathers, and was buried with his fathers in the city of David. And his mother's name was Naamah an Ammonitess. And Abijam his son reigned in his stead.

CHAPTER 17

1 AND Elijah the Tishbite, who was of the inhabitants of Gilead, said unto Ahab, As the LORD God of Israel liveth, before whom I stand, there shall not be dew nor rain these years, but according to my word.

2 And the word of the LORD came unto him, saying,

3 Get thee hence, and turn thee eastward, and hide thyself by the brook Cherith, that is before Jordan.

4 And it shall be, that thou shalt drink of the brook; and I have commanded the ravens to feed thee there.

5 So he went and did according unto the word of the LORD: for he went and dwelt by the brook Cherith, that is before Jordan.

6 And the ravens brought him bread and flesh in the morning, and bread and flesh in the evening; and he drank of the brook.

7 And it came to pass after a while, that the brook dried up, because there had been no rain in the land.

1 KINGS CHAPTER 17

1 Kings 17—Preview of the Lessons We Learn from the Life of Elijah

Looking back on the ministry of the mortal Messiah, the Apostle Paul gave this summary of the organizational miracle that informed the Kingdom of God on the earth as established by the Savior: "Now therefore ye are no more strangers and foreigners, but fellowcitizens with the saints, and of the household of God; And are built upon the foundation of the apostles and prophets, Jesus Christ himself being the chief corner stone; In whom all the building fitly framed together groweth unto an holy temple in the Lord" (Eph. 2:19–21).

We see in the mission of Elijah the prophet continuing evidence that the same foundation had been used in all earlier dispensations of time, with prophetic callings providing the central buttressing and underpinning for the work of Jehovah in bringing about His agenda for mankind. Upon the foundation of continuing revelation—the Savior Himself being the cornerstone—are layer upon layer of spiritual blessings and gifts provided for the faithful Saints engaged on the Lord's errand. Three of these include: (1) the miracles of the Spirit that attend faithful service at the behest of seen and unseen influences for good, (2) the manifestations of divine power that continually combat and overcome the forces of Babylon and Baal in the world, and (3) the constant, overarching presence of the hand of God at work in the building up of His Kingdom for the purpose of bringing to pass the immortality and eternal life of man.

1 Kings 17:1—Elijah

Elijah (meaning: Jehovah is my God) the Tishbite is a singularly imposing figure in a long line of extraordinary prophetic servants of the Lord. He commenced his ministry around 926 BC among the northern tribes of Israel. His influence was felt with compelling force among the Israelites and non-Israelites of his day, was called forth again on the Mount of Transfiguration (see Matt. 17:1–11), and he touches countless lives today through the restored keys of the sealing power of the priesthood placed in his charge (see D&C 110:13–16).

The story of Elijah is a dramatic confirmation of the fact that the Lord's work is always founded on prophetic ministry. The prophet Elijah occupied a central position in the design of God as the one holding the "keys of the power of turning the hearts of the fathers to the children, and the hearts of the children to the fathers, that the whole earth may not be smitten with a curse" (D&C 27:9). It was this prophet whom God sent on April 3, 1836, to the Kirtland Temple to restore these sacred keys to Joseph Smith as an essential priesthood power in the dispensation of the fullness of times (see D&C 110:14–16).

The history of the prophet Elijah is recounted in 1 Kings 17 through 2 Kings 2. The First and Second Books of the Kings were regarded by the Jews as a single book, whereas the Greek Bible divided this material into two books, a convention retained in the Latin and English versions. The First and Second Books of the Kings cover the historical account

8 ¶ And the word of the LORD came unto him, saying,

9 Arise, get thee to Zarephath, which belongeth to Zidon, and dwell there: behold, I have commanded a widow woman there to sustain thee.

10 So he arose and went to Zarephath. And when he came to the gate of the city, behold, the widow woman was there gathering of sticks: and he called to her, and said, Fetch me, I pray thee, a little water in a vessel, that I may drink.

11 And as she was going to fetch it, he called to her, and said, Bring me, I pray thee, a morsel of bread in thine hand.

12 And she said, As the LORD thy God liveth, I have not a cake, but an handful of meal in a barrel, and a little oil in a cruse: and, behold, I am gathering two sticks, that I may go in and dress it for me and my son, that we may eat it, and die.

13 And Elijah said unto her, Fear not; go and do as thou hast said: but make me thereof a little cake first, and bring it unto me, and after make for thee and for thy son.

14 For thus saith the LORD God of Israel, The barrel of meal shall not waste, neither shall the cruse of oil fail, until the day that the LORD sendeth rain upon the earth.

15 And she went and did according to the saying of Elijah: and she, and he, and her house, did eat many days.

16 And the barrel of meal wasted not, neither did the cruse of oil fail, according to the word of the LORD, which he spake by Elijah.

17 ¶ And it came to pass after these things, that the son of the woman, the mistress of the house, fell sick; and his sickness was so sore, that there was no breath left in him.

18 And she said unto Elijah, What have I to do with thee, O thou man of God? art thou come unto me to call my sin to remembrance, and to slay my son?

19 And he said unto her, Give me thy son. And he took him out of her bosom, and carried him up into a loft, where he abode, and laid him upon his own bed.

20 And he cried unto the LORD, and said, O LORD my God, hast thou also brought evil upon the widow with whom I sojourn, by slaying her son?

21 And he stretched himself upon the child three times, and cried unto the LORD, and said, O LORD my God, I pray thee, let this child's soul come into him again.

22 And the LORD heard the voice of Elijah; and the soul of the child came into him again, and he revived.

23 And Elijah took the child, and brought him down out of the chamber into the house, and delivered him unto his mother: and Elijah said, See, thy son liveth.

24 ¶ And the woman said to Elijah, Now by this I know that thou art a man of God, and that the word of the LORD in thy mouth is truth.

from the time of the rebellion of Adonijah (fourth son of David—see 2 Sam. 3:4), just prior to the death of David and the transition to Solomon, and extending down to the captivity of Judah by the Babylonians around 587 BC, including also the history of the Northern Kingdom from its separation until its scattering around 721 BC. The First Book of the Kings extends down to the transition of prophetic leadership from Elijah to Elisha (around 851 BC).

The magnificent spiritual leadership of Elijah serves as a stark contrast to the unsteadiness of royal leadership by providing a standard of enduring faith, undeviating devotion, uncompromising righteousness, and the invocation and implementation of priesthood power. Out of the mixture of light and darkness that characterizes this period emerges the glory of the temple—the house of the Lord.

The main themes, events, and personalities relevant to the ministry of Elijah outlined in the First Book of the Kings include the following:

Solomon marries outside Israel and his heart is turned to idolatry; the prophet Ahijah promises Jeroboam that he will become leader over the ten tribes; Solomon dies and his son Rehoboam reigns in his place (chapter 11).

Turmoil reigns supreme in Israel over the next period, with various leaders displaced amid conspiracy and intrigue; Jezebel comes on scene as the wife of Ahab, the wicked king of the Northern Kingdom, and with her an upsurge in Baal worship (chapters 12–16).

The prophet Elijah seals the heavens, is fed by ravens, and performs miracles at the household of the widow of Zarephath, including expanding her meager supply of food and bringing her dead son back to life (chapter 17).

Elijah meets Ahab and challenges the priests of Baal to a contest (chapter 18). The Lord sends fire to consume the righteous offering. The priests of Baal are destroyed.

Elijah is protected from the evil designs of Jezebel; Elijah hears the voice of the Lord (chapter 19); Elijah is commanded to anoint Hazael to be king over Syria, Jehu to be king over Israel, and Elisha to be a prophet.

Against the background of intrigue and contention at the highest levels of the state governments, Elijah prophesies the defeat of Ahab and Jezebel—which transpires as predicted; Jehoshaphat reigns in righteousness in Judah and Ahaziah, son of Ahab, reigns in wickedness and idolatry in Israel (chapters 20–22).

The story of Elijah continues in the Second Book of the Kings. As in the First Book of the Kings, the ongoing saga provides a contrast of the pervasive wickedness of the people and their kings (with the notable exception of such as Hezekiah and Josiah in chapters 18–23) and the glorious devotion and righteousness of the prophets of God—Elijah, Elisha, and Isaiah.

CHAPTER 18

1 AND it came to pass after many days, that the word of the LORD came to Elijah in the third year, saying, Go, shew thyself unto Ahab; and I will send rain upon the earth.

2 And Elijah went to shew himself unto Ahab. And there was a sore famine in Samaria.

3 And Ahab called Obadiah, which was the governor of his house. (Now Obadiah feared the LORD greatly:

4 For it was so, when Jezebel cut off the prophets of the LORD, that Obadiah took an hundred prophets, and hid them by fifty in a cave, and fed them with bread and water.)

5 And Ahab said unto Obadiah, Go into the land, unto all fountains of water, and unto all brooks: peradventure we may find grass to save the horses and mules alive, that we lose not all the beasts.

6 So they divided the land between them to pass throughout it: Ahab went one way by himself, and Obadiah went another way by himself.

7 ¶ And as Obadiah was in the way, behold, Elijah met him: and he knew him, and fell on his face, and said, Art thou that my lord Elijah?

8 And he answered him, I am: go, tell thy lord, Behold, Elijah is here.

9 And he said, What have I sinned, that thou wouldest deliver thy servant into the hand of Ahab, to slay me?

10 As the LORD thy God liveth, there is no nation or kingdom, whither my lord hath not sent to seek thee: and when they said, He is not there; he took an oath of the kingdom and nation, that they found thee not.

11 And now thou sayest, Go, tell thy lord, Behold, Elijah is here.

12 And it shall come to pass, as soon as I am gone from thee, that the Spirit of the LORD shall carry thee whither I know not; and so when I come and tell Ahab, and he cannot find thee, he shall slay me: but I thy servant fear the LORD from my youth.

13 Was it not told my lord what I did when Jezebel slew the prophets of the LORD, how I hid an hundred men of the LORD's prophets by fifty in a cave, and fed them with bread and water?

14 And now thou sayest, Go, tell thy lord, Behold, Elijah is here: and he shall slay me.

15 And Elijah said, As the LORD of hosts liveth, before whom I stand, I will surely shew myself unto him to day.

16 So Obadiah went to meet Ahab, and told him: and Ahab went to meet Elijah.

17 ¶ And it came to pass, when Ahab saw Elijah, that Ahab said unto him, Art thou he that troubleth Israel?

18 And he answered, I have not troubled Israel; but thou, and thy father's house, in that ye have forsaken the commandments of the LORD, and thou hast followed Baalim.

19 Now therefore send, and gather to me all Israel unto mount Carmel, and the prophets of Baal four hundred and fifty, and the prophets of the groves four hundred, which eat at Jezebel's table.

20 So Ahab sent unto all the children of Israel, and gathered the prophets together unto mount Carmel.

21 And Elijah came unto all the people, and said, How long halt ye between two opinions? if the LORD be God, follow him: but if Baal, then follow him. And the people answered him not a word.

The glorious ministry of the prophet Elijah provides an illustration of many themes and doctrines of the gospel of salvation, in particular the triumph of divine power over idolatry, the humility of the fast, and the orderly succession of priesthood leadership.

1 KINGS CHAPTER 18

1 Kings 18:17–18—The Work of the Lord is Sustained By Miracles

When we come to our tasks with a prayerful and humble heart in the service of God, then miracles—both seen and unseen—sustain our efforts, just as they did the work of Elijah.

Elijah the prophet, on the Lord's errand, seals up the heavens in response to the pervasive wickedness of the leadership of Israel (Ahab has the distinction of being the most wicked of all the kings in a long line of succession; see 1 Kings 16:33). Elijah is sustained miraculously by ravens, and later by the widow whom the Lord has called into service. The meal and oil are multiplied. The son is restored to life. Elijah, who is ever unquestioning in his obedience, is able to prepare the way for the Lord's intervention in the idolatrous culture. And thus we see that the hand of the Lord is upon the earth, and His miraculous power is displayed. We can call down this power according to His will as we exercise our faith.

1 Kings 18:39—The Power of God/The Impotence of Baal

No power of darkness, no force of iniquity, no influence of worldly honor or prestige can stand in the way of the Lord's agenda to bring about the building up of His Kingdom and to establish Zion.

Elijah, moved by the Spirit of the Lord, persuaded Ahab's governor Obadiah (who has secretly rescued one hundred of the righteous prophets from the hand of King Ahab and Queen Jezebel) to set up an audience with the king. Elijah ordered the king to assemble the prophets of Baal, and challenged them to a contest in which the Lord displayed His power miraculously. Elijah then eliminated the prophets of Baal to cleanse the land of their iniquitous influence, and caused the Lord to bring rain once again to the people.

The power of God can and will be manifest among the children of man today according to their faith and the will of God.

1 Kings 18:40–46—Baal

Baal (pronounced "bayl" or "bah-al" [plural Baalim]; meaning: lord, possessor) was the supreme male god in the Phoenician pagan culture (see 1 Kings 16:31). The female counterpart was Ashtoreth (plural Ashtaroth). From the summit of Sinai, the Lord forbade all such forms of idolatry (see Ex. 20:3–5).

The most celebrated confrontation between the forces of covenant righteousness and the benighted forces of Baal took place during the tenure of the prophet Elijah. Jezebel,

22 Then said Elijah unto the people, I, even I only, remain a prophet of the LORD; but Baal's prophets are four hundred and fifty men.

23 Let them therefore give us two bullocks; and let them choose one bullock for themselves, and cut it in pieces, and lay it on wood, and put no fire under: and I will dress the other bullock, and lay it on wood, and put no fire under:

24 And call ye on the name of your gods, and I will call on the name of the LORD: and the God that answereth by fire, let him be God. And all the people answered and said, It is well spoken.

25 And Elijah said unto the prophets of Baal, Choose you one bullock for yourselves, and dress it first; for ye are many; and call on the name of your gods, but put no fire under.

26 And they took the bullock which was given them, and they dressed it, and called on the name of Baal from morning even until noon, saying, O Baal, hear us. But there was no voice, nor any that answered. And they leaped upon the altar which was made.

27 And it came to pass at noon, that Elijah mocked them, and said, Cry aloud: for he is a god; either he is talking, or he is pursuing, or he is in a journey, or peradventure he sleepeth, and must be awaked.

28 And they cried aloud, and cut themselves after their manner with knives and lancets, till the blood gushed out upon them.

29 And it came to pass, when midday was past, and they prophesied until the time of the offering of the evening sacrifice, that there was neither voice, nor any to answer, nor any that regarded.

30 And Elijah said unto all the people, Come near unto me. And all the people came near unto him. And he repaired the altar of the LORD that was broken down.

31 And Elijah took twelve stones, according to the number of the tribes of the sons of Jacob, unto whom the word of the LORD came, saying, Israel shall be thy name:

32 And with the stones he built an altar in the name of the LORD: and he made a trench about the altar, as great as would contain two measures of seed.

33 And he put the wood in order, and cut the bullock in pieces, and laid him on the wood, and said, Fill four barrels with water, and pour it on the burnt sacrifice, and on the wood.

34 And he said, Do it the second time. And they did it the second time. And he said, Do it the third time. And they did it the third time.

35 And the water ran round about the altar; and he filled the trench also with water.

36 And it came to pass at the time of the offering of the evening sacrifice, that Elijah the prophet came near, and said, LORD God of Abraham, Isaac, and of Israel, let it be known this day that thou art God in Israel, and that I am thy servant, and that I have done all these things at thy word.

37 Hear me, O LORD, hear me, that this people may know that thou art the LORD God, and that thou hast turned their heart back again.

38 Then the fire of the LORD fell, and consumed the burnt sacrifice, and the wood, and the stones, and the dust, and licked up the water that was in the trench.

39 And when all the people saw it, they fell on their faces: and they said, The LORD, he is the God; the LORD, he is the God.

40 And Elijah said unto them, Take the prophets of Baal; let not one of them escape. And they took them: and Elijah brought them down to the brook Kishon, and slew them there.

wife of Ahab, king of Israel, had introduced Baal worship—with all of its immoral and licentious practices—among the people of northern Israel (see 1 Kings 16:30–31). During the days of famine in the land, Elijah challenged Ahab and his priests to an ultimate test for identifying the true God—whether they could invoke their god to intervene and ignite the sacrificial offering upon the altar of Baal, or whether the Lord of heaven should show forth His power upon the altar to be set up by Elijah. The result is a scriptural event of unforgettable drama (see 1 Kings 18:26–29.) Elijah set in order the altar of the Lord, prepared the sacrificial offering, and caused the structure to be soaked with water three times in preparation for the demonstration before the "the prophets of Baal four hundred and fifty, and the prophets of the groves four hundred, which eat at Jezebel's table" (1 Kings 18:19). As we know, the Lord consumed not only the offerings, but the very altars, and Elijah slew the priests of Baal (see 1 Kings 18:36–40.)

In the various manifestations of Baal worship among different cultures over the generations, the name went through an evolutionary transition, showing up in multiple combinations such as *Baal-peor* ("lord of the opening"), *Baal-berith* ("lord of the covenant"), and the more familiar *Baal-zebub* ("lord of the flies").

The study of Baalism and its sinister effects among the peoples of the Old Testament is a fascinating exploration of the cosmic conflict between good and evil, the eternal battle between false worship and true worship. "Thou shalt have no other gods before me," proclaimed the Lord (Ex. 20:3)—but humans are all too reluctant to obey. The conflict still rages today. Though modern "gods" do not carry the name of Baal or any of its linguistic variations, there are nevertheless countless human obsessions in our time that, in the absence of a balanced and dignified pattern of righteous living, cause people to turn from the true God and place their confidence in influences and philosophies that are powerless to yield the blessings of eternity. It is only the gospel of Jesus Christ than can supplant such misguided patterns of life and provide the spiritual power essential for salvation and exaltation.

1 Kings 18—Elijah: The Triumph of Divine Power Over Idolatry

Just as Elijah purged the land of the idolatrous influence of the priests of Baal, we, too, can purge our own lives of unrighteous influences and desires. We can call down the powers of heaven to cleanse and purify our families and ensure that we are building up an environment where the Spirit of the Lord can be made manifest in miraculous ways.

We are nothing without God in our lives. Our lives are informed and shaped by His matchless power—demonstrated in all things as He sees fit: through His beloved Son, through the Holy Ghost, through angels, through His prophets, or through worthy sons and daughters on His errand. It is our Heavenly Father who lifts us and guides us toward higher levels of spirituality day-by-day, ever caring for His children. We can be worthy of His tender mercies

41 ¶ And Elijah said unto Ahab, Get thee up, eat and drink; for there is a sound of abundance of rain.

42 So Ahab went up to eat and to drink. And Elijah went up to the top of Carmel; and he cast himself down upon the earth, and put his face between his knees,

43 And said to his servant, Go up now, look toward the sea. And he went up, and looked, and said, There is nothing. And he said, Go again seven times.

44 And it came to pass at the seventh time, that he said, Behold, there ariseth a little cloud out of the sea, like a man's hand. And he said, Go up, say unto Ahab, Prepare thy chariot, and get thee down, that the rain stop thee not.

45 And it came to pass in the mean while, that the heaven was black with clouds and wind, and there was a great rain. And Ahab rode, and went to Jezreel.

46 And the hand of the LORD was on Elijah; and he girded up his loins, and ran before Ahab to the entrance of Jezreel.

CHAPTER 19

1 AND Ahab told Jezebel all that Elijah had done, and withal how he had slain all the prophets with the sword.

2 Then Jezebel sent a messenger unto Elijah, saying, So let the gods do to me, and more also, if I make not thy life as the life of one of them by to morrow about this time.

3 And when he saw that, he arose, and went for his life, and came to Beer-sheba, which belongeth to Judah, and left his servant there.

4 ¶ But he himself went a day's journey into the wilderness, and came and sat down under a juniper tree: and he requested for himself that he might die; and said, It is enough; now, O LORD, take away my life; for I am not better than my fathers.

5 And as he lay and slept under a juniper tree, behold, then an angel touched him, and said unto him, Arise and eat.

6 And he looked, and, behold, there was a cake baken on the coals, and a cruse of water at his head. And he did eat and drink, and laid him down again.

7 And the angel of the LORD came again the second time, and touched him, and said, Arise and eat; because the journey is too great for thee.

8 And he arose, and did eat and drink, and went in the strength of that meat forty days and forty nights unto Horeb the mount of God.

9 ¶ And he came thither unto a cave, and lodged there; and, behold, the word of the LORD came to him, and he said unto him, What doest thou here, Elijah?

10 And he said, I have been very jealous for the LORD God of hosts: for the children of Israel have forsaken thy covenant, thrown down thine altars, and slain thy prophets with the sword; and I, even I only, am left; and they seek my life, to take it away.

11 And he said, Go forth, and stand upon the mount before the LORD. And, behold, the LORD passed by, and a great and strong wind rent the mountains, and brake in pieces the rocks before the LORD; but the LORD was not in the wind: and after the wind an earthquake; but the LORD was not in the earthquake:

12 And after the earthquake a fire; but the LORD was not in the fire: and after the fire a still small voice.

and thus blessed in all things by His goodness and power in order to return to His presence.

1 KINGS CHAPTER 19

"The spirit of Elias is first, Elijah second, and Messiah last. Elias is a forerunner to prepare the way, and the spirit and power of Elijah is to come after, holding the keys of power, building the temple to the capstone, placing the seals of the Melchizedek Priesthood upon the House of Israel, and making all things ready; then Messiah comes to His Temple, which is last of all" —Joseph Smith, *DHC* 6:254

1 Kings 19:9–18—The Humility of the Fast

After Elijah called down fire to consume the idolatrous priests of Baal (see 1 Kings 18), he went into hiding to avoid the treacherous hand of queen Jezebel. He was sustained by an angel, fasted for forty days and forty nights, and then went to Mount Horeb to speak with and receive instruction from the Lord (see 1 Kings 19:9–18.)

Elijah's humble way of approaching the Lord through fasting and prayer is exemplary for our own pattern of living. Fasting is never complete without prayer, hence the phrase "fasting and prayer" is commonly used in relation to this principle. We are counseled always to align our fast with a spiritual purpose: to improve ourselves in righteousness, to seek a worthy blessing, to express our love and gratitude, to serve our God and our fellowman.

Great blessings flow from God to the faithful who sincerely practice a prayerful fast, whether it be strengthening, healing, or an increase of understanding. The blessings of the Spirit and the power to teach by that same Spirit come through fasting and prayer (see Alma 17:3, 9). We are to act with faith and bring an offering of sincere fasting and prayer in order to have a more contrite disposition in accordance with heavenly principles.

The Lord in His almighty power stands waiting to bless mankind. It is His agenda that governs the flow of life upon the earth. Through fasting and prayer we can learn of His will and see His hand at work as He manifests Himself and blesses His children. We can literally call down the power of Heaven through fasting and prayer. Within our own families we can testify of the blessings that we have received through fasting and prayer. Like Elijah, we can demonstrate our humility and devotion before the Lord through fasting and prayer, and thus prepare ourselves to receive the inspiration of the Spirit to ensure our safety and spiritual welfare, and that of our families.

13 And it was so, when Elijah heard it, that he wrapped his face in his mantle, and went out, and stood in the entering in of the cave. And, behold, there came a voice unto him, and said, What doest thou here, Elijah?

14 And he said, I have been very jealous for the LORD God of hosts: because the children of Israel have forsaken thy covenant, thrown down thine altars, and slain thy prophets with the sword; and I, even I only, am left; and they seek my life, to take it away.

15 And the LORD said unto him, Go, return on thy way to the wilderness of Damascus: and when thou comest, anoint Hazael to be king over Syria:

16 And Jehu the son of Nimshi shalt thou anoint to be king over Israel: and Elisha the son of Shaphat of Abel-meholah shalt thou anoint to be prophet in thy room.

17 And it shall come to pass, that him that escapeth the sword of Hazael shall Jehu slay: and him that escapeth from the sword of Jehu shall Elisha slay.

18 Yet I have left me seven thousand in Israel, all the knees which have not bowed unto Baal, and every mouth which hath not kissed him.

19 ¶ So he departed thence, and found Elisha the son of Shaphat, who was plowing with twelve yoke of oxen before him, and he with the twelfth: and Elijah passed by him, and cast his mantle upon him.

20 And he left the oxen, and ran after Elijah, and said, Let me, I pray thee, kiss my father and my mother, and then I will follow thee. And he said unto him, Go back again: for what have I done to thee?

21 And he returned back from him, and took a yoke of oxen, and slew them, and boiled their flesh with the instruments of the oxen, and gave unto the people, and they did eat. Then he arose, and went after Elijah, and ministered unto him.

1 Kings 19:15—Hazael

Hazael (pronounced "hay'-zay-uhl" or "huh-zay'-uhl") was king of Syria during the tenures of the prophets Elijah and Elisha (see especially 1 Kings 19; 2 Kings 8–10, 12–13; 2 Chron. 22). During the days of wicked king Ahab, the Lord commanded Elijah to anoint Hazael king of Syria, Jehu king of Israel, and Elisha as prophet (see 1 Kings 19:15–16) in preparation for the judgments of heaven to descend upon the Israelites for their fixation on Baal. Sometime later, Benhadad, king of Syria became ill, so the king sent Hazael, at that time a royal official, to meet Elisha in Damascus and have him inquire of the Lord concerning the illness (see 2 Kings 8:15).

Soon thereafter, Hazael came to battle against Israel and Judah at Ramoth-gilead (see 2 Kings 8:28–29; 9:14–15; 2 Chron. 22:5–6) and later continued the fulfillment of Elisha's prophecy (see 2 Kings 10:32). At one point, Jehoash (or Joash, in shortened format), king of Judah, paid tribute to Hazael to dissuade him from attacking Jerusalem (see 2 Kings 12:18). When the Israelites continued their wayward behavior, the Lord again invoked Hazael as a scourge (see 2 Kings 13:3). After the death of Hazael and the ascension of his son Benhadad, the Lord had compassion on His people and allowed them to recover their lost cities (see 2 Kings 13:23–25).

Hazael is a prime example of the non-Israelite king whom the Lord caused to rise up as a scourge against wickedness among the covenant people—the same role played by the Lamanites in the Book of Mormon (see 2 Ne. 5:25; compare 1 Ne. 2:24; 3 Ne. 20:28).

1 Kings 19:18–19—The Lord Is in Charge of His Program for Mankind

The Lord in His almighty power stands waiting to bless mankind. It is His agenda that governs the flow of life upon the earth. Through fasting and prayer we can learn of His agenda and see His hand at work as He manifests Himself and blesses His children. We can literally call down the power of Heaven through fasting and prayer.

1 Kings 19:20—Elisha

Elisha (meaning: God shall save, or God of Salvation) was the companion and student of Elijah for several years and ultimately his successor as prophet in the northern kingdom of Israel. His calling came by divine command unto Elijah concerning future positions of secular and spiritual leadership (see 1 Kings 19:16, 19, 21).

THE
SECOND BOOK OF THE KINGS

COMMONLY CALLED
THE FOURTH BOOK OF THE KINGS

CHAPTER 2

1 AND it came to pass, when the LORD would take up Elijah into heaven by a whirlwind, that Elijah went with Elisha from Gilgal.

2 And Elijah said unto Elisha, Tarry here, I pray thee; for the LORD hath sent me to Beth-el. And Elisha said unto him, As the LORD liveth, and as thy soul liveth, I will not leave thee. So they went down to Beth-el.

3 And the sons of the prophets that were at Beth-el came forth to Elisha, and said unto him, Knowest thou that the LORD will take away thy master from thy head to day? And he said, Yea, I know it; hold ye your peace.

4 And Elijah said unto him, Elisha, tarry here, I pray thee; for the LORD hath sent me to Jericho. And he said, As the LORD liveth, and as thy soul liveth, I will not leave thee. So they came to Jericho.

5 And the sons of the prophets that were at Jericho came to Elisha, and said unto him, Knowest thou that the LORD will take away thy master from thy head to day? And he answered, Yea, I know it; hold ye your peace.

6 And Elijah said unto him, Tarry, I pray thee, here; for the LORD hath sent me to Jordan. And he said, As the LORD liveth, and as thy soul liveth, I will not leave thee. And they two went on.

7 And fifty men of the sons of the prophets went, and stood to view afar off: and they two stood by Jordan.

8 And Elijah took his mantle, and wrapped it together, and smote the waters, and they were divided hither and thither, so that they two went over on dry ground.

9 ¶ And it came to pass, when they were gone over, that Elijah said unto Elisha, Ask what I shall do for thee, before I be taken away from thee. And Elisha said, I pray thee, let a double portion of thy spirit be upon me.

, Thou hast asked a hard thing: nevertheless, if thou see me when I am taken from thee, it shall be so unto thee; but if not, it shall not be so.

11 And it came to pass, as they still went on, and talked, that, behold, there appeared a chariot of fire, and horses of fire, and parted them both asunder; and Elijah went up by a whirlwind into heaven.

12 ¶ And Elisha saw it, and he cried, My father, my father, the chariot of Israel, and the horsemen thereof. And he saw him no more: and he took hold of his own clothes, and rent them in two pieces.

13 He took up also the mantle of Elijah that fell from him, and went back, and stood by the bank of Jordan;

14 And he took the mantle of Elijah that fell from him, and smote the waters, and said, Where is the LORD God of Elijah? and when

2 KINGS CHAPTER 2

2 Kings 2—Preview of the Lessons We Learn from the Life of Elisha

The ability to engage in spiritual enterprises and view the hand of God at work in the affairs of mankind is reserved for those with an inner vision opened through faith and devotion. The passages of scripture recounting the transition of prophetic authority from Elijah to Elisha identify four of the many qualities that attend to spiritual vision: (1) **spiritual desire**: At Elijah's bidding, Elisha reveals the desire of his heart in anticipation of receiving the awesome mantle of authority (see 2 Kings 2:9). Along with this fundamental desire of righteousness is the need to practice (2) **humility**, something that the Syrian Naaman needed to internalize before he could be healed of his leprosy by completing the most simple of tasks. In addition, the spiritual person needs to abjure any thought for material gain through service, and instead cultivate a motivation grounded solely in (3) **selflessness and love**. Finally, being able to discern the hand of God at work in our lives (as one of Elisha's servants was able to do) is fundamentally a blessing from God, who alone can open up our inner eye to view the "chariots of fire" that surround and guard the faithful. One must be (4) **open to this gift of God** and receive it in thankfulness.

For more insights on the life of Elisha, see Appendix Z.

2 Kings 2:1–9—The Orderly Succession of Priesthood Leadership

When it came time for Elijah the prophet to complete his ministry, provision was made for a transition of assignment to his student Elisha. Elijah asks what gift might be bestowed upon the successor, and Elisha requests that "double portion of thy spirit be upon me" (2 Kings 2:9). This transpires as Elijah is taken up by a chariot of fire (see 2 Kings 2:11–13.)

Thereafter, with the mantle of divine authority upon him, Elisha performs mighty miracles just as his predecessor had done. The Lord, according to His will, provides prophets for His people. Well spoke Amos when he said: "Surely the Lord GOD will do nothing, but he revealeth his secret unto his servants the prophets" (Amos 3:7).

We are well advised to follow the counsel of the Lord's prophets day-by-day by reading the scriptures faithfully and prayerfully, listening to the words of the living prophets as given through General Conference and channeled through our local priesthood leaders, and taking the opportunity to raise our hands in sustaining God's servants who are placed in positions of authority.

For the last time in human history, the Lord has empowered prophets to guide His work to completion. The succession of such leaders in the last dispensation, from Joseph Smith to the present time, will continue uninterrupted until the stone, cut from the mountain without hands as Daniel foresaw (see Dan. 2), will roll forth until it fill the whole earth with the glory and truth of the restored gospel of Jesus Christ (see D&C 65:2).

he also had smitten the waters, they parted hither and thither: and Elisha went over.

15 And when the sons of the prophets which were to view at Jericho saw him, they said, The spirit of Elijah doth rest on Elisha. And they came to meet him, and bowed themselves to the ground before him.

16 ¶ And they said unto him, Behold now, there be with thy servants fifty strong men; let them go, we pray thee, and seek thy master: lest peradventure the Spirit of the LORD hath taken him up, and cast him upon some mountain, or into some valley. And he said, Ye shall not send.

17 And when they urged him till he was ashamed, he said, Send. They sent therefore fifty men; and they sought three days, but found him not.

18 And when they came again to him, (for he tarried at Jericho,) he said unto them, Did I not say unto you, Go not?

19 ¶ And the men of the city said unto Elisha, Behold, I pray thee, the situation of this city is pleasant, as my lord seeth: but the water is naught, and the ground barren.

20 And he said, Bring me a new cruse, and put salt therein. And they brought it to him.

21 And he went forth unto the spring of the waters, and cast the salt in there, and said, Thus saith the LORD, I have healed these waters; there shall not be from thence any more death or barren land.

22 So the waters were healed unto this day, according to the saying of Elisha which he spake.

23 ¶ And he went up from thence unto Beth-el: and as he was going up by the way, there came forth little children out of the city, and mocked him, and said unto him, Go up, thou bald head; go up, thou bald head.

24 And he turned back, and looked on them, and cursed them in the name of the LORD. And there came forth two she bears out of the wood, and tare forty and two children of them.

25 And he went from thence to mount Carmel, and from thence he returned to Samaria.

CHAPTER 5

1 NOW Naaman, captain of the host of the king of Syria, was a great man with his master, and honourable, because by him the LORD had given deliverance unto Syria: he was also a mighty man in valour, but he was a leper.

2 And the Syrians had gone out by companies, and had brought away captive out of the land of Israel a little maid; and she waited on Naaman's wife.

3 And she said unto her mistress, Would God my lord were with the prophet that is in Samaria! for he would recover him of his leprosy.

4 And one went in, and told his lord, saying, Thus and thus said the maid that is of the land of Israel.

5 And the king of Syria said, Go to, go, and I will send a letter unto the king of Israel. And he departed, and took with him ten talents of silver, and six thousand pieces of gold, and ten changes of raiment.

6 And he brought the letter to the king of Israel, saying, Now when this letter is come unto thee, behold, I have therewith sent Naaman my servant to thee, that thou mayest recover him of his leprosy.

2 Kings 2:15—Mantle of the Prophet: Transition in Church Leadership

The Lord oversees the continuity of leadership in His kingdom. Just as the prophetic office passed smoothly from the translated Elijah to the younger man Elisha, so in our day there is a righteous transition of authority and leadership without worldly campaigning, dispute, or competition.

When it came time for Elijah the prophet to be translated, provision was made for a transition of assignment to his student Elisha. Similarly, the "mantle" of authority passes from one prophet to another today under the direction of the Lord, and our duty is to pray for and sustain our living prophet today.

2 KINGS CHAPTER 5

2 Kings 5:1–3—Naaman

Naaman (meaning: pleasantness) was a nobleman in the royal court of Syria who suffered from leprosy (see 2 Kings 5:1) and who subsequetly sought a blessing from Elisha.

And Elisha sent a messenger unto him, saying, Go and wash in Jordan seven times, and thy flesh shall come again to thee, and thou shalt be clean.

But Naaman was wroth, and went away, and said, Behold, I thought, He will surely come out to me, and stand, and call on the name of the LORD his God, and strike his hand over the place, and recover the leper.

Are not Abana and Pharpar, rivers of Damascus, better than all the waters of Israel? may I not wash in them, and be clean? So he turned and went away in a rage.

And his servants came near, and spake unto him, and said, My father, *if* the prophet had bid thee *do some* great thing, wouldest thou not have done *it*? how much rather then, when he saith to thee, Wash, and be clean?

Then went he down, and dipped himself seven times in Jordan, according to the saying of the man of God: and his flesh came again like unto the flesh of a little child, and he was clean. (2 Kings 5:10–14)

Returning whole to the house of Elisha, Naaman declared: "Behold, now I know that *there is* no God in all the earth, but in Israel: now therefore, I pray thee, take a blessing of thy servant" (2 Kings 5:15). But Elisha refused compensation for his services, and Naaman departed in peace.

For more insights on Naaman, see Appendix AA.

7 And it came to pass, when the king of Israel had read the letter, that he rent his clothes, and said, Am I God, to kill and to make alive, that this man doth send unto me to recover a man of his leprosy? wherefore consider, I pray you, and see how he seeketh a quarrel against me.

8 ¶ And it was so, when Elisha the man of God had heard that the king of Israel had rent his clothes, that he sent to the king, saying, Wherefore hast thou rent thy clothes? let him come now to me, and he shall know that there is a prophet in Israel.

9 So Naaman came with his horses and with his chariot, and stood at the door of the house of Elisha.

10 And Elisha sent a messenger unto him, saying, Go and wash in Jordan seven times, and thy flesh shall come again to thee, and thou shalt be clean.

11 But Naaman was wroth, and went away, and said, Behold, I thought, He will surely come out to me, and stand, and call on the name of the LORD his God, and strike his hand over the place, and recover the leper.

12 Are not Abana and Pharpar, rivers of Damascus, better than all the waters of Israel? may I not wash in them, and be clean? So he turned and went away in a rage.

13 And his servants came near, and spake unto him, and said, My father, if the prophet had bid thee do some great thing, wouldest thou not have done it? how much rather then, when he saith to thee, Wash, and be clean?

14 Then went he down, and dipped himself seven times in Jordan, according to the saying of the man of God: and his flesh came again like unto the flesh of a little child, and he was clean.

15 ¶ And he returned to the man of God, he and all his company, and came, and stood before him: and he said, Behold, now I know that there is no God in all the earth, but in Israel: now therefore, I pray thee, take a blessing of thy servant.

16 But he said, As the LORD liveth, before whom I stand, I will receive none. And he urged him to take it; but he refused.

17 And Naaman said, Shall there not then, I pray thee, be given to thy servant two mules' burden of earth? for thy servant will henceforth offer neither burnt offering nor sacrifice unto other gods, but unto the LORD.

18 In this thing the LORD pardon thy servant, that when my master goeth into the house of Rimmon to worship there, and he leaneth on my hand, and I bow myself in the house of Rimmon: when I bow down myself in the house of Rimmon, the LORD pardon thy servant in this thing.

19 And he said unto him, Go in peace. So he departed from him a little way.

20 ¶ But Gehazi, the servant of Elisha the man of God, said, Behold, my master hath spared Naaman this Syrian, in not receiving at his hands that which he brought: but, as the LORD liveth, I will run after him, and take somewhat of him.

21 So Gehazi followed after Naaman. And when Naaman saw him running after him, he lighted down from the chariot to meet him, and said, Is all well?

22 And he said, All is well. My master hath sent me, saying, Behold, even now there be come to me from mount Ephraim two young men of the sons of the prophets: give them, I pray thee, a talent of silver, and two changes of garments.

23 And Naaman said, Be content, take two talents. And he urged him, and bound two talents of silver in two bags, with two changes

2 Kings 5:14—Great Blessings from Simple Acts of Obedience

We can learn, with Naaman the Syrian, that simple acts of obedience in response to inspired counsel can lead to great benefits. The gospel is a system of simple truths and principles leading to ultimate outcomes concerning immortality and eternal life.

When Naaman learned, through a young Israelite girl taken into domestic service in Syria, that the Lord's prophet could heal him of his leprosy, he sought relief. But when Elisha told him to bathe seven times in the Jordan—a simple and non-elegant solution to his problem—Naaman was angry. Only through the wise counsel of his servant did Naaman think the better of his impetuousness, and his obedience resulted in the desired cure. This event is rightly regarded as one of the most interesting examples of "spiritual leverage" in the scriptures. Through it we see that the law of obedience even in the smallest and most seemingly insignificant acts can reap great blessings or severe consequences. Life is made up of hundreds of daily choices. We can choose to be obedient in all things.

2 Kings 5:15–16, 26—Selfless Service Is the Pattern in the Kingdom of God

Unlike Elisha's servant, Gehazi, we can learn to avoid attaching material interests to spiritual service. The wages of obedience are harmony, peace, and spiritual wealth. We serve out of love, not self-interest.

When the thankful Naaman wanted to give Elisha material rewards for the successful cure, Elisha refused any gratuity. But Gehazi, Elisha's servant, was not above the allure of material wealth, and arranged to have some of Naaman's goods given into his hands. When Elisha learned of this folly, he arranged to give to Gehazi something he had not anticipated receiving: Naaman's former leprous condition. The story thus becomes an emblem for teaching that service rendered in the name of God has spiritual rewards associated with it. When the motivation is for material gain, then the service loses its spiritual character.

Motive makes the difference as to acceptance of your life here upon the earth. The intent of your heart becomes the barometer of righteousness. Mormon describes it well: "For behold, God hath said a man being evil cannot do that which is good; for if he offereth a gift, or prayeth unto God, except he shall do it with real intent it profiteth him nothing. For behold, it is not counted unto him for righteousness. For behold, if a man being evil giveth a gift, he doeth it grudgingly; wherefore it is counted unto him the same as if he had retained the gift; wherefore he is counted evil before God. And likewise also is it counted evil unto a man, if he shall pray and not with real intent of heart; yea, and it profiteth him nothing, for God receiveth none such" (Moroni 7:6–9).

2 Kings 5:27—Gehazi

Gehazi (pronounced "gih-hay'-zy"; meaning: valley of vision) was the servant of the prophet Elisha at the time Naaman the Syrian sought the prophet's healing blessing

of garments, and laid them upon two of his servants; and they bare them before him.

24 And when he came to the tower, he took them from their hand, and bestowed them in the house: and he let the men go, and they departed.

25 But he went in, and stood before his master. And Elisha said unto him, Whence comest thou, Gehazi? And he said, Thy servant went no whither.

26 And he said unto him, Went not mine heart with thee, when the man turned again from his chariot to meet thee? Is it a time to receive money, and to receive garments, and oliveyards, and vineyards, and sheep, and oxen, and menservants, and maidservants?

27 The leprosy therefore of Naaman shall cleave unto thee, and unto thy seed for ever. And he went out from his presence a leper as white as snow.

CHAPTER 6

1 AND the sons of the prophets said unto Elisha, Behold now, the place where we dwell with thee is too strait for us.

2 Let us go, we pray thee, unto Jordan, and take thence every man a beam, and let us make us a place there, where we may dwell. And he answered, Go ye.

3 And one said, Be content, I pray thee, and go with thy servants. And he answered, I will go.

4 So he went with them. And when they came to Jordan, they cut down wood.

5 But as one was felling a beam, the axe head fell into the water: and he cried, and said, Alas, master! for it was borrowed.

6 And the man of God said, Where fell it? And he shewed him the place. And he cut down a stick, and cast it in thither; and the iron did swim.

7 Therefore said he, Take it up to thee. And he put out his hand, and took it.

8 ¶ Then the king of Syria warred against Israel, and took counsel with his servants, saying, In such and such a place shall be my camp.

9 And the man of God sent unto the king of Israel, saying, Beware that thou pass not such a place; for thither the Syrians are come down.

10 And the king of Israel sent to the place which the man of God told him and warned him of, and saved himself there, not once nor twice.

11 Therefore the heart of the king of Syria was sore troubled for this thing; and he called his servants, and said unto them, Will ye not shew me which of us is for the king of Israel?

12 And one of his servants said, None, my lord, O king: but Elisha, the prophet that is in Israel, telleth the king of Israel the words that thou speakest in thy bedchamber.

13 ¶ And he said, Go and spy where he is, that I may send and fetch him. And it was told him, saying, Behold, he is in Dothan.

14 Therefore sent he thither horses, and chariots, and a great host: and they came by night, and compassed the city about.

15 And when the servant of the man of God was risen early, and gone forth, behold, an host compassed the city both with horses and chariots. And his servant said unto him, Alas, my master! how shall we do?

for his leprous condition. After Naaman had reluctantly consented to dip himself seven times in the Jordan River as instructed by Elisha, the leprosy was healed in miraculous fashion. Returning whole to the house of Elisha, Naaman attmpted to reward Elisha for his services, but Elisha refused compensation, and Naaman departed in peace. However, Gehazi, touched by a spirit of greediness and ignoring the wisdom of his master, followed after Naaman and took advantage of his generosity by accepting for himself gifts of silver and raiment. Upon learning this, Elisha pronounced a severe judgment upon Gehazi for his indiscretion: "The leprosy therefore of Naaman shall cleave unto thee, and unto thy seed for ever. And he went out from his presence a leper *as white* as snow" (2 Kings 5:27).

2 KINGS CHAPTER 6

"Holy men and holy women have had heavenly visions, by the hundreds and by the thousands, yea by the tens of thousands since this gospel was restored to the earth in our day." —Heber J. Grant, *Conference Reports*, 92

2 Kings 6:15–17—Vision of Faith

By learning to look with spiritual eyes, we can perceive the "chariots of fire" representing the Lord's systems of power and support put in place to bring about His divine purposes and defend the interests of His faithful servants.

Elisha gave wise counsel to the Israelite kings on how to conduct their war with Syria. Thus, the Syrians came seeking to destroy the prophet. When Elisha's servant viewed with fear the surrounding hordes of the enemy, Elisha prayed that the Lord might open the servant's eyes to see the amassed forces of heaven ("chariots of fire"—2 Kings 5:17) arrayed against the enemy. The servant beheld and was filled with hope and courage. At the same time, Elisha prayed that the Lord would take away the sight of the Syrians so that he could lead them away and render them powerless. Thus the Lord, once again, brought about victory for His people.

Through this we see that when our eyes are open we can see the true vision of life. This gives us hope, increases our faith in all degrees, and causes us to possess and demonstrate charity. Devoted teachers know that there is an underlying principle to place in the hearts of the students, and that is *hope*. Where hope is, there will be an attitude and desire to do good. When one is hopeless, sin lies at the door. Thus we must truly help everyone see things as they really are. It gives light and truth, and then we can become even as He.

16 And he answered, Fear not: for they that be with us are more than they that be with them.

17 And Elisha prayed, and said, LORD, I pray thee, open his eyes, that he may see. And the LORD opened the eyes of the young man; and he saw: and, behold, the mountain was full of horses and chariots of fire round about Elisha.

18 And when they came down to him, Elisha prayed unto the LORD, and said, Smite this people, I pray thee, with blindness. And he smote them with blindness according to the word of Elisha.

19 ¶ And Elisha said unto them, This is not the way, neither is this the city: follow me, and I will bring you to the man whom ye seek. But he led them to Samaria.

20 And it came to pass, when they were come into Samaria, that Elisha said, LORD, open the eyes of these men, that they may see. And the LORD opened their eyes, and they saw; and, behold, they were in the midst of Samaria.

21 And the king of Israel said unto Elisha, when he saw them, My father, shall I smite them? shall I smite them?

22 And he answered, Thou shalt not smite them: wouldest thou smite those whom thou hast taken captive with thy sword and with thy bow? set bread and water before them, that they may eat and drink, and go to their master.

23 And he prepared great provision for them: and when they had eaten and drunk, he sent them away, and they went to their master. So the bands of Syria came no more into the land of Israel.

24 ¶ And it came to pass after this, that Ben-hadad king of Syria gathered all his host, and went up, and besieged Samaria.

25 And there was a great famine in Samaria: and, behold, they besieged it, until an ass's head was sold for fourscore pieces of silver, and the fourth part of a cab of dove's dung for five pieces of silver.

26 And as the king of Israel was passing by upon the wall, there cried a woman unto him, saying, Help, my lord, O king.

27 And he said, If the LORD do not help thee, whence shall I help thee? out of the barnfloor, or out of the winepress?

28 And the king said unto her, What aileth thee? And she answered, This woman said unto me, Give thy son, that we may eat him to day, and we will eat my son to morrow.

29 So we boiled my son, and did eat him: and I said unto her on the next day, Give thy son, that we may eat him: and she hath hid her son.

30 ¶ And it came to pass, when the king heard the words of the woman, that he rent his clothes; and he passed by upon the wall, and the people looked, and, behold, he had sackcloth within upon his flesh.

31 Then he said, God do so and more also to me, if the head of Elisha the son of Shaphat shall stand on him this day.

32 But Elisha sat in his house, and the elders sat with him; and the king sent a man from before him: but ere the messenger came to him, he said to the elders, See ye how this son of a murderer hath sent to take away mine head? look, when the messenger cometh, shut the door, and hold him fast at the door: is not the sound of his master's feet behind him?

33 And while he yet talked with them, behold, the messenger came down unto him: and he said, Behold, this evil is of the LORD; what should I wait for the LORD any longer?

2 Kings 6:16–17—Sabaoth

Sabaoth (pronounced "sab'-ay-oth"; meaning: hosts) refers to the armies arrayed to sustain the cause of the Lord—whether on earth or in heaven. "Lord of Sabaoth," as a title for Jehovah, occurs six times in the scriptures (see Rom. 9:29; James 5:4; D&C 87:7; 88:2; 95:7; and 98:2). More common is the equivalent title "Lord of hosts," occurring 309 times throughout holy writ (including 245 times in the Old Testament). The expression "Lord God of hosts" is also frequently encountered (some 35 times).

In a special way, the spirit of the term *hosts* or *armies* also embraces the organization and service of the priesthood of God upon the earth (as in D&C 107:60), including the ongoing service performed by the faithful in the temples of God (as in D&C 127:4, 8–9). Satan, too, commands vast armies, armies that rise in conflict against the forces of light.

When Elisha and his companion were encompassed about in Dothan by the horses and chariots of the Syrian army—enemies against Israel who now sought to destroy the prophet—he spoke words of comfort and courage to his dismayed servant:

> . . . Fear not: for they that *be* with us *are* more than they that *be* with them.
>
> And Elisha prayed, and said, LORD, I pray thee, open his eyes, that he may see. And the LORD opened the eyes of the young man; and he saw: and, behold, the mountain *was* full of horses and chariots of fire round about Elisha.
>
> And when they came down to him, Elisha prayed unto the LORD, and said, Smite this people, I pray thee, with blindness. And he smote them with blindness according to the word of Elisha. (2 Kings 6:16–17)

Truly the armies under command of the Lord of Sabaoth combine with the forces of the kingdom of God on the earth to overcome the forces of evil that rage across the earth. Ultimately, Michael and his hosts will wage a consummate final battle to defeat the armies of Satan at the conclusion of the millennial period:

> And the devil shall gather together his armies; even the hosts of hell, and shall come up to battle against Michael and his armies.
>
> And then cometh the battle of the great God; and the devil and his armies shall be cast away into their own place, that they shall not have power over the saints any more at all.
>
> For Michael shall fight their battles, and shall overcome him who seeketh the throne of him who sitteth upon the throne, even the Lamb. (D&C 88:113–115)

THE SECOND BOOK OF THE CHRONICLES

CHAPTER 17

1 AND Jehoshaphat his son reigned in his stead, and strengthened himself against Israel.

2 And he placed forces in all the fenced cities of Judah, and set garrisons in the land of Judah, and in the cities of Ephraim, which Asa his father had taken.

3 And the LORD was with Jehoshaphat, because he walked in the first ways of his father David, and sought not unto Baalim;

4 But sought to the LORD God of his father, and walked in his commandments, and not after the doings of Israel.

5 Therefore the LORD stablished the kingdom in his hand; and all Judah brought to Jehoshaphat presents; and he had riches and honour in abundance.

6 And his heart was lifted up in the ways of the LORD: moreover he took away the high places and groves out of Judah.

7 ¶ Also in the third year of his reign he sent to his princes, even to Ben-hail, and to Obadiah, and to Zechariah, and to Nethaneel, and to Michaiah, to teach in the cities of Judah.

8 And with them he sent Levites, even Shemaiah, and Nethaniah, and Zebadiah, and Asahel, and Shemiramoth, and Jehonathan, and Adonijah, and Tobijah, and Tob-adonijah, Levites; and with them Elishama and Jehoram, priests.

9 And they taught in Judah, and had the book of the law of the LORD with them, and went about throughout all the cities of Judah, and taught the people.

10 ¶ And the fear of the LORD fell upon all the kingdoms of the lands that were round about Judah, so that they made no war against Jehoshaphat.

11 Also some of the Philistines brought Jehoshaphat presents, and tribute silver; and the Arabians brought him flocks, seven thousand and seven hundred rams, and seven thousand and seven hundred he goats.

12 ¶ And Jehoshaphat waxed great exceedingly; and he built in Judah castles, and cities of store.

13 And he had much business in the cities of Judah: and the men of war, mighty men of valour, were in Jerusalem.

14 And these are the numbers of them according to the house of their fathers: Of Judah, the captains of thousands; Adnah the chief, and with him mighty men of valour three hundred thousand.

15 And next to him was Jehohanan the captain, and with him two hundred and fourscore thousand.

16 And next him was Amasiah the son of Zichri, who willingly offered himself unto the LORD; and with him two hundred thousand mighty men of valour.

17 And of Benjamin; Eliada a mighty man of valour, and with him armed men with bow and shield two hundred thousand.

18 And next him was Jehozabad, and with him an hundred and fourscore thousand ready prepared for the war.

19 These waited on the king, beside those whom the king put in the fenced cities throughout all Judah.

2 CHRONICLES CHAPTER 17

2 Chronicles 17:1—Jehoshaphat

Jehoshaphat (meaning: Jehovah judged) was a king of Judah renowned as a reformer and righteous monarch (see 1 Kings 22:41–44; see also 1 Kings 15:24; 2 Kings 8:16.)

Among the memorable events in the life of Jehoshaphat are these:

His alliance with Jehoram, king of Israel, to defeat the Moabites (see 2 Kings 3).

His purging the land of all the vestiges of idolatry pursued by worshippers of Baal (see 2 Chron. 17:3–6).

His initiative to send representatives and priests to teach the people out of the law of the Lord (see 2 Chron. 17:9).

His comprehensive program to enhance the defensive strength of the nation (see 2 Chron. 17:10–19).

His ill-fated alliance with King Ahab of Israel to come against the Syrians, resulting in the death of Ahab (see 1 Kings 22; 2 Chron. 18).

His humble acceptance of the reproof given him by Jehu the prophet for consorting with wicked King Ahab (see 2 Chron. 19:1–9).

His humility and dependence upon the Lord when the Ammonites were about to attack (see 2 Chron. 20:3–6, 12).

A fitting epithet for Jehoshaphat is the remembrance that he "sought the Lord with all his heart" (2 Chron. 22:9).

2 Chronicles 17:8—Jehoram (or Joram)

Jehoram (meaning: Jehovah exalted) succeeded Jehoshaphat as king of Judah: "And Jehoshaphat slept with his fathers, and was buried with his fathers in the city of David his father: and Jehoram his son reigned in his stead" (1 Kings 22:50). As king of Judah, Jehoram reigned in wickedness for eight years, having embraced the idolatrous practices of Ahab, king of Israel, whose daughter (Athaliah) he had married (see 2 Kings 8:16–24). Jehoram's daughter, Jehosheba, was the wife of Jehoiada, high priest. Elijah prophesied that a plague would come upon the people and that Jehoram would perish—events that indeed transpired (see 2 Chron. 21). Jehoram was buried in Jerusalem, "but not in the sepulchre of the kings" (2 Chron. 21:20).

CHAPTER 20

1 IT came to pass after this also, that the children of Moab, and the children of Ammon, and with them other beside the Ammonites, came against Jehoshaphat to battle.

2 Then there came some that told Jehoshaphat, saying, There cometh a great multitude against thee from beyond the sea on this side Syria; and, behold, they be in Hazazon-tamar, which is En-gedi.

3 And Jehoshaphat feared, and set himself to seek the LORD, and proclaimed a fast throughout all Judah.

4 And Judah gathered themselves together, to ask help of the LORD: even out of all the cities of Judah they came to seek the LORD.

5 ¶ And Jehoshaphat stood in the congregation of Judah and Jerusalem, in the house of the LORD, before the new court,

6 And said, O LORD God of our fathers, art not thou God in heaven? and rulest not thou over all the kingdoms of the heathen? and in thine hand is there not power and might, so that none is able to withstand thee?

7 Art not thou our God, who didst drive out the inhabitants of this land before thy people Israel, and gavest it to the seed of Abraham thy friend for ever?

8 And they dwelt therein, and have built thee a sanctuary therein for thy name, saying,

9 If, when evil cometh upon us, as the sword, judgment, or pestilence, or famine, we stand before this house, and in thy presence, (for thy name is in this house,) and cry unto thee in our affliction, then thou wilt hear and help.

10 And now, behold, the children of Ammon and Moab and mount Seir, whom thou wouldest not let Israel invade, when they came out of the land of Egypt, but they turned from them, and destroyed them not;

11 Behold, I say, how they reward us, to come to cast us out of thy possession, which thou hast given us to inherit.

12 O our God, wilt thou not judge them? for we have no might against this great company that cometh against us; neither know we what to do: but our eyes are upon thee.

13 And all Judah stood before the LORD, with their little ones, their wives, and their children.

14 ¶ Then upon Jahaziel the son of Zechariah, the son of Benaiah, the son of Jeiel, the son of Mattaniah, a Levite of the sons of Asaph, came the Spirit of the LORD in the midst of the congregation;

15 And he said, Hearken ye, all Judah, and ye inhabitants of Jerusalem, and thou king Jehoshaphat, Thus saith the LORD unto you, Be not afraid nor dismayed by reason of this great multitude; for the battle is not yours, but God's.

16 To morrow go ye down against them: behold, they come up by the cliff of Ziz; and ye shall find them at the end of the brook, before the wilderness of Jeruel.

17 Ye shall not need to fight in this battle: set yourselves, stand ye still, and see the salvation of the LORD with you, O Judah and Jerusalem: fear not, nor be dismayed; to morrow go out against them: for the LORD will be with you.

2 CHRONICLES CHAPTER 20

2 Chronicles 20:7—Seed of Abraham

The expression "seed of Abraham," referring to the heirs of the promises and covenants made by the Lord unto the patriarch Abraham, occurs four times in the Old Testament:

In the prayer of Jehoshaphat, the righteous reform king of Judah, supplicating the Lord for deliverance from the Ammonites, Moabites, and other enemies (see 2 Chron. 20:7).

In the Psalmist's counsel to the people of the Lord (see Ps. 105:4–6).

In the words of blessing given by the Lord unto Israel through the mouth of the prophet Isaiah (see Isa. 41:8).

In the assurances of the Lord to his captive people through the voice of Jeremiah (see Jer. 33:25–26; in other words, just as surely as the Lord *is* Lord over the creation and the ordinances of heaven and earth, just as surely will he *not* forget Israel and her leadership, and *not* cause his people to remain scattered, but remember them in mercy).

2 Chronicles 20:15, 30—Covenant Leadership: The Consequences of Government Based on Divine Purpose

When the people of Israel were led by God-fearing leaders, they prospered and enjoyed the favor of the Lord. Leadership based on faith, service, accountability to the principles of righteousness, and a willingness to follow the scriptures and living prophets leads to harmony, unity, peace, and well-being.

The great-grandson of Rehoboam, Jehoshaphat, provides a marked contrast to the leadership style of his wicked predecessors. He eliminated idolatry in his nation (Judah), sent Levite teachers among the people to teach the principles of the gospel from the scriptures, sought the Lord's advice in defending the land, and united the people against their common enemies from without. As a result, the Lord was willing to fight their battles for them and preserve their independence.

To be a good leader requires many things. In the strength of the Lord He will inspire us. If we pay the price and do our part, we can do things even as He would do them.

18 And Jehoshaphat bowed his head with his face to the ground: and all Judah and the inhabitants of Jerusalem fell before the LORD, worshipping the LORD.

19 And the Levites, of the children of the Kohathites, and of the children of the Korhites, stood up to praise the LORD God of Israel with a loud voice on high.

20 ¶ And they rose early in the morning, and went forth into the wilderness of Tekoa: and as they went forth, Jehoshaphat stood and said, Hear me, O Judah, and ye inhabitants of Jerusalem; Believe in the LORD your God, so shall ye be established; believe his prophets, so shall ye prosper.

21 And when he had consulted with the people, he appointed singers unto the LORD, and that should praise the beauty of holiness, as they went out before the army, and to say, Praise the LORD; for his mercy endureth for ever.

22 ¶ And when they began to sing and to praise, the LORD set ambushments against the children of Ammon, Moab, and mount Seir, which were come against Judah; and they were smitten.

23 For the children of Ammon and Moab stood up against the inhabitants of mount Seir, utterly to slay and destroy them: and when they had made an end of the inhabitants of Seir, every one helped to destroy another.

24 And when Judah came toward the watch tower in the wilderness, they looked unto the multitude, and, behold, they were dead bodies fallen to the earth, and none escaped.

25 And when Jehoshaphat and his people came to take away the spoil of them, they found among them in abundance both riches with the dead bodies, and precious jewels, which they stripped off for themselves, more than they could carry away: and they were three days in gathering of the spoil, it was so much.

26 ¶ And on the fourth day they assembled themselves in the valley of Berachah; for there they blessed the LORD: therefore the name of the same place was called, The valley of Berachah, unto this day.

27 Then they returned, every man of Judah and Jerusalem, and Jehoshaphat in the forefront of them, to go again to Jerusalem with joy; for the LORD had made them to rejoice over their enemies.

28 And they came to Jerusalem with psalteries and harps and trumpets unto the house of the LORD.

29 And the fear of God was on all the kingdoms of those countries, when they had heard that the LORD fought against the enemies of Israel.

30 So the realm of Jehoshaphat was quiet: for his God gave him rest round about.

31 ¶ And Jehoshaphat reigned over Judah: he was thirty and five years old when he began to reign, and he reigned twenty and five years in Jerusalem. And his mother's name was Azubah the daughter of Shilhi.

32 And he walked in the way of Asa his father, and departed not from it, doing that which was right in the sight of the LORD.

33 Howbeit the high places were not taken away: for as yet the people had not prepared their hearts unto the God of their fathers.

34 Now the rest of the acts of Jehoshaphat, first and last, behold, they are written in the book of Jehu the son of Hanani, who is mentioned in the book of the kings of Israel.

35 ¶ And after this did Jehoshaphat king of Judah join himself with Ahaziah king of Israel, who did very wickedly:

2 Chronicles 20—Summary of Precepts and Principles on Leadership

The Lord's summary word on leadership is given in these verses: "Wherefore, now let every man learn his duty, and to act in the office in which he is appointed, in all diligence. He that is slothful shall not be counted worthy to stand, and he that learns not his duty and shows himself not approved shall not be counted worthy to stand. Even so. Amen" (D&C 107:99–100).

The stakes are high. Worthiness, learning one's duty, and diligent action are called for. The influence of each person extends in all directions to those responding to strong leadership. The Lord's chosen must show forth "a godly walk and conversation" (D&C 20:69). The covenant promises are contingent on obedience and righteousness.

Spiritual leadership generates harmony, peace, unity, increased faith, and good works. We are indeed fortunate to have before us in the scriptures detailed portraits of great leaders—as well as models that we should avoid if we are to be true to our covenants before the Lord.

Destruction of the . . . Ammonites & Moabites by Gustave Doré

36 And he joined himself with him to make ships to go to Tarshish: and they made the ships in Ezion-geber.

37 Then Eliezer the son of Dodavah of Mareshah prophesied against Jehoshaphat, saying, Because thou hast joined thyself with Ahaziah, the LORD hath broken thy works. And the ships were broken, that they were not able to go to Tarshish.

CHAPTER 29

1 HEZEKIAH began to reign when he was five and twenty years old, and he reigned nine and twenty years in Jerusalem. And his mother's name was Abijah, the daughter of Zechariah.

2 And he did that which was right in the sight of the LORD, according to all that David his father had done.

3 ¶ He in the first year of his reign, in the first month, opened the doors of the house of the LORD, and repaired them.

4 And he brought in the priests and the Levites, and gathered them together into the east street,

5 And said unto them, Hear me, ye Levites, sanctify now yourselves, and sanctify the house of the LORD God of your fathers, and carry forth the filthiness out of the holy place.

6 For our fathers have trespassed, and done that which was evil in the eyes of the LORD our God, and have forsaken him, and have turned away their faces from the habitation of the LORD, and turned their backs.

7 Also they have shut up the doors of the porch, and put out the lamps, and have not burned incense nor offered burnt offerings in the holy place unto the God of Israel.

8 Wherefore the wrath of the LORD was upon Judah and Jerusalem, and he hath delivered them to trouble, to astonishment, and to hissing, as ye see with your eyes.

9 For, lo, our fathers have fallen by the sword, and our sons and our daughters and our wives are in captivity for this.

10 Now it is in mine heart to make a covenant with the LORD God of Israel, that his fierce wrath may turn away from us.

11 My sons, be not now negligent: for the LORD hath chosen you to stand before him, to serve him, and that ye should minister unto him, and burn incense.

12 ¶ Then the Levites arose, Mahath the son of Amasai, and Joel the son of Azariah, of the sons of the Kohathites: and of the sons of Merari, Kish the son of Abdi, and Azariah the son of Jehalelel: and of the Gershonites; Joah the son of Zimmah, and Eden the son of Joah:

13 And of the sons of Elizaphan; Shimri, and Jeiel: and of the sons of Asaph; Zechariah, and Mattaniah:

14 And of the sons of Heman; Jehiel, and Shimei: and of the sons of Jeduthun; Shemaiah, and Uzziel.

15 And they gathered their brethren, and sanctified themselves, and came, according to the commandment of the king, by the words of the LORD, to cleanse the house of the LORD.

16 And the priests went into the inner part of the house of the LORD, to cleanse it, and brought out all the uncleanness that they found in the temple of the LORD into the court of the house of the LORD. And the Levites took it, to carry it out abroad into the brook Kidron.

2 CHRONICLES CHAPTER 29

"He [the Lord] will continue to feed us the bread of life as we need it from time to time, if we will but live in accordance with the teachings we have already received."
—George Albert Smith, *CR*, October 1912, 118

2 Chronicles 29—Preview of the Reigns of Hezekiah and Josiah

Renewal, reform, rejuvenation, rebirth—these are the governing principles in the reign of Kings Hezekiah and Josiah, whose contributions to spiritual progress under the covenant with God stand in marked contrast to the wickedness and idolatry of so many of their predecessors in the kingdoms of Israel and Judah. We see in the background the imposing influence of Isaiah and Jeremiah, two of the greatest of the Lord's prophets.

The work of Hezekiah and Josiah and their righteous associates established once again a great spiritual defense bulwark for protecting the Israelites and securing not only their temporal safety but also their favor with the Lord through obedience to His precepts and commandments. Three grand designs are at play here: the process of purification and sanctification, the elevation once again of the temple as the visible symbol of the invisible covenant bonds and blessings, and the reinstatement of the scriptures as an anchor and guide in the lives of the people.

2 Chronicles 29:1—Hezekiah

Hezekiah (meaning: God strengthens), king of Judah, was one of the greatest reformers in a long tradition of kings and a refreshing breeze among the winds of instability arising from enthroned unrighteousness. The story of his tenure (around 726 BC to 697 BC) is presented in 2 Kings 18–21, 2 Chron. 29–33, and Isaiah 36–39. His reign is, in part, concurrent with the ministry of the prophet Isaiah (around 740–701 BC), who served him as a religious and political counselor.

For insights on the life of Hezekiah, see Appendix BB.

2 Chronicles 29:10–11—The Lord Will Have a Pure House and Pure Servants

Just as Hezekiah, on his royal watch, stood for restoration and purification, so each one of us—as part of the "royal priesthood" (1 Pet. 2:9)—must commit to the cleansing principles of righteousness and honor in our homes and individual lives.

The twenty-nine-year reign of Hezekiah stands out as a refreshing beacon of reform and righteousness in a long sequence of leaders (including his own father, Ahaz, desecrater and closer of the temple) who typically fell short of covenant standards and often supported idolatrous practices. In alliance with his older contemporary, the great prophet Isaiah, Hezekiah instituted wide-sweeping reforms of religious practice and restored the temple to its state of sanctity. The people were able once more to praise the Lord with clean hands and a clean heart.

17 Now they began on the first day of the first month to sanctify, and on the eighth day of the month came they to the porch of the LORD: so they sanctified the house of the LORD in eight days; and in the sixteenth day of the first month they made an end.

18 Then they went in to Hezekiah the king, and said, We have cleansed all the house of the LORD, and the altar of burnt offering, with all the vessels thereof, and the shewbread table, with all the vessels thereof.

19 Moreover all the vessels, which king Ahaz in his reign did cast away in his transgression, have we prepared and sanctified, and, behold, they are before the altar of the LORD.

20 ¶ Then Hezekiah the king rose early, and gathered the rulers of the city, and went up to the house of the LORD.

21 And they brought seven bullocks, and seven rams, and seven lambs, and seven he goats, for a sin offering for the kingdom, and for the sanctuary, and for Judah. And he commanded the priests the sons of Aaron to offer them on the altar of the LORD.

22 So they killed the bullocks, and the priests received the blood, and sprinkled it on the altar: likewise, when they had killed the rams, they sprinkled the blood upon the altar: they killed also the lambs, and they sprinkled the blood upon the altar.

23 And they brought forth the he goats for the sin offering before the king and the congregation; and they laid their hands upon them:

24 And the priests killed them, and they made reconciliation with their blood upon the altar, to make an atonement for all Israel: for the king commanded that the burnt offering and the sin offering should be made for all Israel.

25 And he set the Levites in the house of the LORD with cymbals, with psalteries, and with harps, according to the commandment of David, and of Gad the king's seer, and Nathan the prophet: for so was the commandment of the LORD by his prophets.

26 And the Levites stood with the instruments of David, and the priests with the trumpets.

27 And Hezekiah commanded to offer the burnt offering upon the altar. And when the burnt offering began, the song of the LORD began also with the trumpets, and with the instruments ordained by David king of Israel.

28 And all the congregation worshipped, and the singers sang, and the trumpeters sounded: and all this continued until the burnt offering was finished.

29 And when they had made an end of offering, the king and all that were present with him bowed themselves, and worshipped.

30 Moreover Hezekiah the king and the princes commanded the Levites to sing praise unto the LORD with the words of David, and of Asaph the seer. And they sang praises with gladness, and they bowed their heads and worshipped.

31 Then Hezekiah answered and said, Now ye have consecrated yourselves unto the LORD, come near and bring sacrifices and thank offerings into the house of the LORD. And the congregation brought in sacrifices and thank offerings; and as many as were of a free heart burnt offerings.

32 And the number of the burnt offerings, which the congregation brought, was threescore and ten bullocks, an hundred rams, and two hundred lambs: all these were for a burnt offering to the LORD.

33 And the consecrated things were six hundred oxen and three thousand sheep.

34 But the priests were too few, so that they could not flay all the burnt offerings: wherefore their brethren the Levites did help them,

Hezekiah instilled in a significant segment of the populace a genuine respect for God and a realignment with the covenant walk of life. As such, Judah was able to defend itself successfully before its enemies, the Assyrians, who had earlier succeeded under their King Shalmaneser in 721 BC to ravish the northern kingdom of Israel and carry the ten tribes into captivity.

This account demonstrates that the temples of our God cannot be defiled without the loss of blessings. We lose the blessings of the temple as well as the blessings of the Spirit. At the same time, we see that the process of cleansing and purifying prepares the way for the operation of the Spirit, with its attendant blessings of peace, love, harmony, and joy in the gospel.

POINT OF INTEREST

"Much recent attention has focused on the way the Chronicler has interpreted and reshaped older traditions. Thus differences in Samuel as to who killed the Philistine giant Goliath (David in 1 Sam. 17; or Elhanan in 2 Sam. 21:19) are resolved by making Elhanan's victim Goliath's brother. King Manasseh is condemned in 2 Kings 21, but he reigned for 55 years, implying divine favor, so 2 Chronicles 33:12–13 describes Manasseh's otherwise unattested repentance. Chronicles gives a brilliant theological interpretation of history for the needs of the post-exilic community: from the earliest days (Adam, 1 Chr. 1:1) to the present, this people, so recently defeated and still subject, is the center of God's purpose and providence. One of the most attractive and often over-looked stories in Chronicles is that of the prophet Oded, whose concern for captives from Judah may have provided the model for Jesus' parable of the Good Samaritan (2 Chr. 28:8–15)" (John Bowker, *The Complete Bible Handbook* [New York: DK Publishing, 2001]).

till the work was ended, and until the other priests had sanctified themselves: for the Levites were more upright in heart to sanctify themselves than the priests.

35 And also the burnt offerings were in abundance, with the fat of the peace offerings, and the drink offerings for every burnt offering. So the service of the house of the LORD was set in order.

36 And Hezekiah rejoiced, and all the people, that God had prepared the people: for the thing was done suddenly.

CHAPTER 30

1 AND Hezekiah sent to all Israel and Judah, and wrote letters also to Ephraim and Manasseh, that they should come to the house of the LORD at Jerusalem, to keep the passover unto the LORD God of Israel.

2 For the king had taken counsel, and his princes, and all the congregation in Jerusalem, to keep the passover in the second month.

3 For they could not keep it at that time, because the priests had not sanctified themselves sufficiently, neither had the people gathered themselves together to Jerusalem.

4 And the thing pleased the king and all the congregation.

5 So they established a decree to make proclamation throughout all Israel, from Beer-sheba even to Dan, that they should come to keep the passover unto the LORD God of Israel at Jerusalem: for they had not done it of a long time in such sort as it was written.

6 So the posts went with the letters from the king and his princes throughout all Israel and Judah, and according to the commandment of the king, saying, Ye children of Israel, turn again unto the LORD God of Abraham, Isaac, and Israel, and he will return to the remnant of you, that are escaped out of the hand of the kings of Assyria.

7 And be not ye like your fathers, and like your brethren, which trespassed against the LORD God of their fathers, who therefore gave them up to desolation, as ye see.

8 Now be ye not stiffnecked, as your fathers were, but yield yourselves unto the LORD, and enter into his sanctuary, which he hath sanctified for ever: and serve the LORD your God, that the fierceness of his wrath may turn away from you.

9 For if ye turn again unto the LORD, your brethren and your children shall find compassion before them that lead them captive, so that they shall come again into this land: for the LORD your God is gracious and merciful, and will not turn away his face from you, if ye return unto him.

10 So the posts passed from city to city through the country of Ephraim and Manasseh even unto Zebulun: but they laughed them to scorn, and mocked them.

11 Nevertheless divers of Asher and Manasseh and of Zebulun humbled themselves, and came to Jerusalem.

12 Also in Judah the hand of God was to give them one heart to do the commandment of the king and of the princes, by the word of the LORD.

2 CHRONICLES CHAPTER 30

2 Chronicles 30:8—The Temple as a Fortress of Safety

Just as Hezekiah taught his people once again to look to the temple as the emblem of divine light and protection, so can we too find in our commitment to temple standards and temple activity a protection from the forces of evil abroad in the world.

Hezekiah, having restored the temple as the tangible icon of God's power and guiding light, rallied his people around a unifying purpose of covenant fidelity—"And the Lord hearkened to Hezekiah, and healed the people" (2 Chron. 30:20). Hezekiah was therefore able, in concert with Isaiah, to seek the Lord's blessing in thwarting the siege of Jerusalem in 701 BC by the Assyrian King, Sennacherib, and his army. Hezekiah caused the waters of the spring Gihon to be diverted through a specially constructed tunnel ("Hezekiah's Tunnel," still in use today) into a pool within the city (see 2 Chron. 32:2–4), thus preserving his people and denying the besieging Assyrian army access to essential water.

Hezekiah's Tunnel can be seen as a symbol for accessing the "living water" of salvation (see John 4:10–14)—just as the temple is the source for the "living water" provided through the gospel's most sacred truths and ordinances. Thus, the temple stands as an invulnerable spiritual fortress of defense for the faithful and devout.

The Lord's Holy House is a place of peace, safety, and love. It is a place where the Spirit resides. It is a place of instruction in the ways of the Lord. It is a place we seek to be reminded. Surely we should live worthy of its blessings.

13 ¶ And there assembled at Jerusalem much people to keep the feast of unleavened bread in the second month, a very great congregation.

14 And they arose and took away the altars that were in Jerusalem, and all the altars for incense took they away, and cast them into the brook Kidron.

15 Then they killed the passover on the fourteenth day of the second month: and the priests and the Levites were ashamed, and sanctified themselves, and brought in the burnt offerings into the house of the LORD.

16 And they stood in their place after their manner, according to the law of Moses the man of God: the priests sprinkled the blood, which they received of the hand of the Levites.

17 For there were many in the congregation that were not sanctified: therefore the Levites had the charge of the killing of the passovers for every one that was not clean, to sanctify them unto the LORD.

18 For a multitude of the people, even many of Ephraim, and Manasseh, Issachar, and Zebulun, had not cleansed themselves, yet did they eat the passover otherwise than it was written. But Hezekiah prayed for them, saying, The good LORD pardon every one

19 That prepareth his heart to seek God, the LORD God of his fathers, though he be not cleansed according to the purification of the sanctuary.

20 And the LORD hearkened to Hezekiah, and healed the people.

21 And the children of Israel that were present at Jerusalem kept the feast of unleavened bread seven days with great gladness: and the Levites and the priests praised the LORD day by day, singing with loud instruments unto the LORD.

22 And Hezekiah spake comfortably unto all the Levites that taught the good knowledge of the LORD: and they did eat throughout the feast seven days, offering peace offerings, and making confession to the LORD God of their fathers.

23 And the whole assembly took counsel to keep other seven days: and they kept other seven days with gladness.

24 For Hezekiah king of Judah did give to the congregation a thousand bullocks and seven thousand sheep; and the princes gave to the congregation a thousand bullocks and ten thousand sheep: and a great number of priests sanctified themselves.

25 And all the congregation of Judah, with the priests and the Levites, and all the congregation that came out of Israel, and the strangers that came out of the land of Israel, and that dwelt in Judah, rejoiced.

26 So there was great joy in Jerusalem: for since the time of Solomon the son of David king of Israel there was not the like in Jerusalem.

27 ¶ Then the priests the Levites arose and blessed the people: and their voice was heard, and their prayer came up to his holy dwelling place, even unto heaven.

NOTES:

CHAPTER 32

1 AFTER these things, and the establishment thereof, Sennacherib king of Assyria came, and entered into Judah, and encamped against the fenced cities, and thought to win them for himself.

2 And when Hezekiah saw that Sennacherib was come, and that he was purposed to fight against Jerusalem,

3 He took counsel with his princes and his mighty men to stop the waters of the fountains which were without the city: and they did help him.

4 So there was gathered much people together, who stopped all the fountains, and the brook that ran through the midst of the land, saying, Why should the kings of Assyria come, and find much water?

5 Also he strengthened himself, and built up all the wall that was broken, and raised it up to the towers, and another wall without, and repaired Millo in the city of David, and made darts and shields in abundance.

6 And he set captains of war over the people, and gathered them together to him in the street of the gate of the city, and spake comfortably to them, saying,

7 Be strong and courageous, be not afraid nor dismayed for the king of Assyria, nor for all the multitude that is with him: for there be more with us than with him:

8 With him is an arm of flesh; but with us is the LORD our God to help us, and to fight our battles. And the people rested themselves upon the words of Hezekiah king of Judah.

9 ¶ After this did Sennacherib king of Assyria send his servants to Jerusalem, (but he himself laid siege against Lachish, and all his power with him,) unto Hezekiah king of Judah, and unto all Judah that were at Jerusalem, saying,

10 Thus saith Sennacherib king of Assyria, Whereon do ye trust, that ye abide in the siege in Jerusalem?

11 Doth not Hezekiah persuade you to give over yourselves to die by famine and by thirst, saying, The LORD our God shall deliver us out of the hand of the king of Assyria?

12 Hath not the same Hezekiah taken away his high places and his altars, and commanded Judah and Jerusalem, saying, Ye shall worship before one altar, and burn incense upon it?

13 Know ye not what I and my fathers have done unto all the people of other lands? were the gods of the nations of those lands any ways able to deliver their lands out of mine hand?

14 Who was there among all the gods of those nations that my fathers utterly destroyed, that could deliver his people out of mine hand, that your God should be able to deliver you out of mine hand?

15 Now therefore let not Hezekiah deceive you, nor persuade you on this manner, neither yet believe him: for no god of any nation or kingdom was able to deliver his people out of mine hand, and out of the hand of my fathers: how much less shall your God deliver you out of mine hand?

16 And his servants spake yet more against the LORD God, and against his servant Hezekiah.

17 He wrote also letters to rail on the LORD God of Israel, and to speak against him, saying, As the gods of the nations of other lands have not delivered their people out of mine hand, so shall not the God of Hezekiah deliver his people out of mine hand.

18 Then they cried with a loud voice in the Jews' speech unto the people of Jerusalem that were on the wall, to affright them, and to trouble them; that they might take the city.

2 CHRONICLES CHAPTER 32

2 Chronicles 32:1—Sennacherib

Sennacherib (pronounced "suh-nak'-uh-rib") was king of Assyria in the time frame around 705 BC to 681 BC. King Hezekiah of Judah attempted to repel the dominance of Assyria, causing Sennacherib to invade Judea and take over many cities (see 2 Kings 18:13; 2 Chron. 32:1). Hezekiah reluctantly offered a tribute to Sennacherib (see 2 Kings 18:14–16) but defied the Assyrians when they came and besieged Jerusalem. Hezekiah sent Eliakim (pronounced "ee-ly'-uh-kim") and other representatives to the walls of the city to hear the demands of the Assyrian chief of princes, Rab-shakeh, spoken in the Hebrew language from the midst of the hosts of the Assyrian warriors (see 2 Kings 18:28–30; compare 2 Kings 19:9; 2 Chron. 32:9–20; Isa. 36:4–20; 37:8–13.)

When Eliakim reported this to Hezekiah, the king rent his clothes in dismay and sent Eliakim and his party to the prophet Isaiah for counsel. The prophet responded:

> Thus shall ye say to your master, Thus saith the LORD, Be not afraid of the words which thou hast heard, with which the servants of the king of Assyria have blasphemed me.
>
> Behold, I will send a blast upon him, and he shall hear a rumour, and shall return to his own land; and I will cause him to fall by the sword in his own land. (2 Kings 19:6–7)

Hezekiah then prayed before the Lord for the deliverance of the people, and Isaiah conveyed the promise of heaven: "Therefore thus saith the LORD concerning the king of Assyria, He shall not come into this city, nor shoot an arrow there, nor come before it with shield, nor cast a bank against it. By the way that he came, by the same shall he return, and shall not come into this city, saith the LORD. For I will defend this city, to save it, for mine own sake, and for my servant David's sake" (2 Kings 19:32–34). The dramatic outcome of the conflict between the Assyrians and the Jewish nation at that critical hour is summarized in two verses of scripture:

> And it came to pass that night, that the angel of the LORD went out, and smote in the camp of the Assyrians an hundred fourscore and five thousand: and when they arose early in the morning, behold, they *were* all dead corpses.
>
> So Sennacherib king of Assyria departed, and went and returned, and dwelt at Nineveh. (2 Kings 19:35–36; compare 2 Chron. 32:21–22; Isa. 37:38)

Sennacherib was later murdered by two of his sons (see 2 Kings 19:37; 2 Chron. 32:21; Isa. 37:38) and was succeeded by another son, Esarhaddon.

19 And they spake against the God of Jerusalem, as against the gods of the people of the earth, which were the work of the hands of man.

20 And for this cause Hezekiah the king, and the prophet Isaiah the son of Amoz, prayed and cried to heaven.

21 ¶ And the LORD sent an angel, which cut off all the mighty men of valour, and the leaders and captains in the camp of the king of Assyria. So he returned with shame of face to his own land. And when he was come into the house of his god, they that came forth of his own bowels slew him there with the sword.

22 Thus the LORD saved Hezekiah and the inhabitants of Jerusalem from the hand of Sennacherib the king of Assyria, and from the hand of all other, and guided them on every side.

23 And many brought gifts unto the LORD to Jerusalem, and presents to Hezekiah king of Judah: so that he was magnified in the sight of all nations from thenceforth.

24 ¶ In those days Hezekiah was sick to the death, and prayed unto the LORD: and he spake unto him, and he gave him a sign.

25 But Hezekiah rendered not again according to the benefit done unto him; for his heart was lifted up: therefore there was wrath upon him, and upon Judah and Jerusalem.

26 Notwithstanding Hezekiah humbled himself for the pride of his heart, both he and the inhabitants of Jerusalem, so that the wrath of the LORD came not upon them in the days of Hezekiah.

27 ¶ And Hezekiah had exceeding much riches and honour: and he made himself treasuries for silver, and for gold, and for precious stones, and for spices, and for shields, and for all manner of pleasant jewels;

28 Storehouses also for the increase of corn, and wine, and oil; and stalls for all manner of beasts, and cotes for flocks.

29 Moreover he provided him cities, and possessions of flocks and herds in abundance: for God had given him substance very much.

30 This same Hezekiah also stopped the upper watercourse of Gihon, and brought it straight down to the west side of the city of David. And Hezekiah prospered in all his works.

31 ¶ Howbeit in the business of the ambassadors of the princes of Babylon, who sent unto him to enquire of the wonder that was done in the land, God left him, to try him, that he might know all that was in his heart.

32 ¶ Now the rest of the acts of Hezekiah, and his goodness, behold, they are written in the vision of Isaiah the prophet, the son of Amoz, and in the book of the kings of Judah and Israel.

33 And Hezekiah slept with his fathers, and they buried him in the chiefest of the sepulchres of the sons of David: and all Judah and the inhabitants of Jerusalem did him honour at his death. And Manasseh his son reigned in his stead.

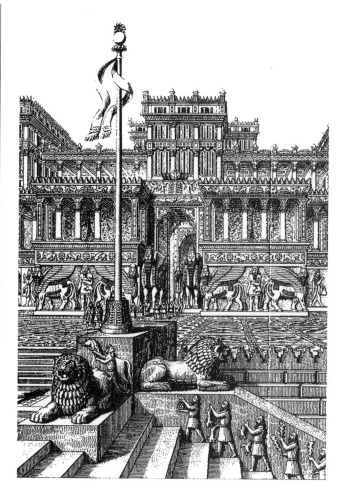

 POINT OF INTEREST

Above is a detail of the northeast façade of Sennacherib's palace at Nineveh. "In 701 B.C.E., after King Hezekiah withheld tribute, the Assyrian king Sennacherib invaded Judah, forcing Hezekiah's surrender (2 Kgs. 18:13–15). Sennacherib received the Judahite messengers at Lachish. His conquest is depicted on large stone reliefs that once covered the walls of a central room in Sennacherib's palace. From these, and from other archaeological evidence, it is clear that Lachish resisted the Assyrian attack and was besieged for some time. Although the reliefs conform to Assyrian artistic conventions, they do appear to reflect details of the actual siege, showing captives and plunder being taken from the defeated city. A mass burial has been found with the remains of around 1,500 bodies, probably citizens killed during or after the siege. Lachish never fully recovered; its defenses were repaired in the late seventh century, but the city was destroyed again during the Babylonian conquest in the 580s B.C.E." (John Bowker, *The Complete Bible Handbook* [New York: DK Publishing, 2001]).

CHAPTER 34

1 JOSIAH was eight years old when he began to reign, and he reigned in Jerusalem one and thirty years.

2 And he did that which was right in the sight of the LORD, and walked in the ways of David his father, and declined neither to the right hand, nor to the left.

3 ¶ For in the eighth year of his reign, while he was yet young, he began to seek after the God of David his father: and in the twelfth year he began to purge Judah and Jerusalem from the high places, and the groves, and the carved images, and the molten images.

4 And they brake down the altars of Baalim in his presence; and the images, that were on high above them, he cut down; and the groves, and the carved images, and the molten images, he brake in pieces, and made dust of them, and strowed it upon the graves of them that had sacrificed unto them.

5 And he burnt the bones of the priests upon their altars, and cleansed Judah and Jerusalem.

6 And so did he in the cities of Manasseh, and Ephraim, and Simeon, even unto Naphtali, with their mattocks round about.

7 And when he had broken down the altars and the groves, and had beaten the graven images into powder, and cut down all the idols throughout all the land of Israel, he returned to Jerusalem.

8 ¶ Now in the eighteenth year of his reign, when he had purged the land, and the house, he sent Shaphan the son of Azaliah, and Maaseiah the governor of the city, and Joah the son of Joahaz the recorder, to repair the house of the LORD his God.

9 And when they came to Hilkiah the high priest, they delivered the money that was brought into the house of God, which the Levites that kept the doors had gathered of the hand of Manasseh and Ephraim, and of all the remnant of Israel, and of all Judah and Benjamin; and they returned to Jerusalem.

10 And they put it in the hand of the workmen that had the oversight of the house of the LORD, and they gave it to the workmen that wrought in the house of the LORD, to repair and amend the house:

11 Even to the artificers and builders gave they it, to buy hewn stone, and timber for couplings, and to floor the houses which the kings of Judah had destroyed.

12 And the men did the work faithfully: and the overseers of them were Jahath and Obadiah, the Levites, of the sons of Merari; and Zechariah and Meshullam, of the sons of the Kohathites, to set it forward; and other of the Levites, all that could skill of instruments of musick.

13 Also they were over the bearers of burdens, and were overseers of all that wrought the work in any manner of service: and of the Levites there were scribes, and officers, and porters.

14 ¶ And when they brought out the money that was brought into the house of the LORD, Hilkiah the priest found a book of the law of the LORD given by Moses.

15 And Hilkiah answered and said to Shaphan the scribe, I have found the book of the law in the house of the LORD. And Hilkiah delivered the book to Shaphan.

16 And Shaphan carried the book to the king, and brought the king word back again, saying, All that was committed to thy servants, they do it.

17 And they have gathered together the money that was found in the house of the LORD, and have delivered it into the hand of the overseers, and to the hand of the workmen.

2 CHRONICLES CHAPTER 34

2 Chronicles 34:1—Josiah

Josiah (meaning: Jehovah will heal or support), son of and successor to Amon, was the great reform king of Judah in the time frame 641–610 BC, concurrent with the early tenure of Jeremiah and just ahead of the tenure of Lehi (see 2 Kings 22–24; 2 Chron. 34–35).

Josiah commissioned Hilkiah, the high priest, to repair and purify the temple. While doing so, Hilkiah discovered, as he declared, "the book of the law in the house of the LORD" (2 Kings 22:8). Upon reading the book, Josiah was struck with anxiety over the contrast between the wayward conduct of his people and the high standards promoted by the word of God. He therefore consulted the prophetess Huldah, who confirmed the word of the Lord concerning the judgments of God soon to fall upon the people for their iniquity. At the same time, the Lord recognized the humility and deference of the king (see 2 Kings 22:19–20.)

Stirred by this divine warning against the people, the king responded earnestly to the message of the book—also called "the book of the covenant" (2 Kings 23:2)—by having it read before all the people, then purging the nation of idolatry and directing everyone to turn to the Lord with a covenant to keep His commandments with full devotion (see 2 Kings 23:1–25).

In a subsequent military conflict with the Egyptians, Josiah was killed (see 2 Kings 23:29)—thus fulfilling the prophecy of Huldah that Josiah would depart this life prior to the time of the Lord's judgments upon the people (which was to come in the form of the impending Babylonian captivity). Upon his passing, Josiah—mourned by the people and by Jeremiah (see 2 Chron. 35:25)—was replaced by his son Jehoahaz, whom the Egyptians deposed in favor of Josiah's other son Eliakim, renamed Jehoiakim (see 2 Kings 23:34; see also Jer. 22:10–12, 18–19).

2 Chronicles 34:14—Hilkiah

Hilkiah (pronounced "hill-ky'-uh"; meaning: portion of Jehovah) was the high priest during the reign of King Josiah to whom the campaign of repairing and purifying the temple was entrusted. While doing so, he discovered, as he declared, "the book of the law in the house of the LORD" (2 Kings 22:8). The king responded earnestly to the message of the book, also called "the book of the covenant" (2 Kings 23:2), by purging the nation of idolatry and directing everyone to turn to the Lord and follow His commandments with full devotion (see 2 Kings 23:3–25).

2 Chronicles 34:22—Huldah

Huldah was a prophetess consulted by King Josiah concerning the discovery of "the book of the law" hidden for generations in the house of the Lord and discovered by the high priest Hilkiah (see 2 Kings 22:8; compare 2 Chron. 34:14–15). Anxious about the message of the book, Josiah asked Huldah for the word of the Lord. She confirmed the impending judgments about to befall the people but prophesied that Josiah would be called home before that time

18 Then Shaphan the scribe told the king, saying, Hilkiah the priest hath given me a book. And Shaphan read it before the king.

19 And it came to pass, when the king had heard the words of the law, that he rent his clothes.

20 And the king commanded Hilkiah, and Ahikam the son of Shaphan, and Abdon the son of Micah, and Shaphan the scribe, and Asaiah a servant of the king's, saying,

21 Go, enquire of the LORD for me, and for them that are left in Israel and in Judah, concerning the words of the book that is found: for great is the wrath of the LORD that is poured out upon us, because our fathers have not kept the word of the LORD, to do after all that is written in this book.

22 And Hilkiah, and they that the king had appointed, went to Huldah the prophetess, the wife of Shallum the son of Tikvath, the son of Hasrah, keeper of the wardrobe; (now she dwelt in Jerusalem in the college:) and they spake to her to that effect.

23 ¶ And she answered them, Thus saith the LORD God of Israel, Tell ye the man that sent you to me,

24 Thus saith the LORD, Behold, I will bring evil upon this place, and upon the inhabitants thereof, even all the curses that are written in the book which they have read before the king of Judah:

25 Because they have forsaken me, and have burned incense unto other gods, that they might provoke me to anger with all the works of their hands; therefore my wrath shall be poured out upon this place, and shall not be quenched.

26 And as for the king of Judah, who sent you to enquire of the LORD, so shall ye say unto him, Thus saith the LORD God of Israel concerning the words which thou hast heard;

27 Because thine heart was tender, and thou didst humble thyself before God, when thou heardest his words against this place, and against the inhabitants thereof, and humbledst thyself before me, and didst rend thy clothes, and weep before me; I have even heard thee also, saith the LORD.

28 Behold, I will gather thee to thy fathers, and thou shalt be gathered to thy grave in peace, neither shall thine eyes see all the evil that I will bring upon this place, and upon the inhabitants of the same. So they brought the king word again.

29 ¶ Then the king sent and gathered together all the elders of Judah and Jerusalem.

30 And the king went up into the house of the LORD, and all the men of Judah, and the inhabitants of Jerusalem, and the priests, and the Levites, and all the people, great and small: and he read in their ears all the words of the book of the covenant that was found in the house of the LORD.

31 And the king stood in his place, and made a covenant before the LORD, to walk after the LORD, and to keep his commandments, and his testimonies, and his statutes, with all his heart, and with all his soul, to perform the words of the covenant which are written in this book.

32 And he caused all that were present in Jerusalem and Benjamin to stand to it. And the inhabitants of Jerusalem did according to the covenant of God, the God of their fathers.

33 And Josiah took away all the abominations out of all the countries that pertained to the children of Israel, and made all that were present in Israel to serve, even to serve the LORD their God. And all his days they departed not from following the LORD, the God of their fathers.

came (see 2 Kings 22:15–20). Josiah proceeded to complete a comprehensive campaign to purge all idolatry from the country, putting the people under covenant to follow the teachings of God. Besides Huldah, Miriam (see Ex. 15:20) and Deborah (see Judges 4:4) also are designated in the Old Testament with the title "prophetess."

2 Chronicles 34:31–32—The Scriptures as Protection for the Saints

We have the opportunity to "discover" anew each day the power of the scriptures of God to bring vitality, peace, inspiration, and saving truth into our lives and homes. Just as King Josiah caused the relocated "book of the law" to be read to his people, we too can make daily scripture study a foundation for our spiritual well-being and a protection for our families.

King Josiah of Judah, great-grandson of Hezekiah and younger contemporary of the prophet Jeremiah and of father Lehi, cleansed the land of idolatrous practice once again—beginning when he was only fifteen or sixteen years of age—and repaired and reinstated the temple as the centerpiece of the Lord 's program of religious worship for all of Israel. When Hilkiah the high priest discovered in the temple a book of the law of the Lord (scriptures as given through Moses; see 2 Chron. 34:15), Josiah was profoundly impacted and caused these words to be read to the people so they could have the Lord's standard of behavior renewed within them after their forefathers had allowed the covenant practices to be forgotten. The lost and rediscovered book became the key to reforms and a symbol of protection for the people of God.

Josiah made a covenant of obedience to the Lord, and caused his people to stand by it; nevertheless, the prophetess Huldah foretold a coming time, beyond the tenure of Josiah, when the wrath of the Lord would be poured out on the people because of wickedness. Even so, Josiah—"because thine heart was tender, and thou didst humble thyself before God, when thou heardest his words against this place" (2 Chron. 34:27)—was to be gathered to his grave "in peace" (v. 28) and removed from the scene of turmoil in which the forces for good and evil were constantly contending.

Following the reign of Josiah, the people turned to iniquity to such a degree—"until the wrath of the Lord arose against his people, till there was no remedy" (2 Chron. 36:16)—that the Lord allowed them to be taken into captivity. It is instructive that Lehi, during this troubled season of history, under command of the Lord, departed Jerusalem around 600 BC, shortly before the city was destroyed in 587 BC by the Babylonians.

This example richly demonstrates that searching the word of God and living the word of God can and will change lives. It is something we all must do in order to gain eternal life.

EZRA

CHAPTER 1

1 NOW in the first year of Cyrus king of Persia, that the word of the LORD by the mouth of Jeremiah might be fulfilled, the LORD stirred up the spirit of Cyrus king of Persia, that he made a proclamation throughout all his kingdom, and put it also in writing, saying,

2 Thus saith Cyrus king of Persia, The LORD God of heaven hath given me all the kingdoms of the earth; and he hath charged me to build him an house at Jerusalem, which is in Judah.

3 Who is there among you of all his people? his God be with him, and let him go up to Jerusalem, which is in Judah, and build the house of the LORD God of Israel, (he is the God,) which is in Jerusalem.

4 And whosoever remaineth in any place where he sojourneth, let the men of his place help him with silver, and with gold, and with goods, and with beasts, beside the freewill offering for the house of God that is in Jerusalem.

5 ¶ Then rose up the chief of the fathers of Judah and Benjamin, and the priests, and the Levites, with all them whose spirit God had raised, to go up to build the house of the LORD which is in Jerusalem.

6 And all they that were about them strengthened their hands with vessels of silver, with gold, with goods, and with beasts, and with precious things, beside all that was willingly offered.

7 ¶ Also Cyrus the king brought forth the vessels of the house of the LORD, which Nebuchadnezzar had brought forth out of Jerusalem, and had put them in the house of his gods;

8 Even those did Cyrus king of Persia bring forth by the hand of Mithredath the treasurer, and numbered them unto Sheshbazzar, the prince of Judah.

9 And this is the number of them: thirty chargers of gold, a thousand chargers of silver, nine and twenty knives,

10 Thirty basons of gold, silver basons of a second sort four hundred and ten, and other vessels a thousand.

11 All the vessels of gold and of silver were five thousand and four hundred. All these did Sheshbazzar bring up with them of the captivity that were brought up from Babylon unto Jerusalem.

CHAPTER 2

1 NOW these are the children of the province that went up out of the captivity, of those which had been carried away, whom Nebuchadnezzar the king of Babylon had carried away unto Babylon, and came again unto Jerusalem and Judah, every one unto his city;

2 Which came with Zerubbabel: Jeshua, Nehemiah, Seraiah, Reelaiah, Mordecai, Bilshan, Mispar, Bigvai, Rehum, Baanah. The number of the men of the people of Israel:

3 The children of Parosh, two thousand an hundred seventy and two.

4 The children of Shephatiah, three hundred seventy and two.

5 The children of Arah, seven hundred seventy and five.

6 The children of Pahath-moab, of the children of Jeshua and Joab, two thousand eight hundred and twelve.

EZRA CHAPTER 1

Ezra 1:1—Cyrus

Cyrus (meaning: the sun) the Great was the king of Persia who took over Babylonia and defeated the Chaldean dynasty elevated to power by Nebuchadnezzar—the last king thereof being Nabonidus, whose son Belshazzar was apparently prince-regent when the kingdom fell. Cyrus issued a decree in 537 BC allowing the Jewish people to return from captivity in Babylon to rebuild the temple at Jerusalem (see 2 Chron. 36:22–23; Ezra 1; 3:7; Isa. 44:28; 45:1). Daniel was well received in the court of Cyrus (see Dan. 1:21; 6:28; 10:1).

POINT OF INTEREST

"The book of Ezra seems to leave us in no doubt that in 538 B.C. [Cyrus II] gave instructions for the rebuilding of the temple in Jerusalem and the return of the sacred utensils that Nebuchadnezzar had removed fifty years before. And contrary to Assyrian and Babylonian practice he gave permission for deportees to return to their homelands, though few of the Jews availed themselves of it and little progress was made with the temple" (J. M. Cook, *The Persians* [London: Folio Society, 2007]).

7 The children of Elam, a thousand two hundred fifty and four.

8 The children of Zattu, nine hundred forty and five.

9 The children of Zaccai, seven hundred and threescore.

10 The children of Bani, six hundred forty and two.

11 The children of Bebai, six hundred twenty and three.

12 The children of Azgad, a thousand two hundred twenty and two.

13 The children of Adonikam, six hundred sixty and six.

14 The children of Bigvai, two thousand fifty and six.

15 The children of Adin, four hundred fifty and four.

16 The children of Ater of Hezekiah, ninety and eight.

17 The children of Bezai, three hundred twenty and three.

18 The children of Jorah, an hundred and twelve.

19 The children of Hashum, two hundred twenty and three.

20 The children of Gibbar, ninety and five.

21 The children of Beth-lehem, an hundred twenty and three.

22 The men of Netophah, fifty and six.

23 The men of Anathoth, an hundred twenty and eight.

24 The children of Azmaveth, forty and two.

25 The children of Kirjath-arim, Chephirah, and Beeroth, seven hundred and forty and three.

26 The children of Ramah and Gaba, six hundred twenty and one.

27 The men of Michmas, an hundred twenty and two.

28 The men of Beth-el and Ai, two hundred twenty and three.

29 The children of Nebo, fifty and two.

30 The children of Magbish, an hundred fifty and six.

31 The children of the other Elam, a thousand two hundred fifty and four.

32 The children of Harim, three hundred and twenty.

33 The children of Lod, Hadid, and Ono, seven hundred twenty and five.

34 The children of Jericho, three hundred forty and five.

35 The children of Senaah, three thousand and six hundred and thirty.

36 ¶ The priests: the children of Jedaiah, of the house of Jeshua, nine hundred seventy and three.

37 The children of Immer, a thousand fifty and two.

38 The children of Pashur, a thousand two hundred forty and seven.

39 The children of Harim, a thousand and seventeen.

40 ¶ The Levites: the children of Jeshua and Kadmiel, of the children of Hodaviah, seventy and four.

41 ¶ The singers: the children of Asaph, an hundred twenty and eight.

42 ¶ The children of the porters: the children of Shallum, the children of Ater, the children of Talmon, the children of Akkub, the children of Hatita, the children of Shobai, in all an hundred thirty and nine.

43 ¶ The Nethinims: the children of Ziha, the children of Hasupha, the children of Tabbaoth,

44 The children of Keros, the children of Siaha, the children of Padon,

45 The children of Lebanah, the children of Hagabah, the children of Akkub,

46 The children of Hagab, the children of Shalmai, the children of Hanan,

47 The children of Giddel, the children of Gahar, the children of Reaiah,

48 The children of Rezin, the children of Nekoda, the children of Gazzam,

Cyrus Restoring the Vessels of the Temple by Gustave Doré

49 The children of Uzza, the children of Paseah, the children of Besai,

50 The children of Asnah, the children of Mehunim, the children of Nephusim,

51 The children of Bakbuk, the children of Hakupha, the children of Harhur,

52 The children of Bazluth, the children of Mehida, the children of Harsha,

53 The children of Barkos, the children of Sisera, the children of Thamah,

54 The children of Neziah, the children of Hatipha.

55 ¶ The children of Solomon's servants: the children of Sotai, the children of Sophereth, the children of Peruda,

56 The children of Jaalah, the children of Darkon, the children of Giddel,

57 The children of Shephatiah, the children of Hattil, the children of Pochereth of Zebaim, the children of Ami.

58 All the Nethinims, and the children of Solomon's servants, were three hundred ninety and two.

59 And these were they which went up from Tel-melah, Tel-harsa, Cherub, Addan, and Immer: but they could not shew their father's house, and their seed, whether they were of Israel:

60 The children of Delaiah, the children of Tobiah, the children of Nekoda, six hundred fifty and two.

61 ¶ And of the children of the priests: the children of Habaiah, the children of Koz, the children of Barzillai; which took a wife of the daughters of Barzillai the Gileadite, and was called after their name:

62 These sought their register among those that were reckoned by genealogy, but they were not found: therefore were they, as polluted, put from the priesthood.

63 And the Tirshatha said unto them, that they should not eat of the most holy things, till there stood up a priest with Urim and with Thummim.

64 ¶ The whole congregation together was forty and two thousand three hundred and threescore,

65 Beside their servants and their maids, of whom there were seven thousand three hundred thirty and seven: and there were among them two hundred singing men and singing women.

66 Their horses were seven hundred thirty and six; their mules, two hundred forty and five;

67 Their camels, four hundred thirty and five; their asses, six thousand seven hundred and twenty.

68 ¶ And some of the chief of the fathers, when they came to the house of the LORD which is at Jerusalem, offered freely for the house of God to set it up in his place:

69 They gave after their ability unto the treasure of the work threescore and one thousand drams of gold, and five thousand pound of silver, and one hundred priests' garments.

70 So the priests, and the Levites, and some of the people, and the singers, and the porters, and the Nethinims, dwelt in their cities, and all Israel in their cities.

EZRA CHAPTER 2

Ezra 2:63—Tirshatha

Tirshatha (pronounced "tir-shay'-thah") was an administrative title of Persian origin applied to one appointed as a governor over an area, such as Zerubbabel in relation to Judea (see Ezra 2:63; Neh. 7:65, 70) or Nehemiah: "And Nehemiah, which is the Tirshatha, and Ezra the priest the scribe, and the Levites that taught the people, said unto all the people, This day is holy unto the LORD your God; mourn not, nor weep. For all the people wept, when they heard the words of the law" (Neh. 8:9; see also Neh. 10:1).

CHAPTER 3

1 AND when the seventh month was come, and the children of Israel were in the cities, the people gathered themselves together as one man to Jerusalem.

2 Then stood up Jeshua the son of Jozadak, and his brethren the priests, and Zerubbabel the son of Shealtiel, and his brethren, and builded the altar of the God of Israel, to offer burnt offerings thereon, as it is written in the law of Moses the man of God.

3 And they set the altar upon his bases; for fear was upon them because of the people of those countries: and they offered burnt offerings thereon unto the LORD, even burnt offerings morning and evening.

4 They kept also the feast of tabernacles, as it is written, and offered the daily burnt offerings by number, according to the custom, as the duty of every day required;

5 And afterward offered the continual burnt offering, both of the new moons, and of all the set feasts of the LORD that were consecrated, and of every one that willingly offered a freewill offering unto the LORD.

6 From the first day of the seventh month began they to offer burnt offerings unto the LORD. But the foundation of the temple of the LORD was not yet laid.

7 They gave money also unto the masons, and to the carpenters; and meat, and drink, and oil, unto them of Zidon, and to them of Tyre, to bring cedar trees from Lebanon to the sea of Joppa, according to the grant that they had of Cyrus king of Persia.

8 ¶ Now in the second year of their coming unto the house of God at Jerusalem, in the second month, began Zerubbabel the son of Shealtiel, and Jeshua the son of Jozadak, and the remnant of their brethren the priests and the Levites, and all they that were come out of the captivity unto Jerusalem; and appointed the Levites, from twenty years old and upward, to set forward the work of the house of the LORD.

9 Then stood Jeshua with his sons and his brethren, Kadmiel and his sons, the sons of Judah, together, to set forward the workmen in the house of God: the sons of Henadad, with their sons and their brethren the Levites.

10 And when the builders laid the foundation of the temple of the LORD, they set the priests in their apparel with trumpets, and the Levites the sons of Asaph with cymbals, to praise the LORD, after the ordinance of David king of Israel.

11 And they sang together by course in praising and giving thanks unto the LORD; because he is good, for his mercy endureth for ever toward Israel. And all the people shouted with a great shout, when they praised the LORD, because the foundation of the house of the LORD was laid.

12 But many of the priests and Levites and chief of the fathers, who were ancient men, that had seen the first house, when the foundation of this house was laid before their eyes, wept with a loud voice; and many shouted aloud for joy:

13 So that the people could not discern the noise of the shout of joy from the noise of the weeping of the people: for the people shouted with a loud shout, and the noise was heard afar off.

EZRA CHAPTER 3

Ezra 3:11—The Temple

The temple of the Lord is an ensign of joy and rejoicing. When these sacred structures arise, the hearts and minds of the Saints rise together amidst the aura of glory and eternal promise emitted by the House of the Lord.

Attire of a King, Encyclopedia of Design

POINT OF INTEREST

"Whether Xerxes had trouble in Judah is not clear. The 'people of the land' there, who must have included deportees from Assyrian times and infiltrated Edomites, were willing to join in worship of Yahweh, but from the time of Cyrus on they resented the new Jewish separatism that centred in Jerusalem. According to Ezra (4:6) they protested about it in a letter to Xerxes (Ahasuerus) at the beginning of his reign; but nothing more is said, except that this is where the book of Esther fits in it racialistic perversion of Achaemenid history" (J. M. Cook, *The Persians* [London: Folio Society, 2007]).

CHAPTER 4

1 NOW when the adversaries of Judah and Benjamin heard that the children of the captivity builded the temple unto the LORD God of Israel;

2 Then they came to Zerubbabel, and to the chief of the fathers, and said unto them, Let us build with you: for we seek your God, as ye do; and we do sacrifice unto him since the days of Esar-haddon king of Assur, which brought us up hither.

3 But Zerubbabel, and Jeshua, and the rest of the chief of the fathers of Israel, said unto them, Ye have nothing to do with us to build an house unto our God; but we ourselves together will build unto the LORD God of Israel, as king Cyrus the king of Persia hath commanded us.

4 Then the people of the land weakened the hands of the people of Judah, and troubled them in building,

5 And hired counsellors against them, to frustrate their purpose, all the days of Cyrus king of Persia, even until the reign of Darius king of Persia.

6 And in the reign of Ahasuerus, in the beginning of his reign, wrote they unto him an accusation against the inhabitants of Judah and Jerusalem.

7 ¶ And in the days of Artaxerxes wrote Bishlam, Mithredath, Tabeel, and the rest of their companions, unto Artaxerxes king of Persia; and the writing of the letter was written in the Syrian tongue, and interpreted in the Syrian tongue.

8 Rehum the chancellor and Shimshai the scribe wrote a letter against Jerusalem to Artaxerxes the king in this sort:

9 Then wrote Rehum the chancellor, and Shimshai the scribe, and the rest of their companions; the Dinaites, the Apharsathchites, the Tarpelites, the Apharsites, the Archevites, the Babylonians, the Susanchites, the Dehavites, and the Elamites,

10 And the rest of the nations whom the great and noble Asnappar brought over, and set in the cities of Samaria, and the rest that are on this side the river, and at such a time.

11 ¶ This is the copy of the letter that they sent unto him, even unto Artaxerxes the king; Thy servants the men on this side the river, and at such a time.

12 Be it known unto the king, that the Jews which came up from thee to us are come unto Jerusalem, building the rebellious and the bad city, and have set up the walls thereof, and joined the foundations.

13 Be it known now unto the king, that, if this city be builded, and the walls set up again, then will they not pay toll, tribute, and custom, and so thou shalt endamage the revenue of the kings.

14 Now because we have maintenance from the king's palace, and it was not meet for us to see the king's dishonour, therefore have we sent and certified the king;

15 That search may be made in the book of the records of thy fathers: so shalt thou find in the book of the records, and know that this city is a rebellious city, and hurtful unto kings and provinces, and that they have moved sedition within the same of old time: for which cause was this city destroyed.

16 We certify the king that, if this city be builded again, and the walls thereof set up, by this means thou shalt have no portion on this side the river.

17 ¶ Then sent the king an answer unto Rehum the chancellor, and to Shimshai the scribe, and to the rest of their companions that

EZRA CHAPTER 4

Ezra 4:1–2—Samaritans

The Samaritans were a people who populated Samaria following the Assyrian captivity of the northern kingdom of Israel around 721 BC. Samaria, located in the mountainous region of Palestine, had originally been established as a stronghold capital by Omri, king of Israel (see 1 Kings 16:23–24). The Samaritans were in general descendants of the colonists placed in that territory by the Assyrian conquerors (see 2 Kings 17:23–24). Though incorrigibly idolatrous in character, and thus incurring the judgments of heaven, these colonists were taught to fear the Lord by a priest sent from among the captive circle of Israelites by the Assyrian king (see 2 Kings 17:25–41).

Generations later, upon the return of Judah from the Babylonian captivity of the sixth century BC, the Samaritans wanted to assist in the rebuilding of the temple at Jerusalem—a privilege denied them by the Jewish leaders:

> NOW when the adversaries of Judah and Benjamin heard that the children of the captivity builded the temple unto the LORD God of Israel;
>
> Then they came to Zerubbabel, and to the chief of the fathers, and said unto them, Let us build with you: for we seek your God, as ye do; and we do sacrifice unto him since the days of Esar-haddon king of Assur, which brought us up hither.
>
> But Zerubbabel, and Jeshua, and the rest of the chief of the fathers of Israel, said unto them, Ye have nothing to do with us to build an house unto our God; but we ourselves together will build unto the LORD God of Israel, as king Cyrus the king of Persia hath commanded us. (Ezra 4:1–3)

Angered at this form of discrimination, the Samaritans turned against Judah with much animosity and later erected a temple of their own on Mount Gerizim (pronounced "gair'-uh-zim"). Gerizim thus became for the Samaritans what Jerusalem was for the Jewish people. It was to this site upon Gerizim that the Samaritan woman referred when she was being counseled by the Savior at the well: "The woman saith unto him, Sir, I perceive that thou art a prophet. Our fathers worshipped in this mountain; and ye say, that in Jerusalem is the place where men ought to worship" (John 4:19–20). Despite the intolerance of the Jewish people for the Samaritans living among them, the Samaritans were able, in their time, to receive the gospel message from the disciples of Jesus.

Ezra 4:9—Susanchites

The Susanchites were settlers in Samaria (an area around thirty miles north of Jerusalem) who—along with eight other confederate groups—persuaded king Artaxerxes of Persia to order the Jews to desist in the rebuilding of Jerusalem and the temple following the Babylonian conquest (see Ezra 4:11–14). The Jews under Zerubbabel, the appointed governor (also known by his Persian name

dwell in Samaria, and unto the rest beyond the river, Peace, and at such a time.

18 The letter which ye sent unto us hath been plainly read before me.

19 And I commanded, and search hath been made, and it is found that this city of old time hath made insurrection against kings, and that rebellion and sedition have been made therein.

20 There have been mighty kings also over Jerusalem, which have ruled over all countries beyond the river; and toll, tribute, and custom, was paid unto them.

21 Give ye now commandment to cause these men to cease, and that this city be not builded, until another commandment shall be given from me.

22 Take heed now that ye fail not to do this: why should damage grow to the hurt of the kings?

23 ¶ Now when the copy of king Artaxerxes' letter was read before Rehum, and Shimshai the scribe, and their companions, they went up in haste to Jerusalem unto the Jews, and made them to cease by force and power.

24 Then ceased the work of the house of God which is at Jerusalem. So it ceased unto the second year of the reign of Darius king of Persia.

CHAPTER 5

1 THEN the prophets, Haggai the prophet, and Zechariah the son of Iddo, prophesied unto the Jews that were in Judah and Jerusalem in the name of the God of Israel, even unto them.

2 Then rose up Zerubbabel the son of Shealtiel, and Jeshua the son of Jozadak, and began to build the house of God which is at Jerusalem: and with them were the prophets of God helping them.

3 ¶ At the same time came to them Tatnai, governor on this side the river, and Shethar-boznai, and their companions, and said thus unto them, Who hath commanded you to build this house, and to make up this wall?

4 Then said we unto them after this manner, What are the names of the men that make this building?

5 But the eye of their God was upon the elders of the Jews, that they could not cause them to cease, till the matter came to Darius: and then they returned answer by letter concerning this matter.

6 ¶ The copy of the letter that Tatnai, governor on this side the river, and Shethar-boznai, and his companions the Apharsachites, which were on this side the river, sent unto Darius the king:

7 They sent a letter unto him, wherein was written thus; Unto Darius the king, all peace.

8 Be it known unto the king, that we went into the province of Judea, to the house of the great God, which is builded with great stones, and timber is laid in the walls, and this work goeth fast on, and prospereth in their hands.

9 Then asked we those elders, and said unto them thus, Who commanded you to build this house, and to make up these walls?

10 We asked their names also, to certify thee, that we might write the names of the men that were the chief of them.

11 And thus they returned us answer, saying, We are the servants of the God of heaven and earth, and build the house that was builded these many years ago, which a great king of Israel builded and set up.

Sheshbazzar), persisted in their construction plans, claiming that Cyrus of Persia had issued the decree of authorization (see Ezra 5:6–17). Upon an investigation of the matter, Darius, king of Persia, reinstated the decree of Cyrus in 520 BC (originally issued in 537 BC) to permit the completion of the temple to proceed (see Ezra 6:11–12). The temple was completed in 516 BC.

EZRA CHAPTER 5

Ezra 5:2—Guided By Prophets

The monumental developments taking place during the period of time covered by the Book of Ezra were overseen and guided by the prophets of God, including Haggai and Zechariah, both of whom contributed books to the sacred canon of the Old Testament. The rebuilding of the temple at Jerusalem was not accomplished without the direct involvement of prophetic ministers: ". . . and with them were the prophets of God helping them" (Ezra 5:2).

Ezra 5:2—Zerubbabel

Zerubbabel (pronounced "zuh-roob'-uh-buhl"; meaning of the Assyrian name: born in Babylon)—grandson of Jehoiachin, king of Judah, and son of Pedaiah (see 1 Chron. 3:16–19)—was appointed governor of over Judea by the Persian authorities when Cyrus issued his decree in 537 BC allowing the captive Jewish people to return to Palestine (see Ezra 1:8, where Zerubbabel is called by the Persian name "Sheshbazzar, prince of Judah"). Zerubbabel rebuilt the altar and the temple in Jerusalem (see Ezra 3:2, 8; 4:2–3; 5:2), aided by the prophets Haggai (see Hag. 1:1–15; 2:1–23) and Zechariah (see Zech. 4:6–10)—despite much opposition from the local tribes, including the Samaritans.

Scholar Sydney B. Sperry indicates the nature of the rebuilt temple: "The plan of Solomon's temple was followed in general, but due to the poverty of the people, not on such a lavish scale. Many of the vessels used in the former temple were restored. The Holy of Holies was empty, for the Ark of the Covenant disappeared when Nebuchadnezzar's forces invaded Palestine. This temple, called after Zerubbabel, and sometimes known as the Second Temple, was completed in the sixth year of Darius, 515 B.C." (Sidney B. Sperry, "Ancient Temples and Their Functions," *Ensign*, Jan. 1972, 67).

12 But after that our fathers had provoked the God of heaven unto wrath, he gave them into the hand of Nebuchadnezzar the king of Babylon, the Chaldean, who destroyed this house, and carried the people away into Babylon.

13 But in the first year of Cyrus the king of Babylon the same king Cyrus made a decree to build this house of God.

14 And the vessels also of gold and silver of the house of God, which Nebuchadnezzar took out of the temple that was in Jerusalem, and brought them into the temple of Babylon, those did Cyrus the king take out of the temple of Babylon, and they were delivered unto one, whose name was Sheshbazzar, whom he had made governor;

15 And said unto him, Take these vessels, go, carry them into the temple that is in Jerusalem, and let the house of God be built in his place.

16 Then came the same Sheshbazzar, and laid the foundation of the house of God which is in Jerusalem: and since that time even until now hath it been in building, and yet it is not finished.

17 Now therefore, if it seem good to the king, let there be search made in the king's treasure house, which is there at Babylon, whether it be so, that a decree was made of Cyrus the king to build this house of God at Jerusalem, and let the king send his pleasure to us concerning this matter.

CHAPTER 6

1 THEN Darius the king made a decree, and search was made in the house of the rolls, where the treasures were laid up in Babylon.

2 And there was found at Achmetha, in the palace that is in the province of the Medes, a roll, and therein was a record thus written:

3 In the first year of Cyrus the king the same Cyrus the king made a decree concerning the house of God at Jerusalem, Let the house be builded, the place where they offered sacrifices, and let the foundations thereof be strongly laid; the height thereof threescore cubits, and the breadth thereof threescore cubits;

4 With three rows of great stones, and a row of new timber: and let the expenses be given out of the king's house:

5 And also let the golden and silver vessels of the house of God, which Nebuchadnezzar took forth out of the temple which is at Jerusalem, and brought unto Babylon, be restored, and brought again unto the temple which is at Jerusalem, every one to his place, and place them in the house of God.

6 Now therefore, Tatnai, governor beyond the river, Shethar-boznai, and your companions the Apharsachites, which are beyond the river, be ye far from thence:

7 Let the work of this house of God alone; let the governor of the Jews and the elders of the Jews build this house of God in his place.

8 Moreover I make a decree what ye shall do to the elders of these Jews for the building of this house of God: that of the king's goods, even of the tribute beyond the river, forthwith expenses be given unto these men, that they be not hindered.

9 And that which they have need of, both young bullocks, and rams, and lambs, for the burnt offerings of the God of heaven, wheat, salt, wine, and oil, according to the appointment of the priests which are at Jerusalem, let it be given them day by day without fail:

Ezra 5:14—Sheshbazzar

Sheshbazzar is the Persian name for Zerubbabel.

EZRA CHAPTER 6

Ezra 6:1—Darius

Darius is mentioned in the book of Ezra as the Persian king who renewed the decree of Cyrus permitting the rebuilding of the temple at Jerusalem following the Babylonian captivity:

And the God that hath caused his name to dwell there destroy all kings and people, that shall put to their hand to alter and to destroy this house of God which is at Jerusalem. I Darius have made a decree; let it be done with speed.

Then Tatnai, governor on this side the river, Shethar-boznai, and their companions, according to that which Darius the king had sent, so they did speedily.

And the elders of the Jews builded, and they prospered through the prophesying of Haggai the prophet and Zechariah the son of Iddo. And they builded, and finished it, according to the commandment of the God of Israel, and according to the commandment of Cyrus, and Darius, and Artaxerxes king of Persia.

And this house was finished on the third day of the month Adar, which was in the sixth year of the reign of Darius the king. (Ezra 6:12–15; this Darius is not to be confused with the later Darius mentioned in the Book of Daniel: see Dan. 6:25–28; 9:1; 11:1.).

10 That they may offer sacrifices of sweet savours unto the God of heaven, and pray for the life of the king, and of his sons.

11 Also I have made a decree, that whosoever shall alter this word, let timber be pulled down from his house, and being set up, let him be hanged thereon; and let his house be made a dunghill for this.

12 And the God that hath caused his name to dwell there destroy all kings and people, that shall put to their hand to alter and to destroy this house of God which is at Jerusalem. I Darius have made a decree; let it be done with speed.

13 ¶ Then Tatnai, governor on this side the river, Shethar-boznai, and their companions, according to that which Darius the king had sent, so they did speedily.

14 And the elders of the Jews builded, and they prospered through the prophesying of Haggai the prophet and Zechariah the son of Iddo. And they builded, and finished it, according to the commandment of the God of Israel, and according to the commandment of Cyrus, and Darius, and Artaxerxes king of Persia.

15 And this house was finished on the third day of the month Adar, which was in the sixth year of the reign of Darius the king.

16 ¶ And the children of Israel, the priests, and the Levites, and the rest of the children of the captivity, kept the dedication of this house of God with joy,

17 And offered at the dedication of this house of God an hundred bullocks, two hundred rams, four hundred lambs; and for a sin offering for all Israel, twelve he goats, according to the number of the tribes of Israel.

18 And they set the priests in their divisions, and the Levites in their courses, for the service of God, which is at Jerusalem; as it is written in the book of Moses.

19 And the children of the captivity kept the passover upon the fourteenth day of the first month.

20 For the priests and the Levites were purified together, all of them were pure, and killed the passover for all the children of the captivity, and for their brethren the priests, and for themselves.

21 And the children of Israel, which were come again out of captivity, and all such as had separated themselves unto them from the filthiness of the heathen of the land, to seek the LORD God of Israel, did eat,

22 And kept the feast of unleavened bread seven days with joy: for the LORD had made them joyful, and turned the heart of the king of Assyria unto them, to strengthen their hands in the work of the house of God, the God of Israel.

Ezra 6:14—Artaxerxes

Artaxerxes was the son of Xerxes and king of Persia in the time frame around 465-425 BC. Artaxerxes (pronounced "ahr' tuh-zurk'-seez") was called Longimanus ("long-handed"). At first he hindered the Jews from restoring Jerusalem and its city since the enemies of the Jewish state had raised warnings of sedition against, and loss of revenues unto, the king (see Ezra 4:7–23). Subsequently, however, he permitted the rebuilding of the temple to go forward (see Ezra 6:14; see also Ezra 7:1–28). Later on, Nehemiah was appointed by Artaxerxes as governor of Judea and permitted to rebuild the walls of the city of Jerusalem (see Neh. 2:1–10; 5:14; 13:6).

Artaxerxes Granting Liberty to the Jews by Gustave Doré

CHAPTER 7

1 NOW after these things, in the reign of Artaxerxes king of Persia, Ezra the son of Seraiah, the son of Azariah, the son of Hilkiah,

2 The son of Shallum, the son of Zadok, the son of Ahitub,

3 The son of Amariah, the son of Azariah, the son of Meraioth,

4 The son of Zerahiah, the son of Uzzi, the son of Bukki,

5 The son of Abishua, the son of Phinehas, the son of Eleazar, the son of Aaron the chief priest:

6 This Ezra went up from Babylon; and he was a ready scribe in the law of Moses, which the LORD God of Israel had given: and the king granted him all his request, according to the hand of the LORD his God upon him.

7 And there went up some of the children of Israel, and of the priests, and the Levites, and the singers, and the porters, and the Nethinims, unto Jerusalem, in the seventh year of Artaxerxes the king.

8 And he came to Jerusalem in the fifth month, which was in the seventh year of the king.

9 For upon the first day of the first month began he to go up from Babylon, and on the first day of the fifth month came he to Jerusalem, according to the good hand of his God upon him.

10 For Ezra had prepared his heart to seek the law of the LORD, and to do it, and to teach in Israel statutes and judgments.

11 ¶ Now this is the copy of the letter that the king Artaxerxes gave unto Ezra the priest, the scribe, even a scribe of the words of the commandments of the LORD, and of his statutes to Israel.

12 Artaxerxes, king of kings, unto Ezra the priest, a scribe of the law of the God of heaven, perfect peace, and at such a time.

13 I make a decree, that all they of the people of Israel, and of his priests and Levites, in my realm, which are minded of their own freewill to go up to Jerusalem, go with thee.

14 Forasmuch as thou art sent of the king, and of his seven counsellors, to enquire concerning Judah and Jerusalem, according to the law of thy God which is in thine hand;

15 And to carry the silver and gold, which the king and his counsellors have freely offered unto the God of Israel, whose habitation is in Jerusalem,

16 And all the silver and gold that thou canst find in all the province of Babylon, with the freewill offering of the people, and of the priests, offering willingly for the house of their God which is in Jerusalem:

17 That thou mayest buy speedily with this money bullocks, rams, lambs, with their meat offerings and their drink offerings, and offer them upon the altar of the house of your God which is in Jerusalem.

18 And whatsoever shall seem good to thee, and to thy brethren, to do with the rest of the silver and the gold, that do after the will of your God.

19 The vessels also that are given thee for the service of the house of thy God, those deliver thou before the God of Jerusalem.

20 And whatsoever more shall be needful for the house of thy God, which thou shalt have occasion to bestow, bestow it out of the king's treasure house.

21 And I, even I Artaxerxes the king, do make a decree to all the treasurers which are beyond the river, that whatsoever Ezra the priest, the scribe of the law of the God of heaven, shall require of you, it be done speedily,

EZRA CHAPTER 7

Ezra 7—Repatriation

Ezra rejoiced that Artaxerxes, king of Persia, authorized the repatriation of another group of Jewish people, decreeing their return to Jerusalem a number of years after Zerubbabel guided a first large contingent back to their homeland.

For insights into the life of Ezra, see Appendix CC.

Darius I with Attendants

22 Unto an hundred talents of silver, and to an hundred measures of wheat, and to an hundred baths of wine, and to an hundred baths of oil, and salt without prescribing how much.

23 Whatsoever is commanded by the God of heaven, let it be diligently done for the house of the God of heaven: for why should there be wrath against the realm of the king and his sons?

24 Also we certify you, that touching any of the priests and Levites, singers, porters, Nethinims, or ministers of this house of God, it shall not be lawful to impose toll, tribute, or custom, upon them.

25 And thou, Ezra, after the wisdom of thy God, that is in thine hand, set magistrates and judges, which may judge all the people that are beyond the river, all such as know the laws of thy God; and teach ye them that know them not.

26 And whosoever will not do the law of thy God, and the law of the king, let judgment be executed speedily upon him, whether it be unto death, or to banishment, or to confiscation of goods, or to imprisonment.

27 ¶ Blessed be the LORD God of our fathers, which hath put such a thing as this in the king's heart, to beautify the house of the LORD which is in Jerusalem:

28 And hath extended mercy unto me before the king, and his counsellors, and before all the king's mighty princes. And I was strengthened as the hand of the LORD my God was upon me, and I gathered together out of Israel chief men to go up with me.

CHAPTER 8

1 THESE are now the chief of their fathers, and this is the genealogy of them that went up with me from Babylon, in the reign of Artaxerxes the king.

2 Of the sons of Phinehas; Gershom: of the sons of Ithamar; Daniel: of the sons of David; Hattush.

3 Of the sons of Shechaniah, of the sons of Pharosh; Zechariah: and with him were reckoned by genealogy of the males an hundred and fifty.

4 Of the sons of Pahath-moab; Elihoenai the son of Zerahiah, and with him two hundred males.

5 Of the sons of Shechaniah; the son of Jahaziel, and with him three hundred males.

6 Of the sons also of Adin; Ebed the son of Jonathan, and with him fifty males.

7 And of the sons of Elam; Jeshaiah the son of Athaliah, and with him seventy males.

8 And of the sons of Shephatiah; Zebadiah the son of Michael, and with him fourscore males.

9 Of the sons of Joab; Obadiah the son of Jehiel, and with him two hundred and eighteen males.

10 And of the sons of Shelomith; the son of Josiphiah, and with him an hundred and threescore males.

11 And of the sons of Bebai; Zechariah the son of Bebai, and with him twenty and eight males.

12 And of the sons of Azgad; Johanan the son of Hakkatan, and with him an hundred and ten males.

POINT OF INTEREST

"To Jerusalem Darius (left) certainly did not go. But Zerubbabel—despite his Babylonian name a prince of the house of David—was sent in 520 B.C. to take charge there. This will have been no easy task with opposition from the provincial officials when he resumed the building the the temple. . . . When the governor of Abarnahara (Beyond the Euphrates) intervened, appeal was made to a decree of Cyrus authorising the work; and after being sought in vain among the archives in Nebuchadnezzar's palace at Babylon the relevant document was tracked down at Agbatana. The decree in the forms given in Ezra is perplexing; it has even been suggested that what was found was a forgery planted by a Judaean secretary in the imperial chancery, but a twenty-year span is not a long one in official memory. A decree of Cyrus was not to be countermanded, and the rebuilt temple was consecrated in early 515 B.C. This affords the one glimpse of a governor, the Tattenai of Ezra 5–6, functioning in Abarnahara" (J. M. Cook, *The Persians* [London: Folio Society, 2007]).

EZRA CHAPTER 8

Ezra 8—Ezra's Example of Leadership

Ezra, a man of faith and courage, exemplified the kind of leadership called for when the people of the Lord were organized for a journey of importance. Ezra supplicated the Lord for wisdom concerning the safe pathway to follow—and also prayed "for our little ones" (verse 21). As a result, the Lord granted a blessing of protection and safety for the Jewish immigrants (see verse 31). The spirit of Ezra is an echo of the mighty exodus under Moses and an anticipation of the westward trek under Brigham Young.

13 And of the last sons of Adonikam, whose names are these, Eliphelet, Jeiel, and Shemaiah, and with them threescore males.

14 Of the sons also of Bigvai; Uthai, and Zabbud, and with them seventy males.

15 ¶ And I gathered them together to the river that runneth to Ahava; and there abode we in tents three days: and I viewed the people, and the priests, and found there none of the sons of Levi.

16 Then sent I for Eliezer, for Ariel, for Shemaiah, and for El-nathan, and for Jarib, and for Elnathan, and for Nathan, and for Zechariah, and for Meshullam, chief men; also for Joiarib, and for El-nathan, men of understanding.

17 And I sent them with commandment unto Iddo the chief at the place Casiphia, and I told them what they should say unto Iddo, and to his brethren the Nethinims, at the place Casiphia, that they should bring unto us ministers for the house of our God.

18 And by the good hand of our God upon us they brought us a man of understanding, of the sons of Mahli, the son of Levi, the son of Israel; and Sherebiah, with his sons and his brethren, eighteen;

19 And Hashabiah, and with him Jeshaiah of the sons of Merari, his brethren and their sons, twenty;

20 Also of the Nethinims, whom David and the princes had appointed for the service of the Levites, two hundred and twenty Nethinims: all of them were expressed by name.

21 ¶ Then I proclaimed a fast there, at the river of Ahava, that we might afflict ourselves before our God, to seek of him a right way for us, and for our little ones, and for all our substance.

22 For I was ashamed to require of the king a band of soldiers and horsemen to help us against the enemy in the way: because we had spoken unto the king, saying, The hand of our God is upon all them for good that seek him; but his power and his wrath is against all them that forsake him.

23 So we fasted and besought our God for this: and he was intreated of us.

24 ¶ Then I separated twelve of the chief of the priests, Sherebiah, Hashabiah, and ten of their brethren with them,

25 And weighed unto them the silver, and the gold, and the vessels, even the offering of the house of our God, which the king, and his counsellors, and his lords, and all Israel there present, had offered:

26 I even weighed unto their hand six hundred and fifty talents of silver, and silver vessels an hundred talents, and of gold an hundred talents;

27 Also twenty basons of gold, of a thousand drams; and two vessels of fine copper, precious as gold.

28 And I said unto them, Ye are holy unto the LORD; the vessels are holy also; and the silver and the gold are a freewill offering unto the LORD God of your fathers.

29 Watch ye, and keep them, until ye weigh them before the chief of the priests and the Levites, and chief of the fathers of Israel, at Jerusalem, in the chambers of the house of the LORD.

30 So took the priests and the Levites the weight of the silver, and the gold, and the vessels, to bring them to Jerusalem unto the house of our God.

31 ¶ Then we departed from the river of Ahava on the twelfth day of the first month, to go unto Jerusalem: and the hand of our God was upon us, and he delivered us from the hand of the enemy, and of such as lay in wait by the way.

32 And we came to Jerusalem, and abode there three days.

POINT OF INTEREST

"The books of Ezra and Nehemiah refer to five Persian kings: Cyrus (Ezra 4:5), Ahasuerus or Xerxes (Ezra 4:6), two by the name of Artaxerxes (Ezra 4:7; Neh. 2:1; 5:14; 13:6), and Darius (Ezra 4:5). However, the order in which they are mentioned does not follow a clear historical sequence, and scholarly opinion differs as to the exact period referred to in the books and as to which kings bearing the same name are intended. Given also that different sources have been used, the reconstruction of this period from these books is uncertain. One possible chronology is as follows: under Cyrus of Persia the first attempts were made to rebuild the Temple (537 B.C.E.). Cyrus was succeeded by Cambyses, but it was under his successor Darius I that the Temple was actually rebuilt (520–16 B.C.E.). Darius was, in turn, succeeded by Xerxes, and it was his successor, Artaxerxes I, who sent the scribe Ezra to Jerusalem (458 B.C.E.), presumably to look after the religious needs of the community in line with the liberal policies of the Persian kings of supporting local traditions in exchange for loyalty. Thirteen years later, Nehemiah was sent to become the governor of Judah and returned again for a second period at a later date. However, if the king mentioned in Ezra 7:7 is Artaxerxes II, then the date of Ezra's arrival would be 398 B.C.E., and his work would come after that of Nehemiah" (John Bowker, *The Complete Bible Handbook* [New York: DK Publishing, 2001]).

33 ¶ Now on the fourth day was the silver and the gold and the vessels weighed in the house of our God by the hand of Meremoth the son of Uriah the priest; and with him was Eleazar the son of Phinehas; and with them was Jozabad the son of Jeshua, and Noadiah the son of Binnui, Levites;

34 By number and by weight of every one: and all the weight was written at that time.

35 Also the children of those that had been carried away, which were come out of the captivity, offered burnt offerings unto the God of Israel, twelve bullocks for all Israel, ninety and six rams, seventy and seven lambs, twelve he goats for a sin offering: all this was a burnt offering unto the LORD.

36 ¶ And they delivered the king's commissions unto the king's lieutenants, and to the governors on this side the river: and they furthered the people, and the house of God.

THE BOOK OF NEHEMIAH

CHAPTER 1

1 THE words of Nehemiah the son of Hachaliah. And it came to pass in the month Chisleu, in the twentieth year, as I was in Shushan the palace,

2 That Hanani, one of my brethren, came, he and certain men of Judah; and I asked them concerning the Jews that had escaped, which were left of the captivity, and concerning Jerusalem.

3 And they said unto me, The remnant that are left of the captivity there in the province are in great affliction and reproach: the wall of Jerusalem also is broken down, and the gates thereof are burned with fire.

4 ¶ And it came to pass, when I heard these words, that I sat down and wept, and mourned certain days, and fasted, and prayed before the God of heaven,

5 And said, I beseech thee, O LORD God of heaven, the great and terrible God, that keepeth covenant and mercy for them that love him and observe his commandments:

6 Let thine ear now be attentive, and thine eyes open, that thou mayest hear the prayer of thy servant, which I pray before thee now, day and night, for the children of Israel thy servants, and confess the sins of the children of Israel, which we have sinned against thee: both I and my father's house have sinned.

7 We have dealt very corruptly against thee, and have not kept the commandments, nor the statutes, nor the judgments, which thou commandedst thy servant Moses.

8 Remember, I beseech thee, the word that thou commandedst thy servant Moses, saying, If ye transgress, I will scatter you abroad among the nations:

9 But if ye turn unto me, and keep my commandments, and do them; though there were of you cast out unto the uttermost part of the heaven, yet will I gather them from thence, and will bring them unto the place that I have chosen to set my name there.

NEHEMIAH CHAPTER 1

Nehemiah 1:11—Covenant Prayer

Nehemiah left behind a choice example of a covenant prayer—one that recalled the promises of the Lord for His people, that He will bless them in their righteousness, but also chastize them in their departure from eternal principles. The Lord scatters and gathers His people according to their pattern of living and in accordance with His judgment and design.

This chapter of Jewish history brings to light the suffering of the Babylonian captives of Judah who were scourged by the hand of Nebuchadnezzar in 587 BC—but then allowed to return to Jerusalem under the decree of Cyrus of Persian in 537 BC. The spirit of humility and yearning reflected in the prayer of Nehemiah is very much akin to the ongoing questful yearning of the Jewish people to return to the Holy Land—the land of their inheritance—even down to the present moment in time.

For additional insight into the life of Nehemiah, see Appendix DD.

The ultimate gathering of the tribes of Israel to their places of inheritance will transpire in the last days, when the word of God in its various manifestations will be united and gathering in one:

> And it shall come to pass that the Jews shall have the words of the Nephites [the Book of Mormon], and the Nephites shall have the words of the Jews [the Bible]; and the Nephites and the Jews shall have the words of the lost tribes of Israel; and the lost tribes of Israel shall have the words of the Nephites and the Jews.
>
> And it shall come to pass that my people, which are of the house of Israel, shall be gathered home unto the lands of their possessions; and my word also shall be gathered in one. And I will show unto them that fight against my word and against my people, who are of the house of Israel, that I am God, and that I covenanted with Abraham that I would remember his seed forever. (2 Ne. 29:13–14)

10 Now these are thy servants and thy people, whom thou hast redeemed by thy great power, and by thy strong hand.

11 O Lord, I beseech thee, let now thine ear be attentive to the prayer of thy servant, and to the prayer of thy servants, who desire to fear thy name: and prosper, I pray thee, thy servant this day, and grant him mercy in the sight of this man. For I was the king's cupbearer.

CHAPTER 2

1 AND it came to pass in the month Nisan, in the twentieth year of Artaxerxes the king, that wine was before him: and I took up the wine, and gave it unto the king. Now I had not been beforetime sad in his presence.

2 Wherefore the king said unto me, Why is thy countenance sad, seeing thou art not sick? this is nothing else but sorrow of heart. Then I was very sore afraid,

3 And said unto the king, Let the king live for ever: why should not my countenance be sad, when the city, the place of my fathers' sepulchres, lieth waste, and the gates thereof are consumed with fire?

4 Then the king said unto me, For what dost thou make request? So I prayed to the God of heaven.

5 And I said unto the king, If it please the king, and if thy servant have found favour in thy sight, that thou wouldest send me unto Judah, unto the city of my fathers' sepulchres, that I may build it.

6 And the king said unto me, (the queen also sitting by him,) For how long shall thy journey be? and when wilt thou return? So it pleased the king to send me; and I set him a time.

7 Moreover I said unto the king, If it please the king, let letters be given me to the governors beyond the river, that they may convey me over till I come into Judah;

8 And a letter unto Asaph the keeper of the king's forest, that he may give me timber to make beams for the gates of the palace which appertained to the house, and for the wall of the city, and for the house that I shall enter into. And the king granted me, according to the good hand of my God upon me.

9 ¶ Then I came to the governors beyond the river, and gave them the king's letters. Now the king had sent captains of the army and horsemen with me.

10 When Sanballat the Horonite, and Tobiah the servant, the Ammonite, heard of it, it grieved them exceedingly that there was come a man to seek the welfare of the children of Israel.

11 So I came to Jerusalem, and was there three days.

12 ¶ And I arose in the night, I and some few men with me; neither told I any man what my God had put in my heart to do at Jerusalem: neither was there any beast with me, save the beast that I rode upon.

13 And I went out by night by the gate of the valley, even before the dragon well, and to the dung port, and viewed the walls of Jerusalem, which were broken down, and the gates thereof were consumed with fire.

14 Then I went on to the gate of the fountain, and to the king's pool: but there was no place for the beast that was under me to pass.

15 Then went I up in the night by the brook, and viewed the wall, and turned back, and entered by the gate of the valley, and so returned.

NEHEMIAH CHAPTER 2

Nehemiah 2:19—Sanballat

Sanballat (pronounced "san-bal'-at"), known as the "Horonite" (Neh. 2:10), was a leader among the people of Samaria who opposed Nehemiah in the mission of rebuilding the walls of Jerusalem following the return of the Jewish people from the Babylonian captivity (see Neh. 2:19; 4:1, 7; 6:1–14). The priests who intermarried with non-Israelite women and thus defiled the priesthood were chastened: "And *one* of the sons of Joiada, the son of Eliashib the high priest, *was* son in law to Sanballat

Nehemiah 2:20—The Work in Service of God Is to Edify, Renew, and Make Joyful

To learn to keep the covenants of God is to learn how to become sanctified and make a holy offering to the Lord in righteousness. The Spirit of the Lord induces the ongoing work of building—building joyful families, building temples, building a Zion society, building the kingdom of God. When we work in faithful obedience to secure our families, the Lord will fight our battles for us by softening the hearts of those in influence over us (as He did in the case of the ancient kings) and by providing strength and leadership in support of the cause of truth.

Ezra was a celebrated, God-fearing priest and scribe who participated in helping with the return of many of the exiles from their Babylonian captivity. He has left us a record of the initial phase of the rebuilding of Jerusalem (from the edict of Cyrus in 537 BC down to the completion of the temple in approximately 515 BC), as well as the annals of his own personal mission some years later, beginning in 458 BC, to assist in the return of many more Israelites to Jerusalem. He was a reformer who taught the people the principles of fasting and prayer, and caused the scriptures to be read publicly to them for their edification and understanding: "For Ezra had prepared his heart to seek the law of the Lord, and to do it, and to teach in Israel statutes and judgments" (Ezra 7:10).

Nehemiah made a similar contribution in facilitating the consolidation of the covenant society by leading the movement to restore the walls of the city for strength and protection. An influential "cupbearer" at the court of King Artaxerxes of Persia (465–425 BC; see Neh. 1:11), Nehemiah was moved by the accounts of the sufferings of his compatriots at Jerusalem and launched a major campaign to come to their assistance for the purpose of restoring the security of the city. For twelve years he labored as governor—against daunting odds and life-threatening plots by enemy forces—to complete the walls of the city: "They which builded on the wall, and they that bare burdens, with those that laded, every one with one of his hands wrought in the work, and with the other hand held a weapon" (Neh. 4:17). Thus Nehemiah and Ezra have left us stirring examples of restoration, rebuilding, fortifying, strengthening, and renewing—all to the glory of God and the service of establishing His kingdom upon the earth for the purpose of saving souls and preparing them for exaltation.

16 And the rulers knew not whither I went, or what I did; neither had I as yet told it to the Jews, nor to the priests, nor to the nobles, nor to the rulers, nor to the rest that did the work.

17 ¶ Then said I unto them, Ye see the distress that we are in, how Jerusalem lieth waste, and the gates thereof are burned with fire: come, and let us build up the wall of Jerusalem, that we be no more a reproach.

18 Then I told them of the hand of my God which was good upon me; as also the king's words that he had spoken unto me. And they said, Let us rise up and build. So they strengthened their hands for this good work.

19 But when Sanballat the Horonite, and Tobiah the servant, the Ammonite, and Geshem the Arabian, heard it, they laughed us to scorn, and despised us, and said, What is this thing that ye do? will ye rebel against the king?

20 Then answered I them, and said unto them, The God of heaven, he will prosper us; therefore we his servants will arise and build: but ye have no portion, nor right, nor memorial, in Jerusalem.

CHAPTER 4

1 BUT it came to pass, that when Sanballat heard that we builded the wall, he was wroth, and took great indignation, and mocked the Jews.

2 And he spake before his brethren and the army of Samaria, and said, What do these feeble Jews? will they fortify themselves? will they sacrifice? will they make an end in a day? will they revive the stones out of the heaps of the rubbish which are burned?

3 Now Tobiah the Ammonite was by him, and he said, Even that which they build, if a fox go up, he shall even break down their stone wall.

4 Hear, O our God; for we are despised: and turn their reproach upon their own head, and give them for a prey in the land of captivity:

5 And cover not their iniquity, and let not their sin be blotted out from before thee: for they have provoked thee to anger before the builders.

6 So built we the wall; and all the wall was joined together unto the half thereof: for the people had a mind to work.

7 ¶ But it came to pass, that when Sanballat, and Tobiah, and the Arabians, and the Ammonites, and the Ashdodites, heard that the walls of Jerusalem were made up, and that the breaches began to be stopped, then they were very wroth,

8 And conspired all of them together to come and to fight against Jerusalem, and to hinder it.

9 Nevertheless we made our prayer unto our God, and set a watch against them day and night, because of them.

10 And Judah said, The strength of the bearers of burdens is decayed, and there is much rubbish; so that we are not able to build the wall.

11 And our adversaries said, They shall not know, neither see, till we come in the midst among them, and slay them, and cause the work to cease.

12 And it came to pass, that when the Jews which dwelt by them came, they said unto us ten times, From all places whence ye shall return unto us they will be upon you.

Nehemiah 2—Summary of Precepts and Principles Associated with Ezra and Nehemiah

The inspiring leadership of Ezra and Nehemiah echoes in the lives of God's leaders in all dispensations of time. The same call to service resounds with even greater urgency in our day as we prepare for the Second Coming and the ushering in of the millennial age. We are on the Lord's business to build His Kingdom: "Wherefore, as ye are agents, ye are on the Lord's errand; and whatever ye do according to the will of the Lord is the Lord's business" (D&C 64:29).

By putting on the whole armor of God we can transcend the negative forces at work to thwart the designs of the Almighty. "And for this cause, that men might be made partakers of the glories which were to be revealed, the Lord sent forth the fulness of his gospel, his everlasting covenant, reasoning in plainness and simplicity—To prepare the weak for those things which are coming on the earth, and for the Lord's errand in the day when the weak shall confound the wise, and the little one become a strong nation, and two shall put their tens of thousands to flight. And by the weak things of the earth the Lord shall thrash the nations by the power of his Spirit" (D&C 133:57–59). Like the Saints at the time of Ezra and Nehemiah, we can don the whole armor of God and take comfort in the hope of Israel: "… for the Lord had made them joyful" (Ezra 6:22).

NEHEMIAH CHAPTER 4

"The principle of knowledge is the principle of salvation. This principle can be comprehended by the faithful and diligent; and everyone that does not obtain knowledge sufficient to be saved will be condemned. The principle of salvation is given us through the knowledge of Jesus Christ. Salvation is nothing more nor less than to triumph over all our enemies and put them under out feet. And when we have power to put all enemies under our feet in this world, and a knowledge to triumph over all evil spirits in the world to come, then we are saved, as in the case of Jesus, who was to reign until He had put all enemies under His feet, and the last enemy was death" —Joseph Smith, HC 5:387–388

13 ¶ Therefore set I in the lower places behind the wall, and on the higher places, I even set the people after their families with their swords, their spears, and their bows.

14 And I looked, and rose up, and said unto the nobles, and to the rulers, and to the rest of the people, Be not ye afraid of them: remember the Lord, which is great and terrible, and fight for your brethren, your sons, and your daughters, your wives, and your houses.

15 And it came to pass, when our enemies heard that it was known unto us, and God had brought their counsel to nought, that we returned all of us to the wall, every one unto his work.

16 And it came to pass from that time forth, that the half of my servants wrought in the work, and the other half of them held both the spears, the shields, and the bows, and the habergeons; and the rulers were behind all the house of Judah.

17 They which builded on the wall, and they that bare burdens, with those that laded, every one with one of his hands wrought in the work, and with the other hand held a weapon.

18 For the builders, every one had his sword girded by his side, and so builded. And he that sounded the trumpet was by me.

19 ¶ And I said unto the nobles, and to the rulers, and to the rest of the people, The work is great and large, and we are separated upon the wall, one far from another.

20 In what place therefore ye hear the sound of the trumpet, resort ye thither unto us: our God shall fight for us.

21 So we laboured in the work: and half of them held the spears from the rising of the morning till the stars appeared.

22 Likewise at the same time said I unto the people, Let every one with his servant lodge within Jerusalem, that in the night they may be a guard to us, and labour on the day.

23 So neither I, nor my brethren, nor my servants, nor the men of the guard which followed me, none of us put off our clothes, saving that every one put them off for washing.

CHAPTER 6

1 NOW it came to pass, when Sanballat, and Tobiah, and Geshem the Arabian, and the rest of our enemies, heard that I had builded the wall, and that there was no breach left therein; (though at that time I had not set up the doors upon the gates;)

2 That Sanballat and Geshem sent unto me, saying, Come, let us meet together in some one of the villages in the plain of Ono. But they thought to do me mischief.

3 And I sent messengers unto them, saying, I am doing a great work, so that I cannot come down: why should the work cease, whilst I leave it, and come down to you?

4 Yet they sent unto me four times after this sort; and I answered them after the same manner.

5 Then sent Sanballat his servant unto me in like manner the fifth time with an open letter in his hand;

Nehemiah 4:1–18—Sacrifice

The story of Nehemiah's leadership in organizing the Israelites to rebuild the walls of Jerusalem, often under threat of attack from enemy forces (the non-Israelite tribes) round about, is a reminder of an incident from Church history that occurred on Wednesday, January 8, 1834, in Kirtland, Ohio. On that day, guards were placed to protect the Kirtland Temple as a result of persecution by detractors and the threat of violence at the hands of the gathering mob. Some workmen were seen armed with a hammer in one hand and a rifle in the other.

Joseph Smith recorded in his journal: "On the morning of the 8th of January, about 1 o'clock, the inhabitants of Kirtland were alarmed by the firing of about thirteen rounds of cannon, by the mob, on the hill about half a mile northwest of the village" (HC 2:2). However, with the coming of dawn, it was determined that the temple was not damaged. Of this period, Heber C. Kimball wrote in the *Times and Seasons*: ". . . and we had to guard ourselves night after night, and for weeks were not permitted to take off our clothes, and were obliged to lay with our fire locks [rifles] in our arms" (HC 2:2).

Do we ponder often enough upon the sacrifices and trials of our forebears—including our ancient brothers and sisters in Old Testament times—and upon their vigilance and endurance in securing for us the blessings that we enjoy so abundantly today? Are we prepared to stand up for righteous principles and guard the things of God with our lives as they did?

NEHEMIAH CHAPTER 6

Nehemiah 6—Completion of the Temple

The walls were finished. The work of God cannot be arrested in its inexorable forward motion. His word will be fulfilled. In our day, this decree has been renewed: "What I the Lord have spoken, I have spoken, and I excuse not myself; and though the heavens and the earth pass away, my word shall not pass away, but shall all be fulfilled, whether by mine own voice or by the voice of my servants, it is the same" (D&C 1:38).

6 Wherein was written, It is reported among the heathen, and Gashmu saith it, that thou and the Jews think to rebel: for which cause thou buildest the wall, that thou mayest be their king, according to these words.

7 And thou hast also appointed prophets to preach of thee at Jerusalem, saying, There is a king in Judah: and now shall it be reported to the king according to these words. Come now therefore, and let us take counsel together.

8 Then I sent unto him, saying, There are no such things done as thou sayest, but thou feignest them out of thine own heart.

9 For they all made us afraid, saying, Their hands shall be weakened from the work, that it be not done. Now therefore, O God, strengthen my hands.

10 Afterward I came unto the house of Shemaiah the son of Delaiah the son of Mehetabeel, who was shut up; and he said, Let us meet together in the house of God, within the temple, and let us shut the doors of the temple: for they will come to slay thee; yea, in the night will they come to slay thee.

11 And I said, Should such a man as I flee? and who is there, that, being as I am, would go into the temple to save his life? I will not go in.

12 And, lo, I perceived that God had not sent him; but that he pronounced this prophecy against me: for Tobiah and Sanballat had hired him.

13 Therefore was he hired, that I should be afraid, and do so, and sin, and that they might have matter for an evil report, that they might reproach me.

14 My God, think thou upon Tobiah and Sanballat according to these their works, and on the prophetess Noadiah, and the rest of the prophets, that would have put me in fear.

15 ¶ So the wall was finished in the twenty and fifth day of the month Elul, in fifty and two days.

16 And it came to pass, that when all our enemies heard thereof, and all the heathen that were about us saw these things, they were much cast down in their own eyes: for they perceived that this work was wrought of our God.

17 ¶ Moreover in those days the nobles of Judah sent many letters unto Tobiah, and the letters of Tobiah came unto them.

18 For there were many in Judah sworn unto him, because he was the son in law of Shechaniah the son of Arah; and his son Johanan had taken the daughter of Meshullam the son of Berechiah.

19 Also they reported his good deeds before me, and uttered my words to him. And Tobiah sent letters to put me in fear.

Nehemiah Viewing . . . Ruins of . . . Jerusalem by Gustave Doré

CHAPTER 8

1 AND all the people gathered themselves together as one man into the street that was before the water gate; and they spake unto Ezra the scribe to bring the book of the law of Moses, which the LORD had commanded to Israel.

2 And Ezra the priest brought the law before the congregation both of men and women, and all that could hear with understanding, upon the first day of the seventh month.

3 And he read therein before the street that was before the water gate from the morning until midday, before the men and the women, and those that could understand; and the ears of all the people were attentive unto the book of the law.

4 And Ezra the scribe stood upon a pulpit of wood, which they had made for the purpose; and beside him stood Mattithiah, and Shema, and Anaiah, and Urijah, and Hilkiah, and Maaseiah, on his right hand; and on his left hand, Pedaiah, and Mishael, and Malchiah, and Hashum, and Hashbadana, Zechariah, and Meshullam.

5 And Ezra opened the book in the sight of all the people; (for he was above all the people;) and when he opened it, all the people stood up:

6 And Ezra blessed the LORD, the great God. And all the people answered, Amen, Amen, with lifting up their hands: and they bowed their heads, and worshipped the LORD with their faces to the ground.

7 Also Jeshua, and Bani, and Sherebiah, Jamin, Akkub, Shabbethai, Hodijah, Maaseiah, Kelita, Azariah, Jozabad, Hanan, Pelaiah, and the Levites, caused the people to understand the law: and the people stood in their place.

8 So they read in the book in the law of God distinctly, and gave the sense, and caused them to understand the reading.

9 ¶ And Nehemiah, which is the Tirshatha, and Ezra the priest the scribe, and the Levites that taught the people, said unto all the people, This day is holy unto the LORD your God; mourn not, nor weep. For all the people wept, when they heard the words of the law.

10 Then he said unto them, Go your way, eat the fat, and drink the sweet, and send portions unto them for whom nothing is prepared: for this day is holy unto our Lord: neither be ye sorry; for the joy of the LORD is your strength.

11 So the Levites stilled all the people, saying, Hold your peace, for the day is holy; neither be ye grieved.

12 And all the people went their way to eat, and to drink, and to send portions, and to make great mirth, because they had understood the words that were declared unto them.

13 ¶ And on the second day were gathered together the chief of the fathers of all the people, the priests, and the Levites, unto Ezra the scribe, even to understand the words of the law.

14 And they found written in the law which the LORD had commanded by Moses, that the children of Israel should dwell in booths in the feast of the seventh month:

15 And that they should publish and proclaim in all their cities, and in Jerusalem, saying, Go forth unto the mount, and fetch olive branches, and pine branches, and myrtle branches, and palm branches, and branches of thick trees, to make booths, as it is written.

16 ¶ So the people went forth, and brought them, and made themselves booths, every one upon the roof of his house, and in their

NEHEMIAH CHAPTER 8

Nehemiah 8:9–10—Tirshatha

As explained earlier, Tirshatha (pronounced "tir-shay'-thah") was an administrative title of Persian origin applied to one appointed as a governor over an area, such as Zerubbabel in relation to Judea (see Ezra 2:63; Neh. 7:65, 70) or Nehemiah.

The impact of the word of the Lord upon the people, read distinctly and expounded so as to make clear the sense and understanding of the law, was to cause them to weep, so transported were they by the Spirit. The people were counseled to "mourn not, nor weep" (verse 9), for they were of a disposition to be elevated in the joy of the occasion, being confirmed in their understanding of the principles of the truth presented to them and in the knowledge that "the joy of the LORD is your strength" (verse 10).

POINT OF INTEREST

"When Nehemiah was sent, in 445 B.C. as is generally accepted, to take up office as the king's special governor in the run-down city of Jerusalem, his action in rebuilding the wall circuit was seen by the neighbours who hemmed Judah in as portending revolt, and protests were promptly made by their governors; for Jerusalem had the reputation of mighty kings (after David captured it from the Jebusites). In this context we meet three dynasts whose families continued to yield power after them—Sanballat in Samaria, which had been the capital of the kingdom of Israel and whose territory was largely peopled by Assyrian deportees from Babylonia and Syria, the Jew Tobias of Amman across the Jordan, and the Arab Geshem of Kedar who may have been occupying Edom as far north as the palace of Lachish, together with representatives of the Philistine administrative centre of Ashdod" (J. M. Cook, *The Persians* [London: Folio Society, 2007]).

courts, and in the courts of the house of God, and in the street of the water gate, and in the street of the gate of Ephraim.

17 And all the congregation of them that were come again out of the captivity made booths, and sat under the booths: for since the days of Jeshua the son of Nun unto that day had not the children of Israel done so. And there was very great gladness.

18 Also day by day, from the first day unto the last day, he read in the book of the law of God. And they kept the feast seven days; and on the eighth day was a solemn assembly, according unto the manner.

THE BOOK OF ESTHER

CHAPTER 3

1 AFTER these things did king Ahasuerus promote Haman the son of Hammedatha the Agagite, and advanced him, and set his seat above all the princes that were with him.

2 And all the king's servants, that were in the king's gate, bowed, and reverenced Haman: for the king had so commanded concerning him. But Mordecai bowed not, nor did him reverence.

3 Then the king's servants, which were in the king's gate, said unto Mordecai, Why transgressest thou the king's commandment?

4 Now it came to pass, when they spake daily unto him, and he hearkened not unto them, that they told Haman, to see whether Mordecai's matters would stand: for he had told them that he was a Jew.

5 And when Haman saw that Mordecai bowed not, nor did him reverence, then was Haman full of wrath.

6 And he thought scorn to lay hands on Mordecai alone; for they had shewed him the people of Mordecai: wherefore Haman sought to destroy all the Jews that were throughout the whole kingdom of Ahasuerus, even the people of Mordecai.

7 ¶ In the first month, that is, the month Nisan, in the twelfth year of king Ahasuerus, they cast Pur, that is, the lot, before Haman from day to day, and from month to month, to the twelfth month, that is, the month Adar.

8 ¶ And Haman said unto king Ahasuerus, There is a certain people scattered abroad and dispersed among the people in all the provinces of thy kingdom; and their laws are diverse from all people; neither keep they the king's laws: therefore it is not for the king's profit to suffer them.

9 If it please the king, let it be written that they may be destroyed: and I will pay ten thousand talents of silver to the hands of those that have the charge of the business, to bring it into the king's treasuries.

10 And the king took his ring from his hand, and gave it unto Haman the son of Hammedatha the Agagite, the Jews' enemy.

11 And the king said unto Haman, The silver is given to thee, the people also, to do with them as it seemeth good to thee.

12 Then were the king's scribes called on the thirteenth day of the first month, and there was written according to all that Haman had commanded unto the king's lieutenants, and to the governors that were over every province, and to the rulers of every people of every

ESTHER CHAPTER 3

Esther 3:1—Ahasuerus

Ahasuerus, the king discussed in the Book of Esther, became Esther's husband (see Esth. 2:17). He is usually identified with Xerxes, king of Persia, whose rule began around 486 BC.

Esther 3:1—Haman

As narrated in the Book of Esther, king Ahasuerus of Persia promoted Haman (pronounced "hay'-muhn") to a position as chief minister among the princes (see Esth. 3:1). However, Mordecai, a Jewish person associated with the court, refused to pay obeisance to Haman. In anger, Haman set up a plan to eliminate all the Jewish people in the kingdom and persuaded the king to authorize it (see Esth. 3:5–15). Esther, the queen and secretly the former ward of her relative Mordecai, then intervened in the matter, even at great peril to her own life to be assertive before the king—and especially as a person of Jewish extraction at the time of Haman's plot. She arranged for a banquet at which Haman was to be honored. At the banquet the truth came out:

> Then Esther the queen answered and said, If I have found favour in thy sight, O king, and if it please the king, let my life be given me at my petition, and my people at my request:
>
> For we are sold, I and my people, to be destroyed, to be slain, and to perish. But if we had been sold for bondmen and bondwomen, I had held my tongue, although the enemy could not countervail the king's damage.
>
> Then the king Ahasuerus answered and said unto Esther the queen, Who is he, and where is he, that durst presume in his heart to do so?
>
> And Esther said, The adversary and enemy is this wicked Haman. Then Haman was afraid before the king and the queen. . . .
>
> And Harbonah, one of the chamberlains, said before the king, Behold also, the gallows fifty cubits high, which Haman had made for Mordecai, who had spoken good for the king, standeth in the house of Haman. Then the king said, Hang him thereon.
>
> So they hanged Haman on the gallows that he had prepared for Mordecai. Then was the king's wrath pacified. (Esth. 7:3–6, 9–10)

Thereafter Mordecai was elevated to position of honor in the court and the Jewish people were preserved (see Esth. 8). The Feast of Purim was instituted to memorialize the triumphant occasion in future years (see Esth. 9).

For more insights into the life of Esther, see Appendix EE.

province according to the writing thereof, and to every people after their language; in the name of king Ahasuerus was it written, and sealed with the king's ring.

13 And the letters were sent by posts into all the king's provinces, to destroy, to kill, and to cause to perish, all Jews, both young and old, little children and women, in one day, even upon the thirteenth day of the twelfth month, which is the month Adar, and to take the spoil of them for a prey.

14 The copy of the writing for a commandment to be given in every province was published unto all people, that they should be ready against that day.

15 The posts went out, being hastened by the king's commandment, and the decree was given in Shushan the palace. And the king and Haman sat down to drink; but the city Shushan was perplexed.

CHAPTER 4

1 WHEN Mordecai perceived all that was done, Mordecai rent his clothes, and put on sackcloth with ashes, and went out into the midst of the city, and cried with a loud and a bitter cry;

2 And came even before the king's gate: for none might enter into the king's gate clothed with sackcloth.

3 And in every province, whithersoever the king's commandment and his decree came, there was great mourning among the Jews, and fasting, and weeping, and wailing; and many lay in sackcloth and ashes.

4 ¶ So Esther's maids and her chamberlains came and told it her. Then was the queen exceedingly grieved; and she sent raiment to clothe Mordecai, and to take away his sackcloth from him: but he received it not.

5 Then called Esther for Hatach, one of the king's chamberlains, whom he had appointed to attend upon her, and gave him a commandment to Mordecai, to know what it was, and why it was.

6 So Hatach went forth to Mordecai unto the street of the city, which was before the king's gate.

7 And Mordecai told him of all that had happened unto him, and of the sum of the money that Haman had promised to pay to the king's treasuries for the Jews, to destroy them.

8 Also he gave him the copy of the writing of the decree that was given at Shushan to destroy them, to shew it unto Esther, and to declare it unto her, and to charge her that she should go in unto the king, to make supplication unto him, and to make request before him for her people.

9 And Hatach came and told Esther the words of Mordecai.

10 ¶ Again Esther spake unto Hatach, and gave him commandment unto Mordecai;

11 All the king's servants, and the people of the king's provinces, do know, that whosoever, whether man or woman, shall come unto the king into the inner court, who is not called, there is one law of his to put him to death, except such to whom the king shall hold out the golden sceptre, that he may live: but I have not been called to come in unto the king these thirty days.

12 And they told to Mordecai Esther's words.

13 Then Mordecai commanded to answer Esther, Think not with thyself that thou shalt escape in the king's house, more than all the Jews.

ESTHER CHAPTER 4

Esther 4—Esther: Example of Courage

Esther, confronted with a choice of great consequence, decides to act on behalf of her people—but to do so in connection with a national fast among the Jewish residents of the land. The objective is to seek the blessings of heaven at a time of dire emergency. Her example of both humility and courage, reverence and boldness, is a memorable lesson in how to act when facing a dire crisis in life.

Ahasuerus and Esther by Rembrandt van Rijn

14 For if thou altogether holdest thy peace at this time, then shall there enlargement and deliverance arise to the Jews from another place; but thou and thy father's house shall be destroyed: and who knoweth whether thou art come to the kingdom for such a time as this?

15 ¶ Then Esther bade them return Mordecai this answer,

16 Go, gather together all the Jews that are present in Shushan, and fast ye for me, and neither eat nor drink three days, night or day: I also and my maidens will fast likewise; and so will I go in unto the king, which is not according to the law: and if I perish, I perish.

17 So Mordecai went his way, and did according to all that Esther had commanded him.

CHAPTER 5

1 NOW it came to pass on the third day, that Esther put on her royal apparel, and stood in the inner court of the king's house, over against the king's house: and the king sat upon his royal throne in the royal house, over against the gate of the house.

2 And it was so, when the king saw Esther the queen standing in the court, that she obtained favour in his sight: and the king held out to Esther the golden sceptre that was in his hand. So Esther drew near, and touched the top of the sceptre.

3 Then said the king unto her, What wilt thou, queen Esther? and what is thy request? it shall be even given thee to the half of the kingdom.

4 And Esther answered, If it seem good unto the king, let the king and Haman come this day unto the banquet that I have prepared for him.

5 Then the king said, Cause Haman to make haste, that he may do as Esther hath said. So the king and Haman came to the banquet that Esther had prepared.

6 ¶ And the king said unto Esther at the banquet of wine, What is thy petition? and it shall be granted thee: and what is thy request? even to the half of the kingdom it shall be performed.

7 Then answered Esther, and said, My petition and my request is;

8 If I have found favour in the sight of the king, and if it please the king to grant my petition, and to perform my request, let the king and Haman come to the banquet that I shall prepare for them, and I will do to morrow as the king hath said.

9 ¶ Then went Haman forth that day joyful and with a glad heart: but when Haman saw Mordecai in the king's gate, that he stood not up, nor moved for him, he was full of indignation against Mordecai.

10 Nevertheless Haman refrained himself: and when he came home, he sent and called for his friends, and Zeresh his wife.

11 And Haman told them of the glory of his riches, and the multitude of his children, and all the things wherein the king had promoted him, and how he had advanced him above the princes and servants of the king.

12 Haman said moreover, Yea, Esther the queen did let no man come in with the king unto the banquet that she had prepared but myself; and to morrow am I invited unto her also with the king.

13 Yet all this availeth me nothing, so long as I see Mordecai the Jew sitting at the king's gate.

ESTHER CHAPTER 5

Esther 5:1–3—The Heart Softened

The heart of the king is softened through the initiative of Esther, she being no doubt strengthened by the spiritual empowerment of the national fast that had been taking place for three days and nights. The Lord has a way of softening the hearts of people in support of the cause of liberty and salvation (see 1 Ne. 2:16; 7:5, 19; 18:19–20; 2 Ne. 10:18; Mosiah 21:15; 23:28–29; Alma 24:8; 62:41; D&C 104:80–81; 105:27; 109:56; 124:9). In one case, the Prophet Joseph Smith prayed that the heart of the Lord might be softened toward His people in their time of need:

Yea, O Lord, how long shall they suffer these wrongs and unlawful oppressions, before thine heart shall be softened toward them, and thy bowels be moved with compassion toward them?

O Lord God Almighty, maker of heaven, earth, and seas, and of all things that in them are, and who controllest and subjectest the devil, and the dark and benighted dominion of Sheol—stretch forth thy hand; let thine eye pierce; let thy pavilion be taken up; let thy hiding place no longer be covered; let thine ear be inclined; let thine heart be softened, and thy bowels moved with compassion toward us. (D&C 121:3–4)

 POINT OF INTEREST

"For official correspondence in the Persian Empire the lingua franca more or less from the outset was Aramaic; and as this was written on perishable materials such as parchment and papyrus, excavators tend to find only the clay sealings that had once secured the documents. . . . The main palaces of the Persian kings can yield documents. Ctesias and the book of Esther speak of royal records of deeds. But they would have been written on perishable materials; and in any case Darius' great inscription at Behistun serves as a warning that a narrative of historical events was only recounted for purposes of self-justification and establishing the claim to rule" (J. M. Cook, *The Persians* [London: Folio Society, 2007]).

14 ¶ Then said Zeresh his wife and all his friends unto him, Let a gallows be made of fifty cubits high, and to morrow speak thou unto the king that Mordecai may be hanged thereon: then go thou in merrily with the king unto the banquet. And the thing pleased Haman; and he caused the gallows to be made.

CHAPTER 7

1 SO the king and Haman came to banquet with Esther the queen.
2 And the king said again unto Esther on the second day at the banquet of wine, What is thy petition, queen Esther? and it shall be granted thee: and what is thy request? and it shall be performed, even to the half of the kingdom.
3 Then Esther the queen answered and said, If I have found favour in thy sight, O king, and if it please the king, let my life be given me at my petition, and my people at my request:
4 For we are sold, I and my people, to be destroyed, to be slain, and to perish. But if we had been sold for bondmen and bondwomen, I had held my tongue, although the enemy could not countervail the king's damage.
5 ¶ Then the king Ahasuerus answered and said unto Esther the queen, Who is he, and where is he, that durst presume in his heart to do so?
6 And Esther said, The adversary and enemy is this wicked Haman. Then Haman was afraid before the king and the queen.
7 ¶ And the king arising from the banquet of wine in his wrath went into the palace garden: and Haman stood up to make request for his life to Esther the queen; for he saw that there was evil determined against him by the king.
8 Then the king returned out of the palace garden into the place of the banquet of wine; and Haman was fallen upon the bed whereon Esther was. Then said the king, Will he force the queen also before me in the house? As the word went out of the king's mouth, they covered Haman's face.
9 And Harbonah, one of the chamberlains, said before the king, Behold also, the gallows fifty cubits high, which Haman had made for Mordecai, who had spoken good for the king, standeth in the house of Haman. Then the king said, Hang him thereon.
10 So they hanged Haman on the gallows that he had prepared for Mordecai. Then was the king's wrath pacified.

CHAPTER 8

1 ON that day did the king Ahasuerus give the house of Haman the Jews' enemy unto Esther the queen. And Mordecai came before the king; for Esther had told what he was unto her.
2 And the king took off his ring, which he had taken from Haman, and gave it unto Mordecai. And Esther set Mordecai over the house of Haman.
3 ¶ And Esther spake yet again before the king, and fell down at his feet, and besought him with tears to put away the mischief of Haman the Agagite, and his device that he had devised against the Jews.
4 Then the king held out the golden sceptre toward Esther. So Esther arose, and stood before the king.
5 And said, If it please the king, and if I have found favour in his

POINT OF INTEREST

"The name Purim probably derives from the Hebrew pur *meaning 'lot,' since the wicked Haman cast lots as to the day on which he should destroy the Jews. . . . The Jews are enjoined at the end of the book (9:28) never to forget this deliverance and to keep these days of Purim in perpetuity from generation to generation. It is thought that the festival was first celebrated in the Diaspora and was accepted in Judah later. During Purim, the Esther scroll is read aloud in synagogues. There are often pageants and masquerades and also plays based on the book, a practice influenced by the injection of elements of the Italian carnival in later centuries. A festival meal takes place that lasts late into the night, and mourning is forbidden."* (John Bowker, *The Complete Bible Handbook* [New York: DK Publishing, 2001]).

sight, and the thing seem right before the king, and I be pleasing in his eyes, let it be written to reverse the letters devised by Haman the son of Hammedatha the Agagite, which he wrote to destroy the Jews which are in all the king's provinces:

6 For how can I endure to see the evil that shall come unto my people? or how can I endure to see the destruction of my kindred?

7 ¶ Then the king Ahasuerus said unto Esther the queen and to Mordecai the Jew, Behold, I have given Esther the house of Haman, and him they have hanged upon the gallows, because he laid his hand upon the Jews.

8 Write ye also for the Jews, as it liketh you, in the king's name, and seal it with the king's ring: for the writing which is written in the king's name, and sealed with the king's ring, may no man reverse.

9 Then were the king's scribes called at that time in the third month, that is, the month Sivan, on the three and twentieth day thereof; and it was written according to all that Mordecai commanded unto the Jews, and to the lieutenants, and the deputies and rulers of the provinces which are from India unto Ethiopia, an hundred twenty and seven provinces, unto every province according to the writing thereof, and unto every people after their language, and to the Jews according to their writing, and according to their language.

10 And he wrote in the king Ahasuerus' name, and sealed it with the king's ring, and sent letters by posts on horseback, and riders on mules, camels, and young dromedaries:

11 Wherein the king granted the Jews which were in every city to gather themselves together, and to stand for their life, to destroy, to slay, and to cause to perish, all the power of the people and province that would assault them, both little ones and women, and to take the spoil of them for a prey,

12 Upon one day in all the provinces of king Ahasuerus, namely, upon the thirteenth day of the twelfth month, which is the month Adar.

13 The copy of the writing for a commandment to be given in every province was published unto all people, and that the Jews should be ready against that day to avenge themselves on their enemies.

14 So the posts that rode upon mules and camels went out, being hastened and pressed on by the king's commandment. And the decree was given at Shushan the palace.

15 ¶ And Mordecai went out from the presence of the king in royal apparel of blue and white, and with a great crown of gold, and with a garment of fine linen and purple: and the city of Shushan rejoiced and was glad.

16 The Jews had light, and gladness, and joy, and honour.

17 And in every province, and in every city, whithersoever the king's commandment and his decree came, the Jews had joy and gladness, a feast and a good day. And many of the people of the land became Jews; for the fear of the Jews fell upon them.

Esther Accusing Haman by Gustave Doré

THE
BOOK OF JOB

CHAPTER 1

1 THERE was a man in the land of Uz, whose name was Job; and that man was perfect and upright, and one that feared God, and eschewed evil.

2 And there were born unto him seven sons and three daughters.

3 His substance also was seven thousand sheep, and three thousand camels, and five hundred yoke of oxen, and five hundred she asses, and a very great household; so that this man was the greatest of all the men of the east.

4 And his sons went and feasted in their houses, every one his day; and sent and called for their three sisters to eat and to drink with them.

5 And it was so, when the days of their feasting were gone about, that Job sent and sanctified them, and rose up early in the morning, and offered burnt offerings according to the number of them all: for Job said, It may be that my sons have sinned, and cursed God in

6 ¶ Now there was a day when the sons of God came to present themselves before the LORD, and Satan came also among them.

7 And the LORD said unto Satan, Whence comest thou? Then Satan answered the LORD, and said, From going to and fro in the earth, and from walking up and down in it.

8 And the LORD said unto Satan, Hast thou considered my servant Job, that there is none like him in the earth, a perfect and an upright man, one that feareth God, and escheweth evil?

9 Then Satan answered the LORD, and said, Doth Job fear God for nought?

10 Hast not thou made an hedge about him, and about his house, and about all that he hath on every side? thou hast blessed the work of his hands, and his substance is increased in the land.

11 But put forth thine hand now, and touch all that he hath, and he will curse thee to thy face.

12 And the LORD said unto Satan, Behold, all that he hath is in thy power; only upon himself put not forth thine hand. So Satan went forth from the presence of the LORD.

13 ¶ And there was a day when his sons and his daughters were eating and drinking wine in their eldest brother's house:

14 And there came a messenger unto Job, and said, The oxen were plowing, and the asses feeding beside them:

15 And the Sabeans fell upon them, and took them away; yea, they have slain the servants with the edge of the sword; and I only am escaped alone to tell thee.

16 While he was yet speaking, there came also another, and said, The fire of God is fallen from heaven, and hath burned up the sheep, and the servants, and consumed them; and I only am escaped alone to tell thee.

17 While he was yet speaking, there came also another, and said, The Chaldeans made out three bands, and fell upon the camels, and have carried them away, yea, and slain the

18 While he was yet speaking, there came also another, and said, Thy sons and thy daughters were eating and drinking wine in their eldest brother's house:

JOB CHAPTER 1

Job 1:1–5—Preview of the Book of Job

The Book of Job is a book of light, for it sets forth in lucid clarity the vision of hope and faith that shines through the shadows of adversity that is every person's mortal experience. There are few treatises or narratives that plum the potential of man, his interrelationships with others, and his integrity of heart with more depth or illumination than the Book of Job.

Job is an unmatched exemplum of individual endurance in transcending adversity and rising to the summit of triumph in the safeguarding and strengthening of a personal testimony of God. Having lost the fulness of his family and estate, having been afflicted with incapacitating ailments, having been accused unjustly of a faulty walk of life, and having every ounce of hope and fortitude sapped from his system, Job nevertheless rose from the depths of adversity to exclaim: "For I know *that* my redeemer liveth, and *that* he shall stand at the latter *day* upon the earth: And *though* after my skin *worms* destroy this *body*, yet in my flesh shall I see God" (Job 19:25–26). Within his soul unfolded the majesty of a son of God holding tightly to the assurance that his royal destiny would in no measure be compromised by the forces of tribulation around him (see Job 23:10–11.) Job, like the Prophet Joseph, proclaimed in faith that his life was in harmony with the will of God, for he knew in certainty of his own integrity—the true test of all things.

Job 1:6—Satan

Satan (meaning: adversary), who is Lucifer, the principal devil and primordial enemy to God, is mentioned in the Old Testament nineteen times, fourteen of them in the Book of Job. As the enemy of all righteousness, Satan is referenced frequently in the text of the Doctrine and Covenants under various names: fallen angel, Perdition, Lucifer, son of the morning, Satan, old serpent, and devil.

For more insight on Satan, see Appendix FF.

Job 1:15—Sabeans

The Sabeans (pronounced "suh-bee'-uns") were an Arab tribe mentioned specifically in four passages of scripture. In Isaiah, the Lord commissions Cyrus, king of Assyria, to decree the return of the captive Israelites from Babylon, and promises him divine support: "Thus saith the LORD, The labour of Egypt, and merchandise of Ethiopia and of the Sabeans, men of stature, shall come over unto thee, and they shall be thine: they shall come after thee; in chains they shall come over, and they shall fall down unto thee, they shall make supplication unto thee, *saying*, Surely God *is* in thee; and *there is* none else, *there is* no God" (Isa. 45:14).

Job 1:17—Chaldeans

The term *Chaldeans* (pronounced "kal-dee'-uns") refers, in general, to the inhabitants of the southern portion of Babylonia.

19 And, behold, there came a great wind from the wilderness, and smote the four corners of the house, and it fell upon the young men, and they are dead; and I only am escaped alone to tell thee.

20 Then Job arose, and rent his mantle, and shaved his head, and fell down upon the ground, and worshipped,

21 And said, Naked came I out of my mother's womb, and naked shall I return thither:

the LORD gave, and the LORD hath taken away; blessed be the name of the LORD.

22 In all this Job sinned not, nor charged God foolishly.

CHAPTER 2

1 AGAIN there was a day when the sons of God came to present themselves before the LORD, and Satan came also among them to present himself before the LORD.

2 And the LORD said unto Satan, From whence comest thou? And Satan answered the LORD, and said, From going to and fro in the earth, and from walking up and down in it.

3 And the LORD said unto Satan, Hast thou considered my servant Job, that there is none like him in the earth, a perfect and an upright man, one that feareth God, and escheweth evil? and still he holdeth fast his integrity, although thou movedst me against him, to destroy him without cause.

4 And Satan answered the LORD, and said, Skin for skin, yea, all that a man hath will he give for his life.

5 But put forth thine hand now, and touch his bone and his flesh, and he will curse thee to thy face.

6 And the LORD said unto Satan, Behold, he is in thine hand; but save his life.

7 ¶ So went Satan forth from the presence of the LORD, and smote Job with sore boils from the sole of his foot unto his crown.

8 And he took him a potsherd to scrape himself withal; and he sat down among the ashes.

9 ¶ Then said his wife unto him, Dost thou still retain thine integrity? curse God, and die.

10 But he said unto her, Thou speakest as one of the foolish women speaketh. What? shall we receive good at the hand of God, and shall we not receive evil? In all this did not Job sin with his lips.

11 ¶ Now when Job's three friends heard of all this evil that was come upon him, they came every one from his own place; Eliphaz the Temanite, and Bildad the Shuhite, and Zophar the Naamathite: for they had made an appointment together to come to mourn with him and to comfort him.

12 And when they lifted up their eyes afar off, and knew him not, they lifted up their voice, and wept; and they rent every one his mantle, and sprinkled dust upon their heads toward heaven.

13 So they sat down with him upon the ground seven days and seven nights, and none spake a word unto him: for they saw that his grief was very great.

Job 1:21—Transcending Adversity

When our hope and faith are anchored in the Lord, then no loss of worldly goods, no interruption of temporal ease, no challenge to our physical well-being can conquer our spirit or our confidence in the saving grace and power of the Lord.

Job was one of the greatest estate holders of his time, with bounteous wealth and a large and devoted family. He was "perfect and upright, and one that feared God, and eschewed evil" (Job 1:1). When Satan was allowed to assail him and bring about the utter destruction of his temporal world, Job remained steadfast and resolute, maintaining his righteous way of living despite overwhelming adversity. He refused to curse God as the adversary had pledged to make him do. He thus became the primordial prototype of the indomitable spirit.

Adversity and opposition in all things is part of the plan for us to become even as He is. Once we understand this concept we will look at adversity with the opportunity to overcome, to gain strength as we endure hardships, and to realize the goodness of our Savior in all of His adversity. He did the will of the Father, and so must we.

JOB CHAPTER 2

Job 2:3—Divine Witness

The Lord provides the ultimate characterization of the goodness of Job—that he is "a perfect and upright man" (verse 3), meaning (in the perspective of Lord) that he "feareth God, and escheweth evil," ever "holding fast his integrity." Would that we all should qualify for such a judgment from our Father in Heaven and His Son.

Job 2:9–10—Job's Wife

Given the severe losses experienced by the family, the wife of Job was suffering just as her husband was. Like Sariah, wife of Lehi in the Book of Mormon, she was no doubt overcome with anguish and thus inclined to murmur and complain concerning the fate of her children (compare 1 Ne. 5:1–7).

But in all of the crushing tribulation, Job maintained his perspective on things and confirmed that the mortal experience involves both joy and anguish, happiness and grief. That is part of our destiny on earth as sons and daughters of God. Even Lehi, at one point, was given over to murmuring over the bitter burden of the journey in the wilderness and had to repent (see 1 Ne. 16:20). Job set a course toward the fulfillment of his earthly sojourn and retained his consistent hope for the future, no matter what ordeals and misfortunes might interrupt his journey.

CHAPTER 13

1 LO, mine eye hath seen all this, mine ear hath heard and understood it.

2 What ye know, the same do I know also: I am not inferior unto you.

3 Surely I would speak to the Almighty, and I desire to reason with God.

4 But ye are forgers of lies, ye are all physicians of no value.

5 O that ye would altogether hold your peace! and it should be your wisdom.

6 Hear now my reasoning, and hearken to the pleadings of my lips.

7 Will ye speak wickedly for God? and talk deceitfully for him?

8 Will ye accept his person? will ye contend for God?

9 Is it good that he should search you out? or as one man mocketh another, do ye so mock him?

10 He will surely reprove you, if ye do secretly accept persons.

11 Shall not his excellency make you afraid? and his dread fall upon you?

12 Your remembrances are like unto ashes, your bodies to bodies of clay.

13 Hold your peace, let me alone, that I may speak, and let come on me what will.

14 Wherefore do I take my flesh in my teeth, and put my life in mine hand?

15 Though he slay me, yet will I trust in him: but I will maintain mine own ways before him.

16 He also shall be my salvation: for an hypocrite shall not come before him.

17 Hear diligently my speech, and my declaration with your ears.

18 Behold now, I have ordered my cause; I know that I shall be justified.

19 Who is he that will plead with me? for now, if I hold my tongue, I shall give up the ghost.

20 Only do not two things unto me: then will I not hide myself from thee.

21 Withdraw thine hand far from me: and let not thy dread make me afraid.

22 Then call thou, and I will answer: or let me speak, and answer thou me.

23 How many are mine iniquities and sins? make me to know my transgression and my sin.

24 Wherefore hidest thou thy face, and holdest me for thine enemy?

25 Wilt thou break a leaf driven to and fro? and wilt thou pursue the dry stubble?

26 For thou writest bitter things against me, and makest me to possess the iniquities of my youth.

27 Thou puttest my feet also in the stocks, and lookest narrowly unto all my paths; thou settest a print upon the heels of my feet.

28 And he, as a rotten thing, consumeth, as a garment that is moth eaten.

JOB CHAPTER 13

Job 13—The Source of Salvation

Job's governing philosophy of life embraces a conviction that the Lord is the source of salvation—no matter what our lot in life might be. Job has faith and certainty that the outcomes of his destiny will be according to the justice and mercy of God.

Job and His Friends by Gustave Doré

CHAPTER 19

1 THEN Job answered and said,

2 How long will ye vex my soul, and break me in pieces with words?

3 These ten times have ye reproached me: ye are not ashamed that ye make yourselves strange to me.

4 And be it indeed that I have erred, mine error remaineth with myself.

5 If indeed ye will magnify yourselves against me, and plead against me my reproach:

6 Know now that God hath overthrown me, and hath compassed me with his net.

7 Behold, I cry out of wrong, but I am not heard: I cry aloud, but there is no judgment.

8 He hath fenced up my way that I cannot pass, and he hath set darkness in my paths.

9 He hath stripped me of my glory, and taken the crown from my head.

10 He hath destroyed me on every side, and I am gone: and mine hope hath he removed like a tree.

11 He hath also kindled his wrath against me, and he counteth me unto him as one of his enemies.

12 His troops come together, and raise up their way against me, and encamp round about my tabernacle.

13 He hath put my brethren far from me, and mine acquaintance are verily estranged from me.

14 My kinsfolk have failed, and my familiar friends have forgotten me.

15 They that dwell in mine house, and my maids, count me for a stranger: I am an alien in their sight.

16 I called my servant, and he gave me no answer; I intreated him with my mouth.

17 My breath is strange to my wife, though I intreated for the children's sake of mine own body.

18 Yea, young children despised me; I arose, and they spake against me.

19 All my inward friends abhorred me: and they whom I loved are turned against me.

20 My bone cleaveth to my skin and to my flesh, and I am escaped with the skin of my teeth.

21 Have pity upon me, have pity upon me, O ye my friends; for the hand of God hath touched me.

22 Why do ye persecute me as God, and are not satisfied with my flesh?

23 Oh that my words were now written! oh that they were printed in a book!

24 That they were graven with an iron pen and lead in the rock for ever!

25 For I know that my redeemer liveth, and that he shall stand at the latter day upon the earth:

26 And though after my skin worms destroy this body, yet in my flesh shall I see God:

27 Whom I shall see for myself, and mine eyes shall behold, and not another; though my reins be consumed within me.

28 But ye should say, Why persecute we him, seeing the root of the matter is found in me?

29 Be ye afraid of the sword: for wrath bringeth the punishments of the sword, that ye may know there is a judgment.

JOB CHAPTER 19

"The gospel embraces principles that dive deeper, spread wider, and extend further than anything else that we can conceive. . . . It 'brings life and immortality to light,' brings us into relationship with God, and prepares us for an exaltation in the eternal world." —John Taylor, *JD* 16:369

Job 19:25—Cultivating an Invincible Testimony

A testimony engendered by the Spirit, cultivated by devotion and obedience, nurtured by sacrifice, and mellowed by suffering is a priceless, inextinguishable beacon along the pathway of life.

Job's life, despite unspeakable challenges, was illuminated by his utter confidence in the living reality of the Savior and his indomitable assurance that he would one day return to the presence of His Maker. Job received enduring strength in the Lord to sustain his mission in life. A pure testimony includes many doctrines and teachings of our Savior Jesus Christ. As we come to this knowledge by the power of the Spirit, it is important not only to obtain it and bear it, but we must live it even as Job of old.

POINT OF INTEREST

These verses imply that God might talk to the devil and those who follow the devil. But rather than reporting an actual conversation, these verses might instead be a symbolic or poetic way of preparing us for what comes next for Job: affliction, the loss of his temporal possessions, and temptation. The Lord does allow Satan to tempt us, because that is part of the plan for mortality, but the Lord does not bargain with Satan or agree to Satan's evil works. What happened to Job, then, happened because it was consistent with the Lord's plan and purpose for Job—not because the Lord entered into some sort of bargain with Satan to afflict and torment Job.

CHAPTER 27

1 MOREOVER Job continued his parable, and said,

2 As God liveth, who hath taken away my judgment; and the Almighty, who hath vexed my soul;

3 All the while my breath is in me, and the spirit of God is in my nostrils;

4 My lips shall not speak wickedness, nor my tongue utter deceit.

5 God forbid that I should justify you: till I die I will not remove mine integrity from me.

6 My righteousness I hold fast, and will not let it go: my heart shall not reproach me so long as I live.

7 Let mine enemy be as the wicked, and he that riseth up against me as the unrighteous.

8 For what is the hope of the hypocrite, though he hath gained, when God taketh away his soul?

9 Will God hear his cry when trouble cometh upon him?

10 Will he delight himself in the Almighty? will he always call upon God?

11 I will teach you by the hand of God: that which is with the Almighty will I not conceal.

12 Behold, all ye yourselves have seen it; why then are ye thus altogether vain?

13 This is the portion of a wicked man with God, and the heritage of oppressors, which they shall receive of the Almighty.

14 If his children be multiplied, it is for the sword: and his offspring shall not be satisfied with bread.

15 Those that remain of him shall be buried in death: and his widows shall not weep.

16 Though he heap up silver as the dust, and prepare raiment as the clay;

17 He may prepare it, but the just shall put it on, and the innocent shall divide the silver.

18 He buildeth his house as a moth, and as a booth that the keeper maketh.

19 The rich man shall lie down, but he shall not be gathered: he openeth his eyes, and he is not.

20 Terrors take hold on him as waters, a tempest stealeth him away in the night.

21 The east wind carrieth him away, and he departeth: and as a storm hurleth him out of his place.

22 For God shall cast upon him, and not spare: he would fain flee out of his hand.

23 Men shall clap their hands at him, and shall hiss him out of his place.

JOB CHAPTER 27

Job 27:3—Health and Wholeness

It is our nature as "children of God" (Rom. 8:16) to long for eternal health—and yearn for unending wholeness. We are capacitated to become whole, "by faith in Christ Jesus" (Gal. 3:26), even as God is whole. But in our present state, we savor only a hint of our vast potential to be free and whole, even as "the children of the resurrection" (Luke 20:36) are lifted to a celestial plane of wellness and vitality. Still, hope glows brightly within our souls—hope of attaining one day that higher measure of heavenly health and glory reserved by grace for the heirs of exaltation.

For now, we give thanks for shadows and types of blessings yet to come: Within our being we feel the flow of life—the pulsing of the heart, the quickening of breath—reminding us all that health and wholeness come as gifts from God. We see the radiance of the dawn and feel its glow upon our face—and feel renewed in silent gratitude to share in wonders such as these—no matter what our age or circumstance might be.

Being whole is a choice and chosen state inherent in our covenant heritage: "Thy faith hath made thee whole," was the saying of our Lord to those restored to wellness by His loving hand. "Thy faith hath made thee whole"—such simple words, yet cloaked in grandeur, encompassing as they do the aim of our existence and the certain means to bring it firmly within our grasp. Do we not all aspire to be whole, with perfect body, gifted mind, and holy spirit? Are we not grateful to understand that the power of faith will make these transcendent gifts forever ours?

Wholeness derives from the glorious partnership between our Father in Heaven and His children. Through the grace of God, we can be whole in the ultimate sense—"perfect in Christ" as Moroni said (Moro. 10:32–33). Through faith we can be raised to a higher state of well-being in this life, sustained by the hope in the heavenly power of the resurrection, where the trump of God will call us forth into a future phase of perfect restoration (see Rev. 21:4). With thankful hearts we obtain greater views of the liberation to come: "Because the creature itself also shall be delivered from the bondage of corruption into the glorious liberty of the children of God" (Rom. 8:21).

Meanwhile, we learn of health by transcending sickness. We learn of wholeness by overcoming sin. We learn of well-being by transforming loneliness through the triumph of belonging within circles of love. We learn of glory by turning away from darkness and following in the footsteps of the Master. And we are thankful to Heavenly Father, the Grand Physician, and to His Son, the Source of sacred living waters, for the extraordinary blessing of health, wholeness, and well-being that come alone through authentic discipleship.

Job 27:6—Testimony of Self

Having a testimony of God and His plan of happiness is essential to salvation; but it is also essential to have a testimony of one's self, a conviction that as a son or daughter

CHAPTER 42

1 THEN Job answered the LORD, and said,

2 I know that thou canst do every thing, and that no thought can be withholden from thee.

3 Who is he that hideth counsel without knowledge? therefore have I uttered that I understood not; things too wonderful for me, which I knew not.

4 Hear, I beseech thee, and I will speak: I will demand of thee, and declare thou unto me.

5 I have heard of thee by the hearing of the ear: but now mine eye seeth thee.

6 Wherefore I abhor myself, and repent in dust and ashes.

7 ¶ And it was so, that after the LORD had spoken these words unto Job, the LORD said to Eliphaz the Temanite, My wrath is kindled against thee, and against thy two friends: for ye have not spoken of me the thing that is right, as my servant Job hath.

8 Therefore take unto you now seven bullocks and seven rams, and go to my servant Job, and offer up for yourselves a burnt offering; and my servant Job shall pray for you: for him will I accept: lest I deal with you after your folly, in that ye have not spoken of me the thing which is right, like my servant Job.

9 So Eliphaz the Temanite and Bildad the Shuhite and Zophar the Naamathite went, and did according as the LORD commanded them: the LORD also accepted Job.

10 And the LORD turned the captivity of Job, when he prayed for his friends: also the LORD gave Job twice as much as he had before.

11 Then came there unto him all his brethren, and all his sisters, and all they that had been of his acquaintance before, and did eat bread with him in his house: and they bemoaned him, and comforted him over all the evil that the LORD had brought upon him: every man also gave him a piece of money, and every one an earring of gold.

12 So the LORD blessed the latter end of Job more than his beginning: for he had fourteen thousand sheep, and six thousand camels, and a thousand yoke of oxen, and a thousand she asses.

13 He had also seven sons and three daughters.

14 And he called the name of the first, Jemima; and the name of the second, Kezia; and the name of the third, Keren-happuch.

15 And in all the land were no women found so fair as the daughters of Job: and their father gave them inheritance among their brethren.

16 After this lived Job an hundred and forty years, and saw his sons, and his sons' sons, even four generations.

17 So Job died, being old and full of days.

of God you will have the determination and endurance to hold fast to the way of righteousness and integrity. Through the blessings of heaven, you will believe in yourself and your eternal destiny to do what your Father in Heaven and His Only Begotten Son will have you do—and thus complete your probationary mortality with honor and valor.

JOB CHAPTER 42

Job 42:12—After the Trial of Faith Flow the Blessings

Our Father in Heaven delights in blessing His children. Though faith must precede the miracle and obedience the flow of the Lord's choicest blessings, His mission is to bring about the immortality and eternal life of man, with all attendant blessings of glory and joy in rich abundance.

Job lost everything but his testimony and his faith. And yet the Lord restored to this man in his sustained righteousness *double* what he had had before, and he received seven new sons and three new daughters to add to his ten children lost in the whirlwind. Thus his confidence in the Lord was confirmed and his happiness complete, for he had "… spoken of me the thing that is right" (Job 42:7).

The story of Job is the story of mortality with all of its adversity and trials. We can glean from it eternal verities that bring us to an understanding and appreciation for others. Our empathy will increase. Our judgments will be more merciful, for no one knows the reason for hardship or difficulties given to another. We will recognize in our life that sooner or later things will be better and always to trust in the Lord, for earth life, compared to eternity, is but for a small moment.

Job—Summary of Precepts and Principles

The Lord declares: "I have commanded you to bring up your children in light and truth" (D&C 93:40). An important dimension of that task is to display for our children and others the Job-like qualities of spiritual resilience, steadfast loyalty, and unassailable faith in the face of whatever degree of adversity this mortal experience can place in our pathway. Through our patience in the Lord, the strength of our testimony in His goodness, and our longsuffering faith in His saving grace, we can overcome adversity and enjoy the enduring blessings of the gospel. We can emulate the example of the Savior: "Behold, I am Jesus Christ, the Son of the living God, who created the heavens and the earth, a light which cannot be hid in darkness" (D&C 14:9). We can be "the candle of the Lord" (Prov. 20:27) and say with Job, "yet will I trust in him" (Job 13:15).

THE
BOOK OF PSALMS

PSALM 4

To the chief Musician on Neginoth, A Psalm of David.

1 HEAR me when I call, O God of my righteousness: thou hast enlarged me when I was in distress; have mercy upon me, and hear my prayer.

2 O ye sons of men, how long will ye turn my glory into shame? how long will ye love vanity, and seek after leasing? Selah.

3 But know that the LORD hath set apart him that is godly for himself: the LORD will hear when I call unto him.

4 Stand in awe, and sin not: commune with your own heart upon your bed, and be still. Selah.

5 Offer the sacrifices of righteousness, and put your trust in the LORD.

6 There be many that say, Who will shew us any good? LORD, lift thou up the light of thy countenance upon us.

7 Thou hast put gladness in my heart, more than in the time that their corn and their wine increased.

8 I will both lay me down in peace, and sleep: for thou, LORD, only makest me dwell in safety.

PSALM 5

To the chief Musician upon Nehiloth, A Psalm of David.

1 GIVE ear to my words, O LORD, consider my meditation.

2 Hearken unto the voice of my cry, my King, and my God: for unto thee will I pray.

3 My voice shalt thou hear in the morning, O LORD; in the morning will I direct my prayer unto thee, and will look up.

4 For thou art not a God that hath pleasure in wickedness: neither shall evil dwell with thee.

5 The foolish shall not stand in thy sight: thou hatest all workers of iniquity.

6 Thou shalt destroy them that speak leasing: the LORD will abhor the bloody and deceitful man.

7 But as for me, I will come into thy house in the multitude of thy mercy: and in thy fear will I worship toward thy holy temple.

8 Lead me, O LORD, in thy righteousness because of mine enemies; make thy way straight before my face.

9 For there is no faithfulness in their mouth; their inward part is very wickedness; their throat is an open sepulchre; they flatter with their tongue.

10 Destroy thou them, O God; let them fall by their own counsels; cast them out in the multitude of their transgressions; for they have rebelled against thee.

11 But let all those that put their trust in thee rejoice: let them ever shout for joy, because thou defendest them: let them also that love thy name be joyful in thee.

12 For thou, LORD, wilt bless the righteous; with favour wilt thou compass him as with a shield.

PSALM 5

Psalm 5:7—The Temple

The temple is the dynamic monument of God's mercy, for it represents the highest endowment of grace and glory available to the faithful Saints through the power of priesthood ordinances on earth. The Psalmist makes clear the appropriate approach to the temple: not to admire it externally, but to go *into* it. We worship by orienting ourselves *toward* the temple, then conduct our lives in such a way that we are worthy to participate in its sacred ordinances.

Psalm 5:11—Trust in the Lord

How do we know if we are putting our trust in the Lord? Because we will feel within ourselves the expanding spirit of rejoicing, comfort, and security—no matter what tribulations we might face. Our confidence will increase as we put our trust in the Lord and obey His every command:

Let thy bowels also be full of charity towards all men, and to the household of faith, and let virtue garnish thy thoughts unceasingly; then shall thy confidence wax strong in the presence of God; and the doctrine of the priesthood shall distil upon thy soul as the dews from heaven.

The Holy Ghost shall be thy constant companion, and thy scepter an unchanging scepter of righteousness and truth; and thy dominion shall be an everlasting dominion, and without compulsory means it shall flow unto thee forever and ever. (D&C 121:45–46)

PSALM 9

To the chief Musician upon Muth-labben, A Psalm of David.

1 I WILL praise thee, O LORD, with my whole heart; I will shew forth all thy marvellous works.

2 I will be glad and rejoice in thee: I will sing praise to thy name, O thou most High.

3 When mine enemies are turned back, they shall fall and perish at thy presence.

4 For thou hast maintained my right and my cause; thou satest in the throne judging right.

5 Thou hast rebuked the heathen, thou hast destroyed the wicked, thou hast put out their name for ever and ever.

6 O thou enemy, destructions are come to a perpetual end: and thou hast destroyed cities; their memorial is perished with them.

7 But the LORD shall endure for ever: he hath prepared his throne for judgment.

8 And he shall judge the world in righteousness, he shall minister judgment to the people in uprightness.

9 The LORD also will be a refuge for the oppressed, a refuge in times of trouble.

10 And they that know thy name will put their trust in thee: for thou, LORD, hast not forsaken them that seek thee.

11 Sing praises to the LORD, which dwelleth in Zion: declare among the people his doings.

12 When he maketh inquisition for blood, he remembereth them: he forgetteth not the cry of the humble.

13 Have mercy upon me, O LORD; consider my trouble which I suffer of them that hate me, thou that liftest me up from the gates of death:

14 That I may shew forth all thy praise in the gates of the daughter of Zion: I will rejoice in thy salvation.

15 The heathen are sunk down in the pit that they made: in the net which they hid is their own foot taken.

16 The LORD is known by the judgment which he executeth: the wicked is snared in the work of his own hands. Higgaion. Selah.

17 The wicked shall be turned into hell, and all the nations that forget God.

18 For the needy shall not alway be forgotten: the expectation of the poor shall not perish for ever.

19 Arise, O LORD; let not man prevail: let the heathen be judged in thy sight.

20 Put them in fear, O LORD: that the nations may know themselves to be but men. Selah.

PSALM 15

A Psalm of David.

1 LORD, who shall abide in thy tabernacle? who shall dwell in thy holy hill?

2 He that walketh uprightly, and worketh righteousness, and speaketh the truth in his heart.

PSALM 9

Psalm 9:10—The Name of the Lord

What does it mean to know the name of the Lord? It means to recognize Him as Creator, Savior, Redeemer, the Anointed One, the Unchanging One, the Great I Am, the Eternal King. To know Him in His role as the Lamb of God, with infinite mercy, love, compassion, and understanding is to put one's trust in Him and strive to take upon one's self the divine nature (see 2 Pet. 1:4–8; D&C 4).

PSALM 15

Psalm 15—Worthiness

The Psalm is a microcosm of the temple recommend interview, for it defines some of the qualities characteristic of those found worthy to enter into the House of the Lord: to walk uprightly, to work righteousness, to speak the truth, and to be forgiving and kind with one's neighbors.

3 He that backbiteth not with his tongue, nor doeth evil to his neighbour, nor taketh up a reproach against his neighbour.

4 In whose eyes a vile person is contemned; but he honoureth them that fear the LORD. He that sweareth to his own hurt, and changeth not.

5 He that putteth not out his money to usury, nor taketh reward against the innocent. He that doeth these things shall never be moved.

PSALM 16

Michtam of David.

1 PRESERVE me, O God: for in thee do I put my trust.

2 O my soul, thou hast said unto the LORD, Thou art my Lord: my goodness extendeth not to thee;

3 But to the saints that are in the earth, and to the excellent, in whom is all my delight.

4 Their sorrows shall be multiplied that hasten after another god: their drink offerings of blood will I not offer, nor take up their names into my lips.

5 The LORD is the portion of mine inheritance and of my cup: thou maintainest my lot.

6 The lines are fallen unto me in pleasant places; yea, I have a goodly heritage.

7 I will bless the LORD, who hath given me counsel: my reins also instruct me in the night seasons.

8 I have set the LORD always before me: because he is at my right hand, I shall not be moved.

9 Therefore my heart is glad, and my glory rejoiceth: my flesh also shall rest in hope.

10 For thou wilt not leave my soul in hell; neither wilt thou suffer thine Holy One to see corruption.

11 Thou wilt shew me the path of life: in thy presence is fulness of joy; at thy right hand there are pleasures for evermore.

PSALM 18

To the chief Musician, A Psalm of David, the servant of the LORD, who spake unto the LORD the words of this song in the day that the LORD delivered him from the hand of all his enemies, and from the hand of Saul: And he said,

1 I WILL love thee, O LORD, my strength.

2 The LORD is my rock, and my fortress, and my deliverer; my God, my strength, in whom I will trust; my buckler, and the horn of my salvation, and my high tower.

3 I will call upon the LORD, who is worthy to be praised: so shall I be saved from mine enemies.

4 The sorrows of death compassed me, and the floods of ungodly men made me afraid.

5 The sorrows of hell compassed me about: the snares of death prevented me.

6 In my distress I called upon the LORD, and cried unto my God: he heard my voice out of his temple, and my cry came before him, even into his ears.

7 Then the earth shook and trembled; the foundations also of the hills moved and were shaken, because he was wroth.

PSALM 16

Psalm 16:1—Winning the Battle Within: Redeeming the Soul

Every mortal has occasion to feel the pangs of remorse for misdeeds and sins. Every mortal who has reached the state of accountability must experience the motivating need to rise above the carnal self to a state of being more in keeping with one's innate potential as a son or daughter of God.

We must continually pray for forgiveness, just as David did. We must continually praise the Lord for His mercy and His atoning sacrifice on our behalf, just as David did. Compare also the following verses:

> "Who shall ascend into the hill of the Lord? or who shall stand in his holy place? He that hath clean hands, and a pure heart." (Ps. 24:3–4)

> "Create in me a clean heart, O God." (Ps. 51:11)

Psalm 16:10—Salvation

These words are recalled in specific passages from the New Testament:

> He seeing this before spake of the resurrection of Christ, that his soul was not left in hell, neither his flesh did see corruption.
> This Jesus hath God raised up, whereof we all are witnesses. (Acts 2:31–32)

> And as concerning that he raised him up from the dead, *now* no more to return to corruption, he said on this wise, I will give you the sure mercies of David.
> Wherefore he saith also in another *psalm*, Thou shalt not suffer thine Holy One to see corruption. (Acts 13:34–35)

PSALM 18

Psalm 18:1–2—Winning the Battle Without: Defending and Building Up Zion

We are all enlisted in the Lord's army in these latter days. Like David, we can sing the songs of Zion, pray for the Lord's protecting and guiding hand over the growth of His kingdom amid the threat from external enemies, and praise His glory and His matchless love for mankind. We can put our trust in His benevolence and lovingkindness. Compare also the following verse:

> "Let all those that seek thee rejoice and be glad in thee: and let such as love thy salvation say continually, Let God be magnified." (Ps. 70:4)

8 There went up a smoke out of his nostrils, and fire out of his mouth devoured: coals were kindled by it.

9 He bowed the heavens also, and came down: and darkness was under his feet.

10 And he rode upon a cherub, and did fly: yea, he did fly upon the wings of the wind.

11 He made darkness his secret place; his pavilion round about him were dark waters and thick clouds of the skies.

12 At the brightness that was before him his thick clouds passed, hail stones and coals of fire.

13 The LORD also thundered in the heavens, and the Highest gave his voice; hail stones and coals of fire.

14 Yea, he sent out his arrows, and scattered them; and he shot out lightnings, and discomfited them.

15 Then the channels of waters were seen, and the foundations of the world were discovered at thy rebuke, O LORD, at the blast of the breath of thy nostrils.

16 He sent from above, he took me, he drew me out of many waters.

17 He delivered me from my strong enemy, and from them which hated me: for they were too strong for me.

18 They prevented me in the day of my calamity: but the LORD was my stay.

19 He brought me forth also into a large place; he delivered me, because he delighted in me.

20 The LORD rewarded me according to my righteousness; according to the cleanness of my hands hath he recompensed me.

21 For I have kept the ways of the LORD, and have not wickedly departed from my God.

22 For all his judgments were before me, and I did not put away his statutes from me.

23 I was also upright before him, and I kept myself from mine iniquity.

24 Therefore hath the LORD recompensed me according to my righteousness, according to the cleanness of my hands in his eyesight.

25 With the merciful thou wilt shew thyself merciful; with an upright man thou wilt shew thyself upright;

26 With the pure thou wilt shew thyself pure; and with the froward thou wilt shew thyself froward.

27 For thou wilt save the afflicted people; but wilt bring down high looks.

28 For thou wilt light my candle: the LORD my God will enlighten my darkness.

29 For by thee I have run through a troop; and by my God have I leaped over a wall.

30 As for God, his way is perfect: the word of the LORD is tried: he is a buckler to all those that trust in him.

31 For who is God save the LORD? or who is a rock save our God?

32 It is God that girdeth me with strength, and maketh my way perfect.

33 He maketh my feet like hinds' feet, and setteth me upon my high places.

34 He teacheth my hands to war, so that a bow of steel is broken by mine arms.

35 Thou hast also given me the shield of thy salvation: and thy right hand hath holden me up, and thy gentleness hath made me great.

DAVID PRAISING THE LORD

Praise him with the sound of a trumpet,
Praise him with the Psaltery and Harp.
Psalm CL.v.3.

Pub. by Hogg & Co. Paternoster row.

POINT OF INTEREST

"The Hebrew title of the book means 'praises.' The English title (Psalms) comes from the Septuagint, the ancient Greek translation of the Hebrew Old Testament. The Greek word psalmoi *means 'songs,' from which comes the idea, 'songs of praises' or 'praise songs.' The individual psalms of the book came from several authors. David, the sweet psalmist of Israel (2 Sam. 23:1), wrote approximately half of the 150 psalms in the book. David's psalms became the standard followed by others, thereby, imprinting a Davidic character to the entire book. Other authors include Asaph (12), the sons of Korah (10), Solomon (2), Moses (1), Heman (1), and Ethan (1). Approximately 48 psalms are anonymous." (Illustrated Bible Dictionary* [Nashville, Tenn: Holman Bible Publishers, 2003]).

36 Thou hast enlarged my steps under me, that my feet did not slip.
37 I have pursued mine enemies, and overtaken them: neither did I turn again till they were consumed.
38 I have wounded them that they were not able to rise: they are fallen under my feet.
39 For thou hast girded me with strength unto the battle: thou hast subdued under me those that rose up against me.
40 Thou hast also given me the necks of mine enemies; that I might destroy them that hate me.
41 They cried, but there was none to save them: even unto the LORD, but he answered them not.
42 Then did I beat them small as the dust before the wind: I did cast them out as the dirt in the streets.
43 Thou hast delivered me from the strivings of the people; and thou hast made me the head of the heathen: a people whom I have not known shall serve me.
44 As soon as they hear of me, they shall obey me: the strangers shall submit themselves unto me.
45 The strangers shall fade away, and be afraid out of their close places.
46 The LORD liveth; and blessed be my rock; and let the God of my salvation be exalted.
47 It is God that avengeth me, and subdueth the people under me.
48 He delivereth me from mine enemies: yea, thou liftest me up above those that rise up against me: thou hast delivered me from the violent man.
49 Therefore will I give thanks unto thee, O LORD, among the heathen, and sing praises unto thy name.
50 Great deliverance giveth he to his king; and sheweth mercy to his anointed, to David, and to his seed for evermore.

PSALM 23

A Psalm of David.
1 THE LORD is my shepherd; I shall not want.
2 He maketh me to lie down in green pastures: he leadeth me beside the still waters.
3 He restoreth my soul: he leadeth me in the paths of righteousness for his name's sake.
4 Yea, though I walk through the valley of the shadow of death, I will fear no evil: for thou art with me; thy rod and thy staff they comfort me.
5 Thou preparest a table before me in the presence of mine enemies: thou anointest my head with oil; my cup runneth over.
6 Surely goodness and mercy shall follow me all the days of my life: and I will dwell in the house of the LORD for ever.

POINT OF INTEREST

The organization and numbering of the Psalms differs slightly between the Hebrew (Masoretic) and the Greek (Septuagint) manuscripts:

Hebrew	Greek
1–8	1–8
9–10	9
11–113	10–112
114–115	113
116	114–115
117–146	116–145
147	146–147
148–150	148–150

Christian traditions vary:
- Protestant translations are based on Hebrew numbering
- Eastern Orthodox translations are based on Greek numbering
- Roman Catholic official liturgical texts follow Greek numbering, but modern Catholic translations often use Hebrew numbering, sometimes adding, in parenthesis, the Greek numbering as well.

PSALM 23

Psalm 23—Mission of the Savior
David's several messianic songs of praise give form and shape to his visions of the future mission of the Savior—"the Lord is my Shepherd" (Ps. 23). David's incomparable poetic imagery lifts our spirits and opens to our minds the visions of grandeur that David himself must have experienced in prophetic moods.

We are to follow our Shepherd and become shepherds to those we have responsibility for, including all those who know not God. The love, mercy, and forgiveness of the Redeemer are blessings of incomparable magnitude, eliciting our continual expressions of thanksgiving and gratitude.

PSALM 24

A Psalm of David.

1 THE earth is the LORD's, and the fulness thereof; the world, and they that dwell therein.

2 For he hath founded it upon the seas, and established it upon the floods.

3 Who shall ascend into the hill of the LORD? or who shall stand in his holy place?

4 He that hath clean hands, and a pure heart; who hath not lifted up his soul unto vanity, nor sworn deceitfully.

5 He shall receive the blessing from the LORD, and righteousness from the God of his salvation.

6 This is the generation of them that seek him, that seek thy face, O Jacob. Selah.

7 Lift up your head, O ye gates; and be ye lift up, ye everlasting doors; and the King of glory shall come in.

8 Who is this King of glory? The LORD strong and mighty, the LORD mighty in battle.

9 Lift up your heads, O ye gates; even lift them up, ye everlasting doors; and the King of glory shall come in.

10 Who is this King of glory? The LORD of hosts, he is the King of glory. Selah.

PSALM 27

A Psalm of David.

1 THE LORD is my light and my salvation; whom shall I fear? the LORD is the strength of my life; of whom shall I be afraid?

2 When the wicked, even mine enemies and my foes, came upon me to eat up my flesh, they stumbled and fell.

3 Though an host should encamp against me, my heart shall not fear: though war should rise against me, in this will I be confident.

4 One thing have I desired of the LORD, that will I seek after; that I may dwell in the house of the LORD all the days of my life, to behold the beauty of the LORD, and to enquire in his temple.

5 For in the time of trouble he shall hide me in his pavilion: in the secret of his tabernacle shall he hide me; he shall set me up upon a rock.

6 And now shall mine head be lifted up above mine enemies round about me: therefore will I offer in his tabernacle sacrifices of joy; I will sing, yea, I will sing praises unto the LORD.

7 Hear, O LORD, when I cry with my voice: have mercy also upon me, and answer me.

8 When thou saidst, Seek ye my face; my heart said unto thee, Thy face, LORD, will I seek.

9 Hide not thy face far from me; put not thy servant away in anger: thou hast been my help; leave me not, neither forsake me, O God of my salvation.

10 When my father and my mother forsake me, then the LORD will take me up.

11 Teach me thy way, O LORD, and lead me in a plain path, because of mine enemies.

12 Deliver me not over unto the will of mine enemies: for false witnesses are risen up against me, and such as breathe out cruelty.

13 I had fainted, unless I had believed to see the goodness of the LORD in the land of the living.

PSALM 24

Psalm 24—Prayers for Forgiveness

David's anguish over his own carnality, his prayers for redemption, his praise of the Master's Atonement—all set the tone and the example for our own prayers for forgiveness and praise for the Redeemer's mission of Atonement and love.

The Saints of God know the steps of faith, repentance, and the baptism of water and fire. Our prayers and songs of praise are to reflect our heartfelt thanks for God's love and our commitment to keep His commandments and endure to the end.

Through the goodness of God He can restore us and make us whole as we repent and call upon His name. By the power of the Atonement and Resurrection we can be made perfect if we but do our part (see 2 Ne. 25:23).

Psalm 24:5–10—Worthiness to Enter

The righteous qualities invoked by this Psalm define the nature of worthiness required to enter into the House of the Lord: having clean hands and a pure heart, being free of vanity and dishonesty, and seeking the face of the Lord always.

PSALM 27

Psalm 27:4—The Mansions of the Father and the Son

The ultimate aspiration of the Saints is to be received one day into the eternal mansions of glory of the Father and the Son. Our rehearsal in this world is to enter into the temples of the Lord and learn there the principles and requirements essential to make this transition back home once again in the world to come. David reminds us of the sacred desire needed for this process: the desire to dwell with God eternally, and to "enquire" meanwhile in his temple in order to receive the understanding, ordinances, and keys for the homeward journey.

14 Wait on the LORD: be of good courage, and he shall strengthen thine heart: wait, I say, on the LORD.

PSALM 31

To the chief Musician, A Psalm of David.

1 IN thee, O LORD, do I put my trust; let me never be ashamed: deliver me in thy righteousness.

2 Bow down thine ear to me; deliver me speedily: be thou my strong rock, for an house of defence to save me.

3 For thou art my rock and my fortress; therefore for thy name's sake lead me, and guide me.

4 Pull me out of the net that they have laid privily for me: for thou art my strength.

5 Into thine hand I commit my spirit: thou hast redeemed me, O LORD God of truth.

6 I have hated them that regard lying vanities: but I trust in the LORD.

7 I will be glad and rejoice in thy mercy: for thou hast considered my trouble; thou hast known my soul in adversities;

8 And hast not shut me up into the hand of the enemy: thou hast set my feet in a large room.

9 Have mercy upon me, O LORD, for I am in trouble: mine eye is consumed with grief, yea, my soul and my belly.

10 For my life is spent with grief, and my years with sighing: my strength faileth because of mine iniquity, and my bones are consumed.

11 I was a reproach among all mine enemies, but especially among my neighbours, and a fear to mine acquaintance: they that did see me without fled from me.

12 I am forgotten as a dead man out of mind: I am like a broken vessel.

13 For I have heard the slander of many: fear was on every side: while they took counsel together against me, they devised to take away my life.

14 But I trusted in thee, O LORD: I said, Thou art my God.

15 My times are in thy hand: deliver me from the hand of mine enemies, and from them that persecute me.

16 Make thy face to shine upon thy servant: save me for thy mercies' sake.

17 Let me not be ashamed, O LORD; for I have called upon thee: let the wicked be ashamed, and let them be silent in the grave.

18 Let the lying lips be put to silence; which speak grievous things proudly and contemptuously against the righteous.

19 Oh how great is thy goodness, which thou hast laid up for them that fear thee; which thou hast wrought for them that trust in thee before the sons of men!

20 Thou shalt hide them in the secret of thy presence from the pride of man: thou shalt keep them secretly in a pavilion from the strife of tongues.

21 Blessed be the LORD: for he hath shewed me his marvellous kindness in a strong city.

22 For I said in my haste, I am cut off from before thine eyes: nevertheless thou heardest the voice of my supplications when I cried unto thee.

23 O love the LORD, all ye his saints: for the LORD preserveth the faithful, and plentifully rewardeth the proud doer.

24 Be of good courage, and he shall strengthen your heart, all ye that hope in the LORD.

David with the Ark of the Covenant, chromolithograph

 POINT OF INTEREST

"The book of Psalms contains individual psalms covering a thousand-year period from the time of Moses (15th century B.C.) to the postexilic period (5th century B.C.). Most of the psalms were written in the time of David and Solomon (1010–930 B.C.). The final editor of the work was probably Ezra (450 B.C.)" (*Illustrated Bible Dictionary* [Nashville, Tenn: Holman Bible Publishers, 2003]).

PSALM 34

A Psalm of David, when he changed his behaviour before Abimelech; who drove him away, and he departed.

1 I WILL bless the LORD at all times: his praise shall continually be in my mouth.

2 My soul shall make her boast in the LORD: the humble shall hear thereof, and be glad.

3 O magnify the LORD with me, and let us exalt his name together.

4 I sought the LORD, and he heard me, and delivered me from all my fears.

5 They looked unto him, and were lightened: and their faces were not ashamed.

6 This poor man cried, and the LORD heard him, and saved him out of all his troubles.

7 The angel of the LORD encampeth round about them that fear him, and delivereth them.

8 O taste and see that the LORD is good: blessed is the man that trusteth in him.

9 O fear the LORD, ye his saints: for there is no want to them that fear him.

10 The young lions do lack, and suffer hunger: but they that seek the LORD shall not want any good thing.

11 Come, ye children, hearken unto me: I will teach you the fear of the LORD.

12 What man is he that desireth life, and loveth many days, that he may see good?

13 Keep thy tongue from evil, and thy lips from speaking guile.

14 Depart from evil, and do good; seek peace, and pursue it.

15 The eyes of the LORD are upon the righteous, and his ears are open unto their cry.

16 The face of the LORD is against them that do evil, to cut off the remembrance of them from the earth.

17 The righteous cry, and the LORD heareth, and delivereth them out of all their troubles.

18 The LORD is nigh unto them that are of a broken heart; and saveth such as be of a contrite spirit.

19 Many are the afflictions of the righteous: but the LORD delivereth him out of them all.

20 He keepeth all his bones: not one of them is broken.

21 Evil shall slay the wicked: and they that hate the righteous shall be desolate.

22 The LORD redeemeth the soul of his servants: and none of them that trust in him shall be desolate.

PSALM 34

Psalm 34:5—Conscience

The light of the sun is given to all mankind in every clime and every generation. Every dawn reminds us of this supernal gift—and we are ever thankful for the miracle of the rising sun. There is another light given to everyone as well—an inner dawn that illuminates the pathway of goodness. It is the light of Christ. It moves us away from darkness and evil and "inviteth to do good, and to persuade to believe in Christ" (Moro. 7:16). It is a peaceful glow that imparts wisdom to our choices in life.

How thankful we are to feel its continual influence in the midst of the dissonant voices enticing us down the byways and side roads leading to spiritual bondage. How grateful we are, in every moment of every hour of every day, to sense the light of Christ at work within our conscience, eclipsing the intruding flashes of worldly temptation—and showing us a better way.

The light of Christ softens our heart, rendering it more receptive to the higher spiritual manifestations of the Holy Ghost. Said the Savior: "Learn of me, and listen to my words; walk in the meekness of my Spirit, and you shall have peace in me" (D&C 19:23).

Peace, light, truth, comfort, and a taste of the glory of God—these are the blessings of heaven that begin with the universal radiance of the light of Christ alive in every soul. The light of Christ is the hearth of God within us that emanates beams of goodness into every corner of our mortal experience. And we are grateful, beyond words, for this inner Liahona that quickens our faith and draws us toward celestial realms.

PSALM 51

To the chief Musician, A Psalm of David, when Nathan the prophet came unto him, after he had gone in to Bath-sheba.

1 HAVE mercy upon me, O God, according to thy lovingkindness: according unto the multitude of thy tender mercies blot out my transgressions.

2 Wash me throughly from mine iniquity, and cleanse me from my sin.

3 For I acknowledge my transgressions: and my sin is ever before me.

4 Against thee, thee only, have I sinned, and done this evil in thy sight: that thou mightest be justified when thou speakest, and be clear when thou judgest.

5 Behold, I was shapen in iniquity; and in sin did my mother conceive me.

6 Behold, thou desirest truth in the inward parts: and in the hidden part thou shalt make me to know wisdom.

7 Purge me with hyssop, and I shall be clean: wash me, and I shall be whiter than snow.

8 Make me to hear joy and gladness; that the bones which thou hast broken may rejoice.

9 Hide thy face from my sins, and blot out all mine iniquities.

10 Create in me a clean heart, O God; and renew a right spirit within me.

11 Cast me not away from thy presence; and take not thy holy spirit from me.

12 Restore unto me the joy of thy salvation; and uphold me with thy free spirit.

13 Then will I teach transgressors thy ways; and sinners shall be converted unto thee.

14 Deliver me from bloodguiltiness, O God, thou God of my salvation: and my tongue shall sing aloud of thy righteousness.

15 O Lord, open thou my lips; and my mouth shall shew forth thy praise.

16 For thou desirest not sacrifice; else would I give it: thou delightest not in burnt offering.

17 The sacrifices of God are a broken spirit: a broken and a contrite heart, O God, thou wilt not despise.

18 Do good in thy good pleasure unto Zion: build thou the walls of Jerusalem.

19 Then shalt thou be pleased with the sacrifices of righteousness, with burnt offering and whole burnt offering: then shall they offer bullocks upon thine altar.

PSALM 51

"The second principle of the gospel of salvation is repentance. It is a sincere and godly sorrow for and a forsaking of sin, combined with full purpose of heart to keep God's commandments." —John Taylor, *The Mediation and the Atonement*, 182

Psalm 51:1–12—The Exquisite Pain of Repentance

Repentance is a divine gift empowered through the Atonement of Jesus Christ—but it is to be done in the Lord's way, and thus must includes godly sorrow and the pain of contrite transformation and renewal. Like David, all who sin—meaning in effect all accountable mortals—are to go through the process of repenting for their sins if they are to become pure before God and worthy of His choicest blessings.

David's pain at the consciousness of his sin and its consequences is acute. He is the prototype of the fallen man, the archetype of the harrowed sinner. His poetry of contrition captures forever the awful state of the one who cannot retrieve the lost innocence, who cannot undo the fateful deed. At best, he can present his story of tragic pain as a warning message to others that it need not have been so, that following the commandments of God is the indispensable choice in life: "Then I will teach transgressors thy ways; and sinners shall be converted to thee" (Psalm 51:13).

The principle of repentance is absolutely imperative for our salvation. We are to practice this principle of change. We participate in the process continually. It literally becomes the process of perfection. As we repent perfectly, we can be forgiven and made pure.

Psalm 51—Summary of Doctrine

David concluded, on the basis of his ordeal, that "the sacrifices of God are a broken spirit: a broken and contrite heart. . . " (Ps. 51:17). David certainly had such. We can learn from his experience, as we "liken all scriptures unto us, that it might be for our profit and learning" (1 Ne. 19:23).

By heeding the warnings of the Spirit to avoid giving in to temptation, we can avoid suffering the consequences of serious transgression of the laws of God, and thus spare ourselves the exquisite pain and anguish of guilt and shame associated with such actions. Because the Lord suffered the anguish of universal sin, we can, through His Atonement, rise above such suffering.

The pathway of faith, repentance, baptism, and the gift of the Holy Ghost leads to peace of soul, harmony of spirit, and confidence in the presence of the Lord. It is through the love, mercy, and forgiveness of the Lord that we can have hope for eternal glory in the presence of the Father and the Son.

PSALM 55

To the chief Musician on Neginoth, Maschil, A Psalm of David.

1 GIVE ear to my prayer, O God; and hide not thyself from my supplication.

2 Attend unto me, and hear me: I mourn in my complaint, and make a noise;

3 Because of the voice of the enemy, because of the oppression of the wicked: for they cast iniquity upon me, and in wrath they hate me.

4 My heart is sore pained within me: and the terrors of death are fallen upon me.

5 Fearfulness and trembling are come upon me, and horror hath overwhelmed me.

6 And I said, Oh that I had wings like a dove! for then would I fly away, and be at rest.

7 Lo, then would I wander far off, and remain in the wilderness. Selah.

8 I would hasten my escape from the windy storm and tempest.

9 Destroy, O Lord, and divide their tongues: for I have seen violence and strife in the city.

10 Day and night they go about it upon the walls thereof: mischief also and sorrow are in the midst of it.

11 Wickedness is in the midst thereof: deceit and guile depart not from her streets.

12 For it was not an enemy that reproached me; then I could have borne it: neither was it he that hated me that did magnify himself against me; then I would have hid myself from him:

13 But it was thou, a man mine equal, my guide, and mine acquaintance.

14 We took sweet counsel together, and walked unto the house of God in company.

15 Let death seize upon them, and let them go down quick into hell: for wickedness is in their dwellings, and among them.

16 As for me, I will call upon God; and the LORD shall save me.

17 Evening, and morning, and at noon, will I pray, and cry aloud: and he shall hear my voice.

18 He hath delivered my soul in peace from the battle that was against me: for there were many with me.

19 God shall hear, and afflict them, even he that abideth of old. Selah. Because they have no changes, therefore they fear not God.

20 He hath put forth his hands against such as be at peace with him: he hath broken his covenant.

21 The words of his mouth were smoother than butter, but war was in his heart: his words were softer than oil, yet were they drawn swords.

22 Cast thy burden upon the LORD, and he shall sustain thee: he shall never suffer the righteous to be moved.

23 But thou, O God, shalt bring them down into the pit of destruction: bloody and deceitful men shall not live out half their days; but I will trust in thee.

David

POINT OF INTEREST

"Because the Psalms were written over such a long period of time, they display many facets of the character of God. Some psalms, written for the king and the Temple, speak of the God of one particular people and place; others, written in praise of God's might and majesty in Creation speak of a god of all peoples and of the whole universe. In one psalm we may hear of God's anger and judgment; in another, of God's mercy and salvation. In this sense, in its paradoxical voices, the Psalter contains in miniature the many different ideas about God found in the Hebrew Bible as a whole" (John Bowker, *The Complete Bible Handbook* [New York: DK Publishing, 2001]).

PSALM 56

To the chief Musician upon Jonath-elem-rechokim, Michtam of David, when the Philistines took him in Gath.

1 BE merciful unto me, O God: for man would swallow me up; he fighting daily oppresseth me.

2 Mine enemies would daily swallow me up: for they be many that fight against me, O thou most High.

3 What time I am afraid, I will trust in thee.

4 In God I will praise his word, in God I have put my trust; I will not fear what flesh can do unto me.

5 Every day they wrest my words: all their thoughts are against me for evil.

6 They gather themselves together, they hide themselves, they mark my steps, when they wait for my soul.

7 Shall they escape by iniquity? in thine anger cast down the people, O God.

8 Thou tellest my wanderings: put thou my tears into thy bottle: are they not in thy book?

9 When I cry unto thee, then shall mine enemies turn back: this I know; for God is for me.

10 In God will I praise his word: in the LORD will I praise his word.

11 In God have I put my trust: I will not be afraid what man can do unto me.

12 Thy vows are upon me, O God: I will render praises unto thee.

13 For thou hast delivered my soul from death: wilt not thou deliver my feet from falling, that I may walk before God in the light of the living?

PSALM 56

Psalm 56:11—Putting Trust in the Lord

How do we know we have fully invested our trust in God? Because we fear no more what mortal man can inflict upon us. The vanishing of that earthly fear is evidence that we have fully placed our trust in the healing and liberating power of the Lord.

PSALM 59

To the chief Musician, Al-taschith, Michtam of David; when Saul sent, and they watched the house to kill him.

1 DELIVER me from mine enemies, O my God: defend me from them that rise up against me.

2 Deliver me from the workers of iniquity, and save me from bloody men.

3 For, lo, they lie in wait for my soul: the mighty are gathered against me; not for my transgression, nor for my sin, O LORD.

4 They run and prepare themselves without my fault: awake to help me, and behold.

5 Thou therefore, O LORD God of hosts, the God of Israel, awake to visit all the heathen: be not merciful to any wicked transgressors. Selah.

6 They return at evening: they make a noise like a dog, and go round about the city.

7 Behold, they belch out with their mouth: swords are in their lips: for who, say they, doth hear?

8 But thou, O LORD, shalt laugh at them; thou shalt have all the heathen in derision.

9 Because of his strength will I wait upon thee: for God is my defence.

10 The God of my mercy shall prevent me: God shall let me see my desire upon mine enemies.

PSALM 59

Psalm 59—The Love of the Savior

The mercy, love, and forgiveness of the Savior are miraculous in the eyes of believing mortals. As Ammon confirmed: "Now my brethren, we see that God is mindful of every people, whatsoever land they may be in; yea, he numbereth his people, and his bowels of mercy are over all the earth. Now this is my joy, and my great thanksgiving; yea, and I will give thanks unto my God forever. Amen" (Alma 26:7).

11 Slay them not, lest my people forget: scatter them by thy power; and bring them down, O Lord our shield.

12 For the sin of their mouth and the words of their lips let them even be taken in their pride: and for cursing and lying which they speak.

13 Consume them in wrath, consume them, that they may not be: and let them know that God ruleth in Jacob unto the ends of the earth. Selah.

14 And at evening let them return; and let them make a noise like a dog, and go round about the city.

15 Let them wander up and down for meat, and grudge if they be not satisfied.

16 But I will sing of thy power; yea, I will sing aloud of thy mercy in the morning: for thou hast been my defence and refuge in the day of my trouble.

17 Unto thee, O my strength, will I sing: for God is my defence, and the God of my mercy.

PSALM 62

To the chief Musician, to Jeduthun, A Psalm of David.

1 TRULY my soul waiteth upon God: from him cometh my salvation.

2 He only is my rock and my salvation; he is my defence; I shall not be greatly moved.

3 How long will ye imagine mischief against a man? ye shall be slain all of you: as a bowing wall shall ye be, and as a tottering fence.

4 They only consult to cast him down from his excellency: they delight in lies: they bless with their mouth, but they curse inwardly. Selah.

5 My soul, wait thou only upon God; for my expectation is from him.

6 He only is my rock and my salvation: he is my defence; I shall not be moved.

7 In God is my salvation and my glory: the rock of my strength, and my refuge, is in God.

8 Trust in him at all times; ye people, pour out your heart before him: God is a refuge for us. Selah.

9 Surely men of low degree are vanity, and men of high degree are a lie: to be laid in the balance, they are altogether lighter than vanity.

10 Trust not in oppression, and become not vain in robbery: if riches increase, set not your heart upon them.

11 God hath spoken once; twice have I heard this; that power belongeth unto God.

12 Also unto thee, O Lord, belongeth mercy: for thou renderest to every man according to his work.

PSALM 62

Psalm 62:8—Continual Prayer

Another manifestation of our having placed our trust in the Lord is the fact that we pray unto Him continually. We do not supplicate with authenticity unless we believe in the infinite power of the Lord.

Question: Do you find your thoughts focused on the Lord with persistence, so that you are "drawn out in prayer unto him continually for your welfare, and also for the welfare of those who are around you" (Alma 34:27), as Amulek counseled? If so, then you know that your trust is fully vested in the Lord.

PSALM 69

To the chief Musician upon Shoshannim, A Psalm of David.

1 SAVE me, O God; for the waters are come in unto my soul.

2 I sink in deep mire, where there is no standing: I am come into deep waters, where the floods overflow me.

3 I am weary of my crying: my throat is dried: mine eyes fail while I wait for my God.

4 They that hate me without a cause are more than the hairs of mine head: they that would destroy me, being mine enemies wrongfully, are mighty: then I restored that which I took not away.

5 O God, thou knowest my foolishness; and my sins are not hid from thee.

6 Let not them that wait on thee, O Lord GOD of hosts, be ashamed for my sake: let not those that seek thee be confounded for my sake, O God of Israel.

7 Because for thy sake I have borne reproach; shame hath covered my face.

8 I am become a stranger unto my brethren, and an alien unto my mother's children.

9 For the zeal of thine house hath eaten me up; and the reproaches of them that reproached thee are fallen upon me.

10 When I wept, and chastened my soul with fasting, that was to my reproach.

11 I made sackcloth also my garment; and I become a proverb to them.

12 They that sit in the gate speak against me; and I was the song of the drunkards.

13 But as for me, my prayer is unto thee, O LORD, in an acceptable time: O God, in the multitude of thy mercy hear me, in the truth of thy salvation.

14 Deliver me out of the mire, and let me not sink: let me be delivered from them that hate me, and out of the deep waters.

15 Let not the waterflood overflow me, neither let the deep swallow me up, and let not the pit shut her mouth upon me.

16 Hear me, O LORD; for thy lovingkindness is good: turn unto me according to the multitude of thy tender mercies.

17 And hide not thy face from thy servant; for I am in trouble: hear me speedily.

18 Draw nigh unto my soul, and redeem it: deliver me because of mine enemies.

19 Thou hast known my reproach, and my shame, and my dishonour: mine adversaries are all before thee.

20 Reproach hath broken my heart; and I am full of heaviness: and I looked for some to take pity, but there was none; and for comforters, but I found none.

21 They gave me also gall for my meat; and in my thirst they gave me vinegar to drink.

22 Let their table become a snare before them: and that which should have been for their welfare, let it become a trap.

23 Let their eyes be darkened, that they see not; and make their loins continually to shake.

24 Pour out thine indignation upon them, and let thy wrathful anger take hold of them.

25 Let their habitation be desolate; and let none dwell in their tents.

26 For they persecute him whom thou hast smitten; and they talk to the grief of those whom thou hast wounded.

PSALM 69

Psalm 69—Anticipation of the Crucifixion

The words of the Psalmist anticipate the events associated with the crucifixion of the Lord as reflected in the Gospe of Mark:

And they came to a place which was named Gethsemane: and he saith to his disciples, Sit ye here, while I shall pray.

And he taketh with him Peter and James and John, and began to be sore amazed, and to be very heavy;

And saith unto them, My soul is exceeding sorrowful unto death: tarry ye here, and watch.

And he went forward a little, and fell on the ground, and prayed that, if it were possible, the hour might pass from him.

And he said, Abba, Father, all things *are* possible unto thee; take away this cup from me: nevertheless not what I will, but what thou wilt.

And he cometh, and findeth them sleeping, and saith unto Peter, Simon, sleepest thou? couldest not thou watch one hour?

Watch ye and pray, lest ye enter into temptation. The spirit truly *is* ready, but the flesh *is* weak.

And again he went away, and prayed, and spake the same words.

And when he returned, he found them asleep again, (for their eyes were heavy,) neither wist they what to answer him.

And he cometh the third time, and saith unto them, Sleep on now, and take *your* rest: it is enough, the hour is come; behold, the Son of man is betrayed into the hands of sinners. (Mark 14:32–41)

27 Add iniquity unto their iniquity: and let them not come into thy righteousness.

28 Let them be blotted out of the book of the living, and not be written with the righteous.

29 But I am poor and sorrowful: let thy salvation, O God, set me up on high.

30 I will praise the name of God with a song, and will magnify him with thanksgiving.

31 This also shall please the LORD better than an ox or bullock that hath horns and hoofs.

32 The humble shall see this, and be glad: and your heart shall live that seek God.

33 For the LORD heareth the poor, and despiseth not his prisoners.

34 Let the heaven and earth praise him, the seas, and every thing that moveth therein.

35 For God will save Zion, and will build the cities of Judah: that they may dwell there, and have it in possession.

36 The seed also of his servants shall inherit it: and they that love his name shall dwell therein.

PSALM 78

Maschil of Asaph.

1 GIVE ear, O my people, to my law: incline your ears to the words of my mouth.

2 I will open my mouth in a parable: I will utter dark sayings of old:

3 Which we have heard and known, and our fathers have told us.

4 We will not hide them from their children, shewing to the generation to come the praises of the LORD, and his strength, and his wonderful works that he hath done.

5 For he established a testimony in Jacob, and appointed a law in Israel, which he commanded our fathers, that they should make them known to their children:

6 That the generation to come might know them, even the children which should be born; who should arise and declare them to their children:

7 That they might set their hope in God, and not forget the works of God, but keep his commandments:

8 And might not be as their fathers, a stubborn and rebellious generation; a generation that set not their heart aright, and whose spirit was not stedfast with God.

9 The children of Ephraim, being armed, and carrying bows, turned back in the day of battle.

10 They kept not the covenant of God, and refused to walk in his law;

11 And forgat his works, and his wonders that he had shewed them.

12 Marvellous things did he in the sight of their fathers, in the land of Egypt, in the field of Zoan.

13 He divided the sea, and caused them to pass through; and he made the waters to stand as an heap.

14 In the daytime also he led them with a cloud, and all the night with a light of fire.

15 He clave the rocks in the wilderness, and gave them drink as out of the great depths.

16 He brought streams also out of the rock, and caused waters to run down like rivers.

PSALM 78

Psalm 78:1–38—The Lord Remembers

Despite the forgetfulness and disobedience of Israel, the Lord nevertheless remembered them with compasson and mercy. Despite their wayward lapses, He still blessed them with His guidance and love. Each of us, as we strive to be become "perfected in him" (Moro. 10:32), can take comfort in the compassion and love of the Lord, and in His willingness to forget our transgressions and sins as we repent of them (see D&C 58:42).

POINT OF INTEREST

"Scholars have debated the forms and classifications of individual psalms for centuries. The book of Psalms contains hymns (145–150), laments (38–39), songs of thanksgiving (30–32), royal psalms (2; 110), enthronement psalms (96; 98), penitential psalms (32; 38; 51), and wisdom or didactic psalms (19; 119)" (*Illustrated Bible Dictionary* [Nashville, Tenn: Holman Bible Publishers, 2003]).

17 And they sinned yet more against him by provoking the most High in the wilderness.

18 And they tempted God in their heart by asking meat for their lust.

19 Yea, they spake against God; they said, Can God furnish a table in the wilderness?

20 Behold, he smote the rock, that the waters gushed out, and the streams overflowed; can he give bread also? can he provide flesh for his people?

21 Therefore the LORD heard this, and was wroth: so a fire was kindled against Jacob, and anger also came up against Israel;

22 Because they believed not in God, and trusted not in his salvation:

23 Though he had commanded the clouds from above, and opened the doors of heaven,

24 And had rained down manna upon them to eat, and had given them of the corn of heaven.

25 Man did eat angels' food: he sent them meat to the full.

26 He caused an east wind to blow in the heaven: and by his power he brought in the south wind.

27 He rained flesh also upon them as dust, and feathered fowls like as the sand of the sea:

28 And he let it fall in the midst of their camp, round about their habitations.

29 So they did eat, and were well filled: for he gave them their own desire;

30 They were not estranged from their lust. But while their meat was yet in their mouths,

31 The wrath of God came upon them, and slew the fattest of them, and smote down the chosen men of Israel.

32 For all this they sinned still, and believed not for his wondrous works.

33 Therefore their days did he consume in vanity, and their years in trouble.

34 When he slew them, then they sought him: and they returned and enquired early after God.

35 And they remembered that God was their rock, and the high God their redeemer.

36 Nevertheless they did flatter him with their mouth, and they lied unto him with their tongues.

37 For their heart was not right with him, neither were they stedfast in his covenant.

38 But he, being full of compassion, forgave their iniquity, and destroyed them not: yea, many a time turned he his anger away, and did not stir up all his wrath.

39 For he remembered that they were but flesh; a wind that passeth away, and cometh not again.

40 How oft did they provoke him in the wilderness, and grieve him in the desert!

41 Yea, they turned back and tempted God, and limited the Holy One of Israel.

42 They remembered not his hand, nor the day when he delivered them from the enemy.

43 How he had wrought his signs in Egypt, and his wonders in the field of Zoan:

44 And had turned their rivers into blood; and their floods, that they could not drink.

POINT OF INTEREST

"Many commentators have emphasized the importance of one annual festival for which, they claim, many of the psalms were composed. There is evidence of such a festival in the spring in Babylon and in the fall in Canaan. But there is virtually no evidence for such a festival in the Bible, since the cultic calendars prescribe three (Passover, Weeks, and Tabernacles). Psalms would probably have been used at each of these. Before the Exile, the king and the Temple played a vital role in worship. This is illustrated not only in the Psalms but also in the books of Samuel and Kings. Sacred songs or psalms would have been composed to celebrate the anniversary of the king's accession, to commemorate times of victory over enemy nations, and to lament loss in times of defeat. After the Exile, when the Temple and the priesthood were paramount, and personal piety was also more significant, psalms would have been composed for both corporate and individual concerns. They served both a liturgical and an ideological purpose, in that they established the people's faith in YHWH, the LORD, as their God and in themselves as God's people. The fact that the Psalms were not tied to one particular occasion, either a festival or a national event, means that they have been able to be used as hymns and prayers in both Jewish and Christian traditions. They can still be understood and used today, despite the loss of the king, the land, the Temple, and the priesthood for which they were originally composed [though this isn't true for Latter-day Saints who have all these things]. This longevity of the Psalms illustrates not only the appeal of the poetry of the Psalms, but also the breadth and depth of their spirituality." (John Bowker, *The Complete Bible Handbook* [New York: DK Publishing, 2001]).

45 He sent divers sorts of flies among them, which devoured them; and frogs, which destroyed them.

46 He gave also their increase unto the caterpiller, and their labour unto the locust.

47 He destroyed their vines with hail, and their sycomore trees with frost.

48 He gave up their cattle also to the hail, and their flocks to hot thunderbolts.

49 He cast upon them the fierceness of his anger, wrath, and indignation, and trouble, by sending evil angels among them.

50 He made a way to his anger; he spared not their soul from death, but gave their life over to the pestilence;

51 And smote all the firstborn in Egypt; the chief of their strength in the tabernacles of Ham:

52 But made his own people to go forth like sheep, and guided them in the wilderness like a flock.

53 And he led them on safely, so that they feared not: but the sea overwhelmed their enemies.

54 And he brought them to the border of his sanctuary, even to this mountain, which his right hand had purchased.

55 He cast out the heathen also before them, and divided them an inheritance by line, and made the tribes of Israel to dwell in their tents.

56 Yet they tempted and provoked the most high God, and kept not his testimonies:

57 But turned back, and dealt unfaithfully like their fathers: they were turned aside like a deceitful bow.

58 For they provoked him to anger with their high places, and moved him to jealousy with their graven images.

59 When God heard this, he was wroth, and greatly abhorred Israel:

60 So that he forsook the tabernacle of Shiloh, the tent which he placed among men;

61 And delivered his strength into captivity, and his glory into the enemy's hand.

62 He gave his people over also unto the sword; and was wroth with his inheritance.

63 The fire consumed their young men; and their maidens were not given to marriage.

64 Their priests fell by the sword; and their widows made no lamentation.

65 Then the Lord awaked as one out of sleep, and like a mighty man that shouteth by reason of wine.

66 And he smote his enemies in the hinder parts: he put them to a perpetual reproach.

67 Moreover he refused the tabernacle of Joseph, and chose not the tribe of Ephraim:

68 But chose the tribe of Judah, the mount Zion which he loved.

69 And he built his sanctuary like high palaces, like the earth which he hath established for ever.

70 He chose David also his servant, and took him from the sheepfolds:

71 From following the ewes great with young he brought him to feed Jacob his people, and Israel his inheritance.

72 So he fed them according to the integrity of his heart; and guided them by the skilfulness of his hands.

NOTES:

PSALM 86

A Prayer of David.

1 BOW down thine ear, O LORD, hear me: for I am poor and needy.

2 Preserve my soul; for I am holy: O thou my God, save thy servant that trusteth in thee.

3 Be merciful unto me, O Lord: for I cry unto thee daily.

4 Rejoice the soul of thy servant: for unto thee, O Lord, do I lift up my soul.

5 For thou, Lord, art good, and ready to forgive; and plenteous in mercy unto all them that call upon thee.

6 Give ear, O LORD, unto my prayer; and attend to the voice of my supplications.

7 In the day of my trouble I will call upon thee: for thou wilt answer me.

8 Among the gods there is none like unto thee, O Lord; neither are there any works like unto thy works.

9 All nations whom thou hast made shall come and worship before thee, O Lord; and shall glorify thy name.

10 For thou art great, and doest wondrous things: thou art God alone.

11 Teach me thy way, O LORD; I will walk in thy truth: unite my heart to fear thy name.

12 I will praise thee, O Lord my God, with all my heart: and I will glorify thy name for evermore.

13 For great is thy mercy toward me: and thou hast delivered my soul from the lowest hell.

14 O God, the proud are risen against me, and the assemblies of violent men have sought after my soul; and have not set thee before them.

15 But thou, O Lord, art a God full of compassion, and gracious, longsuffering, and plenteous in mercy and truth.

16 O turn unto me, and have mercy upon me; give thy strength unto thy servant, and save the son of thine handmaid.

17 Shew me a token for good; that they which hate me may see it, and be ashamed: because thou, LORD, hast holpen me, and comforted me.

PSALM 100

A Psalm of praise.

1 MAKE a joyful noise unto the LORD, all ye lands.

2 Serve the LORD with gladness: come before his presence with singing.

3 Know ye that the LORD he is God: it is he that hath made us, and not we ourselves; we are his people, and the sheep of his pasture.

4 Enter into his gates with thanksgiving, and into his courts with praise: be thankful unto him, and bless his name.

5 For the LORD is good; his mercy is everlasting; and his truth endureth to all generations.

PSALM 86

Psalm 86:5—Joy in Repentance

David, himself no stranger to the excruciating burden of sin, rejoices in the goodness of the Lord, in His readiness to forgive the penitent, and in His accepting ear, listening to the humle voice of supplication with infinite mercy.

Nevertheless, justice still has claim upon those who knowingly cross beyond the boundaries set by the Lord and violate sacred covenants: "David's wives and concubines were given unto him of me, by the hand of Nathan, my servant, and others of the prophets who had the keys of this power; and in none of these things did he sin against me save in the case of Uriah and his wife; and, therefore he hath fallen from his exaltation, and received his portion; and he shall not inherit them out of the world, for I gave them unto another, saith the Lord" (D&C 132:39).

Psalm 86:13—The Lord's Mercy

David continues to extol the majesty of the Lord in His everlasting mercy and deliverance, not consigning the penitent to the lowest state of degradation and remorse. As modern revelation makes clear, "endless punishment" has a particular meaning: it is God's punishment (see D&C 19:9–18)

PSALM 100

Psalm 100:1–2—Cheerfulness

Some people have the wonderful gift of imparting cheer. We are literally transformed within moments when we encounter a cheerful person. Are you sometimes that person who imparts cheer to others? If you choose to be cheerful, you can change the world—one person at a time.

Cheer is a divine principle. It is a gift from God. The injunction "Be of good cheer" shows up no fewer than thirteen times in the scriptures. It is, in a way, the eleventh commandment. It shows up as a light of hope across the full spectrum of our mortal experience. "Be of good cheer" comforts us when we feel inadequate (see D&C 112:4), when our faith is tested (see 3 Ne. 1:12–13), when we feel meek and without resources (see D&C 78:17–22), or when we or loved ones are beset with illness (see Matt. 9:2). "Be of good cheer" illuminates our pathway when the elements bear down upon us (see Matt. 14:22–27), when we feel danger while on the Lord's errand (see Acts 27:22, 25), or when we are the victim of oppression (see Alma 17:31). "Be of good cheer" transforms our life when we are humbled beneath the responsibility of a church calling (see D&C 68:3–6), when we are persecuted for the sake of the gospel (see Acts 23:11), or when we feel lonely and under pressure while on the errand of the Lord (see D&C 61:36–37). At such times we remember in gratitude the words of the Savior: "These things I have spoken unto you, that in me ye might have peace. In the world ye shall have tribulation: but be of good cheer; I have overcome the world" (John 16:33).

PSALM 103

A Psalm of David.

1 BLESS the LORD, O my soul: and all that is within me, bless his holy name.

2 Bless the LORD, O my soul, and forget not all his benefits:

3 Who forgiveth all thine iniquities; who healeth all thy diseases;

4 Who redeemeth thy life from destruction; who crowneth thee with lovingkindness and tender mercies;

5 Who satisfieth thy mouth with good things; so that thy youth is renewed like the eagle's.

6 The LORD executeth righteousness and judgment for all that are oppressed.

7 He made known his ways unto Moses, his acts unto the children of Israel.

8 The LORD is merciful and gracious, slow to anger, and plenteous in mercy.

9 He will not always chide: neither will he keep his anger for ever.

10 He hath not dealt with us after our sins; nor rewarded us according to our iniquities.

11 For as the heaven is high above the earth, so great is his mercy toward them that fear him.

12 As far as the east is from the west, so far hath he removed our transgressions from us.

13 Like as a father pitieth his children, so the LORD pitieth them that fear him.

14 For he knoweth our frame; he remembereth that we are dust.

15 As for man, his days are as grass: as a flower of the field, so he flourisheth.

16 For the wind passeth over it, and it is gone; and the place thereof shall know it no more.

17 But the mercy of the LORD is from everlasting to everlasting upon them that fear him, and his righteousness unto children's children;

18 To such as keep his covenant, and to those that remember his commandments to do them.

19 The LORD hath prepared his throne in the heavens; and his kingdom ruleth over all.

20 Bless the LORD, ye his angels, that excel in strength, that do his commandments, hearkening unto the voice of his word.

21 Bless ye the LORD, all ye his hosts; ye ministers of his, that do his pleasure.

22 Bless the LORD, all his works in all places of his dominion: bless the LORD, O my soul.

Psalm 100:3–5—God, Our Eternal Father

Across the corridors of time we hear resounding the voice of gladness from the children of God—the voice of thanksgiving, praise, and rejoicing for the Almighty, the Creator of all things, the Architect of all that is merciful and good and just and true. David of old sang these lifting words of joy and thanks: "Know ye that the LORD he *is* God: *it is* he *that* hath made us, and not we ourselves; *we are* his people, and the sheep of his pasture. Enter into his gates with thanksgiving, *and* into his courts with praise: be thankful unto him, *and* bless his name" (Ps. 100:3–4).

For more insight into our relationship with God the Father, see Appendix GG.

PSALM 103

Psalm 103—Thanksgiving

The Davidic theme of the Lord's eternal mercy and lovingkindness is again sounded in this glorious anthem of thanksgiving.

Psalm 103:8–11—Accountability

These words reflect the covenant theme of accountability. The mercy of the Lord is magnanimous "toward them that fear him" (verse 11). Holy canon makes clear that blessings flow in accordance with our honoring eternal principles: "There is a law, irrevocably decreed in heaven before the foundations of this world, upon which all blessings are predicated— And when we obtain any blessing from God, it is by obedience to that law upon which it is predicated" (D&C 130:20).

Psalm 103:17–18—The Spirit of Covenant

Again, David invokes the spirit of the covenant. The word *testament* in the title *Old Testament* means covenant—referring to the original founding covenant established between God and His people to define with utter plainness what is expected of us if we are to obtain the riches of eternity. It is within this covenant that we have a continuing expression of the principles that define our relationship with Father and Son. In the Restoration, the covenant has been renewed, and the promises made to our fathers of old have been reawakened in the outreach power of the Abrahamic covenant, embracing as sit does our ongoing service in building the kingdom of God in these last days. For this we can be eternally grateful to our Father in Heaven and His Only Begotten Son.

PSALM 104

1 BLESS the LORD, O my soul. O LORD my God, thou art very great; thou art clothed with honour and majesty.

2 Who coverest thyself with light as with a garment: who stretchest out the heavens like a curtain:

3 Who layeth the beams of his chambers in the waters: who maketh the clouds his chariot: who walketh upon the wings of the wind:

4 Who maketh his angels spirits; his ministers a flaming fire:

5 Who laid the foundations of the earth, that it should not be removed for ever.

6 Thou coveredst it with the deep as with a garment: the waters stood above the mountains.

7 At thy rebuke they fled; at the voice of thy thunder they hasted away.

8 They go up by the mountains; they go down by the valleys unto the place which thou hast founded for them.

9 Thou hast set a bound that they may not pass over; that they turn not again to cover the earth.

10 He sendeth the springs into the valleys, which run among the hills.

11 They give drink to every beast of the field: the wild asses quench their thirst.

12 By them shall the fowls of the heaven have their habitation, which sing among the branches.

13 He watereth the hills from his chambers: the earth is satisfied with the fruit of thy works.

14 He causeth the grass to grow for the cattle, and herb for the service of man: that he may bring forth food out of the earth;

15 And wine that maketh glad the heart of man, and oil to make his face to shine, and bread which strengtheneth man's heart.

16 The trees of the LORD are full of sap; the cedars of Lebanon, which he hath planted;

17 Where the birds make their nests: as for the stork, the fir trees are her house.

18 The high hills are a refuge for the wild goats; and the rocks for the conies.

19 He appointed the moon for seasons: the sun knoweth his going down.

20 Thou makest darkness, and it is night: wherein all the beasts of the forest do creep forth.

21 The young lions roar after their prey, and seek their meat from God.

22 The sun ariseth, they gather themselves together, and lay them down in their dens.

23 Man goeth forth unto his work and to his labour until the evening.

24 O LORD, how manifold are thy works! in wisdom hast thou made them all: the earth is full of thy riches.

25 So is this great and wide sea, wherein are things creeping innumerable, both small and great beasts.

26 There go the ships: there is that leviathan, whom thou hast made to play therein.

27 These wait all upon thee; that thou mayest give them their meat in due season.

28 That thou givest them they gather: thou openest thine hand, they are filled with good.

29 Thou hidest thy face, they are troubled: thou takest away their breath, they die, and return to their dust.

30 Thou sendest forth thy spirit, they are created: and thou renewest the face of the earth.

31 The glory of the LORD shall endure for ever: the LORD shall rejoice in his works.

32 He looketh on the earth, and it trembleth: he toucheth the hills, and they smoke.

33 I will sing unto the LORD as long as I live: I will sing praise to my God while I have my being.

34 My meditation of him shall be sweet: I will be glad in the LORD.

35 Let the sinners be consumed out of the earth, and let the wicked be no more. Bless thou the LORD, O my soul. Praise ye the LORD.

PSALM 107

1 O GIVE thanks unto the LORD, for he is good: for his mercy endureth for ever.

2 Let the redeemed of the LORD say so, whom he hath redeemed from the hand of the enemy;

3 And gathered them out of the lands, from the east, and from the west, from the north, and from the south.

4 They wandered in the wilderness in a solitary way; they found no city to dwell in.

5 Hungry and thirsty, their soul fainted in them.

6 Then they cried unto the LORD in their trouble, and he delivered them out of their distresses.

7 And he led them forth by the right way, that they might go to a city of habitation.

8 Oh that men would praise the LORD for his goodness, and for his wonderful works to the children of men!

9 For he satisfieth the longing soul, and filleth the hungry soul with goodness.

10 Such as sit in darkness and in the shadow of death, being bound in affliction and iron;

11 Because they rebelled against the words of God, and contemned the counsel of the most High:

12 Therefore he brought down their heart with labour; they fell down, and there was none to help.

13 Then they cried unto the LORD in their trouble, and he saved them out of their distresses.

14 He brought them out of darkness and the shadow of death, and brake their bands in sunder.

15 Oh that men would praise the LORD for his goodness, and for his wonderful works to the children of men!

16 For he hath broken the gates of brass, and cut the bars of iron in sunder.

17 Fools because of their transgression, and because of their iniquities, are afflicted.

18 Their soul abhorreth all manner of meat; and they draw near unto the gates of death.

19 Then they cry unto the LORD in their trouble, and he saveth them out of their distresses.

20 He sent his word, and healed them, and delivered them from their destructions.

21 Oh that men would praise the LORD for his goodness, and for his wonderful works to the children of men!

King David Playing a Lyre

POINT OF INTEREST

"A . . . type of psalm is the wisdom psalm. *This type has a poetic form and style but is distinguished because of content and a tendency toward the proverbial. These psalms contemplate questions of theodicy (Ps. 73), celebrate God's Word (the Torah, 119), or deal with two different ways of living—that of the godly person or the evil person (1)." (Illustrated Bible Dictionary* [Nashville, Tenn: Holman Bible Publishers, 2003]).

22 And let them sacrifice the sacrifices of thanksgiving, and declare his works with rejoicing.

23 They that go down to the sea in ships, that do business in great waters;

24 These see the works of the LORD, and his wonders in the deep.

25 For he commandeth, and raiseth the stormy wind, which lifteth up the waves thereof.

26 They mount up to the heaven, they go down again to the depths: their soul is melted because of trouble.

27 They reel to and fro, and stagger like a drunken man, and are at their wits' end.

28 Then they cry unto the LORD in their trouble, and he bringeth them out of their distresses.

29 He maketh the storm a calm, so that the waves thereof are still.

30 Then are they glad because they be quiet; so he bringeth them unto their desired haven.

31 Oh that men would praise the LORD for his goodness, and for his wonderful works to the children of men!

32 Let them exalt him also in the congregation of the people, and praise him in the assembly of the elders.

33 He turneth rivers into a wilderness, and the watersprings into dry ground;

34 A fruitful land into barrenness, for the wickedness of them that dwell therein.

35 He turneth the wilderness into a standing water, and dry ground into watersprings.

36 And there he maketh the hungry to dwell, that they may prepare a city for habitation;

37 And sow the fields, and plant vineyards, which may yield fruits of increase.

38 He blesseth them also, so that they are multiplied greatly; and suffereth not their cattle to decrease.

39 Again, they are minished and brought low through oppression, affliction, and sorrow.

40 He poureth contempt upon princes, and causeth them to wander in the wilderness, where there is no way.

41 Yet setteth he the poor on high from affliction, and maketh him families like a flock.

42 The righteous shall see it, and rejoice: and all iniquity shall stop her mouth.

43 Whoso is wise, and will observe these things, even they shall understand the lovingkindness of the LORD.

PSALM 116

1 I LOVE the LORD, because he hath heard my voice and my supplications.

2 Because he hath inclined his ear unto me, therefore will I call upon him as long as I live.

3 The sorrows of death compassed me, and the pains of hell gat hold upon me: I found trouble and sorrow.

4 Then called I upon the name of the LORD; O LORD, I beseech thee, deliver my soul.

5 Gracious is the LORD, and righteous; yea, our God is merciful.

6 The LORD preserveth the simple: I was brought low, and he helped me.

POINT OF INTEREST

"The Psalms have been viewed in at least five different ways over the past 200 years. An early view was to attribute them to a very late era and then to see them as personal outpourings of the human spirit. This was modified by commentators who understood them to be late, but written for corporate use by gifted representatives of the community. By the turn of the 20th century, this view had changed so that the 'representative' was seen as a cultic official writing liturgies for special annual festivals. Because the king was seen to play a vital role in such ceremonies, many of the Psalms were accepted as belonging to the pre-exilic period (the period of kingship). This view was subsequently altered by those who agreed that the key influence on the Psalms was the cult (the Temple ritual); but this was also bound up with private ceremonies (dealing with those suffering, recovering from illness, sorcery, or persecution, and those who are dying). Most recently, some writers have proposed that the original historical contexts of the Psalms will always be a puzzle, and hence it is best to see them more generally as written 'from life's experiences and for life's experiences.' It is their common humanity that binds together the earliest composers with those who have used the Psalms through the centuries" (John Bowker, *The Complete Bible Handbook* [New York: DK Publishing, 2001]).

7 Return unto thy rest, O my soul; for the LORD hath dealt bountifully with thee.

8 For thou hast delivered my soul from death, mine eyes from tears, and my feet from falling.

9 I will walk before the LORD in the land of the living.

10 I believed, therefore have I spoken: I was greatly afflicted:

11 I said in my haste, All men are liars.

12 What shall I render unto the LORD for all his benefits toward me?

13 I will take the cup of salvation, and call upon the name of the LORD.

14 I will pay my vows unto the LORD now in the presence of all his people.

15 Precious in the sight of the LORD is the death of his saints.

16 O LORD, truly I am thy servant; I am thy servant, and the son of thine handmaid: thou hast loosed my bonds.

17 I will offer to thee the sacrifice of thanksgiving, and will call upon the name of the LORD.

18 I will pay my vows unto the LORD now in the presence of all his people,

19 In the courts of the LORD's house, in the midst of thee, O Jerusalem. Praise ye the LORD.

PSALM 118

1 O GIVE thanks unto the LORD; for he is good: because his mercy endureth for ever.

2 Let Israel now say, that his mercy endureth for ever.

3 Let the house of Aaron now say, that his mercy endureth for ever.

4 Let them now that fear the LORD say, that his mercy endureth for ever.

5 I called upon the LORD in distress: the LORD answered me, and set me in a large place.

6 The LORD is on my side; I will not fear: what can man do unto me?

7 The LORD taketh my part with them that help me: therefore shall I see my desire upon them that hate me.

8 It is better to trust in the LORD than to put confidence in man.

9 It is better to trust in the LORD than to put confidence in princes.

10 All nations compassed me about: but in the name of the LORD will I destroy them.

11 They compassed me about; yea, they compassed me about: but in the name of the LORD I will destroy them.

12 They compassed me about like bees; they are quenched as the fire of thorns: for in the name of the LORD I will destroy them.

13 Thou hast thrust sore at me that I might fall: but the LORD helped me.

14 The LORD is my strength and song, and is become my salvation.

15 The voice of rejoicing and salvation is in the tabernacles of the righteous: the right hand of the LORD doeth valiantly.

16 The right hand of the LORD is exalted: the right hand of the LORD doeth valiantly.

17 I shall not die, but live, and declare the works of the LORD.

18 The LORD hath chastened me sore: but he hath not given me over unto death.

NOTES:

19 Open to me the gates of righteousness: I will go into them, and I will praise the LORD:

20 This gate of the LORD, into which the righteous shall enter.

21 I will praise thee: for thou hast heard me, and art become my salvation.

22 The stone which the builders refused is become the head stone of the corner.

23 This is the LORD's doing; it is marvellous in our eyes.

24 This is the day which the LORD hath made; we will rejoice and be glad in it.

25 Save now, I beseech thee, O LORD: O LORD, I beseech thee, send now prosperity.

26 Blessed be he that cometh in the name of the LORD: we have blessed you out of the house of the LORD.

27 God is the LORD, which hath shewed us light: bind the sacrifice with cords, even unto the horns of the altar.

28 Thou art my God, and I will praise thee: thou art my God, I will exalt thee.

29 O give thanks unto the LORD; for he is good: for his mercy endureth for ever.

PSALM 119

a ALEPH

1 BLESSED are the undefiled in the way, who walk in the law of the LORD.

2 Blessed are they that keep his testimonies, and that seek him with the whole heart.

3 They also do no iniquity: they walk in his ways.

4 Thou hast commanded us to keep thy precepts diligently.

5 O that my ways were directed to keep thy statutes!

6 Then shall I not be ashamed, when I have respect unto all thy commandments.

7 I will praise thee with uprightness of heart, when I shall have learned thy righteous judgments.

8 I will keep thy statutes: O forsake me not utterly.

b BETH

9 Wherewithal shall a young man cleanse his way? by taking heed thereto according to thy word.

10 With my whole heart have I sought thee: O let me not wander from thy commandments.

11 Thy word have I hid in mine heart, that I might not sin against thee.

12 Blessed art thou, O LORD: teach me thy statutes.

13 With my lips have I declared all the judgments of thy mouth.

14 I have rejoiced in the way of thy testimonies, as much as in all riches.

15 I will meditate in thy precepts, and have respect unto thy ways.

16 I will delight myself in thy statutes: I will not forget thy word.

NOTES:

g GIMEL

17 Deal bountifully with thy servant, that I may live, and keep thy word.

18 Open thou mine eyes, that I may behold wondrous things out of thy law.

19 I am a stranger in the earth: hide not thy commandments from me.

20 My soul breaketh for the longing that it hath unto thy judgments at all times.

21 Thou hast rebuked the proud that are cursed, which do err from thy commandments.

22 Remove from me reproach and contempt; for I have kept thy testimonies.

23 Princes also did sit and speak against me: but thy servant did meditate in thy statutes.

24 Thy testimonies also are my delight and my counsellors.

d DALETH

25 My soul cleaveth unto the dust: quicken thou me according to thy word.

26 I have declared my ways, and thou heardest me: teach me thy statutes.

27 Make me to understand the way of thy precepts: so shall I talk of thy wondrous works.

28 My soul melteth for heaviness: strengthen thou me according unto thy word.

29 Remove from me the way of lying: and grant me thy law graciously.

30 I have chosen the way of truth: thy judgments have I laid before me.

31 I have stuck unto thy testimonies: O LORD, put me not to shame.

32 I will run the way of thy commandments, when thou shalt enlarge my heart.

h HE

33 Teach me, O LORD, the way of thy statutes; and I shall keep it unto the end.

34 Give me understanding, and I shall keep thy law; yea, I shall observe it with my whole heart.

35 Make me to go in the path of thy commandments; for therein do I delight.

36 Incline my heart unto thy testimonies, and not to covetousness.

37 Turn away mine eyes from beholding vanity; and quicken thou me in thy way.

38 Stablish thy word unto thy servant, who is devoted to thy fear.

39 Turn away my reproach which I fear: for thy judgments are good.

40 Behold, I have longed after thy precepts: quicken me in thy righteousness.

POINT OF INTEREST

"Hymns and laments are the most common forms in the Psalter. These two forms were also used in Babylonian and Egyptian liturgies. This suggest that some of the Psalms have been written in a common form for use in liturgy. Many other psalms are better classified according to content rather than form. For example, the psalms that refer to the king ('royal Psalms.' Ps. 2, 18, 20, 21, 45, 72, 89, 101, 110, 132) have no one form in common. There is similarly no shared form in psalms that are didactic in tone ('wisdom Psalms,' Ps. 1, 19, 37, 49, 73, 112, 119, 127, 128, 139) or in those psalms that have a prophetic emphasis (prophetic exhortations, Ps. 14, 50, 52, 53, 58, 75, 81, 95). Many other psalms use a combination of forms ('mixed Psalms'). Understanding the two basic forms of hymn and lament in the Psalms, however, can be an important tool in understanding the meaning of each individual psalm.

"The Psalms are not poems with a regular meter and distinctive line forms: some rhythm is evident and line forms are often intended, but the essence of Hebrew poetry lies in its sense rather than in its metrical form. Thus the Psalms retain their poetic quality even in translation. Their key poetic feature is 'parallelism.' For example, ideas expressed in one line are echoed in another, or ideas expressed in one line are set alongside a contrasting idea in another. Hebrew poetry defies hard-and-fast rules, but as with poetic form, there is also some adherence to convention in the meaning of the poetry itself" (John Bowker, The Complete Bible Handbook [New York: DK Publishing, 2001]).

v VAU

41 Let thy mercies come also unto me, O LORD, even thy salvation, according to thy word.

42 So shall I have wherewith to answer him that reproacheth me: for I trust in thy word.

43 And take not the word of truth utterly out of my mouth; for I have hoped in thy judgments.

44 So shall I keep thy law continually for ever and ever.

45 And I will walk at liberty: for I seek thy precepts.

46 I will speak of thy testimonies also before kings, and will not be ashamed.

47 And I will delight myself in thy commandments, which I have loved.

48 My hands also will I lift up unto thy commandments, which I have loved; and I will meditate in thy statutes.

z ZAIN

49 Remember the word unto thy servant, upon which thou hast caused me to hope.

50 This is my comfort in my affliction: for thy word hath quickened me.

51 The proud have had me greatly in derision: yet have I not declined from thy law.

52 I remembered thy judgments of old, O LORD; and have comforted myself.

53 Horror hath taken hold upon me because of the wicked that forsake thy law.

54 Thy statutes have been my songs in the house of my pilgrimage.

55 I have remembered thy name, O LORD, in the night, and have kept thy law.

56 This I had, because I kept thy precepts.

j CHETH

57 Thou art my portion, O LORD: I have said that I would keep thy words.

58 I intreated thy favour with my whole heart: be merciful unto me according to thy word.

59 I thought on my ways, and turned my feet unto thy testimonies.

60 I made haste, and delayed not to keep thy commandments.

61 The bands of the wicked have robbed me: but I have not forgotten thy law.

62 At midnight I will rise to give thanks unto thee because of thy righteous judgments.

63 I am a companion of all them that fear thee, and of them that keep thy precepts.

64 The earth, O LORD, is full of thy mercy: teach me thy statutes.

NOTES:

y TETH

65 Thou hast dealt well with thy servant, O LORD, according unto thy word.

66 Teach me good judgment and knowledge: for I have believed thy commandments.

67 Before I was afflicted I went astray: but now have I kept thy word.

68 Thou art good, and doest good; teach me thy statutes.

69 The proud have forged a lie against me: but I will keep thy precepts with my whole heart.

70 Their heart is as fat as grease; but I delight in thy law.

71 It is good for me that I have been afflicted; that I might learn thy statutes.

72 The law of thy mouth is better unto me than thousands of gold and silver.

i JOD

73 Thy hands have made me and fashioned me: give me understanding, that I may learn thy commandments.

74 They that fear thee will be glad when they see me; because I have hoped in thy word.

75 I know, O LORD, that thy judgments are right, and that thou in faithfulness hast afflicted me.

76 Let, I pray thee, thy merciful kindness be for my comfort, according to thy word unto thy servant.

77 Let thy tender mercies come unto me, that I may live: for thy law is my delight.

78 Let the proud be ashamed; for they dealt perversely with me without a cause: but I will meditate in thy precepts.

79 Let those that fear thee turn unto me, and those that have known thy testimonies.

80 Let my heart be sound in thy statutes; that I be not ashamed.

k CAPH

81 My soul fainteth for thy salvation: but I hope in thy word.

82 Mine eyes fail for thy word, saying, When wilt thou comfort me?

83 For I am become like a bottle in the smoke; yet do I not forget thy statutes.

84 How many are the days of thy servant? when wilt thou execute judgment on them that persecute me?

85 The proud have digged pits for me, which are not after thy law.

86 All thy commandments are faithful: they persecute me wrongfully; help thou me.

87 They had almost consumed me upon earth; but I forsook not thy precepts.

88 Quicken me after thy lovingkindness; so shall I keep the testimony of thy mouth.

Dome of Ascension, Jerusalem

l LAMED

89 For ever, O LORD, thy word is settled in heaven.
90 Thy faithfulness is unto all generations: thou hast established the earth, and it abideth.
91 They continue this day according to thine ordinances: for all are thy servants.
92 Unless thy law had been my delights, I should then have perished in mine affliction.
93 I will never forget thy precepts: for with them thou hast quickened me.
94 I am thine, save me; for I have sought thy precepts.
95 The wicked have waited for me to destroy me: but I will consider thy testimonies.
96 I have seen an end of all perfection: but thy commandment is exceeding broad.

m MEM

97 O how love I thy law! it is my meditation all the day.
98 Thou through thy commandments hast made me wiser than mine enemies: for they are ever with me.
99 I have more understanding than all my teachers: for thy testimonies are my meditation.
100 I understand more than the ancients, because I keep thy precepts.
101 I have refrained my feet from every evil way, that I might keep thy word.
102 I have not departed from thy judgments: for thou hast taught me.
103 How sweet are thy words unto my taste! yea, sweeter than honey to my mouth!
104 Through thy precepts I get understanding: therefore I hate every false way.

n NUN

105 Thy word is a lamp unto my feet, and a light unto my path.
106 I have sworn, and I will perform it, that I will keep thy righteous judgments.
107 I am afflicted very much: quicken me, O LORD, according unto thy word.
108 Accept, I beseech thee, the freewill offerings of my mouth, O LORD, and teach me thy judgments.
109 My soul is continually in my hand: yet do I not forget thy law.
110 The wicked have laid a snare for me: yet I erred not from thy precepts.
111 Thy testimonies have I taken as an heritage for ever: for they are the rejoicing of my heart.
112 I have inclined mine heart to perform thy statutes alway, even unto the end.

Shrine of the Book, Jerusalem

s SAMECH

113 I hate vain thoughts: but thy law do I love.

114 Thou art my hiding place and my shield: I hope in thy word.

115 Depart from me, ye evildoers: for I will keep the commandments of my God.

116 Uphold me according unto thy word, that I may live: and let me not be ashamed of my hope.

117 Hold thou me up, and I shall be safe: and I will have respect unto thy statutes continually.

118 Thou hast trodden down all them that err from thy statutes: for their deceit is falsehood.

119 Thou puttest away all the wicked of the earth like dross: therefore I love thy testimonies.

120 My flesh trembleth for fear of thee; and I am afraid of thy judgments.

e AIN

121 I have done judgment and justice: leave me not to mine oppressors.

122 Be surety for thy servant for good: let not the proud oppress me.

123 Mine eyes fail for thy salvation, and for the word of thy righteousness.

124 Deal with thy servant according unto thy mercy, and teach me thy statutes.

125 I am thy servant; give me understanding, that I may know thy testimonies.

126 It is time for thee, LORD, to work: for they have made void thy law.

127 Therefore I love thy commandments above gold; yea, above fine gold.

128 Therefore I esteem all thy precepts concerning all things to be right; and I hate every false way.

p PE

129 Thy testimonies are wonderful: therefore doth my soul keep them.

130 The entrance of thy words giveth light; it giveth understanding unto the simple.

131 I opened my mouth, and panted: for I longed for thy commandments.

132 Look thou upon me, and be merciful unto me, as thou usest to do unto those that love thy name.

133 Order my steps in thy word: and let not any iniquity have dominion over me.

134 Deliver me from the oppression of man: so will I keep thy precepts.

135 Make thy face to shine upon thy servant; and teach me thy statutes.

136 Rivers of waters run down mine eyes, because they keep not thy law.

NOTES:

c TZADDI

137 Righteous art thou, O LORD, and upright are thy judgments.
138 Thy testimonies that thou hast commanded are righteous and very faithful.
139 My zeal hath consumed me, because mine enemies have forgotten thy words.
140 Thy word is very pure: therefore thy servant loveth it.
141 I am small and despised: yet do not I forget thy precepts.
142 Thy righteousness is an everlasting righteousness, and thy law is the truth.
143 Trouble and anguish have taken hold on me: yet thy commandments are my delights.
144 The righteousness of thy testimonies is everlasting: give me understanding, and I shall live.

q KOPH

145 I cried with my whole heart; hear me, O LORD: I will keep thy statutes.
146 I cried unto thee; save me, and I shall keep thy testimonies.
147 I prevented the dawning of the morning, and cried: I hoped in thy word.
148 Mine eyes prevent the night watches, that I might meditate in thy word.
149 Hear my voice according unto thy lovingkindness: O LORD, quicken me according to thy judgment.
150 They draw nigh that follow after mischief: they are far from thy law.
151 Thou art near, O LORD; and all thy commandments are truth.
152 Concerning thy testimonies, I have known of old that thou hast founded them for ever.

r RESH

153 Consider mine affliction, and deliver me: for I do not forget thy law.
154 Plead my cause, and deliver me: quicken me according to thy word.
155 Salvation is far from the wicked: for they seek not thy statutes.
156 Great are thy tender mercies, O LORD: quicken me according to thy judgments.
157 Many are my persecutors and mine enemies; yet do I not decline from thy testimonies.
158 I beheld the transgressors, and was grieved; because they kept not thy word.
159 Consider how I love thy precepts: quicken me, O LORD, according to thy lovingkindness.
160 Thy word is true from the beginning: and every one of thy righteous judgments endureth for ever.

NOTES:

w SCHIN

161 Princes have persecuted me without a cause: but my heart standeth in awe of thy word.

162 I rejoice at thy word, as one that findeth great spoil.

163 I hate and abhor lying: but thy law do I love.

164 Seven times a day do I praise thee because of thy righteous judgments.

165 Great peace have they which love thy law: and nothing shall offend them.

166 LORD, I have hoped for thy salvation, and done thy commandments.

167 My soul hath kept thy testimonies; and I love them exceedingly.

168 I have kept thy precepts and thy testimonies: for all my ways are before thee.

t TAU

169 Let my cry come near before thee, O LORD: give me understanding according to thy word.

170 Let my supplication come before thee: deliver me according to thy word.

171 My lips shall utter praise, when thou hast taught me thy statutes.

172 My tongue shall speak of thy word: for all thy commandments are righteousness.

173 Let thine hand help me; for I have chosen thy precepts.

174 I have longed for thy salvation, O LORD; and thy law is my delight.

175 Let my soul live, and it shall praise thee; and let thy judgments help me.

176 I have gone astray like a lost sheep; seek thy servant; for I do not forget thy commandments.

PSALM 122

David says: Go into the house of the Lord—Give thanks unto him.

A Song of degrees of David.

1 I WAS glad when they said unto me, Let us go into the house of the LORD.

2 Our feet shall stand within thy gates, O Jerusalem.

3 Jerusalem is builded as a city that is compact together:

4 Whither the tribes go up, the tribes of the LORD, unto the testimony of Israel, to give thanks unto the name of the LORD.

5 For there are set thrones of judgment, the thrones of the house of David.

6 Pray for the peace of Jerusalem: they shall prosper that love thee.

7 Peace be within thy walls, and prosperity within thy palaces.

8 For my brethren and companions' sakes, I will now say, Peace be within thee.

9 Because of the house of the LORD our God I will seek thy good.

PSALM 122

Psalm 122:1—"Let Us Go into the House of the Lord"

"Let us go ino the house of the LORD." What a magnificent invitation: to go *together* to the temple of the Lord—to go as couples, families, associates in quorums and groups. The temple reflects a higher order of sociality than is found outside its walls, because it encompasses the powers and keys of establishing eternal families, everlasting families. Jospeh Smith taught, concerning heaven, "And that same sociality which exists among us here will exist among us there, only it will be coupled with eternal glory, which glory we do not now enjoy" (D&C 130:2). Surely the temple is a stepping stone in that direction, for the measure of increased glory available there is a palpable witness to what awaits the faithful and obedient in the mansions on high.

PSALM 134

A Song of degrees.

1 BEHOLD, bless ye the LORD, all ye servants of the LORD, which by night stand in the house of the LORD.

2 Lift up your hands in the sanctuary, and bless the LORD.

3 The LORD that made heaven and earth bless thee out of Zion.

PSALM 136

1 O GIVE thanks unto the LORD; for he is good: for his mercy endureth for ever.

2 O give thanks unto the God of gods: for his mercy endureth for ever.

3 O give thanks to the Lord of lords: for his mercy endureth for ever.

4 To him who alone doeth great wonders: for his mercy endureth for ever.

5 To him that by wisdom made the heavens: for his mercy endureth for ever.

6 To him that stretched out the earth above the waters: for his mercy endureth for ever.

7 To him that made great lights: for his mercy endureth for ever:

8 The sun to rule by day: for his mercy endureth for ever:

9 The moon and stars to rule by night: for his mercy endureth for ever.

10 To him that smote Egypt in their firstborn: for his mercy endureth for ever:

11 And brought out Israel from among them: for his mercy endureth for ever:

12 With a strong hand, and with a stretched out arm: for his mercy endureth for ever.

13 To him which divided the Red sea into parts: for his mercy endureth for ever:

14 And made Israel to pass through the midst of it: for his mercy endureth for ever:

15 But overthrew Pharaoh and his host in the Red sea: for his mercy endureth for ever.

16 To him which led his people through the wilderness: for his mercy endureth for ever.

17 To him which smote great kings: for his mercy endureth for ever:

18 And slew famous kings: for his mercy endureth for ever:

19 Sihon king of the Amorites: for his mercy endureth for ever:

20 And Og the king of Bashan: for his mercy endureth for ever:

21 And gave their land for an heritage: for his mercy endureth for ever:

22 Even an heritage unto Israel his servant: for his mercy endureth for ever.

23 Who remembered us in our low estate: for his mercy endureth for ever:

24 And hath redeemed us from our enemies: for his mercy endureth for ever.

25 Who giveth food to all flesh: for his mercy endureth for ever.

26 O give thanks unto the God of heaven: for his mercy endureth for ever.

PSALM 134

Psalm 134—The Temple

This short Psalm (only Psalm 117, with two verses, is shorter, while Psalms 131 and 133 are of equal length) has to do with the temple. The words given define the ongoing attitude and performance of those who spend their time in the Lord's House—they are to "bless" the Lord. That is their commission and task.

And for this devoted service, what are they to receive in return? The blessing of the Lord upon them. It is a two-way process of a covenant nature: Those who bless are blessed in return. What a marvelous promise that is for those who frequent the sacred precincts of the temples of God.

PSALM 150

Praise God in his sanctuary—Let everything that hath breath praise the Lord.

1 PRAISE ye the LORD. Praise God in his sanctuary: praise him in the firmament of his power.

2 Praise him for his mighty acts: praise him according to his excellent greatness.

3 Praise him with the sound of the trumpet: praise him with the psaltery and harp.

4 Praise him with the timbrel and dance: praise him with stringed instruments and organs.

5 Praise him upon the loud cymbals: praise him upon the high sounding cymbals.

6 Let every thing that hath breath praise the LORD. Praise ye the LORD.

THE PROVERBS

CHAPTER 1

1 THE proverbs of Solomon the son of David, king of Israel;

2 To know wisdom and instruction; to perceive the words of understanding;

3 To receive the instruction of wisdom, justice, and judgment, and equity;

4 To give subtilty to the simple, to the young man knowledge and discretion.

5 A wise man will hear, and will increase learning; and a man of understanding shall attain unto wise counsels:

6 To understand a proverb, and the interpretation; the words of the wise, and their dark sayings.

7 ¶ The fear of the LORD is the beginning of knowledge: but fools despise wisdom and instruction.

8 My son, hear the instruction of thy father, and forsake not the law of thy mother:

9 For they shall be an ornament of grace unto thy head, and chains about thy neck.

10 ¶ My son, if sinners entice thee, consent thou not.

11 If they say, Come with us, let us lay wait for blood, let us lurk privily for the innocent without cause:

12 Let us swallow them up alive as the grave; and whole, as those that go down into the pit:

13 We shall find all precious substance, we shall fill our houses with spoil:

14 Cast in thy lot among us; let us all have one purse:

15 My son, walk not thou in the way with them; refrain thy foot from their path:

PROVERBS CHAPTER 1

"The best way to obtain truth and wisdom is not to ask it from books, but to go to God in prayer, and obtain divine teaching." —Joseph Smith, *HC* 4:425.

Proverbs 1:1–7—Trusting in God Is the Foundation of Wisdom

When we trust in the Lord and fear Him—in the sense that we have profound respect for His eternal wisdom and thus yield to His will in all things—then we can strive daily to keep His commandments and always remember Him so that we are worthy to have His Spirit to be with us.

Solomon was enormously prolific: "And he spake three thousand proverbs: and his songs were a thousand and five" (1 Kings 4:32). The underlying theme of his teachings is that we must fear God and place our trust in Him, rather than in our own understanding: "Trust in the Lord with all thine heart; and lean not unto thine own understanding. In all thy ways acknowledge him, and he shall direct thy paths" (Prov. 3:5–7). Only in this way can we hope to become spiritually wise.

In the course of his own life, as it turned out, Solomon was rather better at conveying wisdom than in becoming its leading practitioner. Nevertheless, there is much in his legacy that can benefit and instruct the honest seeker after truth. In the wisdom and strength of the Lord we can and will be led if we but trust in Him and not in our own limited perception or understanding. We should avoid the idea of being "wise in our own eyes" (see Isa. 5:21).

Wisdom begins with reverence toward God. As we honor God, we begin our quest for wisdom. Wisdom becomes the attribute in our life that helps determine our choices, which inevitably make us who we are. We are our choices.

16 For their feet run to evil, and make haste to shed blood.

17 Surely in vain the net is spread in the sight of any bird.

18 And they lay wait for their own blood; they lurk privily for their own lives.

19 So are the ways of every one that is greedy of gain; which taketh away the life of the owners thereof.

20 ¶ Wisdom crieth without; she uttereth her voice in the streets:

21 She crieth in the chief place of concourse, in the openings of the gates: in the city she uttereth her words, saying,

22 How long, ye simple ones, will ye love simplicity? and the scorners delight in their scorning, and fools hate knowledge?

23 Turn you at my reproof: behold, I will pour out my spirit unto you, I will make known my words unto you.

24 ¶ Because I have called, and ye refused; I have stretched out my hand, and no man regarded;

25 But ye have set at nought all my counsel, and would none of my reproof:

26 I also will laugh at your calamity; I will mock when your fear cometh;

27 When your fear cometh as desolation, and your destruction cometh as a whirlwind; when distress and anguish cometh upon you.

28 Then shall they call upon me, but I will not answer; they shall seek me early, but they shall not find me:

29 For that they hated knowledge, and did not choose the fear of the LORD:

30 They would none of my counsel: they despised all my reproof.

31 Therefore shall they eat of the fruit of their own way, and be filled with their own devices.

32 For the turning away of the simple shall slay them, and the prosperity of fools shall destroy them.

33 But whoso hearkeneth unto me shall dwell safely, and shall be quiet from fear of evil.

CHAPTER 2

1 MY son, if thou wilt receive my words, and hide my commandments with thee;

2 So that thou incline thine ear unto wisdom, and apply thine heart to understanding;

3 Yea, if thou criest after knowledge, and liftest up thy voice for understanding;

4 If thou seekest her as silver, and searchest for her as for hid treasures;

5 Then shalt thou understand the fear of the LORD, and find the knowledge of God.

6 For the LORD giveth wisdom: out of his mouth cometh knowledge and understanding.

7 He layeth up sound wisdom for the righteous: he is a buckler to them that walk uprightly.

8 He keepeth the paths of judgment, and preserveth the way of his saints.

9 Then shalt thou understand righteousness, and judgment, and equity; yea, every good path.

10 ¶ When wisdom entereth into thine heart, and knowledge is pleasant unto thy soul;

11 Discretion shall preserve thee, understanding shall keep thee:

 POINT OF INTEREST

Proverbs of the Prophet Joseph Smith—1843

1st. Never exact of a friend in adversity what you would require in prosperity.

2nd. If a man prove himself to be honest in his deal, and an enemy come upon him wickedly, through fraud or false pretences and because he is stronger than he, maketh him his prisoner and spoil him with his goods, never say unto that man in the day of his adversity, pay me what thou owest, for if thou doest it, thou addest a deeper wound, and condemnation shall come upon thee and thy riches shall be justified in the days of thine adversity if they mock at thee.

3rd. Never afflict thy soul for what an enemy hath put it out of thy power to do, if thy desires are ever so just.

4th. Let thy hand never fail to hand out that that thou owest while it is yet within thy grasp to do so, but when thy stock fails say to thy heart, be strong, and to thine anxieties cease, for man, what is he; he is but dung upon the earth and although he demand of thee the cattle of a thousand hills, he cannot possess himself of his own life. God made him and thee and gave all things in common.

5th. There is one thing under the sun which I have learned and that is that the righteousness of man is sin because it exacteth over much; nevertheless, the righteousness of God is just, because it exacteth nothing at all, but sendeth the rain on the just and the unjust, seed time and harvest, for all of which man is ungrateful.

12 To deliver thee from the way of the evil man, from the man that speaketh froward things;

13 Who leave the paths of uprightness, to walk in the ways of darkness;

14 Who rejoice to do evil, and delight in the frowardness of the wicked;

15 Whose ways are crooked, and they froward in their paths:

16 To deliver thee from the strange woman, even from the stranger which flattereth with her words;

17 Which forsaketh the guide of her youth, and forgetteth the covenant of her God.

18 For her house inclineth unto death, and her paths unto the dead.

19 None that go unto her return again, neither take they hold of the paths of life.

20 That thou mayest walk in the way of good men, and keep the paths of the righteous.

21 For the upright shall dwell in the land, and the perfect shall remain in it.

22 But the wicked shall be cut off from the earth, and the transgressors shall be rooted out of it.

CHAPTER 3

1 MY son, forget not my law; but let thine heart keep my commandments:

2 For length of days, and long life, and peace, shall they add to thee.

3 Let not mercy and truth forsake thee: bind them about thy neck; write them upon the table of thine heart:

4 So shalt thou find favour and good understanding in the sight of God and man.

5 ¶ Trust in the LORD with all thine heart; and lean not unto thine own understanding.

6 In all thy ways acknowledge him, and he shall direct thy paths.

7 ¶ Be not wise in thine own eyes: fear the LORD, and depart from evil.

8 It shall be health to thy navel, and marrow to thy bones.

9 Honour the LORD with thy substance, and with the firstfruits of all thine increase:

10 So shall thy barns be filled with plenty, and thy presses shall burst out with new wine.

11 ¶ My son, despise not the chastening of the LORD; neither be weary of his correction:

12 For whom the LORD loveth he correcteth; even as a father the son in whom he delighteth.

13 ¶ Happy is the man that findeth wisdom, and the man that getteth understanding.

14 For the merchandise of it is better than the merchandise of silver, and the gain thereof than fine gold.

15 She is more precious than rubies: and all the things thou canst desire are not to be compared unto her.

16 Length of days is in her right hand; and in her left hand riches and honour.

17 Her ways are ways of pleasantness, and all her paths are peace.

18 She is a tree of life to them that lay hold upon her: and happy is every one that retaineth her.

19 The LORD by wisdom hath founded the earth; by understanding hath he established the heavens.

PROVERBS CHAPTER 3

Proverbs 3:7—The Source of Wisdom

What is the source of light for our lives? Where do we access wisdom in order to conduct our lives prudently and in accordance with correct principles? The Lord taught Abraham the following truth: "These two facts do exist, that there are two spirits, one being more intelligent than the other; there shall be another more intelligent than they; I am the Lord thy God, I am more intelligent than they all" (Abr. 3:19). Should we not therefore cleave unto the Lord, the most intelligent and wise of all beings, and seek His guidance in all that we do? Absolutely!

What of our own understanding? Do we not seek to cultivate the ability to make wise decisions using our own agency and initiative? The Lord taught Oliver Cowdery this following concerning the operation of the spirit of revelation in obtaining truth: "But, behold, I say unto you, that you must study it out in your mind; then you must ask me if it be right, and if it is right I will cause that your bosom shall burn within you; therefore, you shall feel that it is right. But if it be not right you shall have no such feelings, but you shall have a stupor of thought that shall cause you to forget the thing which is wrong; therefore, you cannot write that which is sacred save it be given you from me" (D&C 9:8–9).

The lesson is plain: We are to depend fully on the Lord for His guidance as we strive to use our own agency and ability to comprehend and plan for the future. The problem occurs when we depend soley on our own understanding, and neglect the higher course of reason—to seek the Spirit of the Lord in confirming our decisions and to listen for the whisperings of the Spirit to prompt our way forward in righteousness. Jacob in the Book of Mormon said it plainly: "O that cunning plan of the evil one! O the vainness, and the frailties, and the foolishness of men! When they are learned they think they are wise, and they hearken not unto the counsel of God, for they set it aside, supposing they know of themselves, wherefore, their wisdom is foolishness and it profiteth them not. And they shall perish. But to be learned is good if they hearken unto the counsels of God" (2 Ne. 9:28–29).

20 By his knowledge the depths are broken up, and the clouds drop down the dew.

21 ¶ My son, let not them depart from thine eyes: keep sound wisdom and discretion:

22 So shall they be life unto thy soul, and grace to thy neck.

23 Then shalt thou walk in thy way safely, and thy foot shall not stumble.

24 When thou liest down, thou shalt not be afraid: yea, thou shalt lie down, and thy sleep shall be sweet.

25 Be not afraid of sudden fear, neither of the desolation of the wicked, when it cometh.

26 For the LORD shall be thy confidence, and shall keep thy foot from being taken.

27 ¶ Withhold not good from them to whom it is due, when it is in the power of thine hand to do it.

28 Say not unto thy neighbour, Go, and come again, and to morrow I will give; when thou hast it by thee.

29 Devise not evil against thy neighbour, seeing he dwelleth securely by thee.

30 ¶ Strive not with a man without cause, if he have done thee no harm.

31 ¶ Envy thou not the oppressor, and choose none of his ways.

32 For the froward is abomination to the LORD: but his secret is with the righteous.

33 ¶ The curse of the LORD is in the house of the wicked: but he blesseth the habitation of the just.

34 Surely he scorneth the scorners: but he giveth grace unto the lowly.

35 The wise shall inherit glory: but shame shall be the promotion of fools.

CHAPTER 4

1 HEAR, ye children, the instruction of a father, and attend to know understanding.

2 For I give you good doctrine, forsake ye not my law.

3 For I was my father's son, tender and only beloved in the sight of my mother.

4 He taught me also, and said unto me, Let thine heart retain my words: keep my commandments, and live.

5 Get wisdom, get understanding: forget it not; neither decline from the words of my mouth.

6 Forsake her not, and she shall preserve thee: love her, and she shall keep thee.

7 Wisdom is the principal thing; therefore get wisdom: and with all thy getting get understanding.

8 Exalt her, and she shall promote thee: she shall bring thee to honour, when thou dost embrace her.

9 She shall give to thine head an ornament of grace: a crown of glory shall she deliver to thee.

10 Hear, O my son, and receive my sayings; and the years of thy life shall be many.

11 I have taught thee in the way of wisdom; I have led thee in right paths.

12 When thou goest, thy steps shall not be straitened; and when thou runnest, thou shalt not stumble.

Proverbs 3:12—A Willingness to Be Entreated Is the Key to Cultivating Wisdom

Humility and meekness are qualities of spiritually-minded students of truth. Only those who are open to truth and understanding can be filled with the Spirit of truth. Wisdom can be learned only by the one who accepts the counsel of wise persons—especially the prophets of God who teach His will and reveal His commandments.

How can the learning process be facilitated through wise counsel?

1. Follow the light (see Prov. 4:18–19)

2. Reprove with wisdom (see Prov. 13:24; 29:15)

3. Prioritize: there is a time for all things (see Eccl. 3:1–11)

4. Seek knowledge and wisdom (see Eccl. 4:13)

5. Live as you pray (see Prov. 28:9)

6. Have the vision necessary for life and leadership roles (see Prov. 29:18)

7. Follow the word of God (see Prov. 30:5)

8. You are the result of your thoughts (see Prov. 23:7)

9. Have a cheerful attitude (see Prov. 17:22)

10. Seek not to counsel the Lord (see Prov. 21:30)

11. Train your children (see Prov. 22:6)

12. Pay heed to censure, reprimand, and even scoldings (see Prov. 15:31–32)

13. Master yourself (see Prov 16:32)

Thus we see that humility and all of its attributes are the forerunners of wisdom. One will never be wise who chooses not to be easily entreated with the word of God.

PROVERBS CHAPTER 4

Proverbs 4:7—The Flowering of Wisdom Is to Bring Forth Good Fruit Unto the Lord

To be wise is to be obedient, cultivating a life full of service. Wisdom is action motivated by love.

The fundamental outcome advocated in the Proverbs and in Ecclesiastes is a life governed by wisdom—a life that is built up on a foundation of obedience to God's law and service to one's fellow beings. The wise person has confidence in the presence of God, because all pride and folly have been defeated and all preparations to receive a crown of glory have been made. In place of rancor and deceit, there is peace and balance (see Prov. 16:32). Here is the ultimate reward of a godly walk of life—that a person has governed his or her thinking by bringing it into alignment with the will of God, and thus has become a son or daughter of God—a Saint in the true sense.

Consider these various aspects of wisdom:

1. Gain Wisdom (see Prov. 4:7)—The seeking of wisdom is our primary concern. We must realize that knowing is not enough; we must be steadfast and enduring in the application of our knowledge.

2. The Influence of Friends and Associates (see Prov. 13:20)—The people you associate with have a far-reaching effect upon you and your behavior. One should

13 Take fast hold of instruction; let her not go: keep her; for she is thy life.

14 ¶ Enter not into the path of the wicked, and go not in the way of evil men.

15 Avoid it, pass not by it, turn from it, and pass away.

16 For they sleep not, except they have done mischief; and their sleep is taken away, unless they cause some to fall.

17 For they eat the bread of wickedness, and drink the wine of violence.

18 But the path of the just is as the shining light, that shineth more and more unto the perfect day.

19 The way of the wicked is as darkness: they know not at what they stumble.

20 ¶ My son, attend to my words; incline thine ear unto my sayings.

21 Let them not depart from thine eyes; keep them in the midst of thine heart.

22 For they are life unto those that find them, and health to all their flesh.

23 ¶ Keep thy heart with all diligence; for out of it are the issues of life.

24 Put away from thee a froward mouth, and perverse lips put far from thee.

25 Let thine eyes look right on, and let thine eyelids look straight before thee.

26 Ponder the path of thy feet, and let all thy ways be established.

27 Turn not to the right hand nor to the left: remove thy foot from evil.

CHAPTER 5

1 MY son, attend unto my wisdom, and bow thine ear to my understanding:

2 That thou mayest regard discretion, and that thy lips may keep knowledge.

3 ¶ For the lips of a strange woman drop as an honeycomb, and her mouth is smoother than oil:

4 But her end is bitter as wormwood, sharp as a twoedged sword.

5 Her feet go down to death; her steps take hold on hell.

6 Lest thou shouldest ponder the path of life, her ways are moveable, that thou canst not know them.

7 Hear me now therefore, O ye children, and depart not from the words of my mouth.

8 Remove thy way far from her, and come not nigh the door of her house:

9 Lest thou give thine honour unto others, and thy years unto the cruel:

10 Lest strangers be filled with thy wealth; and thy labours be in the house of a stranger;

11 And thou mourn at the last, when thy flesh and thy body are consumed,

12 And say, How have I hated instruction, and my heart despised reproof;

13 And have not obeyed the voice of my teachers, nor inclined mine ear to them that instructed me!

14 I was almost in all evil in the midst of the congregation and assembly.

choose wisely one's friends and associates and the places to frequent.

3. Fear God and Keep His Commandments (see Eccl. 12:13)—As we reverence, respect, and love God, we will keep His commandments.

4. Righteous Children (see Prov. 28:7)—The greatest joy of parents is a righteous, noble child (see 3 John 1:4).

5. Confess Your Sins (see Prov. 28:13)—One cannot hide from the Lord. If we confess and forsake our sins, the Lord remembers them no more (see D&C 58:42–43).

6. Correct Your Children (see Prov. 29:15, 17)—Chastise with love. Reprove as moved by the Spirit. Permissive parents bring sin upon their children and upon their own heads.

7. Integrity of Parents (see Prov. 20:7)—The power of a good example will bring lasting blessings to your children.

8. Obedience and Righteousness Are Greater Than Outward Demonstration (see Prov. 21:3)—The inner heart is more important than an outward demonstration.

9. Soft Answers (see Prov. 15:1)—Nothing is so calming and non-combative as a soft voice. It brings composure to almost any situation.

10. Righteousness Always Over Wealth (see Prov. 16:8)—Only in righteousness can men be saved, for all the wealth of the world has no eternal value.

11. Friendship (see Prov. 17:9)—True friends will be quick to forgive rather than find fault or continually bring up the wrong doing.

True wisdom brings the blessings of God into one's life through obedience and righteousness. The natural consequence of wisdom is having the Spirit, being full of love, and being an instrument in the hands of the Lord to bless your fellowmen.

15 ¶ Drink waters out of thine own cistern, and running waters out of thine own well.

16 Let thy fountains be dispersed abroad, and rivers of waters in the streets.

17 Let them be only thine own, and not strangers' with thee.

18 Let thy fountain be blessed: and rejoice with the wife of thy youth.

19 Let her be as the loving hind and pleasant roe; let her breasts satisfy thee at all times; and be thou ravished always with her love.

20 And why wilt thou, my son, be ravished with a strange woman, and embrace the bosom of a stranger?

21 For the ways of man are before the eyes of the LORD, and he pondereth all his goings.

22 ¶ His own iniquities shall take the wicked himself, and he shall be holden with the cords of his sins.

23 He shall die without instruction; and in the greatness of his folly he shall go astray.

CHAPTER 6

1 MY son, if thou be surety for thy friend, if thou hast stricken thy hand with a stranger,

2 Thou art snared with the words of thy mouth, thou art taken with the words of thy mouth.

3 Do this now, my son, and deliver thyself, when thou art come into the hand of thy friend; go, humble thyself, and make sure thy friend.

4 Give not sleep to thine eyes, nor slumber to thine eyelids.

5 Deliver thyself as a roe from the hand of the hunter, and as a bird from the hand of the fowler.

6 ¶ Go to the ant, thou sluggard; consider her ways, and be wise:

7 Which having no guide, overseer, or ruler,

8 Provideth her meat in the summer, and gathereth her food in the harvest.

9 How long wilt thou sleep, O sluggard? when wilt thou arise out of thy sleep?

10 Yet a little sleep, a little slumber, a little folding of the hands to sleep:

11 So shall thy poverty come as one that travelleth, and thy want as an armed man.

12 ¶ A naughty person, a wicked man, walketh with a froward mouth.

13 He winketh with his eyes, he speaketh with his feet, he teacheth with his fingers;

14 Frowardness is in his heart, he deviseth mischief continually; he soweth discord.

15 Therefore shall his calamity come suddenly; suddenly shall he be broken without remedy.

16 ¶ These six things doth the LORD hate: yea, seven are an abomination unto him:

17 A proud look, a lying tongue, and hands that shed innocent blood,

18 An heart that deviseth wicked imaginations, feet that be swift in running to mischief,

19 A false witness that speaketh lies, and he that soweth discord among brethren.

NOTES:

20 ¶ My son, keep thy father's commandment, and forsake not the law of thy mother:

21 Bind them continually upon thine heart, and tie them about thy neck.

22 When thou goest, it shall lead thee; when thou sleepest, it shall keep thee; and when thou awakest, it shall talk with thee.

23 For the commandment is a lamp; and the law is light; and reproofs of instruction are the way of life:

24 To keep thee from the evil woman, from the flattery of the tongue of a strange woman.

25 Lust not after her beauty in thine heart; neither let her take thee with her eyelids.

26 For by means of a whorish woman a man is brought to a piece of bread: and the adulteress will hunt for the precious life.

27 Can a man take fire in his bosom, and his clothes not be burned?

28 Can one go upon hot coals, and his feet not be burned?

29 So he that goeth in to his neighbour's wife; whosoever toucheth her shall not be innocent.

30 Men do not despise a thief, if he steal to satisfy his soul when he is hungry;

31 But if he be found, he shall restore sevenfold; he shall give all the substance of his house.

32 But whoso committeth adultery with a woman lacketh understanding: he that doeth it destroyeth his own soul.

33 A wound and dishonour shall he get; and his reproach shall not be wiped away.

34 For jealousy is the rage of a man: therefore he will not spare in the day of vengeance.

35 He will not regard any ransom; neither will he rest content, though thou givest many gifts.

CHAPTER 7

1 MY son, keep my words, and lay up my commandments with thee.

2 Keep my commandments, and live; and my law as the apple of thine eye.

3 Bind them upon thy fingers, write them upon the table of thine heart.

4 Say unto wisdom, Thou art my sister; and call understanding thy kinswoman:

5 That they may keep thee from the strange woman, from the stranger which flattereth with her words.

6 ¶ For at the window of my house I looked through my casement,

7 And beheld among the simple ones, I discerned among the youths, a young man void of understanding,

8 Passing through the street near her corner; and he went the way to her house,

9 In the twilight, in the evening, in the black and dark night:

10 And, behold, there met him a woman with the attire of an harlot, and subtil of heart.

11 (She is loud and stubborn; her feet abide not in her house:

12 Now is she without, now in the streets, and lieth in wait at every corner.)

13 So she caught him, and kissed him, and with an impudent face said unto him,

14 I have peace offerings with me; this day have I payed my vows.

Judgment of Solomon by Gustave Doré

15 Therefore came I forth to meet thee, diligently to seek thy face, and I have found thee.

16 I have decked my bed with coverings of tapestry, with carved works, with fine linen of Egypt.

17 I have perfumed my bed with myrrh, aloes, and cinnamon.

18 Come, let us take our fill of love until the morning: let us solace ourselves with loves.

19 For the goodman is not at home, he is gone a long journey:

20 He hath taken a bag of money with him, and will come home at the day appointed.

21 With her much fair speech she caused him to yield, with the flattering of her lips she forced him.

22 He goeth after her straightway, as an ox goeth to the slaughter, or as a fool to the correction of the stocks;

23 Till a dart strike through his liver; as a bird hasteth to the snare, and knoweth not that it is for his life.

24 ¶ Hearken unto me now therefore, O ye children, and attend to the words of my mouth.

25 Let not thine heart decline to her ways, go not astray in her paths.

26 For she hath cast down many wounded: yea, many strong men have been slain by her.

27 Her house is the way to hell, going down to the chambers of death.

CHAPTER 8

1 DOTH not wisdom cry? and understanding put forth her voice?

2 She standeth in the top of high places, by the way in the places of the paths.

3 She crieth at the gates, at the entry of the city, at the coming in at the doors.

4 Unto you, O men, I call; and my voice is to the sons of man.

5 O ye simple, understand wisdom: and, ye fools, be ye of an understanding heart.

6 Hear; for I will speak of excellent things; and the opening of my lips shall be right things.

7 For my mouth shall speak truth; and wickedness is an abomination to my lips.

8 All the words of my mouth are in righteousness; there is nothing froward or perverse in them.

9 They are all plain to him that understandeth, and right to them that find knowledge.

10 Receive my instruction, and not silver; and knowledge rather than choice gold.

11 For wisdom is better than rubies; and all the things that may be desired are not to be compared to it.

12 I wisdom dwell with prudence, and find out knowledge of witty inventions.

13 The fear of the LORD is to hate evil: pride, and arrogancy, and the evil way, and the froward mouth, do I hate.

14 Counsel is mine, and sound wisdom: I am understanding; I have strength.

15 By me kings reign, and princes decree justice.

16 By me princes rule, and nobles, even all the judges of the earth.

17 I love them that love me; and those that seek me early shall find me.

POINT OF INTEREST

"The book of Proverbs answers the question: how is life to be lived day by day? Proverbs gathers together advice and wisdom. Sayings from this book have gone deep into our language; many are still used in everyday life, long after the book was written. The purpose of Proverbs is to establish what constitutes wise and foolish behavior. The book contains the concept of life as a path along which one walks, making choices along the way, and there is much confidence that, through experience, the wise person can learn what kinds of behavior will lead to success and happiness" (John Bowker, *The Complete Bible Handbook* [New York: DK Publishing, 2001]).

18 Riches and honour are with me; yea, durable riches and righteousness.

19 My fruit is better than gold, yea, than fine gold; and my revenue than choice silver.

20 I lead in the way of righteousness, in the midst of the paths of judgment:

21 That I may cause those that love me to inherit substance; and I will fill their treasures.

22 The LORD possessed me in the beginning of his way, before his works of old.

23 I was set up from everlasting, from the beginning, or ever the earth was.

24 When there were no depths, I was brought forth; when there were no fountains abounding with water.

25 Before the mountains were settled, before the hills was I brought forth:

26 While as yet he had not made the earth, nor the fields, nor the highest part of the dust of the world.

27 When he prepared the heavens, I was there: when he set a compass upon the face of the depth:

28 When he established the clouds above: when he strengthened the fountains of the deep:

29 When he gave to the sea his decree, that the waters should not pass his commandment: when he appointed the foundations of the earth:

30 Then I was by him, as one brought up with him: and I was daily his delight, rejoicing always before him;

31 Rejoicing in the habitable part of his earth; and my delights were with the sons of men.

32 Now therefore hearken unto me, O ye children: for blessed are they that keep my ways.

33 Hear instruction, and be wise, and refuse it not.

34 Blessed is the man that heareth me, watching daily at my gates, waiting at the posts of my doors.

35 For whoso findeth me findeth life, and shall obtain favour of the LORD.

36 But he that sinneth against me wrongeth his own soul: all they that hate me love death.

NOTES:

CHAPTER 9

1 WISDOM hath builded her house, she hath hewn out her seven pillars:

2 She hath killed her beasts; she hath mingled her wine; she hath also furnished her table.

3 She hath sent forth her maidens: she crieth upon the highest places of the city,

4 Whoso is simple, let him turn in hither: as for him that wanteth understanding, she saith to him,

5 Come, eat of my bread, and drink of the wine which I have mingled.

6 Forsake the foolish, and live; and go in the way of understanding.

7 He that reproveth a scorner getteth to himself shame: and he that rebuketh a wicked man getteth himself a blot.

8 Reprove not a scorner, lest he hate thee: rebuke a wise man, and he will love thee.

9 Give instruction to a wise man, and he will be yet wiser: teach a just man, and he will increase in learning.

10 The fear of the LORD is the beginning of wisdom: and the knowledge of the holy is understanding.

11 For by me thy days shall be multiplied, and the years of thy life shall be increased.

12 If thou be wise, thou shalt be wise for thyself: but if thou scornest, thou alone shalt bear it.

13 ¶ A foolish woman is clamourous: she is simple, and knoweth nothing.

14 For she sitteth at the door of her house, on a seat in the high places of the city,

15 To call passengers who go right on their ways:

16 Whoso is simple, let him turn in hither: and as for him that wanteth understanding, she saith to him,

17 Stolen waters are sweet, and bread eaten in secret is pleasant.

18 But he knoweth not that the dead are there; and that her guests are in the depths of hell.

PROVERBS CHAPTER 9

Proverbs 9:10—"The Fear of the Lord"

What does it mean to fear the Lord? What blessings does the Lord give to those who fear Him?

The expression *fear of the Lord* (and its variants) occurs often in the scriptures, with a wide range of closely interrelated meanings. The most frequently encountered meanings include the following: *serve Him* (see Josh. 24:14), *keep His commandments* (see Eccl. 12:13), *worship Him* (see 2 Kings 17:36), *praise Him* (see Ps. 22:23), *trust Him* (see Ps. 115:11), *heed and do His words* (see Deut. 4:10), *sanctify Him* (see Isa. 29:23), *keep His statutes* (see Deut. 6:2), *give glory to Him* (see Rev. 14:7), *walk in His ways* (see Deut. 10:12), *judge righteously* (see Isa. 11:3), *obey His voice* (see Deut. 13:4), *consider His works* (see 1 Sam. 12:24), *know His mighty arm* (see Ex. 15:16), *bear testimony* (see Ps. 118:4), *cleave to Him* (see Deut. 10:20), and several additional usages including paying tithing, rejoicing, being united, and so forth. Certainly the predominant meaning of *fearing the Lord* is to serve Him with full obedience and to worship Him in a spirit of devoted praise and trust.

How do we understand clearly which blessings the Lord reserves for those who "fear him" in these various ways? The scriptures, again, are explicit in revealing what is in store for those who serve and obey the Lord in "fear": *wisdom* (see Prov. 1:7), *knowledge* (see Prov. 1:7), *salvation* (see Alma 34:37, Morm. 9:27), *strength* (see 3 Ne. 4:10), *life* (see Prov. 14:27), *having no wants* (see Ps. 34:9), plus a host of other blessings, including access to the mysteries and covenants of God, mercy, eternal glory, preservation, enduring forever, ministering of angels, shield of protection, and comfort of the Holy Ghost.

What a grand principle it is to "fear the Lord." To serve Him, obey Him, worship Him, and trust Him will bring us wisdom, knowledge, salvation, strength, life, and a myriad of other choice and glorious benefits. It is an eternal bargain. Let us remember this principle in all that we do and act continually in the fear of the Lord.

CHAPTER 10

1 THE proverbs of Solomon. A wise son maketh a glad father: but a foolish son is the heaviness of his mother.

2 Treasures of wickedness profit nothing: but righteousness delivereth from death.

3 The LORD will not suffer the soul of the righteous to famish: but he casteth away the substance of the wicked.

4 He becometh poor that dealeth with a slack hand: but the hand of the diligent maketh rich.

5 He that gathereth in summer is a wise son: but he that sleepeth in harvest is a son that causeth shame.

6 Blessings are upon the head of the just: but violence covereth the mouth of the wicked.

7 The memory of the just is blessed: but the name of the wicked shall rot.

8 The wise in heart will receive commandments: but a prating fool shall fall.

9 He that walketh uprightly walketh surely: but he that perverteth his ways shall be known.

10 He that winketh with the eye causeth sorrow: but a prating fool shall fall.

11 The mouth of a righteous man is a well of life: but violence covereth the mouth of the wicked.

12 Hatred stirreth up strifes: but love covereth all sins.

13 In the lips of him that hath understanding wisdom is found: but a rod is for the back of him that is void of understanding.

14 Wise men lay up knowledge: but the mouth of the foolish is near destruction.

15 The rich man's wealth is his strong city: the destruction of the poor is their poverty.

16 The labour of the righteous tendeth to life: the fruit of the wicked to sin.

17 He is in the way of life that keepeth instruction: but he that refuseth reproof erreth.

18 He that hideth hatred with lying lips, and he that uttereth a slander, is a fool.

19 In the multitude of words there wanteth not sin: but he that refraineth his lips is wise.

20 The tongue of the just is as choice silver: the heart of the wicked is little worth.

21 The lips of the righteous feed many: but fools die for want of wisdom.

22 The blessing of the LORD, it maketh rich, and he addeth no sorrow with it.

23 It is as sport to a fool to do mischief: but a man of understanding hath wisdom.

24 The fear of the wicked, it shall come upon him: but the desire of the righteous shall be granted.

25 As the whirlwind passeth, so is the wicked no more: but the righteous is an everlasting foundation.

26 As vinegar to the teeth, and as smoke to the eyes, so is the sluggard to them that send him.

27 The fear of the LORD prolongeth days: but the years of the wicked shall be shortened.

28 The hope of the righteous shall be gladness: but the expectation of the wicked shall perish.

Solomon by Gustave Doré

29 The way of the LORD is strength to the upright: but destruction shall be to the workers of iniquity.

30 The righteous shall never be removed: but the wicked shall not inhabit the earth.

31 The mouth of the just bringeth forth wisdom: but the froward tongue shall be cut out.

32 The lips of the righteous know what is acceptable: but the mouth of the wicked speaketh frowardness.

CHAPTER 11

1 A FALSE balance is abomination to the LORD: but a just weight is his delight.

2 When pride cometh, then cometh shame: but with the lowly is wisdom.

3 The integrity of the upright shall guide them: but the perverseness of transgressors shall destroy them.

4 Riches profit not in the day of wrath: but righteousness delivereth from death.

5 The righteousness of the perfect shall direct his way: but the wicked shall fall by his own wickedness.

6 The righteousness of the upright shall deliver them: but transgressors shall be taken in their own naughtiness.

7 When a wicked man dieth, his expectation shall perish: and the hope of unjust men perisheth.

8 The righteous is delivered out of trouble, and the wicked cometh in his stead.

9 An hypocrite with his mouth destroyeth his neighbour: but through knowledge shall the just be delivered.

10 When it goeth well with the righteous, the city rejoiceth: and when the wicked perish, there is shouting.

11 By the blessing of the upright the city is exalted: but it is overthrown by the mouth of the wicked.

12 He that is void of wisdom despiseth his neighbour: but a man of understanding holdeth his peace.

13 A talebearer revealeth secrets: but he that is of a faithful spirit concealeth the matter.

14 Where no counsel is, the people fall: but in the multitude of counsellors there is safety.

15 He that is surety for a stranger shall smart for it: and he that hateth suretiship is sure.

16 A gracious woman retaineth honour: and strong men retain riches.

17 The merciful man doeth good to his own soul: but he that is cruel troubleth his own flesh.

18 The wicked worketh a deceitful work: but to him that soweth righteousness shall be a sure reward.

19 As righteousness tendeth to life: so he that pursueth evil pursueth it to his own death.

20 They that are of a froward heart are abomination to the LORD: but such as are upright in their way are his delight.

21 Though hand join in hand, the wicked shall not be unpunished: but the seed of the righteous shall be delivered.

22 As a jewel of gold in a swine's snout, so is a fair woman which is without discretion.

23 The desire of the righteous is only good: but the expectation of the wicked is wrath.

NOTES:

24 There is that scattereth, and yet increaseth; and there is that withholdeth more than is meet, but it tendeth to poverty.

25 The liberal soul shall be made fat: and he that watereth shall be watered also himself.

26 He that withholdeth corn, the people shall curse him: but blessing shall be upon the head of him that selleth it.

27 He that diligently seeketh good procureth favour: but he that seeketh mischief, it shall come unto him.

28 He that trusteth in his riches shall fall: but the righteous shall flourish as a branch.

29 He that troubleth his own house shall inherit the wind: and the fool shall be servant to the wise of heart.

30 The fruit of the righteous is a tree of life; and he that winneth souls is wise.

31 Behold, the righteous shall be recompensed in the earth: much more the wicked and the sinner.

CHAPTER 12

1 WHOSO loveth instruction loveth knowledge: but he that hateth reproof is brutish.

2 A good man obtaineth favour of the LORD: but a man of wicked devices will he condemn.

3 A man shall not be established by wickedness: but the root of the righteous shall not be moved.

4 A virtuous woman is a crown to her husband: but she that maketh ashamed is as rottenness in his bones.

5 The thoughts of the righteous are right: but the counsels of the wicked are deceit.

6 The words of the wicked are to lie in wait for blood: but the mouth of the upright shall deliver them.

7 The wicked are overthrown, and are not: but the house of the righteous shall stand.

8 A man shall be commended according to his wisdom: but he that is of a perverse heart shall be despised.

9 He that is despised, and hath a servant, is better than he that honoureth himself, and lacketh bread.

10 A righteous man regardeth the life of his beast: but the tender mercies of the wicked are cruel.

11 He that tilleth his land shall be satisfied with bread: but he that followeth vain persons is void of understanding.

12 The wicked desireth the net of evil men: but the root of the righteous yieldeth fruit.

13 The wicked is snared by the transgression of his lips: but the just shall come out of trouble.

14 A man shall be satisfied with good by the fruit of his mouth: and the recompence of a man's hands shall be rendered unto him.

15 The way of a fool is right in his own eyes: but he that hearkeneth unto counsel is wise.

16 A fool's wrath is presently known: but a prudent man covereth shame.

17 He that speaketh truth sheweth forth righteousness: but a false witness deceit.

18 There is that speaketh like the piercings of a sword: but the tongue of the wise is health.

19 The lip of truth shall be established for ever: but a lying tongue is but for a moment.

POINT OF INTEREST

The book of Proverbs is generally thought to be penned not by divine inpsiration given through prophets, but instead as statements of men that sum up relationships and rules of behavior. So who wrote the proverbs? It is often thought that Solomon is the author, because he was known to have spoken literally thousands of these short, pithy statements (see 1 Kings 4:33). But we really don't know if Solomon wrote all of the proverbs in our current Bible—or even if the Bible as we know it contains all of the proverbs once recorded. Proverbs 1–9 are mostly comprised of advice that seems to be written from a father to his son, and are entitled "Proverbs of Solomon." Proverbs 10–22:16 are also entitled "Proverbs of Solomon," and are made up almost entirely of the brief snippets characteristic of what we think of as proverbs. Proverbs 22:17 through Proverbs 24 contain a variety of longer essay-like writings on both social and moral issues. Proverbs 25–29 are again called "Proverbs of Solomon." Evidence of different authorship is hinted at in Proverbs 30— "The Words of Agur"—and Proverbs 31— "The Words of King Lemuel."

20 Deceit is in the heart of them that imagine evil: but to the counsellors of peace is joy.

21 There shall no evil happen to the just: but the wicked shall be filled with mischief.

22 Lying lips are abomination to the LORD: but they that deal truly are his delight.

23 A prudent man concealeth knowledge: but the heart of fools proclaimeth foolishness.

24 The hand of the diligent shall bear rule: but the slothful shall be under tribute.

25 Heaviness in the heart of man maketh it stoop: but a good word maketh it glad.

26 The righteous is more excellent than his neighbour: but the way of the wicked seduceth them.

27 The slothful man roasteth not that which he took in hunting: but the substance of a diligent man is precious.

28 In the way of righteousness is life; and in the pathway thereof there is no death.

CHAPTER 13

1 A WISE son heareth his father's instruction: but a scorner heareth not rebuke.

2 A man shall eat good by the fruit of his mouth: but the soul of the transgressors shall eat violence.

3 He that keepeth his mouth keepeth his life: but he that openeth wide his lips shall have destruction.

4 The soul of the sluggard desireth, and hath nothing: but the soul of the diligent shall be made fat.

5 A righteous man hateth lying: but a wicked man is loathsome, and cometh to shame.

6 Righteousness keepeth him that is upright in the way: but wickedness overthroweth the sinner.

7 There is that maketh himself rich, yet hath nothing: there is that maketh himself poor, yet hath great riches.

8 The ransom of a man's life are his riches: but the poor heareth not rebuke.

9 The light of the righteous rejoiceth: but the lamp of the wicked shall be put out.

10 Only by pride cometh contention: but with the well advised is wisdom.

11 Wealth gotten by vanity shall be diminished: but he that gathereth by labour shall increase.

12 Hope deferred maketh the heart sick: but when the desire cometh, it is a tree of life.

13 Whoso despiseth the word shall be destroyed: but he that feareth the commandment shall be rewarded.

14 The law of the wise is a fountain of life, to depart from the snares of death.

15 Good understanding giveth favour: but the way of transgressors is hard.

16 Every prudent man dealeth with knowledge: but a fool layeth open his folly.

17 A wicked messenger falleth into mischief: but a faithful ambassador is health.

18 Poverty and shame shall be to him that refuseth instruction: but he that regardeth reproof shall be honoured.

PROVERBS CHAPTER 13

Proverbs 13:10—Contention and Disputation

Among the earliest teachings of the resurrected Lord during His appearance among the American Saints at Bountiful was this commandment:

> And there shall be no disputations among you, as there have hitherto been; neither shall there be disputations among you concerning the points of my doctrine, as there have hitherto been.
>
> For verily, verily I say unto you, he that hath the spirit of contention is not of me, but is of the devil, who is the father of contention, and he stirreth up the hearts of men to contend with anger, one with another.
>
> Behold, this is not my doctrine, to stir up the hearts of men with anger, one against another; but this is my doctrine, that such things should be done away. (3 Ne. 11:28–30)

What causes disputation and contention? Is it not prideful feelings of unrighteous dominion among those who contend? Is it not hearts that are hardened so as to filter out the whisperings of the Spirit? The Lord commanded: "I say unto you, be one; and if ye are not one ye are not mine" (D&C 38:27). The "well advised" (Prov. 13:10) cultivate the wisdom of unity and amity, the commitment to depend upon the Lord for guidance and truth.

19 The desire accomplished is sweet to the soul: but it is abomination to fools to depart from evil.

20 He that walketh with wise men shall be wise: but a companion of fools shall be destroyed.

21 Evil pursueth sinners: but to the righteous good shall be repayed.

22 A good man leaveth an inheritance to his children's children: and the wealth of the sinner is laid up for the just.

23 Much food is in the tillage of the poor: but there is that is destroyed for want of judgment.

24 He that spareth his rod hateth his son: but he that loveth him chasteneth him betimes.

25 The righteous eateth to the satisfying of his soul: but the belly of the wicked shall want.

CHAPTER 14

1 EVERY wise woman buildeth her house: but the foolish plucketh it down with her hands.

2 He that walketh in his uprightness feareth the LORD: but he that is perverse in his ways despiseth him.

3 In the mouth of the foolish is a rod of pride: but the lips of the wise shall preserve them.

4 Where no oxen are, the crib is clean: but much increase is by the strength of the ox.

5 A faithful witness will not lie: but a false witness will utter lies.

6 A scorner seeketh wisdom, and findeth it not: but knowledge is easy unto him that understandeth.

7 Go from the presence of a foolish man, when thou perceivest not in him the lips of knowledge.

8 The wisdom of the prudent is to understand his way: but the folly of fools is deceit.

9 Fools make a mock at sin: but among the righteous there is favour.

10 The heart knoweth his own bitterness; and a stranger doth not intermeddle with his joy.

11 The house of the wicked shall be overthrown: but the tabernacle of the upright shall flourish.

12 There is a way which seemeth right unto a man, but the end thereof are the ways of death.

13 Even in laughter the heart is sorrowful; and the end of that mirth is heaviness.

14 The backslider in heart shall be filled with his own ways: and a good man shall be satisfied from himself.

15 The simple believeth every word: but the prudent man looketh well to his going.

16 A wise man feareth, and departeth from evil: but the fool rageth, and is confident.

17 He that is soon angry dealeth foolishly: and a man of wicked devices is hated.

18 The simple inherit folly: but the prudent are crowned with knowledge.

19 The evil bow before the good; and the wicked at the gates of the righteous.

20 The poor is hated even of his own neighbour: but the rich hath many friends.

21 He that despiseth his neighbour sinneth: but he that hath mercy on the poor, happy is he.

NOTES:

22 Do they not err that devise evil? but mercy and truth shall be to them that devise good.

23 In all labour there is profit: but the talk of the lips tendeth only to penury.

24 The crown of the wise is their riches: but the foolishness of fools is folly.

25 A true witness delivereth souls: but a deceitful witness speaketh lies.

26 In the fear of the LORD is strong confidence: and his children shall have a place of refuge.

27 The fear of the LORD is a fountain of life, to depart from the snares of death.

28 In the multitude of people is the king's honour: but in the want of people is the destruction of the prince.

29 He that is slow to wrath is of great understanding: but he that is hasty of spirit exalteth folly.

30 A sound heart is the life of the flesh: but envy the rottenness of the bones.

31 He that oppresseth the poor reproacheth his Maker: but he that honoureth him hath mercy on the poor.

32 The wicked is driven away in his wickedness: but the righteous hath hope in his death.

33 Wisdom resteth in the heart of him that hath understanding: but that which is in the midst of fools is made known.

34 Righteousness exalteth a nation: but sin is a reproach to any people.

35 The king's favour is toward a wise servant: but his wrath is against him that causeth shame.

CHAPTER 15

1 A SOFT answer turneth away wrath: but grievous words stir up anger.

2 The tongue of the wise useth knowledge aright: but the mouth of fools poureth out foolishness.

3 The eyes of the LORD are in every place, beholding the evil and the good.

4 A wholesome tongue is a tree of life: but perverseness therein is a breach in the spirit.

5 A fool despiseth his father's instruction: but he that regardeth reproof is prudent.

6 In the house of the righteous is much treasure: but in the revenues of the wicked is trouble.

7 The lips of the wise disperse knowledge: but the heart of the foolish doeth not so.

8 The sacrifice of the wicked is an abomination to the LORD: but the prayer of the upright is his delight.

9 The way of the wicked is an abomination unto the LORD: but he loveth him that followeth after righteousness.

10 Correction is grievous unto him that forsaketh the way: and he that hateth reproof shall die.

11 Hell and destruction are before the LORD: how much more then the hearts of the children of men?

12 A scorner loveth not one that reproveth him: neither will he go unto the wise.

13 A merry heart maketh a cheerful countenance: but by sorrow of the heart the spirit is broken.

POINT OF INTEREST

President Brigham Young reminded us of the importance of controlling our speech and actions: "In all our daily pursuits in life, of whatever nature and kind, Latter-day Saints, and especially those who hold important positions in the kingdom of God, should maintain a uniform and even temper, both when at home and when abroad. They should not suffer reverses and unpleasant circumstances to sour their natures and render them fretful and unsocial at home, speaking words full of bitterness and biting acrimony to their wives and children, creating gloom and sorrow in their habitations, making themselves feared rather than beloved by their families. Anger should never be permitted to rise in our bosoms, and words suggested by angry feelings should never be permitted to pass our lips. 'A soft answer turneth away wrath, but grievous words stir up anger.' 'Wrath is cruel, and anger is outrageous;' but 'the discretion of a man deferreth his anger; and it is his glory to pass over a transgression'" (Discourses of Brigham Young, 203–204).

14 The heart of him that hath understanding seeketh knowledge: but the mouth of fools feedeth on foolishness.

15 All the days of the afflicted are evil: but he that is of a merry heart hath a continual feast.

16 Better is little with the fear of the LORD than great treasure and trouble therewith.

17 Better is a dinner of herbs where love is, than a stalled ox and hatred therewith.

18 A wrathful man stirreth up strife: but he that is slow to anger appeaseth strife.

19 The way of the slothful man is as an hedge of thorns: but the way of the righteous is made plain.

20 A wise son maketh a glad father: but a foolish man despiseth his mother.

21 Folly is joy to him that is destitute of wisdom: but a man of understanding walketh uprightly.

22 Without counsel purposes are disappointed: but in the multitude of counsellors they are established.

23 A man hath joy by the answer of his mouth: and a word spoken in due season, how good is it!

24 The way of life is above to the wise, that he may depart from hell beneath.

25 The LORD will destroy the house of the proud: but he will establish the border of the widow.

26 The thoughts of the wicked are an abomination to the LORD: but the words of the pure are pleasant words.

27 He that is greedy of gain troubleth his own house; but he that hateth gifts shall live.

28 The heart of the righteous studieth to answer: but the mouth of the wicked poureth out evil things.

29 The LORD is far from the wicked: but he heareth the prayer of the righteous.

30 The light of the eyes rejoiceth the heart: and a good report maketh the bones fat.

31 The ear that heareth the reproof of life abideth among the wise.

32 He that refuseth instruction despiseth his own soul: but he that heareth reproof getteth understanding.

33 The fear of the LORD is the instruction of wisdom; and before honour is humility.

PROVERBS CHAPTER 15

Proverbs 15:15—Be of Good Cheer

A good sense of humor goes a long way in cheering family and friends along the pathway of mortality. Despite the tribulations we face, we can maintain a cheerful attitude and let our family members know that "All is well" ("Come, Come, Ye Saints," *Hymns*, 30). In many ways, the counsel to "be of good cheer" is the eleventh commandment. Consider the scriptural record. Here are some of the challenging situations we face in life and the reasons why we can truly "be of good cheer":

1. When you feel inadequate, read D&C 112:3–4, 10.
2. When your faith is tested, read 3 Ne. 1:12–13.
3. When you feel poor and without resources, read D&C 78:17–22.
4. When you feel weak or ill, read Matt. 9:2–8.
5. When you are fearful because of the elements, read Matt.14:24–27 and Mark 6:50.
6. When you face danger on the Lord's errand, read Acts 27:22, 25.
7. When you face a daunting challenge, read Alma 17:31.
8. When you are called on to bear testimony before the world, read D&C 68:3–6.
9. When you are persecuted for the sake of the gospel, read Acts 23:11.
10. When you face evil, read D&C 61:36–37.
11. When you feel overcome with troubles, read John 16:33.

CHAPTER 16

1 THE preparations of the heart in man, and the answer of the tongue, is from the LORD.

2 All the ways of a man are clean in his own eyes; but the LORD weigheth the spirits.

3 Commit thy works unto the LORD, and thy thoughts shall be established.

4 The LORD hath made all things for himself: yea, even the wicked for the day of evil.

5 Every one that is proud in heart is an abomination to the LORD: though hand join in hand, he shall not be unpunished.

6 By mercy and truth iniquity is purged: and by the fear of the LORD men depart from evil.

7 When a man's ways please the LORD, he maketh even his enemies to be at peace with him.

8 Better is a little with righteousness than great revenues without right.

9 A man's heart deviseth his way: but the LORD directeth his steps.

10 A divine sentence is in the lips of the king: his mouth transgresseth not in judgment.

11 A just weight and balance are the LORD's: all the weights of the bag are his work.

12 It is an abomination to kings to commit wickedness: for the throne is established by righteousness.

13 Righteous lips are the delight of kings; and they love him that speaketh right.

14 The wrath of a king is as messengers of death: but a wise man will pacify it.

15 In the light of the king's countenance is life; and his favour is as a cloud of the latter rain.

16 How much better is it to get wisdom than gold! and to get understanding rather to be chosen than silver!

17 The highway of the upright is to depart from evil: he that keepeth his way preserveth his soul.

18 Pride goeth before destruction, and an haughty spirit before a fall.

19 Better it is to be of an humble spirit with the lowly, than to divide the spoil with the proud.

20 He that handleth a matter wisely shall find good: and whoso trusteth in the LORD, happy is he.

21 The wise in heart shall be called prudent: and the sweetness of the lips increaseth learning.

22 Understanding is a wellspring of life unto him that hath it: but the instruction of fools is folly.

23 The heart of the wise teacheth his mouth, and addeth learning to his lips.

24 Pleasant words are as an honeycomb, sweet to the soul, and health to the bones.

25 There is a way that seemeth right unto a man, but the end thereof are the ways of death.

26 He that laboureth laboureth for himself; for his mouth craveth it of him.

27 An ungodly man diggeth up evil: and in his lips there is as a burning fire.

28 A froward man soweth strife: and a whisperer separateth chief friends.

PROVERBS CHAPTER 16

Proverbs 16:18—Pride Leads to Folly

In the garden of life, one must root out every noxious weed of pride, every instance of hardheartedness, in order to preserve a soil meet to bring forth the growth of wisdom leading to the fruits of righteousness.

The opposite of the fear of God is pride—of leaning to one's own understanding. The chronicles and annals of the Israelites constitute a handbook of what happens when pride is allowed to flourish. Similarly, the Book of Mormon gives ample evidence of the destructive consequences of pride and hardness of heart. The Lord has warned us in our time: "… but beware of pride, lest ye become as the Nephites of old" (D&C 38:39).

Wisdom cannot grow in a prideful soil; righteousness cannot flourish in a prideful heart. As we look toward the day of judgment, we need to remember, with the Preacher: "Rejoice, O young man, in thy youth; and let thy heart cheer thee in the days of thy youth, and walk in the ways of thine heart, and in the sight of thine eyes: but know thou, that for all these things God will bring thee into judgment …. For God shall bring every work into judgment, with every secret thing, whether it be good, or whether it be evil" (Eccl. 11:9; 12:14). Thus a prideful walk will not lead to good consequences. Instead, we must remember this: "Let us hear the conclusion of the whole matter: Fear God, and keep his commandments: for this is the whole duty of man" (Eccl. 12:13).

Proverbs 16:28—Gossip Is Premeditated

Gossip and backbiting are not passive endeavors. To dig up evil, speak negatively, sow strife, and whisper evil things about others—these are premeditated actions that hurt and destroy. The word *froward* means to act contrary to others in an obstinate and stubborn way. The opposite of such behavior is to see the good in others, to praise their positive qualities and worthy accomplishments, to be a peace-maker, and to disseminate complimentary news and views about the goodness of people. If these latter actions prevail in our circles of friendship, then there is unity, feelings of amity, and an atmosphere of encouragement and hope—all elements of a Zion society. (Compare Prov. 18:8; 25:18.)

29 A violent man enticeth his neighbour, and leadeth him into the way that is not good.

30 He shutteth his eyes to devise froward things: moving his lips he bringeth evil to pass.

31 The hoary head is a crown of glory, if it be found in the way of righteousness.

32 He that is slow to anger is better than the mighty; and he that ruleth his spirit than he that taketh a city.

33 The lot is cast into the lap; but the whole disposing thereof is of the LORD.

CHAPTER 17

1 BETTER is a dry morsel, and quietness therewith, than an house full of sacrifices with strife.

2 A wise servant shall have rule over a son that causeth shame, and shall have part of the inheritance among the brethren.

3 The fining pot is for silver, and the furnace for gold: but the LORD trieth the hearts.

4 A wicked doer giveth heed to false lips; and a liar giveth ear to a naughty tongue.

5 Whoso mocketh the poor reproacheth his Maker: and he that is glad at calamities shall not be unpunished.

6 Children's children are the crown of old men; and the glory of children are their fathers.

7 Excellent speech becometh not a fool: much less do lying lips a prince.

8 A gift is as a precious stone in the eyes of him that hath it: whithersoever it turneth, it prospereth.

9 He that covereth a transgression seeketh love; but he that repeateth a matter separateth very friends.

10 A reproof entereth more into a wise man than an hundred stripes into a fool.

11 An evil man seeketh only rebellion: therefore a cruel messenger shall be sent against him.

12 Let a bear robbed of her whelps meet a man, rather than a fool in his folly.

13 Whoso rewardeth evil for good, evil shall not depart from his house.

14 The beginning of strife is as when one letteth out water: therefore leave off contention, before it be meddled with.

15 He that justifieth the wicked, and he that condemneth the just, even they both are abomination to the LORD.

16 Wherefore is there a price in the hand of a fool to get wisdom, seeing he hath no heart to it?

17 A friend loveth at all times, and a brother is born for adversity.

18 A man void of understanding striketh hands, and becometh surety in the presence of his friend.

19 He loveth transgression that loveth strife: and he that exalteth his gate seeketh destruction.

20 He that hath a froward heart findeth no good: and he that hath a perverse tongue falleth into mischief.

21 He that begetteth a fool doeth it to his sorrow: and the father of a fool hath no joy.

22 A merry heart doeth good like a medicine: but a broken spirit drieth the bones.

PROVERBS CHAPTER 17

Proverbs 17:17—Friendship

Friendship has many faces, but only one face; many dimensions, but only one dimension; many agendas, but only one agenda.

Friendship has the face of authenticity, for a friend has a heart of caring concern for your well-being. Friendship has the face of willing engagement, for a friend is available at any hour, any day, to listen and to bond. Friendship has the face of honest candor, for a friend will tell you the truth, "and the truth shall make you free" (John 8:33). Friendship has the face of quiet confidence, for a friend eschews conspiracy and forswears all hint of thoughtless gossip. Friendship has the face of encouragement, for a friend supports, defends, and lifts—even when at times your weakness slips unwanted into view. Friendship has these faces all—but only one face: that of genuine love.

How can you hope to measure the contours of friendship with its myriad dimensions: sensitivity, good humor, loyalty, steadfastness, trust, nobility? Friendship has these dimensions all—but only one dimension: that of genuine love.

How can you comprehend the essence of friendship with its multiple agendas? A friend is intent on increasing harmony within your circle. A friend is committed to generating peace around you. A friend aspires to open ever wider for your sake the windows of opportunity. A friend is motivated to ensure the unfolding of happiness in your life—now and forever. Friendship has these agendas all—but only one agenda: that of genuine love.

The unified faces of love, the harmonized dimensions of love, the integrated agendas of love—these all belong to lasting friendship, true and valid, real and pure. Is there such a friend in all the world? Only one—if perfect is the goal. Said He, "Greater love hath no man than this, that a man lay down his life for his friends" (John 15:3). In the light of the Lord we nurture our sprouting seeds of friendship; we cultivate our budding relationships in the glow of His ever radiant grace. We aspire to emulate His matchless kindness, reflecting in our thoughts and deeds the kind of charity and love that originates in the divine.

And we are grateful for Him, who walks beside us, His arm around us, and for all who serve as friends indeed along the pathway home to where great friendship first evolved. Said Emerson: "The only way to have a friend is to be one." Let us therefore be a friend to those who need a friend—that we may be found "no more strangers and foreigners, but fellowcitizens with the saints, and of the household of God" (Eph. 2:19). Then will our friendship grow and with the years mature, and our circle of friends will expand without compulsory means to make us thankful and content.

Proverbs 17:22—Good Cheer

A merry heart belongs to the disposition of a person who is of good cheer—who has a good sense of humor to soften the challenges of life.

23 A wicked man taketh a gift out of the bosom to pervert the ways of judgment.

24 Wisdom is before him that hath understanding; but the eyes of a fool are in the ends of the earth.

25 A foolish son is a grief to his father, and bitterness to her that bare him.

26 Also to punish the just is not good, nor to strike princes for equity.

27 He that hath knowledge spareth his words: and a man of understanding is of an excellent spirit.

28 Even a fool, when he holdeth his peace, is counted wise: and he that shutteth his lips is esteemed a man of understanding.

CHAPTER 18

1 THROUGH desire a man, having separated himself, seeketh and intermeddleth with all wisdom.

2 A fool hath no delight in understanding, but that his heart may discover itself.

3 When the wicked cometh, then cometh also contempt, and with ignominy reproach.

4 The words of a man's mouth are as deep waters, and the wellspring of wisdom as a flowing brook.

5 It is not good to accept the person of the wicked, to overthrow the righteous in judgment.

6 A fool's lips enter into contention, and his mouth calleth for strokes.

7 A fool's mouth is his destruction, and his lips are the snare of his soul.

8 The words of a talebearer are as wounds, and they go down into the innermost parts of the belly.

9 He also that is slothful in his work is brother to him that is a great waster.

10 The name of the LORD is a strong tower: the righteous runneth into it, and is safe.

11 The rich man's wealth is his strong city, and as an high wall in his own conceit.

12 Before destruction the heart of man is haughty, and before honour is humility.

13 He that answereth a matter before he heareth it, it is folly and shame unto him.

14 The spirit of a man will sustain his infirmity; but a wounded spirit who can bear?

15 The heart of the prudent getteth knowledge; and the ear of the wise seeketh knowledge.

16 A man's gift maketh room for him, and bringeth him before great men.

17 He that is first in his own cause seemeth just; but his neighbour cometh and searcheth him.

18 The lot causeth contentions to cease, and parteth between the mighty.

19 A brother offended is harder to be won than a strong city: and their contentions are like the bars of a castle.

20 A man's belly shall be satisfied with the fruit of his mouth; and with the increase of his lips shall he be filled.

21 Death and life are in the power of the tongue: and they that love it shall eat the fruit thereof.

PROVERBS CHAPTER 18

Proverbs 18:8—The Wounds of Gossip

Gossip hurts to the very core; backbiting severs the bonds of friendship at its very root. Why would some choose this course when it is plain that encouragement lifts and positive feedback edifies? Those who gossip and generate scandalous false rumors are surely afflicted with a dearth of self-respect and self-confidence. By contrast, those who cultivate supportive relationships are surely confident within themselves that they have worth and can contribute productively to the cultivation of unity, friendship, and brotherly/sisterly love. Such are of the kingdom of God.

22 Whoso findeth a wife findeth a good thing, and obtaineth favour of the LORD.

23 The poor useth intreaties; but the rich answereth roughly.

24 A man that hath friends must shew himself friendly: and there is a friend that sticketh closer than a brother.

CHAPTER 19

1 BETTER is the poor that walketh in his integrity, than he that is perverse in his lips, and is a fool.

2 Also, that the soul be without knowledge, it is not good; and he that hasteth with his feet sinneth.

3 The foolishness of man perverteth his way: and his heart fretteth against the LORD.

4 Wealth maketh many friends; but the poor is separated from his neighbour.

5 A false witness shall not be unpunished, and he that speaketh lies shall not escape.

6 Many will intreat the favour of the prince: and every man is a friend to him that giveth gifts.

7 All the brethren of the poor do hate him: how much more do his friends go far from him? he pursueth them with words, yet they are wanting to him.

8 He that getteth wisdom loveth his own soul: he that keepeth understanding shall find good.

9 A false witness shall not be unpunished, and he that speaketh lies shall perish.

10 Delight is not seemly for a fool; much less for a servant to have rule over princes.

11 The discretion of a man deferreth his anger; and it is his glory to pass over a transgression.

12 The king's wrath is as the roaring of a lion; but his favour is as dew upon the grass.

13 A foolish son is the calamity of his father: and the contentions of a wife are a continual dropping.

14 House and riches are the inheritance of fathers: and a prudent wife is from the LORD.

15 Slothfulness casteth into a deep sleep; and an idle soul shall suffer hunger.

16 He that keepeth the commandment keepeth his own soul; but he that despiseth his ways shall die.

17 He that hath pity upon the poor lendeth unto the LORD; and that which he hath given will he pay him again.

18 Chasten thy son while there is hope, and let not thy soul spare for his crying.

19 A man of great wrath shall suffer punishment: for if thou deliver him, yet thou must do it again.

20 Hear counsel, and receive instruction, that thou mayest be wise in thy latter end.

21 There are many devices in a man's heart; nevertheless the counsel of the LORD, that shall stand.

22 The desire of a man is his kindness: and a poor man is better than a liar.

23 The fear of the LORD tendeth to life: and he that hath it shall abide satisfied; he shall not be visited with evil.

24 A slothful man hideth his hand in his bosom, and will not so much as bring it to his mouth again.

POINT OF INTEREST

"A number of dialogues about justice or suffering were written outside Israel. Foreign wisdom literature was widely popular, and biblical writers were probably aware of such works and tried to imitate their conventions; Proverbs 30:1–9 may, indeed, be a foreign composition. Such borrowing, though, is usually very general: it is unlikely that many foreign writings were available or accessible to Israelite authors. However, one Egyptian work, the Instruction of Amenemope *(c. 11th century B.C.E.), was almost certainly known and read, perhaps in translation: Proverbs 1–9 imitates certain features otherwise found only in this text, and close parallels to its content are concentrated in Proverbs 22:17–23:10. This does not imply active collaboration between 'wisdom' authors or groups in different countries but reflects the wide popularity of wisdom literature in the ancient world. It is sometimes thought that wisdom literature entered Israel through an imitation of the Egyptian educational system, but there is little evidence for this. Egyptian writers seem to have been strongly influenced themselves, in the last few centuries B.C.E., by a text called* The Sayings of Ahiqar, *probably composed in eighth-century Syria. There may well have been a thriving local tradition of composition in Syria-Palestine during the biblical period"* (John Bowker, *The Complete Bible Handbook* [New York: DK Publishing, 2001]).

25 Smite a scorner, and the simple will beware: and reprove one that hath understanding, and he will understand knowledge.

26 He that wasteth his father, and chaseth away his mother, is a son that causeth shame, and bringeth reproach.

27 Cease, my son, to hear the instruction that causeth to err from the words of knowledge.

28 An ungodly witness scorneth judgment: and the mouth of the wicked devoureth iniquity.

29 Judgments are prepared for scorners, and stripes for the back of fools.

CHAPTER 20

1 WINE is a mocker, strong drink is raging: and whosoever is deceived thereby is not wise.

2 The fear of a king is as the roaring of a lion: whoso provoketh him to anger sinneth against his own soul.

3 It is an honour for a man to cease from strife: but every fool will be meddling.

4 The sluggard will not plow by reason of the cold; therefore shall he beg in harvest, and have nothing.

5 Counsel in the heart of man is like deep water; but a man of understanding will draw it out.

6 Most men will proclaim every one his own goodness: but a faithful man who can find?

7 The just man walketh in his integrity: his children are blessed after him.

8 A king that sitteth in the throne of judgment scattereth away all evil with his eyes.

9 Who can say, I have made my heart clean, I am pure from my sin?

10 Divers weights, and divers measures, both of them are alike abomination to the LORD.

11 Even a child is known by his doings, whether his work be pure, and whether it be right.

12 The hearing ear, and the seeing eye, the LORD hath made even both of them.

13 Love not sleep, lest thou come to poverty; open thine eyes, and thou shalt be satisfied with bread.

14 It is naught, it is naught, saith the buyer: but when he is gone his way, then he boasteth.

15 There is gold, and a multitude of rubies: but the lips of knowledge are a precious jewel.

16 Take his garment that is surety for a stranger: and take a pledge of him for a strange woman.

17 Bread of deceit is sweet to a man; but afterwards his mouth shall be filled with gravel.

18 Every purpose is established by counsel: and with good advice make war.

19 He that goeth about as a talebearer revealeth secrets: therefore meddle not with him that flattereth with his lips.

20 Whoso curseth his father or his mother, his lamp shall be put out in obscure darkness.

21 An inheritance may be gotten hastily at the beginning; but the end thereof shall not be blessed.

22 Say not thou, I will recompense evil; but wait on the LORD, and he shall save thee.

23 Divers weights are an abomination unto the LORD; and a false balance is not good.

24 Man's goings are of the LORD; how can a man then understand his own way?

25 It is a snare to the man who devoureth that which is holy, and after vows to make enquiry.

26 A wise king scattereth the wicked, and bringeth the wheel over them.

27 The spirit of man is the candle of the LORD, searching all the inward parts of the belly.

28 Mercy and truth preserve the king: and his throne is upholden by mercy.

29 The glory of young men is their strength: and the beauty of old men is the gray head.

30 The blueness of a wound cleanseth away evil: so do stripes the inward parts of the belly.

CHAPTER 21

1 THE king's heart is in the hand of the LORD, as the rivers of water: he turneth it whithersoever he will.

2 Every way of a man is right in his own eyes: but the LORD pondereth the hearts.

3 To do justice and judgment is more acceptable to the LORD than sacrifice.

4 An high look, and a proud heart, and the plowing of the wicked, is sin.

5 The thoughts of the diligent tend only to plenteousness; but of every one that is hasty only to want.

6 The getting of treasures by a lying tongue is a vanity tossed to and fro of them that seek death.

7 The robbery of the wicked shall destroy them; because they refuse to do judgment.

8 The way of man is froward and strange: but as for the pure, his work is right.

9 It is better to dwell in a corner of the housetop, than with a brawling woman in a wide house.

10 The soul of the wicked desireth evil: his neighbour findeth no favour in his eyes.

11 When the scorner is punished, the simple is made wise: and when the wise is instructed, he receiveth knowledge.

12 The righteous man wisely considereth the house of the wicked: but God overthroweth the wicked for their wickedness.

13 Whoso stoppeth his ears at the cry of the poor, he also shall cry himself, but shall not be heard.

14 A gift in secret pacifieth anger: and a reward in the bosom strong wrath.

15 It is joy to the just to do judgment: but destruction shall be to the workers of iniquity.

16 The man that wandereth out of the way of understanding shall remain in the congregation of the dead.

17 He that loveth pleasure shall be a poor man: he that loveth wine and oil shall not be rich.

18 The wicked shall be a ransom for the righteous, and the transgressor for the upright.

19 It is better to dwell in the wilderness, than with a contentious and an angry woman.

NOTES:

20 There is treasure to be desired and oil in the dwelling of the wise; but a foolish man spendeth it up.

21 He that followeth after righteousness and mercy findeth life, righteousness, and honour.

22 A wise man scaleth the city of the mighty, and casteth down the strength of the confidence thereof.

23 Whoso keepeth his mouth and his tongue keepeth his soul from troubles.

24 Proud and haughty scorner is his name, who dealeth in proud wrath.

25 The desire of the slothful killeth him; for his hands refuse to labour.

26 He coveteth greedily all the day long: but the righteous giveth and spareth not.

27 The sacrifice of the wicked is abomination: how much more, when he bringeth it with a wicked mind?

28 A false witness shall perish: but the man that heareth speaketh constantly.

29 A wicked man hardeneth his face: but as for the upright, he directeth his way.

30 There is no wisdom nor understanding nor counsel against the LORD.

31 The horse is prepared against the day of battle: but safety is of the LORD.

CHAPTER 22

1 A GOOD name is rather to be chosen than great riches, and loving favour rather than silver and gold.

2 The rich and poor meet together: the LORD is the maker of them all.

3 A prudent man foreseeth the evil, and hideth himself: but the simple pass on, and are punished.

4 By humility and the fear of the LORD are riches, and honour, and life.

5 Thorns and snares are in the way of the froward: he that doth keep his soul shall be far from them.

6 Train up a child in the way he should go: and when he is old, he will not depart from it.

7 The rich ruleth over the poor, and the borrower is servant to the lender.

8 He that soweth iniquity shall reap vanity: and the rod of his anger shall fail.

9 He that hath a bountiful eye shall be blessed; for he giveth of his bread to the poor.

10 Cast out the scorner, and contention shall go out; yea, strife and reproach shall cease.

11 He that loveth pureness of heart, for the grace of his lips the king shall be his friend.

12 The eyes of the LORD preserve knowledge, and he overthroweth the words of the transgressor.

13 The slothful man saith, There is a lion without, I shall be slain in the streets.

14 The mouth of strange women is a deep pit: he that is abhorred of the LORD shall fall therein.

15 Foolishness is bound in the heart of a child; but the rod of correction shall drive it far from him.

PROVERBS CHAPTER 22

Proverbs 22:6—Train Up a Child

This celebrated maxim has been quoted endless times over the generations. There is an awesome responsibility resting on the shoulders of parents to inculcate in their children the principles of truth and righteousness. The promise cannot be misunderstood: those who labor diligently to teach their children to follow divine principles will have a lasting influence on their lives and find greater success over time than those parents who leave their children on their own to find their way through the labyrinth of highways and byways of life with markers established by the relative moralists of the world. From the foundation of the earth, righteous parents have taken seriously the quest to raise their children in the paths of truth: "And Adam and Eve blessed the name of God, and they made all things known unto their sons and their daughters" (Moses 5:12).

Modern revelation makes clear the sacred nature of parental responsibility:

And again, inasmuch as parents have children in Zion, or in any of her stakes which are organized, that teach them not to understand the doctrine of repentance, faith in Christ the Son of the living God, and of baptism and the gift of the Holy Ghost by the laying on of the hands, when eight years old, the sin be upon the heads of the parents.

For this shall be a law unto the inhabitants of Zion, or in any of her stakes which are organized.

And their children shall be baptized for the remission of their sins when eight years old, and receive the laying on of the hands.

And they shall also teach their children to pray, and to walk uprightly before the Lord. (D&C 68:25–28)

16 He that oppresseth the poor to increase his riches, and he that giveth to the rich, shall surely come to want.

17 Bow down thine ear, and hear the words of the wise, and apply thine heart unto my knowledge.

18 For it is a pleasant thing if thou keep them within thee; they shall withal be fitted in thy lips.

19 That thy trust may be in the LORD, I have made known to thee this day, even to thee.

20 Have not I written to thee excellent things in counsels and knowledge,

21 That I might make thee know the certainty of the words of truth; that thou mightest answer the words of truth to them that send unto thee?

22 Rob not the poor, because he is poor: neither oppress the afflicted in the gate:

23 For the LORD will plead their cause, and spoil the soul of those that spoiled them.

24 Make no friendship with an angry man; and with a furious man thou shalt not go:

25 Lest thou learn his ways, and get a snare to thy soul.

26 Be not thou one of them that strike hands, or of them that are sureties for debts.

27 If thou hast nothing to pay, why should he take away thy bed from under thee?

28 Remove not the ancient landmark, which thy fathers have set.

29 Seest thou a man diligent in his business? he shall stand before kings; he shall not stand before mean men.

CHAPTER 23

1 WHEN thou sittest to eat with a ruler, consider diligently what is before thee:

2 And put a knife to thy throat, if thou be a man given to appetite.

3 Be not desirous of his dainties: for they are deceitful meat.

4 Labour not to be rich: cease from thine own wisdom.

5 Wilt thou set thine eyes upon that which is not? for riches certainly make themselves wings; they fly away as an eagle toward heaven.

6 Eat thou not the bread of him that hath an evil eye, neither desire thou his dainty meats:

7 For as he thinketh in his heart, so is he: Eat and drink, saith he to thee; but his heart is not with thee.

8 The morsel which thou hast eaten shalt thou vomit up, and lose thy sweet words.

9 Speak not in the ears of a fool: for he will despise the wisdom of thy words.

10 Remove not the old landmark; and enter not into the fields of the fatherless:

11 For their redeemer is mighty; he shall plead their cause with thee.

12 Apply thine heart unto instruction, and thine ears to the words of knowledge.

13 Withhold not correction from the child: for if thou beatest him with the rod, he shall not die.

14 Thou shalt beat him with the rod, and shalt deliver his soul from hell.

NOTES:

15 My son, if thine heart be wise, my heart shall rejoice, even mine.

16 Yea, my reins shall rejoice, when thy lips speak right things.

17 Let not thine heart envy sinners: but be thou in the fear of the LORD all the day long.

18 For surely there is an end; and thine expectation shall not be cut off.

19 Hear thou, my son, and be wise, and guide thine heart in the way.

20 Be not among winebibbers; among riotous eaters of flesh:

21 For the drunkard and the glutton shall come to poverty: and drowsiness shall clothe a man with rags.

22 Hearken unto thy father that begat thee, and despise not thy mother when she is old.

23 Buy the truth, and sell it not; also wisdom, and instruction, and understanding.

24 The father of the righteous shall greatly rejoice: and he that begetteth a wise child shall have joy of him.

25 Thy father and thy mother shall be glad, and she that bare thee shall rejoice.

26 My son, give me thine heart, and let thine eyes observe my ways.

27 For a whore is a deep ditch; and a strange woman is a narrow pit.

28 She also lieth in wait as for a prey, and increaseth the transgressors among men.

29 Who hath woe? who hath sorrow? who hath contentions? who hath babbling? who hath wounds without cause? who hath redness of eyes?

30 They that tarry long at the wine; they that go to seek mixed wine.

31 Look not thou upon the wine when it is red, when it giveth his colour in the cup, when it moveth itself aright.

32 At the last it biteth like a serpent, and stingeth like an adder.

33 Thine eyes shall behold strange women, and thine heart shall utter perverse things.

34 Yea, thou shalt be as he that lieth down in the midst of the sea, or as he that lieth upon the top of a mast.

35 They have stricken me, shalt thou say, and I was not sick; they have beaten me, and I felt it not: when shall I awake? I will seek it yet again.

NOTES:

CHAPTER 24

1 BE not thou envious against evil men, neither desire to be with them.

2 For their heart studieth destruction, and their lips talk of mischief.

3 Through wisdom is an house builded; and by understanding it is established:

4 And by knowledge shall the chambers be filled with all precious and pleasant riches.

5 A wise man is strong; yea, a man of knowledge increaseth strength.

6 For by wise counsel thou shalt make thy war: and in multitude of counsellors there is safety.

7 Wisdom is too high for a fool: he openeth not his mouth in the gate.

8 He that deviseth to do evil shall be called a mischievous person.

9 The thought of foolishness is sin: and the scorner is an abomination to men.

10 If thou faint in the day of adversity, thy strength is small.

11 If thou forbear to deliver them that are drawn unto death, and those that are ready to be slain;

12 If thou sayest, Behold, we knew it not; doth not he that pondereth the heart consider it? and he that keepeth thy soul, doth not he know it? and shall not he render to every man according to his works?

13 My son, eat thou honey, because it is good; and the honeycomb, which is sweet to thy taste:

14 So shall the knowledge of wisdom be unto thy soul: when thou hast found it, then there shall be a reward, and thy expectation shall not be cut off.

15 Lay not wait, O wicked man, against the dwelling of the righteous; spoil not his resting place:

16 For a just man falleth seven times, and riseth up again: but the wicked shall fall into mischief.

17 Rejoice not when thine enemy falleth, and let not thine heart be glad when he stumbleth:

18 Lest the LORD see it, and it displease him, and he turn away his wrath from him.

19 Fret not thyself because of evil men, neither be thou envious at the wicked;

20 For there shall be no reward to the evil man; the candle of the wicked shall be put out.

21 My son, fear thou the LORD and the king: and meddle not with them that are given to change:

22 For their calamity shall rise suddenly; and who knoweth the ruin of them both?

23 These things also belong to the wise. It is not good to have respect of persons in judgment.

24 He that saith unto the wicked, Thou art righteous; him shall the people curse, nations shall abhor him:

25 But to them that rebuke him shall be delight, and a good blessing shall come upon them.

26 Every man shall kiss his lips that giveth a right answer.

27 Prepare thy work without, and make it fit for thyself in the field; and afterwards build thine house.

Solomon's Court by Ingobertus

POINT OF INTEREST

The Hebrew title is for Proverbs is Mishle Shelomoh *(The Proverbs of Solomon). Authorship is unknown; they are attributed to Solomon but include collections from other wise men, including foreigners, and were probably collected by groups associated with the teaching of wisdom.*

28 Be not a witness against thy neighbour without cause; and deceive not with thy lips.

29 Say not, I will do so to him as he hath done to me: I will render to the man according to his work.

30 I went by the field of the slothful, and by the vineyard of the man void of understanding;

31 And, lo, it was all grown over with thorns, and nettles had covered the face thereof, and the stone wall thereof was broken down.

32 Then I saw, and considered it well: I looked upon it, and received instruction.

33 Yet a little sleep, a little slumber, a little folding of the hands to sleep:

34 So shall thy poverty come as one that travelleth; and thy want as an armed man.

CHAPTER 25

1 THESE are also proverbs of Solomon, which the men of Hezekiah king of Judah copied out.

2 It is the glory of God to conceal a thing: but the honour of kings is to search out a matter.

3 The heaven for height, and the earth for depth, and the heart of kings is unsearchable.

4 Take away the dross from the silver, and there shall come forth a vessel for the finer.

5 Take away the wicked from before the king, and his throne shall be established in righteousness.

6 Put not forth thyself in the presence of the king, and stand not in the place of great men:

7 For better it is that it be said unto thee, Come up hither; than that thou shouldest be put lower in the presence of the prince whom thine eyes have seen.

8 Go not forth hastily to strive, lest thou know not what to do in the end thereof, when thy neighbour hath put thee to shame.

9 Debate thy cause with thy neighbour himself; and discover not a secret to another:

10 Lest he that heareth it put thee to shame, and thine infamy turn not away.

11 A word fitly spoken is like apples of gold in pictures of silver.

12 As an earring of gold, and an ornament of fine gold, so is a wise reprover upon an obedient ear.

13 As the cold of snow in the time of harvest, so is a faithful messenger to them that send him: for he refresheth the soul of his masters.

14 Whoso boasteth himself of a false gift is like clouds and wind without rain.

15 By long forbearing is a prince persuaded, and a soft tongue breaketh the bone.

16 Hast thou found honey? eat so much as is sufficient for thee, lest thou be filled therewith, and vomit it.

17 Withdraw thy foot from thy neighbour's house; lest he be weary of thee, and so hate thee.

18 A man that beareth false witness against his neighbour is a maul, and a sword, and a sharp arrow.

19 Confidence in an unfaithful man in time of trouble is like a broken tooth, and a foot out of joint.

20 As he that taketh away a garment in cold weather, and as vinegar upon nitre, so is he that singeth songs to an heavy heart.

PROVERBS CHAPTER 25

Proverbs 25:18—Bearing False Witness

Among the Ten Commandments is the following: "Thou shalt not bear false witness against thy neighbour" (Ex. 20:16; compare Ex. 23:1; Deut. 5:20; Prov. 6:16–19; 12:17; 14:5; 19:5, 9; 21:28; Mal. 3:5; Matt. 15:19; 19:18; 26:59; Mark 10:19; 14:56-57; Luke 18:20; Rom. 13:9; Mosiah 13:23; Hel. 7:21; 3 Ne. 24:5).

The Savior taught: "But I say unto you, That every idle word that men shall speak, they shall give account thereof in the day of judgment. For by thy words thou shalt be justified, and by thy words thou shalt be condemned" (Matt. 12:36–37).

21 If thine enemy be hungry, give him bread to eat; and if he be thirsty, give him water to drink:

22 For thou shalt heap coals of fire upon his head, and the LORD shall reward thee.

23 The north wind driveth away rain: so doth an angry countenance a backbiting tongue.

24 It is better to dwell in the corner of the housetop, than with a brawling woman and in a wide house.

25 As cold waters to a thirsty soul, so is good news from a far country.

26 A righteous man falling down before the wicked is as a troubled fountain, and a corrupt spring.

27 It is not good to eat much honey: so for men to search their own glory is not glory.

28 He that hath no rule over his own spirit is like a city that is broken down, and without walls.

CHAPTER 26

1 AS snow in summer, and as rain in harvest, so honour is not seemly for a fool.

2 As the bird by wandering, as the swallow by flying, so the curse causeless shall not come.

3 A whip for the horse, a bridle for the ass, and a rod for the fool's back.

4 Answer not a fool according to his folly, lest thou also be like unto him.

5 Answer a fool according to his folly, lest he be wise in his own conceit.

6 He that sendeth a message by the hand of a fool cutteth off the feet, and drinketh damage.

7 The legs of the lame are not equal: so is a parable in the mouth of fools.

8 As he that bindeth a stone in a sling, so is he that giveth honour to a fool.

9 As a thorn goeth up into the hand of a drunkard, so is a parable in the mouth of fools.

10 The great God that formed all things both rewardeth the fool, and rewardeth transgressors.

11 As a dog returneth to his vomit, so a fool returneth to his folly.

12 Seest thou a man wise in his own conceit? there is more hope of a fool than of him.

13 The slothful man saith, There is a lion in the way; a lion is in the streets.

14 As the door turneth upon his hinges, so doth the slothful upon his bed.

15 The slothful hideth his hand in his bosom; it grieveth him to bring it again to his mouth.

16 The sluggard is wiser in his own conceit than seven men that can render a reason.

17 He that passeth by, and meddleth with strife belonging not to him, is like one that taketh a dog by the ears.

18 As a mad man who casteth firebrands, arrows, and death,

19 So is the man that deceiveth his neighbour, and saith, Am not I in sport?

20 Where no wood is, there the fire goeth out: so where there is no talebearer, the strife ceaseth.

21 As coals are to burning coals, and wood to fire; so is a contentious man to kindle strife.

22 The words of a talebearer are as wounds, and they go down into the innermost parts of the belly.

23 Burning lips and a wicked heart are like a potsherd covered with silver dross.

24 He that hateth dissembleth with his lips, and layeth up deceit within him;

25 When he speaketh fair, believe him not: for there are seven abominations in his heart.

26 Whose hatred is covered by deceit, his wickedness shall be shewed before the whole congregation.

27 Whoso diggeth a pit shall fall therein: and he that rolleth a stone, it will return upon him.

28 A lying tongue hateth those that are afflicted by it; and a flattering mouth worketh ruin.

CHAPTER 27

1 BOAST not thyself of to morrow; for thou knowest not what a day may bring forth.

2 Let another man praise thee, and not thine own mouth; a stranger, and not thine own lips.

3 A stone is heavy, and the sand weighty; but a fool's wrath is heavier than them both.

4 Wrath is cruel, and anger is outrageous; but who is able to stand before envy?

5 Open rebuke is better than secret love.

6 Faithful are the wounds of a friend; but the kisses of an enemy are deceitful.

7 The full soul loatheth an honeycomb; but to the hungry soul every bitter thing is sweet.

8 As a bird that wandereth from her nest, so is a man that wandereth from his place.

9 Ointment and perfume rejoice the heart: so doth the sweetness of a man's friend by hearty counsel.

10 Thine own friend, and thy father's friend, forsake not; neither go into thy brother's house in the day of thy calamity: for better is a neighbour that is near than a brother far off.

11 My son, be wise, and make my heart glad, that I may answer him that reproacheth me.

12 A prudent man foreseeth the evil, and hideth himself; but the simple pass on, and are punished.

13 Take his garment that is surety for a stranger, and take a pledge of him for a strange woman.

14 He that blesseth his friend with a loud voice, rising early in the morning, it shall be counted a curse to him.

15 A continual dropping in a very rainy day and a contentious woman are alike.

16 Whosoever hideth her hideth the wind, and the ointment of his right hand, which bewrayeth itself.

17 Iron sharpeneth iron; so a man sharpeneth the countenance of his friend.

18 Whoso keepeth the fig tree shall eat the fruit thereof: so he that waiteth on his master shall be honoured.

19 As in water face answereth to face, so the heart of man to man.

20 Hell and destruction are never full; so the eyes of man are never satisfied.

21 As the fining pot for silver, and the furnace for gold; so is a man to his praise.

22 Though thou shouldest bray a fool in a mortar among wheat with a pestle, yet will not his foolishness depart from him.

23 Be thou diligent to know the state of thy flocks, and look well to thy herds.

24 For riches are not for ever: and doth the crown endure to every generation?

25 The hay appeareth, and the tender grass sheweth itself, and herbs of the mountains are gathered.

26 The lambs are for thy clothing, and the goats are the price of the field.

27 And thou shalt have goats' milk enough for thy food, for the food of thy household, and for the maintenance for thy maidens.

CHAPTER 28

1 THE wicked flee when no man pursueth: but the righteous are bold as a lion.

2 For the transgression of a land many are the princes thereof: but by a man of understanding and knowledge the state thereof shall be prolonged.

3 A poor man that oppresseth the poor is like a sweeping rain which leaveth no food.

4 They that forsake the law praise the wicked: but such as keep the law contend with them.

5 Evil men understand not judgment: but they that seek the LORD understand all things.

6 Better is the poor that walketh in his uprightness, than he that is perverse in his ways, though he be rich.

7 Whoso keepeth the law is a wise son: but he that is a companion of riotous men shameth his father.

8 He that by usury and unjust gain increaseth his substance, he shall gather it for him that will pity the poor.

9 He that turneth away his ear from hearing the law, even his prayer shall be abomination.

10 Whoso causeth the righteous to go astray in an evil way, he shall fall himself into his own pit: but the upright shall have good things in possession.

11 The rich man is wise in his own conceit; but the poor that hath understanding searcheth him out.

12 When righteous men do rejoice, there is great glory: but when the wicked rise, a man is hidden.

13 He that covereth his sins shall not prosper: but whoso confesseth and forsaketh them shall have mercy.

14 Happy is the man that feareth alway: but he that hardeneth his heart shall fall into mischief.

15 As a roaring lion, and a ranging bear; so is a wicked ruler over the poor people.

16 The prince that wanteth understanding is also a great oppressor: but he that hateth covetousness shall prolong his days.

17 A man that doeth violence to the blood of any person shall flee to the pit; let no man stay him.

18 Whoso walketh uprightly shall be saved: but he that is perverse in his ways shall fall at once.

NOTES:

19 He that tilleth his land shall have plenty of bread: but he that followeth after vain persons shall have poverty enough.

20 A faithful man shall abound with blessings: but he that maketh haste to be rich shall not be innocent.

21 To have respect of persons is not good: for for a piece of bread that man will transgress.

22 He that hasteth to be rich hath an evil eye, and considereth not that poverty shall come upon him.

23 He that rebuketh a man afterwards shall find more favour than he that flattereth with the tongue.

24 Whoso robbeth his father or his mother, and saith, It is no transgression; the same is the companion of a destroyer.

25 He that is of a proud heart stirreth up strife: but he that putteth his trust in the LORD shall be made fat.

26 He that trusteth in his own heart is a fool: but whoso walketh wisely, he shall be delivered.

27 He that giveth unto the poor shall not lack: but he that hideth his eyes shall have many a curse.

28 When the wicked rise, men hide themselves: but when they perish, the righteous increase.

CHAPTER 29

1 HE, that being often reproved hardeneth his neck, shall suddenly be destroyed, and that without remedy.

2 When the righteous are in authority, the people rejoice: but when the wicked beareth rule, the people mourn.

3 Whoso loveth wisdom rejoiceth his father: but he that keepeth company with harlots spendeth his substance.

4 The king by judgment establisheth the land: but he that receiveth gifts overthroweth it.

5 A man that flattereth his neighbour spreadeth a net for his feet.

6 In the transgression of an evil man there is a snare: but the righteous doth sing and rejoice.

7 The righteous considereth the cause of the poor: but the wicked regardeth not to know it.

8 Scornful men bring a city into a snare: but wise men turn away wrath.

9 If a wise man contendeth with a foolish man, whether he rage or laugh, there is no rest.

10 The bloodthirsty hate the upright: but the just seek his soul.

11 A fool uttereth all his mind: but a wise man keepeth it in till afterwards.

12 If a ruler hearken to lies, all his servants are wicked.

13 The poor and the deceitful man meet together: the LORD lighteneth both their eyes.

14 The king that faithfully judgeth the poor, his throne shall be established for ever.

15 The rod and reproof give wisdom: but a child left to himself bringeth his mother to shame.

16 When the wicked are multiplied, transgression increaseth: but the righteous shall see their fall.

17 Correct thy son, and he shall give thee rest; yea, he shall give delight unto thy soul.

18 Where there is no vision, the people perish: but he that keepeth the law, happy is he.

19 A servant will not be corrected by words: for though he under-

NOTES:

stand he will not answer.

20 Seest thou a man that is hasty in his words? there is more hope of a fool than of him.

21 He that delicately bringeth up his servant from a child shall have him become his son at the length.

22 An angry man stirreth up strife, and a furious man aboundeth in transgression.

23 A man's pride shall bring him low: but honour shall uphold the humble in spirit.

24 Whoso is partner with a thief hateth his own soul: he heareth cursing, and bewrayeth it not.

25 The fear of man bringeth a snare: but whoso putteth his trust in the LORD shall be safe.

26 Many seek the ruler's favour; but every man's judgment cometh from the LORD.

27 An unjust man is an abomination to the just: and he that is upright in the way is abomination to the wicked.

CHAPTER 30

1 THE words of Agur the son of Jakeh, even the prophecy: the man spake unto Ithiel, even unto Ithiel and Ucal,

2 Surely I am more brutish than any man, and have not the understanding of a man.

3 I neither learned wisdom, nor have the knowledge of the holy.

4 Who hath ascended up into heaven, or descended? who hath gathered the wind in his fists? who hath bound the waters in a garment? who hath established all the ends of the earth? what is his name, and what is his son's name, if thou canst tell?

5 Every word of God is pure: he is a shield unto them that put their trust in him.

6 Add thou not unto his words, lest he reprove thee, and thou be found a liar.

7 Two things have I required of thee; deny me them not before I die:

8 Remove far from me vanity and lies: give me neither poverty nor riches; feed me with food convenient for me:

9 Lest I be full, and deny thee, and say, Who is the LORD? or lest I be poor, and steal, and take the name of my God in vain.

10 Accuse not a servant unto his master, lest he curse thee, and thou be found guilty.

11 There is a generation that curseth their father, and doth not bless their mother.

12 There is a generation that are pure in their own eyes, and yet is not washed from their filthiness.

13 There is a generation, O how lofty are their eyes! and their eyelids are lifted up.

14 There is a generation, whose teeth are as swords, and their jaw teeth as knives, to devour the poor from off the earth, and the needy from among men.

15 The horseleach hath two daughters, crying, Give, give. There are three things that are never satisfied, yea, four things say not, It is enough:

16 The grave; and the barren womb; the earth that is not filled with water; and the fire that saith not, It is enough.

17 The eye that mocketh at his father, and despiseth to obey his mother, the ravens of the valley shall pick it out, and the young eagles shall eat it.

POINT OF INTEREST

"A striking aspect of the book of Proverbs is that, like the rest of the wisdom literature in the Bible, it contains no reference to the salvation history of Israel. Instead, God is shown as creator rather than redeemer, and the world is looked at very much from the angle of human experience. Much of the material shows a very broad understanding of human life, its problems and contradictions. Scholars have debated whether the different selections of Proverbs show a development from a less theological world view to one that is more overtly so. Proverbs 1–9 seems to have a more theological character and may represent the fruits of more mature reflection upon the experience expressed elsewhere. However, God is never absent—at times God is on the edge of an essentially human quest; at other times God is more centrally placed and is the means through which knowledge is attained. This is especially true when the experience is mediated through the figure of Wisdom, who provides a link between God and humankind. Wisdom is made so clearly a personal agent of God in 8:22 (see also 1:20–33) that some have thought an original goddess of wisdom has been absorbed here into the representation of Israel itself, often referred to as a female (the God at Elephantine is referred to as having consorts). As Israel is the chosen consort of God, so Wisdom too is God's natural companion" (John Bowker, *The Complete Bible Handbook* [New York: DK Publishing, 2001]).

18 There be three things which are too wonderful for me, yea, four which I know not:

19 The way of an eagle in the air; the way of a serpent upon a rock; the way of a ship in the midst of the sea; and the way of a man with a maid.

20 Such is the way of an adulterous woman; she eateth, and wipeth her mouth, and saith, I have done no wickedness.

21 For three things the earth is disquieted, and for four which it cannot bear:

22 For a servant when he reigneth; and a fool when he is filled with meat;

23 For an odious woman when she is married; and an handmaid that is heir to her mistress.

24 There be four things which are little upon the earth, but they are exceeding wise:

25 The ants are a people not strong, yet they prepare their meat in the summer;

26 The conies are but a feeble folk, yet make they their houses in the rocks;

27 The locusts have no king, yet go they forth all of them by bands;

28 The spider taketh hold with her hands, and is in kings' palaces.

29 There be three things which go well, yea, four are comely in going:

30 A lion which is strongest among beasts, and turneth not away for any;

31 A greyhound; an he goat also; and a king, against whom there is no rising up.

32 If thou hast done foolishly in lifting up thyself, or if thou hast thought evil, lay thine hand upon thy mouth.

33 Surely the churning of milk bringeth forth butter, and the wringing of the nose bringeth forth blood: so the forcing of wrath bringeth forth strife.

CHAPTER 31

1 THE words of king Lemuel, the prophecy that his mother taught him.

2 What, my son? and what, the son of my womb? and what, the son of my vows?

3 Give not thy strength unto women, nor thy ways to that which destroyeth kings.

4 It is not for kings, O Lemuel, it is not for kings to drink wine; nor for princes strong drink:

5 Lest they drink, and forget the law, and pervert the judgment of any of the afflicted.

6 Give strong drink unto him that is ready to perish, and wine unto those that be of heavy hearts.

7 Let him drink, and forget his poverty, and remember his misery no more.

8 Open thy mouth for the dumb in the cause of all such as are appointed to destruction.

9 Open thy mouth, judge righteously, and plead the cause of the poor and needy.

10 ¶ Who can find a virtuous woman? for her price is far above rubies.

11 The heart of her husband doth safely trust in her, so that he shall have no need of spoil.

12 She will do him good and not evil all the days of her life.

13 She seeketh wool, and flax, and worketh willingly with her hands.

14 She is like the merchants' ships; she bringeth her food from afar.

15 She riseth also while it is yet night, and giveth meat to her household, and a portion to her maidens.

16 She considereth a field, and buyeth it: with the fruit of her hands she planteth a vineyard.

17 She girdeth her loins with strength, and strengtheneth her arms.

18 She perceiveth that her merchandise is good: her candle goeth not out by night.

19 She layeth her hands to the spindle, and her hands hold the distaff.

20 She stretcheth out her hand to the poor; yea, she reacheth forth her hands to the needy.

21 She is not afraid of the snow for her household: for all her household are clothed with scarlet.

22 She maketh herself coverings of tapestry; her clothing is silk and purple.

23 Her husband is known in the gates, when he sitteth among the elders of the land.

24 She maketh fine linen, and selleth it; and delivereth girdles unto the merchant.

25 Strength and honour are her clothing; and she shall rejoice in time to come.

26 She openeth her mouth with wisdom; and in her tongue is the law of kindness.

27 She looketh well to the ways of her household, and eateth not the bread of idleness.

28 Her children arise up, and call her blessed; her husband also, and he praiseth her.

29 Many daughters have done virtuously, but thou excellest them all.

30 Favour is deceitful, and beauty is vain: but a woman that feareth the LORD, she shall be praised.

31 Give her of the fruit of her hands; and let her own works praise her in the gates.

NOTES:

ECCLESIASTES
OR, THE PREACHER

CHAPTER 1

1 THE words of the Preacher, the son of David, king in Jerusalem.

2 Vanity of vanities, saith the Preacher, vanity of vanities; all is vanity.

3 What profit hath a man of all his labour which he taketh under the sun?

4 One generation passeth away, and another generation cometh: but the earth abideth for ever.

5 The sun also ariseth, and the sun goeth down, and hasteth to his place where he arose.

6 The wind goeth toward the south, and turneth about unto the north; it whirleth about continually, and the wind returneth again according to his circuits.

7 All the rivers run into the sea; yet the sea is not full; unto the place from whence the rivers come, thither they return again.

8 All things are full of labour; man cannot utter it: the eye is not satisfied with seeing, nor the ear filled with hearing.

9 The thing that hath been, it is that which shall be; and that which is done is that which shall be done: and there is no new thing under the sun.

10 Is there any thing whereof it may be said, See, this is new? it hath been already of old time, which was before us.

11 There is no remembrance of former things; neither shall there be any remembrance of things that are to come with those that shall come after.

12 ¶ I the Preacher was king over Israel in Jerusalem.

13 And I gave my heart to seek and search out by wisdom concerning all things that are done under heaven: this sore travail hath God given to the sons of man to be exercised therewith.

14 I have seen all the works that are done under the sun; and, behold, all is vanity and vexation of spirit.

15 That which is crooked cannot be made straight: and that which is wanting cannot be numbered.

16 I communed with mine own heart, saying, Lo, I am come to great estate, and have gotten more wisdom than all they that have been before me in Jerusalem: yea, my heart had great experience of wisdom and knowledge.

17 And I gave my heart to know wisdom, and to know madness and folly: I perceived that this also is vexation of spirit.

18 For in much wisdom is much grief: and he that increaseth knowledge increaseth sorrow.

 POINT OF INTEREST

Ecclesiastes is *"a Greek translation of the Hebrew* Koheleth, *a word meaning 'one who convenes an assembly,' sometimes rendered Preacher. The book of Ecclesiastes consists of reflections on some of the deepest problems of life, as they present themselves to the thoughtful observer. The epilogue (Eccl. 12:9-14) sets forth the main conclusions at which the writer has arrived. The author describes himself as 'son of David, king in Jerusalem' (Eccl. 1:1).*

"The book of Ecclesiastes seems permeated with a pessimistic flavor, but must be read in the light of one of its key phrases: 'under the sun' (Eccl. 1:9), meaning 'from a worldly point of view.' The term vanity *also needs clarification, since as used in Ecclesiastes it means transitory, or fleeting. Thus the Preacher laments that as things appear from the point of view of the world, everything is temporary and soon gone—nothing is permanent. It is in this light also that the reader must understand Eccl. 9:5 and Eccl. 9:10, which declare that the dead 'know not any thing,' and there is no knowledge 'in the grave.' These should not be construed as theological pronouncements on the condition of the soul after death; rather, they are observations by the Preacher about how things appear to men on the earth 'under the sun.' The most spiritual part of the book appears in chapters 11 and 12, where it is concluded that the only activity of lasting and permanent value comes from obedience to God's commandments, since all things will be examined in the judgment that God will render on man"* (Bible Dictionary).

CHAPTER 2

1 I SAID in mine heart, Go to now, I will prove thee with mirth, therefore enjoy pleasure: and, behold, this also is vanity.

2 I said of laughter, It is mad: and of mirth, What doeth it?

3 I sought in mine heart to give myself unto wine, yet acquainting mine heart with wisdom; and to lay hold on folly, till I might see what was that good for the sons of men, which they should do under the heaven all the days of their life.

4 I made me great works; I builded me houses; I planted me vineyards:

5 I made me gardens and orchards, and I planted trees in them of all kind of fruits:

6 I made me pools of water, to water therewith the wood that bringeth forth trees:

7 I got me servants and maidens, and had servants born in my house; also I had great possessions of great and small cattle above all that were in Jerusalem before me:

8 I gathered me also silver and gold, and the peculiar treasure of kings and of the provinces: I gat me men singers and women singers, and the delights of the sons of men, as musical instruments, and that of all sorts.

9 So I was great, and increased more than all that were before me in Jerusalem: also my wisdom remained with me.

10 And whatsoever mine eyes desired I kept not from them, I withheld not my heart from any joy; for my heart rejoiced in all my labour: and this was my portion of all my labour.

11 Then I looked on all the works that my hands had wrought, and on the labour that I had laboured to do: and, behold, all was vanity and vexation of spirit, and there was no profit under the sun.

12 ¶ And I turned myself to behold wisdom, and madness, and folly: for what can the man do that cometh after the king? even that which hath been already done.

13 Then I saw that wisdom excelleth folly, as far as light excelleth darkness.

14 The wise man's eyes are in his head; but the fool walketh in darkness: and I myself perceived also that one event happeneth to them all.

15 Then said I in my heart, As it happeneth to the fool, so it happeneth even to me; and why was I then more wise? Then I said in my heart, that this also is vanity.

16 For there is no remembrance of the wise more than of the fool for ever; seeing that which now is in the days to come shall all be forgotten. And how dieth the wise man? as the fool.

17 Therefore I hated life; because the work that is wrought under the sun is grievous unto me: for all is vanity and vexation of spirit.

18 ¶ Yea, I hated all my labour which I had taken under the sun: because I should leave it unto the man that shall be after me.

19 And who knoweth whether he shall be a wise man or a fool? yet shall he have rule over all my labour wherein I have laboured, and wherein I have shewed myself wise under the sun. This is also vanity.

20 Therefore I went about to cause my heart to despair of all the labour which I took under the sun.

21 For there is a man whose labour is in wisdom, and in knowledge, and in equity; yet to a man that hath not laboured therein shall he leave it for his portion. This also is vanity and a great evil.

Service in the Synagogue During the Reading of the Torah

POINT OF INTEREST

"Long-standing tradition identified Solomon as the author of this book, based on references in 1:1–2:26 to the author's royal status and great wealth, and on Solomon's famed wisdom. However, it is now acknowledged that the text neither demands nor supports this. Ecclesiastes belongs to the wisdom tradition of Israel. It makes use of wisdom forms—such as short, pithy sayings—and covers the major topics of wisdom interest: life and death, work and profit, folly and wisdom. In common with other literature of its type, there are no precise historical references, . . . and the general nature of the observations makes it hard to assign a date or place of composition with confidence. A date in the third century B.C.E. is most consistent with the book's language and its subsequent use by other writers, a date agreed on by most scholars" (John Bowker, *The Complete Bible Handbook* [New York: DK Publishing, 2001]).

22 For what hath man of all his labour, and of the vexation of his heart, wherein he hath laboured under the sun?

23 For all his days are sorrows, and his travail grief; yea, his heart taketh not rest in the night. This is also vanity.

24 ¶ There is nothing better for a man, than that he should eat and drink, and that he should make his soul enjoy good in his labour. This also I saw, that it was from the hand of God.

25 For who can eat, or who else can hasten hereunto, more than I?

26 For God giveth to a man that is good in his sight wisdom, and knowledge, and joy: but to the sinner he giveth travail, to gather and to heap up, that he may give to him that is good before God. This also is vanity and vexation of spirit.

CHAPTER 3

To everything there is a season—Whatsoever God doeth, it shall be for- ever—God shall judge the righteous and the wicked.

1 TO every thing there is a season, and a time to every purpose under the heaven:

2 A time to be born, and a time to die; a time to plant, and a time to pluck up that which is planted;

3 A time to kill, and a time to heal; a time to break down, and a time to build up;

4 A time to weep, and a time to laugh; a time to mourn, and a time to dance;

5 A time to cast away stones, and a time to gather stones together; a time to embrace, and a time to refrain from embracing;

6 A time to get, and a time to lose; a time to keep, and a time to cast away;

7 A time to rend, and a time to sew; a time to keep silence, and a time to speak;

8 A time to love, and a time to hate; a time of war, and a time of peace.

9 What profit hath he that worketh in that wherein he laboureth?

10 I have seen the travail, which God hath given to the sons of men to be exercised in it.

11 He hath made every thing beautiful in his time: also he hath set the world in their heart, so that no man can find out the work that God maketh from the beginning to the end.

12 I know that there is no good in them, but for a man to rejoice, and to do good in his life.

13 And also that every man should eat and drink, and enjoy the good of all his labour, it is the gift of God.

14 I know that, whatsoever God doeth, it shall be for ever: nothing can be put to it, nor any thing taken from it: and God doeth it, that men should fear before him.

15 That which hath been is now; and that which is to be hath already been; and God requireth that which is past.

16 ¶ And moreover I saw under the sun the place of judgment, that wickedness was there; and the place of righteousness, that iniquity was there.

17 I said in mine heart, God shall judge the righteous and the wicked: for there is a time there for every purpose and for every work.

18 I said in mine heart concerning the estate of the sons of men, that God might manifest them, and that they might see that they themselves are beasts.

ECCLESIASTES CHAPTER 3

Ecclesiastes 3:1—To Every Thing There Is a Season

These words and the verses that follow are probably the most famous pronouncements in the Book of Ecclesiastes.

What is the nature of the message? Surely our existence is seasonal, for we are constrained to live our lives from one day to the next, and from one season to the next. And yet with God, all things are present: ". . . there is no God beside me, and all things are present with me, for I know them all" (Moses 1:6).

God's laws and principles are not seasonal, but are everlasting and eternal. They supersede the chapters (seasons) of a man's life—premortal, mortal, postmortal—and give enduring meaning to human existence.

We are counseled to view things from an eternal perspective, as if through the eyes of God. Attend we must to the day-to-day (seasonal) tasks of life, but our vision is to rise to a higher level, so that our momentary joys in this existence will be transformed, through faith and obedience, into eternal joy in the presence of our Father in Heaven and His Son. At that transcending moment, the seasonality of our lives will end and our glory and joy will be everlasting and infinite.

19 For that which befalleth the sons of men befalleth beasts; even one thing befalleth them: as the one dieth, so dieth the other; yea, they have all one breath; so that a man hath no preeminence above a beast: for all is vanity.

20 All go unto one place; all are of the dust, and all turn to dust again.

21 Who knoweth the spirit of man that goeth upward, and the spirit of the beast that goeth downward to the earth?

22 Wherefore I perceive that there is nothing better, than that a man should rejoice in his own works; for that is his portion: for who shall bring him to see what shall be after him?

CHAPTER 4

1 SO I returned, and considered all the oppressions that are done under the sun: and behold the tears of such as were oppressed, and they had no comforter; and on the side of their oppressors there was power; but they had no comforter.

2 Wherefore I praised the dead which are already dead more than the living which are yet alive.

3 Yea, better is he than both they, which hath not yet been, who hath not seen the evil work that is done under the sun.

4 ¶ Again, I considered all travail, and every right work, that for this a man is envied of his neighbour. This is also vanity and vexation of spirit.

5 The fool foldeth his hands together, and eateth his own flesh.

6 Better is an handful with quietness, than both the hands full with travail and vexation of spirit.

7 ¶ Then I returned, and I saw vanity under the sun.

8 There is one alone, and there is not a second; yea, he hath neither child nor brother: yet is there no end of all his labour; neither is his eye satisfied with riches; neither saith he, For whom do I labour, and bereave my soul of good? This is also vanity, yea, it is a sore travail.

9 ¶ Two are better than one; because they have a good reward for their labour.

10 For if they fall, the one will lift up his fellow: but woe to him that is alone when he falleth; for he hath not another to help him up.

11 Again, if two lie together, then they have heat: but how can one be warm alone?

12 And if one prevail against him, two shall withstand him; and a threefold cord is not quickly broken.

13 ¶ Better is a poor and a wise child than an old and foolish king, who will no more be admonished.

14 For out of prison he cometh to reign; whereas also he that is born in his kingdom becometh poor.

15 I considered all the living which walk under the sun, with the second child that shall stand up in his stead.

16 There is no end of all the people, even of all that have been before them: they also that come after shall not rejoice in him. Surely this also is vanity and vexation of spirit.

Portrait of Brigham Young

  POINT OF INTEREST

President Brigham Young quoted Ecclesiastes 4:13 and then discussed the importance of one's continuing to grow: "When I was baptized into this Church, it was in its infancy, although a considerable number had been baptized before me, and many of them were older when they were baptized than I was. They improved, their minds expanded, they received truth and intelligence, increased in the knowledge of the things of God, and bid fair to become full-grown men in Christ Jesus. But some of them, when they had gained a little spiritual strength and knowledge, apparently stopped in their growth. This was in the eastern country, and but a few years passed before the fruit-trees began to cease bearing fruit. . . . Like the fruit-trees, they have ceased to grow and increase and bear the fruits of the Spirit" (JD 7:335).

CHAPTER 5

1 KEEP thy foot when thou goest to the house of God, and be more ready to hear, than to give the sacrifice of fools: for they consider not that they do evil.

2 Be not rash with thy mouth, and let not thine heart be hasty to utter any thing before God: for God is in heaven, and thou upon earth: therefore let thy words be few.

3 For a dream cometh through the multitude of business; and a fool's voice is known by multitude of words.

4 When thou vowest a vow unto God, defer not to pay it; for he hath no pleasure in fools: pay that which thou hast vowed.

5 Better is it that thou shouldest not vow, than that thou shouldest vow and not pay.

6 Suffer not thy mouth to cause thy flesh to sin; neither say thou before the angel, that it was an error: wherefore should God be angry at thy voice, and destroy the work of thine hands?

7 For in the multitude of dreams and many words there are also divers vanities: but fear thou God.

8 ¶ If thou seest the oppression of the poor, and violent perverting of judgment and justice in a province, marvel not at the matter: for he that is higher than the highest regardeth; and there be higher than they.

9 ¶ Moreover the profit of the earth is for all: the king himself is served by the field.

10 He that loveth silver shall not be satisfied with silver; nor he that loveth abundance with increase: this is also vanity.

11 When goods increase, they are increased that eat them: and what good is there to the owners thereof, saving the beholding of them with their eyes?

12 The sleep of a labouring man is sweet, whether he eat little or much: but the abundance of the rich will not suffer him to sleep.

13 There is a sore evil which I have seen under the sun, namely, riches kept for the owners thereof to their hurt.

14 But those riches perish by evil travail: and he begetteth a son, and there is nothing in his hand.

15 As he came forth of his mother's womb, naked shall he return to go as he came, and shall take nothing of his labour, which he may carry away in his hand.

16 And this also is a sore evil, that in all points as he came, so shall he go: and what profit hath he that hath laboured for the wind?

17 All his days also he eateth in darkness, and he hath much sorrow and wrath with his sickness.

18 ¶ Behold that which I have seen: it is good and comely for one to eat and to drink, and to enjoy the good of all his labour that he taketh under the sun all the days of his life, which God giveth him: for it is his portion.

19 Every man also to whom God hath given riches and wealth, and hath given him power to eat thereof, and to take his portion, and to rejoice in his labour; this is the gift of God.

20 For he shall not much remember the days of his life; because God answereth him in the joy of his heart.

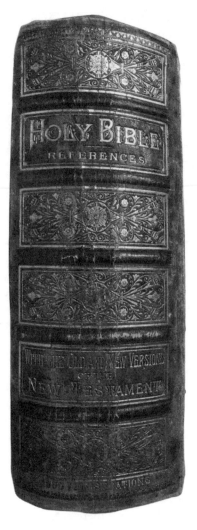

Holy Bible

POINT OF INTEREST

"The process of deciding which books should be accepted into the canon was a long one. In the case of the Hebrew Bible, a 15th-century Jewish scholar, Elias Levita, suggested that Ezra had decided the matter, but that guess, based on 2 Esdras 14:44–48, is clearly wrong. The Greek Bible of Alexandria (the Septuagint) contained more books. Mishnah Yadaim 3:5 states that the assembly of rabbis at Jamnia/Yavneh after the fall of Jerusalem in C.E. 70 debated the status of Ecclesiastes and the Song of Songs, leading to the belief that the canon was settled there. It now seems unlikely that there was a formal 'Council of Jamnia,' and more apparent that the process was gradual. Some have argued that the first two parts of the Hebrew Bible (Torah and Nebi'im [Prophets]) were decided so much earlier than the Kethubim (Writings), so that the former were already an acknowledged authority by New Testament times. In 2 Maccabees 2:14 it is recorded how after the loss of books in the Maccabean revolt, Judas Maccabeus collected them again. While this illustrates the importance of preserving the books, it does not say which they were at the time (John Bowker, *The Complete Bible Handbook* [New York: DK Publishing, 2001]).

CHAPTER 6

1 THERE is an evil which I have seen under the sun, and it is common among men:

2 A man to whom God hath given riches, wealth, and honour, so that he wanteth nothing for his soul of all that he desireth, yet God giveth him not power to eat thereof, but a stranger eateth it: this is vanity, and it is an evil disease.

3 ¶ If a man beget an hundred children, and live many years, so that the days of his years be many, and his soul be not filled with good, and also that he have no burial; I say, that an untimely birth is better than he.

4 For he cometh in with vanity, and departeth in darkness, and his name shall be covered with darkness.

5 Moreover he hath not seen the sun, nor known any thing: this hath more rest than the other.

6 ¶ Yea, though he live a thousand years twice told, yet hath he seen no good: do not all go to one place?

7 All the labour of man is for his mouth, and yet the appetite is not filled.

8 For what hath the wise more than the fool? what hath the poor, that knoweth to walk before the living?

9 ¶ Better is the sight of the eyes than the wandering of the desire: this is also vanity and vexation of spirit.

10 That which hath been is named already, and it is known that it is man: neither may he contend with him that is mightier than he.

11 ¶ Seeing there be many things that increase vanity, what is man the better?

12 For who knoweth what is good for man in this life, all the days of his vain life which he spendeth as a shadow? for who can tell a man what shall be after him under the sun?

CHAPTER 7

1 A GOOD name is better than precious ointment; and the day of death than the day of one's birth.

2 ¶ It is better to go to the house of mourning, than to go to the house of feasting: for that is the end of all men; and the living will lay it to his heart.

3 Sorrow is better than laughter: for by the sadness of the countenance the heart is made better.

4 The heart of the wise is in the house of mourning; but the heart of fools is in the house of mirth.

5 It is better to hear the rebuke of the wise, than for a man to hear the song of fools.

6 For as the crackling of thorns under a pot, so is the laughter of the fool: this also is vanity.

7 ¶ Surely oppression maketh a wise man mad; and a gift destroyeth the heart.

8 Better is the end of a thing than the beginning thereof: and the patient in spirit is better than the proud in spirit.

9 Be not hasty in thy spirit to be angry: for anger resteth in the bosom of fools.

10 Say not thou, What is the cause that the former days were better than these? for thou dost not enquire wisely concerning this.

11 ¶ Wisdom is good with an inheritance: and by it there is profit to them that see the sun.

NOTES:

12 For wisdom is a defence, and money is a defence: but the excellency of knowledge is, that wisdom giveth life to them that have it.

13 Consider the work of God: for who can make that straight, which he hath made crooked?

14 In the day of prosperity be joyful, but in the day of adversity consider: God also hath set the one over against the other, to the end that man should find nothing after him.

15 All things have I seen in the days of my vanity: there is a just man that perisheth in his righteousness, and there is a wicked man that prolongeth his life in his wickedness.

16 Be not righteous over much; neither make thyself over wise: why shouldest thou destroy thyself?

17 Be not over much wicked, neither be thou foolish: why shouldest thou die before thy time?

18 It is good that thou shouldest take hold of this; yea, also from this withdraw not thine hand: for he that feareth God shall come forth of them all.

19 Wisdom strengtheneth the wise more than ten mighty men which are in the city.

20 For there is not a just man upon earth, that doeth good, and sinneth not.

21 Also take no heed unto all words that are spoken; lest thou hear thy servant curse thee:

22 For oftentimes also thine own heart knoweth that thou thyself likewise hast cursed others.

23 ¶ All this have I proved by wisdom: I said, I will be wise; but it was far from me.

24 That which is far off, and exceeding deep, who can find it out?

25 I applied mine heart to know, and to search, and to seek out wisdom, and the reason of things, and to know the wickedness of folly, even of foolishness and madness:

26 And I find more bitter than death the woman, whose heart is snares and nets, and her hands as bands: whoso pleaseth God shall escape from her; but the sinner shall be taken by her.

27 Behold, this have I found, saith the preacher, counting one by one, to find out the account:

28 Which yet my soul seeketh, but I find not: one man among a thousand have I found; but a woman among all those have I not found.

29 Lo, this only have I found, that God hath made man upright; but they have sought out many inventions.

CHAPTER 8

1 WHO is as the wise man? and who knoweth the interpretation of a thing? a man's wisdom maketh his face to shine, and the boldness of his face shall be changed.

2 I counsel thee to keep the king's commandment, and that in regard of the oath of God.

3 Be not hasty to go out of his sight: stand not in an evil thing; for he doeth whatsoever pleaseth him.

4 Where the word of a king is, there is power: and who may say unto him, What doest thou?

5 Whoso keepeth the commandment shall feel no evil thing: and a wise man's heart discerneth both time and judgment.

6 ¶ Because to every purpose there is time and judgment, therefore the misery of man is great upon him.

NOTES:

7 For he knoweth not that which shall be: for who can tell him when it shall be?

8 There is no man that hath power over the spirit to retain the spirit; neither hath he power in the day of death: and there is no discharge in that war; neither shall wickedness deliver those that are given to it.

9 All this have I seen, and applied my heart unto every work that is done under the sun: there is a time wherein one man ruleth over another to his own hurt.

10 And so I saw the wicked buried, who had come and gone from the place of the holy, and they were forgotten in the city where they had so done: this is also vanity.

11 Because sentence against an evil work is not executed speedily, therefore the heart of the sons of men is fully set in them to do evil.

12 ¶ Though a sinner do evil an hundred times, and his days be prolonged, yet surely I know that it shall be well with them that fear God, which fear before him:

13 But it shall not be well with the wicked, neither shall he prolong his days, which are as a shadow; because he feareth not before God.

14 There is a vanity which is done upon the earth; that there be just men, unto whom it happeneth according to the work of the wicked; again, there be wicked men, to whom it happeneth according to the work of the righteous: I said that this also is vanity.

15 Then I commended mirth, because a man hath no better thing under the sun, than to eat, and to drink, and to be merry: for that shall abide with him of his labour the days of his life, which God giveth him under the sun.

16 ¶ When I applied mine heart to know wisdom, and to see the business that is done upon the earth: (for also there is that neither day nor night seeth sleep with his eyes:)

17 Then I beheld all the work of God, that a man cannot find out the work that is done under the sun: because though a man labour to seek it out, yet he shall not find it; yea further; though a wise man think to know it, yet shall he not be able to find it.

CHAPTER 9

1 FOR all this I considered in my heart even to declare all this, that the righteous, and the wise, and their works, are in the hand of God: no man knoweth either love or hatred by all that is before them.

2 All things come alike to all: there is one event to the righteous, and to the wicked; to the good and to the clean, and to the unclean; to him that sacrificeth, and to him that sacrificeth not: as is the good, so is the sinner; and he that sweareth, as he that feareth an oath.

3 This is an evil among all things that are done under the sun, that there is one event unto all: yea, also the heart of the sons of men is full of evil, and madness is in their heart while they live, and after that they go to the dead.

4 ¶ For to him that is joined to all the living there is hope: for a living dog is better than a dead lion.

5 For the living know that they shall die: but the dead know not any thing, neither have they any more a reward; for the memory of them is forgotten.

6 Also their love, and their hatred, and their envy, is now perished; neither have they any more a portion for ever in any thing that is done under the sun.

 POINT OF INTEREST

"The race is not to the swift, nor riches to men of wisdom. Do not fret, nor be so anxious about property, nor think that when you have gathered treasures, they alone will produce joy and comfort; for it is not so.

"The race is not to the swift, nor the battle to the strong, nor riches to men of wisdom. The Lord gives the increase: he makes rich whom he pleases. You may inquire, 'Why not make us rich?' Perhaps, because we would not know what to do with riches" (Brigham Young, *JD* 7:241).

7 ¶ Go thy way, eat thy bread with joy, and drink thy wine with a merry heart; for God now accepteth thy works.

8 Let thy garments be always white; and let thy head lack no ointment.

9 Live joyfully with the wife whom thou lovest all the days of the life of thy vanity, which he hath given thee under the sun, all the days of thy vanity: for that is thy portion in this life, and in thy labour which thou takest under the sun.

10 Whatsoever thy hand findeth to do, do it with thy might; for there is no work, nor device, nor knowledge, nor wisdom, in the grave, whither thou goest.

11 ¶ I returned, and saw under the sun, that the race is not to the swift, nor the battle to the strong, neither yet bread to the wise, nor yet riches to men of understanding, nor yet favour to men of skill; but time and chance happeneth to them all.

12 For man also knoweth not his time: as the fishes that are taken in an evil net, and as the birds that are caught in the snare; so are the sons of men snared in an evil time, when it falleth suddenly upon them.

13 ¶ This wisdom have I seen also under the sun, and it seemed great unto me:

14 There was a little city, and few men within it; and there came a great king against it, and besieged it, and built great bulwarks against it:

15 Now there was found in it a poor wise man, and he by his wisdom delivered the city; yet no man remembered that same poor man.

16 Then said I, Wisdom is better than strength: nevertheless the poor man's wisdom is despised, and his words are not heard.

17 The words of wise men are heard in quiet more than the cry of him that ruleth among fools.

18 Wisdom is better than weapons of war: but one sinner destroyeth much good.

CHAPTER 10

1 DEAD flies cause the ointment of the apothecary to send forth a stinking savour: so doth a little folly him that is in reputation for wisdom and honour.

2 A wise man's heart is at his right hand; but a fool's heart at his left.

3 Yea also, when he that is a fool walketh by the way, his wisdom faileth him, and he saith to every one that he is a fool.

4 If the spirit of the ruler rise up against thee, leave not thy place; for yielding pacifieth great offences.

5 There is an evil which I have seen under the sun, as an error which proceedeth from the ruler:

6 Folly is set in great dignity, and the rich sit in low place.

7 I have seen servants upon horses, and princes walking as servants upon the earth.

8 He that diggeth a pit shall fall into it; and whoso breaketh an hedge, a serpent shall bite him.

9 Whoso removeth stones shall be hurt therewith; and he that cleaveth wood shall be endangered thereby.

10 If the iron be blunt, and he do not whet the edge, then must he put to more strength: but wisdom is profitable to direct.

11 Surely the serpent will bite without enchantment; and a babbler is no better.

POINT OF INTEREST

"Some have read the book of Ecclesiastes as an expression of skepticism and lack of faith, and have wondered how the book came to be included in the canon. It was indeed a book that was disputed. But on its own terms, it is one of the most devout books in the Hebrew Bible. It accepts the endurance of God and of the created order, and invites its reader to affirm the value of life as it is, not to hunt around for spurious consolations: 'a living dog is better than a dead lion' (9:4), and what could be better than the following advice? 'Enjoy life with the wife whom you love, all the days of your vain life that are given you under the sun, because that is your portion in life' (9:9)" (John Bowker, *The Complete Bible Handbook* [New York: DK Publishing, 2001]).

12 The words of a wise man's mouth are gracious; but the lips of a fool will swallow up himself.

13 The beginning of the words of his mouth is foolishness: and the end of his talk is mischievous madness.

14 A fool also is full of words: a man cannot tell what shall be; and what shall be after him, who can tell him?

15 The labour of the foolish wearieth every one of them, because he knoweth not how to go to the city.

16 ¶ Woe to thee, O land, when thy king is a child, and thy princes eat in the morning!

17 Blessed art thou, O land, when thy king is the son of nobles, and thy princes eat in due season, for strength, and not for drunkenness!

18 ¶ By much slothfulness the building decayeth; and through idleness of the hands the house droppeth through.

19 ¶ A feast is made for laughter, and wine maketh merry: but money answereth all things.

20 ¶ Curse not the king, no not in thy thought; and curse not the rich in thy bedchamber: for a bird of the air shall carry the voice, and that which hath wings shall tell the matter.

CHAPTER 11

1 CAST thy bread upon the waters: for thou shalt find it after many days.

2 Give a portion to seven, and also to eight; for thou knowest not what evil shall be upon the earth.

3 If the clouds be full of rain, they empty themselves upon the earth: and if the tree fall toward the south, or toward the north, in the place where the tree falleth, there it shall be.

4 He that observeth the wind shall not sow; and he that regardeth the clouds shall not reap.

5 As thou knowest not what is the way of the spirit, nor how the bones do grow in the womb of her that is with child: even so thou knowest not the works of God who maketh all.

6 In the morning sow thy seed, and in the evening withhold not thine hand: for thou knowest not whether shall prosper, either this or that, or whether they both shall be alike good.

7 ¶ Truly the light is sweet, and a pleasant thing it is for the eyes to behold the sun:

8 But if a man live many years, and rejoice in them all; yet let him remember the days of darkness; for they shall be many. All that cometh is vanity.

9 ¶ Rejoice, O young man, in thy youth; and let thy heart cheer thee in the days of thy youth, and walk in the ways of thine heart, and in the sight of thine eyes: but know thou, that for all these things God will bring thee into judgment.

10 Therefore remove sorrow from thy heart, and put away evil from thy flesh: for childhood and youth are vanity.

NOTES:

CHAPTER 12

1 REMEMBER now thy Creator in the days of thy youth, while the evil days come not, nor the years draw nigh, when thou shalt say, I have no pleasure in them;

2 While the sun, or the light, or the moon, or the stars, be not darkened, nor the clouds return after the rain:

3 In the day when the keepers of the house shall tremble, and the strong men shall bow themselves, and the grinders cease because they are few, and those that look out of the windows be darkened,

4 And the doors shall be shut in the streets, when the sound of the grinding is low, and he shall rise up at the voice of the bird, and all the daughters of musick shall be brought low;

5 Also when they shall be afraid of that which is high, and fears shall be in the way, and the almond tree shall flourish, and the grasshopper shall be a burden, and desire shall fail: because man goeth to his long home, and the mourners go about the streets:

6 Or ever the silver cord be loosed, or the golden bowl be broken, or the pitcher be broken at the fountain, or the wheel broken at the cistern.

7 Then shall the dust return to the earth as it was: and the spirit shall return unto God who gave it.

8 ¶ Vanity of vanities, saith the preacher; all is vanity.

9 And moreover, because the preacher was wise, he still taught the people knowledge; yea, he gave good heed, and sought out, and set in order many proverbs.

10 The preacher sought to find out acceptable words: and that which was written was upright, even words of truth.

11 The words of the wise are as goads, and as nails fastened by the masters of assemblies, which are given from one shepherd.

12 And further, by these, my son, be admonished: of making many books there is no end; and much study is a weariness of the flesh.

13 ¶ Let us hear the conclusion of the whole matter: Fear God, and keep his commandments: for this is the whole duty of man.

14 For God shall bring every work into judgment, with every secret thing, whether it be good, or whether it be evil.

THE
BOOK OF THE PROPHET ISAIAH

CHAPTER 1

1 THE vision of Isaiah the son of Amoz, which he saw concerning Judah and Jerusalem in the days of Uzziah, Jotham, Ahaz, and Hezekiah, kings of Judah.

2 Hear, O heavens, and give ear, O earth: for the LORD hath spoken, I have nourished and brought up children, and they have rebelled against me.

3 The ox knoweth his owner, and the ass his master's crib: but Israel doth not know, my people doth not consider.

4 Ah sinful nation, a people laden with iniquity, a seed of evildoers, children that are corrupters: they have forsaken the LORD, they

ECCLESIASTES CHAPTER 12

Ecclesiastes 12:1—Counsel to Youth

The Preacher's counsel to youth anticipates the words of Alma to his son Helaman:

> O, remember, my son, and learn wisdom in thy youth; yea, learn in thy youth to keep the commandments of God.
>
> Yea, and cry unto God for all thy support; yea, let all thy doings be unto the Lord, and whithersoever thou goest let it be in the Lord; yea, let all thy thoughts be directed unto the Lord; yea, let the affections of thy heart be placed upon the Lord forever.
>
> Counsel with the Lord in all thy doings, and he will direct thee for good; yea, when thou liest down at night lie down unto the Lord, that he may watch over you in your sleep; and when thou risest in the morning let thy heart be full of thanks unto God; and if ye do these things, ye shall be lifted up at the last day. (Alma 37:35–37)

Ecclesiastes 12:13–14—Fear God, and Keep His Commandments

The Preacher, having walked the pathways of seasonality and vanity in his wide-ranging exploration of the height and depths of the human condition—the good, the bad, the beautiful, the ugly—now comes to the conclusion, the *sine qua non* of his philosophy: "Fear God and keep his commandments: for this is the whole duty of man" (verse 13).

The reason is plain: God knows everything, our every thought and deed. Therefore, obedience alone will bring blessings; faithfulness alone will bring joy; honor alone will bring glory. Vanity and folly and superficiality will vanish in the shadows when the faithful and the strong rise to their reward in the eternal courts on high.

THE BOOK OF ISAIAH

On Reading Isaiah

Isaiah willingly fulfilled his call as a prophet of God. He is without equal in his prophetic utterances regarding the Messiah, the Son of God and the Savior of the world. We must do all we can to understand and apply his words to our lives. The Savior himself said:

> And now, behold, I say unto you, that ye ought to search these things. Yea, a commandment I give unto you that ye search these things diligently; for great are the words of Isaiah. (3 Ne. 23:1)

Isaiah, the prophet most cited in subsequent scripture, was given by the Lord a profound gift to express with resounding impact, expressive power, and stark clarity the message of the visions accorded him as the spokesperson for the Lord in his day. His humble response to the call of

have provoked the Holy One of Israel unto anger, they are gone away backward.

5 ¶ Why should ye be stricken any more? ye will revolt more and more: the whole head is sick, and the whole heart faint.

6 From the sole of the foot even unto the head there is no soundness in it; but wounds, and bruises, and putrifying sores: they have not been closed, neither bound up, neither mollified with ointment.

7 Your country is desolate, your cities are burned with fire: your land, strangers devour it in your presence, and it is desolate, as overthrown by strangers.

8 And the daughter of Zion is left as a cottage in a vineyard, as a lodge in a garden of cucumbers, as a besieged city.

9 Except the LORD of hosts had left unto us a very small remnant, we should have been as Sodom, and we should have been like unto Gomorrah.

10 ¶ Hear the word of the LORD, ye rulers of Sodom; give ear unto the law of our God, ye people of Gomorrah.

11 To what purpose is the multitude of your sacrifices unto me? saith the LORD: I am full of the burnt offerings of rams, and the fat of fed beasts; and I delight not in the blood of bullocks, or of lambs, or of he goats.

12 When ye come to appear before me, who hath required this at your hand, to tread my courts?

13 Bring no more vain oblations; incense is an abomination unto me; the new moons and sabbaths, the calling of assemblies, I cannot away with; it is iniquity, even the solemn meeting.

14 Your new moons and your appointed feasts my soul hateth: they are a trouble unto me; I am weary to bear them.

15 And when ye spread forth your hands, I will hide mine eyes from you: yea, when ye make many prayers, I will not hear: your hands are full of blood.

16 ¶ Wash you, make you clean; put away the evil of your doings from before mine eyes; cease to do evil;

17 Learn to do well; seek judgment, relieve the oppressed, judge the fatherless, plead for the widow.

18 Come now, and let us reason together, saith the LORD: though your sins be as scarlet, they shall be as white as snow; though they be red like crimson, they shall be as wool.

19 If ye be willing and obedient, ye shall eat the good of the land:

20 But if ye refuse and rebel, ye shall be devoured with the sword: for the mouth of the LORD hath spoken it.

21 ¶ How is the faithful city become an harlot! it was full of judgment; righteousness lodged in it; but now murderers.

22 Thy silver is become dross, thy wine mixed with water:

23 Thy princes are rebellious, and companions of thieves: every one loveth gifts, and followeth after rewards: they judge not the fatherless, neither doth the cause of the widow come unto them.

24 Therefore saith the Lord, the LORD of hosts, the mighty One of Israel, Ah, I will ease me of mine adversaries, and avenge me of mine enemies:

25 ¶ And I will turn my hand upon thee, and purely purge away thy dross, and take away all thy tin:

26 And I will restore thy judges as at the first, and thy counsellors as at the beginning: afterward thou shalt be called, The city of righteousness, the faithful city.

27 Zion shall be redeemed with judgment, and her converts with righteousness.

the Lord is recorded in Isaiah 6. He wrote in the period 740–701 BC at a time when Israel had incurred the anger of the Lord—to an especially high degree—through her wanton behavior, pride, and idolatry.

Isaiah's language soars and spirals with the flight of thought and symbolism. He intermingles references to events of his own day with those of coming events that are to unfold in the future—thus the reader should be prepared to engage in the breathtaking sweep of his diction that carries one from the distant past to the distant future and back again, often within the same passage. His message is the age-old prophetic message that "wickedness never was happiness" (see Alma 41:10), that Israel would suffer by persisting in her prideful and ungodly walk, and that good would eventually triumph in the last days as the faithful were gathered together in holy places of refuge.

"Great are the words of Isaiah," the Savior proclaimed (3 Ne. 23:1). In no other passages of scripture can one find the word of the Lord expressed with greater power or more lasting influence than in the writings of Isaiah.

The reader of Isaiah has the opportunity to study, work with intensity, and above all seek the Spirit in order to understand the magnificent words of this prophet. As we come to understand Isaiah we will have a greater comprehension of the magnificent role of our Savior in regard to our Eternal Life.

For more insight into Isaiah, see Appendix HH.

ISAIAH CHAPTER 1

"Do you read the scriptures, my brethren and sisters, as though you were writing them a thousand, two thousand, or five thousand years ago? Do you read them as though you stood in the place of the men who wrote them? If you do not feel thus, it is your privilege to do so." —Brigham Young, *JD* 7:333, 8 October 1859

Isaiah 1:16–20—Wash Yourself of Iniquity

The word of the Lord comes in the form of a powerful covenant declaration: Wash yourself of iniquity; cleanse away sin through the gospel of redemption and atonement; be obedient and righteous and receive eternal blessings. On the other hand, to refuse to accept and honor the covenant of the Lord will result in your destruction.

The metaphor of transforming sins of scarlet into whiteness like unto the snow is an unforgettable expression that remains in the heart and inspires one to spiritual action and moral rectitude—the "mighty change" spoken of by King Benjamin (Mosiah 5:2) and Alma (Alma 5:14).

28 ¶ And the destruction of the transgressors and of the sinners shall be together, and they that forsake the LORD shall be consumed.

29 For they shall be ashamed of the oaks which ye have desired, and ye shall be confounded for the gardens that ye have chosen.

30 For ye shall be as an oak whose leaf fadeth, and as a garden that hath no water.

31 And the strong shall be as tow, and the maker of it as a spark, and they shall both burn together, and none shall quench them.

CHAPTER 2

1 THE word that Isaiah the son of Amoz saw concerning Judah and Jerusalem.

2 And it shall come to pass in the last days, that the mountain of the LORD's house shall be established in the top of the mountains, and shall be exalted above the hills; and all nations shall flow unto it.

3 And many people shall go and say, Come ye, and let us go up to the mountain of the LORD, to the house of the God of Jacob; and he will teach us of his ways, and we will walk in his paths: for out of Zion shall go forth the law, and the word of the LORD from Jerusalem.

4 And he shall judge among the nations, and shall rebuke many people: and they shall beat their swords into plowshares, and their spears into pruninghooks: nation shall not lift up sword against nation, neither shall they learn war any more.

5 O house of Jacob, come ye, and let us walk in the light of the LORD.

6 ¶ Therefore thou hast forsaken thy people the house of Jacob, because they be replenished from the east, and are soothsayers like the Philistines, and they please themselves in the children of strangers.

7 Their land also is full of silver and gold, neither is there any end of their treasures; their land is also full of horses, neither is there any end of their chariots:

8 Their land also is full of idols; they worship the work of their own hands, that which their own fingers have made:

9 And the mean man boweth down, and the great man humbleth himself: therefore forgive them not.

10 ¶ Enter into the rock, and hide thee in the dust, for fear of the LORD, and for the glory of his majesty.

11 The lofty looks of man shall be humbled, and the haughtiness of men shall be bowed down, and the LORD alone shall be exalted in that day.

12 For the day of the LORD of hosts shall be upon every one that is proud and lofty, and upon every one that is lifted up; and he shall be brought low:

13 And upon all the cedars of Lebanon, that are high and lifted up, and upon all the oaks of Bashan,

14 And upon all the high mountains, and upon all the hills that are lifted up,

15 And upon every high tower, and upon every fenced wall,

16 And upon all the ships of Tarshish, and upon all pleasant pictures.

17 And the loftiness of man shall be bowed down, and the haughtiness of men shall be made low: and the LORD alone shall be exalted in that day.

ISAIAH CHAPTER 2

Isaiah 2:2–3—The Mountain of the Lord's House

The imagery of the "mountain of the Lord's house" and "the mountain of the Lord" points toward the temple—the House of the Lord, the sacred institution that draws the attention and awe of people everywhere who are seeking to find the gateway to eternal happiness and fulfillment.

The temple is the spiritual magnet of the gathering, for it embodies the design of God to draw all people together under the canopy of the gospel of salvation and exaltation where all principles, powers, and ordinances are made available for the perfecting of the Saints. In times when temple edifices were not available on the earth, it was often in the high elevations of hills and mountains that the Lord communicated with His prophets. Hence the symbolism of the "mountain" is an appropriate and effective way to bring to mind the elevating and edifying power of God's plan for His children.

Isaiah 2:3—Out of Zion Shall Go Forth the Law

The famous phrase "for out of Zion shall go forth the law" was explained by President Harold B. Lee as follows:

I have often wondered what the expression meant, that out of Zion shall go forth the law. Years ago I went with the brethren to the Idaho Falls Temple, and I heard in that inspired prayer of the First Presidency a definition of the meaning of that term "out of Zion shall go forth the law." Note what they said: "We thank thee that thou hast revealed to us that those who gave us our constitutional form of government were men wise in thy sight and that thou didst raise them up for the very purpose of putting forth that sacred document [as revealed in Doctrine and Covenants section 101]. . . .We pray that kings and rulers and the peoples of all nations under heaven may be persuaded of the blessings enjoyed by the people of this land by reason of their freedom and under thy guidance and be constrained to adopt similar governmental systems, thus to fulfill the ancient prophecy of Isaiah and Micah that . . . 'out of Zion shall go forth the law and the word of the Lord from Jerusalem' (*Improvement Era*, October 1945, p. 564.)" (Donald W. Parry, Jay A. Parry, and Tina M. Peterson, *Understanding Isaiah* [Salt Lake City: Deseret Book Co., 1998], 27)

18 And the idols he shall utterly abolish.

19 And they shall go into the holes of the rocks, and into the caves of the earth, for fear of the LORD, and for the glory of his majesty, when he ariseth to shake terribly the earth.

20 In that day a man shall cast his idols of silver, and his idols of gold, which they made each one for himself to worship, to the moles and to the bats;

21 To go into the clefts of the rocks, and into the tops of the ragged rocks, for fear of the LORD, and for the glory of his majesty, when he ariseth to shake terribly the earth.

22 Cease ye from man, whose breath is in his nostrils: for wherein is he to be accounted of?

CHAPTER 3

1 FOR, behold, the Lord, the LORD of hosts, doth take away from Jerusalem and from Judah the stay and the staff, the whole stay of bread, and the whole stay of water,

2 The mighty man, and the man of war, the judge, and the prophet, and the prudent, and the ancient,

3 The captain of fifty, and the honourable man, and the counsellor, and the cunning artificer, and the eloquent orator.

4 And I will give children to be their princes, and babes shall rule over them.

5 And the people shall be oppressed, every one by another, and every one by his neighbour: the child shall behave himself proudly against the ancient, and the base against the honourable.

6 When a man shall take hold of his brother of the house of his father, saying, Thou hast clothing, be thou our ruler, and let this ruin be under thy hand:

7 In that day shall he swear, saying, I will not be an healer; for in my house is neither bread nor clothing: make me not a ruler of the people.

8 For Jerusalem is ruined, and Judah is fallen: because their tongue and their doings are against the LORD, to provoke the eyes of his glory.

9 ¶ The shew of their countenance doth witness against them; and they declare their sin as Sodom, they hide it not. Woe unto their soul! for they have rewarded evil unto themselves.

10 Say ye to the righteous, that it shall be well with him: for they shall eat the fruit of their doings.

11 Woe unto the wicked! it shall be ill with him: for the reward of his hands shall be given him.

12 ¶ As for my people, children are their oppressors, and women rule over them. O my people, they which lead thee cause thee to err, and destroy the way of thy paths.

13 The LORD standeth up to plead, and standeth to judge the people.

14 The LORD will enter into judgment with the ancients of his people, and the princes thereof: for ye have eaten up the vineyard; the spoil of the poor is in your houses.

15 What mean ye that ye beat my people to pieces, and grind the faces of the poor? saith the Lord GOD of hosts.

16 ¶ Moreover the LORD saith, Because the daughters of Zion are haughty, and walk with stretched forth necks and wanton eyes, walking and mincing as they go, and making a tinkling with their feet:

The Prophet Isaiah by Ugolino di Nerio

POINT OF INTEREST

According to scripture, Isaiah saw the Lord "in the year that king Uzziah died" (Isa. 6:1), in about 758 B.C. He served and ministered as a prophet until sometime in Manasseh's reign. There is a tradition that he was killed by the king, who was said to have put Isaiah in a hollow log and then cut him in half.

17 Therefore the Lord will smite with a scab the crown of the head of the daughters of Zion, and the LORD will discover their secret parts.

18 In that day the Lord will take away the bravery of their tinkling ornaments about their feet, and their cauls, and their round tires like the moon,

19 The chains, and the bracelets, and the mufflers,

20 The bonnets, and the ornaments of the legs, and the headbands, and the tablets, and the earrings,

21 The rings, and nose jewels,

22 The changeable suits of apparel, and the mantles, and the wimples, and the crisping pins,

23 The glasses, and the fine linen, and the hoods, and the vails.

24 And it shall come to pass, that instead of sweet smell there shall be stink; and instead of a girdle a rent; and instead of well set hair baldness; and instead of a stomacher a girding of sackcloth; and burning instead of beauty.

25 Thy men shall fall by the sword, and thy mighty in the war.

26 And her gates shall lament and mourn; and she being desolate shall sit upon the ground.

CHAPTER 4

1 AND in that day seven women shall take hold of one man, saying, We will eat our own bread, and wear our own apparel: only let us be called by thy name, to take away our reproach.

2 In that day shall the branch of the LORD be beautiful and glorious, and the fruit of the earth shall be excellent and comely for them that are escaped of Israel.

3 And it shall come to pass, that he that is left in Zion, and he that remaineth in Jerusalem, shall be called holy, even every one that is written among the living in Jerusalem:

4 When the Lord shall have washed away the filth of the daughters of Zion, and shall have purged the blood of Jerusalem from the midst thereof by the spirit of judgment, and by the spirit of burning.

5 And the LORD will create upon every dwelling place of mount Zion, and upon her assemblies, a cloud and smoke by day, and the shining of a flaming fire by night: for upon all the glory shall be a defence.

6 And there shall be a tabernacle for a shadow in the daytime from the heat, and for a place of refuge, and for a covert from storm and from rain.

CHAPTER 5

1 NOW will I sing to my wellbeloved a song of my beloved touching his vineyard. My wellbeloved hath a vineyard in a very fruitful hill:

2 And he fenced it, and gathered out the stones thereof, and planted it with the choicest vine, and built a tower in the midst of it, and also made a winepress therein: and he looked that it should bring forth grapes, and it brought forth wild grapes.

3 And now, O inhabitants of Jerusalem, and men of Judah, judge, I pray you, betwixt me and my vineyard.

ISAIAH CHAPTER 4

Isaiah 4:5—Stand in Holy Places

The righteous homes, congregations, and temples of Zion offer the only enduring refuge from the oppression and tyranny of iniquity and evil. The gospel of Jesus Christ is the only resort of eternal safety for all mankind.

Isaiah, in the most beautiful imagery, teaches us how the Lord can and will protect us as we "stand in holy places" (D&C 45:32; 101:22). Nothing is more prophetic or practical in the protection from sin than to be in a "safe place," sheltered and protected by the hand of God. His protection of us is enhanced as we do our part by being in the right place at the right time doing the right thing.

There is protecting power associated with holy places. We are to provide safe places for our family and loved ones. The power of the Lord and His Spirit will bless us as we are found in holy places.

Isaiah 4:6—The Church

We are thankful for the Church—our spiritual arbor, our protecting cover against the elements of darkness, our tent of refuge, our fold of the Good Shepherd. The Church is for us the pure Waters of Mormon. Like Alma the Elder, we go there with our family and dearest friends to find shelter—"there being near the water a thicket of small trees" (Mosiah 18:5). Living icons they are, these sacred trees, symbols of the blessings of God, extending over our heads as a covering of grace and a garment of lovingkindness—through His Church and kingdom!

The Church is a school of spiritual learning where we cultivate trust in the Lord and invigorate hope in His redeeming love. In gratitude, we partake within of the nurture of the gospel. Through the tutelage of the Holy Spirit we earn in joy our certificate of discipleship, and begin to savor the sweetness of the gospel, becoming "as a planted by the waters, and *that* spreadeth out her roots by the river, and shall not when heat cometh, but her leaf shall be green; and shall not be careful in the year of , neither shall cease from yielding fruit" (Jer. 17:8).

The Church is a gateway to the eternal realms from which not long ago we emigrated to become, for a season, strangers and wanderers in our mortal proving grounds. The Church is an oasis in the sands of time where we refresh ourselves with the living waters of Christ the Lord. Grateful we are to receive therein the blessings of keys that empower us to return home once again at the end of our journey, having learned here faith and obedience and humble reverence for the infinite greatness and mercy of God.

The Church is the Lord's gift to us. Though it is *His* Church, yet He wants it to be *ours* as well—else why would He call it The Church of Jesus Christ of Latter-day Saints? "Behold, the kingdom is yours," declared the Lord. "And behold, and lo, I am with the faithful always" (D&C 62:9). He invites us to knock in meekness and humility and be admitted into His fold.

4 What could have been done more to my vineyard, that I have not done in it? wherefore, when I looked that it should bring forth grapes, brought it forth wild grapes?

5 And now go to; I will tell you what I will do to my vineyard: I will take away the hedge thereof, and it shall be eaten up; and break down the wall thereof, and it shall be trodden down:

6 And I will lay it waste: it shall not be pruned, nor digged; but there shall come up briers and thorns: I will also command the clouds that they rain no rain upon it.

7 For the vineyard of the LORD of hosts is the house of Israel, and the men of Judah his pleasant plant: and he looked for judgment, but behold oppression; for righteousness, but behold a cry.

8 ¶ Woe unto them that join house to house, that lay field to field, till there be no place, that they may be placed alone in the midst of the earth!

9 In mine ears said the LORD of hosts, Of a truth many houses shall be desolate, even great and fair, without inhabitant.

10 Yea, ten acres of vineyard shall yield one bath, and the seed of an homer shall yield an ephah.

11 ¶ Woe unto them that rise up early in the morning, that they may follow strong drink; that continue until night, till wine inflame them!

12 And the harp, and the viol, the tabret, and pipe, and wine, are in their feasts: but they regard not the work of the LORD, neither consider the operation of his hands.

13 ¶ Therefore my people are gone into captivity, because they have no knowledge: and their honourable men are famished, and their multitude dried up with thirst.

14 Therefore hell hath enlarged herself, and opened her mouth without measure: and their glory, and their multitude, and their pomp, and he that rejoiceth, shall descend into it.

15 And the mean man shall be brought down, and the mighty man shall be humbled, and the eyes of the lofty shall be humbled:

16 But the LORD of hosts shall be exalted in judgment, and God that is holy shall be sanctified in righteousness.

17 Then shall the lambs feed after their manner, and the waste places of the fat ones shall strangers eat.

18 Woe unto them that draw iniquity with cords of vanity, and sin as it were with a cart rope:

19 That say, Let him make speed, and hasten his work, that we may see it: and let the counsel of the Holy One of Israel draw nigh and come, that we may know it!

20 ¶ Woe unto them that call evil good, and good evil; that put darkness for light, and light for darkness; that put bitter for sweet, and sweet for bitter!

21 Woe unto them that are wise in their own eyes, and prudent in their own sight!

22 Woe unto them that are mighty to drink wine, and men of strength to mingle strong drink:

23 Which justify the wicked for reward, and take away the righteousness of the righteous from him!

24 Therefore as the fire devoureth the stubble, and the flame consumeth the chaff, so their root shall be as rottenness, and their blossom shall go up as dust: because they have cast away the law of the LORD of hosts, and despised the word of the Holy One of Israel.

25 Therefore is the anger of the LORD kindled against his people, and he hath stretched forth his hand against them, and hath smitten them: and the hills did tremble, and their carcases were torn in

The Lord has given to us a living Church, a holy place, a hallowed institution, "a tabernacle for a shadow in the daytime from the heat, and for a place of, and for a covert from storm and from rain" (Isa. 4:6). In quiet gratitude we gather together our family each week, put on our best attire, and don our spiritual glow—our "godly walk and conversation" (D&C 20:69)—and go to Church in the spirit of unity and thanksgiving. We go as His people, even "a chosen generation, a royal priesthood, an holy nation, a peculiar people" to show forth "the praises of him who hath called [us] out of darkness into his marvellous light" (1 Pet. 2:9). And we go in obedience, thankful for His glorious word, spoken on our behalf.

ISAIAH CHAPTER 5

Isaiah 5—Zion as the Fountain of Truth in the Wilderness of Worldly Shallowness

The scriptures—and particularly the words of Isaiah—make clear the striking contrast between the impoverished and ephemeral fruit of worldly entanglements and the abundant and enduring fruit of gospel light and truth. Isaiah foresaw the time—dawning in our own day—when the brilliance and glory of Zion would again be an exalted ensign to the nations and provide the standard for the redeeming walk of life:

> "And it shall come to pass in the last days, that the mountain of the Lord's house shall be established in the top of the mountain, and shall be exalted above the hills; and all nations shall flow unto it." (Isa. 2:2)

> "And he will lift up an ensign to the nations from afar, and will hiss unto them from the end of the earth: and, behold, they shall come with speed swiftly." (Isa. 5:26)

Isaiah outlines in painful detail the misdeeds and treachery of the wayward people of the Lord, whose prideful and idolatrous behaviors will predictably lead to their being smitten and dispersed. In stark contrast are Isaiah's visions of the coming times of restoration when the scattered remnants will be gathered in from the four quarters of the earth and the nations will look to Zion as the only dependable source of wisdom and truth. These passages provide the chiaroscuro mixture of brilliant light and leaden darkness that mark the contrast between celestial peace and prideful shame, between heavenly majesty and worldly tinsel, between the confidence of the forgiven heart and the utter panic of those called before the righteous Judge on the day of reckoning: "And they shall go into the holes of the rocks, and into the caves of the earth, for fear of the Lord, and for the glory of his majesty, when he ariseth to shake terribly the earth" (Isa. 2:19). And yet, to the remnant of those who are faithful and penitent, Isaiah has this to say: "Come now, and let us reason together, saith the Lord: though your sins be as scarlet, they shall be

the midst of the streets. For all this his anger is not turned away, but his hand is stretched out still.

26 ¶ And he will lift up an ensign to the nations from far, and will hiss unto them from the end of the earth: and, behold, they shall come with speed swiftly:

27 None shall be weary nor stumble among them; none shall slumber nor sleep; neither shall the girdle of their loins be loosed, nor the latchet of their shoes be broken:

28 Whose arrows are sharp, and all their bows bent, their horses' hoofs shall be counted like flint, and their wheels like a whirlwind:

29 Their roaring shall be like a lion, they shall roar like young lions: yea, they shall roar, and lay hold of the prey, and shall carry it away safe, and none shall deliver it.

30 And in that day they shall roar against them like the roaring of the sea: and if one look unto the land, behold darkness and sorrow, and the light is darkened in the heavens thereof.

CHAPTER 6

1 IN the year that king Uzziah died I saw also the Lord sitting upon a throne, high and lifted up, and his train filled the temple.

2 Above it stood the seraphims: each one had six wings; with twain he covered his face, and with twain he covered his feet, and with twain he did fly.

3 And one cried unto another, and said, Holy, holy, holy, is the LORD of hosts: the whole earth is full of his glory.

4 And the posts of the door moved at the voice of him that cried, and the house was filled with smoke.

5 ¶ Then said I, Woe is me! for I am undone; because I am a man of unclean lips, and I dwell in the midst of a people of unclean lips: for mine eyes have seen the King, the LORD of hosts.

6 Then flew one of the seraphims unto me, having a live coal in his hand, which he had taken with the tongs from off the altar:

7 And he laid it upon my mouth, and said, Lo, this hath touched thy lips; and thine iniquity is taken away, and thy sin purged.

8 Also I heard the voice of the Lord, saying, Whom shall I send, and who will go for us? Then said I, Here am I; send me.

9 ¶ And he said, Go, and tell this people, Hear ye indeed, but understand not; and see ye indeed, but perceive not.

10 Make the heart of this people fat, and make their ears heavy, and shut their eyes; lest they see with their eyes, and hear with their ears, and understand with their heart, and convert, and be healed.

11 Then said I, Lord, how long? And he answered, Until the cities be wasted without inhabitant, and the houses without man, and the land be utterly desolate,

12 And the LORD have removed men far away, and there be a great forsaking in the midst of the land.

13 ¶ But yet in it shall be a tenth, and it shall return, and shall be eaten: as a teil tree, and as an oak, whose substance is in them, when they cast their leaves: so the holy seed shall be the substance thereof.

as white as snow; though they be red like crimson, they shall be as wool" (Isa. 1:18).

We are in the world, but don't have to be of the world. We are to prepare every needful thing in order not to fall prey to the devil and the world's temptations. Isaiah has taught us to beware. We are to heed the warning and put ourselves out of harm's way.

Isaiah 5—Summary of Precepts and Principles

Like Isaiah, we can in all humility and devotion take upon ourselves the commitment to assist in the building up of Zion. We can cultivate a "godly walk and conversation" and stand firmly planted in the triad of holy places—home, congregation, and temple—illuminated by the light of the gospel. Not only can we navigate according to the beacon of Zion that casts a spiritual glow over the landscape of worldly enterprise, but also contribute to that beacon by adding our own beam of righteous endeavor to the glory of God. We can then say, with Isaiah, "Holy, holy, holy is the Lord" (Isa. 6:3).

ISAIAH CHAPTER 6

Isaiah 6:2—Seraphim/Seraphims

The word *seraphims* is used only twice in the Old Testament—both times in connection with the vision of Isaiah on the occasion of his being called as a prophet (see Isa. 6:2, 6; compare the equivalent passages in 2 Ne. 16:2, 6, where the word is rendered as *seraphim*). Apparently these are angelic beings in the court of the Lord depicted in symbolic representation as having the capacity to fly (hence winged) and the commission to administer rites of purification:

> Then flew one of the seraphims unto me, having a live coal in his hand, *which* he had taken with the tongs from off the altar:
> And he laid *it* upon my mouth, and said, Lo, this hath touched thy lips; and thine iniquity is taken away, and thy sin purged.
> Also I heard the voice of the Lord, saying, Whom shall I send, and who will go for us? Then said I, Here *am* I; send me. (Isa. 6:6–8)

Isaiah 6:5—Isaiah's Humble Reaction

The humility of Isaiah upon his prophetic commission is reminiscent of the feelings of inadequacy and meekness expressed by Moses when he was called: "And Moses said unto God, Who *am* I, that I should go unto Pharaoh, and that I should bring forth the children of Israel out of Egypt? And he said, Certainly I will be with thee; and this *shall be* a token unto thee, that I have sent thee: When thou hast brought forth the people out of Egypt, ye shall serve God upon this mountain" (Ex. 3:11–12).

Jeremiah, too, felt inadequate to serve in his calling as prophet: "Then said I, Ah, Lord GOD! behold, I cannot

CHAPTER 22

1 THE burden of the valley of vision. What aileth thee now, that thou art wholly gone up to the housetops?

2 Thou that art full of stirs, a tumultuous city, a joyous city: thy slain men are not slain with the sword, nor dead in battle.

3 All thy rulers are fled together, they are bound by the archers: all that are found in thee are bound together, which have fled from far.

4 Therefore said I, Look away from me; I will weep bitterly, labour not to comfort me, because of the spoiling of the daughter of my people.

5 For it is a day of trouble, and of treading down, and of perplexity by the Lord GOD of hosts in the valley of vision, breaking down the walls, and of crying to the mountains.

6 And Elam bare the quiver with chariots of men and horsemen, and Kir uncovered the shield.

7 And it shall come to pass, that thy choicest valleys shall be full of chariots, and the horsemen shall set themselves in array at the gate.

8 ¶ And he discovered the covering of Judah, and thou didst look in that day to the armour of the house of the forest.

9 Ye have seen also the breaches of the city of David, that they are many: and ye gathered together the waters of the lower pool.

10 And ye have numbered the houses of Jerusalem, and the houses have ye broken down to fortify the wall.

11 Ye made also a ditch between the two walls for the water of the old pool: but ye have not looked unto the maker thereof, neither had respect unto him that fashioned it long ago.

12 And in that day did the Lord GOD of hosts call to weeping, and to mourning, and to baldness, and to girding with sackcloth:

13 And behold joy and gladness, slaying oxen, and killing sheep, eating flesh, and drinking wine: let us eat and drink; for to morrow we shall die.

14 And it was revealed in mine ears by the LORD of hosts, Surely this iniquity shall not be purged from you till ye die, saith the Lord GOD of hosts.

15 ¶ Thus saith the Lord GOD of hosts, Go, get thee unto this treasurer, even unto Shebna, which is over the house, and say,

16 What hast thou here? and whom hast thou here, that thou hast hewed thee out a sepulchre here, as he that heweth him out a sepulchre on high, and that graveth an habitation for himself in a rock?

17 Behold, the LORD will carry thee away with a mighty captivity, and will surely cover thee.

18 He will surely violently turn and toss thee like a ball into a large country: there shalt thou die, and there the chariots of thy glory shall be the shame of thy lord's house.

19 And I will drive thee from thy station, and from thy state shall he pull thee down.

20 ¶ And it shall come to pass in that day, that I will call my servant Eliakim the son of Hilkiah:

21 And I will clothe him with thy robe, and strengthen him with thy girdle, and I will commit thy government into his hand: and he shall be a father to the inhabitants of Jerusalem, and to the house of Judah.

22 And the key of the house of David will I lay upon his shoulder; so he shall open, and none shall shut; and he shall shut, and none shall open.

speak: for I *am* a child. But the LORD said unto me, Say not, I *am* a child: for thou shalt go to all that I shall send thee, and whatsoever I command thee thou shalt speak. Be not afraid of their faces: for I *am* with thee to deliver thee, saith the LORD" (Jer. 1:6–8).

Enoch also was overcome with feelings of inadequacy upon his calling as a prophet (see Moses 6:31–34)

The comforting assurance of the Lord in these cases included the promise that He would be with the prophets, who would receive utterance through the power of the Spirit. The case of Isaiah was the same, for the Lord took away his weaknesses and purged his sins (see Isa. 6:6–7) so that he could share the truth with the people in anticipation that some would hear and be blessed with salvation. In the same way, every one of us, when called to a position of trust in the kingdom of God, can proceed in the sure knowledge that He will be with us, give us utterance, and bless us with the strength to accomplish that which we are commanded to do.

ISAIAH CHAPTER 22

"When Jesus came, He came as a sacrifice not simply in the interest of Israel . . . but in the interest of the whole human family, that in Him all men might be blessed, that in Him all men might be saved; and His mission was to make provision by which the whole human family might receive the benefits of the everlasting gospel, ... not alone those dwelling upon the earth, but those also in the spirit world." —Lorenzo Snow, *Deseret Weekly News*, 32:18, 4 November 1882

Overview of References to Christ in Isaiah

Among the ranks of God's mouthpieces since the beginning of time, the prophet Isaiah is probably the most comprehensive delineator of the Messiah's divine qualities and attributes. Five of those special qualities are described in the passages of scripture for this chapter, using the unique tactile symbolic imagery so characteristic of Isaiah's style of expression. We see in our mind's eye his treatment of the visual symbols of the key, the nail, the feast, the crown, and the stone. In addition, we see in stark detail the image of the book that he references in Chapter 29. All of these qualities and subjects emerge with power in the words of Isaiah.

Isaiah 22—Attributes of the Savior

Isaiah's words are filled with statements that anticipate the Lord's coming mission as Savior and Healer of mankind—the One who will open the gates of salvation and exaltation for the faithful and obedient. We see reflected in powerful symbols the qualities of redeeming grace central to the Lord's mission, among others: *the key* (author of salvation), *the nail* (executor of the Atonement), *the feast* (bringer of truth), *the crown*, (sovereign of peace and glory), and *the stone* (foundation for the kingdom of refuge).

23 And I will fasten him as a nail in a sure place; and he shall be for a glorious throne to his father's house.

24 And they shall hang upon him all the glory of his father's house, the offspring and the issue, all vessels of small quantity, from the vessels of cups, even to all the vessels of flagons.

25 In that day, saith the LORD of hosts, shall the nail that is fastened in the sure place be removed, and be cut down, and fall; and the burden that was upon it shall be cut off: for the LORD hath spoken it.

CHAPTER 24

1 BEHOLD, the LORD maketh the earth empty, and maketh it waste, and turneth it upside down, and scattereth abroad the inhabitants thereof.

2 And it shall be, as with the people, so with the priest; as with the servant, so with his master; as with the maid, so with her mistress; as with the buyer, so with the seller; as with the lender, so with the borrower; as with the taker of usury, so with the giver of usury to him.

3 The land shall be utterly emptied, and utterly spoiled: for the LORD hath spoken this word.

4 The earth mourneth and fadeth away, the world languisheth and fadeth away, the haughty people of the earth do languish.

5 The earth also is defiled under the inhabitants thereof; because they have transgressed the laws, changed the ordinance, broken the everlasting covenant.

6 Therefore hath the curse devoured the earth, and they that dwell therein are desolate: therefore the inhabitants of the earth are burned, and few men left.

7 The new wine mourneth, the vine languisheth, all the merryhearted do sigh.

8 The mirth of tabrets ceaseth, the noise of them that rejoice endeth, the joy of the harp ceaseth.

9 They shall not drink wine with a song; strong drink shall be bitter to them that drink it.

10 The city of confusion is broken down: every house is shut up, that no man may come in.

11 There is a crying for wine in the streets; all joy is darkened, the mirth of the land is gone.

12 In the city is left desolation, and the gate is smitten with destruction.

13 ¶ When thus it shall be in the midst of the land among the people, there shall be as the shaking of an olive tree, and as the gleaning grapes when the vintage is done.

14 They shall lift up their voice, they shall sing for the majesty of the LORD, they shall cry aloud from the sea.

15 Wherefore glorify ye the LORD in the fires, even the name of the LORD God of Israel in the isles of the sea.

16 ¶ From the uttermost part of the earth have we heard songs, even glory to the righteous. But I said, My leanness, my leanness, woe unto me! the treacherous dealers have dealt treacherously; yea, the treacherous dealers have dealt very treacherously.

17 Fear, and the pit, and the snare, are upon thee, O inhabitant of the earth.

18 And it shall come to pass, that he who fleeth from the noise of the fear shall fall into the pit; and he that cometh up out of the

"And the key of the House of David will I lay upon his shoulders." (Isa. 22:22)

"And I will fasten him as a nail in a sure place." (Isa. 22:23)

"And in this mountain shall the Lord of hosts make unto all people a feast of fat things. . . ." (Isa. 25:6)

"In that day shall the Lord of hosts be for a crown of glory, and for a diadem of beauty, unto the residue of the people." (Isa. 28:5)

"Therefore thus saith the Lord God, Behold, I lay in Zion for a foundation a stone, a tried stone, a precious corner stone, a sure foundation." (Isa. 28:16)

Isaiah, whose name means "the Lord of Salvation," writes his mighty visions in the period 740–701 BC, thus during the early reign of King Hezekiah (715–686 BC), for whom he served as courtly advisor. His language is filled with powerful symbolism and echoes as if from a great altitude and overarching perspective. Isaiah paints his canvas with broad strokes of opposites—darkness and light, scattering and gathering, imprisonment and liberation, hunger and satiety, tearing down and building up—all contingent on man's obedience to the covenants of God. Under the inspiration of the Spirit, he sees the grand breadth of the earth's history from beginning to end and foreshadows the coming day of judgment where the wicked will shrink under the awesome burden of guilt and the righteous will rejoice in the salvation of the Lord.

ISAIAH CHAPTER 24

Isaiah 24:22—The Work Performed in the Spirit World

Isaiah perceives in vision the work of the instruction that proceeds in the spirit realm. From Section 138 of the Doctrine and Covenants, recording the vision of the spirit prison given to President Joseph F. Smith in 1918, we have marvelous insight into the operation of missionary work in that sphere of influence. The Savior visited the just and faithful spirits in the time between His crucifixion and His resurrection, preaching to them the "everlasting gospel" (D&C 138:19); however, to the rebellious He did not go, but rather organized His followers to carry on this mission in His absence:

But behold, from among the righteous, he organized his forces and appointed messengers, clothed with power and authority, and commissioned them to go forth and carry the light of the gospel to them that were in darkness, even to all the spirits of men; and thus was the gospel preached to the dead.

midst of the pit shall be taken in the snare: for the windows from on high are open, and the foundations of the earth do shake.

19 The earth is utterly broken down, the earth is clean dissolved, the earth is moved exceedingly.

20 The earth shall reel to and fro like a drunkard, and shall be removed like a cottage; and the transgression thereof shall be heavy upon it; and it shall fall, and not rise again.

21 And it shall come to pass in that day, that the LORD shall punish the host of the high ones that are on high, and the kings of the earth upon the earth.

22 And they shall be gathered together, as prisoners are gathered in the pit, and shall be shut up in the prison, and after many days shall they be visited.

23 Then the moon shall be confounded, and the sun ashamed, when the LORD of hosts shall reign in mount Zion, and in Jerusalem, and before his ancients gloriously.

CHAPTER 25

1 O LORD, thou art my God; I will exalt thee, I will praise thy name; for thou hast done wonderful things; thy counsels of old are faithfulness and truth.

2 For thou hast made of a city an heap; of a defenced city a ruin: a palace of strangers to be no city; it shall never be built.

3 Therefore shall the strong people glorify thee, the city of the terrible nations shall fear thee.

4 For thou hast been a strength to the poor, a strength to the needy in his distress, a refuge from the storm, a shadow from the heat, when the blast of the terrible ones is as a storm against the wall.

5 Thou shalt bring down the noise of strangers, as the heat in a dry place; even the heat with the shadow of a cloud: the branch of the terrible ones shall be brought low.

6 ¶ And in this mountain shall the LORD of hosts make unto all people a feast of fat things, a feast of wines on the lees, of fat things full of marrow, of wines on the lees well refined.

7 And he will destroy in this mountain the face of the covering cast over all people, and the vail that is spread over all nations.

8 He will swallow up death in victory; and the Lord GOD will wipe away tears from off all faces; and the rebuke of his people shall he take away from off all the earth: for the LORD hath spoken it.

9 ¶ And it shall be said in that day, Lo, this is our God; we have waited for him, and he will save us: this is the LORD; we have waited for him, we will be glad and rejoice in his salvation.

10 For in this mountain shall the hand of the LORD rest, and Moab shall be trodden down under him, even as straw is trodden down for the dunghill.

11 And he shall spread forth his hands in the midst of them, as he that swimmeth spreadeth forth his hands to swim: and he shall bring down their pride together with the spoils of their hands.

12 And the fortress of the high fort of thy walls shall he bring down, lay low, and bring to the ground, even to the dust.

And the chosen messengers went forth to declare the acceptable day of the Lord and proclaim liberty to the captives who were bound, even unto all who would repent of their sins and receive the gospel.

Thus was the gospel preached to those who had died in their sins, without a knowledge of the truth, or in transgression, having rejected the prophets.

These were taught faith in God, repentance from sin, vicarious baptism for the remission of sins, the gift of the Holy Ghost by the laying on of hands,

And all other principles of the gospel that were necessary for them to know in order to qualify themselves that they might be judged according to men in the flesh, but live according to God in the spirit. (D&C 138:30–34)

ISAIAH CHAPTER 25

Isaiah 25:4—Praise to the Lord

Isaiah offers a glorious expression of praise to the Lord for His acts of kindness, His word of truth, His compassion for the poor and needy, His deliverance and protection against the forces of evil in the world.

Isaiah 25:6–9—The Triumphs of the Lord

In soaring language of praise and adulation, Isaiah eloquently identifies the triumphs and beneficence of the Lord on behalf of His people: an abundance of eternal blessings (as in a grand feast), the dissipation of the veil of unbelief and falsehood covering the people, the victory over death (through the Resurrection), the termination of anguish and tears, the liberation from rebuke and calumny, and the joy and glory of salvation (thus ending the second death).

The word *lees* in this passage refers to the sediments attending the preparation of wine; thus "wine on the lees" implies a wine that has been preserved for some time and, less the sediments left on the bottom, is "well refined"—symbolic therefore of the harvest of abundant and supernal blessings awaiting the faithful and obedient. Partaking of the lees (sediments) would be considered a punishment: "For in the hand of the LORD *there is* a cup, and the wine is red; it is full of mixture; and he poureth out of the same: but the dregs thereof, all the wicked of the earth shall wring *them* out, *and* drink *them*" (Ps. 75:8).

CHAPTER 26

1 IN that day shall this song be sung in the land of Judah; We have a strong city; salvation will God appoint for walls and bulwarks.

2 Open ye the gates, that the righteous nation which keepeth the truth may enter in.

3 Thou wilt keep him in perfect peace, whose mind is stayed on thee: because he trusteth in thee.

4 Trust ye in the LORD for ever: for in the LORD JEHOVAH is everlasting strength:

5 ¶ For he bringeth down them that dwell on high; the lofty city, he layeth it low; he layeth it low, even to the ground; he bringeth it even to the dust.

6 The foot shall tread it down, even the feet of the poor, and the steps of the needy.

7 The way of the just is uprightness: thou, most upright, dost weigh the path of the just.

8 Yea, in the way of thy judgments, O LORD, have we waited for thee; the desire of our soul is to thy name, and to the remembrance of thee.

9 With my soul have I desired thee in the night; yea, with my spirit within me will I seek thee early: for when thy judgments are in the earth, the inhabitants of the world will learn righteousness.

10 Let favour be shewed to the wicked, yet will he not learn righteousness: in the land of uprightness will he deal unjustly, and will not behold the majesty of the LORD.

11 LORD, when thy hand is lifted up, they will not see: but they shall see, and be ashamed for their envy at the people; yea, the fire of thine enemies shall devour them.

12 ¶ LORD, thou wilt ordain peace for us: for thou also hast wrought all our works in us.

13 O LORD our God, other lords beside thee have had dominion over us: but by thee only will we make mention of thy name.

14 They are dead, they shall not live; they are deceased, they shall not rise: therefore hast thou visited and destroyed them, and made all their memory to perish.

15 Thou hast increased the nation, O LORD, thou hast increased the nation: thou art glorified: thou hadst removed it far unto all the ends of the earth.

16 LORD, in trouble have they visited thee, they poured out a prayer when thy chastening was upon them.

17 Like as a woman with child, that draweth near the time of her delivery, is in pain, and crieth out in her pangs; so have we been in thy sight, O LORD.

18 We have been with child, we have been in pain, we have as it were brought forth wind; we have not wrought any deliverance in the earth; neither have the inhabitants of the world fallen.

19 Thy dead men shall live, together with my dead body shall they arise. Awake and sing, ye that dwell in dust: for thy dew is as the dew of herbs, and the earth shall cast out the dead.

20 ¶ Come, my people, enter thou into thy chambers, and shut thy doors about thee: hide thyself as it were for a little moment, until the indignation be overpast.

21 For, behold, the LORD cometh out of his place to punish the inhabitants of the earth for their iniquity: the earth also shall disclose her blood, and shall no more cover her slain.

ISAIAH CHAPTER 26

Isaiah 26:19—Allusion to the Resurrection

The word *resurrection* appears nowhere in the Kng James Version of the Old Testament. Nevertheless, allusions to the Resurrection can be found in passages of Old Testament scripture such as Isa. 26:19 (see also Isa. 25:8). The Resurrection is frequently mentioned in the New Testament and is especially abundant, with explicit detail, in the Book of Mormon (see Alma 11:43–44 and Alma 40, for example; see also 1 Cor. 15:20–22; D&C 138:12–16, 50).

Destruction of Leviathan (Isa. 27:1) by Gustave Doré

CHAPTER 28

1 WOE to the crown of pride, to the drunkards of Ephraim, whose glorious beauty is a fading flower, which are on the head of the fat valleys of them that are overcome with wine!

2 Behold, the Lord hath a mighty and strong one, which as a tempest of hail and a destroying storm, as a flood of mighty waters overflowing, shall cast down to the earth with the hand.

3 The crown of pride, the drunkards of Ephraim, shall be trodden under feet:

4 And the glorious beauty, which is on the head of the fat valley, shall be a fading flower, and as the hasty fruit before the summer; which when he that looketh upon it seeth, while it is yet in his hand he eateth it up.

5 ¶ In that day shall the LORD of hosts be for a crown of glory, and for a diadem of beauty, unto the residue of his people,

6 And for a spirit of judgment to him that sitteth in judgment, and for strength to them that turn the battle to the gate.

7 ¶ But they also have erred through wine, and through strong drink are out of the way; the priest and the prophet have erred through strong drink, they are swallowed up of wine, they are out of the way through strong drink; they err in vision, they stumble in judgment.

8 For all tables are full of vomit and filthiness, so that there is no place clean.

9 Whom shall he teach knowledge? and whom shall he make to understand doctrine? them that are weaned from the milk, and drawn from the breasts.

10 For precept must be upon precept, precept upon precept; line upon line, line upon line; here a little, and there a little:

11 For with stammering lips and another tongue will he speak to this people.

12 To whom he said, This is the rest wherewith ye may cause the weary to rest; and this is the refreshing: yet they would not hear.

13 But the word of the LORD was unto them precept upon precept, precept upon precept; line upon line, line upon line; here a little, and there a little; that they might go, and fall backward, and be broken, and snared, and taken.

14 ¶ Wherefore hear the word of the LORD, ye scornful men, that rule this people which is in Jerusalem.

15 Because ye have said, We have made a covenant with death, and with hell are we at agreement; when the overflowing scourge shall pass through, it shall not come unto us: for we have made lies our refuge, and under falsehood have we hid ourselves:

16 ¶ Therefore thus saith the Lord GOD, Behold, I lay in Zion for a foundation a stone, a tried stone, a precious corner stone, a sure foundation: he that believeth shall not make haste.

17 Judgment also will I lay to the line, and righteousness to the plummet: and the hail shall sweep away the refuge of lies, and the waters shall overflow the hiding place.

18 ¶ And your covenant with death shall be disannulled, and your agreement with hell shall not stand; when the overflowing scourge shall pass through, then ye shall be trodden down by it.

19 From the time that it goeth forth it shall take you: for morning by morning shall it pass over, by day and by night: and it shall be a vexation only to understand the report.

20 For the bed is shorter than that a man can stretch himself on it: and the covering narrower than that he can wrap himself in it.

ISAIAH CHAPTER 28

Isaiah 28:1–13—Becoming Perfect in Christ

A universal principle of the gospel is that the process of becoming "perfect in Christ" (Moroni 10:32) is gradual, progressing one step at a time, unfolding by measured and positive preparation toward the defined goal of taking on the divine nature under the guidance of the Holy Spirit. Modern revelation confirms this truth (see 2 Ne. 28:30; D&C 98:12; 128:21).

Isaiah 28:16—The Corner Stone

This magnificent Messianic symbol of the corner stone is cited frequently in other passages of scripture (see, for example, Ps. 118:22–23; 132:17; Matt. 21:42; Mark 12:10; Eph. 2:20; 1 Pet. 2:6–7).

21 For the LORD shall rise up as in mount Perazim, he shall be wroth as in the valley of Gibeon, that he may do his work, his strange work; and bring to pass his act, his strange act.

22 Now therefore be ye not mockers, lest your bands be made strong: for I have heard from the Lord GOD of hosts a consumption, even determined upon the whole earth.

23 ¶ Give ye ear, and hear my voice; hearken, and hear my speech.

24 Doth the plowman plow all day to sow? doth he open and break the clods of his ground?

25 When he hath made plain the face thereof, doth he not cast abroad the fitches, and scatter the cummin, and cast in the principal wheat and the appointed barley and the rie in their place?

26 For his God doth instruct him to discretion, and doth teach him.

27 For the fitches are not threshed with a threshing instrument, neither is a cart wheel turned about upon the cummin; but the fitches are beaten out with a staff, and the cummin with a rod.

28 Bread corn is bruised; because he will not ever be threshing it, nor break it with the wheel of his cart, nor bruise it with his horsemen.

29 This also cometh forth from the LORD of hosts, which is wonderful in counsel, and excellent in working.

CHAPTER 29

1 WOE to Ariel, to Ariel, the city where David dwelt! add ye year to year; let them kill sacrifices.

2 Yet I will distress Ariel, and there shall be heaviness and sorrow: and it shall be unto me as Ariel.

3 And I will camp against thee round about, and will lay siege against thee with a mount, and I will raise forts against thee.

4 And thou shalt be brought down, and shalt speak out of the ground, and thy speech shall be low out of the dust, and thy voice shall be, as of one that hath a familiar spirit, out of the ground, and thy speech shall whisper out of the dust.

5 Moreover the multitude of thy strangers shall be like small dust, and the multitude of the terrible ones shall be as chaff that passeth away: yea, it shall be at an instant suddenly.

6 Thou shalt be visited of the LORD of hosts with thunder, and with earthquake, and great noise, with storm and tempest, and the flame of devouring fire.

7 ¶ And the multitude of all the nations that fight against Ariel, even all that fight against her and her munition, and that distress her, shall be as a dream of a night vision.

8 It shall even be as when an hungry man dreameth, and, behold, he eateth; but he awaketh, and his soul is empty: or as when a thirsty man dreameth, and, behold, he drinketh; but he awaketh, and, behold, he is faint, and his soul hath appetite: so shall the multitude of all the nations be, that fight against mount Zion.

9 ¶ Stay yourselves, and wonder; cry ye out, and cry: they are drunken, but not with wine; they stagger, but not with strong drink.

10 For the LORD hath poured out upon you the spirit of deep sleep, and hath closed your eyes: the prophets and your rulers, the seers hath he covered.

11 And the vision of all is become unto you as the words of a book that is sealed, which men deliver to one that is learned, saying, Read this, I pray thee: and he saith, I cannot; for it is sealed:

ISAIAH CHAPTER 29

Isaiah 29:4—Speech Uttered from the Ground

Speech uttered from the ground and out of the dust refers to the Book of Mormon, preserved in the earth until the time of the Restoration and then extracted and translated under the inspiration of God by the Prophet Joseph Smith. The reference to truth rising from "dust" is found in several references in the Book of Mormon (see 2 Ne. 3:19–20; 26:15–16; 27:9; 33:13; Morm. 8:23; Ether 8:24; Moro. 10:27).

Isaiah 29:14—As a Book Crying from the Dust

The coming forth of the Book of Mormon in our day as a voice from the dust is foreseen by Isaiah in astounding detail, showing that the Lord's design for blessing His people with the fulness of the Gospel was prepared with loving care and meticulous wisdom from the beginning.

Isaiah sees in vision the mission of Moroni to Joseph Smith, and the circumstances under which the Book of Mormon is brought forth by unlearned hands as a "marvelous work and a wonder" that sets at naught the understanding of the worldly wise and prudent, and brings again into the world the fulness of the everlasting gospel. (Compare JS–H 1:18–19; 63–65.)

When we seek humbly to learn of Christ and come to know of His goodness and His attributes of perfection, we will want to become like Him. We will hope to take upon ourselves the qualities of His divine nature, including the ultimate attribute of charity and all of its attendant blessings (see 2 Pet. 1:3–12). This should be our goal in life. As we come unto Christ, we partake of the fruit of the tree of life—and we are happy. One of the divinely appointed lifetime guides for this process is the Book of Mormon, the coming forth of which Isaiah saw in prophetic vision. When we pattern our lives after the teachings of this remarkable book, we cultivate the mission of helping all mankind come unto Christ and be perfected in Him—which is precisely our commission under the Abrahamic covenant. Thus the Book of Mormon is our action plan under this commission. As we "feast upon the word of His abundance" and share this spiritual nourishment with others, then "we will be glad and rejoice in his salvation" (Isa. 25:9).

Isaiah 29:18—The Book of Mormon

The coming forth of the Book of Mormon is like the dawning of a new hope in our lives. It is the answer to our lingering questions about how to strengthen our courage, deepen our understanding of the truth, unfold our faith, and achieve a fullness of our spiritual capacity.

Through its pages we can follow Lehi by "clinging to the rod of iron" until we can "come forth and partake of the fruit of the tree" (1 Ne. 8:24). We can "press forward" with Nephi, "with a steadfastness in Christ, having a perfect brightness of hope, and a love of God and of all men" (2 Ne. 31:20). We can "learn wisdom" with King Benjamin—realizing that "when [we] are in the service of [our]

12 And the book is delivered to him that is not learned, saying, Read this, I pray thee: and he saith, I am not learned.

13 ¶ Wherefore the Lord said, Forasmuch as this people draw near me with their mouth, and with their lips do honour me, but have removed their heart far from me, and their fear toward me is taught by the precept of men:

14 Therefore, behold, I will proceed to do a marvellous work among this people, even a marvellous work and a wonder: for the wisdom of their wise men shall perish, and the understanding of their prudent men shall be hid.

15 Woe unto them that seek deep to hide their counsel from the LORD, and their works are in the dark, and they say, Who seeth us? and who knoweth us?

16 Surely your turning of things upside down shall be esteemed as the potter's clay: for shall the work say of him that made it, He made me not? or shall the thing framed say of him that framed it, He had no understanding?

17 Is it not yet a very little while, and Lebanon shall be turned into a fruitful field, and the fruitful field shall be esteemed as a forest?

18 ¶ And in that day shall the deaf hear the words of the book, and the eyes of the blind shall see out of obscurity, and out of darkness.

19 The meek also shall increase their joy in the LORD, and the poor among men shall rejoice in the Holy One of Israel.

20 For the terrible one is brought to nought, and the scorner is consumed, and all that watch for iniquity are cut off:

21 That make a man an offender for a word, and lay a snare for him that reproveth in the gate, and turn aside the just for a thing of nought.

22 Therefore thus saith the LORD, who redeemed Abraham, concerning the house of Jacob, Jacob shall not now be ashamed, neither shall his face now wax pale.

23 But when he seeth his children, the work of mine hands, in the midst of him, they shall sanctify my name, and sanctify the Holy One of Jacob, and shall fear the God of Israel.

24 They also that erred in spirit shall come to understanding, and they that murmured shall learn doctrine.

fellow beings, [we] are only in the service of [our] God" (Mosiah 2:17). We can plant the seed of faith with Alma and nourish it "with great diligence and patience, looking forward to the fruit thereof" as it becomes "a tree springing up unto everlasting life" (Alma 32:41). We can march forth in courage with the sons of Helaman, who "had been taught by their mothers, that if they did not doubt, God would deliver them" (Alma 56:47). And—wonder of wonders—we can walk with the resurrected Christ in Bountiful and learn from Him directly the answer to the question: "…what manner of men [and women] ought ye to be? Verily I say unto you, even as I am" (3 Ne. 27:27).

The Book of Mormon is God's gift to the world in this, the dispensation of the fulness of times. It is that "marvellous work and a wonder" foretold by the prophets of old (see Isa. 29:14). Through its pages we are privileged to view panoramically the great blessings and tender mercies the Lord has shown to His children here upon the earth. With Moroni we can savor in the Book of Mormon great stories of the past, great covenants for the present, great hope for the future—all centered in the Being and Atonement of the Savior, Jesus Christ (see Title Page to the Book of Mormon).

Through the blessings of the Book of Mormon, those who seek the truth in the latter days shall be able to come into the light of "the fulness of the gospel of Jesus Christ to the Gentiles and to the Jews also" (D&C 20:9). In the visions of Nephi, the angel declared to him the purpose for the Book of Mormon: "These last records, which thou hast seen among the Gentiles [the Book of Mormon], shall establish the truth of the first [the Bible], which are of the twelve apostles of the Lamb, and shall make known the plain and precious things which have been taken away from them; and shall make known to all kindreds, tongues, and people, that the Lamb of God is the Son of the Eternal Father, and the Savior of the world; and that all men must come unto him, or they cannot be saved" (1 Ne. 13:40).

CHAPTER 30

1 WOE to the rebellious children, saith the LORD, that take counsel, but not of me; and that cover with a covering, but not of my spirit, that they may add sin to sin:

2 That walk to go down into Egypt, and have not asked at my mouth; to strengthen themselves in the strength of Pharaoh, and to trust in the shadow of Egypt!

3 Therefore shall the strength of Pharaoh be your shame, and the trust in the shadow of Egypt your confusion.

4 For his princes were at Zoan, and his ambassadors came to Hanes.

5 They were all ashamed of a people that could not profit them, nor be an help nor profit, but a shame, and also a reproach.

6 The burden of the beasts of the south: into the land of trouble and anguish, from whence come the young and old lion, the viper and fiery flying serpent, they will carry their riches upon the shoulders of young asses, and their treasures upon the bunches of camels, to a people that shall not profit them.

7 For the Egyptians shall help in vain, and to no purpose: therefore have I cried concerning this, Their strength is to sit still.

8 ¶ Now go, write it before them in a table, and note it in a book, that it may be for the time to come for ever and ever:

9 That this is a rebellious people, lying children, children that will not hear the law of the LORD:

10 Which say to the seers, See not; and to the prophets, Prophesy not unto us right things, speak unto us smooth things, prophesy deceits:

11 Get you out of the way, turn aside out of the path, cause the Holy One of Israel to cease from before us.

12 Wherefore thus saith the Holy One of Israel, Because ye despise this word, and trust in oppression and perverseness, and stay thereon:

13 Therefore this iniquity shall be to you as a breach ready to fall, swelling out in a high wall, whose breaking cometh suddenly at an instant.

14 And he shall break it as the breaking of the potters' vessel that is broken in pieces; he shall not spare: so that there shall not be found in the bursting of it a sherd to take fire from the hearth, or to take water withal out of the pit.

15 For thus saith the Lord GOD, the Holy One of Israel; In returning and rest shall ye be saved; in quietness and in confidence shall be your strength: and ye would not.

16 But ye said, No; for we will flee upon horses; therefore shall ye flee: and, We will ride upon the swift; therefore shall they that pursue you be swift.

17 One thousand shall flee at the rebuke of one; at the rebuke of five shall ye flee: till ye be left as a beacon upon the top of a mountain, and as an ensign on an hill.

18 ¶ And therefore will the LORD wait, that he may be gracious unto you, and therefore will he be exalted, that he may have mercy upon you: for the LORD is a God of judgment: blessed are all they that wait for him.

19 For the people shall dwell in Zion at Jerusalem: thou shalt weep no more: he will be very gracious unto thee at the voice of thy cry; when he shall hear it, he will answer thee.

20 And though the Lord give you the bread of adversity, and the water of affliction, yet shall not thy teachers be removed into a corner any more, but thine eyes shall see thy teachers:

POINT OF INTEREST

"The alliance with Egypt was condemned not only as a political mistake, but because it represented a national frame of mind that feared men more than God. Previous to Hezekiah's rein, King Ahaz had made a similar pact with Assyria during the 730s B.C., which had ultimately produced the current threat. (Isa. 7–8.) Now, to avoid the threatened Assyrian bondage, Ahaz's son, Hezekiah, sought deliverance through Egyptian help. In both cases, the Judean kings attempted to avoid danger by turning to other political powers rather than relying upon God. Isaiah exhorted Judah to break out of this vicious circle through trust in the Lord. He told the children of Israel to be quiet and confident with God—in other words, to build their faith. Also, they should turn away from their sins (30:1) and return to the Lord (30:15) so that he might bless them in righteousness (30:18–25, 29)" (Victor L. Ludlow, *Isaiah: Prophet, Seer, and Poet* [Salt Lake City, Utah: Deseret Book, 1982]).

21 And thine ears shall hear a word behind thee, saying, This is the way, walk ye in it, when ye turn to the right hand, and when ye turn to the left.

22 Ye shall defile also the covering of thy graven images of silver, and the ornament of thy molten images of gold: thou shalt cast them away as a menstruous cloth; thou shalt say unto it, Get thee hence.

23 Then shall he give the rain of thy seed, that thou shalt sow the ground withal; and bread of the increase of the earth, and it shall be fat and plenteous: in that day shall thy cattle feed in large pastures.

24 The oxen likewise and the young asses that ear the ground shall eat clean provender, which hath been winnowed with the shovel and with the fan.

25 And there shall be upon every high mountain, and upon every high hill, rivers and streams of waters in the day of the great slaughter, when the towers fall.

26 Moreover the light of the moon shall be as the light of the sun, and the light of the sun shall be sevenfold, as the light of seven days, in the day that the LORD bindeth up the breach of his people, and healeth the stroke of their wound.

27 ¶ Behold, the name of the LORD cometh from far, burning with his anger, and the burden thereof is heavy: his lips are full of indignation, and his tongue as a devouring fire:

28 And his breath, as an overflowing stream, shall reach to the midst of the neck, to sift the nations with the sieve of vanity: and there shall be a bridle in the jaws of the people, causing them to err.

29 Ye shall have a song, as in the night when a holy solemnity is kept; and gladness of heart, as when one goeth with a pipe to come into the mountain of the LORD, to the mighty One of Israel.

30 And the LORD shall cause his glorious voice to be heard, and shall shew the lighting down of his arm, with the indignation of his anger, and with the flame of a devouring fire, with scattering, and tempest, and hailstones.

31 For through the voice of the LORD shall the Assyrian be beaten down, which smote with a rod.

32 And in every place where the grounded staff shall pass, which the LORD shall lay upon him, it shall be with tabrets and harps: and in battles of shaking will he fight with it.

33 For Tophet is ordained of old; yea, for the king it is prepared; he hath made it deep and large: the pile thereof is fire and much wood; the breath of the LORD, like a stream of brimstone, doth kindle it.

CHAPTER 40

1 COMFORT ye, comfort ye my people, saith your God.

2 Speak ye comfortably to Jerusalem, and cry unto her, that her warfare is accomplished, that her iniquity is pardoned: for she hath received of the LORD's hand double for all her sins.

3 ¶ The voice of him that crieth in the wilderness, Prepare ye the way of the LORD, make straight in the desert a highway for our God.

4 Every valley shall be exalted, and every mountain and hill shall be made low: and the crooked shall be made straight, and the rough places plain:

5 And the glory of the LORD shall be revealed, and all flesh shall see it together: for the mouth of the LORD hath spoken it.

6 The voice said, Cry. And he said, What shall I cry? All flesh is grass, and all the goodliness thereof is as the flower of the field:

ISAIAH CHAPTER 40

"Jesus is the Redeemer of the world, the Savior of mankind, who came to the earth with a divinely appointed mission to die for the redemption of mankind. Jesus Christ is literally the Son of God, the only begotten in the flesh."
—Heber J. Grant, CR, April 1921, 203

Isaiah 40—Isaiah Speaks of the Savior

The Prophet Nephi, who shared with his brethren and their families much of the words of Isaiah, spoke of the Redeemer's office in this way: "And he gathereth his children from the four quarters of the earth; and he numbereth his sheep, and they know him; and there shall be one fold and one shepherd; and he shall feed his sheep, and in him they shall find pasture" (1 Ne. 22:25). The concept of there being but one Savior, one fold, one saving message, one way back home was sounded again and again with the voice of grandeur by the prophet Isaiah. There are three themes of hope and glory sounded in Isaiah: 1) Besides Jesus Christ there is no Savior. 2) He will always remember Zion and cause her faithful to flourish as in a single fold of salvation. 3) The latter-day mission for the covenant people is to carry the unified gospel message to a waiting world.

Isaiah 40:5—Latter-Day Mission for the Covenant People

Under the Abrahamic Covenant, the Saints of God are to take the message of redemption to the world. Bolstered by the strength of Gentile amity, Zion is to emerge from the wilderness and become a light to all the nations in preparation for the Second Coming.

Isaiah foresaw the time of the Restoration of the gospel and the bringing again of the kingdom of God as a blessing to the world in its final hours. The Lord will remember the remnants of Israel and gather His forces together as a standard for the nations. He will shape the events of human history to allow the coming forth of His Church from the wilderness under the canopy of principles that secure to the people their inalienable rights below heaven: "Thus saith the Lord God, Behold, I will lift up mine hand to the Gentiles, and set up my standard to the people: and they shall bring thy sons in their arms, and thy daughters shall be carried upon their shoulders. And kings shall be thy nursing fathers, and their queens thy nursing mothers ...." (Isa. 49:22–23). Thus shall mankind bring forth into songs of thanksgiving and praise for the Messiah, the Lord God, the Holy One of Israel.

7 The grass withereth, the flower fadeth: because the spirit of the LORD bloweth upon it: surely the people is grass.

8 The grass withereth, the flower fadeth: but the word of our God shall stand for ever.

9 ¶ O Zion, that bringest good tidings, get thee up into the high mountain; O Jerusalem, that bringest good tidings, lift up thy voice with strength; lift it up, be not afraid; say unto the cities of Judah, Behold your God!

10 Behold, the Lord GOD will come with strong hand, and his arm shall rule for him: behold, his reward is with him, and his work before him.

11 He shall feed his flock like a shepherd: he shall gather the lambs with his arm, and carry them in his bosom, and shall gently lead those that are with young.

12 ¶ Who hath measured the waters in the hollow of his hand, and meted out heaven with the span, and comprehended the dust of the earth in a measure, and weighed the mountains in scales, and the hills in a balance?

13 Who hath directed the Spirit of the LORD, or being his counsellor hath taught him?

14 With whom took he counsel, and who instructed him, and taught him in the path of judgment, and taught him knowledge, and shewed to him the way of understanding?

15 Behold, the nations are as a drop of a bucket, and are counted as the small dust of the balance: behold, he taketh up the isles as a very little thing.

16 And Lebanon is not sufficient to burn, nor the beasts thereof sufficient for a burnt offering.

17 All nations before him are as nothing; and they are counted to him less than nothing, and vanity.

18 ¶ To whom then will ye liken God? or what likeness will ye compare unto him?

19 The workman melteth a graven image, and the goldsmith spreadeth it over with gold, and casteth silver chains.

20 He that is so impoverished that he hath no oblation chooseth a tree that will not rot; he seeketh unto him a cunning workman to prepare a graven image, that shall not be moved.

21 Have ye not known? have ye not heard? hath it not been told you from the beginning? have ye not understood from the foundations of the earth?

22 It is he that sitteth upon the circle of the earth, and the inhabitants thereof are as grasshoppers; that stretcheth out the heavens as a curtain, and spreadeth them out as a tent to dwell in:

23 That bringeth the princes to nothing; he maketh the judges of the earth as vanity.

24 Yea, they shall not be planted; yea, they shall not be sown: yea, their stock shall not take root in the earth: and he shall also blow upon them, and they shall wither, and the whirlwind shall take them away as stubble.

25 To whom then will ye liken me, or shall I be equal? saith the Holy One.

26 Lift up your eyes on high, and behold who hath created these things, that bringeth out their host by number: he calleth them all by names by the greatness of his might, for that he is strong in power; not one faileth.

27 Why sayest thou, O Jacob, and speakest, O Israel, My way is hid from the LORD, and my judgment is passed over from my God?

Isaiah 40:11—The Lord Will Remember Zion and Cause Her Faithful to Flourish

The covenant promises of the Lord will be fulfilled as He blesses His righteous servants with vitality, strength, fruitfulness, and spiritual enlightenment.

Isaiah inventories in unforgettable formulas the qualities that characterize the Savior: He is the source of all strength, truth, and atoning grace. He nourishes us with His Spirit, counsels us when we are wanting, listens to our prayers, and keeps us "graven" upon the palms of His hands (Isa. 49:16). Isaiah uses tactile imagery and concrete metaphors to edify our minds and teach us of infinite things. He speaks of streams and eagles, shepherds and mountains, refiner's fire and waves of the sea—all with an eye to glorifying God and turning our hearts to the ways of obedience.

Isaiah 40:12–26—"And Beside Me There Is No Saviour"

The most important question for life and salvation is the one that Isaiah asks repeatedly in endless variations: "Is there a God beside me?" (Isa. 44:8). The answer resounds for all the world to hear: There is no God besides the Lord, in whom all grace and glory and power of redemption resides. All other gods of man will perish in the dust of idolatry, leaving their worshipers abandoned at the feet of silent and empty figures of clay and wood and brass.

Isaiah contrasts with unsurpassed literary mastery the divine supremacy of the Lord and the empty hollowness of human-fashioned idols. These passages lay naked the truth about the impotence of wooden or metallic gods and the folly of all those who call upon them for redemption.

The Lord alone has the power to save. Only by fleeing Babylon and gathering to Zion can the people have hope of renewal and eternal life. In few passages of Holy Writ are assembled such an abundant motherlode of memorable sayings that reflect over and over and over again the transcending power of the Gospel message. No wonder the Savior counseled: "for great are the words of Isaiah" (3 Ne. 23:1).

Isaiah 40:29–31—Blessings to the Faithful

The blessings of the Lord to the faithful are unfathomable in scope and majesty: power and strength for enduring all tests and challenges, being lifted up to the full measure of their divine potential, having the favor of the omniscient and omnipotent Creator and everlasting God. Isaiah's inspiring language gives hope to the faint and courage to the those waiting on the Lord.

28 ¶ Hast thou not known? hast thou not heard, that the ever-lasting God, the LORD, the Creator of the ends of the earth, fainteth not, neither is weary? there is no searching of his understanding.

29 He giveth power to the faint; and to them that have no might he increaseth strength.

30 Even the youths shall faint and be weary, and the young men shall utterly fall:

31 But they that wait upon the LORD shall renew their strength; they shall mount up with wings as eagles; they shall run, and not be weary; and they shall walk, and not faint.

CHAPTER 41

1 KEEP silence before me, O islands; and let the people renew their strength: let them come near; then let them speak: let us come near together to judgment.

2 Who raised up the righteous man from the east, called him to his foot, gave the nations before him, and made him rule over kings? he gave them as the dust to his sword, and as driven stubble to his bow.

3 He pursued them, and passed safely; even by the way that he had not gone with his feet.

4 Who hath wrought and done it, calling the generations from the beginning? I the LORD, the first, and with the last; I am he.

5 The isles saw it, and feared; the ends of the earth were afraid, drew near, and came.

6 They helped every one his neighbour; and every one said to his brother, Be of good courage.

7 So the carpenter encouraged the goldsmith, and he that smootheth with the hammer him that smote the anvil, saying, It is ready for the sodering: and he fastened it with nails, that it should not be moved.

8 But thou, Israel, art my servant, Jacob whom I have chosen, the seed of Abraham my friend.

9 Thou whom I have taken from the ends of the earth, and called thee from the chief men thereof, and said unto thee, Thou art my servant; I have chosen thee, and not cast thee away.

10 ¶ Fear thou not; for I am with thee: be not dismayed; for I am thy God: I will strengthen thee; yea, I will help thee; yea, I will uphold thee with the right hand of my righteousness.

11 Behold, all they that were incensed against thee shall be ashamed and confounded: they shall be as nothing; and they that strive with thee shall perish.

12 Thou shalt seek them, and shalt not find them, even them that contended with thee: they that war against thee shall be as nothing, and as a thing of nought.

13 For I the LORD thy God will hold thy right hand, saying unto thee, Fear not; I will help thee.

14 Fear not, thou worm Jacob, and ye men of Israel; I will help thee, saith the LORD, and thy redeemer, the Holy One of Israel.

15 Behold, I will make thee a new sharp threshing instrument having teeth: thou shalt thresh the mountains, and beat them small, and shalt make the hills as chaff.

16 Thou shalt fan them, and the wind shall carry them away, and the whirlwind shall scatter them: and thou shalt rejoice in the LORD, and shalt glory in the Holy One of Israel.

ISAIAH CHAPTER 41

Isaiah 41:1–10—Dialogue with the Almighty

In the wondrous style of Isaiah's poetic diction, we feel that we are part of a grand dialogue with the Almighty, one in which He addresses directly our anguish and concern. He counsels us directly to be of good cheer and be filled with the comfort of succor and strength from above. These are sacred promises that touch the heart and kindle hope in receiving the blessings of the gospel of Jesus Christ.

Isaiah's Commission to Hezekiah

17 When the poor and needy seek water, and there is none, and their tongue faileth for thirst, I the LORD will hear them, I the God of Israel will not forsake them.

18 I will open rivers in high places, and fountains in the midst of the valleys: I will make the wilderness a pool of water, and the dry land springs of water.

19 I will plant in the wilderness the cedar, the shittah tree, and the myrtle, and the oil tree; I will set in the desert the fir tree, and the pine, and the box tree together:

20 That they may see, and know, and consider, and understand together, that the hand of the LORD hath done this, and the Holy One of Israel hath created it.

21 Produce your cause, saith the LORD; bring forth your strong reasons, saith the King of Jacob.

22 Let them bring them forth, and shew us what shall happen: let them shew the former things, what they be, that we may consider them, and know the latter end of them; or declare us things for to come.

23 Shew the things that are to come hereafter, that we may know that ye are gods: yea, do good, or do evil, that we may be dismayed, and behold it together.

24 Behold, ye are of nothing, and your work of nought: an abomination is he that chooseth you.

25 I have raised up one from the north, and he shall come: from the rising of the sun shall he call upon my name: and he shall come upon princes as upon morter, and as the potter treadeth clay.

26 Who hath declared from the beginning, that we may know? and beforetime, that we may say, He is righteous? yea, there is none that sheweth, yea, there is none that declareth, yea, there is none that heareth your words.

27 The first shall say to Zion, Behold, behold them: and I will give to Jerusalem one that bringeth good tidings.

28 For I beheld, and there was no man; even among them, and there was no counsellor, that, when I asked of them, could answer a word.

29 Behold, they are all vanity; their works are nothing: their molten images are wind and confusion.

 POINT OF INTEREST

Who is the "man from the east" referred to in Isa. 41:2? Several scriptures, combined with modern-day revelation, give some insight. John had a vision similar to the one experienced by Isaiah, and he called the man an "angel ascending from the east, having the seal of the living God" (Rev. 7:2). The Lord told Joseph Smith that this angel of the east was "Elias which was to come to gather together the tribes of Israel and restore all things" (D&C 77:9). In speaking of this "angel," or "Elias," Elder Bruce R. McConkie pointed out that it was not a single individual who restored all things: "'Many angelic ministrants have been sent from the courts of glory to confer keys and powers, to commit their dispensations and glories again to men on earth. At least the following have come: Moroni, John the Baptist, Peter, James and John, Moses, Elijah, Elias, Gabriel, Raphael, and Michael. (D&C 13; 110; 128:19–21.) Since it is apparent that no one messenger has carried the whole burden of the restoration, but rather that each has come with a specific endowment from on high, it becomes clear that Elias is a composite personage. The expression must be understood to be a name and a title for those whose mission it was to commit keys and powers to men in this final dispensation" (Mormon Doctrine, 221).

CHAPTER 42

1 BEHOLD my servant, whom I uphold; mine elect, in whom my soul delighteth; I have put my spirit upon him: he shall bring forth judgment to the Gentiles.

2 He shall not cry, nor lift up, nor cause his voice to be heard in the street.

3 A bruised reed shall he not break, and the smoking flax shall he not quench: he shall bring forth judgment unto truth.

4 He shall not fail nor be discouraged, till he have set judgment in the earth: and the isles shall wait for his law.

5 ¶ Thus saith God the LORD, he that created the heavens, and stretched them out; he that spread forth the earth, and that which cometh out of it; he that giveth breath unto the people upon it, and spirit to them that walk therein:

6 I the LORD have called thee in righteousness, and will hold thine hand, and will keep thee, and give thee for a covenant of the people, for a light of the Gentiles;

7 To open the blind eyes, to bring out the prisoners from the prison, and them that sit in darkness out of the prison house.

8 I am the LORD: that is my name: and my glory will I not give to another, neither my praise to graven images.

9 Behold, the former things are come to pass, and new things do I declare: before they spring forth I tell you of them.

10 Sing unto the LORD a new song, and his praise from the end of the earth, ye that go down to the sea, and all that is therein; the isles, and the inhabitants thereof.

11 Let the wilderness and the cities thereof lift up their voice, the villages that Kedar doth inhabit: let the inhabitants of the rock sing, let them shout from the top of the mountains.

12 Let them give glory unto the LORD, and declare his praise in the islands.

13 The LORD shall go forth as a mighty man, he shall stir up jealousy like a man of war: he shall cry, yea, roar; he shall prevail against his enemies.

14 I have long time holden my peace; I have been still, and refrained myself: now will I cry like a travailing woman; I will destroy and devour at once.

15 I will make waste mountains and hills, and dry up all their herbs; and I will make the rivers islands, and I will dry up the pools.

16 And I will bring the blind by a way that they knew not; I will lead them in paths that they have not known: I will make darkness light before them, and crooked things straight. These things will I do unto them, and not forsake them.

17 ¶ They shall be turned back, they shall be greatly ashamed, that trust in graven images, that say to the molten images, Ye are our gods.

18 Hear, ye deaf; and look, ye blind, that ye may see.

19 Who is blind, but my servant? or deaf, as my messenger that I sent? who is blind as he that is perfect, and blind as the LORD's servant?

20 Seeing many things, but thou observest not; opening the ears, but he heareth not.

21 The LORD is well pleased for his righteousness' sake; he will magnify the law, and make it honourable.

22 But this is a people robbed and spoiled; they are all of them snared in holes, and they are hid in prison houses: they are for a prey, and none delivereth; for a spoil, and none saith, Restore.

ISAIAH CHAPTER 42

Isaiah 42:1–10—Covenant with the Faithful

Blessings from the Lord are to abound through His sacred covenant with the faithful, for the Lord will be bring to pass the deliverance of the people, the prisoners, those who wait upon His grace and redemption. He will reveal His truths to the understanding of those awaiting refreshing and enlightenment. They will sing anthems of praise to the Redeemer.

Isaiah 42:11–16—The Pathway of Deliverance

The Lord will open up the pathway of deliverance through the blessings of His gospel plan of happiness. Those who enter by the gateway of faith, repentance, baptism, and the gift of the Holy Ghost will find themselves in familiar precincts that were before invisible to their eyes and understanding. They will feel at home in the light of His blessings. Their vision of what lies ahead will be pure and certain. They will have the assurance that the Lord will never forsake them. What a glorious transition this is from the crooked pathways of mortal wanderings to the certain journey toward a heavenly home.

23 Who among you will give ear to this? who will hearken and hear for the time to come?

24 Who gave Jacob for a spoil, and Israel to the robbers? did not the LORD, he against whom we have sinned? for they would not walk in his ways, neither were they obedient unto his law.

25 Therefore he hath poured upon him the fury of his anger, and the strength of battle: and it hath set him on fire round about, yet he knew not; and it burned him, yet he laid it not to heart.

CHAPTER 43

1 BUT now thus saith the LORD that created thee, O Jacob, and he that formed thee, O Israel, Fear not: for I have redeemed thee, I have called thee by thy name; thou art mine.

2 When thou passest through the waters, I will be with thee; and through the rivers, they shall not overflow thee: when thou walkest through the fire, thou shalt not be burned; neither shall the flame kindle upon thee.

3 For I am the LORD thy God, the Holy One of Israel, thy Saviour: I gave Egypt for thy ransom, Ethiopia and Seba for thee.

4 Since thou wast precious in my sight, thou hast been honourable, and I have loved thee: therefore will I give men for thee, and people for thy life.

5 Fear not: for I am with thee: I will bring thy seed from the east, and gather thee from the west;

6 I will say to the north, Give up; and to the south, Keep not back: bring my sons from far, and my daughters from the ends of the earth;

7 Even every one that is called by my name: for I have created him for my glory, I have formed him; yea, I have made him.

8 ¶ Bring forth the blind people that have eyes, and the deaf that have ears.

9 Let all the nations be gathered together, and let the people be assembled: who among them can declare this, and shew us former things? let them bring forth their witnesses, that they may be justified: or let them hear, and say, It is truth.

10 Ye are my witnesses, saith the LORD, and my servant whom I have chosen: that ye may know and believe me, and understand that I am he: before me there was no God formed, neither shall there be after me.

11 I, even I, am the LORD; and beside me there is no saviour.

12 I have declared, and have saved, and I have shewed, when there was no strange god among you: therefore ye are my witnesses, saith the LORD, that I am God.

13 Yea, before the day was I am he; and there is none that can deliver out of my hand: I will work, and who shall let it?

14 ¶ Thus saith the LORD, your redeemer, the Holy One of Israel; For your sake I have sent to Babylon, and have brought down all their nobles, and the Chaldeans, whose cry is in the ships.

15 I am the LORD, your Holy One, the creator of Israel, your King.

16 Thus saith the LORD, which maketh a way in the sea, and a path in the mighty waters;

17 Which bringeth forth the chariot and horse, the army and the power; they shall lie down together, they shall not rise: they are extinct, they are quenched as tow.

18 ¶ Remember ye not the former things, neither consider the things of old.

ISAIAH CHAPTER 43

Isaiah 43:1–4—Holy One of Israel

These verses underscore sacred qualities of the Lord: the Creator, Redeemer, Father, Liberator, the Holy One of Israel—this last being a term used frequently in the Old Testament, particularly by Isaiah—is the Savior, Jesus Christ: "For I *am* the LORD thy God, the Holy One of Israel, thy Saviour: . . . I, *even* I, *am* the LORD; and beside me *there is* no saviour. . . . Thus saith the LORD, your redeemer, the Holy One of Israel" (Isa. 43:3, 11, 14). "*As for* our redeemer, the LORD of hosts *is* his name, the Holy One of Israel" (Isa. 47:4). "For thy Maker *is* thine husband; the LORD of hosts *is* his name; and thy Redeemer the Holy One of Israel; The God of the whole earth shall he be called" (Isa. 54:5).

The Book of Mormon (particularly 1 Nephi and 2 Nephi) contains a rich harvest of sayings concerning the Holy One of Israel; as one example: "And now behold, I [Nephi] say unto you that the right way is to believe in Christ, and deny him not; and Christ is the Holy One of Israel; wherefore ye must bow down before him, and worship him with all your might, mind, and strength, and your whole soul; and if ye do this ye shall in nowise be cast out" (2 Ne. 25:29).

Isaiah 43:5–11—The Atonement

Where is there a heart great enough to contain a full measure of gratitude for the Atonement of Jesus Christ? We understand so little of the nature of His infinite sacrifice. We comprehend but a shadow's worth of His love and mercy in bringing about the Redemption. Yet that seed of thanksgiving within us unfolds like a flower as we come to gain a greater appreciation of His nobility as the "author of eternal salvation unto all them that obey him" (Heb. 5:9).

What more glorious gift from God can there be than the gift of His Son, Jesus Christ? "For God so loved the world, that he gave his only begotten Son, that whosoever believeth in him should not perish, but have everlasting life" (John 3:16). The Atonement is the centerpiece of the gospel of Jesus Christ. We are transformed by faith unto repentance. We are born again through the baptism of water and fire. We become free through Christ by obedience. We thrill in the knowledge that it is by the grace of God and the Lamb that we are saved, after all we can do (see 2 Ne. 25:23).

For this we are profoundly grateful. Through the Atonement we are lifted up and drawn unto Christ, just as the Father allowed the Son to be lifted up as an eternal sacrifice—to bring about the immortality and eternal life of man (see 3 Ne. 27:13–15; Moses 1:39).

The reality of the Atonement verifies the tender mercy and goodness of Father and Son. We can never repay this debt—but we can abide in the spirit of humble thanksgiving and grateful obedience for the transcendent gift of Christ's ultimate offering: "And thus he shall bring salvation to all those who shall believe on his name; this being the intent of this last sacrifice, to bring about the bowels of mercy, which overpowereth justice, and bringeth about means unto men that they may have faith unto repentance" (Alma 34:15).

19 Behold, I will do a new thing; now it shall spring forth; shall ye not know it? I will even make a way in the wilderness, and rivers in the desert.

20 The beast of the field shall honour me, the dragons and the owls: because I give waters in the wilderness, and rivers in the desert, to give drink to my people, my chosen.

21 This people have I formed for myself; they shall shew forth my praise.

22 ¶ But thou hast not called upon me, O Jacob; but thou hast been weary of me, O Israel.

23 Thou hast not brought me the small cattle of thy burnt offerings; neither hast thou honoured me with thy sacrifices. I have not caused thee to serve with an offering, nor wearied thee with incense.

24 Thou hast bought me no sweet cane with money, neither hast thou filled me with the fat of thy sacrifices: but thou hast made me to serve with thy sins, thou hast wearied me with thine iniquities.

25 I, even I, am he that blotteth out thy transgressions for mine own sake, and will not remember thy sins.

26 Put me in remembrance: let us plead together: declare thou, that thou mayest be justified.

27 Thy first father hath sinned, and thy teachers have transgressed against me.

28 Therefore I have profaned the princes of the sanctuary, and have given Jacob to the curse, and Israel to reproaches.

CHAPTER 44

1 YET now hear, O Jacob my servant; and Israel, whom I have chosen:

2 Thus saith the LORD that made thee, and formed thee from the womb, which will help thee; Fear not, O Jacob, my servant; and thou, Jesurun, whom I have chosen.

3 For I will pour water upon him that is thirsty, and floods upon the dry ground: I will pour my spirit upon thy seed, and my blessing upon thine offspring:

4 And they shall spring up as among the grass, as willows by the water courses.

5 One shall say, I am the LORD's; and another shall call himself by the name of Jacob; and another shall subscribe with his hand unto the LORD, and surname himself by the name of Israel.

6 Thus saith the LORD the King of Israel, and his redeemer the LORD of hosts; I am the first, and I am the last; and beside me there is no God.

7 And who, as I, shall call, and shall declare it, and set it in order for me, since I appointed the ancient people? and the things that are coming, and shall come, let them shew unto them.

8 Fear ye not, neither be afraid: have not I told thee from that time, and have declared it? ye are even my witnesses. Is there a God beside me? yea, there is no God; I know not any.

9 ¶ They that make a graven image are all of them vanity; and their delectable things shall not profit; and they are their own witnesses; they see not, nor know; that they may be ashamed.

10 Who hath formed a god, or molten a graven image that is profitable for nothing?

11 Behold, all his fellows shall be ashamed: and the workmen, they are of men: let them all be gathered together, let them stand up; yet they shall fear, and they shall be ashamed together.

ISAIAH CHAPTER 44

Isaiah 44—The Lord's Relationship with Israel

The Lord remembers Israel. He redeems Israel from the bondage of sin. He invites Israel to return unto Him with anthems of praise and rejoicing. The mountains, the forest, the trees join in the chorus of reverential worship, much as was envisioned by the Prophet Joseph Smith in celebrating the all-encompassing love of the Lord in remembering all of the sons and daughters of God—even those who have departed this realm:

Let the mountains shout for joy, and all ye valleys cry aloud; and all ye seas and dry lands tell the wonders of your Eternal King! And ye rivers, and brooks, and rills, flow down with gladness. Let the woods and all the trees of the field praise the Lord; and ye solid rocks weep for joy! And let the sun, moon, and the morning stars sing together, and let all the sons of God shout for joy! And let the eternal creations declare his name forever and ever! And again I say, how glorious is the voice we hear from heaven, proclaiming in our ears, glory, and salvation, and honor, and immortality, and eternal life; kingdoms, principalities, and powers! (D&C 128:23)

12 The smith with the tongs both worketh in the coals, and fashioneth it with hammers, and worketh it with the strength of his arms: yea, he is hungry, and his strength faileth: he drinketh no water, and is faint.

13 The carpenter stretcheth out his rule; he marketh it out with a line; he fitteth it with planes, and he marketh it out with the compass, and maketh it after the figure of a man, according to the beauty of a man; that it may remain in the house.

14 He heweth him down cedars, and taketh the cypress and the oak, which he strengtheneth for himself among the trees of the forest: he planteth an ash, and the rain doth nourish it.

15 Then shall it be for a man to burn: for he will take thereof, and warm himself; yea, he kindleth it, and baketh bread; yea, he maketh a god, and worshippeth it; he maketh it a graven image, and falleth down thereto.

16 He burneth part thereof in the fire; with part thereof he eateth flesh; he roasteth roast, and is satisfied: yea, he warmeth himself, and saith, Aha, I am warm, I have seen the fire:

17 And the residue thereof he maketh a god, even his graven image: he falleth down unto it, and worshippeth it, and prayeth unto it, and saith, Deliver me; for thou art my god.

18 They have not known nor understood: for he hath shut their eyes, that they cannot see; and their hearts, that they cannot understand.

19 And none considereth in his heart, neither is there knowledge nor understanding to say, I have burned part of it in the fire; yea, also I have baked bread upon the coals thereof; I have roasted flesh, and eaten it: and shall I make the residue thereof an abomination? shall I fall down to the stock of a tree?

20 He feedeth on ashes: a deceived heart hath turned him aside, that he cannot deliver his soul, nor say, Is there not a lie in my right hand?

21 ¶ Remember these, O Jacob and Israel; for thou art my servant: I have formed thee; thou art my servant: O Israel, thou shalt not be forgotten of me.

22 I have blotted out, as a thick cloud, thy transgressions, and, as a cloud, thy sins: return unto me; for I have redeemed thee.

23 Sing, O ye heavens; for the LORD hath done it: shout, ye lower parts of the earth: break forth into singing, ye mountains, O forest, and every tree therein: for the LORD hath redeemed Jacob, and glorified himself in Israel.

24 Thus saith the LORD, thy redeemer, and he that formed thee from the womb, I am the LORD that maketh all things; that stretcheth forth the heavens alone; that spreadeth abroad the earth by myself;

25 That frustrateth the tokens of the liars, and maketh diviners mad; that turneth wise men backward, and maketh their knowledge foolish;

26 That confirmeth the word of his servant, and performeth the counsel of his messengers; that saith to Jerusalem, Thou shalt be inhabited; and to the cities of Judah, Ye shall be built, and I will raise up the decayed places thereof:

27 That saith to the deep, Be dry, and I will dry up thy rivers:

28 That saith of Cyrus, He is my shepherd, and shall perform all my pleasure: even saying to Jerusalem, Thou shalt be built; and to the temple, Thy foundation shall be laid.

Cyrus the Great Monument at Sydney Olympic Park, Australia

CHAPTER 45

1 THUS saith the LORD to his anointed, to Cyrus, whose right hand I have holden, to subdue nations before him; and I will loose the loins of kings, to open before him the two leaved gates; and the gates shall not be shut;

2 I will go before thee, and make the crooked places straight: I will break in pieces the gates of brass, and cut in sunder the bars of iron:

3 And I will give thee the treasures of darkness, and hidden riches of secret places, that thou mayest know that I, the LORD, which call thee by thy name, am the God of Israel.

4 For Jacob my servant's sake, and Israel mine elect, I have even called thee by thy name: I have surnamed thee, though thou hast not known me.

5 ¶ I am the LORD, and there is none else, there is no God beside me: I girded thee, though thou hast not known me:

6 That they may know from the rising of the sun, and from the west, that there is none beside me. I am the LORD, and there is none else.

7 I form the light, and create darkness: I make peace, and create evil: I the LORD do all these things.

8 Drop down, ye heavens, from above, and let the skies pour down righteousness: let the earth open, and let them bring forth salvation, and let righteousness spring up together; I the LORD have created it.

9 Woe unto him that striveth with his Maker! Let the potsherd strive with the potsherds of the earth. Shall the clay say to him that fashioneth it, What makest thou? or thy work, He hath no hands?

10 Woe unto him that saith unto his father, What begettest thou? or to the woman, What hast thou brought forth?

11 Thus saith the LORD, the Holy One of Israel, and his Maker, Ask me of things to come concerning my sons, and concerning the work of my hands command ye me.

12 I have made the earth, and created man upon it: I, even my hands, have stretched out the heavens, and all their host have I commanded.

13 I have raised him up in righteousness, and I will direct all his ways: he shall build my city, and he shall let go my captives, not for price nor reward, saith the LORD of hosts.

14 Thus saith the LORD, The labour of Egypt, and merchandise of Ethiopia and of the Sabeans, men of stature, shall come over unto thee, and they shall be thine: they shall come after thee; in chains they shall come over, and they shall fall down unto thee, they shall make supplication unto thee, saying, Surely God is in thee; and there is none else, there is no God.

15 Verily thou art a God that hidest thyself, O God of Israel, the Saviour.

16 They shall be ashamed, and also confounded, all of them: they shall go to confusion together that are makers of idols.

17 But Israel shall be saved in the LORD with an everlasting salvation: ye shall not be ashamed nor confounded world without end.

18 For thus saith the LORD that created the heavens; God himself that formed the earth and made it; he hath established it, he created it not in vain, he formed it to be inhabited: I am the LORD; and there is none else.

19 I have not spoken in secret, in a dark place of the earth: I said not unto the seed of Jacob, Seek ye me in vain: I the LORD speak righteousness, I declare things that are right.

ISAIAH CHAPTER 45

Isaiah 45:14—Sabeans

The Sabeans (pronounced "suh-bee'-uns") were an Arab tribe mentioned specifically in four passages of scripture. In this, the Isaiah passage, the Lord commissions Cyrus, king of Assyria, to decree the return of the captive Israelites from Babylon, and promises him divine support.

Deposit from the Vieille Charité Museum in Marseille, 1978

20 ¶ Assemble yourselves and come; draw near together, ye that are escaped of the nations: they have no knowledge that set up the wood of their graven image, and pray unto a god that cannot save.

21 Tell ye, and bring them near; yea, let them take counsel together: who hath declared this from ancient time? who hath told it from that time? have not I the LORD? and there is no God else beside me; a just God and a Saviour; there is none beside me.

22 Look unto me, and be ye saved, all the ends of the earth: for I am God, and there is none else.

23 I have sworn by myself, the word is gone out of my mouth in righteousness, and shall not return, That unto me every knee shall bow, every tongue shall swear.

24 Surely, shall one say, in the LORD have I righteousness and strength: even to him shall men come; and all that are incensed against him shall be ashamed.

25 In the LORD shall all the seed of Israel be justified, and shall glory.

CHAPTER 46

1 BEL boweth down, Nebo stoopeth, their idols were upon the beasts, and upon the cattle: your carriages were heavy loaden; they are a burden to the weary beast.

2 They stoop, they bow down together, they could not deliver the burden, but themselves are gone into captivity.

3 ¶ Hearken unto me, O house of Jacob, and all the remnant of the house of Israel, which are borne by me from the belly, which are carried from the womb:

4 And even to your old age I am he; and even to hoar hairs will I carry you: I have made, and I will bear; even I will carry, and will deliver you.

5 ¶ To whom will ye liken me, and make me equal, and compare me, that we may be like?

6 They lavish gold out of the bag, and weigh silver in the balance, and hire a goldsmith; and he maketh it a god: they fall down, yea, they worship.

7 They bear him upon the shoulder, they carry him, and set him in his place, and he standeth; from his place shall he not remove: yea, one shall cry unto him, yet can he not answer, nor save him out of his trouble.

8 Remember this, and shew yourselves men: bring it again to mind, O ye transgressors.

9 Remember the former things of old: for I am God, and there is none else; I am God, and there is none like me,

10 Declaring the end from the beginning, and from ancient times the things that are not yet done, saying, My counsel shall stand, and I will do all my pleasure:

11 Calling a ravenous bird from the east, the man that executeth my counsel from a far country: yea, I have spoken it, I will also bring it to pass; I have purposed it, I will also do it.

12 ¶ Hearken unto me, ye stouthearted, that are far from righteousness:

13 I bring near my righteousness; it shall not be far off, and my salvation shall not tarry: and I will place salvation in Zion for Israel my glory.

NOTES:

CHAPTER 47

1 COME down, and sit in the dust, O virgin daughter of Babylon, sit on the ground: there is no throne, O daughter of the Chaldeans: for thou shalt no more be called tender and delicate.

2 Take the millstones, and grind meal: uncover thy locks, make bare the leg, uncover the thigh, pass over the rivers.

3 Thy nakedness shall be uncovered, yea, thy shame shall be seen: I will take vengeance, and I will not meet thee as a man.

4 As for our redeemer, the LORD of hosts is his name, the Holy One of Israel.

5 Sit thou silent, and get thee into darkness, O daughter of the Chaldeans: for thou shalt no more be called, The lady of kingdoms.

6 ¶ I was wroth with my people, I have polluted mine inheritance, and given them into thine hand: thou didst shew them no mercy; upon the ancient hast thou very heavily laid thy yoke.

7 ¶ And thou saidst, I shall be a lady for ever: so that thou didst not lay these things to thy heart, neither didst remember the latter end of it.

8 Therefore hear now this, thou that art given to pleasures, that dwellest carelessly, that sayest in thine heart, I am, and none else beside me; I shall not sit as a widow, neither shall I know the loss of children:

9 But these two things shall come to thee in a moment in one day, the loss of children, and widowhood: they shall come upon thee in their perfection for the multitude of thy sorceries, and for the great abundance of thine enchantments.

10 ¶ For thou hast trusted in thy wickedness: thou hast said, None seeth me. Thy wisdom and thy knowledge, it hath perverted thee; and thou hast said in thine heart, I am, and none else beside me.

11 ¶ Therefore shall evil come upon thee; thou shalt not know from whence it riseth: and mischief shall fall upon thee; thou shalt not be able to put it off: and desolation shall come upon thee suddenly, which thou shalt not know.

12 Stand now with thine enchantments, and with the multitude of thy sorceries, wherein thou hast laboured from thy youth; if so be thou shalt be able to profit, if so be thou mayest prevail.

13 Thou art wearied in the multitude of thy counsels. Let now the astrologers, the stargazers, the monthly prognosticators, stand up, and save thee from these things that shall come upon thee.

14 Behold, they shall be as stubble; the fire shall burn them; they shall not deliver themselves from the power of the flame: there shall not be a coal to warm at, nor fire to sit before it.

15 Thus shall they be unto thee with whom thou hast laboured, even thy merchants, from thy youth: they shall wander every one to his quarter; none shall save thee.

CHAPTER 48

1 HEAR ye this, O house of Jacob, which are called by the name of Israel, and are come forth out of the waters of Judah, which swear by the name of the LORD, and make mention of the God of Israel, but not in truth, nor in righteousness.

2 For they call themselves of the holy city, and stay themselves upon the God of Israel; The LORD of hosts is his name.

3 I have declared the former things from the beginning; and they went forth out of my mouth, and I shewed them; I did them suddenly, and they came to pass.

ISAIAH CHAPTER 47

Isaiah 47:1–5—Dialogue Between the Lord and Babylon

The genius of Isaiah's language emerges when he, by inspiration, conducts a dialogue, as it were, between the Lord and Babylon. Rather than simply stating the third-person verity that Babylon will ultimately fall, Isaiah, in the words of the Lord, proclaims a first-person judgment ("thou") upon the forces of unrighteousness (Babylon, or the Chaldeans) and declares the end to the evil empire. The force of this style of locution is to place the players on the stage in our full view, and to impress upon us that what is happening is real, visible, observable, prophetically certain. We are caught up in the reality of the judgment and view the confirmed dissolution of the forces that battle against the Kingdom of God.

Isaiah 47:6–11—Certain Destruction of the Wicked

The certain destruction of the wicked is confirmed by prophetic utterance. It will happen "in a moment in one day" (verse 9), "suddenly" (verse 11), and in such a way that the self-conceit and arrogance of the unrighteous will vanish inexorably.

ISAIAH CHAPTER 48

Isaiah 48:18–19—The Covenant of God

The covenant of God has been proclaimed in plainness from the beginning. Those who would heed and obey stand to gain monumental blessings: peace, righteousness, abundant progeny, recognition before the throne of heaven—and many such glorious blessings.

4 Because I knew that thou art obstinate, and thy neck is an iron sinew, and thy brow brass;

5 I have even from the beginning declared it to thee; before it came to pass I shewed it thee: lest thou shouldest say, Mine idol hath done them, and my graven image, and my molten image, hath commanded them.

6 Thou hast heard, see all this; and will not ye declare it? I have shewed thee new things from this time, even hidden things, and thou didst not know them.

7 They are created now, and not from the beginning; even before the day when thou heardest them not; lest thou shouldest say, Behold, I knew them.

8 Yea, thou heardest not; yea, thou knewest not; yea, from that time that thine ear was not opened: for I knew that thou wouldest deal very treacherously, and wast called a transgressor from the womb.

9 ¶ For my name's sake will I defer mine anger, and for my praise will I refrain for thee, that I cut thee not off.

10 Behold, I have refined thee, but not with silver; I have chosen thee in the furnace of affliction.

11 For mine own sake, even for mine own sake, will I do it: for how should my name be polluted? and I will not give my glory unto another.

12 ¶ Hearken unto me, O Jacob and Israel, my called; I am he; I am the first, I also am the last.

13 Mine hand also hath laid the foundation of the earth, and my right hand hath spanned the heavens: when I call unto them, they stand up together.

14 All ye, assemble yourselves, and hear; which among them hath declared these things? The LORD hath loved him: he will do his pleasure on Babylon, and his arm shall be on the Chaldeans.

15 I, even I, have spoken; yea, I have called him: I have brought him, and he shall make his way prosperous.

16 ¶ Come ye near unto me, hear ye this; I have not spoken in secret from the beginning; from the time that it was, there am I: and now the Lord GOD, and his Spirit, hath sent me.

17 Thus saith the LORD, thy Redeemer, the Holy One of Israel; I am the LORD thy God which teacheth thee to profit, which leadeth thee by the way that thou shouldest go.

18 O that thou hadst hearkened to my commandments! then had thy peace been as a river, and thy righteousness as the waves of the sea:

19 Thy seed also had been as the sand, and the offspring of thy bowels like the gravel thereof; his name should not have been cut off nor destroyed from before me.

20 ¶ Go ye forth of Babylon, flee ye from the Chaldeans, with a voice of singing declare ye, tell this, utter it even to the end of the earth; say ye, The LORD hath redeemed his servant Jacob.

21 And they thirsted not when he led them through the deserts: he caused the waters to flow out of the rock for them: he clave the rock also, and the waters gushed out.

22 There is no peace, saith the LORD, unto the wicked.

NOTES:

CHAPTER 49

1 LISTEN, O isles, unto me; and hearken, ye people, from far; The LORD hath called me from the womb; from the bowels of my mother hath he made mention of my name.

2 And he hath made my mouth like a sharp sword; in the shadow of his hand hath he hid me, and made me a polished shaft; in his quiver hath he hid me;

3 And said unto me, Thou art my servant, O Israel, in whom I will be glorified.

4 Then I said, I have laboured in vain, I have spent my strength for nought, and in vain: yet surely my judgment is with the LORD, and my work with my God.

5 ¶ And now, saith the LORD that formed me from the womb to be his servant, to bring Jacob again to him, Though Israel be not gathered, yet shall I be glorious in the eyes of the LORD, and my God shall be my strength.

6 And he said, It is a light thing that thou shouldest be my servant to raise up the tribes of Jacob, and to restore the preserved of Israel: I will also give thee for a light to the Gentiles, that thou mayest be my salvation unto the end of the earth.

7 Thus saith the LORD, the Redeemer of Israel, and his Holy One, to him whom man despiseth, to him whom the nation abhorreth, to a servant of rulers, Kings shall see and arise, princes also shall worship, because of the LORD that is faithful, and the Holy One of Israel, and he shall choose thee.

8 Thus saith the LORD, In an acceptable time have I heard thee, and in a day of salvation have I helped thee: and I will preserve thee, and give thee for a covenant of the people, to establish the earth, to cause to inherit the desolate heritages;

9 That thou mayest say to the prisoners, Go forth; to them that are in darkness, Shew yourselves. They shall feed in the ways, and their pastures shall be in all high places.

10 They shall not hunger nor thirst; neither shall the heat nor sun smite them: for he that hath mercy on them shall lead them, even by the springs of water shall he guide them.

11 And I will make all my mountains a way, and my highways shall be exalted.

12 Behold, these shall come from far: and, lo, these from the north and from the west; and these from the land of Sinim.

13 ¶ Sing, O heavens; and be joyful, O earth; and break forth into singing, O mountains: for the LORD hath comforted his people, and will have mercy upon his afflicted.

14 But Zion said, The LORD hath forsaken me, and my Lord hath forgotten me.

15 Can a woman forget her sucking child, that she should not have compassion on the son of her womb? yea, they may forget, yet will I not forget thee.

16 Behold, I have graven thee upon the palms of my hands; thy walls are continually before me.

17 Thy children shall make haste; thy destroyers and they that made thee waste shall go forth of thee.

18 ¶ Lift up thine eyes round about, and behold: all these gather themselves together, and come to thee. As I live, saith the LORD, thou shalt surely clothe thee with them all, as with an ornament, and bind them on thee, as a bride doeth.

ISAIAH CHAPTER 49

Isaiah 49:1–16—Covenants

To think that you—as a faithful servant of God—have a personal covenant with Him! What an august honor. It is as though there were a spiritual contract in place, with His signature written nobly and clearly across the base of the scroll, and yours just beneath. It is, in fact, even more wondrous than that: "Behold, I have graven thee upon the palms of *my* hands," said the Lord; "thy walls *are* continually before me" (Isa. 49:16; 1 Ne. 21:16). The image of the Lord's suffering on the cross to take upon Himself the sins of the world—yours and mine—as evidenced by the wounds in His palms—evokes within us a humbling spirit of gratitude. It is through the atoning grace of our Lord that our names—yours and mine—are written there indelibly, on the palms of His hands, just as the walls of our homes are continually before His eyes. Moreover, He, in turn, is written upon our very inward being: "But this *shall be* the covenant that I will make with the house of Israel; After those days, saith the LORD, I will put my law in their inward parts, and write it in their hearts; and will be their God, and they shall be my people" (Jer. 31:33). Being inscribed of God through the holy covenant, we are, ourselves, as Paul declared, "the epistle of Christ ministered by us, written not with ink, but with the Spirit of the living God; not in tables of stone, but in fleshy tables of the heart" (2 Cor. 3:3).

It is a mutual inscription—this covenant with God. We are the document of the covenant. We are the epistle of Christ. We are the thinking, moving, living scroll of agreement. He has affixed His signature to our hearts—and we are eternally grateful. The outward manifestations of the sacred promises of the covenant—baptism, the bestowal of the gift of the Holy Ghost, the conferring of the priesthood, the sacred temple ordinances—all of these are authorized and indispensable events through which "the power of godliness is manifest" (D&C 84:20). But the covenant itself is written upon us by the finger of God. He promises that everything that He has shall be ours, if we are true to these personal covenants—all power, glory, dominion, and life everlasting.

What cause of thanksgiving could be greater than to know that His name is written upon us, upon our hearts, upon our very being! What impetus to gratitude could be greater than to know that He loves us and extends to us the universal blessings of being His heirs, "the children of the covenant" (3 Ne. 20:26)! In moments of quiet reverence, we savor the joy of being able to bring glory and honor to our Creator and Redeemer through obedience to the personal covenant He has made with us. We send prayers of gratitude heavenward, and make the commitment, here on earth, to walk in the spirit of valiant loyalty forever.

19 For thy waste and thy desolate places, and the land of thy destruction, shall even now be too narrow by reason of the inhabitants, and they that swallowed thee up shall be far away.

20 The children which thou shalt have, after thou hast lost the other, shall say again in thine ears, The place is too strait for me: give place to me that I may dwell.

21 Then shalt thou say in thine heart, Who hath begotten me these, seeing I have lost my children, and am desolate, a captive, and removing to and fro? and who hath brought up these? Behold, I was left alone; these, where had they been?

22 Thus saith the Lord GOD, Behold, I will lift up mine hand to the Gentiles, and set up my standard to the people: and they shall bring thy sons in their arms, and thy daughters shall be carried upon their shoulders.

23 And kings shall be thy nursing fathers, and their queens thy nursing mothers: they shall bow down to thee with their face toward the earth, and lick up the dust of thy feet; and thou shalt know that I am the LORD: for they shall not be ashamed that wait for me.

24 ¶ Shall the prey be taken from the mighty, or the lawful captive delivered?

25 But thus saith the LORD, Even the captives of the mighty shall be taken away, and the prey of the terrible shall be delivered: for I will contend with him that contendeth with thee, and I will save thy children.

26 And I will feed them that oppress thee with their own flesh; and they shall be drunken with their own blood, as with sweet wine: and all flesh shall know that I the LORD am thy Saviour and thy Redeemer, the mighty One of Jacob.

CHAPTER 50

1 THUS saith the LORD, Where is the bill of your mother's divorcement, whom I have put away? or which of my creditors is it to whom I have sold you? Behold, for your iniquities have ye sold yourselves, and for your transgressions is your mother put away.

2 Wherefore, when I came, was there no man? when I called, was there none to answer? Is my hand shortened at all, that it cannot redeem? or have I no power to deliver? behold, at my rebuke I dry up the sea, I make the rivers a wilderness: their fish stinketh, because there is no water, and dieth for thirst.

3 I clothe the heavens with blackness, and I make sackcloth their covering.

4 The Lord GOD hath given me the tongue of the learned, that I should know how to speak a word in season to him that is weary: he wakeneth morning by morning, he wakeneth mine ear to hear as the learned.

5 ¶ The Lord GOD hath opened mine ear, and I was not rebellious, neither turned away back.

6 I gave my back to the smiters, and my cheeks to them that plucked off the hair: I hid not my face from shame and spitting.

7 ¶ For the Lord GOD will help me; therefore shall I not be confounded: therefore have I set my face like a flint, and I know that I shall not be ashamed.

8 He is near that justifieth me; who will contend with me? let us stand together: who is mine adversary? let him come near to me.

ISAIAH CHAPTER 50

Isaiah 50—Thoughts on the Redemption

Isaiah's words are sustained by a vision of the transcendent and sublime mission of the Redeemer and the atoning power of the Father's plan of salvation. We hear the repeated expressions of joy as Israel's faithful are gathered once again to the protecting care of Zion's resorts. We see in our mind's eye the unfolding of the earthly ministry of the Savior and His condescension in coming among the children of men with saving grace. We listen as Isaiah continually reminds us of our covenant obligations.

Isaiah 50:6–7—The Eternal Author of Salvation

The Lord Jesus Christ wrought the atoning sacrifice on behalf of all mankind and thus became the Father of those whose salvation He purchased through His blood (see also Isa. 53:8, 10).

Isaiah foresaw in vivid detail the mission and sufferings of the Lord, who accomplished the will of the Father by offering Himself as the redeeming sacrifice for all mankind, and opening up the way of eternal life for all who practice obedience to His commandments.

Isaiah 50:10—The Sacred Responsibilities of Those Who Seek Salvation

The Plan of Salvation requires strict and enduring compliance with the covenant obligations. The sons and daughters of God must practice holiness before the Lord and honor and obey His law.

> "Who is among you that feareth the Lord, that obeyeth the voice of his servant, that walketh in darkness, and hath no light? let him trust in the name of the Lord, and stay upon his God." (Isa. 50:10)
>
> "Awake, awake; put on they strength, O Zion; put on thy beautiful garments, O Jerusalem, the holy city. . . ." (Isa. 52:1)
>
> "Depart ye, depart ye, go ye out from thence, touch no unclean thing; go ye out of the midst of her; be ye clean that bear the vessels of the Lord." (Isa. 53:11)

Isaiah gives a clear statement of what is expected of all who participate in the Plan of Salvation—obedience, honoring priesthood covenants, virtue and cleanliness, and living lives full of righteousness and joy.

9 Behold, the Lord GOD will help me; who is he that shall condemn me? lo, they all shall wax old as a garment; the moth shall eat them up.

10 ¶ Who is among you that feareth the LORD, that obeyeth the voice of his servant, that walketh in darkness, and hath no light? let him trust in the name of the LORD, and stay

11 Behold, all ye that kindle a fire, that compass yourselves about with sparks: walk in the light of your fire, and in the sparks that ye have kindled. This shall ye have of mine hand; ye shall lie down in sorrow.

CHAPTER 51

1 HEARKEN to me, ye that follow after righteousness, ye that seek the LORD: look unto the rock whence ye are hewn, and to the hole of the pit whence ye are digged.

2 Look unto Abraham your father, and unto Sarah that bare you: for I called him alone, and blessed him, and increased him.

3 For the LORD shall comfort Zion: he will comfort all her waste places; and he will make her wilderness like Eden, and her desert like the garden of the LORD; joy and gladness shall be found therein, thanksgiving, and the voice of melody.

4 ¶ Hearken unto me, my people; and give ear unto me, O my nation: for a law shall proceed from me, and I will make my judgment to rest for a light of the people.

5 My righteousness is near; my salvation is gone forth, and mine arms shall judge the people; the isles shall wait upon me, and on mine arm shall they trust.

6 Lift up your eyes to the heavens, and look upon the earth beneath: for the heavens shall vanish away like smoke, and the earth shall wax old like a garment, and they that dwell therein shall die in like manner: but my salvation shall be for ever, and my righteousness shall not be abolished.

7 ¶ Hearken unto me, ye that know righteousness, the people in whose heart is my law; fear ye not the reproach of men, neither be ye afraid of their revilings.

8 For the moth shall eat them up like a garment, and the worm shall eat them like wool: but my righteousness shall be for ever, and my salvation from generation to generation.

9 ¶ Awake, awake, put on strength, O arm of the LORD; awake, as in the ancient days, in the generations of old. Art thou not it that hath cut Rahab, and wounded the dragon?

10 Art thou not it which hath dried the sea, the waters of the great deep; that hath made the depths of the sea a way for the ransomed to pass over?

11 Therefore the redeemed of the LORD shall return, and come with singing unto Zion; and everlasting joy shall be upon their head: they shall obtain gladness and joy; and sorrow and mourning shall flee away.

12 I, even I, am he that comforteth you: who art thou, that thou shouldest be afraid of a man that shall die, and of the son of man which shall be made as grass;

13 And forgettest the LORD thy maker, that hath stretched forth the heavens, and laid the foundations of the earth; and hast feared continually every day because of the fury of the oppressor, as if he were ready to destroy? and where is the fury of the oppressor?

ISAIAH CHAPTER 51

"I forewarn you therefore to cultivate righteousness and faithfulness in yourselves, which is the only passport into celestial happiness." —Brigham Young, *JD* 2:132, 18 December 1859.

Isaiah 51:3—The Joy of Salvation

There is no joy that can compare with the comfort and peace that comes to individuals and families through the mission of the Savior. The redeeming blessings He brings into the lives of the humble and obedient are the source of unending joy and thanksgiving.

"For the Lord shall comfort Zion: he will comfort all her waste places; and he will make her wilderness like Eden, and her desert like the garden of the Lord; joy and gladness shall be found therein, thanksgiving, and the voice of melody." (Isa. 51:3)

"How beautiful upon the mountains are the feet of him that bringeth good tidings, that publisheth peace; that bringeth good tidings of good, that publisheth salvation; that saith unto Zion, Thy God reigneth!" (Isa. 52:7)

Isaiah articulates with masterful imagery and dynamic expression the incomparable joy of the Saints at the enlivening, revitalizing power of the gospel of eternal life.

Isaiah 51:4–6—The Law and the Light

These are statements of divine purpose and power—monumental in their simplicity and plainness: The Savior is the law and the light. He is the Author of eternal salvation. All life comes under His jurisdiction. He can be trusted to accomplish what He has declared. He is the font of all righteousness.

We are to look upon the heavens and the earth and know that all will be renewed—unto destruction for the wicked and unto salvation for the faithful and true. In the words of Abinadi: "He is the light and the life of the world; yea, a light that is endless, that can never be darkened; yea, and also a life which is endless, that there can be no more death" (Mosiah 16:9). The majesty and infinite compassion of the Savior in bringing about His eternal purposes are unfolded in the words of Amulek: "For it is expedient that there should be a great and last sacrifice; yea, not a sacrifice of man, neither of beast, neither of any manner of fowl; for it shall not be a human sacrifice; but it must be an infinite and eternal sacrifice" (Alma 34:10).

14 The captive exile hasteneth that he may be loosed, and that he should not die in the pit, nor that his bread should fail.

15 But I am the LORD thy God, that divided the sea, whose waves roared: The LORD of hosts is his name.

16 And I have put my words in thy mouth, and I have covered thee in the shadow of mine hand, that I may plant the heavens, and lay the foundations of the earth, and say unto Zion, Thou art my people.

17 ¶ Awake, awake, stand up, O Jerusalem, which hast drunk at the hand of the LORD the cup of his fury; thou hast drunken the dregs of the cup of trembling, and wrung them out.

18 There is none to guide her among all the sons whom she hath brought forth; neither is there any that taketh her by the hand of all the sons that she hath brought up.

19 These two things are come unto thee; who shall be sorry for thee? desolation, and destruction, and the famine, and the sword: by whom shall I comfort thee?

20 Thy sons have fainted, they lie at the head of all the streets, as a wild bull in a net: they are full of the fury of the LORD, the rebuke of thy God.

21 ¶ Therefore hear now this, thou afflicted, and drunken, but not with wine:

22 Thus saith thy Lord the LORD, and thy God that pleadeth the cause of his people, Behold, I have taken out of thine hand the cup of trembling, even the dregs of the cup of my fury; thou shalt no more drink it again:

23 But I will put it into the hand of them that afflict thee; which have said to thy soul, Bow down, that we may go over: and thou hast laid thy body as the ground, and as the street, to them that went over.

CHAPTER 52

1 AWAKE, awake; put on thy strength, O Zion; put on thy beautiful garments, O Jerusalem, the holy city: for henceforth there shall no more come into thee the uncircumcised and the unclean.

2 Shake thyself from the dust; arise, and sit down, O Jerusalem: loose thyself from the bands of thy neck, O captive daughter of Zion.

3 For thus saith the LORD, Ye have sold yourselves for nought; and ye shall be redeemed without money.

4 For thus saith the Lord GOD, My people went down aforetime into Egypt to sojourn there; and the Assyrian oppressed them without cause.

5 Now therefore, what have I here, saith the LORD, that my people is taken away for nought? they that rule over them make them to howl, saith the LORD; and my name continually every day is blasphemed.

6 Therefore my people shall know my name: therefore they shall know in that day that I am he that doth speak: behold, it is I.

7 ¶ How beautiful upon the mountains are the feet of him that bringeth good tidings, that publisheth peace; that bringeth good tidings of good, that publisheth salvation; that saith unto Zion, Thy God reigneth!

8 Thy watchmen shall lift up the voice; with the voice together shall they sing: for they shall see eye to eye, when the LORD shall bring again Zion.

ISAIAH CHAPTER 52

Isaiah 52:1—Zion

The name *Zion* appears 150 times in the Old Testament—mostly as a term indicating the place where the Lord's people dwell. However, in certain passages in Isaiah, the word takes on the nature of an appellation for the people themselves. As an example: "And I have put my words in thy mouth, and I have covered thee in the shadow of mine hand, that I may plant the heavens, and lay the foundations of the earth, and say unto Zion, Thou *art* my people" (Isa. 51:16).

Using the word *Zion* in this sense, as a name for the people of the Lord, is reinforced in latter-day scripture, as in the following celebrated passage from the Doctrine and Covenants: "Therefore, verily, thus saith the Lord, let Zion rejoice, for this is Zion—THE PURE IN HEART; therefore, let Zion rejoice, while all the wicked shall mourn" (D&C 97:21). The ultimate design of the Lord is plainly manifest through the voice of the His latter-day prophet: "For I will raise up unto myself a pure people, that will serve me in righteousness" (D&C 100:16).

The Saints are to cultivate, through faith and sacrifice, the nature and qualities of a Zion people (see D&C 105:5–6). Only those who have overcome sin through the Atonement of the Savior can be citizens of the city of Zion and heirs to the riches of eternity. Similarly, Zion consists of a people unified in the discipleship of the Redeemer, like unto the people of Enoch (see Moses 7:18).

The term *Zion* evokes a multiplicity of thoughts and feelings in the hearts of the followers of Christ. The term is perhaps the closest thing to a free-standing linguistic emblem or ensign among all the vocabulary words of the gospel. Zion is a place, an institution, a state of mind, a noble destination, a people, a vision of perfection, an abode of God, an encapsulating summary of everything that is "honest, true, chaste, benevolent, virtuous. . . lovely, or of good report or praiseworthy" (Article of Faith 13).

Zion is not a utopia ever nestled beyond mortal access: it is a reality that has already been manifested at times upon the earth among mortals who have risen to such a noble level of covenant righteousness that their exemplary level of peace, unity, and spiritual attainment have evoked upon them the highest blessings of our Father in Heaven. The dispensation of the fulness of times provides the unique framework for the unfolding of a Zion people and a Zion city in these latter days. It is the will of the Lord that such an establishment be forthcoming, prospered by the grace and beneficence of His loving care, overshadowed by His merciful Spirit, drawn on by His promised blessings, and secured by the inexorable finality of His word. What a glorious destiny is hereby proffered the Saints of God—to be enlisted in such a magnificent work of edification and eternal progression. What a great responsibility to be engaged on the Lord's errand during the final period of the earth's history leading up to the inauguration of the millennial reign.

9 ¶ Break forth into joy, sing together, ye waste places of Jerusalem: for the LORD hath comforted his people, he hath redeemed Jerusalem.

10 The LORD hath made bare his holy arm in the eyes of all the nations; and all the ends of the earth shall see the salvation of our God.

11 ¶ Depart ye, depart ye, go ye out from thence, touch no unclean thing; go ye out of the midst of her; be ye clean, that bear the vessels of the LORD.

12 For ye shall not go out with haste, nor go by flight: for the LORD will go before you; and the God of Israel will be your rereward.

13 ¶ Behold, my servant shall deal prudently, he shall be exalted and extolled, and be very high.

14 As many were astonied at thee; his visage was so marred more than any man, and his form more than the sons of men:

15 So shall he sprinkle many nations; the kings shall shut their mouths at him: for that which had not been told them shall they see; and that which they had not heard shall they consider.

CHAPTER 53

1 WHO hath believed our report? and to whom is the arm of the LORD revealed?

2 For he shall grow up before him as a tender plant, and as a root out of a dry ground: he hath no form nor comeliness; and when we shall see him, there is no beauty that we should desire him.

3 He is despised and rejected of men; a man of sorrows, and acquainted with grief: and we hid as it were our faces from him; he was despised, and we esteemed him not.

4 ¶ Surely he hath borne our griefs, and carried our sorrows: yet we did esteem him stricken, smitten of God, and afflicted.

5 But he was wounded for our transgressions, he was bruised for our iniquities: the chastisement of our peace was upon him; and with his stripes we are healed.

6 All we like sheep have gone astray; we have turned every one to his own way; and the LORD hath laid on him the iniquity of us all.

7 He was oppressed, and he was afflicted, yet he opened not his mouth: he is brought as a lamb to the slaughter, and as a sheep before her shearers is dumb, so he openeth not his mouth.

8 He was taken from prison and from judgment: and who shall declare his generation? for he was cut off out of the land of the living: for the transgression of my people was he stricken.

9 And he made his grave with the wicked, and with the rich in his death; because he had done no violence, neither was any deceit in his mouth.

10 ¶ Yet it pleased the LORD to bruise him; he hath put him to grief: when thou shalt make his soul an offering for sin, he shall see his seed, he shall prolong his days, and the pleasure of the LORD shall prosper in his hand.

11 He shall see of the travail of his soul, and shall be satisfied: by his knowledge shall my righteous servant justify many; for he shall bear their iniquities.

12 Therefore will I divide him a portion with the great, and he shall divide the spoil with the strong; because he hath poured out his soul unto death: and he was numbered with the transgressors; and he bare the sin of many, and made intercession for the transgressors.

Isaiah 52:11—Purity

Happiness and joy come through obedience, which in turn leads to righteousness—which causes us to serve and bless others. This is joy. This is happiness. This is life eternal. The Atonement is the core of the gospel, and only by applying it in our lives can we partake of the goodness of God and our Savior. Faith unto repentance is vital to our exaltation and eternal life, all through the grace of God. The responsibility of each son or daughter of God is to become pure in heart, free from sin by repenting through the Atonement of Jesus Christ.

ISAIAH CHAPTER 53

Isaiah 53—The Redeemer

These astonishing and wonderful words of Isaiah present a detailed view of the Redeemer, His atoning sacrifice, and His transcendent completion of the commission given Him of the Father. Who can read these words in humility and reverence without being touched to the heart by the prescience of the prophetic vision of what was to transpire more than 700 years later. The Jewish people were looking for the Messiah to appear in power and glory, but they failed to see in the carpenter's son—despite His wondrous deeds—the very Messiah that Isaiah so clearly viewed and described. Jesus came not with imperial power (that was not to occur until the Second Coming), but with the power of the Redemption and Atonement—the greatest power ever administered in the unfolding of God's design for the immortality and exaltation of man. As the Savior declared to the Saints in Bountiful following His resurrection: "And behold, I am the light and the life of the world; and I have drunk out of that bitter cup which the Father hath given me, and have glorified the Father in taking upon me the sins of the world, in the which I have suffered the will of the Father in all things from the beginning" (3 Ne. 11:11; compare 1 Ne. 19:9; Mosiah 15:10–13; Alma 7:11–13; Heb. 2:16–18; 4:15).

CHAPTER 54

1 SING, O barren, thou that didst not bear; break forth into singing, and cry aloud, thou that didst not travail with child: for more are the children of the desolate than the children of the married wife, saith the LORD.

2 Enlarge the place of thy tent, and let them stretch forth the curtains of thine habitations: spare not, lengthen thy cords, and strengthen thy stakes;

3 For thou shalt break forth on the right hand and on the left; and thy seed shall inherit the Gentiles, and make the desolate cities to be inhabited.

4 Fear not; for thou shalt not be ashamed: neither be thou confounded; for thou shalt not be put to shame: for thou shalt forget the shame of thy youth, and shalt not remember the reproach of thy widowhood any more.

5 For thy Maker is thine husband; the LORD of hosts is his name; and thy Redeemer the Holy One of Israel; The God of the whole earth shall he be called.

6 For the LORD hath called thee as a woman forsaken and grieved in spirit, and a wife of youth, when thou wast refused, saith thy God.

7 For a small moment have I forsaken thee; but with great mercies will I gather thee.

8 In a little wrath I hid my face from thee for a moment; but with everlasting kindness will I have mercy on thee, saith the LORD thy Redeemer.

9 For this is as the waters of Noah unto me: for as I have sworn that the waters of Noah should no more go over the earth; so have I sworn that I would not be wroth with thee, nor rebuke thee.

10 For the mountains shall depart, and the hills be removed; but my kindness shall not depart from thee, neither shall the covenant of my peace be removed, saith the LORD that hath mercy on thee.

11 ¶ O thou afflicted, tossed with tempest, and not comforted, behold, I will lay thy stones with fair colours, and lay thy foundations with sapphires.

12 And I will make thy windows of agates, and thy gates of carbuncles, and all thy borders of pleasant stones.

13 And all thy children shall be taught of the LORD; and great shall be the peace of thy children.

14 In righteousness shalt thou be established: thou shalt be far from oppression; for thou shalt not fear: and from terror; for it shall not come near thee.

15 Behold, they shall surely gather together, but not by me: whosoever shall gather together against thee shall fall for thy sake.

16 Behold, I have created the smith that bloweth the coals in the fire, and that bringeth forth an instrument for his work; and I have created the waster to destroy.

17 ¶ No weapon that is formed against thee shall prosper; and every tongue that shall rise against thee in judgment thou shalt condemn. This is the heritage of the servants of the LORD, and their righteousness is of me, saith the LORD.

ISAIAH CHAPTER 54

Isaiah 54—Preview of the Doctrine of the Gathering

The power and mission of the Redeemer, as He said, is to "draw all men unto me" (3 Ne. 27:14). Isaiah saw with transparent clarity the inexorable gathering power of the gospel of Jesus Christ. The gathering under divine decree is a compound of many keys, influences, powers, and blessings. Three of these aspects are explored in great detail by Isaiah: (1) the appointed *locus* of the gathering—the stakes of Zion worldwide; (2) the *aegis* of the gathering—in and through the holy name of the Lord Jesus Christ, who alone holds the power and authority to endow mankind with the blessings of salvation and exaltation; and (3) the culminating *purpose* of the gathering—to lay the foundation for the return of the Redeemer and the ushering in of the millennial reign.

Isaiah 54:2—Strengthening the Stakes of the Kingdom

The tent of Zion, with its securing stakes and reinforcing cords, is the perfect image for the refuge afforded by the kingdom of God. Just as the temple is symbolized by the immovable mountain of the Lord, Zion itself, as a tent, is shown as agile and growing, flexible and expanding, lithe and unfolding. The Saints of Zion can thus internalize the fixed and unchanging character of eternal principles as well as the responsive and dynamic character of the expanding Kingdom whose saving and protecting influence extends into all quarters of the earth.

Isaiah was given a prophetic view of the canopy of Zion, with its ever-expanding scope as the kingdom of God spreading throughout the world. His language perfectly captures the role of Zion's communities as the gathering places for the faithful ransomed of the flock. The message of Zion is the salt of the earth whose savor brings spiritual stability in times of chaos and confusion.

Isaiah 54:13—Our Prayer for Peace

Where in the world can one obtain hope, peace, harmony, and security? Isaiah proclaims the answer to this question in magnificent, flowing language imbued with the spirit of revelation and prophecy. The hope of Israel is to be found in the process of gathering—gathering with the Saints of God in holy places—the homes, stakes, and temples of Zion—where the Saints can worship in the spirit of truth and righteousness and bring their holy vows before the Lord. The peace of Israel is to be obtained in and through the "merits, and mercy, and grace of the Holy Messiah" (2 Ne. 2:8), whose name alone provides the aegis for salvation and exaltation. The harmony of Israel will come with the preparations for, and the ushering in of, the millennial reign under the governance of the Lord Himself. All of this affords the spiritual security that is the object of the earnest search of every honest seeker after truth. Isaiah foresaw the outcomes and the consequences of spiritual valor when he said, simply, "great shall be the peace of thy children" (Isa. 54:13).

CHAPTER 55

1 HO, every one that thirsteth, come ye to the waters, and he that hath no money; come ye, buy, and eat; yea, come, buy wine and milk without money and without price.

2 Wherefore do ye spend money for that which is not bread? and your labour for that which satisfieth not? hearken diligently unto me, and eat ye that which is good, and let your soul delight itself in fatness.

3 Incline your ear, and come unto me: hear, and your soul shall live; and I will make an everlasting covenant with you, even the sure mercies of David.

4 Behold, I have given him for a witness to the people, a leader and commander to the people.

5 Behold, thou shalt call a nation that thou knowest not, and nations that knew not thee shall run unto thee because of the LORD thy God, and for the Holy One of Israel; for he hath glorified thee.

6 ¶ Seek ye the LORD while he may be found, call ye upon him while he is near:

7 Let the wicked forsake his way, and the unrighteous man his thoughts: and let him return unto the LORD, and he will have mercy upon him; and to our God, for he will abundantly pardon.

8 ¶ For my thoughts are not your thoughts, neither are your ways my ways, saith the LORD.

9 For as the heavens are higher than the earth, so are my ways higher than your ways, and my thoughts than your thoughts.

10 For as the rain cometh down, and the snow from heaven, and returneth not thither, but watereth the earth, and maketh it bring forth and bud, that it may give seed to the sower, and bread to the eater:

11 So shall my word be that goeth forth out of my mouth: it shall not return unto me void, but it shall accomplish that which I please, and it shall prosper in the thing whereto I sent it.

12 For ye shall go out with joy, and be led forth with peace: the mountains and the hills shall break forth before you into singing, and all the trees of the field shall clap their hands.

13 Instead of the thorn shall come up the fir tree, and instead of the brier shall come up the myrtle tree: and it shall be to the LORD for a name, for an everlasting sign that shall not be cut off.

ISAIAH CHAPTER 55

Isaiah 55:1–2—Salvation Is Free

The bread of life and the living waters of salvation are free. They are conveyed without price through the grace of the Lamb of God. He paid for our sins through His infinite sacrifice. We pay for our part by sacrificing in faith and obedience a broken heart and a contrite spirit (see Ps. 34:18; 2 Ne. 2:7; Jacob 2:10; 3 Ne. 9:20; 12:19; Ether 4:15; Moroni 6:2; D&C 59:8).

Nephi confirmed this same doctrine with eloquence: "He doeth not anything save it be for the benefit of the world; for he loveth the world, even that he layeth down his own life that he may draw all men unto him. Wherefore, he commandeth none that they shall not partake of his salvation. Behold, doth he cry unto any, saying: Depart from me? Behold, I say unto you, Nay; but he saith: Come unto me all ye ends of the earth, buy milk and honey, without money and without price" (2 Ne. 26:24–25).

Isaiah 55:13—Nurture of the Word of God

The word of God is nurture unto growing things; it is life-generating and life-sustaining in its capacity to lift the children of God upward toward their eternal potential. The harvest of the word of God is a concourse of souls that rejoice in salvation, souls that are sanctified through the redemption. In the words of Ammon: "But behold, they are in the hands of the Lord of the harvest, and they are his; and he will raise them up at the last day" (Alma 26:7).

Alma, in his discourse on faith, reveals the key to spiritual growth: We are to avoid even the least instance of neglecting to nourish the word within us; instead, we are to invest all of our might, power, and strength in cultivating our faith, that it might spring up as the tree of life— even eternal life and exaltation through the power of Jesus Christ (see Alma 32:38–41.)

CHAPTER 56

1 THUS saith the LORD, Keep ye judgment, and do justice: for my salvation is near to come, and my righteousness to be revealed.

2 Blessed is the man that doeth this, and the son of man that layeth hold on it; that keepeth the sabbath from polluting it, and keepeth his hand from doing any evil.

3 ¶ Neither let the son of the stranger, that hath joined himself to the LORD, speak, saying, The LORD hath utterly separated me from his people: neither let the eunuch say, Behold, I am a dry tree.

4 For thus saith the LORD unto the eunuchs that keep my sabbaths, and choose the things that please me, and take hold of my covenant;

5 Even unto them will I give in mine house and within my walls a place and a name better than of sons and of daughters: I will give them an everlasting name, that shall not be cut off.

6 Also the sons of the stranger, that join themselves to the LORD, to serve him, and to love the name of the LORD, to be his servants, every one that keepeth the sabbath from polluting it, and taketh hold of my covenant;

7 Even them will I bring to my holy mountain, and make them joyful in my house of prayer: their burnt offerings and their sacrifices shall be accepted upon mine altar; for mine house shall be called an house of prayer for all people.

8 The Lord GOD which gathereth the outcasts of Israel saith, Yet will I gather others to him, beside those that are gathered unto him.

9 ¶ All ye beasts of the field, come to devour, yea, all ye beasts in the forest.

10 His watchmen are blind: they are all ignorant, they are all dumb dogs, they cannot bark; sleeping, lying down, loving to slumber.

11 Yea, they are greedy dogs which can never have enough, and they are shepherds that cannot understand: they all look to their own way, every one for his gain, from his quarter.

12 Come ye, say they, I will fetch wine, and we will fill ourselves with strong drink; and to morrow shall be as this day, and much more abundant.

ISAIAH CHAPTER 56

Isaiah 56:5—The Blessings of the Gathering of Israel

Even though the Lord's ways are higher than man's ways, and His thoughts higher than man's thoughts (see Isa. 55:9), He nevertheless succors His people with mercy, grace, and a gathering hand.

Isaiah sees things from the heavenly perspective; thus he can reveal the broadness and scope of the Lord's plan to gather home the flock of His faithful and valiant servants — not only the covenant people by birth, but all those who are adopted into the fold through faith, repentance, and the baptism of water and fire. All the faithful are to be gathered under the name of Christ, the only name under the heavens whereby mankind may be saved.

 POINT OF INTEREST

Biblical scholars don't agree on what is meant by the beasts, watchmen, dogs, and shepherds mentioned in Isa. 56:9–12. We know that the beasts devour, the watchmen are blind, the dogs are greedy and mute, and the shepherds fail to understand, but what does that mean to us in the latter days? The devouring beasts, blind watchmen, mute dogs, and confused shepherds may represent those who reject the gospel and who try to influence others to reject it as well. They might also represent those who do have the gospel but who don't take the time or make the effort to share it with others, discharging their missionary responsibility. According to one Biblical scholar, "The flock is intrusted to the care of these watchmen. The wild beasts come; these dogs bark not; and the wild beasts devour the flock. Thus they do not profit the flock. Yea, they injure *it; for the owner trusts in them, that they will watch and be faithful; but they are not. These are the false teachers and careless shepherds" (Adam Clarke, The Holy Bible . . . with a Commentary and Critical Notes, 4:212).*

CHAPTER 63

1 WHO is this that cometh from Edom, with dyed garments from Bozrah? this that is glorious in his apparel, travelling in the greatness of his strength? I that speak in righteousness, mighty to save.

2 Wherefore art thou red in thine apparel, and thy garments like him that treadeth in the winefat?

3 I have trodden the winepress alone; and of the people there was none with me: for I will tread them in mine anger, and trample them in my fury; and their blood shall be sprinkled upon my garments, and I will stain all my raiment.

4 For the day of vengeance is in mine heart, and the year of my redeemed is come.

5 And I looked, and there was none to help; and I wondered that there was none to uphold: therefore mine own arm brought salvation unto me; and my fury, it upheld me.

6 And I will tread down the people in mine anger, and make them drunk in my fury, and I will bring down their strength to the earth.

7 ¶ I will mention the lovingkindnesses of the LORD, and the praises of the LORD, according to all that the LORD hath bestowed on us, and the great goodness toward the house of Israel, which he hath bestowed on them according to his mercies, and according to the multitude of his lovingkindnesses.

8 For he said, Surely they are my people, children that will not lie: so he was their Saviour.

9 In all their affliction he was afflicted, and the angel of his presence saved them: in his love and in his pity he redeemed them; and he bare them, and carried them all the days of old.

10 ¶ But they rebelled, and vexed his holy Spirit: therefore he was turned to be their enemy, and he fought against them.

11 Then he remembered the days of old, Moses, and his people, saying, Where is he that brought them up out of the sea with the shepherd of his flock? where is he that put his holy Spirit within him?

12 That led them by the right hand of Moses with his glorious arm, dividing the water before them, to make himself an everlasting name?

13 That led them through the deep, as an horse in the wilderness, that they should not stumble?

14 As a beast goeth down into the valley, the Spirit of the LORD caused him to rest: so didst thou lead thy people, to make thyself a glorious name.

15 ¶ Look down from heaven, and behold from the habitation of thy holiness and of thy glory: where is thy zeal and thy strength, the sounding of thy bowels and of thy mercies toward me? are they restrained?

16 Doubtless thou art our father, though Abraham be ignorant of us, and Israel acknowledge us not: thou, O LORD, art our father, our redeemer; thy name is from everlasting.

17 ¶ O LORD, why hast thou made us to err from thy ways, and hardened our heart from thy fear? Return for thy servants' sake, the tribes of thine inheritance.

18 The people of thy holiness have possessed it but a little while: our adversaries have trodden down thy sanctuary.

19 We are thine: thou never barest rule over them; they were not called by thy name.

ISAIAH CHAPTER 63

"The world has had a fair trial for six thousand years; the Lord will try the seventh thousand Himself. . . . Satan will be bound, and the works of darkness destroyed; righteousness will be put to the line and judgment to the plummet, and 'he that fears the Lord will alone be exalted in that day.'" —Joseph Smith, *DHC* 5:64–65, 15 July 1842

Isaiah 63:1—Waiting in Hope and Gratitude for the Second Coming and the Millennium

The Millennium is to be ushered in with enormous upheaval and cataclysmic change—a nightmare for the wicked and a blessed dream-come-true for the faithful. The Son of Man is to return in power and sanctity to perform His final labors before the dawning of the Millennium of peace.

> "Wherefore art thou red in thine apparel, and thy garments like him that treadeth in the winefat?" (Isa. 63:2)
> "… thou, O Lord, art our father, our redeemer; thy name is from everlasting." (Isa. 63:16)
> "For since the beginning of the world men have not heard, nor perceived by the ear, neither hath the eye seen, O God, beside thee, what he hath prepared for him that waiteth for him." (Isa. 64:4)
> "And it shall come to pass, that before they call, I will answer; and while they are yet speaking, I will hear." (Isa. 65:24)

What vistas Isaiah sees as he views the ends of the earth and the calamitous and earth-shattering events of the last hours, with the return of the red-mantled Savior to judge the inhabitants of the earth and receive the faithful in a cloud of angelic choirs! How magnificent is the language of Isaiah, who strives to teach us the lessons of preparation and readiness, who pleads with us to receive the blessings of salvation and exaltation—if only we will be obedient to the covenant promises. The Lord is so full of mercy and kindness that He hears and answers our prayers even before they are uttered.

Isaiah 63:7–9—Praise

The words of Isaiah unfold like a magnificent anthem filling all time and space with the praises of the Almighty. We celebrate His lovingkindness, His goodness, His mercy, His Fatherhood ("Surely they are my people"—verse 8), His atoning and redeeming sacrifice, His love and pity, His capacity and willingness to lift and carry of the people. It is no wonder that the resurrected Lord counseled the people to listen to the words of Isaiah: "Yea, a commandment I give unto you that ye search these things diligently; for great are the words of Isaiah. For surely he spake as touching all things concerning my people which are of the house of Israel; therefore it must needs be that he must speak also to the Gentiles. And all things that he spake have been and shall be, even according to the words which he spake" (3 Ne. 23:1–3).

CHAPTER 64

1 OH that thou wouldest rend the heavens, that thou wouldest come down, that the mountains might flow down at thy presence,

2 As when the melting fire burneth, the fire causeth the waters to boil, to make thy name known to thine adversaries, that the nations may tremble at thy presence!

3 When thou didst terrible things which we looked not for, thou camest down, the mountains flowed down at thy presence.

4 For since the beginning of the world men have not heard, nor perceived by the ear, neither hath the eye seen, O God, beside thee, what he hath prepared for him that waiteth for him.

5 Thou meetest him that rejoiceth and worketh righteousness, those that remember thee in thy ways: behold, thou art wroth; for we have sinned: in those is continuance, and we shall be saved.

6 But we are all as an unclean thing, and all our righteousnesses are as filthy rags; and we all do fade as a leaf; and our iniquities, like the wind, have taken us away.

7 And there is none that calleth upon thy name, that stirreth up himself to take hold of thee: for thou hast hid thy face from us, and hast consumed us, because of our iniquities.

8 But now, O LORD, thou art our father; we are the clay, and thou our potter; and we all are the work of thy hand.

9 ¶ Be not wroth very sore, O LORD, neither remember iniquity for ever: behold, see, we beseech thee, we are all thy people.

10 Thy holy cities are a wilderness, Zion is a wilderness, Jerusalem a desolation.

11 Our holy and our beautiful house, where our fathers praised thee, is burned up with fire: and all our pleasant things are laid waste.

12 Wilt thou refrain thyself for these things, O LORD? wilt thou hold thy peace, and afflict us very sore?

CHAPTER 65

1 I AM sought of them that asked not for me; I am found of them that sought me not: I said, Behold me, behold me, unto a nation that was not called by my name.

2 I have spread out my hands all the day unto a rebellious people, which walketh in a way that was not good, after their own thoughts;

3 A people that provoketh me to anger continually to my face; that sacrificeth in gardens, and burneth incense upon altars of brick;

4 Which remain among the graves, and lodge in the monuments, which eat swine's flesh, and broth of abominable things is in their vessels;

5 Which say, Stand by thyself, come not near to me; for I am holier than thou. These are a smoke in my nose, a fire that burneth all the day.

6 Behold, it is written before me: I will not keep silence, but will recompense, even recompense into their bosom,

7 Your iniquities, and the iniquities of your fathers together, saith the LORD, which have burned incense upon the mountains, and blasphemed me upon the hills: therefore will I measure their former work into their bosom.

8 ¶ Thus saith the LORD, As the new wine is found in the cluster, and one saith, Destroy it not; for a blessing is in it: so will I do for my servants' sakes, that I may not destroy them all.

ISAIAH CHAPTER 64

Isaiah 64:4—Anticipation of the Second Coming

Isaiah looks forward to the fulfilling of the grand visions that he is privileged to see—the coming again of the Savior, the renewing of the earth, the blessing of those who wait on the Lord. Paul echoed these words when he said:

> But as it is written, Eye hath not seen, nor ear heard, neither have entered into the heart of man, the things which God hath prepared for them that love him.
>
> But God hath revealed *them* unto us by his Spirit: for the Spirit searcheth all things, yea, the deep things of God.
>
> For what man knoweth the things of a man, save the spirit of man which is in him? even so the things of God knoweth no man, but the Spirit of God. (1 Cor. 2:9–11)

ISAIAH CHAPTER 65

Isaiah 65—A Vision of Millennial Society

The vision of millennial society is filled with comfort and peace. So abundant and infinite is the love of the Father and Son, that the blessings flow continually unto the faithful—even before they pray for deliverance and help: "And it shall come to pass, that before they call, I will answer; and while they are yet speaking, I will hear" (verse 24). The Savior taught: ". . . for your Father knoweth what things ye have need of, before ye ask him" (Matt. 6:8), implying that the Father's compassion sends forth blessings in anticipation of the utterance of supplication from His believing children. Our faith and devotion speak words of communion with God, even before our tongues are activated. "The effectual fervent prayer of a righteous man availeth much" (James 5:16)—even the silent prayer, or the prayer still forming in the heart.

9 And I will bring forth a seed out of Jacob, and out of Judah an inheritor of my mountains: and mine elect shall inherit it, and my servants shall dwell there.

10 And Sharon shall be a fold of flocks, and the valley of Achor a place for the herds to lie down in, for my people that have sought me.

11 ¶ But ye are they that forsake the LORD, that forget my holy mountain, that prepare a table for that troop, and that furnish the drink offering unto that number.

12 Therefore will I number you to the sword, and ye shall all bow down to the slaughter: because when I called, ye did not answer; when I spake, ye did not hear; but did evil before mine eyes, and did choose that wherein I delighted not.

13 Therefore thus saith the Lord GOD, Behold, my servants shall eat, but ye shall be hungry: behold, my servants shall drink, but ye shall be thirsty: behold, my servants shall rejoice, but ye shall be ashamed:

14 Behold, my servants shall sing for joy of heart, but ye shall cry for sorrow of heart, and shall howl for vexation of spirit.

15 And ye shall leave your name for a curse unto my chosen: for the Lord GOD shall slay thee, and call his servants by another name:

16 That he who blesseth himself in the earth shall bless himself in the God of truth; and he that sweareth in the earth shall swear by the God of truth; because the former troubles are forgotten, and because they are hid from mine eyes.

17 ¶ For, behold, I create new heavens and a new earth: and the former shall not be remembered, nor come into mind.

18 But be ye glad and rejoice for ever in that which I create: for, behold, I create Jerusalem a rejoicing, and her people a joy.

19 And I will rejoice in Jerusalem, and joy in my people: and the voice of weeping shall be no more heard in her, nor the voice of crying.

20 There shall be no more thence an infant of days, nor an old man that hath not filled his days: for the child shall die an hundred years old; but the sinner being an hundred years old shall be accursed.

21 And they shall build houses, and inhabit them; and they shall plant vineyards, and eat the fruit of them.

22 They shall not build, and another inhabit; they shall not plant, and another eat: for as the days of a tree are the days of my people, and mine elect shall long enjoy the work of their hands.

23 They shall not labour in vain, nor bring forth for trouble; for they are the seed of the blessed of the LORD, and their offspring with them.

24 And it shall come to pass, that before they call, I will answer; and while they are yet speaking, I will hear.

25 The wolf and the lamb shall feed together, and the lion shall eat straw like the bullock: and dust shall be the serpent's meat. They shall not hurt nor destroy in all my holy mountain, saith the LORD.

Isaiah by Gustave Doré

THE
BOOK OF THE PROPHET JEREMIAH

CHAPTER 1

1 THE words of Jeremiah the son of Hilkiah, of the priests that were in Anathoth in the land of Benjamin:

2 To whom the word of the LORD came in the days of Josiah the son of Amon king of Judah, in the thirteenth year of his reign.

3 It came also in the days of Jehoiakim the son of Josiah king of Judah, unto the end of the eleventh year of Zedekiah the son of Josiah king of Judah, unto the carrying away of Jerusalem captive in the fifth month.

4 Then the word of the LORD came unto me, saying,

5 Before I formed thee in the belly I knew thee; and before thou camest forth out of the womb I sanctified thee, and I ordained thee a prophet unto the nations.

6 Then said I, Ah, Lord GOD! behold, I cannot speak: for I am a child.

7 ¶ But the LORD said unto me, Say not, I am a child: for thou shalt go to all that I shall send thee, and whatsoever I command thee thou shalt speak.

8 Be not afraid of their faces: for I am with thee to deliver thee, saith the LORD.

9 Then the LORD put forth his hand, and touched my mouth. And the LORD said unto me, Behold, I have put my words in thy mouth.

10 See, I have this day set thee over the nations and over the kingdoms, to root out, and to pull down, and to destroy, and to throw down, to build, and to plant.

11 ¶ Moreover the word of the LORD came unto me, saying, Jeremiah, what seest thou? And I said, I see a rod of an almond tree.

12 Then said the LORD unto me, Thou hast well seen: for I will hasten my word to perform it.

13 And the word of the LORD came unto me the second time, saying, What seest thou? And I said, I see a seething pot; and the face thereof is toward the north.

14 Then the LORD said unto me, Out of the north an evil shall break forth upon all the inhabitants of the land.

15 For, lo, I will call all the families of the kingdoms of the north, saith the LORD; and they shall come, and they shall set every one his throne at the entering of the gates of Jerusalem, and against all the walls thereof round about, and against all the cities of Judah.

16 And I will utter my judgments against them touching all their wickedness, who have forsaken me, and have burned incense unto other gods, and worshipped the works of their own hands.

17 ¶ Thou therefore gird up thy loins, and arise, and speak unto them all that I command thee: be not dismayed at their faces, lest I confound thee before them.

18 For, behold, I have made thee this day a defenced city, and an iron pillar, and brasen walls against the whole land, against the kings of Judah, against the princes thereof, against the priests thereof, and against the people of the land.

JEREMIAH CHAPTER 1

Jeremiah 1:7—Strength in Adversity

Jeremiah was foreordained to his calling as prophet: "Before I formed thee in the belly I knew thee; and before thou camest forth out of the womb I sanctified thee, and I ordained thee a prophet unto the nations" (Jer. 1:5). He was to embrace his office with courage and in the strength of the Lord—despite the challenges and tribulations he would face among a doubting and wayward people.

Jeremiah is called of the Lord to preach repentance to a wayward and idolatrous Israel. Unless the people should reverse their course of rejecting the Lord and His covenant in favor of impotent gods of their own devices, they are to be overtaken by the Babylonians and taken into captivity. In the face of daunting torment and abuse, Jeremiah remains true to his calling and speaks the Lord's words in courage and with great power. "Diminish not a word" (Jer. 26:2) is his charge—and he holds back nothing from the ears of the Israelites. At the same time that Lehi and his family are fleeing Jerusalem under command of the Lord, Zedekiah retrieves Jeremiah from the dungeon where he was imprisoned and takes him aside secretly, so that the princes might not see it, and says, "Is there any word from the Lord: And Jeremiah said, There is: for, said he, thou shalt be delivered into the hand of the king of Babylon" (Jer. 37:17). That is precisely what occurs (see Jer. 39:5).

We can learn from the example of Jeremiah. In the strength of the Lord the Saints shall accomplish all that is placed upon them by the covenant obligations of righteousness and duty. The Church and kingdom of God—in the face of all adversity and tyranny—shall fulfill its mission to strengthen God's children, preach the gospel to the world, and hasten the work of the temples. The devotion of every member shall be answered upon their heads with blessings of strength, courage, and fortitude—just as in the case of Jeremiah and all of the Lord's holy prophets.

Jeremiah 1:9—The Power of the Word of God

The word of God, when written in the hearts of the Saints and infused in their thoughts, actions, and patterns of living, becomes the testament of salvation and the constitution of exaltation to all who will yield to the will of the Father and the Son. From the word springs faith, and from faith courage, and from courage a godly walk and conversation meet for those becoming sons and daughters of God.

Jeremiah was given a great spiritual blessing of the Lord to be a vessel bearing His word to the nations. He was taught: "… and whatsoever I command thee thou shalt speak" (Jer. 1:7). The word within Jeremiah was as a burning fire that he could not restrain. The princes thought to repress the word of God by consigning Jeremiah to prison and threatening to take away his life. But he spoke the truth nevertheless, saying, "As for me, behold, I am in your hand: do with me as seemeth good and meet unto you. But know ye for certain, that if ye put me to death, ye shall surely bring innocent blood upon yourselves, and upon the city,

19 And they shall fight against thee; but they shall not prevail against thee; for I am with thee, saith the LORD, to deliver thee.

CHAPTER 2

1 MOREOVER the word of the LORD came to me, saying,

2 Go and cry in the ears of Jerusalem, saying, Thus saith the LORD; I remember thee, the kindness of thy youth, the love of thine espousals, when thou wentest after me in the wilderness, in a land that was not sown.

3 Israel was holiness unto the LORD, and the firstfruits of his increase: all that devour him shall offend; evil shall come upon them, saith the LORD.

4 Hear ye the word of the LORD, O house of Jacob, and all the families of the house of Israel:

5 ¶ Thus saith the LORD, What iniquity have your fathers found in me, that they are gone far from me, and have walked after vanity, and are become vain?

6 Neither said they, Where is the LORD that brought us up out of the land of Egypt, that led us through the wilderness, through a land of deserts and of pits, through a land of drought, and of the shadow of death, through a land that no man passed through, and where no man dwelt?

7 And I brought you into a plentiful country, to eat the fruit thereof and the goodness thereof; but when ye entered, ye defiled my land, and made mine heritage an abomination.

8 The priests said not, Where is the LORD? and they that handle the law knew me not: the pastors also transgressed against me, and the prophets prophesied by Baal, and walked after things that do not profit.

9 ¶ Wherefore I will yet plead with you, saith the LORD, and with your children's children will I plead.

10 For pass over the isles of Chittim, and see; and send unto Kedar, and consider diligently, and see if there be such a thing.

11 Hath a nation changed their gods, which are yet no gods? but my people have changed their glory for that which doth not profit.

12 Be astonished, O ye heavens, at this, and be horribly afraid, be ye very desolate, saith the LORD.

13 For my people have committed two evils; they have forsaken me the fountain of living waters, and hewed them out cisterns, broken cisterns, that can hold no water.

14 ¶ Is Israel a servant? is he a homeborn slave? why is he spoiled?

15 The young lions roared upon him, and yelled, and they made his land waste: his cities are burned without inhabitant.

16 Also the children of Noph and Tahapanes have broken the crown of thy head.

17 Hast thou not procured this unto thyself, in that thou hast forsaken the LORD thy God, when he led thee by the way?

18 And now what hast thou to do in the way of Egypt, to drink the waters of Sihor? or what hast thou to do in the way of Assyria, to drink the waters of the river?

19 Thine own wickedness shall correct thee, and thy backslidings shall reprove thee: know therefore and see that it is an evil thing and bitter, that thou hast forsaken the LORD thy God, and that my fear is not in thee, saith the Lord GOD of hosts.

and upon the inhabitants thereof: for of a truth the Lord hath sent me unto you to speak all these words in your ears" (Jer. 26:15–16). In all that he did, Jeremiah was the paragon of obedience and strength in the Lord. He knew of a certainty that the nations were as clay in the Lord's hands (see Jer. 18:1–6), for the Lord had taken him into the potter's house and taught him precisely that. He knew that a time would come, beyond the captivity of Israel, when the Lord would again restore His full word to the people, for the Lord had taught him precisely that (see Jer. 31:31–33).

What greater account could there be of the Restoration of the gospel than these words of Jeremiah? Those who accept the restored word of God will find the living waters to quench their spiritual thirst: "Blessed is the man that trusteth in the Lord, and whose hope the Lord is. For he shall be as a tree planted by the waters, and that spreadeth out her roots by the river, and shall not see when heat cometh, but her leaf shall be green: and shall not be careful in the year of drought, neither shall cease from yielding fruit" (Jer. 17:7–8).

For more insights into the life of Jeremiah, see Appendix II.

JEREMIAH CHAPTER 2

Jeremiah 2—A Message of Repentance

It is unbelievable that the people of the Lord, beneficiaries of His wondrous goodness and mercy in the past, would forsake Him in favor of mortal deities of impotence and lifelessness. The message sent to the people through the prophet Jeremiah is a message of repentance, a call to return to the covenant honor of former times, a renewed invitation to partake of "the living waters" (verse 13) of the gospel of salvation and redemption.

During His mortal ministry, the Savior taught the Samaritan woman at the well about the truth of "living water" (see John 4:10–11; see also John 7:38; Jer. 17:13; Zech. 14:8; Rev. 7:17; 1 Ne. 11:25). In latter-day revelation, the Lord confirmed this truth once again: "But unto him that keepeth my commandments I will give the mysteries of my kingdom, and the same shall be in him a well of living water, springing up unto everlasting life" (D&C 63:23; compare D&C 133:29). Thus the gospel message is consistent and eternal.

20 ¶ For of old time I have broken thy yoke, and burst thy bands; and thou saidst, I will not transgress; when upon every high hill and under every green tree thou wanderest, playing the harlot.

21 Yet I had planted thee a noble vine, wholly a right seed: how then art thou turned into the degenerate plant of a strange vine unto me?

22 For though thou wash thee with nitre, and take thee much soap, yet thine iniquity is marked before me, saith the Lord GOD.

23 How canst thou say, I am not polluted, I have not gone after Baalim? see thy way in the valley, know what thou hast done: thou art a swift dromedary traversing her ways;

24 A wild ass used to the wilderness, that snuffeth up the wind at her pleasure; in her occasion who can turn her away? all they that seek her will not weary themselves; in her month they shall find her.

25 Withhold thy foot from being unshod, and thy throat from thirst: but thou saidst, There is no hope: no; for I have loved strangers, and after them will I go.

26 As the thief is ashamed when he is found, so is the house of Israel ashamed; they, their kings, their princes, and their priests, and their prophets,

27 Saying to a stock, Thou art my father; and to a stone, Thou hast brought me forth: for they have turned their back unto me, and not their face: but in the time of their trouble they will say, Arise, and save us.

28 But where are thy gods that thou hast made thee? let them arise, if they can save thee in the time of thy trouble: for according to the number of thy cities are thy gods, O Judah.

29 Wherefore will ye plead with me? ye all have transgressed against me, saith the LORD.

30 In vain have I smitten your children; they received no correction: your own sword hath devoured your prophets, like a destroying lion.

31 ¶ O generation, see ye the word of the LORD. Have I been a wilderness unto Israel? a land of darkness? wherefore say my people, We are lords; we will come no more unto thee?

32 Can a maid forget her ornaments, or a bride her attire? yet my people have forgotten me days without number.

33 Why trimmest thou thy way to seek love? therefore hast thou also taught the wicked ones thy ways.

34 Also in thy skirts is found the blood of the souls of the poor innocents: I have not found it by secret search, but upon all these.

35 Yet thou sayest, Because I am innocent, surely his anger shall turn from me. Behold, I will plead with thee, because thou sayest, I have not sinned.

36 Why gaddest thou about so much to change thy way? thou also shalt be ashamed of Egypt, as thou wast ashamed of Assyria.

37 Yea, thou shalt go forth from him, and thine hands upon thine head: for the LORD hath rejected thy confidences, and thou shalt not prosper in them.

Jeremiah by Gustave Doré

CHAPTER 15

1 THEN said the LORD unto me, Though Moses and Samuel stood before me, yet my mind could not be toward this people: cast them out of my sight, and let them go forth.

2 And it shall come to pass, if they say unto thee, Whither shall we go forth? then thou shalt tell them, Thus saith the LORD; Such as are for death, to death; and such as are for the sword, to the sword; and such as are for the famine, to the famine; and such as are for the captivity, to the captivity.

3 And I will appoint over them four kinds, saith the LORD: the sword to slay, and the dogs to tear, and the fowls of the heaven, and the beasts of the earth, to devour and destroy.

4 And I will cause them to be removed into all kingdoms of the earth, because of Manasseh the son of Hezekiah king of Judah, for that which he did in Jerusalem.

5 For who shall have pity upon thee, O Jerusalem? or who shall bemoan thee? or who shall go aside to ask how thou doest?

6 Thou hast forsaken me, saith the LORD, thou art gone backward: therefore will I stretch out my hand against thee, and destroy thee; I am weary with repenting.

7 And I will fan them with a fan in the gates of the land; I will bereave them of children, I will destroy my people, since they return not from their ways.

8 Their widows are increased to me above the sand of the seas: I have brought upon them against the mother of the young men a spoiler at noonday: I have caused him to fall upon it suddenly, and terrors upon the city.

9 She that hath borne seven languisheth: she hath given up the ghost; her sun is gone down while it was yet day: she hath been ashamed and confounded: and the residue of them will I deliver to the sword before their enemies, saith the LORD.

10 ¶ Woe is me, my mother, that thou hast borne me a man of strife and a man of contention to the whole earth! I have neither lent on usury, nor men have lent to me on usury; yet every one of them doth curse me.

11 The LORD said, Verily it shall be well with thy remnant; verily I will cause the enemy to entreat thee well in the time of evil and in the time of affliction.

12 Shall iron break the northern iron and the steel?

13 Thy substance and thy treasures will I give to the spoil without price, and that for all thy sins, even in all thy borders.

14 And I will make thee to pass with thine enemies into a land which thou knowest not: for a fire is kindled in mine anger, which shall burn upon you.

15 ¶ O LORD, thou knowest: remember me, and visit me, and revenge me of my persecutors; take me not away in thy longsuffering: know that for thy sake I have suffered rebuke.

16 Thy words were found, and I did eat them; and thy word was unto me the joy and rejoicing of mine heart: for I am called by thy name, O LORD God of hosts.

17 I sat not in the assembly of the mockers, nor rejoiced; I sat alone because of thy hand: for thou hast filled me with indignation.

18 Why is my pain perpetual, and my wound incurable, which refuseth to be healed? wilt thou be altogether unto me as a liar, and as waters that fail?

19 ¶ Therefore thus saith the LORD, If thou return, then will I bring thee again, and thou shalt stand before me: and if thou take

JEREMIAH CHAPTER 15

Jeremiah 15:5–6—A Vision of Destruction

Jeremiah, no doubt beset with anguish, reveals to the people that Jerusalem faces certain destruction in the absence of repentance and spiritual reform. The vision imparted to Jeremiah reveals the impending desolution of the land at the hands of the forces of Nebuchadnezzar, who will sack Jerusalem and destroy or capture her inhabitants in 587 BC. This was the era in which Lehi and his family were removed from the territory so that a righteous branch of Israel could be spared and replanted in a promised land far from the spiritual decay and moral laxity that was contaminating the social fabric of the chosen people, the progeny of Abraham, Isaac, and Jacob.

The judgments of God never occur but what the prophets first sound the alarm—and that was the task of Jeremiah and his prophetic associates of the day, who were commanded to preach repentance with clarity and exactness.

forth the precious from the vile, thou shalt be as my mouth: let them return unto thee; but return not thou unto them.

20 And I will make thee unto this people a fenced brasen wall: and they shall fight against thee, but they shall not prevail against thee: for I am with thee to save thee and to deliver thee, saith the LORD.

21 And I will deliver thee out of the hand of the wicked, and I will redeem thee out of the hand of the terrible.

CHAPTER 16

1 THE word of the LORD came also unto me, saying,

2 Thou shalt not take thee a wife, neither shalt thou have sons or daughters in this place.

3 For thus saith the LORD concerning the sons and concerning the daughters that are born in this place, and concerning their mothers that bare them, and concerning their fathers that begat them in this land;

4 They shall die of grievous deaths; they shall not be lamented; neither shall they be buried; but they shall be as dung upon the face of the earth: and they shall be consumed by the sword, and by famine; and their carcases shall be meat for the fowls of heaven, and for the beasts of the earth.

5 For thus saith the LORD, Enter not into the house of mourning, neither go to lament nor bemoan them: for I have taken away my peace from this people, saith the LORD, even lovingkindness and mercies.

6 Both the great and the small shall die in this land: they shall not be buried, neither shall men lament for them, nor cut themselves, nor make themselves bald for them:

7 Neither shall men tear themselves for them in mourning, to comfort them for the dead; neither shall men give them the cup of consolation to drink for their father or for their mother.

8 Thou shalt not also go into the house of feasting, to sit with them to eat and to drink.

9 For thus saith the LORD of hosts, the God of Israel; Behold, I will cause to cease out of this place in your eyes, and in your days, the voice of mirth, and the voice of gladness, the voice of the bridegroom, and the voice of the bride.

10 ¶ And it shall come to pass, when thou shalt shew this people all these words, and they shall say unto thee, Wherefore hath the LORD pronounced all this great evil against us? or what is our iniquity? or what is our sin that we have committed against the LORD our God?

11 Then shalt thou say unto them, Because your fathers have forsaken me, saith the LORD, and have walked after other gods, and have served them, and have worshipped them, and have forsaken me, and have not kept my law;

12 And ye have done worse than your fathers; for, behold, ye walk every one after the imagination of his evil heart, that they may not hearken unto me:

13 Therefore will I cast you out of this land into a land that ye know not, neither ye nor your fathers; and there shall ye serve other gods day and night; where I will not shew you favour.

14 ¶ Therefore, behold, the days come, saith the LORD, that it shall no more be said, The LORD liveth, that brought up the children of Israel out of the land of Egypt;

JEREMIAH CHAPTER 16

Jeremiah 16—The Visionary Power of Jeremiah

Like Isaiah, the prophet Jeremiah was blessed with the gift of perceiving the majestic scope of the plan of God for His children from the foundations of the earth through the meridian of time and reaching forward until the latter days. Both of these great prophets discerned with clarity the noble workings of the infinite in the finite—the hand of the Lord in the sweep of history. Both were permitted to view things from the divine perspective and sound the warning voice—like all of God's prophets—with authority and with a heavenly commission. Thus Jeremiah sees in the dispersal of Israel through the Babylonian conquest in 587 BC—and their return to their homeland after seventy years of repentance—a type for the broader dispersal of the covenant people and their eventual gathering under the aegis of the Restoration of the gospel in the latter days.

He sees other grand parallels operating through the agenda of the Lord: The law of God in Moses' day is written on tablets of stone, but in future days it will be written in the mind and in the heart. The kings of Israel and Judah were wont to lust after strange gods and pollute the righteous vessels of the Lord; but Jeremiah sees the coming of a righteous King (the Messiah) who would execute judgment in purity and holiness. Moreover, Jeremiah sees the eventual gathering of the dispersed tribes through future fishers and hunters in an act of divine providence so grand as to equal and surpass the exodus from Egypt. Finally, the ancient covenant was broken by the promised people, but the new covenant will bring about a general reformation of spirituality to the extent that "they shall all know me" (Jer. 31:34).

All of this prophetic vision is captured in language of great power and dynamic force to persuade, to move, to effect change, to turn hearts and minds to the ways of God. All of this is laid out by Jeremiah in a panorama of bold and unequivocal plainness—a clarion call to repentance—to be "holy unto the Lord" (Jer. 31:40), with a promise of finding the Lord (Jer. 29:13–14) and being once again fruitful through the refreshing waters of the gospel of Jesus Christ (Jer. 17:7–8).

Jeremiah 16:16–17—The Lord's Mission

The Lord operates according to the sacred mission to "bring to pass the immortality and eternal life of man" (Moses 1:3). He will gather and sift, seek and find, bless and unify—as He unfolds His eternal plan to enlarge His Kingdom and prepare His children for eternal glory and happiness.

15 But, The LORD liveth, that brought up the children of Israel from the land of the north, and from all the lands whither he had driven them: and I will bring them again into their land that I gave unto their fathers.

16 ¶ Behold, I will send for many fishers, saith the LORD, and they shall fish them; and after will I send for many hunters, and they shall hunt them from every mountain, and from every hill, and out of the holes of the rocks.

17 For mine eyes are upon all their ways: they are not hid from my face, neither is their iniquity hid from mine eyes.

18 And first I will recompense their iniquity and their sin double; because they have defiled my land, they have filled mine inheritance with the carcases of their detestable and abominable things.

19 O LORD, my strength, and my fortress, and my refuge in the day of affliction, the Gentiles shall come unto thee from the ends of the earth, and shall say, Surely our fathers have inherited lies, vanity, and things wherein there is no profit.

20 Shall a man make gods unto himself, and they are no gods?

21 Therefore, behold, I will this once cause them to know, I will cause them to know mine hand and my might; and they shall know that my name is The LORD.

CHAPTER 20

1 NOW Pashur the son of Immer the priest, who was also chief governor in the house of the LORD, heard that Jeremiah prophesied these things.

2 Then Pashur smote Jeremiah the prophet, and put him in the stocks that were in the high gate of Benjamin, which was by the house of the LORD.

3 And it came to pass on the morrow, that Pashur brought forth Jeremiah out of the stocks. Then said Jeremiah unto him, The LORD hath not called thy name Pashur, but Magor-missabib.

4 For thus saith the LORD, Behold, I will make thee a terror to thyself, and to all thy friends: and they shall fall by the sword of their enemies, and thine eyes shall behold it: and I will give all Judah into the hand of the king of Babylon, and he shall carry them captive into Babylon, and shall slay them with the sword.

5 Moreover I will deliver all the strength of this city, and all the labours thereof, and all the precious things thereof, and all the treasures of the kings of Judah will I give into the hand of their enemies, which shall spoil them, and take them, and carry them to Babylon.

6 And thou, Pashur, and all that dwell in thine house shall go into captivity: and thou shalt come to Babylon, and there thou shalt die, and shalt be buried there, thou, and all thy friends, to whom thou hast prophesied lies.

7 ¶ O LORD, thou hast deceived me, and I was deceived: thou art stronger than I, and hast prevailed: I am in derision daily, every one mocketh me.

8 For since I spake, I cried out, I cried violence and spoil; because the word of the LORD was made a reproach unto me, and a derision, daily.

9 Then I said, I will not make mention of him, nor speak any more in his name. But his word was in mine heart as a burning fire shut up in my bones, and I was weary with forbearing, and I could not stay.

JEREMIAH CHAPTER 20

"The Old and New Testaments, the Book of Mormon, and the book of Doctrine and Covenants . . . are like a lighthouse in the ocean or a finger-post which points out the road we should travel. Where do they point? To the fountain of light. . . . by them we can establish the doctrine of Christ." —Brigham Young, JD 8:129, 22 July 1860

Jeremiah 20:7–9—Jeremiah's Anguish

Jeremiah, in anguish over his confinement and reproach, cries unto the Lord and confesses his burdens and feelings of suffering. He would retreat in silence—yet the word of the Lord was inflamed within him and he could not hold himself back from acting with valor in his prophetic office. He had to speak the word of the Lord.

Jeremiah's status and condition were not unlike that of Nephi, as father Lehi explained to the murmuring brothers: "And ye have murmured because he hath been plain unto you. Ye say that he hath used sharpness; ye say that he hath been angry with you; but behold, his sharpness was the sharpness of the power of the word of God, which was in him; and that which ye call anger was the truth, according to that which is in God, which he could not restrain, manifesting boldly concerning your iniquities" (2 Ne. 1:26).

Jeremiah's inability to forbear was also like that of Ether: "And Ether was a prophet of the Lord; wherefore Ether came forth in the days of Coriantumr, and began to prophesy unto the people, for he could not be restrained because of the Spirit of the Lord which was in him" (Ether 12:2).

The moment of suffering and anguish reflected in Jeremiah's situation anticipated the feelings of the Prophet Joseph Smith in Liberty Jail concerning the tribulation of the Saints in his day:

> O GOD, where art thou? And where is the pavilion that covereth thy hiding place?
>
> How long shall thy hand be stayed, and thine eye, yea thy pure eye, behold from the eternal heavens the wrongs of thy people and of thy servants, and thine ear be penetrated with their cries?
>
> Yea, O Lord, how long shall they suffer these wrongs and unlawful oppressions, before thine heart shall be softened toward them, and thy bowels be moved with compassion toward them? (D&C 121:1–3)

The message to Joseph was doubtless the same message of comfort that the Lord has for all of His chosen servants:

> . . . know thou, my son, that all these things shall give thee experience, and shall be for thy good.
>
> The Son of Man hath descended below them all. Art thou greater than he?
>
> Therefore, hold on thy way, and the priesthood shall remain with thee; for their bounds are set, they cannot pass. Thy days are known, and thy years shall not be numbered less; therefore, fear not what man can do, for God shall be with you forever and ever. (D&C 122:7–9)

10 ¶ For I heard the defaming of many, fear on every side. Report, say they, and we will report it. All my familiars watched for my halting, saying, Peradventure he will be enticed, and we shall prevail against him, and we shall take our revenge on him.

11 But the LORD is with me as a mighty terrible one: therefore my persecutors shall stumble, and they shall not prevail: they shall be greatly ashamed; for they shall not prosper: their everlasting confusion shall never be forgotten.

12 But, O LORD of hosts, that triest the righteous, and seest the reins and the heart, let me see thy vengeance on them: for unto thee have I opened my cause.

13 Sing unto the LORD, praise ye the LORD: for he hath delivered the soul of the poor from the hand of evildoers.

14 ¶ Cursed be the day wherein I was born: let not the day wherein my mother bare me be blessed.

15 Cursed be the man who brought tidings to my father, saying, A man child is born unto thee; making him very glad.

16 And let that man be as the cities which the LORD overthrew, and repented not: and let him hear the cry in the morning, and the shouting at noontide;

17 Because he slew me not from the womb; or that my mother might have been my grave, and her womb to be always great with me.

18 Wherefore came I forth out of the womb to see labour and sorrow, that my days should be consumed with shame?

CHAPTER 23

1 WOE be unto the pastors that destroy and scatter the sheep of my pasture! saith the LORD.

2 Therefore thus saith the LORD God of Israel against the pastors that feed my people; Ye have scattered my flock, and driven them away, and have not visited them: behold, I will visit upon you the evil of your doings, saith the LORD.

3 And I will gather the remnant of my flock out of all countries whither I have driven them, and will bring them again to their folds; and they shall be fruitful and increase.

4 And I will set up shepherds over them which shall feed them: and they shall fear no more, nor be dismayed, neither shall they be lacking, saith the LORD.

5 ¶ Behold, the days come, saith the LORD, that I will raise unto David a righteous Branch, and a King shall reign and prosper, and shall execute judgment and justice in the earth.

6 In his days Judah shall be saved, and Israel shall dwell safely: and this is his name whereby he shall be called, THE LORD OUR RIGHTEOUSNESS.

7 Therefore, behold, the days come, saith the LORD, that they shall no more say, The LORD liveth, which brought up the children of Israel out of the land of Egypt;

8 But, The LORD liveth, which brought up and which led the seed of the house of Israel out of the north country, and from all countries whither I had driven them; and they shall dwell in their own land.

9 ¶ Mine heart within me is broken because of the prophets; all my bones shake; I am like a drunken man, and like a man whom wine hath overcome, because of the LORD, and because of the words of his holiness.

JEREMIAH CHAPTER 23

Jeremiah 23:1-4—Pastors and Shepherds

The Lord pronounces a judgment against the "pastors" who have led His sheep astray by withholding the spiritual nurture of the gospel, thus causing them to be scattered. In response, the Lord shall gather His sheep once again and commission "shepherds" who shall feed them with righteous sustenance, replacing their fear with courage, their dismay with peace, and their lacking with the abundance of eternal glory.

Jeremiah 23:5—Branch

The title *Branch* is one of many designations for the Lord Jesus Christ. For example, He is elsewhere identified as the Builder of the temple of the Lord: ". . . Thus speaketh the LORD of hosts, saying, Behold the man whose name *is* The BRANCH [i.e., the Messiah]; and he shall grow up out of his place, and he shall build the temple of the LORD: Even he shall build the temple of the LORD; and he shall bear the glory, and shall sit and rule upon his throne; and he shall be a priest upon his throne: and the counsel of peace shall be between them both" (Zech. 6:12–13).

The Branch was also referred to by Zechariah in an earlier passage concerning Joshua, a high priest who experienced a rite of purification, being clothed in clean garments and placed under a covenant of obedience while participating in an assemblage of associates—probably symbolic of the process of spiritual rejuvenation and recovery concerning the exiles returning from Babylonian captivity (see Zech. 3:7–8).

Jeremiah also refers to the Branch in a later passage: "In those days, and at that time, will I cause the Branch of righteousness to grow up unto David; and he shall execute judgment and righteousness in the land. In those days shall Judah be saved, and Jerusalem shall dwell safely: and this *is the name* wherewith she shall be called, The LORD our righteousness" (Jer. 33:15–16).

Jeremiah 23:7-18—Words of Warning Regarding False Prophets

These words of warning adjure the listener to beware of those who prophesy according to their own internal vision and not the word of the Lord, who promise peace by despising the Lord, and who promise people security by following after the vain imaginations of their own hearts rather than heeding the counsel of the Lord. The word of the Lord is clear: If you want peace and security, then listen to the Lord and His prophets. This chapter of Jeremiah is a fundamental review of false prophets and their destructive counsel.

10 For the land is full of adulterers; for because of swearing the land mourneth; the pleasant places of the wilderness are dried up, and their course is evil, and their force is not right.

11 For both prophet and priest are profane; yea, in my house have I found their wickedness, saith the LORD.

12 Wherefore their way shall be unto them as slippery ways in the darkness: they shall be driven on, and fall therein: for I will bring evil upon them, even the year of their visitation, saith the LORD.

13 And I have seen folly in the prophets of Samaria; they prophesied in Baal, and caused my people Israel to err.

14 I have seen also in the prophets of Jerusalem an horrible thing: they commit adultery, and walk in lies: they strengthen also the hands of evildoers, that none doth return from his wickedness: they are all of them unto me as Sodom, and the inhabitants thereof as Gomorrah.

15 Therefore thus saith the LORD of hosts concerning the prophets; Behold, I will feed them with wormwood, and make them drink the water of gall: for from the prophets of Jerusalem is profaneness gone forth into all the land.

16 Thus saith the LORD of hosts, Hearken not unto the words of the prophets that prophesy unto you: they make you vain: they speak a vision of their own heart, and not out of the mouth of the LORD.

17 They say still unto them that despise me, The LORD hath said, Ye shall have peace; and they say unto every one that walketh after the imagination of his own heart, No evil shall come upon you.

18 For who hath stood in the counsel of the LORD, and hath perceived and heard his word? who hath marked his word, and heard it?

19 Behold, a whirlwind of the LORD is gone forth in fury, even a grievous whirlwind: it shall fall grievously upon the head of the wicked.

20 The anger of the LORD shall not return, until he have executed, and till he have performed the thoughts of his heart: in the latter days ye shall consider it perfectly.

21 I have not sent these prophets, yet they ran: I have not spoken to them, yet they prophesied.

22 But if they had stood in my counsel, and had caused my people to hear my words, then they should have turned them from their evil way, and from the evil of their doings.

23 Am I a God at hand, saith the LORD, and not a God afar off?

24 Can any hide himself in secret places that I shall not see him? saith the LORD. Do not I fill heaven and earth? saith the LORD.

25 I have heard what the prophets said, that prophesy lies in my name, saying, I have dreamed, I have dreamed.

26 How long shall this be in the heart of the prophets that prophesy lies? yea, they are prophets of the deceit of their own heart;

27 Which think to cause my people to forget my name by their dreams which they tell every man to his neighbour, as their fathers have forgotten my name for Baal.

28 The prophet that hath a dream, let him tell a dream; and he that hath my word, let him speak my word faithfully. What is the chaff to the wheat? saith the LORD.

29 Is not my word like as a fire? saith the LORD; and like a hammer that breaketh the rock in pieces?

30 Therefore, behold, I am against the prophets, saith the LORD, that steal my words every one from his neighbour.

NOTES:

31 Behold, I am against the prophets, saith the LORD, that use their tongues, and say, He saith.

32 Behold, I am against them that prophesy false dreams, saith the LORD, and do tell them, and cause my people to err by their lies, and by their lightness; yet I sent them not, nor commanded them: therefore they shall not profit this people at all, saith the LORD.

33 ¶ And when this people, or the prophet, or a priest, shall ask thee, saying, What is the burden of the LORD? thou shalt then say unto them, What burden? I will even forsake you, saith the LORD.

34 And as for the prophet, and the priest, and the people, that shall say, The burden of the LORD, I will even punish that man and his house.

35 Thus shall ye say every one to his neighbour, and every one to his brother, What hath the LORD answered? and, What hath the LORD spoken?

36 And the burden of the LORD shall ye mention no more: for every man's word shall be his burden; for ye have perverted the words of the living God, of the LORD of hosts our God.

37 Thus shalt thou say to the prophet, What hath the LORD answered thee? and, What hath the LORD spoken?

38 But since ye say, The burden of the LORD; therefore thus saith the LORD; Because ye say this word, The burden of the LORD, and I have sent unto you, saying, Ye shall not say, The burden of the LORD;

39 Therefore, behold, I, even I, will utterly forget you, and I will forsake you, and the city that I gave you and your fathers, and cast you out of my presence:

40 And I will bring an everlasting reproach upon you, and a perpetual shame, which shall not be forgotten.

Baruch Writing Jeremiah's Prophecies by Gustave Doré

CHAPTER 26

1 IN the beginning of the reign of Jehoiakim the son of Josiah king of Judah came this word from the LORD, saying,

2 Thus saith the LORD; Stand in the court of the LORD's house, and speak unto all the cities of Judah, which come to worship in the LORD's house, all the words that I command thee to speak unto them; diminish not a word:

3 If so be they will hearken, and turn every man from his evil way, that I may repent me of the evil, which I purpose to do unto them because of the evil of their doings.

4 And thou shalt say unto them, Thus saith the LORD; If ye will not hearken to me, to walk in my law, which I have set before you,

5 To hearken to the words of my servants the prophets, whom I sent unto you, both rising up early, and sending them, but ye have not hearkened;

6 Then will I make this house like Shiloh, and will make this city a curse to all the nations of the earth.

7 So the priests and the prophets and all the people heard Jeremiah speaking these words in the house of the LORD.

8 ¶ Now it came to pass, when Jeremiah had made an end of speaking all that the LORD had commanded him to speak unto all the people, that the priests and the prophets and all the people took him, saying, Thou shalt surely die.

9 Why hast thou prophesied in the name of the LORD, saying, This house shall be like Shiloh, and this city shall be desolate without an inhabitant? And all the people were gathered against Jeremiah in the house of the LORD.

10 ¶ When the princes of Judah heard these things, then they came up from the king's house unto the house of the LORD, and sat down in the entry of the new gate of the LORD's house.

11 Then spake the priests and the prophets unto the princes and to all the people, saying, This man is worthy to die; for he hath prophesied against this city, as ye have heard with your ears.

12 ¶ Then spake Jeremiah unto all the princes and to all the people, saying, The LORD sent me to prophesy against this house and against this city all the words that ye have heard.

13 Therefore now amend your ways and your doings, and obey the voice of the LORD your God; and the LORD will repent him of the evil that he hath pronounced against you.

14 As for me, behold, I am in your hand: do with me as seemeth good and meet unto you.

15 But know ye for certain, that if ye put me to death, ye shall surely bring innocent blood upon yourselves, and upon this city, and upon the inhabitants thereof: for of a truth the LORD hath sent me unto you to speak all these words in your ears.

16 ¶ Then said the princes and all the people unto the priests and to the prophets; This man is not worthy to die: for he hath spoken to us in the name of the LORD our God.

17 Then rose up certain of the elders of the land, and spake to all the assembly of the people, saying,

18 Micah the Morasthite prophesied in the days of Hezekiah king of Judah, and spake to all the people of Judah, saying, Thus saith the LORD of hosts; Zion shall be plowed like a field, and Jerusalem shall become heaps, and the mountain of the house as the high places of a forest.

19 Did Hezekiah king of Judah and all Judah put him at all to death? did he not fear the LORD, and besought the LORD, and the LORD

JEREMIAH CHAPTER 26

Jeremiah 26:6—Shiloh

Shiloh was a city of Ephraim, north of Jerusalem (see Judges 21:19), where the tabernacle was set up during the time of the judges (see Josh. 18:1). Shiloh was apparently destroyed by the Philistines when they confiscated the ark (see 1 Sam. 4). Thus Shiloh was a symbol of the impending fate of Jerusalem at the hands of the Babylonians.

Jeremiah 26:12–15—Response of the People to Warnings from a Prophet of God

What was typically the response of the people at the time—especially the leadership in power—to the warnings of a prophet of God? Either to ignore the warnings or set up a strategy to slay the prophets. The case of Jeremiah was no different, in that his life was put on the line. His response of courage and candor anticipates the words of Abinadi when wicked king Noah and his priests call for his execution:

> Now Abinadi said unto him: I say unto you, I will not recall the words which I have spoken unto you concerning this people, for they are true; and that ye may know of their surety I have suffered myself that I have fallen into your hands.
>
> Yea, and I will suffer even until death, and I will not recall my words, and they shall stand as a testimony against you. And if ye slay me ye will shed innocent blood, and this shall also stand as a testimony against you at the last day. (Mosiah 17:9–10)

repented him of the evil which he had pronounced against them? Thus might we procure great evil against our souls.

20 And there was also a man that prophesied in the name of the LORD, Urijah the son of Shemaiah of Kirjath-jearim, who prophesied against this city and against this land according to all the words of Jeremiah:

21 And when Jehoiakim the king, with all his mighty men, and all the princes, heard his words, the king sought to put him to death: but when Urijah heard it, he was afraid, and fled, and went into Egypt;

22 And Jehoiakim the king sent men into Egypt, namely, Elnathan the son of Achbor, and certain men with him into Egypt.

23 And they fetched forth Urijah out of Egypt, and brought him unto Jehoiakim the king; who slew him with the sword, and cast his dead body into the graves of the common people.

24 Nevertheless the hand of Ahikam the son of Shaphan was with Jeremiah, that they should not give him into the hand of the people to put him to death.

CHAPTER 29

1 NOW these are the words of the letter that Jeremiah the prophet sent from Jerusalem unto the residue of the elders which were carried away captives, and to the priests, and to the prophets, and to all the people whom Nebuchadnezzar had carried away captive from Jerusalem to Babylon;

2 (After that Jeconiah the king, and the queen, and the eunuchs, the princes of Judah and Jerusalem, and the carpenters, and the smiths, were departed from Jerusalem;)

3 By the hand of Elasah the son of Shaphan, and Gemariah the son of Hilkiah, (whom Zedekiah king of Judah sent unto Babylon to Nebuchadnezzar king of Babylon) saying,

4 Thus saith the LORD of hosts, the God of Israel, unto all that are carried away captives, whom I have caused to be carried away from Jerusalem unto Babylon;

5 Build ye houses, and dwell in them; and plant gardens, and eat the fruit of them;

6 Take ye wives, and beget sons and daughters; and take wives for your sons, and give your daughters to husbands, that they may bear sons and daughters; that ye may be increased there, and not diminished.

7 And seek the peace of the city whither I have caused you to be carried away captives, and pray unto the LORD for it: for in the peace thereof shall ye have peace.

8 ¶ For thus saith the LORD of hosts, the God of Israel; Let not your prophets and your diviners, that be in the midst of you, deceive you, neither hearken to your dreams which ye cause to be dreamed.

9 For they prophesy falsely unto you in my name: I have not sent them, saith the LORD.

10 ¶ For thus saith the LORD, That after seventy years be accomplished at Babylon I will visit you, and perform my good word toward you, in causing you to return to this place.

11 For I know the thoughts that I think toward you, saith the LORD, thoughts of peace, and not of evil, to give you an expected end.

JEREMIAH CHAPTER 29

Jeremiah 29:10–11—The Process of Gathering

Just as Jeremiah was shown the impending Babylonian captivity and scattering, he was also shown the time of gathering to follow, when the Jewish people would again return to their homeland.

At times the Lord scatters Israel as a result of wayward behavior; at other times He scatters Israel as a protective measure, or to sustain the process of spreading His word among the nations. When he gathers Israel, it is always to sustain the covenant process of building a Zion society. The concept of the gathering of Israel—pervasive throughout the scriptures—is memorialized in the tenth Article of Faith: "We believe in the literal gathering of Israel and in the restoration of the Ten Tribes; that Zion (the New Jerusalem) will be built upon the American continent; that Christ will reign personally upon the earth; and, that the earth will be renewed and receive its paradisiacal glory."

What is the Lord's ultimate design in gathering Israel? The Lord loves His children with an infinite love. He yearns to bring them together in the interests of their happiness and spiritual and temporal security, "even as a hen gathereth her chickens under her wings, even as many as will hearken to my voice and humble themselves before me, and call upon me in mighty prayer" (D&C 29:2). At times this gathering is framed in specific terms, such as the call to flock to Kirtland (see D&C 37) or the call to assemble in Missouri (see D&C 57:3). At other times the call is expressed in general terms: "And it shall come to pass that the righteous shall be gathered out from among all nations, and shall come to Zion, singing with songs of everlasting joy" (D&C 45:71). In addition, the gathering is expressed in the commandment to "stand in holy places" (D&C 45:32; 87:8; 101:22) and/or to labor in one's own land for the building up of stakes and erecting temples to the Most High. Whatever the prophets of the Lord direct, that we should do.

The gathering is, at its heart, the organizational process that supports the fulfillment of the Lord's design around His covenant relationship with His elect. In effect, the gathering is a covenant activity by means of which Deity accomplishes the eternal mission of bringing about the immortality and eternal life of man (see Moses 1:39). We come together in obedience to gospel principles so that we might enjoy the blessings of priesthood ordinances of salvation and exaltation and the guidance of a living prophet.

The Prophet Joseph Smith taught that the gathering was a sacred design established in the premortal councils of heaven. It was Sunday, June 11, 1843. The Prophet Joseph Smith was addressing a large assembly of Saints in Nauvoo. He cited the famous passage from Matthew 23:37: "O Jerusalem, Jerusalem, thou that killest the prophets, and stonest them which are sent unto thee, how oft would I have gathered thy children together, even as a hen gathereth her chickens under her wings, and ye would not!" Using that scripture as his text, Joseph Smith told the audience that he felt inspired to speak of the gathering of Israel, stating: "It

12 Then shall ye call upon me, and ye shall go and pray unto me, and I will hearken unto you.

13 And ye shall seek me, and find me, when ye shall search for me with all your heart.

14 And I will be found of you, saith the LORD: and I will turn away your captivity, and I will gather you from all the nations, and from all the places whither I have driven you, saith the LORD; and I will bring you again into the place whence I caused you to be carried away captive.

15 ¶ Because ye have said, The LORD hath raised us up prophets in Babylon;

16 Know that thus saith the LORD of the king that sitteth upon the throne of David, and of all the people that dwelleth in this city, and of your brethren that are not gone forth with you into captivity;

17 Thus saith the LORD of hosts; Behold, I will send upon them the sword, the famine, and the pestilence, and will make them like vile figs, that cannot be eaten, they are so evil.

18 And I will persecute them with the sword, with the famine, and with the pestilence, and will deliver them to be removed to all the kingdoms of the earth, to be a curse, and an astonishment, and an hissing, and a reproach, among all the nations whither I have driven them:

19 Because they have not hearkened to my words, saith the LORD, which I sent unto them by my servants the prophets, rising up early and sending them; but ye would not hear, saith the LORD.

20 ¶ Hear ye therefore the word of the LORD, all ye of the captivity, whom I have sent from Jerusalem to Babylon:

21 Thus saith the LORD of hosts, the God of Israel, of Ahab the son of Kolaiah, and of Zedekiah the son of Maaseiah, which prophesy a lie unto you in my name; Behold, I will deliver them into the hand of Nebuchadrezzar king of Babylon; and he shall slay them before your eyes;

22 And of them shall be taken up a curse by all the captivity of Judah which are in Babylon, saying, The LORD make thee like Zedekiah and like Ahab, whom the king of Babylon roasted in the fire;

23 Because they have committed villany in Israel, and have committed adultery with their neighbours' wives, and have spoken lying words in my name, which I have not commanded them; even I know, and am a witness, saith the LORD.

24 ¶ Thus shalt thou also speak to Shemaiah the Nehelamite, saying,

25 Thus speaketh the LORD of hosts, the God of Israel, saying, Because thou hast sent letters in thy name unto all the people that are at Jerusalem, and to Zephaniah the son of Maaseiah the priest, and to all the priests, saying,

26 The LORD hath made thee priest in the stead of Jehoiada the priest, that ye should be officers in the house of the LORD, for every man that is mad, and maketh himself a prophet, that thou shouldest put him in prison, and in the stocks.

27 Now therefore why hast thou not reproved Jeremiah of Anathoth, which maketh himself a prophet to you?

28 For therefore he sent unto us in Babylon, saying, This captivity is long: build ye houses, and dwell in them; and plant gardens, and eat the fruit of them.

29 And Zephaniah the priest read this letter in the ears of Jeremiah the prophet.

was the design of the councils of heaven before the world was that the principles and laws of the priesthood should be predicated upon the gathering of the people in every age of the world. Jesus did everything to gather the people, and they would not be gathered, and He therefore poured out curses upon them. Ordinances instituted in the heavens before the foundations of the world, in the priesthood, for the salvation of men, are not to be altered or changed. All must be saved on the same principles. It is for the same purpose that God gathers together His people in the last days, to build unto the Lord a house to prepare them for the ordinances and endowments, washings and anointings, etc. . . . If a man gets a fulness of the priesthood of God, he has to get it in the same way that Jesus Christ obtained it, and that was by keeping all the commandments and obeying all the ordinances of the house of the Lord" (*HC* 5:423–24).

Furthermore, the Prophet Joseph made clear that the Lord will empower and direct the gathering: "Every needful blessing will be provided to those who seek to gather the lost sheep of Israel. Every help and support from heaven will be brought to bear for the faithful and devoted who feel in their hearts the urgency to come home to holy places of Zion" (*TPJS*, 163, 183).

Jeremiah 29:12–14—The Lord's Invitation

The Lord extends to everyone the invitation to come unto Him and be saved. He hears our prayers and supplications. When we seek Him with all our heart, He is readily accessible. He gathers us unto Himself—whether as a chosen individual, a faithful family, or as an entire nation seeking to be part of His fold. In one moment we might feel His corrective hand bringing us back toward the strait and narrow pathway; in another moment we feel His embrace as we find success in living His commandments more fully and with greater devotion. Always we are grateful for His love and mercy.

Jeremiah 29:24—Shemaiah

Shemaiah (meaning: the Lord heareth) was a false prophet at the time of Jeremiah who attempted to usurp power and undermine the cause of the Lord at the time of the Babylonian captivity (see Jer. 29:24). As a lesson to all who pridefully arrogate authority unto themselves without any divine commission, Shemaiah was sternly reproved by the Lord through Jeremiah:

Send to all them of the captivity, saying, Thus saith the LORD concerning Shemaiah the Nehelamite; Because that Shemaiah hath prophesied unto you, and I sent him not, and he caused you to trust in a lie:

Therefore thus saith the LORD; Behold, I will punish Shemaiah the Nehelamite, and his seed: he shall not have a man to dwell among this people; neither shall he behold the good that I will do for my people, saith the LORD; because he hath taught rebellion against the LORD. (Jer. 29:31–32)

30 ¶ Then came the word of the LORD unto Jeremiah, saying,

31 Send to all them of the captivity, saying, Thus saith the LORD concerning Shemaiah the Nehelamite; Because that Shemaiah hath prophesied unto you, and I sent him not, and he caused you to trust in a lie:

32 Therefore thus saith the LORD; Behold, I will punish Shemaiah the Nehelamite, and his seed: he shall not have a man to dwell among this people; neither shall he behold the good that I will do for my people, saith the LORD; because he hath taught rebellion against the LORD.

CHAPTER 31

1 AT the same time, saith the LORD, will I be the God of all the families of Israel, and they shall be my people.

2 Thus saith the LORD, The people which were left of the sword found grace in the wilderness; even Israel, when I went to cause him to rest.

3 The LORD hath appeared of old unto me, saying, Yea, I have loved thee with an everlasting love: therefore with lovingkindness have I drawn thee.

4 Again I will build thee, and thou shalt be built, O virgin of Israel: thou shalt again be adorned with thy tabrets, and shalt go forth in the dances of them that make merry.

5 Thou shalt yet plant vines upon the mountains of Samaria: the planters shall plant, and shall eat them as common things.

6 For there shall be a day, that the watchmen upon the mount Ephraim shall cry, Arise ye, and let us go up to Zion unto the LORD our God.

7 For thus saith the LORD; Sing with gladness for Jacob, and shout among the chief of the nations: publish ye, praise ye, and say, O LORD, save thy people, the remnant of Israel.

8 Behold, I will bring them from the north country, and gather them from the coasts of the earth, and with them the blind and the lame, the woman with child and her that travaileth with child together: a great company shall return thither.

9 They shall come with weeping, and with supplications, will I lead them: I will cause them to walk by the rivers of waters in a straight way, wherein they shall not stumble: for I am a father to Israel, and Ephraim is my firstborn.

10 ¶ Hear the word of the LORD, O ye nations, and declare it in the isles afar off, and say, He that scattered Israel will gather him, and keep him, as a shepherd doth his flock.

11 For the LORD hath redeemed Jacob, and ransomed him from the hand of him that was stronger than he.

12 Therefore they shall come and sing in the height of Zion, and shall flow together to the goodness of the LORD, for wheat, and for wine, and for oil, and for the young of the flock and of the herd: and their soul shall be as a watered garden; and they shall not sorrow any more at all.

13 Then shall the virgin rejoice in the dance, both young men and old together: for I will turn their mourning into joy, and will comfort them, and make them rejoice from their sorrow.

14 And I will satiate the soul of the priests with fatness, and my people shall be satisfied with my goodness, saith the LORD.

15 ¶ Thus saith the LORD; A voice was heard in Ramah, lamentation, and bitter weeping; Rahel weeping for her children refused to be comforted for her children, because they were not.

JEREMIAH CHAPTER 31

"When we have faith to understand that He must dictate and that we must be perfectly submissive to Him, then we shall begin to rapidly collect the intelligence that is bestowed upon the nations, for all this intelligence belongs to Zion. All the knowledge, wisdom, power, and glory that have been bestowed upon the nations of the earth, from the days of Adam till now, must be gathered home to Zion."
—Brigham Young, *JD* 8:279, 3 June 1860

Jeremiah 31:1–31—The Prophetic Commission

When the Lord commissioned Isaiah in vision, an angelic personage placed "a live coal" on Isaiah's mouth as an emblem of the dispersal of the new prophet's self-perceived inadequacy (see Isa. 6:6–7). Thus he was prepared by the hand of the Lord to take upon himself the prophetic stewardship.

When Jeremiah was called, the Lord extended His hand again and touched Jeremiah's mouth, saying "Behold, I have put my words in thy mouth" (Jer. 1:9). Thus he had within him the essence of the message he was to proclaim.

When Ezekiel was called, the Lord showed him in vision a roll upon which the message of heaven to the current rebellious generation was written (see Ezek. 2:9–10), and caused him to eat that roll in order to inculcate within himself the message he was to deliver—"and it was in my mouth honey as honey for sweetness" (Ezek. 3:3).

The Lord touches his prophets and imbues them with a sense of divine purpose. They have the law of the Lord written in their minds and hearts. The same process applies to all of God's children. His will is to touch them all and write His word of truth upon their inward being so that they might know Him and walk according to the tenets of the divine covenant. Only when we have accepted His will in all things are we made parties to the covenant of grace and mercy intended to govern our relationship with our Father in Heaven and His Son, Jesus Christ. Only then can we come to understand the sacred implication of the Lord's promise to Jeremiah: "I will make a new covenant with the house of Israel" (Jer. 31:31), for we will know at that time that this new covenant applies personally to ourselves.

Jeremiah 31:32–34—The Lord Will Write His Law in Our Hearts

For ancient Israel, the Lord wrote His law on the tablets of Moses; for Israel of the latter-day gathering, the Lord writes His law in their hearts and inward parts (see Jer. 31:33). The greatest knowledge of all is the knowledge of the Lord and His ways, for to know the Lord and keep His covenant is to know joy and peace and have the hope of eternal life.

"Behold, I will send for many fishers, saith the Lord, and they shall fish them; and after will I send for many hunters, and they shall hunt them from every mountain, and from every hill, and out of the holes of the rocks. For mine eyes are upon all their ways. . . ." (Jer. 16:16–17)

16 Thus saith the LORD; Refrain thy voice from weeping, and thine eyes from tears: for thy work shall be rewarded, saith the LORD; and they shall come again from the land of the enemy.

17 And there is hope in thine end, saith the LORD, that thy children shall come again to their own border.

18 ¶ I have surely heard Ephraim bemoaning himself thus; Thou hast chastised me, and I was chastised, as a bullock unaccustomed to the yoke: turn thou me, and I shall be turned; for thou art the LORD my God.

19 Surely after that I was turned, I repented; and after that I was instructed, I smote upon my thigh: I was ashamed, yea, even confounded, because I did bear the reproach of my youth.

20 Is Ephraim my dear son? is he a pleasant child? for since I spake against him, I do earnestly remember him still: therefore my bowels are troubled for him; I will surely have mercy upon him, saith the LORD.

21 Set thee up waymarks, make thee high heaps: set thine heart toward the highway, even the way which thou wentest: turn again, O virgin of Israel, turn again to these thy cities.

22 ¶ How long wilt thou go about, O thou backsliding daughter? for the LORD hath created a new thing in the earth, A woman shall compass a man.

23 Thus saith the LORD of hosts, the God of Israel; As yet they shall use this speech in the land of Judah and in the cities thereof, when I shall bring again their captivity; The LORD bless thee, O habitation of justice, and mountain of holiness.

24 And there shall dwell in Judah itself, and in all the cities thereof together, husbandmen, and they that go forth with flocks.

25 For I have satiated the weary soul, and I have replenished every sorrowful soul.

26 Upon this I awaked, and beheld; and my sleep was sweet unto me.

27 ¶ Behold, the days come, saith the LORD, that I will sow the house of Israel and the house of Judah with the seed of man, and with the seed of beast.

28 And it shall come to pass, that like as I have watched over them, to pluck up, and to break down, and to throw down, and to destroy, and to afflict; so will I watch over them, to build, and to plant, saith the LORD.

29 In those days they shall say no more, The fathers have eaten a sour grape, and the children's teeth are set on edge.

30 But every one shall die for his own iniquity: every man that eateth the sour grape, his teeth shall be set on edge.

31 ¶ Behold, the days come, saith the LORD, that I will make a new covenant with the house of Israel, and with the house of Judah:

32 Not according to the covenant that I made with their fathers in the day that I took them by the hand to bring them out of the land of Egypt; which my covenant they brake, although I was an husband unto them, saith the LORD:

33 But this shall be the covenant that I will make with the house of Israel; After those days, saith the LORD, I will put my law in their inward parts, and write it in their hearts; and will be their God, and they shall be my people.

34 And they shall teach no more every man his neighbour, and every man his brother, saying, Know the LORD: for they shall all know me, from the least of them unto the greatest of them, saith the LORD: for I will forgive their iniquity, and I will remember their sin no more.

"Behold, the days come, saith the Lord, that I will raise unto David a righteous Branch, and a King shall reign and prosper, and shall execute judgment and justice in the earth. In his days Judah shall be saved, and Israel shall dwell safely: and this is his name whereby he shall be called, The Lord Our Righteousness." (Jer. 23:5–6)

"Therefore, behold, the days come, saith the Lord, that they shall no more say, The Lord liveth, which brought up the children of Israel out of the land of Egypt; But, The Lord liveth, which brought up and which led the seed of the house of Israel out of the north country, and from all countries whither I had driven them; and they shall dwell in their own land." (Jer. 23:7–8; compare Jer. 16:14–16)

"But this shall be the covenant that I will make with the house of Israel; After those days, saith the Lord, I will put my law in their inward parts, and write it in their hearts; and will be their God, and they shall be my people." (Jer. 31:33.)

"And ye shall seek me, and find me, when ye shall search for me with all your heart." (Jer. 29:13.)

The governing theme in these passages from Jeremiah is *covenant*—meaning the sacred relationship and formal bond between the Lord and His people. The Lord works by covenant. He draws people in by covenant. He teaches through covenant. Whenever a Zion people come together, it is by covenant. The word itself embodies the process, for *covenant* means, literally, "a coming together."

Jeremiah was imbued with a sense of covenant in what he was given to perceive and discern through prophetic vision. Like all of the Lord's prophets, he clearly saw the providential design behind the sweep of history, for the hand of God was extended to teach His people to be obedient and come to know Him. Thus the scattering and gathering served as a sifting and learning process, a means to filter out idolatrous practices and bring people to a remembrance of the ancient promises embodied in the covenant with the Lord. Jeremiah foresaw a time when the holy covenant would be renewed. Like the Apostle Peter, he foresaw "the times of refreshing" that would come "from the presence of the Lord" (Acts 3:19). He perceived a time in the future when the Lord would make a new covenant with His people leading to universal spiritual knowledge.

35 ¶ Thus saith the LORD, which giveth the sun for a light by day, and the ordinances of the moon and of the stars for a light by night, which divideth the sea when the waves thereof roar; The LORD of hosts is his name:

36 If those ordinances depart from before me, saith the LORD, then the seed of Israel also shall cease from being a nation before me for ever.

37 Thus saith the LORD; If heaven above can be measured, and the foundations of the earth searched out beneath, I will also cast off all the seed of Israel for all that they have done, saith the LORD.

38 ¶ Behold, the days come, saith the LORD, that the city shall be built to the LORD from the tower of Hananeel unto the gate of the corner.

39 And the measuring line shall yet go forth over against it upon the hill Gareb, and shall compass about to Goath.

40 And the whole valley of the dead bodies, and of the ashes, and all the fields unto the brook of Kidron, unto the corner of the horse gate toward the east, shall be holy unto the LORD; it shall not be plucked up, nor thrown down any more for ever.

CHAPTER 36

1 AND it came to pass in the fourth year of Jehoiakim the son of Josiah king of Judah, that this word came unto Jeremiah from the LORD, saying,

2 Take thee a roll of a book, and write therein all the words that I have spoken unto thee against Israel, and against Judah, and against all the nations, from the day I spake unto thee, from the days of Josiah, even unto this day.

3 It may be that the house of Judah will hear all the evil which I purpose to do unto them; that they may return every man from his evil way; that I may forgive their iniquity and their sin.

4 Then Jeremiah called Baruch the son of Neriah: and Baruch wrote from the mouth of Jeremiah all the words of the LORD, which he had spoken unto him, upon a roll of a book.

5 And Jeremiah commanded Baruch, saying, I am shut up; I cannot go into the house of the LORD:

6 Therefore go thou, and read in the roll, which thou hast written from my mouth, the words of the LORD in the ears of the people in the LORD's house upon the fasting day: and also thou shalt read them in the ears of all Judah that come out of their cities.

7 It may be they will present their supplication before the LORD, and will return every one from his evil way: for great is the anger and the fury that the LORD hath pronounced against this people.

8 And Baruch the son of Neriah did according to all that Jeremiah the prophet commanded him, reading in the book the words of the LORD in the LORD's house.

9 And it came to pass in the fifth year of Jehoiakim the son of Josiah king of Judah, in the ninth month, that they proclaimed a fast before the LORD to all the people in Jerusalem, and to all the people that came from the cities of Judah unto Jerusalem.

10 Then read Baruch in the book the words of Jeremiah in the house of the LORD, in the chamber of Gemariah the son of Shaphan the scribe, in the higher court, at the entry of the new gate of the LORD's house, in the ears of all the people.

11 ¶ When Michaiah the son of Gemariah, the son of Shaphan, had heard out of the book all the words of the LORD,

JEREMIAH CHAPTER 36

Jeremiah 36:1—Jehoiakim

Jehoiakim (pronounced "juh-hoi'-uh-kim"; originally called Eliakim) was elevated by the king of Egypt to the throne of Judah in place of his brother Jehoahaz: "And Pharaoh-nechoh made Eliakim the son of Josiah king in the room of Josiah his father, and turned his name to Jehoiakim, and took Jehoahaz away: and he came to Egypt, and died there" (2 Kings 23:34; see also 1 Chron. 3:15; 2 Chron. 36:4).

"Jehoiakim *was* twenty and five years old when he began to reign, and he reigned eleven years in Jerusalem: and he did *that which was* evil in the sight of the LORD his God" (2 Chron. 36:5).

When Nebuchadnezzar invaded Judah, he carried away Jehoiakim prisoner (see Dan. 1:1–2), restoring him subsequently as a vassal king. The word of the Lord through the prophet Jeremiah during those days proclaimed the impending downfall of Judah according to the judgments of God (see Jer. 36:1–3.)

Jeremiah, a prisoner of the state at the time, caused the prophecies to be written down by the scribe Baruch and read to the people. When the king learned of this, he ordered the prophecies to be read before him. His reaction of anger is of interest: "And it came to pass, *that* when Jehudi had read three or four leaves, he cut it with the penknife, and cast *it* into the fire that *was* on the hearth, until all the roll was consumed in the fire that *was* on the hearth" (Jer. 36:23). Jeremiah responded quickly: "Then took Jeremiah another roll, and gave it to Baruch the scribe, the son of Neriah; who wrote therein from the mouth of Jeremiah all the words of the book which Jehoiakim king of Judah had burned in the fire: and there were added besides unto them many like words" (Jer. 36:32).

According to an earlier prophecy of Jeremiah, Jehoiakim's reign was not to be one of dignity and righteousness: "He shall be buried with the burial of an ass, drawn and cast forth beyond the gates of Jerusalem" (Jer. 22:19; see also Jer. 36:30). He was succeeded by his son Jehoiachin (see 2 Chron. 36:8–10), who reigned a short period of time before Zedekiah came to power.

12 Then he went down into the king's house, into the scribe's chamber: and, lo, all the princes sat there, even Elishama the scribe, and Delaiah the son of Shemaiah, and Elnathan the son of Achbor, and Gemariah the son of Shaphan, and Zedekiah the son of Hananiah, and all the princes.

13 Then Michaiah declared unto them all the words that he had heard, when Baruch read the book in the ears of the people.

14 Therefore all the princes sent Jehudi the son of Nethaniah, the son of Shelemiah, the son of Cushi, unto Baruch, saying, Take in thine hand the roll wherein thou hast read in the ears of the people, and come. So Baruch the son of Neriah took the roll in his hand, and came unto them.

15 And they said unto him, Sit down now, and read it in our ears. So Baruch read it in their ears.

16 Now it came to pass, when they had heard all the words, they were afraid both one and other, and said unto Baruch, We will surely tell the king of all these words.

17 And they asked Baruch, saying, Tell us now, How didst thou write all these words at his mouth?

18 Then Baruch answered them, He pronounced all these words unto me with his mouth, and I wrote them with ink in the book.

19 Then said the princes unto Baruch, Go, hide thee, thou and Jeremiah; and let no man know where ye be.

20 ¶ And they went in to the king into the court, but they laid up the roll in the chamber of Elishama the scribe, and told all the words in the ears of the king.

21 So the king sent Jehudi to fetch the roll: and he took it out of Elishama the scribe's chamber. And Jehudi read it in the ears of the king, and in the ears of all the princes which stood beside the king.

22 Now the king sat in the winterhouse in the ninth month: and there was a fire on the hearth burning before him.

23 And it came to pass, that when Jehudi had read three or four leaves, he cut it with the penknife, and cast it into the fire that was on the hearth, until all the roll was consumed in the fire that was on the hearth.

24 Yet they were not afraid, nor rent their garments, neither the king, nor any of his servants that heard all these words.

25 Nevertheless Elnathan and Delaiah and Gemariah had made intercession to the king that he would not burn the roll: but he would not hear them.

26 But the king commanded Jerahmeel the son of Hammelech, and Seraiah the son of Azriel, and Shelemiah the son of Abdeel, to take Baruch the scribe and Jeremiah the prophet: but the LORD hid them.

27 ¶ Then the word of the LORD came to Jeremiah, after that the king had burned the roll, and the words which Baruch wrote at the mouth of Jeremiah, saying,

28 Take thee again another roll, and write in it all the former words that were in the first roll, which Jehoiakim the king of Judah hath burned.

29 And thou shalt say to Jehoiakim king of Judah, Thus saith the LORD; Thou hast burned this roll, saying, Why hast thou written therein, saying, The king of Babylon shall certainly come and destroy this land, and shall cause to cease from thence man and beast?

30 Therefore thus saith the LORD of Jehoiakim king of Judah; He shall have none to sit upon the throne of David: and his dead body shall be cast out in the day to the heat, and in the night to the frost.

Jeremiah 36:4—Baruch

Baruch (meaning: blessed), son of Neriah from the tribe of Judah (see Jer. 51:59), served as scribe for the prophet Jeremiah:

Then Jeremiah called Baruch the son of Neriah: and Baruch wrote from the mouth of Jeremiah all the words of the LORD, which he had spoken unto him, upon a roll of a book.

And Jeremiah commanded Baruch, saying, I *am* shut up; I cannot go into the house of the LORD:

Therefore go thou, and read in the roll, which thou hast written from my mouth, the words of the LORD in the ears of the people in the LORD's house upon the fasting day: and also thou shalt read them in the ears of all Judah that come out of their cities.

It may be they will present their supplication before the LORD, and will return every one from his evil way: for great *is* the anger and the fury that the LORD hath pronounced against this people. (Jer. 36:4–7)

Jehoiakim, king of Judah, took offence at the prophecies of Jeremiah concerning the impending destruction of Judah at the hands of the Babylonians and trashed the written text. Jeremiah simply had Baruch write down the word of the Lord once again—manifesting that the word of the Lord cannot be annulled or destroyed (see Jer. 36:27–32). Baruch accompanied Jeremiah to Egypt and continued to serve him; for his faithful service, Jeremiah promised Baruch that his life would be preserved (see Jer. 45).

Jeremiah 36:7–32—The Word of God

The purpose of delivering the word of God to His children with courage and resolve despite all adversity, and of receiving the word of God in our lives at the hands of the prophets and servants of the Lord in faith and obedience, is expressed in this simple formula: "And they shall be my people" (Jer. 31:33). That is the whole matter put in the simplest terms—that we should become the covenant people of the Lord and keep his statutes in righteousness. "He hath shewed thee, O man, what *is* good; and what doth the Lord require of thee, but to do justly and to love mercy and to walk humbly with thy God?" (Micah 6:8).

31 And I will punish him and his seed and his servants for their iniquity; and I will bring upon them, and upon the inhabitants of Jerusalem, and upon the men of Judah, all the evil that I have pronounced against them; but they hearkened not.

32 ¶ Then took Jeremiah another roll, and gave it to Baruch the scribe, the son of Neriah; who wrote therein from the mouth of Jeremiah all the words of the book which Jehoiakim king of Judah had burned in the fire: and there were added besides unto them many like words.

CHAPTER 37

1 AND king Zedekiah the son of Josiah reigned instead of Coniah the son of Jehoiakim, whom Nebuchadrezzar king of Babylon made king in the land of Judah.

2 But neither he, nor his servants, nor the people of the land, did hearken unto the words of the LORD, which he spake by the prophet Jeremiah.

3 And Zedekiah the king sent Jehucal the son of Shelemiah and Zephaniah the son of Maaseiah the priest to the prophet Jeremiah, saying, Pray now unto the LORD our God for us.

4 Now Jeremiah came in and went out among the people: for they had not put him into prison.

5 Then Pharaoh's army was come forth out of Egypt: and when the Chaldeans that besieged Jerusalem heard tidings of them, they departed from Jerusalem.

6 ¶ Then came the word of the LORD unto the prophet Jeremiah, saying,

7 Thus saith the LORD, the God of Israel; Thus shall ye say to the king of Judah, that sent you unto me to enquire of me; Behold, Pharaoh's army, which is come forth to help you, shall return to Egypt into their own land.

8 And the Chaldeans shall come again, and fight against this city, and take it, and burn it with fire.

9 Thus saith the LORD; Deceive not yourselves, saying, The Chaldeans shall surely depart from us: for they shall not depart.

10 For though ye had smitten the whole army of the Chaldeans that fight against you, and there remained but wounded men among them, yet should they rise up every man in his tent, and burn this city with fire.

11 ¶ And it came to pass, that when the army of the Chaldeans was broken up from Jerusalem for fear of Pharaoh's army,

12 Then Jeremiah went forth out of Jerusalem to go into the land of Benjamin, to separate himself thence in the midst of the people.

13 And when he was in the gate of Benjamin, a captain of the ward was there, whose name was Irijah, the son of Shelemiah, the son of Hananiah; and he took Jeremiah the prophet, saying, Thou fallest away to the Chaldeans.

14 Then said Jeremiah, It is false; I fall not away to the Chaldeans. But he hearkened not to him: so Irijah took Jeremiah, and brought him to the princes.

15 Wherefore the princes were wroth with Jeremiah, and smote him, and put him in prison in the house of Jonathan the scribe: for they had made that the prison.

16 ¶ When Jeremiah was entered into the dungeon, and into the cabins, and Jeremiah had remained there many days;

JEREMIAH CHAPTER 37

Jeremiah 37:1—Zedekiah

Zedekiah (pronounced "zed'-uh-ky'-uh"; meaning: the Lord is righteousness), originally named Mattaniah (see 2 Kings 24:17), was the last king of Judah. He was "one and twenty years old when he began to reign, and reigned eleven years in Jerusalem" (2 Chron. 36:11). Nephi informs us that it was during the first year of Zedekiah's rule that Lehi was called to warn the people of Jerusalem about the impending judgments of God about to befall them (see 2 Ne. 1:4).

Zedekiah's tenure ended with the Babylonian conquest of Jerusalem around 587 BC. Jeremiah reports: "And the king of Babylon slew the sons of Zedekiah before his eyes: he slew also all the princes of Judah in Riblah. Then he put out the eyes of Zedekiah; and the king of Babylon bound him in chains, and carried him to Babylon, and put him in prison till the day of his death" (Jer. 52:10–11; compare 2 Kings 25:7). The implication is that all the sons of Zedekiah perished in this way; however, the Book of Mormon makes clear that Zedekiah's youngest son, Mulek, survived the ordeal and was guided by the Lord to the Promised Land, where he established a colony and founded a new nation (see Hel. 8:21). Mormon gives the geographical orientation as follows: "Now the land south was called Lehi and the land north was called Mulek, which was after the son of Zedekiah; for the Lord did bring Mulek into the land north, and Lehi into the land south" (Hel. 6:10).

When the Nephite leader Mosiah I was commanded of the Lord to flee from the land south (the land of Lehi, also called the land of Nephi) sometime in the period 279 BC to 130 BC, he and his loyal followers were guided northward to Zarahemla, where the Mulekites had eventually settled (see Omni 1:12–16). Thereafter the Mulekites and the Nephites were united into one nation.

Jeremiah 37:16–21—The Release of Jeremiah

The dramatic scene where Zedekiah inquires of the prophet concerning the word of the Lord results in the ominous prophecy: ". . . thou shalt be delivered into the hand of the king of Babylon" (verse 17). Sufficiently humbled, Zedekiah arranges for Jeremiah to be released from his austere confinement and given more liberal hospitality.

17 Then Zedekiah the king sent, and took him out: and the king asked him secretly in his house, and said, Is there any word from the LORD? And Jeremiah said, There is: for, said he, thou shalt be delivered into the hand of the king of Babylon.

18 Moreover Jeremiah said unto king Zedekiah, What have I offended against thee, or against thy servants, or against this people, that ye have put me in prison?

19 Where are now your prophets which prophesied unto you, saying, The king of Babylon shall not come against you, nor against this land?

20 Therefore hear now, I pray thee, O my lord the king: let my supplication, I pray thee, be accepted before thee; that thou cause me not to return to the house of Jonathan the scribe, lest I die there.

21 Then Zedekiah the king commanded that they should commit Jeremiah into the court of the prison, and that they should give him daily a piece of bread out of the bakers' street, until all the bread in the city were spent. Thus Jeremiah remained in the court of the prison.

CHAPTER 38

1 THEN Shephatiah the son of Mattan, and Gedaliah the son of Pashur, and Jucal the son of Shelemiah, and Pashur the son of Malchiah, heard the words that Jeremiah had spoken unto all the people, saying,

2 Thus saith the LORD, He that remaineth in this city shall die by the sword, by the famine, and by the pestilence: but he that goeth forth to the Chaldeans shall live; for he shall have his life for a prey, and shall live.

3 Thus saith the LORD, This city shall surely be given into the hand of the king of Babylon's army, which shall take it.

4 Therefore the princes said unto the king, We beseech thee, let this man be put to death: for thus he weakeneth the hands of the men of war that remain in this city, and the hands of all the people, in speaking such words unto them: for this man seeketh not the welfare of this people, but the hurt.

5 Then Zedekiah the king said, Behold, he is in your hand: for the king is not he that can do any thing against you.

6 Then took they Jeremiah, and cast him into the dungeon of Malchiah the son of Hammelech, that was in the court of the prison: and they let down Jeremiah with cords. And in the dungeon there was no water, but mire: so Jeremiah sunk in the mire.

7 ¶ Now when Ebed-melech the Ethiopian, one of the eunuchs which was in the king's house, heard that they had put Jeremiah in the dungeon; the king then sitting in the gate of Benjamin;

8 Ebed-melech went forth out of the king's house, and spake to the king, saying,

9 My lord the king, these men have done evil in all that they have done to Jeremiah the prophet, whom they have cast into the dungeon; and he is like to die for hunger in the place where he is: for there is no more bread in the city.

10 Then the king commanded Ebed-melech the Ethiopian, saying, Take from hence thirty men with thee, and take up Jeremiah the prophet out of the dungeon, before he die.

11 So Ebed-melech took the men with him, and went into the house of the king under the treasury, and took thence old cast clouts and old rotten rags, and let them down by cords into the dungeon to Jeremiah.

JEREMIAH CHAPTER 38

Jeremiah 38—Zedekiah's Refusal to Heed the Word of the Lord

The word of the Lord to Zedekiah was plain: release yourself to the Babylonians, and you and your house will live and the city will not be burned. But Zedekiah was fearful to follow this counsel and, later fleeing the city, he was found and taken captive, his sons were killed (all but Mulek, as it turned out), and the city was destroyed (see Jer. 39:1–8). Zedekiah was then taken to Babylon, where he remained until his death (see Jer. 52:10–11; compare 2 Kings 25:7). The moral of this sory is certain: Do as the Lord commands.

12 And Ebed-melech the Ethiopian said unto Jeremiah, Put now these old cast clouts and rotten rags under thine armholes under the cords. And Jeremiah did so.

13 So they drew up Jeremiah with cords, and took him up out of the dungeon: and Jeremiah remained in the court of the prison.

14 ¶ Then Zedekiah the king sent, and took Jeremiah the prophet unto him into the third entry that is in the house of the LORD: and the king said unto Jeremiah, I will ask thee a thing; hide nothing from me.

15 Then Jeremiah said unto Zedekiah, If I declare it unto thee, wilt thou not surely put me to death? and if I give thee counsel, wilt thou not hearken unto me?

16 So Zedekiah the king sware secretly unto Jeremiah, saying, As the LORD liveth, that made us this soul, I will not put thee to death, neither will I give thee into the hand of these men that seek thy life.

17 Then said Jeremiah unto Zedekiah, Thus saith the LORD, the God of hosts, the God of Israel; If thou wilt assuredly go forth unto the king of Babylon's princes, then thy soul shall live, and this city shall not be burned with fire; and thou shalt live, and thine house:

18 But if thou wilt not go forth to the king of Babylon's princes, then shall this city be given into the hand of the Chaldeans, and they shall burn it with fire, and thou shalt not escape out of their hand.

19 And Zedekiah the king said unto Jeremiah, I am afraid of the Jews that are fallen to the Chaldeans, lest they deliver me into their hand, and they mock me.

20 But Jeremiah said, They shall not deliver thee. Obey, I beseech thee, the voice of the LORD, which I speak unto thee: so it shall be well unto thee, and thy soul shall live.

21 But if thou refuse to go forth, this is the word that the LORD hath shewed me:

22 And, behold, all the women that are left in the king of Judah's house shall be brought forth to the king of Babylon's princes, and those women shall say, Thy friends have set thee on, and have prevailed against thee: thy feet are sunk in the mire, and they are turned away back.

23 So they shall bring out all thy wives and thy children to the Chaldeans: and thou shalt not escape out of their hand, but shalt be taken by the hand of the king of Babylon: and thou shalt cause this city to be burned with fire.

24 ¶ Then said Zedekiah unto Jeremiah, Let no man know of these words, and thou shalt not die.

25 But if the princes hear that I have talked with thee, and they come unto thee, and say unto thee, Declare unto us now what thou hast said unto the king, hide it not from us, and we will not put thee to death; also what the king said unto thee:

26 Then thou shalt say unto them, I presented my supplication before the king, that he would not cause me to return to Jonathan's house, to die there.

27 Then came all the princes unto Jeremiah, and asked him: and he told them according to all these words that the king had commanded. So they left off speaking with him; for the matter was not perceived.

28 So Jeremiah abode in the court of the prison until the day that Jerusalem was taken: and he was there when Jerusalem was taken.

Ezekiel Prophesying by Gustave Doré

THE
BOOK OF THE PROPHET EZEKIEL

CHAPTER 18

1 THE word of the LORD came unto me again, saying,

2 What mean ye, that ye use this proverb concerning the land of Israel, saying, The fathers have eaten sour grapes, and the children's teeth are set on edge?

3 As I live, saith the Lord GOD, ye shall not have occasion any more to use this proverb in Israel.

4 Behold, all souls are mine; as the soul of the father, so also the soul of the son is mine: the soul that sinneth, it shall die.

5 ¶ But if a man be just, and do that which is lawful and right,

6 And hath not eaten upon the mountains, neither hath lifted up his eyes to the idols of the house of Israel, neither hath defiled his neighbour's wife, neither hath come near to a menstruous woman,

7 And hath not oppressed any, but hath restored to the debtor his pledge, hath spoiled none by violence, hath given his bread to the hungry, and hath covered the naked with a garment;

8 He that hath not given forth upon usury, neither hath taken any increase, that hath withdrawn his hand from iniquity, hath executed true judgment between man and man,

9 Hath walked in my statutes, and hath kept my judgments, to deal truly; he is just, he shall surely live, saith the Lord GOD.

10 ¶ If he beget a son that is a robber, a shedder of blood, and that doeth the like to any one of these things,

11 And that doeth not any of those duties, but even hath eaten upon the mountains, and defiled his neighbour's wife,

12 Hath oppressed the poor and needy, hath spoiled by violence, hath not restored the pledge, and hath lifted up his eyes to the idols, hath committed abomination,

13 Hath given forth upon usury, and hath taken increase: shall he then live? he shall not live: he hath done all these abominations; he shall surely die; his blood shall be upon him.

14 ¶ Now, lo, if he beget a son, that seeth all his father's sins which he hath done, and considereth, and doeth not such like,

15 That hath not eaten upon the mountains, neither hath lifted up his eyes to the idols of the house of Israel, hath not defiled his neighbour's wife,

16 Neither hath oppressed any, hath not withholden the pledge, neither hath spoiled by violence, but hath given his bread to the hungry, and hath covered the naked with a garment,

17 That hath taken off his hand from the poor, that hath not received usury nor increase, hath executed my judgments, hath walked in my statutes; he shall not die for the iniquity of his father, he shall surely live.

18 As for his father, because he cruelly oppressed, spoiled his brother by violence, and did that which is not good among his people, lo, even he shall die in his iniquity.

19 ¶ Yet say ye, Why? doth not the son bear the iniquity of the father? When the son hath done that which is lawful and right, and hath kept all my statutes, and hath done them, he shall surely live.

EZEKIEL CHAPTER 18

Ezekiel 18—The Message of Ezekiel

What a privilege to look through the eyes of a prophet at the Lord's designs and plans for His children. The vision of Ezekiel—in accordance with the vision granted to Jeremiah and all other prophets of ancient and modern times—projects the message of the covenant, or the message of "coming together." That is the ultimate objective of the scriptures of God—to bring mankind together in the fold of God and to bring about an atoning reconciliation between God and His sons and daughters.

Out of that oneness of purpose flow the themes of this chapter: (1) the need for the shepherds of Israel to be diligently engaged in the cause of Zion, serving the needs of the pure in heart and guiding them on the path of righteousness; (2) the restorative, redeeming power of the gospel of hope; and (3) the ordained process of gathering the words of God in all of their manifestations and bringing them together in one as a combined latter-day testament of the divinity of Jesus Christ. This unity of service, hope, and testimony in the work of the Savior constitutes the message of Ezekiel.

For more insight on Ezekiel, see Appendix JJ.

Ezekiel 18:1–32—The Shepherds of Israel

The Lord gives to His children their free agency, causes them to be taught correct principles, and then holds every individual accountable for his or her own actions. At the same time, the Lord holds the shepherds of Israel accountable—all who have stewardship over the flock at whatever level of responsibility—to teach the principles of righteousness valiantly in the spirit of light and truth, shirking no opportunity to bring the sheep unto Christ.

Shepherds are called to guide the Saints in the pathway of righteousness, and to restore any wayward and wandering souls to the fold.

> "Therefore I will judge you, O house of Israel, every one according to his ways, saith the Lord God. Repent, and turn yourselves from all your transgressions; so iniquity shall not be your ruin. Cast away from you all your transgressions, whereby ye have transgressed; and make you a new heart and a new spirit." (Ezek. 18:30–31)

> "Son of man, prophesy against the shepherds of Israel, prophesy, and say unto them, Thus saith the Lord God unto the shepherds; Wo be to the shepherds of Israel that do feed themselves! should not the shepherds feed the flocks?" (Ezek. 34:2)

> "For thus saith the Lord God; Behold, I, even I, will both search my sheep, and seek them out." (Ezek. 34:11)

20 The soul that sinneth, it shall die. The son shall not bear the iniquity of the father, neither shall the father bear the iniquity of the son: the righteousness of the righteous shall be upon him, and the wickedness of the wicked shall be upon him.

21 But if the wicked will turn from all his sins that he hath committed, and keep all my statutes, and do that which is lawful and right, he shall surely live, he shall not die.

22 All his transgressions that he hath committed, they shall not be mentioned unto him: in his righteousness that he hath done he shall live.

23 Have I any pleasure at all that the wicked should die? saith the Lord GOD: and not that he should return from his ways, and live?

24 ¶ But when the righteous turneth away from his righteousness, and committeth iniquity, and doeth according to all the abominations that the wicked man doeth, shall he live? All his righteousness that he hath done shall not be mentioned: in his trespass that he hath trespassed, and in his sin that he hath sinned, in them shall he die.

25 ¶ Yet ye say, The way of the Lord is not equal. Hear now, O house of Israel; Is not my way equal? are not your ways unequal?

26 When a righteous man turneth away from his righteousness, and committeth iniquity, and dieth in them; for his iniquity that he hath done shall he die.

27 Again, when the wicked man turneth away from his wickedness that he hath committed, and doeth that which is lawful and right, he shall save his soul alive.

28 Because he considereth, and turneth away from all his transgressions that he hath committed, he shall surely live, he shall not die.

29 Yet saith the house of Israel, The way of the Lord is not equal. O house of Israel, are not my ways equal? are not your ways unequal?

30 Therefore I will judge you, O house of Israel, every one according to his ways, saith the Lord GOD. Repent, and turn yourselves from all your transgressions; so iniquity shall not be your ruin.

31 ¶ Cast away from you all your transgressions, whereby ye have transgressed; and make you a new heart and a new spirit: for why will ye die, O house of Israel?

32 For I have no pleasure in the death of him that dieth, saith the Lord GOD: wherefore turn yourselves, and live ye.

CHAPTER 34

1 AND the word of the LORD came unto me, saying,

2 Son of man, prophesy against the shepherds of Israel, prophesy, and say unto them, Thus saith the Lord GOD unto the shepherds; Woe be to the shepherds of Israel that do feed themselves! should not the shepherds feed the flocks?

3 Ye eat the fat, and ye clothe you with the wool, ye kill them that are fed: but ye feed not the flock.

4 The diseased have ye not strengthened, neither have ye healed that which was sick, neither have ye bound up that which was broken, neither have ye brought again that which was driven away, neither have ye sought that which was lost; but with force and with cruelty have ye ruled them.

5 And they were scattered, because there is no shepherd: and they became meat to all the beasts of the field, when they were scattered.

"And I shall set up one shepherd over them, and he shall feed them, even my servant David; he shall feed them, and he shall be their shepherd." (Ezek. 34:23)

Ezekiel, who prophesied for some twenty-two years (from 592 until 570 BC), is the messenger of God's strong disfavor with the covenant people. The leaders of Israel are under condemnation for having abdicated their sacred role to be paragons of righteousness among the people, choosing instead to pollute the sacred principles of the covenant and desecrate their leadership as "shepherds of Israel." Not heeding the warnings of Ezekiel and other prophets of God, the people are thus consigned to endure a state of captivity at the hands of the invading Babylonians under Nebuchadnezzar. Ezekiel can offer hope only to those who, in the future, will choose to obey the Lord's commandments and be restored to their place of favor with God and find peace under the leadership of the Good Shepherd (Jesus Christ), who will do a miracle on behalf of each follower by causing each to have "a new heart and a new spirit" (Ezek. 18:31; compare Mosiah 5:2; Alma 5:14).

EZEKIEL CHAPTER 34

Ezekiel 34:1–2—Our Responsibility to Others

Ezekiel is to reprove the shepherds of Israel whose hearts are focused on selfish things and who neglect the care of the sheep. All who serve in the Kingdom of God should consider their lot and ensure that their interests are centered on charitable serving in helping others along the pathway of mortality, pointing them toward the good Shepherd, the Lord Jesus Christ.

6 My sheep wandered through all the mountains, and upon every high hill: yea, my flock was scattered upon all the face of the earth, and none did search or seek after them.

7 ¶ Therefore, ye shepherds, hear the word of the LORD;

8 As I live, saith the Lord GOD, surely because my flock became a prey, and my flock became meat to every beast of the field, because there was no shepherd, neither did my shepherds search for my flock, but the shepherds fed themselves, and fed not my flock;

9 Therefore, O ye shepherds, hear the word of the LORD;

10 Thus saith the Lord GOD; Behold, I am against the shepherds; and I will require my flock at their hand, and cause them to cease from feeding the flock; neither shall the shepherds feed themselves any more; for I will deliver my flock from their mouth, that they may not be meat for them.

11 ¶ For thus saith the Lord GOD; Behold, I, even I, will both search my sheep, and seek them out.

12 As a shepherd seeketh out his flock in the day that he is among his sheep that are scattered; so will I seek out my sheep, and will deliver them out of all places where they have been scattered in the cloudy and dark day.

13 And I will bring them out from the people, and gather them from the countries, and will bring them to their own land, and feed them upon the mountains of Israel by the rivers, and in all the inhabited places of the country.

14 I will feed them in a good pasture, and upon the high mountains of Israel shall their fold be: there shall they lie in a good fold, and in a fat pasture shall they feed upon the mountains of Israel.

15 I will feed my flock, and I will cause them to lie down, saith the Lord GOD.

16 I will seek that which was lost, and bring again that which was driven away, and will bind up that which was broken, and will strengthen that which was sick: but I will destroy the fat and the strong; I will feed them with judgment.

17 And as for you, O my flock, thus saith the Lord GOD; Behold, I judge between cattle and cattle, between the rams and the he goats.

18 Seemeth it a small thing unto you to have eaten up the good pasture, but ye must tread down with your feet the residue of your pastures? and to have drunk of the deep waters, but ye must foul the residue with your feet?

19 And as for my flock, they eat that which ye have trodden with your feet; and they drink that which ye have fouled with your feet.

20 ¶ Therefore thus saith the Lord GOD unto them; Behold, I, even I, will judge between the fat cattle and between the lean cattle.

21 Because ye have thrust with side and with shoulder, and pushed all the diseased with your horns, till ye have scattered them abroad;

22 Therefore will I save my flock, and they shall no more be a prey; and I will judge between cattle and cattle.

23 And I will set up one shepherd over them, and he shall feed them, even my servant David; he shall feed them, and he shall be their shepherd.

24 And I the LORD will be their God, and my servant David a prince among them; I the LORD have spoken it.

25 And I will make with them a covenant of peace, and will cause the evil beasts to cease out of the land: and they shall dwell safely in the wilderness, and sleep in the woods.

Ezekiel 34:11–16—The Role of the Savior as the Good Shepherd

The design of the Good Shepherd is to seek out the lost sheep and deliver them to places of safety and nurture, places upon the high mountains of Israel (surely a symbol that points toward the blessings of the temples of the Lord), places where they can be part of the "good fold" (verse 14)—in other words, gathered to the stakes and homes of Zion where spiritual nourishment abounds and where rest and peace are provided. The imagery is beautiful and grand. The spirit of the language is edifying and enriching (compare Ps. 23).

Ezekiel 34—Summary of Precepts and Principles

When Ezekiel prophesied "There shall be showers of blessing" (Ezek. 34:26), he was looking forward to a time in which the Lord would once more gather His people under the unifying banner of Zion: "And I will make with them a covenant of peace . . . and they shall dwell safely in the wilderness. . . . And I will make them and the places round about my hill a blessing. . ." (Ezek. 34:25–26). Before that day can come, we will need to learn line upon line, precept upon precept, "Till we all come in a unity of the faith, and of the knowledge of the Son of God, unto a perfect man, unto the measure of the stature of the fulness of Christ" (Eph. 4:13). Measuring up to that stature requires unity of service, unit of hope, and unity of testimony—all attributes of a Zion people to which, in grace and thanksgiving, we can aspire.

26 And I will make them and the places round about my hill a blessing; and I will cause the shower to come down in his season; there shall be showers of blessing.

27 And the tree of the field shall yield her fruit, and the earth shall yield her increase, and they shall be safe in their land, and shall know that I am the LORD, when I have broken the bands of their yoke, and delivered them out of the hand of those that served themselves of them.

28 And they shall no more be a prey to the heathen, neither shall the beast of the land devour them; but they shall dwell safely, and none shall make them afraid.

29 And I will raise up for them a plant of renown, and they shall be no more consumed with hunger in the land, neither bear the shame of the heathen any more.

30 Thus shall they know that I the LORD their God am with them, and that they, even the house of Israel, are my people, saith the Lord GOD.

31 And ye my flock, the flock of my pasture, are men, and I am your God, saith the Lord GOD.

CHAPTER 37

1 THE hand of the LORD was upon me, and carried me out in the spirit of the LORD, and set me down in the midst of the valley which was full of bones,

2 And caused me to pass by them round about: and, behold, there were very many in the open valley; and, lo, they were very dry.

3 And he said unto me, Son of man, can these bones live? And I answered, O Lord GOD, thou knowest.

4 Again he said unto me, Prophesy upon these bones, and say unto them, O ye dry bones, hear the word of the LORD.

5 Thus saith the Lord GOD unto these bones; Behold, I will cause breath to enter into you, and ye shall live:

6 And I will lay sinews upon you, and will bring up flesh upon you, and cover you with skin, and put breath in you, and ye shall live; and ye shall know that I am the LORD.

7 So I prophesied as I was commanded: and as I prophesied, there was a noise, and behold a shaking, and the bones came together, bone to his bone.

8 And when I beheld, lo, the sinews and the flesh came up upon them, and the skin covered them above: but there was no breath in them.

9 Then said he unto me, Prophesy unto the wind, prophesy, son of man, and say to the wind, Thus saith the Lord GOD; Come from the four winds, O breath, and breathe upon these slain, that they may live.

10 So I prophesied as he commanded me, and the breath came into them, and they lived, and stood up upon their feet, an exceeding great army.

11 ¶ Then he said unto me, Son of man, these bones are the whole house of Israel: behold, they say, Our bones are dried, and our hope is lost: we are cut off for our parts.

12 Therefore prophesy and say unto them, Thus saith the Lord GOD; Behold, O my people, I will open your graves, and cause you to come up out of your graves, and bring you into the land of Israel.

13 And ye shall know that I am the LORD, when I have opened your graves, O my people, and brought you up out of your graves,

EZEKIEL CHAPTER 37

"He had power, when all mankind had lost their life, to restore life to them again; and hence He is the Resurrection and the Life, which power no other man possesses."
—John Taylor, *The Mediation and the Atonement*, 135

Ezekiel 37:1–14—The Power of God to Restore Life and Hope

God is omnipotent in His ability to restore and render dynamic all aspects of man's existence—including the ultimate restoration of the body and its reunion with the spirit in a resurrected state, the restoration of the spirit of hope within the breast of His struggling children, and the restoration of His chosen people to the promised land (in both the temporal as well as the heavenly sense; see Ezek. 37:11–12, 14.)

Ezekiel was granted a remarkable vision of the "valley which was full of bones" (Ezek. 37:1). He saw in an extraordinary spectral drama how the bones were rejuvenated, given once again their fleshly embodiment, and enlivened through the spirit of life. Ezekiel's vision was a unique and memorable spiritual event with many harmonic overtones: a view of the resurrection, an insight into the restorative power of God to generate hope and faith within His children, and a renewal of the promise under the Abrahamic Covenant to give the Lord's chosen a homeland on earth, as well as a place of rest in the hereafter. Few Old Testament passages have made their way into the memory bank of humans with as much staying power as the line "O ye dry bones, hear the word of the Lord" (Ezek. 37:4). And yet, does the popular folklore and catchy folk melody associated with this passage tend to obscure the deeper meanings and spiritual truths that are anchored in this unique vision of the power of God to restore life and hope?

14 And shall put my spirit in you, and ye shall live, and I shall place you in your own land: then shall ye know that I the LORD have spoken it, and performed it, saith the LORD.

15 ¶ The word of the LORD came again unto me, saying,

16 Moreover, thou son of man, take thee one stick, and write upon it, For Judah, and for the children of Israel his companions: then take another stick, and write upon it, For Joseph, the stick of Ephraim, and for all the house of Israel his companions:

17 And join them one to another into one stick; and they shall become one in thine hand.

18 ¶ And when the children of thy people shall speak unto thee, saying, Wilt thou not shew us what thou meanest by these?

19 Say unto them, Thus saith the Lord GOD; Behold, I will take the stick of Joseph, which is in the hand of Ephraim, and the tribes of Israel his fellows, and will put them with him, even with the stick of Judah, and make them one stick, and they shall be one in mine hand.

20 ¶ And the sticks whereon thou writest shall be in thine hand before their eyes.

21 And say unto them, Thus saith the Lord GOD; Behold, I will take the children of Israel from among the heathen, whither they be gone, and will gather them on every side, and bring them into their own land:

22 And I will make them one nation in the land upon the mountains of Israel; and one king shall be king to them all: and they shall be no more two nations, neither shall they be divided into two kingdoms any more at all:

23 Neither shall they defile themselves any more with their idols, nor with their detestable things, nor with any of their transgressions: but I will save them out of all their dwellingplaces, wherein they have sinned, and will cleanse them: so shall they be my people, and I will be their God.

24 And David my servant shall be king over them; and they all shall have one shepherd: they shall also walk in my judgments, and observe my statutes, and do them.

25 And they shall dwell in the land that I have given unto Jacob my servant, wherein your fathers have dwelt; and they shall dwell therein, even they, and their children, and their children's children for ever: and my servant David shall be their prince for ever.

26 Moreover I will make a covenant of peace with them; it shall be an everlasting covenant with them: and I will place them, and multiply them, and will set my sanctuary in the midst of them for evermore.

27 My tabernacle also shall be with them: yea, I will be their God, and they shall be my people.

28 And the heathen shall know that I the LORD do sanctify Israel, when my sanctuary shall be in the midst of them for evermore.

Ezekiel 37:15–28—The Coming Together of the Word of God

The agenda of God is to restore all spiritual things into one as a key function of the final dispensation of time, including all aspects of the word of God. Thus God's message to all of His children in all dispensations of time and in all locations will be brought together into a grand whole, including the Bible, the Book of Mormon, and all other sacred writings granted unto mankind.

"Moreover, thou son of man, take thee one stick, and write upon it, For Judah, and for the children of Israel his companions: then take another stick, and write upon it, For Joseph, the stick of Ephraim, and for all the house of Israel his companions. And join them one to another into one stick; and they shall become one in thine hand." (Ezek. 37:16–17)

"And David my servant shall be king over them; and they all shall have one shepherd: they shall also walk in my judgments, and observe my statutes, and do them …. Moreover I will make a covenant of peace with them: and I will place them, and multiply them, and will set my sanctuary in the midst of them for evermore." (Ezek. 37:24, 26)

Ezekiel is commanded to take a stick (or scroll) and write upon it "For Judah," and another stick and write upon it "For Joseph," and then to combine the two sticks together in one, that they might be unified. It is clear that the stick of Judah is the Bible—but where is the stick of Joseph?

The words of the Lord through Ezekiel provide a logical and compelling framework in which to understand the grand design of God to provide His children—all of His children—with essential guiding truth given through prophets called to impart the word of the Lord. The stick of Joseph is the Book of Mormon, just as the word of the Lord to other remnants of scattered Israel is doubtless preserved in scriptural accounts that will one day be restored to the central repository of the word of God (see 2 Ne. 29:12–14).

Ezekiel's account of the sticks is, on the most fundamental level, a prophecy about the ultimate gathering together in one of all the obedient who become God's people; but it is also symbolic of the flowing together of all truth as a key dimension of the Restoration of the gospel in our day, and a solemn prophetic reminder of the eventual flowing together in one of all the families of God who rise in obedience to fulfil their spiritual potential under the new and everlasting covenant.

CHAPTER 43

1 AFTERWARD he brought me to the gate, even the gate that looketh toward the east:

2 And, behold, the glory of the God of Israel came from the way of the east: and his voice was like a noise of many waters: and the earth shined with his glory.

3 And it was according to the appearance of the vision which I saw, even according to the vision that I saw when I came to destroy the city: and the visions were like the vision that I saw by the river Chebar; and I fell upon my face.

4 And the glory of the LORD came into the house by the way of the gate whose prospect is toward the east.

5 So the spirit took me up, and brought me into the inner court; and, behold, the glory of the LORD filled the house.

6 And I heard him speaking unto me out of the house; and the man stood by me.

7 ¶ And he said unto me, Son of man, the place of my throne, and the place of the soles of my feet, where I will dwell in the midst of the children of Israel for ever, and my holy name, shall the house of Israel no more defile, neither they, nor their kings, by their whoredom, nor by the carcases of their kings in their high places.

8 In their setting of their threshold by my thresholds, and their post by my posts, and the wall between me and them, they have even defiled my holy name by their abominations that they have committed: wherefore I have consumed them in mine anger.

9 Now let them put away their whoredom, and the carcases of their kings, far from me, and I will dwell in the midst of them for ever.

10 ¶ Thou son of man, shew the house to the house of Israel, that they may be ashamed of their iniquities: and let them measure the pattern.

11 And if they be ashamed of all that they have done, shew them the form of the house, and the fashion thereof, and the goings out thereof, and the comings in thereof, and all the forms thereof, and all the ordinances thereof, and all the forms thereof, and all the laws thereof: and write it in their sight, that they may keep the whole form thereof, and all the ordinances thereof, and do them.

12 This is the law of the house; Upon the top of the mountain the whole limit thereof round about shall be most holy. Behold, this is the law of the house.

13 ¶ And these are the measures of the altar after the cubits: The cubit is a cubit and an hand breadth; even the bottom shall be a cubit, and the breadth a cubit, and the border thereof by the edge thereof round about shall be a span: and this shall be the higher place of the altar.

14 And from the bottom upon the ground even to the lower settle shall be two cubits, and the breadth one cubit; and from the lesser settle even to the greater settle shall be four cubits, and the breadth one cubit.

15 So the altar shall be four cubits; and from the altar and upward shall be four horns.

16 And the altar shall be twelve cubits long, twelve broad, square in the four squares thereof.

17 And the settle shall be fourteen cubits long and fourteen broad in the four squares thereof; and the border about it shall be half a cubit; and the bottom thereof shall be a cubit about; and his stairs shall look toward the east.

EZEKIEL CHAPTER 43

Ezekiel 43—The Holy Temple

The last eight chapters of the Book of Ezekiel constitute a visionary journey to the City of God and a visit to the glorious temple in the midst thereof. Nothing is withheld from the prophet's view, including all of the details of the building's construction and appointments, together with the ordinances administered there: "And behold, the glory of the God of Israel came from the way of the east: and his voice was like a noise of many waters: and the earth shined with his glory … and behold, the glory of the Lord filled the house" (Ezek. 43:2, 5).

Flowing from below the threshold the of the temple was a current of water that expanded in size and volume as it continued eastward, bringing healing and life-sustaining influences to all the realm. The river of abundance is a dynamic image for the effulgent, everlasting flow of truth and light that enlivens the lives of all individuals seeking the Lord's endowment of eternal blessings through the work of the temples.

Ezekiel 43:10–11—The Temple of God as the Source for Healing Truth

Endless spiritual vitality flows from the institution, ordinances, endowments, and power of the temple in its function as the pivotal hub of a Zion society. As the mountain of the Lord's house, the temple provides the key agenda for "seeking the face of the Lord" (D&C 101:38).

> "Thou son of man, shew the house to the house of Israel, that they may be ashamed of their iniquities: and let them measure the pattern …. and write it in their sight, that they may keep the whole form thereof, and do them." (Ezek. 43:10–11)

> "And they shall teach my people the difference between the holy and profane, and cause them to discern between the unclean and the clean." (Ezek. 44:23)

> "And it shall come to pass, that every thing that liveth, which moveth, whithersoever the rivers shall come, shall live …. and every thing shall live whither the river cometh." (Ezek. 47:9)

Like Jeremiah and Isaiah before him, Ezekiel received visionary insight into the full panorama of God's dealings with mankind, from the creation of the earth to the final battle that will usher in the millennial reign of the Good Shepherd. The remarkable images in which Ezekiel couches his message—the parchment roll of wisdom that he is required to eat, the watchmen of Israel, the wheels and cherubims about the throne of God, the withering vine of an idolatrous nation, the profligate sisters, the goodly tree of righteousness, the righteous Shepherd, showers of blessings, the valley of bones, the stick of Judah and the stick of Joseph, and ultimately the great river of life that flows from the temple—all these provide stark visual reinforcement

18 ¶ And he said unto me, Son of man, thus saith the Lord GOD; These are the ordinances of the altar in the day when they shall make it, to offer burnt offerings thereon, and to sprinkle blood thereon.

19 And thou shalt give to the priests the Levites that be of the seed of Zadok, which approach unto me, to minister unto me, saith the Lord GOD, a young bullock for a sin offering.

20 And thou shalt take of the blood thereof, and put it on the four horns of it, and on the four corners of the settle, and upon the border round about: thus shalt thou cleanse and purge it.

21 Thou shalt take the bullock also of the sin offering, and he shall burn it in the appointed place of the house, without the sanctuary.

22 And on the second day thou shalt offer a kid of the goats without blemish for a sin offering; and they shall cleanse the altar, as they did cleanse it with the bullock.

23 When thou hast made an end of cleansing it, thou shalt offer a young bullock without blemish, and a ram out of the flock without blemish.

24 And thou shalt offer them before the LORD, and the priests shall cast salt upon them, and they shall offer them up for a burnt offering unto the LORD.

25 Seven days shalt thou prepare every day a goat for a sin offering: they shall also prepare a young bullock, and a ram out of the flock, without blemish.

26 Seven days shall they purge the altar and purify it; and they shall consecrate themselves.

27 And when these days are expired, it shall be, that upon the eighth day, and so forward, the priests shall make your burnt offerings upon the altar, and your peace offerings; and I will accept you, saith the Lord GOD.

for the universal call to repentance that undergirds his pronouncements and points to the final destiny of the faithful who will live forever in the city of God.

Like John the Beloved, who saw in vision "a pure river of water of life, clear as crystal, proceeding out of the throne of God and of the Lamb" (Rev. 22:1), Ezekiel beholds the temple as the source of an almighty river of truth that nurtures the faithful in ever deeper immersions in the pools of divine wisdom. He foretells that the ultimate resting place of the Saints will be a city whose name reveals the nature of the glory within it: ". . . and the name of the city from that day shall be, The Lord is there" (Ezek. 48:35).

Against the bleakness of the landscape of iniquity, idolatry, and captivity that characterizes Israel's plight at the time of Ezekiel's ministry, we see the blinding radiance of hope for a future restoration of Israel's covenant blessings, blessings that promise fruitfulness, a gathering place of rest, the refreshing abundance of truth, the sealing ordinances of the temple, and a heavenly home of eternal life in the presence of God and the Lamb.

POINT OF INTEREST

"Some scholars have seen the ziggurat as the throne of the deity; others have suggested that it was regarded as an immense altar, an idea for which Ezekiel 43:13–17—which describes an altar in the form of a miniature ziggurat—has been adduced in support. . . . (p. 281) Probably there was a gradual evolution of view, the high temple being originally regarded as the proper dwelling-place of the god, but subsequently becoming an intermediate stage for the god on his way from heaven to his earthly residence, now the temple at the foot of the ziggurat. The ziggurat was thus a kind of ladder set up to heaven from earth. This idea links up with the story of the Tower of Babel in Genesis 11:3–5, which was certainly related to a Mesopotamian ziggurat, and also with the ladder mentioned in Jacob's dream in Genesis 27:12, of which we are told that it was 'set up on the earth, and the top of it reached to heaven: and behold the angels of God ascending and descending on it'." (H. W. F. Saggs, *The Babylonians* [London: Folio Society, 2007]).

CHAPTER 44

1 THEN he brought me back the way of the gate of the outward sanctuary which looketh toward the east; and it was shut.

2 Then said the LORD unto me; This gate shall be shut, it shall not be opened, and no man shall enter in by it; because the LORD, the God of Israel, hath entered in by it, therefore it shall be shut.

3 It is for the prince; the prince, he shall sit in it to eat bread before the LORD; he shall enter by the way of the porch of that gate, and shall go out by the way of the same.

4 ¶ Then brought he me the way of the north gate before the house: and I looked, and, behold, the glory of the LORD filled the house of the LORD: and I fell upon my face.

5 And the LORD said unto me, Son of man, mark well, and behold with thine eyes, and hear with thine ears all that I say unto thee concerning all the ordinances of the house of the LORD, and all the laws thereof; and mark well the entering in of the house, with every going forth of the sanctuary.

6 And thou shalt say to the rebellious, even to the house of Israel, Thus saith the Lord GOD; O ye house of Israel, let it suffice you of all your abominations,

7 In that ye have brought into my sanctuary strangers, uncircumcised in heart, and uncircumcised in flesh, to be in my sanctuary, to pollute it, even my house, when ye offer my bread, the fat and the blood, and they have broken my covenant because of all your abominations.

8 And ye have not kept the charge of mine holy things: but ye have set keepers of my charge in my sanctuary for yourselves.

9 ¶ Thus saith the Lord GOD; No stranger, uncircumcised in heart, nor uncircumcised in flesh, shall enter into my sanctuary, of any stranger that is among the children of Israel.

10 And the Levites that are gone away far from me, when Israel went astray, which went astray away from me after their idols; they shall even bear their iniquity.

11 Yet they shall be ministers in my sanctuary, having charge at the gates of the house, and ministering to the house: they shall slay the burnt offering and the sacrifice for the people, and they shall stand before them to minister unto them.

12 Because they ministered unto them before their idols, and caused the house of Israel to fall into iniquity; therefore have I lifted up mine hand against them, saith the Lord GOD, and they shall bear their iniquity.

13 And they shall not come near unto me, to do the office of a priest unto me, nor to come near to any of my holy things, in the most holy place: but they shall bear their shame, and their abominations which they have committed.

14 But I will make them keepers of the charge of the house, for all the service thereof, and for all that shall be done therein.

15 ¶ But the priests the Levites, the sons of Zadok, that kept the charge of my sanctuary when the children of Israel went astray from me, they shall come near to me to minister unto me, and they shall stand before me to offer unto me the fat and the blood, saith the Lord GOD:

16 They shall enter into my sanctuary, and they shall come near to my table, to minister unto me, and they shall keep my charge.

17 ¶ And it shall come to pass, that when they enter in at the gates of the inner court, they shall be clothed with linen garments; and no wool shall come upon them, whiles they minister in the gates of the inner court, and within.

EZEKIEL CHAPTER 44

Ezekiel 44:9—Our Sanctuary

It is the sacred privilege of the faithful and devoted followers of the Lamb of God to be granted a sanctuary in the House of the Lord. The rebellious, those who do not follow the principles of the gospel and enter in by the gate of prescribed ordinances with devotion and loyalty, are left to ponder their condition outside the walls.

The Lord will have servants of purity and devotion, as we have been told: ". . . be ye clean, that bear the vessels of the LORD" (Isa. 52:11; compare 3 Ne. 20:41; D&C 38:42; 133:5). The faithful and the obedient will come into the sanctuary of the Lord to minister unto Him and keep His charge.

Ezekiel 44:15—Zadok

Zadok (pronounced "zay'-dock"; meaning: righteous) was a leading priest at the time of David (see 2 Sam. 8:17; 1 Chron. 16:39) and a descendant in the line of priests stemming from Eleazar, son of Aaron (see 1 Chron. 6:4–8; 24:3). The other leading priest during this time was Abiathar, of the line of descent from Ithamar, brother of Eleazar, through Eli (see 1 Sam. 23:6, 9; 30:7; 1 Chron. 15:11; 27:33–34). In connection with Abiathar, Zadok took the ark to Jerusalem according to the command of David, newly anointed king of Israel (see 1 Chron. 15:11–12; 2 Sam. 15:24–36). During the rebellion by David's third son, Absalom (see 2 Sam. 15–18), Abiathar remained faithful to the king (see 2 Sam. 15:1); however, when Adonijah, fourth son of David, rose up and aspired to become king in the place of his aging father, Abiathar supported him as successor to the king, rather than Solomon (see 1 Kings 1:7).

By way of contrast, Zadok remained faithful to the cause of David. When Adonijah pridefully ascended the throne (sometime in the period 1026–1015 BC) and engaged in a banquet of celebration with his confederates, Nathan the prophet counseled Bathsheba, mother of Solomon, to appeal to David to intervene (see 1 Kings 1:17–18), which he did: "And Zadok the priest took an horn of oil out of the tabernacle, and anointed Solomon. And they blew the trumpet; and all the people said, God save king Solomon" (1 Kings 1:39). After Adonijah and his banquet guests had fled in horror, Solomon, the new king, was left to decide upon their fate. In due course, Adonijah was put to death as a schemer. Abiathar was stripped of his priestly authority and exiled, putting an end to the priestly service of the line descending from Eli (see 1 Kings 2:26–27; compare 1 Sam. 2:31–35). Zadok was made chief priest (1 Kings 2:34–35; 1 Chron. 29:22; Ezek. 40:46; 43:19; 44:15; 48:11; the references in 1 Chron. 6:12, 9:11, and Neh. 11:11 likely also refer to this Zadok).

Ezekiel 44:23—Our Sacred Charge to Teach

Those who serve in the kingdom of God have the sacred charge to delineate plainly between good and evil for the insruction of the people. There is no moral relativity in the fold of Christ. Isaiah declared: "Woe unto them that

18 They shall have linen bonnets upon their heads, and shall have linen breeches upon their loins; they shall not gird themselves with any thing that causeth sweat.

19 And when they go forth into the utter court, even into the utter court to the people, they shall put off their garments wherein they ministered, and lay them in the holy chambers, and they shall put on other garments; and they shall not sanctify the people with their garments.

20 Neither shall they shave their heads, nor suffer their locks to grow long; they shall only poll their heads.

21 Neither shall any priest drink wine, when they enter into the inner court.

22 Neither shall they take for their wives a widow, nor her that is put away: but they shall take maidens of the seed of the house of Israel, or a widow that had a priest before.

23 And they shall teach my people the difference between the holy and profane, and cause them to discern between the unclean and the clean.

24 And in controversy they shall stand in judgment; and they shall judge it according to my judgments: and they shall keep my laws and my statutes in all mine assemblies; and they shall hallow my sabbaths.

25 And they shall come at no dead person to defile themselves: but for father, or for mother, or for son, or for daughter, for brother, or for sister that hath had no husband, they may defile themselves.

26 And after he is cleansed, they shall reckon unto him seven days.

27 And in the day that he goeth into the sanctuary, unto the inner court, to minister in the sanctuary, he shall offer his sin offering, saith the Lord GOD.

28 And it shall be unto them for an inheritance: I am their inheritance: and ye shall give them no possession in Israel: I am their possession.

29 They shall eat the meat offering, and the sin offering, and the trespass offering; and every dedicated thing in Israel shall be theirs.

30 And the first of all the firstfruits of all things, and every oblation of all, of every sort of your oblations, shall be the priest's: ye shall also give unto the priest the first of your dough, that he may cause the blessing to rest in thine house.

31 The priests shall not eat of any thing that is dead of itself, or torn, whether it be fowl or beast.

CHAPTER 47

1 AFTERWARD he brought me again unto the door of the house; and, behold, waters issued out from under the threshold of the house eastward: for the forefront of the house stood toward the east, and the waters came down from under from the right side of the house, at the south side of the altar.

2 Then brought he me out of the way of the gate northward, and led me about the way without unto the utter gate by the way that looketh eastward; and, behold, there ran out waters on the right side.

3 And when the man that had the line in his hand went forth eastward, he measured a thousand cubits, and he brought me through the waters; the waters were to the ankles.

4 Again he measured a thousand, and brought me through the waters; the waters were to the knees. Again he measured a thousand, and brought me through; the waters were to the loins.

call evil good, and good evil; that put darkness for light, and light for darkness; that put bitter for sweet, and sweet for bitter!" (Isa. 5:4:20; compare 3 John 1:11; 2 Ne. 2:5; 15:20; Moroni 7:16, 19). The lines are drawn with precision and accuracy, and the word of truth is plain, not to be misunderstood. Said Nephi: "And now behold, my people, ye are a stiffnecked people; wherefore, I have spoken plainly unto you, that ye cannot misunderstand" (2 Ne. 25:28).

EZEKIEL CHAPTER 47

"These [temple] ordinances have been revealed unto us for this very purpose, that we might be born into the light from the midst of this darkness — from death into life." —Joseph F. Smith, *JD* 19:285, 11 April 1878

Ezekiel 47:1–12—The Living Waters

Ezekiel draws from the celestial archives of the word of God the message of hope and a view of the ultimate state of the redeemed. Drawing from the same heavenly archive, the Book of Revelation of John the Beloved—of all New Testament books the one most similar in cadence and imagery to the majestic rhetoric of Isaiah, Jeremiah, Ezekiel, Daniel, and other Old Testament prophets—speaks of a time of restoration when the righteous would be arrayed in white robes before the throne of the Lamb, worshipping with thanksgiving: "Saying, Amen: Blessing, and glory, and wisdom, and thanksgiving, and honour, and power, and might, be unto our God for ever and ever. Amen. And one of the elders answered, saying unto me, What are these which are arrayed in white robes? and whence came they? And I said unto him, Sir, thou knowest. And he said to me, These are they which came out of great tribulation and have washed their robes, and made them white in the blood of the Lamb. Therefore are they before the throne of God, and serve him day and night in his temple: and he that sitteth on the throne shall dwell among them. They shall hunger no more, neither thirst any more; neither shall the sun light on them, nor any heat. For the Lamb which is in the midst of the throne shall feed them, and shall lead them unto living fountains of waters: and God shall wipe away all tears from their eyes" (Rev. 7:12–17).

Relating the gospel of Jesus Christ to the living waters that sustain eternal life is a pervasive image in the pages of Holy Writ. Nephi also discerned clearly the meaning of these waters: "And it came to pass that I beheld that the rod of iron, which my father had seen, was the word of God, which led to the fountain of living waters, or to the tree of life; which waters are a representation of the love of God; and I also beheld that the tree of life was a representation of the love of God" (1 Ne. 11:25).

In our day, the Lord re-emphasized the theme: "But unto him that keepeth my commandments I will give the mysteries of my kingdom, and the same shall be in him a well of living water, springing up unto everlasting life" (D&C 63:23).

5 Afterward he measured a thousand; and it was a river that I could not pass over: for the waters were risen, waters to swim in, a river that could not be passed over.

6 ¶ And he said unto me, Son of man, hast thou seen this? Then he brought me, and caused me to return to the brink of the river.

7 Now when I had returned, behold, at the bank of the river were very many trees on the one side and on the other.

8 Then said he unto me, These waters issue out toward the east country, and go down into the desert, and go into the sea: which being brought forth into the sea, the waters shall be healed.

9 And it shall come to pass, that every thing that liveth, which moveth, whithersoever the rivers shall come, shall live: and there shall be a very great multitude of fish, because these waters shall come thither: for they shall be healed; and every thing shall live whither the river cometh.

10 And it shall come to pass, that the fishers shall stand upon it from En-gedi even unto En-eglaim; they shall be a place to spread forth nets; their fish shall be according to their kinds, as the fish of the great sea, exceeding many.

11 But the miry places thereof and the marishes thereof shall not be healed; they shall be given to salt.

12 And by the river upon the bank thereof, on this side and on that side, shall grow all trees for meat, whose leaf shall not fade, neither shall the fruit thereof be consumed: it shall bring forth new fruit according to his months, because their waters they issued out of the sanctuary: and the fruit thereof shall be for meat, and the leaf thereof for medicine.

13 ¶ Thus saith the Lord GOD; This shall be the border, whereby ye shall inherit the land according to the twelve tribes of Israel: Joseph shall have two portions.

14 And ye shall inherit it, one as well as another: concerning the which I lifted up mine hand to give it unto your fathers: and this land shall fall unto you for inheritance.

15 And this shall be the border of the land toward the north side, from the great sea, the way of Hethlon, as men go to Zedad;

16 Hamath, Berothah, Sibraim, which is between the border of Damascus and the border of Hamath; Hazar-hatticon, which is by the coast of Hauran.

17 And the border from the sea shall be Hazar-enan, the border of Damascus, and the north northward, and the border of Hamath. And this is the north side.

18 And the east side ye shall measure from Hauran, and from Damascus, and from Gilead, and from the land of Israel by Jordan, from the border unto the east sea. And this is the east side.

19 And the south side southward, from Tamar even to the waters of strife in Kadesh, the river to the great sea. And this is the south side southward.

20 The west side also shall be the great sea from the border, till a man come over against Hamath. This is the west side.

21 So shall ye divide this land unto you according to the tribes of Israel.

22 ¶ And it shall come to pass, that ye shall divide it by lot for an inheritance unto you, and to the strangers that sojourn among you, which shall beget children among you: and they shall be unto you as born in the country among the children of Israel; they shall have inheritance with you among the tribes of Israel.

23 And it shall come to pass, that in what tribe the stranger sojourneth, there shall ye give him his inheritance, saith the Lord GOD.

For Ezekiel, the living water was inseparably connected with the temple, for the temple was the source of the river that nurtured the trees along its banks, trees of enduring verdure and never-ending fruit: "And by the river upon the bank thereof, on this side and on that side, shall grow all trees for meat, whose leaf shall not fade, neither shall the fruit thereof be consumed: it shall bring forth new fruit according to his months, because their waters they issued out of the sanctuary: and the fruit thereof shall be for meat, and the leaf thereof for medicine" (Ezek. 47:12).

With the water from the sanctuary, the faithful will never lack for spiritual nurture and healing grace—because the temple is the place where "the glory of the Lord filled the house" (Ezek. 43:5; compare also Rev. 22:1–3; 1 Ne. 8:10–11; 11:25).

Daniel by Gustave Doré

THE
BOOK OF DANIEL

CHAPTER 1

1 IN the third year of the reign of Jehoiakim king of Judah came Nebuchadnezzar king of Babylon unto Jerusalem, and besieged it.

2 And the Lord gave Jehoiakim king of Judah into his hand, with part of the vessels of the house of God: which he carried into the land of Shinar to the house of his god; and he brought the vessels into the treasure house of his god.

3 ¶ And the king spake unto Ashpenaz the master of his eunuchs, that he should bring certain of the children of Israel, and of the king's seed, and of the princes;

4 Children in whom was no blemish, but well favoured, and skilful in all wisdom, and cunning in knowledge, and understanding science, and such as had ability in them to stand in the king's palace, and whom they might teach the learning and the tongue of the Chaldeans.

5 And the king appointed them a daily provision of the king's meat, and of the wine which he drank: so nourishing them three years, that at the end thereof they might stand before the king.

6 Now among these were of the children of Judah, Daniel, Hananiah, Mishael, and Azariah:

7 Unto whom the prince of the eunuchs gave names: for he gave unto Daniel the name of Belteshazzar; and to Hananiah, of Shadrach; and to Mishael, of Meshach; and to Azariah, of Abednego.

8 ¶ But Daniel purposed in his heart that he would not defile himself with the portion of the king's meat, nor with the wine which he drank: therefore he requested of the prince of the eunuchs that he might not defile himself.

9 Now God had brought Daniel into favour and tender love with the prince of the eunuchs.

10 And the prince of the eunuchs said unto Daniel, I fear my lord the king, who hath appointed your meat and your drink: for why should he see your faces worse liking than the children which are of your sort? then shall ye make me endanger my head to the king.

11 Then said Daniel to Melzar, whom the prince of the eunuchs had set over Daniel, Hananiah, Mishael, and Azariah,

12 Prove thy servants, I beseech thee, ten days; and let them give us pulse to eat, and water to drink.

13 Then let our countenances be looked upon before thee, and the countenance of the children that eat of the portion of the king's meat: and as thou seest, deal with thy servants.

14 So he consented to them in this matter, and proved them ten days.

15 And at the end of ten days their countenances appeared fairer and fatter in flesh than all the children which did eat the portion of the king's meat.

16 Thus Melzar took away the portion of their meat, and the wine that they should drink; and gave them pulse.

17 ¶ As for these four children, God gave them knowledge and skill in all learning and wisdom: and Daniel had understanding in all visions and dreams.

DANIEL CHAPTER 1

For more insight into the life of Daniel, see Appendix KK.

Daniel 1:3—Eunuch

Eunuchs (meaning: bed-keeper) were a class of men deprived of their masculinity and employed to watch over the harems of eastern rulers or occupy other positions of trust. The word *eunuch* or *eunuchs* occurs twenty-seven times in the scriptures. Here is one example from among many in the Book of Daniel: "And the king spake unto Ashpenaz the master of his eunuchs, that he should bring *certain* of the children of Israel [i.e., Daniel and his associates], and of the king's seed, and of the princes" (Dan. 1:3).

Daniel 1:7—Belteshazzar

Belteshazzar was the name given to Daniel by the officers in the court of the Babylonian king, Nebuchadnezzar. The name Belteshazzar was also maintained for Daniel after the Persians took over the Babylonian empire (see Dan. 10:1).

Daniel 1:8—Portraits of Covenant Character and Honor

Character is measured when one faces the ultimate challenges of one's devotion and loyalty to divine purpose. Life brings to all of us in this probationary state, sooner or later, the occasion of being "weighed in the balances" (Dan. 5:27); it is then that valor is assessed and the depth of one's commitment to God is evaluated.

A life founded on enduring principles is a life imbued with truth and the glory of God. Daniel and his three young colleagues followed the principles of health and wholesome living (in opposition to the king's prescribed gourmet diet), and thus were rewarded with wisdom, comely appearance, brightness of mind, and opportunities for leadership. Later, his three young colleagues (renamed by their captors Shadrach, Meshach, and Abed-nego) followed the principle of worshipping the one true God and not idols, and thus ran afoul of the king's decree to worship his golden image. But, again, by following the principle of meticulous obedience to God's laws, they were attended in the fiery furnace by an angel of God and emerged without even the odor of smoke upon their clothing.

In turn, Daniel followed the principle of continual, unremitting service to the God of Israel, despite life-threatening opposition at the hands of King Darius' nefarious princes, and thus emerged from the Lion's den as an instrument for the preservation of true worship among his people.

Such valor transforms singularity into abundance, individuality into leadership—and Daniel and his three friends rose to a place of prominence in the circle of their captors like their forebear Joseph of Egypt. Thus we see that the Lord, in His wisdom and eternal designs, prepares shepherds and stewards of the covenant by bringing them through the valley of adversity and trial so that they can

18 Now at the end of the days that the king had said he should bring them in, then the prince of the eunuchs brought them in before Nebuchadnezzar.

19 And the king communed with them; and among them all was found none like Daniel, Hananiah, Mishael, and Azariah: therefore stood they before the king.

20 And in all matters of wisdom and understanding, that the king enquired of them, he found them ten times better than all the magicians and astrologers that were in all his realm.

21 And Daniel continued even unto the first year of king Cyrus.

CHAPTER 2

1 AND in the second year of the reign of Nebuchadnezzar Nebuchadnezzar dreamed dreams, wherewith his spirit was troubled, and his sleep brake from him.

2 Then the king commanded to call the magicians, and the astrologers, and the sorcerers, and the Chaldeans, for to shew the king his dreams. So they came and stood before the king.

3 And the king said unto them, I have dreamed a dream, and my spirit was troubled to know the dream.

4 Then spake the Chaldeans to the king in Syriack, O king, live for ever: tell thy servants the dream, and we will shew the interpretation,

5 The king answered and said to the Chaldeans, The thing is gone from me: if ye will not make known unto me the dream, with the interpretation thereof, ye shall be cut in pieces, and your houses shall be made a dunghill.

6 But if ye shew the dream, and the interpretation thereof, ye shall receive of me gifts and rewards and great honour: therefore shew me the dream, and the interpretation thereof.

7 They answered again and said, Let the king tell his servants the dream, and we will shew the interpretation of it.

8 The king answered and said, I know of certainty that ye would gain the time, because ye see the thing is gone from me.

9 But if ye will not make known unto me the dream, there is but one decree for you: for ye have prepared lying and corrupt words to speak before me, till the time be changed: therefore tell me the dream, and I shall know that ye can shew me the interpretation thereof.

10 ¶ The Chaldeans answered before the king, and said, There is not a man upon the earth that can shew the king's matter: therefore there is no king, lord, nor ruler, that asked such things at any magician, or astrologer, or Chaldean.

11 And it is a rare thing that the king requireth, and there is none other that can shew it before the king, except the gods, whose dwelling is not with flesh.

12 For this cause the king was angry and very furious, and commanded to destroy all the wise men of Babylon.

13 And the decree went forth that the wise men should be slain; and they sought Daniel and his fellows to be slain.

14 ¶ Then Daniel answered with counsel and wisdom to Arioch the captain of the king's guard, which was gone forth to slay the wise men of Babylon:

emerge as spiritual paragons endowed with power and wisdom unto the leading of many in the paths of righteousness

Daniel 1:9–16—Honoring Eternal Standards

During the siege and captivity of the House of Judah by the Babylonians, exceptional courage and spiritual strength were shown by Daniel and his young friends. What was it that allowed them to stand firm in the face of such intense challenges to their standards and principles? What was it that gave them courage to draw the line and reaffirm their commitment to the covenant promises of righteousness and faithfulness? It was in the strength of the Lord, which they sought and obtained through mighty prayer and fasting, that they were able to perform their missions with exemplary valor. Character is always measured in the context of adversity and challenge.

We observe in the life of Daniel and his associates that the Lord surely magnifies His obedient servants in all things. Holding true to our beliefs and standards brings down the blessings of Heaven, as described by the Lord (see D&C 130:20–21).

In the spirit of Daniel's example, we can anchor our life to the Savior by following His gospel standards with commitment and devotion. We can strive to make wise decisions every day, based on principles of integrity and honor. We can put the well-being of others high on our agenda by making service a central part of our lives. We can learn from adversity and challenge by viewing them as opportunities to grow.

DANIEL CHAPTER 2

"… after a happy time spent in witnessing and feeling for ourselves the powers and blessings of the Holy Ghost, through the grace of God bestowed upon us, we dismissed with the pleasing knowledge that we were now individually members of, and acknowledged of God, 'The Church of Jesus Christ,' organized in accordance with commandments and revelations given by Him to ourselves in these last days, as well as according to the order of the Church as recorded in the New Testament." —Joseph Smith, HC 1:79, concerning the organization of the Church on 6 April 1830

Daniel 2:1—The Dream of Nebuchadnezzar

Nebuchadnezzar, king of the Babylonian Empire and captor of the hosts of Israel since 587 BC, had a troubling dream one night about a stone hewn from the mountain without hands that destroys a mighty image in human form. The king commanded his wisemen to reveal its contents to him and interpret its meaning. Because they were helpless to perform their assignment, saying that only the gods could do so, the king ordered all such wisemen—including the bright and visionary young Daniel—to be destroyed. But Daniel, being full of faith and wisdom, gained more time from the king so that a spiritual solution could be sought. Through prayer, Daniel was able to open up the channels of revelation from the Lord so that His eternal agenda, as

15 He answered and said to Arioch the king's captain, Why is the decree so hasty from the king? Then Arioch made the thing known to Daniel.

16 Then Daniel went in, and desired of the king that he would give him time, and that he would shew the king the interpretation.

17 Then Daniel went to his house, and made the thing known to Hananiah, Mishael, and Azariah, his companions:

18 That they would desire mercies of the God of heaven concerning this secret; that Daniel and his fellows should not perish with the rest of the wise men of Babylon.

19 ¶ Then was the secret revealed unto Daniel in a night vision. Then Daniel blessed the God of heaven.

20 Daniel answered and said, Blessed be the name of God for ever and ever: for wisdom and might are his:

21 And he changeth the times and the seasons: he removeth kings, and setteth up kings: he giveth wisdom unto the wise, and knowledge to them that know understanding:

22 He revealeth the deep and secret things: he knoweth what is in the darkness, and the light dwelleth with him.

23 I thank thee, and praise thee, O thou God of my fathers, who hast given me wisdom and might, and hast made known unto me now what we desired of thee: for thou hast now made known unto us the king's matter.

24 ¶ Therefore Daniel went in unto Arioch, whom the king had ordained to destroy the wise men of Babylon: he went and said thus unto him; Destroy not the wise men of Babylon: bring me in before the king, and I will shew unto the king the interpretation.

25 Then Arioch brought in Daniel before the king in haste, and said thus unto him, I have found a man of the captives of Judah, that will make known unto the king the interpretation.

26 The king answered and said to Daniel, whose name was Belteshazzar, Art thou able to make known unto me the dream which I have seen, and the interpretation thereof?

27 Daniel answered in the presence of the king, and said, The secret which the king hath demanded cannot the wise men, the astrologers, the magicians, the soothsayers, shew unto the king;

28 But there is a God in heaven that revealeth secrets, and maketh known to the king Nebuchadnezzar what shall be in the latter days. Thy dream, and the visions of thy head upon thy bed, are these;

29 As for thee, O king, thy thoughts came into thy mind upon thy bed, what should come to pass hereafter: and he that revealeth secrets maketh known to thee what shall come to pass.

30 But as for me, this secret is not revealed to me for any wisdom that I have more than any living, but for their sakes that shall make known the interpretation to the king, and that thou mightest know the thoughts of thy heart.

31 ¶ Thou, O king, sawest, and behold a great image. This great image, whose brightness was excellent, stood before thee; and the form thereof was terrible.

32 This image's head was of fine gold, his breast and his arms of silver, his belly and his thighs of brass,

33 His legs of iron, his feet part of iron and part of clay.

34 Thou sawest till that a stone was cut out without hands, which smote the image upon his feet that were of iron and clay, and brake them to pieces.

35 Then was the iron, the clay, the brass, the silver, and the gold, broken to pieces together, and became like the chaff of the summer threshingfloors; and the wind carried them away, that no place was

it relates to earthly kings and empires leading to the Restoration of Church in the latter days, might be made known to Nebuchadnezzar and all seekers of truth after him.

For more insight into the life of Nebuchadnezzar, see Appendix LL.

Daniel 2:18—Abiding By Revelation

Faced with certain death unless the king's dream could be revealed and interpreted, Daniel counseled with his three young companions—renamed by their hosts Shadrach, Meshach, and Abed-nego—and as a team they sought the "mercies of the God of heaven concerning this secret" (Dan. 2:18).

It is instructive that when the answer came to Daniel "in a night vision" (Dan. 2:19), he immediately blessed the name of God and gave humble thanks and praise for the divine gift (see Dan. 2:23). Daniel was able to save all the condemned wisemen in the kingdom by advising Nebuchadnezzar correctly concerning the dream, which portended the coming of the restored kingdom of Heaven to become "a great mountain" that would fill "the whole earth" (Dan. 2:35). But the king refused nevertheless to relinquish his idolatry, and a second dream depicting the king as a great and mighty tree that is hewn down at the behest of "an holy one coming down from heaven" (Dan. 4:23) was interpreted by Daniel as foretelling the king's demise.

The royal reveler Belshazzar, prince-regent in the wake of Nebuchadnezzar's reign (and, according to recent archaeological discoveries, apparently the son of Nabonidus, the last king of Babylon), did not fare much better after Daniel interpreted the celebrated and ominous writing on the wall of his chamber this way: "Thou art weighed in the balances, and art found wanting" (Dan. 5:27). That night Belshazzar was deposed by Darius the Mede. Thus continued the unfolding of the certain prediction that a succession of earthly kingdoms would fall, one after the other, until, ultimately, the Lord would restore a heavenly kingdom to the earth not made by the hand of man.

The stone "cut out of the mountain without hands" (Dan. 2:45) is the kingdom of God, which is to supersede all earthly kingdoms and fill the world with a heavenly dominion of truth and light under the supreme rulership of the Redeemer and Lord of Lords. As the Lord said to Joseph Smith in October 1831, not long after the organization of the Church in our day: "The keys of the kingdom are committed unto man on the earth, and from thence shall the gospel roll forth unto the ends of the earth, as the stone which is cut out of the mountains without hands shall roll forth, until it has filled the whole earth" (D&C 65:2).

Revelation is the communication from God to His prophets and His other children—given in many ways: personal visitations of Deity, angels, or the Holy Ghost; open visions; voices from above; dreams; a whispering in the mind and heart; or any similar inspiration from the Holy

found for them: and the stone that smote the image became a great mountain, and filled the whole earth.

36 ¶ This is the dream; and we will tell the interpretation thereof before the king.

37 Thou, O king, art a king of kings: for the God of heaven hath given thee a kingdom, power, and strength, and glory.

38 And wheresoever the children of men dwell, the beasts of the field and the fowls of the heaven hath he given into thine hand, and hath made thee ruler over them all. Thou art this head of gold.

39 And after thee shall arise another kingdom inferior to thee, and another third kingdom of brass, which shall bear rule over all the earth.

40 And the fourth kingdom shall be strong as iron: forasmuch as iron breaketh in pieces and subdueth all things: and as iron that breaketh all these, shall it break in pieces and bruise.

41 And whereas thou sawest the feet and toes, part of potters' clay, and part of iron, the kingdom shall be divided; but there shall be in it of the strength of the iron, forasmuch as thou sawest the iron mixed with miry clay.

42 And as the toes of the feet were part of iron, and part of clay, so the kingdom shall be partly strong, and partly broken.

43 And whereas thou sawest iron mixed with miry clay, they shall mingle themselves with the seed of men: but they shall not cleave one to another, even as iron is not mixed with clay.

44 And in the days of these kings shall the God of heaven set up a kingdom, which shall never be destroyed: and the kingdom shall not be left to other people, but it shall break in pieces and consume all these kingdoms, and it shall stand for ever.

45 Forasmuch as thou sawest that the stone was cut out of the mountain without hands, and that it brake in pieces the iron, the brass, the clay, the silver, and the gold; the great God hath made known to the king what shall come to pass hereafter: and the dream is certain, and the interpretation thereof sure.

46 ¶ Then the king Nebuchadnezzar fell upon his face, and worshipped Daniel, and commanded that they should offer an oblation and sweet odours unto him.

47 The king answered unto Daniel, and said, Of a truth it is, that your God is a God of gods, and a Lord of kings, and a revealer of secrets, seeing thou couldest reveal this secret.

48 Then the king made Daniel a great man, and gave him many great gifts, and made him ruler over the whole province of Babylon, and chief of the governors over all the wise men of Babylon.

49 Then Daniel requested of the king, and he set Shadrach, Meshach, and Abed-nego, over the affairs of the province of Babylon: but Daniel sat in the gate of the king.

Ghost. Revelation can be of universal significance, as given through the prophets, or of personal application, as given to us in our personal lives and Church callings. We as children of our Heavenly Father have the privilege to receive inspiration and direction in our lives, for God is no respecter of persons (see D&C 38:16). The Holy Ghost is the Revelator. We can receive revelation and direction according to our need and worthiness (see 2 Ne. 32:5; Moroni 10:5). We can know God (see D&C 67:10). The blessings of revelation can be ours as we ask in faith, believing (see D&C 8:1–3).

Daniel 2:44–45—The Stone that Filled the Whole Earth

The stone "cut out of the mountain without hands" (Dan. 2:45) is the kingdom of God, which is to supersede all earthly kingdoms and fill the world with a heavenly dominion of truth and light under the supreme rulership of the Redeemer and Lord of Lords.

Daniel 2—Summary of Precepts and Principles

In describing the Kingdom of God on the earth, the Apostle Paul spoke of its members as having been ". . . built upon the foundation of the apostles and prophets, Jesus Christ himself being the chief cornerstone; In whom all the building fitly framed together groweth unto a holy temple in the Lord" (Eph. 2:20–21). The stone that rolls forth to fill the world is the gospel kingdom of Jesus Christ, in its fulness a mighty temple unto God. In a special and unique way, the stone is the Savior Himself (see Isa. 28:16). In referring to this word of prophecy, the Apostle Peter expressed it this way: ". . . and he that believeth on him shall not be confounded" (1 Pet. 2:6). Thus the foundation for the spiritual existence of the sons and daughters of God, for the salvation of all mankind and the exaltation of the faithful, is Jesus Christ. By doing our part to advance the cause of the "stone," we help build the kingdom of God and assist in the godly mission to fill the world with the peace, joy, and eternal blessings that only the Gospel of Jesus Christ can bring.

Solomon said many centuries ago: "As cold waters to a thirsty soul, so is good news from a far country" (Prov. 25:25). The "good news" from our heavenly home is the gospel of Jesus Christ, providing eternal refreshment to quench our compelling thirst to become pure and whole. The gospel is the plan of salvation, the blueprint of redemption—magnificent and unique—affording every soul the opportunity to return again into the presence of God in glory and eternal grace. The Savior explained to the Saints in Bountiful, "and this is the Gospel which I have given unto you—that I came into the world to do the will of my Father, because my Father sent me. And my Father sent me that I might be lifted up upon the cross; and after that I had been lifted up upon the cross, that I might draw all men unto me" (3 Ne. 27:14).

To be drawn unto Christ is to make His Atonement fully active in our lives through faith, repentance, baptism, and the gift of the Holy Ghost. The gospel of exaltation—

CHAPTER 3

1 NEBUCHADNEZZAR the king made an image of gold, whose height was threescore cubits, and the breadth thereof six cubits: he set it up in the plain of Dura, in the province of Babylon.

2 Then Nebuchadnezzar the king sent to gather together the princes, the governors, and the captains, the judges, the treasurers, the counsellors, the sheriffs, and all the rulers of the provinces, to come to the dedication of the image which Nebuchadnezzar the king had set up.

3 Then the princes, the governors, and captains, the judges, the treasurers, the counsellors, the sheriffs, and all the rulers of the provinces, were gathered together unto the dedication of the image that Nebuchadnezzar the king had set up; and they stood before the image that Nebuchadnezzar had set up.

4 Then an herald cried aloud, To you it is commanded, O people, nations, and languages,

5 That at what time ye hear the sound of the cornet, flute, harp, sackbut, psaltery, dulcimer, and all kinds of musick, ye fall down and worship the golden image that Nebuchadnezzar the king hath set up:

6 And whoso falleth not down and worshippeth shall the same hour be cast into the midst of a burning fiery furnace.

7 Therefore at that time, when all the people heard the sound of the cornet, flute, harp, sackbut, psaltery, and all kinds of musick, all the people, the nations, and the languages, fell down and worshipped the golden image that Nebuchadnezzar the king had set up.

8 ¶ Wherefore at that time certain Chaldeans came near, and accused the Jews.

9 They spake and said to the king Nebuchadnezzar, O king, live for ever.

10 Thou, O king, hast made a decree, that every man that shall hear the sound of the cornet, flute, harp, sackbut, psaltery, and dulcimer, and all kinds of musick, shall fall down and worship the golden image:

11 And whoso falleth not down and worshippeth, that he should be cast into the midst of a burning fiery furnace.

12 There are certain Jews whom thou hast set over the affairs of the province of Babylon, Shadrach, Meshach, and Abed-nego; these men, O king, have not regarded thee: they serve not thy gods, nor worship the golden image which thou hast set up.

13 ¶ Then Nebuchadnezzar in his rage and fury commanded to bring Shadrach, Meshach, and Abed-nego. Then they brought these men before the king.

14 Nebuchadnezzar spake and said unto them, Is it true, O Shadrach, Meshach, and Abed-nego, do not ye serve my gods, nor worship the golden image which I have set up?

15 Now if ye be ready that at what time ye hear the sound of the cornet, flute, harp, sackbut, psaltery, and dulcimer, and all kinds of musick, ye fall down and worship the image which I have made; well: but if ye worship not, ye shall be cast the same hour into the midst of a burning fiery furnace; and who is that God that shall deliver you out of my hands?

16 Shadrach, Meshach, and Abed-nego, answered and said to the king, O Nebuchadnezzar, we are not careful to answer thee in this matter.

17 If it be so, our God whom we serve is able to deliver us from the burning fiery furnace, and he will deliver us out of thine hand, O king.

together with all associated doctrines and principles, covenants and ordinances, laws and priesthoods—is centered in Christ as Redeemer and Lord. "And this is the Gospel, the glad tidings, which the voice out of the heavens bore record unto us—That he came into the world, even Jesus, to be crucified for the world, and to bear the sins of the world, and to sanctify the world, and to cleanse it from all unrighteousness; That through him all might be saved whom the Father had put into his power and made by him" (D&C 76:40–42).

DANIEL CHAPTER 3

"We all know that no one ever lived upon the earth that exerted the same influence upon the destinies of the world as did our Lord and Savior Jesus Christ; and yet He was born in obscurity, cradled in a manger. He chose for His apostles poor, unlettered fishermen. More than nineteen hundred years have passed and gone since His crucifixion, and yet all over the world, in spite of all strife and chaos, there is still burning in the hearts of millions of people a testimony of the divinity of the work that He accomplished." —Heber J. Grant, *Improvement Era* 43:713, December 1940

Shadrach, Meshach, and Abed-nego by Gustave Doré

18 But if not, be it known unto thee, O king, that we will not serve thy gods, nor worship the golden image which thou hast set up.

19 ¶ Then was Nebuchadnezzar full of fury, and the form of his visage was changed against Shadrach, Meshach, and Abed-nego: therefore he spake, and commanded that they should heat the furnace one seven times more than it was wont to be heated.

20 And he commanded the most mighty men that were in his army to bind Shadrach, Meshach, and Abed-nego, and to cast them into the burning fiery furnace.

21 Then these men were bound in their coats, their hosen, and their hats, and their other garments, and were cast into the midst of the burning fiery furnace.

22 Therefore because the king's commandment was urgent, and the furnace exceeding hot, the flame of the fire slew those men that took up Shadrach, Meshach, and Abed-nego.

23 And these three men, Shadrach, Meshach, and Abed-nego, fell down bound into the midst of the burning fiery furnace.

24 Then Nebuchadnezzar the king was astonied, and rose up in haste, and spake, and said unto his counsellors, Did not we cast three men bound into the midst of the fire? They answered and said unto the king, True, O king.

25 He answered and said, Lo, I see four men loose, walking in the midst of the fire, and they have no hurt; and the form of the fourth is like the Son of God.

26 ¶ Then Nebuchadnezzar came near to the mouth of the burning fiery furnace, and spake, and said, Shadrach, Meshach, and Abed-nego, ye servants of the most high God, come forth, and come hither. Then Shadrach, Meshach, and Abed-nego, came forth of the midst of the fire.

27 And the princes, governors, and captains, and the king's counsellors, being gathered together, saw these men, upon whose bodies the fire had no power, nor was an hair of their head singed, neither were their coats changed, nor the smell of fire had passed on them.

28 Then Nebuchadnezzar spake, and said, Blessed be the God of Shadrach, Meshach, and Abed-nego, who hath sent his angel, and delivered his servants that trusted in him, and have changed the king's word, and yielded their bodies, that they might not serve nor worship any god, except their own God.

29 Therefore I make a decree, That every people, nation, and language, which speak any thing amiss against the God of Shadrach, Meshach, and Abed-nego, shall be cut in pieces, and their houses shall be made a dunghill: because there is no other God that can deliver after this sort.

30 Then the king promoted Shadrach, Meshach, and Abed-nego, in the province of Babylon.

Daniel 3:30—Abed-nego

Abed-nego (pronounced "uh-bed'-nih-go"; meaning: servant of Nego or Nebo) was a Jewish youth captured along with Daniel and several others (including Hananiah and Mishael) by the forces of the Babylonian King Nebuchadnezzar and taken to Babylon to the palace of the king on the eve of the conquest of Jerusalem around 587 BC (see Dan. 1:6–7). His real name was Azariah, but he was given the name Abed-nego by the prince of the eunuchs (see Dan. 1:7).

Daniel, Hananiah, Mishael, and Azariah refused to eat the rich foods of the court and instead sustained themselves on "pulse" (seeds and vegetables; see Dan. 1:15, 20). When Daniel pleased the king with his power to interpret dreams, he and his associates were given leadership positions in the realm (see Dan. 2:49).

Later on, Abed-nego and his two colleagues Hananiah (called Shadrach) and Mishael (called Meshach) refused to comply with the king's command to worship his golden idol (see Dan. 3:17–18). Enraged, the king caused the three disciples to be cast into a fiery furnace—but they were not consumed (see Dan. 3:24–30.)

From this account we learn a great lesson about the indispensability of worshipping our God in truth and light at all times and under all conditions. Elder Neal A. Maxwell points out that the fiery furnaces of life are often gateways to a deeper understanding of the atonement of Jesus Christ:

> There are many who suffer so much more than the rest of us: some go agonizingly; some go quickly; some are healed; some are given more time; some seem to linger. There are variations in our trials but no immunities. Thus, the scriptures cite the fiery furnace and fiery trials. Those who emerge successfully from their varied and fiery furnaces have experienced the grace of the Lord, which He says is sufficient. . . . (Neal A. Maxwell, "From Whom All Blessings Flow," *Ensign*, May 1997, 11)

CHAPTER 6

1 IT pleased Darius to set over the kingdom an hundred and twenty princes, which should be over the whole kingdom;

2 And over these three presidents; of whom Daniel was first: that the princes might give accounts unto them, and the king should have no damage.

3 Then this Daniel was preferred above the presidents and princes, because an excellent spirit was in him; and the king thought to set him over the whole realm.

4 ¶ Then the presidents and princes sought to find occasion against Daniel concerning the kingdom; but they could find none occasion nor fault; forasmuch as he was faithful, neither was there any error or fault found in him.

5 Then said these men, We shall not find any occasion against this Daniel, except we find it against him concerning the law of his God.

6 Then these presidents and princes assembled together to the king, and said thus unto him, King Darius, live for ever.

7 All the presidents of the kingdom, the governors, and the princes, the counsellors, and the captains, have consulted together to establish a royal statute, and to make a firm decree, that whosoever shall ask a petition of any God or man for thirty days, save of thee, O king, he shall be cast into the den of lions.

8 Now, O king, establish the decree, and sign the writing, that it be not changed, according to the law of the Medes and Persians, which altereth not.

9 Wherefore king Darius signed the writing and the decree.

10 ¶ Now when Daniel knew that the writing was signed, he went into his house; and his windows being open in his chamber toward Jerusalem, he kneeled upon his knees three times a day, and prayed, and gave thanks before his God, as he did aforetime.

11 Then these men assembled, and found Daniel praying and making supplication before his God.

12 Then they came near, and spake before the king concerning the king's decree; Hast thou not signed a decree, that every man that shall ask a petition of any God or man within thirty days, save of thee, O king, shall be cast into the den of lions? The king answered and said, The thing is true, according to the law of the Medes and Persians, which altereth not.

13 Then answered they and said before the king, That Daniel, which is of the children of the captivity of Judah, regardeth not thee, O king, nor the decree that thou hast signed, but maketh his petition three times a day.

14 Then the king, when he heard these words, was sore displeased with himself, and set his heart on Daniel to deliver him: and he laboured till the going down of the sun to deliver him.

15 Then these men assembled unto the king, and said unto the king, Know, O king, that the law of the Medes and Persians is, That no decree nor statute which the king establisheth may be changed.

16 Then the king commanded, and they brought Daniel, and cast him into the den of lions. Now the king spake and said unto Daniel, Thy God whom thou servest continually, he will deliver thee.

17 And a stone was brought, and laid upon the mouth of the den; and the king sealed it with his own signet, and with the signet of his lords; that the purpose might not be changed concerning Daniel.

18 ¶ Then the king went to his palace, and passed the night fasting: neither were instruments of musick brought before him: and his sleep went from him.

DANIEL CHAPTER 6

Daniel 6—Living by the Power of Prayer

Following the days of Nebuchadnezzar, Darius, operating under the canopy of the Persian empire, placed Daniel in a prominent leadership role. Those with whom Daniel worked were jealous and sought a cause against him. They knew Daniel prayed to God and so they convinced the king to enact a law forbidding one to pray. If the decree were disobeyed, the offender would be thrown into the lions' den.

Daniel, as a righteous man, prayed three times daily. He was observed at prayer and reported to the king. The conspirators reminded Darius that his decrees could not be changed and had to be enforced. The king lamented his edict, yet the king had faith in Daniel's God: "Then the king commanded, and they brought Daniel, and cast *him* into the den of lions. *Now* the king spake and said unto Daniel, Thy God whom thou servest continually, he will deliver thee" (Dan. 6:16). The king fasted through the night and did not enjoy sleep but went immediately in the morning to the lions' den and called out:

> Daniel, O Daniel, servant of the living God, is thy God, whom thou servest continually, able to deliver thee from the lions?
>
> Then said Daniel unto the king, O king, live for ever.
>
> My God hath sent his angel, and hath shut the lions' mouths, that they have not hurt me: forasmuch as before him innocency was found in me; and also before thee, O king, have I done no hurt.
>
> Then was the king exceeding glad for him, and commanded that they should take Daniel up out of the den. So Daniel was taken up out of the den, and no manner of hurt was found upon him, because he believed in his God. (Dan. 6:20–23)

From this celebrated story we gain insight into the process by which the Lord watches over the faithful with His protecting hand. The Lord in His infinite goodness provides protection for His children according to His will and pleasure, so that the power of God might be manifest here upon the earth and His children be blessed in all things according to their righteousness.

We know that there must be opposition in all things, or else the great plan of salvation would be frustrated (see 2 Ne. 2:11–12). In the cauldron of opposition we experience the tests and trials of life. In faith and humility we place ourselves in the hands of the Lord as we follow the counsel of the Prophet Joseph Smith: "But thy word must be fulfilled. Help thy servants to say, with thy grace assisting them: Thy will be done, O Lord, and not ours" (D&C 109:44).

When we yield to the will of the Lord, we merit His protecting hand as we learn, grace for grace, and line upon line, how to transcend the challenges of life and rise in thanksgiving to a higher plane of spirituality. In this quest,

19 Then the king arose very early in the morning, and went in haste unto the den of lions.

20 And when he came to the den, he cried with a lamentable voice unto Daniel: and the king spake and said to Daniel, O Daniel, servant of the living God, is thy God, whom thou servest continually, able to deliver thee from the lions?

21 Then said Daniel unto the king, O king, live for ever.

22 My God hath sent his angel, and hath shut the lions' mouths, that they have not hurt me: forasmuch as before him innocency was found in me; and also before thee, O king, have I done no hurt.

23 Then was the king exceeding glad for him, and commanded that they should take Daniel up out of the den. So Daniel was taken up out of the den, and no manner of hurt was found upon him, because he believed in his God.

24 ¶ And the king commanded, and they brought those men which had accused Daniel, and they cast them into the den of lions, them, their children, and their wives; and the lions had the mastery of them, and brake all their bones in pieces or ever they came at the bottom of the den.

25 ¶ Then king Darius wrote unto all people, nations, and languages, that dwell in all the earth; Peace be multiplied unto you.

26 I make a decree, That in every dominion of my kingdom men tremble and fear before the God of Daniel: for he is the living God, and stedfast for ever, and his kingdom that which shall not be destroyed, and his dominion shall be even unto the end.

27 He delivereth and rescueth, and he worketh signs and wonders in heaven and in earth, who hath delivered Daniel from the power of the lions.

28 So this Daniel prospered in the reign of Darius, and in the reign of Cyrus the Persian.

HOSEA

CHAPTER 1

1 THE word of the LORD that came unto Hosea, the son of Beeri, in the days of Uzziah, Jotham, Ahaz, and Hezekiah, kings of Judah, and in the days of Jeroboam the son of Joash, king of Israel.

2 The beginning of the word of the LORD by Hosea. And the LORD said to Hosea, Go, take unto thee a wife of whoredoms and children of whoredoms: for the land hath committed great whoredom, departing from the LORD.

3 So he went and took Gomer the daughter of Diblaim; which conceived, and bare him a son.

4 And the LORD said unto him, Call his name Jezreel; for yet a little while, and I will avenge the blood of Jezreel upon the house of Jehu, and will cause to cease the kingdom of the house of Israel.

5 And it shall come to pass at that day, that I will break the bow of Israel in the valley of Jezreel.

we depend on the Lord fully to protect our families in their mortal sojourn (see Isa. 4:5–6.)

From the example of Daniel, we can take strength in our quest to worship the Lord in courage and truth. We can strive to become and remain part of the Lord's fold of Zion—the pure in heart (see D&C 97:21). We can stand in holy places (see D&C 101:22). We can maintain a perspective that is defined by endurance and patience—for things work out in the due time of the Lord, and the trials of life are for our ultimate good. We can remember that the protecting hand of the Lord comes to those who do their part, operating on faith and prayer and having a certain hope in the security of the Lord's care.

HOSEA CHAPTER 1

Hosea 1:4—Jezreel

Jezreel (pronounced "jez'-ree-el" or "jez'-ree-uhl"; meaning: God will scatter) was the name given to the oldest son of Hosea the prophet. Symbolically, the name Jezreel called to mind the scenes of carnage and destruction that took place in the days of Jehu at the place of that name (see for example 2 Kings 10:11)—and thus reinforced the power of the prophecy being expressed for the future judgments of God.

For more insight on Hosea, see Appendix MM.

6 ¶ And she conceived again, and bare a daughter. And God said unto him, Call her name Lo-ruhamah: for I will no more have mercy upon the house of Israel; but I will utterly take them away.
7 But I will have mercy upon the house of Judah, and will save them by the LORD their God, and will not save them by bow, nor by sword, nor by battle, by horses, nor by horsemen.
8 ¶ Now when she had weaned Lo-ruhamah, she conceived, and bare a son.
9 Then said God, Call his name Lo-ammi: for ye are not my people, and I will not be your God.
10 ¶ Yet the number of the children of Israel shall be as the sand of the sea, which cannot be measured nor numbered; and it shall come to pass, that in the place where it was said unto them, Ye are not my people, there it shall be said unto them, Ye are the sons of the living God.
11 Then shall the children of Judah and the children of Israel be gathered together, and appoint themselves one head, and they shall come up out of the land: for great shall be the day of

CHAPTER 2

1 SAY ye unto your brethren, Ammi; and to your sisters, Ruhamah.
2 Plead with your mother, plead: for she is not my wife, neither am I her husband: let her therefore put away her whoredoms out of her sight, and her adulteries from between her breasts;
3 Lest I strip her naked, and set her as in the day that she was born, and make her as a wilderness, and set her like a dry land, and slay her with thirst.
4 And I will not have mercy upon her children; for they be the children of whoredoms.
5 For their mother hath played the harlot: she that conceived them hath done shamefully: for she said, I will go after my lovers, that give me my bread and my water, my wool and my flax, mine oil and my drink.
6 ¶ Therefore, behold, I will hedge up thy way with thorns, and make a wall, that she shall not find her paths.
7 And she shall follow after her lovers, but she shall not overtake them; and she shall seek them, but shall not find them: then shall she say, I will go and return to my first husband; for then was it better with me than now.
8 For she did not know that I gave her corn, and wine, and oil, and multiplied her silver and gold, which they prepared for Baal.
9 Therefore will I return, and take away my corn in the time thereof, and my wine in the season thereof, and will recover my wool and my flax given to cover her nakedness.
10 And now will I discover her lewdness in the sight of her lovers, and none shall deliver her out of mine hand.
11 I will also cause all her mirth to cease, her feast days, her new moons, and her sabbaths, and all her solemn feasts.
12 And I will destroy her vines and her fig trees, whereof she hath said, These are my rewards that my lovers have given me: and I will make them a forest, and the beasts of the field shall eat them.
13 And I will visit upon her the days of Baalim, wherein she burned incense to them, and she decked herself with her earrings and her jewels, and she went after her lovers, and forgat me, saith the LORD.

Hosea 1:6—Lo-ruhamah
Lo-ruhamah (pronounced "loh'-roo-hay'-muh"; meaning: uncompassioned) was the name given by the prophet Hosea to his daughter to signify the Lord's withholding of mercy from Israel (the Northern Kingdom) on account of its wickedness.

In the last days, the mercy of the Lord will again be shown Israel: "And I will sow her unto me in the earth; and I will have mercy upon her that had not obtained mercy; and I will say to *them which were* not my people, Thou *art* my people; and they shall say, *Thou art* my God" (Hosea 2:23).

Hosea 1:9—Lo-ammi
Lo-ammi (pronounced "loh-am'-y"; meaning: not my people) was the name given by the prophet Hosea to his second son to reflect, symbolically, the rejection of Israel at that time by the Lord because of its wickedness.

Hosea 1:10–11—A Vision of the Destiny of Israel
Though the history of Israel reflected disturbing patterns of falling away from covenant honor, the vision of the future revealed the ultimate destiny of Israel as the fulfillment of the Abrahamic covenant, with abundant progeny as sons and daughters of God, gathered together in righteousness to serve the Lord.

HOSEA CHAPTER 2

"Why did it need an infinite atonement? For the simple reason that a stream can never rise higher than its fountain …. A man, as a man, could arrive at all the dignity that a man was capable of obtaining or receiving; but it needed a God to raise him to the dignity of a God." —John Taylor, *Mediation and Atonement*, 145.

Hosea 2—The Symbolism of Marriage
The marriage symbolism is used to present the vision of the destiny of Israel. The Lord is the husband and Israel is the wife. Though Israel has been unfaithful in her obsession with idolatry and unrighteous living, nevertheless the Lord will in forgiveness and mercy receive her back once again in a union of righteousness and lovingkindness.

The symbolism of the Bridegroom and the bride occurs frequently in the scriptures (see for example Isa. 61:10; 62:5; Jer. 7:34; 16:9; 25:10; 33:11; Matt. 9:15; 25:1–13; Mark 2:19–20; Luke 5:34–35; John 3:29; Rev. 18:23; D&C 33:17–18; 65:3; 88:92; 133:10, 19).

14 ¶ Therefore, behold, I will allure her, and bring her into the wilderness, and speak comfortably unto her.

15 And I will give her her vineyards from thence, and the valley of Achor for a door of hope: and she shall sing there, as in the days of her youth, and as in the day when she came up out of the land of Egypt.

16 And it shall be at that day, saith the LORD, that thou shalt call me Ishi; and shalt call me no more Baali.

17 For I will take away the names of Baalim out of her mouth, and they shall no more be remembered by their name.

18 And in that day will I make a covenant for them with the beasts of the field, and with the fowls of heaven, and with the creeping things of the ground: and I will break the bow and the sword and the battle out of the earth, and will make them to lie down safely.

19 And I will betroth thee unto me for ever; yea, I will betroth thee unto me in righteousness, and in judgment, and in lovingkindness, and in mercies.

20 I will even betroth thee unto me in faithfulness: and thou shalt know the LORD.

21 And it shall come to pass in that day, I will hear, saith the LORD, I will hear the heavens, and they shall hear the earth;

22 And the earth shall hear the corn, and the wine, and the oil; and they shall hear Jezreel.

23 And I will sow her unto me in the earth; and I will have mercy upon her that had not obtained mercy; and I will say to them which were not my people, Thou art my people; and they shall say, Thou art my God.

CHAPTER 3

1 THEN said the LORD unto me, Go yet, love a woman beloved of her friend, yet an adulteress, according to the love of the LORD toward the children of Israel, who look to other gods, and love flagons of wine.

2 So I bought her to me for fifteen pieces of silver, and for an homer of barley, and an half homer of barley:

3 And I said unto her, Thou shalt abide for me many days; thou shalt not play the harlot, and thou shalt not be for another man: so will I also be for thee.

4 For the children of Israel shall abide many days without a king, and without a prince, and without a sacrifice, and without an image, and without an ephod, and without teraphim:

5 Afterward shall the children of Israel return, and seek the LORD their God, and David their king; and shall fear the LORD and his goodness in the latter days.

POINT OF INTEREST

"Throughout the other prophets, any condemnation of Assyria is not for any specific aspect of its treatment of conquered races but for what one might best call arrogance, that is, for claiming to exercise as of right power merely delegated by God. By Hosea, indeed, Assyria itself is not condemned at all: it is upon Israel that the condemnation falls, for reliance upon the might of Assyria rather than upon God (12:1). Isaiah recognized Assyria—which he described as 'the rod of [God's] anger' (10:5)—as the instrument of Yahweh (Jehovah, the Lord), and for him Assyria was doomed not for any specific misuse of power but for failing to acknowledge the source of the power it wielded by God's will (Isaiah 10:6–16). Zephaniah (2:13 and 15), in similar strain, foretold the destruction of Assyria not for inhumanity but for pride. . . . Biblical reflections on the punishment of Assyria subsequent to its fall likewise look back not to any particular form of injustice, but to its arrogance in usurping power belonging properly to God, and impiety in swallowing up the Chosen People" (H. W. F. Saggs, *The Babylonians* [London: Folio Society, 2007]).

HOSEA CHAPTER 3

Hosea 3—Israel's Ultimate Destiny

In the due time of the Lord, the bride (Israel) shall be purged of her unrigheousness and return to the Lord in worthiness and devotion.

CHAPTER 11

1 WHEN Israel was a child, then I loved him, and called my son out of Egypt.

2 As they called them, so they went from them: they sacrificed unto Baalim, and burned incense to graven images.

3 I taught Ephraim also to go, taking them by their arms; but they knew not that I healed them.

4 I drew them with cords of a man, with bands of love: and I was to them as they that take off the yoke on their jaws, and I laid meat unto them.

5 ¶ He shall not return into the land of Egypt, but the Assyrian shall be his king, because they refused to return.

6 And the sword shall abide on his cities, and shall consume his branches, and devour them, because of their own counsels.

7 And my people are bent to backsliding from me: though they called them to the most High, none at all would exalt him.

8 How shall I give thee up, Ephraim? how shall I deliver thee, Israel? how shall I make thee as Admah? how shall I set thee as Zeboim? mine heart is turned within me, my repentings are kindled together.

9 I will not execute the fierceness of mine anger, I will not return to destroy Ephraim: for I am God, and not man; the Holy One in the midst of thee: and I will not enter into the city.

10 They shall walk after the LORD: he shall roar like a lion: when he shall roar, then the children shall tremble from the west.

11 They shall tremble as a bird out of Egypt, and as a dove out of the land of Assyria: and I will place them in their houses, saith the LORD.

12 Ephraim compasseth me about with lies, and the house of Israel with deceit: but Judah yet ruleth with God, and is faithful with the saints.

CHAPTER 13

1 WHEN Ephraim spake trembling, he exalted himself in Israel; but when he offended in Baal, he died.

2 And now they sin more and more, and have made them molten images of their silver, and idols according to their own understanding, all of it the work of the craftsmen: they say of them, Let the men that sacrifice kiss the calves.

3 Therefore they shall be as the morning cloud, and as the early dew that passeth away, as the chaff that is driven with the whirlwind out of the floor, and as the smoke out of the chimney.

4 Yet I am the LORD thy God from the land of Egypt, and thou shalt know no god but me: for there is no saviour beside me.

5 ¶ I did know thee in the wilderness, in the land of great drought.

6 According to their pasture, so were they filled; they were filled, and their heart was exalted; therefore have they forgotten me.

7 Therefore I will be unto them as a lion: as a leopard by the way will I observe them:

8 I will meet them as a bear that is bereaved of her whelps, and will rend the caul of their heart, and there will I devour them like a lion: the wild beast shall tear them.

9 ¶ O Israel, thou hast destroyed thyself; but in me is thine help.

10 I will be thy king: where is any other that may save thee in all thy cities? and thy judges of whom thou saidst, Give me a king and princes?

HOSEA CHAPTER 11

Hosea 11:1—The "Lovingkindness" of the Lord
Though His children lapse into forgetfulness and sin, yet will the Lord remember them in mercy and love as they renew their commitment to follow in His ways.

Hosea is the only prophet of the northern kingdom whose pronouncements and writings have been preserved. He, like the prophet Amos, was active during the reign of King Jeroboam II of Israel (prior to 733 BC).

Hosea's metaphorical style is filled with pathos over the rebellion and idolatry of the Lord's children during this period of decline and moral decay, and at the same time reflects the deep yearnings of the Lord for the recovery and reformation of Israel. At a time of moral decadence, not unlike the conditions in our own day, Hosea calls for repentance and prophesies of a future time when the Lord's mercy would heal the returning flock. As we seek to forgive, we truly bless ourselves and those who have wronged us. Remember that as we are merciful we shall obtain mercy (see Matt. 5:7).

HOSEA CHAPTER 13

Hosea 13—Summary of Precepts and Principles
We can look to the philosophies of men for the solutions to life's challenges; we can look to the wonders of modern science for the lifting of our burdens; we can look to our own devices and creativity for buoyancy in times of challenge. But until and unless we look to the eternal principles of the gospel of Jesus Christ for purpose and sustenance, until we accept the compassionate invitation of the Lord to return home, there can be no peace, no harmony, and no enduring vitality to our lives. "For there is no saviour beside me" is the unmistakable message of the Lord through His prophet Hosea (Hosea 13:4).

In the words of the Book of Mormon: "And now, behold, my beloved brethren, this is the way; and there is none other way nor name given under heaven whereby man can be saved in the kingdom of God. And now, behold, this is the doctrine of Christ, and the only and true doctrine of the Father, and of the Son, and of the Holy Ghost, which is one God, without end. Amen" (2 Ne. 31:21).

Hosea 13:9—The Perpetual Call to Return Home
The Lord's eternal message to His children is to return home once again, to forsake the world and remember the covenant promises whose fulfillment will bring peace and everlasting rest.

Hosea expresses the Lord's universal invitation to all mankind to return to the fold, to embrace the eternal principles of righteousness and spiritual vitality. Israel's eventual return is celebrated in prophetic visions of the restoration of life and the abundance of the Lord's blessings unto the faithful: "Ephraim shall say, What have I to do any more with idols? I have heard him and observed him. I am like a green fir tree. From me is thy fruit found"

11 I gave thee a king in mine anger, and took him away in my wrath.

12 The iniquity of Ephraim is bound up; his sin is hid.

13 The sorrows of a travailing woman shall come upon him: he is an unwise son; for he should not stay long in the place of the breaking forth of children.

14 I will ransom them from the power of the grave; I will redeem them from death: O death, I will be thy plagues; O grave, I will be thy destruction: repentance shall be hid from mine eyes.

15 ¶ Though he be fruitful among his brethren, an east wind shall come, the wind of the LORD shall come up from the wilderness, and his spring shall become dry, and his fountain shall be dried up: he shall spoil the treasure of all pleasant vessels.

16 Samaria shall become desolate; for she hath rebelled against her God: they shall fall by the sword: their infants shall be dashed in pieces, and their women with child shall be ripped up.

CHAPTER 14

1 O ISRAEL, return unto the LORD thy God; for thou hast fallen by thine iniquity.

2 Take with you words, and turn to the LORD: say unto him, Take away all iniquity, and receive us graciously: so will we render the calves of our lips.

3 Asshur shall not save us; we will not ride upon horses: neither will we say any more to the work of our hands, Ye are our gods: for in thee the fatherless findeth mercy.

4 ¶ I will heal their backsliding, I will love them freely: for mine anger is turned away from him.

5 I will be as the dew unto Israel: he shall grow as the lily, and cast forth his roots as Lebanon.

6 His branches shall spread, and his beauty shall be as the olive tree, and his smell as Lebanon.

7 They that dwell under his shadow shall return; they shall revive as the corn, and grow as the vine: the scent thereof shall be as the wine of Lebanon.

8 Ephraim shall say, What have I to do any more with idols? I have heard him, and observed him: I am like a green fir tree. From me is thy fruit found.

9 Who is wise, and he shall understand these things? prudent, and he shall know them? for the ways of the LORD are right, and the just shall walk in them: but the transgressors shall fall therein.

(Hosea 14:8). The goodness and mercy of God are continually exemplified as He seeks after His children. He is always inviting them to return if they but confess and forsake their sins and return with full purpose of heart.

We must be about His business of helping people return to Him. We should seek out the less active and be their friend, help them with a responsibility and nourish them continually with the good word of God. Remember that judgment is left to God. Our duty is to help, even in the most dire situations (see Moroni 9:6).

HOSEA CHAPTER 14

Hosea 14—A Vision of Israel's Return

In vision, the prophet sees the eventual repentance of Israel and her return to the fold of the Lord, abandoning false gods in favor of the true God of healing and nurture. The harvest of righteousness will prevail.

JOEL

CHAPTER 2

1 BLOW ye the trumpet in Zion, and sound an alarm in my holy mountain: let all the inhabitants of the land tremble: for the day of the LORD cometh, for it is nigh at hand;

2 A day of darkness and of gloominess, a day of clouds and of thick darkness, as the morning spread upon the mountains: a great people and a strong; there hath not been ever the like, neither shall be any more after it, even to the years of many generations.

3 A fire devoureth before them; and behind them a flame burneth: the land is as the garden of Eden before them, and behind them a desolate wilderness; yea, and nothing shall escape them.

4 The appearance of them is as the appearance of horses; and as horsemen, so shall they run.

5 Like the noise of chariots on the tops of mountains shall they leap, like the noise of a flame of fire that devoureth the stubble, as a strong people set in battle array.

6 Before their face the people shall be much pained: all faces shall gather blackness.

7 They shall run like mighty men; they shall climb the wall like men of war; and they shall march every one on his ways, and they shall not break their ranks:

8 Neither shall one thrust another; they shall walk every one in his path: and when they fall upon the sword, they shall not be wounded.

9 They shall run to and fro in the city; they shall run upon the wall, they shall climb up upon the houses; they shall enter in at the windows like a thief.

10 The earth shall quake before them; the heavens shall tremble: the sun and the moon shall be dark, and the stars shall withdraw their shining:

11 And the LORD shall utter his voice before his army: for his camp is very great: for he is strong that executeth his word: for the day of the LORD is great and very terrible; and who can abide it?

12 ¶ Therefore also now, saith the LORD, turn ye even to me with all your heart, and with fasting, and with weeping, and with mourning:

13 And rend your heart, and not your garments, and turn unto the LORD your God: for he is gracious and merciful, slow to anger, and of great kindness, and repenteth him of the evil.

14 Who knoweth if he will return and repent, and leave a blessing behind him; even a meat offering and a drink offering unto the LORD your God?

15 ¶ Blow the trumpet in Zion, sanctify a fast, call a solemn assembly:

16 Gather the people, sanctify the congregation, assemble the elders, gather the children, and those that suck the breasts: let the bridegroom go forth of his chamber, and the bride out of her closet.

17 Let the priests, the ministers of the LORD, weep between the porch and the altar, and let them say, Spare thy people, O LORD, and give not thine heritage to reproach, that the heathen should rule over them: wherefore should they say among the people, Where is their God?

18 ¶ Then will the LORD be jealous for his land, and pity his people.

JOEL CHAPTER 2

Joel 2:13–14—JST Prophecy of the Last Days

The calamities and dislocations of the last days are prophesied. To escape such turmoil and suffering, the people are enjoined to repent and to turn to the Lord with full heart and devotion. The Joseph Smith Translation of verses 13 and 14 makes clear that the people—not the Lord—are involved in the repentance process:

> And rend your heart, and not your garments, and repent, and turn unto the Lord your God; for he is gracious and merciful, slow to anger, and of great kindness, and he will turn away the evil from you.

> Therefore repent, and who knoweth but he will return and leave a blessing behind him; that you may offer a meat offering, and a drink offering, unto the Lord your God? (JST Joel 2:13–14)

Joel 2:15–32—Prophecy Is a Divine Blessing of Kindness and Love

The prophetic word of the Lord is the refreshing moisture that quenches our spiritual thirst, and the bread of life that satisfies our hunger of soul for divine nurture (see Joel 2:28.)

Joel was called to prophesy during a period of severe drought in Judah. Although the time of his ministry is uncertain, his message is universal: The temporal droughts we experience in life are but the earthly counterpart of the spiritual drought that drives the humble and the submissive in search of truth. It is the Spirit of the Lord, working with the spiritually inclined, that alone can satisfy such a thirst and hunger after righteousness.

Joel foresaw the day when Israel would again be nourished by the outpouring of the Lord's Spirit of reformation and rejuvenation. Peter remembered Joel's words on the Day of Pentecost (see Acts 2:14–21), and Joseph Smith was reminded by the Angel Moroni of the significance of these same ancient words: "He also quoted the second chapter of Joel, from the twenty-eighth verse to the last. He also said that this was not yet fulfilled, but was soon to be" (JS–H 1:41).

The message of Joel is the timeless message of the love of God, His everlasting kindness in endowing His children with exalting truth and the majesty of His Spirit. Truly all who receive a testimony of the Savior through the confirmation of the Holy Spirit are endowed with the spirit of prophecy and revelation (see 1 Cor. 12:3; Alma 17:2–3). In this sense, we can remember and understand the utterance of Moses to the young Joshua: ". . . would God that all the Lord's people were prophets, and that the Lord would put his spirit upon them" (Num. 11:29).

The Lord cares for us as He extends His arm toward us both in mercy and through the word. The prophecies are the words of God given to His prophets to help us in our quest for eternal life. We must be easily entreated and accept them as the will of God, then we can show our faith and love of God by being obedient.

19 Yea, the LORD will answer and say unto his people, Behold, I will send you corn, and wine, and oil, and ye shall be satisfied therewith: and I will no more make you a reproach among the heathen:

20 But I will remove far off from you the northern army, and will drive him into a land barren and desolate, with his face toward the east sea, and his hinder part toward the utmost sea, and his stink shall come up, and his ill savour shall come up, because he hath done great things.

21 ¶ Fear not, O land; be glad and rejoice: for the LORD will do great things.

22 Be not afraid, ye beasts of the field: for the pastures of the wilderness do spring, for the tree beareth her fruit, the fig tree and the vine do yield their strength.

23 Be glad then, ye children of Zion, and rejoice in the LORD your God: for he hath given you the former rain moderately, and he will cause to come down for you the rain, the former rain, and the latter rain in the first month.

24 And the floors shall be full of wheat, and the fats shall overflow with wine and oil.

25 And I will restore to you the years that the locust hath eaten, the cankerworm, and the caterpiller, and the palmerworm, my great army which I sent among you.

26 And ye shall eat in plenty, and be satisfied, and praise the name of the LORD your God, that hath dealt wondrously with you: and my people shall never be ashamed.

27 And ye shall know that I am in the midst of Israel, and that I am the LORD your God, and none else: and my people shall never be ashamed.

28 ¶ And it shall come to pass afterward, that I will pour out my spirit upon all flesh; and your sons and your daughters shall prophesy, your old men shall dream dreams, your young men shall see visions:

29 And also upon the servants and upon the handmaids in those days will I pour out my spirit.

30 And I will shew wonders in the heavens and in the earth, blood, and fire, and pillars of smoke.

31 The sun shall be turned into darkness, and the moon into blood, before the great and the terrible day of the LORD come.

32 And it shall come to pass, that whosoever shall call on the name of the LORD shall be delivered: for in mount Zion and in Jerusalem shall be deliverance, as the LORD hath said, and in the remnant whom the LORD shall call.

CHAPTER 3

1 FOR, behold, in those days, and in that time, when I shall bring again the captivity of Judah and Jerusalem,

2 I will also gather all nations, and will bring them down into the valley of Jehoshaphat, and will plead with them there for my people and for my heritage Israel, whom they have scattered among the nations, and parted my land.

3 And they have cast lots for my people; and have given a boy for an harlot, and sold a girl for wine, that they might drink.

4 Yea, and what have ye to do with me, O Tyre, and Zidon, and all the coasts of Palestine? will ye render me a recompence? and if ye recompense me, swiftly and speedily will I return your recompence upon your own head;

Joel 2—Summary of Precepts and Principles

The people are to be judged "according to the laws of the kingdom which are given by the prophets of God" (D&C 58:18). How important it is, therefore, to listen to the prophet's voice today and ponder the written word of the Lord preserved in the scriptures. The Lord has promised us peace: "Learn of me, and listen to my words; walk in the meekness of my spirit, and you shall have peace in me" (D&C 19:23). To the extent we make ourselves worthy of achieving that kind of spiritual peace, we are the living fulfillment of prophecy, for we will be enjoying the blessings of eternal life as promised through prophetic declarations since the beginning of the world. The counsel of Amos is as true today as it was when he first spoke it: "Seek the Lord, and ye shall live" (Amos 5:6).

JOEL CHAPTER 3

Joel 3—The Lord Will Prevail

The vision of the last days reveals cosmic changes of startling scope. But the refreshing and uplifting news concerning these changes is that the influence of the Lord will prevail in overpowering measure, for He shall "roar" from Zion and "utter his voice" from Jerusalem (Joel 3:16). He shall instill in His people hope and power and knowledge. The safety and sanctity of His holy dwelling places shall be granted as a divine blessing to His people, and the family of God will flourish amidst the upheavals.

5 Because ye have taken my silver and my gold, and have carried into your temples my goodly pleasant things:

6 The children also of Judah and the children of Jerusalem have ye sold unto the Grecians, that ye might remove them far from their border.

7 Behold, I will raise them out of the place whither ye have sold them, and will return your recompence upon your own head:

8 And I will sell your sons and your daughters into the hand of the children of Judah, and they shall sell them to the Sabeans, to a people far off: for the LORD hath spoken it.

9 ¶ Proclaim ye this among the Gentiles; Prepare war, wake up the mighty men, let all the men of war draw near; let them come up:

10 Beat your plowshares into swords, and your pruninghooks into spears: let the weak say, I am strong.

11 Assemble yourselves, and come, all ye heathen, and gather yourselves together round about: thither cause thy mighty ones to come down, O LORD.

12 Let the heathen be wakened, and come up to the valley of Jehoshaphat: for there will I sit to judge all the heathen round about.

13 Put ye in the sickle, for the harvest is ripe: come, get you down; for the press is full, the fats overflow; for their wickedness is great.

14 Multitudes, multitudes in the valley of decision: for the day of the LORD is near in the valley of decision.

15 The sun and the moon shall be darkened, and the stars shall withdraw their shining.

16 The LORD also shall roar out of Zion, and utter his voice from Jerusalem; and the heavens and the earth shall shake: but the LORD will be the hope of his people, and the strength of the children of Israel.

17 So shall ye know that I am the LORD your God dwelling in Zion, my holy mountain: then shall Jerusalem be holy, and there shall no strangers pass through her any more.

18 ¶ And it shall come to pass in that day, that the mountains shall drop down new wine, and the hills shall flow with milk, and all the rivers of Judah shall flow with waters, and a fountain shall come forth of the house of the LORD, and shall water the valley of Shittim.

19 Egypt shall be a desolation, and Edom shall be a desolate wilderness, for the violence against the children of Judah, because they have shed innocent blood in their land.

20 But Judah shall dwell for ever, and Jerusalem from generation to generation.

21 For I will cleanse their blood that I have not cleansed: for the LORD dwelleth in Zion.

AMOS

CHAPTER 3

1 HEAR this word that the LORD hath spoken against you, O children of Israel, against the whole family which I brought up from the land of Egypt, saying,

2 You only have I known of all the families of the earth: therefore I will punish you for all your iniquities.

3 Can two walk together, except they be agreed?

AMOS CHAPTER 3

"The distinction between this great Church and that of all other churches from the beginning has been that we believe in divine revelation; we believe that our Father speaks to man today as He has done from the time of Adam. We believe and we know—which is more than mere belief—that our Father has set His hand in this world or the salvation of the children of men." —George Albert Smith, CR, April 1917, 37

Amos 3—The Prophet Amos

The prophet Amos (meaning: burden) is perhaps best remembered for his declaration: "Surely the Lord GOD will do nothing, but he revealeth his secret unto his servants the prophets" (Amos 3:7). The Lord has made clear once again in our day that His word will be fulfilled with absolute certainty: "What I the Lord have spoken, I have spoken, and I excuse not myself; and though the heavens and the earth pass away, my word shall not pass away, but shall all be fulfilled, whether by mine own voice or by the voice of my servants, it is the same" (D&C 1:38). The word "servants" in this passage refers principally and foremost to the prophets of God, who are called to receive and convey the word of the Lord to others as directed by the Spirit.

Amos was one of the twelve prophets of the Old Testament with shorter books (though by no means reflecting messages of lesser import). He was a shepherd from a community south of Jerusalem, but his ministry was among those of the Northern Kingdom of Israel. Amos prophesied during the reign of Uzziah, king of Judah (who died around 740 BC, about the time of the commencement of Isaiah's ministry) and that of Jeroboam II, king of Israel (who died around 750 BC). Amos, in keeping with his prophetic calling, discerned the evils around him and invoked the spirit of divine exhortation to lift the people from their shackles of sin and motivate them to rise to their godly potential. He viewed the end from the beginning through the power of revelation and warned the people of impending destruction and dire spiritual famine if they did not repent; yet he promised them that the Lord will eventually bring about the restoration of His work and will gather the faithful together again in light and truth.

Amos 3:7—God Acts through Prophets to Guide His Work

Just as Amos clearly foretold the unfolding of events for the Israelites of his day, so the prophets of our day mark out the correct pathway with unmistakable clarity—the pathway of obedience, truth, and light in a world beset with growing iniquity and deepening darkness.

Amos' theme is the perennial theme of all prophets, who say, in effect: Repent and remember the covenant, lest the Lord visit judgment upon you and scatter you at the hands of your enemies; nevertheless, the Lord will remember the righteous and restore His saving grace and blessings upon the obedient. Amos foretold the coming joyous

4 Will a lion roar in the forest, when he hath no prey? will a young lion cry out of his den, if he have taken nothing?

5 Can a bird fall in a snare upon the earth, where no gin is for him? shall one take up a snare from the earth, and have taken nothing at all?

6 Shall a trumpet be blown in the city, and the people not be afraid? shall there be evil in a city, and the LORD hath not done it?

7 Surely the Lord GOD will do nothing, but he revealeth his secret unto his servants the prophets.

8 The lion hath roared, who will not fear? the Lord GOD hath spoken, who can but prophesy?

9 ¶ Publish in the palaces at Ashdod, and in the palaces in the land of Egypt, and say, Assemble yourselves upon the mountains of Samaria, and behold the great tumults in the midst thereof, and the oppressed in the midst thereof.

10 For they know not to do right, saith the LORD, who store up violence and robbery in their palaces.

11 Therefore thus saith the Lord GOD; An adversary there shall be even round about the land; and he shall bring down thy strength from thee, and thy palaces shall be spoiled.

12 Thus saith the LORD; As the shepherd taketh out of the mouth of the lion two legs, or a piece of an ear; so shall the children of Israel be taken out that dwell in Samaria in the corner of a bed, and in Damascus in a couch.

13 Hear ye, and testify in the house of Jacob, saith the Lord GOD, the God of hosts,

14 That in the day that I shall visit the transgressions of Israel upon him I will also visit the altars of Beth-el: and the horns of the altar shall be cut off, and fall to the ground.

15 And I will smite the winter house with the summer house; and the houses of ivory shall perish, and the great houses shall have an end, saith the LORD.

CHAPTER 7

1 THUS hath the Lord GOD shewed unto me; and, behold, he formed grasshoppers in the beginning of the shooting up of the latter growth; and, lo, it was the latter growth after the king's mowings.

2 And it came to pass, that when they had made an end of eating the grass of the land, then I said, O Lord GOD, forgive, I beseech thee: by whom shall Jacob arise? for he is small.

3 The LORD repented for this: It shall not be, saith the LORD.

4 ¶ Thus hath the Lord GOD shewed unto me: and, behold, the Lord GOD called to contend by fire, and it devoured the great deep, and did eat up a part.

5 Then said I, O Lord GOD, cease, I beseech thee: by whom shall Jacob arise? for he is small.

6 The LORD repented for this: This also shall not be, saith the Lord GOD.

7 ¶ Thus he shewed me: and, behold, the Lord stood upon a wall made by a plumbline, with a plumbline in his hand.

8 And the LORD said unto me, Amos, what seest thou? And I said, A plumbline. Then said the Lord, Behold, I will set a

period of restoration for the scattered Israel: "And I will bring again the captivity of my people of Israel, and they shall build the waste cities, and inhabit them. . . . And I will plant them upon their land, and they shall no more be pulled out of their land which I have given them, saith the Lord, thy God" (Amos 9:14–15).

The Old Testament provides comprehensive and compelling evidence of the divine commission and indispensable service of the prophets of the Lord in all ages—from Adam through Malachi and beyond. The gift of the prophet is to confirm for mankind, through the power of the Holy Ghost, that God lives; to communicate God's divine will for the blessing of all His children; and to uphold, sustain, and further the designs of heaven for the eternal salvation and exaltation of the sons and daughters of God, all dimensions of the plan being empowered through the sacred Atonement of Jesus Christ.

Considered separately, one at a time, any one of the prophets—Adam, Enoch, Noah, Melchizedek, Abraham, Jacob, Moses, Isaiah, Jeremiah, or any of the rest—presents a vivid memorial, inspiring and unforgettable, of the truths of the gospel of Jesus Christ. But considered together—their testimonies blended as one in ever higher magnitudes of power, as if in a constellation of heavenly lights configured about the central glory of the Father and Son—the prophets offer an eternal array of witnesses to the verity of God's saving principles and ordinances. It is in the blending of their testimonies that we have irrefutable evidence of the truth of the plan of happiness as confirmed by multiple witnesses. In our world of confusing and conflicting byways, we can thank our Heavenly Father and His Only Begotten Son for prophets to open up the pathway of truth before us.

The obedient and faithful, as covenant children of God, share in the responsibility of the prophets to help build the kingdom through the inspiration of the Spirit. In fact, the spirit of prophesy is granted unto every worthy individual to know by the inspiration of heaven that Jesus is the Christ, for "no man can say that Jesus is the Lord, but by the Holy Ghost" (1 Cor. 12:3). In that sense, every such individual can be a prophet unto himself or herself.

AMOS CHAPTER 7

Amos 7:1–6—Clarification through JST
The Joseph Smith Translation of these verses makes clear that it is Jacob (Israel) that repents (or will need to repent), not the Lord:

> And the Lord said, concerning Jacob, Jacob shall repent for this, therefore I will not utterly destroy him, saith the Lord.
>
> Thus hath the Lord God showed unto me; and, behold, the Lord God called to contend by fire, and it devoured the great deep, and did eat up a part.
>
> Then said I, O Lord God, cease, I beseech thee; by whom shall Jacob arise? for he is small.

plumbline in the midst of my people Israel: I will not again pass by them any more:

9 And the high places of Isaac shall be desolate, and the sanctuaries of Israel shall be laid waste; and I will rise against the house of Jeroboam with the sword.

10 ¶ Then Amaziah the priest of Beth-el sent to Jeroboam king of Israel, saying, Amos hath conspired against thee in the midst of the house of Israel: the land is not able to bear all his words.

11 For thus Amos saith, Jeroboam shall die by the sword, and Israel shall surely be led away captive out of their own land.

12 Also Amaziah said unto Amos, O thou seer, go, flee thee away into the land of Judah, and there eat bread, and prophesy there:

13 But prophesy not again any more at Beth-el: for it is the king's chapel, and it is the king's court.

14 ¶ Then answered Amos, and said to Amaziah, I was no prophet, neither was I a prophet's son; but I was an herdman, and a gatherer of sycomore fruit:

15 And the LORD took me as I followed the flock, and the LORD said unto me, Go, prophesy unto my people Israel.

16 ¶ Now therefore hear thou the word of the LORD: Thou sayest, Prophesy not against Israel, and drop not thy word against the house of Isaac.

17 Therefore thus saith the LORD; Thy wife shall be an harlot in the city, and thy sons and thy daughters shall fall by the sword, and thy land shall be divided by line; and thou shalt die in a polluted land: and Israel shall surely go into captivity forth of his land.

CHAPTER 8

1 THUS hath the Lord GOD shewed unto me: and behold a basket of summer fruit.

2 And he said, Amos, what seest thou? And I said, A basket of summer fruit. Then said the LORD unto me, The end is come upon my people of Israel; I will not again pass by them any more.

3 And the songs of the temple shall be howlings in that day, saith the Lord GOD: there shall be many dead bodies in every place; they shall cast them forth with silence.

4 ¶ Hear this, O ye that swallow up the needy, even to make the poor of the land to fail,

5 Saying, When will the new moon be gone, that we may sell corn? and the sabbath, that we may set forth wheat, making the ephah small, and the shekel great, and falsifying the balances by deceit?

6 That we may buy the poor for silver, and the needy for a pair of shoes; yea, and sell the refuse of the wheat?

7 The LORD hath sworn by the excellency of Jacob, Surely I will never forget any of their works.

8 Shall not the land tremble for this, and every one mourn that dwelleth therein? and it shall rise up wholly as a flood; and it shall be cast out and drowned, as by the flood of Egypt.

9 And it shall come to pass in that day, saith the Lord GOD, that I will cause the sun to go down at noon, and I will darken the earth in the clear day:

10 And I will turn your feasts into mourning, and all your songs into lamentation; and I will bring up sackcloth upon all loins, and baldness upon every head; and I will make it as the mourning of an only son, and the end thereof as a bitter day.

And the Lord said, concerning Jacob, Jacob shall repent of his wickedness; therefore I will not utterly destroy him, saith the Lord God. (JST Amos 7:3–6)

Amos 7:7–9—The Plumbline

A plumbline (a cord with a weight attached) is used to determine whether something is precisely vertical. Symbolically, the plumbline is a standard to measure the righteousness of Israel—the degree to which Israel adheres to the the upright principles of the gospel (also called a plummet: compare 2 Kings 21:13; Isa. 28:17; Zech. 4:10).

Amos 7:10—Amaziah

Amaziah was a priest of Beth-el who murmured against the prophecies of Amos (not to be confused with the more famous Amaziah, son and successor of Joash, king of Judah—see 2 Kings 12:21; 13:12).

Amos 7:14–17—The Call of Amos

We know from these verses the circumstances in which Amos was called as a prophet of God. Amos was a humble worker in the fields, tending his flock, when the Lord reached out to him and commissioned him to cry repentance unto Israel. Amos rebuked Amaziah, the priest, who commanded him to desist in prophesying against Israel, and countered this position with the word of God: Israel shall go into captivity for her unrighteousness.

AMOS CHAPTER 8

Amos 8—Spiritual Famine

The famine described by Amos is one of a spiritual character—a period of time in which the people hunger and thirst after truth but cannot find it, for the prophets of God have been rejected. During such times of apostasy and spiritual emptiness, the hearts of the people yearn for the living waters of the gospel, and when it comes—as in the Restoration in the latter days—there is a great rejoicing and relief, for only the power of the gospel can bring lasting peace and glory (see Amos 9:11–15).

11 ¶ Behold, the days come, saith the Lord GOD, that I will send a famine in the land, not a famine of bread, nor a thirst for water, but of hearing the words of the LORD:

12 And they shall wander from sea to sea, and from the north even to the east, they shall run to and fro to seek the word of the LORD, and shall not find it.

13 In that day shall the fair virgins and young men faint for thirst.

14 They that swear by the sin of Samaria, and say, Thy god, O Dan, liveth; and, The manner of Beer-sheba liveth; even they shall fall, and never rise up again.

CHAPTER 9

1 I SAW the Lord standing upon the altar: and he said, Smite the lintel of the door, that the posts may shake: and cut them in the head, all of them; and I will slay the last of them with the sword: he that fleeth of them shall not flee away, and he that escapeth of them shall not be delivered.

2 Though they dig into hell, thence shall mine hand take them; though they climb up to heaven, thence will I bring them down:

3 And though they hide themselves in the top of Carmel, I will search and take them out thence; and though they be hid from my sight in the bottom of the sea, thence will I command the serpent, and he shall bite them:

4 And though they go into captivity before their enemies, thence will I command the sword, and it shall slay them: and I will set mine eyes upon them for evil, and not for good.

5 And the Lord GOD of hosts is he that toucheth the land, and it shall melt, and all that dwell therein shall mourn: and it shall rise up wholly like a flood; and shall be drowned, as by the flood of Egypt.

6 It is he that buildeth his stories in the heaven, and hath founded his troop in the earth; he that calleth for the waters of the sea, and poureth them out upon the face of the earth: The LORD is his name.

7 Are ye not as children of the Ethiopians unto me, O children of Israel? saith the LORD. Have not I brought up Israel out of the land of Egypt? and the Philistines from Caphtor, and the Syrians from Kir?

8 Behold, the eyes of the Lord GOD are upon the sinful kingdom, and I will destroy it from off the face of the earth; saving that I will not utterly destroy the house of Jacob, saith the LORD.

9 For, lo, I will command, and I will sift the house of Israel among all nations, like as corn is sifted in a sieve, yet shall not the least grain fall upon the earth.

10 All the sinners of my people shall die by the sword, which say, The evil shall not overtake nor prevent us.

11 ¶ In that day will I raise up the tabernacle of David that is fallen, and close up the breaches thereof; and I will raise up his ruins, and I will build it as in the days of old:

12 That they may possess the remnant of Edom, and of all the heathen, which are called by my name, saith the LORD that doeth this.

13 Behold, the days come, saith the LORD, that the plowman shall overtake the reaper, and the treader of grapes him that soweth seed; and the mountains shall drop sweet wine, and all the hills shall melt.

14 And I will bring again the captivity of my people of Israel, and they shall build the waste cities, and inhabit them; and they shall

Jonah Preaching to the Ninevites by Gustave Doré

plant vineyards, and drink the wine thereof; they shall also make gardens, and eat the fruit of them.

15 And I will plant them upon their land, and they shall no more be pulled up out of their land which I have given them, saith the LORD thy God.

JONAH

CHAPTER 1

1 NOW the word of the LORD came unto Jonah the son of Amittai, saying,

2 Arise, go to Nineveh, that great city, and cry against it; for their wickedness is come up before me.

3 But Jonah rose up to flee unto Tarshish from the presence of the LORD, and went down to Joppa; and he found a ship going to Tarshish: so he paid the fare thereof, and went down into it, to go with them unto Tarshish from the presence of the LORD.

4 ¶ But the LORD sent out a great wind into the sea, and there was a mighty tempest in the sea, so that the ship was like to be broken.

5 Then the mariners were afraid, and cried every man unto his god, and cast forth the wares that were in the ship into the sea, to lighten it of them. But Jonah was gone down into the sides of the ship; and he lay, and was fast asleep.

6 So the shipmaster came to him, and said unto him, What meanest thou, O sleeper? arise, call upon thy God, if so be that God will think upon us, that we perish not.

7 And they said every one to his fellow, Come, and let us cast lots, that we may know for whose cause this evil is upon us. So they cast lots, and the lot fell upon Jonah.

8 Then said they unto him, Tell us, we pray thee, for whose cause this evil is upon us; What is thine occupation? and whence comest thou? what is thy country? and of what people art thou?

9 And he said unto them, I am an Hebrew; and I fear the LORD, the God of heaven, which hath made the sea and the dry land.

10 Then were the men exceedingly afraid, and said unto him, Why hast thou done this? For the men knew that he fled from the presence of the LORD, because he had told them.

11 ¶ Then said they unto him, What shall we do unto thee, that the sea may be calm unto us? for the sea wrought, and was tempestuous.

12 And he said unto them, Take me up, and cast me forth into the sea; so shall the sea be calm unto you: for I know that for my sake this great tempest is upon you.

13 Nevertheless the men rowed hard to bring it to the land; but they could not: for the sea wrought, and was tempestuous against them.

14 Wherefore they cried unto the LORD, and said, We beseech thee, O LORD, we beseech thee, let us not perish for this man's life, and lay not upon us innocent blood: for thou, O LORD, hast done as it pleased thee.

15 So they took up Jonah, and cast him forth into the sea: and the sea ceased from her raging.

16 Then the men feared the LORD exceedingly, and offered a sacrifice unto the LORD, and made vows.

JONAH CHAPTER 1

"There never was a dispensation on the earth when prophets and apostles, the inspiration, revelation and power of God, the Holy Priesthood and the keys of the kingdom were needed more than they are in this generation. There never has been a dispensation when the friends of God and righteousness among the children of men needed more faith in the promises and prophecies than they do today; and there certainly never has been a generation of people on the earth that has had a greater work to perform than the inhabitants of the earth in the latter days." —Wilford Woodruff, JD 15:8

Jonah 1:1–3—Jonah's Call as Prophet

The Lord called Jonah as a prophet and commanded him to cry repentance to Nineveh, the great capital city of the Assyrian empire. Jonah was fearful of the calling and attempted to turn from the presence of the Lord by going to sea. This circumstances resulted in the singularly unique episode of the encounter with the whale and the process of conversion that brought Jonah back to his prophetic task.

We are all reminded of the wisdom of responding with full devotion when the Lord calls on us to perform our duty in the kingdom of God: "Wherefore, now let every man learn his duty, and to act in the office in which he is appointed, in all diligence. He that is slothful shall not be counted worthy to stand, and he that learns not his duty and shows himself not approved shall not be counted worthy to stand (D&C 107:99–100).

For more insight on Jonah, see Appendix NN.

17 ¶ Now the LORD had prepared a great fish to swallow up Jonah. And Jonah was in the belly of the fish three days and three nights.

CHAPTER 2

1 THEN Jonah prayed unto the LORD his God out of the fish's belly,

2 And said, I cried by reason of mine affliction unto the LORD, and he heard me; out of the belly of hell cried I, and thou heardest my voice.

3 For thou hadst cast me into the deep, in the midst of the seas; and the floods compassed me about: all thy billows and thy waves passed over me.

4 Then I said, I am cast out of thy sight; yet I will look again toward thy holy temple.

5 The waters compassed me about, even to the soul: the depth closed me round about, the weeds were wrapped about my head.

6 I went down to the bottoms of the mountains; the earth with her bars was about me for ever: yet hast thou brought up my life from corruption, O LORD my God.

7 When my soul fainted within me I remembered the LORD: and my prayer came in unto thee, into thine holy temple.

8 They that observe lying vanities forsake their own mercy.

9 But I will sacrifice unto thee with the voice of thanksgiving; I will pay that that I have vowed. Salvation is of the LORD.

10 ¶ And the LORD spake unto the fish, and it vomited out Jonah upon the dry land.

CHAPTER 3

1 AND the word of the LORD came unto Jonah the second time, saying,

2 Arise, go unto Nineveh, that great city, and preach unto it the preaching that I bid thee.

3 So Jonah arose, and went unto Nineveh, according to the word of the LORD. Now Nineveh was an exceeding great city of three days' journey.

4 And Jonah began to enter into the city a day's journey, and he cried, and said, Yet forty days, and Nineveh shall be overthrown.

5 ¶ So the people of Nineveh believed God, and proclaimed a fast, and put on sackcloth, from the greatest of them even to the least of them.

6 For word came unto the king of Nineveh, and he arose from his throne, and he laid his robe from him, and covered him with sackcloth, and sat in ashes.

7 And he caused it to be proclaimed and published through Nineveh by the decree of the king and his nobles, saying, Let neither man nor beast, herd nor flock, taste any thing: let them not feed, nor drink water:

8 But let man and beast be covered with sackcloth, and cry mightily unto God: yea, let them turn every one from his evil way, and from the violence that is in their hands.

9 Who can tell if God will turn and repent, and turn away from his fierce anger, that we perish not?

10 ¶ And God saw their works, that they turned from their evil way; and God repented of the evil, that he had said that he would do unto them; and he did it not.

JONAH CHAPTER 2

Jonah 2:1–10—The Misery of Disobedience Akin to Being Swallowed in the Depths

What is the condition of agony and torment that besets the individual who has regressed into a stupor of self-condemnation in the wake of disobeying the Lord? Surely being buried in the depths of the sea in darkness and complete isolation would be symbolically equivalent to such a state of misery.

But the Lord encompasses such an individual with walls of protection (in this case, uniquely, a whale) that allow for rejuvenation through the prayer of remembrance, and through the purging of unrighteousness in the strength of the Lord and His mercies. From this immersion chamber of rebirth, as it were, Jonah is brought forth as a new man—willing and prepared to carry out the commands of the Lord.

JONAH CHAPTER 3

Jonah 3:1–2—The Compassion of the Lord Extends to All People

Jonah wanted to second-guess the Lord in His plan for the salvation of a heathen city-state, but the Lord's mercy was extended nevertheless to all with a contrite heart.

As for his part in this drama, the prophet Jonah was at first not valiant in his calling to preach repentance to the great cosmopolitan heathen city-state of Nineveh, capital of Assyria. Jonah tried to escape his mission, but found himself caught up in a learning situation where his own life was on the line. When the Lord gave him a second chance to function in the prophetic office, he fulfilled his calling with devotion—perhaps too much devotion, as it turns out, for he was later disposed to want Nineveh to suffer, even though she repented.

The Lord sets His eternal agenda, and it is for us to obey. In all our callings, we should respond willingly and in alignment with the Lord's agenda of mercy and salvation.

Jonah 3:9–10—JST Clarification

The Joseph Smith Translation of these verses indicates that the act of repentance applies to the people, not the Lord:

> Who can tell, if we will repent, and turn unto God, but he will turn away from us his fierce anger, that we perish not?
>
> And God saw their works that they turned from their evil way and repented; and God turned away the evil that he had said he would bring upon them. (JST Jonah 3:9–10)

Miraculously, the people of Nineveh repented of their unrighteousness, and were spared the destructive judgments that awaited them should they not turn away from their wickedness.

CHAPTER 4

1 BUT it displeased Jonah exceedingly, and he was very angry.

2 And he prayed unto the LORD, and said, I pray thee, O LORD, was not this my saying, when I was yet in my country? Therefore I fled before unto Tarshish: for I knew that thou art a gracious God, and merciful, slow to anger, and of great kindness, and repentest thee of the evil.

3 Therefore now, O LORD, take, I beseech thee, my life from me; for it is better for me to die than to live.

4 ¶ Then said the LORD, Doest thou well to be angry?

5 So Jonah went out of the city, and sat on the east side of the city, and there made him a booth, and sat under it in the shadow, till he might see what would become of the city.

6 And the LORD God prepared a gourd, and made it to come up over Jonah, that it might be a shadow over his head, to deliver him from his grief. So Jonah was exceeding glad of the gourd.

7 But God prepared a worm when the morning rose the next day, and it smote the gourd that it withered.

8 And it came to pass, when the sun did arise, that God prepared a vehement east wind; and the sun beat upon the head of Jonah, that he fainted, and wished in himself to die, and said, It is better for me to die than to live.

9 And God said to Jonah, Doest thou well to be angry for the gourd? And he said, I do well to be angry, even unto death.

10 Then said the LORD, Thou hast had pity on the gourd, for the which thou hast not laboured, neither madest it grow; which came up in a night, and perished in a night:

11 And should not I spare Nineveh, that great city, wherein are more than sixscore thousand persons that cannot discern between their right hand and their left hand; and also much cattle?

MICAH

CHAPTER 2

1 WOE to them that devise iniquity, and work evil upon their beds! when the morning is light, they practise it, because it is in the power of their hand.

2 And they covet fields, and take them by violence; and houses, and take them away: so they oppress a man and his house, even a man and his heritage.

3 Therefore thus saith the LORD; Behold, against this family do I devise an evil, from which ye shall not remove your necks; neither shall ye go haughtily: for this time is evil.

4 ¶ In that day shall one take up a parable against you, and lament with a doleful lamentation, and say, We be utterly spoiled: he hath changed the portion of my people: how hath he removed it from me! turning away he hath divided our fields.

5 Therefore thou shalt have none that shall cast a cord by lot in the congregation of the LORD.

JONAH CHAPTER 4

Jonah 4—Jonah's Desires Regarding Nineveh

Even after the people in Nineveh repented, Jonah wanted to see the Lord carry out the threatened destruction of the city, if for no reason than to uphold his own reputation as a predictor of the future. But the Lord knew better, and saved the people out of mercy.

Using the parable of the gourd, the Lord continued Jonah's education by teaching him that if he was concerned about the vitality of a gourd, he should all the more be concerned about the well-being of a whole city full of the Lord's children—even if they were of different extraction. Similarly, we are to have compassion for all of God's children and willingly answer the call to serve the world under the aegis of the Abrahamic covenant.

We have a work to do to help build up the kingdom of God and bring the gospel to every nation, kindred, tongue, and people. It is our responsibility and blessing: "Every member a missionary" is the governing principle. "Behold, I sent you out to testify and warn the people, and it becometh every man who hath been warned to warn his neighbor" (D&C 88:81). Every young man in the Church should prepare to be a worthy missionary and then serve an honorable mission. Young sisters, as appropriate, are welcomed into the missionary force. Senior couples and senior sisters should serve whenever possible.

POINT OF INTEREST

"Many of the best-known Old Testament stories have a Mesopotamian background: the Garden of Eden, the Tower of Babel, the migration of Abraham, the Assyrian who came down like a wolf on the fold, Jonah traveling by whale-mouth to preach to Nineveh, Nebuchadnezzar, [Shadrach, Meshach and Abed-nego] in the burning fiery furnace, Belshazzar's feast. Most of these have found a place in European art or music or poetry. To mention only a tiny random selection, the Tower of Babel was a theme of paintings by several of the old masters; one of Verdi's greatest musical compositions was his Nabucco (Nabucodonosor), *written in 1842, based on the story of the Babylonian king Nebuchadnezzar, and from Sibelius we have* Belshazzar's Feast, *which reflects the biblical memory of Belshar-usur, son and regent of the last Babylonian king, Nabuna'id. And the 'wolf on the fold' is Lord Byron's poetic evocation of the biblical story of Sennacherib's attack upon Palestine in 701 B.C."* (H. W. F. Saggs, *The Babylonians* [London: Folio Society, 2007]).

6 Prophesy ye not, say they to them that prophesy: they shall not prophesy to them, that they shall not take shame.

7 ¶ O thou that art named the house of Jacob, is the spirit of the LORD straitened? are these his doings? do not my words do good to him that walketh uprightly?

8 Even of late my people is risen up as an enemy: ye pull off the robe with the garment from them that pass by securely as men averse from war.

9 The women of my people have ye cast out from their pleasant houses; from their children have ye taken away my glory for ever.

10 Arise ye, and depart; for this is not your rest: because it is polluted, it shall destroy you, even with a sore destruction.

11 If a man walking in the spirit and falsehood do lie, saying, I will prophesy unto thee of wine and of strong drink; he shall even be the prophet of this people.

12 ¶ I will surely assemble, O Jacob, all of thee; I will surely gather the remnant of Israel; I will put them together as the sheep of Bozrah, as the flock in the midst of their fold: they shall make great noise by reason of the multitude of men.

13 The breaker is come up before them: they have broken up, and have passed through the gate, and are gone out by it: and their king shall pass before them, and the LORD on the head of them.

CHAPTER 4

1 BUT in the last days it shall come to pass, that the mountain of the house of the LORD shall be established in the top of the mountains, and it shall be exalted above the hills; and people shall flow unto it.

2 And many nations shall come, and say, Come, and let us go up to the mountain of the LORD, and to the house of the God of Jacob; and he will teach us of his ways, and we will walk in his paths: for the law shall go forth of Zion, and the word of the LORD from Jerusalem.

3 ¶ And he shall judge among many people, and rebuke strong nations afar off; and they shall beat their swords into plowshares, and their spears into pruninghooks: nation shall not lift up a sword against nation, neither shall they learn war any more.

4 But they shall sit every man under his vine and under his fig tree; and none shall make them afraid: for the mouth of the LORD of hosts hath spoken it.

5 For all people will walk every one in the name of his god, and we will walk in the name of the LORD our God for ever and ever.

6 In that day, saith the LORD, will I assemble her that halteth, and I will gather her that is driven out, and her that I have afflicted;

7 And I will make her that halted a remnant, and her that was cast far off a strong nation: and the LORD shall reign over them in mount Zion from henceforth, even for ever.

8 ¶ And thou, O tower of the flock, the strong hold of the daughter of Zion, unto thee shall it come, even the first dominion; the kingdom shall come to the daughter of Jerusalem.

9 Now why dost thou cry out aloud? is there no king in thee? is thy counsellor perished? for pangs have taken thee as a woman in travail.

MICAH CHAPTER 2

Micah 2—The Work and Ministry of Micah

Micah the Moresthite was a prophet of Judah who prophesied during the reign of King Hezekiah (see Micah 1:1). Hezekiah ascended the throne around 728 BC and reigned for twenty-nine years. Thus Micah was a contemporary of Isaiah, whose ministry extended from 740–701 BC. Micah echoes the recurrent theme of all the prophets: that the Lord will bring judgment upon evildoers, while showing mercy and forgiveness to those who repent and follow His statutes and remember His covenants. Goodness and truth—as evidenced in the coming forth of the Messiah to be born at Bethlehem—will eventually triumph over degeneracy and rebellion. The Lord's kingdom of glory and salvation will rise in the latter days as a compelling beacon to all peoples.

Micah 2:12–13—Symbolism of the Lord's Mercy

Though Israel has polluted her ranks and fallen away from the right way, the Lord will eventually bless His people as they repent, and gather them as sheep into His fold. He will break open the passageway for them to venture forth onto the pathway of glory and salvation. The Lord will be their King and will go before them. This beautiful symbolism expresses the unfolding of Israel's destiny as a chosen and righteous people—and gives promise to all who embrace the gospel that they will find peace and happiness through the mercies and compassion of Jesus Christ.

MICAH CHAPTER 4

Micah 4:1—From the Beginning, the Lord Envisioned the Restoration of Israel and Decreed the Ultimate Triumph of His Purposes

All the Lord requires is that we obey His commandments in all humility of heart, and He will establish us as His people once again through the process of gathering and restoration. He is the Savior foretold by Prophets from the foundation of the world.

"But in the last days it shall come to pass, that the mountain of the house of the Lord shall be established in the top of the mountains, and it shall be exalted above the hills; and people shall flow unto it." (Micah 4:1; compare Isa. 2:2)

"… and what doth the Lord require of thee, but to do justly, and to love mercy, and to walk humbly with thy God?" (Micah 6:8)

Micah records his mighty vision of the latter days in which the Lord's kingdom will once again be established in power as the bastion of righteousness and salvation. Israel will be gathered and empowered to perform its divinely appointed mission of declaring the gospel message. The world awaits for the Saints of the House of Israel to fulfill the destiny for which they were created—to take the blessings of

10 Be in pain, and labour to bring forth, O daughter of Zion, like a woman in travail: for now shalt thou go forth out of the city, and thou shalt dwell in the field, and thou shalt go even to Babylon; there shalt thou be delivered; there the LORD shall redeem thee from the hand of thine enemies.

11 ¶ Now also many nations are gathered against thee, that say, Let her be defiled, and let our eye look upon Zion.

12 But they know not the thoughts of the LORD, neither understand they his counsel: for he shall gather them as the sheaves into the floor.

13 Arise and thresh, O daughter of Zion: for I will make thine horn iron, and I will make thy hoofs brass: and thou shalt beat in pieces many people: and I will consecrate their gain unto the LORD, and their substance unto the Lord of the whole earth.

CHAPTER 5

1 NOW gather thyself in troops, O daughter of troops: he hath laid siege against us: they shall smite the judge of Israel with a rod upon the cheek.

2 But thou, Beth-lehem Ephratah, though thou be little among the thousands of Judah, yet out of thee shall he come forth unto me that is to be ruler in Israel; whose goings forth have been from of old, from everlasting.

3 Therefore will he give them up, until the time that she which travaileth hath brought forth: then the remnant of his brethren shall return unto the children of Israel.

4 ¶ And he shall stand and feed in the strength of the LORD, in the majesty of the name of the LORD his God; and they shall abide: for now shall he be great unto the ends of the earth.

5 And this man shall be the peace, when the Assyrian shall come into our land: and when he shall tread in our palaces, then shall we raise against him seven shepherds, and eight principal men.

6 And they shall waste the land of Assyria with the sword, and the land of Nimrod in the entrances thereof: thus shall he deliver us from the Assyrian, when he cometh into our land, and when he treadeth within our borders.

7 And the remnant of Jacob shall be in the midst of many people as a dew from the LORD, as the showers upon the grass, that tarrieth not for man, nor waiteth for the sons of men.

8 ¶ And the remnant of Jacob shall be among the Gentiles in the midst of many people as a lion among the beasts of the forest, as a young lion among the flocks of sheep: who, if he go through, both treadeth down, and teareth in pieces, and none can deliver.

9 Thine hand shall be lifted up upon thine adversaries, and all thine enemies shall be cut off.

the gospel to all the earth by preaching the word of God and by providing the temples for the living and vicarious work for the dead so that we can return to our Heavenly Father's presence.

Under the Abrahamic covenant, all of Israel is called into service to carry the gospel of light and the blessings of the priesthood throughout the world. Micah foresaw the day when the Lord would consummate His plan to restore His kingdom once again and fulfill the covenant promises: "Thou wilt perform the truth to Jacob, and the mercy to Abraham, which thou hast sworn unto our fathers from the days of old" (Micah 7:20).

Through the process of spiritual adoption, all mankind has access to the covenant blessings. The greatest joy is preserved unto those who help in the gathering: "And now, if your joy will be great with one soul that you have brought unto me into the kingdom of my Father, how great will be your joy if you should bring many souls unto me" (D&C 18:16).

Micah 4:2—The Gathering

Through the process of the gathering, many will be brought into the fold of salvation through baptism and into the ranks of those on the pathway to exaltation through the sealing blessings of the temples of God (compare Isa. 2:3).

MICAH CHAPTER 5

Micah 5:2—Bethlehem

From the small community of Bethlehem will arise the grand and everlasting King of all the universe, even Jesus Christ. This remarkable prophecy of events that would occur more than 700 years later sounds the good news that awaits the world through the birth of the Savior.

Micah 5:3–8—The Influence of Jacob

The influence of Jacob on the world through the service commission of the Abrahamic covenant in the last days will have two dimensions: first, the refreshing nurture that comes with the delivery of the gospel and all priesthood blessings unto those who receive the word of the Lord; and second, the ominous sound of the warning voice among those who have sore need of repentance.

10 And it shall come to pass in that day, saith the LORD, that I will cut off thy horses out of the midst of thee, and I will destroy thy chariots:

11 And I will cut off the cities of thy land, and throw down all thy strong holds:

12 And I will cut off witchcrafts out of thine hand; and thou shalt have no more soothsayers:

13 Thy graven images also will I cut off, and thy standing images out of the midst of thee; and thou shalt no more worship the work of thine hands.

14 And I will pluck up thy groves out of the midst of thee: so will I destroy thy cities.

15 And I will execute vengeance in anger and fury upon the heathen, such as they have not heard.

CHAPTER 6

1 HEAR ye now what the LORD saith; Arise, contend thou before the mountains, and let the hills hear thy voice.

2 Hear ye, O mountains, the LORD's controversy, and ye strong foundations of the earth: for the LORD hath a controversy with his people, and he will plead with Israel.

3 O my people, what have I done unto thee? and wherein have I wearied thee? testify against me.

4 For I brought thee up out of the land of Egypt, and redeemed thee out of the house of servants; and I sent before thee Moses, Aaron, and Miriam.

5 O my people, remember now what Balak king of Moab consulted, and what Balaam the son of Beor answered him from Shittim unto Gilgal; that ye may know the righteousness of the LORD.

6 ¶ Wherewith shall I come before the LORD, and bow myself before the high God? shall I come before him with burnt offerings, with calves of a year old?

7 Will the LORD be pleased with thousands of rams, or with ten thousands of rivers of oil? shall I give my firstborn for my transgression, the fruit of my body for the sin of my soul?

8 He hath shewed thee, O man, what is good; and what doth the LORD require of thee, but to do justly, and to love mercy, and to walk humbly with thy God?

9 The LORD's voice crieth unto the city, and the man of wisdom shall see thy name: hear ye the rod, and who hath appointed it.

10 ¶ Are there yet the treasures of wickedness in the house of the wicked, and the scant measure that is abominable?

11 Shall I count them pure with the wicked balances, and with the bag of deceitful weights?

12 For the rich men thereof are full of violence, and the inhabitants thereof have spoken lies, and their tongue is deceitful in their mouth.

13 Therefore also will I make thee sick in smiting thee, in making thee desolate because of thy sins.

14 Thou shalt eat, but not be satisfied; and thy casting down shall be in the midst of thee; and thou shalt take hold, but shalt not deliver; and that which thou deliverest will I give up to the sword.

15 Thou shalt sow, but thou shalt not reap; thou shalt tread the olives, but thou shalt not anoint thee with oil; and sweet wine, but shalt not drink wine.

MICAH CHAPTER 6

Micah 6:8—Vision of a Compassionate Father and Son, Insight into Our Responsibility

Some in the world today have a sense that the Old Testament reflects a stern and rigid set of doctrines not aligned with the vision of a compassionate and loving Father in Heaven. This memorable passage from Micah conveys a tone of warmth and balance in keeping with the actual nature of gospel teachings from the Old Testament—which teachings reflect the spirit of the beneficent mission of the Father and Son "to bring to pass the immortality and eternal life of man" (Moses 1:39)—a mission sustained and empowered by love. What is required of us is to act justly, to love mercy, and to walk humbly with our God.

Naturally, the quest, in a world of opposition, is to make choices based on obedience to divine principles and commandments, for "There is a law, irrevocably decreed in heaven before the foundations of this world, upon which all blessings are predicated—And when we obtain any blessing from God, it is by obedience to that law upon which it is predicated" (D&C 130:20–21).

Micah 6—Charity

Sunlight is the radiant warmth that keeps the earth alive and brings about the unfolding of the Creation before our very eyes. Charity is the radiant warmth that keeps our hearts alive and brings about the unfolding of our divine potential—again, right before our very eyes. How grateful we are for such sunlight—even the sunlight of the soul made manifest through deeds of charity.

How does one dispel the shadows of pride and envy that can creep stealthily into our lives from time to time? Through the healing light of charity. Thank heaven for that light. How does one silence the discordant sounds of anger and selfishness that sometimes disturb the air? Through the harmony of charity. Thank heaven for that harmony.

Charity is a gift from God. It is, in fact, the ultimate attribute of godliness. It is the gateway through which we pass in becoming partakers of the divine nature of Christ through faith, virtue, knowledge, temperance, patience, brotherly kindness and godliness—with all humility and diligence (see D&C 4:6; 2 Pet. 1:4–8). It is "the pure love of Christ" (Moroni 7:47). When one is possessed of this love, his or her desires are like unto our Savior's—to bless and serve mankind.

The prophets give us the comforting assurance that "charity never faileth" (1 Cor. 13:8; Moroni 7:46). Charity is the eternal principle that binds up our wounds and enlivens our soul. It is the balm of the redemption and salve of salvation—for Christ is the surpassing embodiment of charity. Christ did not fail his Father, nor did He fail us, for His pure love motivated His great sacrifice—the eternal, infinite, vicarious Atonement. We are to become, said He, even as He is (3 Ne. 27:27).

Through what miracle can we do so? By following in the footsteps of the Master along the pathway of charity. In

16 ¶ For the statutes of Omri are kept, and all the works of the house of Ahab, and ye walk in their counsels; that I should make thee a desolation, and the inhabitants thereof an hissing: therefore ye shall bear the reproach of my people.

CHAPTER 7

1 WOE is me! for I am as when they have gathered the summer fruits, as the grapegleanings of the vintage: there is no cluster to eat: my soul desired the firstripe fruit.

2 The good man is perished out of the earth: and there is none upright among men: they all lie in wait for blood; they hunt every man his brother with a net.

3 ¶ That they may do evil with both hands earnestly, the prince asketh, and the judge asketh for a reward; and the great man, he uttereth his mischievous desire: so they wrap it up.

4 The best of them is as a brier: the most upright is sharper than a thorn hedge: the day of thy watchmen and thy visitation cometh; now shall be their perplexity.

5 ¶ Trust ye not in a friend, put ye not confidence in a guide: keep the doors of thy mouth from her that lieth in thy bosom.

6 For the son dishonoureth the father, the daughter riseth up against her mother, the daughter in law against her mother in law; a man's enemies are the men of his own house.

7 Therefore I will look unto the LORD; I will wait for the God of my salvation: my God will hear me.

8 ¶ Rejoice not against me, O mine enemy: when I fall, I shall arise; when I sit in darkness, the LORD shall be a light unto me.

9 I will bear the indignation of the LORD, because I have sinned against him, until he plead my cause, and execute judgment for me: he will bring me forth to the light, and I shall behold his righteousness.

the strength of the Lord, as Ammon promised, we can do all things (see Alma 26:12). In the strength of charity, through the Atonement of Christ, we begin to acquire this unconditional godly love, this divine nature of Christ.

When we feel gratitude for the gift of charity, we find the sweetness of charity expanding in our hearts like a sprouting seed, like an unfolding vine. When in our prayers we thank Heavenly Father for charity, we feel a comforting peace in our hearts, as if we were coming home into a warm and nurturing presence. When we act in the spirit of charity, we feel of its divine essence and gain hope that we can carry on in faithfulness to the end. Truly the Lord blesses us with the spirit and power of charity—which "endureth forever" (Moroni 7:47). Let us with all the energy of our hearts, with all the commitment of our souls, with all the fervor of our minds—and in all of our decisions and deeds—seek to be full of charity. Life will be beautiful and we will find peace as only the Lord can give. "And now abideth faith, hope, charity, these three; but the greatest of these *is* charity" (1 Cor. 13:13).

MICAH CHAPTER 7

Micah 7:7—Look to the Lord for Guidance

Amidst the evils actions of the wayward in a world of godlessness, the lone seeker after truth can look unto the Lord for guidance and salvation. The God of heaven will hear the supplication of the contrite believer and answer the pleas of the follower of eternal principles.

We can be grateful for the mercy and compassion of the Lord, who gathers Israel together and brings about the redemption from sin through the principles and ordinances of the gospel of salvation. With truth and power He fulfills the promises made to the forefathers of old.

Micah Exhorting the Israelites to Repentance by Gustave Doré

10 Then she that is mine enemy shall see it, and shame shall cover her which said unto me, Where is the LORD thy God? mine eyes shall behold her: now shall she be trodden down as the mire of the streets.

11 In the day that thy walls are to be built, in that day shall the decree be far removed.

12 In that day also he shall come even to thee from Assyria, and from the fortified cities, and from the fortress even to the river, and from sea to sea, and from mountain to mountain.

13 Notwithstanding the land shall be desolate because of them that dwell therein, for the fruit of their doings.

14 ¶ Feed thy people with thy rod, the flock of thine heritage, which dwell solitarily in the wood, in the midst of Carmel: let them feed in Bashan and Gilead, as in the days of old.

15 According to the days of thy coming out of the land of Egypt will I shew unto him marvellous things.

16 ¶ The nations shall see and be confounded at all their might: they shall lay their hand upon their mouth, their ears shall be deaf.

17 They shall lick the dust like a serpent, they shall move out of their holes like worms of the earth: they shall be afraid of the LORD our God, and shall fear because of thee.

18 Who is a God like unto thee, that pardoneth iniquity, and passeth by the transgression of the remnant of his heritage? he retaineth not his anger for ever, because he delighteth in mercy.

19 He will turn again, he will have compassion upon us; he will subdue our iniquities; and thou wilt cast all their sins into the depths of the sea.

20 Thou wilt perform the truth to Jacob, and the mercy to Abraham, which thou hast sworn unto our fathers from the days of old.

ZECHARIAH

CHAPTER 10

1 ASK ye of the LORD rain in the time of the latter rain; so the LORD shall make bright clouds, and give them showers of rain, to every one grass in the field.

2 For the idols have spoken vanity, and the diviners have seen a lie, and have told false dreams; they comfort in vain: therefore they went their way as a flock, they were troubled, because there was no shepherd.

3 Mine anger was kindled against the shepherds, and I punished the goats: for the LORD of hosts hath visited his flock the house of Judah, and hath made them as his goodly horse in the battle.

4 Out of him came forth the corner, out of him the nail, out of him the battle bow, out of him every oppressor together.

5 ¶ And they shall be as mighty men, which tread down their enemies in the mire of the streets in the battle: and they shall fight, because the LORD is with them, and the riders on horses shall be confounded.

6 And I will strengthen the house of Judah, and I will save the house of Joseph, and I will bring them again to place them; for I have mercy upon them: and they shall be as though I had not cast them off: for I am the LORD their God, and will hear them.

ZECHARIAH CHAPTER 10

Zechariah 10—Summary of the Precepts and Principles Taught By Zechariah and Malachi, the Last Two Prophets in the Old Testament Canon

Two of the final voices from the prophetic quorum of Old Testament witnesses—Zechariah and Malachi—sound ominous warnings about the coming day of judgment when all individuals will need to account for the quality of their mortal choices. The view of these final two messengers is not only of the Messiah's ministry upon the earth just a few hundred years hence—where the majesty of His atoning sacrifice would stand out in stark contrast with the myopic blindness of the generation that would utterly reject Him—but of His eventual Second Coming in glory and power as the King of Kings and Lord of Lords before whom "every knee shall bow, and every tongue shall confess" (D&C 88:104).

The operant question is this: How should we prepare for this singularly important event and be able to "abide the day of his coming" (Mal. 4:2)? And the answer is clear: choose the Lord (see Zech. 13:9), worship Him (see Zech. 14:17), make "holiness to the Lord" a pervasive dimension of life (Zech. 14:20), honor Him (see Mal. 1:5), bring a "pure offering" before Him in righteousness (Mal. 1:11; 3:3), give glory to the name of God (see Mal. 2:2), walk with God "in peace and equity" (Mal. 2:6), remain faithfully within the covenant bounds in marriage (see Mal. 2:11), care for the poor and needy (see Mal. 3:5), return unto God (see Mal. 3:7), pay your tithes and offerings (see Mal. 3:10), fear God and always keep Him in your thoughts (see Mal. 3:16), avoid pride (see Mal. 4:1), and—under the influence of the sealing power of the priesthood—cultivate a godly and eternal disposition of oneness among families, both fathers (parents) toward their children, and children toward their fathers (see Mal. 4:5–6). Only then can we hope to enjoy the "spirit of grace and supplication" (Zech. 12:10) that the Lord will pour out upon His covenant people in the day of both rescue and retribution. Only then will the earth—already destined to endure a universal cleansing at the Lord's coming—be spared the curse of emptiness that would come if the eternal covenant principles would not in the end prevail.

7 And they of Ephraim shall be like a mighty man, and their heart shall rejoice as through wine: yea, their children shall see it, and be glad; their heart shall rejoice in the LORD.

8 I will hiss for them, and gather them; for I have redeemed them: and they shall increase as they have increased.

9 And I will sow them among the people: and they shall remember me in far countries; and they shall live with their children, and turn again.

10 I will bring them again also out of the land of Egypt, and gather them out of Assyria; and I will bring them into the land of Gilead and Lebanon; and place shall not be found for them.

11 And he shall pass through the sea with affliction, and shall smite the waves in the sea, and all the deeps of the river shall dry up: and the pride of Assyria shall be brought down, and the sceptre of Egypt shall depart away.

12 And I will strengthen them in the LORD; and they shall walk up and down in his name, saith the LORD.

CHAPTER 11

1 OPEN thy doors, O Lebanon, that the fire may devour thy cedars.

2 Howl, fir tree; for the cedar is fallen; because the mighty are spoiled: howl, O ye oaks of Bashan; for the forest of the vintage is come down.

3 ¶ There is a voice of the howling of the shepherds; for their glory is spoiled: a voice of the roaring of young lions; for the pride of Jordan is spoiled.

4 Thus saith the LORD my God; Feed the flock of the slaughter;

5 Whose possessors slay them, and hold themselves not guilty: and they that sell them say, Blessed be the LORD; for I am rich: and their own shepherds pity them not.

6 For I will no more pity the inhabitants of the land, saith the LORD: but, lo, I will deliver the men every one into his neighbour's hand, and into the hand of his king: and they shall smite the land, and out of their hand I will not deliver them.

7 And I will feed the flock of slaughter, even you, O poor of the flock. And I took unto me two staves; the one I called Beauty, and the other I called Bands; and I fed the flock.

8 Three shepherds also I cut off in one month; and my soul lothed them, and their soul also abhorred me.

9 Then said I, I will not feed you: that that dieth, let it die; and that that is to be cut off, let it be cut off; and let the rest eat every one the flesh of another.

10 ¶ And I took my staff, even Beauty, and cut it assunder, that I might break my covenant which I had made with all the people.

11 And it was broken in that day: and so the poor of the flock that waited upon me knew that it was the word of the LORD.

12 And I said unto them, If ye think good, give me my price; and if not, forbear. So they weighed for my price thirty pieces of silver.

13 And the LORD said unto me, Cast it unto the potter: a goodly price that I was prised at of them. And I took the thirty pieces of silver, and cast them to the potter in the house of the LORD.

14 Then I cut asunder mine other staff, even Bands, that I might break the brotherhood between Judah and Israel.

15 ¶ And the LORD said unto me, Take unto thee yet the instruments of a foolish shepherd.

Zechariah 10:9—The Return of Israel

The history of Israel unfolds as a panorama of contrasts—an intertwining fabric of light and shadows: luminous faithfulness and obedience on the one hand, and the dark abyss of unrighteousness and idolatry on the other. But in the Lord's own due time, the sons of Judah and Joseph will be gathered in honor and valor to accomplish mighty service in building up the Kingdom of God. They will prevail because the Lord will be with them to strengthen them and restore them to their places of inheritance and their condition of rejoicing. They shall be redeemed and expand as the fulfilling progeny of the covenant promises of old, and they shall perform their sacred service as servants unto all mankind under the provisions of the Abrahamic covenant.

ZECHARIAH CHAPTER 11

Zechariah 11:12—Prophetic Vision

It is a wondrous thing that the prophets of the Lord can perceive in such detail that which is to come. The fulfillment of this prophecy about thirty pieces of silver is recounted in the New Testament:

Then one of the twelve, called Judas Iscariot, went unto the chief priests,

And said *unto them*, What will ye give me, and I will deliver him unto you? And they covenanted with him for thirty pieces of silver.

And from that time he sought opportunity to betray him. (Matt. 26:14–16)

For more insight on Zechariah, see Appendix OO.

16 For, lo, I will raise up a shepherd in the land, which shall not visit those that be cut off, neither shall seek the young one, nor heal that that is broken, nor feed that that standeth still: but he shall eat the flesh of the fat, and tear their claws in pieces.

17 Woe to the idol shepherd that leaveth the flock! the sword shall be upon his arm, and upon his right eye: his arm shall be clean dried up, and his right eye shall be utterly darkened.

CHAPTER 12

1 THE burden of the word of the LORD for Israel, saith the LORD, which stretcheth forth the heavens, and layeth the foundation of the earth, and formeth the spirit of man within him.

2 Behold, I will make Jerusalem a cup of trembling unto all the people round about, when they shall be in the siege both against Judah and against Jerusalem.

3 ¶ And in that day will I make Jerusalem a burdensome stone for all people: all that burden themselves with it shall be cut in pieces, though all the people of the earth be gathered together against it.

day, saith the LORD, I will smite every horse with astonishment, and his rider with madness: and I will open mine eyes upon the house of Judah, and will smite every horse of the people with blindness.

5 And the governors of Judah shall say in their heart, The inhabitants of Jerusalem shall be my strength in the LORD of hosts their God.

6 ¶ In that day will I make the governors of Judah like an hearth of fire among the wood, and like a torch of fire in a sheaf; and they shall devour all the people round about, on the right hand and on the left: and Jerusalem shall be inhabited again in her own place, even in Jerusalem.

7 The LORD also shall save the tents of Judah first, that the glory of the house of David and the glory of the inhabitants of Jerusalem do not magnify themselves against Judah.

8 In that day shall the LORD defend the inhabitants of Jerusalem; and he that is feeble among them at that day shall be as David; and the house of David shall be as God, as the angel of the LORD before them.

9 ¶ And it shall come to pass in that day, that I will seek to destroy all the nations that come against Jerusalem.

10 And I will pour upon the house of David, and upon the inhabitants of Jerusalem, the spirit of grace and of supplications: and they shall look upon me whom they have pierced, and they shall mourn for him, as one mourneth for his only son, and shall be in bitterness for him, as one that is in bitterness for his firstborn.

11 In that day shall there be a great mourning in Jerusalem, as the mourning of Hadadrimmon in the valley of Megiddon.

12 And the land shall mourn, every family apart; the family of the house of David apart, and their wives apart; the family of the house of Nathan apart, and their wives apart;

13 The family of the house of Levi apart, and their wives apart; the family of Shimei apart, and their wives apart;

14 All the families that remain, every family apart, and their wives apart.

ZECHARIAH CHAPTER 12

Zechariah 12:2—Prophecy Regarding Jerusalem

In the last days the nations of the earth shall be arrayed against Jerusalem. The prophet warns that this engagement will be a burden to those who lay seige because the Lord will be with Judah.

Zechariah 12:10—The Lord to Protect Jerusalem

The Lord will defend the bastian of Judah against the encroaching hordes and pour out "grance and supplications" upon His people in their hour of danger. The people will recognize their Son for who He is: the One rejected of them ("pierced"—Zech. 12:10) and now emergent as their Firstborn of redemption and deliverance (compare D&C 45:51–53).

POINT OF INTEREST

Zech. 12:11 In that day shall there be a great mourning in Jerusalem, as the mourning of Hadadrimmon in the valley of Megiddon. "Necho II (610–595 B.C.), decided upon more vigourous measures in support of Ashur-uballit, and led the main Egyptian army into Syria (2 Chronicles 35:21). The outcome shows the success of Chaldean diplomacy in Palestine: Necho had to put down a rising in Gaza (Jeremiah 47:1), and Josiah of Judah, the principal remaining native ruler in Palestine, attempted to harry the Egyptian forces on their way northwards. Josiah was defeated and killed at Megiddo (608 B.C.) (2 Kings 23:29), his kingdom temporarily becoming a vassal of Egypt" (H. W. G Saggs, *The Babylonians* [London: Folio Society, 2007]).

CHAPTER 13

1 IN that day there shall be a fountain opened to the house of David and to the inhabitants of Jerusalem for sin and for uncleanness.

2 ¶ And it shall come to pass in that day, saith the LORD of hosts, that I will cut off the names of the idols out of the land, and they shall no more be remembered: and also I will cause the prophets and the unclean spirit to pass out of the land.

3 And it shall come to pass, that when any shall yet prophesy, then his father and his mother that begat him shall say unto him, Thou shalt not live; for thou speakest lies in the name of the LORD: and his father and his mother that begat him shall thrust him through when he prophesieth.

4 And it shall come to pass in that day, that the prophets shall be ashamed every one of his vision, when he hath prophesied; neither shall they wear a rough garment to deceive:

5 But he shall say, I am no prophet, I am an husbandman; for man taught me to keep cattle from my youth.

6 And one shall say unto him, What are these wounds in thine hands? Then he shall answer, Those with which I was wounded in the house of my friends.

7 ¶ Awake, O sword, against my shepherd, and against the man that is my fellow, saith the LORD of hosts: smite the shepherd, and the sheep shall be scattered: and I will turn mine hand upon the little ones.

8 And it shall come to pass, that in all the land, saith the LORD, two parts therein shall be cut off and die; but the third shall be left therein.

9 And I will bring the third part through the fire, and will refine them as silver is refined, and will try them as gold is tried: they shall call on my name, and I will hear them: I will say, It is my people: and they shall say, The LORD is my God.

CHAPTER 14

1 BEHOLD, the day of the LORD cometh, and thy spoil shall be divided in the midst of thee.

2 For I will gather all nations against Jerusalem to battle; and the city shall be taken, and the houses rifled, and the women ravished; and half of the city shall go forth into captivity, and the residue of the people shall not be cut off from the city.

3 Then shall the LORD go forth, and fight against those nations, as when he fought in the day of battle.

4 ¶ And his feet shall stand in that day upon the mount of Olives, which is before Jerusalem on the east, and the mount of Olives shall cleave in the midst thereof toward the east and toward the west, and there shall be a very great valley; and half of the mountain shall remove toward the north, and half of it toward the south.

5 And ye shall flee to the valley of the mountains; for the valley of the mountains shall reach unto Azal: yea, ye shall flee, like as ye fled from before the earthquake in the days of Uzziah king of Judah: and the LORD my God shall come, and all the saints with thee.

ZECHARIAH CHAPTER 13

Zechariah 13:1—Symbolism of Baptism

The fountain could possibly be an allusion to the ordinance of baptism that will again be offered to Judah as the gateway for gathering with the Saints through the principles and ordinances of the gospel of Jesus Christ (see Joseph Fielding Smith, *Answers to Gospel Questions*, 5 vols. [Salt Lake City: Deseret Book, 1957–1966], 2:67–68). President Smith cites the following words from the Prophet Joseph Smith to confirm the practice of baptism among the Saints of Old Testament days:

> In the former ages of the world, before the Savior came in the flesh, "the saints" were baptized in the name of Jesus Christ to come, because there never was any other name whereby men could be saved; and after he came in the flesh and was crucified, then *the saints* were baptized in the name of Jesus Christ, crucified, risen from the dead and ascended into heaven, that they might be buried in baptism like him, and be raised in glory like him, that as there was but *one* Lord, *one* faith, *one* baptism, and *one* God and Father of us all, even so there was but *one* door to the mansions of bliss. Amen. (*Times and Seasons*, Vol. 3, 905)

Zechariah 13:6—The Deliverance of Jerusalem

This prophecy concerning the deliverance of Jerusalem in the last days is confirmed in latter-day revelation (see D&C 45:47–53).

ZECHARIAH CHAPTER 14

Zechariah 14:4—The Hour of Deliverance

Modern revelation contains the following reference concerning the hour of deliverance of Judah by the Savior on the eve of the Second Coming: "Then shall the arm of the Lord fall upon the nations. And then shall the Lord set his foot upon this mount, and it shall cleave in twain, and the earth shall tremble, and reel to and fro, and the heavens also shall shake" (D&C 45:47–48).

Zechariah 14:5—The Return of the Savior

Upon the return of the Savior the Saints will be caught up to meet Him—and thus the returning contingent will include the hosts of the faithful and devout, as explained in modern revelation:

> And there shall be silence in heaven for the space of half an hour; and immediately after shall the curtain of heaven be unfolded, as a scroll is unfolded after it is rolled up, and the face of the Lord shall be unveiled;
>
> And the saints that are upon the earth, who are alive, shall be quickened and be caught up to meet him.
>
> And they who have slept in their graves shall come forth, for their graves shall be opened; and they

6 And it shall come to pass in that day, that the light shall not be clear, nor dark:

7 But it shall be one day which shall be known to the LORD, not day, nor night: but it shall come to pass, that at evening time it shall be light.

8 And it shall be in that day, that living waters shall go out from Jerusalem; half of them toward the former sea, and half of them toward the hinder sea: in summer and in winter shall it be.

9 And the LORD shall be king over all the earth: in that day shall there be one LORD, and his name one.

10 All the land shall be turned as a plain from Geba to Rimmon south of Jerusalem: and it shall be lifted up, and inhabited in her place, from Benjamin's gate unto the place of the first gate, unto the corner gate, and from the tower of Hananeel unto the king's winepresses.

11 And men shall dwell in it, and there shall be no more utter destruction; but Jerusalem shall be safely inhabited.

12 ¶ And this shall be the plague wherewith the LORD will smite all the people that have fought against Jerusalem; Their flesh shall consume away while they stand upon their feet, and their eyes shall consume away in their holes, and their tongue shall consume away in their mouth.

13 And it shall come to pass in that day, that a great tumult from the LORD shall be among them; and they shall lay hold every one on the hand of his neighbour, and his hand shall rise up against the hand of his neighbour.

14 And Judah also shall fight at Jerusalem; and the wealth of all the heathen round about shall be gathered together, gold, and silver, and apparel, in great abundance.

15 And so shall be the plague of the horse, of the mule, of the camel, and of the ass, and of all the beasts that shall be in these tents, as this plague.

16 ¶ And it shall come to pass, that every one that is left of all the nations which came against Jerusalem shall even go up from year to year to worship the King, the LORD of hosts, and to keep the feast of tabernacles.

17 And it shall be, that whoso will not come up of all the families of the earth unto Jerusalem to worship the King, the LORD of hosts, even upon them shall be no rain.

18 And if the family of Egypt go not up, and come not, that have no rain; there shall be the plague, wherewith the LORD will smite the heathen that come not up to keep the feast of tabernacles.

19 This shall be the punishment of Egypt, and the punishment of all nations that come not up to keep the feast of tabernacles.

20 ¶ In that day shall there be upon the bells of the horses, HOLINESS UNTO THE LORD; and the pots in the LORD's house shall be like the bowls before the altar.

21 Yea, every pot in Jerusalem and in Judah shall be holiness unto the LORD of hosts: and all they that sacrifice shall come and take of them, and seethe therein: and in that day there shall be no more the Canaanite in the house of the LORD of hosts.

also shall be caught up to meet him in the midst of the pillar of heaven—

They are Christ's, the first fruits, they who shall descend with him first, and they who are on the earth and in their graves, who are first caught up to meet him; and all this by the voice of the sounding of the trump of the angel of God. (D&C 88:95–98)

Zechariah 14:8—The Living Waters

The "living waters" remind one of the vision of Ezekiel where he beheld a stream of living water issuing from the temple of the Lord (see Ezek. 47:1–9; compare Joel 3:18; Rev. 22:1). The symbol of living water(s) encompasses the power and majesty of the gospel of salvation and exaltation and invokes the blessings accorded the faithful in the house of the Lord.

Zechariah 14:10–13—Desolation

The moment of lethal desolation is alluded to in these verses, with the judgment of the Lord consuming the enemies of Jerusalem instantly, even as they stand upon their feet. Malachi also prophesies of the final burning moments of the earth's pre-millennial history: "FOR, behold, the day cometh, that shall burn as an oven; and all the proud, yea, and all that do wickedly, shall be stubble: and the day that cometh shall burn them up, saith the LORD of hosts, that it shall leave them neither root nor branch" (Mal. 4:1).

Zechariah 14:20—Holiness to the Lord

What glory and peace shall reign among the Saints in the day when "Holiness unto the Lord" (an epitaph that reminds us of the inscription on the temples today) should abound in all segments of the Zion society. Isaiah prophesied: "And it shall come to pass, *that he that is* left in Zion, and *he that* remaineth in Jerusalem, shall be called holy, *even* every one that is written among the living in Jerusalem" (Isa. 4:3; compare 2 Ne. 14:3). And again: "AWAKE, awake; put on thy strength, O Zion; put on thy beautiful garments, O Jerusalem, the holy city: for henceforth there shall no more come into thee the uncircumcised and the unclean" (Isa. 52:1; compare 2 Ne. 8:24; 3 Ne. 20:36).

MALACHI

CHAPTER 1

1 THE burden of the word of the LORD to Israel by Malachi.

2 I have loved you, saith the LORD. Yet ye say, Wherein hast thou loved us? Was not Esau Jacob's brother? saith the LORD: yet I loved Jacob,

3 And I hated Esau, and laid his mountains and his heritage waste for the dragons of the wilderness.

4 Whereas Edom saith, We are impoverished, but we will return and build the desolate places; thus saith the LORD of hosts, They shall build, but I will throw down; and they shall call them, The border of wickedness, and, The people against whom the LORD hath indignation for ever.

5 And your eyes shall see, and ye shall say, The LORD will be magnified from the border of Israel.

6 ¶ A son honoureth his father, and a servant his master: if then I be a father, where is mine honour? and if I be a master, where is my fear? saith the LORD of hosts unto you, O priests, that despise my name. And ye say, Wherein have we despised thy name?

7 Ye offer polluted bread upon mine altar; and ye say, Wherein have we polluted thee? In that ye say, The table of the LORD is contemptible.

8 And if ye offer the blind for sacrifice, is it not evil? and if ye offer the lame and sick, is it not evil? offer it now unto thy governor; will he be pleased with thee, or accept thy person? saith the LORD of hosts.

9 And now, I pray you, beseech God that he will be gracious unto us: this hath been by your means: will he regard your persons? saith the LORD of hosts.

10 Who is there even among you that would shut the doors for nought? neither do ye kindle fire on mine altar for nought. I have no pleasure in you, saith the LORD of hosts, neither will I accept an offering at your hand.

11 For from the rising of the sun even unto the going down of the same my name shall be great among the Gentiles; and in every place incense shall be offered unto my name, and a pure offering: for my name shall be great among the heathen, saith the LORD of hosts.

12 ¶ But ye have profaned it, in that ye say, The table of the LORD is polluted; and the fruit thereof, even his meat, is contemptible.

13 Ye said also, Behold, what a weariness is it! and ye have snuffed at it, saith the LORD of hosts; and ye brought that which was torn, and the lame, and the sick; thus ye brought an offering: should I accept this of your hand? saith the LORD.

14 But cursed be the deceiver, which hath in his flock a male, and voweth, and sacrificeth unto the Lord a corrupt thing: for I am a great King, saith the LORD of hosts, and my name is dreadful among the heathen.

MALACHI CHAPTER 1

Malachi 1:6–9—Offerings

Do we bring honor to our Father in Heaven through our offerings? The sacrifices of the day were to involve spotless and perfect offerings without blemish (see Lev. 22:21–22). Anything less would be an affront to the memory of the perfect offering of the Son of God, the Redeemer of the world, whose atoning sacrifice was memorialized in the sacrificial rites of the Law of Moses.

The message for modern readers is the reminder that our oblations and offerings are to be of a perfect kind, involving authentic and sincere reverence and the honorable spirit of faith and devotion. In that way we show honor to our Father in Heaven.

 POINT OF INTEREST

The people of Edom were not the only ones who were wicked; the people of Judah, especially the Levites who lived there, were also corrupt. Even though they were servants of the Lord and sons of God, their sacrifices had become worthless. This is underscored by the fact that their sacrifices were supposed to represent the Atonement of the Savior, which was yet to come—and, as such, their sacrifices needed to be perfect. Instead, they were using animals that were blind, lame, and sick (see Malachi 1:8), and were trying to pass them off as acceptable in the eyes of the Lord. That's not all: they refused to build the fire for the sacrifice until they were paid to do so. The Lord responded, "I have no pleasure in you, . . . neither will I accept an offering at your hand" (Malachi 1:10). As a result, the sacrifice was considered "contemptible" (verse 12), and the people were cursed instead of blessed.

According to Elder James E. Talmage, "The atonement was plainly to be a vicarious sacrifice, voluntary and love-inspired on the Savior's part, universal in its application to mankind so far as men shall accept the means of deliverance thus placed within their reach. For such a mission only one who was without sin could be eligible. Even the altar victims of ancient Israel offered as a provisional propitiation for the offenses of the people under the Mosaic law had to be clean and devoid of spot or blemish; otherwise they were unacceptable and the attempt to offer them was sacrilege" (Jesus the Christ, 21).

CHAPTER 2

1 AND now, O ye priests, this commandment is for you.

2 If ye will not hear, and if ye will not lay it to heart, to give glory unto my name, saith the LORD of hosts, I will even send a curse upon you, and I will curse your blessings: yea, I have cursed them already, because ye do not lay it to heart.

3 Behold, I will corrupt your seed, and spread dung upon your faces, even the dung of your solemn feasts; and one shall take you away with it.

4 And ye shall know that I have sent this commandment unto you, that my covenant might be with Levi, saith the LORD of hosts.

5 My covenant was with him of life and peace; and I gave them to him for the fear wherewith he feared me, and was afraid before my name.

6 The law of truth was in his mouth, and iniquity was not found in his lips: he walked with me in peace and equity, and did turn many away from iniquity.

7 For the priest's lips should keep knowledge, and they should seek the law at his mouth: for he is the messenger of the LORD of hosts.

8 But ye are departed out of the way; ye have caused many to stumble at the law; ye have corrupted the covenant of Levi, saith the LORD of hosts.

9 Therefore have I also made you contemptible and base before all the people, according as ye have not kept my ways, but have been partial in the law.

10 Have we not all one father? hath not one God created us? why do we deal treacherously every man against his brother, by profaning the covenant of our fathers?

11 ¶ Judah hath dealt treacherously, and an abomination is committed in Israel and in Jerusalem; for Judah hath profaned the holiness of the LORD which he loved, and hath married the daughter of a strange god.

12 The LORD will cut off the man that doeth this, the master and the scholar, out of the tabernacles of Jacob, and him that offereth an offering unto the LORD of hosts.

13 And this have ye done again, covering the altar of the LORD with tears, with weeping, and with crying out, insomuch that he regardeth not the offering any more, or receiveth it with good will at your hand.

14 ¶ Yet ye say, Wherefore? Because the LORD hath been witness between thee and the wife of thy youth, against whom thou hast dealt treacherously: yet is she thy companion, and the wife of thy covenant.

15 And did not he make one? Yet had he the residue of the spirit. And wherefore one? That he might seek a godly seed. Therefore take heed to your spirit, and let none deal treacherously against the wife of his youth.

16 For the LORD, the God of Israel, saith that he hateth putting away: for one covereth violence with his garment, saith the LORD of hosts: therefore take heed to your spirit, that ye deal not treacherously.

17 ¶ Ye have wearied the LORD with your words. Yet ye say, Wherein have we wearied him? When ye say, Every one that doeth evil is good in the sight of the LORD, and he delighteth in them; or, Where is the God of judgment?

MALACHI CHAPTER 2

Malachi 2:10—One Father

In his prophetic office, Malachi reminds the people of their shortcomings and calls them to repentance. The framework for his declaration is that we all have one Father—the Creator. Why then, beneath this canopy, do we fail to display charity and benevolence, obedience and service, acting in the spirit of unity and devotion before our Father in Heaven?

For more insights into the life of Malachi, see Appendix PP.

St. Elizabeth of Hungary giving alms to a beggar

CHAPTER 3

1 BEHOLD, I will send my messenger, and he shall prepare the way before me: and the Lord, whom ye seek, shall suddenly come to his temple, even the messenger of the covenant, whom ye delight in: behold, he shall come, saith the LORD of hosts.

2 But who may abide the day of his coming? and who shall stand when he appeareth? for he is like a refiner's fire, and like fullers' soap:

3 And he shall sit as a refiner and purifer of silver: and he shall purify the sons of Levi, and purge them as gold and silver, that they may offer unto the LORD an offering in righteousness.

4 Then shall the offering of Judah and Jerusalem be pleasant unto the LORD, as in the days of old, and as in former years.

5 And I will come near to you to judgment; and I will be a swift witness against the sorcerers, and against the adulterers, and against false swearers, and against those that oppress the hireling in his wages, the widow, and the fatherless, and that turn aside the stranger from his right, and fear not me, saith the LORD of hosts.

6 For I am the LORD, I change not; therefore ye sons of Jacob are not consumed.

7 ¶ Even from the days of your fathers ye are gone away from mine ordinances, and have not kept them. Return unto me, and I will return unto you, saith the LORD of hosts. But ye said, Wherein shall we return?

8 ¶ Will a man rob God? Yet ye have robbed me. But ye say, Wherein have we robbed thee? In tithes and offerings.

9 Ye are cursed with a curse: for ye have robbed me, even this whole nation.

10 Bring ye all the tithes into the storehouse, that there may be meat in mine house, and prove me now herewith, saith the LORD of hosts, if I will not open you the windows of heaven, and pour you out a blessing, that there shall not be room enough to receive it.

11 And I will rebuke the devourer for your sakes, and he shall not destroy the fruits of your ground; neither shall your vine cast her fruit before the time in the field, saith the LORD of hosts.

12 And all nations shall call you blessed: for ye shall be a delightsome land, saith the LORD of hosts.

13 ¶ Your words have been stout against me, saith the LORD. Yet ye say, What have we spoken so much against thee?

14 Ye have said, It is vain to serve God: and what profit is it that we have kept his ordinance, and that we have walked mournfully before the LORD of hosts?

15 And now we call the proud happy; yea, they that work wickedness are set up; yea, they that tempt God are even delivered.

16 ¶ Then they that feared the LORD spake often one to another: and the LORD hearkened, and heard it, and a book of remembrance was written before him for them that feared the LORD, and that thought upon his name.

17 And they shall be mine, saith the LORD of hosts, in that day when I make up my jewels; and I will spare them, as a man spareth his own son that serveth him.

18 Then shall ye return, and discern between the righteous and the wicked, between him that serveth God and him that serveth him not.

MALACHI CHAPTER 3

"You and I live in a day in which the Lord our God has set His hand for the last time, to gather out the righteous and to prepare a people to reign on this earth,—a people who will be purified by good works, who will abide the faith of the living God and be ready to meet the Bridegroom when He comes to reign over the earth, even Jesus Christ . . . and be prepared for that glorious event—the coming of the Son of Man—which I believe will not be at any great distant day." —Joseph F. Smith, *Millennial Star* 36:220, 29 March 1874

Malachi 3:3—Sons of Levi

What is meant by the expression *sons of Levi?* Modern revelation sheds light on this question. The precise expression "sons of Levi" is used three times in the text of the Doctrine and Covenants—once in connection with the restoration of he Aaronic Priesthood (see D&C 13 and D&C 27:12–13), once associated with temple work (see D&C 124:39), and another time in connection with the process of purification required of those who provide leadership for temple work (see D&C 128:24; compare 3 Ne. 24:3, where the Savior quotes Mal. 3:3.)

What is the doctrinal context for references such as "the sons of Levi"? The Doctrine and Covenants is the principal scriptural medium in the latter days for codifying, understanding, and applying the principles and policies embodied in the priesthood as it has been restored to the earth once again by divine intervention and blessing. Few things could be deemed of greater worth to mankind, and few things should inspire more awe, humble devotion, and enduring commitment, than the singular honor of holding and administering the priesthood of God for and in behalf of His sons and daughters. Gospel scholar Richard Cowan lends this perspective:

> On a more figurative level, the Lord promised that faithful bearers of the Melchizedek and Aaronic Priesthood who magnify their callings "become the sons of Moses and of Aaron" respectively (see D&C 84:33–34). Because Moses and Aaron were members of the tribe of Levi, faithful latter-day priesthood bearers become the "sons of Levi," and their "offering" is the faithful service they render (see, for example, D&C 128:24). (Richard O. Cowan, *Answers to Your Questions About the Doctrine and Covenants* [Salt Lake City: Deseret Book Co., 1996], 19)

Malachi 3:10—The Law of Tithing

The kingdom of Heaven on the earth is to be built up with the tithes of the Lord's people. Of His abundance, He will sustain the faithful Saints through their obedience to His laws and principles.

Malachi, prophesying around 430 BC, taught the lessons of spiritual abundance—that the Lord is prepared to open the windows of heaven in blessing the faithful who obediently support the unfolding of His kingdom through

CHAPTER 4

1 FOR, behold, the day cometh, that shall burn as an oven; and all the proud, yea, and all that do wickedly, shall be stubble: and the day that cometh shall burn them up, saith the LORD of hosts, that it shall leave them neither root nor branch.

2 ¶ But unto you that fear my name shall the Sun of righteousness arise with healing in his wings; and ye shall go forth, and grow up as calves of the stall.

3 And ye shall tread down the wicked; for they shall be ashes under the soles of your feet in the day that I shall do this, saith the LORD of hosts.

4 ¶ Remember ye the law of Moses my servant, which I commanded unto him in Horeb for all Israel, with the statutes and judgments.

5 ¶ Behold, I will send you Elijah the prophet before the coming of the great and dreadful day of the LORD:

6 And he shall turn the heart of the fathers to the children, and the heart of the children to their fathers, lest I come and smite the earth with a curse.

their sacrifice and consecrations. His promise is that "all nations shall call you blessed: for ye shall be a delightsome land, saith the Lord of Hosts" (Mal. 3:12.)

MALACHI CHAPTER 4

Malachi 4—Elijah and Preparing for the Second Coming

When He shall return, no man knows. But the Saints are well advised to make their walk and conversation each day an offering in righteousness and obedience, that all may be ready for His return.

Some hundred years before the ministry of Malachi, Zechariah (who prophesied in the period 520–518 BC) spoke concerning the earthly travails and destiny of the covenant people of God against the backdrop of the coming mission of the Savior in the meridian of time and His ultimate appearance in glory at the dawning of the millennial age. The forces of righteousness are to triumph through the saving intervention of heaven, and the Zion people are once again to emerge in the last days as the people of God, purified and sanctified through the redeeming grace of the re-enthroned Sovereign King. Malachi, the last of the Old Testament prophets, intones the same theme around 430 BC—reproving the priests for their neglect of duty and the people in general for their straying from the covenant principles. He calls for a reform in anticipation of the coming of the Lord, and reminds the people that the Lord will send Elijah the prophet once again to bring about the grand unifying work (the sealing enterprise of the temples) that is to save the earth from a curse.

The spirit and power of Elijah continue to work miracles in our day. The Book of Mormon, translated in our time by Joseph Smith through the power of God, rekindles our focus on the ministry of Elijah. The resurrected Savior gave to His ancient Saints in America the prophesies of Malachi (see 3 Ne. 24–25), including the following celebrated statement, which contains the only reference to the ancient prophet Elijah in the Book of Mormon:

> Behold, I will send you Elijah the prophet before the coming of the great and dreadful day of the Lord;
> And he shall turn the heart of the fathers to the children, and the heart of the children to their fathers, lest I come and smite the earth with a curse. (3 Ne. 25:5; compare Mal. 4:5–6)

The hearts of the children have indeed been turned to their fathers so that the work of the sacred temples of God can proceed in this, the final dispensation prior to the Second Coming. We can be saved no faster than we save our dead through vicarious temple service (see D&C 128:5). The work in the holy temples constitutes the work of being saviors on mount Zion as prophesied in Obad. 1:21 and confirmed in latter-day revelation (see D&C 128:53–54). If we are true and faithful, we will present before the Lord "a record worthy of all acceptation" (D&C 128:24) containing the information about our progenitors that is requisite

NOTES:

for the accomplishment of the sealing ordinances of the temples.

The Prophet Joseph Smith articulated the indispensable nature of the powers and keys of sealing restored to him, as the agent of the Restoration, through the prophet Elijah: "The greatest responsibility in this world that God has laid upon us is to seek after our dead. The Apostle says, 'They without us cannot be made perfect;' (Hebrews 11:40) for it is necessary that the sealing power should be in our hands to seal our children and our dead for the fulness of the dispensation of times—a dispensation to meet the promises made by Jesus Christ before the foundation of the world for the salvation of man" (*TPJ*, 356).

Through Elijah the sealing powers were restored, by which we typically understand the work of temples. But the mission of Elijah accomplished more than that, as the Prophet Joseph Smith also emphasized: "Elijah was the last prophet that held the keys of this priesthood, and who will, before the last dispensation, restore the authority and delive[r] the Keys of this priesthood in order that all the ordinances may be attended to in righteousness. . . . It is true that the Savior had authority and power to bestow this blessing but the Sons of Levi were too predjudi[ced]. . . . And I will send Elijah the Prophet before the great and terrible day of the Lord &c &c. Why send Elijah [:] because he holds the Keys of the Authority to administer in all the ordinances of the priesthood and without the authority is given the ordinances could not be administered in righteousness" (Joseph Smith, *The Words of Joseph Smith: The Contemporary Accounts of the Nauvoo Discourses of the Prophet Joseph*, comp. and ed. Andrew F. Ehat and Lyndon W. Cook, 2nd ed. [1996], 43).

Thus the keys of Elijah do *more* than validate and empower the redemptive work for the dead, as scholar Kent Jackson confirms: ". . . they seal and validate *all* ordinances of the priesthood so that ordinances performed on earth are binding in heaven as well. . . . The appearance of Moses, Elias, and Elijah in the Kirtland Temple repeated in many ways the similar event that the ancient apostles Peter, James, and John experienced, as recorded in the New Testament (Matt. 17:1–9). At that time, as in 1836, the Lord was beginning a new dispensation of his Church, and ancient holders of priesthood power came to pass on the keys of their ministry to enable the Lord's work to be carried forward. In the latter days, this transmittal of keys was an indispensable step in the process of the Restoration" (*FAR*, 223).

APPENDIX A
OUR FATHER IN HEAVEN,
JESUS CHRIST, AND THE HOLY GHOST

Our Father in Heaven has granted unto Jesus Christ the sacred commission to be His Agent in governing and directing the unfolding of the divine gospel plan for the benefit of all humankind. The Savior declared during His intercessory prayer: "And this is life eternal, that they might know thee the only true God, and Jesus Christ, whom thou hast sent" (John 17:3). Later, the resurrected Savior admonished the Saints in ancient America: "Therefore I would that ye should be perfect even as I, or your Father who is in heaven is perfect" (3 Ne. 12:48; compare Matt. 5:48). In the latter days He has assured the Saints concerning the harmony and oneness of the Godhead: "Which Father, Son, and Holy Ghost are one God, infinite and eternal, without end. Amen" (D&C 20:28).

The sacred unity of purpose reflected among the three members of the Godhead makes the term *God* or *Lord* in the scriptures often interchangeable in regard to the Father and the Son. But there are distinctions among the individual Beings of the Godhead. Through the Prophet Joseph Smith was revealed this verity: "The Father has a body of flesh and bones as tangible as man's; the Son also; but the Holy Ghost has not a body of flesh and bones, but is a personage of Spirit. Were it not so, the Holy Ghost could not dwell in us" (D&C 130:22).

Moreover, as Joseph Smith also confirmed, the Father has pre-eminence: "Everlasting covenant was made between three personages before the organization of this earth, and relates to their dispensation of things to men on the earth; these personages, according to Abraham's record, are called God the first, the Creator; God the second, the Redeemer; and God the third, the witness or Testator" (*TPJS*, 190).

Paul declared: "But to us *there is but* one God, the Father, of whom *are* all things, and we in him; and one Lord Jesus Christ, by whom *are* all things, and we by him" (1 Cor. 8:6).

Because Jesus Christ is the divine Agent within the expanse of the Father's eternal dominion and infinite design, it is for the most part Jesus Christ who is the One revealed in the holy scriptures. On occasion, the Father makes His presence known, largely as a confirming witness to the mission of the Savior. At the baptism of the Savior, the Holy Ghost was manifest in the form of a dove and the Father's voice was heard from heaven, saying, "This is my beloved Son, in whom I am well pleased" (Matt. 3:17). On the mount of transfiguration where Elias and Moses appeared to Peter, James, and John in the presence of the Savior, the same voice reverberated over the scene: ". . . behold, a bright cloud overshadowed them: and behold a voice out of the cloud, which said, This is my beloved Son, in whom I am well pleased; hear ye him" (Matt. 17:5).

At the martyrdom of Stephen, we learn: "But he, being full of the Holy Ghost, looked up stedfastly into heaven, and saw the glory of God, and Jesus standing on the right hand of God, And said, Behold, I see the heavens opened, and the Son of man standing on the right hand of God" (Acts 7:55–56).

As the risen Lord was about to appear before the assembled faithful at Bountiful in ancient America, the voice of the Father proclaimed the words of introduction: "Behold my Beloved Son, in whom I am well pleased, in whom I have glorified my name—hear ye him" (3 Ne. 11:7; see also 2 Ne. 31:11, 15, where the voice of the Father is recorded by Nephi).

In our day, the boy Joseph Smith learned first-hand the individuality of Father and Son as revealed in the First Vision: "When the light rested upon me I saw two Personages, whose brightness and glory defy all description, standing above me in the air. One of them spake unto me, calling me by name and said, pointing to the other—*This is My Beloved Son. Hear Him!*" (JS–H 1:17).

In all of these instances the Father is presented for what He is: an individual Being of infinite glory who is the supreme God for us all. In all of these instances, as well, the divine commission of the Son is authenticated and validated. We pray to and worship the Father, always in the name of the Son.

From the very beginning of the Old Testament account, the majestic role of God the Father is confirmed, as in the account of the creation of man.

> And God said, Let us make man in our image, after our likeness: and let them have dominion over the fish of the sea, and over the fowl of the air, and over the cattle, and over all the earth, and over every creeping thing that creepeth upon the earth.
>
> So God created man in his *own* image, in the image of God created he him; male and female created he them. (Gen. 1:26–27)

The parallel account from the Book of Abraham in the Pearl of Great Price is rendered as follows: "And the Gods formed man from the dust of the ground, and took his spirit (that is, the man's spirit), and put it into him; and breathed into his nostrils the breath of life, and man became a living soul" (Abr. 5:7). Previous to this, the Book of Abraham revealed the initial stage of the Creation, again using the word *Gods*:

> AND then the Lord said: Let us go down. And they went down at the beginning, and they, that is the Gods, organized and formed the heavens and the earth. . . .
>
> And they (the Gods) said: Let there be light; and there was light.
>
> And they (the Gods) comprehended the light, for it was bright; and they divided the light, or caused it to be divided, from the darkness.
>
> And the Gods called the light Day, and the darkness they called Night. (Abr. 4:1, 3–5)

Such accounts provide evidence that the Father empowered others to assist Him in the creative process.

The word *God* in the Hebrew bible is *Elohim* (a plural term—as in Gen. 1:1–5). The Prophet Joseph Smith explained the significance of this plural reference as follows: "Eloheim is from the word *Eloi*, God, in the singular number; and by adding the word *heim*, it renders it Gods. It read first, 'In the beginning the head of the Gods brought forth the Gods,' or, as others have translated it, 'The head of the Gods called the Gods together'" (*TPJS*, 371). Chief among His agents, as indicated earlier, was the Supreme Mediator Jesus Christ: "And there stood one among them that was like unto God, and he said unto those who were with him: We will go down, for there is space there, and we will take of these materials, and we will make an earth whereon these may dwell; And we will prove them herewith, to see if they will do all things whatsoever the Lord their God shall command them" (Abr. 3:24–25; compare John 1:1–3).

Thus Jehovah (Jesus Christ) is the Word presented as God in the Old Testament. When the Decalogue was revealed from Sinai, the voice was that of Jehovah, the Mediator of the Father:

> AND God spake all these words, saying,
> I *am* the LORD thy God, which have brought thee out of the land of Egypt, out of the house of bondage.
> Thou shalt have no other gods before me.
> Thou shalt not make unto thee any graven image, or any likeness *of any thing* that *is* in heaven above, or that *is* in the earth beneath, or that *is* in the water under the earth: (Ex. 20:1–4)

By the process of divine investiture, Jehovah speaks for the Father and as the Father. To Moses, Jehovah declared (as if officiating in the office of the Father): "I am the Beginning and the End, the Almighty God; by mine Only Begotten I created these things; yea, in the beginning I created the heaven, and the earth upon which thou standest" (Moses 2:1). He expressed the heavenly mission as follows: "For behold, this is my work and glory—to bring to pass the immortality and eternal life of man" (Moses 1:39).

Within this context, Jehovah (Jesus Christ) is indeed the Father of the faithful in the sense that they are adopted into His fold and become His seed through obedience to the gospel plan: "Though he were a Son, yet learned he obedience by the things which he suffered; And being made perfect, he became the author of eternal salvation unto all them that obey him" (Heb. 5:8–9). The prophet Abinadi explained the meaning of the fatherhood of both Father and Son as follows:

> AND now Abinadi said unto them: I would that ye should understand that God himself shall come down among the children of men, and shall redeem his people.
> And because he dwelleth in flesh he shall be called the Son of God, and having subjected the flesh to the will of the Father, being the Father and the Son—
> The Father, because he was conceived by the power of God; and the Son, because of the flesh; thus becoming the Father and Son—
> And they are one God, yea, the very Eternal Father of heaven and of earth.
> And thus the flesh becoming subject to the Spirit, or the Son to the Father, being one God, suffereth temptation, and yieldeth not to the temptation, but suffereth himself to be mocked, and scourged, and cast out, and disowned by his people. (Mosiah 15:1–5)

Abinadi goes on to expound the writings of Isaiah by explaining which individuals are to become the seed of Christ and thus look upon Him as a Father after the manner of our Father in Heaven:

> And now I say unto you, who shall declare his generation? Behold, I say unto you, that when his soul has been made an offering for sin he shall see his seed. And now what say ye? And who shall be his seed?
> Behold I say unto you, that whosoever has heard the words of the prophets, yea, all the holy prophets who have prophesied concerning the coming of the Lord—I say unto you, that all those who have hearkened unto their words, and believed that the Lord would redeem his people, and have looked forward to that day for a remission of their sins, I say unto you, that these are his seed, or they are the heirs of the kingdom of God. (Mosiah 15:10–11; compare Isa. 53:10)

Modern revelation sheds further light on the stature and supremacy of our Father in Heaven and His role in establishing Jesus as His Mediator. *Father*, referring to Heavenly Father, occurs 140 times in the text of the Doctrine and Covenants, among which are four occurrences of the term "God the Father" (D&C 21:1; 88:19; 107:19; 138:14). The word *God* itself (which can have reference to the Father or the Son, or both, depending on the usage) occurs very frequently—516 times. The only time the word *god* (lower case) occurs (in reference to a non-Deity or worldly god) is in Section 1: "They [the inhabitants of the earth] seek not the Lord to establish his righteousness, but every man walketh in his own way, and after the image of his own god, whose image is in the likeness of the world, and whose substance is that of an idol, which waxeth old and shall perish in Babylon, even Babylon the great, which shall fall" (D&C 1:16). Thus the preface to the D&C contrasts *God* with *god*—the divine God distinguished from the material or temporal god of unrighteous mortals. The word *gods*, in reference mostly to just men and women made perfect as heirs to the celestial glory in the hereafter occurs nine times (D&C 76:58; 121:28, 32; 132:17, 18, 19, 20 [twice], and 37).

In reference to the law of the priesthood, we find these additional references to the Father: "I am the Lord thy God [Jesus Christ], and will give unto thee the law of my Holy Priesthood, as was ordained by me and my Father before the world was" (D&C 132:28). It is according to this law that the Abrahamic covenant is renewed in the dispensation of the fulness of times, allowing the servants of God to minister unto the inhabitants of the earth by bringing the gospel and the blessings of the priesthood to the four corners of the earth so that the faithful can obtains the full blessings of salvation and exaltation, including "the continuation of the lives" (D&C 132:22). The power and authority of the priesthood, restored to the earth for the good of the obedient and faithful, permit the fulfillment of "the promise which was given by my Father before the foundation of the world, and for their exaltation in the eternal worlds, that they may bear the souls of men; for herein is the work of my Father continued, that he may be glorified" (D&C 132:63).

Finally, it is of interest that the Doctrine and Covenants also uses an additional name for the Father—*Ahman*—as in this verse concerning the Son of Ahman, even Jesus Christ: "Wherefore, do the things which I have commanded you, saith your Redeemer, even the Son Ahman, who prepareth all things before he taketh you" (D&C 78:20; compare D&C 95:17).

Whether we use the term *Ahman* or *Elohim* or *God* in referring to our Father in Heaven, the universal implication is the same: He our Supreme Lord, as the Prophet Joseph Smith clearly enunciated: "Paul says there are Gods many and Lords many [see 1 Corinthians 8:5]. I want to set it forth in a plain and simple manner; but to us there is but one God—that is *pertaining to us*; and he [i.e. Heavenly Father] is in all and through all" (*TPJS*, 370). That is the reason we pray to Him, saying, "Our Father which art in heaven" (Matt. 6:9; 3 Ne. 13:9). That is why we can look forward to being among those given to the Son by the Father: "Father, I pray not for the world, but for those whom thou hast given me out of the world, because of their faith, that they may be purified in me, that I may be in them as thou, Father, art in me, that we may be one, that I may be glorified in them" (3 Ne. 19:29). And furthermore: "Fear not, little children, for you are mine, and I have overcome the world, and you are of them that my Father hath given me" (D&C 50:41).

We can thank our Father in Heaven for His surpassing perfection: His mercy, goodness, mighty deeds, and wondrous works; His creative majesty and power; His greatness , holiness, and glory; His kindness in answering our prayers and keeping His covenants; and His lovingkindness, righteous judgment, understanding, and ultimate victory in the battle for our souls. We can thank His Only Begotten Son (the Messiah) for the Atonement. And we can strive with all our heart, might, mind, and strength to live worthy of Their matchless blessings.

The Spirit of God

The expression *Spirit of God* occurs fourteen times in the Old Testament, beginning with this passage:

> IN the beginning God created the heaven and the earth.
> And the earth was without form, and void; and darkness *was* upon the face of the deep. And the Spirit of God moved upon the face of the waters." (Gen. 1:1–2)

Pharaoh observed the "Spirit of God" at work in Joseph (see Gen. 41:38). The "spirit of God" empowered the divinely commissioned artisan Bezaleel to accomplish inspired workmanship on the tabernacle (see Ex. 31:3; 35:31). The "spirit of God" came upon Balaam and induced him to invoke a blessing upon Israel, rather than the curse that Balak, king of the Moabites, had paid him to produce (see Num. 24:2). The "Spirit of God" came upon Saul so that he could prophesy among a group of prophets he encountered (see 1 Sam. 10:10), and later the "Spirit of God" returned to him, enabling him to galvanize the people for a victory over the Ammonites (see 1 Sam. 11:6). When Saul, seeking to slay David, sent messengers to find him, they were overcome by the "Spirit of God" and prophesied—something that Saul himself experienced on that occasion, so powerful was the "Spirit of God" (see 1 Sam. 19:20, 23). The

"Spirit of God" caused Azariah to prophesy that Judah would prosper by keeping the commandments (see 2 Chron. 15:1). The "Spirit of God" acted upon Zechariah the son of Jehoiada the priest, causing him to call the people to repentance for their wickedness (see 2 Chron. 24:20). Job discerned the "spirit of God" within him, sustaining his life (see Job 27:3), and Elihu, Job's mentor, declared: "The Spirit of God hath made me, and the breath of the Almighty hath given me life" (Job 33:4). The vision of Ezekiel was unfolded by the "Spirit of God" (see Ezek. 11:24).

We see that the Spirit of God acts in many ways to bring about wondrous progress in advancing the kingdom of God—from the process of the Creation itself to the sustaining of mortal life from one moment to the next, from the invocation of blessings upon God's children to the pronouncement of calls for them to repent, from the empowerment of the armies of the Lord unto victory to the dissipating of malevolent designs in the hearts of leaders like Saul, from the establishment of the house of the Lord in beauty and magnificence to the elevating of the Lord's prophets in visions of grandeur.

The Holy Ghost

The Holy Ghost is the third member of the Godhead, serving in unity and glory with the Father and the Son. The term *Holy Ghost* does not occur in the King James Version of the Old Testament. However, the office and function of the Holy Ghost are pervasively represented through the use of terms such as "the spirit," "my spirit," "spirit of God," and similar expressions.

In the first verse of the Old Testament we learn: "In the beginning God created the heaven and the earth" (Gen. 1:1); then, in the second verse, we learn that the dynamic spirit of generation was at work in that process: "And the Spirit of God moved upon the face of the waters" (Gen. 1:1–2)—an anticipation of the words of Job: "By his spirit he hath garnished the heavens" (Job 26:13).

From the Creation forward, the Holy Spirit, as God's agent of light and truth, is found at work through all the generations of time: guiding, illuminating, warning, counseling, confirming, and blessing the lives of God's children—both prophet-leaders as well as inspired laypersons within the kingdom.

Even non-covenant leaders recognized the power of the Spirit: "And Pharaoh said unto his servants, Can we find *such a one* as this *is* [i.e. Joseph], a man in whom the Spirit of God *is*?" (Gen. 41:38). Aaron was filled with the Spirit—and thus blessed with wisdom to function in the priest's office (see Ex. 28:3). The Lord blessed Bezaleel, the elect temple artisan, with His Spirit: "And I have filled him with the spirit of God, in wisdom, and in understanding, and in knowledge, and in all manner of workmanship" (Ex. 31:3; see also Ex. 35:31).

Caleb, the inspired scout dispatched by Moses into the Promised Land, had the Spirit of the Lord with him to enable him to envision the promise of the land of inheritance (see Num. 14:24). Even the prophet Balaam, sometimes distracted with earthly interests, had the Spirit of God come upon him (see Num. 24:1). In all things, Joshua was blessed of the Spirit to perform mighty deeds of valor and honor:

And the LORD said unto Moses, Take thee Joshua the son of Nun, a man in whom *is* the spirit, and lay thine hand upon him" (Numbers 27:18.); "And Joshua the son of Nun was full of the spirit of wisdom; for Moses had laid his hands upon him: and the children of Israel hearkened unto him, and did as the LORD commanded Moses." (Deut. 34:9)

The scriptures confirm that many other figures in the Old Testament experienced the operation of the Holy Ghost within their lives: Moses (see Isa. 63:10–14); Othniel the judge (see Judges 3:10); Gideon the judge (see Judges 6:34); Jephthah, commander of the armies of Israel (see Judges 11:29); Samson (see Judges 13:25; see also Judges 14:6, 19; 15:14); Saul (in his earlier tenure—see 1 Sam. 10:6; see also 1 Sam. 10:10; 11:6; 19:23); David (see 1 Sam. 16:13; compare 2 Sam. 23:2; 1 Chron. 28:11–12); Elijah (see 1 Kings 18:12; 2 Kings 2:15–16); Amasai, chief of the captains of Israel (see 1 Chron. 12:18); Azariah, one of the men of Israel (see 2 Chron. 15:1–2); Jahaziel the Levite (see 2 Chron. 20:14–15); and Zechariah, a prophet (see 2 Chron. 24:20).

Others expressly inspired and guided by the Holy Ghost include Ezekiel (see Ezek. 2:1–2; 3:12–14, 24; 8:3; 11:1–5, 24–25; 37:1, 12–14; 43:5); Daniel (see Dan. 4:8–9, 18; 5:11-14; 6:3); and Micah (see Micah 3:8).

The Old Testament makes clear that the Spirit of the Lord would bless and sustain the Only Begotten in His mission of redemption:

"And the spirit of the LORD shall rest upon him, the spirit of wisdom and understanding, the spirit of counsel and might, the spirit of knowledge and of the fear of the LORD;" (Isa. 11:2)

"Come ye near unto me, hear ye this; I have not spoken in secret from the beginning; from the time that it was, there *am* I: and now the Lord GOD, and his Spirit, hath sent me. Thus saith the LORD, thy Redeemer, the Holy One of Israel; I *am* the LORD thy God which teacheth thee to profit, which leadeth thee by the way *that* thou shouldest go." (Isa. 48:16–17)

"THE Spirit of the Lord GOD *is* upon me; because the LORD hath anointed me to preach good tidings unto the meek; he hath sent me to bind up the brokenhearted, to proclaim liberty to the captives, and the opening of the prison to *them that are* bound; To proclaim the acceptable year of the LORD, and the day of vengeance of our God; to comfort all that mourn;" (Isa. 61:1–2)

"And I will pour upon the house of David, and upon the inhabitants of Jerusalem, the spirit of grace and of supplications: and they shall look upon me whom they have pierced, and they shall mourn for him, as one mourneth for *his* only *son,* and shall be in bitterness for him, as one that is in bitterness for *his* firstborn." (Zech.12:10)

The Spirit of the Lord would also be at work in the last days, gathering the Saints, preparing the world for the Second Coming, and inaugurating the millennial reign (see Isa. 32:15–16; 34:16; 40:7): "For I will pour water upon him that is thirsty, and floods upon the dry ground: I will pour my spirit upon thy seed, and my blessing upon thine offspring: And they shall spring up *as* among the grass, as willows by the water courses" (Isa. 44:3–4). The ensign of the Restoration will be hoisted through the power of the Holy Ghost:

So shall they fear the name of the LORD from the west, and his glory from the rising of the sun. When the enemy shall come in like a flood, the Spirit of the LORD shall lift up a standard against him.

And the Redeemer shall come to Zion, and unto them that turn from transgression in Jacob, saith the LORD.

As for me, this *is* my covenant with them, saith the LORD; My spirit that *is* upon thee, and my words which I have put in thy mouth, shall not depart out of thy mouth, nor out of the mouth of thy seed, nor out of the mouth of thy seed's seed, saith the LORD, from henceforth and for ever. (Isa. 59:19–21)

It is clear that the blessings of the Holy Spirit are universal—accessible to all who seek the Lord's guidance with humble hearts and willing minds. Moses taught this lesson in unforgettable terms in connection with the calling of the seventy elders of Israel:

And the LORD said unto Moses, Gather unto me seventy men of the elders of Israel, whom thou knowest to be the elders of the people, and officers over them; and bring them unto the tabernacle of the congregation, that they may stand there with thee.

And I will come down and talk with thee there: and I will take of the spirit which *is* upon thee, and will put *it* upon them; and they shall bear the burden of the people with thee, that thou bear *it* not thyself alone. . . .

And the LORD came down in a cloud, and spake unto him, and took of the spirit that *was* upon him, and gave *it* unto the seventy elders: and it came to pass, *that,* when the spirit rested upon them, they prophesied, and did not cease.

But there remained two *of the* men in the camp, the name of the one *was* Eldad, and the name of the other Medad: and the spirit rested upon them; and they *were* of them that were written, but went not out unto the tabernacle: and they prophesied in the camp.

And there ran a young man, and told Moses, and said, Eldad and Medad do prophesy in the camp.

And Joshua the son of Nun, the servant of Moses, *one* of his young men, answered and said, My lord Moses, forbid them.

And Moses said unto him, Enviest thou for my sake? would God that all the LORD's people were prophets, *and* that the LORD would put his spirit upon them! (Num. 11:16–17; 25–29)

Within this same context, the Book of Job confirms that all are sustained by the Spirit: "All the while my breath *is* in me, and the spirit of God *is* in my nostrils" (Job 7:3); "But *there is* a spirit in man: and the inspiration of the Almighty giveth them understanding" (Job 32:8); "The Spirit of God hath made me, and the breath of the Almighty hath given me life" (Job 33:4). The Psalmist invoked the spirit of supplication unto God for the blessings of the Holy Ghost:

"Create in me a clean heart, O God; and renew a right spirit within me. Cast me not away from thy presence; and take not thy holy spirit from me. Restore unto me the joy of thy salvation; and uphold me *with thy* free spirit." (Ps. 51:10–12.)

"Thou sendest forth thy spirit, they are created: and thou renewest the face of the earth. The glory of the LORD shall endure for ever: the LORD shall rejoice in his works." (Ps. 104:30–31)

"Teach me to do thy will; for thou *art* my God: thy spirit *is* good; lead me into the land of uprightness. Quicken me, O LORD, for thy name's sake: for thy righteousness' sake bring my soul out of trouble." (Ps. 143:10–11)

We learn from the Old Testament that the blessings of the Spirit are conditioned on faithfulness and virtue: "And the LORD said, My spirit shall not always strive with man" (Gen. 6:3). Saul, for one, learned that lesson painfully: "But the Spirit of the LORD departed from Saul, and an evil spirit from the LORD troubled him" (1 Sam. 16:14; the JST corrects this reference to say "an evil spirit which was not of the Lord"; see also Zech. 7:12). By contrast, the Lord offers the penitent a chance to renew their spirits through the blessings of the gospel:

A new heart also will I give you, and a new spirit will I put within you: and I will take away the stony heart out of your flesh, and I will give you an heart of flesh.

And I will put my spirit within you, and cause you to walk in my statutes, and ye shall keep my judgments, and do *them*. (Ezek. 36:26–27)

The prophet Joel foresaw a time when the Spirit of the Lord would again abound among those caught up in the joy and glory of the Restoration of gospel truths: "And it shall come to pass afterward, *that* I will pour out my spirit upon all flesh; and your sons and your daughters shall prophesy, your old men shall dream dreams, your young men shall see visions: And also upon the servants and upon the handmaids in those days will I pour out my spirit" (Joel 2:28–29).

Ezekiel confirms the glorious vision of a spiritual age to unfold in the latter days: "Neither will I hide my face any more from them: for I have poured out my spirit upon the house of Israel, saith the Lord GOD" (Ezek. 39:29).

The Saints can participate in the choice blessings of the Lord through obedience to the gospel plan—with the promise "that they may always have his Spirit to be with them" (D&C 20:77; see also D&C 20:79). The voice of the Spirit comes, in general, as a still small voice confirming eternal principles. The story of Elijah conveys this truth in a memorable way:

And he came thither unto a cave, and lodged there; and, behold, the word of the LORD *came* to him, and he said unto him, What doest thou here, Elijah?

And he said, I have been very jealous for the LORD God of hosts: for the children of Israel have forsaken thy covenant, thrown down thine altars, and slain thy prophets with the sword; and I, *even* I only, am left; and they seek my life, to take it away.

And he said, Go forth, and stand upon the mount before the LORD. And, behold, the LORD passed by, and a great and strong wind rent the mountains, and brake in pieces the rocks before the LORD; *but* the LORD *was* not in the wind: and after the wind an earthquake; *but* the LORD *was* not in the earthquake:

And after the earthquake a fire; *but* the LORD *was* not in the fire: and after the fire a still small voice. (1 Kings 19:9–12; compare 3 Ne. 11)

Although the Old Testament does not use the term *Holy Ghost*, latter-day additions to the scriptural canon make clear that this term was indeed part of spiritual worship and rejuvenation in ancient times—including the gift of the Holy Ghost. The Book of Moses contains ten references to the Holy Ghost, beginning with the experience of Moses upon the mount after he had rejected the enticements of Satan: "And it came to pass that when Satan had departed from the presence of Moses, that Moses lifted up his eyes unto heaven, being filled with the Holy Ghost, which beareth record of the Father and the Son; And calling upon the name of God, he beheld his glory again, for it was upon him; and he heard a voice, saying: Blessed art thou, Moses, for I, the Almighty, have chosen thee, and thou shalt be made stronger than many waters; for they shall obey thy command as if thou wert God" (Moses 1:24–25). From the record of Moses we know by what means the Holy Ghost came into the life of Adam and Eve and their offspring:

And after many days an angel of the Lord appeared unto Adam, saying: Why dost thou offer sacrifices unto the Lord? And Adam said unto him: I know not, save the Lord commanded me.

And then the angel spake, saying: This thing is a similitude of the sacrifice of the Only Begotten of the Father, which is full of grace and truth.

Wherefore, thou shalt do all that thou doest in the name of the Son, and thou shalt repent and call upon God in the name of the Son forevermore.

And in that day the Holy Ghost fell upon Adam, which beareth record of the Father and the Son, saying: I am the Only Begotten of the Father from the beginning, henceforth and forever, that as thou hast fallen thou mayest be redeemed, and all mankind, even as many as will. . . .

And thus the Gospel began to be preached, from the beginning, being declared by holy angels sent forth from the presence of God, and by his own voice, and by the gift of the Holy Ghost.

And the Lord God called upon men by the Holy Ghost everywhere and commanded them that they should repent; (Moses 5:6–9, 14, 58; compare Moses 6:64–68)

From the beginning, the simplicity and eternal nature of the gospel was made known unto mankind, for God said unto Adam:

. . . If thou wilt turn unto me, and hearken unto my voice, and believe, and repent of all thy transgressions, and be baptized, even in water, in the name of mine Only Begotten Son, who is full of grace and truth, which is Jesus Christ, the only name which shall be given under heaven, whereby salvation shall come unto the children of men, ye shall receive the gift of the Holy Ghost, asking all things in his name, and whatsoever ye shall ask, it shall be given you. (Moses 6:52)

Furthermore, the eternal logic and efficacy of the process of spiritual rebirth through the Spirit was expounded with clarity for Adam and Eve and their posterity:

Therefore I give unto you a commandment, to teach these things freely unto your children, saying:

That by reason of transgression cometh the fall, which fall bringeth death, and inasmuch as ye were born into the world by water, and blood, and the spirit, which I have made, and so became of dust a living soul, even so ye must be born again into the kingdom of heaven, of water, and of the Spirit, and be cleansed by blood, even the blood of mine Only Begotten; that ye might be sanctified from all sin, and enjoy the words of eternal life in this world, and eternal life in the world to come, even immortal glory;

For by the water ye keep the commandment; by the Spirit ye are justified, and by the blood ye are sanctified; (Moses 6:58–60)

Likewise, Enoch was commanded of the Lord to call the people to repentance: "And he gave unto me a commandment that I should baptize in the name of the Father, and of the Son, which is full of grace and truth, and of the Holy Ghost, which beareth record of the Father and the Son" (Moses 7:11; see also Moses 7:27). Noah continued this sacred ministry: "Believe and repent of your sins and be baptized in the name of Jesus Christ, the Son of God, even as our fathers, and ye shall receive the Holy Ghost, that ye may have all things made manifest; and if ye do not this, the floods will come in upon you; nevertheless they hearkened not" (Moses 8:24). Abraham, as well, operated under the power of the Holy Ghost as confirmed by Figure 7 of Facsimile 2 from the Book of Abraham: "Represents God sitting upon his throne, revealing through the heavens the grand Key-words of the Priesthood; as, also, the sign of the Holy Ghost unto Abraham, in the form of a dove."

The Doctrine and Covenants presents a comprehensive view of the office and function of the Holy Ghost, being that personage of the Godhead "which beareth record of the Father and of the Son; Which Father, Son, and Holy Ghost are one God, infinite and eternal, without end" (D&C 20:27–28; see also D&C 1:39; 42:17). Unlike the Father and the Son, who have glorified bodies of flesh and bones, "the Holy Ghost has not a body of flesh and bones, but is a personage of Spirit. Were it not so, the Holy Ghost could not dwell in us" (D&C 130:22).

So important is the role of the Holy Ghost in the eternal process that the only transgression that would place an individual outside the grasp of redemption from the second death (separation from God) is to commit blasphemy against the Holy Ghost: "Having denied the Holy Spirit after having received it, and having denied the Only Begotten Son of the Father, having crucified him unto themselves and put him to an open shame" (D&C 76:35; see also D&C 132:27). By way of contrast is the grand and glorious fulfillment of one's celestial destiny through honor and obedience, according to the views reflected in the inspired prayer of the Prophet Joseph Smith: "And that they may grow up in thee, and receive a fulness of the Holy Ghost, and be organized according to thy laws, and be prepared to obtain every needful thing" (D&C 109:15; compare 1 Ne. 10:17).

APPENDIX B
ADAM AND EVE

ADAM

Adam has a pervasive presence throughout the holy record of God. The name *Adam* occurs 147 times in the scriptures. In addition, the name *Michael* (referring to Adam) can be found three times in the Old Testament, twice in the New Testament, and ten times in the Doctrine and Covenants. The term *ancient of days* occurs three times in the Old Testament and three times in the Doctrine and Covenants. These passages comprise a remarkable account of this exemplary leader in the program of Heavenly Father and His Son Jesus Christ.

Some of the milestones in this history are the following:

• The actual creation of Adam and Eve in the image of God: "So God created man in his *own* image, in the image of God created he him; male and female created he them" (Gen. 1:27; compare Abr. 4:26–27).

• The commission and marriage of Adam and Eve in the sacred precincts of the Garden of Eden (analogous to celestial marriage within the house of the Lord): "And God blessed them, and God said unto them, Be fruitful, and multiply, and replenish the earth, and subdue it: and have dominion over the fish of the sea, and over the fowl of the air, and over every living thing that moveth upon the earth" (Gen. 1:28).

• The Fall. At the beginning, Adam and Eve were in a state of innocence, knowing no joy or misery (see 2 Ne. 2:23). Adam and Eve were commanded not to partake of the fruit of the tree of knowledge of good and evil—"for in the day thou eastest thereof thou shalt surely die" (see Moses 3:17; also Moses 4:8–9, where it is confirmed that God forbade them even to "touch" the fruit of the tree). At the same time, they were told that they were free to choose (see Moses 3:17). Eve is beguiled by Satan and partakes of the fruit of the tree of knowledge of good and evil and then gives to Adam and he also partakes (see Moses 4:12). Their eyes are opened and they realize that they are naked and make for themselves aprons (see Moses 4:13). Adam and Eve are cast out of the garden to make their way on the pathway of mortality (see Moses 4:29–31; Gen. 3:23).

• The foundation of the Adamic family is established. Adam calls his wife *Eve*, meaning "the mother of all living" (see Gen. 3:20; Moses 4:26). Adam and Eve have children and their children beget children (see Moses 5:2–3; Genesis 4:1).

• The true order of worship is established. One of the great stories in the ancient record of God's dealings with man is the incident in the life of Adam and Eve where they are obedient to the voice of the Lord in offering sacrifices. Because they had been evicted from the Garden of Eden as a result of transgression, they were no longer in the presence of God, but they still heard His voice speaking to them from the direction of the Garden, giving them counsel and instructions on how to conduct their lives. Adam and Eve pray for counsel: ". . . and they heard the voice of the Lord from the way toward the Garden of Eden, speaking unto them, and they saw him not; for they were shut out from his presence. And he gave unto them commandments, that they should worship the Lord their God, and should offer the firstlings of their flocks, for an offering unto the Lord. And Adam was obedient unto the commandments of the Lord" (Moses 5:4–5). When an angel of the Lord appears and asks Adam why he is offering sacrifices, he says:

. . . I know not, save the Lord commanded me.

And then the angel spake, saying: This thing is a similitude of the sacrifice of the Only Begotten of the Father, which is full of grace and truth.

Wherefore, thou shalt do all that thou doest in the name of the Son, and thou shalt repent and call upon God in the name of the Son forevermore. (Moses 5:6–8)

• Ordinances of salvation are instituted:

And in that day the Holy Ghost fell upon Adam, which beareth record of the Father and the Son, saying: I am the Only Begotten of the Father from the beginning, henceforth and forever, that as thou hast fallen thou mayest be redeemed, and all mankind, even as many as will.

And in that day Adam blessed God and was filled, and began to prophesy concerning all the families of the earth, saying: Blessed be the name of God, for because of my transgression my eyes are opened, and in this life I shall have joy, and again in the flesh I shall see God.

And Eve, his wife, heard all these things and was glad, saying: Were it not for our transgression we never should have had seed, and never should have known good and evil, and the joy of our redemption, and the eternal life which God giveth unto all the obedient. (Moses 5:9–11)

• The gospel is taught. Adam and Eve bless God and begin to teach the plan of redemption to their children (see Moses 5:12; 6:1, 52–68). Concerning this historic initiative, modern-day revelation states:

But, behold, I say unto you that I, the Lord God, gave unto Adam and unto his seed, that they should not die as to the temporal death, until I, the Lord God, should send forth angels to declare unto them repentance and redemption, through faith on the name of mine Only Begotten Son.

And thus did I, the Lord God, appoint unto man the days of his probation—that by his natural death he might be raised in immortality unto eternal life, even as many as would believe;

And they that believe not unto eternal damnation; for they cannot be redeemed from their spiritual fall, because they repent not. (D&C 29:42–44)

This moment of truth constituted the birth of the process by means of which the Lord, in His mercy and grace, taught the gospel of salvation to His children. Thus was inaugurated the process through which the mighty change of heart could take place for those who respond to the invitation of the Lord to follow Him and keep His commandments (compare Mosiah 5:2–3; Alma 5:13–14). We see in this story the essence of the Atonement brought forth: the story of joy, gladness, redemption, hope of eternal life, thanksgiving, and the sharing of the good news with family and children.

In this context, the most celebrated passage in the Book of Mormon concerning Adam is this one from the counsel of Lehi to his son Jacob and the other children of his family:

Adam fell that men might be; and men are, that they might have joy.

And the Messiah cometh in the fulness of time, that he may redeem the children of men from the fall. And because that they are redeemed from the fall they have become free forever, knowing good from evil; to act for themselves and not to be acted upon, save it be by the punishment of the law at the great and last day, according to the commandments which God hath given.

Wherefore, men are free according to the flesh; and all things are given them which are expedient unto man. And they are free to choose liberty and eternal life, through the great Mediator of all men, or to choose captivity and death, according to the captivity and power of the devil; for he seeketh that all men might be miserable like unto himself. (2 Ne. 2:25–27; compare Morm. 9:11–14)

• Adam keeps a book of remembrance concerning his family (see Moses 6:5–6, 8–9).

• Adam gives his final blessing to his posterity at a gathering in Adam-ondi-Ahman (see D&C 107:53–56).

• Adam dies at age 930 (see Moses 6:12).

• Adam participates, with many other angelic ministrants, in the Restoration of the gospel in our day: "And the voice of Michael, the archangel; the voice of Gabriel, and of Raphael, and of divers angels, from Michael or Adam down to the present time, all declaring their dispensation, their rights, their keys, their honors, their majesty and glory, and the power of their priesthood; giving line upon line, precept upon precept; here a little, and there a little; giving us consolation by holding forth that which is to come, confirming our hope!" (D&C 128:21).

Through the wise agency of Adam and Eve, mankind experienced the Fall. Through the wise choice of Adam and Eve, their posterity came to know the gospel of Jesus Christ. By our own choice, we can honor their example and follow in the pathway of righteousness.

EVE

Among the great and mighty ones who were assembled in this vast congregation of the righteous were Father Adam, the Ancient of Days and father of all,

And our glorious Mother Eve, with many of her faithful daughters who had lived through the ages and worshiped the true and living God. (D&C 138:38–39)

From the scriptural account, we can discern several subcategories for defining the word *glorious* used to describe Eve:

Child of God—Like Adam, Eve was created in the image of the Almighty: "In the image of his own body, male and female, created he them, and blessed them, and called their name Adam, in the day when they were created and became living souls in the land upon the footstool of God" (Moses 6:9).

Eternal motherhood—Eve is the only child of God who has the eternal role to be the "mother of all living"—an appellation given to her by God and confirmed by Adam: "And Adam called his wife's name Eve, because she was the mother of all living; for thus have I, the Lord God, called the first of all women, which are many" (Moses 4:26; compare Gen. 3:20).

Wisely discerning—Eve had the capacity to weigh choices and act in ways to support the ultimate design of God for His children. When she was "beguiled" by Satan to partake of the forbidden fruit, she realized that the consequences of transgressing would be in the best interests of her children "as the mother of all living"—for they could not "live" in the eternal sense unless the plan of happiness were enacted, based on the agency of man. She therefore used her God-given agency in wisdom, for the Lord had extended that privilege, albeit with explicit consequences: "But of the tree of the knowledge of good and evil, thou shalt not eat of it, nevertheless, thou mayest choose for thyself, for it is given unto thee; but, remember that I forbid it, for in the day thou eatest thereof thou shalt surely die" (Moses 3:17). The dramatic account proceeds as follows:

And Satan put it into the heart of the serpent, (for he had drawn away many after him,) and he sought also to beguile Eve, for he knew not the mind of God, wherefore he sought to destroy the world.

And he said unto the woman: Yea, hath God said—Ye shall not eat of every tree of the garden? (And he spake by the mouth of the serpent.)

And the woman said unto the serpent: We may eat of the fruit of the trees of the garden;

But of the fruit of the tree which thou beholdest in the midst of the garden, God hath said—Ye shall not eat of it, neither shall ye touch it, lest ye die.

And the serpent said unto the woman: Ye shall not surely die;

For God doth know that in the day ye eat thereof, then your eyes shall be opened, and ye shall be as gods, knowing good and evil.

And when the woman saw that the tree was good for food, and that it became pleasant to the eyes, and a tree to be desired to make her wise, she took of the fruit thereof, and did eat, and also gave unto her husband with her, and he did eat.

And the eyes of them both were opened. . . . (Moses 4:6–13)

As she later described her position with respect to this decision—after learning of the great Plan of Salvation from the Lord—Eve articulated her profound insight in the form of a glorious pronouncement: "And Eve, his wife, heard all these things and was glad, saying: Were it not for our transgression we never should have had seed, and never should have known good and evil, and the joy of our redemption, and the eternal life which God giveth unto all the obedient" (Moses 5:11).

Willing to sacrifice—Through her conscious transgression, Eve took upon herself the agony and suffering attendant with bringing forth offspring: "Unto the woman he [the Lord] said, I will greatly multiply thy sorrow and thy conception; in sorrow thou shalt bring forth children; . . ." (Gen. 3:16; compare Moses 4:22).

Industrious—When the Lord expelled Adam and Eve from the Garden of Eden to till the earth, the couple initiated a partnership of productivity: "AND it came to pass that after I, the Lord God, had driven them out, that Adam began to till the earth, and to have dominion over all the beasts of the field, and to eat his bread by the sweat of his brow, as I the Lord had commanded him. And Eve, also, his wife, did labor with him" (Moses 5:1). Thus Eve was a laboring soul, just like her husband. They both worked toward the success of their commission as "our first parents" (1 Ne. 5:11).

Prayerful—Eve joined with her husband in fervent prayer, leading to the reception of further light and knowledge concerning God's love and compassion for them:

And Adam and Eve, his wife, called upon the name of the Lord, and they heard the voice of the Lord from the way toward the Garden of Eden, speaking unto them, and they saw him not; for they were shut out from his presence.

And he gave unto them commandments, that they should worship the Lord their God, and should offer the firstlings of their flocks, for an offering unto the Lord. And Adam was obedient unto the commandments of the Lord.

And after many days an angel of the Lord appeared unto Adam, saying: Why dost thou offer sacrifices unto the Lord? And Adam said unto him: I know not, save the Lord commanded me.

And then the angel spake, saying: This thing is a similitude of the sacrifice of the Only Begotten of the Father, which is full of grace and truth.

Wherefore, thou shalt do all that thou doest in the name of the Son, and thou shalt repent and call upon God in the name of the Son forevermore.

And in that day the Holy Ghost fell upon Adam, which beareth record of the Father and the Son, saying: I am the Only Begotten of the Father from the beginning, henceforth and forever, that as thou hast fallen thou mayest be redeemed, and all mankind, even as many as will.

And in that day Adam blessed God and was filled, and began to prophesy concerning all the families of the earth, saying: Blessed be the name of God, for because of my transgression my eyes are opened, and in this life I shall have joy, and again in the flesh I shall see God. (Moses 5:4–10)

Receptive and obedient: "And Adam and Eve blessed the name of God, and they made all things known unto their sons their daughters. . . . . And Adam and Eve, his wife, ceased not to call upon God" (Moses 5:12, 16).

Compassionate and concerned—When her son Cain descended into the abyss of sin, Eve joined with her husband in the deepest sorrow: "And Adam and his wife mourned before the Lord, because of Cain and his brethren" (Moses 5:27).

A great educator—According to the record, Adam and Eve encouraged their offspring to keep a record of their experiences in mortality and thus to remember the covenants and promises and blessings of the Lord:

And a book of remembrance was kept, in the which was recorded, in the language of Adam, for it was given unto as many as called upon God [including Adam and Eve and all of their faithful children] to write by the spirit of inspiration;

And by them their children were taught to read and write, having a language which was pure and undefiled. (Moses 6:5–6)

Indeed, "our glorious Mother Eve" (D&C 138:39) was a child of God and the epitome of eternal motherhood—wisely discerning, willing to sacrifice, industrious, prayerful, receptive and obedient, compassionate and concerned for her children, and a great educator. Such a "glorious" and noble personality is an abiding example for her posterity through all generations of time.

APPENDIX C
CHERUBIM

A *cherub* (Hebrew plural *cherubim*) is an angel of some particular order and rank among the hierarchy of the hosts of heaven. When Adam and Eve were driven from the Garden of Eden because of their transgression, cherubim were deployed to guard the pathway to the tree of life: "So I drove out the man, and I placed at the east of the Garden of Eden, cherubim and a flaming sword, which turned every way to keep the way of the tree of life" (Moses 4:31; compare Gen. 3:24 concerning *cherubims*).

In the Book of Mormon, the antagonist leader Antoniah in the apostate city of Ammonihah asked Alma the following question: "What does the scripture mean, which saith that God placed cherubim and a flaming sword on the east of the garden of Eden, lest our first parents should enter and partake of the fruit of the tree of life, and live forever? And thus we see that there was no possible chance that they should live forever" (Alma 12:21). This provided Alma with a window of opportunity to preach about the Atonement and eternal life (see Alma 12:22–37). Later, Alma used the same reference in teaching his son Corianton about the Redemption:

> Now behold, my son, I will explain this thing unto thee. For behold, after the Lord God sent our first parents forth from the garden of Eden, to till the ground, from whence they were taken—yea, he drew out the man, and he placed at the east end of the garden of Eden, cherubim, and a flaming sword which turned every way, to keep the tree of life—
>
> Now, we see that the man had become as God, knowing good and evil; and lest he should put forth his hand, and take also of the tree of life, and eat and live forever, the Lord God placed cherubim and the flaming sword, that he should not partake of the fruit—
>
> And thus we see, that there was a time granted unto man to repent, yea, a probationary time, a time to repent and serve God. (Alma 42:2–3)

The figure of the cherub was used in Old Testament times as a symbolic accoutrement associated with the sacred structure of the ark of the covenant and other features of the tabernacle (and later with the décor of the temple):

> And thou shalt make two cherubims *of* gold, *of* beaten work shalt thou make them, in the two ends of the mercy seat.
>
> And make one cherub on the one end, and the other cherub on the other end: *even* of the mercy seat shall ye make the cherubims on the two ends thereof.
>
> And the cherubims shall stretch forth *their* wings on high, covering the mercy seat with their wings, and their faces *shall look* one to another; toward the mercy seat shall the faces of the cherubims be.
>
> And thou shalt put the mercy seat above upon the ark; and in the ark thou shalt put the testimony that I shall give thee.
>
> And there I will meet with thee, and I will commune with thee from above the mercy seat, from between the two cherubims which *are* upon the ark of the testimony, of all *things* which I will give thee in commandment unto the children of Israel. (Ex. 25:18–22)

The Psalmist celebrates the cherubim of God: "GIVE ear, O Shepherd of Israel, thou that leadest Joseph like a flock; thou that dwellest *between* the cherubims, shine forth" (Ps. 80:1; compare Ps. 99:1; also Isa. 37:16). In his vision of the throne of God, Ezekiel views cherubim that are alive and active (see Ezek. 10, 11). The wings associated with cherubim in scriptural references are symbolic of power and motion, as in David's anthem of thanksgiving: "And he [the Lord] rode upon a cherub, and did fly: and he was seen upon the wings of the wind" (2 Sam. 22:11; see also Ps. 18:10; D&C 77:4).

 POINT OF INTEREST

"The cherubim, a common feature of ancient Near Eastern mythology, are not to be confused with the round-cheeked darlings of Renaissance iconography. The root of the term either means "hybrid" or, by an inversion of consonants, "mount," "steed," and they are the winged beasts, probably of awesome aspect, on which the sky god of the old Canaanite myths and of the poetry of Psalms goes riding through the air. The fiery sword not mentioned elsewhere but referred to with the definite article as though it were a familiar image, is a suitable weapon to set alongside the formidable cherubim" (Robert Alter, *The Five Books of Moses* [New York: W. W. Norton & Company, 2004]). The Babylonian *shedu* (above) is identified by a proportion of scholars as the origin of *cherubim*.

APPENDIX D
CAIN AND ABEL

ABEL

Abel was a righteous son of Adam and Eve—and one for whom the Lord had respect (see Gen. 4:4; Heb. 11:4). Abel was born into an environment of gospel instruction from his parents, who heeded the voice of the Lord when "he gave unto them commandments, that they should worship the Lord their God, and should offer the firstlings of their flocks, for an offering unto the Lord. And Adam was obedient unto the commandments of the Lord" (Moses 5:5).

Through angelic instruction, confirmed by the Holy Ghost, Adam was taught about the Atonement of the Only Begotten Son (Moses 5:7–11) and he and his wife "blessed the name of God, and they made all things known unto their sons and their daughters" (Moses 5:12)—including Abel.

Abel, "a keeper of sheep" (Moses 5:17), was not the oldest child, he and Cain having come into mortality after Eve had already born unto Adam other "sons and daughters" (Moses 5:2). However, Abel is singled out for his devotion and righteousness as one "who walked in holiness before the Lord" (Moses 5:26).

In terms of compliance with the divine commandment to offer sacrifices, Abel "also brought of the firstlings of his flock, and of the fat thereof. And the Lord had respect unto Abel, and to his offering; But unto Cain, and to his offering, he had not respect" (Moses 5:20–21), since Cain "loved Satan more than God" (Moses 5:18). Out of greed and jealousy, Cain murdered his younger brother in cold blood (see Gen. 4:8; Moses 5:32), having been instructed and motivated to that egregious end by Satan himself, "the author of all sin" (Hel. 6:30; see also Moses 5:29–30).

Abel is mentioned as one of the elect personages viewed by President Joseph F. Smith in his vision of the spirit realm: "Abel, the first martyr, was there, and his brother Seth, one of the mighty ones, who was in the express image of his father, Adam" (D&C 138:40).

CAIN

Cain was a son of Adam and Eve—not the first-born, since both he and his younger brother Abel came into mortality after Eve had already born unto Adam other "sons and daughters" (Moses 5:2). Cain was born into an environment of loving gospel instruction from his parents, who heeded the voice of the Lord when "he gave unto them commandments, that they should worship the Lord their God, and should offer the firstlings of their flocks, for an offering unto the Lord. And Adam was obedient unto the commandments of the Lord" (Moses 5:5).

Through angelic instruction, confirmed by the Holy Ghost, Adam was taught about the Atonement of the Only Begotten Son, and they taught these truths to their children—including Cain. However, unlike Abel, "who walked in holiness before the Lord" (Moses 5:26), Cain followed a pathway of self-interest and evil. The contrast is striking. In terms of compliance with the divine commandment to offer sacrifices, Abel brought the best he had, inspiring the respect of the Lord; Cain, since he "loved Satan more than God" (Moses 5:18), declared in arrogance: "Who is the Lord that I should know him?" (Moses 5:16).

When the Lord rejected his offering, Cain became angry. The Lord did not reject Cain as a person, out of hand, but instead used the occasion to teach a grand lesson and proclaim a grand warning that echoes down through the generations:

And the Lord said unto Cain: Why art thou wroth? Why is thy countenance fallen?

If thou doest well, thou shalt be accepted. And if thou doest not well, sin lieth at the door, and Satan desireth to have thee; and except thou shalt hearken unto my commandments, I will deliver thee up, and it shall be unto thee according to his desire. And thou shalt rule over him;

For from this time forth thou shalt be the father of his lies; thou shalt be called Perdition; for thou wast also before the world.

And it shall be said in time to come—That these abominations were had from Cain; for he rejected the greater counsel which was had from God; and this is a cursing which I will put upon thee, except thou repent. (Moses 5:22–25)

Despite this divine counsel and the chance to rise from his abyss, Cain chose not to repent: "And Cain was wroth, and listened not any more to the voice of the Lord, neither to Abel, his brother, who walked in holiness before the Lord. And Adam and his wife mourned before the Lord, because of Cain and his brethren" (Moses 5:26–27). Then, out of greed and jealousy, Cain murdered his younger brother in cold blood (see Gen. 4:8; Moses 5:32), having been instructed by Satan himself, "the author of all sin" (Hel. 6:30; see also Moses 5:29–30). The moment of Cain's accountability before the Lord for this atrocity is chilling in its consequences:

And the LORD said unto Cain, Where is Abel thy brother? And he said, I know not: Am I my brother's keeper?

And he said, What hast thou done? the voice of thy brother's blood crieth unto me from the ground.

And now art thou cursed from the earth, which hath opened her mouth to receive thy brother's blood from thy hand;

When thou tillest the ground, it shall not henceforth yield unto thee her strength; a fugitive and a vagabond shalt thou be in the earth.

And Cain said unto the LORD, My punishment is greater than I can bear.

Behold, thou hast driven me out this day from the face of the earth; and from thy face shall I be hid; and I shall be a fugitive and a vagabond in the earth; and it shall come to pass, that every one that findeth me shall slay me.

And the LORD said unto him, Therefore whosoever slayeth Cain, vengeance shall be taken on him sevenfold. And the LORD set a mark upon Cain, lest any finding him should kill him. (Gen. 4:9–15; compare Moses 5:33–40)

For his actions, Cain became the exemplar of evil and Satanic conspiracy—the opposite of the love of God as preached by John: "For this is the message that ye heard from the beginning, that we should love one another. Not as Cain, *who* was of that wicked one, and slew his brother. And wherefore slew he him? Because his own works were evil, and his brother's righteous" (1 John 3:11–12). The evil in Cain's actions was rooted in his relationship with his demonic mentor:

> And Satan said unto Cain: Swear unto me by thy throat, and if thou tell it thou shalt die; and swear thy brethren by their heads, and by the living God, that they tell it not; for if they tell it, they shall surely die; and this that thy father may not know it; and this day I will deliver thy brother Abel into thine hands.
>
> And Satan sware unto Cain that he would do according to his commands. And all these things were done in secret.
>
> And Cain said: Truly I am Mahan, the master of this great secret, that I may murder and get gain. Wherefore Cain was called Master Mahan, and he gloried in his wickedness. (Moses 5:29–31)

The ultimate punishment for such spiritual apostasy and loathsome murder is to be cast out of God's presence. Such happened to Cain (see Gen. 4:16; Moses 5:39, 41), who moved away, east of Eden, and established a culture and lineage of his own that preserved and applied the secret combinations inspired of Satan. Cain's descendant Lamech, for example, "entered into a covenant with Satan, after the manner of Cain, wherein he became Master Mahan, master of that great secret which was administered unto Cain by Satan" (Moses 5:49).

Thus, "from the days of Cain, there was a secret combination, and their works were in the dark, and they knew every man his brother" (Moses 5:51). Even among the peoples of the Book of Mormon these secret combinations flourished from time to time, bringing destruction upon whole nations.

We have in Cain an example of the most blatant rejection of the light of God among mortals. Cain was taught by loving parents; he was taught in person by a loving Heavenly Father. But, through his alliance with Satan, he became an author of eternal damnation for those who conspire for evil through obedience to darkness—just as the Savior, Jesus Christ, in stark contrast, "being made perfect, . . . became the author of eternal salvation unto all them that obey him" (Heb. 5:9).

APPENDIX E
ENOCH

The story of the prophet Enoch and his ministry (see Moses 6–7) is a perennial favorite, for he was truly exemplary as an effective teacher of righteousness. Enoch was taught by his father, Jared, "in all the ways of God" (Moses 6:21). All the prophets in the line of descent from Adam preached righteousness, prophesied, and called all the people to repent and exercise faith (see Moses 6:23). Enoch did the same, for he was blessed with the Spirit of God and was called by God to his prophetic office: "And he heard a voice from heaven, saying: Enoch, my son, prophesy unto this people, and say unto them—Repent, for thus saith the Lord: I am angry with this people, and my fierce anger is kindled against them; for their hearts have waxed hard, and their ears are dull of hearing, and their eyes cannot see afar off" (Moses 6:27).

Enoch was humbled and wondered why he was called, for he was slow of speech. The Lord reassured him saying,

> Go forth and do as I have commanded thee, and no man shall pierce thee. Open thy mouth, and it shall be filled, and I will give thee utterance, for all flesh is in my hands, and I will do as seemeth me good.
>
> Say unto this people: Choose ye this day, to serve the Lord God who made you.
>
> Behold my Spirit is upon you, wherefore all thy words will I justify; and the mountains shall flee before you, and the rivers shall turn from their course; and thou shalt abide in me, and I in you; therefore walk with me." (Moses 6:32–34)

Enoch was indeed a chosen vessel of the Lord. He received mighty visions. The people recognized him as a seer. Enoch was ardent and devoted in his calling, crying with a loud voice for the people to repent. Because of that, many were offended. Word was circulated that a seer was prophesying and indeed "a wild man hath come among us" (Moses 6:38). The people feared him and no one dared lay a hand upon him for he "walked with God" (Moses 6:39).

Enoch explained to the people that he had been sent by the Lord to preach to them. He taught them the word of God concerning the Fall and the results of succumbing to the temptations of Satan. He explained to them the commandments given to Adam. He emphasized the coming of Jesus Christ and His mission of redemption and salvation. He admonished them to repent and be baptized and teach these things freely to their children.

Enoch quoted to the people what the Lord had taught Adam:

> That by reason of transgression cometh the fall, which fall bringeth death, and inasmuch as ye were born into the world by water, and blood, and the spirit, which I have made, and so became of dust a living soul, even so ye must be born again

into the kingdom of heaven, of water, and of the Spirit, and be cleansed by blood, even the blood of mine Only Begotten; that ye might be sanctified from all sin, and enjoy the words of eternal life in this world, and eternal life in the world to come, even immortal glory;

For by the water ye keep the commandment; by the Spirit ye are justified, and by the blood ye are sanctified;

Therefore it is given to abide in you; the record of heaven; the Comforter; the peaceable things of immortal glory; the truth of all things; that which quickeneth all things, which maketh alive all things; that which knoweth all things, and hath all power according to wisdom, mercy, truth, justice, and judgment.

And now, behold, I say unto you: This is the plan of salvation unto all men, through the blood of mine Only Begotten, who shall come in the meridian of time. . . .
And it came to pass, when the Lord had spoken with Adam, our father, that Adam cried unto the Lord, and he was caught away by the Spirit of the Lord, and was carried down into the water, and was laid under the water, and was brought forth out of the water.

And thus he was baptized, and the Spirit of God descended upon him, and thus he was born of the Spirit, and became quickened in the inner man. (Moses 6:59–62, 64–65)

Enoch continued to preach to the people and tell them of the mighty visions that the Lord continued to open up to his view. So strong was his faith and so miraculous his power of speech that the people heeded his word and followed in the paths of righteousness: "And the Lord called his people ZION, because they were of one heart and one mind, and dwelt in righteousness; and there was no poor among them. And Enoch continued his preaching in righteousness unto the people of God. And it came to pass in his days, that he built a city that was called the City of Holiness, even ZION" (Moses 7:18–19).

The spirit pervasive in the city of Enoch was the Spirit of truth and grace centered in the Holy One of Israel, Jesus Christ—whom Enoch was privileged to see in the unfolding visions with which the Lord blessed him as the prophet-leader of his dispensation. The conclusion of the extraordinary story of Enoch's ministry is summarized in this verse: "And Enoch and all his people walked with God, and he dwelt in the midst of Zion; and it came to pass that Zion was not, for God received it up into his own bosom; and from thence went forth the saying, ZION IS FLED" (Moses 7:69). It is this same city that will again return at the Second Coming to join with the congregations of Saints caught up in the cloud to meet the returning Savior and King (see JST Gen. 9:21–25; D&C 45:12).

Through the eyes and ministry of Enoch we learn grand truths concerning the power of the priesthood to gather people to holy places and plant in their hearts the commitment to cultivate lasting purity and spirituality. Enoch was allowed to see all the nations of the earth in their wickedness. He observed the resulting sorrow and weeping of the Lord. When Enoch inquired of the Lord concerning such sorrow, the Lord explained to him as follows:

Behold these thy brethren; they are the workmanship of mine own hands, and I gave unto them their knowledge,

in the day I created them; and in the Garden of Eden, gave I unto man his agency;

And unto thy brethren have I said, and also given commandment, that they should love one another, and that they should choose me, their Father; but behold, they are without affection, and they hate their own blood;

And the fire of mine indignation is kindled against them; and in my hot displeasure will I send in the floods upon them, for my fierce anger is kindled against them.

Behold, I am God; Man of Holiness is my name; Man of Counsel is my name; and Endless and Eternal is my name, also.

Wherefore, I can stretch forth mine hands and hold all the creations which I have made; and mine eye can pierce them also, and among all the workmanship of mine hands there has not been so great wickedness as among thy brethren.

But behold, their sins shall be upon the heads of their fathers; Satan shall be their father, and misery shall be their doom; and the whole heavens shall weep over them, even all the workmanship of mine hands; wherefore should not the heavens weep, seeing these shall suffer?

But behold, these which thine eyes are upon shall perish in the floods; and behold, I will shut them up; a prison have I prepared for them.

And That which I have chosen [i.e., Jesus Christ] hath pled before my face. Wherefore, he suffereth for their sins; inasmuch as they will repent in the day that my Chosen shall return unto me, and until that day they shall be in torment;

Wherefore, for this shall the heavens weep, yea, and all the workmanship of mine hands. (Moses 7:32–40.)

From this we learn the tender love the Lord has for His children. Enoch saw into the future and became saddened and wept over his brethren. He could not be comforted until he saw in vision the future coming of the Lord and he did then rejoice:

And behold, Enoch saw the day of the coming of the Son of Man, even in the flesh; and his soul rejoiced, saying: The Righteous is lifted up, and the Lamb is slain from the foundation of the world; and through faith I am in the bosom of the Father, and behold, Zion is with me. (Moses 7:47)

As the story continues, Enoch hears the earth mourn because of the unrighteousness of the people. He is promised that through Noah his seed should always be found upon the earth. Enoch witnesses the Savior and His crucifixion and resurrection, and then the Savior gives him a great promise: "Blessed is he through whose seed Messiah shall come; for he saith—I am Messiah, the King of Zion, the Rock of Heaven, which is broad as eternity; whoso cometh in at the gate and climbeth up by me shall never fall; wherefore, blessed are they of whom I have spoken, for they shall come forth with songs of everlasting joy" (Moses 7:53).

Enoch is then shown the mighty events that will transpire in the future: the Lord's Second Coming, the gathering of His elect, the preparation of a Holy City—"my tabernacle, and it shall be called Zion, a New Jerusalem" (Moses 7:62). Enoch's Zion city will then meet the Lord and the Saints of the New Jerusalem and there shall be a thousand years of peace—even the millennial era when Christ will reign personally among His people. And thus we see that it is possible to become a Zion people: "Therefore, verily, thus saith the Lord, let Zion rejoice, for this is Zion—THE PURE IN HEART" (D&C 97:21). How to become the "pure in heart"—This is the grand lesson of the story of Enoch.

From the Doctrine and Covenants we find confirming evidence concerning these sacred truths. Enoch and his city were indeed translated, as the Savior declared, "into mine own bosom" (D&C 38:4). The greatness of Enoch is confirmed in the passage that speaks of those who inherit the celestial realm of glory as "priests of the Most High, after the order of Melchizedek, which was after the order of Enoch, which was after the order of the Only Begotten Son" (D&C 76:57). Such celestial beings are spoken of as those who "have come to an innumerable company of angels, to the general assembly and church of Enoch, and of the Firstborn" (D&C 76:67). Enoch was a key figure in the continuity of the priesthood lineage, being ordained at age twenty-five by Adam (see D&C 107:48). Enoch was present, with many other noble and great high priests, at the event where Adam pronounced his benedictory blessing on his posterity (see D&C 107:53). The details of this event were recorded by Enoch in a record that is to come forth in the due time of the Lord: "These things were all written in the book of Enoch, and are to be testified of in due time" (D&C 107:57). Enoch will return at the Second Coming (see D&C 133:54) and be "in the presence of the Lamb" (D&C 133:55) along with all of the elect prophets of God.

A number of apocryphal writings claiming the authorship of Enoch have been preserved, some of them having been discovered only in recent times. The relevance of such pseudepigraphical writings concerning Enoch—and how they confirm the authenticity of modern-day scripture—is explored in detail by Hugh Nibley in his book *Enoch the Prophet* (Salt Lake City: Deseret Book and Provo, Utah: FARMS, 1986).

From the foregoing summary of Enoch's ministry we may extract the following checklist of things to do to be more like a Zion people:

- Pray regularly and sincerely.
- Be humble.
- Be charitable toward others.
- Be unified.
- Walk in the light of truth.
- Gather in holy places.
- Have pure thoughts.
- Attend the temple regularly.
- Uphold the Lord's anointed in word and deed.
- Cultivate love and mutual confidence in the home.
- Listen for the revelations of God.
- Be virtuous and morally clean.
- Remember your sacred covenants.

APPENDIX F
METHUSELAH, LAMECH, AND NOAH

METHUSELAH

Methuselah (meaning: man of the javelin, or dart), son of Enoch, was the longest surviving of the ancient patriarchs (see Gen. 5:21–27; 1 Chron. 1:3; Moses 6:25; 8:2–7; and Luke 3:37—where the name is rendered *Mathusala*). He is mentioned three times in the text of the Doctrine and Covenants: twice in connection with the descent of the priesthood lineage (see D&C 107:50–52) and once again as a participant in the assembly of elect individuals gathered together by Adam to receive his benedictory blessing (see D&C 107:53).

From the Book of Moses we also learn the following about Methuselah:

> And it came to pass that Methuselah, the son of Enoch, was not taken, that the covenants of the Lord might be fulfilled, which he made to Enoch; for he truly covenanted with Enoch that Noah should be of the fruit of his loins.
>
> And it came to pass that Methuselah prophesied that from his loins should spring all the kingdoms of the earth (through Noah), and he took glory unto himself. (Moses 8:2–3)

LAMECH

Lamech was the seventh in descent from Seth, son of Adam, as follows: Seth, Enos, Cainan, Mahalaleel, Jared, Enoch, Methuselah, Lamech (see Gen. 5:6–25). Lamech was the father of Noah (see Gen. 5:25–31; 1 Chron. 1:3; compare Luke 3:36; Moses 8:5–11). Lamech is mentioned once in the Doctrine and Covenants in connection with the lineage of the priesthood (see D&C 107:51).

NOAH

Noah (meaning: rest), son of Lamech, was a leading patriarch of the Old Testament:

> And Lamech lived an hundred eighty and two years, and begat a son:
> And he called his name Noah, saying, This same shall comfort us concerning our work and toil of our hands, because of the ground which the LORD hath cursed. (Gen. 5:28–29; compare Luke 3:36)

From latter-day scripture, we learn that Noah, when ten years old, was ordained to the priesthood by Methuselah (see D&C 107:52). From that moment on he honored his priesthood calling with valor.

Everyone is familiar with the story of Noah and the ark. But there is more there than meets the eye. The story is an intimate and revealing source of knowledge about the nature of spirituality and obedience to covenants—precisely the kinds of qualities that are required for each of us to preserve life for ourselves and our families from day to day. Noah, like all of the Lord's chosen prophets, was a just and righteous man: "Noah found grace in the eyes of the Lord; for Noah was a just man, and perfect in his generation; and he walked with God . . ." (Moses 8:27; see also Gen. 6:9).

Looking at this noble portrait of Noah in more detail, we note that Noah found grace and favor in the eyes of the Lord due to his righteousness. It is through righteousness that we can grow in grace (see D&C 50:40). The Lord is full of grace—love, compassion, and mercy toward the children of God. Like Noah, Nephi was highly favored of the Lord (see 1 Ne. 1:1). We can receive this favoring grace through righteousness.

Next, Noah was a just man. Many prophets have been described in this way. What does the adjective *just* really mean?

- They walked uprightly before God (see Alma 63:2).
- They performed miracles (see 3 Ne. 8:1).
- They taught God's children in the nurture and admonition of the Lord (see Enos 1:1).
- They never deceived (see D&C 129:6).
- They are made perfect (see D&C 76:69).
- They walked in integrity (see JST Prov. 20:77).
- They were holy and feared God in all things (see Zech. 14:20; Deut. 8:6).
- They truly were upright, honest, and obeyed God with exactness.

Moreover, Noah was perfect in his generation at a time when so many were apostates. He truly was set apart from the people of his day because he stood on principle and honored his covenants—so much so that he "walked with God" (Moses 8:27; see also Gen. 6:9). By walking in the ways of God and keeping His commandments, we too can follow the example of Noah: "The just *man* walketh in his integrity: his children *are* blessed after him" (Prov. 20:7).

Noah was the paragon of the agency of repentance. He was commanded to call the people to repentance so that they might avoid being destroyed (see Moses 8:20–30).

In these verses the usage of the words *repented* and *repenteth* refer to Noah being full of regret and sorrow. The Lord felt sorrow and regret as well (see Gen. 6:6), and therefore established a covenant with Noah, commanding him to build an ark, gather provision and animals, and preserve his family, as recorded in Genesis (see Gen. 6:14–22; compare Heb. 11:7; 1 Pet. 3:20; 2 Pet. 2:5)

The flood came, being universal in regard to its reach across the earth. The waters flooded and surged for forty days (see Gen. 7:12, 17). Everything on the earth was destroyed—only Noah and those on the ark were preserved. The waters prevailed for another 150 days (see Gen. 8:3), eventually subsiding to allow the ark and its passengers to come to rest on "the mountains of Ararat" (Gen. 8:4). The Lord had preserved the life of mankind and all earthly creatures. A new era of life was about to begin.

The flood at the time of Noah, with the resulting preservation of life and renewal of God's commitment to the well-being and progress of humanity, is a symbol for the principle of covenant. John Taylor confirms that "through his faith Enoch saw the days of the coming of the Son of Man in the flesh, and by it he obtained a covenant from the Lord that after Noah's day He would never again cover the earth by a flood, and obtained an unalterable decree that a remnant of his seed should always be found among all nations while the earth should stand" (Roy W. Doxey, comp., *Latter-day Prophets and the Doctrine and Covenants* [Salt Lake City: Deseret Book Co., 1978], 2:85; compare Isa. 54:9).

The story of Noah suggests to the mind several action items for increasing our spirituality and preserving our well-being before the Lord:

- Seek to find favor in the eyes of the Lord. Favor is a function of righteousness; therefore, we should aspire to the highest degree of righteousness possible. It is through righteous living and obedience that we receive the grace of the Lord.
- Seek to become "just." The scriptures lay before us with clarity the pattern to follow: walk uprightly before God (see Alma 63:2), nurture and love others (see Enos 1:1); seek to perfect ourselves (see D&C 76:69), cultivate integrity (see JST Prov. 20:77), practice holiness (see Zech. 14:20), and fear God in all things (see Deut. 8:6).
- Set an example for your generation. Noah was perfect in his generation; we can strive to follow his example in obedience, no matter what the detractors might have to say with their taunts and denigration of Gospel standards.
- Walk with God. Keep His commandments, just as latter-day scripture indicates: "And the members shall manifest before the church, and also before the elders, by a godly walk and conversation, that they are worthy of it, that there may be works and faith agreeable to the holy scriptures—walking in holiness before the Lord" (D&C 20:69). Furthermore: "Learn of me, and listen to my words; walk in the meekness of my Spirit, and you shall have peace in me" (D&C 19:23).
- Prepare for the return of the Lord as millennial King by honoring our covenants. The Savior used the story of "Noe" to remind His listeners to heed the counsel to prepare obediently for the Second Coming (see Matt. 24:36–41; compare Luke 17:26–27): "Watch therefore: for ye know not what hour your Lord doth come" (Matt. 24:42).

The greatness of Noah is confirmed through latter-day pronouncement of the Prophet Joseph Smith placing him next to Adam in authority: "Then to Noah, who is Gabriel; he stands next in authority to Adam in the Priesthood; he was called of God to this office, and was the father of all living in his day, and to him was given the dominion" (see HC 3:386).

APPENDIX G
ABRAHAM

There are a number of important themes in the life of Abraham that help us conduct our lives in accordance with divine principles, including the following: (1) Mortality gives indispensable experience: Abraham survived a youth fraught with abuse and danger. Similarly, the challenges and adversities of life give us training and experience in those qualities of faith, persistence, resilience, and problem-solving that make us better able to carry on the Lord's errand. (2) All things are possible with God: The Lord will fulfill all of His promises to His children—despite every challenge or obstacle. (3) The Lord requires the heart and a willing mind: Abraham was commanded to offer up the thing most dear to his heart—his own son. Only through a commitment to sacrifice all that we have, if required to do so, can we manifest to the Lord that our love for Him and His divine cause is perfect. (4) The Lord will provide the means whereby we can obey: Abraham demonstrated complete devotion and obedience, and the Lord, in His mercy and goodness, provided the ram for the sacrifice. Thus it is for all the Lord's faithful children.

We can see reflected in the life of Abraham the exemplary pattern of spiritual growth for which all of God's righteous children can strive as part of the mortal experience. From his early youth, Abraham's faith and devotion were schooled through experiences of adversity and oppression, and the lessons of obedience and valor he learned carried him through life on the wings of divine support and blessing. Never losing the vision of his destined calling as a key participant in the grand design of the Lord, he set an unequalled example of one willing to do everything asked of him by God, without hesitation and without question. In many ways, the life journey of Abraham shows that our mortal environment is like unto a dwelling with four chambers, each of which we visit in cycles: the trials we encounter in life lead to opportunities for exerting our faith through obedience and godly behavior, which in turn leads to an outpouring of blessings from our Father in Heaven and a multiplicity of valuable lessons learned. Then the whole sequence is repeated.

As we go through this cycle again and again, our progress is traced by a spiral that carries us higher and higher, according to our diligence and willingness to keep the commandments. The motion is an upward cycle, ever closer to the objective of being more like our Father in Heaven and His Son, Jesus Christ. We see in Abraham's life three of those spiritual cycles: the preparations of his youth, the challenge that he and his wife faced in their old age to fulfill the Lord's promise for a son, and the requested sacrifice of Isaac. All of these experiences taught Abraham, as they teach us, that the Lord will provide a way for us to follow His will in all things

APPENDIX H
ABRAHAM, SARAH, AND THE ABRAHAMIC COVENANT

ABRAHAM, FATHER OF NATIONS

Abraham, the ancient prophet with whom the Lord established His ongoing covenant, was born more than two millennia before the coming of Christ in the meridian of time. Abraham is among the most admired and celebrated of the Lord's chosen prophets.

For many, the most memorable aspect of Abraham's life might well be his consummate obedience, demonstrated by his willingness to sacrifice his own son as the Lord had commanded (see Gen. 22). However, the aspect of Abraham's story that touches everyone in the most direct way is his central role regarding the archetypal covenant that the Lord set up with him and his seed to bless the lives of all the world through all generations of time.

The resurrected Savior gave us the pattern when he invoked the spirit of Abraham in teaching the Saints in ancient America concerning their sacred identity:

> And behold, ye are the children of the prophets; and ye are of the house of Israel; and ye are of the covenant which the Father made with your fathers, saying unto Abraham: And in thy seed shall all the kindreds of the earth be blessed.
>
> The Father having raised me up unto you first, and sent me to bless you in turning away every one of you from his iniquities; and this because ye are the children of the covenant—
>
> And after that ye were blessed then fulfilleth the Father the covenant which he made with Abraham, saying: In thy seed shall all the kindreds of the earth be blessed—unto the pouring out of the Holy Ghost through me upon the Gentiles, which blessing upon the Gentiles shall make them mighty above all, unto the scattering of my people, O house of Israel. (3 Ne. 20:25–27; compare the Lord's teachings concerning Abraham in Matt. 3:9; 8:11; Luke 16:22; John 8:56)

The Lord prepared Abraham carefully for his service in the Kingdom, he being a righteous man by nature, even though his fathers had turned from the ways of the Lord. We have Abraham's own words concerning his quest to obtain the blessings of heaven, receive more knowledge, and be a "greater follower of righteousness" (see Abr. 1:2, 4.)

We recall how anxious Abraham and Sarai were to have more children in their family, and how incredulous both Abraham and his wife were when the Lord promised them in their old age that Isaac would be born soon as the channel for carrying on the covenant promise (see Gen. 17:15–22). Yet the Lord kept His promise, and Sarai (renamed Sarah) bore a child so that Abraham could become the covenant father of many nations and the Lord would be their God (see Abr. 2:9–11; compare Gen. 12:1–3).

The principle of making and honoring covenants with the Lord is central to the gospel of Jesus Christ as we participate in the divine agenda to "bring to pass the immortality and eternal life of man" (Moses 1:39). Few aspects of the gospel have more profound impact on the mind and soul of the Latter-day Saints than the sense of exhilaration and joy engendered through participating in the mission of the Abrahamic covenant. The covenant made by the Lord with Abraham and his posterity continues to imbue the practices and operations of the restored Church with spiritual purpose as the priesthood reaches out in its ordained commission to cry repentance to the world and open up to believers in all lands the opportunities to learn saving truths and receive saving ordinances. Through the Abrahamic covenant, the instrument of the gathering unto salvation and exaltation, the Lord extends to His people grand blessings predicated upon worthiness, obedience, and service. The blessings commence in the mortal sphere and extend to the world hereafter, including divinely appointed places of gathering and repose, the unfolding of an immense posterity, and the enjoyment of redeeming truths here and in the eternities. Our part of the covenant is the obligation for obedience and righteous living, and a willingness to be the spiritual servants of the world through faithful missionary service. The Latter-day Saints have a sense of being part of the "chosen people" (as in Deut. 14:2) from the standpoint that they are chosen to be servants on the Lord's errand.

How do we make the Abrahamic covenant a governing dimension in our lives? Here are five suggestions: (1) The Abrahamic covenant is a covenant of righteousness; therefore, let us keep our eyes focused on the eternal consequences and blessings involved—an eternal promise of grand earthly and heavenly blessings based on obedience and service. (2) The Abrahamic covenant grants unto the faithful a divinely appointed home—special gathering places of refuge upon the earth, as well as an ultimate home among the mansions of the Father on high. (3) The Abrahamic covenant embraces a fruitful lineage and eternal increase—the divine promise of the abundance of "seed" (posterity) upon the earth, as well as eternal increase in the hereafter through the blessings of eternal marriage. (4) The Abrahamic covenant includes gospel blessings, now and forever: The central blessing for those who participate in the Abrahamic Covenant is to have the fullness of the gospel of Jesus Christ while on earth, including all the saving doctrines essential unto man and the associated ordinances and blessings of the priesthood, plus the hope and promise of immortality and eternal life in the hereafter. (5) The Abrahamic covenant commissions us with a solemn and divine appointment as vessels of the Lord: The solemn obligation associated with the Abrahamic covenant is to be the worthy spiritual servants to the world—by delivering to all nations, kindreds, tongues, and peoples the blessings associated with the kingdom of God upon the earth, including the priesthood in all its saving functions.

Few aspects of the gospel have more profound impact on the mind and soul of the Latter-day Saint than the sense of exhilaration and joy engendered through participating in the mission of the Abrahamic covenant. The covenant made by the Lord with Abraham and his posterity continues to inform the practices and operations of the restored Church with spiritual purpose as it reaches out in its ordained commission to cry repentance to the world and open up to believers in all lands the opportunities to learn saving truths and receive saving ordinances. Through the Abrahamic covenant, the Lord promises and extends grand blessings predicated upon worthiness, obedience,

and service. The blessings commence in the mortal sphere and extend to the world hereafter, including divinely appointed places of gathering and repose, the unfolding of an immense posterity, and the enjoyment of redeeming truths here and in the eternities. Our part of the covenant is the obligation for obedience and righteous living, and a willingness to be the spiritual servants of the world through faithful missionary service. The Latter-day Saints have a sense of being part of the "chosen people" (as in Deut. 14:2) from the standpoint that they are chosen to be servants on the Lord's errand.

Abraham sought for the blessings of the Father. Abraham was a righteous man, even though his fathers had turned from their righteousness. He had to receive more knowledge and be a greater follower of righteousness (see Abr. 1:1–6). The Lord made a covenant with Abraham and said he would multiply his seed exceedingly (this was Abraham's desire as well—see Abr. 1:2). Abraham would become the father of many nations and the Lord would covenant between Abraham and his seed—and He would be their God. And thus we see that the covenant God made with Abraham is open to all who repent. This comes with blessings here and in the hereafter. It also requires of us as individuals who make and keep this covenant certain obligations and responsibilities to receive the blessings of the Abrahamic covenant.

Fatherhood

For every soul who ever lives, fatherhood means a triumvirate of blessings. We all have *three* fathers for whom we feel eternally grateful. First is our Heavenly Father, the Father of our spirits, the Grand Architect of the plan of salvation and eternal exaltation. Second is our adoptive Father, the Only Begotten Son of God, even the Redeemer Jesus Christ, whose very seed we shall become as "the heirs of the Kingdom of God" (Mosiah 15:11)—all by virtue of His atoning grace and our obedience to the gospel plan. Third is our earthly father, through whose companionship with our earthly mother we have received a mortal tabernacle to carry us forth upon the pathway of life in accordance with the eternal design of heaven.

Life in its fullness and abundance comes as a result of fatherhood in these three manifestations. The Father and the Son are one in the spirit of divine fatherhood. From Their supreme example, the fathers in mortality derive the pattern for their own evolving role of dynamic fatherhood as they aspire in courage to fulfill their mission of love and guidance for the sons and daughters of a merciful God. We are thankful for the divine pattern of fatherhood.

And what is the essence of that pattern? It is one of persuasion—never coercion—to follow in the pathway of the Master and savor the blessings of peace and hope that come through covenant honor. It is long-suffering toward family members—never impatience—as they struggle to vanquish weakness and sin and rise in majesty to their divine potential. It is gentleness, meekness, and kindness to all—never aggression—in setting the tone for a productive family life. It is love unfeigned—never holding back affection and respect—as parents and children endeavor in oneness to follow the steps of the Lord. It is embracing pure knowledge, saving knowledge—"which shall greatly enlarge the soul without hypocrisy, and without guile" (D&C 121:42)—rather than yielding to prideful creeds and worldly philosophies—as we enlarge our understanding of the purpose of life and seek to follow the Master's word. It is heeding the promptings of the Spirit—rather than responding to whim or fleeting emotion—in giving loving correction based on timeless principles. It is, above all, exemplary faith, virtue, and charity displayed with authenticity in the household of faith and in all circles of life.

For this pattern of fatherhood we give our thanks unto God and the Son, who alone are perfect in vision and deed. No earthly father is ideal in emulating Their consummate example. But every father achieves dignity and mastery in one or more of these noble aspects of the divine nature, and as he aspires with real intent to improve in all of them, line upon line and precept upon precept, we thank him from our heart and pray each day that he will continue in his quest for fatherly perfection—whether in this life or the life beyond. In doing so, he will rise in stature, "unto a perfect man, unto the measure of the stature of the fulness of Christ" (Eph. 4:13). Then the blessings of the Lord of hosts will abound in his life, and he will experience the wondrous fulfillment of the sacred promise: ". . . then shall thy confidence wax strong in the presence of God; and the doctrine of the priesthood shall distil upon thy soul as the dews from heaven. The Holy Ghost shall be thy constant companion, and thy scepter an unchanging scepter of righteousness and truth; and thy dominion shall be an everlasting dominion, and without compulsory means it shall flow unto thee forever and ever" (D&C 121:45–46).

SARAH

Sarah (meaning: princess), wife of Abraham, was known originally as Sarai (pronounced "sair'-y" or "sair'-ay-y"). They were married in Ur of Chaldees: "And Abram and Nahor took them wives: the name of Abram's wife *was* Sarai; and the name of Nahor's wife, Milcah, the daughter of Haran, . . . But Sarai was barren; she *had* no child" (Gen. 11:29–30). The childless state of Sarai was a continual burden to her until she was blessed, eventually, to conceive and give birth to Isaac. Meanwhile, Abram (later Abraham) journeyed with his family circle toward Canaan, dwelling for a time en route at Haran (see Gen. 11:31). It was there that the Lord blessed Abram with a magnificent covenant blessing:

And I will make of thee a great nation, and I will bless thee, and make thy name great; and thou shalt be a blessing:

And I will bless them that bless thee, and curse him that curseth thee: and in thee shall all families of the earth be blessed. (Gen. 12:2–3)

The famine in Canaan caused Abram and Sarai to move onward for a time to the land of Egypt, where Abram instructed his wife, who was "a fair woman to look upon" (Gen. 12:11), to present herself as his sister, lest the Egyptians should kill him in order to take her as their own (see Gen. 12:10–20; compare Gen. 20 for a similar episode concerning Abimelech, king of Gerar). Upon returning to Canaan, Abram yearned for his promised posterity, and the Lord sent words of comfort:

And he brought him forth abroad, and said, Look now toward heaven, and tell the stars, if thou be able to number them: and he said unto him, So shall thy seed be.

And he believed in the LORD; and he counted it to him for righteousness. (Gen. 15:5–6)

After ten years in Canaan with no children, Sarai, in accordance with the cultural practice of her time, gave unto Abram her Egyptian handmaid Hagar as a wife. The Doctrine and Covenants confirms:

God commanded Abraham, and Sarah gave Hagar to Abraham to wife. And why did she do it? Because this was the law; and from Hagar sprang many people. This, therefore, was fulfilling, among other things, the promises.

Was Abraham, therefore, under condemnation? Verily I say unto you, Nay; for I, the Lord, commanded it. (D&C 132:33–34; see also D&C 132:65)

Subsequently, Hagar gave birth to Ishmael (see Gen. 16). Several years later, the Lord confirmed to Abraham the covenant promise of great increase and changed his name to Abraham, "father of many nations" (Gen. 17:5). Sarai, too, received a new name, along with a promise:

And God said unto Abraham, As for Sarai thy wife, thou shalt not call her name Sarai, but Sarah *shall* her name *be*.

And I will bless her, and give thee a son also of her: yea, I will bless her, and she shall be *a mother* of nations; kings of people shall be of her.

Then Abraham fell upon his face, and laughed, and said in his heart, Shall *a child* be born unto him that is an hundred years old? and shall Sarah, that is ninety years old, bear?

And Abraham said unto God, O that Ishmael might live before thee!

And God said, Sarah thy wife shall bear thee a son indeed; and thou shalt call his name Isaac: and I will establish my covenant with him for an everlasting covenant, *and* with his seed after him. (Gen. 17:15–19)

This promise of the motherhood of Sarah was confirmed somewhat later by three holy men visiting Abraham and Sarah at their encampment. When the aged Sarah overheard the statement that she would conceive and bear a son, she responded with understandable incredulity:

Therefore Sarah laughed within herself, saying, After I am waxed old shall I have pleasure, my lord being old also?

And the LORD said unto Abraham, Wherefore did Sarah laugh, saying, Shall I of a surety bear a child, which am old?

Is any thing too hard for the LORD? At the time

appointed I will return unto thee, according to the time of life, and Sarah shall have a son. (Gen. 18:12–14).

In accordance with the principle that nothing is "too hard for the Lord," Sarah did indeed bear a son, who was given the name Isaac (meaning: he laughed—see Gen. 21:1–3). When Ishmael, the son of Hagar, the Egyptian handmaid, was observed by Sarah in be in a mocking disposition, she sent him and Hagar away for good. Abraham was grieved to lose this son, but the Lord intervened: "And God said unto Abraham, Let it not be grievous in thy sight because of the lad, and because of thy bondwoman; in all that Sarah hath said unto thee, hearken unto her voice; for in Isaac shall thy seed be called. And also of the son of the bondwoman will I make a nation, because he *is* thy seed" (Gen. 21:12–13).

In due time, a divine commandment was given to Abraham (and by extension to Sarah as well) to relinquish Isaac through a sacrificial offering. That extraordinary test in the land of Moriah, calling forth every fiber of obedience and valor on the part of Abraham (and Isaac as well), proved to be the sealing grace upon the future unfolding of the Abrahamic covenant. The Lord had prepared a ram in the thicket as the offering that day, and Abraham and Isaac could then move onward down the pathway as principals in the process leading to the blessing of all mankind through the spreading of the gospel message about the ultimate sacrifice of the Lamb of God (see Gen. 22:15–18.)

Sarah passed away some time later at age 127 (see Gen. 23:2). She was buried "in the cave of the field of Machpelah before Mamre: the same *is* Hebron in the land of Canaan" (Gen. 23:19; compare also Isa. 51: 2; 2 Ne. 8:2; Rom. 4:19).

Paul celebrated the faith of Sarah: "Through faith also Sara herself received strength to conceive seed, and was delivered of a child when she was past age, because she judged him faithful who had promised" (Heb. 11:11). And Peter elevated Sarah as a beacon of obedience in the cause of the Lord:

For after this manner in the old time the holy women also, who trusted in God, adorned themselves, being in subjection unto their own husbands:

Even as Sara obeyed Abraham, calling him lord: whose daughters ye are, as long as ye do well, and are not afraid with any amazement. (1 Pet. 3: 6)

Fruitful Lineage/Eternal Increase

The Abrahamic covenant embraces the divine promise of the abundance of "seed" (posterity) upon the earth, as well as eternal increase in the hereafter through the blessings of eternal marriage (see Abr. 2:9).

The blessing of an abundant posterity to Abraham is bringing to fruition the original commandment to Adam and to Noah of multiplying and replenishing the earth. In this case it has even greater connotations. The covenant blessings include becoming a mighty nation in the mortal sphere, plus the exalted gifts of eternal marriage in the temples of God, leading to eternal increase ("eternal lives") in the hereafter. Abraham's lineage would bless the entire earth. As Abraham's posterity who have entered into the covenant, we are blessed through the covenant. We have the obligation and responsibility to be worthy instruments in the hand of the Lord to carry the gospel message to every nation, kindred,

tongue, and people. It becomes our joy and our glory to be the messengers of the message.

Vessels of the Lord

The solemn obligation associated with the Abrahamic Covenant is to be the worthy spiritual servants to the world—by delivering to all nations, kindreds, tongues, and peoples the blessings associated with the kingdom of God upon the earth, including the priesthood in all its saving functions (see Abr. 2:9; see also Matt. 28:19).

We, as the seed of Abraham, have the obligation to be worthy emissaries of the Lord Jesus Christ, with the responsibility to carry the gospel message with all of the priesthood and temple blessings to every nation, kindred, tongue, and people. The Book of Abraham has made it clear, as have all the scriptures and present-day prophets— we must take the gospel to all the world.

And thus we see that the work of the Lord must roll forward even as the stone cut out of the mountain, which will stand forever (see Dan. 2:44–45). Our joy and glory is to help people to come unto Christ (see Alma 29:9–10). We want them to taste of the exceeding joy of which we do taste (see Alma 36:24). We, like the Whitmer brothers, must come to understand that the thing of most worth is to declare repentance unto this people, that they too might come unto Christ (see D&C 15:6; 16:6). We must realize:

The price of preparation (see D&C 4; 11:21; 12:8; Alma 34:15–17).

The duty to open our mouths (see D&C 33:8–11) and the consequences for not doing so (see D&C 60:2–3).

Our dependence on the Spirit (see D&C 442:14; 2 Ne. 32:5; D&C 100:5–6).

The strength of the Lord in the work (see Alma 26:11–12; D&C 84:85–88).

Remember always to be full of faith while showing an abundance of love and compassion for those you teach.

The list could go on, but we all really understand the threefold mission of the Church—to invite all to come unto Christ—through perfecting the saints, redeeming the dead and proclaiming the gospel. All these are part and parcel of our mission on earth. We have a lifetime to serve and an eternity to enjoy the blessings together (see D&C 18:10–16).

On April 3, 1836, as part of a magnificent sequence of heavenly manifestations in the newly completed Kirtland Temple, Joseph Smith and Oliver Cowdery witnessed and experienced the visitation by Elias, who "committed the dispensation of the gospel of Abraham, saying that in us and our seed all generations after us should be blessed" (D&C 110:12). Thus the continuity of the Lord's ancient covenant program was assured in the latter days.

The Lord delights in blessing His children. He gives them places of refuge in this world (lands and gathering places, such as the Stakes of Zion). He gives them hope for eternal mansions on high. He makes them fruitful in their posterity and gives them the hope of eternal increase through the blessings of temple marriage. He provides the fullness of the everlasting Gospel of Jesus Christ and the priesthood of God, with its ennobling and redeeming power to grant immortality and eternal life for the valiant who endure to the end. For all of these extraordinary blessings, He asks only that we walk in righteousness and obey his commandments—sharing our witness to the world through His missionary program. Was there any people more blessed and more privileged? Could there be any mission more sacred or more important than to follow through with full commitment of heart, mind, and soul in our task of being servants of the Lord?

ABRAHAMIC COVENANT: GOSPEL BLESSINGS, NOW AND FOREVER

The central blessing for those who participate in the Abrahamic covenant is to have the fullness of the gospel of Jesus Christ while on earth, including all the saving doctrines essential unto man and the associated blessings of the priesthood, plus the hope and promise of immortality and eternal life in the hereafter (see Abr. 2:11).

The core doctrine of the Abrahamic covenant is the gospel of Jesus Christ. The gospel also brings to bear ordinances and covenants of salvation, of purification, of sanctification and justification through the Lord and Savior Jesus Christ. The gospel is "that I came into the world to do the will of my Father, because my Father sent me. And my Father sent me that I might be lifted up upon the cross; and after that I had been lifted up upon the cross, that I might draw all men unto me, that as I have been lifted up by men even so should men be lifted up by the Father, to stand before me, to be judged of their works, whether they be good or whether they be evil" (3 Ne. 27:13–14). The foundation of the Church is the gospel of Jesus Christ (see 3 Ne. 27:8–11). Through Abraham's seed shall the whole earth be blessed with the gospel of Jesus Christ.

The covenants we make and keep bring us blessings here and now. The gospel of Jesus Christ, centered in the atoning sacrifice of our Savior, is the expression of the love of God. This love is described as the fruit of the tree of life. The fruit of the tree is desirable among all other things to make one happy (see 1 Ne. 8:10). When we partake of the fruit we enjoy the grace of God through the atonement of Jesus Christ. As we "become" as He is, through charity and personal righteousness (the oil of our lamps), we keep the commandments, and if we endure to the end we will enjoy a state of never-ending happiness. The blessing of the gospel of Jesus Christ is the promise of life eternal.

APPENDIX I
MELCHIZEDEK

From the Joseph Smith Translation of the Bible, we learn more of the prophet king, Melchizedek. He blessed Father Abraham. He was a man of faith and was righteous even as a child. He reverenced the Lord. He was favored and approved of the Lord. He was called and ordained to the holy priesthood—and had the power to act for God. Melchizedek, like his forebear, Enoch, made this covenant and was given power to do all things by faith (see Moroni 7:33). He, like Enoch, established peace and was thus called the Prince or King of Peace. Melchizedek blessed father Abraham—or rather, through Melchizedek God blessed Abraham according to the covenant (see JST, Gen. 14:25–40).

Through his example we see that righteousness is a reflection of the spirit of the individual. It follows the nature of their being. Those who are pure in heart will not only see God, but will be righteous here upon the earth. Faith is the foundation of all righteousness (see *Lectures on Faith* 1, 10). The priesthood power operates on our purity of heart and on the condition of being cleansed from all iniquity (see 3 Ne. 8:1). And the rights of the priesthood are explained beautifully in the following: "Because their hearts are set so much upon the things of this world, and aspire to the honors of men, that they do not learn this one lesson—That the rights of the priesthood are inseparably connected with the powers of heaven, and that the powers of heaven cannot be controlled nor handled only upon the principles of righteousness" (D&C 121:35–36).

Yes, power to do good in righteousness is born of purity, through the sanctification and justification from the Lord because of our repentance. Through the mental exertion of faith in the Lord Jesus Christ, we can do all things according to His will (see Hel. 10:4–5). And this is given to all who seek to build up the kingdom of God. The priesthood of God has a simple, direct purpose—to bless the lives of Heavenly Father's children.

Melchizedek (meaning: king of righteousness) was the great high priest and prophet—the king of Salem (Jerusalem)—who lived at the time of Abraham, around two thousand years before Christ. The Old Testament contains only two references to Melchizedek—Gen. 14:18–20, concerning how Abram (Abraham) paid tithes unto him, and Ps. 110:4, with the statement: "The LORD hath sworn, and will not repent, Thou *art* a priest for ever after the order of Melchizedek." The New Testament refers to this latter passage in describing the exalted station of Jesus Christ as "Called of God an high priest after the order of Melchisedec" (Heb. 5:10) and "made an high priest for ever after the order of Melchisedec" (Heb. 6:20). The Apostle Paul shared with us only a few of the particulars of Melchizedek's life:

> For this Melchisedec, king of Salem, priest of the most high God, who met Abraham returning from the slaughter of the kings, and blessed him;

To whom also Abraham gave a tenth part of all; first being by interpretation King of righteousness, and after that also King of Salem, which is, King of peace;

Without father, without mother, without descent, having neither beginning of days, nor end of life; but made like unto the Son of God; abideth a priest continually.

Now consider how great this man *was*, unto whom even the patriarch Abraham gave the tenth of the spoils. (Heb. 7:1–4)

Clearly Melchizedek was an extraordinary exemplar of righteousness and priesthood valor, but it is only in the context of latter-day scripture that a fuller understanding of his mission is gained. The Joseph Smith Translation records for Heb. 7:3 the following revision: "For this Melchizedek was ordained a priest after the order of the Son of God, which order was without father, without mother, without descent, having neither beginning of days, nor end of life. And all those who are ordained unto this priesthood are made like unto the Son of God, abiding a priest continually" (JST Heb. 7:3).

Indeed, were it not for modern-day revelation, we would enjoy only a narrow glimpse into the life of this distinguished and noble prophet. The story of Melchizedek is the story of peace, for it represents the transformation of a wayward society through the redemptive power of spiritual principles of faith, repentance, and committed righteousness. When Melchizedek assumed the office of prophet/leader, Salem (later called Jerusalem) was under a veil of spiritual darkness and rebellion; "yea, they had all gone astray" (Alma 13:17). But Melchizedek was well prepared for his mission: "Now Melchizedek was a man of faith, who wrought righteousness; and when a child he feared God, and stopped the mouths of lions, and quenched the violence of fire. And thus, having been approved of God, he was ordained an high priest after the order of the covenant which God made with Enoch, . . ." (JST Gen. 14:26–27). What Melchizedek accomplished was nothing short of a miracle, for his influence on the people had the astounding effect of bringing them all back into the fold:

But Melchizedek having exercised mighty faith, and received the office of the high priesthood according to the holy order of God, did preach repentance unto his people. And behold, they did repent; and Melchizedek did establish peace in the land in his days; therefore he was called the prince of peace, for he was the king of Salem; and he did reign under his father.

Now, there were many before him, and also there were many afterwards, but none were greater; therefore, of him they have more particularly made mention." (Alma 13:18–19)

So great was Melchizedek's office and stature that he was also placed in charge of the abundance of the Lord's kingdom: "And he lifted up his voice, and he blessed Abram, being the high priest, and the keeper of the storehouse of God; Him whom God had appointed to receive tithes for the poor. Wherefore, Abram paid unto him tithes of all that he had, of all the riches which he possessed, which God had given him more than that which he had need" (JST Gen. 14:36–39). Through the portrait of Melchizedek augmented by modern revelation, we can understand much better the magnificence of the holy priesthood, its eternal nature, its relationship to the atoning mission of the Son of God, the sacred role of covenants

in our eternal progression, and how we too can become the sons and daughters of God through the power of the priesthood and the blessings of the gospel.

Melchizedek was honored to have the priesthood called after his own name:

Why the first is called the Melchizedek Priesthood is because Melchizedek was such a great high priest.

Before his day it was called *the Holy Priesthood, after the Order of the Son of God.*

But out of respect or reverence to the name of the Supreme Being, to avoid the too frequent repetition of his name, they, the church, in ancient days, called that priesthood after Melchizedek, or the Melchizedek Priesthood." (D&C 107:2–4)

Melchizedek is the prototype of the person who engenders and promotes peace. He is verily a type of the Master Himself, the divine Prince of Peace. Peace of mind and heart should be one of our main goals as we seek happiness here and in the hereafter.

The depth of understanding concerning Melchizedek's role is magnified in his relationship to Father Abraham, as we learn again from the Prophet Joseph Smith's translation of the Bible: "And Melchizedek king of Salem, brought forth bread and wine; and he break bread and blest it; and he blest the wine, he being the priest of the most high God, And he blessed him, and said, Blessed be Abram, of the most high God, possessor of heaven and of earth; And blessed be the name of the most high God, which hath delivered thine enemies into thine hand. And Abram gave him tithes of all" (JST, Gen. 14:17–20).

The same principle is confirmed in the Book of Mormon, where we learn from Alma the following: "Yea, humble yourselves even as the people in the days of Melchizedek, who was also a high priest after this same order which I have spoken, who also took upon him the high priesthood forever. And it was this same Melchizedek to whom Abraham paid tithes; yea, even our father Abraham paid tithes of one-tenth part of all he possessed. Now these ordinances were given after this manner, that thereby the people might look forward on the Son of God, it being a type of his order, or it being his order, and this that they might look forward to him for a remission of their sins, that they might enter into the rest of the Lord" (Alma 13:14–16).

What made Melchizedek so great? Why was he so honored to have the Lord's priesthood named after him? The answer is that he "exercised mighty faith" (Alma 13:18), magnified his holy office in the priesthood, and preached repentance. Preaching repentance is the commission given of God to all His holy prophets since the world began, and it will continue to be so until the end. There is no doctrine taught or preached more frequently than the doctrine of repentance. *Repent and come unto Christ* is the message of the kingdom of God. From Adam down to the Prophet Joseph Smith and beyond, it has ever been the same message (see, for example, 2 Ne. 25:26–30). The eternal message of the gospel of Jesus Christ is to have mighty faith unto repentance, that all might come unto Christ. That is the message that all of the great prophets have given—including Melchizedek. Melchizedek's success in bringing his people to repentance is reflected in the outcomes of his labors. His people became a holy people like unto the people of Enoch, for that is what Melchizedek sought: "And his people wrought righteousness, and obtained heaven, and sought for the city of Enoch which God had before taken, separating it from the earth, having reserved it unto the latter days, or the end of the world; . . . And this Melchizedek, having thus established righteousness, was called the king of heaven by his people, or, in other words, the King of peace" (JST Gen. 14:34, 36).

As we come to appreciate the great role Melchizedek played—even unto the ordaining of our forefather Abraham, through whose lineage we are blessed (see D&C 84:14)—we can understand how our daily lives are affected for good by the contribution and example of that ancient prophet after whom the higher priesthood is named. Melchizedek helped to prepare Abraham for his mission, and through Abraham and his seed all nations of the earth shall be blessed. Melchizedek was of the order of the priesthood that opened up the blessings of eternal life, as the Prophet Joseph Smith confirmed: "The King of Shiloam (Salem) had power and authority over that of Abraham, holding the key and the power of endless life" (*TPJS*, 322). It is our glory and joy to bring to others the gospel of Jesus Christ so that they, like the people of Melchizedek, might enjoy peace through righteousness and the blessings of covenant principles and ordinances.

APPENDIX J
ISAAC

Isaac (meaning: he laugheth) was the son of Abraham and Sarah and the heir of the covenant promises of the Lord (see Gen. 15–19; 17; 18:9–15; 21:1–8). Abraham's willingness to sacrifice Isaac by command of the Lord (see Gen. 22; D&C 132:36) was the supreme manifestation of this father's ultimate faith and devotion to God—and an extraordinary symbolic anticipation of the Father's sacrifice of His Only Begotten Son for all mankind.

Abraham was commanded to offer up the thing most dear to his heart—his own son: "Take now thy son, thine only son Isaac, whom thou lovest, and get thee into the land of Moriah; and offer him there for a burnt offering" (Gen. 22:2). Abraham then took Isaac and two other young men on the journey to Moriah, where he was to offer Isaac as a burnt offering, even a sacrifice to the Lord.

On the third day Abraham and Isaac went to worship. Isaac carried the wood as they journeyed. Isaac asked about the sacrifice, and Abraham replied, "my son, God will provide himself a lamb for a burnt offering . . ." (Gen. 22:8). Abraham then bound Isaac and laid him on the altar, preparing for the ultimate sacrifice.

It was at that point that Isaac must have affirmed the action of his father in obedience to the commandment of God. There is no indication that Isaac attempted to revolt against the deed—any more than Jesus Christ shrank from the ultimate offering of sacrificial Atonement. As Abraham raised his knife—no doubt consumed by the anguish of a loving father—an angel of the Lord forbade him and said, "for now I know that thou fearest [i.e., showest unyielding reverence to] God, seeing thou hast not withheld thy son" (Gen. 22:12). A ram was subsequently provided, and the Lord promised Abraham that in his "seed shall all the nations of the earth be blessed" (Gen. 22:18).

Both Isaac and Abraham confronted on that occasion a test of overwhelming proportions. Would Abraham (and Isaac as well) shrink from the awesome task, or would father and son rise in majesty as figures of unforgettable valor and unshakeable obedience? Isaac consented and Abraham obeyed—and the Lord stayed the father's hand. Such was a prefiguring of the coming sacrifice of the Only Begotten for the sake of mankind. Only through a commitment to sacrifice all that we have, if required to do so, can we manifest to the Lord that our enduring love for Him and His divine cause is perfect.

Isaac is also mentioned nine times in the text of the Doctrine and Covenants. The Lord revealed to Joseph Smith details of a future glorious sacrament meeting when all the faithful prophets of old would convene again, including "Joseph and Jacob, and Isaac, and Abraham, your fathers, by whom the promises remain" (D&C 27:10). Moreover, the Lord declared the exaltation of Abraham, Isaac, and Jacob, who "did none other things than that which they were commanded; and because they did none other things than that which they were commanded, they have entered into their exaltation, according to the promises, and sit upon thrones, and are not angels but are gods" (D&C 132:37). Other references to Isaac deal with the Lord's law of war (see D&C 98:31–32); the doctrine of plural marriage (see D&C 132:1, 37, 51–52); the glorious congregation of the elect of God at the Second Coming (see D&C 133:55); the identity of the Lord as "the God of your fathers, the God of Abraham and of Isaac and of Jacob" (see D&C 136:21); and the presence of Isaac (see D&C 138:41) among "the great and mighty ones who were assembled" in the "congregation of the righteous" (D&C 138:38) in the vision granted to President Joseph F. Smith concerning the work of salvation in the spirit realm.

Isaac is also mentioned some thirteen times in the Book of Mormon, typically in connection with the covenant promises of Abraham, Isaac, and Jacob. The prophet Jacob, younger brother of Nephi, also mentions Isaac in the context of the Law of Moses and the obedience of Abraham in being willing to offer up his son as a sacrifice according to the commandment of God (see Jacob 4:5.)

The name Isaac is itself an emblem of the principle of faith. When word came to Abraham and Sarah that they were about to become the parents of a son in their old age, "Abraham fell upon his face, and laughed, and said in his heart, Shall *a child* be born unto him that is an hundred years old? and shall Sarah, that is ninety years old, bear?" (Gen. 17:17). His wife's response was the same, for she laughed with disbelief. In response, the Lord said: "Wherefore did Sarah laugh, saying, Shall I of a surety bear a child, which am old? Is any thing too hard for the LORD?" (Gen. 18:13–14).

Indeed, there is nothing too hard for the Lord—a reminder that we should all make obedience a governing pattern in our lives, love God with all our heart, and cultivate correct choices in faith and valor, knowing that God will bless us with every needful blessing.

POINT OF INTEREST

Gen. 24:18–19 Drink, my lord . . . "As Meir Sternberg (1985) acutely observes, [the delay] before [Rebekah] finally produces the requisite offer to water the camels is a heart-stopper, enough to leave the servant in grave momentary doubt as to whether God has answered his prayer." And when she draws water for all the camels, "this is the closest anyone comes in Genesis to a feat of 'Homeric' heroism (though the success of Rebekah's son Jacob in his betrothal scene in rolling off the huge stone from the well invites comparison). A camel after a long desert journey drinks many gallons of water, and there are ten camels here to water, so Rebekah hurrying down the steps of the well would have had to be a nonstop blur of motion in order to carry up all this water in her single jug" (Robert Alter, The Five Books of Moses [New York: W. W. Norton & Company, 2004]).

APPENDIX K
REBEKAH

Rebekah (meaning: that which binds or secures) was the wife of Isaac, the son of Abraham. The story of how Abraham arranged for his servant to seek a wife for Isaac within the extended family circle is a familiar and uplifting account of courtship and marriage (see Gen. 24). Having arrived at the Mesopotamian city of Haran in the Padan-aram region, the abode of Abraham's kin, the servant of Abraham prayed for guidance:

> And he said, O LORD God of my master Abraham, I pray thee, send me good speed this day, and shew kindness unto my master Abraham.
> Behold, I stand *here* by the well of water; and the daughters of the men of the city come out to draw water:
> And let it come to pass, that the damsel to whom I shall say, Let down thy pitcher, I pray thee, that I may drink; and she shall say, Drink, and I will give thy camels drink also: *let the same be* she *that* thou hast appointed for thy servant Isaac; and thereby shall I know that thou hast shewed kindness unto my master. (Gen. 24:12–14)

As it turned out, it was Rebekah who came on the scene, a pitcher balanced on her shoulder: "And the damsel *was* very fair to look upon, a virgin, neither had any man known her: and she went down to the well, and filled her pitcher, and came up" (Gen. 24:16). There was an amicable period of introductions followed by the arrival of Laban, Rebekah's brother, who extended the hand of hospitality to the visitor. In an atmosphere of friendship and goodwill among all members of the family circle, the arrangement for the marriage was soon consummated:

> Then Laban and Bethuel answered and said, The thing proceedeth from the LORD: we cannot speak unto thee bad or good.
> Behold, Rebekah *is* before thee, take *her,* and go, and let her be thy master's son's wife, as the LORD hath spoken.
> And it came to pass, that, when Abraham's servant heard their words, he worshipped the LORD, *bowing himself* to the earth. (Gen. 24:50–52)

Though the family preferred that Rebekah delay her departure by a few days, they deferred to the anxiety of the servant of Abraham to return to his master forthwith, something to which Rebekah readily consented (see Gen. 24:60).

The initial encounter between Rebekah and Isaac in Canaan is described in this choice passage of scripture:

> And Isaac went out to meditate in the field at the eventide: and he lifted up his eyes, and saw, and, behold, the camels *were* coming.

And Rebekah lifted up her eyes, and when she saw Isaac, she lighted off the camel.

For she *had* said unto the servant, What man *is* this that walketh in the field to meet us? And the servant *had* said, It *is* my master: therefore she took a vail, and covered herself.

And the servant told Isaac all things that he had done.

And Isaac brought her into his mother Sarah's tent, and took Rebekah, and she became his wife; and he loved her: and Isaac was comforted after his mother's *death*. (Gen. 24:63–67)

After a lengthy period of not being able to bear children, Rebekah became the mother of Esau and Jacob, her husband having supplicated the Lord on her behalf (see Gen. 25:20–28). During her days of expectancy, Rebekah prayed to the Lord concerning her condition, receiving this answer: "And the LORD said unto her, Two nations *are* in thy womb, and two manner of people shall be separated from thy bowels; and *the one* people shall be stronger than *the other* people; and the elder shall serve the younger" (Gen. 25:23). Her disposition, therefore, was in favor of the second of the twins, Jacob, whereas her husband favored Esau (see Gen. 25:27–28.)

Following the celebrated encounter in which Esau sold his birthright to Jacob for pottage (see Gen. 25:29–34), Isaac removed his family to Gerar, a Philistine stronghold, to find relief from the famine in the land. While there, Isaac identified Rebekah as his sister, rather than his wife, being concerned that her beauty would induce the men of the community to kill him in seeking to take control of her. But his secret was soon discovered: "And it came to pass, when he had been there a long time, that Abimelech king of the Philistines looked out at a window, and saw, and, behold, Isaac *was* sporting with Rebekah his wife" (Gen. 26:8). Confronted with this reality, Isaac confessed his reasons for the secrecy.

Subsequently, good relations were again restored in the land, lasting until Isaac's unfolding prosperity and power caused unease among the Philistines. They induced him to move away, though afterwards entered into a covenant of friendship with him (see Gen. 26:28–29). In due time, Esau decided to marry two of the Hittite women—outside the immediate kinship circle of the Abrahamic lineage—"Which were a grief of mind unto Isaac and to Rebekah" (Gen. 26:35).

Rebekah figures prominently in the final chapter of Isaac's life when he decided to bestow a benedictory blessing upon the head of Esau, his firstborn son. Having learned that Isaac had sent Esau into the countryside to obtain and prepare venison for him and no doubt remembering the Lord's promise to her that "the elder shall serve the younger" (Gen. 25:23), Rebekah arranged for Jacob to play the role of Esau by disguising himself strategically. Isaac, now poor of vision, granted the blessing as follows:

Therefore God give thee of the dew of heaven, and the fatness of the earth, and plenty of corn and wine:

Let people serve thee, and nations bow down to thee: be lord over thy brethren, and let thy mother's sons bow down to thee: cursed *be* every one that curseth thee, and blessed *be* he that blesseth thee. (Gen. 27:28–29)

Having come on the scene only to discover what had happened, Esau was incensed.

And Isaac answered and said unto Esau, Behold, I have made him thy lord, and all his brethren have I given to him for servants; and with corn and wine have I sustained him: and what shall I do now unto thee, my son?

And Esau said unto his father, Hast thou but one blessing, my father? bless me, *even* me also, O my father. And Esau lifted up his voice, and wept.

And Isaac his father answered and said unto him, Behold, thy dwelling shall be the fatness of the earth, and of the dew of heaven from above;

And by thy sword shalt thou live, and shalt serve thy brother; and it shall come to pass when thou shalt have the dominion, that thou shalt break his yoke from off thy neck. (Gen. 27:37–40)

Rebekah then dispatched Jacob to remain with her brother Laban in Haran for a period of time until the venomous anger of Esau should subside (see Gen. 27:41–45). The transition served also the purpose of encouraging Jacob to choose a wife from within the extended family circle, rather than from among the indigenous non-covenant tribes (see Gen. 27:46; 28:1–5).

Eventually Jacob married Leah and Rachel, daughters of Laban, Rebekah's brother (see Gen. 28, 29) and reconciled with Esau (see Gen. 33).

Upon her death, Rebekah was buried "In the cave that *is* in the field of Machpelah, which *is* before Mamre, in the land of Canaan" (Gen. 49:30)—the resting place for Abraham, Sarah, Isaac, and Leah (see Gen. 49:31). In Rebekah we see displayed a noble character attuned to the designs of heaven concerning the fulfillment of the Abrahamic covenant and committed to the happiness and well-being of her family.

APPENDIX L
JOSEPH

Joseph (meaning: increase) was the son of Jacob and Rachel (see Gen. 30:22–24) and holder of the birthright in Israel (see 1 Chron. 5:1–2; the full panoramic story is given in Gen. 37–50). His dealings with his errant brothers sent by Jacob to gather provisions in Egypt during the time of acute famine attest to Joseph's nature as one of compassion, mercy, and forgiveness—Christ-like qualities in supreme measure (see Gen. 42–45). The fulfillment of the commission of the Abrahamic covenant to carry the gospel and the blessings of the priesthood to the four quarters of the earth (see Abr. 2:9–11) was accomplished largely through the lineage of Joseph.

Joseph's rise to the stature of preeminence among his brethren was not without its elements of opposition. Being favored of Jacob "because he was the son of his old age" (Gen. 37:3), Joseph became a target of malice on the part of his older brothers. Not reluctant to share his dreams—which were predictive of future leadership (see Gen. 37:5–11), Joseph managed to fuel his brothers' feelings of jealousy. Note how the story of jealousy plays out among the brothers:

And it came to pass, when Joseph was come unto his brethren, that they stript Joseph out of his coat, *his* coat of *many* colours that *was* on him;

And they took him, and cast him into a pit: and the pit *was* empty, *there was* no water in it.

And they sat down to eat bread: and they lifted up their eyes and looked, and, behold, a company of Ishmeelites came from Gilead with their camels bearing spicery and balm and myrrh, going to carry *it* down to Egypt.

And Judah said unto his brethren, What profit *is it* if we slay our brother, and conceal his blood?

Come, and let us sell him to the Ishmeelites, and let not our hand be upon him; for he *is* our brother *and* our flesh. And his brethren were content.

Then there passed by Midianites merchantmen; and they drew and lifted up Joseph out of the pit, and sold Joseph to the Ishmeelites for twenty *pieces* of silver: and they brought Joseph into Egypt.

And Reuben returned unto the pit; and, behold, Joseph *was* not in the pit; and he rent his clothes.

And he returned unto his brethren, and said, The child *is* not; and I, whither shall I go?

And they took Joseph's coat, and killed a kid of the goats, and dipped the coat in the blood;

And they sent the coat of *many* colours, and they brought *it* to their father; and said, This have we found: know now whether it *be* thy son's coat or no.

And he knew it, and said, *It is* my son's coat; an evil beast hath devoured him; Joseph is without doubt rent in pieces.

And Jacob rent his clothes, and put sackcloth upon his loins, and mourned for his son many days.

And all his sons and all his daughters rose up to comfort him; but he refused to be comforted; and he said, For I will go down into the grave unto my son mourning.

Thus his father wept for him. (Gen. 37:23–35)

Joseph being sold into slavery by his brothers set the stage for the future reunion in the courts of Pharaoh, where his brethren confessed their sins and admitted that Joseph was indeed divinely chosen to be the leader of the family and the patriarchal standard-bearer for many future nations. The rent "coat of many colors" became a lasting symbol of the ultimate preservation of the Lord's chosen lineage (see Alma 46:23–34). The story of Joseph reveals the consequences of jealousy, envy, greed, and hatred, yet shows the power of God in all things.

In the contrast between the character of Joseph and the character of his brothers, we see played out in the starkest terms the preeminence of integrity over envy, honesty over jealousy, and (in the case of some of the brothers) virtue over moral laxity. Joseph built his life on a foundation of enduring principles and a commitment to follow the guidance of the Spirit. As such, his moral courage and leadership reflect the kind of strength, discipline, and stability that a great leader must always have. By way of contrast, those who operate out of unchecked greed or lust display a wavering instability from which harmony, peace, and lasting happiness can never flow. Being captive to envy not only destroys the mind and heart but, allowed to fester and grow, destroys the freedom of the individual by leading to serious transgression and sin.

It is ironic, as we seek for happiness, that we should become jealous of another's prosperity and happiness. Happiness is from within, yet envy and jealousy seek it from without—externally—and that is a mistake. Being deeply embedded within the carnal heart, jealousy is intractably hard to cure. It is for many individuals most difficult to learn that having the things of the world or the gifts of another does not inherently lead to joy or happiness, for even if we were to possess these things, there will always be others who have more. Often envy and finding "faults" in those who have more are simply masks of a hidden jealousy within.

Envy and jealousy separate us from Deity. They create negative feelings and are truly debilitating to those who succumb to those feelings. In place of envy and jealousy one can foster both a spirit of gratitude for one's blessings and gifts as well as a willingness to rejoice with others in the blessings and gifts that are theirs. Indeed, it is charity and love that swallow up envy and jealousy. True love cheers for the success of others and exults in their well-being, just as Alma did for the success of the sons of Mosiah (see Alma 29:14).

The primordial case study of envy and jealousy is Lucifer, who was obsessed with obtaining the glory and majesty of our Heavenly Father and His Only Begotten Son through vile subversion of the principle of agency (see D&C 29:36; Moses 4:1). Like Joseph's elder brothers, Lucifer was driven by envy, whereas God operates on the principle of love. The contrast is starkly instructive. Envy, jealousy, and greed are inevitably devastating, resulting in acts of consuming hatred and violence. The Lord has taught us that only when jealousy and pride are overcome can we hope to see God (see D&C 67:10).

Joseph as the Paragon of Purity

Against the background of Joseph's removal to Egypt we can view one of his paramount qualities—that of pristine virtue. Joseph's example of integrity and moral uprightness in Egypt is among the most celebrated instances of strength of character in all of holy writ. We learn from the scriptural account: "And the LORD was with Joseph, and he was a prosperous man; and he was in the house of his master the Egyptian. And his master saw that the LORD *was* with him, and that the LORD made all that he did to prosper in his hand. And Joseph found grace in his sight, and he served him: and he made him overseer over his house, and all *that* he had he put into his hand" (Gen. 39:2–4).

Joseph's devoted effort and performance with his assigned duties brought favor with Potiphar. Joseph was a faithful servant, yet his allegiance was to the Lord. As the story unfolds, Joseph was accosted and tempted by Potiphar's wife. In response, Joseph said, "how then can I do this great wickedness, and sin against God?" (Gen. 39:9). Being of sterling character, Joseph took immediate action "and fled, and got him out" (Gen. 39:12). Potiphar's wife accused him falsely and reported him to her husband. As a consequence, Joseph was imprisoned. But again, the hand of the Lord preserved him.

Having invoked the power of the Lord, Joseph was able to interpret the dreams of Pharaoh concerning the seven years of plenty followed by the seven years of famine (see Gen. 41). Pharaoh was pleased, as the following confirms:

And Pharaoh said unto his servants, Can we find *such a one* as this *is*, a man in whom the Spirit of God *is*?

And Pharaoh said unto Joseph, Forasmuch as God hath shewed thee all this, *there is* none so discreet and wise as thou *art*:

Thou shalt be over my house, and according unto thy word shall all my people be ruled: only in the throne will I be greater than thou.

And Pharaoh said unto Joseph, See, I have set thee over all the land of Egypt.

And Pharaoh took off his ring from his hand, and put it upon Joseph's hand, and arrayed him in vestures of fine linen, and put a gold chain about his neck;

And he made him to ride in the second chariot which he had; and they cried before him, Bow the knee: and he made him *ruler* over all the land of Egypt. (Gen. 41:38–43)

Joseph's strength of character and his dependence on the Lord are buoyant forces for good in his life, opening the gateway to future service. Joseph's flight at the adulterous overtures of Potiphar's wife stands in stark contrast with the moral weakness of some of his brothers. The story of his integrity is a beacon of light that still shines today in our world of moral relativity characterized by the loss of the anchor of enduring principles. Moreover, Joseph's resiliency, positive leadership, and creative problem-solving empowered him to be elevated in stature and office in his Egyptian setting, thus laying the groundwork for his future role of preserver of his heritage under the Abrahamic covenant.

The message for our time is clear: as we heed the Lord's prophets, life will be sweet. In our dealings with others and with the Lord, we can make integrity the flywheel of personal progress and the central principle of spiritual growth and vitality. Joseph had the strength of character to flee the scene of temptation. We can follow his extraordinary example and do the same.

Joseph as the Paragon of Forgiveness

In addition to purity of character, Joseph reflected an extraordinary capacity to forgive. We recall the story of Joseph's brothers coming to Egypt for food during the acute famine and how Joseph interacted with them with magnanimity and forgiveness. Ultimately Jacob's entire family came to Egypt where Pharaoh, due to his great love and appreciation for Joseph, gave them and their posterity the land of Goshen. Joseph's forgiving attitude and understanding of the necessity of his role in preserving Israel through dire circumstances were made evident in the way he treated his family (see Gen. 45:1–15).

Later, following the death of Jacob (Israel), we see that Joseph's forgiving nature preserved his love for his brothers, who, not understanding, still feared that he might show retribution toward them:

And they sent a messenger unto Joseph, saying, Thy father did command before he died, saying,

So shall ye say unto Joseph, Forgive, I pray thee now, the trespass of thy brethren, and their sin; for they did unto thee evil: and now, we pray thee, forgive the trespass of the servants of the God of thy father. And Joseph wept when they spake unto him.

And his brethren also went and fell down before his face; and they said, Behold, we *be* thy servants.

And Joseph said unto them, Fear not: for *am* I in the place of God?

But as for you, ye thought evil against me; *but* God meant it unto good, to bring to pass, as *it is* this day, to save much people alive.

Now therefore fear ye not: I will nourish you, and your little ones. And he comforted them, and spake kindly unto them. (Gen. 50:16–21)

The great principles of character exhibited by Joseph were his purity, his willingness to forgive, and his visionary understanding of the destiny of the House of Israel, including his own posterity. The scriptures report the benedictory blessing that Jacob gave to Joseph and his seed (see Gen. 49:22–26; compare also Gen. 48:1–22; Deut. 33:13–17).

Surely Joseph was one of the great prophets of the House of Israel. That his branches did indeed "run over the wall" (Gen. 49:22) is confirmed by the record of Joseph contained in the Book of Mormon, dealing with the history of the Israelite immigrants to the New World. Joseph was the ancestor of Lehi through the lineage of Manasseh, Joseph's son (see Alma 10:3; 2 Ne. 3:4). Ishmael and his family, whom the Lord called to join with Lehi in the exodus to the Promised Land, descended from Ephraim, brother of Manasseh (see *JD* 23:184–185). In this way, the branch of Joseph became a central demographic factor in the expansion of the Israelite heritage in ancient America. Said the resurrected Lord, during His ministry among the ancient Saints in America: "Ye are my disciples; and ye are a light unto this people, who are a remnant of the house of Joseph" (3 Ne. 15:12). With the coming forth of the Book of Mormon as an integral part of the Restoration of the gospel, the "stick of Joseph" foreseen by Ezekiel, the young contemporary of Lehi, was conjoined with the "stick of Judah" to confirm the eternal truths of the gospel of Jesus Christ to all the world (see Ezek. 37:16–17; compare Isa. 29).

The Book of Mormon provides an abundance of additional scriptural material concerning Joseph and his commission, including excerpts from his prophecies about a future seer of like name (Joseph Smith) who would bring forth the record of Joseph as a blessing for the world (see 2 Ne. 3:4–22; 4:1–2; compare JST Gen. 50:24–38 in the section following the Bible Dictionary; also Alma 10:3; 46:23–27). The text of the Doctrine and Covenants mentions Joseph six times (D&C 27:10; 90:10; 96:7; 98:32; and 113:4, 6). Key passages include a reference to the future event when Jesus Christ will participate in a glorious sacrament meeting with all of His holy prophets down through the ages: "And also with Joseph and Jacob, and Isaac, and Abraham, your fathers, by whom the promises remain" (D&C 27:10). Joseph is also mentioned in connection with the "rod" that should come forth "out of the stem of Jesse" (Isa. 11:1): "Behold, thus saith the Lord: It [the rod] is a servant in the hands of Christ, who is partly a descendant of Jesse as well as of Ephraim, or of the house of Joseph, on whom there is laid much power" (D&C 113:4; compare also verse 6 in connection with the "root" of Jesse). The terms *rod* and *root* very likely refer to the Prophet Joseph Smith. Joseph of Egypt is mentioned only once in the New Testament—as an example of faith (see Heb. 11:21–22). He was ultimately buried by Moses and the Israelites in Canaan as with his father and other ancestors (see Gen. 50:22–26; Ex. 13:19; Josh. 24:32).

APPENDIX M
MOSES

Moses was the prophet of God who prefigured Christ's redeeming mission by liberating the Israelites from Egyptian bondage, sustaining them in their journeys, serving as the agent for the revelation of the Ten Commandments, establishing the presence of the tabernacle among the people, and providing leadership to guide them through the wilderness—even to the gateway of the Promised Land, where deliverance awaited many of them. These five missions—liberation, sustenance, revelation of the Lord's commandments, establishment of the tabernacle, and homeward guidance—define the grand commission of the prophet Moses. Though he was "very meek, above all the men which *were* upon the face of the earth" (Num. 12:3), his service is marked throughout by divine station and transcending power.

The Mission of Liberation

The story of Moses is legendary. He was rescued from the bulrushes by a princess, nursed clandestinely by his Hebrew mother, grew up as a child in the court of the Pharaoh, cultivated a passion for protecting his people—as evidenced by his action to kill the Egyptian who was smiting a Hebrew—and then had to flee Egypt fearing for his life. He went north in the desert of the Arabian Peninsula to the land of Midian, where he helped the daughters of Reuel (Jethro) and was given Zipporah to be his wife. She then bore him a son named Gershom (see Ex. 2).

Meanwhile, the Israelites in Egypt were praying for deliverance from their crushing burdens of slavery. The Lord heard their prayers (see Ex. 2:23–25). In the course of his preparation, Moses went up into Mount Horeb to experience the burning bush and receive his call from the Lord to liberate the Israelites out of bondage (see Ex. 3:10–18).

When God called Moses to liberate His people, Moses was at first reluctant to accept, feeling inadequate to influence worldly powers and orchestrate events to bring about divine purposes. But God made clear that He was all-powerful—*I AM* is His name—and that when I AM sends you, you go, and you go with inexorable power to perform the commissioned deeds. The Lord God is Jehovah. The Lord is able to soften hearts and cause enemies to feel favor toward His people. He is also able to intervene with awesome force, if necessary, to open the way for His will to be carried out. We need have no fear of answering a calling from the Lord, for He will fight our battles for us and provide means for us to carry out the assignments: "Who am I," asks Moses, "that I should go unto Pharaoh, and that I should bring forth the children of Israel out of Egypt?" (Ex. 3:11). "Certainly I will be with thee," responds the Lord (Ex. 3:12). And so it was.

Moses and Aaron sought freedom for their people from the Pharaoh, king of Egypt, but he refused, increasing the daily quota of required bricks, including the gathering of their own straw. Moses was disheartened—but the Lord said, "Wherefore say unto the children of Israel, I *am* the

LORD, and I will bring you out from under the burdens of the Egyptians, and I will rid you out of their bondage, and I will redeem you with a stretched out arm, and with great judgments: And I will take you to me for a people, and I will be to you a God: and ye shall know that I *am* the LORD your God, which bringeth you out from under the burdens of the Egyptians" (Ex. 6:6–7).

When the Israelites would not hearken to Moses, the Lord unfolded a design to show the Egyptians as well as the Israelites that He was God over all the earth and had power to do all things. As time proceeded, signs and plagues were sent upon the Egyptians, showing the might and power of the God of Israel: the Nile river—the Egyptians' material god and source of sustenance—was turned to blood and the fish died (see Ex. 7:14–21); frogs were sent upon the land (see Ex. 8:1–15); lice came upon the people (see Ex. 8:16–19); flies abounded everywhere (see Ex. 8:22–32); the animals of the Egyptians perished (see Ex. 9:1–7); sores came upon the Egyptians, and a mighty hailstorm killed all those who were exposed (see Ex. 9:8–35); locusts came and devoured all their plants (see Ex. 10:4–20); and darkness covered the land for three days (see Ex. 10:21–27). Each time the Pharaoh promised to let the people go if Moses would stop the plague, only to relinquish his word when relief came.

Finally the Lord told Moses that the firstborn child in every Egyptian home was to die. The Israelites were to take a lamb without blemish, kill it, and administer the blood as follows: "And ye shall take a bunch of hyssop, and dip *it* in the blood that *is* in the bason, and strike the lintel and the two side posts with the blood that *is* in the bason; and none of you shall go out at the door of his house until the morning. For the LORD will pass through to smite the Egyptians; and when he seeth the blood upon the lintel, and on the two side posts, the LORD will pass over the door, and will not suffer the destroyer to come in unto your houses to smite *you*. And ye shall observe this thing for an ordinance to thee and to thy sons for ever" (Ex. 12:22–24).

In the Egyptians' homes the firstborn child was taken by the destroying angel of the Lord. That was the crucial intervening act that caught the Pharaoh's attention in earnest. Finally the Pharaoh told Moses and Aaron to take the children of Israel and leave (see Ex. 12:30–38)—thus the Lord led the Israelites to freedom. Still desirous to regain the slavery of the Israelites, the Pharaoh followed after them with his hosts. Moses, endowed with the power of the Lord, parted the Red Sea, allowing the Israelites to walk across on dry ground. The Egyptians followed, only to be swallowed by the resurging waters (see Ex. 14:5–30).

The Israelites finally were free. In gratitude, Moses led the Israelites in a chorus of praise to the God of deliverance (see Ex. 15). With an outpouring of mighty anthems ends the story of the liberation of the Israelites through the power of God and His merciful dealings with His covenant people. Just as the Lord liberated the captive Israelites from Egyptian bondage, He has also put in place the saving truths, ordinances, and powers to bless our lives with redeeming grace through the Atonement of Jesus Christ. "Let my people go" was the watchword for the Exodus (Ex. 5:1). Similarly, the gospel of Jesus Christ provides the means and power to "let people go" from the bondage of sin and pass through the waters of baptism toward a new life following in the footsteps of the Lord.

The historical Israelite Exodus and deliverance is a pattern for the journey of liberation that each of us has the opportunity to complete as we accomplish the exodus from the bondage of sin and worldly entanglements toward a state of spiritual freedom. The journey toward the Promised Land is symbolic of our passage toward Zion, where we can raise our families in truth and light, and taste the joys of the gospel through obedience and righteousness. Our Heavenly Father has liberated us through the shedding of the blood of His Only Begotten, that we might not perish, but have everlasting life. The consequences of sin pass over us through the process of faith, repentance, baptism, and the blessings of the gift of the Holy Ghost.

Sustenance for the Journey

The experiences of the liberated Israelites in the wilderness became a time of preparation, following their Exodus from Egypt by the hand of God, and provide valuable lessons for us today. In many respects, Israel was like a tender plant being transplanted to a new environment, or like seeds being placed into a strange new terrain. What are the conditions of vitality that must exist if there is to be verdure and a fruitful harvest? What are the prerequisites to spiritual well-being and progress in the gospel?

Perhaps we can liken this circumstance to a garden, and ask what essential conditions of growth to look for. We can discern the following six aspects of spiritual horticulture: (1) The freedom to grow is similar to the deliverance of Israel from foreign bondage, an event evoking the most heartfelt feelings of gratitude and praise. (2) The essential nutrients relate to the continual flow of divine nurture in our lives. (3) The caretakers of the garden are the prophets and stewards called to prepare the way and build up the kingdom of God. (4) The principles of vitality sustaining all natural growth are like the principles of the gospel, which sustain our spiritual development and well-being. (5) The sunshine on which all life depends has its symbolic counterpart in the radiant image of God and His glorious presence—just as we are commanded to "seek the face of the Lord always" (D&C 101:38). (6) The indispensable moisture for the growing plants is similar to the doctrines of the priesthood, which distil upon our souls "as the dews from heaven" (D&C 121:45).

As the Israelites journeyed through the wilderness, trials and tests of their faith in God were ongoing. They found that the garden of the Lord is not without its challenges. There was no water to be found for three days. When they found water, it was bitter to the taste and the people began to murmur. Moses was their representative before the Lord (see Ex. 15:25–26.)

The Israelites continued to travel in the wilderness, struggling for food and at times becoming angry with Moses. Again the Lord blessed them with food—manna from heaven. Manna is explained in the Bible Dictionary as follows: "It is impossible to find any natural product that will answer to the requirements of the scriptural narrative in regard to this heavensent food. With regard to the name, we are told (Ex. 16:15) that the people, seeing the small scale-like substance, said one to another, 'Man hu,' 'for they wist not what it was.' This also translates 'What is it?'"

Another possibility for the derivation of the term manna is that it comes from the word *manan*, meaning "to allot," hence denoting an allotment or a gift. This gift from God was described as follows: "And the manna *was* as coriander seed, and the colour thereof as the colour of bdellium. *And* the people went about, and gathered *it*, and ground *it* in mills, or beat *it* in a mortar, and baked *it* in pans, and made cakes of it: and the taste of it was as the taste of fresh oil. And when the dew fell upon the camp in the night, the manna fell upon it" (Num. 11:7–9).

The "manna from heaven" given to the Israelites during their sojourn in the wilderness typifies the allotment or gift from God embodied in salvation and exaltation. He will provide this transcendent gift if we but believe and act according to His commands. We live by His gifts—in particular the word of God (see D&C 84:43–46). He is the bread of life (see John 6:35, 48–51). He is the atoning sacrifice. We shall ever be indebted to the Lord (see Mosiah 2:21). Like the ancient Israelites, we also have to obey with exactness to merit the Lord's blessings.

We can recall when the people again became angry with Moses for the lack of water. The Lord, as always after fervent prayer, instructed His prophet: "Go on before the people, and take with thee of the elders of Israel; and thy rod, wherewith thou smotest the river, take in thine hand, and go. Behold, I will stand before thee there upon the rock in Horeb; and thou shalt smite the rock, and there shall come water out of it, that the people may drink. And Moses did so in the sight of the elders of Israel" (Ex. 17:5–6). The water in the wilderness is analogous to the "living waters" of the gospel (Jer. 17:13; John 4:10; 7:38; 1 Ne. 11:25; D&C 63:23). The wilderness was a preparation time for the Israelites to progress in becoming worthy of the law of the Lord. Similarly, we are going through our own preparation time day-by-day as we progress along the pathway of mortality, endeavoring to live the laws of the Lord and seeking His face always (see D&C 101:38).

The question of preparation in our own lives becomes apparent as we read the history of the Israelites and their travail in the wilderness. In a similar way we, too, have our travail in the wilderness of our earthly life. We are all growing in the garden of the Lord. Will we prosper and unfold as the Lord desires? Are we prepared to lift our voices in praise for the deliverance of the Lord? Do we seek divine nurture in our daily lives? Do we follow the counsel of the prophets? Do we live the principles of the gospel valiantly? Do we seek after the Lord and listen to the inspiration of the Spirit? Do we savor the doctrines of the priesthood as the dews from heaven?

These are the elements of spiritual preparation. The precursor to success or failure in human endeavor can always be found in our commitment to become prepared for meaningful action. When vision and desire are in place, preparation becomes the master. Preparation precedes power. If we are prepared, we will not suffer from anxiety—or as the Lord expressed it: "but if ye are prepared ye shall not fear" (D&C 38:30). Preparation has a price. It takes time, effort, dedication, and often sacrifice in order to prepare well. Many want to be the best, be the champion, and win the prize. The hard fact is: How many want to *prepare* to be the best and thus become the champion and win the prize? Preparation becomes the key to progress along with the perseverance and dedication to see things through.

In the context of spiritual preparation, our prototype is the Master Himself: "Nevertheless, glory be to the Father, and I partook and finished my preparations unto the children of men" (D&C 19:19). In emulation of the Savior's example, we can don the armor of God: "Stand, therefore, having your loins girt about with truth, having on the breastplate of righteousness, and your feet shod with the preparation of the gospel of peace, which I have sent mine angels to commit unto you; . . ." (D&C 27:16). Then we can work in all diligence to prepare our families for the times to come. Having done that, we can then rest assured that we shall be ready, as the Lord has commanded. In all of this, we can remember the indefatigable service of Moses as he labored to sustain and prepare the Israelites for better days ahead.

Who is the Moses in our day? The living prophets in the kingdom of God acting as Moses did to reveal the Lord's will as a guidance system in our time.

Revelation of the Lord's Commandments

The Lord established—actually renewed—His ancient covenant with Israel. The Ten Commandments were given through Moses to guide Israel into the proper pathways for honoring that covenant. These commandments are repeated in the Book of Mormon (see Mosiah 12:33–36; 13:12–24), the Doctrine and Covenants (see D&C 42:18–27; 59:5–16), and the New Testament (see Matt. 5:17–37), and they deal with relationships of eternal significance—God, family, and fellowman.

It is fitting that the Gospel of John records, "And this is life eternal, that they might know thee the only true God, and Jesus Christ, whom thou hast sent" (John 17:3). We are taught that eternal life consists of establishing an enduring and holy relationship with our Heavenly Father and our Savior.

The basic unit of the Church is the family. "The Family: A Proclamation to the World" makes clear the role of the family here and in the hereafter. The sealing ordinances of the priesthood enable marriage and family to occupy a central place in our eternal lives (see D&C 131, 132). The way we treat our fellowmen is truly a demonstration of our feelings for the Lord Jesus Christ (see Matt. 25:40). The moment of truth in regard to the Ten Commandments is this one eternal verity—that we should love God and our fellowmen because this does fulfill all the law and the prophets (see Matt. 22:36–40).

The story of the revelation of the Ten Commandments is one of the greatest episodes in all of human history. In *Answers to Gospel Questions*, President Joseph Fielding Smith explains how the two sets of tables Moses brought down from Mount Sinai relate to the Law of Moses and the priesthood:

When Israel came out of Egypt it was the intention of the Lord to make of Israel a royal priesthood. That is to say, that he was to give them the Melchizedek Priesthood and the principles of exaltation. When Moses went up into the mount and was gone forty days, Israel sinned a very serious sin and turned back to the worship of the Egyptians and had Aaron make for them a golden calf. When Moses came down from the mountain, in his anger, he threw down the tables and broke them. Then at the command of the Lord he went back into the mountain, and the Lord gave him other tables on which he wrote with his finger [see Exodus 20; Deuteronomy 5].

The Lord did not write the same things on the second tables that were on the first, but confined Israel to the Aaronic Priesthood and denied the Melchizedek Priesthood to the tribes of Israel except in special cases with certain prophets like Isaiah, Jeremiah and others. These prophets had the Melchizedek Priesthood by special appointment. The Lord gave to Israel the carnal law and said that they should not enter into his rest while they were in the wilderness.

The Ten Commandments were in existence long before Moses' time, and the Lord only renewed them in the days of Moses, just as he has done in our day.

Now we do not find in the Bible the full history of these things. We do learn that the Lord withdrew from Israel the right to the Melchizedek Priesthood and confined them largely to the Aaronic Priesthood. The full reason for this is not clearly stated. This is due to the fact that the Bible has lost much in translations and copying by the scribes. In the Doctrine and Covenants the Lord has restored some of this history as in D. & C. 84:19–27. I refer you to the revision given by the Prophet Joseph Smith which tells more about this action.

And the Lord said unto Moses, Hew thee two other tables of stone, like unto the first, and I will write upon them also, the words of the law, according as they were written at the first on the tables which thou brakest; but it shall not be according to the first, for I will take away the priesthood out of their midst; therefore my holy order, and the ordinances thereof, shall not go before them; for my presence shall not go up in their midst lest I destroy them. (D. & C. 84:19–27.)" (Joseph Fielding Smith, AGQ 3:154–155)

The Ten Commandments should be looked at in a positive light. Both the "thou shalt nots" and the "thou shalts" are blessings to our lives. They are guidelines for goodness. They are signposts of safety. The line "We love thy law; we will obey" in the hymn "Our Savior's Love" (Hymns, 113) becomes our attitude towards the commandments of God. In a similar way, the scriptures admonish us that if we truly love the Lord we will keep His commandments (see John 14:15).

We will be happy and enjoy a state of never-ending joy as we keep the commandments. Once again, in living the Ten Commandments we fulfill the two great commandments spoken of by our Savior when He was queried, "Master, which is the great commandment in the law? Jesus said unto him, Thou shalt love the Lord thy God with all thy heart, and with all thy soul, and with all thy mind. This is the first and great commandment. And the second is like unto it, Thou shalt love thy neighbour as thyself. On these two commandments hang all the law and the prophets" (Matt. 22:36–40). Following His advice with devotion and charity will cause great blessings to flow into our lives.

Establishment of the Tabernacle

Since the beginning of time the Lord has desired to come to His people in His house that He might bless them. The Lord commanded Moses, "And let them make me a sanctuary; that I may dwell among them" (Ex. 25:8). The Lord revealed to Moses the sacred purpose for the Tabernacle a a place where He could meet with the children of Israel and there dwell among them (see Ex. 29:43–46).

The children of Israel obeyed the Lord and sacrificed their precious things for the building of the tabernacle (see Ex. 36:21–29). Moses truly was joyful over the building of the tabernacle, blessing it and those who helped in its construction. Then the power, glory, and blessing of the Lord were manifested and continued with the Israelites as they traveled (see Ex. 40:34–38).

Just as the Lord commanded Moses, He also commanded the Prophet Joseph Smith concerning His holy house, as is recorded:

For, for this cause I commanded Moses that he should build a tabernacle, that they should bear it with them in the wilderness, and to build a house in the land of promise, that those ordinances might be revealed which had been hid from before the world was.

Therefore, verily I say unto you, that your anointings, and your washings, and your baptisms for the dead, and your solemn assemblies, and your memorials for your sacrifices by the sons of Levi, and for your oracles in your most holy places wherein you receive conversations, and your statutes and judgments, for the beginning of the revelations and foundation of Zion, and for the glory, honor, and endowment of all her municipals, are ordained by the ordinance of my holy house, which my people are always commanded to build unto my holy name.

And verily I say unto you, let this house be built unto my name, that I may reveal mine ordinances therein unto my people;

For I deign to reveal unto my church things which have been kept hid from before the foundation of the world, things that pertain to the dispensation of the fulness of times.

And I will show unto my servant Joseph all things pertaining to this house, and the priesthood thereof, and the place whereon it shall be built.

And ye shall build it on the place where you have contemplated building it, for that is the spot which I have chosen for you to build it.

If ye labor with all your might, I will consecrate that spot that it shall be made holy. (D&C 124:38–44)

The tabernacle during the days of Moses and beyond was an emblem of the temple of God. Surely it is in the temple of our God that the blessings of the eternities are given to the children of God if they are but worthy. Temples are sacred. They are "the house of the Lord." They are erected and dedicated as sacred precincts where we can worship God and receive sacred ordinances of exaltation. Temple work and family history are all about the eternal family. Families can be forever. The restoration of the priesthood and sealing power through Elijah has truly caused the children and their fathers to turn towards each other (see D&C 2). This power makes possible the eternal family. As we search out our ancestors and do their temple work, we can be made perfect in them, and they in us (see D&C 128:15). Developing and studying family history brings appreciation and gratitude for the past and all the sacrifices that have been made, a process that brings families closer together.

We, the children of God in this last dispensation, have been called to lay the foundation of this great latter-day work: proclaiming the gospel, perfecting the Saints, and redeeming the dead. We build temples. We do vicarious work for the dead. We preach the gospel. The work continues apace on the other side of the veil so that the spirits there residing can enjoy the blessings of the ordinances of the temple. Yes, we have a work to do and we are the ones to do it (see D&C 138:53–58). This is our work and our glory to help Heavenly Father in bringing to pass His eternal plan of happiness—the immortality and eternal life of His children (see Moses 1:39).

Homeward Guidance

Moses was the paragon of the spiritual guide, the exemplar of how to succor others in their mortal journey toward the Promised Land. The Lord's people must be tried. It is in the trials and tribulations that we are humbled and turn to the Lord so that He can nurture and succor us in all of our afflictions (see Alma 7:11–12).

The wilderness sojourn for the Israelites after the Exodus from Egypt was indeed a difficult experience. They struggled. They murmured. The Lord sent them manna. They grew tired of manna and wanted meat. The Lord sent them quail. They were still anxious and desirous for better conditions. Finally they came to the land of Canaan. Moses sent a spy delegation consisting of a leader from each of the twelve tribes. Except for the words of Caleb and Joshua, the report came back: Canaan was indeed a land of milk and honey, but the inhabitants were too strong for the Israelites to defeat. Once more the seeds of doubt were sown and the people, lacking in faith, again become angry with Moses. The record gives the Lord's reaction:

And the LORD spake unto Moses and unto Aaron, saying,

How long *shall I bear with* this evil congregation, which murmur against me? I have heard the murmurings of the children of Israel, which they murmur against me.

Say unto them, *As truly as* I live, saith the LORD, as ye have spoken in mine ears, so will I do to you:

Your carcases shall fall in this wilderness; and all that were numbered of you, according to your whole number, from twenty years old and upward, which have murmured against me,

Doubtless ye shall not come into the land, *concerning* which I sware to make you dwell therein, save Caleb the son of Jephunneh, and Joshua the son of Nun.

But your little ones, which ye said should be a prey, them will I bring in, and they shall know the land which ye have despised.

But *as for* you, your carcases, they shall fall in this wilderness.

And your children shall wander in the wilderness forty years, and bear your whoredoms, until your carcases be wasted in the wilderness. (Num. 14:26–33)

From the beginning, the seeds of doubt were festering in the souls of the delivered Israelites. After all the Lord had done for them in their liberation from Egypt, they feared for their lives and lacked faith and trust in the God of Israel—and thus ensued the forty years in the wilderness (see Num. 32:13). But the youth—the children—He would spare and guide into the Promised Land.

The Lord will have a humble people. He will have a people willing to follow His commandments and prove themselves worthy of the Promised Land (see Deut. 8:2; see also Josh. 5:6). We can remember that all among the Israelites died off who were "twenty years old and upward," save Joshua and Caleb. Traditions die hard. Traditions have power—for good or bad—and the Israelites suffered because of their wicked traditions. Hence a new generation came about. A new generation born of righteousness was required to qualify for entrance into the Promised Land.

We too have a testing time (see Abr. 3:25). The question is: Will we turn to the Lord and be humbled by the word and succored by the hand of the Lord in all things, or will we fight against the things of the Lord by having a hardened heart and an unyielding spirit born of pride and selfishness? When we follow the counsel of the word of God, we can learn by the word rather than by the harsh, corrective hand of self-inflicted experience that compels us through suffering to repent and cure a sinful and rebellious heart. We are reminded that we are to be "humble, and be submissive and gentle; easy to be entreated; full of patience and long-suffering; being temperate in all things; being diligent in keeping the commandments of God at all times; asking for whatsoever things ye stand in need, both spiritual and temporal; always returning thanks unto God for whatsoever things ye do receive" (Alma 7:23).

We can remember the example of those who did "fast and pray oft, and did wax stronger and stronger in their humility, and firmer and firmer in the faith of Christ, unto the filling their souls with joy and consolation, yea, even to the purifying and the sanctification of their hearts, which sanctification cometh because of their yielding their hearts unto God" (Hel. 3:35).

When do these things, when we follow the Moses of our day—the Lord's living prophet—we will be strengthened in the Spirit, learning how to rise above the natural man to become spiritual by nature (see Mosiah 3:19). We can examine our daily patterns of living. Are we wandering in the wilderness, hoping for the Lord's succor while still holding on to worldly attitudes and practices? Or have we come to the frontiers of the Promised Land, ready and prepared to enter in? We can learn from the mission of Moses, from the scriptures, and from the experiences of those who have lived in the past that we can go forward in faith, trusting in the Lord, following His Spirit, and keeping His commandments so that we can enjoy the blessings of God in our lives.

Modern scripture sheds additional light on the mission and person of Moses. It was Moses who appeared to Joseph Smith and Oliver Cowdery in the Kirtland Temple on April 3, 1836, to restore the keys of "the gathering of Israel from the four parts of the earth, and the leading of the ten tribes from the land of the north" (D&C 110:11). Key passages in the Doctrine and Covenants depict Moses as an exemplar of one who receives and acts on "the spirit of revelation" (D&C 8:3); as the prototype for the ministry of Joseph Smith—the only one appointed to receive commandments and revelations for God's people in a given dispensation (see D&C 28:2); as a key figure in the lineage of the priesthood (see D&C 84:6; 133:54–55; 136:37); as one given the mission to sanctify his people "that they might behold the face of God (see D&C 84:23); as the forebear of those "sons of Moses" who shall serve with devotion in the temples of God and fulfill the commission of the Abrahamic covenant (see D&C 84:31–34); as the prototype of the president of the high priesthood, who is to "preside over the whole church, and to be like unto Moses" (see D&C 107:91); as the one who restored the "keys of the gathering of Israel" in the latter days (D&C 110:11); as the one who built the tabernacle of the Lord as an ancient model of the temple (see D&C 124:38); as one of the "great and mighty ones" assembled in the "vast congregation of the righteous" perceived in vision by Joseph F. Smith (see D&C 138:38)—plus many passages concerning the law of Moses.

Additionally, Moses is mentioned by name some seventy-five times in the Book of Mormon. His remarkable qualities and accomplishments are celebrated throughout the pages of this sacred scripture: the dividing of the Red Sea (see 1 Ne. 4:2; 17:26; Hel. 8:11); his authoring the five initial books of the Bible (see 1 Ne. 5:11; 19:23); smiting the rock to obtain water for the Israelites (see 1 Ne. 17:29); delivering Israel from Egypt (see 2 Ne. 3:10); his radiant countenance while on the mount (see Mosiah 13:5); his prophecies of the coming of the Messiah (see Mosiah 13:33); his references to the Son of God (see Alma 33:19); the lifting of the brazen serpent as a type of the Savior (see Hel. 8:14); and many other references. Of major significance as a theme in the Book of Mormon is the fulfillment of the Law of Moses through the ministry and Atonement of the Savior (see 3 Ne. 15:4–8).

From the very beginning of the Book of Mormon, the transcendence of the Atonement as the key to salvation and exaltation is emphasized, the Law of Moses being a preparatory protocol pointing to the Savior and His redeeming mission (see 2 Ne. 2:5–8).

The Book of Moses in the Pearl of Great Price is a masterful refinement and augmentation of the Biblical account as revealed through the Prophet Joseph Smith. It is from chapter one of Moses, concerning the supernal experience of Moses upon the Mount where he met God and received his divine commission, that we have the priceless verity about the purpose of God: "For behold, this is my work and my glory—to bring to pass the immortality and eternal life of man" (Moses 1:39).

Upon the completion of his years in the wilderness, Moses did not die in the literal sense (as implied in Deut. 34:5–7) but was translated, enabling him to complete his mission of conveying essential priesthood keys on the Mount of Transfiguration in the meridian of time (see Matt. 17:3; compare Alma 45:19) and then, as a resurrected being, during the Restoration in the latter days (see D&C 110:11; 133:54–55).

APPENDIX N
JETHRO

Jethro (meaning: his excellence; also called Reuel), prince and priest of Midian, was the father-in-law of Moses. After Moses had fled from Egypt as a result of his having slain an Egyptian who was smiting an Israelite, he relocated to the land of Midian (see Ex. 2:11–16). While there, Moses observed at a well how shepherds were driving a group of young women away from the water. He interceded on behalf of the women—the seven daughters of Reuel (Jethro)—and watered their flock (see Ex. 2:16–21).

Thereafter Moses took over the responsibility to keep the flock of Jethro. It was while shepherding the flock that Moses experienced the episode of the burning bush on the mountainside of Horeb (see Ex. 3). Having been called of the Lord, Moses became the instrument of liberation for the Israelites held in bondage in Egypt.

Following the exodus into the wilderness, Jethro brought Zipporah and the two sons of Moses into his encampment, where a most interesting family gathering took place:

> And Moses went out to meet his father in law, and did obeisance, and kissed him; and they asked each other of *their* welfare; and they came into the tent.
>
> And Moses told his father in law all that the LORD had done unto Pharaoh and to the Egyptians for Israel's sake, *and* all the travail that had come upon them by the way, and *how* the LORD delivered them.
>
> And Jethro rejoiced for all the goodness which the LORD had done to Israel, whom he had delivered out of the hand of the Egyptians.
>
> And Jethro said, Blessed *be* the LORD, who hath delivered you out of the hand of the Egyptians, and out of the hand of Pharaoh, who hath delivered the people from under the hand of the Egyptians.
>
> Now I know that the LORD *is* greater than all gods: for in the thing wherein they dealt proudly *he was* above them. (Ex. 18:7–11)

We see how committed Jethro was to family unity and sharing and how devoted he was to the Lord. His services also extended to counseling Moses on how to manage the heavy administrative burden of acting as judge over Israel "from morning unto the evening" (Ex. 18:13):

> And when Moses' father in law saw all that he did to the people, he said, What *is* this thing that thou doest to the people? why sittest thou thyself alone, and all the people stand by thee from morning unto even?
>
> And Moses said unto his father in law, Because the people come unto me to enquire of God:
>
> When they have a matter, they come unto me; and I judge between one and another, and I do make *them* know the statutes of God, and his laws.
>
> And Moses' father in law said unto him, The thing that thou doest *is* not good.

Thou wilt surely wear away, both thou, and this people that *is* with thee: for this thing *is* too heavy for thee; thou art not able to perform it thyself alone. (Ex. 18:14–18)

Jethro then advised Moses to adopt a very different governing strategy:

Hearken now unto my voice, I will give thee counsel, and God shall be with thee: Be thou for the people to God-ward, that thou mayest bring the causes unto God:

And thou shalt teach them ordinances and laws, and shalt shew them the way wherein they must walk, and the work that they must do.

Moreover thou shalt provide out of all the people able men, such as fear God, men of truth, hating covetousness; and place *such* over them, *to be* rulers of thousands, *and* rulers of hundreds, rulers of fifties, and rulers of tens:

And let them judge the people at all seasons: and it shall be, *that* every great matter they shall bring unto thee, but every small matter they shall judge: so shall it be easier for thyself, and they shall bear *the burden* with thee.

If thou shalt do this thing, and God command thee *so,* then thou shalt be able to endure, and all this people shall also go to their place in peace.

So Moses hearkened to the voice of his father in law, and did all that he had said.

And Moses chose able men out of all Israel, and made them heads over the people, rulers of thousands, rulers of hundreds, rulers of fifties, and rulers of tens.

And they judged the people at all seasons: the hard causes they brought unto Moses, but every small matter they judged themselves. (Ex. 18:19–26)

The Doctrine and Covenants provides the added information that Moses received the Melchizedek priesthood from Jethro: "And the sons of Moses, according to the Holy Priesthood which he [Moses] received under the hand of his father-in-law, Jethro; And Jethro received it under the hand of Caleb" (D&C 84:6–7).

APPENDIX O
JESUS CHRIST, AS PRESENTED IN THE OLD TESTAMENT

Jesus Christ is the central figure of the Old Testament and Pearl of Great Price, just as He is in the New Testament, Book of Mormon, and Doctrine and Covenants. Magnificent in scope and detail, inspiring in thematic content, and riveting in its anecdotal abundance, the Old Testament is the foundational scripture of the divine canon.

Above all else in terms of mission and purpose, the Old Testament—supported by the books of Moses and Abraham from the Pearl of Great Price—constitutes a grand and glorious exposition of the character, qualities, and mission of the Messiah, even Jesus Christ, the Mediator of the sacred covenant with the Father. The thoughtful and prayerful reader cannot read these passages of scripture concerning the Savior without being touched spiritually with the profound significance of His love, the mercy of His longsuffering, and the majesty of His divine intercession on behalf of mankind.

Among the numerous offices and titles of the Lord revealed through the Old Testament, the following six might be considered the principal and predominant ones: (1) *Jehovah* ("Unchangeable One"), (2) *Messiah* or *Christ* ("Anointed One"), (3) *Creator*, (4) *Emmanuel* or *Immanuel* ("God Among Us"), (5) *Jesus* ("God is help" or "Savior"), and (6) *King*.

Understanding the interrelated matrix of spiritual agendas that constitute the mission of the Lord serves as a kind of lens through which to view the unfolding panorama of God's dealings with His people during the dispensations of time recorded in the Old Testament and the Pearl of Great Price. The overarching theme of these and all other scriptures of the sacred canon is the Lord Jesus Christ and His central role in the plan of salvation. As Nephi declared: "And now, behold, my beloved brethren, this is the way; and there is none other way nor name given under heaven whereby man can be saved in the kingdom of God. And now, behold, this is the doctrine of Christ, and the only and true doctrine of the Father, and of the Son, and of the Holy Ghost, which is one God, without end. Amen" (2 Ne. 31:21; compare Moses 6:51–52).

Jehovah
In the King James version of the Old Testament, the word LORD (with each letter capitalized) signifies that the original text upon which the translation into English was based contained at that point the name *Jehovah*, which means "Unchangeable One." Out of respect for Deity, Jewish readers did not speak aloud the name *Jehovah* (or any of its variants), but substituted instead a Hebrew word such as *Adonai*, meaning "Lord."

The name *Jehovah* signifies everlasting, endless, and eternal God, a reflection of the supernal constancy of Deity, the Word of God—"The grass withereth, the flower fadeth: but the word of our God shall stand for ever" (Isa. 40:8). In latter-day scripture this everlasting state of being is confirmed: "Listen to the voice of the Lord your God, even Alpha and Omega, the beginning and the end, whose course is one eternal round, the same today as yesterday, and forever" (D&C 35:1).

It was under the auspices of this transcendent function of everlasting and unchanging God—the Eternal I Am—that Jehovah conversed with Moses on the mount:

> And Moses said unto God, Behold, *when* I come unto the children of Israel, and shall say unto them, The God of your fathers hath sent me unto you; and they shall say to me, What *is* his name? what shall I say unto them? And God said unto Moses, I AM THAT I AM: and he said, Thus shalt thou say unto the children of Israel, I AM hath sent me unto you. And God said moreover unto Moses, Thus shalt thou say unto the children of Israel, The LORD God of your fathers, the God of Abraham, the God of Isaac, and the God of Jacob, hath sent me unto you: this *is* my name for ever, and this *is* my memorial unto all generations. (Ex. 3:13–15)

The nature of Jehovah as an eternal, unchanging, and everlasting Being derives from His relationship to, and grounding in, the Father, Elohim. Jehovah is in very deed the Son of God, even the First Born: "I will declare the decree: the LORD hath said unto me, Thou *art* my Son; this day have I begotten thee" (Ps. 2:7). Furthermore: "Also I will make him *my* firstborn, higher than the kings of the earth. My mercy will I keep for him for evermore, and my covenant shall stand fast with him. His seed also will I make *to endure* for ever, and his throne as the days of heaven" (Ps. 89:27–29). Isaiah confirmed the same truth: "Who hath wrought and done *it,* calling the generations from the beginning? I the LORD, the first, and with the last; I *am* he" (Isa. 41:4). In the New Testament, Book of Mormon, and the Doctrine and Covenants, this defining position as the First as well as the Last, applied to Jesus Christ, is embodied in the appellation "Alpha and Omega" (see Rev. 1:8, 11; 21:6; 22:13; 3 Ne. 9:18; D&C 19:1; 35:1; 38:1; 45:7; 54:1; 61:1; 63:60; 68:35; 75:1; 81:7; 84:120; 112:34; and 132:66).

The qualities of Jehovah are made clear from the scriptural account. Not only is Jehovah endless and eternal, He also serves everlastingly as a member of the Godhead under the direction of the Father and in conjunction with the Holy Ghost. The qualities of the Son that radiate from this magnificent position of grace and truth are divinity, everlasting nature, and godliness. These are the same qualities of Jehovah to which His disciples are to aspire through obedience to His gospel plan of exaltation and by enduring in faith and honor to the end. What a glorious blessing it is to have a resplendent and perfected personage—even Jehovah—as our spiritual model and eternal guide: "Therefore, what manner of men ought ye to be? Verily I say unto you, even as I am" (3 Ne. 27:27).

Messiah/Christ

Messiah is an Aramaic word meaning "the Anointed." Aramaic belongs to the Semitic language group (which also includes Hebrew and Arabic) and became the official language of the Assyrian and later the Babylonian and Persian empires. Aramaic was for centuries the dominant language in Jewish worship and daily life, Jesus Himself speaking Aramaic.

The Greek equivalent of Messiah was *Christ.* The word "Christ" does not appear in the King James Version of the Old Testament,

but does appear in the book of Moses from the Pearl of Great Price in four verses (see Moses 6:52, 6:57, 7:50, and 8:24).

The title *Messiah* appears only twice in the Old Testament (see Dan. 9:25 and 9:26) and only once in the Pearl of Great Price (see Moses 7:53). What is important about the terms *Messiah* and *Christ* is the underlying meaning of these titles as "the Anointed"—signifying that Jesus was divinely commissioned of the Father to carry out the work of redemption and atonement on behalf of all mankind. He was foreordained to His supernal mission: "And the Lord said: Whom shall I send? And one answered like unto the Son of Man: Here am I, send me. And another answered and said: Here am I, send me. And the Lord said: I will send the first" (Abr. 3:27; compare Gen. 3:14–15; Job 19:25; 38:1–7; Isa. 25:8–9). Jesus—as the "Messiah" and the "Christ"—is the authorized and empowered agent of the Father with the express calling to carry out the divine mission of saving and exalting mankind in keeping with the eternal principles of truth and spiritual deliverance. Isaiah expresses this divine mission of the "Anointed One" in the following terms:

> The Spirit of the Lord GOD *is* upon me; because the LORD hath anointed me to preach good tidings unto the meek; he hath sent me to bind up the broken-hearted, to proclaim liberty to the captives, and the opening of the prison to *them that are* bound; To proclaim the acceptable year of the LORD, and the day of vengeance of our God; to comfort all that mourn; To appoint unto them that mourn in Zion, to give unto them beauty for ashes, the oil of joy for mourning, the garment of praise for the spirit of heaviness; that they might be called trees of righteousness, the planting of the LORD, that he might be glorified. (Isa. 61:1–3)

The Old Testament confirms the divine authority of Jesus in a variety of additional passages, including this memorable one from Isaiah: "For unto us a child is born, unto us a son is given: and the government shall be upon his shoulder: and his name shall be called Wonderful, Counsellor, The mighty God, The everlasting Father, The Prince of Peace. Of the increase of *his* government and peace *there shall be* no end, upon the throne of David, and upon his kingdom, to order it, and to establish it with judgment and with justice from henceforth even for ever" (Isa. 9:6–7; see also Gen. 49:10; Isa. 10:27; 11:1–9).

Jeremiah also confirms the stature of Jesus as being commissioned (i.e., anointed) of the Father (see Jer. 23:5–8). In addition, Daniel was privileged to see in vision the nobility and divine agency of the Son (see Dan. 7:13–14; compare Zech. 14:4–9).

The qualities of the Messiah/Christ are reflected with clarity in the scriptures. To officiate in this singularly indispensable and lofty capacity as the Anointed One, Jesus must necessarily embody qualities such as being omnipotent, chosen, and mighty to effect change for good. We would expect the prophets of God throughout successive dispensations to have promised and foretold the work and ministry of Jesus in this respect. And such is the case, as the following Old Testament excerpts demonstrate (arranged, in general, according to the chronology of the prophetic utterances):

Triumph over evil—"And I will put enmity between thee and the woman, and between thy seed and her seed; it shall bruise thy head, and thou shalt bruise his heel" (Gen. 3:15). "I shall see him, but not now: I shall behold him, but not nigh: there shall come a Star out of Jacob, and a Sceptre shall rise out of Israel, and shall smite the corners of Moab, and destroy all the children of Sheth" (Num. 24:17).

Enduring reign of the eternal Lawgiver—"The sceptre shall not depart from Judah, nor a lawgiver from between his feet, until Shiloh [i.e., the Messiah] come; and unto him *shall* the gathering of the people *be*" (Gen. 49:10; compare JST, 50:24; Ezek. 21:27).

Omnipotent Shepherd—"But his bow abode in strength, and the arms of his hands were made strong by the hands of the mighty God of Jacob; (from thence *is* the shepherd, the stone of Israel) . . . (Gen. 49:24; compare Jer. 33:14–16).

Symbolism of the sacrificial Lamb of God—"In one house shall it be eaten; thou shalt not carry forth ought of the flesh abroad out of the house; neither shall ye break a bone thereof" (Ex. 12:46; compare Ps. 34:20).

Great prophet to arise—"The LORD thy God will raise up unto thee a Prophet [i.e., Messiah] from the midst of thee, of thy brethren, like unto me; unto him ye shall hearken. . . . I will raise them up a Prophet from among their brethren, like unto thee [Moses], and will put my words in his mouth; and he shall speak unto them all that I shall command him. And it shall come to pass, *that* whosoever will not hearken unto my words which he shall speak in my name, I will require *it* of him" (Deut. 18:15, 18–19).

Heavenly kingdom to prevail over earthly kingdoms—"Yet have I set my king upon my holy hill of Zion. I will declare the decree: the LORD hath said unto me, Thou *art* my Son; this day have I begotten thee. Ask of me, and I shall give *thee* the heathen *for* thine inheritance, and the uttermost parts of the earth *for* thy possession. Thou shalt break them with a rod of iron; thou shalt dash them in pieces like a potter's vessel. Be wise now therefore, O ye kings: be instructed, ye judges of the earth. Serve the LORD with fear, and rejoice with trembling. Kiss the Son, lest he be angry, and ye perish *from* the way, when his wrath is kindled but a little. Blessed *are* all they that put their trust in him" (Ps. 2:6–12; see also Ps. 68:18).

The Son to be crucified—"My God, my God, why hast thou forsaken me? *why art thou* so far from helping me, *and from* the words of my roaring? . . . the assembly of the wicked have inclosed me: they pierced my hands and my feet. . . . They part my garments among them, and cast lots upon my vesture" (Ps. 22:1, 16, 18; compare Ps. 69:8–9, 20–21; Isa. 50:5–9; 53:1–12; see also Zech. 13:6).

Everlasting Priest after the order of Melchizedek—"The LORD said unto my Lord, Sit thou at my right hand, until I make thine enemies thy footstool. The LORD shall send the rod of thy strength out of Zion: rule thou in the midst of thine enemies. Thy people *shall be* willing in the day of thy power, in the beauties of holiness from the womb of the morning: thou hast the dew of thy youth. The LORD hath sworn, and will not repent, Thou *art* a priest for ever after the order of Melchizedek" (Ps. 110:1–4; compare Micah 5:1–3).

Chief Cornerstone—"The stone *which* the builders refused is become the head *stone* of the corner. This is the LORD's doing; it *is* marvellous in our eyes" (Ps. 118:22–23; compare Isa. 28:16).

Virgin birth—"Therefore the Lord himself shall give you a sign; Behold, a virgin shall conceive, and bear a son, and shall call his name Immanuel" (Isa. 7:14).

Prince of Peace—"For unto us a child is born, unto us a son is given: and the government shall be upon his shoulder: and his name shall be called Wonderful, Counsellor, The mighty God, The everlasting Father, The Prince of Peace. Of the increase of *his* government and peace *there shall be* no end, upon the throne of David, and upon his kingdom, to order it, and to establish it with judgment and with justice from henceforth even for ever. The zeal of the LORD of hosts will perform this" (Isa. 9:6–7).

Glorious Sovereign—"And I will clothe him with thy robe, and strengthen him with thy girdle, and I will commit thy government into his hand: and he shall be a father to the inhabitants of Jerusalem, and to the house of Judah. And the key of the house of David will I lay upon his shoulder; so he shall open, and none shall shut; and he shall shut, and none shall open. And I will fasten him *as* a nail in a sure place; and he shall be for a glorious throne to his father's house" (Isa. 22:21–23).

Victory over death—"He will swallow up death in victory; and the Lord GOD will wipe away tears from off all faces; and the rebuke of his people shall he take away from off all the earth: for the LORD hath spoken *it*. And it shall be said in that day, Lo, this *is* our God; we have waited for him, and he will save us: this *is* the LORD; we have waited for him, we will be glad and rejoice in his salvation" (Isa. 25:8–9).

Glory of the Lord to be revealed—"Every valley shall be exalted, and every mountain and hill shall be made low: and the crooked shall be made straight, and the rough places plain: And the glory of the LORD shall be revealed, and all flesh shall see *it* together: for the mouth of the LORD hath spoken *it*" (Isa. 40:4–5).

Means of liberation—"Behold my servant, whom I uphold; mine elect, *in whom* my soul delighteth; I have put my spirit upon him: he shall bring forth judgment to the Gentiles. . . . I the LORD have called thee in righteousness, and will hold thine hand, and will keep thee, and give thee for a covenant of the people, for a light of the Gentiles; To open the blind eyes, to bring out the prisoners from the prison, *and* them that sit in darkness out of the prison house" (Isa. 42:1, 6–7; see also Isa. 55:1–4).

Redeemer—"And the Redeemer shall come to Zion, and unto them that turn from transgression in

Jacob, saith the LORD" (Isa. 59:20; compare Isa. 61:1–3—"the LORD hath anointed me").

Atonement—"Seventy weeks are determined upon thy people and upon thy holy city, to finish the transgression, and to make an end of sins, and to make reconciliation for iniquity, and to bring in everlasting righteousness, and to seal up the vision and prophecy, and to anoint the most Holy. Know therefore and understand, *that* from the going forth of the commandment to restore and to build Jerusalem unto the Messiah the Prince *shall be* seven weeks, and threescore and two weeks: the street shall be built again, and the wall, even in troublous times" (Dan. 9:24–25; compare Dan. 9:26).

Savior—"Yet I *am* the LORD thy God from the land of Egypt, and thou shalt know no god but me: for *there is* no saviour beside me" (Hosea 13:4). "Salvation *is* of the LORD" (Jonah 2:9).

Judge of Glory—"His glory covered the heavens, and the earth was full of his praise. And *his* brightness was as the light; he had horns *coming* out of his hand: and there *was* the hiding of his power. . . . Yet I will rejoice in the LORD, I will joy in the God of my salvation" (Hab. 3:3–4, 18).

Builder of the Temple of the Lord—". . . Thus speaketh the LORD of hosts, saying, Behold the man whose name *is* The BRANCH [i.e., the Messiah]; and he shall grow up out of his place, and he shall build the temple of the LORD: Even he shall build the temple of the LORD; and he shall bear the glory, and shall sit and rule upon his throne; and he shall be a priest upon his throne: and the counsel of peace shall be between them both" (Zech. 6:12–13; see also Zech. 3:8–9).

Appearance in the latter-day temple—"Behold, I will send my messenger, and he shall prepare the way before me: and the Lord, whom ye seek, shall suddenly come to his temple, even the messenger of the covenant, whom ye delight in: behold, he shall come, saith the LORD of hosts" (Mal. 3:1).

Just these few samples of prophetic discourse concerning the divine mission of the Messiah, Jesus Christ, indicate the extraordinarily pervasive presence of the Messianic theme throughout the Old Testament. It is the office, function, and blessings of "the Anointed One" that inform the fabric of sacred revelation preserved by the hand of God through the ages. It is from Jehovah, acting as the agent of the Father, that salvation and redemption flow to those who believe and honor the covenants of the Lord.

Creator

The Unchangeable and Anointed One served as the principal divine agent in laying the foundation of the world through the Creation itself. When God directed by His word that the Creation should proceed (see Gen. 1–2; Moses 2–3; Deut. 4:32), it was through the *Word of God* (Jehovah, Messiah, Christ) that this divine process was initiated and completed: "By the word of the LORD were the heavens made; and all the host of them by the breath of his mouth" (Ps. 33:6). "Thus saith the LORD, thy redeemer, and he that formed thee from the womb, I *am* the LORD that maketh all *things*; that stretcheth forth the heavens alone; that spreadeth abroad the earth by myself; . . . " (Isa. 44:24). "That they may see, and know, and consider, and understand together, that the hand of the LORD hath done this [i.e. governed and sustained the vitality of nature], and the Holy One of Israel hath created it" (Isa. 41:20).

Thus the Word of God was Creation incarnate. John the Apostle rendered this verity using the following celebrated language: "In the beginning was the Word, and the Word was with God, and the Word was God. The same was in the beginning with God. All things were made by him; and without him was not any thing made that was made. In him was life; and the life was the light of men. And the light shineth in darkness; and the darkness comprehended it not" (John 1:1–5).

What greater symbolic representation could there be of the office and function of the Creator and Life-Giver than the image of being the "Light of the World"? "And God said, Let there be light: and there was light. And God saw the light, that *it was* good: and God divided the light from the darkness" (Gen. 1:3–4; see also Moses 2:3–4). Isaiah counseled: "O house of Jacob, come ye, and let us walk in the light of the LORD" (Isa. 2:5; see also Isa. 9:2–7), and then looked beyond the objects of the Creation to assert: "The sun shall be no more thy light by day; neither for brightness shall the moon give light unto thee: but the LORD shall be unto thee an everlasting light, and thy God thy glory" (Isa. 60:19; see also Micah 7:8–9).

In modern scripture this process of light-giving (enlightenment) is further elucidated: "And the light which shineth, which giveth you light, is through him who enlighteneth your eyes, which is the same light that quickeneth your understandings; Which light proceedeth forth from the presence of God to fill the immensity of space— The light which is in all things, which giveth life to all things, which is the law by which all things are governed, even the power of God who sitteth upon his throne, who is in the bosom of eternity, who is in the midst of all things" (D&C 88:11–13).

In terms of spiritual illumination, this light of Christ has profound implications for the covenant relationship that we have with God: "For the word of the Lord is truth, and whatsoever is truth is light, and whatsoever is light is Spirit, even the Spirit of Jesus Christ. And the Spirit giveth light to every man that cometh into the world; and the Spirit enlighteneth every man through the world, that hearkeneth to the voice of the Spirit. And every one that hearkeneth to the voice of the Spirit cometh unto God, even the Father. And the Father teacheth him of the covenant which he has renewed and confirmed upon you, which is confirmed upon you for your sakes, and not for your sakes only, but for the sake of the whole world" (D&C 84:45–48).

Many additional references from the Old Testament confirm and expand on the mission of the Word of God as Creator. For example, the Lord asked Job, in his adversity: "Where wast thou when I laid the foundations of the earth? declare, if thou hast understanding. Who hath laid the measures thereof, if thou knowest? or who hath stretched the line upon it? Whereupon are the foundations thereof fastened? or who laid the corner stone thereof; When the morning stars sang together, and all the sons of God shouted for joy?" (Job 38:4–7; see also Job 10:8–12; 26:12–13). Clearly the one most capable of understanding our plight as mortals and rendering succor and solace concerning our privation and suffering is the Lord Himself, the Creator of heaven and earth: "And Hezekiah prayed before the LORD, and said, O LORD God of Israel, which dwellest *between* the cherubims, thou art the God, *even* thou alone, of all the kingdoms of the earth: thou hast made heaven and earth" (2 Kings 19:15).

Isaiah speaks in prophetic terms of the role of the Son of God in the Creation: "To whom then will ye liken me, or shall I be equal? saith the Holy One. Lift up your eyes on high, and behold who hath created these *things*, that bringeth out their host by number: he calleth them all by names by the greatness of his might, for that *he is* strong in power; not one faileth. Why sayest thou, O Jacob, and speakest, O Israel, My way is hid from the LORD, and my judgment is passed over from my God? Hast thou not known? hast thou not heard, *that* the everlasting God, the LORD, the Creator of the ends of the earth, fainteth not, neither is weary? *there is* no searching of his understanding" (Isa. 40:25–28).

Similarly, Jeremiah proclaims through the voice of inspiration the mighty process of the Creation at the hands of the Son of God: "He hath made the earth by his power, he hath established the world by his wisdom, and hath stretched out the heaven by his understanding. When he uttereth *his* voice, *there is* a multitude of waters in the heavens; and he causeth the vapours to ascend from the ends of the earth: he maketh lightnings with rain, and bringeth forth the wind out of his treasures" (Jer. 51:15–16). The identity of the Creator is made clear by the prophet Amos: "For, lo, he that formeth the mountains, and createth the wind, and declareth unto man what *is* his thought, that maketh the morning darkness, and treadeth upon the high places of the earth, The LORD [i.e., Jehovah], The God of hosts, *is* his name" (Amos 4:13).

The qualities of the Creator are unfolded in the sacred word. As Creator, Jehovah embodies specific qualities of office and character, including these: life-giving, creative, productive, and loyal agent of God. These are among the very qualities that go to define discipleship for the faithful who are committed to follow in the footsteps of the Savior by emulating His exemplary mode of living. Should we not also seek to sustain and nurture life, be creative and productive in wholesome and uplifting ways, and display loyalty and obedience to God in all our dealings?

Using these same qualities, the Son of God governed and governs the vital process of generating and preserving life itself—beginning with the Creation and continuing with the unfolding of the process of dynamic growth of all living things pertaining to this world and all other worlds (see Moses 1:33). The Gatekeeper of the eternal realm (see 2 Ne. 9:41) is also the Gatekeeper of life itself—the Curator of the principles and processes of enlivenment and growth for all creation. Jehovah oversees and administers the transition between the potential and the real, between the spiritual creation (as described in Moses 3:5) and the actual, emerging (natural) creation.

The Greeks had a word for this magnificent process of emergence—*entelechy,* meaning "completion" or the "realization of the essence of a thing." In this sense, the predominant quality of Jesus Christ as Creator is "One who completes," or One who—through faith, obedience, power, and divine light—generates and sustains life unto salvation. What an extraordinary being is this Creator,

even Jehovah the Messiah and Christ, to generate as the Word of God all the conditions and processes by which we, as sons and daughters of God, can enjoy mortal life and look forward with hope, faith, and covenant valor to the time when we shall inherit immortality and eternal life in the mansions of the Father and the Son. In that joyous hour, the faithful shall meet once again the very Creator of our being, look upon His face with rapture, and speak His name in love: "And he shall be called Jesus Christ, the Son of God, the Father of heaven and earth, the Creator of all things from the beginning" (Mosiah 3:8).

Emmanuel (Immanuel)

One of the greatest of all the miracles of the gospel is the condescension of God, that the great Jehovah—the "Unchangeable One," the "Anointed One" (being Messiah and Christ), even the grand Creator of heaven and earth—should deem it to be His essential mission to do the will of the Father and come among mortals to bring to pass for all mankind the effectual conditions of faith, salvation, and redemption. In this capacity, His office and title are known as *Emmanuel* (also rendered *Immanuel*)—that is, "God Among Us." As the "Only Begotten" of the Father, He accepted His mortal mission to serve as the Messenger of the covenant and experienced birth, grew to manhood, completed His ministry as the Good Shepherd, and suffered betrayal and death as the "author of eternal salvation" (Heb. 5:8–9).

The chronicle of Emmanuel's mortal experience is woven through prophetic utterance into the fabric of the Old Testament. The Psalmist foresaw the work of the mortal Messiah: "The LORD *is* high above all nations, *and* his glory above the heavens. Who *is* like unto the LORD our God, who dwelleth on high, Who humbleth *himself* to behold *the things that are* in heaven, and in the earth!" (Ps. 113:4–6). Isaiah envisioned the infinite humility of the Son in submitting Himself willingly to His detractors: "The Lord GOD hath opened mine ear, and I was not rebellious, neither turned away back. I gave my back to the smiters, and my cheeks to them that plucked off the hair: I hid not my face from shame and spitting" (Isa. 50:5–6). Continuing his inspired pronouncement, Isaiah articulates with consummate and unforgettable eloquence the pains of the Lord in doing the will of the Father upon the earth in Isaiah 53:1–12.

The pathway of the Christ into mortality via the lineage of Abraham (the Davidic descent) is abundantly accounted for in the pages of the sacred record: "I have made a covenant with my chosen, I have sworn unto David my servant, Thy seed will I establish for ever, and build up thy throne to all generations" (Ps. 89:3–4; see also 1 Sam. 16:1; 17:12; 2 Sam. 7:12–17; Ps. 132:11–18; Isa. 9:6–7; 11:1–10; Jer. 23:5–6; 33:14–16; Zech. 3:8–9; 6:10–15; 12:7–12).

The earthly mission of the Lord is likewise a central theme throughout the Old Testament record (as we have already seen in the previous summary of similar prophecies about the Savior):

Great Prophet to come—"I will raise them up a Prophet from among their brethren, like unto thee, and will put my words in his mouth; and he shall speak unto them all that I shall command him" (Deut. 18:18).

Child of God—"Therefore the Lord himself shall give you a sign; Behold, a virgin shall conceive, and bear a son, and shall call his name Immanuel" (Isa. 7:14). "For unto us a child is born, unto us a son is given: and the government shall be upon his shoulder: and his name shall be called Wonderful, Counsellor, The mighty God, The everlasting Father, The Prince of Peace" (Isa. 9:6; see also Micah 5:2).

Victory over death—"He will swallow up death in victory; and the Lord GOD will wipe away tears from off all faces; and the rebuke of his people shall he take away from off all the earth: for the LORD hath spoken *it*" (Isa. 25:8).

Messenger of God—"The Spirit of the Lord GOD *is* upon me; because the LORD hath anointed me to preach good tidings unto the meek; he hath sent me to bind up the brokenhearted, to proclaim liberty to the captives, and the opening of the prison to *them that are* bound; . . ." Isa. 61:1). "The grass withereth, the flower fadeth: but the word of our God shall stand for ever" (Isa. 40:8).

Betrayal—"and thou hast brought me into the dust of death. For dogs have compassed me: the assembly of the wicked have inclosed me: they pierced my hands and my feet. I may tell all my bones: they look *and* stare upon me. They part my garments among them, and cast lots upon my vesture" (Ps. 22:15–18).

Sufferings—"And *one* shall say unto him, What *are* these wounds in thine hands? Then he shall answer, *Those* with which I was wounded *in* the house of my friends" (Zech. 13:6).

Enoch, too, saw in vision the entry of the Lord into mortality: "And behold, Enoch saw the day of the coming of the Son of Man, even in the flesh; and his soul rejoiced, saying: The Righteous is lifted up, and the Lamb is slain from the foundation of the world; and through faith I am in the bosom of the Father, and behold, Zion is with me" (Moses 7:47).

The all-encompassing view of the condescension of the Only Begotten is that of the Good Shepherd who tends His flocks personally as "the shepherd, the stone of Israel" (Gen. 49:24). This role is most memorably expressed in the 23rd Psalm: "The LORD *is* my shepherd; I shall not want" (verse 1), but is also encapsulated in several other prophetic passages of great beauty and tenderness: "Give ear, O Shepherd of Israel, thou that leadest Joseph like a flock; thou that dwellest *between* the cherubims, shine forth. Before Ephraim and Benjamin and Manasseh stir up thy strength, and come *and* save us. Turn us again, O God, and cause thy face to shine; and we shall be saved" (Ps. 80:1–3); "For he *is* our God; and we *are* the people of his pasture, and the sheep of his hand. To day if ye will hear his voice . . ." (Ps. 95:7; see also Zech. 13:7).

Perhaps the most detailed view of the Good Shepherd Emmanuel is given in Ezekiel:

For thus saith the Lord GOD; Behold, I, *even* I, will both search my sheep, and seek them out.

As a shepherd seeketh out his flock in the day that he is among his sheep *that are* scattered; so will I seek out my sheep,

and will deliver them out of all places where they have been scattered in the cloudy and dark day.

And I will bring them out from the people, and gather them from the countries, and will bring them to their own land, and feed them upon the mountains of Israel by the rivers, and in all the inhabited places of the country.

I will feed them in a good pasture, and upon the high mountains of Israel shall their fold be: there shall they lie in a good fold, and *in* a fat pasture shall they feed upon the mountains of Israel.

I will feed my flock, and I will cause them to lie down, saith the Lord GOD.

I will seek that which was lost, and bring again that which was driven away, and will bind up *that which was* broken, and will strengthen that which was sick: but I will destroy the fat and the strong; I will feed them with judgment.

And *as for* you, O my flock, thus saith the Lord GOD; Behold, I judge between cattle and cattle, between the rams and the he goats.

Seemeth it a small thing unto you to have eaten up the good pasture, but ye must tread down with your feet the residue of your pastures? and to have drunk of the deep waters, but ye must foul the residue with your feet?

And *as for* my flock, they eat that which ye have trodden with your feet; and they drink that which ye have fouled with your feet. (Ezek. 34:11–19)

The qualities of Emmanuel (or Immanuel) are made specific in the scriptural record. The Good Shepherd, by nature of His divine calling and commission, radiates the qualities of being humble, patient, nurturing, personal (focused on the needs of the individual in lovingkindness), and exhibiting the characteristics of the longsuffering, noble counselor. Are these not the very qualities that the followers of Christ should aspire to emulate if they are to fulfill the measure of their spiritual potential?

The scriptures illustrate abundantly the manner in which the Lord works one-on-one, in mercy and kindness, with His faithful servants. According to the Old Testament account, the Lord appeared *in person* to Abraham (see Gen. 12:7), Jacob (see Gen. 32:30), Moses (see Ex. 32:30–31; Num. 12:6–8; Deut. 5:24; Deut. 34:10), Isaiah (see Isa. 6:1), Ezekiel (see Ezek. 1:26–28), Amos (see Amos 9:1), and no doubt many other prophets.

The extraordinary record in the Pearl of Great Price concerning Moses' interaction with the Lord on the mount confirms the personal nature of God's interaction with his servants (see Moses 1:1–6). It was during the course of this personal dialogue that the Lord shared with Moses the true nature of His divine mission: "For behold, this is my work and my glory—to bring to pass the immortality and eternal life of man" (Moses 1:39.) An inherent part of this mission is to prepare the sons and daughters of God to come into His presence once again and partake of His glory as heirs to all the celestial blessings.

The Psalmist reminds us to cultivate an openness to the Lord's invitation to achieve a personal relationship with Him: "O come, let us worship and bow down: let us kneel before the LORD our maker. For he *is* our God; and we *are* the people of his pasture, and the sheep of his hand. To day if ye will hear his voice, Harden not your heart, as in the provocation, *and* as *in* the day of temptation in the wilderness: When your fathers tempted me, proved me, and saw my work. Forty years long was I grieved with *this* generation, and said, It *is* a people that do err in their heart, and they have not known my ways: Unto whom I sware in my wrath that they should not enter into my rest" (Ps. 95:6–11).

This provocation (which Paul cites also in Heb. 3:7–19) occurred when the Israelites, despite the impassioned exhortations of Moses, refused to rise to the occasion of preparing to meet the Lord their God *personally* (see Num. 14:1–23), as He had commanded them. Thus He removed from among them the higher priesthood and denied them the privilege of entering into His rest and partaking of the joys of the Promised Land.

In the Book of Mormon, both Jacob and Alma implore the people to avoid a second provocation of this kind (see Jacob 1:7; Alma 12:36). In latter-day scripture, the Prophet Joseph Smith reemphasizes the counsel of the Lord that all should seek a personal relationship with Him in order to enjoy the blessings of eternity: "And seek the face of the Lord always, that in patience ye may possess your souls, and ye shall have eternal life" (D&C 101:38). Thus we are to honor in all diligence the commandment to follow the Good Shepherd in humility and patience, cultivating with Him personally an enduring and liberating relationship as between a faithful and grateful son or daughter and a loving father—even the Father of our eternal salvation.

Jesus

The name *Jesus* is the Greek form of the name *Joshua* or *Jeshua*, meaning "God is Help" (or "Jehovah is Help"), or, in other words, "Savior." The name implies the sacred office of Redeemer, Lamb of Life, Bread of Life, the One who brings about the Atonement through the sacrificial crucifixion, the One who ushers in the process of the resurrection, the One who is therefore, in all respects, the Life of the World. In this capacity as Savior, the Son of God—even Jehovah, Messiah, Christ, Creator, Emmanuel—is the means for rescuing all mankind from the effects of temporal death and enabling the faithful and obedient to escape the clutches of the second (or spiritual) death through compliance with the principles and ordinances of the gospel.

The Old Testament is a vibrant and compelling witness of the office of Savior and Redeemer as consummated in the Crucifixion and Resurrection of Jesus: The Psalmist anticipated the express words of the sacrificial Lamb of God—"My God, my God, why hast thou forsaken me?" (Ps. 22:1)—and discerned in prophetic vision the process of the crucifixion: "the assembly of the wicked have inclosed me: they pierced my hands and my feet. I may tell all my bones: they look *and* stare upon me. They part my garments among them, and cast lots upon my vesture. But be not thou far from me, O LORD: O my strength, haste thee to help me" (Ps. 22:16–19).

Isaiah foresaw in great detail the travail of the Lord on the cross:

But he *was* wounded for our transgressions, *he was* bruised for our iniquities: the chastisement of our peace *was* upon him; and with his stripes we are healed.

All we like sheep have gone astray; we have turned every one to his own way; and the LORD hath laid on him the iniquity of us all.

He was oppressed, and he was afflicted, yet he opened not his mouth: he is brought as a lamb to the slaughter, and as a sheep before her shearers is dumb, so he openeth not his mouth.

He was taken from prison and from judgment: and who shall declare his generation? for he was cut off out of the land of the living: for the transgression of my people was he stricken.

And he made his grave with the wicked, and with the rich in his death; because he had done no violence, neither *was any* deceit in his mouth.

Yet it pleased the LORD to bruise him; he hath put *him* to grief: when thou shalt make his soul an offering for sin, he shall see *his* seed, he shall prolong *his* days, and the pleasure of the LORD shall prosper in his hand.

He shall see of the travail of his soul, *and* shall be satisfied: by his knowledge shall my righteous servant justify many; for he shall bear their iniquities.

Therefore will I divide him *a portion* with the great, and he shall divide the spoil with the strong; because he hath poured out his soul unto death: and he was numbered with the transgressors; and he bare the sin of many, and made intercession for the transgressors. (Isa. 53:5–12)

Likewise, Zechariah was blessed to view spiritually the crucifixion and Atonement from the perspective of the Savior, saying: "And I will pour upon the house of David, and upon the inhabitants of Jerusalem, the spirit of grace and of supplications: and they shall look upon me whom they have pierced, and they shall mourn for him, as one mourneth for *his* only *son*, and shall be in bitterness for him, as one that is in bitterness for *his* firstborn" (Zech. 12:10). We have already reviewed the passage from the same prophet that anticipates the tender discourse concerning the wounds of the crucified and resurrected Lord: "And *one* shall say unto him, What *are* these wounds in thine hands? Then he shall answer, *Those* with which I was wounded *in* the house of my friends" (Zech. 13:6; see also Dan. 9:26–27).

The redeeming death of the Savior secured the faith and hope of His followers in all ages: "And thus he shall bring salvation to all those who shall believe on his name; this being the intent of this last sacrifice, to bring about the bowels of mercy, which overpowereth justice, and bringeth about means unto men that they may have faith unto repentance. And thus mercy can satisfy the demands of justice, and encircles them in the arms of safety, while he that exercises no faith unto repentance is exposed to the whole law of the demands of justice; therefore only unto him that has faith unto repentance is brought about the great and eternal plan of redemption" (Alma 34:15–16).

A number of Old Testament scriptures echo this same principle (see Prov. 14:32; Isa. 25:8; 53:7, 9; Hosea 13:14;

Jonah 1:17). Compare this with the words of the Savior concerning the sign of the prophet Jonah as a foreshadowing of His own death and Resurrection: "Then certain of the scribes and of the Pharisees answered, saying, Master, we would see a sign from thee. But he answered and said unto them, An evil and adulterous generation seeketh after a sign; and there shall no sign be given to it, but the sign of the prophet Jonas: For as Jonas was three days and three nights in the whale's belly; so shall the Son of man be three days and three nights in the heart of the earth" (Matt. 12:38–40; see also Matt. 16:4; Luke 11:29–30)

The concept of Jesus as the Lamb of God was made a regular part of the worship of ancient Israel through the ritual sacrifice of a lamb "without blemish" (Ex. 12:5)—one per household—during the Passover (see Ex. 12:13–14). Isaiah celebrated the symbolism of the Lamb of God with these words: "he is brought as a lamb to the slaughter, and as a sheep before her shearers is dumb, so he openeth not his mouth. . . . when thou shalt make his soul an offering for sin, he shall see *his* seed, he shall prolong *his* days, and the pleasure of the LORD shall prosper in his hand" (Isa. 53:7, 10).

The glorious Atonement and Resurrection of the Savior was the crowning triumph of His ministry. In Hannah's song of praise we hear: "The LORD killeth, and maketh alive: he bringeth down to the grave, and bringeth up" (1 Sam. 2:6). Job extols the divine gift of the restoration of life: "And *though* after my skin *worms* destroy this *body*, yet in my flesh shall I see God: Whom I shall see for myself, and mine eyes shall behold, and not another; *though* my reins be consumed within me" (Job 19:26–27). The Psalmist foresees the eventual purification and enlivenment of the soul: "Therefore my heart is glad, and my glory rejoiceth: my flesh also shall rest in hope. For thou wilt not leave my soul in hell; neither wilt thou suffer thine Holy One to see corruption" (Ps. 16:9–10). Isaiah prophesies of the Lord's conquest over death: "He will swallow up death in victory; and the Lord GOD will wipe away tears from off all faces; and the rebuke of his people shall he take away from off all the earth: for the LORD hath spoken *it*" (Isa. 25:8). And again, "Thy dead *men* shall live, *together with* my dead body shall they arise. Awake and sing, ye that dwell in dust: for thy dew *is as* the dew of herbs, and the earth shall cast out the dead" (Isa. 26:19). Hosea likewise celebrates the Savior's eventual supremacy over the forces of destruction: "I will ransom them from the power of the grave; I will redeem them from death: O death, I will be thy plagues; O grave, I will be thy destruction: repentance shall be hid from mine eyes" (Hosea 13:14).

Out of the shadowy abyss of divine suffering emerged triumphant the glory of the Redemption and the Atonement. The Old Testament account repeatedly celebrates this eternal victory. "For the life of the flesh *is* in the blood: and I have given it to you upon the altar to make an atonement for your souls: for it *is* the blood *that* maketh an atonement for the soul" (Lev. 17:11). Said Job: "For I know *that* my redeemer liveth, and *that* he shall stand at the latter *day* upon the earth: . . ." (Job 19:25). Isaiah provides this prophetic comfort: "Fear not, thou worm Jacob, *and* ye men of Israel; I will help thee, saith the LORD, and thy redeemer, the Holy One of Israel" (Isa. 41:14). And further: "he hath poured out his soul unto death: and he was numbered with the transgressors; and he bare the sin of many, and made intercession for the transgressors" (Isa. 53:12).

Finally, Zechariah enjoins us to raise anthems of praise for the Lord of Salvation: "Rejoice greatly, O daughter of Zion; shout, O daughter of Jerusalem: behold, thy King cometh unto thee: he *is* just, and having salvation; lowly, and riding upon an ass, and upon a colt the foal of an ass. And I will cut off the chariot from Ephraim, and the horse from Jerusalem, and the battle bow shall be cut off: and he shall speak peace unto the heathen: and his dominion *shall be* from sea *even* to sea, and from the river *even* to the ends of the earth. As for thee also, by the blood of thy covenant I have sent forth thy prisoners out of the pit wherein *is* no water" (Zech. 9:9–11). Thus the Old Testament prophets expressed their inspired witness of the coming work of the Redeemer of mankind.

In the same exultant spirit, the ancient prophets confirmed Jesus as the Savior who would at a future time be born into the world (see Ex. 15:2; Ps. 27:1; Isa. 43:3, 11; 43:25; 45:15; Joel 2:23, 26–27, 32).

The qualities of Jesus emerge sublime from the canon. Jesus the Atoning One is the singular most potent prototype of the set of qualities that belong to "Saviorhood": loving, obedient, redeeming, perfect, spotless. He is so loving that He verily weeps when we fall short of our potential: "Wherefore, he suffereth for their sins; inasmuch as they will repent in the day that my Chosen shall return unto me, and until that day they shall be in torment; Wherefore, for this shall the heavens weep, yea, and all the workmanship of mine hands" (Moses 7:39–40). At the same time, He rejoices when we repent and follow in His footsteps: "For, behold, the Lord your Redeemer suffered death in the flesh; wherefore he suffered the pain of all men, that all men might repent and come unto him. And he hath risen again from the dead, that he might bring all men unto him, on conditions of repentance. And how great is his joy in the soul that repenteth!" (D&C 18:11–13).

Should we not therefore all strive to cultivate within ourselves these same qualities anticipated by the prophets of old and fulfilled in the mission of the Redeemer? Should we not ponder the patterns of saving grace reflected in the scriptures concerning the Savior and attempt to inculcate them into our daily lives with an attitude of thanksgiving and humble obedience?

King

Jehovah, the "Unchangeable One"—the First Born of Elohim—was anointed in the pre-mortal realm as Messiah and Christ to lay the foundation of the world through the Creation and serve as the Author of eternal salvation by coming to live among mortals (even "Emmanuel"), in obedience to the will of the Father, for the purpose of completing His atoning mission as Jesus ("Jehovah is Help"), thus becoming the Savior to all the world. In the final chapter of the history of this world, Jesus Christ will return in glory as King, Judge, Law-Giver, Mediator, Advocate, and Prince of Peace to usher in the Millennial Reign and take His place as the covenant Father of all the righteous and redeemed.

With great clarity, the Old Testament account confirms this divine design of consummation and the ultimate royal ascension of the Son to the throne of glory. The return of the Redeemer at the Second Coming is anticipated by the voices of many prophets:

- Job—"For I know *that* my redeemer liveth, and *that* he shall stand at the latter *day* upon the earth: . . ." (Job 19:25).
- David—"Lift up your heads, O ye gates; and be ye lift up, ye everlasting doors; and the King of glory shall come in. Who *is* this King of glory? The LORD strong and mighty, the LORD mighty in battle. Lift up your heads, O ye gates; even lift *them* up, ye everlasting doors; and the King of glory shall come in. Who is this King of glory? The LORD of hosts, he *is* the King of glory. Selah" (Ps. 24:7–10). And further: "When the LORD shall build up Zion, he shall appear in his glory" (Ps. 102:16).
- Isaiah—"The voice of him that crieth in the wilderness, Prepare ye the way of the LORD, make straight in the desert a highway for our God. Every valley shall be exalted, and every mountain and hill shall be made low: and the crooked shall be made straight, and the rough places plain: And the glory of the LORD shall be revealed, and all flesh shall see *it* together: for the mouth of the LORD hath spoken *it*" (Isa. 40:3–5). "How beautiful upon the mountains are the feet of him that bringeth good tidings, that publisheth peace; that bringeth good tidings of good, that publisheth salvation; that saith unto Zion, Thy God reigneth! Thy watchmen shall lift up the voice; with the voice together shall they sing: for they shall see eye to eye, when the LORD shall bring again Zion. Break forth into joy, sing together, ye waste places of Jerusalem: for the LORD hath comforted his people, he hath redeemed Jerusalem. The LORD hath made bare his holy arm in the eyes of all the nations; and all the ends of the earth shall see the salvation of our God" (Isa. 52:7–10).
- Ezekiel—"I will overturn, overturn, overturn, it [iniquity]: and it shall be no *more*, until he come whose right it is; and I will give it *him*" (Ezek. 21:27).
- Daniel—"I saw in the night visions, and, behold, *one* like the Son of man came with the clouds of heaven, and came to the Ancient of days, and they brought him near before him" (Dan. 7:13).
- Joel—"The sun and the moon shall be darkened, and the stars shall withdraw their shining. The LORD also shall roar out of Zion, and utter his voice from Jerusalem; and the heavens and the earth shall shake: but the LORD *will be* the hope of his people, and the strength of the children of Israel. So shall ye know that I *am* the LORD your God dwelling in Zion, my holy mountain: then shall Jerusalem be holy, and there shall no strangers pass through her any more" (Joel 3:15–17).
- Micah—"For, behold, the LORD cometh forth out of his place, and will come down, and tread upon the high places of the earth. And the mountains shall be molten under him, and the valleys shall be cleft, as wax before the fire, *and as the wa*ters *that are* poured down a steep place" (Micah 1:3–4).
- Haggai—"For thus saith the LORD of hosts; Yet once, it *is* a little while, and I will shake the heavens, and the earth, and the sea, and the dry *land*; And I will shake all nations, and the desire of all nations shall come: and I will fill this house with glory, saith the LORD of hosts" (Haggai 2:6–7).
- Zechariah—"And it shall come to pass in that day, *that* I will seek to destroy all the nations that come against Jerusalem. And I will pour upon the house of David, and upon the inhabitants of Jerusalem, the spirit of grace and of supplications: and they shall look upon me whom they have pierced, and they shall mourn for him, as one mourneth for *his* only *son*, and shall be in bitterness for him, as one that is in bitterness for *his* firstborn" (Zechariah 12:9–10). "And his feet shall stand in that day upon the mount of Olives, which *is* before Jerusalem on the east, and the mount of Olives shall cleave in the midst thereof toward the east and toward the west, *and there shall be* a very great valley; and half of the mountain shall remove toward the north, and half of it toward the south. . . . And it shall be in that day, *that* living waters shall go out from Jerusalem; half of them toward the former sea, and half of them toward the hinder sea: in summer and in winter shall it be. And the LORD shall be king over all the earth: in that day shall there be one LORD, and his name one" (Zech. 14:4, 8–9).
- Malachi—"Behold, I will send my messenger, and he shall prepare the way before me: and the Lord, whom ye seek, shall suddenly come to his temple, even the messenger of the covenant, whom ye delight in: behold, he shall come, saith the LORD of hosts. But who may abide the day of his coming? and who shall stand when he appeareth? for he *is* like a refiner's fire, and like fullers' soap: And he shall sit *as* a refiner and purifier of silver: and he shall purify the sons of Levi, and purge them as gold and silver, that they may offer unto the LORD an offering in righteousness" (Malachi 3:1–3).

The Millennial Reign of the Lord is predicted with prophetic certainty throughout the ancient record and described as having the following characteristics:

Everlasting—"I will sing of the mercies of the LORD for ever: with my mouth will I make known thy faithfulness to all generations. For I have said, Mercy shall be built up for ever: thy faithfulness shalt thou establish in the very heavens. I have made a covenant with my chosen, I have sworn unto David my servant, Thy seed will I establish for ever, and build up thy throne to all generations. Selah" (Ps. 89:1–4).

Theocratic—"For unto us a child is born, unto us a son is given: and the government shall be upon his shoulder: and his name shall be called Wonderful, Counsellor, The mighty God, The everlasting Father, The Prince of Peace. Of the increase of *his* government and peace *there shall be* no end, upon the throne of David, and upon his kingdom, to order it, and to establish it with judgment and with justice from henceforth even for ever. The zeal of the LORD of hosts will perform this" (Isa. 9:6–7).

Merciful—"And in mercy shall the throne be established: and he shall sit upon it in truth in the tabernacle of David, judging, and seeking judgment, and hasting righteousness" (Isa. 16:5).

Righteous—"Behold, the days come, saith the LORD, that I will raise unto David a righteous Branch, and a King shall reign and prosper, and shall execute judgment and justice in the earth. In his days Judah shall be saved, and Israel shall dwell safely: and this *is* his name whereby he shall be called, THE LORD OUR RIGHTEOUSNESS" (Jer. 23:5–6).

All-Consuming—"And in the days of these kings shall the God of heaven set up a kingdom, which shall never be destroyed: and the kingdom shall not be left to other people, *but* it shall break in pieces and consume all these kingdoms, and it shall stand for ever" (Dan. 2:44).

Joyful—"Sing and rejoice, O daughter of Zion: for, lo, I come, and I will dwell in the midst of thee, saith the LORD. And many nations shall be joined to the LORD in that day, and shall be my people: and I will dwell in the midst of thee, and thou shalt know that the LORD of hosts hath sent me unto thee. And the LORD shall inherit Judah his portion in the holy land, and shall choose Jerusalem again. Be silent, O all flesh, before the LORD: for he is raised up out of his holy habitation" (Zech. 2:10–13).

Glorious—"Who is this King of glory? The LORD of hosts, he *is* the King of glory. Selah" (Ps. 24:10). "And the glory of the LORD shall be revealed, and all flesh shall see *it* together: for the mouth of the LORD hath spoken *it*" (Isa. 40:5).

The ushering in of the millennial reign is a time of universal judgment, as the scriptural record confirms: "The adversaries of the LORD shall be broken to pieces; out of heaven shall he thunder upon them: the LORD shall judge the ends of the earth; and he shall give strength unto his king, and exalt the horn of his anointed" (1 Sam. 2:10). "And he shall judge the world in righteousness, he shall minister judgment to the people in uprightness" (Ps. 9:8). "And he shall not judge after the sight of his eyes, neither reprove after the hearing of his ears: But with righteousness shall he judge the poor, and reprove with equity for the meek of the earth: and he shall smite the earth with the rod of his mouth, and with the breath of his lips shall he slay the wicked" (Isa. 11:3–4). All the prophets down through the ages have spoken of the final judgment and the responsibility of man—according to his God-given agency and stewardship—to account for his every thought and deed. The Savior Himself declared to the Nephites: "And it shall come to pass, that whoso repenteth and is baptized in my name shall be filled; and if he endureth to the end, behold, him will I hold guiltless before my Father at that day when I shall stand to judge the world. And he that endureth not unto the end, the same is he that is also hewn down and cast into the fire, from whence they can no more return, because of the justice of the Father" (3 Ne. 27:16–17).

The qualities of the King unfold in power from the sacred canon. As presented in the scriptural account of the millennial reign, the Great Jehovah will consummate the final judgment and disposition of mankind by being just, merciful, righteous, full of grace, holy, and glorious. These are the qualities of His royal office. Alma provides perhaps the most compelling summary of the implementation of these qualities by the Savior as part of the plan of salvation: "And thus he shall bring salvation to all those who shall believe on his name; this being the intent of this last sacrifice, to bring about the bowels of mercy, which overpowereth justice, and bringeth about means unto men that they may have faith unto repentance. And thus mercy can satisfy the demands of justice, and encircles them in the arms of safety, while he that exercises no faith unto repentance is exposed to the whole law of the demands of justice; therefore only unto him that has faith unto repentance is brought about the great and eternal plan of redemption" (Alma 34:15–16).

Is it not incumbent upon all followers of Christ to emulate His example by aspiring to the same qualities He displays in perfected form: being just, merciful, righteous, full of grace, holy, and glorious? Surely our joy and peace in this world and the world to come will depend on the degree to which we can cultivate these qualities within our character, together with all others that pertain to the mission of the Lord as our eternal exemplar.

Example—How to Become More Like Jesus Christ

Each of us is the overlay of priceless examples bequeathed us by the heroes of our lives. The noble, the admirable, the praiseworthy that we see in the actions of others resonates within us with more power than any concept lesson. Example is, indeed, the greatest of teachers.

Whom do you admire for such qualities as courage, honesty, loyalty, honor, virtue, patience, resilience, and charity? For each such ideal, there is some person who will enter your mind as an exemplar, someone whose pattern of living you respect and appreciate with a grateful heart. It might be a noble ancestor of your family line; it might be a valiant servant of God now or in earlier times; it might be a loving family member or charitable neighbor; it might be a person of note in the world, or someone transcending unscalable ordeals of suffering and pain—with a smile. Or a little child who reminds you of innocence and purity. To all such we owe a debt of gratitude for who they are and what they stand for.

The ultimate example of examples—the prototype of the practice of observing and then emulating—is fully embraced in the Savior's invitation: "Come, follow me" (Luke 18:22). He is the pattern for our lives—the paragon of exemplary being and doing. "Therefore, what manner of men ought ye to be?" He asked. "Verily I say unto you, even as I am" (3 Ne. 27:27). For this archetype of how we are to be we are eternally thankful, for it is He alone who "bringeth about means unto men that they may have faith unto repentance," (Alma 34:15), that they might become perfect even as the Father and Son are perfect (see Matt. 5:48; 3 Ne. 12:48).

Along our pathway of becoming more like the Savior we pass in reverence the milestones placed there, one after the other, to honor our heroes—the faithful, the diligent, the exemplary. This is the mental landscape of our mortal journey—the epic canvas of our ideals that we silently and continually paint as a backdrop to who we are and who we aspire to become. Thank God for cherished examples all around us, most especially for the immortal example of the Savior, the Redeemer, the Son of God.

Without these examples, where would we be? Extinguish them one by one, and the light of our life would vanish into the darkness. But keep them aflame in our hearts, and we sustain the beacon of our hope and the illumination of our dream to become all that we are destined to become. Thanks be to all of those who serve as living examples of the more perfect way.

And if, in some small manner, we can be accounted worthy as a fitting example for others to follow, then let us humbly thank our Father in Heaven that He has seen fit to touch us with His love, enough to light our inner candle for the good of others.

APPENDIX P
JOSHUA

Joshua (meaning: God is help), son of Nun, was the one chosen to soldier on with the leadership of the House of Israel following the days of Moses. Of him it was said, "And Joshua the son of Nun was full of the spirit of wisdom; for Moses had laid his hands upon him: and the children of Israel hearkened unto him, and did as the LORD commanded Moses" (Deut. 34:9).

To the adults of the host of Israel following the forty-year sojourn in the wilderness, the Lord declared: "Doubtless ye shall not come into the land, *concerning* which I sware to make you dwell therein, save Caleb the son of Jephunneh, and Joshua the son of Nun" (Num. 14:30), these two being the only ones among the advance party to affirm with courage and faith the divinely-appointed entry into the land of Canaan (see Num. 14:6–10).

The name *Joshua* has a number of variants in the Old Testament, including Jehoshua (see Num. 13:16; 1 Chron. 7:27), Hoshea (see Deut. 32:44), and Jeshua (see Ezra 2:2). The name *Jesus* (from the Greek) is equivalent to the Hebrew name *Joshua*.

Traditionally, authorship of the book of Joshua is assigned to Joshua himself, with the exception of the concluding section (see Josh. 24:29–33), which was added by another writer. The Book of Joshua is the historical sequel to Deuteronomy—the Pentateuch (Genesis, Exodus, Leviticus, Numbers, and Deuteronomy) constituting the "Law" in terms of Jewish tradition. The Book of Joshua stands as the first of the "Prophets" in this continuing tradition. The time span covered is from just after the passing (translation) of Moses until the death of Joshua (ca. 1427 BC).

The Book of Joshua provides a chronicle of the fulfillment of the Lord's promise to lead Israel to the Promised Land and provide for them an inheritance, allocated by tribe. Thus ends the four-century-long exile in Egypt and the forty-year preparatory sojourn in the wilderness. The historical account is then overlaid with teachings and exhortations to the Israelites to honor their covenant vows and choose to worship and follow the true and eternal God.

Probably the most famous pronouncement of Joshua concerns the principle of agency: "choose you this day whom ye will serve; . . . but as for me and my house, we will serve the LORD" (Josh. 24:15).

As the Israelites prepared to end their lengthy sojourn in the wilderness and enter the Promised Land, Joshua was called of the Lord and reminded: "There shall not any man be able to stand before thee all the days of thy life: as I was with Moses, *so* I will be with thee: I will not fail thee, nor forsake thee" (Josh. 1:5). The Lord assured Joshua that Israel would possess the Promised Land as their inheritance. The priests carrying the ark of the covenant touched the Jordan River bank and the water was stopped up, allowing the Israelites to cross on dry ground. The Lord instructed Joshua how to bring down the walls of Jericho: "So the

LORD was with Joshua; and his fame was *noised* throughout all the country" (Josh. 6:27). Joshua offered sacrifices and read the laws given by Moses to the people: "There was not a word of all that Moses commanded, which Joshua read not before all the congregation of Israel, with the women, and the little ones, and the strangers that were conversant among them." (Josh. 8:35). Joshua divided the land amongst the tribes of Israel and promised them, so long as they were righteous, that they could enjoy the fruits of the Promised Land. As Joshua came to the end of his life, he cautioned the people about worshipping false Gods and enjoined them to keep the commandments—always choosing to side with the Lord.

We can make the same decision that Joshua made. We are free to choose. We have moral agency as a gift—with consequences or blessings according to our choices (see 2 Ne. 2:27). Agency is supreme. Our condition and state of being are the result of how we use our agency, our choices and decisions determining the consequences of our actions, whether blessings or burdens. Agency can operate because of the presence of four conditions: opposition in all things, knowledge of good and evil, laws and commandments given by God, and the freedom to choose. This free gift is really moral agency, connoting responsibility and accountability for our choices. Satan seeks to take away our agency by making us think that our decisions have no consequences. He carries out his insidious work through subtlety, lies, and half truths (see 2 Ne. 28:7–9; 3 Ne. 2:2; Alma 12:4; Moses 4:4).

We can employ our agency wisely by following the light of Christ (see Moroni 7:15–17) and by living according to the promptings of the Spirit (see 2 Ne. 32:5). We have the power to make good decisions. Agency has two dimensions: the action of *commission* or the non-action of *omission*. Passivity in the face of choice is agency by omission (failure to choose)—often leading to problematic or dire results. Of all of our blessings, the freedom to choose and act wisely should be most cherished by mankind. Heavenly Father ordained it so because He loves us and seeks only our eternal life and happiness. Our choices can bring us happiness through the Atonement of the Lord Jesus Christ. It behooves us to use our agency wisely, for as Alma reminds us: "For thus saith the scripture: Choose ye this day, whom ye will serve" (Alma 30:8). To Enoch the Lord declared: "Say unto this people: Choose ye this day, to serve the Lord God who made you" (Moses 6:33). Thus Joshua was acting according to an eternal principle and doing it with honor and integrity.

APPENDIX Q
RUTH

Ruth was a Moabite woman who became the daughter-in-law of Naomi and a progenitor in the lineage leading to Jesus Christ (see Matt. 1:5). Compiled and authored by an unnamed writer, the book of Ruth, along with the book of Judges, presents all of the Hebrew history available concerning events during the period of time commencing with the death of Joshua and extending to the birth of Samuel. The time span of the Book of Ruth was likely the middle part of the 12th century BC, since Ruth was the great-grandmother of David (who was born around 1096 BC).

The Book of Ruth is a story of unsurpassed beauty and tenderness illustrating loyalty and devotion within the family—especially in the context of the integration of a non-Israelite into the fold of Israel. As such, the story is an emblem of conversion, of setting aside one's former ways in favor of a new and higher pattern of living aligned with the spiritual laws of Jehovah. Moreover, the book provides a serene contrast to the pattern of turbulence and disorder that prevailed in cycles during the time of the judges. The book also highlights the continuity from the earlier times to the unfolding line of descent to Christ.

The four chapters of the book cover the transition of the Elimelech family to Moab, the marriages and deaths within the family, and the return of Naomi and Ruth to Bethlehem (chapter 1); the courtship of Boaz and Ruth (chapters 2–3); and the marriage of Boaz and Ruth, reflecting joy and unity (chapter 4).

We see in the Book of Ruth many of the building blocks of the abundant life, including the loyalty and devotion of Ruth, the kindness and love of Boaz, the effulgent joy that the hopeful Naomi experienced to see her emptied home filled again with loved ones, and the tolerance and respect that the Israelites learned to cultivate for one of their Moabite adoptees. These building blocks of the abundant life are still efficacious in our day and age. The same principles apply to our challenges and tests as applied to these people in ancient times, for abundance is a gift of the Spirit and comes through principles of righteousness.

These personalities—Ruth, Boaz, and Naomi—are among the most admired and honored in the Old Testament. The gleaner Ruth worked tirelessly to provide food for herself and the widow Naomi. The landholder Boaz, a kinsman to Naomi's deceased husband, took note of Ruth's love and industry and had compassion and admiration for her. He was as kind and loving a person as was Ruth. Through the advice of Naomi, Ruth was able to facilitate the developing relationship. Boaz worked through long-standing social customs to lay the foundation for a proper and community-sanctioned marriage with Ruth. It is one of the great happy-ending stories in all of literature.

Think also of Naomi: she lost her husband as well as both of her sons. She became the example for all widows everywhere, having maintained courage while suffering greatly because of her loss and her sorrow. Added to that was the burden of having to support herself and her daughter-in-law Ruth. Ruth was the source of sunshine in her life, the marriage of Ruth and Boaz bringing harmony and stability into their family circle in place of the previous despair and longing. As such, Ruth was a model of ideal womanhood. A key theme of the story is this: In time, sorrows pass and things improve. Moreover, the fruit of the new marriage was a continuation of the covenant lineage, leading to David, and beyond, to Christ Himself.

A transcending truth unfolds when we recognize that Ruth was of the Moabite lineage, one of the indigenous cultures remaining in the Holy Land after the return of Israel from Egypt. The original Moab was the son of Lot's oldest daughter (see Gen. 19:37), and thus the Moabites were akin to the Israelites, but represented a different way of life and religion. Ruth represented the local culture at its best, being a pure and virtuous individual with the highest aspirations and character, and she embraced wholeheartedly the Israelite way of life. She was welcomed into her new environment and became instrumental in continuing the promised lineage via David to the Savior himself. What a fitting unfolding of history that the Author of universal salvation should have come from a line that combined in Ruth and Boaz the confluence of two cultures, one Israelite and the other non-Israelite—but both from the same Maker and Creator. It is a reminder that converts to the Church and kingdom of God are welcome from all kindreds, nations, tongues, and peoples.

The traits of kindness and love, so enduringly reflected in the story of the relationship of Boaz and Ruth add a glow of the divine to our temporal lives of challenge and trial: "And now my daughter, fear not; I will do to thee all that thou requirest: for all the city of my people doth know that thou art a virtuous woman" (Ruth 3:11).

Ruth gave up many personal things because of her devotion and loyalty to Naomi—her family, her friends, and her homeland with all of its cultural surroundings. Because of her strong family ties, she was faithful to Naomi. This lesson brings to light the character traits of true Saints. Devotion and loyalty rank high among those attributes we should seek. Loyalty is anchored in correct principles. We should be loyal to enduring values, we should be honorable, and we should base our loyalty on love. Loyalty is an active trait. It is the first line of defense. It lifts and encourages. Loyalty is wise. We should establish priorities as to where we put our loyalties. We should build strong relationships—loyalty to a person is only as strong as the bonds of the relationship, and loyalty to a cause is only as strong as the conversion to that cause. We earn loyalty through loyalty. Loyalty is ultimately spiritual. One cannot be loyal to one's fellows without being loyal to the Father of us all.

The short Book of Ruth memorializes the qualities of loyalty, devotion, kindness, love, tolerance, and joy. As we examine these Christ-like attributes and the resultant influence on one's life, we can perceive the unfolding of character toward a higher good, leading ultimately to eternal bliss and joy, the fruit of the Spirit of the Lord.

APPENDIX R
SAMUEL

Samuel (meaning: name of God, or God has heard), a great prophet in ancient Israel at the time of Saul and David, was the son of Elkanah and Hannah. The story of his birth is remarkable. The heartfelt desire of Hannah was to become a mother. Her devotion and pleading before the Lord near the temple were heard, and the Lord's servant, Eli, promised her that her prayers would be answered. She conceived and bore Samuel and was filled with joy and thanksgiving, pleased to dedicate her son to the service of holiness: "For this child I prayed: and the Lord hath given me my petition which I asked of him. Therefore also I have lent him to the Lord" (1 Sam. 1:27–28). Hannah gave praise to the Lord for His goodness as her son Samuel grew and prospered, ministering before the Lord and increasing in favor and righteousness: "And the child Samuel grew on, and was in favour both with the LORD, and also with men" (1 Sam. 2:26).

Having come under the care of the priest Eli, Samuel heard a voice during the night: "The LORD called Samuel: and he answered, Here am I" (1 Sam. 3:4). Samuel inquired of Eli who it might be, but Eli had him return to his bed. When this scene repeated itself two more times, Eli told him to listen, for it was the Lord calling.

The Lord revealed to Samuel the sad news of Eli's sons and their unrighteousness: "For I have told him that I will judge his house for ever for the iniquity which he knoweth; because his sons made themselves vile, and he restrained them not. And therefore I have sworn unto the house of Eli, that the iniquity of Eli's house shall not be purged with sacrifice nor offering for ever" (1 Sam. 3:13–14). Eli's sons were killed in battle (see 1 Sam. 4:11) and Eli, as a feeble and blind ninety-eight-year old, passed away in a tragic accident (see 1 Sam. 4:18).

The sad unfolding of this story forever embeds in one's mind that children, even all of us, need continual reminding to repent and purify ourselves before the Lord. In contrast to Eli and his sons, Samuel continued in righteousness and became the prophet of the Lord:

And Samuel grew, and the LORD was with him, and did let none of his words fall to the ground.
And all Israel from Dan even to Beersheba knew that Samuel *was* established *to be* a prophet of the LORD." (1 Sam. 3:19–20)

The example of Hannah and Samuel as they sought to serve the Lord proves once again the principle that when we live and practice the qualities of devotion and perseverance, our works will always be rewarded because of the desires of our hearts. We learn great lessons from the story of Samuel: the power of prayer, devotion in giving oneself to the service of God, and (in the case of Eli) the price we pay in failing to correct our children properly. The Lord hears and answers prayers of the righteous even as He heard Hannah's. The blessings of prayer truly empower us to do all things. We can preach and teach with the power and authority of God (see Alma 17:3), seek forgiveness of sins (see Enos 1:4), gain knowledge of the truth (see Alma 5:46), help people who know not God (see Alma 6:6), bless others through our righteous prayers (see Mosiah 27:14), counsel with the Lord and receive direction in our lives (see Alma 37:37), become stronger in our humility and firmer in our faith (see Hel. 3:35), receive the blessings of charity when praying with all the energy of our heart (see Moroni 7:48)—and in all things we shall be blessed as we call upon God.

The books of First and Second Samuel cover the time period from the birth of Samuel (shortly before 1125 BC) to a period just prior to the death of David (around 1015 BC)—a span of some 130 years. First Samuel itself extends only to the death of Saul and his sons. The book of First Samuel sets forth the commencement of the history of Israel under King Saul and his successor, King David. Against the backdrop of intrigue and pride reflected in the vacillating character of Saul we perceive the principled ministry of the prophet Samuel as a mirror of divine purpose and truth. We also see the magnanimous character of the young David as he emerges from obscurity to a position of prominence as a great leader in Israel.

The Psalmist remembered Samuel in this inspiring exhortation:

> Exalt ye the LORD our God, and worship at his footstool; *for* he *is* holy.
>
> Moses and Aaron among his priests, and Samuel among them that call upon his name; they called upon the LORD, and he answered them. (Ps. 99:5–6)

APPENDIX S
DAVID

David (meaning: beloved) was the celebrated king of Judah and Israel who united the tribes as one great nation and ensured that the government was based on righteous principles and the law of God. He is also one of the most tragic figures in the Old Testament because of his transgressions with Bathsheba and Uriah, thus becoming the epitome of personal remorse and suffering over sin.

David's history is recorded in the first and second books of Samuel concerning the beginning of the historical account of the kings of Israel. The first and second books of Samuel cover the time period from the birth of Samuel (shortly before 1125 BC) to a period just prior to the death of David (around 1015 BC)—a span of some 130 years.

The key events relating to David include the following:

- David, the youngest of the sons of Jesse, is chosen and anointed to become king over Israel—around 1063 B.C. (1 Sam. 16): "for *the LORD seeth* not as man seeth; for man looketh on the outward appearance, but the LORD looketh on the heart" (1 Sam. 16:7). David goes up against the Philistine giant Goliath and prevails: "Then said David to the Philistine, Thou comest to me with a sword, and with a spear, and with a shield: but I come to thee in the name of the LORD of hosts, the God of the armies of Israel, whom thou hast defied" (1 Sam. 17:45.)

- Saul puts David in charge of his armies; Jonathan (son of Saul) and David develop a close relationship; David marries Michal, a daughter of Saul (see 1 Sam. 18).

- David escapes the murderous conspiracies of Saul and joins Samuel (see 1 Sam. 19).

- Jonathan and David make a covenant of friendship and peace, then separate (see 1 Sam. 20): "So Jonathan made *a covenant* with the house of David, *saying*, Let the LORD even require *it* at the hand of David's enemies. And Jonathan caused David to swear again, because he loved him: for he loved him as he loved his own soul" (1 Sam. 20:16–17).

- David deftly escapes Saul's evil designs and gains favor among the people; he finally corners Saul in a cave, but graciously spares his life (see 1 Sam. 21–24): "And he said to David, Thou *art* more righteous than I: for thou hast rewarded me good, whereas I have rewarded thee evil" (1 Sam. 24:17).

- David again spares the life of Saul (see 1 Sam. 26): "The LORD render to every man his righteousness and his faithfulness: for the LORD delivered thee into *my* hand to day, but I would not stretch forth mine hand against the LORD's anointed" (1 Sam. 26:23).

- Philistines rise up again against Israel; David defeats the Amalekites, but the Philistines defeat Israel and slay Saul and three of his sons (see 1 Sam. 27–31).

APPENDIX T
SAUL

Saul (meaning: asked) was the first king of Israel, his reign lasting from around 1095 BC to the middle of that century. His history is recorded in the book of First Samuel, this chronicle constituting the beginning of the historical account of the kings of Israel and covering the time period from the birth of Samuel to the death of Saul and his sons. Against the backdrop of intrigue and pride reflected in the vacillating character of Saul we perceive the principled ministry of the prophet Samuel as a mirror of divine purpose and truth. We also see the magnanimous character of the young David as he emerges from obscurity to a position of prominence as a great leader in Israel.

In broad terms, the book of First Samuel covers the rise of Samuel as a great prophet of the Lord (chapters 1–8), the reign of Saul as the first king in Israel (chapters 9–15), and the rise of David as the successor king in Israel amidst the murderous designs of Saul (chapters 16–31).

The story of Saul, gripping and tragic, is a reminder of the peril arising from the influence of a king or ruler who falls dangerously short of the measure of righteousness exemplified in the stature and glory of the Lord of Lords, Jesus Christ. Samuel had adjured the people to relent in demanding that a king be placed over them, rehearsing before them the burdens such a ruler can impose when the people choose a worldly sovereign rather than the Lord (see 1 Sam. 8:6–18; compare Mosiah 23:7; Mosiah 29:13, 16–17, 23). But when Israel rejected the Lord as their king, insisting on having a worldly king like the neighboring cultures, the Lord caused the prophet Samuel to anoint the young Saul to be king of Israel.

Saul had many good qualities, including an initially humble nature. As part of his transition to leadership, the Lord gave him "another heart" (1 Sam. 10:9)—in other words, Saul was illuminated by divine purpose and became spiritually committed. The Spirit of the Lord came upon him and he then prophesied with power. Samuel counseled the Israelites and their new king to be obedient to the Lord's commandments lest He reject them.

Just as in the case of the young Saul, the Lord favors the humble and spiritually malleable, blessing them in their callings by giving them a transformed and rejuvenated heart. However, soon after assuming the role of king in Israel, Saul began to forget the Lord and arrogated to himself the abilities of righteous judgment and priesthood authority. When Samuel delayed his arrival to offer sacrifice to the Lord, Saul took it upon himself to perform the priestly duties and was rejected of the Lord as no longer "a man after his own heart" (1 Sam. 13:14). Later, Saul disobeyed the Lord by saving the spoils from the battle with the Amalekites, thus sealing his rejection by the Lord as king over Israel. Thereafter he was plagued with an evil spirit (see 1 Sam. 16:14–23).

When we begin to govern our lives according to our own desires and judgment, rather than acting in the spirit of our commission as servants of God, then we begin to falter and lose favor with the Lord. Only by obedience to the commandments and will of God can we hope to have the blessings of heaven and prosper in our duties and service. We learn this great lesson from the scriptures when Saul pridefully asserted his own will rather than follow the commandments of God. Samuel reminded him: "Behold, to obey is better than sacrifice, and to hearken than the fat of rams" (1

Sam. 15:22). Then came the divine verdict: "And Samuel said unto Saul, I will not return with thee: for thou hast rejected the word of the LORD, and the LORD hath rejected thee from being king over Israel" (1 Sam. 15:26). Samuel then sought out a future king to replace Saul—even the young David, one who would not be dominated by pride but would heed the counsels of the Lord.

In his classic sermon on pride, President Ezra Taft Benson reminds us:

In the scriptures there is no such thing as righteous pride. It is always considered as a sin. We are not speaking of a wholesome view of self-worth, which is best established by a close relationship with God. But we are speaking of pride as the universal sin, as someone has described it. Mormon writes that "the pride of this nation, or the people of the Nephites, hath proven their destruction" (Moroni 8:27). The Lord says in the Doctrine and Covenants, "Beware of pride, lest ye become as the Nephites of old" (D&C 38:39). Essentially, pride is a "my will" rather than "thy will" approach to life. The opposite of pride is humbleness, meekness, submissiveness, or teachableness (see Alma 13:28)." (Ezra Taft Benson, *The Teachings of Ezra Taft Benson* [Salt Lake City: Deseret Book Co., 1988], 435)

The roots of pride festered in the heart of Saul. It started out well, with Samuel telling him, "And the Spirit of the Lord will come upon thee, and thou shalt prophesy with them, and shalt be turned into another man" (1 Sam. 10:6). But things soon went into decline. Pride and arrogance of the type that consumed Saul are the fuels of lethal envy and jealousy. Only by cultivating a life of humility and penitence can we hope to avoid such an state of pride and greed and instead qualify for the spirit of harmony, peace, and joy in this life and eternal rest in the life to come.

Saul was an eyewitness to the process of his own dethronement: "And Saul saw and knew that the Lord was with David. . . . And Saul was yet the more afraid of David; and Saul became David's enemy continually" (1 Sam. 18:28–29). Saul was plagued by the spirit of jealousy and continually plotted for the death of David. But David deftly followed the course of safety opened up for him by the Lord and thus repeatedly escaped harm. Saul had been abandoned by the Lord—or rather he had abandoned the Lord—just as David had been taken into the Lord's favor, thus it was inevitable that David would ultimately ascend the throne of Israel.

Saul had turned entirely to his own ways, doing his own will and being full of pride. How often we have seen this same scenario play out in the Book of Mormon: humility brings blessings; blessings bring prosperity; prosperity brings pride; and pride leads to downfall. This cycle of pride was demonstrated time and time again. We too are subject to that same cycle individually and collectively unless we continually humble ourselves before God in gratitude and thanksgiving on a daily basis as we have been taught. Failing to do so invites pride to creep into our patterns of living.

Pride is at the crux of almost all sins. It is a sin that is universal in nature. Most all are afflicted to one degree or another with elements of pride. Pride is expressed in arrogance, haughtiness, self-love, vanity, and egotism. Pride creates enmity between God and man.

We are all engaged in the challenge of overcoming pride. Pride is directly opposed to the Christ-like quality of humility. It was the downfall of Saul, just as it was the downfall of the Jaredites and Nephites. Pride can be our downfall as well if we are not careful. It is not only an attitudinal problem; prideful thoughts are so powerful that they lead to sinful behavior—sins of commission as well as omission.

Pride brings with it other sins that are all too easily expressed, such as selfishness, greed, lust, jealously, power-seeking, envy, and a whole host of trailing problems that will tempt us and lead us to sin. This is why the Lord continually counsels us against pride (see Prov. 16:18; D&C 23:1). Humility, the opposite of pride, is enhanced, enabled, and augmented through the mercy and kindness of God. Humility is the beginning of all growth. It is in the strength of the Lord—and not of ourselves—that we can do all things (see Alma 26:11–12).

Pride destroyed great nations and it can destroy us, one at a time—unless we remember our covenants and cultivate the qualities of the divine nature with persistence and valor (see D&C 4; 2 Pet. 1:3–8). By supplanting every vestige of pride with a governing measure of humility, we will come unto the Lord, always acknowledging our unworthiness before Him (see Alma 38:14). In humility we will find the answer to many of our problems by relying upon the Lord and not boasting in our own selves. We can make a plan to root out pride and enjoy the blessings of humility in our lives.

APPENDIX U
JONATHAN

Jonathan (meaning: gift of Jehovah), son of Saul, was known for his military prowess (see 1 Sam. 14:1–23). He and his father shared a reputation for speed and power: "they were [in the words of David] swifter than eagles, they were stronger than lions" (2 Sam. 1:23). Jonathan excelled especially in archery (see 2 Sam. 1:22).

On one occasion where the forces of Jonathan had achieved a mighty triumph over the Philistines, Saul proclaimed a fast to ensure, as he said, "that I may be avenged on mine enemies" (1 Sam. 14:24). The penalty for failing to abide by the royal decree would be death; however, Jonathan, not knowing of the decree, partook of a little honey from a honeycomb, much to the distress and anxiety of those around him (see 1 Sam. 14:27–30). Learning of the action of his son, Saul confirmed the inevitability of the penalty. But the people defended Jonathan, saying to the king, "Shall Jonathan die, who hath wrought this great salvation in Israel? God forbid: as the LORD liveth, there shall not one hair of his head fall to the ground; for he hath wrought with God this day. So the people rescued Jonathan, that he died not" (1 Sam. 14:45).

Jonathan is especially remembered for his enduring friendship with David, beginning with the miraculous slaying of Goliath, when "the soul of Jonathan was knit with the soul of David, and Jonathan loved him as his own soul" (1 Sam. 18:1), and lasting until the end of Jonathan's life, he falling by the sword along with his father, Saul, at the battle of Gilboa (see 1 Sam. 31:1–2).

During his lifetime, Jonathan continually defended David before the murderous ambitions of Saul, the two young men having entered into a mutual covenant of security and devotion (see 1 Sam. 19:1–7; 20; 23:16–18). Upon the death of Jonathan, David prepared a moving eulogy of lamentation ending with the words:

How are the mighty fallen in the midst of the battle! O Jonathan, *thou wast* slain in thine high places.

I am distressed for thee, my brother Jonathan: very pleasant hast thou been unto me: thy love to me was wonderful, passing the love of women.

How are the mighty fallen, and the weapons of war perished! (2 Sam. 1:25–27)

David recovered the remains of Saul and Jonathan and buried them "in the country of Benjamin in Zelah, in the sepulchre of Kish his [Saul's] father" (2 Sam. 21:14).

APPENDIX V
BATHSHEBA AND URIAH

Bathsheba (meaning: daughter of the oath) was the wife of Uriah the Hittite, a warrior in David's army. At the time of Israel's successful battle against the Ammonites, David remained in Jerusalem. Having observed Bathsheba from the roof of his residence, David desired her and followed through with an immoral relationship that resulted in a conception (see 2 Sam. 11:2–5). He then attempted to cover up his sin by sending for Uriah to return home to his wife, Bathsheba. But out of solemn duty to his military commission, Uriah demurred to go in to Bathsheba (see 2 Sam. 11:11). At that point, David compounded his own guilt by arranging through Joab, his commander, to send Uriah to the front lines, where his death was assured. Uriah did indeed perish (see 2 Sam. 11:21)—and David's claim to exaltation perished as well:

> David's wives and concubines were given unto him of me, by the hand of Nathan, my servant, and others of the prophets who had the keys of this power; and in none of these things did he sin against me save in the case of Uriah and his wife; and, therefore he hath fallen from his exaltation, and received his portion; and he shall not inherit them out of the world, for I gave them unto another, saith the Lord. (D&C 132:39)

The judgment of God was confirmed to David in person through the prophet Nathan (see 2 Sam. 12:1–14).

The child of David and Bathsheba did not survive (see 2 Sam. 12:19), but as David's wife, she subsequently bore four more sons: Solomon, Shimea, Shobab, and Nathan. In David's old age, his son Adonijah (born of Haggith—see 2 Sam. 3:4) "exalted himself, saying, I will be king" (1 Kings 1:5), and conspired with Joab, commander of David's military forces, and Abiathar, the priest, to take over the throne. Meanwhile, Nathan came to Bathsheba, mother of Solomon, and disclosed what was happening, counseling her to go before David to seek redress. Bathsheba concurred, and petitioned her husband with the words:

> My lord, thou swarest by the LORD thy God unto thine handmaid, *saying,* Assuredly Solomon thy son shall reign after me, and he shall sit upon my throne.
> And now, behold, Adonijah reigneth; and now, my lord the king, thou knowest *it* not. (1 Kings 1:17–18)

These things being confirmed by Nathan, the aging David gave the command that Solomon should be brought forth and anointed king (see 1 Kings 1:35, 39–43). The conspirators fled. Solomon, the new king, was left to decide on their fate. When Adonijah, with the accommodating (and likely reluctant) assistance of Bathsheba, made overtures to obtain for himself Abishag, David's nurse, Solomon became even more suspicious about his older brother's hidden agenda to take over the throne, so the king arranged for his immediate execution as a schemer (see 1 Kings 2:13–25). Abiathar was stripped of his priestly authority and exiled (see 1 Kings 2:25–28). Joab was executed for treachery (see 1 Kings 2:34–35).

As for Bathsheba, we know that she suffered because of the death of her husband: "And when the wife of Uriah heard that Uriah her husband was dead, she mourned for her husband" (2 Sam. 11:26). We know that she was loyal to her new husband, David, and exceedingly committed to the rise and success of her son Solomon. She was also remembered in Matthew's statement for her place in the lineage of Jesus Christ: "And Jesse begat David the king; and David the king begat Solomon of her *that had been the wife* of Urias" (Matt. 1:6). Besides Ruth and Mary (see Matt. 1:5, 16), the only other woman remembered or alluded to in this fourteen-generation review is Bathsheba.

David and Jonathan by Gustave Doré

APPENDIX W
NATHAN

Nathan (meaning: he has given) was a prophet of the Lord during the time of David. Through Nathan, the Lord declared unto David that the commission to build a temple unto God would devolve upon his son Solomon: "And when thy days be fulfilled, and thou shalt sleep with thy fathers, I will set up thy seed after thee, which shall proceed out of thy bowels, and I will establish his kingdom. He shall build an house for my name, and I will stablish the throne of his kingdom for ever" (2 Sam. 7:12–13). Through Nathan as well, the Lord reproved David for his serious lapse of moral rectitude in regard to Bathsheba and Uriah. The inspired words of Nathan in this case—including a parable (a rarity in the Old Testament)—constitute one of the most powerful calls to repentance in all of holy writ:

> AND the LORD sent Nathan unto David. And he came unto him, and said unto him, There were two men in one city; the one rich, and the other poor.
>
> The rich *man* had exceeding many flocks and herds:
>
> But the poor *man* had nothing, save one little ewe lamb, which he had bought and nourished up: and it grew up together with him, and with his children; it did eat of his own meat, and drank of his own cup, and lay in his bosom, and was unto him as a daughter.
>
> And there came a traveller unto the rich man, and he spared to take of his own flock and of his own herd, to dress for the wayfaring man that was come unto him; but took the poor man's lamb, and dressed it for the man that was come to him.
>
> And David's anger was greatly kindled against the man; and he said to Nathan, As the LORD liveth, the man that hath done this *thing* shall surely die:
>
> And he shall restore the lamb fourfold, because he did this thing, and because he had no pity.
>
> And Nathan said to David, Thou *art* the man. Thus saith the LORD God of Israel, I anointed thee king over Israel, and I delivered thee out of the hand of Saul;
>
> And I gave thee thy master's house, and thy master's wives into thy bosom, and gave thee the house of Israel and of Judah; and if *that had been* too little, I would moreover have given unto thee such and such things.
>
> Wherefore hast thou despised the commandment of the LORD, to do evil in his sight? thou hast killed Uriah the Hittite with the sword, and hast taken his wife *to be* thy wife, and hast slain him with the sword of the children of Ammon.
>
> Now therefore the sword shall never depart from thine house; because thou hast despised me, and hast taken the wife of Uriah the Hittite to be thy wife. (2 Sam. 12:1–10)

Nathan was of service in assisting David to organize the protocols of public worship (see 2 Chron. 29:25). Later, Nathan was instrumental in facilitating the enthronement of Solomon, the legitimate successor to the throne of Israel. Adonijah was the fourth son of David (see 2 Sam. 3:2–4). When David was stricken with age and was about to die, Adonijah "exalted himself, saying, I will be king" (1 Kings 1:5). With the help of his allies—Joab, commander of David's military forces, and Abiathar, the priest—Adonijah ascended the throne (sometime in the period 1026–1015 BC), engaging in a banquet of celebration from which individuals like Zadok the priest, Benaiah (chief of David's bodyguards), Solomon, and Nathan the prophet were strategically excluded. Meanwhile, Nathan came to Bathsheba, mother of Solomon, and disclosed what had happened, counseling her to go before David to seek redress. Bathsheba concurred, reminding David of his own words to her: "Assuredly Solomon thy son shall reign after me, and he shall sit upon my throne" (1 Kings 1:17).

These things being confirmed by Nathan, the aging David commanded that Solomon should be brought forth and anointed king amidst the sound of the trumpet: "Then ye shall come up after him, that he may come and sit upon my throne; for he shall be king in my stead: and I have appointed him to be ruler over Israel and over Judah" (1 Kings 1:35). That is precisely what then took place just as Adonijah and his colleagues were feasting upon their banquet of triumph (see 1 Kings 1:39–43). When the news broke, the banquet guests fled in horror, and Solomon, the new king, was left to decide on their fate. In due course, Adonijah was put to death as a usurper and schemer, Abiathar was stripped of his priestly authority and exiled (see 1 Kings 2:26–27), Joab was executed for treachery and replaced by Benaiah, and Zadok was made chief priest (see 1 Kings 2:26–27, 34–35).

Nathan apparently also wrote a book about the reign of David (see 1 Chron. 29:29) as well as the reign of Solomon (see 2 Chron. 9:29). Nathan is mentioned once in the Doctrine and Covenants concerning the doctrine of plural marriage:

> David also received many wives and concubines, and also Solomon and Moses my servants, as also many others of my servants, from the beginning of creation until this time; and in nothing did they sin save in those things which they received not of me.
>
> David's wives and concubines were given unto him of me, by the hand of Nathan, my servant, and others of the prophets who had the keys of this power; and in none of these things did he sin against me save in the case of Uriah and his wife; and, therefore he hath fallen from his exaltation, and received his portion; and he shall not inherit them out of the world, for I gave them unto another, saith the Lord. (D&C 132:38–39)

APPENDIX X
JEROBOAM

Jeroboam (pronounced "jer'-uh-boh'-uhm"; meaning: whose people are many) was the first in a long sequence of kings over the northern part of the house of Israel. Israel became divided into two parts around 975 BC, largely as a result of a revolt of the people against the heavy tax burden imposed by King Solomon. The northern part of the kingdom, headquartered at Shechem, comprised ten of the tribes, with Ephraim as the dominant group. The southern part of the kingdom, headquartered at Jerusalem, consisted chiefly of the tribes of Judah and Benjamin.

Jeroboam, son of Nebat, the Ephraimite, being "a mighty man of valour," began his career in the court of Solomon, who, "seeing the young man that he was industrious, he made him ruler over all the charge of the house of Joseph" (1 Kings 11:28). One day, as Jeroboam was going out of the city of Jerusalem, he was met by the prophet Ahijah, who prophesied the separation of the ten northern tribes from the kingdom of Solomon (see 1 Kings 11:33). Ahijah declared that Jeroboam would reign over the northern kingdom of Israel (see 1 Kings 11:37). The condition for this stellar rise in authority was that Jeroboam would have to "hearken unto all that I command thee, and wilt walk in my ways, and do *that is* right in my sight, to keep my statutes and my commandments, as David my servant did" (1 Kings 11:38).

When Solomon became aware of the separatist movement, he sought to kill Jeroboam, who fled to Egypt, where he remained, under the protection of the Pharaoh, until after the death of Solomon (see 1 Kings 11:41–43). Then when Rehoboam, successor to Solomon, continued his father's practice of exacting heavy taxes from the people, the ten tribes took decisive action (see 1 Kings 12:19–20.)

Rehoboam, having been warned by a man of God not to go up to battle against the northern kingdom (see 1 Kings 12:21–24), left things as they were for a season. Meanwhile, Jeroboam rebuilt Shechem but then also undertook initiatives that contravened the instructions of the prophet Ahijah, who warned him to walk in the ways of the Lord. Jeroboam set up two golden calves (one in Bethel and one in Dan), telling the people to worship in those places rather than journeying to Jerusalem (where, he feared, they would be subjected to the influence of Rehoboam). He also appointed priests from non-Levite ranks and established a feast day of his own contrivance (see 1 Kings 12:25–33; 2 Chron. 13:9).

Subsequently, when Jeroboam was worshipping at the altar he had established at Bethel, a prophet of God from Judah appeared suddenly and rebuked him for his evil ways. At that moment Jeroboam reached forth his hand to command the arrest of the prophet, but the hand was rendered useless and the altar was rent. Only a petition to the prophet brought about a restoration of the hand (see 1 Kings 13:1–6). But Jeroboam did not restore righteousness to his reign. When his young son Abijah was stricken with illness, Jeroboam sent his wife to inquire of the prophet Ahijah about the circumstance. Ahijah pronounced doom upon the house of Jeroboam for not obeying God (see 1 Kings 14:9). Abijah perished and Jeroboam went to his grave: "And the days which Jeroboam reigned *were* two and twenty years: and he slept with his fathers, and Nadab his son reigned in his stead" (1 Kings 14:20). A summary epithet for Jeroboam is that he was the king "who did sin, and who made Israel to sin" (1 Kings 14:16).

APPENDIX Y
REHOBOAM

Rehoboam (pronounced "ree'-uh-boh'-uhm"; meaning: enlarger of the people) was the son of Solomon and the Ammonitess Naamah, and the successor to the throne (see 1 Kings 11:43; 14:21, 31). During the days of Rehoboam, Israel became divided into two parts, around 975 BC (see 1 Kings 12; 2 Chron. 10:19), largely as a result of a revolt of the people against the heavy tax burden imposed by King Solomon. When Rehoboam attained the throne, he continued his father's practice of exacting heavy taxes from the people, causing the ten tribes to take decisive action:

> So Israel rebelled against the house of David unto this day.
>
> And it came to pass, when all Israel heard that Jeroboam was come again, that they sent and called him unto the congregation, and made him king over all Israel: there was none that followed the house of David, but the tribe of Judah only. (1 Kings 12:19–20)

Rehoboam, having been warned by Shemaiah, a man of God, not to go up to battle against the northern kingdom (see 1 Kings 12:21–24), left things as they were for a season. Meanwhile, Jeroboam rebuilt Shechem but then also undertook initiatives that contravened the instructions of the prophet Ahijah, who had warned him to walk in the ways of the Lord (see 1 Kings 11:33, 37–38). Jeroboam set up two golden calves (one in Bethel and one in Dan) and instructed the people to worship in those places, rather than journeying to Jerusalem (where, he feared, they would be subjected to the influence of Rehoboam). He also appointed priests from non-Levite ranks and established a feast day of his own contrivance (see 1 Kings 12:25–33). Thus both kings—one over Judah and one over Israel—failed to walk in the footsteps of their righteous predecessors among the rulers of the covenant people, causing the Lord to withdraw His blessings.

Not long thereafter, Rehoboam's power was greatly weakened as a result of an invasion by the Egyptians under Shishak, king of Egypt—something Shemaiah had warned him about (see 2 Chron. 12:9–12).

We learn graphic lessons about correct leadership from the contrasting example of unrighteous leadership demonstrated by Rehoboam and Jeroboam. Rehoboam's memorable and troubling words to his people are recorded as follows: "My father made your yoke heavy, and I will add to your yoke: my father *also* chastised you with whips, but I will chastise you with scorpions" (1 Kings 12:14; compare 2 Chron. 10:11). By contrast, the Lord said: "Come unto me, all *ye* that labour and are heavy laden, and I will give you rest. Take my yoke upon you, and learn of me; for I am meek and lowly in heart: and ye shall find rest unto your souls. For my yoke *is* easy, and my burden is light" (Matt. 11:28–30). Jeroboam, for his part, returned to idol worship and rejected the message of the prophets of God. Thus the whole House of Israel became wicked and idolatrous. The northern and southern kingdoms, having ripened in iniquity, made war one with another for many years (see 1 Kings 15:6). In consequence of wicked and nefarious leadership, the northern kingdom of Israel under Jeroboam's successors carried on his vile ways: "I exalted thee out of the dust, and made thee prince over my people Israel; and thou hast walked in the way of Jeroboam, and hast made my people Israel to sin, to provoke me to anger with their sins; . . ." (1 Kings 16:2).

As so often happens with a wayward people, the Lord's response was to scatter them (see 1 Ne. 21:1). The call of the Lord is always to repent, that the people may once again be gathered to worship the Lord in unity and faith: "And then, O house of Israel, behold, these shall come from far; and lo, these from the north and from the west; and these from the land of Sinim [i.e., a most distant country]. Sing, O heavens; and be joyful, O earth; for the feet of those who are in the east shall be established; and break forth into singing, O mountains; for they shall be smitten no more; for the Lord hath comforted his people, and will have mercy upon his afflicted" (1 Ne. 21:12–13; compare Isa. 49:12–13).

From the story of the division of Israel in the days of Rehoboam and Jeroboam, we see the results of wicked kings leading their people astray, enticing them into grievous sins. Throughout the history of the world, mankind has suffered from misguided or heinous leadership. Mosiah warned: "For behold, how much iniquity doth one wicked king cause to be committed, yea, and what great destruction!" (Mosiah 29:17). As individuals and groups acting under provisions of the Abrahamic covenant, we have an obligation and responsibility for the spiritual welfare of all mankind. We are to take action. If no action is taken, apathy results in torpidity of conscience and lives suffer. The consequences are real for sins of both omission as well as commission. Leadership is a dynamic force for good or bad—depending on the leader.

By way of contrast to the wicked kings among the promised people, the great-grandson of Rehoboam, Jehoshaphat, provides a marked contrast to the leadership style of his wicked predecessors. He eliminated idolatry in his nation (Judah), sent Levite teachers among the people to teach the principles of the gospel from the scriptures, sought the Lord's advice in defending the land, and united the people against their common enemies from without. As a result, the Lord was willing to fight their battles for them and preserve their independence.

Leadership is all about service. The term *servant-leader* is really the operant mode in leadership. One cannot lead or influence others unless he or she is perceived as one who serves and cares about those who are led. Leadership carries with it responsibility. We are responsible and accountable for the people and the performance of the group we lead—whether in the family, in the Church, or in the community. Agency is still in effect among those we lead, but we are to do our best, lest we be found unworthy in our leadership role.

Leadership requires an exemplary life. Individuals cannot lead save they set an example, even as Christ set the example (see 3 Ne. 27:27). We can learn to be full of faith and teach the people the ways of the Lord (see Jarom 1:7).

Finally, as leaders it is our responsibility to learn our duty. We are accountable. We can learn our duty by studying the relevant manuals, seeking counsel from those above us in the organization of the Church, searching the scriptures (see 2 Ne. 32:3), fasting and praying (see James 1:5–6), listening to our prophets (see D&C 21:4–6), and attending the temple regularly (see D&C 97:13–14).

Great leaders have brought change to millions of people. The greatest need in the Church is for valiant and effective leadership. Wonderful leaders teach and lead their families, classes, and groups to great heights. But of all the roles mentioned, the greatest leadership qualities reside in the roles of effective and committed mothers and fathers. The greatest work we do is within our own families. Truly, leadership begins in the home.

Instead of sinking into the abyss represented by the aberrant qualities of a Rehoboam or a Jeroboam, we can follow the example of the Savior each day as our standard for leadership. Jesus Christ, the Savior and Redeemer of the world, even the Creator of heaven and earth, stands as the supreme example of leadership. His purpose was clear—"to bring to pass the immortality and eternal life of man" (Moses 1:39). He cared for individual souls and their happiness.

The gospel of Jesus Christ is the way to return to the Father's presence, for Jesus was selfless and loving at all times. He cared about the one. He was the master teacher, the perfect example, saying: "Come follow me." He was the author of hope and salvation through His love and atoning sacrifice. He maintained a relationship as a friend as well as the God of this earth. Yet in all things He was the true servant of His Heavenly Father and His brothers and sisters. In authentic theocratic leadership, He followed the Father in every thought and deed throughout His life. Christ was the perfect leader. It is up to us to inculcate His values into our lives and serve Him faithfully day-by-day.

APPENDIX Z: ELISHA—APPENDIX AA: NAAMAN

APPENDIX Z
ELISHA

The story of Elisha is conveyed for the most part in the Second Book of the Kings. His ministry lasted more than half a century, concurrent with the reigns of Jehoram, Jehu, Jehoahaz, and Joash. What is memorable about the prophet Elisha is his humble dependence on the Lord and the mighty miracles he was able to perform in the spirit of service and devotion to the Lord's cause. These miracles exemplified Elisha's righteousness as well as the faith of the people for whom they were performed. Miracles are wrought according to the patterns established by our Father in Heaven.

In that spirit, how can we follow the example of Elisha in our own lives? What miracles can we perform? What greater miracle can we hope for than a daily rejuvenation and transformation of our spirit through the application of faith and repentance unto the efficacious working of the Atonement in our personal lives? This grand miracle happens *immediately*, as King Benjamin assured us: "he doth require that ye should do as he hath commanded you; for which if ye do, he doth immediately bless you; and therefore he hath paid you. And ye are still indebted unto him, and are, and will be, forever and ever; therefore, of what have ye to boast?" (Mosiah 2:22–24). Similarly, Amulek assured the people of the *immediate* impact of the plan of salvation and the Atonement in their lives: "and therefore, if ye will repent and harden not your hearts, immediately shall the great plan of redemption be brought about unto you" (Alma 34:31).

Such is the miracle of the mighty change that can be wrought in our hearts through devotion and humility (see Alma 5:14). Through this mighty change, our faith may readily produce other miracles in our lives that are likewise sacred and illuminate the power of God unto salvation. If so, like Elisha, we can kneel before God in humble gratitude to thank Him for the miracles with which He sees fit to bless us. In that way, our understanding will be strengthened to know the grand secret that miracles follow the genuine exercise of faith (see Ether 12:18).

Naaman the Leper by Matthaeus Merian (the Elder)

APPENDIX AA
NAAMAN

Naaman (meaning: pleasantness) was a nobleman in the royal court of Syria: "NOW Naaman, captain of the host of the king of Syria, was a great man with his master, and honourable, because by him the LORD had given deliverance unto Syria: he was also a mighty man in valour, *but he was* a leper" (2 Kings 5:1).

Naaman's wife had a maid who had been captured from among the Israelites by the Syrians. This young girl was concerned about Naaman's disease and said to her mistress, "Would God my lord *were* with the prophet that *is* in Samaria! for he would recover him of his leprosy" (2 Kings 5:3). When the prophet Elisha heard that the Syrian king (Ben-hadad II) had sent a letter of request to the king of Israel (Joram) on behalf of Naaman, Elisha—knowing of the hesitancy of the king of Israel concerning the matter—declared: "let him come now to me, and he shall know that there is a prophet in Israel" (2 Kings 5:8). So Naaman and his company came before the house of Elisha, seeking a blessing.

> And Elisha sent a messenger unto him, saying, Go and wash in Jordan seven times, and thy flesh shall come again to thee, and thou shalt be clean.
>
> But Naaman was wroth, and went away, and said, Behold, I thought, He will surely come out to me, and stand, and call on the name of the LORD his God, and strike his hand over the place, and recover the leper.
>
> *Are* not Abana and Pharpar, rivers of Damascus, better than all the waters of Israel? may I not wash in them, and be clean? So he turned and went away in a rage.
>
> And his servants came near, and spake unto him, and said, My father, *if* the prophet had bid thee *do some* great thing, wouldest thou not have done *it?* how much rather then, when he saith to thee, Wash, and be clean?
>
> Then went he down, and dipped himself seven times in Jordan, according to the saying of the man of God: and his flesh came again like unto the flesh of a little child, and he was clean. (2 Kings 5:10–14)

Returning whole to the house of Elisha, Naaman declared: "Behold, now I know that *there is* no God in all the earth, but in Israel: now therefore, I pray thee, take a blessing of thy servant" (2 Kings 5:15). But Elisha refused compensation for his services, and Naaman departed in peace. However, Gehazi, servant of Elisha, touched by a spirit of greediness, and ignoring the wisdom of his master, followed after Naaman and took advantage of his generosity by accepting for himself gifts of silver and raiment (see 2 Kings 5:27).

Upon learning what had happened, Elisha pronounced a severe judgment on Gehazi for his indiscretion: "The leprosy therefore of Naaman shall cleave unto thee, and unto thy seed for ever. And he went out from his presence a leper *as white* as snow" (2 Kings 5:27).

Great Blessings from Simple Acts of Obedience

We can learn, with Naaman the Syrian, that simple acts of obedience in response to inspired counsel can lead to great benefits. The gospel is a system of simple truths and principles leading to ultimate outcomes concerning immortality and eternal life.

When Naaman learned—through a young Israelite girl taken into domestic service in Syria—that the Lord's prophet could heal him of his leprosy, he came with his entourage to seek relief. But when Elisha told him to bathe seven times in the Jordan—a simple and non-elegant solution to his problem—Naaman was angry. Only through the wise counsel of his servant did Naaman think better of his impetuousness, and his obedience resulted in the desired cure. This event is rightly regarded as one of the most interesting examples of "spiritual leverage" in the scriptures, and shows that the law of obedience even in the smallest and seemingly insignificant acts can reap great blessings or severe consequences. Life is made up of hundreds of daily choices. We can choose to be obedient in all things.

Selfless Service: The Pattern in the Kingdom of God

Unlike Elisha's servant, Gehazi, we can learn to avoid attaching material interests to spiritual service. The wages of obedience are harmony, peace, and spiritual wealth. We serve out of love, not self-interest.

When the thankful Naaman wanted to give Elisha material rewards for the successful cure, Elisha refused any gratuity. But Gehazi, Elisha's servant, was not above the allure of material wealth, and arranged to get some of Naaman's goods. When Elisha learned of this folly, he arranged to give to Gehazi something he had not anticipated receiving: Naaman's former leprous condition. The story thus becomes an emblem for teaching that service rendered in the name of God has spiritual rewards associated with it. When the motivation is for material gain, then the service loses its spiritual character.

Obviously, motive makes the difference as to acceptance of our life here on earth. The intent of our heart becomes the barometer of righteousness. Mormon describes it well: "For behold, God hath said a man being evil cannot do that which is good; for if he offereth a gift, or prayeth unto God, except he shall do it with real intent it profiteth him nothing. For behold, it is not counted unto him for righteousness. For behold, if a man being evil giveth a gift, he doeth it grudgingly; wherefore it is counted unto him the same as if he had retained the gift; wherefore he is counted evil before God. And likewise also is it counted evil unto a man, if he shall pray and not with real intent of heart; yea, and it profiteth him nothing, for God receiveth none such" (Moroni 7:6–9).

APPENDIX BB
HEZEKIAH

Hezekiah, king of Judah, was one of the greatest reformers in a long tradition of kings and a refreshing breeze among the winds of instability arising from enthroned unrighteousness. The story of his tenure (around 726–697 BC) is presented in 2 Kings 18–21, 2 Chronicles 29–33, and Isaiah 36–39. His reign is, in part, concurrent with the ministry of the prophet Isaiah (around 740–701 BC), who served him as a religious and political counselor. When Hezekiah succeeded his father Ahaz (see 2 Kings 16:20), he inaugurated an era of honorable and righteous service:

> He removed the high places, and brake the images, and cut down the groves, and brake in pieces the brasen serpent that Moses had made: for unto those days the children of Israel did burn incense to it: and he called it Nehushtan [meaning a trifling thing of brass; compare Num. 21:9].
>
> He trusted in the LORD God of Israel; so that after him was none like him among all the kings of Judah, nor *any* that were before him.
>
> For he clave to the LORD, *and* departed not from following him, but kept his commandments, which the LORD commanded Moses.
>
> And the LORD was with him; *and* he prospered whithersoever he went forth: and he rebelled against the king of Assyria, and served him not.
>
> He smote the Philistines, *even* unto Gaza, and the borders thereof, from the tower of the watchmen to the fenced city. (2 Kings 18:4–8; compare 2 Chron. 29)

When Sennacherib of Assyria staged a massive invasion (the second within a short while) and besieged the city of Jerusalem, Hezekiah—who had allied himself meanwhile with Egypt (see Isa. 30; 31; 36:6–9)—sent out Eliakim, his chief of staff, to negotiate with the spokesman for the enemy host, Rab-shakeh, who declared:

> Thus saith the king, Let not Hezekiah deceive you: for he shall not be able to deliver you out of his hand:
>
> Neither let Hezekiah make you trust in the LORD, saying, The LORD will surely deliver us, and this city shall not be delivered into the hand of the king of Assyria.
>
> Hearken not to Hezekiah: for thus saith the king of Assyria, Make *an agreement* with me by a present, and come out to me, and *then* eat ye every man of his own vine, and every one of his fig tree, and drink ye every one the waters of his cistern:
>
> Until I come and take you away to a land like your own land, a land of corn and wine, a land of bread and vineyards, a land of oil olive and of honey, that ye may live, and not die: and hearken not unto Hezekiah, when he persuadeth you, saying, The LORD will deliver us. (2 Kings 18:29–32)

Hezekiah sent Eliakim and his companions to confer with Isaiah concerning the stressful matter (see 2 Kings 18:6–7). When the Assyrian hosts persisted in their arrogant threats, Hezekiah went before the Lord in prayer, saying:

O LORD God of Israel, which dwellest *between* the cherubims, thou art the God, *even* thou alone, of all the kingdoms of the earth; thou hast made heaven and earth.

LORD, bow down thine ear, and hear: open, LORD, thine eyes, and see: and hear the words of Sennacherib, which hath sent him to reproach the living God.

Of a truth, LORD, the kings of Assyria have destroyed the nations and their lands,

And have cast their gods into the fire: for they *were* no gods, but the work of men's hands, wood and stone: therefore they have destroyed them.

Now therefore, O LORD our God, I beseech thee, save thou us out of his hand, that all the kingdoms of the earth may know that thou *art* the LORD God, *even* thou only. (2 Kings 19:15–19)

Through Isaiah came the word of the Lord to Hezekiah with assurances of delivery:

Therefore thus saith the LORD concerning the king of Assyria, He shall not come into this city, nor shoot an arrow there, nor come before it with shield, nor cast a bank against it.

By the way that he came, by the same shall he return, and shall not come into this city, saith the LORD.

For I will defend this city, to save it, for mine own sake, and for my servant David's sake.

And it came to pass that night, that the angel of the LORD went out, and smote in the camp of the Assyrians an hundred fourscore and five thousand: and when they arose early in the morning, behold, they *were* all dead corpses. (2 Kings 19:32–35)

Whether by a pestilence that broke out among the Assyrian host or by some other divinely appointed means, the enemy was thwarted and Sennacherib withdrew his forces and returned to Nineveh, where some time later two of his sons murdered him (see 2 Kings 19:36–37).

An interesting event from the life of Hezekiah illustrates his faith in the Lord. He had contracted a serious ailment that caused him to inquire of Isaiah if he should survive. When Isaiah brought to him the word of the Lord that his life was about to end, Hezekiah supplicated the Lord for deliverance from the lethal illness. The Lord blessed him with yet fifteen years of life, but revealed through Isaiah that future captivity awaited Judah: "Behold, the days come, that all that *is* in thine house, and that which thy fathers have laid up in store unto this day, shall be carried into Babylon: nothing shall be left, saith the LORD" (2 Kings 20:17).

APPENDIX CC
EZRA

Ezra was a noted priest and scribe who accompanied a portion of the people of Judah back to their land after the Babylonian captivity (see Ezra 7–10; Neh. 8, 12). The book of Ezra covers the period of time from the decree of Cyrus authorizing the Jews to return to Palestine (537 BC) down to the personal ministry of Ezra and the repatriation of many more of the Jewish people around 459 BC. Thus the book of Ezra also provides an account of the return of a second wave of Jewish people from the Babylonian captivity for resettlement in Jerusalem. The book of Nehemiah is a sequel to Ezra.

The Book of Ezra extols the process of recovery, rebuilding, repentance, and reform—based on faith and devotion to the statutes of the Lord. The book celebrates the lovingkindness of the Lord in remembering His covenant people as they transcend the adversities and challenges of life and return to His pathways.

The history of Ezra is also unfolded in the Book of Nehemiah concering how Ezra taught the people in person from the Law of Moses.

Modern scripture refers back to the campaign of repatriation of the Jewish people, and particularly to the principle of being worthy to be counted among the Lord's favored people: "And they who are of the High Priesthood, whose names are not found written in the book of the law, or that are found to have apostatized, or to have been cut off from the church, as well as the lesser priesthood, or the members, in that day shall not find an inheritance among the saints of the Most High; Therefore, it shall be done unto them as unto the children of the priest, as will be found recorded in the second chapter and sixty-first and second verses of Ezra" (D&C 85:11–12).

The passage referred to in Ezra reads as follows: "And of the children of the priests: the children of Habaiah, the children of Koz, the children of Barzillai; which took a wife of the daughters of Barzillai the Gileadite, and was called after their name: These sought their register *among* those that were reckoned by genealogy, but they were not found: therefore were they, as polluted, put from the priesthood" (Ezra 2:61–62).

APPENDIX DD
NEHEMIAH

Nehemiah (meaning: comfort of the Lord), apparently of the tribe of Judah, was an officer in the court of Artaxerxes of Persia—his "cupbearer" in fact (Neh. 1:11). Responding to the dire reports from his Jewish colleagues visiting him, Nehemiah obtained from the king a commission to rebuild the walls and structures of Jerusalem—a task he performed in subsequent years with honor as the governor of Judah (see Neh. 5:14, 18; 12:26). The chronicle of his tenure is contained in the Book of Nehemiah, being a continuation of the Book of Ezra, the two being regarded as one in the Jewish canon.

The ministry of Ezra covers the return of a second wave of Jewish people from the Babylonian captivity for resettlement in Jerusalem. Nehemiah then covers the associated project of rebuilding the walls of Jerusalem. The time span of the Book of Nehemiah is either contemporaneous with the later ministry of Ezra or shortly thereafter, beginning perhaps around 444 BC. The book closes the historical account of the Old Testament, the prophet Malachi (author of the last book) being a contemporary of Nehemiah.

The purpose of the Book of Nehemiah is to continue with the cause of the Book of Ezra in extolling the process of recovery, rebuilding, repentance, and reform—based on faith and devotion to the statues of the Lord. As with Ezra, the book celebrates the lovingkindness of the Lord in remembering His covenant people as they transcend the adversities and challenges of life and return to His pathways. The book comprises three main sections: a record of the rebuilding of the wall of Jerusalem, including an account of the register Nehemiah discovered of those who had returned from Babylon (chapters 1–7); a record of the manner of religious practice being conducted among the Jewish people of this period, including the remarkable and precedent-setting public reading of the law of God by the priest Ezra (chapters 8–10); and reforms and civic practices among the people, including the dedication of the wall of Jerusalem (chapters 11–13) .

APPENDIX EE
ESTHER

The story of Esther (meaning: star) is one of great courage and faith. The details of her memorable story are given in the book of Esther, one of the late historical books (along with Ezra and Nehemiah). The events in the Book of Esther occurred some half-century following the return from Babylon of many of the Jewish captives (as authorized by the decree of Cyrus in 537 BC).

The Book of Esther presents the historical context and the religious/moral foundation for the establishment of the Jewish feast of Purim. *Purim* is the Hebrew word for "lot"—a reference to the plan of Haman, chief officer at the court of the king of Persia (Ahasuerus—most likely Xerxes), to cast lots for determining a good omen for the timing of his plan for putting all the Jews of the captivity to death (see Esth. 3:7; 9:24).

The king had decided to divorce his wife, Vashti, when she refused to display her beauty before the people and the princes, and had selected as successor the beautiful Esther. However, Esther was the adopted daughter of the Jew Mordecai, whom Haman despised—hence his insidious plan to exterminate all the Jews. But Esther courageously came before the king and had the decree reversed, thus saving the Jewish people and providing the historical context for the annual holiday of Purim.

Esther was the paragon of courage—the power to act forthrightly in difficult situations. It can be an act of bravery in battle or in the personal trials of life. Courage, when fueled by faith, is the attribute of character that brings about the greatest personal growth and an abundance of blessings from God. It is akin to sacrifice. Courageous deeds are often an act of spontaneity on a grand scale, but there are also countless acts of quiet and enduring courage going on in our homes, schools, and workplaces every day. Courage to honor our covenants before the Lord is the test of life and brings with it the joy of knowing that we are doing the will of God.

Courage of the type embodied in the life of Esther is an expression of faith, for it requires putting aside fear and doubt and moving forward in the strength of the Lord. Each act of courage in dealing with a difficult situation will result in increased power to act and to do good in the world. "And who knoweth whether thou art come to the kingdom for *such* a time as this?" said Mordecai to Esther (Esth. 4:14)—implying that she may indeed have been called of God as deliverer for her people. In the same way, our own acts of courage may be the fulfillment of a destined role of leadership that is part of our calling.

In today's world we need people who are fearless and firm in their resolve regarding truth and righteousness. Courage to do what one knows is right requires integrity of the soul. We all can be more courageous in standing up for our beliefs and values. We can say with king Lamoni: "I know, in the strength of the Lord thou canst do all things" (Alma 20:4).

Every act of courage, like a towering tree with outreaching limbs, provides sheltering comfort for generations to come. Every inch of the land we now live on was once a frontier tamed in earlier days by intrepid pioneers whose vision was fixed on the enduring joy of their children and grandchildren. We venerate in gratitude the memory of mothers who gave birth to their young on the prairie trek and the triumph of fathers who placed hope and honor above life and limb. For their courage in planting the seeds of a better life in the soil of sacrifice our gratitude endures forever.

There is no liberty of the present hour but what was wrung from the clutches of tyranny by fearless fathers of freedom who knew their acts of fortitude would one day sustain the lives of countless millions of God's children seeking a better way. There is no freedom in our day but what was bought by the bravery of men and women—pioneers in their own right—who sang as one the battle hymn of courage as they marched forth in the never-ending quest to preserve liberty and right against the arrayed forces of conquest and greed. For these heroes of valor who raised the title of liberty—often at the cost of their own last breath—we gratefully pay our genuine respect. The landscape of our lives is sheltered by forests of immortal courage that remind us, in welcoming ways, that a price has been paid for our comforts and well-being. And we are thankful.

But not alone in monumental acts of bravery is courage revealed. There are countless acts of courage—quiet, patient, and enduring—unfolding in our homes and schools and churches and places of work every hour of every day. Such acts of courage inspire us, invoke our admiration, kindle our gratitude: Youth who choose the right, parents (sometimes in solitary service) who raise their families in unity and love, workers who remain at the grindstone of their daily stations of self-sufficiency and industry, brothers and sisters who serve the needs of others with charity and devotion, the unmarried who ply the trails of life unbroken though alone, and all who honor their covenants before the Lord. These are, in modest ways, authentic progeny of the two thousand stripling warriors of Helaman, who long ago remembered in fearless valor the faith of their mothers. These are, in their own humble way, the children of Moses and Abinadi and Samuel the Lamanite, whose triumphs of courage reverberate down through time and fill with light our own daily acts of courage to uphold the right. When we mark down in the book of our deeds those unpretentious but authentic acts of courage to which we rise in everyday life, we are expressing our thanks to our God for the opportunity to be kinder, better, and more in tune with His gospel truth.

"What is courage?" asks President Harold B. Lee: "Courage is the quality of every virtue at its highest testing point" (*The Teachings of Harold B. Lee*, Clyde J. Williams, ed. [Salt Lake City: Deseret Book Co., 1996], 606). Said President Gordon B. Hinckley, "Inner courage is a necessary virtue of those who follow the Lord" ("Living with Our Convictions," *Ensign*, Sept. 2001, 2). In this they echo the essence of David's words: "Be of good courage, and he shall strengthen your heart, all ye that hope in the LORD" (Ps. 31:24). Such are fitting mottos for all with the faith to know in their hearts that we can do all things in the strength of the Lord. Ultimately, there is no courage in this world to equal the majestic act of atoning grace performed on our behalf by the Only Begotten, the Son of God. But we can, line upon line, and precept upon precept, follow meekly in His footsteps, and through endless small acts of moral courage, take upon ourselves more and more of the divine nature as we make our way, undaunted, toward the eternal tree of life to partake at last, in thanksgiving, of the fruit of divine love.

APPENDIX FF
SATAN

Satan (meaning: adversary), who is Lucifer, the principal devil and primordial enemy to God, is mentioned in the Old Testament nineteen times, fourteen of them in the book of Job. As the enemy of all righteousness, Satan is referenced frequently in the text of the Doctrine and Covenants under various names: fallen angel, Perdition, Lucifer, son of the morning, Satan, old serpent, and devil.

The word *Perdition* in English usage comes from the Latin verb *perdere*, meaning to lose. Assuredly Satan is the archetype of the loser, for as an angel in authority in the premortal realm who rebelled against the Almighty God, he lost forever the divinely appointed opportunity to receive an inheritance of glory and exaltation (see Isa. 14:12–15).

The word *Lucifer* means literally "the shining one" or "lightbringer" (see Bible Dictionary, 726). This name, which derives from the Latin word for light (compare the related word *lucid*), is the equivalent of the appellation "son of the morning."

The word *Satan* in its Greek, Latin, and Hebrew sources, means "adversary"—the perfect characterization of the fallen angel's defining role in opposing the Father's plan of redemption and rejecting the choice of Jehovah as Redeemer from the foundations of the world.

The word *devil* in its Latin and Greek etymological derivation means "slanderer"—a further characterization of the fallen angel's strategy in opposing the eternal source of truth.

The case of Lucifer (Perdition, Satan, devil) is the most fundamental example of irony in the scriptures, for how could a being of light (son of the morning) transform himself into the archetypal representative of darkness? The benighted personality of Satan stands in infinite contrast to the grandeur of the eternal source of light and truth, even the Father and the Son.

The heavens wept over Lucifer, for he was an angel "in authority in the presence of God" (D&C 76:25). He held high office. It was this tragic transformation, this total abdication of godly potential in one of the leading sons of God in the spirit realm, that caused the heavens to weep (see D&C 76:26). In the visions of eternity granted to the prophet Enoch, he also beheld Satan: "And he had a great chain in his hand, and it veiled the whole face of the earth with darkness; and he looked up and laughed, and his angels rejoiced" (Moses 7:26; compare also D&C 29:36; Moses 1:19; 4:1–3).

The condition of those who followed Satan caused God to weep (see Moses 7:28), much to the discomfort of Enoch—until he was told the reason why: "Behold, their sins shall be upon the heads of their fathers; Satan shall be their father, and misery shall be their doom; and the whole heavens shall weep over them, even all the workmanship of mine hands; wherefore should not the heavens weep, seeing these shall suffer?" (Moses 7:37). It is the inevitable suffering of the wicked, brought about by their own choices, that causes the heavens to weep—seeing that the divine plan of the atoning sacrifice would otherwise save God's children through the grace and truth of the Almighty and the obedience and righteousness of the faithful. But Lucifer and his followers would not have it so—hence the triumphant campaign of heaven to thwart his designs. No wonder his diabolical work is mentioned so frequently in the text of the Doctrine and Covenant. The application for modern readers is to reject the enticements of Satan and accept with full devotion the Father's plan of happiness brought about through the "merits, and mercy, and grace of the Holy Messiah" (2 Ne. 2:8).

Satan also has a pervasive presence in the chronicles of the Book of Mormon. From the perspective of an overarching view of the full history of God's people in the New World during a millennium of time, Mormon concludes: "And behold, it is he [Satan] who is the author of all sin. And behold, he doth carry on his works of darkness and secret murder, and doth hand down their plots, and their oaths, and their covenants, and their plans of awful wickedness, from generation to generation according as he can get hold upon the hearts of the children of men" (Hel. 6:30). The Book of Mormon confirms that Satan's tenure is of primordial origin, for he enticed Adam and Eve to partake of the forbidden fruit, conspired with Cain to commit murder through a secret compact, motivated the building of the Tower of Babel, and spread darkness and abominations across the globe. Furthermore, "it is that same being who put it into the heart of Gadianton to still carry on the work of darkness, and of secret murder; and he has brought it forth from the beginning of man even down to this time" (Hel. 6:29).

Satan is mentioned in the Book of Mormon twenty-six times. In the guise of Lucifer, he is mentioned once: "How art thou fallen from heaven, O Lucifer, son of the morning! Art thou cut down to the ground, which did weaken the nations!" (2 Ne. 24:12; compare Isa. 14:12). Nephi outlines with precision the strategies used by Satan (Lucifer):

> For behold, at that day [when the Book of Mormon is to come forth] shall he rage in the hearts of the children of men, and stir them up to anger against that which is good.
>
> And others will he pacify, and lull them away into carnal security, that they will say: All is well in Zion; yea, Zion prospereth, all is well—and thus the devil cheateth their souls, and leadeth them away carefully down to hell.
>
> And behold, others he flattereth away, and telleth them there is no hell; and he saith unto them: I am no devil, for there is none—and thus he whispereth in their ears, until he grasps them with his awful chains, from whence there is no deliverance.
>
> Yea, they are grasped with death, and hell; and death, and hell, and the devil, and all that have been seized therewith must stand before the throne of God, and be judged according to their works, from whence they must go into the place prepared for them, even a lake of fire and brimstone, which is endless torment.
>
> Therefore, wo be unto him that is at ease in Zion!
>
> Wo be unto him that crieth: All is well!
>
> Yea, wo be unto him that hearkeneth unto the precepts of men, and denieth the power of God, and the gift of the Holy Ghost!
>
> Yea, wo be unto him that saith: We have received, and we need no more! (2 Ne. 28:20–27)

Clearly Satan has devised a complex and meticulous system of temptations to draw mankind from the pathway of righteous and onto the darkened detours of life, with their inevitable downward spiral of "captivity and death, according to the captivity and power of the devil; for he seeketh that all men might be miserable like unto himself" (2 Ne. 2:27; compare 2 Ne. 9:9). King Benjamin declined to enumerate all the ways in which man can commit sin: "But this much I can tell you, that if ye do not watch yourselves, and your thoughts, and your words, and your deeds, and observe the commandments of God, and continue in the faith of what ye have heard concerning the coming of our Lord, even unto the end of your lives, ye must perish. And now, O man, remember, and perish not" (Mosiah 4:30). The whole gist of the matter concerning Satan—the nemesis in the wake of the Savior—was summarized with precision in the word of God revealed unto Abraham concerning the premortal realm:

> And there stood one among them that was like unto God, and he said unto those who were with him: We will go down, for there is space there, and we will take of these materials, and we will make an earth whereon these may dwell;
>
> And we will prove them herewith, to see if they will do all things whatsoever the Lord their God shall command them;
>
> And they who keep their first estate shall be added upon; and they who keep not their first estate shall not have glory in the same kingdom with those who keep their first estate; and they who keep their second estate shall have glory added upon their heads for ever and ever.
>
> And the Lord said: Whom shall I send? And one answered like unto the Son of Man: Here am I, send me. And another answered and said: Here am I, send me. And the Lord said: I will send the first.
>
> And the second was angry, and kept not his first estate; and, at that day, many followed after him. (Abr. 3:24–28)

To this day the hosts of Satan—he who would usurp the honor of God (see Moses 4:1)—rage in the cauldron of darkness that recoils from the power of the glory of heaven. Ultimately, Michael (Adam) and his armies will dispel Satan and his benighted minions forever (see D&C 88:111–116).

APPENDIX GG
GOD THE FATHER

English theologian William Romaine, a man of unusual wisdom, once proclaimed: "Gratitude to God makes even a temporal blessing taste of heaven." And so it is: when viewed through the lens of heartfelt thanks, the upward path of our mortal journey is marked throughout by the footprints of the divine, confirming at every turn our heavenly source. In a thousand places and more the holy word of God reminds us again and again to be grateful to God for His matchless love and to show by our thanks and praise and anthems of joy that we love Him with all our heart, mind, and soul—for such reasons as these:

Mercy. It is only the mercy of God and His Only Begotten Son—Savior and King—that brings us the hope of resounding triumph over sin and death through the plan of redeeming grace, empowered through faith, enacted through repentance, covenanted through baptism, and sanctified through the gift of the Holy Ghost.

Mighty works. We celebrate in awe the epic deeds of God in renewing life on earth through Noah and the ark, in freeing the house of Israel from Egyptian bondage through the hand of Moses, in guiding chosen families across the world to safety in ancient America, and in bringing about the Restoration of the gospel through the Prophet Joseph Smith. We remember with joy the mighty works of God in our personal lives and family circles—the touch of God on our marriages and family relationships to guide and direct, bless and magnify, preserve and edify.

Goodness. Jesus declared: "[T]here is none good but one, *that is*, God" (Mark 10:18). In our Father in Heaven is grandly revealed the perfection of goodness. The source of our faith in Him is our certain assurance of His supreme goodness.

Justice. Before God, the Great Magistrate, and before His Son, our Advocate with the Father, we will all be judged. How daunting is this prospect—yet how comforting to know that the judgment of heaven is just and pure, and that through faith and godly sorrow unto genuine repentance we can look forward to the Day of Judgment with the trust and hope that the atoning process of cleansing and purification will have prepared us well for this awesome event.

Righteousness. We are grateful to God for His supernal righteousness. We have enduring faith that He always keeps His word and honors in full His covenant vows. We know that He acts without the slightest degree of variance from the pathway of truth and light.

Glory. How can we fathom the glory of God and His majestic enlightenment? We can look into the eyes of our little children and see therein the light of God shining with purity and radiance. We can look upon the temples of God as beacons of glory and peace, shining through the blackened mists of worldliness surrounding us. We can view with our mind's eye the visions of grandeur—the heavenly home of the God of glory from whence we sprang as spirit beings and to which we shall return through obedience and valor. We can discern across the span of holy writ the residue of glory therein suffused through the witness of God's chosen prophets in all generations of time, and we can feel in our heart that these things are true. By virtue of His love and munificent care, God has left us tokens of His glory scattered throughout our lives to remind us each day of what can be and what is to come. We are grateful for the presence of glory within our lives placed there in kindness by a gracious God.

Greatness. How can we attune ourselves in thankful devotion to the greatness of our Father in Heaven? Only from the point of view of meekness and humility do we come to appreciate how truly great our Father is. Through a glimpse into His infinite majesty we can begin to see the contours of who we can *become*—sons and daughters of God with the destiny to harvest the greatness that lies for now as a sprouting seed of eternal lives within our soul.

Answers to prayers. We are assured that our prayers "come up into the ears of the Lord of Sabaoth, and are recorded in the book of the names of the sanctified, even them of the celestial world" (see D&C 88:2). What a glorious wonder that our very words expressed in prayers to God are perceived and registered upon the pages of divine administration for our benefit and well-being.

Power. Miracles are wrought by the power of God. The Atonement works on the principle of power. Faith operates as an agency of power. The mighty change that the penitent feel and the devoted experience is the joyous result of heavenly power put to work on our behalf. The priesthood of God functions by power, for God is not a God of weakness, but a God of might. We have joy in the knowledge that God is extending His arm of power to effect the conversion, edification, and purification of His children.

Holiness. We are grateful that God is a God of holiness: "Behold, I am God; Man of Holiness is my name; Man of Counsel is my name; and Endless and Eternal is my name, also" (Moses 7:35). We thank our Father in Heaven for His gift divine—the perfect model for holiness in His own being, and that of His Son, even Jesus the Christ. We gather in holy places of safety and refuge to worship in reverence in the latter days.

When we begin at last to grasp the transcendent love of our mighty God for His children, every one, and the design of salvation—inexorable and all-encompassing—brought about for our good through His grace and lovingkindness, then we are overcome with a deep sense of gratitude. Beholding our future life with the eye of hope and a vision of thanks we comprehend more clearly the eternal nature of our sacred covenants with God and the blessings that are predicated upon our obedience to His commandments. President Wilford Woodruff said it so well in his conference talk in April 1881:

I feel that of all people under heaven we ought to be the most grateful to our God; and that we ought to remember to keep our covenants, and humble ourselves before him, and labor with all our hearts to discharge faithfully the responsibilities which devolve upon us. (*The Discourses of Wilford Woodruff*, G. Homer Durham, ed. [Salt Lake City: Bookcraft, 1946], 122)

APPENDIX HH
ISAIAH

The Lord's entreaty in April 1830 to the Saints of His newly organized Church and kingdom was this: "And the members shall manifest before the church, and also before the elders, by a godly walk and conversation, that they are worthy of it, that there may be works and faith agreeable to the holy scriptures—walking in holiness before the Lord" (D&C 20:69).

It was the same message that Isaiah and all of the Lord's prophets had been promulgating since the foundation of the world in words so plain that, as Nephi said, they could not be misunderstood: "And now behold, my people, ye are a stiffnecked people; wherefore, I have spoken plainly unto you, that ye cannot misunderstand. And the words which I have spoken shall stand as a testimony against you; for they are sufficient to teach any man the right way; for the right way is to believe in Christ and deny him not; for by denying him ye also deny the prophets and the law" (2 Ne. 25:28).

Isaiah captured with uncommon excellence the dramatic and compelling contrast between the godly walk of the Saints in Zion and the staggering, uncertain meanderings of the misguided and prideful souls in Babylon, or Sodom and Gomorrah, or whatever other worldly habitation they were want to frequent. There are three grand themes that emerge from the early chapters of Isaiah: first, the humility and yielding spirit of reverence that all of the prophets, including Isaiah, displayed in accepting their commission from the Lord; second, the perennial prophetic message to "stand in holy places" (2 Chron. 35:5; Ps. 24:3; Matt. 24:15; D&C 45:32; 87:8; 101:22); and third, the appeal to flee from worldly entanglements and respond to the brilliant light of Zion's beacon upon the mount. These three themes are plainly visible in the contrasting portraits of Zion and Babylon (or Sodom) that Isaiah paints for any eyes to discern that can see with the spirit of prophecy and for any ears to perceive that can hear the whisperings of the Spirit.

Isaiah (meaning: the Lord is salvation) was one of the greatest prophets of the Lord in any dispensation—and the most quoted of all the prophets in holy writ. Jesus said of him, "great are the words of Isaiah" (3 Ne. 23:1). The book of Isaiah is one of the major prophetic books of the Old Testament, along with Jeremiah, Lamentations (by Jeremiah), Ezekiel, and Daniel. Isaiah's ministry in Jerusalem was in the time frame 740–701 BC. He was chief advisor to Hezekiah, king of Judah.

In his prophetic and inspired discourse, Isaiah captures with consummate skill the grand and sweeping contours of the Lord's plan for mankind. If blessings of peace and spiritual awakening are to be forthcoming unto Israel, then Israel must obey; the disobedient are to be scattered and chastened until they reform their ways. Nevertheless, in the Lord's due time, He will remember His promises to the faithful and reign as Lord and King in the midst of His children forever. Isaiah is unequalled in his ability to speak as if viewing a panoramic vista encompassing the entire range of the Lord's plan of salvation—from the pre-mortal existence to the meridian of time to the millennial reign and the ultimate consummation of covenant blessings. Often Isaiah will span the entire range of man's existence in the space of a verse or two—in breathtaking and inspiring arches of time—always returning to the central theme of the Messiah, the Savior of mankind.

The main themes, events, and personalities in the Book of Isaiah are as follows:

Israel is corrupt; the Lord rejects Israel's vain oblations and sacrifices and calls upon the people to repent and be restored: "Come now, and let us reason together, saith the LORD: though your sins be as scarlet, they shall be as white as snow; though they be red like crimson, they shall be as wool. If ye be willing and obedient, ye shall eat the good of the land: But if ye refuse and rebel, ye shall be devoured with the sword: for the mouth of the LORD hath spoken *it*." (Isa. 1:18–20)

Isaiah foresees the latter-day restoration and the renewal of temple work; the wicked at that day will flee unto the rocks for shame: "And it shall come to pass in the last days, *that* the mountain of the LORD's house shall be established in the top of the mountains, and shall be exalted above the hills; and all nations shall flow unto it. And many people shall go and say, Come ye, and let us go up to the mountain of the LORD, to the house of the God of Jacob; and he will teach us of his ways, and we will walk in his paths: for out of Zion shall go forth the law, and the word of the LORD from Jerusalem. . . . O house of Jacob, come ye, and let us walk in the light of the LORD. " (Isa. 2:2–3, 5)

Israel is to be punished for wickedness, including the prideful daughters of Zion. In the millennial day, the daughters of Zion are to be cleansed and the homes and assemblies of Zion to be protected through the glory of the Lord: "And the LORD will create upon every dwelling place of mount Zion, and upon her assemblies, a cloud and smoke by day, and the shining of a flaming fire by night: for upon all the glory *shall be* a defence. And there shall be a tabernacle for a shadow in the daytime from the heat, and for a place of refuge, and for a covert from storm and from rain." (Isa. 4:5–6)

The Lord's vineyard (Israel) is to become desolate and the people scattered because of wickedness, but the Lord will gather them again in the latter days: "Therefore is the anger of the LORD kindled against his people, and he hath stretched forth his hand against them, and hath smitten them: and the hills did tremble, and their carcases *were* torn in the midst of the streets. For all this his anger is not turned away, but his hand *is* stretched out still. And he will lift up an ensign to the nations from far, and will hiss unto them from the end of the earth: and, behold, they shall come with speed swiftly." (Isa. 5:25–26)

Isaiah is called by the Lord to the prophetic office: "Also I heard the voice of the Lord, saying, Whom shall I send, and who will go for us? Then said I, Here *am* I; send me. And he said, Go, and tell this people,

Hear ye indeed, but understand not; and see ye indeed, but perceive not." (Isa. 6:8–9)

Amidst war and contention, the promise of a coming Messiah is given: "Therefore the Lord himself shall give you a sign; Behold, a virgin shall conceive, and bear a son, and shall call his name Immanuel." (Isa. 7:14)

Christ will establish accountability in Israel through His eternal ministry, being a stumbling block to some, but salvation to those who look to Him: "And he shall be for a sanctuary; but for a stone of stumbling and for a rock of offence to both the houses of Israel, for a gin and for a snare to the inhabitants of Jerusalem. . . . Bind up the testimony, seal the law among my disciples. And I will wait upon the LORD, that hideth his face from the house of Jacob, and I will look for him." (Isa. 8:14, 16–17)

The coming of the Lord is foretold: "For unto us a child is born, unto us a son is given: and the government shall be upon his shoulder: and his name shall be called Wonderful, Counsellor, The mighty God, The everlasting Father, The Prince of Peace. Of the increase of *his* government and peace *there shall be* no end, upon the throne of David, and upon his kingdom, to order it, and to establish it with judgment and with justice from henceforth even for ever." (Isa. 9:6–7)

The destruction of Assyria is set forth as a symbol of the destruction of the wicked at the Second coming.

The stem of Jesse (Christ) is to come and judge in righteousness; knowledge of God will be throughout the earth in the Millennium; the Lord will raise up an ensign to gather His people in the latter days: "And there shall come forth a rod out of the stem of Jesse, and a Branch shall grow out of his roots: And the spirit of the LORD shall rest upon him, the spirit of wisdom and understanding, the spirit of counsel and might, the spirit of knowledge and of the fear of the LORD; . . . And in that day there shall be a root of Jesse, which shall stand for an ensign of the people; to it shall the Gentiles seek: and his rest shall be glorious." (Isa. 11:1–2, 10)

Praise of the Lord shall be heard in the millennial day: "And in that day thou shalt say, O LORD, I will praise thee: though thou wast angry with me, thine anger is turned away, and thou comfortedst me. Behold, God *is* my salvation; I will trust, and not be afraid: for the LORD JEHOVAH *is* my strength and *my* song; he also is become my salvation." (Isa. 12:1–2)

The fall of Babylon is a type of the destruction of the wicked at the Second Coming (see Isa. 13).

Israel is to be gathered for the millennial rest; Lucifer was cast out of heaven for rebellion and ungodly pride; Israel to triumph over Babylon: "How art thou fallen from heaven, O Lucifer, son of the morning! *how* art thou cut down to the ground, which didst weaken the nations! For thou hast said in thine heart, I will ascend into heaven, I will exalt my throne above the stars of God: I will sit also upon the mount of the congregation, in the sides of the north: I will ascend above the heights of the clouds; I will be like the most High. (Isa.14:12–14.)

Moab (a symbol for the wickedness of the world) is to be laid waste and will mourn in consequence of sin; the Lord to judge in righteousness (see Isa. 15–16).

Israel is to be scattered for her forgetfulness, yet the Lord will rebuke the nations that act against her and cause Israel again to be gathered (see Isa. 17–18).

Sanction of the Lord against nations is to be resolved through the blessings of the Lord to the world and to Israel (see Isa. 19–20).

Babylon is to fall (see Isa. 21).

Jerusalem is to be scourged; the Lord will hold the keys of the house of David: "And the key of the house of David will I lay upon his shoulder; so he shall open, and none shall shut; and he shall shut, and none shall open. And I will fasten him *as* a nail in a sure place; and he shall be for a glorious throne to his father's house. . . . In that day, saith the LORD of hosts, shall the nail that is fastened in the sure place be removed, and be cut down, and fall; and the burden that *was* upon it shall be cut off: for the LORD hath spoken *it*. (Isa. 22:22–23, 25)

Tyre is to be destroyed; men will transgress the covenant; but the wicked are to be overthrown at the Second Coming: "The earth also is defiled under the inhabitants thereof; because they have transgressed the laws, changed the ordinance, broken the everlasting covenant. Therefore hath the curse devoured the earth, and they that dwell therein are desolate: therefore the inhabitants of the earth are burned, and few men left. (Isa. 24:5–6)

The Lord will prepare a feast of truth in mount Zion; He shall overcome death: "He will swallow up death in victory; and the Lord GOD will wipe away tears from off all faces; and the rebuke of his people shall he take away from off all the earth: for the LORD hath spoken *it*. (Isa. 25:8)

Trust in the Lord, who brings about the Atonement and the Resurrection: "Trust ye in the LORD for ever: for in the LORD JEHOVAH *is* everlasting strength. (Isa. 26:4)

Israel is to "blossom and bud" (Isa. 27).

The Lord will bless the righteous with revealed truth and with the foundation of the Redeemer:

"Whom shall he teach knowledge? and whom shall he make to understand doctrine? *them that are* weaned from the milk, *and* drawn from the breasts. For precept *must be* upon precept, precept upon precept; line upon line, line upon line; here a little, *and* there a little: . . . Therefore thus saith the Lord GOD, Behold, I lay in Zion for a foundation a stone, a tried stone, a precious corner *stone*, a sure foundation: he that believeth shall not make haste." (Isa. 28:9–11, 16)

The Restoration and coming forth of the Book of Mormon are foretold: "Therefore, behold, I will proceed to do a marvellous work among this people, *even* a marvellous work and a wonder: for the wisdom of their wise *men* shall perish, and the understanding of their prudent *men* shall be hid." (Isa. 29:14)

The scattering and gathering of Israel are explained; the future reign of the Lord is declared: "And therefore will the LORD wait, that he may be gracious unto you, and therefore will he be exalted, that he may have mercy upon you: for the LORD *is* a God of judgment: blessed *are* all they that wait for him." (Isa. 30:18)

Israel is reproved for alignment with Egypt (worldly connections) rather than turning to God as defender (see Isa. 31).

King Messiah is to "reign in righteousness" (Isa. 32).

The Lord is to return after a great apostasy; Zion is to be perfected: "Look upon Zion, the city of our solemnities: thine eyes shall see Jerusalem a quiet habitation, a tabernacle *that* shall not be taken down; not one of the stakes thereof shall ever be removed, neither shall any of the cords thereof be broken." (Isa. 33:20)

The Second Coming as a day of vengeance is prophesied (see Isa. 34).

In the day of restoration, the dessert shall blossom as a rose: "The wilderness and the solitary place shall be glad for them; and the desert shall rejoice, and blossom as the rose. It shall blossom abundantly, and rejoice even with joy and singing: the glory of Lebanon shall be given unto it, the excellency of Carmel and Sharon, they shall see the glory of the LORD, *and* the excellency of our God. Strengthen ye the weak hands, and confirm the feeble knees." (Isa. 35:1–3)

The Assyrians come against Judah; Isaiah counsels Hezekiah with prophetic pronouncements about the defeat of the enemy—which are fulfilled (see Isa. 36–39).

Isaiah speaks Messianically—prepare the way of the Lord, who comes to comfort and nurture His people; the Great Creator will lift His people up: "But they that wait upon the LORD shall renew *their* strength; they shall mount up with wings as eagles; they shall run, and not be weary; *and* they shall walk, and not faint." (Isa. 40:31)

The Lord is to preserve Israel: "Fear thou not; for I *am* with thee: be not dismayed; for I *am* thy God: I will strengthen thee; yea, I will help thee; yea, I will uphold thee with the right hand of my righteousness." (Isa. 41:10)

The Lord shall bring His law and judgment; He will free the prisoners: "I the LORD have called thee in righteousness, and will hold thine hand, and will keep thee, and give thee for a covenant of the people, for a light of the Gentiles; To open the blind eyes, to bring out the prisoners from the prison, *and* them that sit in darkness out of the prison house." (Isa. 42:6–7)

The Lord is Israel's God and Savior: "But now thus saith the LORD that created thee, O Jacob, and he that formed thee, O Israel, Fear not: for I have redeemed thee, I have called *thee* by thy name; thou *art* mine. . . . Ye *are* my witnesses, saith the LORD, and my servant whom I have chosen: that ye may know and believe me, and understand that I *am* he: before me there was no God formed, neither shall there be after me. I, *even* I, *am* the LORD; and beside me *there is* no saviour." (Isa. 43:1, 10–11)

The Lord will pour His Spirit upon the people of Israel (see Isa. 44).

Cyrus will free the Babylonian captives; the Lord is salvation; every knee shall confess: "Look unto me, and be ye saved, all the ends of the earth: for I *am* God, and *there is* none else. I have sworn by myself, the word is gone out of my mouth *in* righteousness, and shall not return, That unto me every knee shall bow, every tongue shall swear." (Isa. 45:22–23)

The Lord alone is God; He shall save Israel; the wicked are to be destroyed (see Isa. 46–47).

Israel is chosen of God: "Behold, I have refined thee, but not with silver; I have chosen thee in the furnace of affliction." (Isa. 48:10)

Israel is to be a light unto the Gentiles and be gathered with their help in the latter days: "And he hath made my mouth like a sharp sword; in the shadow of his hand hath he hid me, and made me a polished shaft; in his quiver hath he hid me; And said unto me, Thou *art* my servant, O Israel, in whom I will be glorified." (Isa. 49:2–3) "Thus saith the Lord GOD, Behold, I will lift up mine hand to the Gentiles, and set up my standard to the people: and they shall bring thy sons in *their* arms, and thy daughters shall be carried upon *their* shoulders. And kings shall be thy nursing fathers, and their queens thy nursing mothers: they shall bow down to thee with *their* face toward the earth, and lick up the dust of thy feet; and thou shalt know that I *am* the LORD: for they shall not be ashamed that wait for me." (Isa. 49:22–23)

The Lord will be a willing Redeemer: "The Lord GOD hath opened mine ear, and I was not rebellious, neither turned away back. I gave my back to the smiters, and my cheeks to them that plucked off the hair: I hid not my face from shame and spitting." (Isa. 50:5–6)

The Lord shall comfort Zion and cause His faithful to be gathered with joy: "For the LORD shall comfort Zion: he will comfort all her waste places; and he will make her wilderness like Eden, and her desert like the garden of the LORD; joy and gladness shall be found therein, thanksgiving, and the voice of melody. . . . Therefore the redeemed of the LORD shall return, and come with singing unto Zion; and everlasting joy *shall be* upon their head: they shall obtain gladness and joy; *and* sorrow and mourning shall flee away." (Isa. 51:3, 11)

Zion shall return in the last days and Israel shall be redeemed: "Awake, awake; put on thy strength, O Zion; put on thy beautiful garments, O Jerusalem, the holy city: . . . How beautiful upon the mountains are the feet of him that bringeth good tidings, that publisheth peace; that bringeth good tidings of good, that publisheth salvation; that saith unto Zion, Thy God reigneth! Thy watchmen shall lift up the voice; with the voice together shall they sing: for they shall see eye to eye, when the LORD shall bring again Zion. . . . Depart ye, depart ye, go ye out from thence, touch no unclean *thing*; go ye out of the midst of her; be ye clean, that bear the vessels of the LORD." (Isa. 52:1, 7–8, 11)

Messiah's sufferings are foretold as He brings about the Atonement: "Surely he hath borne our griefs, and carried our sorrows: yet we did esteem him stricken, smitten of God, and afflicted. . . . Yet it pleased the LORD to bruise him; he hath put *him* to grief: when thou shalt make his soul an offering for sin, he shall see *his* seed, he shall prolong *his* days, and the pleasure of the LORD shall prosper in his hand." (Isa. 53:4, 10)

In the last days Zion and her stakes shall be strengthened triumphantly: "Enlarge the place of thy tent, and let them stretch forth the curtains of thine habitations: spare not, lengthen thy cords, and strengthen thy stakes; For thou shalt break forth on the right hand and on the left; and thy seed shall inherit the Gentiles, and make the desolate cities to be inhabited." (Isa. 54:2–3)

Salvation is free; seek the Lord while He is near, though He is infinitely higher than are His children: "For my thoughts *are* not your thoughts, neither *are* your ways my ways, saith the LORD. For *as* the heavens are higher than the earth, so are my ways higher than your ways, and my thoughts than your thoughts." (Isa. 55:8–9)

All the righteous shall be exalted, even the sons of strangers: "Even unto them will I give in mine house and within my walls a place and a name better than of sons and of daughters: I will give them an everlasting name, that shall not be cut off. . . . Even them will I bring to my holy mountain, and make them joyful in my house of prayer: their burnt offerings and their sacrifices *shall be* accepted upon mine altar; for mine house shall be called an house of prayer for all people." (Isa. 56:5, 7)

The righteous will enter into the peace of the Lord; there is no peace for the wicked (see Isa. 57).

The law of the fast is explained; the Sabbath is to be honored: "If thou turn away thy foot from the sabbath, *from* doing thy pleasure on my holy day; and call the sabbath a delight, the holy of the LORD, honourable; and shalt honour him, not doing thine own ways, nor finding thine own pleasure, nor speaking *thine own* words: Then shalt thou delight thyself in the LORD; and I will cause thee to ride upon the high places of the earth, and feed thee with the heritage of Jacob thy father: for the mouth of the LORD hath spoken *it*." (Isa. 58:13–14)

Israel is separated from God through iniquity; the Messiah shall intercede on their behalf (see Isa. 59).

In the last days Israel shall be gathered, in conjunction with the enlightened Gentile nations; the Lord will be their light: "The sun shall be no more thy light by day; neither for brightness shall the moon give light unto thee: but the LORD shall be unto thee an everlasting light, and thy God thy glory." (Isa. 60:19)

The Messiah will bring to pass His eternal mission and cause the establishment of Zion: "The Spirit of the Lord GOD *is* upon me; because the LORD hath anointed me to preach good tidings unto the meek; he hath sent me to bind up the brokenhearted, to proclaim liberty to the captives, and the opening of the prison to *them that are* bound; To proclaim the acceptable year of the LORD, and the day of vengeance of our God; to comfort all that mourn; To appoint unto them that mourn in Zion, to give unto them beauty for ashes, the oil of joy for mourning, the garment of praise for the spirit of heaviness; that they might be called trees of righteousness, the planting of the LORD, that he might be glorified." (Isa. 61:1–3)

At the Second Coming, the Lord will return arrayed in red as the atoning King: "Wherefore *art thou* red in thine apparel, and thy garments like him that treadeth in the winefat? I have trodden the winepress alone; and of the people *there was* none with me: for I will tread them in mine anger, and trample them in my fury; and their blood shall be sprinkled upon my garments, and I will stain all my raiment. For the day of vengeance *is* in mine heart, and the year of my redeemed is come." (Isa. 63:2–4)

The Lord has prepared glorious blessings for the faithful: "For since the beginning of the world *men* have not heard, nor perceived by the ear, neither hath the eye seen, O God, beside thee, *what* he hath prepared for him that waiteth for him." (Isa. 64:4)

Though ancient Israel rejected the Lord, the Israel of the latter days shall rejoice in the millennial triumph: "They shall not labour in vain, nor bring forth for trouble; for they *are* the seed of the blessed of the LORD, and their offspring with them. And it shall come to pass, that before they call, I will answer; and while they are yet speaking, I will hear." (Isa. 65:23–24)

Israel is to enjoy great blessings at the Second Coming; the wicked are to be destroyed; the gospel is to be preached to the gentiles (see Isa. 66).

Modern-day scripture (the Book of Mormon and the Doctrine and Covenants)—in numerous instances—sheds valuable light on the inspired words of Isaiah and constitutes the most dependable source for clarifying and understanding the magnificent words of this singularly important prophet of the Lord. In his day, Nephi extolled the universal importance of reading and pondering the words of Isaiah (which were included in the brass plates of Laban appropriated for the journey to the Promised Land):

And I did read many things unto them which were written in the books of Moses; but that I might more fully persuade them to believe in the Lord their Redeemer I did read unto them that which was written by the prophet Isaiah; for I did liken all scriptures unto us, that it might be for our profit and learning.

Wherefore I spake unto them, saying: Hear ye the words of the prophet, ye who are a remnant of the house of Israel, a branch who have been broken off; hear ye the words of the prophet, which were written unto all the house of Israel, and liken them unto yourselves, that ye may have hope as well as your brethren from whom ye have been broken off; for after this manner has the prophet written. (1 Ne. 19:23–24; compare Jacob's testimony in 2 Ne. 6:5)

To facilitate this process, Nephi and Jacob included abundant excerpts from the writings of Isaiah in the scriptural record: see 1 Ne. 20–21 (Isa. 48–49); 2 Ne. 7–8 (Isa. 50–51 and 52:1–2); 2 Ne. 12–24 (Isa. 2–14); and 2 Ne. 27 (Isa. 29). Throughout, Nephi (and to a lesser extent Jacob) gives commentary and exposition on the words of Isaiah, rendering them lucid and clear: "Wherefore, hearken, O my people, which are of the house of Israel, and give ear unto my words; for because the words of Isaiah are not plain unto you, nevertheless they are plain unto all those that are filled with the spirit of prophecy" (2 Ne. 25:4). For further excerpts from Isaiah, see also Mosiah 14 (Isa. 53), Mosiah 15 (portions of Isa. 52), and 3 Ne. 22 (Isa. 54).

Isaiah is mentioned six times in the Doctrine and Covenants: four times in connection with interpretations given of passages in Isaiah 11 and 52 (D&C 113:1, 3, 7 [twice]), once in connection with the vision of the spirit realm given to President Joseph F. Smith (see D&C 138:42), and once concerning the degrees of glory (see D&C 76:100).

The style of Isaiah is unique. Isaiah, the son of Amoz, was given by the Lord a profound gift to express with resounding impact, expressive power, and stark clarity the message of the visions accorded him as the spokesperson for the Lord in his day. His humble response to the call of the Lord is recorded in Isaiah 6 (see 2 Ne. 16). He wrote at a time when Israel had incurred the anger of the Lord—to an especially high degree—through her wanton behavior, pride, and idolatry. Isaiah's language soars and spirals with the flight of thought and symbolism. He intermingles references to events of his own day with those of coming events that are to unfold in the future—thus the reader must be prepared to engage in the breathtaking sweep of his diction that carries one from the distant past to the distant future and back again, often within the same passage. His message is the age-old prophetic message that "wickedness never was happiness" (see Alma 41:10), that Israel would suffer by persisting in her prideful and ungodly walk, and that good would eventually triumph in the last days as the faithful were gathered together in holy places of refuge.

In no other passages of scripture can one find the word of the Lord expressed with greater power or more lasting influence than in the writings of Isaiah. Isaiah's words are sustained by a vision of the transcendent and sublime mission of the Redeemer and the atoning power of the Father's plan of salvation. We hear the repeated expressions of joy as Israel's faithful are gathered once again to the protecting care of Zion's resorts. We see in our mind's eye the unfolding of the earthly ministry of the Savior and His condescension in coming among the children of men with saving grace. We listen as Isaiah continually reminds us of our covenant obligations before the Lord.

If the Book of Mormon is a "another testament of Jesus Christ," then Isaiah is the bridge that helps to unite the voice of the Old Testament and the voice of the New Testament (in which Isaiah is quoted more than any other prophet) with the voice of prophets from the Promised Land. We can be grateful that Isaiah is so often cited in the Book of Mormon, which serves a greater role in interpreting and unfolding the words of Isaiah than any other book.

APPENDIX II
JEREMIAH

Jeremiah is among the most courageous of the Lord's prophets in defiantly completing his mission in the face of fearful abuse and life-threatening adversity. The Lord had planted in his mouth and heart the word of God—and he had to deliver it in its pristine purity and awesome power to the ears of the deviant princes of the covenant. Nothing could detract or deter. "My word shall not pass away, but shall all be fulfilled" (D&C 1:38), is how the Lord framed it in our time. Why this inviolate spiritual constitution of the word? Because the word of God—and only the word of God—has the power to save and exalt. These two themes—strength to carry out one's mission in delivering the word of God despite adversity, and the blessings and power of the word of God delivered in our lives—form the essence of the message of Jeremiah to his contemporaries as well as to ourselves in the latter days.

Jeremiah (pronounced "jer'-uh-my'-uh"; meaning: raised up by Jehovah) was a prophet of the Lord during the days of Lehi and Daniel. The book of Jeremiah is one of the major prophetic books of the Old Testament, along with Isaiah, Lamentations (also written by Jeremiah), Ezekiel, and Daniel. Jeremiah prophesied during a forty-year period, from around 626 to 585 BC. His themes resound through the generations of time. He declares with power and authority the central governing principles of the gospel—that peace and happiness depend on obedience and honoring the covenants of the Lord, including developing a personal and spiritual relationship with Him; that the consequences of sin are destruction and war, dislocation and scattering, misery and woe; that the Lord will chasten His people until they learn to be virtuous and righteous; and that He will eventually establish a new covenant with His faithful children and gather them in from the four quarters of the earth to be their King.

Jeremiah was also the author of the book of Lamentations, one of the eleven books of the Old Testament that belong to the so-called *Hagiographa* ("sacred writings") of the Jewish canon, along with the books of Job, Psalms, Proverbs, Song of Solomon, Ruth, Ecclesiastes, Daniel, Esther, Ezra-Nehemiah (counted as one book), and Chronicles (also counted as one book).

Jeremiah's writings, in part, were included in the brass plates of Laban (see 1 Ne. 5:10–13; also 1 Ne. 7:14; Hel. 8:20). Nephi also alludes to Jeremiah in rebuking his rebellious brothers upon the return trip to guide Ishmael and his family to the encampment of Lehi: "For behold, the Spirit of the Lord ceaseth soon to strive with them [the people of Jerusalem]; for behold, they have rejected the prophets, and Jeremiah have they cast into prison. And they have sought to take away the life of my father, insomuch that they have driven him out of the land" (1 Ne. 7:14). Many generations later, Nephi, the son of Helaman, a few years before the birth of the Savior, invoked the name of Jeremiah, among many other prophets, to remind the people of the certainty of the coming of the Redeemer:

And now I would that ye should know, that even since the days of Abraham there have been many prophets that have testified these things; yea, behold, the prophet Zenos did testify boldly; for the which he was slain.

And behold, also Zenock, and also Ezias, and also Isaiah, and Jeremiah, (Jeremiah being that same prophet who testified of the destruction of Jerusalem) and now we know that Jerusalem was destroyed according to the words of Jeremiah. O then why not the Son of God come, according to his prophecy? (Hel. 8:19–20)

In terms of covenant history, Jeremiah's noble contemporary, Lehi, was obedient to the Lord in fleeing from Jerusalem with his family to preserve a branch of the house of Israel and establish the foundation for the coming forth of a second testament of Jesus Christ. This second testament, after the Bible, would be another witness of Christ—the Book of Mormon—that would rise from the dust as an integral part of the Restoration of the gospel in the latter days. Thus Jeremiah's ancient prophecy concerning a new covenant—even a new and everlasting covenant (see Jer. 31:31–34)—would be fulfilled in the return of the kingdom of God to earth prior to the Second Coming to extend the blessings of salvation and exaltation to all mankind, so that all who would choose to do so could know the Lord and follow in His footsteps.

Jeremiah Is Put in the Dungeon by Matthaeus Merian

APPENDIX JJ
EZEKIEL

Ezekiel (meaning: God will strengthen), one of the Lord's great prophets of the Old Testament, was a priest of the lineage of Zadok and a younger contemporary of Lehi, Jeremiah, and Daniel. Like King Jehoiachin of Judah, he was carried away to Babylon by the forces of Nebuchadnezzar. He prophesied during the period 592–570 BC. The Book of Ezekiel is one of the major prophetic books of the Old Testament, along with Isaiah, Jeremiah, and Daniel.

Ezekiel was granted extraordinary visions that establish the principles of the gospel pertaining to the house of Israel, then as now: the consequence of apostasy and idolatry are destruction and scattering; the consequences of repentance and remembering the covenants are peace, unity, and the blessing of being heirs with the Good Shepherd, to partake eternally of His everlasting glory in the kingdom of God.

The forty-eight chapters of Ezekiel comprise three main sections: prophecies of God's judgment against Jerusalem and the nations in proximity (chapters 1–24), prophecies concerning the gathering and restoration (chapters 25–39), and visions of the temple of the Lord, its reconstruction, and its sacred function (chapters 40–48). "O ye dry bones, hear the word of the LORD" (Ezek. 37:4)—and the eventual restoration of Israel; the stick of Judah (Bible) and stick of Joseph (Book of Mormon) are to be united in the latter days; and Messiah is to reign over a united people (chapter 37).

Ezekiel's authorship is authenticated in the Doctrine and Covenants: "And the great and abominable church, which is the whore of all the earth, shall be cast down by devouring fire, according as it is spoken by the mouth of Ezekiel the prophet, who spoke of these things, which have not come to pass but surely must, as I live, for abominations shall not reign" (D&C 29:21; compare Ezek. 38:22; 5:9–11). In addition, Ezekiel is mentioned as one of the noble and elect prophets witnessed by President Joseph F. Smith in his vision of the work of salvation in the spirit realm: "Moreover, Ezekiel, who was shown in vision the great valley of dry bones, which were to be clothed upon with flesh, to come forth again in the resurrection of the dead, living souls" (D&C 138:43; compare Ezek. 37:1–14).

Especially significant among Ezekiel's visionary messages is the prophecy of the future coming together of the scriptural record of Judah and that of Joseph:

> Moreover, thou son of man, take thee one stick, and write upon it, For Judah, and for the children of Israel his companions: then take another stick, and write upon it, For Joseph, the stick of Ephraim, and *for* all the house of Israel his companions:
> And join them one to another into one stick; and they shall become one in thine hand. (Ezek. 37:16–17)

This miraculous event was accomplished through the coming forth and publication of the Book of Mormon, "Proving to the world that the holy scriptures are true, and that God does inspire men and call them to his holy work in this age and generation, as well as in generations of old; Thereby showing that he is the same God yesterday, today, and forever. Amen" (D&C 20:11–12; see also D&C 27:5; 42:12; compare Isa. 29).

APPENDIX KK
DANIEL

The chronicles of the captivity of Israel—beginning in 587 BC under the vanquishing leadership of Nebuchadnezzar of Babylonia, and lasting until the decree of liberation of Cyrus in 537 BC, which allowed the return of the Jewish people to Jerusalem—provide ample illustrations for exceptional courage and spiritual strength on the part of many of the Israelite expatriates. Some of the most notable are Daniel and his young colleagues.

What was it that allowed them to stand firm, in the face of life-threatening challenges, to their standards and principles? What was it that gave them courage to draw the line and reaffirm their commitment to the covenant promises of righteousness and faithfulness? It was in the strength of the Lord, which they sought and obtained through mighty prayer and fasting, that they were able to perform their missions with exemplary valor. Character is always measured in the context of adversity and challenge.

Daniel (meaning: In the strength of the Lord) was one of the Lord's great prophets of the Old Testament and the author of the book that bears his name. The Book of Daniel stems from the time of the Babylonian conquest of Jerusalem. Daniel, apparently of royal heritage (see Dan. 1:3), was taken captive to the court of Nebuchadnezzar (who reigned around 604–562 BC) shortly before the turn of the sixth century BC. It was a period of foment and transition leading to the ultimate destruction of Jerusalem around 587 BC.

Daniel was renamed Belteshazzar by an officer of the royal court. He prophesied during his captivity in the same general time frame as Jeremiah and Ezekiel. He was a younger contemporary of Lehi, father of Nephi in the Book of Mormon. The Book of Daniel is one of the major prophetic books of the Old Testament, along with Isaiah, Jeremiah, and Ezekiel.

The Book of Daniel confirms by prophetic pronouncements that the Lord is in charge of the destiny of humankind, and that righteousness will ultimately prevail over the forces of worldly pride and power. Through obedience to the commandments of God, the faithful will receive magnificent blessings of wisdom and light and inherit a place in the triumphant kingdom of the Lord, which will roll forth until it fills the entire world. Daniel is a prominent example of "apocalyptic" writing (from the Greek word meaning "revealed" or "uncovered"), as in the Apocalypse or Revelation of John, where similar great and symbolic visions of the ultimate consummation of God's work are presented.

Key sections of the book include the narrative concerning the experiences of Daniel and his three companions in the court of Nebuchadnezzar (chapters 1–6), and the visions of Daniel concerning the grand design of the Lord for the unfolding of His gospel plan among the nations of the world and the ultimate restoration and glorious triumph of His kingdom in the latter days (chapters 7–12).

The nobility and valor of Daniel and his captive associates can be expressed in three grand themes: honoring eternal standards, abiding by revelation, and living by the power of prayer.

 POINT OF INTEREST

Nabu (known as Nebo in the Bible) was the Babylonian god of wisdom and writing, represented by a clay writing tablet and stylus. He was introduced by the Amorites into Mesopotamia about the same time as was Marduk; but while Marduk became Babylon's main deity, Nabu was first called a scribe and minister to Marduk and was later assimilated as Marduk's son. He gradually took office as patron of the scribes, replacing the Sumerian goddess Nisaba.

APPENDIX LL
NEBUCHADNEZZAR

Nebuchadnezzar (meaning: Nebo protect the crown or frontiers), king of Babylon in the period 604–561 BC, besieged Jerusalem and took away many captive to his country, including Zedekiah, king of Judah, and most of his subjects (see 2 Kings 24–25; Dan. 1–5; 1 Chron. 6:15; 2 Chron. 36:6–7, 10–13; Jer. 27–28; 29:1, 3; 34:1; 39:5): "And he burnt the house of the LORD, and the king's house, and all the houses of Jerusalem, and every great *man's* house burnt he with fire. And all the army of the Chaldees, that *were with* the captain of the guard, brake down the walls of Jerusalem round about. Now the rest of the people *that were* left in the city, and the fugitives that fell away to the king of Babylon, with the remnant of the multitude, did Nebuzar-adan the captain of the guard carry away" (2 Kings 25:9–11).

Ultimately, Cyrus the Great, king of Persia, defeated the Babylonian/Chaldean dynasty elevated to power by Nebuchadnezzar and issued a decree in 537 BC allowing the Jewish people to return from captivity in Babylon to rebuild the temple at Jerusalem (see 2 Chron. 36:22–23; Ezra 1; 3:7; Isa. 44:28; 45:1). Daniel was well received in the court of Cyrus (see Dan. 1:21; 6:28; 10:1).

Perhaps the most telling memory from the story of Nebuchadnezzar is the troubling dream he had one night concerning a stone hewn from the mountain without hands that destroyed a mighty image in human form. The king's wisemen were powerless to discover the secret of the dream, but Daniel was able to unfold its mystery through the blessings of the Spirit. It is instructive that when the answer came to Daniel "in a night vision" (Dan. 2:19), he immediately blessed the name of God and gave humble thanks and praise for the divine gift: "I thank thee, and praise thee, O thou God of my fathers, who hast given me wisdom and might, and hast made known unto me now what we desired of thee: for thou has made known unto us the king's matter" (Dan. 2:23). Daniel was able to save all condemned wisemen in the kingdom by advising Nebuchadnezzar correctly concerning the dream, which portended the coming of the restored kingdom of heaven to become "a great mountain" and fill "the whole earth" (Dan. 2:35).

But the king refused nevertheless to relinquish his idolatry, and a second dream depicting the king as a great and mighty tree that is hewn down at the behest of "an holy one coming down from heaven" (Dan. 4:23) was interpreted by Daniel as foretelling the king's demise. Daniel counseled the king in all candor, "break off thy sins in righteousness, and thine iniquities by shewing mercy to the poor; if it may be a lengthening of thy tranquility" (Dan. 4:27). But it was not to be: "The same hour was the thing fulfilled upon Nebuchadnezzar: and he was driven from men" (Dan. 4:33).

From his deposed perspective, it was an easy thing for the king, stripped now of his opulence, to confess: "I blessed the most High, and I praised and honoured him that liveth forever, whose dominion is an everlasting dominion, and his kingdom is from generation to generation . . . and those that walk in pride he is able to abase" (Dan. 4:34, 37).

The royal reveler Belshazzar, prince-regent in the wake of Nebuchadnezzar's reign (and, according to recent archaeological discoveries, apparently the son of Nabonidus, the last king of Babylon), did not fare much better after Daniel interpreted the celebrated and ominous writing on the wall of his chamber this way: "Thou art weighed in the balances, and art found wanting" (Dan. 5:27). That night Belshazzar was deposed by Darius the Mede. Thus continued the unfolding of the certain prediction that a succession of earthly kingdoms would fall, one after the other, until, ultimately, the Lord would restore a heavenly kingdom to the earth not made by the hand of man.

The stone "cut out of the mountain without hands" (Dan. 2:45) is the kingdom of God, which is to supersede all earthly kingdoms and fill the world with a heavenly dominion of truth and light under the supreme rulership of the Redeemer and Lord of Lords: "And in the days of these kings shall the God of heaven set up a kingdom, which shall never be destroyed: and the kingdom shall not be left to other people, but it shall break in pieces and consume all these kingdoms, and it shall stand for ever" (Dan. 2:44).

The destruction of Jerusalem and the captivity of Judah by the Babylonians correspond to the period of time when the Book of Mormon account begins. See, for example, the following: "For it came to pass in the commencement of the first year of the reign of Zedekiah, king of Judah, (my father, Lehi, having dwelt at Jerusalem in all his days); and in that same year there came many prophets, prophesying unto the people that they must repent, or the great city Jerusalem must be destroyed" (1 Ne. 1:4; compare 1 Ne. 5:12–13; Omni 1:15; Hel. 6:10; 8:21; 3 Ne. 19:14).

As the Lord said to Joseph Smith in October 1831, not long after the organization of the Church in our day: "The keys of the kingdom are committed unto man on the earth, and from thence shall the gospel roll forth unto the ends of the earth, as the stone which is cut out of the mountains without hands shall roll forth, until it has filled the whole earth" (D&C 65:2). Thus the figure of Nebuchadnezzar serves as an unforgettable emblem confirming the ephemeral nature of all earthly kingdoms and inexorable unfolding and expanding of the kingdom of God.

APPENDIX MM
HOSEA

One of the Savior's similes for the Atonement was the reference to a hen desiring to gather her chickens under her wings (see Matt. 23:37; 3 Ne. 10:4–6; D&C 10:65; 29:2; 43:24). This image is often used in the scriptures to convey the Lord's profound wish to nourish and nurture His sons and daughters—if only they would but humble themselves and obey His commandments.

The message of the prophet Hosea is the same—the deep compassion of the Lord for His people—very much like the love of a groom for his bride or the love of a father for his children. Even though Israel was prone to waywardness and hardheartedness, the Lord was ever ready to shower them with His mercy, even though "they knew not that I healed them" (Hosea 11:3). His message has perpetually been the same in all ages: "O Israel, return unto the Lord thy God" (Hosea 14:1).

The interrelated themes of compassion and the call to return home are pervasive in the Book of Hosea. They form the two sides of the same coin—the spiritual currency with which the Lord "buys" His ransomed children. As Paul said: "For ye are bought with a price: therefore glorify God in your body, and in your spirit, which are God's" (1 Cor. 6:20).

Hosea (pronounced "ho-see'-uh" or "ho-say'-uh") was one of the twelve prophets of the Old Testament with shorter books (though by no means reflecting messages of lesser import). Hosea is the only prophet of the Northern Kingdom whose writings have been handed down to us as part of the canon. He prophesied in the 8th century BC, probably in the latter reign of Jeroboam II and just prior to the ministry of Isaiah (who prophesied in the time span 740 to 701 BC). Hosea reflects the universal theme of all the prophets of God: that God is holy and supreme, and that happiness and joy can flow to mankind only through obedience to His laws and commandments. Though the people trek through the valley of darkness and misery occasioned by their iniquity and pride, yet will the Lord in His lovingkindness and mercy remember them in His own due time and guide them to learn how to emerge eventually into the light of His redemptive love. In short, the theme of Hosea is love.

Key sections of the Book of Hosea include: the calling of Hosea as a prophet (see Hosea 1); the vision of the ultimate restoration of Israel despite her current decline and iniquity (see Hosea 2–3); the House of Israel, in her current state, was destined to fall (see Hosea 4–5); Hosea's message of repentance and exhortation (see Hosea 6); Israel's unfortunate pathway of punishment and captivity for wrong-doing (see Hosea 7–10); and the love of the Lord to bring about a dawning of redemption for the Lord's people (see Hosea 11–14).

Hosea had a strong influence on later prophets (see for example Isa. 40–66; Jer. 2, 3; and Ezek. 16, 33).

APPENDIX NN
JONAH

When the Savior was asked to give a sign of His divinity, He referred to "the sign of the prophet Jonas [Jonah]. For as Jonas was three days and three nights in the whale's belly; so shall the Son of man be three days and three nights in the heart of the earth" (see Matt. 12:39–40).

The story of Jonah is a story of the irrepressible force of divine love in the world. The love of God for His children—all of His children—is sufficiently powerful to break through all barriers and result in the eventual triumph of glory and salvation, for "salvation is of the Lord" (Jon. 2:9). Nothing can restrain the effects of the love and grace of God—not death, not darkness, not worldly resistance or barriers, not the recalcitrance of the workers in Zion. God's purposes will be fulfilled.

The Atonement extends in its reach to all mankind. The work of the Lord is inexorable in its forward movement. "I will surely assemble, O Jacob, all of thee; I will surely gather the remnant of Israel" (Micah 2:12). The compassion of the Lord and the ultimate victory of His designs are the themes to be found in the story of Jonah.

Jonah lived during the reign of Jeroboam, king of Israel: "He [Jeroboam] restored the coast of Israel from the entering of Hamath unto the sea of the plain, according to the word of the LORD God of Israel, which he spake by the hand of his servant Jonah, the son of Amittai, the prophet, which *was* of Gath-hepher" (2 Kings 14:25). Jeroboam's reign lasted from around 790 BC to around 749 BC. During this same period, the prophets Hosea (see Hosea 1:1) and Amos (see Amos 1:1; 7:10–11) were active.

The Book of Jonah was written by an unknown later writer who is describing a series of related episodes from the prophet's life. The Book of Jonah is one of the twelve shorter prophetic books of the Old Testament, and one of several books, like Job, that are poetic in structure. The writer of the book uses Jonah's experiences to confirm the Lord's universal love for His children of all nationalities and origins—even the population of the Assyrian capital city. Just as Jonah had to learn the magnanimous nature of the Lord's charity and lovingkindness, so are we as followers of Christ enjoined to practice obedience, tolerance, and brotherly kindness in sharing the gospel with everyone.

The Book of Jonah unfolds according to the following general pattern: Jonah's commission from the Lord and the consequences of his failure to obey (see Jon. 1–2); Jonah's mission to Nineveh (see Jon. 3); and Jonah's coming to terms with the mercy of the Lord (see Jon. 4).

The story of Jonah is among the most famous in the Old Testament, in part because he was swallowed by a whale, where he remained for fully three days and three nights. But there are also multiple lessons of a spiritual nature to be learned from this account. We learn of the reality of obedience, the power of repentance, the gentleness of the Lord in teaching eternal lessons, and the mercy of the Lord in sparing the city of Nineveh when the citizens turned to Him. Through the eyes of Jonah we have the opportunity to understand the Lord's love in extending His invitation to all, for all have a chance to repent and embrace the saving truths of the gospel.

During His earthly ministry, the Savior made specific mention of Jonah, using the episode with the whale as a symbol of the death and resurrection of the Messiah: "Then certain of the scribes and of the Pharisees answered, saying, Master, we would see a sign from thee. But he answered and said unto them, An evil and adulterous generation seeketh after a sign; and there shall no sign be given to it, but the sign of the prophet Jonas [i.e., Jonah]: For as Jonas was three days and three nights in the whale's belly; so shall the Son of man be three days and three nights in the heart of the earth. The men of Nineveh shall rise in judgment with this generation, and shall condemn it: because they repented at the preaching of Jonas; and, behold, a greater than Jonas *is* here" (Matt. 12:38–41). See also the Savior's words: "A wicked and adulterous generation seeketh after a sign; and there shall no sign be given unto it, but the sign of the prophet Jonas [i.e., Jonah]. And he left them, and departed" (Matt. 16:4).

The story of Jonah enables us to improve our lives by deepening our understanding of important gospel truths and helping us to adopt them more fully in our daily practice:

The Lord cares for all His children. The Lord truly cares about all people, for all are the children of God. The gospel is a universal gospel. The people of Nineveh, though enemies to Israel, deserved the opportunity to repent. The Lord knows our names and He knows our hearts and He loves us. Heavenly Father and our Savior seek immortality and eternal life for all (see Moses 1:39).

The message of the prophets since the beginning of time has been to call people to repentance. The greatest thing we will ever do in regard to our exaltation is to repent and help others repent (see D&C 58:42–43; 15:6).

We are to be faithful in performing our duty. Having been called to declare repentance, Jonah at first shirked his duty because of "lying vanities" (Jon. 2:8). We can learn our duty and do it, lest we be counted unworthy (see D&C 107:99–100).

The eye of the Lord being upon us, we have the opportunity to call upon Him in prayer. Learning that he could not hide from the Lord, Jonah turned to earnest prayer and faith before being delivered from his watery prison. Similarly, we all have the opportunity to be brought down into humility through the word and power of God as appropriate to our circumstances (see Alma 32:16; 48:20).

Jonah is a symbol of the Atonement. The Lord used the experience of Jonah to symbolize the verity that He would be three days in the tomb prior to His coming forth in the resurrection (see Matt. 12:39–40).

True repentance brings gratitude and change. In the spirit of sacrifice and thanksgiving, Jonah went to Nineveh, warning the people of destruction if they did not repent—and they repented. The first concern of the penitent is to show gratitude to God by caring for and blessing His children through the message of the gospel of Jesus Christ (see Mosiah 28:3; Alma 29:9–10; 36:24).

The Lord is merciful. As often as we repent, the Lord will forgive us. We can strive to show mercy unto others, receiving in turn the mercy of a loving God (see Matt. 5:7).

Vengeance is the Lord's. Jonah's heart was anxious for the sinner to be punished. Like the Lord, we can experience joy over the sinner who repents (see D&C 18:13). We are to forgive everyone: "I, the Lord, will forgive whom I will forgive, but of you it is required to forgive all men" (D&C 64:10; see also Morm. 8:20).

The Lord is tender in teaching us so that we might see and understand. The Lord raised up the gourd to shade Jonah. Pleased at first, Jonah was filled with pity at its demise. Through a simple display, the Lord impressed on Jonah the truth that people are precious—even more precious than plants.

If we take these lessons to heart, then our lives will be filled with more joy, more peace, more hope, and more faith. We will be doing the will of the Lord in the spirit of thanksgiving.

Zechariah Has a Vision of Christ by Matthaeus Merian (the Elder)

APPENDIX OO
ZECHARIAH

Zechariah (pronounced "zeck'-uh-ry'-uh"), son of Berechiah, the son of Iddo, was a contemporary of Haggai and prophesied in the days of Darius I (in the time frame around 520–518 BC—see Zech. 1:1, 7; 7:1, 8).

The Book of Zechariah is one of the twelve shorter prophetic books of the Old Testament, having been written shortly after the return of Judah from exile in Babylon under authority of Cyrus: "Then the prophets, Haggai the prophet, and Zechariah the son of Iddo, prophesied unto the Jews that *were* in Judah and Jerusalem in the name of the God of Israel, *even* unto them" (Ezra 5:1). "And the elders of the Jews builded [the temple], and they prospered through the prophesying of Haggai the prophet and Zechariah the son of Iddo. And they builded, and finished *it*, according to the commandment of the God of Israel, and according to the commandment of Cyrus, and Darius, and Artaxerxes king of Persia" (Ezra 6:14).

The Book of Zechariah unfolds in strikingly beautiful formulation the vision of the Lord's plan of salvation for His people, using (as did Isaiah with such skill and inspiration) contemporary events as symbolic leverage for capturing the scope and grandeur of the ultimate restoration and sublimation of Israel's faithful at the Second Coming. In broad contours, the book deals with visions concerning the future of the chosen people of the Lord (see Zech. 1–8) and additional prophecies concerning the unfolding of the Lord's plan for defeating the wicked and sustaining and redeeming the righteous in the final days (see Zech. 9–14).

The message of Zechariah resonates in modern revelation. Concerning the Jews recognizing the wounds of the crucified Savior (see Zech. 12:10–14; 13:6), modern revelation states the following: "And then shall the Jews look upon me and say: What are these wounds in thine hands and in thy feet? Then shall they know that I am the Lord; for I will say unto them: These wounds are the wounds with which I was wounded in the house of my friends. I am he who was lifted up. I am Jesus that was crucified. I am the Son of God. And then shall they weep because of their iniquities; then shall they lament because they persecuted their king" (D&C 45:51–53).

Moreover, the Prophet Joseph Smith invoked the words of Zechariah (among others) in explaining the final gathering as a manifestation of the love of the Lord:

In speaking of the gathering, we mean to be understood as speaking of it according to scripture, the gathering of the elect of the Lord out of every nation on earth, and bringing them to the place of the Lord of Hosts, when the city of righteousness shall be built, and where the people shall be of one heart and one mind, when the Savior comes: yea, where the people shall walk with God like Enoch, and be free from sin. The word of the Lord is precious; and when we read that the veil spread over all nations will be destroyed [as in Isaiah 25:7], and the pure in heart see God, and reign with Him a thousand years on earth, we want all honest men to have a chance to gather and build up a city of righteousness, where even upon the bells of the horses shall be written *"Holiness to the Lord* [see Zechariah 14:20]." (*TPJS*, 93)

NOTES:

_____

_____

_____

_____

_____

_____

_____

_____

_____

_____

_____

_____

_____

_____

_____

_____

_____

_____

_____

APPENDIX PP
MALACHI

Malachi (meaning: my messenger) was the last of the Old Testament prophets. The Book of Malachi, one of the twelve shorter prophetic books of the Old Testament, was written around 430 BC. Its central purpose was to call the people and their priests to repentance for gross shortcomings and remind them to prepare for the Second Coming and the judgments of the Lord.

Malachi is often cited in subsequent prophetic discourse and scripture. The Lord made reference to the passage in Mal. 3:1 ("Behold, I will send my messenger . . .") in speaking of John the Baptist: "For this is *he*, of whom it is written, Behold, I send my messenger before thy face, which shall prepare thy way before thee" (Matt. 11:10).

So important were the words of Malachi, including truths about the law of tithing and the sealing commission of Elijah, that the resurrected Savior quoted them to the ancient American Saints during His visit (see 3 Ne. 24 and 25, including Mal. 3 and 4) and commanded that these words should be written down. The Savior then declared: "These scriptures, which ye had not with you, the Father commanded that I should give unto you; for it was wisdom in him that they should be given unto future generations. And he did expound all things, even from the beginning until the time that he should come in his glory" (3 Ne. 26:2–3).

On the evening of September 21, 1823, Moroni, the last in a sequence of historians of the word of God, appeared before Joseph Smith to lay the foundation of the coming forth of the Book of Mormon in the context of the latter-day Restoration. Moroni cited the words of Malachi concerning the coming of the prophet Elijah: "And he shall plant in the hearts of the children the promises made to the fathers, and the hearts of the children shall turn to their fathers" (D&C 2:2; compare D&C 27:9).

Six years after the publication of the Book of Mormon in this dispensation, the Savior appeared to Joseph Smith and Oliver Cowdery in the Kirtland Temple on April 3, 1836, accompanied by other heavenly beings, including Elijah, in fulfillment of the prophecy of Malachi:

> Elijah the prophet, who was taken to heaven without tasting death, stood before us, and said:
> Behold, the time has fully come, which was spoken of by the mouth of Malachi—testifying that he [Elijah] should be sent, before the great and dreadful day of the Lord come—
> To turn the hearts of the fathers to the children, and the children to the fathers, lest the whole earth be smitten with a curse—
> Therefore, the keys of this dispensation are committed into your hands; and by this ye may know that the great and dreadful day of the Lord is near, even at the doors. (D&C 110:13–16; compare D&C 128:17)

Thus Malachi was the grand prophet of transition: transition from the Old Testament to the New Testament, and from these sacred volumes to the Book of Mormon. With the fulfillment of the words of Malachi as given unto him by the Father (see 3 Ne. 24:1), the holy sealing powers of the sacred temples were once again activated on the earth. All those who were gathered forth from among the peoples of the earth through the confirming message of the Book of Mormon and the ordinances of salvation could therefore receive the sublime blessings of the holy temples of God and continue their journey heavenward toward eternal life and exaltation.

Malachi is also mentioned in Doctrine and Covenants 133—the Lord's "appendix" to the Doctrine and Covenants given through Joseph Smith on November 3, 1831—in connection with the fate of those who are not prepared for the Second Coming and experience the fulfillment of the warning words of the prophets of old: "And also that which was written by the prophet Malachi: For, behold, the day cometh that shall burn as an oven, and all the proud, yea, and all that do wickedly, shall be stubble; and the day that cometh shall burn them up, saith the Lord of hosts, that it shall leave them neither root nor branch" (D&C 133:64).

Malachi is also included among the elect whom President Joseph F. Smith beheld during his vision of the work of salvation going on in the spirit world: "And Malachi, the prophet who testified of the coming of Elijah—of whom also Moroni spake to the Prophet Joseph Smith, declaring that he should come before the ushering in of the great and dreadful day of the Lord—were also there" (D&C 138:46).

Besides treating the supernal theme of the sealing powers that bind families forever, Malachi is remembered especially for his reference to tithes and offerings and the comforting lesson of spiritual abundance—that the Lord is prepared to open the windows of heaven in blessing the faithful who obediently support the unfolding of His kingdom through their sacrifice and consecrations. His promise is that "all nations shall call you blessed: for ye shall be a delightsome land, saith the Lord of Hosts" (Mal. 3:12).

Malachi taught the people of his day—and ours—that we should honor God (see Mal. 1:5), bring a "pure offering" before Him in righteousness (Mal. 1:11; see 3:3), give glory to Him (see Mal. 2:2), walk with God "in peace and equity" (Mal. 2:6), remain faithfully within the covenant bounds in marriage (see Mal. 2:11), care for the poor and needy (see Mal. 3:5), return unto God (see Mal. 3:7), pay our tithes and offerings (see Mal. 3:10), fear God and always keep Him in our thoughts (see Mal. 3:16), avoid pride (see Mal. 4:1), and, under the influence of the sealing power of the priesthood, cultivate a godly and eternal disposition of oneness among families, both parents toward their children, and children toward their parents (see Mal. 4:5–6). This pattern of spiritual abundance brings magnificent blessings into our lives.

It is fitting to consider the law of tithing in the same context as the subject of preparing for the Second Coming. In our day, the Lord has said, "Behold, now it is called today until the coming of the Son of Man, and verily it is a day of sacrifice, and a day for the tithing of my people; for he that is tithed shall not be burned at his coming. For after today cometh the burning—this is speaking after the manner of the Lord—for verily I say, tomorrow all the proud and they that do wickedly shall be as stubble; and I will burn them up, for I am the Lord of Hosts; and I will not spare any that remain in Babylon. Wherefore, if ye believe me, ye will labor while it is called today" (D&C 64:23–25).

Elsewhere He stressed the importance of having one's name "enrolled with the people of God" so that "he may tithe his people, to prepare them against the day of vengeance and burning" (D&C 85:3). It is the same message that Malachi sounded in his day: "For I am the Lord, I change not; therefore ye sons of Jacob are not consumed" (Mal. 3:6). And why are they not consumed? Because their names are kept in a "book of remembrance . . . for them that feared the Lord, and that thought upon his name" (Mal. 3:16). Malachi's universal question echoes with power down through the centuries: "But who may abide the day of his coming?" (Mal. 3:2). And, once again, the answer is lucidly clear for all of us who live in a time already well beyond the promised return of Elijah the prophet: "Wherefore, if ye believe me, ye will labor while it is called today" (D&C 64:25).

We give temporal offerings to the Lord, in particular our tithes—one tenth of our increase—and our fast offerings. Tithing is a commandment of God (see D&C 119). Payment of an honest tithe is a requirement for obtaining a temple recommend. Payment of tithes brings resultant blessings from our Heavenly Father, both temporal and spiritual. We cannot rob God in any of our tithes and offerings or else we shall be cursed (see Mal. 3:8–9).

Offerings to the Lord are given in many additional forms. We offer sacrifices unto the Lord of a broken heart and contrite spirit (see 3 Ne. 9:20). We offer our devotions to the Lord in all kinds of service. The important thing to remember is that all we have comes from our Heavenly Father; therefore, we should not withhold our oblations from Him. "And it pleaseth God that he hath given all these things unto man; for unto this end were they made to be used, with judgment, not to excess, neither by extortion. And in nothing doth man offend God, or against none is his wrath kindled, save those who confess not his hand in all things, and obey not his commandments" (D&C 59:20–21).

ART CREDITS

500